Make the Grade.
Your Atomic Dog Online Edition.

The Atomic Dog Online Edition includes proven study tools that expand and enhance key concepts in your text. Reinforce and review the information you absolutely 'need to know' with features like:

- **Review Quizzes**
- Key term Assessments
- Interactive Animations and Simulations
- Notes and Information from Your Instructor
- Pop-up Glossary Terms
- A Full Text Search Engine

Ensure that you 'make the grade'. Follow your lectures, complete assignments, and take advantage of all your available study resources like the Atomic Dog Online Edition.

How to Access Your Online Edition

- **If you purchased this text directly from Atomic Dog ....**
  Visit atomicdog.com and enter your email address and password in the login box at the top-right corner of the page.

- **If you purchased this text NEW from another source....**
  Visit our Students' Page on atomicdog.com and enter the **activation key located below** to register and access your Online Edition.

- **If you purchased this text USED from another source....**
  Using the Book Activation key below you can access the Online Edition at a discounted rate. Visit our Students' Page on atomicdog.com and enter the **Book Activation Key in** the field provided to register and gain access to the Online Edition.

Be sure to download our **How to Use Your Online Edition** guide located on atomicdog.com to learn about additional features!

This key activates your online edition. Visit atomicdog.com to enter your Book Activation Key and start accessing your online resources. For more information, give us a call at (800) 310-5661 or send us an email at support@atomicdog.com

21225XBNH

W9-ATZ-537

PKG

CENGAGE
Learning™

*Some online Editions do not contain all features.

Dynamics of Democracy

SIXTH EDITION

Dynamics of Democracy

Peverill Squire | James M. Lindsay | Cary R. Covington | Eric R.A.N. Smith

Dynamics of Democracy

Peverill Squire, James M. Lindsay, Cary R. Covington and Eric R.A.N. Smith

Executive Editor: Michele Baird, Maureen Staudt and Michael Stranz

Product Development Manager: Greg Albert

Marketing Coordinators: Sara Mercurio

Production/Manufacturing Manager: Donna M. Brown

Custom Production Editor: K.A. Espy

Rights and Permissions Specialists: Todd Osborne

Cover Image: © Getty Images

For product information and technology assistance, contact us at **Cengage Learning Customer & Sales Support, 1-800-354-9706**

For permission to use material from this text or product, submit all requests online at **cengage.com/permissions** Further permissions questions can be emailed to **permissionrequest@cengage.com**

Library of Congress Control Number: 2009924883

Book ISBN 13: 978-1-424-06877-7
Book ISBN 10: 1-424-06877-0

Package ISBN-13: 978-1-424-08042-7
Package ISBN-10: 1-424-08042-8

Cengage Learning
5191 Natorp Boulevard
Mason, OH 45040
USA

Cengage Learning is a leading provider of customized learning solutions with office locations around the globe, including Singapore, the United Kingdom, Australia, Mexico, Brazil, and Japan. Locate your local office at: **international.cengage.com/region**

Cengage Learning products are represented in Canada by Nelson Education, Ltd.

Visit our corporate website at **cengage.com**.

Printed in the United States of America
1 2 3 4 5 6 7 13 12 11 10 09

To
  Russell and Emma
  Ian, Cameron, Flora, and Malcolm
  Sarah, Michael, and David
  Katharine and Stephanie

Contents

 PART 1 THE CONTEXT OF AMERICAN POLITICS   1

PART 2 INDIVIDUALS AND GROUPS IN AMERICAN POLITICS   253

PART 3 THE INSTITUTIONS OF AMERICAN POLITICS   493

PART 4 THE POLICY PROCESS IN AMERICAN POLITICS   733

List of Boxes

THE PEOPLE BEHIND THE RULES

POINT OF ORDER

Preface

American politics can often seem a confusing swirl of personalities and issues: Will Barack Obama transform American politics for the better, or will he fuel greater partisan bickering? Are budget deficits a good thing because they will stimulate a troubled economy or a bad thing because we are running up huge debts that will come back to haunt us? Each of us could add issues that we consider important—and ones that we do not understand or care about as well.

Politics and the political system touch the lives of every American every day in many ways. But how do we make sense of it all? This book is our attempt to help you understand the political structures and forces that shape your lives.

APPROACH

We address the issue of government and politics by emphasizing two lessons that appear in virtually every chapter. First, *politics arises from conflict.* The variety of interests in society makes conflicts virtually inevitable. Government seeks to manage (though not necessarily resolve) some of those conflicts by creating procedures and institutions. The Constitution, for instance, establishes many of the fundamental rules that structure politics in the United States. The second lesson we emphasize is that *the rules that stipulate how the government makes its decisions help determine the winners and losers in particular conflicts.* Rules are not neutral. Inevitably, the rules that structure the political process help some participants and harm others. That is why the rules themselves are often the target of vociferous debate and why changing the rules can change the outcome of a conflict. Thus, throughout *Dynamics of Democracy,* we show how the rules of politics and government reflect and shape conflicts in society.

ONLINE AND IN PRINT

This new edition of *Dynamics of Democracy* is available online as well as in print. The Online Edition offers a full range of interactivity, including full search capability, glossary terms defined immediately, pop-up references, end-of-chapter study questions, and Flash animations that bring concepts to life. Each chapter of the Online Edition ends with an interactive study guide that provides tools for learning, such as interactive key-term matching and the ability to review customized content in one place. In addition, with both Online and Print Editions of the text materials, you have the flexibility to choose which combination of resources works best for you.

The primary heads and subheads in each chapter in both the Online and Print Editions are numbered. For example, the first primary head in Chapter 1 is labeled 1-1, the second primary head in this chapter is labeled 1-2, and so on. The subheads build from the designation of their corresponding primary head: 1-1a, 1-1b, etc. This numbering system is designed to make moving between the Online and Print Editions as seamless as possible. So if you need to read the material in 2-3 and 2-4 for tomorrow's assignment, you will know that the information appears in Chapter 2 of both the Online and Print Editions of the text, and you can then choose the best way for you to complete the assignment. The Contents for both the Online and Print Editions also show the numbering system.

Finally, next to a number of figures and tables in this Print Edition of the text are interactive icons like those in the margin on the right. These icons indicate that this figure or table in the Online Edition of the text is an interactive animation that is designed to apply, illustrate, or reinforce the concept.

PEDAGOGICAL FEATURES

A number of features within each chapter facilitate learning. First, each chapter is previewed with an outline of the main points covered in the text. These outlines provide an overview of the chapter and help you see how the various topics fit together. Second, each chapter opens with a brief story that highlights the key themes of the chapter and shows in concrete terms why they matter. Third, we have placed the text of the Constitution at the end of the chapter 2 discussion of the Constitution, so you can refer to it as needed. To ease your exploration of the Constitution, we have supplied marginal annotations that summarize the key points of each section.

In addition to these in-text features, you will find two types of boxes in each chapter. The first type of box, called "Point of Order," focuses on rules in government. You will read about how rules were adopted, how they changed over time, and how those changes affect the workings of the government. The second type of box, called "The People behind the Rules," focuses on the people in government and politics. It, too, emphasizes change, showing how changes in the people involved in politics can affect the outcomes of political conflicts. Thus, each chapter contains in-depth examples that illustrate how rules and participants shape the political process.

Finally, at the end of each chapter, you will find a summary of the chapter and an alphabetized and page-referenced list of key terms. The key terms appear within the chapter text in boldface type, with marginal definitions provided on the same page. The key terms and definitions are also compiled in the glossary at the end of the book. The Online Edition of the text has "pop-up" definitions of key terms, as well as a key-term matching quiz in each end-of-chapter study guide. The key terms also serve as a list of core concepts for study and review.

Also provided at the end of each chapter is an annotated list of suggested readings for further study. By its very nature, an introductory textbook can only introduce the many important subjects of American politics. The readings at the end of each chapter suggest ways to explore further those topics that you find particularly interesting. Finally, review questions at the end of the chapter allow for self-testing.

In the appendixes at the end of the book, you will find a rich array of supplemental readings and historical materials. They provide an important resource for independent study and research. How did the *Federalist Papers* explain the Constitution's solution to the threat of majority tyranny? Find the answer in Federalist No. 10 in appendix C. How frequently have we experienced periods of "divided" government (when Congress is controlled by one party and the presidency by the other)? Analyze appendix I for the answer. Thus, in a variety of ways, we have tried to ensure that reading the book will be a rewarding and enjoyable experience.

WHAT'S NEW TO THIS EDITION

This new edition of *Dynamics of Democracy* includes fully updated census and study data, as well as coverage of recent events:

- Chapter 1 discusses presidential term limits and the ramifications of the Twenty-Second Amendment on George W. Bush's second term. The chapter also explores why popular governors Arnold Schwarzenegger and Jennifer Granholm will not be able to run for the highest office in the country.

- Chapters 2 and 3 include the latest census figures and demographic data in portraying the "average American" so that readers have the most current information available. Chapter 3 also includes expanded discussions on immigration and religion.

- Chapter 4 contains a completely revamped discussion of the second amendment in light of the Court's decision in *District of fColumbia v. Heller*, as well as updated discussions on the application of the death penalty and on the use of prior restraint.

- Chapter 5 provides up-to-date information on gay marriage and the effects of "don't ask—don't tell" on military operations. Also included is a new examination of Asian Americans and reverse discrimination in higher education.

- Chapter 6 coverage includes learning about politics from the Internet, media encouragement of tolerance of gays and lesbians, and how the attitudes of the young are becoming more positive toward gays and lesbians.

- Chapter 7 discusses the 2004 and 2008 election in terms of voter turnout (including breakdown by demographic groups) and the possible effects, including splits between men and women, and between urban and rural. Figure 7–5 has been updated to show partisan perceptions of who told the truth about Iraq. The chapter also includes discussion of the ongoing U.S. involvement in the Middle East.

- Chapter 8 begins with a new vignette highlighting complaints about how the new media do their job, reviews the career of media baron Rupert Murdoch, and discusses how broadcast television companies are increasingly contesting fines levied by the Federal Communications Commissions for violating federal decency standards.

- Chapter 9 begins with a discussion of the 2008 election and party politics, and also includes fully updated data from the election and coverage of third-party influence, including the effect of Ralph Nader's presidential bids.

- Chapters 10 offers numerous new examples highlighting interest-group activity, provides updated data on federal campaign contributions, reviews Nancy Dorn's emergence as one of Washington's "superlobbyists," and discusses netroots lobbying and the Honest Leadership and Open Government Act of 2007.

- Chapter 11 opens with a new story on breaking a filibuster, and contains in depth examinations of Speaker Pelosi's role as leader of the House. In addition, the chapter is updated with data on the results of the 2008 elections.

- Chapter 12 has updated coverage of the presidency that includes the historic 2008 presidential election, and a preview of Barack Obama's plans for organizing the White House staff and creating significant breaks with many of the policies of George W. Bush. It provides updated accounts for the controversies surrounding George W. Bush's efforts to expand presidential authority, and presidential approval ratings through 2008.

- Chapter 13 incorporates recent developments in the Food and Drug Administration as an example of bureaucratic politics and includes a thorough account of President George W. Bush's attempts to reform the federal bureaucracy and President Barack Obama's early efforts to reverse those policies.

- Chapter 14 has a new opening vignette on a recent racial discrimination case and is thoroughly updated to reflect the current membership of the Supreme Court. In addition, there is a new figure and discussion of the declining number of cases decided by the Court in recent years.

- Chapter 15 incorporates the results of the 2008 elections and has an extensive discussion of the debate over the implementation of Real ID. Also incorporated is an updated discussion of privatization.

- Chapter 16 is updated to reflect the new budget realities faced by the Obama administration. The chapter also includes new discussions of pork and earmarks and contains completely updated federal budget data.

- Chapter 17 includes an explanation of the 2008 housing bubble and financial crisis. It also looks into Bill Clinton's claim that "Big Government is over" and discusses the Kyoto Treaty controversy and other environmental policies.

- Chapter 18 discusses the "surge" of U.S. troops to Iraq ordered by President George W. Bush, President Barack Obama's plans to withdraw U.S. troops from Iraq, and growing public opposition to free-trade agreements.

ANCILLARY MATERIALS

Atomic Dog is pleased to offer a competitive suite of supplemental materials for instructors using its textbooks. These ancillaries include a Test Bank, PowerPoint® slides, Instructor's Manual, and Lecture Animations. Some titles may also have WebCT E-Packs and Blackboard Course Cartridges available. Please contact your Atomic Dog sales representative if you are interested in these products.

The Test Bank for this book includes over 2,500 multiple-choice questions in a wide range of difficulty levels for each chapter. All Atomic Dog Test Banks offer not only the correct answer for each question, but also a rationale or explanation for the correct answer and a reference—the location in the chapter where materials addressing the question content can be found. This Test Bank comes with ExamViewPro software for easily creating customized or multiple versions of a test, and includes the option of editing or adding to the existing question bank.

A full set of PowerPoint® Slides is available for this text and has been updated to reflect changes to this edition. This is designed to provide instructors with comprehensive visual aids for each chapter in the book. These slides include outlines of each chapter, highlighting important terms, concepts, and discussion points.

The Instructor's Manual for this book has also recently been updated to cover all of the new materials and topics in the text. It offers suggested syllabi for 10- and 14-week terms; lecture outlines and notes; in-class and take-home assignments; recommendations for multimedia resources such as films and websites; and long and short essay questions and their answers, appropriate for use on tests.

ACKNOWLEDGMENTS

We wish to thank Atomic Dog Publishing for its enthusiasm and innovative approach to college publishing. We also wish to thank our many colleagues around the country who read and commented on our draft chapters. *Dynamics of Democracy* has become a much better book because of the care and thought our readers put into their reviews.

Finally, we would like to thank our families. They supported and encouraged us throughout the many ups and downs that attended the writing of *Dynamics of Democracy*. We deeply appreciate their love and understanding.

About the Authors

PEVERILL SQUIRE

Peverill Squire is Hicks and Martha Griffiths Chair in American Political Institutions at the University of Missouri and co-editor of *Legislative Studies Quarterly*. Previously, he was on the faculty of the University of Iowa for many years. Professor Squire received his A.B., M.A., and Ph.D. from the University of California, Berkeley. He has been a visiting professor at Meiji University in Tokyo, Japan, and a Fulbright Distinguished Lecturer, holding the John Marshall Chair in Political Science at the Budapest (Hungary) University of Economic Sciences. Professor Squire is the co-author of *The Politics of California Coastal Legislation* (Institute of Governmental Studies), *Who Runs for the Legislature?* (Prentice Hall), and *101 Chambers: Congress, State Legislatures, and the Future of Legislative Studies* (Ohio State University Press); editor of *The Iowa Caucuses and the Presidential Nominating Process* (Westview Press); and co-editor of *Legislatures: Comparative Perspectives on Representative Assemblies* (University of Michigan Press). His articles on legislatures and elections at both the state and national levels, and on other aspects of American politics, have appeared in *American Political Science Review, Annual Review of Political Science, British Journal of Political Science, Canadian Journal of Political Science, Congress & the Presidency, Legislative Studies Quarterly, Journal of Politics, Political Behavior, Political Research Quarterly, Polity, Public Opinion Quarterly, State and Local Government Review, State Politics and Policy Quarterly*, and other leading journals. He has served on the planning committees for the 1992 National Election Study, Senate Election Study, and the 1994 National Election Study; as Senior Consulting Editor (Politics) for *The American Midwest: An Interpretive Encyclopedia; and on the editorial boards for American Politics Quarterly, Congress and the Presidency, Legislative*

Studies Quarterly, Political Research Quarterly, State Politics and Policy Quarterly, and *State and Local Government Review*. Professor Squire regularly teaches introduction to American politics, legislative process, and American state politics. While on the faculty at the University of Iowa he received a Collegiate Teaching Award and was the recipient of a Regent's Award for Faculty Excellence given by the Board of Regents, State of Iowa.

JAMES M. LINDSAY

James M. Lindsay is Senior Vice President, Director of Studies, and Maurice R. Greenberg Chair at the Council of Foreign Relations. From 2003-2006 he was the inaugural director of the Robert S. Strauss Center for International Security and Law at the University of Texas at Austin, where he was the first to hold the Tom Slick Chair for International Affairs at the Lyndon B. Johnson School of Public Affairs. He was previously Vice President, Director of Studies, and Maurice R. Greenberg Chair at the Council on Foreign Relations and Deputy Director and Senior Fellow in the Foreign Policy Studies Program at the Brookings Institution. Lindsay has authored, co-authored, or edited more than fifteen books and fifty journal articles and book chapters on various aspects of American foreign policy and international relations. He is the co-author of *America Unbound: The Bush Revolution in Foreign Policy* (Brookings Institution Press), which won the 2003 Lionel Gelber Prize and was named a top book of 2003 by *The Economist*. He is also co-editor of *Agenda for the Nation* (Brookings Institution Press), which *Choice Magazine* selected as an Outstanding Academic Book for 2004. He is the author of *Congress and the Politics of U.S. Foreign Policy* (Johns Hopkins University Press) and *Congress and Nuclear Weapons* (Johns Hopkins University Press). He has contributed articles to the op-ed pages of many major newspapers, including the *New York Times*, the *Washington Post*, and the *Los Angeles Times*. Earlier in his career, he was a professor of political science at the University of Iowa, where he received the Collegiate Teaching Award, the James N. Murray Faculty Teaching Award, and a Pew Faculty Fellowship in International Affairs. In 1996–1997, Lindsay served as Director for Global Issues and Multilateral Affairs at the National Security Council. He received his A.B. from the University of Michigan and his M.A., M.Phil., and Ph.D. from Yale University.

CARY R. COVINGTON

Cary R. Covington is associate professor of political science at the University of Iowa. He received his B.A. from Whittier College and his A.M. and Ph.D. from the University of Illinois at Urbana–Champaign. He is co-author of *The Coalitional Presidency*

(Brooks/Cole Publishing Company), and his research on the institution of the presidency and on presidential-congressional relations has been published in such journals as *American Journal of Political Science, Journal of Politics, Political Research Quarterly, Legislative Studies Quarterly*, and *American Politics Quarterly*. Professor Covington has had a long and abiding interest in teaching, both in and out of the classroom. He has worked as a consultant for the Educational Testing Service (ETS) as a member of its Test Development Committee for the College Level Examination Program (CLEP) in American government and served as a faculty instructor for The Washington Center's Campaign 2000 Internship Program at the Republican National Convention in Philadelphia. At the University of Iowa, Professor Covington received the Collegiate Teaching Award in 2002 for his teaching of both large- and small-enrollment courses on introductory American politics, and courses on the American presidency, the legislative process, and bureaucratic politics. In addition to his activities in the classroom, he has assisted many students by serving at various times as the political science department's Director of Undergraduate Studies, Director of Graduate Studies, and Director of Government Internships.

ERIC R.A.N. SMITH

Eric R.A.N. Smith is professor of political science and environmental studies at the University of California, Santa Barbara. He received his A.B., M.A., and Ph.D. degrees from the University of California, Berkeley. He taught at Brandeis University and then at Columbia University before moving to U.C. Santa Barbara. From 1996 to 1997, he was the director of U.C. Santa Barbara's Washington, D.C. Center. Professor Smith is also affiliated with the Bren School of Environmental Science and Management, and the Environmental Studies Program at U.C. Santa Barbara. His research focuses on public opinion, elections, and environmental politics. He is the author of *The Unchanging American Voter* (University of California Press), *Energy, the Environment, and Public Opinion* (Rowman & Littlefield), and numerous articles in such journals as *American Political Science Review, Journal of Politics, Legislative Studies Quarterly, Public Opinion Quarterly, Political Research Quarterly, Political Psychology,* and *Society and Natural Resources*. Professor Smith enjoys teaching and has taught a wide range of classes—including introduction to American government and politics, public opinion and elections, political parties, Congress, and environmental politics. He believes that to understand and appreciate politics, students should both study academic theories about politics and be exposed to real politics and politicians. Toward that end, Professor Smith teaches his Congress course based on a simulation of the U.S. House of Representatives; he regularly brings politicians into his classes to talk with his students; and he sponsors dozens of internships in local, state, and national politics. Smith is not only a scholar who studies politics, he is also an active participant in politics. He sponsors one of the political clubs on his campus and has worked in campaigns ranging from local to national office.

Part 1

The Context of American Politics

1

Studying the Dynamics of Democracy
Conflict, Rules, and Change

CHAPTER OUTLINE

George W. Bush and Al Gore both looked forward to November 7, 2000. For months, the two men had crisscrossed the country in pursuit of the presidency. They had shaken hands with thousands of Americans, given hundreds of speeches, attended dozens of fund-raising dinners, and participated in three high-stakes debates on national television. After surviving this electoral marathon, both men assumed that shortly after the polls closed that Tuesday night they would know whether they had succeeded in their bid to become the next president of the United States.

But election 2000 had a surprise for Bush and Gore, as well as the rest of America. When dawn broke on November 8, the election was still too close to call. Gore led by several hundred thousand votes in the popular vote, a slim margin in an election in which more than 105 million votes were cast and more than 1 million absentee ballots remained to be counted. More important, neither Bush nor Gore had a majority in the **electoral college**, which is the body that, under the Constitution, actually elects the president. Candidates get votes in the electoral college for each state in which they get the most votes; the more populous the state, the more electoral votes they get. Even though the popular vote was close in many states and absentee ballots still had to be counted, most experts figured that Gore had 267 electoral votes locked up and Bush had 246. But 271 votes were needed to win. Everything came down to Florida's 25 electoral votes. And in the Sunshine State, Bush led Gore in the initial vote tallies by only 1,784 votes out of the more than 6 million cast. In short, the country had flipped a coin in the presidential election, and the coin had landed on its edge.

The election's narrowness immediately focused attention on the mechanics of how America, and especially Florida, votes. Americans soon discovered that in the United States, individual states rather than the federal government set most election rules, and states, not the federal government, operate the polling places. Moreover, the states have considerable freedom in the rules they create. Everything from the layout of the ballot to the type of machine that counts the votes to the identification a voter needs to be allowed in the voting booth varies across the country. In some states, including Florida, the rules vary from county to county. Some Floridians vote by filling out ballots that look like the standardized tests that schoolchildren hate. Others vote by punching out squares (or chads) in the ballot next to the names of the candidates they want to elect.

As people examined the mechanics of voting in Florida, they saw things they did not like. In Palm Beach County, a poorly designed ballot misled hundreds of voters into voting for third-party candidate Patrick Buchanan rather than Gore. In Miami-Dade County, overworked election officials mistakenly prevented some African Americans from voting even though they were registered to vote.[1] More generally, Americans learned what voting experts had known for years: Many vote-counting machines, particularly the ones that process the punch-card ballots used by nearly one in three counties in America, fail to record some votes (see Box 1–1). These missing votes are not a problem in most

electoral college
The body of electors, whose composition is determined by the results of the general election, that chooses the president and vice president. To win in the electoral college, candidates must secure a majority of the electoral vote.

POINT OF ORDER

Box 1–1 How the United States Counts Votes

Florida's disputed 2000 presidential election taught Americans something that experts on the mechanics of voting have known for years: The machines used to count ballots regularly miss some votes. Florida also taught Americans another important lesson: The rules governing how to count votes that machines miss vary from state to state, and even from county to county. Moreover, these recount rules are often maddeningly unclear, even though the way they are applied can affect who wins an election.

VOTING MACHINES AND DEVICES

In the American electoral system, the responsibility for deciding how ballots are cast rests with the states rather than the federal government. Most states, in turn, leave the decision up to individual counties. So if you move across county lines, you may encounter entirely different voting technology.

Four types of voting technology are used in American elections. The oldest type is the mechanical lever machine. Each candidate's name is assigned to a particular lever. Voters move the levers to indicate a choice, and when they have made all their choices, they pull another lever that tells the machine to record the votes. Mechanical voting machines were first used in Lockport, New York, in 1892, and by the 1960s, more than half of all votes were cast using them. Because the machines are expensive to maintain and frequently break down, other voting technologies are slowly replacing them. In 2004, 14 percent of all registered voters lived in counties that used mechanical lever machines.

The voting device that helped drive mechanical lever machine companies out of business was the punch-card ballot, which was first used in 1964. With punch-card systems, voters insert a ballot into a ballot holder. They then use a stylus to punch a hole in the ballot opposite their candidate's name. A machine then reads the punched ballot. Punch-card systems are popular because they are inexpensive. In 2004, 14 percent of all registered voters lived in counties that used punch-card ballots. (At least eleven states and more than 250 counties abandoned punch-card balloting after the 2000 election.)

Optical-scanning ballots use the same technology as the standardized tests you take in school. Voters record their vote by filling in a rectangle, circle, or oval, or by completing an arrow. A computer then scans the ballots and records the votes. In 2004, 34 percent of all registered voters lived in counties that used optical-scanning ballots.

Electronic voting is the most recent voting technology. It resembles a bank automated teller machine (ATM). Voters register their preferences by using buttons or touch-screen technology. In 2004, 31 percent of registered voters lived in counties that used electronic voting.

In addition to the four voting methods just described, voters can also vote the old-fashioned way, by filling out paper ballots. In 2004, less than 1 percent of registered voters lived in counties that used hand-counted paper ballots. (Many advanced industrialized democracies, including Canada and Great Britain, continue to count all votes by hand.)

THE SHORTCOMINGS OF VOTING MACHINES

Voting machines have supplanted hand counts almost everywhere in the United States because they count votes quickly—not because they are more accurate. Indeed, no voting machine is flawless. All of them can break down, all are vulnerable to electoral fraud, and all can be misused by voters who do not follow the directions or understand the voting technology.

The disputed 2000 election in Florida focused particular attention on two potential problems with voting machines: undervotes and overvotes. Undervotes occur when a machine records no candidate preference in a given race. Undervotes may be intentional or unintentional. They may occur because voters decide not to select a candidate in a particular race. (They presumably record their preferences in the other races on the ballot.) But an undervote may occur accidentally, even when a voter intended to cast a vote. This can happen with a punch-card ballot if a voter inserts the punch card into the ballot holder improperly, or if the voter fails to punch all the way through the ballot. An undervote can happen with an optical-scanning ballot if a voter fails to fill in the oval completely or uses a pen instead of a pencil.

Overvotes occur when a voter votes for more than one candidate in a race. (Machine lever and electronic voting machines are designed to make it impossible to overvote.) Sometimes, voters do this intentionally, perhaps to indicate their displeasure with the candidates. One survey of voting patterns in eight of Florida's largest counties in the 2000 election discovered that 4,300 voters punched the holes next to at least seven of the ten names listed for the presidential race.

Overvotes can also occur accidentally. Voting experts have found that the percentage of overvotes rises with punch-card and optical-scanning systems when the ballots split the list of candidate names into two columns. (Many voters mistakenly think that split-column ballots require them to vote for one candidate in each column.)

Overvotes can also occur with optical-scanning ballots if voters fail to erase a mark completely, leave a stray mark on the ballot, or fill in the oval next to a candidate's name and then write the same candidate's name on the write-in line. An analysis of the ballots in nine Florida counties with the highest rate of discarded votes found 962 cases in which a voter selected Bush or Gore and then also wrote in the candidate's name. The voting machines read those ballots as double votes and discarded them. (If these ballots had been counted, Gore would have gained 194 votes.)

POINT OF ORDER   (continued)

RECOUNTS

Experts on the mechanics of voting have known for years that voting machines do not provide perfect counts. Indeed, one common type of punch-card system—the Votomatic—may misread 4 percent or more of the ballots it processes. But these errors are usually overlooked for two reasons. One is that most elections are not close, so getting a precise count would take great effort and not change the result. The other reason is the assumption that Republicans are as likely to make mistakes as Democrats are, so an imprecise vote count does not favor one party over the other.

The case for relying on machine counts weakens, however, when the election results are close and one party's voters are more likely to have made mistakes. The former was clearly true in Florida in 2000; Bush's final margin of 537 votes amounted to 0.0005 percent of all the votes cast in the state's presidential contest. The latter also appears to have been true. Florida counties with Democratic majorities were more likely than Republican counties to use the punch-card system, which is the voting technology most prone to producing undervotes. As a result, even if the same percentage of Democratic and Republican voters erred in punching their ballots, the greater number of Democrats in these counties meant that more Democratic votes were discarded. At the same time, a confusing ballot layout in Palm Beach misled as many as 2,800 Democratic voters into voting for Pat Buchanan.

Voting machines routinely treat undervotes and overvotes as spoiled ballots, and in some cases, determining how the voter intended to vote is impossible. For instance, a voter may have double-punched a ballot by mistake, but there is no way to know for which candidate he or she wanted to vote. In some instances, however, the voter's intent can be determined by looking at the ballot. This is especially true of optical-scanning ballots. Visual inspection might reveal that a voter

Figure 1–1   Hypothetical Recount Example. To view this figure, please go to the online text.

had erased one oval and filled in another, or that the voter voted for a candidate and then wrote the candidate's name on the write-in line.

Whether these votes should count as legal ballots and be tabulated in a recount is another matter. (See Figure 1–1 for an example of a hypothetical election recount.)

The rules vary from state to state, and their application often varies by county. One of the ironies of the 2000 Florida election is that Texas had the most specific (and generous) laws regarding recounts. The Texas statute, which George W. Bush signed into law when he was governor, specifically states that so-called dimpled chads (punch-card ballots that are indented but not punctured) can be counted as legal votes.

Many states, however, including Florida in 2000, are vague or silent on which ballots should count as legal votes. They instead allow individual counties to set the standard for what constitutes a vote. So what counts for a vote in one county may be discarded as a spoiled ballot in another. In Florida in 2000, for example, some counties examined spoiled ballots and counted as legitimate votes those where a voter filled in the oval for a candidate and then wrote the same name on the write-in line. Other counties never examined the spoiled ballots or decided that they did not count as votes.

FINDING A SOLUTION

Florida's 2000 presidential election prompted Congress to pass the Help America Vote Act of 2002, which encouraged states to replace outdated voting systems. But buying new machines costs money, and the Help America Vote Act did not foot the entire bill. Most counties prefer to spend their dollars on items that residents use frequently, such as roads and parks, rather than voting machines that are used only occasionally. That is one reason why roughly three out of four voters who went to polls in November 2004 used the same type voting system they had used three years earlier.

Yet, better technology by itself will not entirely solve the problems that the Florida vote highlighted. States also need to develop more precise rules about how recounts should be conducted and what the standards should be for determining legal votes. (Indeed, numerous recounts in other states in 2000 did not encounter the same problems as Florida because the rules governing the recounts in those states were more detailed and specific.) If Florida had had more specific rules in place in November 2000, the recount would have been far less controversial and probably could have been concluded more rapidly. In short, rules matter.

Sources: Kimball W. Brace, "Overview of Voting Equipment Usage in the United States, Direct Recording Electronic (DRE) Voting," testimony before the United States Election Commission Assistance Commission, May 5, 2004, available at www.electiondataservices.com/EDSInc_DREover-view.pdf#search='kimball%20brace%20voting%20machines%202004' (accessed February 2005); "Clearly Marked Confusion," *Washington Post*, January 27, 2001; Election Data Services, "New Study Shows 50 Million Voters Will Use Electronic Voting Systems, 32 Million Still with Punch Cards in 2004," February 12, 2004, available at www.electiondataservices.com/EDSInc_VEstudy2004.pdf#search='kimball%20brace%20-voting%20machines%202004' (accessed February 2004); Dan Keating, "Fla. 'Overvotes' Hit Democrats the Hardest," *Washington Post*, January 27, 2001; John Mintz, "Most States Don't Count Dimples," *Washington Post*, November 24, 2000; Roger Roy and David Damron, "Small Counties Wasted More Than 1,700 Votes," *Orlando Sentinel*, January 28, 2001; Jonathan Wand, Kenneth Shotts, Jasjeet S. Sekhon, Walter R. Mebane, Jr., Michael Herron, and Henry E. Brady, "The Butterfly Did It: The Aberrant Vote for Buchanan in Palm Beach County, Florida," *American Political Science Review* 95 (December 2001): 793–810, available at www.elections.fas.harvard.edu/election2000/butterfly.pdf (accessed February 2005); David Von Drehle, Dan Balz, Ellen Nakashima, and Jo Becker, "A Wild Ride into Uncharted Territory," *Washington Post*, January 28, 2001.

elections because the margin of victory usually exceeds the number of missed votes. But in a close election, these missed votes can mean the difference between victory and defeat.

The problems with the mechanics of American voting prompted a great deal of talk about devising standardized ballots and building better voting machines for the next election. But the immediate question on the morning of November 8 was whether the vote count on election night had been accurate. Florida law requires that all ballots be recounted by machine whenever the winning margin is less than one-half of 1 percent of the total vote, which it was. When the machine recount was completed on November 9, Bush's lead had shrunk to 327 votes with several thousand overseas absentee ballots still to be counted. These ballots figured to increase Bush's lead when they were counted. They were mostly from American servicemen and servicewomen serving abroad, who in past elections had favored Republican candidates.

The election was far from over, however. Gore exercised his rights under Florida law to ask the four Florida counties with the most obvious voting problems to recount their ballots by hand. That seemingly simple request touched off more than a month of bitter partisan and legal wrangling. The rest of the nation watched as Florida struggled to determine who would get its electoral votes. Previously obscure government officials in the Sunshine State soon became famous (or infamous) from Maine to Maui (see Box 1–2). Commentators either mocked or praised pictures of election officials holding ballots up to the light as they tried to determine whether a partially detached chad should count as a legal vote.

As happens in so many disputes in the United States, the battle over how (and whether) to count votes quickly moved to the courts. The courts only fueled the controversy. Several Florida lower courts handed Bush legal victories. The Florida Supreme Court, however, handed down rulings that favored Gore, including one that directed all sixty-seven Florida counties to manually review all undervotes, which are ballots that registered no presidential vote when they were first passed through the voting machines. Although the U.S. Supreme Court usually defers to state supreme courts on how to interpret state law, on the reasonable assumption that they know it better, it too joined the fray. As a result, Americans who followed the news in late November and early December 2000 got a free legal education. Expert commentators valiantly tried to explain the complexities of state and federal electoral law, the nuances of court rulings, and the relative authorities of state and federal courts.

All this political and legal wrangling culminated in a dramatic hearing before the U.S. Supreme Court on December 11, 2000. Bush and Gore supporters stood on the courtroom steps waving signs, trading insults, and mugging for the television cameras. Inside, the nine justices grilled the lawyers for each side and indirectly each other. Bush's legal team argued that the vote recount violated the law and should be halted. Gore's lawyers countered that the vote recount was being conducted according to the law

The People behind the Rules

Box 1–2   Katherine Harris and Carol Roberts

Attention in the days following a presidential election usually focuses on the candidates and their running mates. Reporters speculate about who the winning candidate will appoint to key government posts, and they analyze why the defeated candidate lost. But in the days following the 2000 election, attention focused on a whole cast of ordinarily obscure government officials in Florida. In trying to implement Florida's laws on recounting disputed elections, these officials helped shape the election's ultimate outcome, as the experiences of Katherine Harris and Carol Roberts attest.

KATHERINE HARRIS

Katherine Harris, Florida Secretary of State.

Republican Katherine Harris hardly figured to be a major figure in the 2000 presidential election. Six years earlier, she was a wealthy but obscure socialite, the granddaughter of a powerful cattle and citrus baron for whom the University of Florida's football stadium is named. She had held a series of jobs, including a stint in a nightclub act in which she tried to persuade audience members to join her in flapping their arms in a "chicken dance." In 1994, she used her wealth to win election to the Florida state senate. Four years later, she was elected

secretary of state, a post considered so inconsequential that it was abolished in 2002.

But Florida's secretary of state has one key responsibility: administering the state's election laws. Thus, when the Gore campaign demanded hand recounts in four predominantly Democratic counties, Harris became a key player. She insisted that Florida law required the counties, which ran the polling places and tabulated the vote, to complete the hand recounts by November 14. She would then use those results to certify the official vote count for Florida, and with it, the winner of the presidential election. She also told the counties that they could conduct hand recounts only if voting machines had malfunctioned and not because the vote was close.

The Florida Supreme Court ultimately ruled that Harris had misapplied the law. It ordered the hand recounts to begin, and it directed her to hold off certifying the election until November 26. When that day came, two counties had finished their recounts, one had given up counting because it could not meet the deadline, and another was struggling to finish. Harris refused its request for a few extra hours. At 7 p.m. on November 26, she certified that George W. Bush had defeated Al Gore in Florida by a mere 537 votes.

Was Katherine Harris a hero or a villain? The answer depends on whom you ask. Republicans hailed her for judiciously applying the law and flooded her office with flowers. Democrats accused her of *giving* the election to George W. Bush. However, voters in Florida's thirteenth congressional district did not hold the dispute against Harris. In 2002, and again in 2004, they elected her to the U.S. House of Representatives. In 2006, though, Harris was soundly defeated in her bid to become a U.S. Senator.

CAROL ROBERTS

Carol Roberts, Palm Beach, Florida, County Election Canvassing Board.

Democrat Carol Roberts was no newcomer to politics or to close elections. The 64-year-old collector of donkey figurines had held a variety of elected posts in Palm Beach County. She won her first public office as a young mother when she decided to challenge an incumbent county official who was running unopposed. She was later elected the mayor of West Palm Beach. And she once lost an election by a single vote.

In 2000, Roberts was completing her fourteenth year on the Palm Beach County Commission. More important, she also served on the Palm Beach County Election Canvassing Board, which is responsible for overseeing all elections in the county for public office. Few people want to serve on canvassing boards—most counties in the United States have them in one form or another—even though they play an important role in elections. The reason is simple: It is a dull job. Most elections aren't close, so canvassing boards spend most of their time on mundane matters.

But the 2000 presidential election was different, and Roberts seized her moment in the sun. After the canvassing board recounted a few thousand votes and found 19 votes for

The People behind the Rules *(continued)*

Al Gore that the machine count had missed, she demanded that all 450,000 of the county's votes be recounted by hand. When her fellow canvassing board members waffled on what to do, Roberts pushed them to go ahead with the recount. She also took to the television airwaves to defend the need for the recount. Despite Roberts's efforts, Palm Beach finished its hand recount two hours after the November 26 deadline, and that count did not make it into the figure Katherine Harris certified.

Much like Harris, Roberts was a hero to some and a villain to others. Democrats praised her courage in fighting for a recount. Republicans had less kind words. One critic e-mailed her to say, "You are such a Democratic hack. People are laughing at you all over the U.S. You are an old, old hag." Unlike Harris, Roberts failed in her bid in 2002 to win a seat in the U.S. House of Representatives.

Sources: Tim Padgett, "Woman on the Verge of Certifying," *Time* (November 27, 2000): 42–45; Timothy Roche, "Punch-Out in Palm Beach," *Time* (November 27, 2000): 44–45.

and that a completed recount was necessary so that all Americans could have faith in the legitimacy of the election results.

The next day, the U.S. Supreme Court handed down its decision in *Bush v. Gore*. The ruling was complicated. But the bottom line was simple: Seven justices concluded that Florida lacked a clear, uniform standard for conducting hand recounts, which raised serious constitutional questions about conducting a statewide manual recount. More important, the Court ruled by a 5–4 margin that there was no time left to create a new standard that would pass constitutional muster. The Court's majority defended its decision by emphasizing that it had not sought to be a kingmaker. "When contending parties invoke the process of the courts . . . it becomes our unsought responsibility to resolve the federal and constitutional issues the judicial system has been forced to confront."[2] But the justices in the minority, who believed that the Court had acted for political and not legal reasons, denounced the decision. Justice John Paul Stevens, a Republican, wrote: "Although we may never know with complete certainty the identity of the winner of this year's presidential election, the identity of the loser is perfectly clear. It is the nation's confidence in the judge as an impartial guardian of the law."[3]

Constitutional scholars will be dissecting the U.S. Supreme Court's decision in *Bush v. Gore* for years to come. But its immediate effect was to settle the outcome of the 2000 presidential election. On December 13, thirty-seven days after Election Day, Al Gore told the nation that "For the sake of the unity of the people and the strength of our democracy, I offer my concession."[4] In defeat, Gore gained a dubious honor. He became only the fourth man, and the first since 1888, to win the popular vote but lose the presidency. As for President-elect George W. Bush, he used his victory speech to pledge "to do my best to serve your interests and. . .to earn your respect."[5] Like Gore, he also gained an unusual distinction. He joined John Quincy Adams as only the second son of a president to be elected president. What made this historical link all the more curious was that Bush, like Adams, won the presidency while losing the popular vote.

The fight over who won the 2000 presidential election illustrates two important lessons about politics and government in the United States. First, politics arises from conflict. That is not to say that politics means violence. It doesn't. Rather, politics occurs because people disagree over what they want their communities to do and to be. Every day, long-standing disagreements over issues (who should be the next president?) erupt into specific policy questions (were the votes counted accurately?). As the public, interest groups, and government officials express their opinions and pressure the government to adopt the policy they favor, the government must respond by making some decision to resolve the issue—or at least, to keep the conflict within manageable boundaries. (In the case of the 2000 presidential election, the U.S. Supreme Court's ruling made George W. Bush the victor.)

Second, the rules of government help determine who wins the political battle. In the United States, the rules allow politicians, judges, political activists, and individual Americans to express their opinions on an issue. The rules also set forth how political decisions are to be made by allocating power among the three branches of the federal government—the executive, the legislature, and the judiciary—and between the federal government and the state governments. The 2000 presidential election was no exception. It was affected at every step by our rules of government. The fact that the winner of the popular vote is not automatically elected president kept Bush's presidential hopes alive. The fact that Florida counties used voting machines that missed votes raised serious questions about the accuracy of the vote. The fact that Florida's election laws were vague and contradictory on how to conduct recounts helped fuel a five-week-long legal battle. The fact that a ruling by the U.S. Supreme Court requires only five justices to agree allowed the high court to decide the election's outcome. If any of these rules of government had been different—if, for example, the winner of the popular vote won the White House—then the outcome of the 2000 presidential election would have been different as well.

1-1 POLITICS AND CONFLICT

The wide variety of activities that constitute politics all have one important characteristic in common: They arise from conflict. We conduct elections because we disagree about who should represent us in Congress and the White House. We have a set of rules for turning bills into laws because we disagree on which pieces of legislation will best serve the public interest, and we need a way to determine whether a bill's supporters or opponents have more public support. We write letters of complaint to elected officials and demonstrate against government policies because we disagree with the government's actions. In short, politics arises from conflict over both resources—that is, who will get what—and values—that is, how we will govern ourselves, what rules we will follow to make our decisions, and what sort of society we hope to have. In turn, government provides the primary means for managing, if not always resolving, conflict in society.

1-1a The Roots of Conflict

Conflict is an inherent feature of all societies because it springs from two roots that cannot be eradicated: material scarcity and disagreement over values. **Material scarcity** simply means that no country can provide its citizens with everything they may need or desire. To be sure, nations vary greatly in the relative scarcity they experience. For instance, we have all seen photographs of the famines that killed tens of thousands of Ethiopians, Somalis, and Sudanese. The lack of adequate quantities of food, water, and medicine in these countries represents an extreme example of scarce resources. But even in a wealthy country such as the United States, many citizens are underfed, underemployed, ill-housed, and poorly educated. Because societies cannot meet the physical needs and wants of all their citizens, conflict inevitably arises over who should get how much of the resources that are available.

Scarcity, and thus conflict, are also found in government itself. If it were practical to give seats in Congress to everyone who wished to serve, there would be no conflict and therefore no need for elections. If the federal budget were based on an unlimited number of dollars, then interest groups, government agencies, and committees in Congress would not compete over taxpayer dollars. Thus, in both its private and public spheres, society is unable to provide resources adequate to satisfy the wishes of all its members. As a result, those members inevitably compete with one another over the distribution of resources.

The second reason political conflict is inevitable is that people disagree over the kind of society they want for themselves and their fellow citizens. Put another way, civilization has yet to produce a political community whose members all share the same values, principles, and beliefs. The conflicts that have arisen when large numbers of American citizens have held sharply different ideas about what constitutes good public policy have profoundly affected the political history of the United States. The Civil War was fought in large part because northern and southern states disagreed over the morality of slavery. In the early 1900s, Americans disagreed over whether women should be allowed to vote. In the 1950s and 1960s, Americans disagreed over whether private businesses and state and local governments should be allowed to discriminate against African Americans and other minorities. In the late 1960s and early 1970s, Americans disagreed over U.S. involvement in the Vietnam War. And today, Americans disagree over issues ranging from a woman's right to an abortion to whether everyone has a right to medical care to how best to win the war on terrorism.

Because material resources are scarce and because people often hold very different values, principles, and beliefs, political conflict

material scarcity
The inability of a society to provide its citizens with all the goods and services they may want or need.

typically produces outcomes that create winners and losers. For example, either John McCain or Barack Obama would be inaugurated president on January 20, 2009. Both men could not win the 2008 presidential election. And although on some issues it may be possible to reach a compromise that gives all the interested parties at least some of what they seek, by its very nature, compromise requires people to give up something they want.

As you might imagine, the hope in a democracy usually is that the outcome of a political conflict will create many more winners than losers. (As we shall see in Chapter 2, in some circumstances, the goals of democratic government are served only when the rights of the minority triumph over the preferences of the majority.) But nothing guarantees that winners will outnumber losers. Indeed, politicians and the public alike frequently complain that special interests dominate government. This raises the possibility that political conflict may create more losers than winners.

1-1b The Role of Government in Managing Conflict

If conflict is an enduring feature of society, what prevents conflict from degenerating into political violence and civil war? The answer is government. A government provides a society with a way to manage, and sometimes solve, its internal conflicts. In societies in which the government collapses entirely, chaos and warfare typically erupt. This happened in the early 1990s in Somalia and in several of the republics in the former Soviet Union and Yugoslavia.

Governments are uniquely empowered to manage conflict because they can authoritatively allocate values in society; that is, they can decide who wins, who loses, and by how much.[6] The decisions of government are authoritative in the sense that government is the only institution in society that can enforce its decisions on the participants in a conflict. No other institution possesses such power. The authority of a government derives from both its legitimacy and its ability to control the use of coercive force in society.[7]

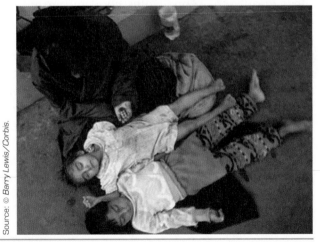

Source: © Joseph Sohm/Visions of America./Corbis.   Source: © Barry Lewis./Corbis.

Material scarcity, a feature of all societies, is a source of much political conflict.

Legitimacy refers to the willingness of citizens to obey the decisions of their government. In essence, then, legitimacy is a self-imposed obligation on the part of the people to obey their government. Legitimacy can derive from a variety of sources. In fifteenth-through eighteenth-century Europe, for example, monarchs ruled because their subjects accepted the doctrine of divine right, which is the idea that God had ordained that the royal family would rule. In Germany under Adolf Hitler, the legitimacy of the government was based on its promotion of German nationalism, which is the belief that the German people had special traits that set them apart from other people. And in communist countries such as the People's Republic of China, the legitimacy of the government rests on the public's acceptance of the principles of communism.

legitimacy
A self-imposed willingness of citizens to respect and obey the decisions of their government.

In the United States, as in all democracies, the legitimacy of the government is based on the consent of the governed—that is, the people. Because Americans choose their leaders in elections, they believe they can hold the government accountable for its actions. In theory, they can influence the work of the government by writing to their elected officials, donating money to an interest group, participating in a protest march, or engaging in a host of other activities. If the government fails to respond to their concerns, the people can vote to elect new officials. Thus, most Americans believe their government is legitimate because they believe it usually responds to their wishes. But even in democratic societies, the government's legitimacy can be called into question, or even lost, if the public comes to believe that its wishes are being ignored. That is why so many media pundits openly worried that the closeness of the 2000 presidential election would cause some Americans to doubt that George W. Bush was legitimately elected president.

If legitimacy provides one source of government authority, the other stems from the government's usual monopoly on the use of **coercive force** against the members of society. Through its police, judicial, and military institutions, a government can force its citizens to comply with its decisions and punish those who refuse to obey. For example, the government can arrest and jail criminals, force people to pay taxes, and deny people the right to enter or leave the country. Although many individuals or organizations in society may use force, as when a mugger robs someone or a drug gang shoots its rivals, typically no group or institution in society can successfully challenge the government's dominance in the use of force on a national scale.

coercive force
The ability of a government to compel its citizens to obey its decisions.

To succeed in managing conflict in society, a government needs to possess both legitimacy and coercive force. Legitimacy in the absence of the threat of coercion cannot ensure that people will obey the decisions of government. For example, many people would refuse to pay taxes if they knew the government was unable or unwilling to enforce the tax laws. Likewise, more people would be inclined to steal if they knew their crimes would go unpunished. Only the threat of penalties and imprisonment ensures that most people will comply with government directions.

By the same token, no government can endure for long if it possesses coercive force but lacks legitimacy. A government may be able to frighten its citizens into submission for a time, but eventually they will challenge its authority and demand a more legitimate basis for governing. One example of this challenge to authority was the collapse of the communist governments in Eastern Europe and the Soviet Union in the late 1980s and early 1990s. Their threats to use physical violence finally failed to compensate for their growing lack of legitimacy. Likewise, the system of apartheid, or white rule, in South Africa came to an end in the early 1990s because white South Africans finally recognized that they could not compel the obedience of non-white South Africans indefinitely. Thus, government must possess both legitimacy and coercive force to manage conflict in society successfully.

1-2 GOVERNMENT AS RULE MAKER

How does a government manage conflict and make choices about how society will function? The answer is by devising rules that structure how political decisions will be made and then by issuing rules that determine the winners and losers on specific issues. As we shall see time and time again in this book, the rules that a government adopts and follows are not neutral; rather, they create winners and losers by helping some groups and hurting others.

1-2a Structural Rules

structural rules
Rules that establish the organization, procedures, and powers of government.

The rules of government consist of two types: structural rules and policy rules. **Structural rules** establish the organization, procedures, and powers of government. They tell us how we are to choose government officials, what steps government officials must follow when they make policy decisions, and what actions government officials can and cannot take. In the United States, the most important structural rules come from the Constitution. But structural rules also stem from the constitutions of the fifty states, from the laws passed by Congress and the state legislatures, and from the decisions of both state and federal courts.

The 2000 presidential election illustrates the idea of a structural rule. How do we know when someone has been elected president? The answer lies in the Constitution. It clearly states that the president shall be the candidate who wins a majority of the votes in the electoral college. But what if no candidate receives a majority of the electoral college votes? That scenario is highly unlikely, but as we saw in 2000, not unthinkable. Should it happen, the Constitution says that the newly elected members of the House of Representatives must decide who will be the next president. The Constitution stipulates that the House must choose from among the three presidential candidates who won the most electoral votes, with the delegation from each state casting one vote. (Although most state delegations in the House consist of more than one member, the

Source: © United Features Syndicate, Inc.

Rules matter—they benefit some and disadvantage others.

Constitution says nothing about the rules representatives must follow in deciding how their state delegation will vote.)

Another way to make the idea of structural rules concrete is to think about how many terms presidents and members of Congress can serve. Ever since the Constitution was ratified in 1788, the structural rules of American government have allowed senators and representatives to serve as long as their constituents are willing to reelect them. The same was true until 1951 for the presidency, although presidents traditionally declined to serve for more than two terms. After Franklin Delano Roosevelt was elected president four times between 1932 and 1944, Congress passed and the states ratified a constitutional amendment barring anyone from being elected president more than twice (see Box 1–3). If congressional term limits ever become a reality in the future—attempts to do just that so far have failed—new structural rules will govern how long members can serve in Congress.

As the procedure for selecting presidents attests, the structural rules of American government can be quite complicated. Despite their occasional complexity, however, structural rules tell us how government is to be organized and operated, and they tell us what powers government can and cannot exercise. Because these structural rules exist, we know how to choose government officials, we know what rules government officials must follow when they decide public policy issues, and we know which actions government officials can and cannot take. In short, structural rules give government stability and continuity.

1-2b Policy Rules

The second type of government rule is the **policy rule**, which is simply the decision that a government institution reaches on a specific political question within its jurisdiction. For example, how

policy rule
A decision a government institution reaches on a specific political question within its jurisdiction.

POINT OF ORDER

Box 1–3 Presidential Term Limits: The Twenty-Second Amendment

George W. Bush's supporters cheered his 2004 reelection victory. They confidently proclaimed he had won a mandate to remake American politics. Bush, however, recognized that the opportunity created by his reelection would fade quickly because he could not run again in 2008. As he told top Republican donors, we have "two years, at least, until the next midterm. We have to move quickly, because after that I'll be quacking like a duck."

Source: © White House Photo by Eric Draper.

George W. Bush.

So why couldn't Bush run for a third term and thereby put off the prospect of becoming a lame duck? The answer lies in the Twenty-Second Amendment to the Constitution. It bars anyone from being elected president more than twice.

The decision to limit presidents to no more than two terms in office reversed the decision that the Founders made at the Constitutional Convention in 1787. After much debate, the Founders decided that presidents should serve four-year terms with no limits on how many terms they might serve. In deciding against term limits, many of the Founders agreed with George Washington that it made no sense at all

"in precluding ourselves from the services of any man who on some emergency shall be deemed universally most capable of serving the public."

Although the Constitution did not limit the number of terms a president might serve, the early presidents established a custom that no president should serve more than two terms. George Washington rejected suggestions that he seek a third term, telling the country in his Farewell Address that he preferred "the shade of retirement." Thomas Jefferson elevated Washington's pragmatic decision to the level of principle: "If some termination of the services of the Chief Magistrate be not fixed by the Constitution, or supplied by practice, his office, nominally four years, will in fact become for life." Although the two-term tradition was deeply rooted for more than 100 years, Congress often revisited the issue of presidential term limits. Between 1789 and 1947, members of Congress introduced 270 resolutions seeking to limit the president's eligibility for reelection.

The tradition of serving no more than two terms ended with the presidency of Franklin Delano Roosevelt (FDR). First elected in 1932 and then reelected in 1936, FDR was in his seventh year as president when World War II began in Europe. Faced with a perilous threat to American national interests, and despite substantial public support for the two-term tradition, he announced in July 1940 that he would seek a third term. Reelected by a wide margin (although smaller than his first two victories), he ran again in 1944 and won. Less than three months after his inauguration as president for the fourth time, FDR died.

The congressional elections of 1946 saw Republicans win control of Congress for the first time in fourteen years. The new majority, determined that no future president should serve more than two terms in office, passed a proposed constitutional amendment. It read:

No person shall be elected to the office of the President more than twice, and no person who has held the office of President, or acted as President, for more than two years of a term to which some other person was elected President shall be elected to the office of the President more than once.

Proponents of presidential term limits spoke eloquently of the need to protect the country from an unscrupulous president who would use his powers to secure repeated reelection to the detriment of the country's best interests. Thus, limiting the freedom of Americans to vote for whomever they wanted for president would in the long run prevent "autocracy" and result in "the destruction of the real freedom of the people."

Despite the claims of principle, Republicans passed the Twenty-Second Amendment largely because they wanted to inflict posthumous revenge on FDR. No public hearings were held on the proposed amendment, debate in the House lasted only two hours, and no Republican in either the House or the Senate voted against it. Moreover, when a motion was offered in the Senate to protect the American public from unscrupulous representatives and senators by limiting the terms of members of Congress as well, senators voted down the motion 82 to 1.

The Twenty-Second Amendment carries with it some irony. Of the four presidents barred from running for reelection since it came into force— Dwight Eisenhower, Ronald Reagan, Bill Clinton, and George W. Bush— three were Republicans.

Sources: Calvin C. Jillson, *Constitution Making: Conflict and Consensus in the Federal Convention of 1787* (New York: Agathon Press, 1988), 104–20; Sidney M. Milkis and Michael Nelson, *The American Presidency: Origins and Development*, 2nd ed. (Washington, D.C.: CQ Press, 1994), 303–5; Clinton Rossiter, *The American Presidency*, rev. ed. (New York: Mentor Books, 1960), 220–27; Ron Suskind, "Without a Doubt," *New York Times* (October 17, 2004): 44; Paul G. Willis and George L. Willis, "The Politics of the Twenty-Second Amendment," *Western Political Quarterly* 5 (September 1952): 469–82.

much money shall the government spend on defense? At what rate shall it tax incomes? By what means and to what extent shall the government act to improve the quality of the environment? Shall American citizens be allowed to travel to communist countries such as Cuba, North Korea, and Vietnam? The answer to each of these questions, and many more as well, constitutes a policy rule of government, or what we can call more simply a *policy*. (Throughout the remainder of the book, we will use the shorter term *policy* when referring to a policy rule. We are using the full term here because we want to emphasize that all government policies are rules that allocate costs and benefits among citizens.) All of a government's policy rules taken together constitute what we call *public policy*.

Unlike structural rules, policy rules generally do not spring from the Constitution or from the constitutions of the fifty states. Instead, the government makes policy rules whenever an institution of government decides a question about public policy. Thus, when Congress or a state legislature passes a law, when a president issues an executive order, when a government agency writes a new regulation, or when a state or federal court hands down a decision, another policy rule is created. As you might imagine, federal, state, and local governments in the United States produce tens of thousands of policy rules each year. Despite the large number of policy rules, each must be developed according to the relevant procedures called for by the structural rules of government. But policy rules, because they address specific issues at specific times, give government flexibility to meet society's changing desires and needs.

1-2c The Biased Character of Rules

Governments are responsible for devising structural and policy rules that will manage conflict in society. Yet rules are not neutral in their effect. They inevitably create winners and losers because, compared with other possible rules, they benefit the interests of some parties and harm the interests of others. The inescapable fact that different rules have different effects means that structural rules and policy rules are inherently biased. Of course, recognizing that all rules are biased does not mean that rules are bad or unfair or that they inevitably serve the interests of one group (say, the wealthy) over another (say, the poor). The point is that any rule, even one adopted for the best of reasons, inevitably will help some citizens and hurt others.

The biased character of rules applies to both structural and policy rules. To see the biased nature of structural rules, just recall the 2000 presidential election. If the Constitution stipulated that the winner of the popular vote won the presidency, Al Gore would have become president. Or consider the consequences that flow from the provision in the Constitution that "the Senate of the United States shall be composed of two Senators from each State." As a result of this structural rule, the 20 million people living in the eight Mountain states (Arizona, Colorado, Idaho, Montana, Nevada, New Mexico, Utah, and Wyoming) send sixteen senators to Washington, D.C. In contrast, the 37 million people living in California send only two senators to Washington, D.C. Because the people living in the Mountain states have Senate representation disproportionate to their share of the American population, they also wield disproportionate influence in Senate decisions, and as a result, over which laws are passed. If representation in the Senate were instead based on the size of each state's population, as is the case with the House of Representatives, people living in the Mountain states would see their representation in Congress shrink and, along with it, their influence over public policy. Thus, the structural rule that stipulates that two senators will represent each state benefits states with small populations and hurts those with large ones.

The fact that rules are not neutral explains why structural rules, as well as policy rules, often become the target of vociferous debate. One structural rule of American politics that is likely to get increased scrutiny in coming years as the foreign-born share of the American population grows involves who is eligible to be president. Jennifer Granholm, the two-term governor of Michigan, and Arnold Schwarzenegger, the two-term governor of California, would, under normal circumstances, be considered strong candidates for their party's presidential or vice presidential nomination. But neither Granholm nor Schwarzenegger is eligible to run for president or to be selected as a vice presidential nominee. Why? Because the Constitution stipulates that the president must be an American by birth. Granholm was born in Canada, and Schwarzenegger was born in Austria.

Source: © Underwood & Underwood/Corbis.

The structural rules of American politics have changed over the past 200 years. In 1920, for example, American women won the right to vote.

The biased character of rules also reveals a critical lesson about politics that we will return to time and again in the pages that follow: Changing either structural or policy rules can alter which groups win and which groups lose in a political conflict. The political history of the United States would look much different if the structural rules dictated that Congress can pass laws without submitting them to the president, that representation in the Senate is based on population, or that states could secede from the union as they saw fit. Likewise, the composition of the American military would look quite different today if the Defense Department's policy rules segregated African American and white soldiers and denied women the right to serve in the armed forces. In short, different rules benefit different groups in society. That is why groups compete with such great intensity over the decisions government makes.

1-2d The Changing Rules of Government

If the rules of government are inherently biased, they also are subject to great change. Indeed, the rules of American government have changed frequently, and often dramatically, over the past 200 years. It is a mistake to assume that today's policies and governmental arrangements resemble yesterday's and that tomorrow's will look much like those we have today. Governmental institutions, procedures, and policies are not handed down unchanged by past generations, and they are not etched in stone for future generations. A review of our nation's history reveals that change is the one constant of American politics.

Take, for example, the structural rules that determine who can vote in the United States. Although today virtually every American citizen over the age of eighteen is entitled to vote, this was not always the case. The Constitution originally stipulated that "the Electors in each State shall have the Qualifications requisite for Electors of the most numerous Branch of the State Legislature." Given the common practice of the time, this meant only white men over the age of twenty-one were allowed to vote. With the passage of the Fifteenth Amendment to the Constitution after the Civil War, the right to vote was extended to all male citizens over the age of twenty-one, regardless of race or color. In 1920, with the ratification of the Nineteenth Amendment, the right to vote was extended to all women over the age of twenty-one. And in 1971, with the ratification of the Twenty-Sixth Amendment, the right to vote was extended to all Americans from ages eighteen through twenty.

The rules of government change not by magic but because the American people and government officials make choices. When they make choices, by definition, they reject other alternatives. For example, the Constitution assigns the president important powers and responsibilities because a little more than 200 years ago some delegates to the Constitutional Convention sought to create an independent presidency. If those delegates had been less persuasive and less adept at manipulating the rules of parliamentary debate in their favor, the office of the presidency might look quite different today.

Their opponents wanted to fill the office of the president with a committee of presidents, each elected by Congress, and without the power to appoint judges and make foreign treaties.[8] Thus, governmental institutions, procedures, and policies that might appear inevitable in hindsight turn out on closer examination to be only one of a number of possible outcomes.

1-3 PUTTING IT ALL TOGETHER: CONTEXT, PARTICIPANTS, INSTITUTIONS, AND PROCESSES

The objective of *Dynamics of Democracy* is to describe and explain how the rules of politics operate in the United States. Although we will talk from time to time about state and local government, our focus is primarily on the rules that govern the operation of our national government, or as it is more commonly called, the federal government. To accomplish our goal of explaining how the rules of American politics operate, we have divided the chapters that follow into four distinct categories: the context of American politics, the participants in American politics, the institutions of American politics, and the policy process in American politics.

1-3a The Context of American Politics

In Part 1, we examine the context of American politics. We begin in Chapter 2 by discussing the origins of the Constitution and the reasoning behind the basic structural rules that define the American political system. Here, we explore issues such as the division of power among the legislative, executive, and judicial branches of government and the federal relationship between the national and state governments. We continue in Chapter 3 by describing the social context of American politics—that is, the people who make up our nation. We profile the changing demographic and social characteristics of the United States so that you can better understand what sorts of political conflicts arise and what sorts of demands people make on the government. In Chapter 4, we review the structural rules that specify the civil liberties of the American people. Although the words in the Constitution's Bill of Rights—which set forth many of the basic rules about civil liberties—have not changed since their adoption, their interpretation has changed a good deal. We conclude our discussion of the context of American politics in Chapter 5 by examining the civil rights movement and the structural rules that specify the civil rights of the American people. We carefully trace the evolving nature of civil rights over the course of our nation's history.

1-3b Individuals and Groups in American Politics

Part 2 of *Dynamics of Democracy* explores the "input" side of American politics, the individuals and groups that place demands on government and influence its decisions. We begin in Chapter 6 with a discussion of public opinion—what people want from government, why they want it, and how their opinions and desires fit together to form ideologies. We continue our focus on individuals in Chapter 7 by examining individual political participation. The act of voting is of special importance, so we discuss who does or does not vote and why, and we analyze how voters make up their minds once they step into the voting booth. We also consider other forms of participation, such as writing letters to members of Congress and joining marches to protest government policy.

In Chapters 8, 9, and 10, we shift our focus from individuals to groups as we examine the political roles the news media, political parties, and interest groups play. All three of these groups act as intermediaries in American politics; they help people to make demands on the government, and they help the government to explain itself to the people. Chapter 8 examines the role of the media, the principal source of information about government and politics for most people. We look at the relationship between the media and the government, and we discuss how a robust media is essential to a healthy democracy. In Chapters 9 and 10, we discuss the history and current behavior of political parties and interest groups—the two primary forms of organized mass political participation in the United States. In each case, we explain how people use these groups to influence the government, and we explore the limits each group faces on its ability to shape government policy.

1-3c The Institutions of American Politics

After setting the context for American national government and describing the individuals and groups who seek to influence the government, *Dynamics of Democracy* turns in Part 3 to the core institutions of the federal government: Congress, the presidency, the bureaucracy, and the courts. These institutions handle the "output" side of the system—they make the decisions, or policy rules, of the federal government.

We begin in Chapter 11 with what has been called the first branch of government—Congress. We describe the institution, its history, and its policy-making processes. We also discuss congressional elections because the unique aspects of these elections strongly influence how members of Congress behave once they are in office. We move on to the presidency in Chapter 12, discussing its historical development and the ways in which the Constitution and the actions of past presidents have defined the nature of the office. We examine the organization, operation, powers, and functions of the modern presidency. In this chapter, we also discuss how the United States chooses its presidents because changes in the rules governing presidential selection have significantly affected how presidents relate to the rest of government. Throughout both Chapters 11 and 12, we devote special attention to the way Congress and the president respond to the pressures the American people, the news media, political parties, and interest groups place on them.

In Chapter 13, we turn to a key set of government officials who are not elected—the bureaucrats in the executive branch of government. Although government agencies are sometimes considered politically neutral, we show that because part of their job is to make rules and to resolve conflicts, they are inherently political institutions. We conclude our discussion of the institutions of the federal government in Chapter 14 by examining the court system in the United States. We both describe the judicial system and explain the unique role the courts play as an undemocratic institution operating within a larger democratic political system.

1-3d The Policy Process in American Politics

Part 4 of *Dynamics of Democracy* examines different processes the national government is involved in and some of the policies it produces. We begin in Chapter 15 by discussing state governments, the roles they play in domestic policy formation, and the way they relate to the federal government. In Chapter 16, we turn to the federal budget process—a process that has become central to American politics in recent years. We examine the debates over tax and spending policy, and we explain how the rules of the budgetary process operate. In Chapter 17, we examine the federal government's role in domestic policy. We examine how the federal government has become responsible for managing the economy, regulating the business practices of private firms, and providing a social safety net for the American people. We complete our tour of American politics in Chapter 18 with a look at foreign policy. After briefly reviewing the history of American foreign policy, we discuss how foreign policy decisions are made in the United States, as well as how the distribution of political power pertaining to foreign policy differs from what we are accustomed to seeing in domestic policy.

SUMMARY

In this chapter, we have learned two lessons about American politics and government: Politics arises from conflict, and the rules of government help determine the winners and losers in particular conflicts. The 2000 presidential election illustrates both lessons. When the polls finally closed in Florida on Election Day, George W. Bush had a slender lead over Al Gore. Considerable uncertainty surrounded the accuracy of the vote, and both sides argued that if the rules were applied fairly, their man would win. The debate over Florida's vote eventually wound up in the courts. In the end, the U.S. Supreme Court handed down a decision that benefited Bush.

Throughout the next seventeen chapters, we try to emphasize that the rules and institutions of government provide society with a way to cope with its internal conflicts. Moreover, because the

rules help determine who wins and who loses, the rules themselves often become the subject of intense political conflict.
Indeed, the rules—and government itself—are continually undergoing dynamic change. These three factors—conflict, rules, and
change—underlie the dynamics of democracy.

KEY TERMS

coercive force   material scarcity

electoral college   policy rule

legitimacy   structural rules

READINGS FOR FURTHER STUDY

Dahl, Robert A., and Bruce Stinebricker. *Modern Political Analysis*, 6th ed. (Englewood Cliffs, NJ: Prentice-Hall, 2003). Dahl,
whom many consider the most influential political scientist of
the past fifty years, offers a concise introduction to the fundamental concepts of political science.

Dionne, E. J., Jr., and William Kristol, eds. *Bush v. Gore: The Court
Cases and the Commentary* (Washington, D.C.: Brookings,
2001). A collection of court rulings and political commentary
on the historic 2000 presidential election.

Lasswell, Harold. *Politics: Who Gets What, When, How* (New
York: Whittlesey House, 1936). A classic study of the nature of
politics by a scholar who helped found the modern discipline
of political science.

Morris, Roy, Jr. *Fraud of the Century: Rutherford B. Hayes,
Samuel Tilden, and the Stolen Election of 1876* (New York:
Simon & Schuster, 2003). An entertaining and informative
account of the partisan machinations surrounding the disputed
1876 presidential election.

Safire, William. *Safire's Political Dictionary* (New York: Oxford
University Press, 2008). A longtime columnist for the *New
York Times* provides an engaging tour of the American politi-
cal lexicon, with entries ranging from Abolitionist to Zulu.

Schattschneider, E. E. *The Semi-Sovereign People* (New York:
Holt, 1960). A classic study that provides simple yet powerful
concepts for understanding politics in the United States.

Tocqueville, Alexis de. *Democracy in America*, ed. J. P. Mayer
(New York: Anchor Books, 1969). One of the most insightful
studies ever made of American democracy, written by a
French aristocrat who traveled around the United States in
the 1830s.

Zelden, Charles L. *Bush v. Gore: Exposing the Hidden Crisis in
American Democracy* (Lawrence: University of Kansas Press,
2008). A historian argues that *Bush v. Gore* exposed major
flaws in our electoral system that remain with us today.

REVIEW QUESTIONS

1. What did the Supreme Court rule on state laws limiting service in Congress?
   a. Nothing.
   b. The justices ruled that such laws were constitutional.
   c. The justices ruled that such laws were unconstitutional.
   d. The justices called for a constitutional convention to settle the term limits dispute.

2. What does the fight over term limits illustrate?
   a. Politics arises from conflict.
   b. The rules of government help determine who wins political battles.
   c. Both a and b.
   d. Public opinion is the decisive factor in all congressional debates.

3. Conflict is an inherent feature of all societies because
   a. of the existence of material scarcity.
   b. people disagree over core values.
   c. there are rich and poor people.
   d. all of the above.

4. Which of the following is the ultimate authority in the United States?
   a. the president
   b. the Internal Revenue Service
   c. Congress
   d. the people

5. To succeed at managing conflict, a government needs
   a. a strong army.
   b. a popular leader.
   c. legitimacy and coercive force.
   d. favorable public opinion ratings and low taxes.

6. Where do we find the most important structural rules in the United States?
   a. the Declaration of Independence
   b. the U.S. Constitution
   c. the laws passed by Congress
   d. rulings handed down by the Supreme Court

7. Rules create
   a. winners and losers.
   b. equality for all.
   c. a society with little or no conflict.
   d. fair representation in the U.S. Congress.

8. In the United States, presidents are elected by
   a. the electoral college.
   b. the popular vote.
   c. the Senate.
   d. the state legislatures.

9. People who participate in politics are all motivated by
   a. conflict.
   b. greed.
   c. the desire to serve the greater public interest.
   d. the desire to become powerful politicians.

NOTES

1. David Gonzalez, "Counting the Vote: The Race Factor," *New York Times*, November 11, 2000; Mireya Navarro and Somini Sengupta, "Contesting the Vote: Black Voters," *New York Times*, November 30, 2000. On how race influenced the vote outside Florida, see John Mintz and Dan Keating, "A Racial Gap in Voided Votes," *Washington Post*, December 27, 2000.
2. Quoted in Dan Balz and Charles Lane, "In Blow to Gore, Court Overturns Recounts," *Washington Post*, December 13, 2000.
3. Ibid.
4. Quoted in Dan Balz, "Gore Concedes; Bush Reaches Out," *Washington Post*, December 14, 2000.
5. Ibid.
6. David Easton, *The Political System: An Inquiry into the State of Political Science*, 2nd ed. (New York: Knopf, 1971); Harold Lasswell, *Politics: Who Gets What, When, How* (New York: Whittlesey House, 1936).
7. Robert A. Dahl, *Modern Political Analysis*, 2nd ed. (Englewood Cliffs, NJ: Prentice-Hall, 1970).
8. Gregor Reinhard, "The Origins of the Presidency," in *The American Presidency: A Policy Perspective from Readings and Documents*, ed. David C. Kozak and Kenneth N. Ciboski (Chicago: Nelson-Hall, 1985), 1–13.

2

The Constitution

CHAPTER OUTLINE

In 2001, the United States went to war in Afghanistan to topple the Taliban government and seek the capture of Osama bin Laden and other leaders of Al Qaeda. During that war, the American military detained hundreds of individuals who it claimed fought against the United States. The George W. Bush administration defined many of these individuals as "unlawful enemy combatants" and sent them to a detention center at the military base in Guantanamo Bay, Cuba. President Bush claimed that his authority as commander in chief and the absence of federal court jurisdiction over the base empowered him to hold those detainees indefinitely without trial. This claim denied the detainees the protection of the Constitution's right of habeas corpus, which is an individual's right to be charged with a crime in court or released from detention.

When the Supreme Court ruled that the detainees possessed some constitutional protections, Congress bolstered the President's authority with the Military Commissions Act of 2006. It held that the detainees had no habeas corpus rights and could appeal only their classification as enemy combatants. Thus, the two democratically elected branches of government stood united in the claim that the president had the authority to hold these individuals indefinitely, so long as a court upheld their status as enemy combatants. Because Congress is often described as "the people's branch," and presidents are traditionally granted great leeway in conducting foreign and military policy, the matter appeared to be settled.

However, lawyers for the detainees filed claims before the Supreme Court. Despite the assertions of authority by Congress and the president, in 2008 the Court ruled that the detainees did possess some right of habeas corpus and that the military tribunals' law did not satisfy those protections. As a result, many observers expected a "flood of cases" into the federal court system as the detainees sought the protections of a court hearing.[1]

This confrontation between the democratically elected branches of government and the Supreme Court illustrates the importance of the Constitution as it defines the powers and roles of the three branches. As this case illustrates, the Constitution empowers each branch; yet at the same time, it constrains each branch. In fundamentally important ways, the Constitution provides the rules that help determine who wins and who loses in a wide variety of such conflicts. Therefore, to understand government in the United States, we must first know something about the Constitution, the rules it sets forth, and how those rules are interpreted in practice.

We begin by considering why the Founders wrote the document as they did. As we shall see, the Constitution—and thus the structure of this country's government—was shaped by both the political experiences and objectives of those who wrote it and by the underlying philosophical values they held. We will also discuss the core provisions of the Constitution: the rules that govern the operation of Congress, the presidency, and the judiciary, as well as the relations between the federal and state governments. We will show how these rules have affected the way politics operates in the United States. Finally, we will review the changing relationship between the federal and state governments to illustrate how the interpretation of the Constitution changes over time and how its rules have shaped our nation's history.

2-1 THE CONSTITUTION AS A REFLECTION OF POLITICAL CONFLICT

The Constitution reflects the political values and choices of the people who wrote it. To understand why, we need to recognize that the delegates to the Constitutional Convention, like politicians of today, represented states with competing political interests. The years as English colonies left each of the thirteen states jealously protective of its independence and fearful of conceding power to a national government. Previous efforts "to build one government out of thirteen" had foundered because individual states refused to surrender supreme power over events within their borders.[2] The need to reconcile the states' competing political interests profoundly affected the rules the Founders set down in the Constitution. As a result, our constitutional rules of government are rooted not only in high-minded philosophical concepts such as democracy and liberty, but also in the political maneuverings of eighteenth-century politicians.

2-1a The Colonial Experience

The relationship between England and the colonies shaped the political outlook of the Founders. England had created each of the original thirteen colonies, and the King of England appointed most colonial governors to govern on his behalf. Because the governors owed their jobs to the king, they put England's interests ahead of the interests of the colonists. Nonetheless, most of the colonies had relatively powerful legislatures. For almost a century and a half, these elected bodies exercised considerable authority, and many colonists grew accustomed to substantial independence from England.

This freedom began to diminish in the middle of the eighteenth century. Under the leadership of King George III, England began to exert more direct control over the colonies. During the 1760s, England imposed a number of taxes on the colonies to help pay for the French and Indian War. The colonists deeply resented the taxes but quickly discovered that the English government felt no obligation to heed the colonial legislatures' requests that the taxes be repealed. The fact that the colonists had no voice in the decisions to impose the taxes they were required to pay gave rise to the famous claim of "no taxation without representation."

As a result of the lack of representation in decision-making that affected their lives, many colonists became disillusioned with the English government. To use the terms introduced in Chapter 1, the English government was losing *legitimacy* in the eyes of the colonists. As more and more colonists began to regard the English government as illegitimate, England increasingly relied on *coercive force* to compel the colonies to obey. The resulting conflicts culminated, of course, in the American Revolutionary War, which, as one eminent historian has observed, "was not fought to *obtain* freedom, but to *preserve* the liberties that Americans already had as colonials."[3] With the defeat of the English at Yorktown in 1781 and the signing of the Treaty of Paris in 1783, the American colonies achieved their independence.

The leaders of the newly independent states drew two important lessons from their years under English rule. The first was that a political system that put political power in the hands of state government would better guarantee liberty and representation than a system that concentrated power in a national government. Having thrown off what they viewed as English tyranny, the leaders of the newly independent colonies wanted nothing to do with another distant and unresponsive national government. The fact that many colonists had a strong sense of identity and loyalty to their own states reinforced their preference for state government. They saw themselves not as Britons or Americans, but as Pennsylvanians, Virginians, and New Yorkers. The combination of a negative experience with a powerful national government and a strong identification with their individual states led the colonists to place their confidence in governments at the state rather than national level.

The second important lesson the leaders of the newly independent colonies drew from their colonial experience was that a new national government should have a strong legislature but not a strong executive leader. The years under English rule left many colonists with a deep distrust of executive authority. The new states would not give leaders of the new nation the powers that King George had. At the same time, the leaders of the newly independent states had an abiding respect for elected legislatures. Many had served in the colonial legislatures, which had forcefully expressed the views of the colonies in their disputes with the colonial governors and the king. In sum, the colonial era "ended with the belief prevalent that 'the executive magistry' was the natural enemy, the legislative assembly the natural friend of liberty."[4]

2-1b The Articles of Confederation

Articles of Confederation

The document written by the states following their declaration of independence from England and adopted in 1781. It established a system of strong states and a weak national government with a legislative branch but no separate executive or judicial branches and few powers beyond the sphere of foreign relations.

The preference the leaders of the newly independent colonies had for strong state government and their aversion to creating a powerful national executive government guided the writing of the **Articles of Confederation**, which represented the first attempt to create a political system for the newly independent country. Written in 1777 and ratified in 1781, the Articles of Confederation contained the rules that governed our nation until the Constitution was adopted in 1789.

Because the colonial experience left many colonists with a deep distrust of powerful national government, the authors of the

Articles of Confederation chose to create a *confederal government.* In this form of government, the states retain their sovereignty, that is, supreme power over events within their borders. In turn, the national government exercises only those powers the states choose to give it. The one major task the state governments gave the national government under the Articles of Confederation was responsibility for managing most of the country's foreign relations. Beyond this, however, the national government received few powers. For example, it was not allowed to impose taxes or regulate economic relations among the states or between individual states and foreign countries. Moreover, to prevent any possible tyranny by the national government, the Articles of Confederation provided for no executive branch. Instead, all the powers of the national government were vested in Congress. As a result of the decision to erect a confederal government lacking an executive branch, the Articles of Confederation established a weak national government.

The confederal government the Articles of Confederation created quickly proved inadequate to meet the needs of the new country. The national government could not represent itself effectively in foreign affairs because Congress was unable to respond quickly and decisively to other governments. Individual states negotiated their own trading relationships with Europe, which undermined efforts to construct a national economic policy. States sought to protect their own industries by imposing tariffs (or taxes) on goods from other states, which in turn hurt economic growth throughout the country. Wealthy citizens complained when state legislatures passed laws that enhanced the interests of the working and debtor classes at the expense of the wealthy.

Several efforts were made to revise the Articles of Confederation. The most important was the Annapolis Convention, held in 1786, which produced a resolution calling for another convention in Philadelphia to discuss proposed revisions. The call for another convention took on special urgency when farmers in western Massachusetts took up arms in what became known as **Shays' Rebellion** to protest the state's economic policies. The governor of Massachusetts asked the national government for help in putting down the revolt, but none came. Massachusetts eventually contained the revolt, but Shays' Rebellion heightened concerns that the national government could not govern effectively. In light of growing dissatisfaction with the status quo, delegates from every state but Rhode Island met in Philadelphia in the summer of 1787. The convention began as a discussion of how best to revise the Articles of Confederation, but it quickly became the forum for drafting what would become the U.S. Constitution.

Shays' Rebellion

A protest, staged by small farmers from western Massachusetts and led by Daniel Shays, an officer in the American Revolutionary War, against the state's taxes and policy of foreclosing on debtor farmers.

2-1c The Politics of the Constitutional Convention

The colonial experience led many Americans to prefer a weak, decentralized national government and to place considerable political power in the state legislatures. But a few years' experience with the Articles of Confederation showed that the country needed a national government that could act on behalf of the entire nation and settle disputes between the states. Those two lessons came to the forefront as the Founders met in Philadelphia in 1787 to discuss revisions in the Articles of Confederation. When James Madison and Edmund Randolph immediately proposed, on behalf of the Virginia delegation, an entirely new plan of government, the convention quickly abandoned the Articles of Confederation and began to write a new constitution.

How should we understand the weeks of debate that ultimately produced the Constitution? A review of the proceedings shows that the delegates held strong beliefs about the principles that should form the basis of a new government. We would be greatly mistaken, however, to think of the writing of the Constitution as simply the process of great minds debating the merits of various forms of government. The delegates to the Constitutional Convention were self-interested politicians who understood that the decisions they made would have enormous consequences. Some of them were even prepared to let the Convention fail if delegates could not reach acceptable compromises.[5] Yet in the end, the delegates produced a document that they accepted as an improvement over the Articles of Confederation.

What were some of the critical political disputes at the Constitutional Convention? Three issues were especially divisive: how to allocate representation in the new Congress, how to deal with the question of slavery, and how to define the powers of the new office of the presidency. The Founders managed to resolve these disputes through a mix of compromise and calculated ambiguity. Let's consider each dispute in turn.

Representation in the National Legislature

The plan that Madison and Randolph introduced is known as the **Virginia Plan**. The main elements of the plan appear in Table 2–1. As originally proposed, it called for dividing the powers of government among three separate branches: a legislative branch for making laws; an executive branch for enforcing laws; and a judicial branch for interpreting laws. The Virginia Plan called for the national legislature to consist of two houses. Seats in each house would be allocated among the states in proportion to each state's population. The voters would directly elect the members of the lower chamber, and the lower chamber would in turn elect the members of the upper chamber from a slate of nominees each state legislature would submit. The Virginia Plan had a simple appeal: Every voter in the United States would be represented equally in the national legislature. What could be fairer?

As it turned out, many delegates thought the Virginia Plan was unfair. In what became known as the **New Jersey Plan**, whose main elements also appear in Table 2–1, critics of the Virginia Plan proposed that rather than representing each *citizen* equally, the new national legislature should represent each *state* equally. Proponents of the New Jersey Plan argued for treating states equally

Virginia Plan

A plan for a new national government that the Virginia delegation proposed at the Constitutional Convention in 1787. It called for a strong, essentially unitary national government, with separate executive and judicial branches, and a two-house legislative branch with representation based on each state's population.

New Jersey Plan

A plan for a new national government that the New Jersey delegation proposed at the Constitutional Convention in 1787. Its key feature consisted of giving each state equal representation in the national legislature, regardless of its population.

The Constitutional Convention considered substantially different plans for structuring the new government.			
Characteristic	**Virginia Plan**	**New Jersey Plan**	**Constitution**
Congress	Two houses	One house	Two houses
Representation in Congress	Both houses based on population	Equal representation for each state	One house based on population; other house two seats per state
Decision rule	Simple majority	Extraordinary majority	Concurrent majority
Executive	Single, elected by Congress	More than one person	Single, elected by electoral college
Removal of executive	By Congress	By a majority of states	By Congress
Courts	National judiciary, elected by Congress	Judiciary, appointed by executive to hear appeals on violations of national laws in state courts	National judiciary, nominated by president and confirmed by Senate
Ratification	By the people	By the states	By state conventions
State laws	Congress can override	National supremacy	National supremacy

Table 2–1   The Virginia Plan, the New Jersey Plan, and the Constitution

on the grounds of both precedent and principle. In terms of precedent, they argued that the states were equally represented in the national legislature under the Articles of Confederation. As for principle, proponents of the New Jersey Plan pointed out that the states, and not the people, were writing and ratifying the new government, so the states should have equal voices in the legislature.

Although both sides in the debate over the Virginia and New Jersey Plans invoked principle, the debate involved much more than simply deciding which principle held greater merit. Also at stake was the political power some states would gain and some would lose under the new national government. The more populous states such as Massachusetts, Pennsylvania, and Virginia favored the Virginia Plan because it would give them the most seats in the new Congress. Conversely, less populous states such as New Jersey, Connecticut, and Delaware favored the "one state-one vote" principle embodied in the New Jersey Plan because it preserved their political power. The small states feared that if representation in the new national government were based solely on population, their interests would become secondary to those of the more populous states. The small states felt strongly about this issue and threatened to leave the convention if it did not address their concerns.

The dispute between large and small states was resolved by the **Connecticut Compromise** (also known as the Great Compromise), which combined elements of both the Virginia and New Jersey Plans and formed the basis for the Constitution (see Table 2–1). In the House of Representatives, seats would be allocated on the basis of population, thereby satisfying the concerns of the more populous states. In contrast, in the Senate, two seats would be allocated to each state, thereby satisfying

Connecticut Compromise

A plan the Connecticut delegation proposed at the Constitutional Convention. This plan sought to manage the dispute between large- and small-population states by creating a two-house legislature with representation in one house based on population and representation in the second house set at two seats per state.

the concerns of the less populous states. The Connecticut Compromise also required that both the House of Representatives and the Senate had to pass a bill before it could become law. This provision gave both large and small states further assurance that the new Congress would not disregard their interests. Thus, in the end, both large and small states gained some, but not all, of what they had wanted.

Slavery and the Three-Fifths Compromise

The second divisive issue the delegates at the Constitutional Convention faced was how the new government should deal with the question of slavery. This time, geography rather than population divided the states. Southern delegates staunchly defended slavery, whereas northern delegates favored limiting and eventually terminating the practice. Southern delegates made it clear they would desert the convention rather than accept rules that would outlaw slavery.

The debate over slavery quickly became tied to the debate over representation. Southern delegates recognized that because the northern states outnumbered the southern states, and because more white people lived in the North than the South, northern states would have more representation in Congress, which might enable them to limit or even outlaw slavery. Southern delegates could not simply create new states to strengthen the South's position in the Senate, so they proposed counting slaves as part of a state's population when seats were allocated in the House of Representatives. Northern delegates, however, opposed counting people that Southerners themselves considered property. In a clear example of compromising to accomplish a larger purpose, the northern states agreed to count each slave as three-fifths of a person. The Constitution also extended other protections to slave owners. Article I prevented the government from ending the importation of slaves until 1808, and Article IV required that the states respect the rights of slave owners from other states by returning escaped slaves to their masters.

Northern delegates found the three-fifths compromise easier to accept when southern delegates agreed that slaves would also be counted on a three-fifths basis if the national government imposed a per capita tax on each state. Under such a tax system, states with larger populations would carry a higher tax burden than smaller states. Southern states were willing to pay higher taxes in return for the political advantage of inflating the size of their populations.

Defining the Powers of the President

In addition to struggling with the issues of representation and slavery, the Founders struggled with the question of how much power to give the president of the new national government, or what is more commonly called the federal government. The dismal experience with the Articles of Confederation convinced the Founders that they needed to create an executive branch of government

Slavery was a recurring source of conflict in the new nation. Northern and southern delegates clashed at the Constitutional Convention over whether to count slaves as part of the population when allocating seats in the House of Representatives. The contending factions sidestepped the issue by counting each slave as three-fifths of a person.

headed by a president. The delegates agreed that the president should have the power to veto legislation Congress had passed, as well as powers to appoint officials in the executive branch, to negotiate treaties on behalf of the United States, and to grant pardons. Beyond this point, however, the delegates disagreed. Some wanted to bestow substantial powers on the president, whereas others feared that creating a powerful presidency would promote tyranny.

Although the Founders disagreed on the powers to be given to the presidency, they all believed its first occupant would be George Washington. Widely admired and trusted, Washington was expected to serve with integrity and balance. Because of their immense respect for Washington, the Founders agreed to finesse their differences over the presidency by being ambiguous about the precise boundaries of presidential power; thus, the Constitution discusses the powers of the presidency in fairly vague terms. The Founders were willing to use ambiguity to settle their differences because they trusted President Washington to give acceptable concrete meaning to the abstract language of the Constitution.

To see how reluctant the Founders were to define the powers of the presidency, compare Articles I and II of the Constitution. Article I lays out the structure, operation, and powers of Congress. It begins: "All legislative Powers *herein granted* shall be vested in a Congress of the United States" (emphasis added). The remainder of Article I enumerates the many powers of Congress. Article II of the Constitution lays out the structure, operation, and powers of the presidency, but it looks quite different from Article I. It begins with the simple statement: "The executive Power shall be vested in a President of the United States of America." Nothing in Article

II defines what is meant by the term *executive power,* and Article II avoids enumerating the powers of the presidency as Article I does for Congress.

The Founders resorted to ambiguity because it enabled them to disguise their differences on the question of presidential power. But as is true, any time people resort to ambiguity to mask their differences, the underlying conflict remains. In the case of the Constitution, the Founders' failure to define the precise limits of presidential power sowed the seeds of much future conflict. For more than 200 years, presidents and congresses have struggled to define the proper limits of presidential power on issues ranging from who can send U.S. troops into combat to when the president can disregard the directives of Congress. Historically, presidents argue for expansive readings of their constitutional powers, whereas members of Congress usually prefer restrictive interpretations.

As the debates over representation, slavery, and the powers of the presidency all show, both principle and self-interest greatly influenced the content of the Constitution. By the end of the summer of 1787, after weeks of debate, compromise, and appeals to ambiguity, the Constitutional Convention approved the final draft of the Constitution. The Constitutional Convention had ended, but the struggle to create a new federal government had just begun because the states had to ratify, or approve, the Constitution before it could replace the Articles of Confederation.

2-1d The Politics of Ratification

The fight to ratify the Constitution pitted two groups against each other. People who supported ratification, known as **Federalists**, had as their most vocal leaders James Madison and Alexander Hamilton. Federalists argued that the new Constitution was needed to remedy the problems the new nation had experienced under the Articles of Confederation. People who opposed ratification, including such leading figures in the American Revolution as Samuel Adams and Patrick Henry, were known as **Antifederalists** (see Box 2–1). Fearful that the Constitution gave too much power to the national government, Antifederalists denounced the document as a "political monster," a "*Colossus of Despotism,*" and the "most daring attempt to establish a despotic aristocracy among freemen, that the world has ever witnessed."[6] Because the Antifederalists were well represented in the state legislatures, the Federalists took two steps to increase the chances of ratification: They wrote rules of ratification that favored the supporters of the Constitution, and they sought to undercut support for the Antifederalists by agreeing to amend the Constitution to include a specific list of guarantees for individual rights.

The Rules for Ratification

For the Constitution to replace the Articles of Confederation, the states first had to give their approval. But who in each state had the authority to approve or reject the Constitution? And how many states would need to ratify the Constitution before it could

Federalists
The label describing those who supported adoption of the Constitution. They believed in the need for a national government stronger than the one provided under the Articles of Confederation.

Antifederalists
The label describing those who opposed adoption of the Constitution. While opponents gave a variety of reasons for rejecting the Constitution, their main concern was that a strong national government would jeopardize individual rights.

The People behind the Rules

Box 2–1   Antifederalists versus Federalists: Patrick Henry and James Madison

The success the American political system has enjoyed for more than two centuries makes the wisdom of the Constitution and its authors seem obvious. Yet when it was written, the Constitution was a controversial document that divided the American people. The leading voices in the Antifederalist and Federalist camps included two of the most important political figures in eighteenth-century America: Patrick Henry and James Madison.

PATRICK HENRY

Henry was born in Virginia in 1736. First as a lawyer and then as a member of Virginia's colonial legislature, Henry made a name for himself as a brilliant orator. He frequently used his oratorical gifts to criticize English rule. By the mid-1770s, Henry had become convinced that the colonies had no choice but to rebel against England. In a speech in 1775, he urged his fellow Virginians to arm the state militia for the inevitable fight against the English. Henry ended the speech with a line that galvanized his compatriots and that remains well known to American schoolchildren more than two centuries later: "I know not what course others may take, but as for me, give me liberty or give me death."

During the American Revolutionary War, Henry served three one-year terms as the governor of Virginia. In 1786, he was selected as a delegate to what would become the Constitutional Convention. However, he declined the offer to go to Philadelphia. When the Convention produced a new political blueprint for the United States, Henry became a leading Antifederalist. He denounced the Constitution for reasons involving both political philosophy and practical politics. He believed the document was grievously flawed because it failed to guarantee the rights of either states or individuals, and he worried that in the new political system the northern states would cede navigation rights on the lower Mississippi to Spain.

(Navigation on the lower reaches of the Mississippi was an issue of great concern to Americans then living on the Western frontier.)

Although Henry opposed ratification of the Constitution, he is largely responsible for the passage of the Bill of Rights. To blunt his criticisms and those of other Antifederalists, the Federalists promised to attach a list of individual rights and liberties to the Constitution once the new Congress met. When the states ratified the Constitution, Henry turned his energies toward seeing that the Federalists kept their promise. With the eventual adoption of the Bill of Rights, Henry dropped his opposition to the new federal government.

Despite Henry's efforts to block ratification of the Constitution, he retained the respect of Federalist leaders. George Washington offered to appoint him as secretary of state or as chief justice of the Supreme Court. He declined both offers, citing poor health and family duties. Henry gave his last public speech during an election campaign in 1799 for a seat in the Virginia state legislature. The topic of his speech: a call for American unity.

JAMES MADISON

Like Henry, Madison was a son of Virginia. Born in 1751, he was elected to Virginia's Revolutionary Convention at the age of twenty-five. There he helped to draft legislation that guaranteed religious freedom to all Virginians, as well as legislation that effectively abolished Virginia's state church. Madison ran for reelection to what had become the Virginia state legislature, but he was defeated when he refused to follow the customary practice of wooing voters with free whiskey.

In 1780, Madison became one of Virginia's delegates to the Continental Congress. He soon established himself as a leading proponent of a strong national government. Following the passage of the Articles of

Confederation, which concentrated power in the hands of the states, Madison searched unsuccessfully for ways to strengthen the national government. In 1784, he rejoined the Virginia state legislature, where, among other things, he helped defeat a bill sponsored by Henry that would have directed the state of Virginia to provide financial support to "teachers of the Christian religion."

Despite his return to Virginia, Madison remained deeply involved in national affairs. When the states refused to cede power to the national government despite the obvious failings of the Articles of Confederation, he helped lead the calls for holding the Annapolis Convention and, eventually, the Constitutional Convention. In Philadelphia, Virginia Governor Edmund Randolph introduced Madison's vision of a new political system for the thirteen states. Although the Connecticut Compromise and other changes modified the Virginia Plan in many of its particulars, Madison, more than anyone else, deserves the title of architect of the Constitution.

Madison continued his efforts on behalf of the Constitution once the Constitutional Convention adjourned. When ratification appeared in doubt in New York, he joined with Alexander Hamilton and John Jay to write the *Federalist Papers.* (Madison wrote twenty-nine of the eighty-five essays in the series.) He also played a key role in convincing the Virginia state convention to ratify the Constitution, despite Henry's impassioned pleas to reject it. Madison subsequently won election to the first Congress, and he used his seat in the House of Representatives to push passage of the Bill of Rights. He later served as secretary of state under Thomas Jefferson and then as president of the United States from 1809 to 1817.

Source: Robert Douthat Meade, *Patrick Henry: Practical Revolutionary* (Philadelphia: J. B. Lippincott, 1969); Ralph Ketcham, *James Madison: A Biography* (New York: Macmillan, 1971).

take effect? The Founders answered these two questions in Article VII of the Constitution: "The Ratification of the Conventions of nine States, shall be sufficient for the Establishment of this Constitution between the States so ratifying the Same."

The Founders chose to make the Constitution subject to ratification by conventions in nine states because this was the one rule that was both politically acceptable and likely to lead to ratification.[7] The Founders could have put the Constitution to a vote among the state legislatures, but many Antifederalists served as state legislators. Thus, to minimize any organizational advantage the Antifederalists might have, the Founders opted to rely on special state conventions. (This decision had some precedent. In 1780, Massachusetts had put its new constitution to the vote of a special state convention rather than to a vote of the state legislature.) Because they were already well organized and the Antifederalists were not, the Federalists calculated that they could gain the upper hand in the state conventions. At the same time, the reliance on state conventions made the Constitution seem more democratic; the people of each state would elect delegates to the conventions.

Like the decision to make the Constitution subject to the approval of special state conventions, the decision to require the approval of nine states reflected shrewd political calculation. The Founders could have made the Constitution subject to unanimous approval. After all, such a rule had precedent; the Articles of Confederation, for example, required that every state approve all amendments. Adoption of a unanimity rule, however, would have doomed the Constitution to defeat. Rhode Island had refused even to send delegates to the Convention, and it would have blocked adoption of the Constitution if it had had been given the chance to do so. Given that the Antifederalists opposed the Constitution, it is not surprising they criticized the abandonment of the unanimity rule as an illegitimate change in the rules governing the relations among the thirteen states.

At the other extreme, the Founders might have made ratification of the Constitution subject to a simple majority vote. But they recognized that ratification by a majority vote was simply not politically acceptable to most of the voting public. Although in principle the Constitution applied only to the states that ratified it, in practice its adoption would effectively end the national government created by the Articles of Confederation. The decision to dissolve one union and initiate a second would have lacked legitimacy with the American electorate if only seven of the thirteen states had endorsed the new system of government.

Because the Founders deemed ratification by both unanimous consent and simple majority unacceptable, they settled on the rule of nine. A precedent for requiring a majority of nine states existed in the Articles of Confederation, which required that nine states had to approve a bill before it became law. Additional support for the rule of nine came from Article V of the Constitution, which states that three-fourths of the states must ratify amendments to the Constitution. Because Rhode Island was virtually certain to reject the Constitution, only twelve states were seriously willing to entertain the notion of adopting it. Thus, by requiring the approval of nine of thirteen states, the Founders, in essence, were subjecting the Constitution to a three-fourths majority standard similar to the one proposed for adopting amendments.

The Bill of Rights

The Founders wrote the rules of ratification in response to prevailing political realities and their desire to maximize the chances the Constitution would be ratified. But once the text of the Constitution became public, the Federalists found themselves on the defensive. Antifederalists began to complain that the Constitution failed to protect the rights of individual citizens. To undercut these criticisms, the Federalists promised to amend the Constitution to include a list of provisions guaranteeing certain individual rights. These amendments would eventually become known as the **Bill of Rights**.

Bill of Rights
The name given to the first ten amendments of the Constitution. They outline a large number of important individual rights.

At the Constitutional Convention, delegates such as Madison and Hamilton had strongly opposed incorporating an explicit statement of rights into the Constitution for a number of reasons. They argued that such a list could never be complete, and that if the statement enumerated only some rights, the government could use the existence of such a list to deny the people other rights. Moreover, they claimed that because the government had not been given the power to regulate these rights, there was no need to protect against abusive uses of such powers. Finally, Madison and Hamilton preferred a system of structural protections. They persuaded the other delegates to structure the new government so that groups and individuals could defend their own interests. As we shall see in the next section, the belief that a properly structured government could promote individual rights was part of the philosophical justification for the doctrines of separation of powers and checks and balances.

Antifederalists put little stock in the structural protections Madison and Hamilton favored. They instead called for a second convention that would revise the Constitution to include a statement of rights. Not surprisingly, Federalists reacted to such a proposal with alarm. They knew the delegates to a second constitutional convention might scrap the proposed Constitution, just as they had scrapped the Articles of Confederation. To defeat calls for a new convention, the Federalists promised the new government's first task would be to amend the Constitution to include a list specifying a wide variety of individual rights. The willingness of the Federalists to provide explicit guarantees of individual rights persuaded some Antifederalists, including Samuel Adams, to drop their opposition to the Constitution. As a result, the bid to convene a second constitutional convention failed.

Ratification of the Constitution

The Federalists' strategy of writing favorable rules of ratification and offering to add a Bill of Rights to the Constitution succeeded in blunting the challenge the Antifederalists posed. In December 1787, Delaware became the first state to ratify the Constitution, and eight months later, New Hampshire became the ninth. (Three other states ratified the Constitution before the end of 1788, and Rhode Island withheld its approval until May 1790, after the first Congress convened, Washington was inaugurated, and the Supreme Court was established.) Although the Federalists had triumphed, their victory had depended on narrow margins in several states. New York, for example, approved the Constitution by a vote of 30 to 27, and in Rhode Island the vote was 34 to 32.

The new Congress of the United States met for the first time in March 1789. The Federalists quickly made good their pledge to formulate a list of individual rights to append to the Constitution. By September, Congress had approved twelve amendments for consideration by the states. The states ratified ten of the twelve in short order, and these ten amendments make up what we know as the Bill of Rights. (One of the two remaining amendments, which requires members of Congress to stand for reelection before receiving a pay raise, was ratified in 1992.) Thus, the Bill of Rights was created not to correct a philosophical oversight in the Constitution, but as a political tactic designed to strip the Constitution's critics of their most potent weapon.

2-2 THE CONSTITUTION AS A REFLECTION OF THE FOUNDERS' PHILOSOPHY

Although many sharp political conflicts influenced the writing of the Constitution, the document is not the product of politics alone. The philosophical principles the Founders shared also profoundly influenced the Constitution. These philosophical principles led the Founders to create rules of government that seek to protect individual rights and prevent the majority from unfairly imposing its will on the minority. We use the term *minority* here not to denote racial or ethnic minorities such as African Americans or Arab Americans, but rather to refer to any group in society whose numbers fall short of a majority. Indeed, many of the Founders felt that they, as members of the wealthier classes, were a minority threatened by the more numerous poor. The root beliefs of the Founders, then, provide the Constitution with its essential structuring principles.

2-2a Individual Rights and Democratic Rule

The principle that stood first and foremost in the thinking of the Founders was the need to protect the rights of the individual. In strongly emphasizing individual rights, the Founders leaned heavily on the **classical liberalism** of philosophers such as John Locke. (Classical liberalism, which emphasizes the rights of individuals, should not be confused with modern liberalism, which

classical liberalism

A political philosophy, particularly strong in the eighteenth century, that claims that the rights of the individual predate the existence of government and take priority over government policy. This philosophy advocates the protection of individual freedoms from the government.

emphasizes using government to solve problems in society.) The willingness of the Founders to embrace the arguments of classical liberalism had roots in and was reinforced by the Judeo-Christian beliefs prominent among the colonies at the time. These beliefs contended that people are created in the image of God and thus possess an intrinsic value deserving of protection.

Classical liberals believed in the doctrine of *natural rights,* the idea that individuals possess certain rights that are inherent and inalienable—that is, that cannot be taken away. In his *Two Treatises of Government,* Locke argued that all humans possess the rights to life, liberty, and property.[8] The influence of the doctrine of natural rights is evident in the Declaration of Independence (1776), which declares that people are "endowed by their Creator with certain unalienable rights, that among these are Life, Liberty, and the pursuit of Happiness."

Although Locke and other classical liberals claimed that these individual rights were self-evident and could not be denied, they nonetheless recognized that these rights could be suppressed. Locke argued that in a society without any government, or what he called the "state of nature," the strong in all likelihood would suppress the rights of the weak. According to classical liberals, then, government was needed to ensure liberty for everyone so that all could enjoy the freedom to fully exercise their rights. Beyond this duty, the responsibilities of government were extremely limited. Indeed, Locke argued that even the government itself was subordinate to these rights because God had given the people the right to revolt against unjust governments that violated their rights. Thomas Jefferson drew on precisely this argument when he wrote in the Declaration of Independence that citizens have the right to rebel when their government "becomes destructive of" the free exercise of the rights of citizens.

The twin beliefs in individual rights and the need for a government that would protect them led the Founders to favor a way of making government decisions that was quite radical for the eighteenth century: majority rule. If everyone possesses the same rights and possesses them to the same degree, then claims that kings have a divine right to rule or that only aristocrats can govern are fundamentally illegitimate. Instead, all citizens (which to the Founders meant all white males who owned property) should have a voice in government. At the same time, if every citizen has an equal voice in government, it follows that government should act on the basis of what most citizens desire. A minority should not be allowed to impose its wishes on the majority. Yet as appealing as the Founders found the argument for majority rule, it posed a potential paradox. What if the majority's wishes conflicted with an individual's rights? Who should prevail—the majority or the individual?

2-2b Majority Tyranny: The Paradox of Majority Rule

The great disadvantage of government by majority rule is that it may produce **majority tyranny**: a situation in which the majority

majority tyranny
A situation in which the majority uses its advantage in numbers to suppress the rights of the minority.

uses its advantage in numbers to suppress the rights of the minority. The problem of majority tyranny is not simply that a majority prevails on a given issue. By definition, majority rule always produces minorities because every decision has a losing side. Because the existence of a losing side is unavoidable, the fact that some people find themselves in a minority on any given decision does not mean that majority tyranny exists. Rather, majority tyranny arises, threatening individual rights, when the same groups repeatedly find themselves in the majority and minority. Under these conditions, the majority has little reason to constrain its behavior and the minority has few means to protect itself.

Madison recognized the paradox of majority rule in "Federalist No. 10," the most influential of the many *Federalist Papers* that he, Hamilton, and John Jay wrote to persuade the New York state convention to ratify the Constitution: "The form of popular government...enables [the majority] to sacrifice to its ruling passion or interest, both the public good and rights of other citizens."[9] Thus, in writing the Constitution, the Founders had to find a way to reconcile their dedication to government by majority rule with their commitment to individual rights. They did so by modifying the concept of majority rule to make it unlikely that a single majority would govern consistently on many issues over an extended period.

2-2c Preventing Majority Tyranny

To prevent the emergence of a permanent majority that could suppress the rights of the minority, the Founders took three important steps: (1) They wrote electoral rules into the Constitution that make it difficult for permanent electoral majorities to form; (2) they divided authority among government institutions, as well as between the federal and state governments; and (3) they placed formal boundaries on what the government may do. Each of these three steps created a barrier to majority tyranny.

Electoral Rules

The Founders settled on elections as the mechanism for choosing most government leaders because of their commitment to the principles of democracy and republicanism. **Democracy** recognizes that the authority to create and run a government rests with the people. As we saw, the doctrine of classical liberalism justifies a democratic system of government. **Republicanism** is a specific form of government run by representatives of the people. Elections thus make the American political system a democratic republic because the people run the government through their chosen representatives. (Note that a democracy need not be a republic. In a so-called pure, or participatory, democracy, the people govern themselves directly rather than through elected representatives.)

Although elections make American politics democratic, the Founders chose to subject elections to rules that inhibit the

democracy

A form of government in which the people (defined broadly to include all adults or narrowly to exclude women or slaves, for example) are the ultimate political authority.

republicanism

A system of government in which the people's selected representatives run the government.

formation of permanent electoral majorities. These rules include indirect elections, fixed terms of office, and geographically defined representation.

Indirect Elections Under the original provisions of the Constitution, only members of the House of Representatives were to be elected directly by the people. All other government officials were to be elected indirectly or appointed by the president and Congress. Although today the people directly elect senators, the Constitution originally stipulated that state legislatures were to elect the members of the Senate. The nation moved to direct election of senators only with the passage of the Seventeenth Amendment in 1913.

As the 2000 presidential election reminded Americans, the president is not elected by the people but by an electoral college. Each state sends electors to the electoral college (see Chapter 12), and the Constitution leaves it up to the legislature in each state to decide how it will choose them. In early American history, many state legislatures decided who the electors would be. The practice of letting voters pick electors eventually spread—the last time a state legislature chose electors itself was in Colorado in 1876. Unlike the direct election of senators, though, which became a constitutional requirement by virtue of the passage of the Seventeenth Amendment, the practice of using the popular vote to determine presidential electors is not enshrined in the Constitution. (One U.S. Supreme Court justice noted this fact—that there is no constitutional right to vote for president—during the lawsuit over the Florida recount.) If a state legislature decided that it wanted to revert to the tradition of picking electors itself, it could. (The Republican-controlled Florida state legislature was apparently prepared to do so following the 2000 presidential election if a recount had given Al Gore a victory in the state.) However the electors are chosen in each state, they are expected to vote for the candidate to whom they are pledged. But no constitutional requirement exists that they do so. (As a practical matter, so-called faithless electors are rare.)

The president (who is not directly elected) in turn nominates, and the Senate (which originally was not directly elected) confirms, all federal court judges who serve life terms. Figure 2–1 depicts the structure of the electoral system that the Founders created. The Founders wrote the Constitution so that only members of the House of Representatives were directly elected by the people.

The Founders resorted to indirect elections because they feared having government officials who were too responsive to the wishes of the majority. The Founders believed that if government officials were somewhat insulated from the passions of the public, they would find it easier to protect the rights of the minority and to promote the common good.

Fixed Terms of Office The second set of electoral rules that helps prevent the creation of a permanent electoral majority is fixed terms of office. In the United States, unlike most other industrial democracies, elections are set on fixed dates. The president and

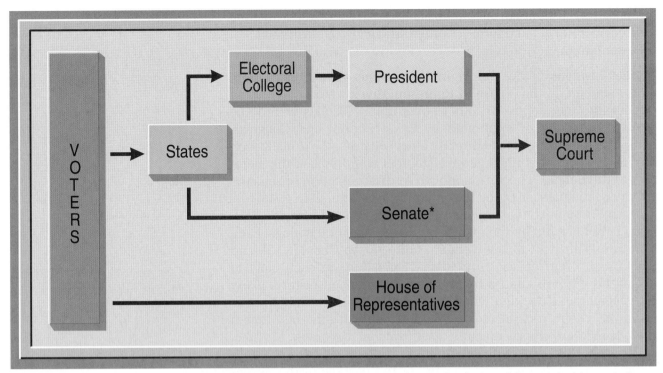

*The Seventeenth Amendment, which provided for direct election of senators by the people, eliminated the state legislatures' role in choosing senators in 1913.

Figure 2-1   The Use of Indirect Elections in the Constitution. The Founders wrote the Constitution so that only
members of the House of Representatives were directly elected by the people.

members of Congress cannot reschedule an election to take advantage of favorable circumstances or avoid unfavorable ones. At the same time, the Founders varied the length of the different fixed terms. Representatives are elected every two years, presidents every four years, and senators every six years, with only one-third up for election every two years. The Founders calculated that staggering elections would make it impossible for a passionate majority to seize control of both Congress and the White House in a single election.

Geographically Defined Representation The third set of electoral rules that helps deter the formation of permanent electoral majorities is the geographically defined system of representation. Whereas in some countries people vote for the national legislature in nationwide elections, in the United States, elections to Congress are tied to where we live; each state elects its own senators and representatives. (In the case of elections to the House of Representatives, each state is divided into a number of districts based on its population, with each district electing a single representative. Although a district is another example of a geographically defined system of representation, a federal law passed in 1842, rather than the Constitution, mandates districts.) Because each district and state contains a different mix of economic, social, and political interests, the Founders doubted that the same groups could win a majority of congressional elections. At the same time, although presidents are elected in a nationwide election, they must win a majority of the electoral college votes rather than a majority of the popular vote. Again, because each state contains such a different mix of interests, candidates for president are discouraged from attending exclusively to the interests of any one group.

Divided Authority

The Founders created a second line of defense against majority tyranny by dividing authority among government institutions, as well as between the federal government and state governments. Thus, even if voters elect a permanent majority, the fact that authority is dispersed among government institutions makes it difficult for that majority to govern because minorities have many opportunities to protect their own interests. In dividing authority among government institutions, the Founders embraced the doctrines of separation of powers, checks and balances, bicameralism, and federalism.

Separation of Powers One way the Founders sought to block majority tyranny was to divide the power to govern among three separate branches of government. This doctrine of **separation of powers**, which the Founders took from the work of French philosopher Montesquieu, holds that separate branches of government should exercise the legislative, executive, and judicial powers of government.[10] Thus, in the United States, unlike many other countries, Congress, the president, and the judiciary are independent of each other, meaning that none of the three can control the decisions of the others. The separation of powers seeks to prevent majority tyranny by making it impossible for any majority to control government simply by gaining control of one or even two sources of political power.

separation of powers
The principle that each of the three powers of government—legislative, executive, and judicial—should be held by a separate branch of government.

Checks and Balances Closely aligned with the doctrine of separation of powers is the principle of **checks and balances**. Checks and balances are negative powers each branch of government can use to block the actions of another branch. For example, only Congress can pass laws, but the president can use the veto power to cancel them. In turn, if two-thirds of both the House and Senate wish to, Congress can override a presidential veto. Checks and balances put teeth into the separation of powers by allowing a group that controls one branch of government to protect itself from groups controlling the other branches of government. Figure 2–2 illustrates the relationship between the doctrine of separation of powers and the system of checks and balances.

checks and balances
The powers each branch of government can use to block the actions of other branches.

By combining checks and balances with the principle of the separation of powers, the Founders actually created a political system in which the separation of powers is incomplete. The practice of checks and balances means that more than one branch of government is involved in exercising a particular power. For example, as we just mentioned, the structural rules of American politics give Congress the power to write laws, but these rules also give the

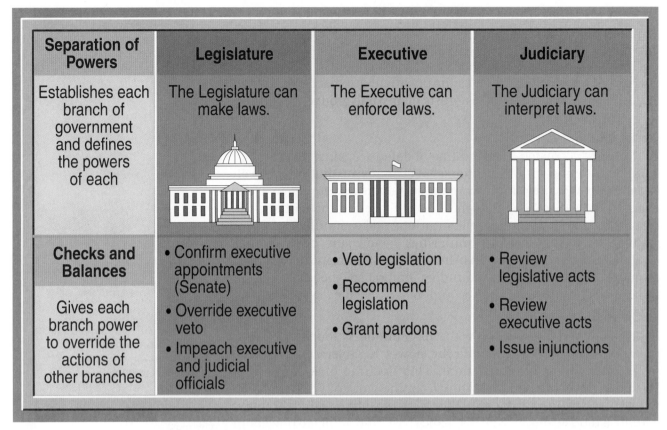

Separation of Powers	Legislature	Executive	Judiciary
Establishes each branch of government and defines the powers of each	The Legislature can make laws.	The Executive can enforce laws.	The Judiciary can interpret laws.
Checks and Balances Gives each branch power to override the actions of other branches	• Confirm executive appointments (Senate) • Override executive veto • Impeach executive and judicial officials	• Veto legislation • Recommend legislation • Grant pardons	• Review legislative acts • Review executive acts • Issue injunctions

Figure 2–2   Separation of Powers and Checks and Balances. To protect against majority tyranny, the Founders created a system based on two principles: separation of powers, and checks and balances. Separation of powers divides the federal government into three equal branches, and the principle of checks and balances gives each branch powers that enable it to prevent the other branches from taking actions that it opposes.

bicameral legislature

A legislature with two houses—such as the House and the Senate.

president the power to veto any law Congress passes. Thus, both the legislative and executive branches of government participate in the lawmaking process. Because some political powers belong to more than one branch of government, we can most accurately describe the federal government as "separated institutions *sharing* powers."[11]

Bicameralism The third step the Founders took to make it difficult for permanent majorities to govern was to create a **bicameral legislature**, which divides lawmaking authority between two legislative houses. Thus, in most circumstances, no proposal can become law unless *concurrent majorities*—that is, majority votes in both the House and Senate—approve it. This means that if a majority of the members of the House favor a bill to cut income taxes but a majority of the Senate opposes it (or vice versa), the bill does not become law. In the few circumstances in which the Founders did not require a majority vote in both House and Senate, they required that a *supermajority* of one house approve legislation, or some number greater than a simple majority. For example, no treaty can go into effect unless two-thirds of the members of the Senate give their consent.

In some circumstances, the Founders combined the requirements of concurrent and supermajorities to make it especially difficult for a single majority to impose its will. For example, Congress can propose an amendment to the Constitution only if two-thirds of the members of the House *and* two-thirds of the members of the Senate vote to do so. Likewise, to override a presidential veto, two-thirds of both the House and the Senate must vote to reverse the president's decision. In today's Congress, the combination of concurrent and supermajorities means that thirty-four senators who agree with the president can frustrate the will of 501 members of Congress who do not. Because the combination of concurrent and supermajorities poses such a formidable barrier, Congress has overridden only 7 percent of all presidential vetoes.[12]

Federalism With the separation of powers, the Constitution divides political power among the three branches of the federal government. To further deter the operation of permanent majorities, the Founders developed the doctrine of **federalism**, which is the idea that a country should have different levels of government, each with its own set of sovereign or independent political powers. In the United States, the Constitution divides power between the federal and state governments. Federalism initially emerged at the Constitutional Convention as an imaginative compromise between those who wanted a more powerful national government and those who feared that a strong national government might tyrannize small states and other minorities. By reserving powers to the states, the Founders established a basis for groups that are a majority within a state but a minority within the nation to exercise some degree of local self-government.

federalism
A two-tiered form of government in which governments on both levels are sovereign and share authority over the same geographic jurisdiction.

Formal Boundaries on Government Action

The final barrier the Founders erected to prevent a permanent majority from suppressing the rights of the minority was to place formal boundaries on the powers of the national government. In general, leading supporters of the Constitution, such as Madison, were not sympathetic to this approach. They argued that a determined majority could easily ignore any formal rules protecting minority rights. Moreover, they argued that a failure to mention some rights might later allow others to argue that those rights did not exist or did not need protection. In deference to other delegates at the Constitutional Convention, the Constitution does include several specific limitations on government power. As we have seen, the Founders also agreed to add a Bill of Rights to the Constitution to win ratification.

Limits in the Original Constitution One specific limitation the Constitution places on the powers of government is that government officials cannot suspend an individual's right to *habeas corpus,* that is, an individual's right not to be imprisoned unless charged with a crime, except in time of "rebellion or invasion." Thus, in normal circumstances, the government cannot imprison people unless it can produce credible evidence that they may have committed a crime. The Constitution further forbids the government from passing *bills of attainder,* which means Congress cannot punish an individual for a crime without first providing a trial in court. Finally, the Constitution forbids Congress from passing *ex post facto* laws, which are laws that declare an act criminal after the act was committed. More recently, the courts have interpreted the prohibition against ex post facto laws to mean that the government cannot impose a punishment greater than the punishment in effect when the crime was committed.[13] Thus, if a state reinstated the death penalty, officials could not apply it to prisoners who had been convicted of committing murder before the law was changed.

Limits in the Bill of Rights The Bill of Rights adds an extensive list of prohibitions to government actions (see Chapter 4). As we learned previously, Antifederalists feared that a strong national government would suppress individual rights. Thus, they insisted on, and the Federalists ultimately agreed to, the inclusion of a list of rights that individuals possess and that limit the government's jurisdiction. They serve as a final defense of individual rights by proclaiming that, even if all parts of the government wish to act, the government cannot take an action if it violates the rights of an individual.

In erecting the three barriers we have just discussed to prevent majority tyranny, the Founders placed a higher value on preventing "bad" government decisions (i.e., the suppression of the rights of the minority) than on encouraging "good" government decisions (i.e., achieving the wishes of the majority). In a practical sense, this means it is easier to block action than to accomplish it in our system of government; this causes the wheels of government to lumber along slowly. Although today's politicians decry gridlock, the Constitution clearly sets forth rules that are designed to prevent the government from making hasty, unilateral decisions that might harm the rights of the minority.

2-3 THE CORE PROVISIONS OF THE CONSTITUTION

We have seen that a combination of political imperatives and philosophical beliefs influenced the writing of the Constitution. But what exactly does the Constitution say? Its core provisions set forth the rules governing Congress, the presidency, and the judiciary, as well as the rules governing relations between the federal and state governments.

2-3a Congress

Although the Constitution discusses Congress in several places, the most thorough discussion of the rules, structures, and powers of Congress appears in Article I. The ten sections that make up

Source: © Digital Stock 1996.

The Capitol—home to the U.S. Congress.

Article I specify the rules for electing members of Congress, the procedures for turning bills into laws, and the powers of Congress.

We already have discussed some of the details of Article I that regulate congressional elections. For example, Article I stipulates that Congress shall consist of two chambers, the House of Representatives and the Senate. Each state is represented in the House of Representatives in proportion to its population, and all representatives are elected to two-year terms. Every state has two seats in the Senate, and senators serve six-year terms. Other election rules that Article I lays out are less well known. For instance, each state sets its own rules for electing members of Congress, subject to the provision that it must permit every person it allows to vote in the election for the most numerous branch of the state legislature to vote in the election for the House. The responsibility for resolving any disputes that arise over the outcome or validity of an election lies with the chamber in which the dispute occurs, and no member of Congress may hold a position in another branch of government during his or her congressional service.

Besides establishing the rules for electing people to Congress, Article I also specifies the rules that Congress must follow to turn a bill into a law. Under Article I, the House and Senate must first approve identical versions of a bill. Then the bill goes to the president. If the president signs the bill, it becomes law; if the president vetoes the bill, it returns to Congress. Members of Congress have the option of trying to override the president's veto, but, as we mentioned, two-thirds of each house must vote to override the veto. If members of Congress decide not to override the veto or fail in their attempt to do so, the bill does not become law. Finally, if the president neither signs the bill nor vetoes it, the bill becomes law after ten days, provided Congress does not adjourn during that time. If Congress does adjourn within that ten-day period, however, the bill does not become law. Allowing a bill to die when Congress adjourns is known as the *pocket veto*.

The Constitution lays out other powers of Congress (many of which are subject to a presidential veto). Congress controls the finances of government because it has the power to write tax laws, appropriate money, and borrow and coin money. Congress is centrally involved in establishing the structure of the government through its power to create, fund, and set the jurisdictions of agencies in the executive branch and courts in the judicial branch. Congress influences the state of the economy through its powers to regulate foreign and interstate commerce. It is integrally involved in the nation's defense and foreign policies through its power to declare war; through its powers to raise, support, and establish rules of conduct for the army and navy; and through the Senate's responsibility to approve treaties and confirm ambassadors.

The Constitution also empowers Congress "To make all Laws which shall be necessary and proper for carrying into Execution the foregoing Powers." Often referred to as the **necessary and proper clause** (or the *elastic clause*), this provision enables Congress to act in ways the Constitution does not specify, provided Congress can show that such acts are appropriate in fulfilling its duties. As we shall see, the Supreme Court's decision in *McCulloch v. Maryland* (1819) gave Congress wide latitude to define the realm of the elastic clause.

Still, the powers of Congress are not infinite. As we saw in the discussion of habeas corpus, bills of attainder, and ex post facto laws, the Constitution withholds some powers from Congress. Likewise, the Constitution requires Congress to give a public accounting of all public expenditures. But in general, the Constitution assigns Congress a great deal of power, consistent with the Founders' belief in empowering the legislative rather than the executive branch of government.

2-3b The Presidency and the Executive Branch

As with Congress, the Constitution specifies the rules for electing presidents, as well as the powers of the presidency. Most of the discussion of the presidency and the executive branch is in Article II.

As we previously discussed, presidents are elected by the vote of the electoral college rather than by the direct vote of the people. Article II sets the number of electoral votes assigned to each state at a figure equal to the number of senators and representatives that state has in Congress. The Constitution authorizes each individual state to decide how to select its electors. Article II also requires that the president be a natural-born citizen of the United States. Thus, the Constitution bars immigrants who become naturalized citizens from becoming president. (No constitutional provisions bar naturalized citizens from holding other government offices.)

In keeping with the Founders' wariness about giving too much power to any one branch of government, the Constitution gives the

necessary and proper clause
The provision in Article I of the Constitution that states that Congress possesses whatever additional and unspecified powers it needs to fulfill its responsibilities.

Source: © Digital Stock 1996.

The White House—where the president of the United States lives and works.

president powers it denies Congress. Perhaps the most important presidential power is the executive power. As we previously discussed, the Founders so disagreed over the proper boundaries of presidential power that they refused to define the exact meaning of the executive power. At a minimum, it was meant to give presidents the authority they would need to implement congressional directives and to fulfill the other duties of the executive branch. Over the past 200 years, however, presidents have successfully argued that the executive power confers a broad range of additional powers. Presidents have also expanded their political power by expanding the meaning of the so-called commander-in-chief clause, which designates the president as the commander in chief of American military forces. The Founders intended the position of commander in chief to be simply an office rather than an independent source of political power. For much of U.S. history, however, and especially since World War II, presidents have argued that the commander-in-chief clause gives them wide powers in foreign policy.[14]

In addition to the broad grant of executive power and the special foreign policy powers that successive presidents have read into the commander-in-chief clause, Article II of the Constitution gives the president several specific powers. These presidential powers include the right to negotiate treaties with other countries (provided that two-thirds of the Senate concurs), the right to appoint people to positions in the executive and judicial branches of government (provided that a majority of the Senate concurs), the right to grant pardons and reprieves to people convicted of crimes, and the right to receive foreign ambassadors. Article II also grants the president special powers relative to Congress. Presidents are required to inform Congress of the state of the union, and they may recommend legislation for its consideration. Presidents also have the authority to call Congress into session and to adjourn Congress

Source: © Digital Stock 1996.

The Supreme Court—where the highest judicial body in the land interprets the law.

if the House and Senate fail to agree on those dates. As you can see, the Constitution creates an executive whose powers are checked and balanced by the other branches, and who can in turn check and balance the powers of those branches.

2-3c The Federal Judiciary

The Constitution specifies the rules and powers of the federal judiciary in Article III. (The constitution of each state sets forth rules governing that state's courts.) As a quick glance at Article III shows, the Constitution only briefly discusses the federal courts. Article III creates the Supreme Court and gives Congress the power to create all lower federal courts. Federal court judges are appointed for life, so long as they remain on "good Behaviour." If federal judges act unethically or illegally, Congress can remove them from office. The Constitution requires the federal courts to hear all cases under the Constitution, and it specifies that in some special circumstances the Supreme Court must be the first court to hear a case.

2-3d Interstate Relations

Article IV of the Constitution sets forth the rules that govern interstate relations, that is, the relationship between the national and state governments and the relationship among the states themselves. Article IV requires each state to respect, honor, and cooperate with the decisions of other states. For example, the Constitution requires the state of New York to respect a divorce granted in the state of California. This requirement is one reason why twenty-five states have written prohibitions to "gay marriage" into their constitutions.[15] They fear that without those provisions, they will be required to recognize marriage licenses that other states have granted to gay or lesbian couples. Article IV also bars states from discriminating against citizens of other states. Finally, Article IV lays out the rules governing the admission of new states to the Union, and it guarantees that the national government will come to the aid of the states in the event of a foreign invasion or domestic violence.

2-3e Other Provisions

The remaining three articles in the Constitution establish rules for amending the Constitution, for resolving conflicts between the states and the federal government, and for ratifying the Constitution. Article V prescribes four methods for amending the Constitution. Figure 2–3 describes how each method works. In practice, amendments are almost always enacted through the first route in the figure; twenty-six of the first twenty-seven amendments to the Constitution were approved by two-thirds vote of both houses of Congress and then ratified by state legislatures in three-fourths of the states. The other successful amendment, the Twenty-First, originated in Congress, which then sent it to state conventions for ratification by three-fourths of the states. Most amendments are enacted within a few years of being proposed to the states, and in recent years, most proposed amendments have included a time limit for ratification. The exception was the Twenty-Seventh Amendment, which was proposed by Congress in 1789 but not ratified by the states until 1992.[16]

The key provision of Article VI establishes that the laws of the federal government are the "supreme law of the land" and that the states must adhere to them. The practical import of this provision is that federal law, which encompasses the entire text of the Constitution, all laws Congress passes, and all legal obligations that duly ratified treaties impose, takes precedence when it conflicts with state or local law. Article VI also requires all federal and state officials, whether elected or appointed, to swear an oath to support the Constitution, and it stipulates that "no religious test shall ever be required as a qualification" for any government office. Finally, Article VII lays out the rules for ratifying the Constitution itself, which were previously discussed.

As you can see, the core provisions of the Constitution set out the basic rules for each branch of government, as well as for the relationship between the national and state governments. Let's look now at what consequences these rules have had for politics in the United States.

2-4 THREE CONSEQUENCES OF THE CONSTITUTION

The Constitution is more than a quaint relic kept under glass at the National Archives. It contains the principles and rules that have guided Congress, the executive branch, and the federal judiciary

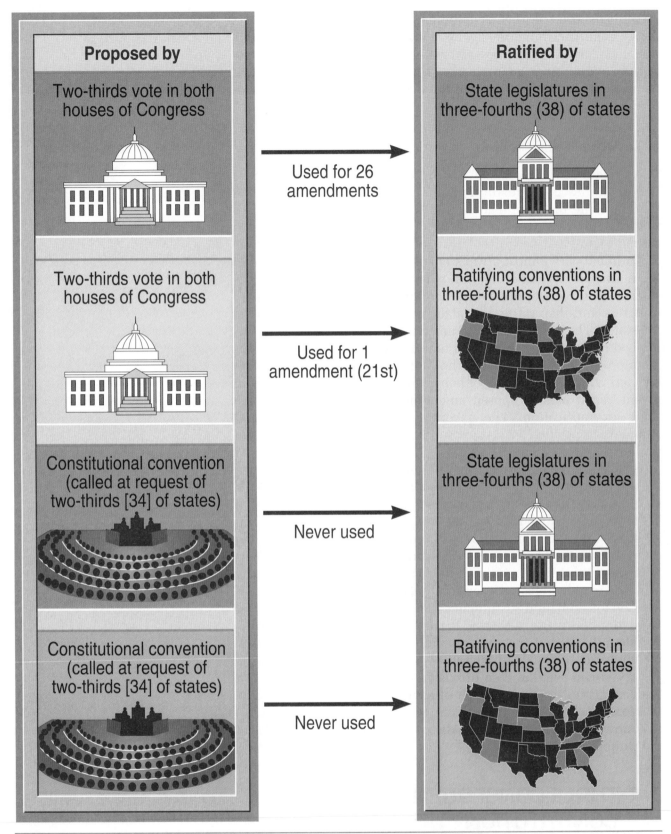

Figure 2–3   Amending the Constitution. The Founders provided four different methods to amend the Constitution, but twenty-six of the twenty-seven amendments were proposed by Congress and ratified by three-fourths of the states' legislatures.

over the past two centuries. These principles and rules, in turn, have had significant effects on politics in the United States. The three most important effects warrant specific consideration. First, the rights of the individual enjoy such strong legal protection that at times they frustrate the will of the majority. Second, the obstacles placed in the way of passing legislation create a strong bias in American politics in favor of the existing state of affairs, or status quo, even when a majority of Americans would prefer otherwise. Third, even though the Constitution makes it difficult to pass new laws, it has created a political system that is sufficiently flexible to meet the country's changing needs.

2-4a The Protection of Individual Rights

As the statement of the rules of politics in the United States, the Constitution clearly favors protecting the rights of the individual over respecting the wishes of the majority. We have already seen how ideas such as the separation of powers, checks and balances, and federalism had their roots in the Founders' desire to prevent majorities in the federal government from suppressing the rights and interests of individuals and minorities. The intention to protect individuals became even more pronounced once the Bill of Rights and other amendments were adopted. Amendments protect the rights of individuals to express and inform themselves (the First Amendment), ensure they receive fair treatment in the criminal and civil justice system (the Fourth through Eighth Amendments), prevent states from violating rights protected by the Constitution (the Fourteenth Amendment), expand the rights of citizenship in general (the Thirteenth Amendment), and extend the right to vote (the Fifteenth, Nineteenth, Twenty-Fourth, and Twenty-Sixth Amendments).

The most important consequence of the Constitution's protection of individual rights is that the power of government is limited. Initially, however, the Constitution was understood only to limit the power of the *federal government.* As Chapter 4 discusses at greater length, the protections afforded to individuals by the Constitution in general and the Bill of Rights in particular did not extend to the actions of *state and local government* for more than 100 years. Only in 1897 did the Supreme Court begin to use the due process clause of the Fourteenth Amendment to argue that the Bill of Rights limited the ability of state and local government to infringe on the rights of individuals.

Because the Supreme Court's interpretation of how to apply the Bill of Rights has changed, federal, state, and local governments are limited today in their ability to pass laws that infringe on an individual's rights under the Constitution. Take, for example, the controversy over prayer in public schools. In two landmark cases in 1962 and 1963, the Supreme Court ruled that government-sponsored prayer in public schools violates the **establishment clause** of the First Amendment, which states that "Congress shall make no law respecting an establishment of religion." (Although the First

establishment clause
The provision in the First Amendment of the Constitution that "Congress shall make no law respecting an establishment of religion."

Source: © Bettmann/Corbis.

For nearly 200 years, organized prayer in public schools was a common event. In 1962, the Supreme Court ruled in *Engel v. Vitale* that the practice violated the establishment clause of the First Amendment. The issue of prayer in public schools has raised controversy ever since.

Amendment literally bars only Congress from making such laws, for half a century the courts have interpreted the Amendment to apply to state and local governments as well.) As Table 2–2 shows, public opinion surveys consistently show that a majority of Americans wants to reinstate the practice of official school prayer. Despite strong public support for school prayer, the Constitution protects dissenting minorities from the majority's preference for public prayer. (Of course, to say that the Constitution protects individual rights is not to say that these rights are absolute or never violated. As Chapters 4 and 14 discuss, sometimes the courts rule that compelling reasons justify a governmental decision to suppress individual rights, and sometimes federal, state, and local governments refuse to abide by court rulings.)

2-4b A Bias in Favor of the Status Quo

The obstacles the Constitution places in the way of passing legislation make it difficult to change the political status quo in the United States. As we previously discussed, bills seldom become law unless the House of Representatives, the Senate, and the president all agree. And the three often do not agree on the best course of action for the country. Thus, it should not be surprising that most bills never become law. For example, during the 109th Congress (2005–2006), members of the House of Representatives and the Senate introduced over 10,000 bills but less than 400 became law.[17] The Founders constructed a political system that favors the status quo because they believed that the status quo embodies important values that merit protection from the momentary passions of politics.

Year	Favor (%)*	Oppose (%)*	Don't Know or No Opinion (%)*
1963	24	70	6
1971	28	67	6
1974	31	66	3
1975	35	62	3
1977	33	64	2
1981	31	66	3
1982	37	60	3
1983	40	57	4
1985 (March)	43	54	3
1985 (September)	37	62	1
1986	37	61	2
1988	37	59	4
1989	41	56	3
1990	40	56	5
1991	38	58	4
1993	39	58	4
1994	37	58	4
1996	40	56	4
1998	43	53	5
2000	37	58	5
2002	38	57	5

Table 2–2 Public Opinion on Banning School Prayer

Question posed: "The U.S. Supreme Court has ruled that no state or local government may require the reading of the Lord's Prayer or Bible verses in public schools. What are your views on this—do you approve or disapprove of the court ruling?"

Source: Data for 1963–1998 from Harold W. Stanley and Richard G. Niemi, Vital Statistics on American Politics 1999–2000 (Washington, D.C.: Congressional Quarterly, 2000), 148; data for 2000–2002 from Harold W. Stanley and Richard G. Niemi, Vital Statistics on American Politics 2003–2004 (Washington, D.C.: Congressional Quarterly, 2003), 154.

*Percentage of respondents; numbers may not add up to 100 percent because of rounding.

The bias in American politics toward the status quo persists even when a majority of Americans would prefer to make changes. Take, for instance, the failed effort to pass the Equal Rights Amendment (ERA), which would have amended the Constitution to guarantee equal rights to men and women. In 1972, Congress passed the ERA and gave the states seven years to ratify it. Over the next decade, public opinion surveys consistently showed that more than 50 percent of the American public supported ratification of ERA. In 1979, the last year in which the amendment could be ratified under the terms Congress originally laid out, public support stood at 58 percent, but only thirty-five states had ratified it—three short of the required three-fourths. Congress then voted to extend the ratification deadline until 1982, but even though public support for the ERA continued to exceed 50 percent, the measure failed to secure support from three additional states. (As Box 2–2 shows, this experience is not unique.) The example of the ERA shows once again how the rules that govern the political decision-making process can determine the eventual outcome.

POINT OF ORDER

Box 2–2 Obstacles to Amending the Constitution

Imagine the confusion that would result if you were playing a game in which players could change the rules as they went to help them win. No one could ever be sure what the rules are or whether they have been broken. Eventually, most people would probably decide not to play. The Founders wanted to protect the Constitution from this kind of easy manipulation. Public confidence in the stability of the rules encourages confidence in the fairness of the government itself.

The rules the Founders put in place for amending the Constitution reflect this desire for stability. These rules require extraordinary support to pass an amendment (see Figure 2–3). As a result, although many amendments have been proposed, few have been adopted. Over the past two centuries, members of Congress have proposed nearly 11,000 amendments, but only 27 have made their way into the Constitution.

This degree of stability is unusual, as we can see when we compare the experience of state constitutions. Twenty-two states have had three or more constitutions. Twenty-three states have amended their constitutions more than 100 times, with Alabama leading the way with 556 amendments. Only five states have amended their constitutions fewer than the twenty-seven times the U.S. Constitution has been amended.

Although many people take comfort in the stability of the Constitution, others find its resistance to change frustrating. For several decades, for example, conservatives have called for the adoption of amendments to require a balanced budget, give the president a line-item veto, permit organized school prayer, impose term limits on members of Congress, and prohibit abortions. Yet none of these proposals has found its way into the Constitution.

Proponents of constitutional change criticize Congress for failing to approve their favored amendments, and some of them seek alternative ways to bring constitutional amendments before the states. One possibility is for Congress to convene a constitutional convention in which state delegations could propose amendments. Congress can by a simple majority vote convene such a convention whenever two-thirds (or thirty-four) of the states request it. By one count, as many as forty-five states have formally called for a constitutional convention over the past 200 years. Yet we have had no constitutional convention. Why?

The answer involves both legal and political concerns. Although at least thirty-four states may have formally called for a constitutional convention—the number the Constitution requires—not all thirty-four requests for a convention may be legally valid. Some states requested a constitutional convention more than 100 years ago, and many legal scholars argue that such requests are too old to count. At the same time, states have specified a wide range of reasons for calling a constitutional convention, from passing a balanced budget amendment to banning the burning of the American flag. Legal scholars argue over whether all requests must agree on the reason for seeking a convention, and the courts have never settled the matter.

As for the political concerns involved, the questionable validity of state requests for a constitutional convention makes it easy for Congress to avoid convening a convention. As you might imagine, members of Congress have a self-interest in keeping the power to propose amendments to themselves. Once a constitutional convention is convened, they would no longer monopolize that power. Thus, until and unless Congress is forced to call for a convention, say, because of a Supreme Court ruling, the prospects for one are virtually nonexistent.

What would happen if a constitutional convention were convened is anyone's guess. Some observers fear that it would result in a "runaway" convention that would rewrite the Constitution, thereby tampering with our basic rights and government procedures. Such an outcome is not totally out of the realm of possibility. After all, this is precisely what the Founders did to the Articles of Confederation when they met in Philadelphia in the summer of 1787.

So we are left with a situation that the Founders no doubt intended. Passionate groups, even majorities, come and go, seeking to embed their preferences into the fundamental rules that structure our nation's government. But unless those preferences enjoy the consensus support of the public, they stand little chance of surmounting the difficult challenges the Constitution lays down.

Source: Terry Eastland "To Amend or Not to Amend?" *Wall Street Journal* (November 23, 1994); Michael Stokes Paulsen, "The Case for a Constitutional Convention, *Wall Street Journal* (May 3, 1995); Harold W. Stanley and Richard G. Niemi, *Vital Statistics on American Politics*, 5th ed. (Washington, D.C.: CQ Press, 1995), 13–15.

By favoring the status quo, the Constitution helps some Americans and hurts others. Some Americans benefit from existing laws. To protect their interests, they need only to block changes in the status quo. In contrast, Americans who dislike existing laws face the more difficult task of steering new legislation through Congress and winning the president's approval, a task made all the more difficult by the need to assemble supermajorities in some circumstances. In short, defenders and critics of the status quo face dramatically different tasks. Defenders of the status quo usually need to win only once at some point in the process. If they defeat a proposal to change existing law at any point in the policy-making process, they win. Critics of the status quo, on the other hand, face exactly the opposite task: They must win at every point in the policy-making process if they want to see their proposal become law. Once again, the rules of American politics shape the outcome of political debates.

2-4c Political Flexibility

Although efforts to write new laws must overcome many obstacles, the Constitution nonetheless created a political system capable of considerable flexibility. Americans' understanding of the Constitution has changed greatly over the past 200 years. The flexibility of the Constitution and, in turn, the American political system stems partly from the provisions that allow the Constitution to be amended, partly from the general nature of the text, and partly from the Constitution's silence on many of the practical aspects of government.

The Founders recognized that when they wrote the Constitution they could not foresee what the future would hold for the new nation. To ensure that the new political system could meet the needs of future generations, the Founders provided that the Constitution could be amended and that the amendments would be as binding as the original text. However, to prevent the Constitution from constant revision to reflect every majority whim, they imposed stringent requirements on the passage of amendments (see Figure 2–3). As a result, only twenty-seven amendments have been added to the Constitution over the past 200 years, and ten of those—the Bill of Rights—were adopted as part of the political agreement that made the ratification of the Constitution itself possible. The flexibility that the amending process provides applies even to correcting mistakes made in previous amendments. In 1933, for example, the country decided that it had erred with Prohibition and passed the Twenty-First Amendment, which repealed the Eighteenth Amendment's ban on the manufacture and sale of intoxicating liquors.

In addition to the flexibility the amending process provides, the American political system gains flexibility from the very ambiguity of the Constitution. A quick glance at the Constitution shows that the Founders did not specify their plan for a new government in great detail. They instead wrote in general language. For example, the necessary and proper clause in Article I empowers Congress "to make all Laws which shall be necessary and proper," but it says nothing about what constitutes necessity or propriety. Likewise, Article II directs the president to make treaties with the "Advice and Consent" of the Senate, but it fails to explain precisely how senators are to give their advice. As we previously mentioned, sometimes the Founders resorted to ambiguity as a way of disguising their differences on key issues. Elsewhere, however, the ambiguity reflects the Founders' recognition that much of the effort to apply the principles of the Constitution would inevitably depend on the good judgment of elected officials rather than on a lengthy explanation of the rules of the political system.

The final source of flexibility in the Constitution is its silence on many of the practical aspects of government. Although Article II vests the executive power in the president, it says nothing about what the structure of the executive branch should look like. Nor does the Constitution say anything about political parties and their role in government. Although the omission of these and other aspects of government might seem strange, it has contributed to the strength of the American political system by enabling the government to adapt more easily to changes in the nation and in public expectations.

As this discussion shows, certain broad features of the Constitution—protecting individual rights and making it difficult to change existing laws—have stood the test of time and continue to shape our government today. Yet amendments, as well as the ambiguity and silences of the Constitution, allow the operational specifics of government to change as our needs as a nation evolve. One of the areas in which the flexibility of the Constitution is most evident is in the so-called vertical dimension of the Constitution—the way in which the federal and state governments interact.

2-5 FEDERALISM: THE VERTICAL DIMENSION TO THE CONSTITUTION

Any discussion of the Constitution would be incomplete without a discussion of the principle of federalism and how it has changed over time. You may recall that federalism is the idea that a country should have different levels of government, each with its own set of sovereign political powers. The Founders settled on a federal political system because they wanted to avoid the problems that had undermined the Articles of Confederation without creating a national government that could impose its will on the states. Exactly how the new federal political system was meant to work, however, has been the subject of bitter political debate. For most of U.S. history, federal law has been interpreted to be superior to state law. At other times, however, some people have forcefully challenged the claim that the federal government is the dominant partner in its relationship with the states.

2-5a Confederal, Unitary, and Federal Governments

As we previously discussed, one of the most important decisions the delegates to the Constitutional Convention had to make was how to structure the relationship between the national and state governments. Neither of the two most likely options had much political appeal. On one hand, the confederal government the Articles of Confederation had created had proved inadequate to meet the needs of the new country. On the other hand, the fear many Americans had of a tyrannical national government ruled out the possibility of creating a *unitary* government in which political power was concentrated in the hands of a national government. Faced with two unpalatable options, the Founders created a third: the federal form of government, in which the national and state governments share political power. Figure 2–4 illustrates how the national government, state governments, and citizens relate to one another under each arrangement of authority.

In a confederal government, authority rests fundamentally with the members of the union; as a result, political power essentially flows from the bottom up. A contemporary example of a confederal government is the United Nations, which can exercise only the powers its member states choose to give it. In contrast, in a unitary government, power is centralized in the national government.

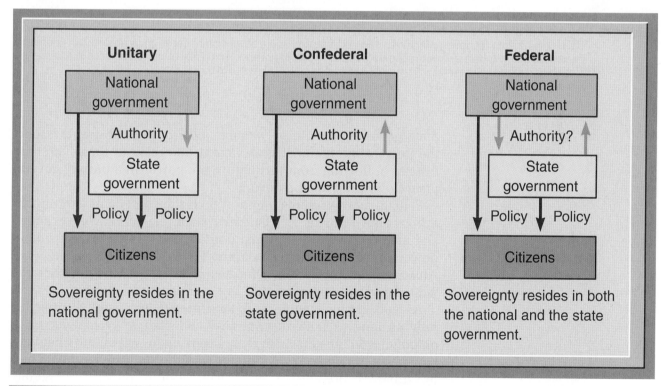

Figure 2–4 Power Arrangements in the Unitary, Confederal, and Federal Forms of Government. The Founders rejected unitary government because their experience with it as colonists convinced them that an all-powerful national government was dangerous. They also rejected confederal government because their experience under the Articles of Confederation convinced them that a national government without sufficient authority was ineffective. Federalism was their attempt to balance the authority of the national and state governments so that neither would be too powerful.

	State Governments	National Government	Both Governments
Powers Denied to:	• Cannot refuse to abide by lawful acts of other states • Cannot enter into treaties or alliances with foreign governments	• Cannot challenge state power to govern • Cannot return indictments without grand jury • Cannot tax goods transported from state to state	• Cannot pass bills of attainder or *ex post facto* laws • Cannot deprive individuals of rights guaranteed in Constitution
Powers Granted to:	• Can supervise elections within state • Can provide local government, public health, and public safety	• Can declare war and raise and support an army and a navy • Can establish post office and coin money	• Can tax and can spend funds for general welfare

Figure 2-5   Examples of the Constitution's Distribution of Powers between State and National Governments. To create a federal system of government with sovereign states and a sovereign national government, the Founders granted and withheld a variety of powers to each level of government. They allocated powers in an attempt to create a strong national government without seriously weakening the states.

State governments are subsidiary entities that can exercise only the powers the national government delegates to them. In short, instead of flowing from the bottom up, power in a unitary government flows from the top down.

Federalism represents a mix of both the confederal and unitary forms of government. In a federal system, the national government and member states share some political powers and possess other powers independent of each other. Figure 2–5 illustrates how the American federal system allocates political powers between the federal and state governments.

As you might imagine, a federal system can work in practice only as long as both the national and state governments agree on policies in the areas where their powers overlap. But what happens when the federal government and the state governments prefer different policies? Which level should prevail? A review of U.S. history shows that the answers to these questions have changed over the years. Federalism in the United States has meant different things at different times, and as these meanings change, so does the relative balance of power between the federal government and the state governments.

2-5b Establishing National Supremacy

The Supreme Court provided its first (but not last) definitive interpretation of federalism in the case of *McCulloch v. Maryland* (1819). Chief Justice John Marshall, a proponent of a strong national government, wrote the opinion for the Court (see Box 2–3). The genesis for the case lay in a law Congress passed creating a national bank. Federalists favored the law, arguing that it would help integrate the economies of the individual states into a single national economy. Many states, however, opposed what they saw as an unwarranted federal intrusion into their affairs. Maryland sought to limit the bank's operations within its borders by taxing the bank's transactions. The federal government argued that Maryland's tax was improper on the grounds that states could not adopt policies that contradicted national goals. In ruling that Maryland's tax was unconstitutional, the Supreme Court set forth the doctrine of **national supremacy**, the argument that federal law is superior to state law.

In deciding *McCulloch v. Maryland,* the Supreme Court had to answer two important questions. First, did the federal government have the authority to create such a bank? Maryland argued that the Constitution did not specifically authorize the federal government to do so. It reasoned that the federal government must show that a

national supremacy

An interpretation of federalism that holds that the national government's laws should take precedence over state law. This idea is based on the provision in Article VI of the Constitution that the national government's laws are the "supreme law of the land."

The People behind the Rules

Box 2–3   The Impact of Individuals on the Meaning of Federalism: Chief Justices John Marshall and Roger Taney

John Marshall and Roger Taney are two of the acknowledged great Chief Justices of the U.S. Supreme Court. Both believed in a strong national judiciary. Yet differences in their views on the respective roles of the national and state governments created major shifts in the nature of federalism during the first half of the nineteenth century.

President John Adams appointed John Marshall as Chief Justice in 1801. Marshall was a dedicated Federalist, committed to the principle of a strong national government. He served thirty-four years (longer than all but three other justices) and authored 519 of the 1,215 decisions his court rendered. In those cases, he established the principle of national supremacy over the states, most clearly in the case *McCulloch v. Maryland* (1819). For a unanimous Court, he wrote: "the

constitution and the laws made in pursuance thereof are supreme;. . .they control the constitution and laws of the respective states, and cannot be controlled by them."

President Andrew Jackson appointed Roger Taney as Chief Justice in 1836 to fill the vacancy created by Marshall's death. Although he shared Marshall's belief in a strong and independent judiciary, Taney repeatedly sought to "enhance the role of the states as governmental and philosophical entities." Although he is held in high esteem by scholars, Taney's decision in *Dred Scott v. Sandford* (1857) is widely acknowledged to be one of the "most disastrous" decisions the Court ever rendered. In it, he held that the Missouri Compromise was unconstitutional because the national government lacked the authority to

outlaw slavery in the territories. He argued further that blacks were "of an inferior order" and that no black was a part of "the American people."

The *Dred Scott* decision was Taney's effort to avert civil war over slavery by redefining Marshall's interpretation of federalism. Taney's unsuccessful attempt to uphold the rights of the states and slave owners against the authority of the national government and the rights of black Americans confused the meaning of federalism in the tumultuous period leading up to the Civil War. The roles of the national and state governments were not to be clearly reestablished until the Union defeated the South in the Civil War.

Source: Henry J. Abraham, *Justices and Presidents,* 2nd ed. (New York: Oxford University Press, 1985).

national bank was the only or best means of accomplishing its goal of integrating the states' economies. The federal government argued that the necessary and proper clause of Article I implied the power to create a national bank. At issue was the meaning of that clause. The Supreme Court agreed with the federal government, thereby greatly expanding the scope of federal power.

The second question dealt more directly with federalism. Given that the bank was constitutional, could Maryland tax its operations? Maryland had the power to tax, so shouldn't it tax the national bank? The federal government argued that such a tax would effectively allow the states to negate federal laws, contrary to the provision in Article VI of the Constitution that federal laws "shall be the supreme Law of the Land." Again, the Supreme Court sided with the federal government, striking down the Maryland tax on the grounds that "the States have no power, by taxation or otherwise, to retard, impede, burden, or in any manner control, the operations of the constitutional laws enacted by Congress to carry into execution the powers vested in the general government."[18] The Court's decision established the first authoritative interpretation of federalism—the federal government ruled supreme. The victory, however, would not go unchallenged.

2-5c The Assertion of States' Rights

The Supreme Court's decision in *McCulloch v. Maryland* angered people who opposed the emergence of a dominant federal government. These opponents argued for a different interpretation of the proper relationship between the federal and state governments. In the years before the Civil War, the most prominent challenge to the doctrine of national supremacy was the doctrine of **states' rights**. Advocates of states' rights turned the argument for national supremacy on its head; they claimed that properly interpreted federalism made the states, not the federal government, supreme.

Advocates of states' rights based their argument on two principles: the *doctrine of interposition* and the *doctrine of nullification*. According to the doctrine of interposition, states are placed between the people and the federal government; hence, states have the right to intervene on behalf of their citizens to evaluate federal policies. The doctrine of nullification held that states have the right to block the application of federal policies that affect their citizens. Figure 2–6 illustrates the logic behind the argument made by advocates of states' rights. The interposition and nullification doctrines both dated back to the 1790s, and they both enjoyed broad support. In 1798, for example, Madison and Jefferson argued that states could nullify federal laws that punished newspaper editors for writing stories criticizing the federal government. Andrew Jackson was a strong supporter of states' rights, and as president he sought to protect the states from the federal government by forcing the 1832 collapse of the national bank that had spawned the Supreme Court's ruling in *McCulloch v. Maryland.*

states' rights

An interpretation of federalism which claimed that states possessed the right to accept or reject federal laws.

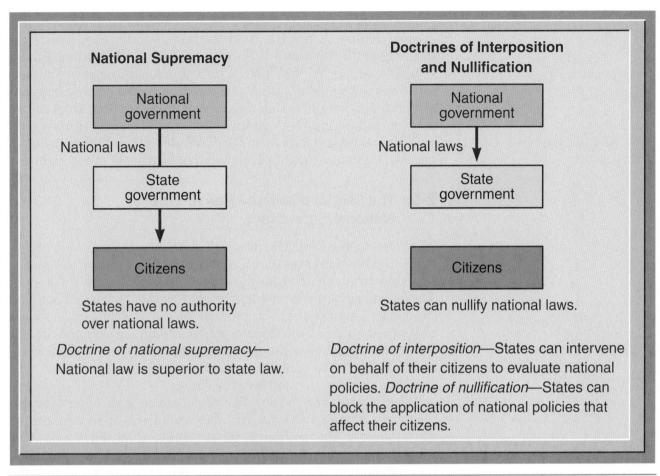

Figure 2-6 Illustrating the States' Rights Doctrine. Advocates of the states' rights doctrine claimed that because the Constitution interposed state government between the national government and the citizens of the states, each state had the right to nullify, or invalidate, the national government's laws. As a result, citizens would not have to obey those national laws that their states had nullified.

The doctrine of states' rights took on special urgency in the 1830s and 1840s as southern states came to fear that the federal government would use its supremacy to outlaw slavery. Those fears were mollified when the Supreme Court strengthened the cause of states' rights in *Dred Scott v. Sandford* (1857). In this case, Scott, a slave, was taken from Missouri, a slave state, to a federal territory in which slavery was illegal. A dispute then arose over whether Scott had gained his freedom or remained a slave. The case eventually reached the Supreme Court, where Chief Justice Roger Taney wrote the majority opinion (see Box 2–3). Taney, whom Jackson had appointed to succeed John Marshall, the author of *McCulloch v. Maryland,* was widely known to be a supporter of states' rights. Taney held that Scott had lost whatever freedom he had gained when he returned to Missouri to file his lawsuit. Taney went further to rule that the federal ban on slavery in the territories was unconstitutional because it violated the right of slave owners to own property (that is, slaves). In short, the *Dred Scott* case placed state law above federal law.

As a result of the *Dred Scott* case, the meaning of federalism was in great dispute during the years leading up to the Civil War. To a large extent, the dispute fell along geographic lines. Northern states generally supported the doctrine of national supremacy; southern states supported the doctrine of states' rights. The dispute between northern and southern states grew increasingly bitter, so much so that the southern states eventually sought to secede. It was only with the North's victory in the Civil War that the doctrine of national supremacy triumphed over the doctrine of states' rights.

2-5d The Civil War and the Reassertion of National Supremacy

In one sense, the Civil War was a dispute over the meaning of federalism. The southern states, embracing the logic of the states' rights doctrine, claimed they were free to secede from the Union. The federal government, which insisted on the doctrine of national supremacy, argued that the citizens of the southern states were also citizens of the United States and could not be stripped of their national citizenship without the permission of the federal government. Because the federal government rejected secession, the southern states could not leave the Union.

The dispute over the legality of secession had important implications for the behavior of other countries. If they accepted the argument the southern states made, then the Civil War was a conflict between independent nations and the norms of international relations would allow other countries to aid the Confederacy. If other countries accepted the argument the federal government made, however, the Civil War was a domestic insurrection and the norms of international relations would discourage other nations from becoming entangled in the internal affairs of the United States. The Confederacy desperately sought support from European countries in general and Britain in particular, but President Abraham Lincoln convinced Europe that the Civil War was a domestic matter. Unable to obtain outside help, Confederate forces slowly wore down against the superior military and industrial might of the Union.

Once the southern states surrendered at Appomattox, the federal government tried to drive the last nail in the coffin of the states' rights doctrine. The "nail" was the Fourteenth Amendment. Enacted along with the Thirteenth and Fifteenth Amendments, which outlawed slavery and guaranteed former male slaves the right to vote, the Fourteenth Amendment provided that "No State shall make or enforce any law which shall abridge the privileges or immunities of citizens of the United States; nor shall any State deprive any person of life, liberty, or property, without due process of law; nor deny to any person within its jurisdiction the equal protection of the laws." In other words, no state could violate or abridge the rights the Constitution accorded to citizens of the United States. With the passage of the Fourteenth Amendment, the federal government again reigned supreme.

2-5e Dual Federalism

Although the Civil War marked the eclipse of the doctrine of states' rights, it did not mark the end of challenges to national supremacy. American political culture continued to reflect the long-standing mistrust of a strong national government. These fears surfaced in the decades after the Civil War in a second challenge to the claims of national supremacy: the doctrine of **dual federalism**.

The doctrine of dual federalism held that the federal and state governments possessed complementary spheres of influence, within which each was supreme. According to this view, the federal government was supreme when it came to conducting those tasks that the Constitution explicitly assigned to it. For example, the Constitution made it clear that only the federal government could manage foreign affairs, impose tariffs on foreign goods, coin the country's money, and create a postal system. On the other hand, the doctrine of dual federalism argued that state governments were supreme in conducting tasks the Constitution did not explicitly give to the federal government. Proponents of dual federalism argued that the states were supreme when it came to education, fire and police protection, and welfare programs.

The doctrine of dual federalism, then, held that the federal and state governments would each exercise responsibility within their own sphere of activity without interference from the other. Because of the idea of noninterference, dual federalism is sometimes called the "layer cake" model of federalism.[19] As Figure 2–7 illustrates, in this model, the two levels of government operate like separate layers of a cake. Each possesses its own independent character. The two layers are joined as a single entity, but they retain their respective roles within that union. Because advocates of dual federalism were able to tap Americans' long-standing distrust of a powerful national government, the doctrine of dual federalism held sway in the half-century after 1880. In the 1930s, however, the doctrine of national supremacy would once again become ascendant.

2-5f The Present Era—National Supremacy as Fiscal Federalism

The 1930s gave rise to yet another interpretation of the meaning of federalism, an interpretation that prevails to this day. Under this new version of federalism, not only are federal laws superior to state laws, but the federal government also has a responsibility for providing financial assistance to state governments. Because federal aid has emerged as a major source of state revenue over the past seventy years, this newest form of federalism is known as **fiscal federalism**.

The **Great Depression** triggered the shift away from dual federalism toward fiscal federalism. During the early 1930s, unemployment reached 25 percent in the United States, national income fell by 50 percent, and the people turned to their state governments for

dual federalism
An interpretation of federalism that held that the national government was supreme within those areas specifically assigned to it in the Constitution, and the states were supreme in all other areas of public policy.

fiscal federalism
The principle that the federal government should play a major role in financing some of the activities of state and local governments.

Great Depression
The worst economic crisis in U.S. history, with unemployment rates reaching 25 percent. It began in 1929 and lasted until the start of World War II.

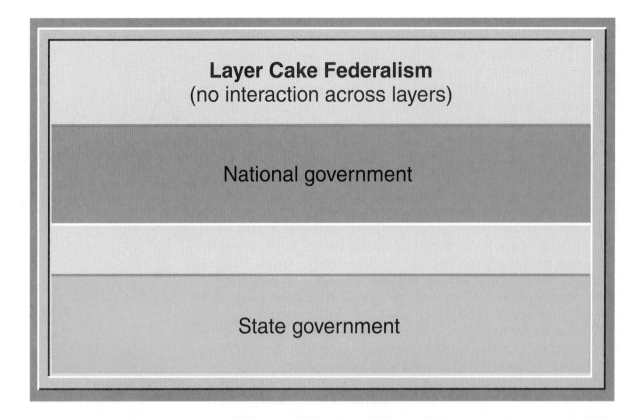

Layer Cake Federalism
(no interaction across layers)

National government

State government

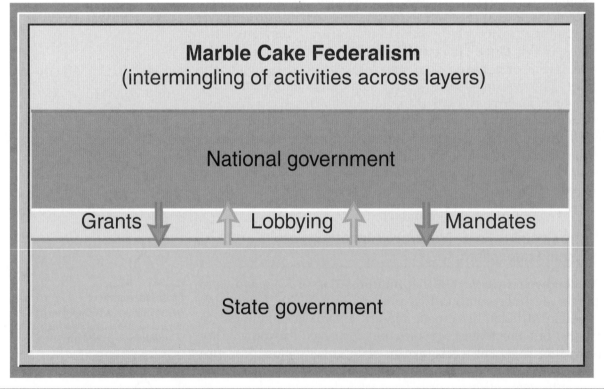

Marble Cake Federalism
(intermingling of activities across layers)

National government

Grants   Lobbying   Mandates

State government

Figure 2–7   "Layer Cake" versus "Marble Cake": Two Versions of Federalism. Before the New Deal, the layer cake model of federalism described a system in which states and the national government performed their respective duties with little interaction. In the 1930s, New Deal programs gave the national government a key role in funding services that the states handle. In turn, the states now try to influence national government decisions about the forms federal aid takes. The resulting intermingling of state and national government activities describes the marble cake model of federalism.

INTERACTIVE FIGURE

relief. The states, however, could not cope with the demand. The Great Depression had reduced their tax revenues, and most state constitutions barred the states from spending more than they took in. With the states unable to get the economy going again, all eyes turned to the federal government.

In Washington, D.C., President Franklin Delano Roosevelt (FDR) was quick to respond. During FDR's presidency, the federal government assumed a new role as a provider of services to states and individuals. Together with Congress, FDR's administration created a number of federal programs, known collectively as the **New Deal**, which were designed to provide federal assistance to the states and unemployment compensation and retirement insurance to individuals.

New Deal
The economic and social programs Congress enacted during Franklin Roosevelt's presidency before World War II.

The federal role in providing services to states and individuals would grow even larger three decades later. In the 1960s, President Lyndon Johnson persuaded Congress to launch the **Great Society**, which included federal programs designed to end poverty in the United States, make health care accessible to more people, and revitalize America's cities. With the creation of these programs, federal aid emerged as a primary source of revenue for state and local governments.

Great Society
The economic and social programs Congress enacted during Lyndon Johnson's presidency, from 1963 to 1969.

As federal aid to the states has grown, federal involvement in activities once thought to be the domain of the states has grown as well. Because many government services today represent a mix of federal and state activities, fiscal federalism is sometimes called "marble cake" federalism (see Figure 2–7).[20] In many instances, the federal government stipulates what sorts of services should be provided and gives the states the money they need to carry out its mandates. In turn, the states accept the money, meet the requirements, and provide the services.

The shift to fiscal federalism in some ways represents the most profound change in our understanding of federalism. Before the 1930s, the relationship between the federal and state governments was highly contentious. Washington, D.C., and the state capitals frequently jockeyed for legal authority and for dominance over one another. Since the 1930s, however, the focus has shifted from legal to fiscal concerns because the states have accepted federal preeminence in exchange for needed financial support. (We will discuss fiscal federalism more fully in Chapter 15.)

However, beginning in 1995, the Supreme Court handed down a series of decisions that place limits on the range of activities subject to national supremacy that have not been seen since the 1930s. Some cases limit the scope of the **interstate commerce clause** of the Constitution, which gives Congress the authority to "regulate commerce…among the several states." Beginning in the 1930s, the Court interpreted this power to include not only the regulation of interstate commerce, but also activities that merely affect interstate commerce. With this broad mandate, the federal government enacted laws giving itself power over a growing range of activities traditionally reserved to the states. One such law, the Gun-Free School Zones Act, prohibited the possession of guns

interstate commerce clause
The provision in Article I of the Constitution granting Congress the power to "regulate commerce . . . among the several states."

within 1,000 feet of a school. A second, the Violence Against Women Act, prohibited violence motivated by gender bias. In both cases, the Court ruled the laws were unconstitutional because neither possession of a gun at school nor acts of violence against women were sufficiently related to interstate commerce to justify the federal government's intrusion into the states' jurisdiction.[21] Another series of decisions have protected states from being sued under federal law. For example, in 1999, the Court protected states from suit by state employees seeking overtime pay mandated by the Fair Labor Standards Act of 1938, and in 2000, it concluded that states cannot be sued by employees under the federal government's Age Discrimination in Employment Act.[22] If the Court continues to follow this line of reasoning in subsequent rulings, it will place increasingly important constraints on the authority of the federal government, moving the nation closer to the dual federalism that existed at the start of the twentieth century.

The continually changing interpretations of the meaning of federalism remind us that the Constitution is not a rigid document. Although it sets forth the basic rules structuring the American political system, our understanding of what those rules mean has changed over time. As our interpretations of the rules change, so do the sorts of policies the government pursues. It is this flexibility of the Constitution that has enabled the federal government to meet the changing needs of the country.

SUMMARY

The need for the U.S. Constitution grew out of the failure of the confederal government established by the Articles of Confederation. The Founders brought conflicting political ambitions and objectives to the Constitutional Convention, and as a result, politics greatly influenced the content of the Constitution. Three issues were especially divisive: how to allocate representation in the new Congress, how to deal with the question of slavery, and how to define the powers of the new office of the presidency. The Founders managed to settle their differences through a mix of compromise and ambiguity. The states eventually ratified the Constitution after its proponents agreed to add a series of amendments, now known as the Bill of Rights, that would guarantee individual rights.

As they wrote the Constitution, the Founders were influenced by their philosophical principles, as well as by politics. The principle that stood first and foremost in their thinking was the need to protect individual rights. The importance the Founders attached to individual rights led them to favor democratic government by majority rule. The Founders recognized, however, that if left unchecked, a majority could use its advantage in numbers to suppress individual rights. To limit the potential for majority tyranny, the Founders modified the principle of majority rule in three important ways. First, they wrote electoral rules into the Constitution that make it difficult for permanent majorities to form. Second, they divided authority among branches of government, as well as between the federal government and state governments. Third, they placed formal boundaries on government action.

The Constitution specifies the fundamental structural rules that govern how the federal government is organized, how its officials are selected, the procedures by which it makes decisions, and how it relates to the state governments. Article I of the Constitution discusses the structure and powers of the legislative branch of government. Among other things, it stipulates that Congress shall consist of two chambers, the House and Senate, both of which must approve identical versions of a bill before it can become law. Article II discusses the powers of the presidency. Among other things, it assigns the president the power to run the executive branch, as well as the right to veto legislation Congress has passed. The Constitution says little about either the federal court system or relations among the states. Article III creates a Supreme Court and authorizes Congress to create other federal courts as needed. Article IV requires each state to respect, honor, and cooperate with other states, and it guarantees that the federal government will protect the states in time of foreign and domestic violence. Articles V, VI, and VII establish rules for amending the Constitution, for resolving conflicts between the states and the federal government, and for ratifying the Constitution.

The principles and rules contained in the Constitution have had three important consequences for politics in the United States. First, the rights of the individual enjoy such strong legal protection that the will of the majority may be frustrated at times. Second, the obstacles placed in the way of passing legislation create a strong bias in American politics in favor of the status quo, or the existing state of affairs, even when a majority of Americans would prefer change. Third, even though the Constitution makes it difficult to pass new laws, it has created a political system sufficiently flexible to meet the country's changing needs.

The flexibility of the Constitution shows clearly in the changing nature of federalism, the rules governing the relationship between the federal and state governments. The Founders chose to construct a federal political system because they wanted to remedy the problems that had undermined the Articles of Confederation without creating a national government that could impose its will on the states. Exactly how they meant the new federal political system to work, however, has stirred bitter political debate. For most of American history, federal law has been interpreted to be superior to state law. At other times, however, states have challenged the claim that the federal government is the dominant partner in the relationship between Washington, D.C., and the states. The continually changing meaning of federalism reminds us that the Constitution is not a rigid document, but a flexible set of rules still relevant to a dynamic society and political system.

KEY TERMS

Antifederalists

Articles of Confederation

bicameral legislature

Bill of Rights

checks and balances

classical liberalism

Connecticut Compromise

democracy

dual federalism

establishment clause

federalism

Federalists

fiscal federalism

Great Depression

Great Society

interstate commerce clause

majority tyranny

national supremacy

necessary and proper clause

New Deal

New Jersey Plan

republicanism

separation of powers

Shays' Rebellion

states' rights

Virginia Plan

READINGS FOR FURTHER STUDY

Bailyn, Bernard, ed. *The Debate on the Constitution: Federalist and Antifederalist Speeches, Articles, and Letters during the Struggle over Ratification* (New York: Library of America, 1993). A collection of speeches, articles, and letters by both supporters and critics of the Constitution as they debated its ratification.

———. *The Ideological Origins of the American Revolution* (Cambridge: Harvard University Press, 1967). The most widely accepted account of the development of support for independence in the American colonies.

Beard, Charles. *An Economic Interpretation of the Constitution of the United States* (New York: Macmillan, 1913). The classic treatment depicting how the Constitution reflects the economic self-interest of the Founders.

Brookhiser, Richard. *What Would the Founders Do?* (New York, Basic Books, 2006). In this book, Brookhiser examines how the Founders might handle contemporary problems like stem cell research and the drug wars.

Ellis, Joseph J. *Founding Brothers: The Revolutionary Generation* (New York: Alfred A. Knopf, 2000). This book tells the story of the Founders from their perspective. It emphasizes that neither independence nor the Constitution were foreordained but were the result of choices and circumstances that could easily have produced different outcomes.

Grodzins, Morton. *The American System* (New Brunswick, NJ: Transaction Books, 1984). A comprehensive discussion of the federal relationship in the United States.

Alexander Hamilton, James Madison, and John Jay, *The Federalist Papers,* ed. Garry Wills (New York: Bantam Books, 1982). The collection of articles these three Federalists wrote. The papers contain the essential arguments used to justify adoption of the Constitution.

Storing, Herbert J. *What the Antifederalists Were For* (Chicago: University of Chicago Press, 1981). A well-documented presentation of the arguments the losers made in the constitutional debate.

Wills, Garry. *Explaining America* (New York: Doubleday & Company, 1981). An interesting exploration of the themes of the *Federalist Papers.*

REVIEW QUESTIONS

1. The Founders of the U.S. Constitution wanted to
   a. ensure majority rule over the minority.
   b. prevent the suppression of minority rights.
   c. keep the states more powerful than the federal government.
   d. both b and c.
2. Which of the following is TRUE about the Articles of Confederation?
   a. All foreign policy power was vested in the states.
   b. Congress had the power to regulate interstate commerce.
   c. All powers of the national government were vested in Congress.
   d. The domestic economy prospered during this time.
3. Why did King George III decide to exert more control over the colonies in the middle of the eighteenth century?
   a. He grew tired of the radical colonists.
   b. He wanted to punish the colonists for dumping tea in Boston Harbor.
   c. He needed revenue to pay the costs of the French and Indian War.
   d. He wanted revenue to expand his palace.
4. The American Revolutionary War was fought because the colonists wanted
   a. to preserve the liberties that they already enjoyed.
   b. to obtain freedom from Great Britain.
   c. Samuel Adams to be their leader.
   d. a republican form of government.
5. Shays' Rebellion demonstrated that
   a. Congress could govern effectively in periods of crises.
   b. Congress could not govern effectively in periods of crises.
   c. state governments could always rely on the national government to assist them in dealing with armed rebellions.
   d. the president would help state governors with violence within their borders.
6. Under the Virginia Plan,
   a. every voter in the United States would be represented equally in the national legislature.

    b. every state in the United States would be represented equally in the national legislature.

    c. slavery would be abolished.

    d. the less populous states would have as much political power as Massachusetts, Pennsylvania, and Virginia.

7. In the three-fifths compromise, the debate over slavery became intertwined with the debate over

    a. the natural rights of African Americans.

    b. federalism.

    c. state boundaries.

    d. representation in the U.S. House of Representatives.

8. Classical liberalism emphasizes

    a. the rights of individuals.

    b. using the federal government to solve problems in society.

    c. using state governments to solve problems in society.

    d. none of the above.

9. The factual basis of *McCulloch v. Maryland* (1819) was the question, "Does Congress have the power to

    a. regulate interstate commerce?"

    b. tax personal income?"

    c. create a national bank?"

    d. build lighthouses?"

10. The shift from dual to fiscal federalism was triggered by

    a. the Civil War.

    b. the *Dred Scott* decision.

    c. the Great Depression.

    d. World War II.

NOTES

1. Emma Schwartz, "A Third Rebuke to Bush on Guantanamo Bay," *usnews.com*, posted June 12, 2008, available at www.usnews.com/articles/news/world/2008/06/12/a-third-rebuke-to-bush-on-guantnamo-bay.html (accessed August 8, 2008). The Obama administration has ordered the closure of the Guantanamo detention center by 2010 and has stopped using the term 'enemy combatant', but it has not clearly defined its position on indefinite detention. See William Douglas and Carol Rosenberg, "White House scraps term 'enemy combatant'", miamiherald.com, posted March 13, 2009, available at http://www.miamiherald.com/509/story/949019.html (accessed April 4, 2009).

2. Theodore Draper, "The Constitution Was Made, Not Born," *New York Times Book Review*, October 10, 1993, 3.

3. Samuel Eliot Morrison, *Oxford History of the American People* (New York: Oxford University Press, 1965), 182.

4. Edward S. Corwin, *The President: Office and Powers, 1787–1957*, 4th rev. ed. (New York: New York University Press, 1957), 5–6.

5. John Roche, "The Founding Fathers: A Reform Caucus in Action," *American Political Review* 55 (December 1961): 799–816.

6. Quoted in Draper, "The Constitution Was Made, Not Born," 25.

7. See Calvin C. Jillson, *Constitution Making: Conflict and Consensus in the Federal Convention of 1787* (New York: Agathon Press, 1988), 164–65.

8. John Locke, *Two Treatises of Government* (1630).

9. James Madison, "Federalist No. 10," in Alexander Hamilton, James Madison, and John Jay, *The Federalist Papers*, ed. Garry Wills (New York: Bantam Books, 1982), 45.

10. Charles de Montesquieu, *The Spirit of the Laws* (1734).

11. Richard E. Neustadt, *Presidential Power and the Modern Presidents: The Politics of Leadership from Roosevelt to Reagan* (New York: Free Press, 1990), 29. (Emphasis in the original.)

12. "Table 6-9 Presidential Vetoes, 1789–2006, and Signing Statements, 1929–2006," *CQ Press Electronic Library, CQ's Vital Statistics on American Politics Online Edition*, available at www.library.cqpress.com/vsap/document.php?id=vsap07_tab6-9&type=toc&num=10} (accessed August 1, 2008).

13. Jay Shafritz, *The Dorsey Dictionary of American Government and Politics* (Chicago: Dorsey, 1988), 206.

14. See David Gray Adler, "The Constitution and Presidential Warmaking," *Political Science Quarterly* 103 (Spring 1988): 8–13; Alexander Hamilton, "Federalist No. 69," in Alexander Hamilton, James Madison, and John Jay, *The Federalist Papers,* ed. Garry Wills (New York: Bantam Books, 1982); Louis Henkin, *Foreign Affairs and the Constitution* (Mineola, NY: Foundation Press, 1972), 50–51; Arthur M. Schlesinger, Jr., *The Imperial Presidency* (Boston: Houghton Mifflin, 1989), 6, 61–62.

15. For information on state laws and constitutional amendments affecting the rights of gays and lesbians to marry, go to www.hrc.org/issues/marriage/marriage_laws.asp.

16. See Ruth Ann Strickland, "The Twenty-seventh Amendment and Constitutional Change by Stealth," *PS: Political Science & Politics* 24 (December 1993): 716–21.

17. "Table 5-6 Congressional Measures Introduced and Enacted, 1947–2007," *CQ Press Electronic Library, CQ's Vital Statistics on American Politics Online Edition*, www.library.cqpress.com/vsap/document.php?id=vsap07_tab5-6&type=toc&num=9} (accessed August 1, 2008).

18. *McCulloch v. Maryland*, 4 Wheat. 316 (1819).

19. Morton Grodzins, "The Federal System," in *Goals for Americans: The Report of the President's Commission on National Goals* (Englewood Cliffs, NJ: Prentice-Hall, 1960), 265.

20. Ibid.

21. United States v. Lopez, 514 U.S. 549 (1995); see Aric Press and Bruce Shenitz, "The Limits of Commerce," *U.S. News & World Report,* May 8, 1995; *United States v. Morrison*, 529 U.S. 598 (2000).

22. *Alden v. Maine*, 527 U.S. 706 (1999); *Kimel v. Florida Bd of Regents*, 528 U.S. 62 (2000).

Constitution

CONSTITUTION OF THE UNITED STATES

Preamble

We the People of the United States, in Order to form a more perfect Union, establish Justice, insure domestic Tranquility, provide for the common defense, promote the general Welfare, and secure the Blessings of Liberty to ourselves and our Posterity, do ordain and establish this Constitution for the United States of America.

Article I.

Section 1.

Bicameral Congress

All legislative Powers herein granted shall be vested in a Congress of the United States, which shall consist of a Senate and House of Representatives.

Section 2.

Membership of the House

The House of Representatives shall be composed of Members chosen every second Year by the People of the several States, and the Electors in each State shall have the Qualifications requisite for Electors of the most numerous Branch of the State Legislature.

No Person shall be a Representative who shall not have attained to the age of twenty-five Years, and been seven Years a Citizen of the United States, and who shall not, when elected, be an Inhabitant of that State in which he shall be chosen.

Representatives and direct Taxes shall be apportioned among the several States which may be included within this Union, according to their respective Numbers, which shall be determined by adding to the whole Number of free Persons, including those bound to Service for a Term of Years, and excluding Indians not taxed, three fifths of all other Persons.[1] The actual Enumeration shall be made within three Years after the first Meeting of the Congress of the United States, and within every subsequent Term of ten Years, in such Manner as they shall by Law direct. The Number of Representatives shall not exceed one for every thirty Thousand, but each State shall have at Least one Representative; and until such enumeration shall be made, the State of New Hampshire shall be entitled to chose three, Massachusetts eight, Rhode-Island and Providence Plantations one, Connecticut five, New-York six, New Jersey four, Pennsylvania eight, Delaware one, Maryland six, Virginia ten, North Carolina five, South Carolina five, and Georgia three.

When vacancies happen in the Representation from any State, the Executive Authority thereof shall issue Writs of Election to fill such Vacancies.

The House of Representatives shall chuse their Speaker and other Officers; and shall have the sole Power of Impeachment.

Power to impeach

Section 3.

The Senate of the United States shall be composed of two Senators from each State, chosen by the Legislature thereof,[2] for six Years; and each Senator shall have one Vote.

Membership of the Senate

Immediately after they shall be assembled in Consequence of the first Election, they shall be divided as equally as may be into three Classes. The Seats of the Senators of the first class shall be vacated at the Expiration of the second Year, of the second Class at the Expiration of the fourth Year, and of the third Class at the Expiration of the sixth Year, so that one third may be chosen every second Year; *and if Vacancies happen by Resignation, or otherwise, during the Recess of the Legislature of any State, the Executive thereof may make temporary Appointments until the next Meeting of the Legislature, which shall then fill such Vacancies.*[3]

No Person shall be a Senator who shall not have attained to the Age of thirty Years, and been nine Years a Citizen of the United States, and who shall not, when elected, be an Inhabitant of that State for which he shall be chosen.

The Vice President of the United States shall be President of the Senate, but shall have no Vote, unless they be equally divided.

The Senate shall chuse their other Officers, and also a President pro tempore, in the Absence of the Vice President, or when he shall exercise the Office of President of the United States.

The Senate shall have the sole Power to try all Impeachments. When sitting for that Purpose, they shall be on Oath or Affirmation. When the President of the United States is tried the Chief Justice shall preside: and no Person shall be convicted without the Concurrence of two thirds of the Members present.

Power to try impeachments

Judgment in Cases of Impeachment shall not extend further than to removal from Office, and disqualification to hold and enjoy any Office of honor, Trust or Profit under the United States: but the Party convicted shall nevertheless be liable and subject to Indictment, Trial, Judgment and Punishment, according to Law.

Section 4.

Laws governing elections

The Times, Places and Manner of holding elections for Senators and Representatives, shall be prescribed in each State by the Legislature thereof; but the Congress may at any time by Law make or alter such Regulations, except as to the Places of choosing Senators.

The Congress shall assemble at least once in every Year, and such Meeting shall be on the *first Monday in December, unless they shall by Law appoint a different Day.*[4]

Section 5.

Rules of Congress

Each House shall be the Judge of the Elections, Returns and Qualifications of its own Members, and a Majority of each shall constitute a Quorum to do Business; but a smaller Number may adjourn from day to day, and may be authorized to compel the Attendance of absent Members, in such Manner, and under such Penalties as each House may provide.

Each House may determine the Rules of its Proceedings, punish its Members for disorderly Behavior, and, with the Concurrence of two thirds, expel a Member.

Each House shall keep a Journal of its Proceedings, and from time to time publish the same, excepting such Parts as may in their Judgment require Secrecy; and the Yeas and Nays of the Members of either House on any question shall, at the Desire of one fifth of those Present, be entered on the Journal.

Neither House, during the Session of Congress, shall, without the Consent of the other, adjourn for more than three days, nor to any other Place than that in which the two Houses shall be sitting.

Section 6.

Salaries and immunities of members

The Senators and Representatives shall receive a Compensation for their Services, to be ascertained by Law, and paid out of the Treasury of the United States. They shall in all Cases, except Treason, Felony and Breach of the Peace, be privileged from Arrest during their Attendance at the Session of their respective Houses, and in going to and returning from the same; and for any Speech or Debate in either House, they shall not be questioned in any other Place.

Ban on members of Congress holding federal appointive office

No Senator or Representative shall, during the Time for which he was elected, be appointed to any civil Office under the Authority of the United States, which shall have been created, or the Emoluments whereof shall have been increased during such time; and no Person holding any Office under the United States, shall be a Member of either House during his Continuance in Office.

Section 7.

All Bills for raising Revenue shall originate in the House of Representatives; but the Senate may propose or concur with Amendments as on other Bills.

Money bills originate in House

Every Bill which shall have passed the House of Representatives and the Senate, shall, before it become a Law, be presented to the President of the United States; If he approve he shall sign it, but if not he shall return it, with his Objections to that House in which it shall have originated, who shall enter the Objections at large on their Journal, and proceed to reconsider it. If after such Reconsideration two thirds of that House shall agree to pass the Bill, it shall be sent, together with the Objections, to the other House, by which it shall likewise be reconsidered, and if approved by two thirds of that House, it shall become a Law. But in all such Cases the Votes of both Houses shall be determined by yeas and Nays, and the Names of the Persons voting for and against the Bill shall be entered on the Journal of each House respectively. If any Bill shall not be returned by the President within ten Days (Sundays excepted) after it shall have been presented to him, the Same shall be a Law, in like Manner as if he had signed it, unless the Congress by their Adjournment prevent its Return, in which Case it shall not be a Law.

Every Order, Resolution, or Vote to which the concurrence of the Senate and House of Representatives may be necessary (except on a question of Adjournment) shall be presented to the President of the United States; and before the Same shall take Effect, shall be approved by him, or being disapproved by him, shall be repassed by two thirds of the Senate and House of Representatives, according to the Rules and Limitations prescribed in the Case of a Bill.

Section 8.

The Congress shall have Power To lay and collect Taxes, Duties, Imposts and Excises, to pay the Debts and provide for the common Defence and general Welfare of the United States; but all Duties, Imposts and Excises shall be uniform throughout the United States;

Powers of Congress

raise taxes

To borrow Money on the credit of the United States;

To regulate Commerce with foreign Nations, and among the several States, and with the Indian Tribes;

borrow money
regulate foreign commerce

To establish an uniform Rule of Naturalization, and uniform Laws on the subject of Bankruptcies throughout the United States;

To coin Money, regulate the Value thereof, and of foreign Coin, and fix the Standard of Weights and Measures;

*write naturalization and
bankruptcy laws*
coin money

To provide for the Punishment of counterfeiting the Securities and current Coin of the United States;

To establish Post Offices and post Roads;

punish counterfeiting

establish post offices

To promote the Progress of Science and useful Arts, by securing for limited Times to Authors and Inventors the exclusive Right to their respective Writings and Discoveries;

To constitute Tribunals inferior to the Supreme Court;

*provide for patents and
copyrights*
create courts

punish piracies

To define and punish Piracies and Felonies committed on the high Seas, and Offenses against the Law of Nations;

declare war

To declare War, grant Letters of Marque and Reprisal, and make Rules concerning Captures on Land and Water;

To raise and support Armies, but no Appropriation of Money to that Use shall be for a longer Term than two Years;

create army and navy

To provide and maintain a Navy;

To make Rules for the Government and Regulation of the land and naval Forces;

call forth the militia

To provide for calling forth the Militia to execute the Laws of the Union, suppress Insurrections and repel Invasions;

To provide for organizing, arming, and disciplining, the Militia, and for governing such Part of them as may be employed in the Service of the United States, reserving to the States respectively, the Appointment of the Officers, and the Authority of training the Militia according to the discipline prescribed by Congress;

govern District of Columbia

To exercise exclusive Legislation in all Cases whatsoever, over such District (not exceeding ten Miles square) as may, by Cession of particular States, and the Acceptance of Congress, become the Seat of the Government of the United States, and to exercise like Authority over all Places purchased by the Consent of the Legislature of the State in which the Same shall be, for the Erection of Forts, Magazines, Arsenals, dock-Yards and other needful Buildings;—And

necessary and proper clause

To make all Laws which shall be necessary and proper for carrying into Execution the foregoing Powers, and all other Powers vested by this Constitution in the Government of the United States, or in any Department or Officer thereof.

Section 9.

Restrictions on powers of Congress

The Migration or Importation of such Persons as any of the States now existing shall think proper to admit, shall not be prohibited by the Congress prior to the Year one thousand eight hundred and eight, but a Tax or duty may be imposed on such Importation, not exceeding ten dollars for each Person.

slave trade

habeas corpus

The Privilege of the Writ of Habeas Corpus shall not be suspended, unless when in Cases of Rebellion or Invasion the public Safety may require it.

no bill of attainder or ex post facto law

No bill of Attainder or ex post facto Law shall be passed.

No Capitation, or other direct, Tax shall be laid, *unless in Proportion to the Census or Enumeration herein before directed to be taken.*[5]

no interstate tariffs

No Tax or Duty shall be laid on Articles exported from any State.

no preferential treatment for some states

No Preference shall be given by any Regulation of Commerce or Revenue to the Ports of one State over those of another; nor shall Vessels bound to, or from, one State, be obliged to enter, clear or pay Duties in another.

no spending without appropriations

No Money shall be drawn from the Treasury, but in Consequence of Appropriations made by Law; and a regular Statement and Account of the Receipts and Expenditures of all public Money shall be published from time to time.

No Title of Nobility shall be granted by the United States: And no person holding any Office of Profit or Trust under them, shall, without the Consent of the Congress, accept of any present, Emolument, Office, or Title, of any kind whatever, from any King, Prince, or foreign State.

no titles of nobility

Section 10.

No State shall enter into any Treaty, Alliance, or Confederation; grant Letters of Marque and Reprisal; coin Money; emit Bills of Credit; make any Thing but gold and silver Coin a Tender in Payment of Debts; pass any Bill of Attainder, ex post facto Law, or Law impairing the Obligation of Contracts, or grant any Title of Nobility.

Restrictions on powers of states

No State shall, without the Consent of the Congress, lay any Imposts or Duties on Imports or Exports, except what may be absolutely necessary for executing its inspection Laws: and the net Produce of all Duties and Imposts, laid by any State on Imports or Exports, shall be for the Use of the Treasury of the United States; and all such Laws shall be subject to the Revision and Control of the Congress.

No State shall, without the Consent of Congress, lay any Duty of Tonnage, keep Troops, or Ships of War in time of Peace, enter into any Agreement or Compact with another State, or with a foreign Power, or engage in War, unless actually invaded, or in such imminent Danger as will not admit of delay.

Article II.

Section 1.

The executive Power shall be vested in a President of the United States of America. He shall hold his Office during the Term of four Years, and, together with the Vice President, chosen for the same Term, be elected, as follows

Office of President

the executive power

Each State shall appoint, in such Manner as the Legislature thereof may direct, a Number of Electors, equal to the whole Number of Senators and Representatives to which the State may be entitled in the Congress: but no Senator or Representative, or Person holding an Office of Trust or Profit under the United States, shall be appointed an Elector.

Election of President

The Electors shall meet in their respective States, and vote by Ballot for two Persons, of whom one at least shall not be an Inhabitant of the same State with themselves. And they shall make a List of all the Persons voted for, and of the Number of Votes for each; which List they shall sign and certify, and transmit sealed to the Seat of the Government of the United States, directed to the President of the Senate. The President of the Senate shall, in the Presence of the Senate and House of Representatives, open all the Certificates, and the Votes shall then be counted. The Person having the greatest Number of Votes shall be the President, if such Number be a Majority of the whole Number of Electors appointed;

and if there be more than one who have such Majority, and have an equal Number of Votes, then the House of Representatives shall immediately chuse by Ballot one of them for President; and if no Person have a Majority, then from the five highest on the List the said House shall in like Manner chuse the President. But in chusing the President, the Votes shall be taken by States, the Representation from each State having one Vote; a quorum for this Purpose shall consist of a Member or Members from two thirds of the States, and a Majority of all the States shall be necessary to a Choice. In every Case, after the Choice of the President, the Person having the greatest Number of Votes of the Electors shall be the Vice President. But if there should remain two or more who have equal Votes, the Senate shall chuse from them by Ballot the Vice President.[6]

The Congress may determine the Time of chusing the Electors, and the Day on which they shall give their Votes; which Day shall be the same throughout the United States.

Requirements to be President

No Person except a natural born Citizen, or a Citizen of the United States, at the time of the Adoption of this Constitution, shall be eligible to the Office of President; neither shall any person be eligible to that Office who shall not have attained to the Age of thirty-five Years, and been fourteen Years a Resident within the United States.

In Case of the Removal of the President from Office, or of his Death, Resignation, or Inability to discharge the Powers and Duties of the said Office, the Same shall devolve on the Vice President, and the Congress may by Law provide for the Case of Removal, Death, Resignation or Inability, both of the President and Vice President, declaring what Officer shall then act as President, and such Officer shall act accordingly, until the Disability be removed, or a President shall be elected.[7]

Pay of President

The President shall, at stated Times, receive for his Services, a Compensation, which shall neither be increased nor diminished during the Period for which he shall have been elected, and he shall not receive within that Period any other Emolument from the United States, or any of them.

Before he enter on the Execution of his Office, he shall take the following Oath or Affirmation:—"I do solemnly swear (or affirm) that I will faithfully execute the Office of President of the United States, and will to the best of my Ability, preserve, protect and defend the Constitution of the United States."

Section 2.

Powers of President

commander-in-chief clause require opinion of departmental officers

The President shall be Commander in Chief of the Army and Navy of the United States, and of the Militia of the several States, when called into the actual Service of the United States; he may require the Opinion, in writing, of the principal Officer in each of the executive Departments, upon any Subject relating to the Duties of their respective Offices, and he shall have Power to grant Reprieves and Pardons for Offences against the United States, except in Cases of Impeachment.

grant pardons

He shall have Power, by and with the Advice and Consent of the Senate, to make Treaties, provided two thirds of the Senators present concur; and he shall nominate, and by and with the Advice and Consent of the Senate, shall appoint Ambassadors, other public Ministers and Consuls, Judges of the supreme Court, and all other Officers of the United States, whose Appointments are not herein otherwise provided for, and which shall be established by Law: but the Congress may by Law vest the Appointment of such inferior Officers, as they think proper, in the President alone, in the Courts of Law, or in the Heads of Departments.

make treaties and appointments

The President shall have Power to fill up all Vacancies that may happen during the Recess of the Senate, by granting Commissions which shall expire at the End of their next Session.

Section 3.

He shall from time to time give to the Congress Information of the State of the Union, and recommend to their Consideration such Measures as he shall judge necessary and expedient; he may, on extraordinary Occasions, convene both Houses, or either of them, and in Case of Disagreement between them, with Respect to the Time of Adjournment, he may adjourn them to such Time as he shall think proper; he shall receive Ambassadors and other public Ministers; he shall take Care that the Laws be faithfully executed, and shall Commission all the Officers of the United States.

Relations of President with Congress

Section 4.

The President, Vice President and all civil Officers of the United States, shall be removed from Office on Impeachment for, and Conviction of, Treason, Bribery, or other high Crimes and Misdemeanors.

Impeachment

Article III.

Section 1.

The judicial Power of the United States, shall be vested in one supreme Court, and in such inferior Courts as the Congress may from time to time ordain and establish. The Judges, both of the supreme and inferior Courts, shall hold their Offices during good Behaviour, and shall, at stated Times, receive for their Services, a Compensation, which shall not be diminished during their Continuance in Office.

Federal courts

Section 2.

The judicial Power shall extend to all Cases, in Law and Equity, arising under this Constitution, the Laws of the United States, and Treaties made, or which shall be made, under their Authority;—to all Cases affecting Ambassadors, other public Ministers and Consuls;—to all Cases of admiralty and maritime Jurisdiction;—to Controversies to which the United States shall be a Party;—to

Jurisdiction of courts

Controversies between two or more States;—*between a State and Citizens of another State*,[8]—between Citizens of different States;—between Citizens of the same State claiming Lands under Grants of different States, and between a State, or the Citizens thereof, and foreign States, Citizens or Subjects.

original
appellate

In all Cases affecting Ambassadors, other public Ministers and Consuls, and those in which a State shall be Party, the supreme Court shall have original Jurisdiction. In all the other Cases before mentioned, the supreme Court shall have appellate Jurisdiction, both as to Law and Fact, with such Exceptions, and under such Regulations as the Congress shall make.

The Trial of all Crimes, except in Cases of Impeachment, shall be by Jury; and such Trial shall be held in the State where the said Crimes shall have been committed; but when not committed within any State, the Trial shall be at such Place or Places as the Congress may by Law have directed.

Section 3.

Treason

Treason against the United States, shall consist only in levying War against them, or in adhering to their Enemies, giving them Aid and Comfort. No Person shall be convicted of Treason unless on the Testimony of two Witnesses to the same overt Act, or on Confession in open Court.

The Congress shall have Power to declare the Punishment of Treason, but no Attainder of Treason shall work Corruption of Blood, or Forfeiture except during the Life of the Person attainted.

Article IV.

Section 1.

Full faith and credit

Full Faith and Credit shall be given in each State to the public Acts, Records, and judicial Proceedings of every other State. And the Congress may by general Laws prescribe the Manner in which such Acts, Records and Proceedings shall be proved, and the Effect thereof.

Section 2.

Privileges and immunities

The Citizens of each State shall be entitled to all Privileges and Immunities of Citizens in the several States.

A person charged in any State with Treason, Felony, or other Crime, who shall flee from Justice, and be found in another State, shall on Demand of the executive Authority of the State from which he fled, be delivered up, to be removed to the State having Jurisdiction of the Crime.

Extradition

No Person held to Service or Labour in one State, under the Laws thereof, escaping into another, shall, in Consequence of any Law or Regulation therein, be discharged from such Service or Labour, but shall be delivered up on Claim of the Party to whom such Service or Labour may be due.[9]

Section 3.

New States may be admitted by the Congress into this Union; but no new State shall be formed or erected within the Jurisdiction of any other State; nor any State be formed by the Junction of two or more States, or Parts of States, without the consent of the Legislatures of the States concerned as well as of the Congress.

Creation of new states

The Congress shall have Power to dispose of and make all needful Rules and Regulations respecting the Territory or other Property belonging to the United States; and nothing in this Constitution shall be so construed as to Prejudice any Claims of the United States, or of any particular State.

Governing territories

Section 4.

The United States shall guarantee to every State in this Union a Republican Form of Government, and shall protect each of them against Invasion; and on Application of the Legislature, or of the Executive (when the Legislature cannot be convened) against domestic Violence.

Protection of states

Article V.

The Congress, whenever two thirds of both Houses shall deem it necessary, shall propose Amendments to this Constitution, or, on the Application of the Legislatures of two thirds of the several States, shall call a Convention for proposing Amendments, which, in either Case, shall be valid to all Intents and Purposes, as Part of this Constitution, when ratified by the Legislatures of three fourths of the several States, or by Conventions in three fourths thereof, as the one or the other Mode of Ratification may be proposed by the Congress; Provided that no Amendment which may be made prior to the Year One Thousand eight hundred and eight shall in any Manner affect the first and fourth Clauses in the Ninth Section of the first Article; and that no State, without its Consent, shall be deprived of its equal Suffrage in the Senate.

Amending the Constitution

Article VI.

All Debts contracted and Engagements entered into, before the Adoption of this Constitution, shall be as valid against the United States under this Constitution, as under the Confederation.

Assumption of debts of Confederation

This Constitution, and the Laws of the United States which shall be made in Pursuance thereof; and all Treaties made, or which shall be made, under the Authority of the United States, shall be the supreme Law of the Land; and the Judges in every State shall be bound thereby, any Thing in the Constitution or Laws of any State to the Contrary notwithstanding.

Supremacy of federal laws and treaties

The Senators and Representatives before mentioned, and the Members of the several State Legislatures, and all executive and judicial Officers, both of the United States and of the several States, shall be bound by Oath or Affirmation, to support this Constitution; but no religious Test shall ever be required as a Qualification to any Office or public Trust under the United States.

No religious test

Article VII.

Ratification procedure

The Ratification of the Conventions of nine States, shall be sufficient for the Establishment of this Constitution between the States so ratifying the Same.

Done in Convention by the Unanimous Consent of the States present the Seventeenth Day of September in the Year of our Lord one thousand seven hundred and Eighty seven and of the Independence of the United States of America the Twelfth In witness whereof We have hereunto subscribed our Names,

G° Washington—Presid^t and deputy from Virginia			
New Hampshire	John Langdon	Pennsylvania	Geo. Clymer
	Nicholas Gilman		Thos FitzSimons
			B Franklin
			Thomas Mifflin
			Robt Morris
Massachusetts	Nathaniel Gorham		Jared Ingersoll
	Rufus King		James Wilson
Connecticut	W^m. Saml Johnson		Gouv. Morris
	Roger Sherman	Delaware	Geo. Read
New York	Alexander Hamilton		Gunning Bedford
New Jersey	Wil. Livingston		John Dickinson
	David Brearley		Richard Bassett
	Wm Paterson		Jaco. Broom
	Jona. Dayton	Maryland	James McHenry
			Dan of St Thos Jenifer
			Danl Carroll
Virginia	John Blair	South Carolina	Pinckney
	James Madison Jr.		Charles Pinckney
North Carolina	Wm Blount		Pierce Butler
			J. Rutledge
			Charles Cotesworth Pinckney
	Richd Dobbs Spaight	Georgia	William Few
	Hu Williamson		Abr Baldwin

[The first ten amendments, known as the "Bill or Rights," were ratified in 1791.]

Amendment I.

Freedom of religion, speech, press, assembly

Congress shall make no law respecting an establishment of religion, or prohibiting the free exercise thereof; or abridging the freedom of speech, or of the press; or the right of the people peaceably to assemble, and to petition the Government for a redress of grievances.

Amendment II.

A well regulated Militia, being necessary to the security of a free State, the right of the people to keep and bear Arms, shall not be infringed.

Right to bear arms

Amendment III.

No Soldier shall, in time of peace be quartered in any house, without the consent of the Owner, nor in time of war, but in a manner prescribed by law.

No quartering of troops in private homes

Amendment IV.

The right of the people to be secure in their persons, houses, papers, and effects, against unreasonable searches and seizures, shall not be violated, and no Warrants shall issue, but upon probable cause, supported by Oath or affirmation, and particularly describing the place to be searched, and the persons or things to be seized.

Unreasonable searches and seizures prohibited

Amendment V.

No person shall be held to answer for a capital, or otherwise infamous crime, unless on a presentment or indictment of a Grand Jury, except in cases arising in the land or naval forces, or in the Militia, when in actual service in time of War or public danger; nor shall any person be subject for the same offence to be twice put in jeopardy of life or limb; nor shall be compelled in any criminal case to be a witness against himself, nor be deprived of life, liberty, or property, without due process of law, nor shall private property be taken for public use, without just compensation.

Rights when accused; due process clause

Amendment VI.

In all criminal prosecutions, the accused shall enjoy the right to a speedy and public trial, by an impartial jury of the State and district wherein the crime shall have been committed, which district shall have been previously ascertained by law, and to be informed of the nature and cause of the accusation; to be confronted with the witnesses against him; to have compulsory process for obtaining witnesses in his favor, and to have Assistance of Counsel for his defence.

Rights when on trial

Amendment VII.

In Suits at common law, where the value in controversy shall exceed twenty dollars, the right of trial by jury shall be preserved, and no fact tried by a jury, shall be other-wise reexamined in any Court of the United States, than according to the rules of the common law.

Common-law suits

Amendment VIII.

Bail; no cruel and unusual punishments

Excessive bail shall not be required, nor excessive fines imposed, nor cruel and unusual punishments inflicted.

Amendment IX.

Unenumerated rights protected

The enumeration in the Constitution, of certain rights, shall not be construed to deny or disparage others retained by the people.

Amendment X.

Powers reserved for states

The powers not delegated to the United States by the Constitution, nor prohibited by it to the States, are reserved to the States respectively, or to the people.

Amendment XI. [Ratified in 1795.]

Limits on suits against states

The Judicial power of the United States shall not be construed to extend to any suit in law or equity, commenced or prosecuted against one of the United States by Citizens of another State, or by Citizens or Subjects of any Foreign State.

Amendment XII. [Ratified in 1804.]

Revision of electoral college procedure

The Electors shall meet in their respective states and vote by ballot for President and Vice President, one of whom, at least, shall not be an inhabitant of the same state with themselves; they shall name in their ballots the person voted for as President, and in distinct ballots the person voted for as Vice President, and they shall make distinct lists of all persons voted for as President, and of all persons voted for as Vice President, and of the number of votes for each, which lists they shall sign and certify, and transmit sealed to the seat of the government of the United States, directed to the President of the Senate;—The President of the Senate shall, in the presence of the Senate and House of Representatives, open all the certificates and the votes shall then be counted;—The person having the greatest number of votes for President, shall be the President, if such number be a majority of the whole number of Electors appointed; and if no person have such majority, then from the persons having the highest numbers not exceeding three on the list of those voted for as President, the House of Representatives shall choose immediately, by ballot, the President. But in choosing the President, the votes shall be taken by states, the representation from each state having one vote; a quorum for this purpose shall consist of a member or members from two-thirds of the states, and a majority of all the states shall be necessary to a choice. *And if the House of Representatives shall not choose a President whenever the right of choice shall devolve upon them, before the fourth day of March next following, then the Vice President shall act as President, as in the case of the death or other constitutional disability of the President.*—[10] The person having the greatest number of votes as Vice President, shall be the Vice President, if such number be a majority of the whole number of Electors appointed, and if no person have a majority, then from the two highest numbers on the list, the Senate shall choose the Vice President; a quorum for the purpose shall consist of two-thirds of the whole number of Senators, and a majority of the whole number shall be necessary to a choice. But no person constitutionally ineligible to the office of President shall be eligible to that of Vice President of the United States.

Amendment XIII. [Ratified in 1865.]

Section 1.

Neither slavery nor involuntary servitude, except as a punishment for crime whereof the party shall have been duly convicted, shall exist within the United States, or any place subject to their jurisdiction.

Slavery prohibited

Section 2.

Congress shall have power to enforce this article by appropriate legislation.

Amendment XIV. [Ratified in 1868.]

Section 1.

All persons born or naturalized in the United States and subject to the jurisdiction thereof, are citizens of the United States and of the State wherein they reside. No State shall make or enforce any law which shall abridge the privileges or immunities of citizens of the United States; nor shall any State deprive any person of life, liberty, or property, without due process of law; nor deny to any person within its jurisdiction the equal protection of the laws.

Ex-slaves made citizens
Due process clause
Equal protection clause

Section 2.

Representatives shall be apportioned among the several States according to their respective numbers, counting the whole number of persons in each State, excluding Indians not taxed. But when the right to vote at any election for the choice of electors for President and Vice President of the United States, Representatives in Congress, the Executive and Judicial officers of a State, or the members of the Legislature thereof, is denied to any of the male inhabitants of such State, being *twenty-one*[11] years of age, and citizens of the United States, or in any way abridged, except for participation in rebellion, or other crime, the basis of representation therein shall be reduced in the proportion which the number of such male citizens shall bear to the whole number of male citizens twenty-one years of age in such State.

Rules for reducing congressional representation for states that deny adult males the right to vote

Section 3.

No person shall be a Senator or Representative in Congress, or elector of President and Vice President, or hold any office, civil or

Southern rebels denied federal office

military, under the United States, or under any State, who, having previously taken an oath, as a member of Congress, or as an officer of the United States, or as a member of any State legislature, or as an executive or judicial officer of any State, to support the Constitution of the United States, shall have engaged in insurrection or rebellion against the same, or given aid or comfort to the enemies thereof. But Congress may by a vote of two-thirds of each House, remove such disability.

Section 4.

Rebel debts repudiated

The validity of the public debt of the United States, authorized by law, including debts incurred for payment of pensions and bounties for services in suppressing insurrection or rebellion, shall not be questioned. But neither the United States nor any State shall assume or pay any debt or obligation incurred in aid of insurrection or rebellion against the United States, or any claim for the loss or emancipation of any slave; but all such debts, obligations and claims shall be held illegal and void.

Section 5.

The Congress shall have power to enforce, by appropriate legislation, the provisions of this article.

Amendment XV. [Ratified in 1870.]

Section 1.

African American males given right to vote

The right of citizens of the United States to vote shall not be denied or abridged by the United States or by any State on account of race, color, or previous condition of servitude.

Section 2.

The Congress shall have power to enforce this article by appropriate legislation.

Amendment XVI. [Ratified in 1913.]

Federal income tax authorized

The Congress shall have power to lay and collect taxes on incomes, from whatever source derived, without apportionment among the several States, and without regard to any census or enumeration.

Amendment XVII. [Ratified in 1913.]

Popular election of senators required

The Senate of the United States shall be composed of two Senators from each State, elected by the people thereof, for six years; and each Senator shall have one vote. The electors in each State shall have the qualifications requisite for electors of the most numerous branch of the State legislatures.

When vacancies happen in the representation of any State in the Senate, the executive authority of such State shall issue writs of election to fill such vacancies: *Provided*, That the legislature of any State may empower the executive thereof to make temporary appointments until the people fill the vacancies by election as the legislature may direct.

This amendment shall not be so construed as to affect the election or term of any Senator chosen before it becomes valid as part of the Constitution.

Amendment XVIII. [Ratified in 1919.]

Section 1.

After one year from the ratification of this article the manufacture, sale, or transportation of intoxicating liquors within, the importation thereof into, or the exportation thereof from the United States and all territory subject to the jurisdiction thereof for beverage purposes is hereby prohibited.

Manufacture and sale of liquor prohibited (Prohibition)

Section 2.

The Congress and the several States shall have concurrent power to enforce this article by appropriate legislation.

Section 3.

This article shall be inoperative unless it shall have been ratified as an amendment to the Constitution by the legislatures of the several States, as provided in the Constitution, within seven years from the date of the submission hereof to the States by the Congress.[12]

Amendment XIX. [Ratified in 1920.]

The right of citizens of the United States to vote shall not be denied or abridged by the United States or by any State on account of sex.

Women given right to vote

Congress shall have power to enforce this article by appropriate legislation.

Amendment XX. [Ratified in 1933.]

Section 1.

The terms of the President and Vice President shall end at noon on the 20th day of January, and the terms of Senators and Representatives at noon on the 3d day of January, of the years in which such terms would have ended if this article had not been ratified; and the terms of their successors shall then begin.

Federal terms of office to begin in January

Section 2.

The Congress shall assemble at least once in every year, and such meeting shall begin at noon on the 3d day of January, unless they shall by law appoint a different day.

Emergency presidential
succession

Section 3.

If, at the time fixed for the beginning of the term of the President, the President elect shall have died, the Vice President elect shall become President. If a President shall not have been chosen before the time fixed for the beginning of his term, or if the President elect shall have failed to qualify, then the Vice President elect shall act as President until a President shall have qualified; and the Congress may by law provide for the case wherein neither a President elect nor a Vice President elect shall have qualified, declaring who shall then act as President, or the manner in which one who is to act shall be selected, and such person shall act accordingly until a President or Vice President shall have qualified.

Section 4.

The Congress may by law provide for the case of the death of any of the persons from whom the House of Representatives may choose a President whenever the right of choice shall have devolved upon them, and for the case of the death of any of the persons from whom the Senate may choose a Vice President whenever the right of choice shall have devolved upon them.

Section 5.

Sections 1 and 2 shall take effect on the 15th day of October following the ratification of this article.

Section 6.

This article shall be inoperative unless it shall have been ratified as an amendment to the Constitution by the legislatures of three-fourths of the several States within seven years from the date of its submission.

Amendment XXI. [Ratified in 1933.]

Section 1.

Ban on manufacture and sale of
liquor (Prohibition) repealed

The eighteenth article of amendment to the Constitution of the United States is hereby repealed.

Section 2.

The transportation or importation into any State, Territory, or possession of the United States for delivery or use therein of intoxicating liquors, in violation of the laws thereof, is hereby prohibited.

Section 3.

This article shall be inoperative unless it shall have been ratified as an amendment to the Constitution by conventions in the several States, as provided in the Constitution, within seven years from the date of the submission hereof to the States by the Congress.

Amendment XXII. [Ratified in 1951.]

Section 1.

No person shall be elected to the office of the President more than twice, and no person who has held the office of President, or acted as President, for more than two years of a term to which some other person was elected President shall be elected to the office of the President more than once. But this Article shall not apply to any person holding the office of President when this Article was proposed by the Congress, and shall not prevent any person who may be holding the office of President, or acting as President, during the term within which this Article becomes operative from holding the office of President or acting as President during the remainder of such term.

Two-term limit for President

Section 2.

This article shall be inoperative unless it shall have been ratified as an amendment to the Constitution by the legislatures of three-fourths of the several States within seven years from the date of its submission to the States by the Congress.

Amendment XXIII. [Ratified in 1961.]

Section 1.

The District constituting the seat of Government of the United States shall appoint in such manner as the Congress may direct:

A number of electors of President and Vice President equal to the whole number of Senators and Representatives in Congress to which the District would be entitled if it were a State, but in no event more than the least populous State; they shall be in addition to those appointed by the States, but they shall be considered, for the purposes of the election of President and Vice President, to be electors appointed by a State; and they shall meet in the District and perform such duties as provided by the twelfth article of amendment.

Residents of the District of Columbia given right to vote for president

Section 2.

The Congress shall have power to enforce this article by appropriate legislation.

Amendment XXIV. [Ratified in 1964.]

Section 1.

The right of citizens of the United States to vote in any primary or other election for President or Vice President, for electors for President or Vice President, or for Senator or Representative in Congress, shall not be denied or abridged by the United States or any State by reason of failure to pay any poll tax or other tax.

Poll taxes in federal elections prohibited

Section 2.

The Congress shall have power to enforce this article by appropriate legislation.

Presidential disability and succession

Amendment XXV. [Ratified in 1967.]

Section 1.
In case of the removal of the President from office or of his death or resignation, the Vice President shall become President.

Section 2.
Whenever there is a vacancy in the office of the Vice President, the President shall nominate a Vice President who shall take office upon confirmation by a majority vote of both Houses of Congress.

Section 3.
Whenever the President transmits to the president pro tempore of the Senate and the Speaker of the House of Representatives his written declaration that he is unable to discharge the powers and duties of his office, and until he transmits to them a written declaration to the contrary, such powers and duties shall be discharged by the Vice President as Acting President.

Section 4.
Whenever the Vice President and a majority of either the principal officers of the executive departments or of such other body as Congress may by law provide, transmit to the President pro tempore of the Senate and the Speaker of the House of Representatives their written declaration that the President is unable to discharge the powers and duties of his office, the Vice President shall immediately assume the powers and duties of the office as Acting President.

Thereafter, when the President transmits to the President pro tempore of the Senate and the Speaker of the House of Representatives his written declaration that no inability exists, he shall resume the powers and duties of his office unless the Vice President and a majority of either the principal officers of the executive department[s] or of such other body as Congress may by law provide, transmit within four days to the President pro tempore of the Senate and the Speaker of the House of Representatives their written declaration that the President is unable to discharge the powers and duties of his office. Thereupon Congress shall decide the issue, assembling within forty-eight hours for that purpose if not in session. If the Congress, within twenty-one days after receipt of the latter written declaration, or, if Congress is not in session, within twenty-one days after Congress is required to assemble, determines by two-thirds vote of both Houses that the President is unable to discharge the powers and duties of his office, the Vice President shall continue to discharge the same as Acting President; otherwise, the President shall resume the powers and duties of his office.

Amendment XXVI. [Ratified in 1971.]

Section 1.
The right of citizens of the United States, who are 18 years of age or older, to vote shall not be denied or abridged by the United States or by any State on account of age.

Voting age lowered to eighteen

Section 2.
The Congress shall have power to enforce this article by appropriate legislation.

Amendment XXVII. [Ratified in 1992.]

Section 1.
No law, varying the compensation for the services of the senators and representatives, shall take effect until an election of representatives shall have intervened.

No congressional pay increase within a term

[1] Changed by the Fourteenth Amendment, section 2.

[2] Changed by the Seventeenth Amendment.

[3] Changed by the Seventeenth Amendment.

[4] Changed by the Twentieth Amendment, section 2.

[5] Changed by the Sixteenth Amendment.

[6] Superseded by the Twelfth Amendment.

[7] Modified by the Twenty-fifth Amendment.

[8] Modified by the Eleventh Amendment.

[9] Changed by the Thirteenth Amendment.

[10] Changed by the Twentieth Amendment, section 3.

[11] Changed by the Twenty-sixth Amendment.

[12] Repealed by the Twenty-first Amendment.

3

The Social Context of American Politics

CHAPTER OUTLINE

INTRODUCTION

In the spring of 2008, the U.S. Census Bureau announced that the American population had reached a milestone: More than 100 million Americans were considered members of minority groups, and they constituted 34 percent of the national population.[1] The country was becoming more diverse in large part because of the rapid growth of the Hispanic and Asian populations. The number of Hispanics grew by 3.3 percent between 2006 and 2007 alone. Over that same time span, the Asian population grew by 2.9 percent. The number of non-Hispanic whites, African Americans, and American Indians grew at much slower rates. Given different birth rates and immigration levels among racial and ethnic groups, the composition of the American population will continue to change rapidly over the next several decades, raising a number of interesting questions about the potential consequences for the country's politics.[2]

Although dramatic demographic changes have occurred in recent years, it is not at all clear that most Americans really know what America looks like. A recent survey of eighteen- to twenty-four-year olds, for example, revealed considerable ignorance of even the most basic population number. When asked how many people were living in the United States, only 30 percent of young people could give the right answer, even with the broad category of 150 million people to 350 million people being considered correct. (The actual figure is 300 million. The majority of young Americans guessed that the population was between 500 million people and a billion people.) Along similar lines, a *Washington Post* survey from a decade previous showed that white Americans underestimated their own numbers and exaggerated the numbers for minority groups. African Americans, Hispanics, and Asian Americans also greatly underestimated the number of white Americans and exaggerated their own numbers.[3]

Survey results such as these are by no means unusual. Public opinion polls repeatedly find that many Americans do not have an accurate idea of the demographic, economic, or social composition of the country. This lack of awareness is particularly prevalent among the young, the less educated, and those who live in areas with large concentrations of minorities. More importantly, these misconceptions are not innocuous; people who think more Americans are minorities than is really the case also feel more threatened by minorities.[4]

Is it necessary to know the makeup of the American population to understand politics in the United States? In a word, yes. The preamble to the Constitution makes it clear that governing authority in the United States rests ultimately in the hands of "We the People." And for more than 200 years observers have lauded the American commitment to, in Abraham Lincoln's immortal words, "government of the people, by the people, for the people." In short, the Founders sought to create a representative government.

But representative of what or whom? The United States is an extraordinarily diverse society. Whether Americans identify themselves in terms of their race, ethnicity, religion, or some other characteristic determines how they see their political interests, and in turn, shapes the demands they make on government and the kinds of political rules they favor. At the same time, many voters now doubt that the American political system lives up to Lincoln's lofty vision of a government by the people. Callers to radio talk shows frequently complain that the average American has no effective voice in politics, and some scholars argue that a power elite dominates American politics. So to evaluate whether American government in the twenty-first century fulfills the Founders' vision of representative government, we need to understand the diverse nature of American society.

In this chapter, we look at who the American people are and at which groups wield political power in the United States. We begin by examining the basic demographic characteristics of American society, such as the size of the population, its racial and ethnic makeup, the proportion of immigrants, and how these characteristics have changed over the past two centuries. We then explore some of the current social and economic characteristics of American society, including religion, education, and wealth. We go on to discuss why the United States, unlike so many other countries, has dampened social conflict and succeeded in combining social diversity with political stability. We show that the answer lies in the overlapping memberships of groups in the United States, a phenomenon that enables the government to respond to at least some of the needs of nearly all groups or individuals. We argue that our political system is pluralistic—that is, responsive to many groups, although these groups neither wield equal political power nor share equally in government benefits. These two characteristics—group overlap and pluralism—enable our political system to manage the inevitable conflicts that arise among different groups.

3-1 WHO ARE AMERICANS?

Political commentators like to speak about the average American, usually using colorful terms such as Joe Sixpack, and John or Jane Q. Public. And it is a relatively simple matter to generate a statistical profile of the average American (see Box 3–1), yet focusing on statistical averages obscures much more than it reveals. Because American society is remarkably diverse, most Americans look anything but average. To begin to draw a more accurate picture of who Americans are as a people, we look first at the growth of the American population over the past 220 years and at the shift the population made from rural to urban life. We then examine American society along several key demographic dimensions: race, ethnicity, language, age, family households, and sexual orientation.

3-1a A Growing and Changing Population

In July 2007, the U.S. Census Bureau estimated that 301,621,157 people were living in the United States, making it the third most

The People behind the Rules

Box 3–1   The Average American, 1900 and 2008

Source: © Bettmann/CORBIS

Source: © The Image Works.

The average American in 1900 *(left)* and 2000 *(right)*.

A look at the statistically average American is enlightening because it reveals some of the general ways our society is changing (see Table 3–1).

The average American has changed in significant ways since 1900. Over the last century, the population has, on average, grown older, but the majority of the population is still white. Since 1950, women have outnumbered men—in large part because women live longer than men do. The number of men and women is virtually the same in most age groups, with the only major difference occurring among people older than sixty-five years of age.

In 1900, the average American was a twenty-three-year-old man, three years away from marriage. In 2005, the average American was a thirty-five-year-old woman, married and with children. In 1900, a slight majority of Americans were renters, whereas in 2008 the average American owned his or her home.

Finally, the average American household in 1900 earned $651 a year, whereas in 2007, the average household income exceeded $50,233 a year. Comparing relative buying power is, of course, difficult because so many things we take for granted as expenses—such as cars, televisions,

DVD players (86 percent of homes own one or more), cell phones (74 percent), iPods or other music players (25 percent), digital video recorders (23 percent), and other items—were either not invented or not generally available in 1900. Indeed, more changes are in the offing; by 2006, 73 percent of homes had a personal computer and 67 percent of Americans had home access to the Internet. All these technological advances change the way we live and, in many cases, the way we interact with each other and conduct politics. During the 2008 presidential campaign, for example, every candidate had a home page on the World Wide Web, and several of them were remarkably successful in using the Internet to raise campaign funds.

Sources: *Historical Statistics of the United States: Colonial Times to 1970* (Washington, D.C.: U.S. Census Bureau, 1975), 14, 19, 20, 381; "People, Opinions, & Polls," *Public Perspective,* 6 (August/September 1995): 45; *Statistical Abstract of the United States, 2006,* 125th ed. (Washington, D.C.: U.S. Census Bureau, 2006); Carmen DeNavas-Walt, Bernadette D. Proctor, and Cheryl Hill Lee, *U.S. Census Bureau, Current Population Reports, P60-229, Income, Poverty, and Health Insurance in the United States: 2004* (Washington, D.C: U.S. Government Printing Office, 2005); Pew Center for the People and the Press, "Online Papers Modestly Boost Newspaper Readership," July 30, 2006, available at www.people-press.org/report/282/online-papers-modestly-boost-newspaper-readership

Characteristic	1900	2008
Race and ethnicity	White	White
Sex	Male	Female
Age	22.9	36.4
Marital status	Unmarried	Married
Education	8.2 years	Some college (but no degree)
Household income	$651	$50,233
Homeownership	Renter	Owner

Table 3–1   The Average American, 1900 and 2008

populous country in the world, after China and India.[5] The vast majority of these 302 million people are American citizens, but not all are. The Census Bureau attempts to count everyone who lives in the United States, regardless of whether they are citizens. By the same token, the census does not count the thousands of American citizens who live abroad.

In practice, the Census Bureau's figure probably misestimates the true number of people living in the United States. (The Census Bureau estimates that in 2000, the census takers overcounted the total population by 1.3 million people but undercounted African Americans.) Nonetheless, the figure represents incredible growth since the first census was taken in 1790. When George Washington was president, fewer than 4 million people lived in the United States, a figure roughly equal to 10 percent of California's population today. As Figure 3–1 shows, population growth exploded over the next half century, as the United States grew westward and new immigrants arrived. The rate of population growth was actually higher during the nineteenth century than it is today. Nonetheless, in last decade, the United States added more than 30 million

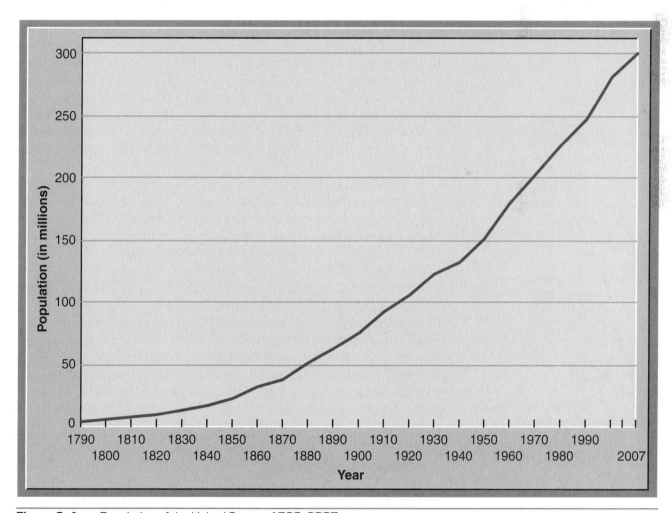

Figure 3–1 Population of the United States, 1790–2007.
Source: *U.S. Census Bureau.*

people. (Of course, because the United States is so large today, even a small percentage increase adds millions of people to our population.) This increase has outstripped our geographic growth: In 1790, there were 4.5 people per square mile, and in 2000, there were 79.6. A growing population affects the political system because it usually entails more demands on government and more problems for government to solve.

The dramatic growth in the population of the United States over the past two centuries has been accompanied by equally dramatic changes in the places where Americans live. The United States has changed from being predominantly rural to predominantly urban. (An urban area encompasses a central or inner city, as well as surrounding suburbs.) For much of American history, rural-urban migration meant that people moved to a central city. In recent decades, however, both rural areas and cities have seen migration to the suburbs. In 1910, only 12 percent of Americans lived in suburbs, whereas in 2000, 52 percent did.[6]

The movement of Americans from towns to cities and from cities to suburbs has had important political consequences. City dwellers, suburbanites, and rural voters have different interests on many issues. Take, for example, government spending on transportation. City dwellers may wish to spend their tax dollars on mass transit, suburbanites may prefer to build more freeways for their commute to work, and rural voters may want better county roads. Because American legislatures are designed to be representative and because they usually cannot satisfy every group, they generally are most responsive to whichever group commands the most votes. Thus, as the U.S. population has become more suburban, the interests of rural areas and inner cities have become secondary.

In addition to moving from towns to cities, the population growth has shifted away from the Eastern seaboard (and the original thirteen colonies) to other areas of the country. The country's mean center of population—the point on an imaginary flat map of the United States where the country would balance—has moved from twenty-three miles east of Baltimore, Maryland, in 1790, to Phelps County, Missouri, southwest of St. Louis, today. Again, because the population has grown faster in the South and West, these areas have gained representation at the expense of the more established (and slower growing) East and Midwest. Because the so-called **Sun Belt** states (those states in the South and West) have different economic and social conditions, their growth has meant that the concerns of the **Rust Belt** states (the older industrial states in the Northeast and around the Great Lakes) have been given less government attention than they would otherwise command.

Sun Belt
The states in the South, Southwest, and West Coast—areas that have experienced tremendous population and economic growth since 1950.

Rust Belt
The major industrial states of the Northeast and Midwest that did not enjoy great population or economic growth in the second half of the twentieth century.

3-1b Race and Ethnicity

Americans often think of the United States as a melting pot of people from many different backgrounds. Yet the melting pot image misleads. Rather than becoming generic Americans, many people have maintained their sense of racial or ethnic identity. Indeed, the nation's population is becoming increasingly heterogeneous, with important implications for American politics.

White Americans

White Americans continue to be the country's largest racial group. Their percentage of the population, however, is dropping, to 66 percent in 2007 from 70 percent just seven years before. The original white colonists came from northern Europe. (Keep in mind, of course, that American Indians lived here long before Europeans arrived.) Although the United States saw large-scale immigration from southern Europe at the beginning of the twentieth century, northern Europeans remain the largest ethnic groups in the United States. Germany claims the honor of providing the largest contribution to the U.S. population; 15 percent of all Americans say they are of German descent. Other major European ethnic groups are Irish (11 percent), English (9 percent), Italian (6 percent), French (3 percent), and Polish (3 percent).

African Americans

In 2007, African Americans constituted the second largest minority group in the United States at 12.8 percent of the population, although they were the largest minority group in 24 states.[7] (Surveys suggest that there is little agreement in the African American community over the label to be attached to their group. One recent poll shows a preference for *African American*, another a predilection for *black*, a third suggests an even split between the two terms, and a fourth concluded it does not matter either way.)[8] Until quite recently, African Americans had always been the country's largest minority group, having constituted 19 percent of the population in 1790.

African Americans are a significant political bloc not just because of their numbers, but because their social and economic heritage forged a common political orientation. From the end of the Civil War to the New Deal era, African Americans who were able to vote overwhelmingly supported Republican candidates because Lincoln, who issued the Emancipation Proclamation, was a Republican and because the Democrats were linked to segregationist policies in the South. African Americans began to shift their allegiance to the Democratic Party in the 1930s, when northern Democrats began to push civil rights legislation over the opposition of many Republicans and southern Democrats. The African American identification with the Democratic Party was cemented in 1964, when the Republicans ran Arizona Senator Barry Goldwater, an ardent foe of the Civil Rights Act of 1964, for president against the incumbent, Lyndon Johnson, who had pushed hard for the legislation.[9] Now, because of their political cohesiveness, African Americans form a significant component of the Democratic Party.[10] But there is some evidence that political differences between middle class and lower class African Americans are starting to appear. Indeed, over a third of African Americans now say that they can no longer be thought of as a single race. These differences, however, have yet to shift any substantial number of African Americans away from their liberal leanings and toward the more conservative Republican Party.[11]

The political influence of African Americans is concentrated in the South and in large cities. A majority of African Americans live in the South. They constitute more than 30 percent of the voting age population in Mississippi; more than 25 percent in Georgia, Louisiana, Maryland, and South Carolina; and more than 20 percent in Alabama and North Carolina.[12] As Chapter 5 discusses in some detail, the civil rights movement has succeeded in ending the discriminatory practices that prevented African Americans from exercising their right to vote, and as a result, they have become an important political force in the South. African Americans also have enjoyed great electoral success in cities where they form a significant portion of the population. Over the past three decades, for example, most major cities, among them Atlanta, Baltimore, Buffalo, Chicago, Cincinnati, Cleveland, Columbus, Dallas, Denver, Detroit, Houston, Los Angeles, Memphis, New Orleans, New York, Philadelphia, San Francisco, and Washington, D.C., have elected African American mayors.

Outside the South and large cities, African Americans exercise much less political clout. In twenty states, most of which are in the North and West, African Americans constitute less than 5 percent of the population. Likewise, only 25 percent of African Americans live in the suburbs. Where African Americans are few in number, they have a harder time achieving their political goals, not necessarily because of racism, but because they lack the votes needed to command the attention of elected officials. Simply put, elected officials respond to voters.[13]

Hispanic Americans

In 2001, Hispanics became the largest minority group in the United States. (The U.S. Census Bureau defines Hispanics as people of Spanish background, who may be of any race. Many Hispanics also call themselves white; thus, in census figures, some whites are also Hispanics.) The Census Bureau estimated that in 2007 there were 45.5 million Hispanics and 38.7 million blacks (the designation used on the census forms). Moreover, Hispanics now outnumber African Americans in seven of America's largest cities: Dallas, Houston, Los Angeles, New York City, Phoenix, San Antonio, and San Diego.[14]

The rise in the number of Hispanics living in the United States has been dramatic. In 1980, they constituted 6 percent of the population; twenty-seven years later, they constituted 15.1 percent. The primary reason for this rapid growth is that the average Hispanic woman has more children during her lifetime (roughly three) than the average non-Hispanic woman (roughly two). Another reason (and the one that gets the most attention) is that large numbers of people have immigrated to the United States from Latin America over the past three decades. The high rate of immigration means that many Hispanics—no one knows for sure but perhaps as many as one out of three—are not U.S. citizens and thus do not have the right to vote. This helps explain why Hispanics often do not exercise political power commensurate with their share of the population.

In the 2006 American Community Survey, 64 percent of Hispanics traced their heritage to Mexico. The rest came from Central and South America (13 percent), Puerto Rico (9 percent), Cuba (3 percent), the Dominican Republic (3 percent) and other Latin countries.[15] The fact that Hispanic Americans trace their roots to so many different countries carries with it a crucial lesson: Hispanics cannot be treated as a monolithic group. They hold a wide variety of political attitudes and concerns. Indeed, Americans of Latin descent even disagree over whether they should be called *Hispanics* (a term adopted by the federal government in 1975), *Latinos* (a term that is inclusive of Portuguese-speaking Brazilians), or a more country-specific term like *Chicanos* for Mexican Americans. A 2003 survey found that roughly 34 percent of Hispanics preferred the term *Hispanic*, whereas 13 percent liked *Latino*. The rest did not express a preference. Hispanics in Texas preferred *Hispanic*; those in California leaned toward *Latino*.[16]

Hispanics of Mexican origin have tended to settle in states bordering Mexico. Just under half of the nation's Hispanic Americans live in California and Texas, where they make up roughly one-third of the total population. For decades, Mexican Americans living in California and Texas endured substantial economic, political, and social discrimination. Only over the past two decades have they begun to move toward gaining political clout equal to their numbers in the population. In both California and Texas, the majority of Mexican Americans vote for Democratic candidates.[17] But, although their attachment to Democratic candidates has been maintained over time, Mexican Americans remain less devoted to the Democratic Party and to liberal political causes than African Americans.[18]

In contrast to the political experience of Mexican Americans in California and Texas, Mexican Americans in New Mexico have long been integrated into that state's political (but not economic) elite. At 44 percent of New Mexico's population, Mexican Americans have been elected to every political office, including governor and both houses of Congress. As is true of Mexican Americans living in Texas and California, Mexican Americans in New Mexico favor the Democratic Party.

Most Hispanics of Cuban descent live in Florida. Many Cuban Americans fled their homeland to escape Fidel Castro and communist rule. Because of their strong anticommunist beliefs, most Cuban Americans identify themselves as Republicans; relatively few belong to the Democratic Party.[19]

Asian Americans

Like Hispanic Americans, Asian Americans are a fast-growing and diverse community. Between 1980 and 2007, the number of Asians living in the United States more than tripled, rising from 3.7 million to 13.4 million. Asian Americans constitute almost 5 percent of all Americans. More than 33 percent of Asian Americans live in California, making them the second largest minority group in the state (behind Hispanic Americans and ahead of African Americans). The state where Asian Americans constitute the greatest share of the population (at 55 percent with 21 percent native Hawaiian and Pacific Islander) is Hawaii; there they have enjoyed the most political success, electing governors and members of Congress.

The Asian community in the United States is like the Hispanic community in another way as well—immigration has played a major role in its rapid growth. And as is the case with many Hispanics living in the United States, many people of Asian descent—the exact percentage is unclear—are not citizens and do not have the right to vote. This, in turn, helps diminish their potential political power.

Although earlier Asian immigrants hailed primarily from China, Japan, and the Philippines, Figure 3–2 shows that many now come

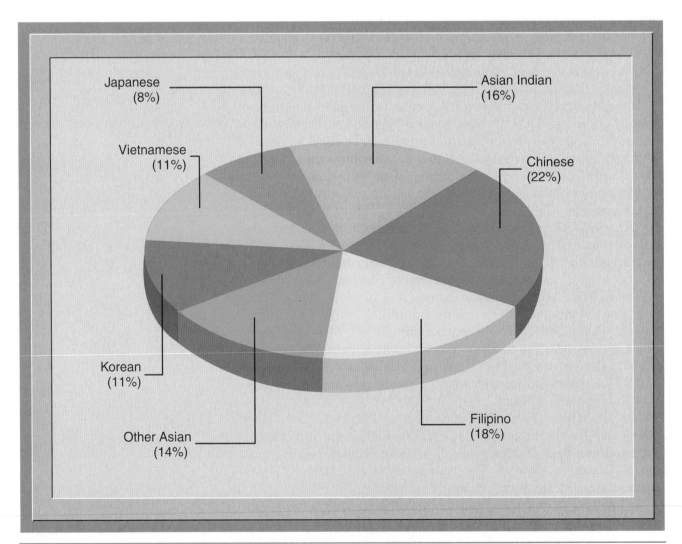

Figure 3–2 Asian American Population, 2000. Asian Americans have remarkably diverse backgrounds.

Source: Jessica S. Barnes and Claudette E. Bennett, "The Asian Population: 2000," February 2002, available at www.census.gov/prod/2002pubs/c2kbr01-16.pdf

from India, Korea, and Vietnam.[20] (The Census Bureau counts forty-eight different ethnic groups among Asian Americans and Pacific Islanders.) Like Cuban Americans, Asian Americans from Vietnam and Korea—nations that are partly or entirely communist ruled—have been supportive of the Republican Party because of its hard-line anticommunist policies. Other Asian Americans, however, do not exhibit any strong partisan preferences. Asian Indians, for example, although becoming very active politically, are not tied to a particular political party.[21] Obviously, Asian Americans do not always share common political interests. In Hawaii, for example, those of Hawaiian heritage often spar with Japanese Americans over political offices and other issues.[22]

American Indians and Alaska Natives

American Indians and Alaska natives together constitute 1 percent of the nation's population. (A strong plurality of *American Indians* prefers that label over the name *Native American*.)[23] From 1980 to 2007, their numbers grew from 1.4 million to just over 2.9 million. The state where American Indians constitute the largest proportion of the population is Alaska, at 18 percent, followed by Oklahoma at 11 percent. Most American Indians live in the western and southern states; few live in the Northeast. About 34 percent of American Indians reside in "American Indian Areas" such as reservations and trust lands. Thus, many American Indians have a relationship with the federal government that differs greatly from that of the rest of the population, as we will discuss in Chapter 5. Voter turnout rates are low among American Indians. Most of those who do vote favor the Democrats.[24]

3-2 A MULTICULTURAL UNITED STATES

The United States is becoming an increasingly multicultural society. As noted at the start of this chapter, minorities now constitute one-third of the population. Given current population trends, the Census Bureau projects that figure will reach 50 percent by 2042 and 54 percent by 2050. By 2023, minorities will constitute half of all children in the country.[25] Already, California, Hawaii, New Mexico, and Texas are "majority-minority" states, where no one racial or ethnic group constitutes a majority, and Georgia, Maryland, and Nevada are closing in on that status.[26] Almost one out of every ten counties across the country is now majority-minority.[27] Such massive changes may, of course, alter the political landscape in important ways. But three things suggest that the changes are more likely to be subtle than startling.

First, as we have noted several times in this chapter, ethnic and racial groups are not monolithic—their members do not always think and act alike. Each group harbors a wide variety of opinions on political, social, and economic issues. Moreover, differences within groups appear to be widening, not narrowing. Indeed, we often lump people together into a group that they themselves do not identify with. As a small-business owner in Los Angeles commented, "My family has had trouble understanding that we are now Asians, and not Koreans, or people from Korea, or Korean Americans, or just plain Americans. Sometimes we laugh about it. Oh, the Asian students are so smart! The Asians have no interest in politics! But we don't know what people are talking about. Who are the Asians?"[28]

Second, different minority groups that might be thought to share common ground do not always make common cause. For example, the African American and Hispanic American communities in Los Angeles often compete rather than cooperate, even though (or perhaps because) both can claim to be a disadvantaged minority group. Thus, African American labor leaders in that city have complained that affirmative action programs benefit Hispanic Americans rather than African Americans.[29] And when Los Angeles residents voted for mayor in 2005, African Americans and Asian Americans supported the white candidate, whereas Hispanic Americans voted heavily for the Hispanic candidate. Indeed, African Americans voters were more supportive of the white candidate than were white voters.[30] More generally, Hispanic Americans and African Americans express conflicting views on a number of social and political issues.[31]

In addition to divisions within and between minority communities, a third reason that the increasingly multicultural nature of American society may not bring about dramatic change is that increased multiculturalism is blurring the lines between different ethnic and racial groups. In recent years, the United States has witnessed a sharp rise in the number of interracial couples—now numbering 3.1 million. This number represents 5.4 percent of all married couples, up from less than 1 percent of married couples in 1970. Intermarriage between whites and Asian Americans and whites and Hispanic Americans is particularly common, but intermarriage among all groups is rising.[32]

The rise of interracial and interethnic marriage means that more children are born who belong to multiple racial and ethnic groups. As pollsters have discovered, many of these people and others no longer know how they ought to be categorized, and many have requested the inclusion of a "multiracial" category in surveys and on public forms.[33] Indeed, a third of African Americans consider themselves to be multiracial.[34]

The rise of interracial marriage and the growing number of multiracial children have prompted calls for the federal government to rethink its racial and ethnic categories. The Census Bureau considered changing its racial categories when it conducted the 2000 census. But proposals to change the current set of racial and ethnic categories stirred up considerable political controversy. Some civil rights groups opposed adding a separate multiracial category because they believed it would reduce the number of people counted as belonging to their group and thereby diminish their community's political clout. In a similar vein, the National Congress of American Indians opposed Senator Daniel Akaka's (D-HI) efforts to reclassify native Hawaiians as Native Americans instead of Asian and Pacific Islanders because the move would have entitled native Hawaiians to certain privileges currently restricted to American Indians. Indeed, one concession Sen. Akaka had to make to generate support for his bill was to incorporate a provision that would prevent native Hawaiians from legally operating gambling facilities. (Despite Sen. Akaka's efforts, the bill failed to pass the Senate in 2006.)[35]

How much the census numbers would change if people were allowed to choose a separate multiracial category is unclear. Only 2 percent of African Americans say they would choose the multiracial category if it were an option.[36] The number of people who identify themselves as Asian Americans and American Indians might fall substantially, however. The controversy over tinkering with existing racial and ethnic categories ultimately persuaded the Census Bureau not to create a separate multiracial category. Instead, it allowed people to "mark or select one or more races" in response to the racial category question on the 2000 Census form. More people than anticipated checked more than one race on the 2000 Census form. Among African American respondents, for example, 5 percent also checked at least one other race. The figure was even higher for African American children under the age of 18: more than 8 percent. Thus, Americans may think of themselves as being more multiracial than demographic experts had thought.[37] People who identify themselves as multiracial, however, appear to adopt political views similar to those held by their minority counterparts.[38]

3-2a Immigration

It is trite but true to say that the United States is a country of immigrants. The rate of immigration, however, has fluctuated over time. Between 1901 and 1910, for example, almost 9 million people came to the United States as immigrants, a rate of 10 immigrants per 1,000 people in the U.S. population. The number of immigrants then declined, fluctuating between 500,000 to 4.5 million immigrants per decade from 1930 to 1980. Since then, the number of immigrants has increased dramatically, numbering 19,568,402 from 1988 to 2007. The change in American society has been remarkable. In 1980, 6.2 percent of the country's population was foreign born. In 2006 that percentage had leaped to 12.5 percent. Even with that increased number, however, the proportion of immigrants to the rest of the population is much less than it was at the beginning of the twentieth century. And many immigrants eventually become American citizens. Of those who arrived prior to 1970, for example, 83 percent had become citizens by 2004.

Immigrants come to the United States from around the world. As Figure 3–3 shows, of the 1,052,415 people legally admitted to the country in 2007, about 12 percent came from Europe, 36 percent from Asia, 10 percent from South America, 9 percent from Africa, and only 1 percent from Oceania. The rest came from North

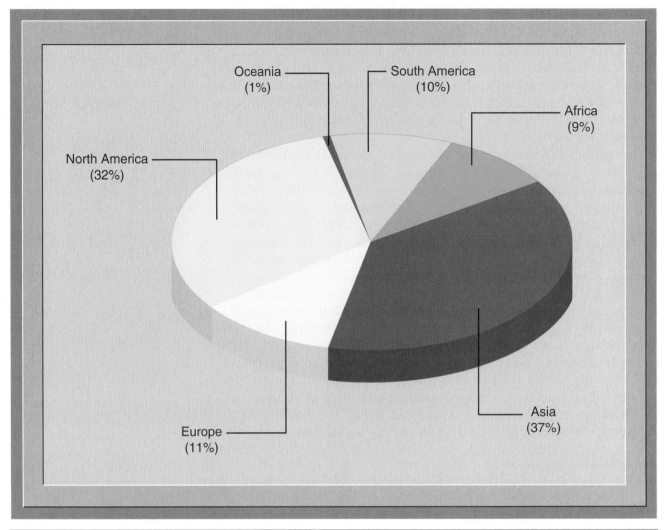

Figure 3-3   American Immigration by World Region, 2007. Immigrants come to the United States from around the world.

Source: *Department of Homeland Security, Yearbook of Immigration Statistics: 2007 (www.dhs.gov/ximgtn/statistics/publications/LPR07.shtm).*

America, particularly Mexico and countries in the Caribbean. Almost two-thirds of the people admitted in 2007 were close family members of people who were already U.S. citizens or legal permanent residents. Another 15 percent were allowed in for employment purposes because they possessed special or unusual skills. The rest fell under other special circumstances, including fleeing political persecution in their homeland.[39]

Immigration has long been an explosive political issue. As Chapter 5 discusses in greater detail, over the years Congress has responded to political pressures to limit immigration by establishing quotas designating how many people from a particular country may come to this country, or in some cases, passing laws preventing any people from a particular country from immigrating. Currently, the political debate over immigration breaks down into two main issues. The first involves the appropriate level of legal immigration. Congress has addressed that issue several times in the past

America is a nation of immigrants and their descendents.

few decades. The most recent legislation, the Immigration Act of 1990, established a limit of about 700,000 new arrivals each year, but loopholes have allowed far more people to enter the country in some years. One reason Congress has been unable to agree on a new immigration law despite years of political wrangling is the undetermined number of immigrants that voters are willing to allow to enter the country legally.[40]

The second and more politically divisive issue involves how best to stem illegal immigration. Estimates of the number of illegal immigrants in the country are imprecise because such people are unlikely to volunteer information about themselves to government agents such as census takers. In 2006, the Pew Hispanic Center estimated that between 11.5 and 12 million people were in the country illegally, a majority of them having arrived since 1995. More than three-fourths of all illegal immigrants are thought to come from Latin American countries—primarily from Mexico; the rest come from all other parts of the world.[41] But the image of illegal immigrants scurrying across the border may be somewhat exaggerated. Credible estimates suggest that between 33 and 45 percent of all illegal immigrants are "visa overstays"—that is, people who enter the country with a legal visa but then fail to leave when the visa expires.[42]

Significant concerns have been raised about the impact illegal immigrants have on the American economy and society. Some of the perceived threats may be overblown. Many illegal immigrants manage to transition to permanent legal status. One recent study estimated that less than 40 percent of legal permanent residents are new to the United States when they attain legal status; most legal permanent residents have been in the country illegally at least once in the past.[43] Another study found that immigrants who arrived in the last 25 years have actually assimilated into American society more quickly than their counterparts of a century ago,[44] and they are much less likely to be imprisoned than are native-born

Americans.[45] Finally, although some currently unemployed workers would find employment if illegal workers were fired, many of the vacated positions would go unfilled or would require legal residents to relocate and acquire new job skills.[46] Indeed, some analyses suggest that the long-term vitality of the American economy, and the Social Security and Medicare systems it supports, will depend heavily on the influx of immigrant workers.[47]

About 24 percent of illegal immigrants reside in California, with most of the rest living in Texas, Florida, New York, Arizona, and Illinois.[48] Each of those states has felt the financial burden of providing social services to illegal immigrants, and California and five other states went so far as to sue the federal government to cover those costs. And illegal immigration continues to be a contentious political issue. In 2004, for example, Arizona voters passed Proposition 200, a measure requiring proof of legal immigration status for anyone trying to obtain state welfare benefits and proof of American citizenship to register to vote. In 2006, Arizonans passed four more measures targeting illegal immigrants to, among other things, deny them bail in serious felony cases and in-state tuition at public universities. All four measures passed with at least 70 percent of the vote.

3-2b Language

One source of great conflict in many countries with diverse populations is language. Predominantly English-speaking Canada, for example, has struggled with the problem of accommodating the interests of its French-speaking citizens in Quebec. Other countries, such as Belgium and India, have had ongoing problems between citizens of different language groups.

The United States' changing social composition has pushed language concerns onto the American political agenda. The 2006 American Community Survey conducted by the U.S Census Bureau found that 20 percent of Americans speak a language other than English at home. The most commonly spoken language besides English was Spanish. The other most commonly spoken languages were (in order) Chinese, French, Tagalog (a language spoken in the Philippines), German, Vietnamese, and Korean. California had the highest percentage of residents speaking another language at home: 43 percent. New Mexico had the second highest percentage at 37 percent, with Texas close behind at 34 percent.

Recent immigrants to the United States do not appear to be less likely to learn English than their predecessors were. Almost all Hispanic Americans, for example, believe that everyone should learn to speak English.[49] And 92 percent of second-generation Hispanic Americans and 96 percent of second-generation Asian Americans speak English either well or very well.[50] Nonetheless, language has become a political issue in the United States. Groups such as U.S. ENGLISH have lobbied to make English the official language, thereby abolishing multilingual ballots, forms, and educational programs.[51] By 2008, 30 states had adopted some version of an English-only amendment to their state constitutions. In 1998, however, the Arizona State Supreme Court declared Arizona's English-only amendment unconstitutional. A year later, the U.S. Supreme Court refused to hear the case, leaving the state supreme court's decision in place.[52] Nonetheless, during consideration of a controversial immigration bill in 2006, the U.S. Senate voted to make English "the national language."

3-2c Age

Over the course of American history, the average age of the population has increased dramatically. In 1820, the median age was less than 17; by 2006, it was 36.4. (The median age means that half of all people are older and half are younger.) The median age has risen in part because improvements in nutrition and medical care are cutting infant mortality rates and enabling adult Americans to live longer. It also has risen because Americans are marrying at later ages and having fewer children.

Changes in the age of the population have important political consequences. As Figure 3–4 shows, the proportion of the nation's population that is sixty-five years of age or older increased significantly over the last century. By 2008, 13 percent of the population was age 65 or older; 2 percent was age 85 or older.[53] Moreover, that

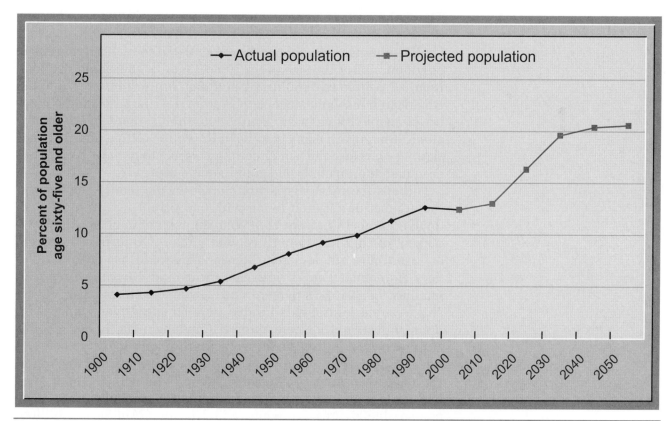

Figure 3–4 Percentage of American Population Age Sixty-Five and Older.

Source: *Data taken from Wan He, Manisha Sengupta, Victoria A. Velkoff, and Kimberly A. DeBarros, U.S. Census Bureau, Current Population Reports, P23-209, 65+ in the United States, 2005* (Washington, D.C.: U.S. Government Printing Office, 2005).

baby boomers
The generation of Americans born between 1946 and 1964.

trend is expected to continue in the twenty-first century as the **baby boomers**—usually defined as the large number of people born between the end of World War II and 1964—start to gray.

As the population becomes older, more demands are made on the health-care system and Social Security. Moreover, there are (and will be) fewer people in the workforce in proportion to those who are retired. This means relatively fewer workers are available to pay the taxes needed to finance these programs. In 1950, for instance, there were 16.5 workers for every retiree drawing Social Security; in 2005, there were 3.3; and by 2035—well before most of today's college students start retiring—experts project there will be only 2.1.[54] (The populations of other major industrialized democracies are aging even faster. For example, in 2050, when 26 percent of Americans are expected to be more than sixty years old, the proportion in the United Kingdom will be 29 percent; in France, 33 percent; in Germany, 35 percent; and in Japan, 42 percent. Even China and Russia will have a larger proportion of their populations age sixty and older than will the United States.)[55]

On the flip side, when the proportion of younger people grows, the government devotes more attention to other problems, notably education (because the young are the primary consumers) and crime (because the young are much more likely to commit crimes).

3-2d Family Households

The social units in which Americans live their lives have changed in recent decades. About 68 percent of Americans still live in a family—that is, with people they are related to by birth, marriage, or adoption. But the size of the typical family household declined from 3.7 people in 1960 to 3.1 in 2006. The declining size of the American household stems in part from the sharp rise in the number of people living in nonfamily households, many of whom live alone. Moreover, many people now delay getting married and starting families, and when couples marry, they have fewer children than their parents and grandparents did.

Perhaps the most significant change in the family has been in the number of children living with one parent, which more than doubled from 13 percent in 1970 to 28 percent in 2006. Another 5 percent of children do not live with either of their parents. Mothers head most single-parent homes. This trend has been particularly pronounced in African American and Hispanic American families: In 2006, 51 percent and 25 percent, respectively, were single-parent households headed by a female. Divorce and abandonment account for part of the rise in single-family households. A third reason is that single women are increasingly choosing to have children. For example, in 2006, 32 percent of African- American children younger than age eighteen lived with a mother who had never been married, up steeply from 4 percent in 1970. The comparable figures for white and Hispanic American children were 6 percent and 11 percent, respectively, both up from negligible percentages in 1970.

Although African American women have a higher rate of out-of-wedlock births, far more children are born to unwed white mothers than to African American mothers every year. (Keep in mind that whites far outnumber African Americans in the general population.) Moreover, only around 23 percent of out-of-wedlock births are to teenage mothers; the vast majority are to women in their twenties. And although the rising number of children born to unwed mothers is a significant social problem in the United States (39 percent of all births in 2006), the rate of such births is even higher in several other industrialized countries, including Iceland (64 percent of all births in 2003), Sweden (56 percent), Denmark (45 percent), France (44 percent), and the United Kingdom (42 percent).[56]

The rising number of single-parent households is important because it places greater demands on government. Single-parent households are much more likely to be poor, and as a result, to require welfare or other government assistance. At the same time, a working parent in a single-parent household needs greater access to affordable child care.

3-2e Sexual Orientation

Since the early 1970s, the gay rights movement has actively sought to extend civil rights protections to gay and lesbian Americans (Chapter 5 will discuss this in greater detail). Yet the number of people who can be considered gay or lesbian is in question. For several decades, the most widely accepted estimate was that 10 percent of the population was gay or lesbian. Studies done in the 1990s, however, suggested that the percentage of gays and lesbians in the population is smaller, probably less than 3 percent. An analysis of the 2005 American Community Study put the percentage at 2.9 percent of the population.[57]

Does it matter if gays and lesbians constitute only 3 percent of the population rather than 10 percent? In politics, the answer is usually yes. Groups on both sides of the gay rights battle have fought over which estimates to use because they believe that public acceptance of gay rights depends on perceptions of the size of the gay and lesbian community. A representative of the National Gay and Lesbian Task Force said about the conflicting estimates, "Politically, it's a very sensitive subject. Our opponents would like to say there are thirty-nine of us and we all live in the Castro in San Francisco or Greenwich Village in New York." In the same vein, a member of the conservative Family Research Council complained that the 10 percent figure "has been used with great effect by the gay rights lobby to press for political power and extra civil rights protections. It's been used to tell businessmen that 10 percent of their workforce is gay and that they should accommodate them like they do African Americans."[58] Interestingly, Americans are able to correctly estimate the size of the gay population in their local communities.[59]

Politically, gays, lesbians, and bisexuals lean heavily toward the Democratic Party. In 2004, for example, 4 percent of voters were gay. Of gay voters in that election, 77 percent supported John Kerry; only 23 percent backed George W. Bush. But the gay vote is not always so heavily tilted to the Democrats. In the watershed 1994 midterm elections, which put the Republicans in control of both houses of Congress for the first time in 40 years, 40 percent of gays, lesbians, and bisexuals voted for Republican congressional candidates.[60] As a leader of the Log Cabin Republicans—a group of gay Republicans—observed, "Among all minority groups, the gay vote showed the greatest shift toward the GOP in 1994."[61]

3-3 SOCIAL AND ECONOMIC CHARACTERISTICS

Race, ethnicity, immigration, language, age, household makeup, and sexual orientation tell only one part of the story of who Americans are as a people. Another way to tell the story is to examine the social and economic makeup of the United States. In this section, we explore five social and economic characteristics that have great political relevance: religion, education, wealth, home ownership, and occupation.

3-3a Religion

A quick glance around the world is all it takes to understand the importance of religion in politics. Different religious beliefs continue to fuel conflict between countries (e.g., predominantly Hindu India and Muslim Pakistan) and within countries (e.g., Protestants and Catholics in Northern Ireland). But religion has generated little civil strife in the United States.

The United States is based, in theory if not always in practice, on a strong belief in religious freedom. Religious activity of all sorts abounds. The number of active religious denominations is difficult to pin down, but one credible estimate put it at 2,630 in 2003.[62] According to a 2007 national survey, 92 percent of Americans believe in God or a universal spirit; 56 percent said religion is a very important part of their lives. Only 39 percent of Americans, however, say they attend religious services at least once a week. Those who attend more regularly and who hold more traditional religious beliefs tend to be more conservative politically.[63]

Christians in the United States constitute 78 percent of the population, and they belong to a staggering number of different churches. Roman Catholics form the single largest group, with almost 24 percent of the population. Catholics are found in the largest numbers in the Northeast and industrial Midwest, and with the influx of Hispanic immigrants, in the Southwest. Slightly more than 50 percent of Americans are Protestant; 26 percent identify with evangelical churches, 18 percent with so-called mainline churches, and 7 percent with historical black churches.[64] Most other denominations are small, and only the Mormons (1.7 percent of the population nationally) are geographically concentrated in significant enough numbers to dominate politics in a state (Utah, where in 2007 they were estimated to be 60 percent of the population, and to a lesser extent, Idaho and Nevada).[65]

Jewish Americans represent a small percentage of the adult American population: 1.7 percent. But as with minority groups, people often greatly exaggerate the number of Jewish Americans. Roughly half of all Americans think that more than 20 percent of Americans are Jewish.[66] But New York is the only state where Jewish Americans constitute even 9 percent of the population.

Although the Jewish population in the United States is slightly larger than the Muslim population, Jewish organizations are much more active and widely thought to influence politics, particularly American policy toward Israel. But over the last decade, Muslims have increased their importance in American politics, although they still constitute less than 1 percent of the national population. A 2007 survey found that 65 percent of Muslims in the United States were foreign born. Only one-third were from Arab countries; others came from Iran, Pakistan, other South Asian countries, Africa, and Europe. Evidence suggests that foreign-born Muslims have largely assimilated into American society.[67] Indeed, Muslims have become noteworthy voting blocs in California and Michigan.[68] Evidence of their growing electoral importance came when President George W. Bush became the first president to mention the word "mosque" in his 2001 inaugural address.[69] And in 2006, Keith Ellison (D-MN) became the first Muslim elected to Congress, followed in 2008 by Andre Carson (D-IN).

Religion matters because religious beliefs influence the political behavior of many Americans. But the ability of religious leaders to influence the political beliefs of their followers varies. Catholics, for example, are split on the issues of abortion rights and stem cell research despite their church's unequivocal opposition to both.[70] Similarly, the liberal policy preferences of the leaders of mainline Protestant churches diverge from the thinking of many of their members.[71] Indeed, an important point to remember about religion in American politics is that major political differences exist not only *among* religious groups, but also *within* them.[72] Only a few denominations—predominantly, but not exclusively, fundamentalist churches aligned with the Republican Party—possess the social characteristics necessary to produce political conformity among their members.[73] Otherwise, religious groups do not form cohesive political blocs.

3-3b Education

Education is a critical issue in American politics. For the individual, education is usually the key to getting a better job and earning more money over a lifetime. For the nation, education is an important factor in making the country competitive in the world economy. Not surprisingly, education is one of the most important activities the government undertakes. Roughly 90 percent of all primary and secondary students are enrolled in public schools, and public colleges and universities account for 75 percent of all college students. Federal, state, and local governments spend almost $900 billion on education each year.

Americans today have completed far more years of schooling than their parents and grandparents did. As recently as 1940, only about 25 percent of American adults had finished four years of high school. Now that figure stands at more than 86 percent. The percentage of the population with at least four years of college also has gone up dramatically, from less than 5 percent in 1940 to 29 percent in 2007. Education levels are higher in the Northeast and West than in the rest of the country and are higher in metropolitan areas than in rural areas.

Educational attainment also varies by race and sex. Whites graduate from high school at a higher rate than do African Americans and Hispanic Americans, although over the past two decades African Americans have narrowed that gap. In 2007, 82 percent of African American adults had graduated from high school, whereas 91 percent of non-Hispanic whites, 88 percent of Asian Americans, and 60 percent of Hispanics had high school degrees. (The most recent data on American Indians are from 2004, and they show that 77 percent are high school graduates.)[74] At the college level, non-Hispanic whites graduate at a higher rate (32 percent) than do African Americans (19 percent), Hispanic Americans (13 percent), and American Indians (14 percent). But Asian American graduation rates (52 percent) far surpass those of whites.[75]

Over the past fifty years, women, like men, have increased their average educational level. Up until 1980, women were more likely than men to have graduated from high school. Now they graduate at virtually the same rate. Men have always been more likely than women to graduate from college, and in 2005, 30 percent of men older than age twenty-five had at least a bachelor's degree, compared with 28 percent of women. But these numbers are changing. Among people age twenty-five to twenty-nine in 2007, more women than men have at least a bachelor's degree, 34 percent versus 26 percent, a trend that is likely to continue in the future because women currently constitute 57 percent of enrolled college students.[76]

3-3c Wealth and Income

The distribution of wealth and income in a country often reflects social class. Many critics of capitalism, for example, argue that the upper class benefits by exploiting the labor of the lower class. Indeed, in many countries politics is organized around class conflict.

But class rarely has been an important political issue in the United States. Despite objective evidence to suggest that lower, middle, and upper classes do exist in this country, Americans generally do not think in class terms. The Census Bureau does not have an official measure of middle class, and social scientists also have failed to agree on one.[77] But in the 2006 General Social Survey, 92 percent of respondents identified themselves as either middle class or working class. Only 5 percent saw themselves as being lower class, and just 3 percent claimed to be upper class. These figures have held constant for more than a generation.[78] Exploiting class distinctions holds little political payoff when most people see themselves as members of the same group. Nor does knowing that someone is middle class tell us anything about his or her politics because in the United States social class usually has not been an important basis for beliefs or action.

Still, *middle class* is a term loaded with political meaning. Because most Americans think of themselves as middle class, elected officials usually try to pitch their pet programs as being good for the middle class. In 2008, for example, both John McCain, the Republican presidential candidate, and Barack Obama, the Democratic presidential candidate, offered tax cut proposals that they each said was targeted at the middle class. Americans, however, do not always agree on who qualifies as middle class. In a 2007 national survey, for example, just over 60 percent of respondents agreed that a family of four with an income of $50,000 to $60,000 was middle class.[79] A third of respondents thought that a family with an annual income of $100,000 should be considered middle class. Perhaps not surprisingly, politicians fumble around for a definition of the middle class. When asked for his characterization, New Mexico Governor Bill Richardson offered that the middle class is "about a lot more than money" and applies to "anybody who has to work for a living."[80]

Wealth and income are distributed unevenly in the United States, and the gap between the richest and poorest Americans appears to have grown over the last two decades.[81] Wealth (the difference between a family's net assets, such as equity in a home, savings accounts, and other financial assets, and net liabilities, such as a home mortgage and car or student loans) is highly

Source: © Moodboard./Corbis.

Although movies and television often portray Americans as rich, the median household income in 2007 was only $50,233—and even less for most minority households—hardly lending itself to the lifestyle of the rich and famous.

concentrated in the hands of relatively few Americans. In 2004, the wealthiest 1 percent of the country's population controlled 33 percent of the country's total net worth. In contrast, the poorest 50 percent controlled just 2.5 percent of the country's wealth. Even more striking is that more than 60 percent of all business assets are owned by the richest 1 percent of Americans. Wealth is, of course, strongly related to income and education. The median net worth for a family with an income in the lowest 20 percent is just $7,500, whereas the comparable figure for a family with an income in the top 10 percent is $924,100. Families headed by someone with a college degree have a median net worth that is $206,000 greater than that for a family headed by someone lacking a high school degree. There are also differences by race. The median non-Hispanic white family has $140,700 in financial assets, compared with $24,800 for all other families. Over the last decade, however, every demographic group increased its net worth.[82]

National income is a bit more evenly distributed, although the share received by the highest-paid 20 percent of the American public has increased in recent years, from 43 percent in 1970 to 51 percent in 2006. The income share of the poorest 20 percent of the country declined during that same period, from 4.1 percent to 3.4 percent. Figure 3–5 shows another way to look at income distribution in the United States. The median household income in 2007 was $50,233. Just over 20 percent of the households in the country earned more than $100,000, whereas just over 13 percent made less than $15,000.

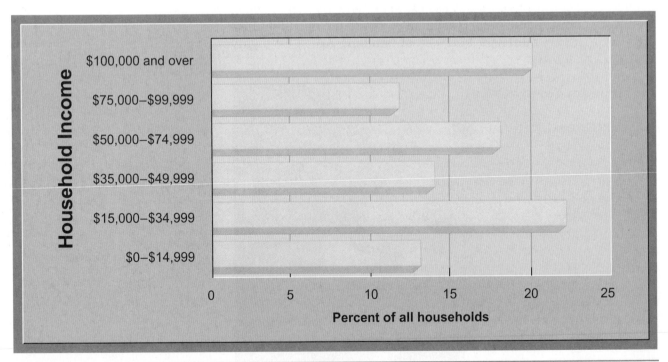

Figure 3–5   American Household Income, 2007. Most Americans are middle class; relatively few are very poor or very rich.

Source: *Carmen DeNavas-Walt, Bernadette D. Proctor, and Jessica Smith, U.S. Census Bureau, Current Population Reports, P60-235, Income, Poverty, and Health Insurance Coverage in the United States: 2007* (Washington, D.C.: U.S. Government Printing Office, 2008).

Income in the United States also is strongly linked to race and education. The median income for white, non-Hispanic households in 2007 was $54,920, whereas Hispanic-American households averaged $38,679 and African American households just $33,916. Asian American households earned the most: $66,103.[83] The impact of education on income is even more striking. In 2006, an individual who had a bachelor's degree earned an average of $56,788, whereas a person who had no more than a high school degree averaged $31,071. A person with an advanced degree made an average of $82,320. Even when the increasing cost of obtaining a college education is taken into account, higher education still pays off in the long run.[84]

The income figures in Figure 3–5 show that many Americans are poor. In 2007, the Census Bureau considered a family of four with two children under the age of 18 earning less than $21,027 a year to be below the poverty line. Figure 3–6 shows the percentage of all Americans living in poverty since 1960 (based on the yearly poverty line established by the Census Bureau, discussed in Box 3–2). From 1960 to 1970, the percentage of poor people dropped almost in half, in large part because of the success of the federal government's concerted attack on the problem, including many of the Great Society programs President Lyndon Johnson initiated.[85]

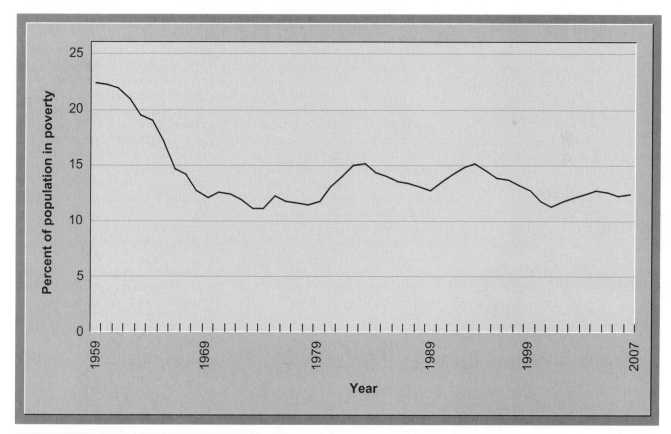

Figure 3–6   American Poverty Rate, 1959–2007. After declining during the 1960s, the poverty rate has stabilized at between 10 and 15 percent.

Source: *Carmen DeNavas-Walt, Bernadette D. Proctor, and Jessica Smith, U.S. Census Bureau, Current Population Reports, P60-235, Income, Poverty, and Health Insurance Coverage in the United States: 2007* (Washington, D.C.: U.S. Government Printing Office, 2008).

POINT OF ORDER

Box 3–2 Figuring the Poverty Rate

In the early 1960s, Mollie Orshansky, an economist with the Social Security Administration, developed a crude measure of poverty to assess how many older Americans lived in dire financial conditions. The poverty measure she created was relatively simple. It took the Agriculture Department's estimate of how much money an individual needed for food each year and multiplied that number by three to account for all other basic living expenses. The final figure was then adjusted to take different family sizes into account.

The measure might have languished in obscurity had President Lyndon Johnson not needed a national measure of poverty as part of his War on Poverty. Johnson seized on Orshansky's measure, and ever since, each October brings the Census Bureau's announcement of the poverty figure for the previous year, triggering a debate about the improving or deteriorating financial well-being of the American public. But more hangs on the poverty figure than just the image of how well Americans are faring. The numbers are used to help determine eligibility standards for a number of federal programs, including food stamps, Head Start, Medicaid, and school lunches.

Mollie Orshansky developed the basic measure the federal government uses to calculate the poverty line in the United States.

Source: © AP Photo/World Wide Photo.

But does this simple measure really capture the level of poverty in the United Sates? Surprisingly, given the figure's long history and political importance, no one argues that it does. One liberal critic asserts the measure is "completely outdated, with a technique that makes no sense." A conservative economist exclaims, "The Census Bureau stuff isn't even on the right planet." Prominent social scientists who study poverty have dismissed the measure as "truly awful" and "absolutely wrong." The Census Bureau official in charge of compiling data on poverty admits, "the current measure is flawed." Even Orshansky said in 2001 that "Anyone who thinks we ought to change it is perfectly right." But that does not mean that people agree on a replacement measure, or even how much poverty exists in the United States. Some people think the real poverty figure is higher than what is currently reported, whereas others think fewer people live in poverty than the official figure suggests.

People who think that Orshansky's measure for calculating the poverty line understates poverty note that it does not take into account regional differences in the cost of living. As a result, it probably underestimates the number of poor people residing in more expensive urban areas and overestimates the number of poor people living in lower-cost rural areas. One study in New York City, for example, found that the cost of basic necessities there was two to five times higher than the national poverty level. Similarly, the measure does not assess the rising costs of child care, medical coverage, and transportation. Many economists think families now spend only one-fourth of their income on food, not the one-third that Orshansky's measure assumes. Including better estimates of such expenses might swell the ranks of the poor by several percentage points.

People who think that Orshansky's measure overstates poverty point out that it fails to take into account "in-kind" benefits the government

provides, such as food stamps, subsidized housing, school lunches, and home energy assistance. The measure also fails to take into account the effect of tax credits such as the Earned Income Tax Credit that help boost the incomes of the working poor. If these benefits were counted, the number of people thought to live in poverty would fall. The Census Bureau estimates that including in-kind and credit benefits would have reduced the poverty level in 2004 from 12.7 percent to 8.3 percent.

In 1995, a committee of thirteen professors, charged by the government with studying the issue, produced a 500-page report suggesting changes to the way the government measures poverty. The report responded to many of the criticisms leveled against Orshansky's measure. It proposed a new poverty measure that would take into account in-kind benefits, as well as expenses such as child care and medical care that are not incorporated in the current measure. A number of other studies along these lines have been conducted in the last decade.

But the federal government has not adopted any of the new measures that have been developed. It has, however, begun issuing reports that give the poverty rates generated by alternatives to Orshansky's measure. The findings thus far suggest that many of the "experimental poverty rates are higher than the official rate mainly because expenses subtracted from resources outweigh transfers added." Some measures, however, produce a lower poverty rate. The differences between Orshansky's measure and many of the alternative measures are not particularly large, but they do raise the possibility that poverty is slightly worse than the current measure suggests. Indeed, if the United States measured poverty in the same way most countries in Western Europe do, more people would be considered poor than the current measure suggests. In any event, calls to revamp the poverty measure continue from both Republicans and Democrats.

POINT OF ORDER *(continued)*

Sources: Neela Banerjee, "Debate Over Measuring the Poverty Line Will Come to a Head in Senate Hearing," *Wall Street Journal*, May 12, 1994; Jared Bernstein, "Who's Poor? Don't Ask the Census Bureau," *New York Times*, September 26, 2003; Nina Bernstein, "Family Needs Far Exceed the Official Poverty Line," *New York Times*, September 13, 2000; John Cassidy, "Relatively Deprived," *The New Yorker*, April 3, 2006; Constance F. Citro and Robert T. Michael, eds., *Measuring Poverty: A New Approach* (Washington, D.C.: National Academy Press, 1995); Erik Eckholm, "Report on Impact of Federal Benefits on Curbing Poverty Reignites a Debate,"

New York Times, February 18, 2006; Gordon M. Fisher, "The Development of the Orshansky Poverty Thresholds and Their Subsequent History as the Official U.S. Poverty Measure," *U.S. Census Bureau, Poverty Measurement Working Papers*, September 1997; Dana Milbank, "Old Flaws Undermine New Poverty-Level Data," *Wall Street Journal*, October 5, 1995; Robert Pear, "Experts' Concept of Poverty Makes More People Poor," *Des Moines Register*, April 30, 1995; Kathleen Short, John Iceland, and Thesia I. Garner, "Experimental Poverty Measures: 1998," September 1999; *Statistical Abstract of the United States 2000*, 120th ed. (Washington, D.C.: U.S. Bureau of the

Census, 2001), 450; Rachel L. Swarns, "Bipartisan Calls for New Federal Poverty Measure," *New York Times*, September 1, 2008; U.S. Census Bureau, "The Effects of Government Taxes and Transfers on Income and Poverty: 2004," February 14, 2006, available at www.census.gov/hhes/www/poverty/effect2004/effectofgovtandt2004.pdf Jonathan Weisman, Measuring the Economy May Not Be as Simple as 1, 2, 3," *Washington Post*, August 29, 2005; David Wessell, "Counting the Poor: Methods and Controversy," *Wall Street Journal*, June 15, 2006.

Since 1970, the percentage of Americans living below the poverty line has fluctuated between 11 and 15 percent of the population, dipping to 11.3 percent in 2000 before rising to 12.7 in 2004 and dipping slightly since then.

Figure 3–7*A* shows that African Americans and Hispanic Americans are roughly three times more likely than whites to live in poverty. (The most impoverished group in America comprises American Indians who live on reservations without gambling operations, where 25 percent of families live in "deep poverty" with incomes reaching only 75 percent of the poverty level.)[86] But

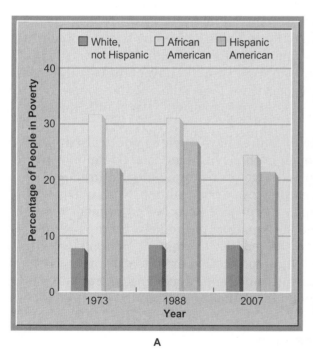 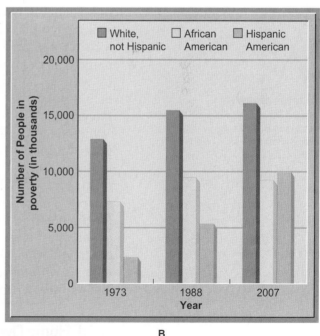

A   B

Figure 3-7 *A*, Percentage of American Poor by Race and Ethnicity. A smaller percentage of white Americans are poor than African and Hispanic Americans. *B*, Number of American Poor by Race and Ethnicity. The number of poor white Americans is much larger than the number of poor African and Hispanic Americans.

Source: *Carmen DeNavas-Walt, Bernadette D. Proctor, and Jessica Smith, U.S. Census Bureau, Current Population Reports, P60-235, Income, Poverty, and Health Insurance Coverage in the United States: 2007* (Washington, D.C.: U.S. Government Printing Office, 2008).

although minorities do not fare as well as whites, the problem of poverty is not limited to minorities. As Figure 3–7B shows, *far more poor people are white than African American or Hispanic American.* The reason that whites constitute the single largest group of poor Americans is that they are by far the largest group in the country, so even a small percentage of whites in poverty translates into a large number. Moreover, poverty is not limited to the inner cities, but affects rural areas and the suburbs as well. Indeed, one study found that in 2005, a million more poor people were living in the nation's suburbs than in large cities.[87] Politically, these figures suggest that characterizations of poverty as a problem facing only minorities are dead wrong.

Poverty in the United States is associated with age, as well as with race. Children are much more likely to be poor than older people. In 2007, 18 percent of children younger than age eighteen lived in poverty. African American and Hispanic American children were particularly hard pressed, with 35 percent and 29 percent of them, respectively, living in poverty. In contrast, the poverty rate for people older than sixty-five years of age is lower than the national average, at 9.7 percent in 2007. As recently as 1970, almost 25 percent of older Americans lived in poverty. Social Security, Medicare, and other government programs have, in large part, lifted senior citizens out of poverty.[88]

Another important characteristic of poverty is its strong association with sex and family status. Women are more likely than men to be poor, particularly women heading single-parent households. In 2006, for example, 30 percent of households headed by single non-Hispanic white women fell under the poverty line. Even more striking, 45 percent of households headed by single African American women and 42 percent of households headed by single Hispanic American women were poor.[89] The fact that families headed by women account for such a large share of the people who live below the poverty line is often referred to as the **feminization of poverty.**

Income and wealth figures have obvious political implications. For example, although millions of Americans live in poverty, they form too small a percentage of the population to influence policy making except when they can form coalitions with other groups in society. For example, the poor are too few in number to account for the creation and continuation of the Food Stamps program, an expensive but successful federal government program to limit hunger in America. But those promoting the interests of the poor have aligned with agricultural and food processing interests to develop and support a program that benefits each group.

feminization of poverty
The trend in the United States in which families headed by women account for a growing share of the people who live below the poverty line.

3-3d Home Ownership

A big part of the American Dream has always been to own one's own home. According to Census Bureau figures, in the first quarter of 2008, 67.8 percent of households lived in homes they owned, a decline from the record of 69.1 percent set in 2005. Not surprisingly, given the income figures we discussed in Section 3–3, a much higher percentage of non-Hispanic whites (75 percent) own their own home than do African Americans (47 percent) or Hispanic Americans (49 percent). A much higher percentage of older people are homeowners than younger people: 41 percent of those younger than thirty-five years of age, compared with 80 percent of those fifty-five years and older.[90]

Not all Americans have a place to live. The number of homeless people is difficult to pin down. One recent study estimated that up to 3.5 million Americans—1.35 million of whom are children—experience homelessness each year, with between 444,000 and 842,000 being homeless each night.[91] According to a 2007 survey of homelessness in twenty-three cities, individuals constitute 76 percent of the homeless; families with children, 23 percent; and unaccompanied children, 1 percent. Some 17 percent of the homeless families had an employed family member, and 17 percent of individuals who were homeless were military veterans. Among individual homeless people many suffer from mental illness (65 percent) and from substance abuse (61 percent).[92] Families remain homeless for an average of six months and individuals for five months. In 2005 a survey of twenty-seven city governments in this study spent more than $420 million on programs to provide shelter and services for the homeless, a sum that still left 18 percent of the need unmet.[93]

Home ownership and homelessness have important political consequences. For example, tax policy favors homeowners because of the generous tax deduction for the interest paid on mortgages. Renters do not get a similar break. But property taxes, the main source of revenue for local governments and school districts, fall directly on landowners. Homeowners also differ politically from renters in that homeowners are more likely to vote, and ownership may make people more conservative in their political outlook.[94]

3-3e Occupation

The most important change in the American economic landscape over the past century has been in what Americans do for a living. In 1880, 44 percent of the population lived and worked on farms. By 2000, that number had dwindled to less than 1 percent. The number of farms has declined from 4 million in 1880 to just 2.1 million in 2006. At first, Americans left the farm to work in manufacturing industries such as steel and automobiles. In recent years, however, jobs in service industries, which may be as simple as flipping hamburgers and as complex as working in health-care, computer, and education fields, have eclipsed manufacturing jobs. By some estimates, the service industries now employ upward of 75 percent of Americans.

The shift from a manufacturing economy to a service economy has been accompanied by a change in the places where Americans work. Fewer Americans work for large companies today than in years past. By 2005, 56 percent of workers were employed by firms with fewer than 500 employees, whereas only a little more than one-third of workers were employed by firms with 1,000 or more employees.[95] The growing importance of small business to the American economy has many implications for politics. For example, small firms are less able to provide health benefits than large ones. Only 45 percent of businesses with fewer than 10 employees offered health benefits in 2007, compared with 99 percent of companies with 200 or more workers. The lack of health-care plans at smaller firms puts more pressure on the government to provide some form of coverage.[96]

Along with the shift from manufacturing to services and the increased importance of small businesses, a third major change in the American workforce has been the declining importance of unions. In 1955, the percentage of all nonagricultural workers belonging to unions stood at 32 percent, but this figure has fallen steadily since then, dropping to 12 percent in 2007.[97] As Figure 3–8 shows, union membership has been strong in the public sector in recent years. This trend is particularly evident among local government workers, 42 percent of whom are unionized, largely because of unions representing teachers, fire fighters, and police officers. But union membership is weak and getting weaker in the private sector. Overall membership in labor unions fell in part because highly organized manufacturing industries such as automobiles and steel laid off many workers and in part because government policies favored management at the expense of unions. The decline in union membership, in turn, has diminished the ability of organized labor to influence government policy. And because most unions favor Democratic candidates, dwindling union membership has weakened the Democratic Party.

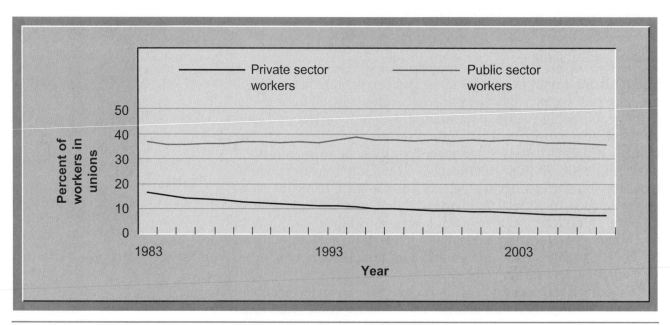

Figure 3–8   Unionization Trends, Public versus Private Sector, 1983–2007.

Sources: Bureau of Labor Statistics, "Union Members in 2007," January 25, 2008; *Statistical Abstract of the United States,* 119th ed., 453.

A fourth major change in the American labor force is the increasing number of working women. As Figure 3–9 shows, the percentage of women either working outside the home or actively seeking such employment almost doubled between 1948 and 2007. Perhaps even more striking, the percentage of women with children younger than age six who work outside the home rose from 19 percent in 1960 to 65 percent in 2000 before dropping slightly to 63 percent by 2005. On average, women still do not make as much money as men, but that gap has narrowed in recent years. In 1973, women made 57 percent of what men earned; in 2006, they made 77 percent of what men made.[98] Among younger age cohorts, where women and men have more comparable educational and work experience, the gap narrows significantly. For example, according to one study, "Among people age 27 to 33 who have never had a child, the earnings of women are close to 98 percent of men's."[99] Indeed, it has been argued that the widening income gap in the United States is in large part the result of two-income families, particularly those with two high-income earners.[100] The influx of women into the labor force has forced a host of new issues, such as child care, sexual harassment in the workplace, and comparable pay, onto the political agenda.

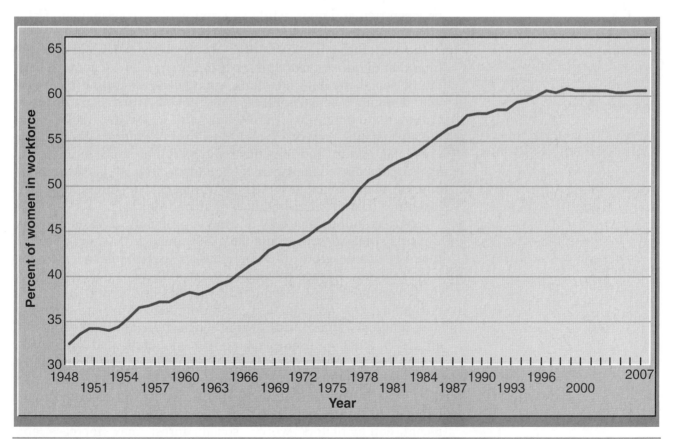

Figure 3–9   Percent of Women Twenty Years and Older in the Workforce, 1948–2007.

Source: *Bureau of Labor Statistics, Labor Force Participation Rate–20 years and Over, Women.*

Finally, over the past three decades, unemployment rates have fluctuated between 3 and 10 percent. Unemployment rates are higher for minorities than for whites, and higher for younger people than for older people. Typically, the highest rate is among African American males between the ages of sixteen and nineteen. Unemployment is, of course, a politically sensitive issue. Presidents and members of Congress often see their political fortunes tied to the unemployment rate. Unemployment has budgetary costs as well. People out of work may draw unemployment compensation, and they do not pay many taxes.

3-4 DIVERSITY AND SOCIAL HARMONY

The diversity of American society is unparalleled in the world. Yet in many other countries diversity has been the source of political conflict and instability. Although the United States' murder rate shows it to be a violent society and although civil disorders such as the 1992 Los Angeles riots occasionally occur, perhaps the most exceptional fact about American society is that, with the tragic exception of the Civil War, its diverse population has managed to avoid widespread social unrest. One reason for this stability is that, for the most part, the social and economic cleavages or divisions that might threaten American society do not coincide to create sharply distinct, homogeneous groups. That is, differences between rich and poor, white and non-white, Protestant and Catholic, and labor and management are not the same.

cross-cutting cleavages
Divisions that split society into small groups so that in different policy areas, people have different allies and opponents, and so that no group forms a majority on all issues.

We call these divisions **cross-cutting cleavages** because the lines that divide, for example, rich and poor, may cut across a variety of social, racial, and ethnic groups. Cross-cutting cleavages tend to dampen social conflict. Thus, not all African Americans or Catholics are poor, not all Protestants and whites are wealthy, and not all Hispanic Americans and Muslims hold blue-collar jobs. Every racial, ethnic, and religious group is represented (but not necessarily equally) in management and labor. Indeed, most members of every major social group in the United States (and group membership is overlapping) are likely to be middle class.

The tremendous diversity of American society, then, is in many ways its strength. It prevents the government from catering to the interests of one group of Americans to the exclusion of others, which thereby lessens the chances for political violence. Instead, the government must respond to a number of different, and often competing, concerns. In turn, both political parties are forced to seek political support in the same social, religious, and economic groups. In 2008, for example, both the Democratic and Republican candidates for president gained substantial support from almost every social and economic group in the United States. Conflict does exist in the United States, but cross-cutting cleavages help dampen it. If cleavages begin to reinforce one another, as some recent commentators worry, social unrest may increase and threaten the United States' social and political stability.

3-5 POLITICAL POWER IN THE UNITED STATES

Regardless of background, many Americans share the belief that the government does not take their interests into account. One does not have to look too hard to find complaints that what was intended to be government by the people has become government by an elite group. Who plays the villain in such complaints depends on who is doing the complaining. People on the political left often complain that multinational corporations dominate political and economic life. Those on the political right complain about an intellectual and cultural elite that controls the media, entertainment industry, and universities.[101]

Who, then, wields political power in the United States? Is political power distributed equally, or do some groups of people have more than others? We argue that **pluralism** characterizes our political system; that is, on different issues, different groups tend to exercise power.

pluralism
The theory that political power is spread widely and that on different issues different groups of people exercise power.

Defining and measuring power are difficult and controversial tasks that lie well beyond the scope of this book. For our purposes here, however, power can be defined simply as the ability of person A to get person B to do something person B would not otherwise do. For instance, if the National Rifle Association persuades a senator to drop her support for gun control or if the National Association of Manufacturers convinces the president to push for lower corporate taxes, we normally say that each group has exercised power.

Comparing two landmark studies of power in American cities is a useful way to examine the distribution of political influence because the basics of what is learned at the local level can be transferred easily to the national level. Moreover, although these studies are now dated and other researchers have since done much more work on these questions, we discuss them because they draw a simple and stark distinction between competing notions of how American politics works.[102] One study found that power is concentrated in the hands of a few elite leaders, whereas the other found power distributed among different groups—a finding consistent with the idea of pluralism.

The first study, Floyd Hunter's investigation of Atlanta in the early 1950s, argued that a power elite composed of a small group of powerful white men who interacted socially at country clubs and churches dominated the city.[103] Most of the members of the power elite were business leaders; very few were politicians. Hunter claimed that these men acted behind the scenes to enact policies that benefited their economic interests and protected the city's political and social status quo.

Hunter's findings are consistent with a belief many Americans express, that they are politically powerless because a small elite dominates politics. Before accepting Hunter's conclusions as fact, however, it is important to understand how he reached them. Hunter identified Atlanta's power elite by first asking community leaders (e.g., the chamber of commerce, League of Women Voters, and newspaper editors) to provide names of people they thought were powerful. Using these names, other community observers were then asked to develop a list of the forty people Hunter would then examine as the power elite. One might question why Hunter settled on 40 people and not 20 or 100 or 1,000, but an even more important objection can be raised. By asking people who they thought composed Atlanta's power elite, Hunter assumed that such an elite group existed; yet he never showed that this elite group actually influenced city government. Because reputations often bear little relation to reality, Hunter's findings should be treated with skepticism.

One of the many studies to follow Hunter's was Robert Dahl's examination of political power in New Haven, Connecticut.[104] As Hunter had done in Atlanta, Dahl tried to determine who belonged to New Haven's power elite. But he went further to see if the elite actually exercised power across a broad range of issues in the city. He found that no single power elite controlled New Haven. The people and groups that influenced urban renewal differed from those who influenced educational issues, who in turn differed from those who influenced nominations for political office. As for New Haven's business leaders, Dahl found that they exercised power on relatively few issues.

Dahl's findings are consistent with the idea of pluralism, which holds that political power is widely dispersed in the United States and that different groups of people exercise power on different issues. *Although pluralism rejects the claim that a single political elite wields power in the United States, it recognizes that Americans do not share political or economic power equally.* No one would argue, for example, that the homeless have as much influence on government policy as do corporate executives or that politicians pay as much attention to the views of college students as they do to senior citizens. Yet, although it acknowledges that political inequalities exist in the United States, pluralism holds that American politics can be best understood as the result of bargaining among competing groups rather than the result of decisions by some small political elite.

In the context of national politics, then, pluralism tells us that the voices heard on gun control differ from those heard on farm subsidies, which in turn differ from those that influence welfare policies or defense spending. As we will show in later chapters, especially in the discussion of interest group politics in Chapter 10, American society has produced a dizzying array of groups designed to promote the political, economic, and social interests of their members. These so-called interest groups tend to focus their attention on their narrow area of concern and generally try to influence government policy only within that limited area. Thus, only a small number of interest groups are active on most issues that come before government. And those groups, regardless of the interests they represent, tend to be dominated by wealthier and better educated people.

Because the wealthy and the well educated tend to dominate interest groups, pluralism can be thought of as a system of competing elites. Yet the membership of these elite groups varies across policy issues, and the identity and composition of the elite on any policy issue is likely to change over time. Consider the situation in Atlanta, for example. In many important respects, Atlanta in the 2000s looks nothing like the Atlanta that Hunter described in the early 1950s. Although Atlanta's African American community still does not share equally in the city's economic wealth, it does dominate city politics. Indeed, since the 1970s, African Americans have held every major elected position in Atlanta. In 2001, Shirley Franklin became the first African American woman to be elected mayor. She was reelected in 2005 with more than 90 percent of the vote. And perhaps most symbolic of the power shift in Atlanta, in 2003 the name of the city's airport was changed to Hartsfield-Jackson, adding the name of the first African American mayor, Maynard Jackson, to that of one of his notable white predecessors, William Hartsfield.

American politics is pluralist because it involves competition and bargaining among groups. But it is important to remember that not all groups are equal; some groups have more resources than other groups, and some groups win more often than other groups. When groups begin to see themselves losing most of the time or when cleavages reinforce rather than overlap, political conflict or even violence may result, as with the civil unrest in many urban areas in the early 1990s showed. Although American politics does respond to the country's changing population, the changes tend to lag, and they may never produce a society that achieves equality on every social, economic, or political dimension.

SUMMARY

The United States has changed dramatically over its 200-year history. The population has grown and become incredibly diverse on almost every social dimension. What was once a country of immigrants from a handful of northern European countries now draws citizens from every country in the world. The basis of the American economy has shifted from agriculture to industry to services. As it stands today, there are great social and economic differences in American society, including differences in religion, education, and wealth. These and other economic characteristics, such as the numbers of Americans who own homes and who work, have important political implications.

Despite the tremendous diversity of American society, Americans for the most part have avoided the sort of political violence that has ripped apart many other multicultural countries. The reason for the United States' success is that social and economic divisions in the United States tend to be cross-cutting cleavages in which the have-nots on one issue are the haves on another. In addition, the American political process is pluralistic. It gives access to unlimited numbers of people and groups, although they do not enjoy equal success in getting what they want from government.

KEY TERMS

baby boomers   pluralism

cross-cutting cleavages   Rust Belt

feminization of poverty   Sun Belt

READINGS FOR FURTHER STUDY

Alba, Richard, and Victor Nee. *Remaking the American Mainstream: Assimilation and Contemporary Immigration* (Cambridge: Harvard University Press, 2003). A thorough examination of how immigrants become integrated into American political, social, and economic life by two noted sociologists.

Caplow, Theodore, Louis Hicks, and Ben J. Wattenberg. *The First Measured Century* (Washington, D.C.: AEI Press, 2001). A statistical guide to social, demographic, and economic changes across twentieth-century America.

Daniels, Roger. *Guarding the Golden Door: American Immigration Policy and Immigrants since 1882* (New York: Hill and Wang, 2004). A historical examination of American immigration policy and the convoluted politics driving it.

Dawson, Michael C. *Behind the Mule: Race and Class in African-American Politics* (Princeton, NJ: Princeton University Press, 1994). An exhaustive look at the political consequences of the development of an African American middle class.

Greenhouse, Steven. *The Big Squeeze: Tough Times for the American Worker* (New York: Knopf, 2008). A *New York Times* reporter examines the impact of globalization, immigration, and other social and economic forces on the lives of working Americans.

Lien, Pie-te, M. Margaret Conway, and Janelle Wong. *The Politics of Asian Americans: Diversity and Community* (New York: Routledge, 2004). A rigorous analysis of the political behavior of Asian Americans based on unique survey data.

Segura, Gary M., and Shaun Bowler, eds. *Diversity in Democracy: Minority Representation in the United States* (Charlottesville: University of Virginia Press, 2005). An excellent collection of essays that examines African American and Hispanic American representation in the political system.

Suro, Roberto. *Strangers among Us: Latinos Living in a Changing America* (New York: Random House, 1998). A *Washington Post* reporter charts the variety of Hispanic experiences in the United States and how a growing Latino population is changing the way America views itself.

Takaki, Ronald T. *A Different Mirror: A History of Multicultural America* (Boston: Little, Brown, 1993). A reexamination of American history and race relations from a multicultural perspective.

REVIEW QUESTIONS

1. According to the U.S. Census Bureau, _____ percent of Americans identify themselves as white.
   a. 36
   b. 50
   c. 67
   d. 89

2. According to the U.S. Census Bureau, _____ percent of Americans identify themselves as African American, and _____ percent of Americans identify themselves as Hispanic American.
   a. 5, 13
   b. 13, 14
   c. 13, 38
   d. 13, 2

3. According to the U.S. Census Bureau, what was the approximate population in the United States in 2005?
   a. 150 million
   b. 200 million
   c. 302 million
   d. 338 million

4. How has the American population changed since 1900?
   a. The average age is higher.
   b. The average American is a homeowner.
   c. Women outnumber men.
   d. All of the above

5. Which ethnic group is the largest in the United States?
   a. Northern Europeans
   b. African Americans
   c. Hispanic Americans
   d. Asian Americans

6. What is the largest religious denomination in the United States?
   a. Baptists
   b. Roman Catholics
   c. Lutherans
   d. Jews

7. Income in the United States is strongly linked to
   a. ideology and motivation.
   b. hobbies and marital status.
   c. race and education.
   d. religion and education.

8. Which of the following does *not* represent a dramatic change in the American economic landscape?
   a. The economy has shifted from a manufacturing to a service economy.
   b. Almost 40 percent of the population makes a living by farming the land.
   c. The number of union workers is declining.
   d. More than 60 percent of married women work outside the home.

9. Which of the following is *true* about contemporary America?
   a. More Americans work for large companies than ever before.
   b. There are fewer people in the workforce in proportion to those who are retired than in 1950.
   c. Families headed by men account for the largest share of the people who live below the poverty line.
   d. Wealth is fairly equally distributed in the United States.
10. In Robert Dahl's study of New Haven, he concluded that
    a. public policy making was dominated by a power elite.
    b. public policy making was pluralistic.
    c. business leaders controlled most public policy issues.
    d. none of the above.

NOTES

1. U.S. Census Bureau, "U.S. Hispanic Population Surpasses 45 Million, Now 15 Percent of Total," May 1, 2008. www.census.gov/Press-Release/www/releases/archives/population/011910.html

2. Paula D. McClain and Joseph Stewart, Jr., *"Can We All Get Along?" Racial and Ethnic Minorities in American Politics,* 4th edition (Boulder, CO: Westview, 2006); June Kronholz, "Hispanics Gain in Census," *Wall Street Journal,* May 10, 2006.

3. The 2006 data are from the National Geographic-Roper Public Affairs 2006 Geographic Literacy Study. On the previous survey see Malcolm Gladwell, "Fundamental Ignorance about Numbers," *Washington Post National Weekly Edition,* October 16–22, 1995. See also George Gallup, Jr., and Frank Newport, "Americans Ignorant of Basic Census Facts," *Gallup Poll Monthly,* no. 294 (1990): 2; Benjamin Highton and Raymond E. Wolfinger, "Report to the National Election Studies Board of Overseers," January 24, 1992; Richard Nadeau, Richard G. Niemi, and Jeffrey Levine, "Innumeracy about Minority Populations," *Public Opinion Quarterly* 57 (Fall 1993): 332–47.

4. Nadeau, Niemi, and Levine, "Innumeracy about Minority Populations," 340–43; Gladwell, "Fundamental Ignorance."

5. The numbers reported in this chapter are drawn from U.S. Census figures, as reported in several different sources, including the *2008 Statistical Abstract* (www.census.gov/compendia/statab/); *Historical Statistics of the United States: Colonial Times to 1970* (Washington, D.C.: U.S. Bureau of the Census, 1975); Theodore Caplow, Louis Hicks, and Ben J. Wattenberg, *The First Measured Century* (Washington, D.C.: AEI Press, 2001); *New York Times 2001 Almanac* (New York: Penguin, 2000); Harold W. Stanley and Richard G. Niemi, *Vital Statistics on American Politics, 1999–2000* (Washington, D.C.: CQ Press, 2000).

6. Caplow, Hicks, and Wattenberg, *First Measured Century,* 11–12.

7. Calculated by the authors from U.S. Census Bureau, "Table 1. Estimates of the Population by Race Alone or in Combination and Hispanic Origin for the United States and States: July 1, 2007."

8. A Yankelovich poll taken in October 1995 revealed a preference for *African American. Black* was the preferred label in a 1995 U.S. Department of Labor

survey, and *doesn't matter* was the top choice in a July 1995 Gallup Poll. The even split was reported in Lee Sigelman, Steven A. Tuch, and Jack K. Martin, "What's in a Name: Preference for 'Black' Versus 'African-American' Among Americans of African Descent," *Public Opinion Quarterly* 69 (Fall 2005): 429–38. For reports on the first and forth surveys, see "People, Opinions, & Polls," *Public Perspective* 7 (February/March 1996): 25. The Labor Department survey is discussed in Asra Q. Nomani, "Work Week," *Wall Street Journal*, November 7, 1995; "Outlook: American Pie," *U.S. News & World Report,* November 20, 1995, 28.

9. Edward G. Carmines and James A. Stimson, *Issue Evolution: Race and the Transformation of American Politics* (Princeton, NJ: Princeton University Press, 1989), 27–58.

10. Harold W. Stanley and Richard G. Niemi, "Partisanship and Group Support Over Time," in *Controversies in Voting Behavior,* 3rd ed., ed. Richard G. Niemi and Herbert F. Weisberg (Washington, D.C.: CQ Press, 1993).

11. Pew Research Center, "Optimism About Black Progress Declines: Blacks See Growing Values Gap Between Poor and Middle Class," November 13, 2007. www.pewsocialtrends.org/pubs/700/black-public-opinion See also Michael Dawson, *Behind the Mule: Race and Class in African-American Politics* (Princeton, NJ: Princeton University Press, 1994); Franklin D. Gilliam, Jr., and Kenny J. Whitby, Jr., "Race, Class, and Attitudes Toward Social Welfare Spending: An Ethclass Interpretation," *Social Science Quarterly* 70 (March 1989): 88–100; Byran O. Jackson, Elisabeth R. Gerber, and Bruce E. Cain, "Coalitional Prospects in a Multi-Racial Society: African-American Attitudes Toward Other Minority Groups," *Political Research Quarterly* 47 (June 1994): 277–94.

12. David A. Bositis, "Politics and the 2004 Election," *The Joint Center for Political and Economic Studies,* February 2005; David A. Bositis, "The Black Vote in 2000," *The Joint Center for Political and Economic Studies,* December 2000; Michael K. Frisby, "Jesse Jackson Ponders Another Presidential Bid, But Decision Hinges on Clinton's Tilt to Right," *Wall Street Journal,* July 7, 1995.

13. See Kim Quaile Hill and Jan Leighley, "Lower-Class Mobilization and Policy Linkage in the U.S. States," *American Journal of Political Science* 39 (February 1995): 75–86.

14. *Statistical Abstract of the United States, 2002*, 122nd ed. (Washington, D.C.: U.S. Census Bureau, 2002): 39–40.

15. U.S. Census Bureau, "Hispanics in the United States," www.census.gov/population/www/socdemo/hispanic/files/Internet_Hispanic_in_US_2006.pdf.

16. Pew Hispanic Center/Kaiser Family Foundation, *2002 National Survey of Latinos,* December 2002, 30. See also Darryl Fears, "The Roots of 'Hispanic,'" *Washington Post,* October 15, 2003, and Darryl Fears, "Latinos or Hispanics? A Debate about Identity," *Washington Post,* August 25, 2003.

17. See James Fay and Kay Lawson, "Is California Going Republican?" in *Party Realignment and State Politics,* ed. Maureen Moakley (Columbus: Ohio State University Press, 1992); Jeanie R. Stanley, "Party Realignment in Texas," in *Party Realignment and State Politics,* ed. Maureen Moakley (Columbus: Ohio State University Press, 1992).

18. Bruce Cain and D. Roderick Kiewiet, "Ethnicity and Electoral Choice: Mexican-American Voting Behavior in the California 30th Congressional

District," *Social Science Quarterly* 65 (June 1984): 315–27; Bruce E. Cain, D. Roderick Kiewiet, and Carole J. Uhlaner, "The Acquisition of Partisanship by Latinos and Asian Americans," *American Journal of Political Science* 35 (May 1991): 390–422; Pew Hispanic Center/Kaiser Family Foundation, *The 2004 National Survey of Latinos: Politics and Civic Participation.* www.kff.org/kaiserpolls/upload/The-2004-National-Survey-of-Latinos-Politics-and-Civic-Participation-Summary-and-Chart-Pack.pdf

19. The Pew Forum on Religion & Public Life and Pew Hispanic Center, "Changing Faiths: Latinos and the Transformation of American Religion," 2007, 80; Pew Hispanic Center/Kaiser Family Foundation, *2004 National Survey of Latinos: Politics and Civic Participation*; Rodolfo O. De la Garza, Louis DeSipio, Chris Garcia, John Garcia, and Angelo Falcon, *Latino Voices* (Boulder, CO: Westview, 1992), 127; Christopher L. Warren, "Hispanics," in *Florida's Politics and Government,* 2nd ed., ed. Manning J. Dauer (Gainesville: University of Florida Presses, 1984).

20. Jessica S. Barnes and Claudette E. Bennett, "The Asian Population: 2000," U.S. Census Bureau, February 2002. www.census.gov/prod/2002pubs/c2kbr01-16.pdf

21. Wendy K. Tam Cho and Suneet P. Lad, "Subcontinental Divide: Asian Indians and Asian American Politics," *American Politics Research* 32 (May 2004): 239–63; James S. Lai, Wendy K. Tam Cho, Thomas P. Kim, and Okiyoshi Takeda, "Asian Pacific-American Campaigns, Elections, and Elected Officials," *PS: Political Science and Politics,* 34 (September 2001): 611–17; Nishad H. Majmudar, "In the U.S., Indians Gain Campaign Clout," *Wall Street Journal,* August 17, 2004. See also Cain, Kiewiet, and Uhlaner, "The Acquisition of Partisanship," 390–422; Fay and Lawson, "Is California Going Republican?" 30–33.

22. Wendy K. Tam Cho, "Foreshadowing Strategic Pan-Ethnic Politics: Asian American Campaign Finance Activity in Varying Multicultural Contexts," *State Politics and Policy Quarterly* 1 (Fall 2001): 273–94.

23. Nomani, "Work Week"; "Outlook: American Pie."

24. Geoffrey D. Peterson, "Native American Turnout in the 1990 and 1992 Elections," *American Indian Quarterly* 21 (Spring 1997): 321–31.

25. U.S. Census Bureau, "An Older, More Diverse Nation by Midcentury," August 14, 2008. www.census.gov/Press-Release/www/releases/archives/population/012496.html

26. U.S. Census Bureau, "U.S. Hispanic Population Surpasses 45 Million, Now 15 Percent of Total," www.census.gov/Press-Release/www/releases/archives/population/011910.html

27. U.S. Census Bureau, "La Paz, Ariz., Population is Nation's Oldest County," August 7, 2008.

28. Quoted in William Booth, "Diversity and Division," *Washington Post National Weekly Edition*, March 2, 1998.

29. See D'Vera Cohn and Darryl Fears, "Hispanics Draw Even with Blacks in New Census," *Washington Post,* March 7, 2001; Franklin D. Gilliam, "Exploring Minority Empowerment: Symbolic Politics, Governing Coalitions and Traces of Political Style in Los Angeles," *American Journal of Political Science* (February 1996): 56–81; Tanya K. Hernandez, "Roots of Latino/Black Anger," *Los Angeles Times,* January 7, 2007; Miriam Jordan, "Blacks vs. Latinos at Work," *Wall Street Journal,* January 24, 2006; Jackson, Gerber, and Cain, "Coalitional Prospects."

30. Data are from the *Los Angeles Times,* "LA City Exit Poll, Mayoral Runoff Election, May 17, 2005." For an analysis of the 2001 race between the same two candidates that makes a similar point, see Sharon D. Wright Austin and Richard T. Middleton, IV, "The Limitations of the Deracialization Concept in the 2001 Los Angeles Mayoral Election," *Political Research Quarterly* 57 (June 2004): 283–93. See also Raphael J. Sonenshein and Susan H. Pinkus, "The Dynamics of Latino Political Incorporation: The 2001 Los Angeles Mayoral Election as Seen in 'Los Angeles Times' Exit Polls," *PS: Political Science and Politics* 35 (March 2002): 67–74.

31. Richard Morin, "Do Blacks and Hispanics Get Along?" January 31, 2008. www.pewresearch.org/pubs/713/blacks-hispanics

32. Sharon M. Lee, and Barry Edmonston, "New Marriages, New Families: U.S. Racial and Hispanic Intermarriage," *Population Bulletin* 60, no. 2 (Washington, D.C.: Population Reference Bureau, 2005). See also Amitai Etzioni, "The Monochrome Society," *Public Interest* 137 (Fall 1999): 42–55; and Roland G. Fryer, "Guess Who's Been Coming to Dinner: Trends in Interracial Marriage over the 20th Century," *Journal of Economic Perspectives* 21 (Spring 2007): 71–90.

33. Richard Morin, "Who Wants to Know?" *Washington Post National Weekly Edition,* August 28–September 3, 1995, 36.

34. See "People, Opinions & Polls" *The Public Perspective* 7 (February/March 1996): 25; Rochelle L. Stanfield, "Multiple Choice," *National Journal,* November 22, 1997.

35. Richard Borreca, "Proposed Akaka Bill Changes Get Federal OK, Lingle Says," *Honolulu Star-Bulletin,* August 24, 2005; Dennis Camire, "Akaka Vows to Offer Bill Again," *The Honolulu Advertiser,* June 9, 2006; Daniel Seligman, "Talking Back to the IQ Test, Guess Who's in Love with Lefties, More Casino Wars, and Other Matters," *Fortune,* October 16, 1995, 246.

36. Stanfield, "Multiple Choice."

37. Cohn and Fears, "Hispanics Draw Even with Blacks in New Census."

38. Natalie Masuoka, "Political Attitudes and Ideologies of Multiracial Americans," *Political Research Quarterly* 61 (June 2008): 253–67.

39. U.S. Department of Homeland Security, *Yearbook of Immigration Statistics, 2007* (www.dhs.gov/ximgtn/statistics/publications/LPR07.shtml). See also U.S. Census Bureau, "Foreign-Born Population of the United States, Current Population Survey—March 2004," Detailed Tables (PPL-176), Table 2.6; and Pew Hispanic Center, "Statistical Portrait of the Foreign-Born Population in the United States, 2006," January 23, 2008. www.pewhispanic.org/factsheets/factsheet.php?FactsheetID=36

40. Carolyn Lochhead, "Senate Swayed by Analyst's Immigrant Count: How Conservative Think Tank's Estimate Led to Changes in Bill," *San Francisco Chronicle,* June 20, 2006.

41. Jeffrey S. Passel, "The Size and Characteristics of the Unauthorized Migrant Population in the U.S.: Estimates Based on the March 2005 Current Population Survey," March 7, 2006. www.pewhispanic.org/files/reports/61.pdf

42. General Accounting Office, "Tracking," GAO 04-82, May 2004; Pew Hispanic Center, "Modes of Entry Overstay for the Unauthorized Migrant Population," May 22, 2006; www.pewhispanic.org/files/factsheets/19.pdf and U.S. Immigration and Naturalization Service, "Estimates of the Unauthorized Immigrant Population Residing in the United States: 1990 to 2000," 2003. www.dhs.gov/xlibrary/assets/statistics/publications/Ill_Report_1211.pdf

43. Joseph M. Hayes and Laura E. Hill, "Immigrant Pathways to Legal Permanent Residence," *California Counts* 9 (June 2008).

44. Jacob L. Vigdor, "Measuring Immigrant Assimilation in the United States," *Civic Report* 53 (May 2008).

45. Kristin F. Butcher and Anne Morrison Piehl, "Crime, Corrections, and California," *California Counts* 9 (February 2008).

46. Center for Continuing Study of the California Economy, "Can the Unemployed Replace Unauthorized Workers?" August 2007. www.ccsce.com/pdf/Numbers-aug07-unemployed.pdf

47. Dowell Myers, "Thinking Ahead about Our Immigrant Future: New Trends and Mutual Benefits in Our Aging Society," *Immigration Policy in Focus* 6 (January 2008).

48. Jeffrey S. Passell, "Estimates of the Size and Characteristics of the Undocumented Population," March 21, 2005. www.pewhispanic.org/files/reports/44.pdf

49. De la Garza, DeSipio, Garcia, Garcia, and Falcon, *Latino Voices,* 97–98.

50. Sydney J. Freedberg Jr., "Issues & Ideas—English Spoken Here?" *National Journal*, January 7, 2006. Similar figures are reported by Shirin Hakimzadeh and D'Vera Cohn, "English Usage among Hispanics in the United States," November 29, 2007, revised December 6, 2007. www.pewhispanic.org/files/reports/82.pdf

51. Teresa Watanabe, "Growing Diversity Fuels a War of Words," *Los Angeles Times,* March 19, 2006; William M. Welch, "English Language Legislation Gathers Steam Across the USA," *USA TODAY*, June 19, 2008.

52. Data from U.S. ENGLISH, Inc. *Ruiz et al. v. Hull et al.* 191 Ariz. 441, 957 P.2d 984 (1998).

53. U.S. Census Bureau, "US Hispanic Population Surpasses 45 Million, Now 15 Percent of Total." www.census.gov/Press-Release/www/releases/archives/population/011910.html

54. The Board of Trustees, Federal Old-Age and Survivors Insurance and Federal Disability Insurance Trust Funds, "2008 Annual Report of the Board of Trustees of the Federal Old-Age and Survivors Insurance and Disability Insurance Trust Funds," Table IV.B2. www.ssa.gov/OACT/TR/TR08/trTOC.html

55. Frederick Kempe, "Demographic Time Bomb Ticks On," *Wall Street Journal,* June 6, 2006.

56. Brady E. Hamilton, Joyce A. Martin, and Stephanie J. Ventura, "Births: Preliminary Data for 2006," *National Vital Statistics Report* 56 (December 5, 2007); Council of Europe, "Recent Demographic Developments in Europe 2004," January 2005; Richard Morin, "The Face of the Single Mother," *Washington Post National Weekly Edition,* May 1–7, 1995, 34.

57. Dan Black, Gary J. Gates, Seth G. Sanders, and Lowell Taylor. "Demographics of the Gay and Lesbian Population in the United States: Evidence from Available Systematic Data Sources," *Demography* 37 (May 2000): 139–54; Gary J. Gates, "Same-sex Couples and the Gay, Lesbian, Bisexual Population: New Estimates from the American Community Survey," October 2006; Tamar Lewin, "New Sex Survey Finds Little of the Wild Life," *Des Moines Register,* October 7, 1994; Boyce Rensberger, "Playing Politics by the Numbers," *Washington Post National Weekly Edition,* April 26–May 2, 1993.

58. "Gays Finding '10%' Statistic Questioned," *Iowa City Press-Citizen*, April 19, 1993.

59. L. Marvin Overby and Jay Barth, "Numeracy about Minority Populations: Americans' Estimations of *Local* Gay Population Size," *Polity* 38 (April 2006): 194–210.

60. The data on the 2004 vote are from exit polls conducted by Edison Media Research (EMR) and Mitofsky International for the major networks and the Associated Press. For 1994, see the data reported in "Portrait of the Electorate: Who Voted for Whom in the House," November 13, 1994.

61. Rich Tafel quoted in "Gingrich's Thoughts on Gays," *Des Moines Register,* November 24, 1994.

62. The number of denominations is from the *Encyclopedia of American Religion.*

63. The Pew Forum on Religion & Public Life, "U.S. Religious Landscape Survey, Religious Beliefs and Practices: Diverse and Politically Relevant," June 2008. www.religions.pewforum.org/pdf/report2-religious-landscape-study-full.pdf

64. Religious affiliation numbers are from the Pew Forum on Religion & Public Life, "U.S. Religious Landscape Survey." www.religions.pewforum.org/reports

65. The Utah numbers are from Vauhini Vara, "Utah on Verge of a Tippling Point," *Wall Street Journal,* June 3, 2008.

66. Highton and Wolfinger, "Report to the National Election Studies Board of Overseers.".

67. Pew Research Center, "Muslim Americans: Middle Class and Mostly Mainstream," May 22, 2007. www.pewresearch.org/assets/pdf/muslim-americans.pdf

68. Joel Millman, "Delayed Recognition," *Wall Street Journal,* November 14, 2005; John Sherry, "California Muslims Flex Electoral Muscles," *The Hill,* July 12, 2000.

69. See Bill Broadway, "God's Place on the Dais," *Washington Post,* January 27, 2001.

70. The Pew Forum on Religion & Public Life, "U.S. Religious Landscape Survey." See also Barbara Hinkson Craig and David M. O'Brien, *Abortion and American Politics* (Chatham, NJ: Chatham House, 1993), 258; Laurie Goodstein and Richard Morin, "Love the Messenger, Not His Message," *Washington Post National Weekly Edition,* October 9–15, 1995, 37; and James L. Guth, Corwin E. Smidt, Lyman A. Kellstedt, and John C. Green, "The Sources of Antiabortion Attitudes: The Case of Religious Political Activists," in *Understanding the New Politics of Abortion,* ed. Malcolm Goggin (Newbury Park, CA: Sage, 1993), 49.

71. A. James Reichley, *Religion in American Public Life* (Washington, D.C.: Brookings Institution, 1985), 267–81; Paul A. Djupe and Christopher P. Gilbert, *The Prophetic Pulpit: Clergy, Churches, and Communities in American Politics* (Lanham, MD: Rowman & Littlefield, 2003).

72. Kenneth D. Wald, "Assessing the Religious Factor in Electoral Behavior," in *Religion in American Politics,* ed. Charles W. Dunn (Washington, D.C.: CQ Press, 1989).

73. Kenneth D. Wald, Dennis E. Owen, and Samuel S. Hill, Jr., "Political Cohesion in Churches," *Journal of Politics* 52 (February 1990): 197–215.

74. U.S. Census Bureau, Educational Attainment, "Table A-2. Percent of People 25 Years and Over Who Have Completed High School or College, by Race, Hispanic Origin and Sex: Selected Years 1940 to 2007," March 15, 2007;

www.census.gov/population/socdemo/education/cps2007/tabA-2.xls   U.S. Census Bureau, "The American Community—American Indians and Alaska Natives: 2004," May 2007; www.census.gov/prod/2007pubs/acs-07.pdf U.S. Census Bureau, "College Degree Nearly Doubles Annual Earnings, Census Bureau Reports," March 28, 2005. www.census.gov/Press-Release/www/releases/archives/education/004214.html

75. U.S. Census Bureau, "Table A-2. Percent of People 25 Years and Over Who Have Completed High School or College, by Race, Hispanic Origin and Sex: Selected Years 1940 to 2007,"; www.census.gov/population/socdemo/education/cps2007/tabA-2.xls U.S. Census Bureau, "The American Community—American Indians and Alaska Natives: 2004. www.census.gov/prod/2007pubs/acs-07.pdf

76. U.S. Census Bureau, School Enrollment—Social and Economic Characteristics of Students: October 2006, "Table 1. Enrollment Status of the Population 3 Years Old and Over, by Sex, Age, Race, Hispanic Origin, Foreign Born, and Foreign-Born Parentage: October 2006," www.census.gov/population/www/socdemo/school/cps2006.html

77. Chris Baker, "What is Middle Class?" *Washington Times,* November 30, 2003.

78. The General Social Survey data were calculated by the authors using the General Social Survey cumulative file.

79. NPR/Kaiser Family Foundation/Harvard School of Public Health, "Public Views on SCHIP Reauthorization," October 2007. www.kff.org/kaiserpolls/upload/7704.pdf

80. Quoted in Jessica Holzer, "Dems Grapple with 'Rich," *The Hill,* July 13, 2007.

81. See, for example, the 2007 comments of Federal Reserve Board Chairman Ben S. Bernanke (www.federalreserve.gov/newsevents/speech/Bernanke20070206a.htm). See also, Thomas Piketty and Emmanuel Saez, "Income Inequality in the United States, 1913–1998," *Quarterly Journal of Economics* 118 (February 2003): 1–39. For a contrarian position, see Alan Reynolds, "Has U.S. Income Inequality *Really* Increased?" Cato Institute *Policy Analysis* 586, January 8, 2007.

82. Arthur B. Kennickell, "Currents and Undercurrents: Changes in the Distribution of Wealth, 1989–2004," *Federal Reserve Board,* January 30, 2006; and Brian K. Bucks, Arthur B. Kennickell, and Kevin B. Moore, "Recent Changes in U.S. Family Finances: Evidence from the 2001 and 2004 Survey of Consumer Finances," *Federal Reserve Bulletin,* 2006.

83. Carmen DeNavas-Walt, Bernadette D. Proctor, and Jessica Smith, *U.S. Census Bureau, Current Population Reports, P60-235, Income, Poverty, and Health Insurance Coverage in the United States: 2007* (Washington, DC: U.S. Government Printing Office, Washington, DC, 2008).

84. U.S. Census Bureau, Educational Attainment, "Table A-3. Mean Earnings of Workers 18 Years and Over, by Educational Attainment, Race, Hispanic Origin, and Sex: 1975 to 2006," March 15, 2007; www.census.gov/population/socdemo/education/cps2007/tabA-3.xls and Lisa Barrow and Cecilia Elena Rouse, "Does College Still Pay?" *The Economists' Voice,* 2 (no. 4, 2005): article 3.

85. John E. Schwarz, *America's Hidden Success,* rev. ed. (New York: Norton, 1988).

86. Jonathan B. Taylor and Joseph P. Kalt, "American Indians on Reservations: A Databook of Socioeconomic Change between the 1990 and 2000

Censuses," *The Harvard Project on American Indian Economic Development,* January 2005, 24–25.

87. Alan Berube and Elizabeth Kneebone, "Two Steps Back: City and Suburban Poverty Trends 1999–2005," *The Brookings Institution, Metropolitan Policy Program,* December 2006.

88. Eric R. Kingson and Edward D. Berkowitz, *Social Security and Medicare* (Westport, CT: Auburn House, 1993), 75–81.

89. U.S. Census Bureau, "POV03. People in Families with Related Children under 18 by Family Structure, Age, Sex, Iterated by Income-to-Poverty Ratio and Race, Below 100 Percent of Poverty," August 29, 2007. www.pubdb3. census.gov/macro/032008/pov/new03_100.htm

90. U.S. Bureau of the Census, "Census Bureau Reports on Residential Vacancies and Homeownership," April 28, 2008. www.census.gov/hhes/www/ housing/hvs/qtr108/q108press.pdf

91. National Coalition for the Homeless, "How Many People Experience Homelessness?" NCH Fact Sheet #2. August 2007.

92. United States Conference of Mayors—Sodexho USA, "Hunger and Homelessness Survey," December 2007. www.usmayors.org/HHSurvey2007/ hhsurvey07.pdf

93. United States Conference of Mayors—Sodexho USA, "Hunger and Homelessness Survey," December 2007. www.usmayors.org/HHSurvey2007/ hhsurvey07.pdf

94. Peverill Squire, Raymond E. Wolfinger, and David P. Glass, "Residential Mobility and Voter Turnout," *American Political Science Review* 81 (March 1987): 45–65. See also Ted G. Jelen, "The Impact of Home Ownership on Whites' Racial Attitudes," *American Politics Quarterly* 18 (April 1990): 208–14; Paul William Kingston, John L. P. Thompson, and Douglas M. Eichar, "The Politics of Homeownership," *American Politics Quarterly* 12 (April 1984): 131–50.

95. Bureau of Labor Statistics, "New Quarterly Data from BLS on Business Employment Dynamics by Size of Firm," December 8, 2005. www.bls.gov/ news.release/cewfs.nr0.htm

96. The Kaiser Family Foundation and Health Research and Educational Trust, "Employee Health Benefits, 2007 Annual Survey," www.kff.org/insurance/ 7672/upload/76723.pdf

97. Bureau of Labor Statistics, "Union Members in 2007," January 25, 2008. www.bls.gov/news.release/pdf/union2.pdf

98. On women with children under the age of six, see Bureau of Labor Statistics, "Employment Characteristics of Families in 2005," April 27, 2006. Wage data reported DeNavas-Walt, Proctor, and Smith, *U.S. Census Bureau, Current Population Reports, P60-233, Income, Poverty, and Health Insurance Coverage in the United States: 2006.*

99. June Ellenoff O'Neill, "The Shrinking Pay Gap," *Wall Street Journal,* October 7, 1994. See also June O'Neill, "The Gender Gap in Wages, circa 2000," *AEA Papers and Proceedings,* 93 (May 2003): 309–14.

100. Diana Furchtgott-Roth, "Working Wives Widen 'Income Gap,'" *Wall Street Journal,* June 20, 1995.

101. See Nicholas Lemann, "A Cartoon Elite," Atlantic Monthly (November 1996): 109–16; and Geoffrey Nunberg, *Talking Right: How Conservatives Turned Liberalism into a Tax-Raising, Latte-Drinking, Sushi-Eating, Volvo-*

Driving, New York Times-Reading, Body-Piercing, Hollywood-Loving, Left-Wing Freak Show (New York: Public Affairs, 2006), chapter 7.

102. For examples of more recent work, see Nelson W. Polsby, *Community Power and Political Theory,* rev. ed. (New Haven: Yale University Press, 1980); Clarence N. Stone, "Systemic Power in Community Decision-Making: A Restatement of Stratification Theory," *American Political Science Review* 74 (December 1980): 978–90; and Clarence N. Stone, "Pre-emptive Power: Floyd Hunter's 'Community Power Structure' Reconsidered," *American Journal of Political Science* 32 (February 1988): 82–104.

103. Floyd Hunter, *Community Power Structure* (Chapel Hill: University of North Carolina Press, 1953). In the style of the time, Hunter disguises Atlanta by calling it Regional City.

104. Robert A. Dahl, *Who Governs* (New Haven: Yale University Press, 1960).

4

Civil Liberties

During the evening of May 21, 2000, a deputy sheriff from Humboldt County, Nevada, approached a man standing beside a pickup truck sitting on the shoulder of Grass Valley Road.[1] The deputy had received a report that a man had struck a woman in the cab of a pickup while driving on the road. The man fit the description of the alleged perpetrator; a woman was sitting in the pickup; and skid marks were on the road. The suspicious deputy asked eleven times to see the man's identification. Eleven times the man refused. The deputy concluded from the man's behavior that he had been involved in domestic violence and had possibly been drinking and driving. But the deputy did not arrest him on those charges. Instead, he arrested him for violating a Nevada state law that requires people to identify themselves when a police officer has reason to believe they committed a crime.

The man who was arrested, Larry Dudley Hiibel, was never charged with any other crime. (The woman in the pickup turned out to be Hiibel's teenage daughter. She had been driving, and they had been arguing over a boy she was seeing. The daughter had hit Hiibel in the shoulder. A driver in another car had seen the fight and called the police.) The local justice of the peace determined that the deputy sheriff had acted properly and fined Hiibel $250 plus a $70 court fee.[2] Believing that the Constitution did not require him to identify himself to the police, Hiibel appealed his case. Both the Sixth Judicial District Court and Nevada Supreme Court sided with the police. Hiibel then took his case to the U.S. Supreme Court.

Surprisingly, the U.S. Supreme Court had never ruled on whether the police could require individuals suspected of a crime to identify themselves on demand. Consequently, Hiibel's case generated considerable interest in the legal community, even though it involved a minor incident and a small fine. A wide range of organizations, including the American Civil Liberties Union (ACLU), the Cato Institute, the National Law Center on Homelessness and Poverty, and the Electronic Frontier Foundation, supported Hiibel's position that he was not required to identify himself to the police. Groups such as the National Association of Police Organizations backed the state of Nevada's contention that such requests are permitted by the Constitution.

In 2004, the U.S. Supreme Court, on a 5–4 vote, upheld the Nevada law requiring people under suspicion to provide officers their names. (By extension, similar laws in twenty other states also are presumed to be constitutional.) The Court's decision, written by Justice Anthony Kennedy, rejected Hiibel's claim that his Fourth Amendment rights against unreasonable search and seizure were violated. The Court ruled that the police request for identification properly balanced the government's interests against those of the individual wanting to prevent unreasonable intrusions. The Court also held that the police did not violate Hiibel's Fifth Amendment protections against self-incrimination, arguing that in this case, providing a name would not be incriminating. After the decision was announced, Hiibel's lawyers issued a statement saying, "A

Nevada cowboy courageously fought for his right to be left alone but lost."[3]

The questions the *Hiibel* case raises are complex. For more than 200 years, Americans have struggled to define what the freedoms set forth in the Constitution mean in practice. Disagreements have frequently arisen over how to interpret these structural rules of American politics, and many of these disputes have led to bitter political conflict. Moreover, the way the government and the public have interpreted phrases such as "freedom of religion," "freedom of speech," and "freedom of the press" has changed over time.

Although we like to think that the Constitution guarantees certain and absolute **civil liberties**, the truth is that our interpretations of these freedoms constantly change. The question of how to settle conflicts between competing liberties is a tricky one, akin to achieving a delicate balance between two items on a scale. On one side of the scale are individual liberties, and on the other, societal rights; in the *Hiibel* case, the rights of individuals rested on one side and the rights of the police acting on behalf of society on the other. The balance constantly shifts, and politics often dictates the final results. In other words, the rules governing our liberties change, and politics helps determine the changes.

In this chapter, we examine the evolution of civil liberties in the United States and the role politics plays in defining them. We look at how the Founders introduced the concept of individual rights in the Bill of Rights, which forms the foundation for the civil liberties we enjoy today. We then discuss specific changes in the way our political system has interpreted the Bill of Rights over the past two centuries, tracing its relationship to state government and to the still-evolving rules that mediate conflict in areas such as First Amendment rights, the right to bear arms, government treatment of criminal suspects, and the right to privacy.

civil liberties
The freedoms guaranteed to all Americans in the Bill of Rights (although some are in the body of the Constitution). These liberties include freedom of speech, freedom of religion, and the right to assemble peaceably.

In 2004, Dudley Hiibel's conviction for not identifying himself to police when asked as required under a Nevada law was upheld as constitutional by the Supreme Court.

4-1 INTERPRETING THE CONSTITUTION

As we saw in Chapter 2, the vague, ambiguous language of the Constitution allows a flexible interpretation of its provisions. Most of the ten amendments in the Bill of Rights are short in length and broad in scope. A few, particularly the Ninth and Tenth Amendments, are so vague that we still have not reached a consensus about what they mean. How, then, are we to interpret the meaning of the Constitution and its amendments? How can we apply it to resolve or manage conflicts over rights—to balance, as in the *Hiibel* case, the rights of the individual against the rights of the larger society?

Some people believe in interpreting the Constitution in light of original intent—in other words, according to what its writers originally had in mind.[4] This approach requires a judge to comb the historical record to learn what the Founders or the sponsors of constitutional amendments intended when they adopted the specific words in the Constitution. For example, in the famous *Dred Scott v. Sandford* (1858) case, in which the Supreme Court ruled that, short of a constitutional amendment, the federal government lacked the authority to outlaw slavery (see Chapter 2), Chief Justice Roger Taney wrote:

> No one, we presume, supposes that any change in public opinion or feeling . . . should induce the court to give to the words of the Constitution a more liberal construction . . . than they were intended to bear when the instrument was framed and adopted. . . . [I]t must be construed now as it was understood at the time of its adoption. It is not only the same in words, but the same in meaning.[5]

As you can see, using original intent as a rule limits a judge's discretion in deciding what the Constitution means. It requires the judge to settle legal challenges on the basis of what the Founders meant, not what the judge might think is reasonable or justified.[6] The idea of **original intent** promises a stable interpretation of the Constitution, with decisions about whether to change the law left to legislators rather than judges.

Although original intent offers one way to interpret the Constitution, by necessity it cannot be the only way. Determining original intent raises a host of thorny questions. One problem involves the question of whose original intent one should examine. Should it be the people who wrote the applicable clause in the Constitution or the people in the state conventions or legislatures that ratified it? Many people believe that the intent of the people who wrote the language is crucial. However, several of the Founders believed that to determine the meaning of the Constitution, one should look not to their views, but to the views of the ratifying conventions. Albert Gallatin, a key ally of Thomas Jefferson and a major political figure in the early years of the Republic, argued that "the gentlemen who formed the general [Constitutional] Convention . . . only drew it and proposed it. The people and the State Conventions who ratified and who adopted the instrument, are alone parties to it, and their intentions alone might, with any degree of

original intent

The theory that judges should interpret the Constitution by determining what the Founders intended when they wrote it.

propriety, be resorted to."[7] James Madison, who is generally considered the main architect of the Constitution, agreed with Gallatin: "If we were to look ... for the [Constitution's] meaning beyond the face of the instrument, we must look for it, not in the General Convention which proposed, but in the State Conventions which accepted and ratified the Constitution."[8]

Even when one decides whose intent to examine, it is not always possible to determine their intent. Ferreting out the intent of the Founders can be arduous work. After all, their deliberations were conducted in secret; thus, we have limited information about their discussions. Moreover, when it came to applying the text of the Constitution to concrete issues, the Founders frequently disagreed over what the document they had drafted meant. In a similar vein, determining the intent of the delegates attending the state conventions or the members of the state legislatures that ratified the Constitution is easier said than done. Disagreements about what those who wrote and ratified the Constitution intended by their handiwork can leave Supreme Court justices scratching their heads. For example, in the famous case of *Brown v. Board of Education* (see Chapter 5), which found that laws requiring segregated public schools are unconstitutional, Chief Justice Earl Warren wrote that he and his fellow justices heard extensive arguments about the meaning of the equal protection clause of the Fourteenth Amendment.

> These arguments covered exhaustively consideration of the Amendment in Congress, ratification by the states, then existing practices in racial segregation, and the view of the proponents and opponents of the Amendment. This discussion and our own investigation convince us that, although these sources cast some light, it is not enough to resolve the problem with which we are faced. At best, they are inconclusive.[9]

As a result of their inability to determine original intent, Warren and his fellow Supreme Court justices had to look elsewhere when deciding how to rule.

Beyond the problems of whose intent to examine and how to determine that intent, the idea of original intent may run into another obstacle: The precise meanings of many of the words used in the Constitution and the Bill of Rights are open to debate. When, for instance, does a police search become *unreasonable* in the eyes of the Fourth Amendment? When do punishments become *cruel and unusual* under the Eighth Amendment? No dictionary will help here.

A final problem with original intent is the fact that American society in the twenty-first century faces many issues that no one envisioned 200 years ago. Do the free speech protections the Founders instituted for the print press extend to electronic media, such as radio, television, and the Internet? What does the Fourth Amendment's prohibition against unreasonable search and seizure mean in a world with electronic eavesdropping and DNA testing? With the world having changed so much over two centuries, the Founders' thinking may not be relevant, even when we know what they thought. As a result, many people agree with Justice Oliver

Wendell Holmes that the Constitution must be interpreted "in light of our whole experience and not merely in the light of what was said a hundred years ago."[10]

In the end, decisions about the extent of our civil liberties rest with our governmental institutions. Congress, the president, and state governments have, over time, taken a number of important steps to protect and extend civil liberties. But the members of the Supreme Court have an especially important role in defining civil liberties. As Charles Evans Hughes said in 1907, a few years before he joined the Supreme Court, "The Constitution is what the judges say it is." In making their decisions, individual justices are free to rely on their own judgments, whatever the thoughts of the Founders or other justices may be. Thus, the meanings of the words in the Constitution can, and do, change as the membership of the Court and other governmental institutions and society at large change.

This constant redefinition of our civil liberties helps our government respond to the needs and desires of a changing, increasingly diverse population. What Americans take civil liberties to mean at the start of the twenty-first century differs markedly from what most people took them to mean in 1789. This very flexibility, as we discussed in Chapter 2, may be a major reason the Constitution is still relevant (and relatively unchanged by amendments) after two centuries; it may become even more important as a diverse American society enters the next century. As society changes, the rules of American politics change as well.

4-2 THE BILL OF RIGHTS AND STATE GOVERNMENT

Recall that the Bill of Rights encompasses the first ten amendments to the Constitution and guarantees some of our most treasured individual rights, including freedom of speech, freedom of religion, and the right to legal protections when charged with a crime. When the Bill of Rights was adopted, it applied only to the relations between the federal government and the people, not to those between the states and their citizens (although many states incorporated similar rights into their own constitutions). During congressional deliberations on the Bill of Rights, some members of the House of Representatives, most notably James Madison, wanted to protect some individual rights against intrusion by the state governments, but the Senate rebuffed the effort.

In 1833, the Supreme Court was asked to extend the Bill of Rights to relations between state governments and the people by applying the "just compensation" clause in the Fifth Amendment to a dispute between a wharf owner and the city of Baltimore. (This clause says simply that the government may not seize private property without providing "just compensation," or fair payment, for it.) The Court refused to apply the clause to the Baltimore case. The Court's reasoning was that each state had adopted its own constitution and that document determined the mix of restrictions on government powers it thought appropriate. The Bill of Rights applied only to the relationship between the federal government and the citizenry. The Court's ruling set a precedent that stood for more than sixty years.[11]

Over time, however, the courts gradually began to extend the Bill of Rights to the states; although after 200 years, the application remains incomplete. The ratification of the Fourteenth Amendment in 1868 prompted the change. That amendment, one of three passed in the immediate aftermath of the Civil War, declares that no state shall "deprive any person of life, liberty, or property, without due process of law." As early as 1873, justices argued in dissenting opinions that these words meant that the Bill of Rights should apply to the states.[12] In 1897, the Court first applied part of the Bill of Rights to the states, overturning its 1833 ruling that the just compensation clause did not apply to the states.[13] A few years later in 1925, the Court began assuming that states had to protect free speech rights, meaning that they finally explicitly applied the First Amendment's guarantee of free speech to the states.[14] As Table 4–1 shows, other rights have been extended to the state level since then, although a few still have not. Indeed, in *District of Columbia v. Heller* (2008), the case in which the Supreme Court held that the Second Amendment protects an individual's right to bear arms, the majority opinion explicitly sidestepped the question of whether the ruling applied to state laws, and it left open the possibility that it might not be in future decisions.[15]

4-3 THE FIRST AMENDMENT: FREEDOM OF SPEECH, ASSEMBLY, PRESS, AND RELIGION

Interpretations of First Amendment rights have also changed over the years. Many of our political and religious rights flow directly from the First Amendment. Yet it has never been taken to mean an absolute guarantee of political or religious freedom. In determining whether a law violates the First Amendment, the Supreme Court usually balances what it sees as the rights of the individual against the interests of society. Moreover, as the political and societal climate changes with time, the Supreme Court changes its interpretation of what the First Amendment means in practice.

The First Amendment guarantees Americans freedom of speech, freedom to assemble peaceably, freedom of the press, and freedom of religion. Let's look at each in turn, focusing on past and present interpretations and how they affect our rights in a practical sense today.

4-3a Freedom of Speech

The Founders believed that the health of a democracy rested on the ability of its citizens to speak their minds without fear of

Amendment Right	Supreme Court Case (Year)*
First	
Speech	*Gitlow v. New York* (1925)
Press	*Near v. Minnesota* (1931)
Assembly	*De Jonge v. Oregon* (1937)
Free exercise of religion	*Cantwell v. Connecticut* (1940)
Establishment of religion	*Everson v. Board of Education* (1947)
Second	Not applied
Third	Not applied
Fourth	
Search and seizure	*Wolf v. Colorado* (1949)
Exclusionary rule	*Mapp v. Ohio* (1961)
Fifth	
Grand jury	Not applied
Just compensation	*Chicago, Burlington & Quincy Railroad Co. v. Chicago* (1897)
Self-incrimination	*Malloy v. Hogan* (1964)
Double jeopardy	*Benton v. Maryland* (1969)
Sixth	
Public trial	*in re* Oliver (1948)
Assistance of counsel	*Gideon v. Wainwright* (1963)
	Argersinger v. Hamlin (1972)
Confrontation	*Pointer v. Texas* (1965)
Impartial jury	*Parker v. Gladden* (1966)
Speedy trial	*Klopfer v. North Carolina* (1967)
Seventh	Not applied
Eighth	
Excessive bail and fines	Not expressly applied
	(see *Shilb v. Kuebel*, 1971)
Cruel and unusual punishment	*Robinson v. California* (1962)
Ninth	Not applicable
Tenth	Not applicable

Table 4–1   Application of the Bill of Rights to the States

*Not all parts of the Bill of Rights have been applied to the states.

government reprisal. Yet Congress has passed laws outlawing or limiting certain speech, and the Supreme Court has upheld many of these limitations. For example, truth-in-advertising laws limit what advertisers can say about their products, and truth-in-lending laws limit what banks can say about their services. As we move away from commercial speech and toward political and symbolic speech, however, in the past fifty years the Court has looked more and more skeptically on laws that infringe on the freedom of speech.

Political Speech

One civil liberty that amply demonstrates the effects of changes in rules and policies is the freedom of political speech. The balance between the individual right to freely criticize the U.S. government and society's right to ensure political stability has shifted back and forth as circumstances have changed over the past two centuries.

To the Founders, the freedom of speech that the First Amendment provides for meant, first and foremost, freedom of *political* speech. But whether Americans actually had a right to speak their minds on the major political matters of the day became an issue early in American history. In 1798, Congress passed the Alien and Sedition Acts, which made it illegal for anyone to write, speak, or publish defamatory statements about the federal government. One motive behind the passage of the acts was political: The Federalists, the party in control of the government, wanted to destroy the opposition Democrat-Republican Party.[16]

The first person convicted under the Alien and Sedition Acts was Matthew Lyon, a Democrat-Republican member of the U.S. House of Representatives from Vermont. He was sentenced to four months in jail and fined $1,000 (a huge sum in 1798) for having written a letter to the editor criticizing President John Adams for his "unbounded thirst for ridiculous pomp, foolish adulation and selfish avarice."[17] Nine other people were eventually convicted under the act. As a practical matter, the Alien and Sedition Acts backfired on the Federalists. The convictions caused great popular concern and helped to derail Adams's bid for reelection. The laws expired in 1801, and one of Thomas Jefferson's first decisions as president was to pardon all those convicted under them.

Although the Alien and Sedition Acts clearly conflicted with the First Amendment, the lower federal courts upheld them, and the Supreme Court never heard a direct challenge to their legality. (However, in a 1964 case, the Court did, in passing, finally call the acts unconstitutional!)[18] Indeed, the Court did not rule on the extent to which the First Amendment protects political speech until the early twentieth century, when it ruled on the constitutionality of the Espionage Act of 1917 and the Sedition Act of 1918. Written amid the heated political atmosphere of World War I and the communist revolution in Russia, the Espionage Act made it illegal to interfere with any military activity, including recruitment and induction, or to advocate insubordination or mutiny. The Sedition Act was even more sweeping. It made it "a federal crime to ... say, print, write, or publish anything intended to cause contempt or scorn for the federal government, the Constitution, the flag, or the uniform of the armed forces, or to say or write anything that

Source: © Bettmann/Corbis. Reproduced by permission.

One of the most influential justices ever to serve on the Supreme Court was Oliver Wendell Holmes. His opinions and dissents on free speech cases still help frame our understanding of First Amendment rights.

clear and present danger standard
The doctrine that Congress may limit speech if it causes a clear and present danger to the interests of the country.

interfered with defense production."[19] These two laws outlawed some political speech because of its supposed subversive content.

Almost 1,000 people were convicted under the Espionage and Sedition Acts, and several appealed to the Supreme Court. The first case to reach the Court involved Carl Schenck, the general secretary of the Socialist party. Schenck had mailed leaflets urging American men to resist the draft, and as a result, he was convicted of violating the Espionage Act. The Supreme Court upheld the conviction even though Schenck had failed to obstruct the induction of draftees. Writing for a unanimous Court in *Schenck v. United States,* Justice Oliver Wendell Holmes set forth the **clear and present danger standard**, which allows Congress to impose restrictions on political speech when it thinks such speech threatens the interests of the country. Holmes wrote that

> in many places and in ordinary times the defendants in saying all that was said in the circular would have been within their constitutional rights. But the character of every act depends upon the circumstances in which it is done. . . . The question in every case is whether the words used are used in such circumstances and are of such a nature as to create a clear and present danger that they will bring about the substantive evils that Congress has a right to prevent.[20]

Thus, with the *Schenck* decision, the Supreme Court established that freedom of speech is not an absolute right. They
removed some weight from the individual side of the scale, deciding that in some circumstances government can restrict or punish
some kinds of political speech.

A few months after the *Schenck* decision, the Supreme Court
placed conditions on political speech that were even more restrictive
than the clear and present danger standard. In *Abrams v. United
States,* the Court upheld the conviction of five Russian immigrants
for violating the Espionage Act.[21] The accused, all of whom had lived
in the United States for at least five years, were prosecuted for writing
political pamphlets that criticized United States' interference in the
Russian revolution and claimed, among other things, that President
Woodrow Wilson was a coward and a hypocrite. The Court's majority opinion set forth the **bad tendency doctrine**. This doctrine held
that the clear and present danger standard required the government
to show only that certain speech was likely to lead to the negative
consequences that Congress thought must be avoided; the government was not obligated to demonstrate that danger was imminent.

bad tendency doctrine
The doctrine that speech need only be likely to lead
to negative consequences, in Congress's judgment,
for it to be illegal.

Justice Holmes disagreed with the bad tendency doctrine. In his
written dissent, he argued that Abrams and his associates did not
pose the sort of imminent danger that had led him to propose the
clear and present danger standard:

> It is only the present danger of immediate evil or an intent to bring
> it about that warrants Congress in setting a limit to the expression of
> opinion where private rights are not concerned.... Now nobody can
> suppose that the surreptitious publishing of a silly leaflet by an
> unknown man, without more, would present any immediate danger
> that its opinions would hinder the success of government arms or
> have any appreciable tendency to do so.[22]

Justice Holmes went on to argue that in most circumstances,
speech is constitutionally protected because facts ultimately will triumph over falsehoods in the marketplace of ideas. But a majority of
the Supreme Court would not heed Holmes's call for a return to a
strict interpretation of clear and present danger for many years.

The Supreme Court again shifted the balance, giving individual
rights more weight in the late 1930s, when it developed a standard
that gave preferred status to the liberties granted by the Bill of
Rights.[23] In the context of the First Amendment, this preferred status meant that free speech was so fundamental to the health of a democracy that the Court would assume any measure that limited it
was unconstitutional unless the government could prove otherwise.

The government's chance to test the preferred status of free
speech came quickly. World War II and the perceived resurgence
of the communist threat to the United States led to legislation
restricting political speech similar to that passed during World
War I. In 1940, Congress passed the Alien Registration Act, also
known as the Smith Act, after its main congressional sponsor. The
act made it illegal to advocate the overthrow of the government
through force or violence or to organize or even be a member of

any group that espoused such ideas. The McCarran Act, passed in 1950, required communist organizations to register with the federal government and to disclose the names of their members. The Communist Control Act of 1954 barred all communist party organizations from participating in elections.

In deciding the cases these laws prompted, the Supreme Court weighed the rights of the individual against the interests of society. Given the immense concern at the time over the threat that communism posed to the United States, it is perhaps not surprising that the Court placed less value on individual rights in favor of protecting society as a whole. In *Dennis v. United States* (1951), the Court upheld the conviction of top members of the Communist party of the United States for violating several provisions of the Smith Act. The majority opinion again employed the clear and present danger standard, but they defined it in a way that brought it very close to the bad tendency doctrine. The application of the clear and present danger standard in *Dennis* has sometimes been called the "sliding scale rule." Chief Justice Fred Vinson wrote that academic discussions of revolution were protected, but he went on to state that the government did not have to "wait until the *putsch* [overthrow] is about to be executed, the plans have been laid and the signal is awaited" to prohibit speech. "In each case [courts] must ask whether the gravity of the 'evil,' discounted by its improbability, justifies such invasion of free speech as is necessary to avoid the danger."[24] In this case, the Court believed that an organized group's threat to overthrow the government was sufficient to override the group's right to free speech, even if justices did not think the group actually had the ability to overthrow the government.

In the two decades after the *Dennis* case, the Supreme Court moved toward a less restrictive interpretation of the clear and present danger standard, granting more weight to the individual right to freedom of speech. In the early 1960s, it found several provisions of the McCarran Act unconstitutional, and Congress subsequently repealed the act's registration requirement. In the 1969 case, *Brandenburg v. Ohio,* which involved a top Ku Klux Klan (KKK) official, the Court returned to a rule close to Holmes's original clear and present danger standard, rejecting the more restrictive bad tendency doctrine. In *Brandenburg,* the Court erected the **incitement standard**. Under this test, the government has to prove the speech in question is likely to produce immediate illegal activity. The Court judged that the law under which the Klan leader had been convicted was unconstitutional because it "purports to punish mere advocacy."[25] In other words, the Court held that it is acceptable to express opinions as long as the speaker does not incite listeners to commit illegal acts.

Over time, the Supreme Court's views on how to balance the rights of individuals and the interests of society have changed. In general, the Court has moved to reduce restrictions on the exercise of free speech (see Box 4–1). This movement has not occurred in a vacuum; it has often paralleled changes in public opinion about

incitement standard

The doctrine that speech must cause listeners to be likely to commit immediate illegal acts for the speech itself to be illegal.

free speech and other civil liberties.[26] For example, as Congress and the courts have removed restrictions on the free speech of avowed communists, the public has also become more tolerant of such speech. As Figure 4–1 shows, the public has become more willing since the 1950s to allow admitted communists to speak, teach college, and have their books remain on library bookshelves. As perceptions of a communist threat receded, people, including judges and legislators, became more willing to allow unpopular political speech. Over time, our understanding of our liberties changes.

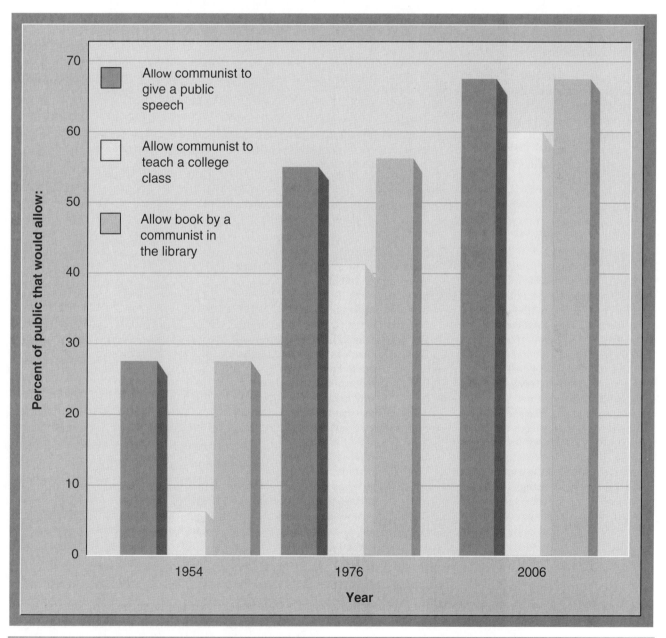

Figure 4–1 Public Tolerance of Communists, 1954–2006. Americans are much more tolerant of communists in public life now than they were forty or more years ago.

Source: *Data from Harold W. Stanley and Richard G. Niemi, Vital Statistics on American Politics, 2007–2008* (Washington, D.C.: CQ Press, 2008), 156–57.

The People behind the Rules

Box 4–1   The Ku Klux Klan and the Right to Adopt a Highway

The first adopt-a-highway program was developed in Texas in 1984. The idea behind it was to create a partnership between government and the private sector to help keep state roadways litter free. The government would provide equipment and training and in return get clean roads at an affordable price, while private organizations would donate labor and have their efforts recognized by roadside signs.

The Texas program was an immediate success and quickly spread to forty-eight other states. (Vermont, the lone holdout, has a similar litter removal program, but it does not allow for the posting of signs.) Missouri established its program in 1987 and was swamped by applicants. By late 2008, 3,772 groups were picking up garbage along 5,281 miles of the state's roads.

The application of one group, however, sparked enormous controversy. In 1994, the Knights of the Ku Klux Klan (KKK) applied to keep clean a half-mile stretch of Interstate 55 in St. Louis. Missouri highway officials rejected the Klan's application, reasoning that the organization was more interested in generating publicity for its unpopular cause than in picking up trash. The KKK took its case to federal court, claiming that the state's decision to bar it from the adopt-a-highway program violated its members' First Amendment right of free speech. Legal support for the Klan was provided by the American Civil Liberties Union (ACLU).

In April 1999, U.S. District Court Judge Stephen N. Limbaugh held that "as lacking as the Klansman's ideology may be of any redeeming social, intellectual or spiritual value, the Constitution of the United States protects his right to express that ideology as freely as one whose views society embraces." The KKK's two adopt-a-highway program signs were put up in November 1999. The first night, one sign was knocked down. The next night, after the downed sign had been repaired, both signs were stolen.

Missouri appealed Judge Limbaugh's decision all the way to the Supreme Court, losing at each step. Although the state failed to keep the Klan from participating in the adopt-a-highway program, Missouri legislators fashioned a clever retort. In 2000, legislation was passed and signed into law naming the KKK's section of Interstate 55 in honor of Rosa Parks, the civil rights pioneer.

The legislature's action, however, did not end the story. In 2001, Missouri dropped the KKK from the program for failing to pick up any trash. The Klan's response was to reapply, setting off another round of court battles. The state's legal position was again rejected all the way to the Supreme Court, allowing the KKK to this time adopt a portion of Highway 21 north of Potosi, a small town in eastern Missouri. The Klan continues to have responsibility for cleaning that stretch of road, but no signs to that effect remain because they have all been stolen or vandalized. (Under regulations that apply to every group participating in the program, the state will only pay for two replacement signs.)

The opportunity to exploit the adopt-a-highway program has not been lost on other fringe groups. In 2005, for example, the American Nazi Party was allowed to adopt a road in Marion County, Oregon, because county supervisors reasoned that the Missouri court decisions left them no alternative. For similar reasons, in 2008, the San Diego Minutemen (an anti-illegal immigrant organization) were able to force the California Department of Transportation to allow them to continue picking up trash with a sign recognizing their contribution on a stretch of Interstate 5 near a major U.S. Border Patrol checkpoint. Current interpretations of the First Amendment do not allow the government to pick and choose the speech it will promote or protect, even that which most Americans find objectionable. Consequently, even something as seemingly innocuous as an adopt-a-highway program can become a flashpoint in the debate over free speech.

Sources: Leslie Berestein, "Minutemen's Highway Cleanup Sign Replaced Near Checkpoint," *San Diego Union*, July 25, 2008; Tim Bryant, "Klan Wins Fight to Pick Up Road Litter," *St Louis Post-Dispatch*, June 12, 1996; Tim Bryant, "KKK Is Free to Pick Up Litter," *St Louis Post-Dispatch*, April 14, 1999; Bill Lambrecht, "Effort to Bar Klan from Adopting Highway Fails," *St Louis Post-Dispatch*, January 11, 2005; Ken Leiser, "State Drops Klan from Trash Pickup Program; Officials Say Group Failed to Collect Litter Along Section of I-55," *St Louis Post-Dispatch*, April 5, 2001; David Lieb, "MoDOT Changes Litter Cleanup Rules in Response to Klan Ruling," Associated Press State Local Wire &, July 31, 2006; The Oregonian, "County Should Have Rejected Nazis," February 4, 2005; "The Pick of the Litter," *Pittsburgh Post-Gazette*, January 11, 2005; Robert D. Richards and Clay Calvert, "Counter speech 2000: A New Look at the Old Remedy for 'Bad' Speech," *Brigham Young University Law Review* 2000: 553–62; "Answering the KKK," *St Louis Post-Dispatch*, May 29, 2000. Information on the Texas Adopt-A-Highway program is taken from www.dontmesswithtexas.org/adopt_history.php. Information on the Missouri Adopt-A-Highway program is taken from www.modot.org/services/community/adoptahighway.htm. On Vermont, see www.aot.state.vt.us/Maint/green%20up%20roadside.htm.

Symbolic Speech

Not all questions about free speech revolve around spoken or written words. Some "speech" takes the form of symbols or actions instead of words, and important questions have arisen about how far the right to free speech extends to protect symbolic speech. The Supreme Court generally has sought to draw a distinction (sometimes quite murky) between acts that constitute speech, and thus are constitutionally protected, and acts that constitute conduct, and thus are not.

The Supreme Court first tackled symbolic speech in a 1931 case in which the state of California had made it illegal to use a red flag "as a sign, symbol, or emblem of opposition to organized government." As before, communists were the target of the law. The Court threw out their convictions, claiming the law was too vague and denied people "the opportunity for a free political discussion."[27]

During the Vietnam War, the Supreme Court decided several more cases involving symbolic speech. In *United States v. O'Brien,* the Court upheld the conviction of a man who burned his draft registration card to protest the war. The Court decided that the government's interest in seeing that draft-age men had continual access to the information on their draft card outweighed the individual's right to burn the card as an act of political protest.[28] Thus, the Court recognized some restrictions on symbolic speech. But one year later in *Tinker v. Des Moines School District,* the Court ruled that students could not be suspended for wearing black armbands to protest the Vietnam War because their actions were *not* disruptive and they were entitled to express their political opinions.

The most heated symbolic speech case in recent years was *Texas v. Johnson,* decided in 1989. Johnson, a member of a radical left-wing organization, burned an American flag outside the 1984 Republican National Convention in Dallas. Texas (and forty-seven other states) had made it illegal to deface an American flag. But, in a 5–4 decision, the Supreme Court overturned Johnson's conviction, supporting his right to burn the flag. The majority opinion harkened back to Justice Holmes's marketplace argument of seven decades before:

> We can imagine no more appropriate response to burning a flag than waving one's own, no better way to counter a flag burner's message than by saluting the flag that burns…. We do not consecrate the flag by punishing its desecration, for in doing so we dilute the freedom that this cherished emblem represents.[29]

The Court's decision to overturn Johnson's conviction was deeply unpopular with the American public, but efforts to amend the Constitution to ban flag burning have failed, albeit by the narrowest of margins in recent years.

So-called *hate crimes* are at the core of another controversial issue that touches on symbolic speech. In recent years, many state and local governments have outlawed the use of symbols thought to be deeply offensive to minorities. The first Supreme Court ruling on these laws involved an ordinance in St. Paul, Minnesota, that made it illegal to burn crosses or place swastikas on public or private property. In *R.A.V. v. City of St. Paul* (1992), the Court overturned the conviction of several teenagers for burning a cross in the yard of an African American family. The Court noted that St. Paul could have punished the conduct of the cross burners by charging them with an offense, such as trespassing or arson, but that the city instead sought to punish the teenagers for the words and thoughts behind their actions. Because the ordinance forbade only certain offensive words and symbols and not others, the Court ruled that the city had "no such authority to license one side of a debate to fight freestyle, while requiring the other to follow Marquis of Queensbury Rules."[30] Because of the First Amendment, American courts are far more tolerant of hate speech than are their counterparts in other advanced democracies.[31]

But actions are treated differently than speech. Although the Supreme Court overturned the St. Paul ordinance on First Amendment grounds, the following year it upheld a Wisconsin law that imposed harsher penalties for violent crimes in which the victims were selected because of their race, religion, color, disability, sexual orientation, national origin, or ancestry. The Court noted in its opinion that, whereas the St. Paul ordinance was explicitly directed at speech, the Wisconsin law was "aimed at conduct unprotected by the First Amendment." Thus, the Court ruled that cross burning qualified as legitimate symbolic speech, but violent offenses did not. Indeed, in 2003 the Court held that cross burning carried out with the intent to intimidate may be banned.[32]

4-3b Freedom of Assembly and Association

The First Amendment establishes "the right of the people peaceably to assemble, and to petition the Government for the redress of grievances." The Supreme Court first upheld the constitutional right to assemble peaceably in 1875.[33] In *Hague v. Committee of Industrial Organization* (1939), the Court ruled that the government cannot limit the right to assemble in public places in ways that favor one group over another. The government can, however, control the time, place, and manner of the assembly, so long as the rules apply to all groups equally.[34] As one justice wrote in a later decision, the government can prevent "a street meeting in the middle of Times Square during rush hour."[35]

A critical test of the right to assemble peaceably came in 1978, when a group of American Nazis proposed to march in Skokie, Illinois.[36] After being denied an opportunity to march in nearby Chicago, the Nazis chose Skokie, a town in which many people had family members who had survived the Jewish Holocaust of World War II. Most residents of Skokie vehemently opposed the proposed march, even though the Nazis posed no threat to the community. As a result, town officials demanded that the Nazis post a $350,000 bond before holding their rally, an amount everyone knew the Nazis could not raise. The Nazis responded by announcing that they would hold a quiet gathering outside Skokie Village Hall to protest what they saw as the town's violation of their rights of assembly and free speech. City officials asked the courts to bar the proposed demonstration.

The legal battle dragged on for months, and a federal district court eventually sided with the Nazis. It ruled that the bond requirement and other impediments Skokie had imposed were unconstitutional because they infringed on free speech. After their legal victory, the Nazis held two marches in Chicago, their original target. On both occasions, the handful of Nazis who marched were greatly outnumbered by the people who came to protest against them.

In recent decades, the Supreme Court has also interpreted the First Amendment to include an implicit right of political associa-tion.[37] In 1958, the Court decided a case challenging an Alabama law that required the National Association for the Advancement of Colored People (NAACP) to disclose its membership lists. In its ruling, the Court noted the importance of group membership in promoting and protecting the political interests of different groups, and it noted that previous disclosures of the NAACP's membership lists had exposed its members to various kinds of harassment. As a result, the Court concluded that forced disclosure was unconstitu-tional because it would hinder the ability of the NAACP and its members "to pursue their collective effort to foster beliefs which they admittedly have a right to advocate."[38] With this ruling, the Court expanded our understanding of what the right to "peaceably assemble" means as well as our understanding of the right of an individual to associate with the group of his or her choice.

4-3c Freedom of the Press

The First Amendment not only protects the rights of individual citizens to speak freely and assemble peaceably, but it also stipu-lates that "Congress shall make no law ... abridging the freedom ... of the press." In the more than 200 years since these words were penned, the Supreme Court has extended the freedom of the press to include the modern media of television, radio, and film as well as the printed media so familiar to the Founders. Regardless of the medium used to convey information, three potential checks can restrict the freedom of the press: prior restraint, libel law, and ob-scenity law.

Prior Restraint

One of the central questions in the debate over freedom of the press is whether the government has the right to suppress a story before it has been published or broadcast. The Supreme Court first addressed the constitutionality of **prior restraint** in *Near v. Minne-sota,* a 1931 case in which the Court used the due process clause of the Fourteenth Amendment to apply the First Amendment's freedom of the press guarantee to state governments for the first time. Jay Near was the publisher of a small-circulation newspaper convicted of violating a Minnesota law that prohibited malicious and scandalous publications. Although the Court showed no admi-ration for Near's anti-Semitic scandal sheet, it overturned his con-viction on the grounds that the First Amendment gives enormous leeway to the press in deciding what to publish: "The fact that lib-erty of the press may be used by miscreant purveyors of scandal

prior restraint
An act of government preventing publication or broadcast of a story or document.

Pentagon Papers

A set of secret government documents—leaked to the press in 1971—showing that Presidents Kennedy and Johnson misled the public about U.S. involvement in Vietnam.

does not make any the less necessary the immunity of the press from previous restraint in dealing with official misconduct."[39] Using logic similar to the clear and present danger doctrine presented in the *Schenck* case, the Court indicated that prior restraint was constitutional only in exceptional cases. The Court weighed the right to freedom of the press against society's right to suppress offensive publications, and the justices favored freedom of the press in their decision.

During the Vietnam War, the Supreme Court had an opportunity to specify exactly when the government's interest in suppressing a story is strong enough to override the press's freedom to publish it. In June 1971, the *New York Times* began publishing a series of secret government documents known as the **Pentagon Papers**. The documents, which showed that Presidents John F. Kennedy and Lyndon Johnson had misled the American public about U.S. policy in Vietnam, were leaked to the *Times* by a former Defense Department official who opposed the war. Although the papers dealt with historical material and did not jeopardize existing diplomatic or military plans, the Richard Nixon administration asked a federal court to bar the *Times* from publishing any more of the documents on the grounds that their publication violated the Espionage Act of 1917. The lower court granted the request, marking the first time in U.S. history that a newspaper had been barred from printing a specific article. Two weeks later, however, the Supreme Court ruled that the government had failed to prove its claim that the threat to national security justified prior restraint. The Court lifted the ban, and the *Times* was free to resume publishing the documents.[40]

Despite the political importance of the Pentagon Papers case, it broke no new ground on the circumstances under which prior restraint is constitutional. Indeed, the *New York Times* did not claim that the First Amendment made prior restraint unconstitutional. Instead, the paper chose to defend itself by arguing that the government had failed to prove that publication of the Pentagon Papers would harm national security. The justices disagreed so strongly over the merits of the government's case and the propriety of prior restraint that they wrote nine separate opinions. Although some justices argued that freedom of the press is absolute, others held that some circumstances justify prior restraint. As a result, it remains unclear exactly when the government can obtain an order for prior restraint.

A 2003 case highlights the uncertainty surrounding prior restraint. In July 2003, Kobe Bryant, a star basketball player with the Los Angeles Lakers, was charged with sexually assaulting a hotel employee in Colorado. A court transcript of a hearing held to determine the relevance of the victim's alleged past sexual conduct to the criminal proceedings was mistakenly e-mailed by a court clerk to seven news outlets, among them the *Denver Post* and the *Los Angeles Times*. Once the blunder became known, the Colorado district court ordered the news organizations not to disclose any of the information they had learned from the transcript. The news organizations reasoned that they had obtained the transcript legally, so they challenged the district court's order as an unconstitutional imposition of prior restraint.[41] Ultimately, Colorado's Supreme Court upheld the district court's order, finding that protecting both the victim's privacy rights under the state's rape shield laws and the state's interest in making rape victims comfortable with reporting the crime outweighed the media's constitutional concerns.[42]

Libel

A more common check on the freedom of the press than prior restraint is **libel law**, which governs any written or visual publication that unjustly injures a person's reputation. (*Slander* applies to *spoken* words that unjustly injure a person's reputation.) Simply stated, these laws prohibit the press as well as individuals from writing (or uttering) false and damaging statements about people. Because it usually is impractical to prevent people from speaking, writing, or broadcasting offensive words, legal action comes only after someone believes those words have injured his or her reputation.

libel law
Laws governing written or visual publications that unjustly injure a person's reputation.

The landmark case in libel law is *New York Times Co. v. Sullivan* (1964).[43] L. B. Sullivan, a city commissioner in Montgomery, Alabama, sued the *Times* for printing an advertisement that condemned the way the police in Montgomery had treated civil rights protesters. When a state court awarded Sullivan $500,000 in damages because of factual errors in the ad, other officials filed lawsuits of their own. Suddenly, it looked as if segregationists would be able to use libel laws to discourage the press from covering the civil rights movement.

The Supreme Court, however, overturned the Alabama court's ruling. For the first time in its history, the Court held that a libel judgment violated the First Amendment. The Court ruled that robust political debate will suffer unless public officials carry a higher burden of proof in libel cases than do ordinary citizens. The Court ruled that public officials must not only prove that a news report contained a damaging error—the standard for a private citizen—but also that the falsehood "was made with 'actual malice'— that is, with knowledge that it was false or with reckless disregard of whether it was false or not."[44] In later rulings, the Court extended its requirement that certain plaintiffs suing for libel prove the press acted with actual malice. These plaintiffs include all government officials, who have substantial control over public policy making; candidates for public office; and people whose prominence places them in the public eye. In general, public figures, whether they are members of Congress, heads of foreign governments, or entertainers, have a harder time establishing libel than do private citizens because freedom of the press is a civil liberty given considerable weight by Supreme Court rulings.

Obscenity

No issue has proved more vexing for members of the Supreme Court than **obscenity law**, which forbids materials whose predominant

obscenity law
Laws governing materials whose predominant appeal is to a prurient interest in nudity, sex, or excretion.

appeal is to a prurient interest in nudity, sex, or excretion. Again, the Court usually tries to balance society's interests against personal liberties. Although Congress first passed legislation on obscenity in 1842, and the Court upheld later obscenity legislation in 1878, it was not until 1942 that the Court held that obscenity did not enjoy First Amendment protection.[45] Since then, the Court has had great difficulty, however, establishing standards by which to judge material obscene. For example, in *Roth v. the United States* (1957), the Court held that the appropriate test was "whether to the average person, applying contemporary community standards, the dominant theme of the material taken as a whole appeals to prurient interest."[46] But determining who qualifies as an "average" person or what prevailing "community standards" are has proved difficult. Other standards have since been offered, but none has gained wide acceptance.[47] So difficult is the definition problem that Justice Potter Stewart was reduced in one 1964 case to stating that although he could not define obscenity, he knew it when he saw it.[48]

In the 1973 case, *Miller v. California,* the Supreme Court established a three-part test to determine whether material is obscene, which is a standard that is still in place. The first part of the test is the "average person applying community standards" rule from *Roth.* The second component is "whether the work depicts or describes, in a patently offensive way, sexual conduct specifically defined by the applicable law." The third part of the test is "whether the work, taken as a whole, lacks serious literary, artistic, political, or scientific value."[49] In essence, with the *Miller* decision, the Court turned the question of defining obscenity back to the states. The Court continues to hear obscenity cases—although the number has declined dramatically since the early 1970s—and it has overturned some community-based obscenity standards as too strict or too vague.[50] In obscenity cases, as in prior restraint and libel cases, the Court has generally favored press freedom over restraint.

4-3d Freedom of Religion

The First Amendment states that "Congress shall make no law respecting an establishment of religion, or prohibiting the free exercise thereof." These two clauses—referred to as the **establishment clause** and the **free exercise clause**—were intended to keep the government separate from religion and to allow Americans to practice whatever religion they choose. But as is often the case with civil liberties, the Supreme Court's attitude toward the separation of church and state and the free exercise of religion has changed with the times.

The Establishment Clause

The establishment clause has always been taken to mean that the federal government cannot create an official state church, such as the Church of England. This interpretation reflects political reality as much as grand theories about individual rights; even when the

establishment clause

The provision in the First Amendment of the Constitution that "Congress shall make no law respecting an establishment of religion."

free exercise clause

The provision in the First Amendment of the Constitution that "Congress shall make no law . . . prohibiting the free exercise" of religion.

Constitution was adopted, Americans adhered to a wide array of religious practices, and as Chapter 3 shows, the diversity of religious beliefs has only increased. But the establishment clause did represent something of a breakthrough in political thought. Even after the federal Constitution was enacted, five states continued to have state churches, with Massachusetts having an official church (Congregational) until 1833.[51]

Although there has never been much doubt that the government cannot establish a state religion, considerable debate surrounds the government's treatment of religion. The Supreme Court has never taken the position that the federal government must adopt a pure hands-off approach. We still print "IN GOD WE TRUST" on our money, swear presidents into office using a Bible, and ask chaplains to open sessions of Congress with prayer. But beyond these symbolic acts lie a host of complex constitutional issues. Can the government assist, promote, or hinder the practice of any religion? Must the government treat all religions alike? What happens if a religious practice runs contrary to other public policy goals? Just precisely where do we draw the line between church and state? In recent decades, many of the cases dealing with separation of church and state have involved the constitutionality of public assistance to religious schools. The Supreme Court has allowed the expenditure of some public money on students attending religious schools for books, lunch programs, transportation, computers, software, projectors, and even the provision of an interpreter for a deaf student. The Court approves such expenditures when the aid is deemed to benefit the *student* and not the religious entity that operates the school.[52] Indeed, in recent years, the Court has relaxed the barriers between public funds and

Source: © AP Photo/World Wide Photo.

In 1995, the Supreme Court ruled 7 to 2 that the Ku Klux Klan (KKK) had a right to erect a cross in a public park near the state capitol in Columbus, Ohio. The KKK and its opponents wrestled over erecting the cross in 1993.

religious schools, even going so far in a 2002 decision as to allow the use of public money or vouchers to pay tuition for religious schools.[53] The Court generally has ruled that public aid to religious colleges is constitutional, in part because "college students are less impressionable and less susceptible to religious indoctrination."[54] But in a 2004 case, *Locke v. Davey,* the Court held that the state of Washington was not required to grant a state-funded scholarship to a college student studying for the ministry, even though it provides such financial support to students pursuing secular studies.[55]

More controversial than public assistance for religious schools has been the issue of religious activities in the public schools. In 1962, the Supreme Court ruled that a school district in New York could not require the daily reading of a state-written nondenominational prayer, even though students who did not want to say the prayer could leave the room.[56] The next year, the Court held that a Pennsylvania law requiring the reading aloud of ten Bible selections each school day and a Maryland law requiring the recitation of a Bible chapter or the Lord's Prayer during school were both unconstitutional.[57] Although opinion surveys consistently show strong public support for allowing prayer in the classroom, the Court continues to resist. In recent years, it has tossed out an Alabama law requiring a moment of meditation, a Rhode Island practice in which ministers offered prayers at public school graduations, and in a case from Texas, organized, student-led prayer at public high school football games.[58]

A 1995 case involving the establishment clause shows the complexity of the civil liberties cases that the Supreme Court confronts. During the 1993 Christmas season, members of the KKK asked to place a cross in a public plaza located near the Ohio statehouse, a place often used for speeches and demonstrations. A state agency denied the Klan a permit to raise a cross because it feared doing so would represent government endorsement of a particular religion. In a 7–2 decision in *Capitol Square v. Pinette* (1995), the Supreme Court held that religious speech is fully protected under the First Amendment and that as long as other groups were allowed to use the plaza, the Klan had to have equal access.[59] The Court majority, however, splintered on one point. Four of the justices did not think that the question of state endorsement of religion applied to this case, whereas the three others thought it did apply but that no reasonable person would think that the state of Ohio was affirming the KKK's message. Among the groups that praised the Court's decision protecting the Klan's rights was Luba-vitch, an organization of Orthodox Jews that has long campaigned for the right to erect Hanukkah menorahs on public grounds.[60]

The Supreme Court has set forth a number of arguments for determining where to draw the line between church and state, but for many years the most influential opinion came from a 1971 case, *Lemon v. Kurtzman.* In that decision, the Court overturned a Rhode Island law allowing the state to supplement the salaries of teachers at private elementary schools by up to 15 percent. The Court established a three-part test for judging the constitutionality of such measures: "First, the statute must have a secular legislative purpose; second, its principal or primary effect must be one that neither advances nor inhibits religion ... [and] finally, the statute must not foster 'an excessive government entanglement with religion.'"[61] The Court believed that allowing the state and any particular religion to become "entangled" might eventually endanger an individual's right to freely exercise his or her religious beliefs. But for the past few years, the more conservative justices on the Court have tried to overturn the test devised in *Lemon,* thinking it is too unfriendly toward religious activities. The Court has yet to devise a replacement rule, and it has occasionally decided important state and religion cases without any serious reference to *Lemon.* The Court's reasoning in other cases, however, suggests that it still uses the basic *Lemon* framework and is only tinkering with it at the margins. In 2005, for example, the Court relied heavily on *Lemon* in determining that a display of the Ten Commandments in a Kentucky county courthouse was unconstitutional. But in another decision announced that same day, the Court mentioned *Lemon* only in passing when finding a Ten Commandments monument on the Texas state capitol grounds to be constitutional.[62] As our nation's populace changes, we may need the flexibility to fine-tune and modify the rules that prevent the establishment of a state religion.

The Free Exercise Clause

Debate over the free exercise clause largely revolves around the distinction between beliefs and action. The Supreme Court's initial decision on the free exercise clause came in an 1878 case involving a polygamist from the Utah territory.[63] Although polygamy violated federal law, the defendant, a Mormon, argued that it was an important part of his religion, and he was therefore exercising his First Amendment rights. In upholding his conviction, the Court drew a sharp distinction between belief, which the government could not impede, and action based on those beliefs, which the government had a clear right to outlaw.

Since the 1940s, the Supreme Court has generally moved away from the distinction it drew in 1878 between belief and action, holding that some actions are protected by the free exercise clause.[64] In 1943, the Court ruled that Jehovah's Witnesses could not be compelled to salute the flag, thereby reversing the position it had taken in a similar case only three years previously.[65] In 1972, the Court allowed Amish children in Wisconsin to ignore a state law requiring public school attendance until age sixteen.[66] The Court reasoned that the right of the Amish to practice their religious beliefs, which call for minimizing contact with people from other faiths, outweighed the state's interest in requiring children to receive an education. And in 1993, the Court found that the city of Hialeah, Florida, had violated the First Amendment when it passed a series of ordinances designed to prevent practitioners of the Santeria faith from conducting animal sacrifices.[67]

The Supreme Court does not, however, always rule in favor of those exercising their religious beliefs. In a 1990 decision, the

Court upheld the denial of unemployment benefits to two men fired by a private drug rehabilitation organization for using peyote, a hallucinogenic drug, during an American Indian religious ritual.[68] In that ruling, the Court abandoned its previous principle that the government had to demonstrate a compelling state interest to restrict religious practices and held that the state could restrict activities as long as the restrictions were not directed at religious groups alone. Therefore, the state of Oregon could outlaw the use of peyote, even for religious purposes. (A number of other states did exempt religious use of the drug.)

Congress and the president, however, joined together in 1993 to force the Supreme Court to tip the balance back toward individual religious liberties, returning to the stricter compelling state interest standard it had used before 1990 to judge whether a law restricting religious practices passed constitutional scrutiny. The Religious Freedom Restoration Act also held that even when the government could meet the compelling interest standard, it must institute laws that would restrict religious practices the least.[69] The Court ruled the Religious Freedom Restoration Act unconstitutional in 1997, restoring the balance to what it had established in its 1990 decision. Congress later responded by passing the Religious Land Use and Institutionalized Persons Act of 2000, which partially restored Congress's preferred position. The battle over the extent of governmental control over religious practices demonstrates that the elected branches of government also play a role in determining the boundaries of our civil liberties.

The First Amendment is a cornerstone of American politics and American society. Yet a constant tension exists between the rights of the individual and the interests of society. Because the balance between these two competing rights shifts with changes in political events and social mores, our understanding of the liberties embedded in the First Amendment has evolved over the past two centuries. No doubt the balance will continue to change over the next two as well.

4-4 THE SECOND AMENDMENT: THE RIGHT TO BEAR ARMS?

The Second Amendment states: "A well regulated Militia, being necessary to the security of a free state, the right of the people to keep and bear Arms, shall not be infringed." Although many Americans believe that the Constitution gives them the right to own guns, the Supreme Court never recognized such a constitutional right until 2008.

4-4a Supreme Court Rulings

Before its decision in *District of Columbia v. Heller* in 2008, the Court had argued that the Second Amendment was intended to prevent federal interference with state militias rather than to guarantee the right of individuals to own guns. Indeed, in 1991, retired Chief Justice Warren E. Burger publicly criticized the National Rifle Association (NRA) for perpetuating the myth that Americans had a constitutional right to keep and bear arms. According to Burger, the Second Amendment "has been the subject of one of the greatest pieces of fraud, I repeat the word 'fraud,' on the American public."[70]

The Supreme Court's first major Second Amendment case was *United States v. Cruikshank,* decided in 1876. In that case, the Supreme Court ruled that gun ownership "is not a right guaranteed by the Constitution. Neither is it in any manner dependent upon that instrument for its existence. The Second Amendment declares that it shall not be infringed; but this, as has been seen, means no more than that it shall not be infringed on by Congress."[71] In subsequent cases, "the Court [had] consistently held to the *Cruikshank* doctrine that the Second Amendment does not apply to the states" (see Table 4–1).[72] This meant that the states were free to restrict or regulate gun ownership.

Ten years after *Cruikshank,* the Supreme Court ruled unanimously in *Presser v. Illinois* (1886) that states can ban "private armies" and otherwise regulate militias. The Court again held that the Second Amendment grants states, and not individuals, the right to form well-regulated militias: "We think it clear that the sections under consideration, which only forbid bodies of men to associate together as military organizations, or to drill or parade with arms in cities and towns unless authorized by law, do not infringe the right of the people to keep and bear arms."[73] With this ruling, the Court rejected the claim that individuals can create their own militias. In 1894 and again in 1897, the Court repeated its view that the Second Amendment does not guarantee individuals the right to own guns.[74]

Whereas all the nineteenth-century cases dealt with the validity of *state* laws, the Supreme Court first considered the constitutionality of *federal* laws regulating firearms in the 1939 case of *United States v. Miller.* Jack Miller had been charged with violating the National Firearms Act of 1934 when he carried a sawed-off shotgun across state lines. Miller contended that the Firearms Act violated the Second Amendment. The Court disagreed, arguing that the "obvious purpose" of the Second Amendment was "to assure the continuation and render possible the effectiveness of state militia forces." As a result, "in the absence of any evidence tending to show that possession or use of a 'shotgun having a barrel of less than eighteen inches in length' at this time has some reasonable relationship to the preservation or efficiency of a well regulated militia, we cannot say that the Second Amendment guarantees the right to keep and bear such an instrument."[75]

The Supreme Court revisited the question of the constitutionality of federal gun-control laws in 1980. In its decision, the Court said: "These legislative restrictions are neither based on constitutionally suspect criteria, nor do they trench upon any constitutionally protected liberties."[76] Three years later, the Court let stand, without comment or dissent, a lower court ruling that the town of Morton Grove, Illinois, had the authority to ban handguns within the city limits. The lower court flatly rejected the argument that Americans have a constitutional right to own guns: "We conclude that the right to keep and bear handguns is not guaranteed by the Second Amendment."[77]

In 2008, however, the Supreme Court declared for the first time that the Second Amendment protects an individual's right to own guns.[78] The case before the Court involved the District of Columbia's strict gun-control law that banned private possession of handguns. In a 5-to-4 decision, the majority took the position that "the District's ban on handgun possession in the home violates the Second Amendment, as does its prohibition against rendering any lawful firearm in the home operable for the purpose of immediate self-defense."[79] Somewhat self-consciously, the decision went on to acknowledge, "We are aware of the problem of handgun violence in this country.... But the enshrinement of constitutional rights necessarily takes certain policy choices off the table. These include the absolute prohibition of handguns held and used for self-defense in the home."[80]

Although holding that private ownership of guns for self-defense was protected by the Second Amendment, the majority decision went to some lengths to assert that "nothing in our opinion should be taken to cast doubt on longstanding prohibitions on the possession of firearms by felons and the mentally ill, or laws forbidding the carrying of firearms in sensitive places such as schools and government buildings, or laws imposing conditions and qualifications on the commercial sale of arms."[81] The decision also stated that laws prohibiting private ownership of "dangerous and unusual weapons" were still deemed constitutional.[82] But in the immediate aftermath of the Court's decision on the Second Amendment, numerous cases were filed around the country to test the new limits of federal and state gun-control laws.[83]

4-4b Gun-Control Laws

Although the Supreme Court has interpreted the Second Amendment as allowing federal, state, and local government to regulate the sale, possession, and use of firearms, federal gun-control laws impose only modest restrictions on gun ownership. The federal government did not pass its first gun-control law until 1919.[84] Over the next seventy years, Congress enacted a variety of laws that placed relatively minor restrictions on gun ownership.

In the 1990s, efforts to enact more stringent federal gun-control laws picked up steam. In 1993, Congress passed the Brady Bill, named after James Brady, the press secretary who was gravely wounded in 1981 when John Hinckley tried to assassinate President Ronald Reagan. The Brady Bill requires a five-day waiting period for the purchase of a gun so that authorities can conduct a background check to see if the purchaser is a convicted felon or has a history of mental illness. In 1994, Congress passed a law banning various types of assault weapons. Despite these laws, however, the federal government places relatively few limits on gun ownership, especially when compared with the stringent laws found in other advanced industrialized democracies. Indeed, the assault weapons ban lapsed at the end of 2004 without Congress taking any action to extend it. The lack of restrictive federal gun-control laws stems from the political clout of groups such as the NRA; this is a good example of a situation in which political power determines the effective rules of the political system.

Partially in response to local and state politics, the restrictive-ness of state and local gun-control laws varies widely. As Figure 4–2 shows, in 2008, thirty-five states granted almost all nonfelons a permit to carry a concealed weapon. In another eleven states, concealed weapons permits were given only to people who could demonstrate a specific need. Two states, Vermont and Alaska, allowed anyone to carry a concealed weapon without any permit or license, whereas two other states, Illinois and Wisconsin, pro-hibited concealed weapons altogether. Most state constitutions have provisions relating to the right to keep and bear arms, but the texts of those provisions differ, as do the interpretations state courts give to them. In general, highly urbanized states, such as New York and Massachusetts, tend to have the most restrictive gun laws, whereas highly rural states, such as New Mexico and Idaho, tend to have the least restrictive gun laws. Moreover, most

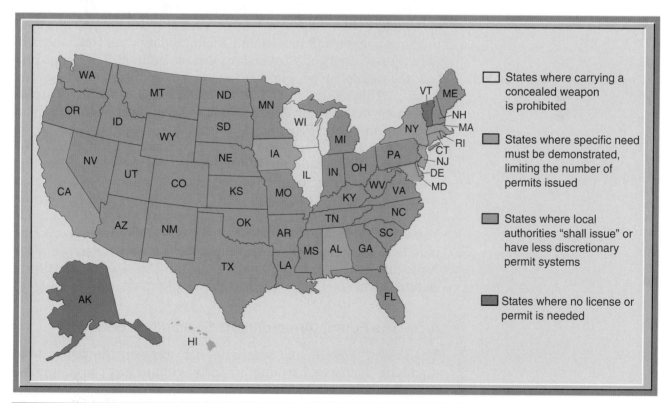

Figure 4–2   States Allowing Concealed Weapons, 2008. A citizen's legal right to carry a concealed weapon varies by state.

Sources: *National Rifle Association, "Right-to-Carry Laws 2008." www.nraila.org/Issues/FactSheets/Read.aspx?ID=18*

states have also enacted so-called preemption legislation, which bars county and local government from imposing gun laws stricter than those the state has passed.[85]

In addition to regulating individual gun ownership, states may, in keeping with the Supreme Court's decision in *Presser,* regulate the activities of militias. Currently, forty-two states ban or regulate private militias and paramilitary groups. These anti-militia laws became the subject of debate in 1995 when the Oklahoma City bombing focused public attention on the widespread growth of paramilitary groups in the United States. Critics of the militia movement argue that groups, such as the Michigan Militia and the U.S. Militia Association, have flourished because states have refused to enforce anti-militia laws. Many law enforcement officials and legal scholars argue, however, that these groups do not meet the legal definition of a militia. To quote one legal scholar: "What is called the Michigan Militia is a private organization. They could call themselves the Michigan Nuts. They are not a militia in any legal sense. There is no law against grown men dressing up in camouflage uniforms and playing soldier with legally acquired weapons."[86]

4-5 GOVERNMENT AND THE RIGHTS OF CRIMINAL SUSPECTS

Whereas the First Amendment protects the rights of people to speak and write freely, to assemble peaceably, and to practice their religious beliefs, and the Second Amendment protects the individual's right to own guns, several provisions in the Bill of Rights protect the rights of people suspected of committing crimes. The Fourth, Fifth, Sixth, and Eighth Amendments set forth the rules governing the relationship between the federal government and criminal suspects. Proponents of the Bill of Rights insisted on these provisions to limit the federal government's ability to abuse its powers. As a result, the Bill of Rights contains many rules that limit what the government can do to fight crime. As with the First Amendment, however, and unlike the Second Amendment, the limits imposed on government behavior have changed over time. Moreover, the conflict between the rights of the individual and the interests of society that is so prominent in debates over the First Amendment also figures prominently in the area of criminal procedure. As the conflict rages on, the rules keep changing.

4-5a The Fourth Amendment: Search and Seizure

The Fourth Amendment was written to prevent the police from searching homes and seizing property without just cause. In most circumstances, police officers must obtain a search warrant before they can search someone's home for evidence of a crime, and judges are to grant a warrant only when the police can show probable cause exists to believe they might find incriminating evidence.

In *Wolf v. Colorado* (1949), the Supreme Court extended the Fourth Amendment's requirement for a search warrant to the states.[87] But the *Wolf* decision had no power because it did not forbid states from using information they obtained from illegal searches in court. The *Mapp v. Ohio* decision in 1961 changed that.[88]

In establishing rules to govern the conduct of searches, the Supreme Court has sought to balance the protection the Fourth Amendment offers the individual against the realities of police work. The Court has recognized that in many situations, it is unrealistic to expect the police to obtain a search warrant before they look for incriminating evidence. As a result, the Court has created numerous exceptions to the requirement that the police obtain a warrant before conducting a search.

One such exception applies to the ability of police officers to stop motorists. Since 1925, the Supreme Court has allowed police officers to stop and search a car based on probable cause—that is, when they have good reason to think they will find evidence of a crime. But does the police officers' right to stop and search a car extend to searching the package on the backseat or the luggage in the trunk? The Court has changed its view of the constitutionality of such searches over the years, with the most recent ruling giving the police considerable latitude to search a car and its contents. The Court also has given the police the right to search mobile homes, airplanes, and other motor vehicles in most instances. But in a 1998 decision, the Court held that merely issuing a driver a citation, in this case for speeding, does not give the police the right to conduct a full search of the vehicle.[89]

Police officers also do not need a search warrant to act on evidence in plain view. What constitutes plain view? The Supreme Court confronted this question in a 1968 case in which it held that officers who are legally in a position to see items in plain view may seize those items and use them as evidence.[90] The Court later established three standards for plain view search and seizure: The police must be in position lawfully, the evidence in plain view must be found inadvertently, and it should be immediately obvious to the police that the items in question are illicit.[91]

The Supreme Court has found that aerial surveillance does not violate Fourth Amendment protections. In *California v. Ciraolo* (1986), the police, acting on a tip, used a helicopter to fly over a suspect's backyard to see a marijuana crop they could not see from the ground. They used their visual inspection to get a search warrant, and they arrested Ciraolo. The Court upheld Ciraolo's conviction, noting the police were free to use public airspace to gain incriminating information.[92]

In addition to balancing the protection of the Fourth Amendment with the realities of police work, the Supreme Court has had to reconcile it with the advent of new technology. Take, for instance, the question of whether the police need a search warrant to tap someone's phone. When the Court first addressed the issue in 1928, it held that no search warrant was necessary because

exclusionary rule

The doctrine, stemming from the Fourth Amendment, that the government cannot use illegally obtained evidence in court.

electronic eavesdropping fell outside the scope of the unreasonable search and seizure clause.[93] Over time, however, the Court changed its position; in 1967, it held that people "had a reasonable expectation of privacy," which therefore required the police to obtain a search warrant before listening in on a conversation.[94] In 1968, Congress passed a law requiring the Attorney General to obtain court approval for wiretapping.[95] Almost all government requests for wiretaps are approved; in 2007, for example, every one of the 2,208 applications for intercepts was authorized. In recent years, the courts have required search warrants for eavesdropping on cellular phone conversations. Not surprisingly (given their increasing use in American society), 99 percent of all wiretaps in 2007 were for electronic devices, and only 1 percent involved planting microphones or having law enforcement agents eavesdrop.[96] The expectation of privacy has become an important standard in determining unreasonable search and seizure (and, as we will see, in other areas of the law as well), but this expectation is subject to limits. For example, the Court has held that individuals cannot expect to maintain the privacy of garbage left at the curb.[97]

What happens when the police gather evidence illegally? The answer lies in the **exclusionary rule**, which bars government officials from using evidence obtained in violation of the Fourth Amendment. It is a rule that only exists in the United States; judicial systems elsewhere in the world have nothing like it.[98] The Supreme Court created the exclusionary rule at the federal level in 1914, but they did not apply it to the states until 1961.[99] In recent years, the Court has whittled away at the absolute nature of the exclusionary rule, in some cases allowing tainted evidence to enter court if the police acted in good faith.[100] In 1995, for example, the Supreme Court ruled that police in Phoenix, Arizona, could use evidence of criminal conduct they found in a search triggered by a computer's erroneous report that a valid arrest warrant was in place.[101] And in 2006, the Court held that the failure of the police to knock and announce their presence did not invalidate the evidence they collected in a raid.[102]

The exclusionary rule gives the police an incentive to follow proper legal procedure when they conduct a search; if they do not, they risk losing a conviction. Many Americans, however, believe that the exclusionary rule enables criminals to go free on a "technicality." A federal government report found that only around 1 percent of all federal cases involve questions about improper collection of evidence.[103] (Other studies report similar numbers, ranging from 0.6 percent to 2.4 percent.)[104] Still, in recent years, both Democrats and Republicans have introduced bills in Congress that would limit the exclusionary rule.

A recent challenge to the Fourth Amendment's protections is the Uniting and Strengthening America by Providing Appropriate Tools Required to Intercept and Obstruct Terrorism Act (USA Patriot Act). This law, passed quickly after the September 11, 2001, terrorist attacks, allows the government to more easily

'I'M SEARCHING YOUR POCKETS, IF IT'S ANY OF YOUR DAMN BUSINESS.'

In recent years, Congress has debated legislation to expand police powers.

engage in "sneak and peek" searches in which federal agents with a warrant can enter (either physically or electronically), examine various kinds of evidence, and delay notifying the subject of the search for weeks. The act also makes it easier for police and intelligence agencies to share information and to intercept cell phone conversations, e-mail, and Internet traffic. Civil libertarians worry about the extensive powers the act grants to the government, and by August 2008, 406 local governments and eight states had passed resolutions opposing it.[105] Nonetheless, in 2006 Congress voted overwhelmingly in favor of reauthorizing the Patriot Act, and President George W. Bush swiftly signed it into law. In response to concerns raised by civil libertarians, the reauthorized law restricted a few governmental intelligence-gathering activities allowed under the original version.

Other actions taken by the Bush administration in the aftermath of the terrorist attacks also raised Fourth Amendment concerns. In late 2005, it was revealed that the National Security Agency—a technologically sophisticated government agency charged with gathering and analyzing communications—had been authorized to conduct warrantless searches of Americans' international electronic communications. Domestic communications, however, still required a warrant.[106] A few months later it was learned that the agency also was assembling a massive database of some two trillion phone calls made by Americans since September 11, 2001, again without warrants.[107] Although some were comforted that the phone records consisted simply of the numbers called and not the content of the conversations, these actions and others were decried by civil libertarians who raised strong constitutional objections to them. In 2008, however, Congress passed and President Bush signed legislation expanding the government's surveillance powers, while also granting legal immunity for phone companies that had cooperated with the National Security Agency in wiretapping.[108]

4-5b The Fifth Amendment: Criminal Procedure for a Person Accused

The Fifth Amendment lays out several liberties designed to protect a person accused of committing a crime. Among the most prominent is that no person "shall be compelled in any criminal case to be a witness against himself." Although individuals can refuse to testify against themselves by invoking the Fifth Amendment, they can voluntarily confess, and prosecutors can use "nontestimonial" evidence such as fingerprints and DNA samples. In addition, if a person is granted immunity from prosecution—that is, the government promises to waive charges for the specific crime at issue—he or she can be compelled to testify.

Because individuals have an absolute right to refuse to incriminate themselves, debate has focused on the circumstances under which confessions may be considered voluntary. The Supreme Court first held in 1936 that law enforcement officials cannot use physical torture to force a confession.[109] By 1959, the Court was examining the "totality of the situation" to see if the police had coerced a confession by "third degree" tactics, such as long interrogations by teams of interviewers that wear down a suspect's will to resist.[110]

In 1966, the Supreme Court issued a landmark decision in *Miranda v. Arizona* that established procedural rules to protect people subjected to police interrogations.[111] As anyone who watches television knows, the police must inform suspects of their Miranda rights: the right to remain silent during questioning, the right to know that any statement may be used as evidence against them, and the right to speak to an attorney before questioning. The police not only must inform a suspect of these rights, but they must also establish that he or she understands them.

Miranda rights
The rights against self-incrimination that the Fifth Amendment guarantees. Miranda rights include the right to remain silent during questioning, the right to know that any statements suspects make may be used as evidence against them, and the right to speak to an attorney before questioning.

Since 1966, the Supreme Court has identified situations in which the violation of a suspect's **Miranda rights** does not automatically invalidate an arrest. If a suspect provides evidence without being informed of his or her Miranda rights, the evidence may still be used if it inevitably would have been uncovered.[112] In a similar vein, the Court has held that a suspect may be jailed despite a coerced confession if other evidence at the trial would sustain a guilty verdict.[113] The Court has also created a public-safety exemption that allows the police to gain information and act on it if public safety is threatened. But when the Supreme Court had the opportunity to completely overturn Miranda in a 2000 case, they declined to do so, in part because the rule has become so ingrained into our legal system and popular culture. But the Court continues to grapple with questions about the application of Miranda. In 2004, the Court held that police could not delay administering the warning in the hope of first securing an admission of guilt. In another case, however, they determined that police could use physical evidence they discover as the result of an admission given by a suspect before hearing the warning.[114]

What difference does the requirement to issue a Miranda warning make to law enforcement? One estimate is that the obligation to read Miranda rights to suspects has caused confession rates to drop by around 17 percent.[115] That suggests that perhaps as many as 4 percent of all criminal cases are not successfully prosecuted because of Miranda requirements. Like the exclusionary rule, the Miranda requirement has been the subject of political debate. Some legislators want to limit it or abolish it altogether.[116]

In addition to establishing a right against self-incrimination, the Fifth Amendment also provides protection against double jeopardy—trying a person acquitted of a crime on the same charge a second time. The protection against double jeopardy was adopted to prevent the government from harassing innocent people by repeatedly trying them for the same offense.

Some situations might seem to suggest that a person has been placed in double jeopardy, but the Supreme Court does not agree that these situations constitute double jeopardy. For instance, individuals who commit an act that breaks both state and federal laws can be tried by both jurisdictions. Take, for example, the trials of the four Los Angeles police officers accused of beating motorist Rodney King in the early 1990s. The officers were acquitted in state court of criminal charges that they had used excessive force in arresting King. They were then tried (and two of the officers were convicted) in federal court for violating King's civil rights. The officers were tried twice for the same act, but under different laws in different jurisdictions.

4-5c The Sixth Amendment: Procedures for People Charged with a Crime

The Sixth Amendment extends several protections to people charged with committing crimes, including the right to an attorney, the right to a jury trial, and the right to confront witnesses. The Supreme Court recognized a right to legal counsel for people charged with capital crimes for the first time in 1932. In that ruling, the Court directed state governments to provide an attorney for defendants who could not afford one if the defendant might face the death penalty.[117] Not until 1963, however, in *Gideon v. Wainwright*, did the Court require the states to provide legal counsel in all felony cases. The *Gideon* decision marked an important change in policy because most criminal prosecutions take place in state courts.[118] In 1972, the Court extended the guarantee of legal counsel to most misdemeanor cases involving possible jail time.[119] As a result of these rulings, people charged with committing a crime are now guaranteed access to legal counsel at most, but not all, pretrial, trial, and posttrial stages, including one appeal after a felony conviction.

The Supreme Court did not apply the Sixth Amendment's guarantee of a jury trial to state courts until 1968, and even then it required jury trials only in "serious" cases.[120] State trials do not have to follow the procedures used in federal trials in other regards as well. Juries in criminal cases in state courts do not have to have twelve members, as they do in federal courts, although the Court

> In The Supreme Court of The United States
> _ _ _ Washington D.C.
> Clarence Earl Gideon
>   Petitioner   Petition for a writ
>   vs.   of Certiorari Directed
> H.G. Cochran, Jr, as   To The Supreme Court
> Director, Divisions   State of Florida.
> of corrections State   No. - 890   Misc.
> of Florida. _ _ _   OCT. TERM 1961
>   U. S. Supreme Court
> To. The Honorable Earl Warren, Chief
>   Justice of the United States
>   Comes now The petitioner, Clarence
> Earl Gideon, a citizen of The United States
> of America, in proper person, and appearing
> as his own counsel. Who petitions this
> Honorable Court for a Writ of Certiorari
> directed to The Supreme Court of The State
> of Florida. To review the order and Judge-
> ment of the court below denying The
> petitioner a Writ of Habeas Corpus.

Clarence Gideon's pencil-written petition to the Supreme Court led to the *Gideon v. Wainwright* decision, which guaranteed a lawyer to anyone accused of a felony.

has declared five-member juries are too small.[121] In a similar vein, state courts do not need a unanimous jury vote to convict a person of a crime, although federal courts require unanimity.[122]

The Supreme Court has applied the Sixth Amendment right to confront one's accusers to state courts since 1965.[123] In recent years, the most explosive question involving the right to confront witnesses is whether a person accused of child molestation has the right to confront the child making the accusation. In 1988, the Court held that a screen that had been placed between a defendant and the teenage girls who accused him of molesting them violated his right to confront his accusers. The Court held open the possibility, however, that some protection might be afforded children who needed it. Indeed, in 1990, the Court upheld the conviction of a man in a Maryland case in which a six-year-old child testified by closed-circuit television.[124] Again, although the Court upholds the rights of the individual (even one charged with a crime), those rights are not absolute and unlimited. They must always be weighed against the rights of the larger community.

4-5d The Eighth Amendment: Cruel and Unusual Punishment

Whereas the Fourth Amendment deals with gathering evidence, the Fifth with persons accused of a crime, and the Sixth with charging a person with a crime, the Eighth Amendment addresses what comes after a conviction—it prohibits "cruel and unusual punishment." The Supreme Court has never found capital punishment cruel and unusual. In 1972, the Court did find that death sentences were being imposed in an arbitrary, and therefore, unconstitutional manner.[125] Four years later, the Court upheld a death penalty law that had been rewritten in response to its previous objections.[126] Since the late 1970s, executions have increased, and the public has maintained its support for the death penalty. Indeed, the number of states with a death penalty has increased, and the federal government has increased the number of federal crimes punishable by death. Recent capital punishment cases have challenged *how* the death penalty is applied. In the late 1980s, the Court had held that someone as young as sixteen years old may be put to death, but not someone fifteen years old. In 2005, the Court reversed itself, determining that the laws of nineteen states, which permitted the execution of people convicted of committing crimes while under the age of eighteen, were unconstitutional. And citing society's "evolving standards of decency," in 2002, the Court barred the execution of the mentally retarded, as it already had done for the legally insane in 1986. The same line of reasoning was employed in 2008 to overturn laws in Louisiana and five other states that allowed the death penalty for people convicted of raping children.[127] Yet, in another 2008 case, the Court ruled that Kentucky's method of lethal injection for executions did not violate the Constitution's "cruel and unusual" standard. But, although Justice John Paul Stevens sided with the majority in that decision as a matter of law, his concurring opinion called for the abolition of the death penalty.[128]

In recent years the Court has also been asked to decide whether "three-strike" laws constitute cruel and unusual punishment. Three-strike laws have been adopted by the federal government and more than twenty states. These laws typically require that a person convicted of a third violent felony be sent to prison for an extended sentence—often twenty-five years or more. In California, only the first two of three felony convictions need to be for violent crimes to invoke the state's third-strike law. In two 2003 cases from California, the Supreme Court found that the punishments for third-strike violations—twenty-five years without parole for stealing two golf clubs in one case *(Ewing v California)* and fifty years without parole for twice shoplifting children's videos in the other case *(Lockyer v. Andrade)*—were not sufficiently disproportionate to the crimes to trigger a violation of the Eighth Amendment.[129]

In writing the Bill of Rights, the Founders took several steps to protect the rights of criminal suspects and to prevent the federal government from abusing its police powers. Over the past two centuries, the Supreme Court's interpretation of the rights conveyed by the Fourth, Fifth, Sixth, and Eighth Amendments has changed. The Court has struggled to find the appropriate balance between the rights of the individual and the rights of society. In the past, changes in the political and social climate of the country have influenced the balance between these competing rights. No doubt the same will hold true in the future, and the rules governing the rights of criminal suspects will continue to change.

4-6 PRIVACY AS A CONSTITUTIONAL RIGHT

Americans take their right to privacy as a given. But is there a *constitutional* right to privacy? The Constitution does not mention privacy, although hints of such a right appear in the Bill of Rights. Because most Americans cherish their right to privacy and although the Constitution says nothing about the scope of that right, privacy issues have fueled some of the country's most bitter political and legal battles.

The Supreme Court's most complete discussion of the right of privacy came in *Griswold v. Connecticut* (1965).[130] At that time, Connecticut had a law forbidding the use of birth control, although the ban was not regularly enforced. When an activist challenged the law, the Supreme Court declared it unconstitutional. The justices supporting the Court's majority position found a right to privacy in several places in the Constitution: the First Amendment's right to association, the Third Amendment's prohibition against quartering soldiers, the Fourth Amendment's ban on unreasonable search and seizure, the Fifth Amendment's self-incrimination clause, and the Ninth Amendment's declaration that the Constitution did not explicitly enumerate all individual rights. (As Box 4–2 discusses, the use of the Ninth Amendment was somewhat unusual and controversial in this particular context.) The Court then determined that the zone of privacy a married couple enjoys makes a law prohibiting the use of contraceptives unconstitutional. Several years later, the Court extended the zone of privacy to cover the use of birth control by unmarried couples.[131]

The *Griswold* decision laid the foundation for the Supreme Court's most controversial decision in recent decades: ***Roe v. Wade*** (1973).[132] In *Roe,* the Court held that a woman's right to privacy allows her to obtain an abortion during the first trimester of pregnancy. The Court further held that states can impose reasonable regulations on abortions during the second trimester and can prohibit abortions under most circumstances in the third trimester.

The political furor *Roe* created cannot be exaggerated. Pro-life organizations have tried to convince the Supreme Court to overturn the decision, and they have lobbied state legislatures to impose stringent restrictions on abortions. Pro-choice groups, on the other hand, have fought to preserve (and expand) the abortion rights *Roe* established. For its part, the Court has allowed states to impose some restrictions, such as barring government funds from being used to pay for abortions and requiring women under the age of eighteen to notify their parents before having an abortion.[133] The Court also appears to have abandoned the trimester system set forth in *Roe.* But thus far, the Court has refused to overturn *Roe* and thereby leave it up to the states to decide whether abortion should be legal. Indeed, in a 2000 case, *Stenberg v. Carhart,* the Court declared a law in Nebraska and thirty other states banning an abortion procedure known as partial-birth abortion

Roe v. Wade

A 1973 Supreme Court decision that a woman's right to privacy prevents states from barring her from having an abortion during the first trimester of pregnancy. States can impose reasonable regulations on abortions during the second trimester and can prohibit abortions under most circumstances in the third trimester.

POINT OF ORDER

Box 4–2 The Ninth Amendment: What Does It Mean?

Amendment IX.

The enumeration in the Constitution, of certain rights, shall not be construed to deny or disparage others retained by the people.

The first eight amendments to the Constitution enumerate specific rights granted to individuals to protect them from the federal government. The Ninth Amendment breaks from that pattern. It states, "The enumeration in the Constitution, of certain rights, shall not be construed to deny or disparage others retained by the people." In other words, the Ninth Amendment states that the people have rights the Constitution does not list, but it also says nothing about what those rights are. Thus, rather than granting more or fewer specific rights, the Ninth Amendment is ambiguous. What does it mean, and how have the courts used it to define our civil liberties?

It is easier to answer the second part of the question than the first. From the adoption of the Bill of Rights until the New Deal era, the Ninth Amendment played a useful but now forgotten role, not in protecting individual rights, but in protecting the autonomy of the states from federal interference. With the advent of the New Deal and its expansion of federal government powers, this interpretation of the Ninth Amendment disappeared. Only in 1965 did the Supreme Court resurrect the Ninth Amendment in legal argument, this time with a focus on individual rights, in *Griswold v. Connecticut,* which was a case involving the constitutionality of a Connecticut law banning the use of birth control. In finding Connecticut's law unconstitutional—and thereby expanding each American's right to privacy—the Court relied heavily on

the Ninth Amendment. But some legal scholars sharply criticized the Court's decision, so much so that in recent years the Court has tended to make decisions on privacy issues based on other provisions of the Constitution.

The reason for the Court's reluctance to invoke the Ninth Amendment takes us back to our first question—what does the amendment mean? The answer is that no one knows for sure. Indeed, legal scholars disagree vehemently over how the Ninth Amendment affects our civil liberties. A major reason this disagreement exists is that we know relatively little about the history of the amendment, why it was written the way it was, and what the people who supported it thought it would do.

In the absence of a shared understanding of the history of the Ninth Amendment, legal scholars have had considerable freedom to speculate about the amendment's meaning and purpose. Some prominent legal scholars take an expansive view of the Ninth Amendment, arguing that it gives federal judges the authority to establish rights not specifically mentioned in the Constitution or its amendments. This is essentially the approach that Justice William Douglas took in writing the Supreme Court's opinion in the *Griswold* case. As you might imagine, this expansive interpretation of the Ninth Amendment places tremendous power in the hands of the Supreme Court.

Other prominent legal scholars reject an expansive reading of the Ninth Amendment. They argue that such an interpretation would allow judges to open up a "Pandora's box" of new constitutional rights. In rejecting an expansive interpretation, critics point out that the Ninth Amendment explicitly refers to other rights "retained by the people." They argue that this phrase indicates that the

Founders intended for the amendment to refer to well-known rights that the American people already had. If one accepts this interpretation, then the meaning of the Ninth Amendment depends on our understanding of what rights people had at the time the amendment was written. And to determine what those known rights were, we need to look at both state constitutions and at common law of that time. (Common law is the collection of rules and principles long used in custom and the judicial recognition of those customs.) Under this restricted interpretation, the Founders intended the Ninth Amendment merely to reassure Americans that the enumeration of rights contained in the first eight amendments did not threaten their existing rights.

The ongoing debate over the meaning of the Ninth Amendment reflects the importance of the rules in American politics. One interpretation gives judges broad powers that can change how government and citizens may interact, whereas the other limits the powers judges may exercise. This all underscores the enduring power of rules.

Sources: Randy E. Barnett, "Karl Lash's Majoritarian Difficulty: A Response to *A Textual-Historical Theory of the Ninth Amendment,*" *Stanford Law Review* 60 (February 2008): 937–68; Robert Bork, *The Tempting of America: The Political Seduction of the Law* (New York: Touchstone, 1990), 183–85; James A. Curry, Richard B. Riley, and Richard M. Battistoni, *Constitutional Government: The American Experience* (St. Paul, MN: West, 1989), 410; Kurt T. Lash, "The Lost Original Meaning of the Ninth Amendment," *Texas Law Review* 83 (December 2004): 331–430; Kurt T. Lash, "The Lost Jurisprudence of the Ninth Amendment," *Texas Law Review* 83 (February 2005): 597–716; Kurt T. Lash, "A Textual-Historical Theory of the Ninth Amendment," *Stanford Law Review* 60 (February 2008): 895–936; Kurt T. Lash, "On Federalism, Freedom, and the Founders' View of Retained Rights," *Stanford Law Review* 60 (February 2008): 969–88; H. L. Pohlman, *Constitutional Debate in Action: Civil Rights and Liberties* (New York: HarperCollins, 1995), 131–37.

unconstitutional. In this 5-to-4 decision, the Court articulated perhaps its clearest statement of the right to an abortion.[134] Yet, just seven years later and by another 5-to-4 vote, the Court upheld the Partial-Birth Abortion Ban Act of 2003, essentially reversing its previous decision in *Stenberg* and once again raising the possibility that *Roe* will be overturned at some point in the future.[135]

Although the Supreme Court has established that the right to privacy applies to birth control and abortions, it has only slowly extended privacy rights to other areas of personal activity. For example, in 1986 the Court ruled that a Georgia law against sodomy was constitutional, thereby rebuffing the defendant's argument that his sexual practices were covered by a right to privacy. In 2003, the Court reversed itself and on privacy grounds struck down a Texas law outlawing same-sex sodomy.[136] The Court has also indicated that the right to privacy does not necessarily mean a right to die, finding that the state may have a right to regulate the circumstances under which decisions about life support or euthanasia are made. In a 1997 case, the Court concluded that there is no constitutional right to die with the help of a physician, and it upheld state bans on assisted suicide. That decision, however, allowed the possibility that states could experiment with right-to-die laws. Nine years later the Court held Oregon's law allowing for physician-assisted suicide to be constitutional.[137]

Our concepts of the civil liberties guaranteed by the Bill of Rights are quite different from what the Founders envisioned in the late eighteenth century. At times, the Supreme Court and the elected branches of government have expanded civil liberties; at other times, they have narrowed them. In most cases, however, the Court, Congress, and other governmental institutions have recognized that individual freedoms must be balanced against the rights of society.

SUMMARY

The Constitution sets forth the fundamental rules governing the relationship between the government and its citizens. These rules attempt to guarantee certain civil liberties, most of which Americans cherish as fundamental rights and freedoms. But although we think of these liberties as absolute and fixed concepts, they are neither. Part of government's task is to balance competing rights, and in doing so, it must continually redefine the rules that govern our civil liberties.

Our civil liberties are rooted in the Bill of Rights. The Bill of Rights guarantees all Americans an extensive set of civil liberties, including freedom of speech, the right to assemble peaceably, and protection against unreasonable search and seizure (although not the right to own guns). Yet none of our civil liberties is absolute. The Supreme Court and Congress have long recognized that the rights of the individual must be weighed against the rights of society. One of the Court's tasks is to decide how to balance competing rights—where to draw the line when individual rights conflict with the common good.

If the civil liberties the Constitution provides are not absolute, they are not fixed, either. As the membership of the Supreme Court and the values of society both change, so does the meaning of the Constitution. For many years, for example, the Court declined to apply the Bill of Rights to state government. In 1897, however, the Court changed its mind; over the past 110 years, the justices have gradually used the due process clause of the Fourteenth Amendment to extend the civil liberties guaranteed in the Bill of Rights to limit state and local laws.

The civil liberties we enjoy are quite different from what the Founders envisioned because of the flexibility of the Constitution and the dynamics of a growing, changing society. At times our civil liberties have expanded, and at other times, they have narrowed. Throughout our history as a nation, however, we have striven to find a fair balance between the rights of the individual and the rights of society, and we will undoubtedly continue to do so.

KEY TERMS

bad tendency doctrine

civil liberties

clear and present danger
   standard

establishment clause

exclusionary rule

free exercise clause

incitement standard

libel law

Miranda rights

obscenity law

original intent

Pentagon Papers

prior restraint

Roe v. Wade

READINGS FOR FURTHER STUDY

Bedau, Hugo, and Paul Cassell, eds. *Debating the Death Penalty: Should America Have Capital Punishment? The Experts on Both Sides Make Their Best Case* (New York: Oxford University Press, 2004). A thorough examination of the range of arguments for and against the death penalty by noted scholars.

Krotoszynski, Ronald J., Jr. *The First Amendment in Cross-Cultural Perspective* (New York: New York University Press, 2006). An informative analysis of free speech protections in Canada, Germany, Japan, and the United Kingdom.

Labunski, Richard, *James Madison and the Struggle for the Bill of Rights* (New York: Oxford University Press, 2006). Labunski examines the political and policy disputes over the ratification of the Constitution and the Bill of Rights.

Levy, Leonard W. *Original Intent and the Framers' Constitution* (New York: Macmillan, 1988). Levy examines the historical evidence on original intent and analyzes court decisions on each major right the Bill of Rights grants.

Lewis, Anthony. *Gideon's Trumpet* (New York: Vintage, 1964). The story of Clarence Earl Gideon's successful Supreme Court appeal, which overturned his conviction for burglary on the grounds that he had no legal counsel at his trial.

Johnson, John W. *Griswold v. Connecticut: Birth Control and the Constitutional Right of Privacy* (Lawrence: University Press of Kansas, 2005). Johnson traces the acceptance of birth control rights for women and examines their legal implications.

Stone, Geoffrey. *Perilous Times: Free Speech in Wartime from the Sedition Act of 1798 to the War on Terrorism* (New York: W. W. Norton, 2004). A detailed legal history of the suppression of free speech rights during wartime in America.

Strossen, Nadine. *Defending Pornography: Free Speech, Sex, and the Fight for Women's Rights* (New York: New York University Press, 2000). The president of the American Civil Liberties Union argues that censorship, not pornography, poses the greatest danger to women's rights.

REVIEW QUESTIONS

1. The *Hiibel* (2004) decision illustrated the importance of
   a. the doctrine of original intent.
   b. the First Amendment's protection of free speech.
   c. the living Constitution philosophy.
   d. the Court's balancing of individual rights and the rights of society.
2. The Alien and Sedition Acts
   a. violated the First Amendment.
   b. made it illegal to publish material that criticized the federal government.
   c. helped to keep the Federalists in control of the presidency.
   d. both a and b.
3. Which of the following is *true* about the Ninth Amendment?
   a. There is little consensus by legal scholars as to its meaning.
   b. The Supreme Court justices refer to it extensively during oral argument.
   c. It is the primary constitutional basis for the right to privacy.
   d. None of the above.
4. State governments
   a. are not bound by the Bill of Rights.
   b. have had to respect free speech since 1925.
   c. have always had to respect free speech.
   d. are not bound by the double jeopardy clause.
5. The Supreme Court first used the clear and present danger standard in
   a. *Schenck v. United States.*
   b. *Near v. Minnesota.*
   c. *New York Times Co. v. Sullivan.*
   d. *Gideon v. Wainwright.*
6. Prior restraint is used
   a. frequently.
   b. a great deal in the United States, but not much in the People's Republic of China.

   c. only in exceptional cases.

   d. more by Democratic presidents than by Republican presidents.

7. How have the justices of the Supreme Court consistently interpreted the Second Amendment?

   a. Individuals have the right to bear arms.

   b. Individuals have a constitutional right to own a machine gun.

   c. The people are guaranteed the right to maintain militias.

   d. Capital punishment is not cruel and unusual punishment.

8. The Fifth Amendment

   a. protects individuals from self-incrimination.

   b. protects freedom of religion.

   c. guarantees the right to counsel for all citizens.

   d. protects individuals from illegal searches and seizures.

9. The justices of the Supreme Court

   a. have never found the death penalty to be unconstitutional.

   b. ruled that the death penalty was imposed in an arbitrary, and therefore, unconstitutional manner in 1972.

   c. have ruled that executing mentally retarded citizens is unconstitutional.

   d. both a and b.

10. The establishment clause pertains to

   a. speech.

   b. privacy.

   c. religion.

   d. peaceful assembly.

NOTES

1. Dudley Hiibel maintains a Web page with the video of the incident and other relevant information. See www.papersplease.org/hiibel/facts.html. See also Linda Greenhouse, "Justices Uphold a Nevada Law Requiring Citizens to Identify Themselves to the Police," *New York Times,* June 22, 2004; Anne M. Coughlin, "Simple Questions, Big Implications," *Washington Post,* March 28, 2004.

2. Information gathered from Lydia Sargent, "*Hiibel, Larry v. 6th Judicial District Court of Nevada, Humboldt, et al.,*" June 23, 2004. www.onthedocket .org/cases/identification/hiibel-larry-v-6th-judicial-district-court-nevada-humboldt-county-et-al

3. The Court's decision is *Hiibel v. Sixth Judicial District Court of Nevada, Humboldt County*, 542 U.S. 177 (2004). The lawyers' statement is from the Nevada State Public Defender and is available on Hiibel's Web page (www.papersplease.org/hiibel/).

4. See Robert Bork, *The Tempting of America* (New York: Simon & Schuster, 1990); Daniel Levin, "Federalists in the Attic: Original Intent, the Heritage Movement, and Democratic Theory," *Law and Social Inquiry* 29 (2004): 105–26; Antonin Scalia, *A Matter of Interpretation: Federal Courts and the Law* (Princeton: Princeton University Press, 1997).

5. *Dred Scott v. Sandford*, 19 Howard 393 (1857).

6. See the excellent discussion in Thomas G. Walker and Lee Epstein, *The Supreme Court of the United States* (New York: St. Martin's, 1993), 118–20.

7. *5 Annals of Congress 734* (April 6, 1796).

8. *5 Annals of Congress 776* (April 6, 1796).

9. *Brown et al. v. Board of Education*, 347 U.S. 483 (1954).

10. Quoted in *The Supreme Court A to Z* (Washington, D.C.: Congressional Quarterly, 1994), 283.

11. *Barron v. the Mayor and City Council of Baltimore*, 7 Peters (32 U.S.) (1833). See the discussion in Henry J. Abraham and Barbara A. Perry, *Freedom and the Court: Civil Rights and Liberties in the United States,* 6th ed. (New York: Oxford University Press, 1994), 30–32.

12. See *The Slaughterhouse Cases*, 16 Wall. (83 U.S.) 36 (1872); *Hurtado v. California*, 110 U.S. 516 (1884).

13. *Chicago, Burlington & Quincy Railroad Co. v. Chicago*, 166 U.S. 226 (1897).

14. See Mark A. Graber, *Transforming Free Speech: The Ambiguous Legacy of Civil Libertarianism* (Berkeley: University of California Press, 1991); *Gitlow v. New York*, 268 U.S. 652 (1925).

15. See footnote 23 in *District of Columbia v. Heller*, No. 07-290 (2008).

16. Richard Hofstadter, *The Idea of a Party System* (Berkeley: University of California Press, 1969), 106–8.

17. Quoted in Edwin Emery, *The Press and America: An Interpretative History of the Mass Media,* 3rd ed. (Englewood Cliffs, NJ: Prentice-Hall, 1972), 123.

18. *New York Times Co. v. Sullivan*, 376 U.S. 254 (1964).

19. James A. Curry, Richard B. Riley, and Richard M. Battistoni, *Constitutional Government* (St. Paul, MN: West, 1989), 444.

20. *Schenck v. United States*, 249 U.S. 47 (1919).

21. *Abrams v. United States*, 250 U.S. 16 (1919).

22. Ibid.

23. See Justice Stone's footnote in *United States v. Carolene Products Co.*, 304 U.S. 144 (1938).

24. *Dennis v. United States*, 341 U.S. 494 (1951).

25. *Brandenburg v. Ohio*, 395 U.S. 444 (1969).

26. For some evidence, see Thomas R. Marshall, *Public Opinion and the Supreme Court* (Boston: Unwin Hyman, 1989), 173–81; Thomas R. Marshall, "Public Opinion, Representation, and the Modern Supreme Court," *American Politics Quarterly* 16 (July 1988): 296–316.

27. *Stromberg v. California*, 283 U.S. 359 (1931).

28. *United States v. O'Brien*, 391 U.S. 367 (1968).

29. *Texas v. Johnson*, 491 U.S. 397 (1989).

30. *R.A.V. v. City of St. Paul*, 505 U.S. 377 (1992).

31. Adam Liptak, "Unlike Others, U.S. Defends Freedom to Offend in Speech," *New York Times,* June 12, 2008; Ronald J. Krotoszynski, Jr. *The First Amendment in Cross-Cultural Perspective* (New York: New York University Press, 2006).

32. *Wisconsin v. Mitchell*, 508 U.S. 47 (1993); *Virginia v. Black*, 538 U.S. 343 (2003).

33. See *United States v. Cruikshank*, 92 U.S. 542 (1875).

34. *Hague v. Committee of Industrial Organization*, 307 U.S. 496 (1939).

35. *Cox v. Louisiana*, 379 U.S. 536 (1965).

36. This account draws on Fred W. Friendly and Martha J.H. Elliott, *The Constitution—That Delicate Balance* (New York: Random House, 1984), 81–88.

37. See the discussion in Curry, Riley, and Battistoni, *Constitutional Government,* 477–78.

38. *National Association for the Advancement of Colored People v. Alabama ex rel Patterson*, 357 U.S. 449 (1958).

39. *Near v. Minnesota*, 283 U.S. 697 (1931).

40. See *New York Times Company v. United States* and *United States v. The Washington Post Company*, 403 U.S. 713 (1971).

41. Jeffrey Matrullo, "*People v. Bryant* and Prior Restraint: The Unsettling of a Settled Area of Law," *Connecticut Public Interest Law Journal* 4 (Spring 2005): 320–50.

42. Ibid.

43. See Anthony Lewis, *Make No Law: The Sullivan Case and the First Amendment* (New York: Random House, 1991).

44. *New York Times Co. v. Sullivan*, 376 U.S. 254 (1964).

45. *Chaplinsky v. New Hampshire*, 315 U.S. 568 (1942). The Court upheld the Comstock Act in *Ex Parte Jackson*, 96 U.S. 727(1878).

46. *Roth v. United States*, 354 U.S. 476 (1957).

47. See the discussion in Curry, Riley, and Battistoni, *Constitutional Government,* 510–11.

48. *Jacobellis v. Ohio*, 378 U.S. 194 (1964).

49. *Miller v. California*, 413 U.S. 15 (1973).

50. See especially *Jenkins v. Georgia*, 418 U.S. 153 (1974).

51. A. James Reichley, *Religion in American Public Life* (Washington, D.C.: Brookings Institution, 1985), 111.

52. See *Everson v. Board of Education*, 330 U.S. 1 (1947); *Agostini v. Felton*, 521 U.S. 203 (1997).

53. *Zelman v. Simmons-Harris*, 536 U.S. 639 (2002).

54. *Tilton v. Richardson*, 403 U.S. 672 (1971); *Roemer v. Board of Public Works*, 426 U.S. 736 (1976).

55. *Locke v. Davey*, 540 U.S. 712 (2004).

56. *Engel v. Vitale*, 370 U.S. 421 (1962).

57. *Abington School District v. Schempp*, (1963); *Murray v. Curlett*, 374 U.S. 203 (1963).

58. *Wallace v. Jaffe*, 472 U.S. 38 (1985); *Lee v. Weisman*, 505 U.S. 577 (1992); *Santa Fe Independent School District v. Doe*, individually and as next friend for her minor children, et al., 530 U.S. 290 (2000).

59. *Capitol Square Review Board v. Pinette*, 515 U.S. 753 (1995).

60. Linda Greenhouse, "The Supreme Court: Church-State Relations," *New York Times,* June 30, 1995.

61. *Lemon v. Kurtzman*, 403 U.S. 602 (1971).

62. The Kentucky case was *McCreary County v. ACLU of Kentucky*, 545 U. S. 844 (2005); the Texas case was *Van Orden v. Perry*, 545 U. S. 677 (2005).

63. *Reynolds v. United States*, 98 U.S. 145 (1878).

64. This movement started with *Cantwell v. Connecticut*, 310 U.S. 296 (1940).

65. *West Virginia State Board of Education v. Barnette*, 319 U.S. 624 (1943). This ruling over-turned *Minersville School District v. Gobitis*, 310 U.S. 586 (1940).

66. *Wisconsin v. Yoder*, 406 U.S. 205 (1972).

67. *Church of the Lukumi BabaluAye Inc. v. Hialeah, Fla.*, 508 U.S. 520 (1993).

68. *Employment Division, Department of Human Resources v. Smith*, 494 U.S. 872 (1990).

69. Peter Steinfels, "New Law Protects Religious Practices," *New York Times*, November 17, 1993.

70. Quoted in Joan Biskupic, "A Second (Amendment) Look at Bearing Arms," *Washington Post National Weekly Edition*, May 15–21, 1995, 33.

71. *United States v. Cruikshank*, 92 U.S. 542, 553 (1876).

72. Cohen and Kaplan, *Constitutional Law*, 785.

73. *Presser v. Illinois*, 116 U.S. 252 (1886).

74. *Miller v. Texas*, 153 U.S. 535 (1894); *Robertson v. Baldwin*, 165 U.S. 275 (1897).

75. *United States v. Miller*, 307 U.S. 174 (1939).

76. *Lewis v. United States*, 455 U.S. 55 (1980).

77. *Quilici v. Village of Morton Grove*, 695 F. 2d 261 (1982); *Quilici v. Village of Morton Grove*, 464 U.S. 863 (1983).

78. *District of Columbia v. Heller*, No. 07-290 (2008).

79. Ibid., 64.

80. Ibid., 64.

81. Ibid., 54–55.

82. Ibid., 55.

83. Adam Liptak, "Coming Next, Court Fights on Guns in Cities," *New York Times*, June 27, 2008.

84. Gordon Witkin, "The Fight to Bear Arms," *U.S. News and World Report*, May 22, 1995, 30.

85. Andrew Kirby, "A Smoking Gun: Relations between the State and Local State in the Case of Firearms Control," *Policy Studies Journal* 18 (Spring 1990): 739–54.

86. Quoted in Peter Applebome, "Paramilitary Groups Are Presenting Delicate Legal Choices for the States," *New York Times*, May 10, 1995.

87. *Wolf v. Colorado*, 338 U.S. 25 (1949).

88. *Mapp v. Ohio*, 367 U.S. 643 (1961).

89. On latitude given, see *United States v. Ross*, 456 U.S. 798 (1982); on citation as opposed to arrest as a limitation, see *Knowles v. Iowa*, 525 U.S. 113 (1998).

90. *Harris v. United States*, 390 U.S. 294 (1968).

91. *Coolidge v. New Hampshire*, 403 U.S. 433 (1971).

92. *California v. Ciraolo*, 476 U.S. 207 (1986).

93. *Olmstead v. United States*, 277 U.S. 438 (1928).

94. *Katz v. United States*, 389 U.S. 347 (1967).

95. See Title III of the Omnibus Crime Control and Safe Streets Act of 1968.

96. The 2007 data are taken from Administrative Office of the United States Courts, "Report of the Director of the Administrative Office of the United States Courts on Applications for Orders Authorizing or Approving the Interception of Wire, Oral, or Electronic Communications," April 2008. See also *Plasencia v. U.S.*, 921 F2d 1557 (1991).

97. *California v. Greenwood*, 486 U.S. 35 (1988).

98. Adam Liptak, "U.S. is Alone in Rejecting All Evidence if Police Err," *New York Times*, July 19, 2008.

99. See *Weeks v. United States*, 232 U.S. 383 (1914); *Mapp v. Ohio*, 367 U.S. 643 (1961).

100. See *United States v. Peltier*, 422 U.S. 531 (1975); *United States v. Leon*, 468 U.S. 897 (1984).

101. *Arizona v. Evans*, 514 U.S. 1 (1995); Linda Greenhouse, "Justices Validate Seizure Based on Error on Warrant," *New York Times*, March 2, 1995.

102. *Hudson v. Michigan*, 547 U. S. 586 (2006).

103. General Accounting Office data reported in Kenneth J. Cooper and John F. Harris, "Admissible Evidence Expanded," *Des Moines Register*, February 9, 1995.

104. Donald A. Dripps, "Miscarriages of Justice and the Constitution," *Buffalo Criminal Law Review* 2 (no. 2, 1999): 645–46; Paul G. Cassell, "How Many Criminals Has *Miranda* Set Free?" *Wall Street Journal*, March 1, 1995.

105. Data on opposition are taken from Bill of Rights Defense Committee, Inc., as of August 2008.

106. James Risen and Eric Lichtblau, "Bush Lets U.S. Spy on Callers without Courts," *New York Times*, December 16, 2005.

107. Leslie Cauley, "NSA Has Massive Database of Americans' Phone Calls," *USA Today*, May 11, 2006.

108. Eric Lichtblau, "Senate Approves Bill to Broaden Wiretap Powers," *New York Times*, July 10, 2008.

109. *Brown v. Mississippi*, 297 U.S. 278 (1936).

110. *Spano v. New York*, 360 U.S. 315 (1959).

111. *Miranda v. Arizona*, 384 U.S. 436 (1966).

112. *Nix v. Williams*, 467 U.S. 431 (1984).

113. *Arizona v. Fulminante*, 499 U.S. 279 (1991).

114. *New York v. Quarles*, 467 U.S. 649 (1984); *Dickerson v. United States*, 530 U.S. 428 (2000); Linda Greenhouse, "A Turf Battle's Unlikely Victim," *New York Times*, June 28, 2000. The 2004 cases are *Missouri v. Siebert*, 542 U.S. 600 (2004), and *United States v. Patane*, 542 U.S. 630 (2004).

115. Cassell, "How Many Criminals Has *Miranda* Set Free?"; Paul G. Cassell, "Handcuffing the Cops: Miranda's Harmful Effects on Law Enforcement," *National Center for Policy Analysis*, August 1998.

116. Jo Davidson, "Senators Weigh Plan, Backed by Hatch, to End 'Miranda,'" *Wall Street Journal*, March 8, 1995.

117. *Powell v. Alabama*, 287 U.S. 45 (1932).

118. *Gideon v. Wainwright*, 372 U.S. 335 (1963). This decision explicitly overturned the previous ruling in *Betts v. Brady*, 316 U.S. 455 (1942).

119. *Argersinger v. Hamlin*, 407 U.S. 25 (1972).

120. *Duncan v. Louisiana*, 391 U.S. 145 (1968).

121. See *Williams v. Florida*, 399 U.S. 78 (1970); *Colgrove v. Battin*, 413 U.S. 149 (1973).

122. *Apodaca v. Oregon*, 406 U.S. 404 (1972).

123. *Pointer v. Texas*, 380 U.S. 400 (1965).

124. See the excellent discussion of *Coy v. Iowa*, 487 U.S. 1012 (1988), and *Maryland v. Craig*, 497 U.S. 836 (1990), in Ellen Alderman and Caroline Kennedy, *In Our Defense: The Bill of Rights in Action* (New York: Avon Books, 1991).

125. *Furman v. Georgia*, 408 U.S. 238 (1972).

126. *Gregg v. Georgia*, 428 U.S. 153 (1976).

127. See *Stanford v. Kentucky*, 492 U.S. 361 (1989) for executing sixteen-year-olds; *Thompson v. Oklahoma*, 487 U.S. 815 (1988) on not putting fifteen-year-olds to death; *Roper v. Simmons*, 543 U.S. 551 (2005) on not putting sixteen- and seventeen-year-olds to death. On not imposing the death penalty on the insane, see *Ford v. Wainwright*, 477 U.S. 399 (1986). On not

executing the mentally retarded, see *Atkins v. Virginia*, 536 U.S. 304 (2002). On not applying the death penalty to child rapists, see *Kennedy v. Louisiana*, no. 07-343 (2008).

128. *Baze v. Rees*, No. 07-5439 (2008). See Justice Stevens's concurring opinion.

129. *Ewing v. California*, 538 U.S. 11 (2003); *Lockyer v. Andrade*, 538 U.S. 63 (2003).

130. *Griswold v. Connecticut*, 381 U.S. 479 (1965).

131. *Eisenstadt v. Baird*, 405 U.S. 438 (1972).

132. *Roe v. Wade*, 410 U.S. 113 (1973).

133. *Webster v. Reproductive Health Services*, 492 U.S. 490 (1989); *Hodgson v. Minnesota*, 497 U.S. 417 (1990).

134. *Planned Parenthood of Southeastern Pennsylvania v. Casey*, 505 U.S. 833 (1992); *Stenberg v. Carhart*, 530 U.S. 914 (2000).

135. *Gonzalez v. Carhart*, No. 05-380 (2007).

136. *Bowers v. Hardwick*, 478 U.S. 186 (1986); *Lawrence v. Texas*, 539 U. S. 558 (2003).

137. *Cruzan v. Director, Missouri Department of Health*, 497 U.S. 261 (1990); *Washington v. Glucksberg*, 521 U.S. 702 (1997); *Gonzales v. Oregon*, 546 U.S. 243 (2006).

5

Civil Rights

CHAPTER OUTLINE

In 2006, Nebraska State Senator Ernie Chambers offered a seemingly innocuous amendment to a bill designed to provide more money for the financially troubled Omaha Public Schools. He proposed dividing the existing school district into three separate districts, arguing that smaller units would allow parents to have greater say over how financial resources would be used to educate their children. Within days his amendment, along with the rest of the measure, was passed by the legislature and signed into law by the governor.

The reality of what Chamber's amendment would mean in practice, however, touched off political and legal firestorms. Given housing patterns in Omaha, the only way three districts could be drawn would be to establish one predominantly white district, one majority African American district, and one district that was heavily Hispanic. In essence, the bill would authorize the resegregation of the city's schools, overturning the results of a painful desegregation battle fought in the 1970s.[1]

Chambers, the state legislature's only African American member, fully understood the implications of his proposal. A product of the Omaha school system in the 1940s, he could recall the racial taunts hurled at him by white classmates after a teacher read *Little Black Sambo* to the class. During the legislature's debate on his amendment, Chambers asserted that the current system had failed minority students and stated that his "intent is not to have an exclusionary system, but [one that] we, meaning black people, whose children make up the vast majority of the student population, would control."[2] Support for the resegregation plan was given by the *Omaha Star,* the city's only black-owned newspaper.[3]

Source: © Bill Wolf/AP Photo.

Nebraska State Senator Ernie Chambers offered the controversial proposal to break up the Omaha Public Schools.

Opposition came from the white superintendent of the Omaha Public Schools, who called the plan unconstitutional. The state attorney general, also white, weighed in with similar concerns, writing to state legislators before their final vote that, "We believe that the state may face serious risk due to the potential constitutional problems raised...." He went on to say that because of the Fourteenth Amendment to the U.S. Constitution, the government cannot sanction segregation, "even if the state believes that 'separate but equal' is superior for minority children."[4] Given the legal problems surrounding the plan, most observers predicted it would never go into effect. They were right. In 2007, the state legislature passed and the governor signed legislation repealing the breakup of the Omaha Public Schools. In its place, they created a new voting structure for the district that was expected to provide more representation for minorities.[5]

The city of Omaha and the state of Nebraska found themselves debating questions about race because discrimination has a long and tragic history in American society. Despite a promise to "establish justice" and "secure the blessings of liberty," the original text of the Constitution made discrimination legally permissible. Although the word *slavery* was not used, Article I, Section 9 and Article IV, Section 2 essentially condoned the bondage of African Americans. Moreover, Article I, Section 2 stipulated that when counting the population to apportion seats in the House of Representatives, slaves should be considered equal to three-fifths of a free person; American Indians (called Indians in the Constitution) were not to be counted at all unless they paid taxes (that is, lived off their tribal reservations). None of the articles guaranteed equal rights for women, and the Supreme Court would later rule that the Constitution did not require that women be allowed to vote.[6]

Ever since the signing of the Constitution, some people have fought to see the blessings of liberty extended to all Americans, regardless of race, sex, or ethnicity. In many battles they have succeeded, and government has changed the rules that govern our civil rights. American citizens can no longer buy and sell slaves. Women, African Americans, American Indians, and members of other groups can vote. The battle over civil rights has at times exposed the ugly side of American society, but it also has demonstrated the capacity of the courts and other governmental institutions to translate the promises of the Constitution into reality, at least in some areas. Today, many Americans find themselves debating, as the Omaha community does, the question of what steps the government should take to aid the victims of discrimination.

In this chapter, we examine the evolution of civil rights in the United States and the role politics plays in defining them. We explore how African Americans pioneered the civil rights movement and how other groups—including Asian Americans, Hispanic Americans, American Indians, women, people with disabilities, people with age claims, and gays and lesbians—have fought to ensure that they, too, enjoy the freedoms the Constitution promises. We conclude the chapter with a look at affirmative action, demonstrating the conflicts that may arise when two sets of rights collide. When this happens, our interpretations of civil rights change as government seeks to manage the conflict; often, as we shall see, political considerations determine the final balance. Groups on both sides battle hard to establish rules that favor their side. They know the rules matter—because the rules determine the rights real people exercise every day in the United States.

5-1 CIVIL LIBERTIES AND CIVIL RIGHTS

The distinction between civil liberties and civil rights is difficult to draw. Both involve the federal government's relationship with individuals. As we discussed in Chapter 4, the term *civil liberties* usually applies to the freedoms the Bill of Rights guarantees (although some are in the body of the Constitution). These liberties include freedom of speech, freedom of religion, and the right to assemble peaceably. In a general sense, the civil liberties listed in the Bill of Rights restrain government—they prohibit government from taking negative actions that tread on individual rights.

The term **civil rights** usually refers to the notion of equality of rights for all people regardless of race, sex, ethnicity, religion, sexual orientation, and so on. Civil rights are rooted in the courts' interpretation of the Fourteenth Amendment and in laws that Congress and the state legislatures pass. Broadly speaking, civil rights require government to take positive actions to protect individual rights—for example, to desegregate public schools.

In practice, civil liberties and civil rights are closely linked. But sometimes the two can conflict. For example, laws designed to protect minorities from so-called hate speech can infringe on the rights of others to exercise their freedom of speech. (As we saw in Chapter 4, the First Amendment applies even to speech that many Americans find reprehensible.) How can we balance the rights of some individuals to be protected from discrimination with the rights of other individuals to speak their minds as they see fit? Finding such a balance is not always an easy task. As we will see, the pursuit of civil rights—government's attempt to ensure equality of rights—can sometimes conflict with civil liberties.

5-2 DISCRIMINATION AGAINST AFRICAN AMERICANS

Although many groups have participated in the struggle to ensure equal rights for all Americans, the battle for civil rights is most closely identified with African Americans, and their victories have been extended to benefit other groups. The leading role African Americans have played in the push for civil rights reflects their unique experience in the United States. The United States did not ban slavery until the end of the Civil War, and many African

civil rights

The equality of rights for all people regardless of race, sex, ethnicity, religion, and sexual orientation. Civil rights are rooted in the courts' interpretation of the Fourteenth Amendment and in laws that Congress and the state legislatures pass.

Americans were denied full political rights until well into the twentieth century. The experience with slavery and racism has shaped the relationship between African Americans as a group and the legal system.

To examine the problem of discrimination against African Americans, we must review the African American journey from slavery to emancipation and then explore the steps that many states took to deny African Americans the rights they won at the end of the Civil War. We will then discuss the appearance of the first civil rights organizations, their success in challenging discriminatory laws, and the birth of the civil rights movement. We will conclude the section by examining the steps Congress has taken to protect and promote the civil rights of African Americans and by discussing the continuing controversy over what steps the government may properly take to help the victims of discrimination. Though African Americans have made great strides in changing the rules to expand their civil rights, these rule changes have yet to bring them social and economic equality.

5-2a From Slavery to Emancipation

African Americans first arrived in what would become the United States in 1619. Many came initially as indentured servants who agreed to work for an employer for a fixed number of years to pay for their passage. By the latter half of the seventeenth century, however, slavery had taken hold in the thirteen colonies, especially in the South. As we discussed in Chapter 2, the status of African Americans was a major issue at the Constitutional Convention in 1787. Delegates from southern states strongly defended slavery, whereas delegates from northern states were inclined to limit and eventually terminate the practice. Because southern delegates made it clear that they would desert the convention rather than accept a constitution that abolished slavery, northern delegates dropped their efforts to insert a provision in the Constitution that would have banned slavery. In this case, as would be true many times in later years, political pressures molded the rules that denied African Americans their civil rights.

In addition to allowing the practice of slavery to continue, the Founders inserted language into the Constitution that barred Congress from stopping the slave trade before 1808. As soon as the ban lapsed, Congress made the importation of slaves illegal. The buying and selling of slaves already in the country continued unabated, however, until the Civil War. Although slavery became an increasingly divisive and unpopular policy, the Supreme Court continued to find it constitutional, most notably (as we saw in Chapter 2) in the *Dred Scott v. Sandford* decision of 1857.[7] In that case, the Court held that African Americans were not citizens of the United States and therefore were not entitled to the liberties granted in the Constitution.

During the Civil War, President Abraham Lincoln issued the Emancipation Proclamation, which freed only those slaves living in the Confederacy. Slavery was finally made illegal everywhere in the country with the ratification of the Thirteenth Amendment in 1865. (Mississippi did not ratify the amendment until 1995, making it the last state to do so.) Although the Thirteenth Amendment made slavery unconstitutional, it did not guarantee that African Americans would be able to exercise the political rights available to other Americans. Many southern states quickly passed laws, called *Black Codes,* that barred African Americans from buying and selling property, signing business contracts, and serving on juries (among other things). By severely limiting the legal rights of African Americans, the southern states were effectively forcing them back into slavery.

Congress responded to the Black Codes by passing a series of civil rights laws between 1866 and 1875. Congress also proposed the Fourteenth Amendment, which the states ratified in 1868. That amendment granted citizenship to "all persons born or naturalized in the United States," thereby nullifying the *Dred Scott* decision. The amendment also stipulated, among other things, that no state shall "deprive any person of life, liberty, or property, without due process of law," and it promised that all people would receive equal protection under the law. As we discussed in Chapter 4, since the turn of the century, the Supreme Court has used the language of the Fourteenth Amendment to extend the Bill of Rights to cover the actions of state governments. The Court has also used it to advance the civil rights of African Americans and other groups.

Source: © *Bettmann/Corbis. Reproduced by permission.*

With the passage of the Thirteenth, Fourteenth, and Fifteenth Amendments, African Americans initially enjoyed a measure of political equality with whites. Between 1869 and 1877, two African Americans were elected to the Senate and fourteen were elected to the House.

But in the second half of the nineteenth century, the Court would not take to heart the Fourteenth Amendment's injunction to provide all Americans with "equal protection of the laws." In effect, the Court ignored the spirit of this rule.

In addition to the Thirteenth and Fourteenth Amendments, Congress proposed the Fifteenth Amendment as another way to protect the civil rights of African Americans. Ratified by the states in 1870, the Fifteenth Amendment gave African American men the right to vote for the first time. For a brief time, many African American men enjoyed a measure of political equality with white men. Between 1869 and 1877, two African Americans from the South were elected to the Senate and fourteen were elected to the House. (Until the early twentieth century, the vast majority of African Americans lived in the South.) A major reason the Fifteenth Amendment succeeded initially was that the federal troops still occupied the southern states, and although their record was by no means perfect, they did much to protect African Americans from intimidation and retaliation by white Southerners. (Federal troops occupied the South from 1865 to 1877, a period known as *Reconstruction*.)

Although Congress acted in the years immediately following the Civil War to guarantee (at least in writing) the *political* rights of African Americans, it did little to protect or improve their *economic* condition. Despite a promise Union General William Tecumseh Sherman made to African Americans in the last months of the Civil War, Congress refused to pass legislation to confiscate southern plantations and give each former slave "forty acres and a mule."[8] Without land of their own to farm or an education to fall back on—slave owners generally prevented their slaves from learning to read and write—and faced with the hostility of most white Southerners, African Americans had few opportunities to escape poverty. As a result, at least in terms of economic conditions, their lives as free citizens in many respects resembled the lives they had led as slaves.

5-2b Jim Crow

The political victories that African Americans won in the heady days immediately following the Civil War began to dissipate during the mid-1870s. In 1876, the outcome of the presidential election between Republican Rutherford B. Hayes and Democrat Samuel J. Tilden was disputed. (Tilden had won a majority of the popular vote, but the question of who had won a majority of the electoral votes was open to debate.) In the end, southern Democrats agreed to support Hayes for president in return for a Republican promise to withdraw federal troops from southern states and to drop the federal government's efforts to protect African Americans living in the South. With the end of Reconstruction came the end of congressional efforts, which spanned nearly half a century, to bar discrimination against African Americans—a sad instance when political deal making resulted in new rules that restricted the civil rights of African Americans.

Just as African Americans found themselves abandoned by the political branches of the federal government, they also found the federal courts equally unwilling to give life to the spirit of the Civil War amendments and legislation. In 1873, the Supreme Court handed down a ruling that interpreted the Fourteenth Amendment in a narrow fashion—so narrow, in fact, that it virtually nullified the amendment as a source of legal protection for African Americans.[9] In its decision, the Court noted that the Fourteenth Amendment distinguished between national citizenship and state citizenship. The Court used this distinction to argue that, with the exception of a few broad rights such as the right to travel and the right to enter into contracts, the amendment was not intended to guarantee individual rights against state government actions. In essence, then, the Court held that state governments were not obliged to honor the rights (such as those set forth in the Bill of Rights) conferred on Americans as a result of their national citizenship.

Three years later, the Supreme Court handed down two rulings on the same day that curtailed the political rights of African Americans even further. In one case, the Court ruled that federal laws that punished individuals who violated the rights of African Americans were unconstitutional.[10] This ruling gutted Congress's ability to extend equal rights to African Americans. In the other case, the Court ruled that the Fifteenth Amendment did not guarantee all men over age twenty-one the right to vote. Instead, the Court argued, the amendment simply listed reasons that could not be used to deny citizens the right to vote.[11] The Court's decision gave the states permission to enact laws, such as literacy tests and poll taxes, that effectively denied African Americans the right to vote. The net result was to rob the Fifteenth Amendment of much of its meaning. It would be nearly a century before African Americans in the South (and in some parts of the North) would regain the right to vote. (Indeed, no African American from the South would serve in Congress from 1901 until 1973.)[12]

With the federal government no longer willing to protect the rights of African Americans, legal discrimination became a constant part of African American life despite the promises contained in the Thirteenth, Fourteenth, and Fifteenth Amendments. Many southern states adopted **Jim Crow laws** that suppressed the rights of African Americans. (The term *Jim Crow* came from an early eighteenth-century Kentucky plantation song. By the mid-nineteenth century, the term was synonymous with the legal suppression of African American rights.)[13] The result was **de jure segregation**, with African Americans required by law to live and work separately from white Americans. Many state governments actually maintained segregation in the workplace by making it illegal to hire African Americans for many jobs. Other laws barred African Americans from using the same public accommodations as whites. Throughout the South, hospitals, public parks, cemeteries, prisons, and even drinking fountains and restrooms were all segregated by race. In the North, meanwhile, Jim Crow laws were far less common, but social practices effectively discriminated

Jim Crow laws

Laws that discriminated against African Americans, usually by enforcing segregation.

de jure segregation

Government-imposed laws that required African Americans to live and work separately from white Americans.

against African Americans, and thereby limited their opportunities for education and employment.

African Americans periodically challenged the constitutionality of Jim Crow laws in court, but they repeatedly came away disappointed. The most important such case was *Plessy v. Ferguson* (1896), in which the Supreme Court upheld segregated public facilities. This ruling established the **separate-but-equal standard** (see Box 5–1), which declared that segregated facilities were acceptable as long as they were "equal."[14] Most prominent among the public facilities where the Court sanctioned segregation was the public school system. School segregation was so common, the Court noted in *Plessy*, that Congress had created and supported segregated schools in the District of Columbia. Only Justice John

separate-but-equal standard
The now-rejected Supreme Court doctrine that separation of the races was acceptable as long as each race was treated equally.

The People behind the Rules

Box 5–1   Who Were Plessy and Brown?

Few names loom larger in the history of American civil rights than Plessy and Brown, the names in two of the most important Supreme Court decisions. Yet most people know little about these two individuals. Who were they, and how did they become such important actors on the stage of American history?

HOMER ADOLPH PLESSY
Homer Adolph Plessy was an African American civil rights activist from New Orleans who chose to challenge one of Louisiana's Jim Crow laws, which were state statutes that legalized segregated public facilities. In 1890, the Louisiana state legislature had

In the 1890s, Homer Adolph Plessy challenged the Louisiana law requiring "equal but separate accommodations for the white and colored races." He lost.

followed the lead of several other southern states and passed a law requiring that "all railway companies carrying passengers in their coaches in this State, shall provide equal but separate accommodations for the white, and colored, races." Until a few years previous, most southern railroads had allowed African Americans to mix with whites in second class, though not in first class. Although the railroads in Louisiana were not actively enforcing the law, Plessy's fellow activists arranged for him to be arrested in the whites-only passenger car of the East Louisiana Railway. The first judge he faced was John H. Ferguson of the Criminal District Court of New Orleans. Ferguson ruled that the law did not violate the Fourteenth Amendment, as Plessy had argued; the Supreme Court ultimately upheld his decision in the infamous case that preserved both their names, *Plessy v. Ferguson*. From this case stemmed the separate-but-equal standard that legitimized discrimination for the next half century.

OLIVER BROWN
The case that led the Supreme Court to repeal the separate-but-equal standard was *Brown v. Board of Education*. Oliver Brown was a railroad worker in Topeka, Kansas. In September 1950, he attempted to enroll his daughter Linda

in the third grade at the Sumner School, which was located four blocks from the Browns' home. The Sumner School was for white children only, however, and the Brown family was African American. Because Topeka, like many other American cities, had a segregated school system, Linda had been forced to attend the Monroe School, which was located about a mile from her home. After officials at the Sumner School refused to accept Linda as a student, Brown sued the local school board at the urging of the local chapter of the National Association for the Advancement of Colored People (NAACP). Brown's legal challenge wound its way through the legal system, eventually winding up in the Supreme Court. Chief Justice Earl Warren, writing on behalf of a unanimous Court, held that segregated school systems denied African American children equal protection under the law.

Both *Plessy v. Ferguson* and *Brown v. Board of Education* pitted individual rights against the rights of society. Although the outcome of each case was very different, Plessy and Brown share one distinction: Few Americans have had a greater impact on the rules that govern our civil rights than Homer Plessy and Oliver Brown.

Source: See Richard Kluger, *Simple Justice* (New York: Vintage Books, 1975).

Harlan, a former slave owner himself, disagreed with the ruling of the majority. In a dissent that would remain famous long after his death, Harlan wrote: "Our Constitution is color blind, and neither knows nor tolerates classes among citizens. In respect of civil rights, all citizens are equal before the law."

State-sanctioned discrimination made it easy for private groups, most notably the Ku Klux Klan (KKK), to terrorize African Americans. The Klan was originally formed in 1865 in Tennessee by a small group of ex-Confederate soldiers who wanted to resist the Union occupation. The KKK's practice of terrorizing African Americans prompted Congress to pass a law in 1872 (which the Supreme Court declared unconstitutional in 1883), making it a crime for any individual to deprive another of his or her rights. The original Klan collapsed shortly after it was founded, but it was revived in 1915. Its membership grew rapidly, peaking at 5 million in 1924. The power of the KKK in the southern states led to its label as "the invisible empire of the South."[15]

The Klan frequently used violence to intimidate African Americans as well as any whites who opposed segregation. To serve as a warning of impending violence, KKK members initiated the practice of cross burning. Beatings were the most common form of violence, but at times, the violence escalated to murder. Klan members (and nonmembers as well) often practiced **lynching**—that is, the unlawful killing, usually by hanging, of a person by a mob. Lynchings were exceptionally brutal and sadistic events, perhaps none more so than one that took place in Livermore, Kentucky, in 1911:

> A Negro charged with murdering a white man was seized and hauled to a local theater, where an audience was invited to witness his hanging. Receipts were to go to the murdered white man's family. To add interest to the benefit performance, seatholders in the orchestra were invited to empty their revolvers into the swaying black body while those in the gallery were restricted to a single shot.[16]

Lynchings were especially common in the 1890s, with an average of one African American lynched every two-and-a-half days.[17] In all, more than 3,000 African Americans were lynched in the South and elsewhere in the United States between 1880 and 1960.[18]

Despite the barbarity of the attacks on African Americans, the federal government repeatedly refused to step in to protect them. Successive presidents insisted that state and local governments must control mob violence, and Congress refused to pass legislation that would have made lynching a federal crime. State and local officials, however, usually failed to prosecute whites who lynched or otherwise terrorized African Americans, either because they approved of the attacks—many government officials belonged to the KKK or sympathized with it—or because they feared that doing so would cost them their jobs.

5-2c The First Civil Rights Organizations

In response to the spread of Jim Crow laws, several organizations formed to fight for the rights of African Americans. The most

lynching
The unlawful killing, usually by hanging, of a person by a mob.

important was the National Association for the Advancement of Colored People (NAACP), founded in 1909 by black sociologist W. E. B. Dubois and others. The goal of the NAACP, whose founding members included African Americans and whites, was to end racial discrimination and legal segregation. The organization began a slow but steady battle to rewrite the rules and policies discriminating against African Americans.

The NAACP used many different strategies to advance the cause of African Americans, but it achieved the most success by filing lawsuits. In seeking vindication in the courts, the NAACP's legal team faced daunting odds. In many parts of the country, the deck was clearly stacked against African Americans. Take, for example, the prosecution of black sharecroppers in Arkansas in 1919. Their attempts to unionize had brought a violent response from landowners and local authorities, culminating in a pitched battle between the two sides. One account shows that

> Nearly one hundred blacks were indicted by an all-white grand jury on various charges; twelve were charged with murder. (A lone white man arrested was considered to be a Union sympathizer.) Though the trials were brisk—none lasted more than forty-five minutes—they positively meandered compared to the five minutes (on average) required of the juries to return the guilty verdicts. In five days, twelve men were sentenced to die in the electric chair and eighty others were sentenced to prison terms from one to twenty years.[19]

NAACP lawyers appealed the death sentences, and the Supreme Court later overturned each sentence because the sharecroppers had been denied due process, or the right to be tried according to fundamental, established legal principles.[20] Here, the existing rules of government were newly applied to protect the rights of African Americans.

Despite facing a hostile legal environment, the NAACP won some important victories. In 1915, the Supreme Court accepted its argument that election laws containing *grandfather clauses* were unconstitutional.[21] (When southern states adopted literacy tests to deny African Americans the right to vote, they protected the voting rights of illiterate whites by stipulating that those who failed a literacy test could still vote if their grandfathers had had the right to vote before 1867—that is, before African Americans could legally vote in the South.) In 1917, the NAACP persuaded the Court that laws barring African Americans from buying homes in white neighborhoods were unconstitutional.[22] In 1938, the NAACP convinced the Court that the state of Missouri's refusal either to admit African Americans to the University of Missouri law school or to establish a separate African American law school violated the Constitution. (Missouri's policy had been to pay for its African American citizens to attend law school in other states.) The decision meant that, at a minimum, states were obligated to establish law schools for African Americans "substantially equal to those which the State there offered for persons of the white race."[23]

In 1944, the NAACP Legal Defense and Education Fund—created out of the NAACP in 1939 so that the NAACP itself could concentrate on lobbying the political branches of government—won a major victory in the fight to secure voting rights for African Americans. That year, the Supreme Court ruled that the southern practice of white-only primaries was unconstitutional.[24] At the time, Republican candidates seldom won elections in the South, so the real political battles generally took place in the Democratic primaries. Because they were barred from voting in the primaries, African Americans were denied the right to help pick candidates, and thereby effectively denied the right to help choose elected officials. The states had argued that the political parties administered the white primary and that the parties were private organizations and thus entitled to discriminate if they wished. The Court disagreed.

In addition to its victories in the courts, the NAACP and other civil rights organizations won some victories by working through the other branches of government. For example, despite the heroic contributions of African American soldiers throughout American history, the armed forces remained segregated at the end of World War II. One of President Harry Truman's top advisors later recalled that by the late 1940s,

> the Army and the Air Force had only one black Colonel each, and no one of higher rank. The Navy had a grand total of four black officers, the Marine Corps only one.... I thought the Navy at times resembled a Southern plantation that had somehow escaped the Civil War. Blacks swabbed the decks, shined the shoes, did the cooking, washed the dishes, and served the food. Virtually no other jobs were open to them. The Army ... had established a quota for black Americans in the Army of 10 percent—a policy Army leaders actually thought of as progressive. They trained with white troops but lived in segregated barracks, shopped at segregated stores, rode on segregated trains, and served in segregated units.[25]

Civil rights organizations campaigned to end such discrimination, taking their case to the White House and Congress, and President Truman responded. In 1948, he issued landmark executive orders ending segregation in the armed services and in all other parts of the federal government.[26]

Finally, civil rights activists pushed on social and economic fronts as well. During World War II, for example, African American leaders increased pressure on major league baseball to break the color barrier and sign African American ballplayers.[27] In October 1945, the Brooklyn Dodgers took the lead by signing Jackie Robinson, a UCLA alumnus and World War II army officer playing in the Negro baseball leagues. When Robinson broke into the majors in 1947, African Americans around the country greeted his arrival as a major step forward.[28] Few teams, however, rushed to sign other African American ballplayers, and only a handful joined Robinson in the majors over the next few years. Those that followed in Robinson's footsteps found playing in minor league cities, especially in the South, a humiliating experience. Curt Flood, an outstanding player with the St. Louis Cardinals, said of his days in the minor leagues that

> of the many indignities to which I was subject, few angered me more than the routine in [the] bus. When we were in transit and the team made a dinner stop, I wasn't permitted in the dining room. I had to go to the back door of the restaurant, like a beggar.... If I had to relieve myself, the bus would stop along the highway and I would hide from traffic as best I could.[29]

Because legal and social discrimination remained, African Americans continued to suffer a multitude of indignities in everyday life to remind them of their second-class status in the United States.

5-2d The *Brown* Decision

Even though by the late 1940s the NAACP had won important legal victories and President Truman had ended segregation in the armed forces, segregation remained firmly embedded in American life. That would finally begin to change in the 1950s because the Supreme Court handed down a series of rulings that recognized the promise of equal protection the Fourteenth Amendment made to all Americans. In other words, the Court began enforcing the rules and policies already in place for white Americans.

The main legal battleground was the issue of segregated schooling. In two important rulings handed down in 1950, the Supreme Court effectively ended racial segregation in law schools and graduate schools. In the first case, the Court found that the state of Texas had established an African American law school clearly inferior to the white law school at the University of Texas "in terms of number of faculty, variety of courses and opportunities for specialization, size of the student body, scope of the library, [and] availability of law review and similar activities."[30] In the second case, the Court ruled against the state of Oklahoma's decision to allow an African American student to attend graduate school at the University of Oklahoma only if he sat in separate sections of the classroom, library, and cafeteria facilities. In the Court's view, these restrictions impermissibly impaired the student's "ability to study, to engage in discussions and exchange views with other students, and, in general, to learn his profession."[31]

The two decisions the Supreme Court handed down in 1950 failed to overturn the separate-but-equal standard set forth in *Plessy.* Instead, they set the standard for judging whether a state or local government had provided "substantially equal" facilities so high that it was nearly impossible to meet. It would not be until 1954, and the landmark case of ***Brown v. Board of Education,*** that the Court would finally overturn *Plessy.*[32] (The lead lawyer for the NAACP Legal Defense and Education Fund in the case was Thurgood Marshall, who thirteen years later would become the first African American appointed to the Supreme Court.)

The *Brown* case addressed the fundamental question of whether segregated schools are constitutional (see Box 5–1). A unanimous

Brown v. Board of Education
The landmark 1954 Supreme Court decision holding that separate was not equal and public schools must be desegregated.

Source: © Bettmann/Corbis.

Thurgood Marshall first established himself as a national figure through his work as the director of the National Association for the Advanced of Colored People (NAACP) Counsel of Legal Defense and Education Fund. In that capacity, he led the legal team that argued the landmark *Brown v. Board of Education* case before the Supreme Court. He was later named a Supreme Court justice.

Supreme Court ruled they are not. In the words of Chief Justice Earl Warren:

> We conclude that in the field of public education the doctrine of "separate but equal" has no place. Separate educational facilities are inherently unequal. Therefore, we hold that the plaintiffs and others similarly situated...are, by reason of the segregation complained of, deprived of the equal protection of the laws guaranteed by the Fourteenth Amendment.[33]

The Court held that separate educational facilities are inherently unequal because they irreparably damage the self-esteem of African American children—"To separate [African American children] from others of similar age and qualifications solely because of their race generates a feeling of inferiority ... that may affect their hearts and minds in a way unlikely ever to be undone."[34] Thus, fifty-eight years later, the Court redressed the historic wrong it had done to African Americans in *Plessy*.

The Supreme Court's ruling in *Brown v. Board of Education* was courageous in many respects. Many people, both inside and outside government, wanted the Court to find school segregation constitutional. Chief Justice Warren found himself overtly pressured to rule against the NAACP's position. President Dwight Eisenhower, who had nominated Warren to the Court only a year previous, invited the chief justice to dinner at the White House. He used the dinner to defend segregationists: "These are not bad people. All they are concerned about is to see that their sweet little girls are not required to sit in schools alongside some big overgrown Negroes."[35] Despite the pressure from Eisenhower, Warren actively worked to convince justices who were initially inclined to find segregation constitutional to vote with the majority, thereby allowing the Court to speak in a unified voice on a highly controversial issue.

Although the Supreme Court ruled against school segregation in *Brown v. Board of Education,* the case left open the question of *how* to dismantle the nation's entrenched system of segregated schools. In 1955, in a case known as ***Brown v. Board of Education II,*** the Court settled that question by stating that schools were to desegregate with "all deliberate speed."[36] The Court also assigned the lower federal courts the task of supervising school desegregation.

Although some states began the desegregation process the *Brown* decision mandated, many did not. State and local governments throughout the South initially engaged in **massive resistance**, the policy of fiercely resisting desegregation.[37] Confrontations between the federal courts and state and local officials erupted. In 1957 the governor of Arkansas ordered the state's National Guard to prevent nine African American students from enrolling at an all-white high school in Little Rock. When the governor's actions led to mob violence, President Eisenhower, who had long been reluctant to have the federal government enforce desegregation orders the federal courts had issued, finally sent American troops to Little Rock to restore order and to allow the nine students to enroll.[38] Elsewhere, states passed laws "requiring state schools to be closed if blacks and whites were placed in the same facilities."[39] The state of Virginia closed down the public schools in Norfolk for the entire 1958–1959 school year rather than integrate them. Some states set up programs that paid the tuition of white students who attended private schools, which at that time had a legal right to discriminate against African Americans. (The Supreme Court eventually ruled that private school segregation was unconstitutional as well.)[40] As a result of these and other tactics, in 1964, ten years after the Supreme Court handed down its decision in *Brown,* "97.75 percent of the South's black schoolchildren still attended all-black schools."[41] And in 1969, the Court was still pushing schools to obey its desegregation orders from a decade and a half previous.[42]

Resistance to desegregation was equally fierce on college campuses. In 1962, the governor of Mississippi personally tried to prevent James Meredith from registering as the first African American student at the University of Mississippi in Oxford. When President John F. Kennedy announced in a televised address that Meredith must be allowed to register, segregationists in Oxford began to riot and two people were killed. Peace was restored, and Meredith was allowed to register only after Kennedy ordered nearly 20,000 troops to the town.[43] The refusal to desegregate an all-white college until the federal government threatened to use force was repeated the following year in Alabama. Governor George Wallace, who at his inauguration months earlier had vowed "segregation now, segregation tomorrow, segregation forever," blocked the door to the registration building at the University of Alabama to keep the first two African

Brown v. Board of Education II
The 1955 Supreme Court decision which stated that the nation's entrenched system of segregated schools should desegregate with "all deliberate speed."

massive resistance
The policy many southern states followed in the wake of the first Brown decision of fiercely resisting desegregation.

Americans from registering.[44] Wallace quickly backed down, however, when Kennedy issued the order to send troops to the campus.

As the federal courts sought to desegregate public schools in the first decade after the *Brown* decision, the Supreme Court extended the principle that separate is inherently unequal by striking down laws that mandated segregation in public places such as parks, swimming pools, and courtrooms. Yet because of public resistance to the Court's rulings, especially intense in the South but by no means unique to that region, the day-to-day lives of African Americans changed remarkably little. African Americans who insisted on their rights often faced beatings and even murder at the hands of ardent segregationists, and law enforcement officials often turned a blind eye to such crimes. The Court's promises would become reality only as a result of the rise of the civil rights movement.

5-2e The Civil Rights Movement

civil rights movement
The mobilization of people to push for racial equality.

Following the initial *Brown* decision, African Americans, as well as many white Americans, joined civil rights protests that generated significant public pressure to put an end to segregation. The **civil rights movement** organized protests that would eventually reshape public opinion and lead Congress to take action to protect the rights of African Americans.

The civil rights movement was born in 1955 in Montgomery, Alabama, with a simple act of defiance. Rosa Parks, a forty-three-year-old seamstress and active member of the NAACP, boarded a city bus and sat in a front seat reserved for whites. When the bus driver ordered her to move to the back of the bus, as the law required her to do, Parks refused. She was arrested and fined $10 for violating the city ordinance. Parks's arrest prompted Montgomery's African American community to boycott the city's buses. The boycott lasted for a year, ending only when the Supreme Court affirmed a lower court ruling that laws requiring segregation on city buses are unconstitutional.[45]

civil disobedience
The nonviolent refusal to obey what one perceives to be unjust laws.

The Montgomery bus boycott thrust its leader, the Rev. Dr. Martin Luther King, Jr., into the national spotlight. King and the organization he led, the Southern Christian Leadership Conference (SCLC), pioneered the idea of **civil disobedience**—the nonviolent refusal to obey what one perceives to be unjust laws—as a means to force an end to racial discrimination. In his famed "Letter from Birmingham Jail"—he was arrested in Birmingham, Alabama, in April 1963 for parading without a permit—King explained that civil disobedience "seeks to create such a crisis and foster such a tension that a community which has constantly refused to negotiate is forced to confront the issue [of segregation]. It seeks so to dramatize the issue that it can no longer be ignored."[46] Thus, King and the SCLC hoped that civil disobedience would make the plight of the African American community a national (and even worldwide) concern and force changes in American law.

One type of civil disobedience was the sit-in. In 1960, four first-year African American students at North Carolina Agricultural and

Technical College in Greensboro sat down to eat at a white-only lunch counter at a local Woolworth's store. The African American waitress refused to serve them, saying that "fellows like you make our race look bad."[47] The four students sat at the lunch counter all afternoon and then returned the next day to continue their sit-in protest. Despite threats of violence, other students quickly joined the sit-in—by the sixth day of the protest, some 400 students showed up at Woolworth's. Others in the South, and later elsewhere, quickly emulated the Greensboro sit-in to protest segregation.[48]

The Greensboro sit-in inspired the "freedom rides" of the summer of 1961. Organized by the leaders of the Congress of Racial Equality (commonly referred to by its acronym, CORE, and at the time, a more militant civil rights organization than the NAACP), the freedom rides were intended to pressure government to desegregate public facilities such as bus stations. In May, two buses containing African American and white volunteers left Washington, D.C., to travel around the South, challenging local and state Jim Crow laws. Concentrating their initial efforts on Alabama, the "freedom riders," as they came to be called, met strong resistance; a mob in Birmingham beat them (the local police chief said that police could not protect them because it was Mother's Day and most police officers were off-duty visiting their mothers), and white supremacists in Anniston burned one of their buses. President Kennedy and his brother, Attorney General Robert Kennedy, responded to the violence by sending 600 federal marshals to protect the riders. Later that summer, the Interstate Commerce Commission (ICC) ordered the desegregation of all terminals used in interstate transportation.[49]

Another tactic the civil rights movement used to promote the cause of African American rights was the protest march. Sometimes the marches turned violent because police officers and segregationists attacked the protesters. In a 1963 march organized by Rev. King, more than 1,000 African American students marched to protest the segregation of public facilities in Birmingham, Alabama. Rather than ignore or arrest the demonstrators, Birmingham authorities doused them with water from high-pressure fire hoses and then unleashed police dogs on them. The following year in Selma, Alabama, King organized another march to demand that restrictions on African American voting rights be lifted. The march broke up when Alabama state troopers clubbed some marchers and segregationists beat and shot others.

In addition to practicing civil disobedience, the civil rights movement also worked within the law to promote the rights of African Americans. Many civil rights organizations launched efforts in the South to register African Americans to vote, calculating that if more African Americans voted, they could elect officials opposed to discriminatory laws. As with civil disobedience, however, their attempts to register African Americans to vote often made civil rights workers the targets of segregationist violence. For example, African American and white college students mounted a voter registration drive in Mississippi in the summer of 1964. By the end of the summer, eighty had been beaten, thirty-five shot, and at least six killed, including three who were apparently murdered with the help of a local sheriff and his deputy.[50]

As you can see, the people who took part in the civil rights protests of the early 1960s often did so at great personal risk. Yet the courage these protesters demonstrated helped to change public opinion—and ultimately the rules and policies that perpetuated legalized discrimination—throughout the United States. Many white Americans who initially believed that the protesters were asking for too much too soon found the violent attacks on demonstrators repulsive and concluded that segregation had to end.

5-2f Congress Responds

The *Brown* decision and the rise of the civil rights movement placed early pressure on Congress and President Eisenhower to enact stronger civil rights legislation. In 1957, Congress responded by passing the Civil Rights Act. From the viewpoint of substance, the bill accomplished little. Its major provision created a Civil Rights Commission, a nonpartisan and temporary body charged with investigating and documenting civil rights violations. From a symbolic viewpoint, however, the bill was tremendously important. It marked the first time in the twentieth century that a coalition of northern Democrats and Republicans had been able to overcome the adamant opposition of southern Democrats to civil rights legislation. Three years later, Congress passed another civil rights bill. Among other things, the Civil Rights Act of 1960 established criminal penalties for people who used the threat of force to obstruct federal court orders on civil rights matters. The rules were changing because the federal government responded to the steady pressure of the civil rights movement.

The Civil Rights Acts of 1957 and 1960 fell far short of guaranteeing African Americans their constitutional rights. But support among the American public for stronger civil rights legislation grew, especially in the wake of the television and newspaper photos of police dogs and fire hoses unleashed on demonstrators in Birmingham. Many members of Congress agreed it was time to take stronger action, including some not known for liberal views on matters of race; for example, as civil rights protests spread, the generally conservative Senate Minority Leader Everett Dirksen (R-IL) remarked that equality before the law was "an idea whose time had come."[51] The push for stronger civil rights legislation also gained momentum following the assassination of President Kennedy in November 1963. Not only did many in Congress regret not acting on a civil rights bill the slain president had introduced in Congress, but his successor, Lyndon Johnson, made civil rights his top legislative priority.

With strong backing from President Johnson, himself a southerner, Congress passed the **Civil Rights Act of 1964**. The landmark bill outlawed segregation in public accommodations such as theaters, restaurants, and motels, and it barred tax dollars from going

Civil Rights Act of 1964

An act of Congress that outlaws racial segregation in public accommodations and employment and prevents tax dollars from going to organizations that discriminate on the basis of race, color, or national origin.

to organizations that discriminated on the basis of race, color, or national origin. The act also made job discrimination illegal, and it created the Equal Employment Opportunity Commission (EEOC) to enforce fair employment policies. The Civil Rights Act of 1964 is by far the strongest piece of civil rights legislation ever passed. It gave African Americans and others who had been denied full rights greater opportunities to participate in the mainstream of American social and economic life.

Equal rights for all Americans were enhanced the following year with the passage of the **Voting Rights Act of 1965**. Although the Fifteenth Amendment was adopted to guarantee African Americans the right to vote, as we have seen and as Chapter 7 discusses further, many southern states adopted registration laws that made it difficult, if not impossible, for most African Americans to vote. The Voting Rights Act outlawed most registration and voting practices that discriminated against African Americans and other minorities. Perhaps even more important, it gave the Justice Department authority to review registration and voting laws in states in which less than 50 percent of the population was registered. During the following two decades, the Voting Rights Act led to a dramatic increase in the number of African Americans registered to vote. As the number of African American voters increased, so did the number of African Americans elected to political office, especially at the local level.[52] As Figure 5–1 shows, changes in registration and voting laws have had a real and profound effect on the political power of African American men and women.

Congress has passed other civil rights legislation since the mid-1960s, but none has matched the importance of the Civil Rights Act of 1964 and the Voting Rights Act of 1965. In 1968, Congress banned racial discrimination in housing, and in 1974 it outlawed discrimination in the extension of credit. The most recent civil rights bill, the Civil Rights Act of 1991, essentially clarified disputed provisions of previous legislation and expanded several interpretations of previous laws that the Supreme Court had narrowed. Of course, passing a law does not in itself root out discrimination. As much attention is now devoted to enforcing existing laws as to writing new ones.

Voting Rights Act of 1965
An act of Congress that bars states from creating voting and registration practices that discriminate against African Americans and other minorities.

5-2g The Continuing Fight against Discrimination

Have African Americans won their fight for equal rights under the law? As with many questions, the answer depends on one's vantage point and one's expectations.

In some respects, the change in race relations in the United States since the mid-twentieth century is nothing short of remarkable. In 1954, the year the Supreme Court handed down its decision in *Brown,* African Americans in many parts of the country were barred from attending school with whites, forced to ride in segregated buses, and effectively denied the right to vote. Moreover, African Americans were virtually absent from national political life. Fifty years later, racial discrimination is no longer legal; African

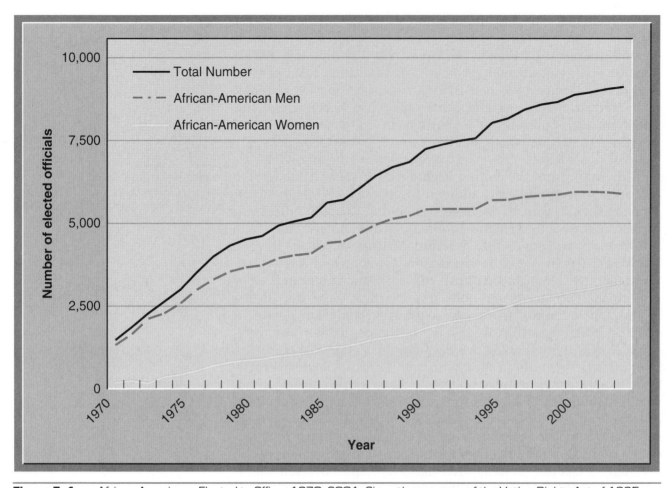

Figure 5-1      African Americans Elected to Office, 1970–2001. Since the passage of the Voting Rights Act of 1965, the number of African Americans, both men and women, elected to political office at the federal, state, and local levels has increased substantially.

Source: *Data from David Bositis, "Black Elected Officials: A Statistical Summary 2000," Joint Center for Political and Economic Studies, 2002.* www.jointcenter.org/publications_recent_publications/black_elected_officials/black_elected_officials_a_statistical_summary_2000

de facto segregation

Segregation that results from the actions of individuals rather than the government.

Americans serve prominently in Congress, the Supreme Court, and in 2008, the first African American was elected president.

Yet, if the United States has moved dramatically away from the segregated society it once was, it has by no means become a society in which, to borrow the famous words of the Rev. King's "I Have a Dream" speech, people are judged not "by the color of their skin, but by the content of their character."[53] Despite the fact that government-mandated segregation is illegal, **de facto segregation**—that is, segregation that results from the acts of individuals rather than the government—persists. For example, as Figure 5–2 shows, the average African American student attends a school where the majority of students are African Americans. Similarly, Hispanic American children go to schools where Hispanic Americans constitute a majority of the students. Substantial concerns about the use of racial profiling and police brutality continue to be raised by African Americans in many communities. Moreover, various measures of education, income, and health reveal that African Americans continue to lag behind white Americans. Indeed, as shown by differing evaluations of the government's response to

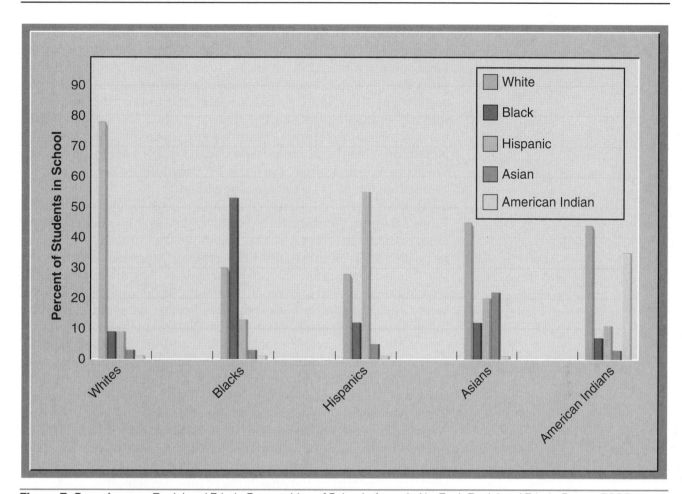

Figure 5–2   Average Racial and Ethnic Composition of Schools Attended by Each Racial and Ethnic Group, 2003–2004. Whites, African Americans, and Hispanic Americans typically attend schools where a majority of students are from their own group. Asian Americans attend the most integrated schools.

Source: *Data from Gary Orfield and Chungmei Lee, "Racial Transformation and the Changing Nature of Segregation," Harvard University, The Civil Rights Project, January 2006. www.civilrightsproject.ucla.edu/research/deseg/Racial_Transformation.pdf*

the plight of the victims of Hurricane Katrina in 2005, or the state of race relations in 2008, African Americans and white Americans seem at times almost to inhabit two very different United States.[54]

Thus, racial discrimination remains a potent issue in American politics, raising thorny political, legal, and moral questions. As we will discuss at greater length in this chapter, much debate surrounds the question of what steps the government may properly take to fight discrimination. This debate has been just as difficult for judges as it has been for elected officials. For example, ever since handing down its *Brown* decision, the Supreme Court has struggled with the question of how to achieve desegregated schools. For many years, the Court supported forced busing as a way to achieve school desegregation, but in recent years, it has moved to limit the practice.[55] The Court's change in direction in part reflects the public's backlash against busing and other remedial programs that are viewed as special treatment for African Americans, but it also reflects the tremendous difficulty the justices have in balancing the rights of African Americans (and other ethnic and racial minorities as well) against the rights of the white majority.

The complexity of many civil rights issues and the lack of easy answers helps to explain why the civil rights movement is not the force it once was in American politics. Most civil rights organizations have watched their memberships decline sharply since the early 1970s. The NAACP almost went bankrupt in 1995 amidst an internal squabble over charges that its leaders had engaged in financial mismanagement. Continuing management problems and a lack of organizational focus have caused the NAACP to lose both members and donations since then.[56] Meanwhile, Rev. King's organization, the SCLC, exists in name only.[57]

As traditional civil rights organizations seek to rejuvenate themselves, they are finding their claim to leadership challenged by other voices in the African American community. In some respects, this is nothing new. The African American community, like other communities in American society, has always harbored a wide range of views. Even at the height of the civil rights movement, Rev. King and other civil rights leaders were challenged on the one hand by conservative African Americans who argued that they were asking for too much too fast, and on the other hand by militant African Americans who argued that they were too eager to accept the rules of white society. Among the most important militants was Malcolm X, a leading member of the Nation of Islam (or Black Muslim faith), who called for creating a separate African American nation built apart from white society and paid for by white reparations for slavery.[58] Shortly before he was assassinated in 1965, Malcolm X left the Nation of Islam and modified his views on black separatism, admitting the possibility of interracial brotherhood.

Many of these same divisions remain in the African American community. Conservative African American intellectuals argue that many of the problems currently facing African Americans are rooted in the African American community itself and that most government programs designed to help African Americans perpetuate the problems rather than solve them.[59] Although recognizing that racism exists in the United States, conservative African Americans contend that African Americans must rely more on themselves and on the opportunities available to them. As the writer Shelby Steele puts it, "There is today, despite America's residual racism, an enormous range of opportunity open to blacks in this society. The nexus of this new [African American] identity must be a meeting of black individual initiative and American possibility."[60]

For their part, militants continue to advocate radical steps such as the creation of an independent African American nation separate from white America. The most prominent advocate of black separatism for many years has been Louis Farrakhan, the head of the Nation of Islam, though in recent years he has taken some steps toward the political mainstream. Farrakhan is an enormously controversial figure; his supporters hail him as an unbending defender of African American interests, and his critics denounce him as a racist and an anti-Semite. African Americans themselves are deeply divided over Farrakhan; a poll conducted in 1995 found that 41 percent of African Americans viewed him unfavorably, whereas 41 percent viewed him favorably.[61] Moreover, few African Americans believe that Farrakhan's views reflect what they think—the same 1995 poll found that only 14 percent of African Americans think he reflects the mainstream of African American thought. Nonetheless, Farrakhan successfully organized the Million Man March, which brought hundreds of thousands of African American men to Washington, D.C., in October 1995 to participate in the largest civil rights demonstration in American history. Even with that success, a 2000 survey reported that only 6 percent of African Americans considered him the leader "who best represents the interests of the black community today."[62] Moreover, where 12 percent of African Americans named Farrakhan the most important leader in the black community in 1995, less than 1 percent did by 2003.[63]

It remains to be seen whether traditional civil rights organizations will succeed in rejuvenating themselves to tackle the civil rights issues of the twenty-first century or whether they will cede their leadership of the African American community to other groups. However, no one can deny the successes that civil rights organizations achieved during the twentieth century in securing rule changes that protect the civil rights of African Americans. Moreover, these changes benefited many other minority groups in the United States in the years to follow.

5-3 DISCRIMINATION AGAINST ASIAN AMERICANS, HISPANIC AMERICANS, AMERICAN INDIANS, AND OTHERS

Although African Americans were the only group of Americans forced into slavery, Asian Americans, Hispanic Americans, and American Indians have also endured virulent racism, legal under our political rules for many years, that has denied them their political rights. The advances of the African American civil rights movement have benefited each of these groups, but their own unique histories give them somewhat different problems to solve. Each of their victories, whether in the courts or other political arenas, has improved not only their own prospects for gaining civil rights, but also the prospects of other groups.

5-3a Asian Americans

Like African Americans, Asian Americans have long endured official discrimination. A particular source of discrimination for many years was immigration policy, which, like the rules governing the rights of African Americans, has changed as American society has changed. For much of the nineteenth century, the United States had no immigration laws; indeed, the young nation openly welcomed immigrants. In the 1850s, many Chinese came to the United States to seek their fortunes in California's gold fields.

> But California law discriminated against them.... They were not allowed to work on the "Mother Lode." To work the "tailings" they

had to pay a "miner's tax," a $4-per-head so-called permissions tax, plus a $2 water tax. In addition, the Chinese had to pay a personal tax, a hospital tax, a $2 school tax, and a property tax. But they could not go to public school, they were denied citizenship, they could not vote, nor could they testify in court.[64]

Later, they and other Chinese who followed them to the United States worked in large numbers building railroads in the West. In the 1870s, railroad construction slowed, and as the competition for jobs increased, anti-Chinese sentiment and violence increased even more. In 1882, Congress passed the Exclusion Act, which barred all immigrants from China for ten years. Rather than diminish anti-Chinese violence, however, the law seemed only to fuel it. In 1892, Congress passed legislation that prohibited Chinese immigration indefinitely.[65]

American immigration policy also discriminated against immigrants from Japan. In 1890, the government of Japan allowed its citizens to emigrate for the first time, and by 1900, 24,000 Japanese immigrants had arrived in California.[66] Although Japanese immigrants constituted less than 2 percent of the state's population, anti-Japanese racism quickly surfaced, and the California state legislature began to consider proposals to restrict their rights. To head off legislation that he feared would damage the United States standing in Asia, President Theodore Roosevelt negotiated a "Gentleman's Agreement" with Japan in 1907. Under the terms of the agreement, Tokyo "voluntarily" agreed to restrict Japanese emigration to the United States.[67]

In 1921 and 1924, Congress formally changed the rules and revamped the country's immigration laws, this time by imposing a "national origins quota system" that limited the number of immigrants allowed into the United States from outside the Western Hemisphere. The quotas were tied to the percentage of each ethnic group already living in the United States, but people from Asia (and Africa) were barred from immigrating. In 1952, Congress relaxed the ban on immigration from some Asian countries, but it retained the national origins quota system. Despite the change, Asian immigrants continued to be penalized because Asian Americans constituted such a small share of the American population; hence, the number of Asians admitted into the United States was correspondingly small. Congress abolished the national origins quota system in 1968 and replaced it with a first-come, first-served system that gives preference to foreign relatives of American citizens and to people with special skills.

Once in the United States, immigrants from Asia often found themselves subjected to official discrimination. In 1913, the California state legislature passed a law that effectively barred Japanese immigrants—as well as immigrants from other Asian countries—from owning agricultural land in the state.[68] Racism was the motivating factor behind the law—state legislators railed against the prospect of interracial marriage, and the governor openly worried that the Japanese were "driving the root of their civilization deep in

California soil."[69] The state legislature had targeted land ownership because Japanese immigrants to California had been extraordinarily successful as farmers—by 1910, they accounted for 20 percent of the state's agricultural output.[70] Over the next ten years, more than half a dozen states would follow California's lead and pass laws barring Asian immigrants from owning land.[71]

Asian immigrants were vulnerable to discriminatory laws because American laws had long designated them, unlike immigrants from Europe, as "aliens ineligible to citizenship." (Children born in the United States of Asian immigrant parents were, however, considered American citizens.) In 1914, Takao Ozawa, a Japanese immigrant who had come to the United States as a student to learn about democracy, was turned down when he applied for citizenship. Ozawa, who had studied law at the University of California, prepared his own case, challenging the constitutionality of laws denying Asian immigrants the right to be naturalized—that is, to become American citizens. Ozawa's case wound its way through the legal system for eight years before finally reaching the Supreme Court. In a landmark decision, the Court held that immigrants from Asia could not become American citizens because the Constitution limited naturalization to "free white persons and to aliens of African nativity and persons of African descent."[72] Immigrants from Asia would remain ineligible for American citizenship until 1952, when Congress finally passed legislation removing all racial discrimination from the country's immigration laws.

Even when people of Asian ancestry held American citizenship because they had been born in the United States, they could not count on equal protection under the law. During World War II, President Franklin Roosevelt ordered the relocation of all people

Source: © AP/Wide World Photos

In the 1944 *Korematsu v. United States* decision, the Supreme Court upheld the government's right to imprison American citizens in internment camps, such as this one at Manzanar, California, solely because of their Japanese ancestry. In 1988, Congress formally apologized for these actions.

of Japanese ancestry living on the West Coast—most of whom were American citizens because Japanese immigration had long since ended—to detention camps. The government did not force Americans of German and Italian heritage to relocate.[73] The Supreme Court upheld the legality of the relocation order as well as several other directives that restricted the rights of people of Japanese ancestry. In its rulings, the Court gave much greater weight to the government's claims that Japanese Americans posed a potential risk to national security than to the internees' argument that the orders violated their civil rights.[74] Not until 1988 did Congress pass a law that formally apologized for the internment and provided financial compensation to the survivors.[75]

Although the legal system discriminated against Asian Americans until well into the twentieth century, they did on occasion win legal vindication. In one landmark civil rights case in 1886, for example, the Supreme Court overturned a San Francisco ordinance intended to prevent Chinese from operating laundries.[76] As rules protecting the rights of minority groups accumulated with the key civil rights decisions of the 1950s and the congressional legislation of the 1960s, Asian Americans gained a fuller measure of protection for their civil rights.

Like many other non-English-speaking minorities, Asian Americans have often faced discrimination because of their language. In the early 1970s, Chinese parents in San Francisco sued the local school district because it had failed to establish a program to help students who were not native English speakers to overcome the language barrier. The case eventually reached the Supreme Court, which agreed with the parents, concluding that the Civil Rights Act of 1964 required school districts to provide special assistance to Chinese-speaking students.[77] The basic principle behind the Court's ruling—that public schools should teach students in a language they can understand—has been extended to other non-English-speaking minority groups, including Hispanic Americans, Filipino Americans, and Vietnamese Americans. The result has been the rapid growth of bilingual education throughout the United States—a good example of how a change in rules can influence policy outcomes that affect everyday lives.

In recent years, Asian Americans have worried that because they have been so successful economically—as Chapter 3 discussed, Asian American households are on average the wealthiest in the United States—they are now subject to discrimination of a different sort. In 1994, for example, Chinese Americans in San Francisco filed suit against the city school district to overturn a court-ordered desegregation plan. That plan, which went into effect in 1983, defined nine racial groups among San Francisco's students and mandated that no group may compose more than 45 percent of the student body in any school. To maintain that balance, administrators had to shuffle students among schools. In one instance, the school district set different standards for members of various ethnic groups seeking admission to the city's premier high school. Thus, Chinese-American applicants had to score higher than whites, other Asian Americans, and students from the other six ethnic groups on the school's admissions test. The lawsuit the Chinese Americans filed challenged the legality of the school district's policy. In 1999, after a prolonged legal battle, the suit was settled out of court. It was agreed that race would no longer be used in assigning students to particular schools. Since the settlement, San Francisco schools have begun to resegregate.[78]

As we noted in Chapter 3, Asian Americans are, on average, better educated than other racial and ethnic groups. Their success in the classroom has led to charges of reverse discrimination that academic institutions limit the number of Asian American applicants they admit. In 2008, for example, the United States Department of Education investigated Princeton University for having denied admission to a Chinese-American student who scored the maximum on the SAT and came within ten points of the combined maximum score on his SAT2 subject tests in calculus, chemistry, and physics. (The student was also turned down by Stanford, MIT, and two other Ivy League universities.)[79] Yet, as we also pointed out in Chapter 3, Asian Americans should not be seen as a monolithic group. Although many Asian Indians and Pakistanis have done remarkably well in attaining higher education (64 percent of the former and 54 percent of the latter have at least a bachelor's degree), other groups, such as Cambodians, Hmong, Laotians, and Vietnamese still lag behind the national mean in educational achievement.[80]

5-3b Hispanic Americans

Like African Americans, many Hispanic Americans have been the victims of rules and policies that perpetuate discrimination. In states with large Hispanic populations, such as California and Texas, many Hispanic children were forced for many years to attend segregated schools. Like African Americans, Hispanic Americans had to turn to the courts to force desegregation.[81]

Many Hispanic Americans have also been discriminated against because they speak Spanish rather than English. This was long a particular problem at the ballot box because many states had laws requiring voters to pass an English literacy test. In 1966, the Supreme Court upheld the constitutionality of a provision of the Voting Rights Act of 1965 that outlawed such tests.[82] And as we saw as the result of a case involving Chinese Americans, school districts are now required to provide bilingual education programs to Hispanic American children.

Immigration issues affect many Hispanic Americans, especially those living in the Southwest. Hispanic Americans have applauded some court rulings on immigration matters. In 1971, for example, the Supreme Court ruled that legal residents—people living legally in the United States who are not citizens—are entitled to welfare benefits (a right that 1996 legislation significantly reduces), and eleven years later, it ruled that the children of illegal residents have the right to attend public schools.[83] Hispanic Americans have criticized other court rulings, however. Most notably, the Court has ruled that the federal government has broad powers to arrest and search illegal aliens.[84] Many Hispanic Americans worry that such power will be abused, and as a result, that the rights of Hispanic citizens will be violated.

The Hispanic community's concerns about immigration issues intensified in 1986 after Congress passed the Immigration Reform and Control Act, which among other things imposed substantial fines on employers who hire illegal residents. Many Hispanic Americans fear that employers will make it a rule not to hire any Hispanic, even if he or she is an American citizen or a legal resident, to avoid inadvertently violating the 1986 law. A 1996 law reinforced these concerns by making it harder to sue employers for discrimination in hiring. About two-thirds of Hispanics say that recent political battles over national immigration policy and the resulting state and local government efforts to crack down on illegal immigrants have made life more difficult for them in the United States.[85]

5-3c American Indians

American Indians have had a unique relationship with the federal government and have lived under a unique set of laws and rules. The Constitution did not grant them citizenship. Instead, for more than 100 years after the writing of the Constitution, the prevailing belief was that American Indian tribes constituted their own political communities separate from the United States. As a result, the federal government pushed American Indians onto reservations, the dimensions of which continually shrank as the United States enveloped and devoured their land.

The passage of the Civil War amendments did not change the relationship between American Indians and the federal government. In 1884, the Supreme Court ruled that American Indians were not citizens of the United States; hence, neither the Fourteenth nor Fifteenth Amendments applied to them.[86] In 1924 Congress passed the Indian Citizenship Act, which finally gave American Indians the right to vote. Despite passage of the act, however, some state laws effectively prevented American Indians from voting. For example, Arizona and New Mexico denied them the right to vote until 1948, and Utah did so until 1956.[87]

The success African Americans had in ending years of rules that allowed legalized discrimination also affected American Indians. In 1968, Congress passed the Indian Civil Rights Act, which finally extended most of the rights contained in the Bill of Rights to American Indians living on reservations. The 1960s also saw American Indians begin to emulate the tactics of the civil rights movement. They occupied government buildings, held sit-ins, and staged demonstrations to bring attention to discrimination against American Indians. In 1969, for example, several American Indian groups seized Alcatraz Island, an island in San Francisco Bay that was home to an abandoned federal prison. The groups argued that according to the terms of a treaty the American government had signed with the Sioux Nation in 1868, American Indians were entitled to all unused federal lands. Although the occupation lasted for nineteen months, it failed to produce significant changes in federal policy toward American Indians.

Sometimes protests by American Indians led to violence, as happened in 1973, when members of the American Indian Movement (AIM) seized hostages in the town of Wounded Knee, South Dakota, the site at which the American Cavalry had massacred more than 200 Sioux prisoners in 1890. The occupation lasted more than two months and left two members of AIM dead and one federal marshal seriously wounded. When the federal government agreed to review the implementation of treaties it had signed with American Indian tribes, the occupation ended.

In addition to engaging in civil disobedience, American Indians, like African Americans and other groups, have also turned to the courts for redress. A major objective of their litigation has been to force the federal government to abide by the terms of the many treaties it has signed with American Indian tribes. In a series of cases, American Indians have won the return of parts of their ancestral lands in the western United States. In other cases, the government has had to compensate them financially for their lost lands. In 1980, for example, the Supreme Court upheld the decision of a lower court to award the Sioux Nation $17.1 million plus interest as compensation for the government's seizure of the Black Hills of South Dakota a century previous.[88] American Indians have also won court cases that have forced the federal government as well as state governments to abide by treaty obligations that give them special hunting and fishing rights.

The idea that the United States and the American Indian community form separate nations persists. Many American Indians continue to live on reservations where tribal courts rather than state courts enforce tribal law. In 1987, the Supreme Court cited the special status of American Indians under American law in upholding the right of a California tribe to run a high-stakes bingo parlor without state regulation.[89] Congress responded to the Court's decision by passing the Indian Gaming Regulatory Act, which stipulates that if a state allows some form of gambling, American Indian tribes must be allowed to run their own gambling operations on tribal lands.[90] (The tribes must negotiate the precise details of the gambling operations with the government of the state where the tribal lands are located.) Many tribes have taken advantage of the Indian Gaming Regulatory Act to open casinos, thereby generating considerable revenue for tribal coffers. Despite this new influx of money, American Indians as a group remain among the poorest in the United States. Their unique political status and the unique rules that govern them have not benefited them socially or economically.

5-3d Other Minorities

Traditionally, the courts held that civil rights laws did not apply to members of white ethnic groups, such as Arab Americans, Irish

Americans, and Polish Americans. In 1987, however, the Supreme Court expanded the scope of minority groups that are protected by civil rights laws. In a case involving an Arab American who was denied tenure at a private college in Pennsylvania, a unanimous Supreme Court ruled that the Civil Rights Act of 1866 protects members of all minority groups against a wide range of discriminatory acts.[91] As a result of the Court's ruling, members of any ethnic group can now sue if they believe they have been discriminated against in violation of the law on the basis of their race or ethnicity. If they can establish that the law has been broken, the courts can award them monetary damages.

5-4 DISCRIMINATION AGAINST WOMEN

Although women constitute slightly more than half the population in the United States, the rules set forth in the Constitution originally did not guarantee them political rights. For more than 100 years, women were denied the right to vote and were discriminated against in many other ways as well. For example, in 1873 the Supreme Court upheld a decision by the Illinois state supreme court to reject a woman's application for a license to practice law simply because of her sex.[92] A few decades later, the Court held that Oregon could set the maximum number of hours a woman could work (noting "that a woman's physical structure and the performance of maternal functions place her at a disadvantage") and that New York could bar women from working as waitresses at night (though the state allowed them to work as entertainers).[93]

The Supreme Court's rulings in these and other cases were based on a belief widely shared in American society in the nineteenth and for much of the twentieth century: Women are a weaker sex that men need to protect. The Court made its views on the proper place of women explicit when it upheld the Illinois law denying women the right to practice law:

> Man is, or should be, woman's protector and defender. The natural and proper timidity and delicacy which belongs to the female sex evidently unfits it for many of the occupations of civil life. The constitution of the family organization, which is founded in the divine ordinance, as well as in the nature of things, indicates the domestic as that which properly belongs to the domain and functions of womanhood. The harmony . . . of interests and views which belong, or should belong, to the family institution is repugnant to the idea of a woman adopting a distinct and independent career from that of her husband. . . .
>
> . . .The paramount destiny and mission of woman are to fulfill the noble and benign offices of wife and mother. This is the law of the Creator.[94]

In keeping with this line of thinking, laws were designed both to protect women from activities believed harmful to them and to keep them from breaking out of the roles society deemed proper for them.

For more than 100 years, women's rights activists have challenged the idea that women need the protection of men and have fought to repeal laws that endorse sex discrimination. The focus of their efforts, though, has changed over time. Throughout the nineteenth century and during the first two decades of the twentieth century, the women's movement focused on securing the right to vote. Since the rebirth of the women's movement in the 1960s, women's rights activists have focused on eliminating discriminatory laws and practices. The women's movement has had many successes, first on Capitol Hill and then in the courts. As a result of these victories, women now play a more prominent role in American economic and political life.

5-4a Campaigning for the Right to Vote

The **women's movement**—the effort to guarantee equal rights for women—first surfaced on a national scale in 1848, when Elizabeth Cady Stanton and Lucretia Mott organized the first women's rights convention in Seneca Falls, New York. The convention delegates endorsed a manifesto written by Stanton that catalogued a long list of "injuries and usurpations" men had inflicted on women. Borrowing heavily from the language of the Declaration of Independence, this Declaration of Sentiments proclaimed:

women's movement
The mobilization of people to push for equality between the sexes.

> We hold these truths to be self-evident: that all men and women are created equal; that they are endowed by their Creator with certain inalienable rights, that among these are life, liberty, and the pursuit of happiness; that to secure these rights governments are instituted, deriving their just powers from the consent of the governed. Whenever any form of government becomes destructive of these ends, it is the right of those who suffer from it to refuse allegiance to it, and to insist upon the institution of a new government, laying its foundation on such principles, and organizing its powers in such form as to them shall seem most likely to effect their safety and happiness....
>
> Now, in view of this entire disenfranchisement of one-half of the people of this country, their social and religious degradation—in view of the unjust laws ... and because women do feel themselves aggrieved, oppressed, and fraudulently deprived of their most sacred rights, we insist that they have immediate admission to all the rights and privileges which belong to them as citizens of the United States.[95]

The women's movement met with at best mixed success in the first two decades after the Seneca Falls convention. For example, the state of New York passed several laws allowing women to own property and to enter into contracts as well as to guarantee them shares of their husbands' estates. By the beginning of the Civil War, however, most of these laws had been modified or repealed under pressure from men who opposed expanding the rights of women.[96] Likewise, in 1861, Kansas became the first state to give women the right to vote in elections involving local schools, but it would be many years before more than a handful of states would follow Kansas's lead.[97]

Following the Civil War, women's groups allied themselves with the movement to give African Americans the right to vote, hoping that women would attain the same right as well. This hope came to naught, however. The Fourteenth Amendment introduced the word *male* into the Constitution for the first time, and it explicitly spoke of the right to vote as a right belonging to men. Meanwhile, the Fifteenth Amendment guaranteed the right to vote regardless of "race, color, or previous condition of servitude," but it made no mention of sex.

Disappointed with the results of their alliance with the movement to recognize the rights of African Americans, women's rights activists formed their own organizations to push for the extension of **suffrage**, or the right to vote, to women (see Box 5–2). The first success came in 1869, when the Wyoming Territory gave women full suffrage. The Utah Territory followed suit the next year. Victories were in short supply during the next four decades, however, and by the end of 1910, only five states (Colorado, Idaho, Utah, Washington, and Wyoming) had given women the right to vote. The movement for women's suffrage gained steam throughout the next half dozen years—as women's rights activists repeatedly picketed the White House and Congress—and by 1918, fifteen states had given women the right to vote. Finally, in 1919 Congress passed a constitutional amendment giving women the right to vote, and in 1920, the states ratified the Nineteenth Amendment. The constitutional rules on suffrage were finally extended to the female half of the American population. As both women and African Americans discovered, though, securing the right to vote was merely a first step in the fight for civil rights.

5-4b The Fight for Equal Rights on Capitol Hill

The passage of the Nineteenth Amendment gave women the right to vote, but it did not eliminate laws and social practices that discriminated against them. Yet for several decades the women's movement lay dormant, partly because some groups were satisfied with having won the right to vote and partly because other groups argued over the movement's proper objectives and tactics.

The women's movement reemerged in the 1960s. Betty Friedan's immensely influential book, *The Feminine Mystique,* prompted many women to begin to question how society allocated roles according to sex. The actions of the civil rights movement also provided a powerful example to emulate. In 1966, a group of professional women founded the National Organization for Women (NOW) with Friedan as their first president. NOW dedicated itself to winning equal rights for women (see Box 5–2).

Unlike the civil rights movement, the women's movement won its first major victories on Capitol Hill rather than in court. For decades, women had worked alongside men in many occupations, often performing the same work for less pay. With the **Equal Pay Act of 1963**, Congress recognized the equal-pay-for-equal-work movement by banning wage discrimination based on sex as well as race religion, and national origin. The initial impact of the Equal Pay Act was limited, however, because it required equal pay only

suffrage
The right to vote.

Equal Pay Act of 1963
An act of Congress that banned wage discrimination based on sex, race, religion, and national origin.

Although the Constitution is frequently hailed for guaranteeing individual rights, as originally written, it denied equal rights to women. As the work of the woman suffrage movement and the National Organization for Women (NOW) both illustrate, for more than 100 years, women's rights activists have fought to ensure that our fundamental rules of government extend equal rights to women as well as to men.

THE WOMAN SUFFRAGE MOVEMENT

The Constitution as it was written in 1789 did not grant women the right to vote. In 1869, two organizations formed to lobby for a change in the rules: the extension of suffrage (the right to vote) to women. These two organizations were the National Woman Suffrage Association (NWSA) and the American Woman Suffrage Association (AWSA).

The two groups had different philosophies. NWSA was the more militant; it sought to win passage of a federal amendment giving women the right to vote and to advance women's rights more generally. In contrast, AWSA worked solely on suffrage issues, and it concentrated its efforts on the state level. AWSA won its first major victory in 1890, when Wyoming's admission to the Union made it the first state to give women the right to vote.

In 1890, NWSA and AWSA finally joined ranks, creating the National American Woman Suffrage Association (NAWSA). The new organization lobbied both federal and state governments. By 1912, NAWSA had more than 75,000 members, and it had persuaded nine states to give women the right to vote. NAWSA gained more momentum when the Woman's Christian Temperance Union, a conservative group with great influence in the South, began to advocate woman suffrage.

The turning point for the cause of woman suffrage came with the American entry into World War I. When President Woodrow Wilson said the United States would make the "world safe for democracy," NAWSA demanded that he begin at home by giving women the right to vote. Under growing public pressure to live up to his rhetoric, Wilson abandoned his opposition to woman suffrage. In the meantime, NAWSA's persistent efforts to influence congressional elections had paid off by producing a pro-suffragist Congress.

NAWSA finally achieved its goal in 1920 after Congress passed and the states ratified the Nineteenth Amendment. With its primary objective accomplished, NAWSA formally disbanded. Much of its membership was absorbed into a new organization dedicated to educating women about their new political responsibilities, the League of Women Voters.

NATIONAL ORGANIZATION FOR WOMEN

Despite the successes of NAWSA, when NOW was founded in 1966, American women were in many ways second-class citizens. Airlines could fire stewardesses simply for gaining weight or marrying, newspapers had separate listings for male and female jobs, and almost no women held political office. The founding members of NOW resolved at their first meeting to take all necessary "action to bring women into full participation of American society now."

During the next quarter century, NOW fulfilled its vow to push women's issues to the forefront of the political debate and to rewrite the rules of the political game in ways that broadened the freedom of women. NOW no longer dominates the women's movement as it once did. Its very success inspired the formation of many other women's groups, including groups such as Concerned Women for America that oppose NOW on almost every issue. However, NOW's 500,000 members and 550 chapters still make it the largest feminist organization in the United States.

NOW has fought legislative battles on a wide range of issues, including abortion rights, paid maternity leave, and more vigorous enforcement of civil rights. But NOW is most closely associated with efforts to make the Equal Rights Amendment (ERA) a part of the Constitution. Congress passed the ERA in 1972. When it appeared in 1978 that the required three-fourths of the states would not ratify the ERA within the seven-year time limit set by law, NOW persuaded Congress to extend the ratification period for another three years. Despite the extension, the proposed constitutional amendment expired on June 30, 1982, without being ratified.

Conservative critics regularly denounce NOW as a militant fringe group. Although attacks from the right are to be expected, NOW also draws criticism from other groups in the women's movement. They complain that NOW is too enamored with its rhetoric and too busy fighting old battles to recognize that new problems face women at the beginning of the twenty-first century. Even Betty Friedan, the first president of NOW, argues that the organization has "too narrow a focus."

A few years ago Patricia Ireland, then president of NOW, was unbowed in the face of the organization's critics. "We lead public opinion, we do not follow it. That's who we are. Sure, it has its down side. Taking a leadership position makes people uncomfortable. But my ultimate value isn't comfort. My ultimate value is progress for women." Along similar lines, Ireland's successor as NOW president, Kim Gandy, recently observed of the group's detractors, "They've been writing headlines about the death of feminism since the '70s. It's a lot of wishful thinking on their part." And many women do rally to NOW's causes. Participation in NOW's 2004 March for Women's Lives in Washington, D.C., was estimated at upward of one million.

Sources: "Now a Tough Political Time, Feminists Say," *Columbia Daily Tribune,* January 16, 2005; Jane Gross, "Does She Speak for Today's Women?" *New York Times Magazine,* March 1, 1992; L. Sandy Maisel, ed., *Political Parties and Elections in the United States: An Encyclopedia* (New York: Garland Publishing, 1991); Edward L. Schapsmeier and Frederick H. Schapsmeier, *Political Parties and Civic Action Groups* (Westport, CT: Greenwood Press, 1981); National Organization for Women, "NOW History," and "How Many Members Does NOW Currently Have?" www.now.org/organization/faq.html#member

for substantially equivalent jobs rather than those merely comparable. As a result, employers had considerable freedom to classify positions in ways that kept women in lower-paying jobs. Moreover, state laws and employer practices that barred women from holding jobs that might expose them to physical danger or to toxic substances remained legal.

A more important victory in the cause of equal rights for women came with the passage of the Civil Rights Act of 1964. Although the primary purpose of the act was to guarantee the civil rights of African Americans, it included a section prohibiting job discrimination on the basis of sex. Ironically, the provision was to have been introduced by Rep. Martha Griffiths (D-MI), but she strategically deferred to Rep. Howard Smith (D-VA), an opponent of equal rights for African Americans. Rep. Smith sponsored the provision prohibiting job discrimination on the basis of sex because he believed that the prospect of extending civil rights protection to women would make the entire civil rights bill unacceptable to his male colleagues. Much to Smith's surprise and to Griffiths's delight, the House passed the amendment, and it became law.[98]

In the 1970s, Congress passed several other pieces of legislation that the women's movement favored. Title IX of the 1972 Higher Education Act bars colleges and universities that receive federal funds from discriminating on the basis of sex. Title IX has been a prominent issue on the nation's sports pages in recent years because it has been used to gain equal standing for women's collegiate athletic programs. The Equal Opportunity Credit Act of 1974 prohibits financial companies from discriminating on the basis of sex or marital status when lending money or issuing credit cards. This act removed most of the legal barriers that had traditionally made it very difficult for women to borrow money in their own name. Finally, in 1978 Congress enacted legislation that prohibits job discrimination against pregnant women.

The women's movement had renewed legislative success following Bill Clinton's election in 1992, which restored control of both the White House and Capitol Hill to the Democrats for the first time in a dozen years. In 1993, Congress passed the Family and Medical Leave Act. This law requires employers to give eligible employees up to twelve weeks of unpaid leave each year if the employee or the employee's spouse has a baby, or if the employee or a family member becomes seriously ill.[99] In 1994, Congress passed the Violence Against Women Act. This law contains a variety of provisions designed to punish domestic violence and other attacks against women, to help women who have been victims of violence, and to prevent violence in the future. The most controversial provision of the law holds that anyone who commits a violent crime motivated by sex bias is guilty of a federal civil rights violation and that the victim of such an attack can sue his or her attacker for damages.[100] Critics of the provision—which applies to both sexes but was primarily intended to protect female crime victims—argued that it would overwhelm the federal courts with domestic abuse cases better handled by state courts. During its first two years in operation, however, relatively few cases were filed under the Violence Against Women Act. In 2000, however, the Supreme Court held that Congress had overstepped its powers in the Violence Against Women Act when it granted rape victims the right to sue their attackers.[101] But that same year Congress strengthened the original act when it passed the Violence Against Women Act of 2000. That Act was reauthorized in 2006.

Although the women's movement has enjoyed great success on Capitol Hill, it has fallen short of its goals in the state legislatures. In 1972 Congress passed the Equal Rights Amendment (ERA), which simply stated: "Equality of rights under the law shall not be denied or abridged by the United States or by any state on account of sex." Within a few years, thirty-five states had ratified the amendment. Despite the considerable political efforts of NOW and other groups in the women's movement, the ERA failed to win the approval of the three additional states needed for the amendment to enter into force. The ERA died largely because conservative women's groups mobilized to defeat it.

Although the effort to pass a national equal rights amendment failed, twenty states include an equal rights provision in their state constitution.[102] In recent years, however, supporters of the ERA have failed to make additional headway on the state level. In 1992, for example, voters in Iowa rejected a proposal to add an equal rights amendment to their state constitution. (In 1998, however, Iowans voted overwhelmingly to add the phrase "and women" to the state constitution section on the rights of persons.) Despite the failure of the ERA, its opponents and supporters agree that many, though not all, of its intended benefits already have been achieved through legislation, and judicial decisions that have rewritten the rules to prohibit many types of sex discrimination.

5-4c The Fight for Equal Rights in the Courts

The courts were relatively slow to join the fight against sex discrimination. It was not until 1971 that the Supreme Court first struck down a law on the grounds that it discriminated against women.[103] The case in question involved an Idaho law that mandated that a man should always be chosen before an equally qualified woman to be the executor of a will. The law's intent was to limit the need to hold hearings on who should be the executor. In invalidating Idaho's law, the Court ruled that giving a "mandatory preference to either sex over members of the other, merely to accomplish the elimination of hearings on the merits, is to make the very kind of arbitrary legislative choice forbidden by the equal protection clause of the Fourteenth Amendment."[104]

The Supreme Court followed its 1971 ruling with a string of decisions that outlawed different classes of sex discrimination. Many of these rulings affect the treatment of women in the workplace. For example, newspapers cannot designate jobs listed in help-wanted ads as *male* and *female*.[105] Companies cannot refuse to hire mothers because they fear these women will need to take time off to take care of their children, and they cannot force pregnant women to take maternity leave or punish women who do take maternity leave.[106] Companies cannot force women to pay more into their pension plans each month while they are working or pay them less out of their pension plans each month after they retire simply because they are likely to live longer than male employees.[107] And companies cannot bar women of childbearing age from working in jobs that might render them infertile or harm their fetus should they become pregnant.[108] In this latter case, the Court demonstrated unequivocally that it had shed the once-dominant notion that the law has a special obligation to protect women from dangers to their well-being. Other Supreme Court rulings affect how government treats women. For example, in 1996, the Court ruled that states cannot maintain all-male colleges.[109]

In applying the principle of equality between the sexes, the Supreme Court has thrown out several laws that discriminate against men. In a 1976 case, the Court held that an Oklahoma law that required women to be at least eighteen to buy beer but required men to be at least twenty-one was unconstitutional.[110] In 1979, the Court struck down an Alabama law that barred men from suing for alimony in a divorce, and in 1982, it struck down a Mississippi law that barred men from attending a state nursing school.[111]

Although the Supreme Court has struck down many laws that discriminate on the basis of sex, it has held that discrimination is legal in some areas. For example, the Court has upheld the law that requires men but not women to register for the military draft.[112] Laws for statutory rape that apply to men need not apply to women.[113] The government can give property tax exemptions to widows that it does not give to widowers, and it can treat men and women differently when allocating Social Security benefits.[114] Government agencies and private employers may take sex into account in certain hiring and promotion decisions.[115] And in 2007, the Supreme Court made it much more difficult for women to sue over discriminatory pay.[116] (In early 2009, Congress passed legislation effectively overturning the Court's decision.) The general trend, however, has been to remove sex-based distinctions from the law.

5-4d The Continuing Struggle against Sex Discrimination

We noted that the civil rights movement has achieved substantial but by no means complete success in ensuring that African Americans enjoy an equal place in American society. The same may be said about the women's movement. Today, as a result of changes in the rules of American politics, American women enjoy more equality than ever before, but in many areas their opportunities continue to lag behind those of men.

On the positive side, women have broken into fields that for many years were denied to them. This has been especially true in the political arena. Women now play a prominent role as lobbyists (see Chapter 10), members of Congress (see Chapter 11), Supreme Court justices (see Chapter 14), and governors and state legislators (see Chapter 15). Women also hold important positions in the federal bureaucracy, both as political appointees and as members of the civil service. For example, women now constitute 27 percent of the members of the federal government's Senior Executive Service, the highest-level management positions.[117]

Women have also made impressive gains in gaining access to education. All-male colleges have all but disappeared, and women now attend prestigious undergraduate schools such as Ivy League colleges and the U.S. military academies. Women have made similar gains in graduate education. For example, as late as 1971, women constituted only 9 percent of law school students; in 1992, the figure reached 50 percent, before falling slightly to 47 percent by 2007.[118] As a result of greater access to education, women have made rapid inroads into high-paying and traditionally male-dominated professions such as law and medicine. For example, the percentage of female lawyers has grown steadily since the mid-1970s; now women constitute 44 percent of all associates, 17 percent of all partners in law firms, and 17 percent of general counsel positions in Fortune 500 corporations.[119] Women currently account for 24 percent of all physicians, and in 2004, they earned 47 percent of all the doctorates given in the biological and biomedical sciences.[120]

Finally, women have made great strides as entrepreneurs. Since the mid-1970s, the number of female-owned businesses has tripled. In 2006, women owned an estimated 10.4 million businesses, employing 12.8 million people and generating sales of $1.9 trillion. The number of women-owned businesses grew at a much faster rate between 1997 and 2006 than private businesses in general. Women have also climbed the corporate ladder. In 1980, none of the Fortune 100's top corporate executives were women; by 2003, 6 percent were and their pay was virtually identical to that of their male counterparts. And women held 15 percent of the corporate board of director seats for the Fortune 500 companies in 2005, up from 10 percent in 1995. The growing number of female-owned businesses has led to the formation of groups, such as the National Association of Women Business Owners, that are dedicated to translating women's increased economic power into increased political power.[121]

On the negative side, however, women are still underrepresented in government and in corporate workplaces as a percentage of their share of the American population. For example, although slightly more than one in every two Americans is a woman, in 2008, only about one in seven members of Congress was a woman. Similarly, women account for only one of the nine Supreme Court justices and just 24 percent of all federal court judges.[122] And, of course, no woman has yet been elected president or vice president. Things aren't much better at the upper echelons of America's colleges and universities. In law schools in the United States, for example, women constitute only 20 percent of the deans and 35 percent of the faculty.[123]

In the private sector, women who enter the labor force often find themselves shunted into low-paying jobs, such as secretaries, maids, and child-care workers, that have traditionally been held

by women. When women take a professional job, they often encounter an invisible "glass ceiling" that limits their ability to rise
to the top of the corporate ladder. For example, a federal commission reported in 1995 that even though women make up almost
one-half of the American workforce, they hold just 5 percent of senior management jobs. (Women have had more success obtaining
middle management jobs such as assistant vice president and office
manager; women now hold roughly 45 percent of these slots.) Five
years later, another report found that women managers in ten major
industries had made scant progress.[124] Moreover, as women climb
through the corporate ranks, they frequently find they are rewarded
less handsomely than men are. For example, national surveys show
that women who work as lawyers for Fortune 500 companies earn
"less than their male counterparts at every level of seniority, with
pay gaps that range as high as 35 percent," a discrepancy that also
appeared between the pay of high-ranking men and women in a
study of 1,500 major companies.[125] Similarly, women's pay on Wall
Street and among lawyers has been found to lag that of men with
comparable characteristics.[126]

In light of the hardships women continue to confront in the
workplace, women's rights activists continue to push for new rules
of government that will redress inequalities between the sexes. But
what the precise problems are and what steps the government
should take are matters of considerable controversy. For example,
sexism is only one possible explanation for why women on average earn only 77 percent of what men make (which is up from 59
percent in 1963).[127] Because many women take lower-paying jobs
such as child-care provider or school teacher, suspend their
schooling or careers to have and raise children, or choose not to
enter the workforce at all, women's average earnings may never
match those of men and the percentage of women in senior management positions may never mirror the percentage of women in
the population. Moreover, as we have seen in this chapter and in
Chapter 3 many of the differences between men and women in the
workplace have narrowed over the years. This suggests that, with
time, many of the inequalities in today's workplace will diminish
further. For example, one reason we see so few women in senior
management jobs today may be that for many years women could
not rise to middle management jobs. Now that so many women
hold middle management positions, the number of women in senior management positions is likely to increase in the future.
Indeed, with women forging ahead of men in getting college
degrees, as discussed in Chapter 3, recent data have revealed that
young women living in New York and other major cities are earning higher salaries than young men in the same locales.[128] Still,
although the wage gap may be narrowing in the near term, it is not
apt to disappear altogether.[129]

The debate over what to do to promote equality between the
sexes is further complicated by disagreements, even among
women, over what constitutes impermissible sexual discrimination and what government should do about it. Much as we saw in

our discussion of the African American community, women disagree among themselves over the nature of the problems they face and the proper solutions. Take, for example, the issue of pornography. Feminists such as law school professor Catharine MacKinnon argue that pornography exploits women and denies them the equal protection promised by the Fourteenth Amendment. As a result, they argue on civil rights grounds that the First Amendment should not be interpreted to protect "sexually explicit materials that subordinate women through pictures or words."[130] In contrast, other feminists, such as Nadine Strossen, the president of the American Civil Liberties Union (ACLU), argue that censorship, not pornography, poses the greater danger to women's rights.[131] These feminists oppose any effort to narrow the protections the First Amendment provides.

At the same time, some women are highly critical of some of the goals the women's movement has sought to accomplish.[132] Groups such as Concerned Women for America and the Independent Women's Forum reject policies such as affirmative action and sex equity in education as unfair, misdirected, and counterproductive.[133] Moreover, these groups, which many women support, argue that if the cause of equal rights is pushed too far, women will suffer rather than benefit. For example, they argue that pure equality would deprive women of important protections in divorce proceedings and child custody cases. As a result of these divergent views on what is best for women, the question of how far the rules of government should go to promote women's rights will remain a hotly debated topic for years to come.

5-5 EXTENDING CIVIL RIGHTS

Since the 1970s, many groups have pressed federal and state governments to recognize their status as victims of discrimination and to recognize and protect their civil rights. Three groups in particular stand out: (1) people with disabilities, (2) people with age claims, and (3) gays and lesbians. The push to extend civil rights to new groups poses a particular problem for the Supreme Court, which must decide at what point a discriminatory law becomes unconstitutional. To help it decide, the Court has developed a set of rules for determining who bears the burden of showing that a discriminatory law fails to pass constitutional muster.

5-5a People with Disabilities

In recent years, people with physical or mental disabilities have appealed to Congress and the Supreme Court for recognition and guarantees of their civil rights. They have met with some success in advancing their cause, although more through congressional action than court decisions. In 1968, Congress passed the Architectural Barriers Act, which required buildings built with federal funds to be accessible to persons with physical difficulties. In

Americans with Disabilities Act of 1990
An act of Congress that seeks to minimize job discrimination, maximize access to government programs, and ensure access to public accommodations for people with disabilities.

addition, several other pieces of legislation in the 1970s and 1980s attempted to make public transportation more accessible to people with physical disabilities.[134]

The most significant legislation advancing the rights of people with disabilities is the **Americans with Disabilities Act (ADA) of 1990**. The ADA is a comprehensive bill that seeks to minimize job discrimination, maximize access to government programs, and ensure access to public accommodations such as hotels, restaurants, and museums. This legislation is a good example of government taking a positive step to ensure equal rights. But unlike the Civil Rights Act of 1964, which stipulates that racial discrimination must be eliminated regardless of cost, the ADA allows cost to be considered in the search for a remedy when people with disabilities face discrimination. This compromise is meant to balance the right of persons with disabilities to gain access to a building or facility against the right of a business owner to avoid unreasonable costs. For example, under the ADA, "restaurants do not have to provide menus in Braille; waiters can read them to blind customers."[135]

Experience with the ADA shows that it has not led to the explosion of lawsuits that some opponents feared. The EEOC, for example, resolved 236,724 ADA complaints from 1992 to 2007, an average of slightly less than 17,000 cases annually. Moreover, those bringing the ADA claims were successful in only 19 percent of the cases.[136] Still, concerns about the scope of the legislation arise occasionally as new groups push for coverage under the ADA's provisions. For example, activists on behalf of Multiple Chemical Sensitivity sufferers—people who say that various scents, odors, and chemicals make them ill—have been pushing to have their ailments covered even though little scientific evidence supports the existence of their condition.[137] Initially, their concerns were not taken seriously.[138] However, in recent years public policy has shifted a bit in their favor. One 2007 analysis reported at least 18 court cases alleging perfume sensitivities under the ADA and a few of the decisions found for the complainant.[139] The United States Department of Labor's Office of Disability Employment Policy has even gone so far as to issue a pamphlet on how to accommodate Multiple Chemical Sensitivity sufferers in the workplace.[140] Indeed, in 2008, Congress was considering legislation to substantially broaden the population covered by the ADA, partly in response to a series of Supreme Court decisions that had narrowed coverage.[141]

5-5b People with Age Claims

Another class of people occasionally seeking civil rights guarantees is people of certain ages. Older Americans have been the most successful in this regard; they have gained substantial protection from discrimination, again more because of acts of Congress (responding, no doubt, to the political pressures older Americans can bring to bear in the voting booth) than from the courts. In 1967, Congress passed the Age Discrimination in Employment Act, which bars job discrimination based on age. The Age Discrimination Act of 1975 extended protection against age discrimination to any program receiving federal money. And Congress has also made mandatory retirement ages illegal in most circumstances, though the Supreme Court has upheld them in certain job categories in which convincing cases can be made that older people as a class are less able to perform the required work.[142]

Younger people have had less success in overturning laws that discriminate against them. States have passed and the courts have upheld a wide variety of laws that discriminate against the young, including drinking laws, driving laws, parental consent requirements for contracts, marriage laws, and in some states, abortion laws. And in 2004, the Supreme Court in *General Dynamics Land Systems v. Clines,* held that retirement health benefit plans can be changed in ways that disfavor younger workers without violating age discrimination laws. Thus, such laws protect older workers from discriminatory acts, not younger workers.[143] In 2005, the Court allowed older workers claiming discrimination to demonstrate only that a company's policies had a "disparate impact," and not the harder-to-prove standard that it acted with "discriminatory intent."[144] Another Court decision in 2008 placed the burden on employers to prove that actions against workers were based on "reasonable factors other than age."[145] The one major success younger Americans won came in 1971, when the states ratified the Twenty-Sixth Amendment, which lowered the minimum voting age to eighteen.

5-5c Gays and Lesbians

In June 1969, homosexual patrons of the Stonewall bar in New York City finally tired of police harassment and fought back. What became known as the Stonewall riots resulted in the mobilization of a previously unorganized group and gave birth to the modern gay rights movement. In the years since Stonewall, gay rights organizations have pressed to extend civil rights laws that protect other groups to cover gays and lesbians. Although the movement has enjoyed some success at the state and local levels, it has won few victories at the national level.

President Clinton showed some sympathy for gay rights, but Congress was reluctant to follow his lead. During the 1992 presidential campaign, for example, Clinton pledged that if elected, he would overturn the Defense Department policy that banned gays and lesbians from serving openly in the military. Following the election, members of Congress, officials in the Defense Department, and leaders of conservative interest groups attacked Clinton's pledge. After a bitter political fight, Congress passed legislation that relaxed the military's policy of discriminating against gays and lesbians only slightly. Under the "Don't Ask, Don't Tell, Don't Pursue" policy, the military is barred from asking soldiers about their sexual orientation and from initiating inquiries into the subject, but gay and lesbian soldiers are allowed to remain in the armed forces only if they do not reveal their sexual orientation to other members of the military. The constitutionality of the Don't Ask, Don't Tell, Don't Pursue policy has been challenged in court, but thus far, no court has struck it down.

Since its adoption, some 12,500 service members have been forced to leave the service. Among them were fifty-five Arab language specialists and nine Farsi linguists. A 2005 Government Accountability Office report found that almost 800 mission specialists had been required to leave military service because of Don't Ask, Don't Tell. The policy is estimated to have kept an additional 45,000 people from either joining the military or extending their enlistments.[146] Public opinion appears to be turning against the policy. In 1993, only 44 percent of Americans supported allowing homosexuals to serve openly in the armed forces. By 2008 that number had increased dramatically to 75 percent.[147]

In 1995, President Clinton became the first president to publicly endorse gay rights legislation when he endorsed a legislative proposal known as the Employment Non-Discrimination Act. In writing to Senator Ted Kennedy (D-MA) in support of the bill, Clinton noted that "discrimination in employment on the basis of sexual orientation is currently legal in forty-one states. This is wrong."[148] Despite President Clinton's support, the Employment Non-Discrimination Act never became law while he was in office. Indeed, efforts to get the measure passed were still being made in 2008. In May 1998, President Clinton issued an executive order banning discrimination against employees in the executive branch of the federal government on the basis of their sexual orientation. A vote in the Republican-controlled House a few months later to overturn President Clinton's executive order was defeated by a vote of 252 to 176. This was the first time the House had voted to support a policy protecting against discrimination based on sexual orientation.

Although Congress and the president have argued over whether gays and lesbians merit civil rights protection, the Supreme Court has not recognized any special standing for gay rights. As we discussed in Chapter 3, in a 1986 case involving the right to privacy, the Court upheld a Georgia law outlawing sodomy. (The man who had been arrested under the sodomy statute had not been prosecuted for the crime—no one had been for years—but he chose to pursue the case to have the law declared unconstitutional.) A majority of the justices concluded that the right to privacy does not extend to consensual homosexual sex because the Court recognizes fundamental rights only when they are based on values "deeply rooted in this Nation's history and tradition." The claim that the right to privacy extended to homosexual sex failed to meet this standard because "proscriptions against [sodomy] have ancient roots." Many observers took the Court's decision in this civil liberties case to mean that the justices were unlikely to rule that gays and lesbians enjoy the civil rights protections that some other groups, such as African Americans and women, enjoy. Indeed, in 2000 the Court handed down a decision allowing the Boy Scouts of America to ban gay members, holding that the First

Amendment's right to freedom of assembly permitted such discrimination by a private organization. In 2003, however, the Court on privacy grounds struck down a Texas law outlawing same-sex sodomy, invalidating similar laws in several other states, and overturning their Georgia decision of seventeen years previous. Speaking for the Court, Justice Anthony Kennedy observed, "The petitioners are entitled to respect for their private lives. The State cannot demean their existence or control their destiny by making their private sexual conduct a crime. Their right to liberty under the Due Process Clause gives them the full right to engage in their conduct without intervention of the government."[149]

Outside Washington, D.C., many states and communities have taken steps to limit discrimination against gays and lesbians. At the beginning of 2007, 52 percent of Americans lived in a state, county, or city with laws banning discrimination against gays and lesbians, up from 7 percent in 1987. In passing such laws, local officials can point to public opinion polls that show that a majority of Americans favor legal safeguards against discrimination on the basis of sexual orientation.[150]

Despite the support expressed in public opinion polls, state and local government decisions in recent years to extend civil rights protections to gays and lesbians have sometimes provoked backlashes and elections have produced mixed results. In 2000, for example, Oregon voters defeated an initiative intended to prevent homosexuality from being discussed in public schools, a vote consistent with positions the state's voters had taken on other gay rights proposals in previous years.[151] Voters in Maine repealed gay rights bills the state legislature had passed and the governor had signed in 1998 and 2000, but in 2005 they declined to overturn legislation outlawing discrimination on the basis of sexual orientation.[152]

Gay rights has been a similarly controversial issue in Colorado. In 1992, the citizens of Colorado voted to amend the state's constitution to forbid state and local government from passing laws that would extend civil rights protections to gays and lesbians. The constitutional amendment invalidated ordinances in Denver and other Colorado communities banning discrimination against homosexuals. Gay and lesbian groups challenged the new amendment in the Colorado courts, arguing that it would effectively deny them equal participation in the political process. In 1994, the Colorado Supreme Court agreed, although it did not go so far as to rule that gays and lesbians are a legally protected minority. The state of Colorado appealed the case to the Supreme Court, which in 1996 found the amendment unconstitutional because it "classifies homosexuals not to further a proper legislative end but to make them unequal to everyone else."[153]

The precise impact of the Court's decision is a matter of dispute. Gay and lesbian groups hailed the ruling in the Colorado case as a landmark legal victory that made it likely that other laws discriminating against homosexuals will be found unconstitutional. Supporters of the Colorado amendment argued, however, that the Court had left open the possibility that laws discriminating against homosexuals will pass constitutional muster if they serve some legitimate government purpose.

The gay rights issue that has moved to the forefront of political debate in recent years is same-sex marriage (see Figure 5–3). In 1993, the Supreme Court of Hawaii ruled that unless the state of Hawaii demonstrated that it had a compelling reason for denying homosexual couples the right to marry, the practice violated the state's constitution. This led to a long political fight in the state. In 1998, Hawaii voters passed a constitutional amendment that gave the legislature the power to reserve marriage for opposite-sex couples. A year later the state Supreme Court dismissed the original lawsuit as being moot because of the voter-approved constitutional amendment.

Had Hawaii recognized a right for gays and lesbians to marry in the mid-1990s, the other forty-nine states might have had to grant legal recognition to same-sex marriages performed in Hawaii— whether they wanted to or not—because the Constitution stipulates that "full faith and credit shall be given in each state to the public acts, records and judicial proceedings of every other state." To fend off the possibility of being forced to recognize same-sex marriages, Utah passed a law in 1995 that denies recognition to all out-of-state marriages that do not conform to Utah law. In 1996,

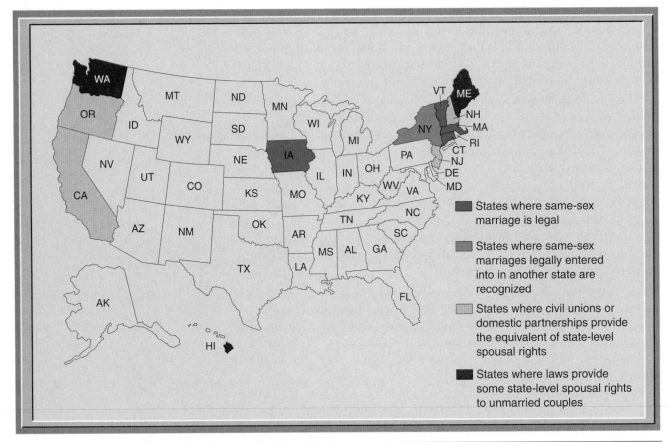

Figure 5–3   Legal Recognition of Same-Sex Relationships by State, 2009. Relatively few states currently provide any legal recognition to relationships between same sex couples.

Source: *Human Rights Campaign, "Relationship Recognition in the U.S.," October 15, 2008 and 2008 election news reports.*

Congress passed the Defense of Marriage Act, which bars federal recognition of same-sex marriages and permits states to disregard same-sex marriages performed in other states.

In 2000, Vermont passed legislation allowing same-sex partners to establish a civil union, giving them the same legal rights granted to married couples under state (but not federal) law. A few years later the prospect of legislation creating civil unions along the lines of the Vermont model led the Massachusetts state Senate to seek an advisory opinion from the state's supreme court as to whether such unions would be legal under the Massachusetts constitution. The court's advisory opinion, delivered in February 2004, stated that any measure that fell short of allowing same-sex marriage would be unconstitutional because it would be discriminatory. The opinion set the stage for same-sex marriages in Massachusetts and unleashed a political firestorm nationally.

The same day the Massachusetts opinion was rendered, President George W. Bush called on Congress to "promptly pass, and to send to the states for ratification, an amendment to our Constitution defining and protecting marriage as a union of man and woman as husband and wife." Although clearly opposing same-sex marriage, the president left open the possibility of accepting civil unions, saying that state legislatures should be left "free to make their own choices in defining legal arrangements other than marriage." Although the president and a several members of Congress backed the Federal Marriage Amendment, it failed to come close to passing in the Senate, and it made no headway in 2007 or 2008. But same-sex marriage opponents enjoyed much greater success at the state level, with bans passing in all thirteen states where they appeared on the ballot in 2004, and two more states in 2005. Although bans passed in seven additional states in 2006, voters in Arizona rejected such a measure. Two years later, however, Arizonans passed a gay marriage ban, along with voters in California and Florida.

By 2009, forty-four states had either constitutional provisions or laws on the books that prevented same-sex marriages. Only in Connecticut, Iowa, Massachusetts, and Vermont were such marriages legal. After the state supreme court allowed gay marriage in California in early 2008, the state's voters narrowly voted to amend the state constitution to ban them in the November general election. New Jersey established civil unions in 2007, followed by New Hampshire in 2008. Oregon established domestic partnerships with state-recognized spousal rights equivalent to those given straight couples in 2008. Some spousal rights are granted by state law to same-sex couples in Hawaii, Maine, Maryland, and Washington. Public opinion surveys show a majority of Americans still oppose same-sex marriages. At the same time, a majority support some form of civil unions.[154] It is likely, however, that federal courts will be called on to decide whether or not the "full faith and credit" clause of the Constitution trumps the Defense of Marriage Act and requires other states and the federal government to grant legal recognition to same-sex marriages legally performed in Massachusetts. The initial federal court decision on the question, in Florida in early 2005, upheld the Defense of Marriage Act. Several other cases touching on the issue are working their way through the court system.[155]

5-5d The Burden of Proof

As you can see, since the 1970s, many different groups have asked the Supreme Court to recognize their status as victims of discrimination and to recognize and protect their civil rights. Because the Court has held that discrimination per se is not unconstitutional—recall, for example, that it has found some laws that discriminate on the basis of sex and age are constitutional—it has had to develop rules to determine which parties bear the burden of proof in determining when a discriminatory law is unconstitutional.

As the law now stands, the Supreme Court employs a three-tiered standard for evaluating the constitutionality of a discriminatory law. Under the standard of **rational scrutiny**, the government needs only to show that a law is reasonable and not arbitrary. Here, the burden of proof rests with the individual or group challenging the government to prove that a law is unreasonable or arbitrary. Under the standard of **strict scrutiny**, the government must show a compelling reason for a discriminatory law. Here, the burden of proof rests with the government, and it usually finds it difficult to meet this burden of proof. The standard of **intermediate scrutiny** lies somewhere between the rational and strict scrutiny standards.[156] Under the intermediate scrutiny standard, a discriminatory law must "serve important governmental interests and must be substantially related to the achievement of those objectives."[157] Here, the government and the group challenging the law share the burden of proof. (In a 1996 case, the Court raised questions about the continued validity of the three-tiered standard for judging the constitutionality of a discriminatory law when it introduced the idea of "skeptical scrutiny." As Box 5–3 discusses, it remains to be seen whether skeptical scrutiny represents an entirely new standard or simply restates the intermediate scrutiny standard more forcefully.)

Rational, intermediate, and strict scrutiny apply different standards to different groups of people, as Box 5–3 discusses in greater detail. Even with these standards, however, civil rights law remains one of the most complex aspects of American law, and it may become more complex in the future. For example, researchers have found persuasive evidence that businesses routinely discriminate against people on the basis of height, weight, and looks in making hiring decisions. As a result, people who are short, overweight, or unattractive earn less than other Americans.[158] People who believe they have been discriminated against on the basis of their height, weight, or looks are now testing their legal claims to protection against discrimination in the courts.

rational scrutiny
A legal standard for judging whether a discriminatory law is unconstitutional. Rational scrutiny requires the government only to show that a law is reasonable and not arbitrary.

strict scrutiny
A legal standard for judging whether a discriminatory law is unconstitutional. Strict scrutiny requires the government to show a compelling reason for a discriminatory law.

intermediate scrutiny
A legal standard for judging whether a discriminatory law is unconstitutional. Intermediate scrutiny lies somewhere between the rational and strict scrutiny standards. It requires the government to show that a discriminatory law serves important governmental interests and is substantially related to the achievement of those objectives, or a group to show that the law does not meet these two standards.

POINT OF ORDER

Box 5–3 Standards of Judicial Scrutiny: Who Is Protected under Civil Rights Laws

Civil rights are not absolute. In its attempt to balance society's rights and the individual's rights, government constructs rules or standards that sometimes place limits on individual rights. One example of such a set of rules is the Supreme Court's three-tiered standard for proving a law does not discriminate improperly against a certain person or group: rational scrutiny, strict scrutiny, and intermediate scrutiny. The political climate of the times influences the way the Court applies this three-tiered standard.

Since the early years of the twentieth century, the Supreme Court has held that any method of classification that groups people by some characteristic must be rational (that is, reasonable and not arbitrary) and must be directly related to some legitimate state goal. This is a relatively easy standard for the government to meet, and the Court

almost never overturns a law it subjects to so-called rational scrutiny. (One exception is the 1996 case *Romer v. Evans,* which involved an amendment to the Colorado Constitution barring state and local government from giving civil rights protections to homosexuals. The Court held that the amendment was unconstitutional because it did not "bear a rational relationship to a legitimate government purpose.")

Later, the Court developed a much tougher rule—the strict scrutiny standard. This standard says that in certain cases, government must work much harder to prove that a law that differentiates between groups is constitutional. For example, the Court has ruled that differentiating on the basis of race or national origin is a suspect classification scheme. In such cases, the Court will automatically assume that any law that classifies people according to race or ethnicity is unconstitutional unless the government can prove otherwise. The Court almost always overturns laws that differentiate between people on the basis of race or nationality. (Two exceptions to this rule were *Korematsu v. United States* and *Hirabayashi v. United States.* These cases upheld President Franklin Roosevelt's decision to order the internment of more than 75,000 Japanese Americans in detention camps during World War II.)

In 1976, the Supreme Court created a third standard, known as intermediate scrutiny, for determining whether a law improperly distinguishes between different groups in society. Current Supreme Court Justice Ruth Bader Ginsburg filed a brief at that time as an attorney, asking the Court to apply the strict scrutiny standard to any law that discriminates between men and women—in effect, to make sex a suspect classification. The Court declined the request, but it did agree that sex-based laws should meet

a standard somewhere between the easy-to-meet standard of rational scrutiny and the difficult-to-meet standard of strict scrutiny. Hence, it created the intermediate scrutiny standard. The Court subsequently subjected laws that distinguish between children born in and out of wedlock to intermediate scrutiny. Laws subjected to intermediate scrutiny have a fair chance of being upheld.

In a 1996 case involving the Virginia Military Institute (VMI), a state-supported, all-male military college, the Supreme Court threw the three-tiered standard of rational, intermediate, and strict scrutiny into some doubt. In ruling that VMI's ban on women was unconstitutional, the Court, in an opinion written by Justice Ginsburg, applied a "skeptical scrutiny" standard, which holds that a state must demonstrate an "exceedingly persuasive justification" for any official action that treats men and women differently. It remains to be seen, however, whether the skeptical scrutiny standard marks an entirely new standard or simply restates the idea of intermediate scrutiny in more forceful terms. As Chief Justice William Rehnquist noted in his concurring opinion, the Court's new verbal formulation has injected an "element of uncertainty" in the legal analysis of sex discrimination.

Since the 1970s, the Supreme Court has been asked to rule that other classification schemes require strict or intermediate scrutiny. So far, the Court has refused to do so. Among those groups that have argued for protected status but that have never been granted strict or intermediate scrutiny are age groups, people with disabilities, and gays and lesbians. These groups seek the protection of such rules because the rules matter. The rules on rational, intermediate, and strict scrutiny radically affect the civil rights of real people in everyday life.

5-6 AFFIRMATIVE ACTION: EQUAL OPPORTUNITY OR EQUAL OUTCOMES?

Civil rights laws are intended to guarantee equal rights for all Americans. But what exactly does it mean to say that the government should ensure equal rights? You will recall that civil rights legislation generally requires government to take positive steps to ensure equality. But what specific steps should government take? And how far should it go? These questions are at the crux of many disputes over civil rights.

Ensuring equality of rights is a demanding task. One way to understand the problem of how to ensure equal rights is to think of rights as items on a scale. On one side of the scale are the rights of an individual or group and on the other, the rights of the rest of society. Exactly how to achieve a balance is often a matter of considerable debate. For example, most Americans believe the government should protect against discrimination in the workplace. But what steps should the government take to achieve this goal? The question of whether equal rights means *equality of opportunity* or *equality of outcome* has been at the heart of civil rights debates since the mid-1960s.

The issue that most clearly exemplifies the conflict between equality of opportunity and equality of outcome is **affirmative action**. Affirmative action programs require government to take positive actions to increase the number of underrepresented groups in certain positions, usually in the workplace. Using the scale analogy, imagine that on one side of the balance we have disadvantaged minority groups; on the other, the advantaged majority. Most people agree the balance has long been weighted on the side of the majority and that it needs to be tipped toward the minority side. But the question is, how far? What is the proper balance? Is it enough to make rules that *try* to ensure equal opportunity? Or do we need to establish rules that *guarantee* equal outcomes?

Which positive actions are desirable and permissible lies at the heart of the affirmative action dispute. At a minimum, positive action means taking steps to notify people that an equal opportunity exists. Many large American corporations, for instance, put the phrase "equal opportunity employer" on their stationery. At the other end of the spectrum, affirmative action takes the form of quotas or set-asides—rules that guarantee a number of positions for members of certain groups.

The affirmative action movement began under President Johnson in the mid-1960s, as the federal government directed organizations that received public money to take affirmative steps to increase the participation of underrepresented groups. This led to a series of programs designed to bring more minorities and women into the nation's educational system as well as its workplace. In the years since then, affirmative action programs frequently have triggered heated political and legal debate.

affirmative action
Programs designed to take positive actions to increase the number of women and minorities in jobs and educational programs.

The debate over affirmative action centers on whether the law should treat everyone equally regardless of personal characteristics other than ability, or whether it should compensate groups that have faced discrimination in the past by giving them special advantages. Proponents of affirmative action contend that only positive actions can redress the effects of decades of discrimination. Opponents argue, however, that affirmative action creates a system of **reverse discrimination** in which whites, and especially white men, are denied equal protection under the law, or, as noted earlier in this chapter, when Asian Americans students are denied admission to prestigious universities. This demonstrates the complex problems that can arise when competing sets of rights collide. Minorities should have a right to an equal chance at education and employment, but the white majority should also have this right. How can government create rules that balance these two sets of rights—that ensure the underrepresented group an equal chance without violating the rights of the rest of society?

reverse discrimination
Laws and policies that discriminate against whites, especially white males.

The Supreme Court has had numerous opportunities to judge the constitutionality of affirmative action. The Court's first major ruling came in the case of Allan Bakke, a white male who was denied admission to the medical school at the University of California–Davis even though his grades and test scores were higher than those of several minority students admitted under a special program. The Court ruled that the school could consider minority status a factor when making its admissions decisions, but that it could not impose a quota system. In two 2003 cases, the Court essentially reinforced its previous decision in *Regents of the University of California v. Bakke* (1978). The Court upheld the use of race as one variable in determining admission to the University of Michigan's law school but overturned the explicit point system the university used to decide undergraduate admissions.[159]

Other Supreme Court decisions also have left the constitutionality of affirmative action programs somewhat unclear. The Court has upheld voluntary affirmative action programs, and it has allowed quotas in instances in which past discrimination was proved.[160] The Court has also allowed affirmative action programs for women when a "manifest imbalance" exists in a specific workforce.[161] The Court has ruled, however, that some set-aside programs, such as Richmond, Virginia's requirement that 30 percent of all city contracts must go to minority contractors, are unconstitutional because no past discrimination was demonstrated.[162] And in 1995, the Court, in a majority opinion written by Justice Sandra Day O'Connor, suggested that federal affirmative action programs must meet a strict scrutiny test.[163] This decision forced the Clinton administration to review government programs to see what, if any, changes should be made for them to survive legal challenge.[164] In initiating the review, President Clinton promised that his goal was to "mend, not end" the government's affirmative action programs.[165]

What sorts of affirmative action policies does the federal government pursue? A list compiled in 1995 identified more than 100 programs with some affirmative action component.[166] They ranged from "programs as precise as setting aside a fixed percentage of crime assistance grants for minority or female-owned institutions, and as general as urging recipients of federal agriculture or housing assistance to use minority-owned banks."[167] The Clinton administration reduced the number of federal affirmative action programs in 1996, when it imposed a three-year moratorium on all government set-aside programs. Although the administration left open the possibility that it might revive set-asides at the end of the three years, it set such stringent conditions for reviving the programs that revival is unlikely. As one Clinton administration official put it, "as a practical matter, set-asides are gone."[168] The Bush administration was even less inclined to resurrect set-asides.

What differences have the government's affirmative action programs made? The answer is not clear, in large part because it is difficult to collect and judge evidence on the question. Minority-owned firms are disproportionately few in number and small in size, and a significant number of them depend heavily on government set-asides to direct business their way.[169] Many minority business owners fear that if the government's affirmative action rules change, they will lose their businesses, in part because discriminatory practices will reemerge, but also because their firms are too small or not well enough connected to land government contracts.[170] But many of these federal government programs, although they once enjoyed bipartisan support, are now under attack as the owners of nonminority firms raise reverse discrimination claims.[171]

In the end, the government is searching for policies that correct for past discrimination without producing reverse discrimination. Developing such policies, which would achieve a balance between both sets of rights, is crucial as increasing numbers of individuals and groups seek rules that give them equality of status and rights under the law. One possible solution is "place, not race," a notion the Clinton administration discussed. Such a policy might steer government contracts to companies located in economically distressed areas rather than to businesses whose owners represent certain races.[172]

Some state university systems have developed a variant of the "place, not race" approach. After a federal court struck down the University of Texas's race-based admissions policy in 1996, the Texas legislature passed, and then-Governor George W. Bush signed, a law guaranteeing that any student who ranks in "the top ten percent" of his or her high school graduating class would automatically be admitted to a Texas public university.[173] The Regents of the University of California subsequently developed a similar admissions policy. Their policy would base admissions on factors such as "unusual persistence and determination" in overcoming disadvantaged social and educational circumstances in addition to grades and standardized test scores. Since 2001, the top 4 percent of each high school class is guaranteed admission to the University of California system, although not necessarily to the campus of their choice. The number of Hispanic Americans admitted to the University of California system has increased in the wake of these policies, while the number of African American and American Indian applicants has increased to a lesser extent. On a percentage basis, Hispanic Americans now comprise a larger proportion of the students admitted than before 2001; the percentage of admitted students who are African Americans has increased only slightly; and the percentage of students who are American Indian has stayed the same.[174]

Pressure on governments to change affirmative action programs is likely to continue. Indeed, affirmative action opponents seized on Barack Obama's successful campaign in 2008 as evidence that such programs were no longer needed.[175] Voters appear to agree with that position. In 1996, for example, California voters passed Proposition 209, ending all the state's affirmative action programs. Voters in Washington State passed a similar measure two years later, as did Michigan voters in 2006 and Nebraska voters in 2008. Voters in Colorado, however, narrowly rejected a comparable measure in 2008. In 2000, Florida's state government became the first to voluntarily ban affirmative action in both college admissions and state contracts. The state put into place a college admissions policy guaranteeing students who finish in the top 20 percent of their high school class a place in one of the state's ten public universities.

Is the Constitution flexible enough to allow the federal government to create rules that correct for the lingering effects of past discrimination without triggering claims of reverse discrimination? History suggests it is. Exactly what rules will the Court and Congress establish to attain this balance? Realistically, political pressures will probably determine which rules are created and how they work.

SUMMARY

The Constitution sets forth the fundamental rules governing the relationship between the government and its citizens. These rules attempt to guarantee certain civil rights. But although we think of these rights as fixed concepts, they are not. Part of government's task is to balance competing rights; in doing so, it must continually redefine the rules that govern our civil rights. And these rights matter greatly to real people in everyday life.

The flexibility of the Constitution is evident in the struggle of the civil rights movement. Throughout the nineteenth century and much of the twentieth century, the Supreme Court refused to recognize that all Americans were entitled to equal protection under the law regardless of race, creed, color, or sex.

African Americans found themselves disenfranchised first by rulings that sanctioned slavery, and then, after slavery was abolished, by rulings that insisted that separate treatment was equal treatment. American Indians were denied citizenship rights, and Hispanic Americans and Asian Americans frequently confronted laws that limited their right to work and educate their children. Even women, who constituted half the American population, found that they were not full citizens in the eyes of the law.

Since the mid-twentieth century, the civil rights movement has breathed life into the promise of the Fourteenth Amendment that no person shall be denied equal protection under the law. Working through both the legal and political systems, African American civil rights leaders succeeded in forcing both the Supreme Court and Congress to take steps to end legalized discrimination. The success of African Americans at forcing changes in rules and policies in turn inspired other minorities as well as women to demand that the government protect their rights as well. And in recent years, other groups, most notably people with disabilities, have been motivated by the civil rights movement to demand that they, too, be allowed to enjoy the full fruits of American citizenship. Gays and lesbians, however, have generally been unable to gain specific coverage under civil rights laws.

The very success of the civil rights movement has created new tensions and conflicts in American politics because protecting the rights of one group may infringe on the rights of another. These tensions and conflicts are most obvious in affirmative action programs. Proponents argue that we need affirmative action to reverse the effects of decades of discrimination, whereas opponents contend it curtails the rights of the majority. The Supreme Court has sought to chart a middle course between both camps, looking on the one hand to promote the interests of groups that have suffered discrimination, while on the other hand attempting to avoid charges that it is promoting reverse discrimination. Undoubtedly, the Court will eventually define new rules in response to these new tensions in our increasingly diverse society. Just what those rules will be, however, is hard to predict. They will most likely be ushered in on the prevailing political winds as new members join the Court and new issues take center stage in American politics.

KEY TERMS

affirmative action

Americans with Disabilities
   Act (ADA) of 1990

Brown v. Board of Education

Brown v. Board of Education II

civil disobedience

civil rights

Civil Rights Act of 1964

civil rights movement

de facto segregation

de jure segregation

Equal Pay Act of 1963

intermediate scrutiny

Jim Crow laws

lynching

massive resistance

rational scrutiny

reverse discrimination

separate-but-equal standard

strict scrutiny

suffrage

Voting Rights Act of 1965

women's movement

READINGS FOR FURTHER STUDY

Branch, Taylor. *Parting the Waters: America in the King Years, 1954–1963* (New York: Simon & Schuster, 1988). An award-winning account of the civil rights movement in the decade leading up to the passage of the Civil Rights Act of 1964.

Gerstmann, Evan. *Same Sex Marriage and the Constitution* (New York: Cambridge University Press, 2004). A thoughtful and thorough examination of the legal, political, and social implications of the movement for gay marriage.

Irons, Peter. *The Courage of Their Convictions: Sixteen Americans Who Fought Their Way to the Supreme Court* (New York: Free Press, 1988). Compelling stories of sixteen people whose lawsuits challenged, and in many cases changed, our conception of civil rights.

Klarman, Michael J. *From Jim Crow to Civil Rights: The Supreme Court and the Struggle for Racial Equality* (New York: Oxford University Press, 2004). A sweeping examination of the Supreme Court's role in inhibiting and advancing civil rights from the 1890s to the 1960s.

Kluger, Richard. *Simple Justice* (New York: Vintage Books, 1975). A now-classic examination of the African American struggle for civil rights, with particular attention paid to the history of *Brown v. Board of Education.*

Nakanishi, Don T., and James S. Lai, eds. *Asian American Politics: Law, Participation, and Policy* (Lanham, MD: Rowman & Littlefield, 2003). An edited volume analyzing a wide range of historical materials on the Asian American political and legal experience.

Sniderman, Paul M., and Thomas Piazza. *The Scar of Race* (Cambridge: Harvard University Press, 1993). A first-rate work of social science showing the complexity of racial attitudes current in American politics.

Switzer, Jacqueline Vaughn. *Disabled Rights: American Disability Policy and the Fight for Equality* (Washington, D.C.: Georgetown University Press, 2003). A political scientist documents the rise of the civil rights movement for people with disabilities.

Wilkins, David E. *American Indian Politics and the American Political System* (Lanham, MD: Rowman & Littlefield, 2002). An interesting study of the tensions between tribal government and the federal government in the lives of American Indians.

Wolbrecht, Christina. *The Politics of Women's Rights: Parties, Positions, and Change* (Princeton, NJ: Princeton University Press, 2000). A scholarly examination detailing how the Democratic and Republican parties' positions on women's rights have evolved and polarized over time.

REVIEW QUESTIONS

1. Which of the following statements is *true?*
   a. Civil liberties typically come before civil rights.
   b. Civil rights typically come before civil liberties.

    c. Civil rights are rooted in courts' interpretation of the Fourteenth Amendment.

    d. Both a and c.

2. What was Reconstruction?

    a. when federal troops occupied the South (1865–1877)

    b. a time followed by Jim Crow laws

    c. a time that ended with a compromise that made Rutherford B. Hayes president

    d. all of the above

3. What was the "invisible empire of the South"?

    a. Ku Klux Klan

    b. National Association for the Advancement of Colored People

    c. Democratic Party

    d. Republican Party

4. Who wrote, "Our Constitution is color blind, and neither knows nor tolerates classes among citizens"?

    a. Dr. Martin Luther King, Jr.

    b. President John Kennedy

    c. Justice John Harlan

    d. President Abraham Lincoln

5. The _____ gave African Americans greater opportunities to participate in the main stream of American economic and social life.

    a. Civil Rights Act of 1957

    b. Civil Rights Act of 1964

    c. Voting Rights Act of 1965

    d. Civil Rights Act of 1991

6. Which of the following is *true* about *Plessy v. Ferguson* (1896)?

    a. It sanctioned apartheid in the United States.

    b. It ended de jure, but not de facto, segregation.

    c. It started the civil rights struggle in the United States.

    d. It ended Jim Crow laws in the United States.

7. The Supreme Court justices

    a. upheld the use of quotas as constitutional in the *Bakke* decision.

    b. ruled that the use of quotas was unconstitutional in the *Bakke* decision.

    c. have never ruled on the constitutionality of quotas.

    d. have always ruled that racial set-aside programs are constitutional.

8. Under _____ scrutiny, the burden of proof rests with the individual or group challenging the government to prove that a law is unreasonable or arbitrary.

    a. rational

    b. intermediate

    c. strict

    d. liberal

9. Affirmative action
    a. began during the Nixon administration.
    b. is designed to increase the number of women and minorities in employment and education.
    c. ended during the Clinton administration.
    d. always guarantees equal outcomes.
10. Congress gave American Indians citizenship in
    a. 1789.
    b. 1865.
    c. 1924.
    d. 1971.

NOTES

1. Rick Montgomery, "School Law has Omaha on Edge," *Kansas City Star*, April 23, 2006.
2. Sam Dillon, "Law to Segregate Omaha Schools," *New York Times*, April 15, 2006.
3. Montgomery, "School Law has Omaha on Edge"; Dillon, "Law to Segregate Omaha Divides Nebraska."
4. Nate Jenkins, "Omaha School Division Bill Passes," *Lincoln Journal Star*, April 14, 2006.
5. Michaela Saunders, "In with New Law, Out with Old Lawsuits, Attorneys Say They'll End Challenges to the Old Law's OPS Breakup and the Governing Structure for the Learning Community," *Omaha World-Herald*, May 25, 2007.
6. Minor v. Happersett, 21 Wall 162 (1875).
7. Dred Scott v. Sandford, 19 Howard 393 (1857).
8. William Safire, *Safire's New Political Dictionary* (New York: Random House, 1993), 262.
9. The Slaughterhouse Cases, 68 (1 Wall) 36 (1873).
10. United States v. Cruikshank, 92 U.S. 542 (1876).
11. United States v. Reese, 12 U.S. 214 (1876).
12. *Congress A to Z* (Washington, D.C.: Congressional Quarterly, 1993), 31; Michael Barone, Grant Ujifusa, and Douglas Matthews, *The Almanac of American Politics 1976* (New York: Dutton, 1975), 198.
13. Safire, *Safire's New Political Dictionary*, 377–78.
14. Plessy v. Ferguson, 163 U.S. 537 (1896).
15. Safire, *Safire's New Political Dictionary*, 368.
16. Richard Kluger, *Simple Justice* (New York: Knopf, 1975), 111.
17. Walter LaFeber, *The Cambridge History of American Foreign Relations, Volume II: The American Search for Opportunity, 1865–1913* (New York: Cambridge University Press, 1993), 49.
18. *The Concise Columbia Encyclopedia* (New York: Columbia University Press, 1983), 498.
19. William M. Adler, *Land of Opportunity* (New York: Atlantic Monthly Press, 1995), 176–77.
20. Ibid., 177. The Supreme Court's decision is Moore v. Dempsey, 261 U.S. 86 (1923). See also Richard C. Cortner, *A Mob Intent on Death: The NAACP and the Arkansas Riot Cases* (Middletown, CT: Wesleyan University Press, 1988).
21. Guinn v. United States, 238 U.S. 347 (1915).

22. Buchanan v. Warley, 245 U.S. 60 (1917).

23. Missouri ex rel. Gaines v. Canada, 305 U.S. 337 (1938).

24. Smith v. Allwright, 321 U.S. 649 (1944).

25. Clark Clifford, *Counsel to the President: A Memoir* (New York: Anchor Books, 1991), 208–9.

26. Ibid., 210–11.

27. Jules Tygiel, *Baseball's Great Experiment* (New York: Oxford University Press, 1983), 37–43.

28. Ibid., 195–200.

29. Quoted in Ibid., 280.

30. Sweatt v. Painter, 339 U.S. 629 (1950).

31. McLaurin v. Oklahoma State Regents, 339 U.S. 637 (1950).

32. Brown v. Board of Education, 347 U.S. 483 (1954).

33. Ibid. For an argument that the *Brown* decision was less important than is commonly thought, see Gerald N. Rosenberg, *The Hollow Hope: Can Courts Bring About Social Change?* (Chicago: University of Chicago Press, 1991).

34. Brown v. Board of Education, 347 U.S. 483 (1954).

35. Quoted in Earl Warren, *The Memoirs of Earl Warren* (Garden City, NY: Doubleday, 1977), 291.

36. Brown v. Board of Education (Brown II), 349 U.S. 294 (1955).

37. See Numan V. Bartley, *The Rise of Massive Resistance* (Baton Rouge: Louisiana State University Press, 1969); Robbins L. Gates, *The Making of Massive Resistance* (Chapel Hill: University of North Carolina Press, 1964); Benjamin Muse, *Virginia's Massive Resistance* (Bloomington: Indiana University Press, 1961); Francis M. Wilhoit, *The Politics of Massive Resistance* (New York: Braziller, 1973).

38. See Taylor Branch, *Parting the Waters: America in the King Years, 1954–63* (New York: Simon & Schuster, 1988), 222–24.

39. Earl Black and Merle Black, *Politics and Society in the South* (Cambridge: Harvard University Press, 1987), 95.

40. Griffin v. County School Board of Prince Edward County, 377 U.S. 218 (1964).

41. Black and Black, *Politics and Society in the South*, 96.

42. See Green v. County School Board, 391 U.S. 430 (1968); Alexander v. Holmes County Board of Education, 396 U.S. 19 (1969).

43. See Arthur M. Schlesinger, Jr., *A Thousand Days: John F. Kennedy in the White House* (New York: Greenwich House, 1983), 940–49; Theodore C. Sorensen, *Kennedy* (New York: Harper & Row, 1965), 483–88.

44. See Stephen Lesher, *George Wallace: American Populist* (Reading, MA: Addison-Wesley, 1994), 174, 211–34.

45. Gayle v. Browder, 352 U.S. 903 (1956).

46. "Letter from Birmingham Jail," reprinted in Peverill Squire, James M. Lindsay, Cary R. Covington, and Eric R.A.N. Smith, *Dynamics of Democracy*, 2nd ed. (Madison, WI: Brown & Benchmark, 1997), 650.

47. Quoted in Branch, *Parting the Waters*, 271.

48. Ibid., 271–74.

49. Lerone Bennett, Jr., *Before the Mayflower* (Baltimore: Penguin, 1964), 322–23; Godfrey Hodgson, *America in Our Time* (New York: Vintage, 1976), 189–91; Safire, *Safire's New Political Dictionary*, 266–67.

50. C. Vann Woodward, *The Strange Career of Jim Crow*, 3rd rev. ed. (New York: Oxford University Press, 1974), 184.

51. Quoted in *The Encyclopedic Dictionary of American Government*, 4th ed. (Guilford, CT: Dushkin, 1991), 47.

52. See, for example, Black and Black, *Politics and Society in the South*, 126–51.

53. Quoted in *Bartlett's Familiar Quotations*, 15th ed. (Boston: Little, Brown, 1980), 909.

54. On Hurricane Katrina, see Lydia Saad, "Blacks Blast Bush for Katrina Response," September 14, 2005. www.gallup.com/poll/18526/Blacks-Blast-Bush-Katrina-Response.aspx On race relations, see the New York Times/CBS News poll of July 7-14, 2008. www.nytimes.com/2008/07/16/us/politics/16poll.html

55. See, for example, Missouri v. Jenkins, 515 U.S. 70 (1995); David Armor, *Forced Justice: School Desegregation and the Law* (New York: Oxford University Press, 1995).

56. DeWayne Wickham, "NAACP Loses another Leader, and More Luster," *USA TODAY*, March 6, 2007.

57. See Steven A. Holmes, "For the Civil Rights Movement, A New Reason for Living," *New York Times*, July 9, 1995; Steven A. Holmes, "In a Southern City, Many Blacks Question the N.A.A.C.P.'s Role," *New York Times*, January 9, 1996.

58. See Malcolm X, *The Autobiography of Malcolm X* (New York: Grove Press, 1965).

59. See Glenn C. Loury, *One by One from the Inside Out: Essays and Reviews on Race and Responsibility* (New York: Free Press, 1995); Thomas Sowell, *Race and Culture: A World View* (New York: Basic Books, 1994); Shelby Steele, *The Content of Our Character: A New Vision of Race in America* (New York: St. Martin's, 1990).

60. Steele, *The Content of Our Character*, 174.

61. Howard Fineman and Vern E. Smith, "An Angry 'Charmer,'" *Newsweek* (October 30, 1995): 33.

62. David Maraniss, "A March of Contradictions," *Washington Post National Weekly Edition*, October 23–29, 1995, 8; NBC News/Wall Street Journal Poll, March 2–5, 2000.

63. Frank Newport, "Jackson and Powell Top List of Most Important Black Leaders," July 18, 2003. www.gallup.com/poll/8866/Jackson-Powell-Top-List-Most-Important-Black-Leaders.aspx

64. The quote is from Stephen E. Ambrose, *Nothing Like It in the World: The Men Who Built the Transcontinental Railroad 1863–1969* (New York: Simon & Schuster, 2000), 150. See also Charles McClain, ed., *Asian Indians, Filipinos, Other Asian Communities and the Law* (New York: Garland, 1994); Charles McClain, ed., *Chinese Immigrants and American Law* (New York: Garland, 1994); Charles McClain, ed., *Japanese Immigrants and American Law: The Alien Land Laws and Other Issues* (New York: Garland, 1994).

65. LaFeber, *Cambridge History of American Foreign Relations*, II: 51–52; Charles J. McClain, *In Search of Equality: The Chinese Struggle against Discrimination in Nineteenth-Century America* (Berkeley: University of California Press, 1994), chap. 6.

66. Page Smith, *Democracy on Trial: The Japanese American Evacuation and Relocation in World War II* (New York: Simon & Schuster, 1995), 48.

67. See Thomas G. Paterson, J. Garry Clifford, and Kenneth J. Hagan, *American Foreign Relations, A History: Since 1895*, 4th ed. (Lexington, MA: Heath, 1995), 62.

68. See Thomas A. Bailey, "California, Japan, and the Alien Land Legislation of 1913," *Pacific Historical Review* 1, no. 1 (1932): 36–59; Paolo E. Coletta, "'The Most Thankless Task': Bryan and the California Alien Land Legislation," *Pacific Historical Review* 36 (May 1967): 163–87; Herbert P. LePore, "Prelude to Prejudice: Hiram Johnson, Woodrow Wilson, and the California Land Law Controversy of 1913," *Southern California Quarterly* 61 (Spring 1979): 99–110.

69. Quoted in Paterson, Clifford, and Hagan, *American Foreign Relations*, 65.

70. Smith, *Democracy on Trial*, 49.

71. Dudley O. McGovney, "The Anti-Japanese Land Laws of California and Ten Other States," *California Law Review* 35 (March 1947): 7–60.

72. Takao Ozawa v. United States, 260 U.S. 178 (1922); see also Yuji Ichioka, "The Early Japanese Immigrant Quest for Citizenship: The Background of the 1922 Ozawa Case," *Amerasia Journal* 4, no. 2 (1977): 1–22.

73. See Roger Daniels, Sandra C. Taylor, and Harry H.L. Kitano, eds., *Japanese Americans: From Relocation to Redress*, 2nd ed. (Seattle: University of Washington Press, 1991); Charles McClain, ed., *The Mass Internment of Japanese Americans and the Quest for Legal Redress* (New York: Garland, 1994); Smith, *Democracy on Trial*, esp. chaps. 7–15.

74. Hirabayashi v. United States, 320 U.S. 81 (1943); Korematsu v. United States, 323 U.S. 214 (1944); Ex parte Endo, 323 U.S. 283 (1944).

75. See Roger Daniels, "Redress Achieved, 1983–1990," in *Japanese Americans: From Relocation to Redress*, 2nd ed., ed. Roger Daniels, Sandra C. Taylor, and Harry H.L. Kitano (Seattle: University of Washington Press, 1991).

76. Yick Wo v. Hopkins, 118 U.S. 356 (1886); see also McClain, *In Search of Equality*, chap. 4.

77. Lau v. Nichols, 414 U.S. 563 (1974).

78. Nanette Asimov, "Proposal to Alter Lowell Admissions," *San Francisco Chronicle*, January 10, 1996; Jonathan D. Glater and Alan Finder, "School Diversity Based on Income Segregates Some," *New York Times*, July 15, 2007; "New Admissions Policy Offered for San Francisco's Top School," *New York Times*, January 11, 1996; Lawrence J. Siskind, "A Year Later in San Francisco, the Schools Are Still Segregated," *Wall Street Journal*, July 12, 1995; Nanette Asimov, "S.F. Schools Can't Use Race in Admissions," *San Francisco Chronicle*, December 18, 1999; Sara Zaske, "Desegregation Still Divisive in Schools," *San Francisco Examiner*, March 9, 2004.

79. John Hechinger, "U.S. Widens Princeton Bias Probe," *Wall Street Journal*, June 12, 2008.

80. The Asian/Pacific/American Institute at New York University, and The Steinhardt Institute for Higher Education Policy at New York University, "Asian Americans and Pacific Islanders, Facts, Not Fiction: Setting the Record Straight," 2008. www.professionals.collegeboard.com/profdownload/08-0608-AAPI.pdf

81. Guadalupe San Miguel, Jr., "Mexican-American Organizations and the Changing Politics of School Desegregation in Texas, 1945–1980," *Social Science Quarterly* 63 (December 1982): 701–15.

82. Katzenbach v. Morgan, 384 U.S. 641 (1966).

83. Graham v. Richardson, 403 U.S. 365 (1971); Plyler v. Doe, 457 U.S. 202 (1982).

84. U.S. v. Brignoni-Ponce, 422 U.S. 873 (1975); INS v. Delgado, 466 U.S. 210 (1984); INS v. Lopez-Mendoza, 486 U.S. 1032 (1984).

85. Pew Hispanic Center. *2007 National Survey of Latinos: As Illegal Immigration Issue Heats Up, Hispanics Feel A Chill*, December 2007. www.pewhispanic .org/reports/report.php?ReportID=84

86. Elk v. Wilkins, 112 U.S. 94 (1884).

87. Vine Deloria, Jr., and Clifford M. Lytle, *American Indians, American Justice* (Austin: University of Texas Press, 1983), 222–25.

88. United States v. Sioux Nation of Indians et al, 448 U.S. 371 (1980). See also Edward Lazarus, *Black Hills/White Justice: The Sioux Nation versus the United States, 1775 to the Present* (New York: HarperCollins, 1991).

89. California v. Cabazon Band of Mission Indians, 480 U.S. 202(1987).

90. George Johnson, "Indians Take on the U.S. in a 90's Battle for Control," *New York Times*, February 11, 1996.

91. Saint Francis College v. Al-Khazraji, 481 U.S. 604 (1987).

92. Bradwell v. Illinois, 16 Wall. 130 (1873).

93. Muller v. Oregon, 208 U.S. 412 (1908); Radice v. New York, 264 U.S. 292 (1924).

94. Justice Joseph Bradley quoted in Gerald Gunther, *Constitutional Law: Cases and Materials* (Mineola, NY: Foundation Press, 1975), 766.

95. Declaration of Sentiments, reprinted in Pat Andrews, ed., *Voices of Diversity: Perspectives on American Political Ideals and Institutions* (Guilford, CT: Dushkin, 1995), 46–47.

96. Nancy E. McGlen and Karen O'Connor, *Women's Rights: The Struggle for Equality in the Nineteenth and Twentieth Centuries* (New York: Praeger, 1983), 272–74.

97. V.O. Key, Jr., *Politics, Parties, and Pressure Groups*, 5th ed. (New York: Crowell, 1964), 614–15.

98. Carl M. Brauer, "Women Activists, Southern Conservatives, and the Prohibition of Sex Discrimination in Title VII of the 1964 Civil Rights Act," *Journal of Southern History* 49 (February 1983): 37–56.

99. See Jill Zuckman, "As Family Leave Is Enacted, Some See End to Logjam," *Congressional Quarterly Weekly Report*, February 6, 1993, 267–69.

100. Holly Idelson, "A Tougher Domestic Violence Law," *Congressional Quarterly Weekly Report*, June 25, 1995, 1714.

101. Nina Bernstein, "Civil Rights Lawsuit in a Rape Case Challenges Integrity of a Campus," *New York Times*, February 11, 1996; U.S. v. Morrison, 529 U.S. 598 (2000).

102. Leslie W. Gladstone, "Equal Rights Amendments: State Provisions," RS20217, Updated August 23, 2004.. www.digital.library.unt.edu/govdocs/crs/permalink/meta-crs-7397:1

103. Reed v. Reed, 404 U.S. 71 (1971).

104. Ibid., 76.

105. Pittsburgh Press v. Pittsburgh Commission on Human Relations, 413 U.S. 376 (1973).

106. Phillips v. Martin-Marietta, 400 U.S. 542 (1971); Cleveland Board of Education v. LaFleur, 413 U.S. 632 (1974); Nashville Gas v. Satty, 434 U.S. 136 (1976).

107. Los Angeles Department of Water and Power v. Manhart, 435 U.S. 702 (1978); Arizona Governing Committee v. Norris, 463 U.S. 1073 (1983).

108. Automobile Workers v. Johnson Controls, 499 U.S. 187 (1991). See also Sally J. Kenney, *For Whose Protection? Reproductive Hazards and Exclusionary Policies in the United States and Britain* (Ann Arbor: University of Michigan Press, 1992).

109. United States v. Virginia, 518 U.S. 515 (1996).

110. Craig v. Boren, 429 U.S. 190 (1976).

111. Orr v. Orr, 440 U.S. 268 (1979); Mississippi University for Women v. Hogan, 458 U.S. 718 (1982).

112. Rostker v. Goldberg, 453 U.S. 57 (1981).

113. Michael M. v. Superior Court of Sonoma County, 450 U.S. 464 (1981).

114. Kahn v. Shevin, 416 U.S. 351 (1974); Califano v. Webster, 430 U.S. 313 (1977); Heckler v. Mathews, 465 U.S. 728 (1984).

115. Johnson v. Transportation Agency, Santa Clara County, 480 U.S. 616 (1987).

116. Ledbetter v. Goodyear Tire & Rubber Company Co., Inc., 127 S. Ct. 2162 (2007).

117. The United States Office of Personnel Management, "Federal Civilian Workforce Statistics: The Fact Book 2005 Edition," www.opm.gov/feddata/factbook/2005/factbook2005.pdf

118. These data are taken from American Bar Association Section of Legal Education and Admissions to the Bar, "First Year and Total J.D. Enrollment by Gender, 1947–2007," www.abanet.org/legaled/statistics/charts/stats%20-%206.pdf.

119. American Bar Association, Commission on Women in the Profession, "A Current Glance at Women in the Law 2006," www.abanet.org/women/CurrentGlanceStatistics2006.pdf

120. American Medical Association, "Physician Statistics Now: Table Physicians in the United States and Possessions by Selected Characteristics." The data are for 2000. www.ama-assn.org/ama1/pub/upload/images/373/internettable.gif. See also U.S. Department of Education, National Center for Education Statistics, "The Condition of Education 2006," 176. www.nces.ed.gov/pubs2006/2006071.pdf

121. Center for Women's Business Research, "Women-Owned Businesses in the United States, 2006: A Fact Sheet," www.cfwbr.org/assets/344_statesoverviewwebcolorfac.pdf; Charles E. Jordan, Stanley J. Clark, and Marilyn A. Waldron, "Gender Bias and Compensation in the Executive Suite of the Fortune 100," *Journal of Organizational Culture, Communications and Conflict* (January 2007) www.findarticles.com/p/articles/mi_m1TOT/is_1_11/ai_n25009738; Phred Dvorak, "Women Slowly Break Into Boardroom," *Wall Street Journal*, March 27, 2006; "Farewell, Organization Man," *Wall Street Journal*, December 31, 2004.

122. Judicial figures calculated by the authors from Alliance for Justice data. www.judicialselectionproject.org/

123. American Bar Association, Commission on Women in the Profession, "A Current Glance at Women in the Law 2006," www.abanet.org/women/CurrentGlanceStatistics2006.pdf

124. See The Offices of Representative John D. Dingell and Representative Carolyn M. Maloney, "A New Look Through the Glass Ceiling: Where Are the Women?" January 2002. www.house.gov/dingell/documents/pdfs/dingellmaloneyreport.pdf See also Steven A. Holmes, "Programs Based on Race and Sex Are Challenged," *New York Times*, March 16, 1995; Peter T. Kilborn, "For Many in Workforce, 'Glass Ceiling' Still Exists," *New York Times*, March 16, 1995; Peter T. Kilborn, "White Males and Management," *New York Times*, March 17, 1995; Deborah Stead, "Breaking the Glass Ceiling with the Power of Words," *New York Times*, January 7, 1996.

125. Nina Bernstein, "Equal Opportunity Recedes for Most Female Lawyers," *New York Times*, January 8, 1996; Pamela Mendels, "Equal Pay in Top Jobs," *Business Week*, August 16, 2000.

126. Mary C. Noonan, Mary E. Corcoran, and Paul N. Courant, "Pay Differences among the Highly Trained: Cohort Differences in the Sex Gap in Lawyers' Earnings," *Social Forces* 84 (December 2005): 853–72; Louise Marie Roth, "Selling Women Short: A Research Note on Gender Differences in Compensation on Wall Street," *Social Forces* 82 (December 2003): 783–802.

127. Wage data reported in National Women's Law Center, "Congress Must Act to Close the Wage Gap for Women," April 2008 www.pay-equity.org/PDFs/PayEquityFactSheet_May2008.pdf, and Institute for Women's Policy Research, "The Gender Wage Ratio: Women's and Men's Earnings," Updated August 2008 www.iwpr.org/pdf/C350.pdf.

128. Sam Roberts, "For Young Earners in Big City, a Gap in Women's Favor," *New York Times*, August 3, 2007.

129. Francine D. Blau and Lawrence M. Kahn, "The Gender Pay Gap," *The Economists' Voice* 4 (June 2007). Available at www.bepress.com/ev/vol4/iss4/art5.

130. Catharine A. MacKinnon, *Only Words* (Cambridge: Harvard University Press, 1993), 22. See also Andrea Dworkin and Catharine A. MacKinnon, *Pornography and Civil Rights: A New Day for Women's Equality* (Minneapolis: Organizing Against Pornography, 1988).

131. Nadine Strossen, *Defending Pornography: Free Speech, Sex, and the Fight for Women's Rights* (New York: Scribner, 1995).

132. See, for example, Christina Hoff Sommers, *Who Stole Feminism: How Women Have Betrayed Women* (New York: Simon & Schuster, 1994); Daphne Patai and Noretta Koertge, *Professing Feminism: Cautionary Tales from the Strange World of Women's Studies* (New York: Basic Books, 1994); Katie Roiphe, *Sex, Fear, and Feminism on Campus* (Boston: Little, Brown, 1993).

133. See, for example, Anita K. Blair, "Separate But Equal," *New York Times*, November 20, 1995; Laura Ingraham, "Enter, Women," *New York Times*, April 19, 1995; Megan Rosenfeld, "Feminist Fatales: This Conservative Women's Group Has Traditionalists Seething," *Washington Post*, November 30, 1995.

134. See Robert A. Katzmann, *Institutional Disability* (Washington, D.C.: Brookings Institution, 1986).

135. Janet Reno and Dick Thornburgh, "ADA—Not a Disabling Mandate," *Wall Street Journal*, July 26, 1995.

136. Data calculated by the authors from U.S. Equal Employment Opportunity Commission, "Americans with Disabilities Act of 1990 (ADA) Charges FY 1997–FY 2007," April 24, 2008. www.eeoc.gov/stats/ada-charges.html

137. James Bovard, "Get a Whiff of This!" *Wall Street Journal*, December 27, 1995.

138. See Michael H. Fox and KyungMe Kim, "Understanding Emerging Disabilities," *Disability and Society* 19 (June 2004): 323–37; Pamela Reed Gibson and Amanda Lindberg, "Work Accomodation for People with Multiple Chemical Sensitivity, *Disability and Society* 22 (December 2007): 717–32.

139. Michael Moore, "Perfume Sensitivity: ADA Claim of Office Nonsense?" July 6, 2007. On the Pennsylvania Employment Law Blog, www.paemploymentblog.com/2007/07/articles/discrimination/perfume-sensitivity-ada-claim-or-office-nonsense/.

140. Job Accomodation Network, "Accomodation and Compliance Series: Employees with Multiple Chemical Sensitivity and Environmental Illness," February 1, 2006. www.cleanerindoorair.org/JANaccommodations.pdf

141. Elizabeth Williamson and Kris Maher, "Businessess Face Push to Expand Disabled Access," *Wall Street Journal*, June 17, 2008.

142. Massachusetts Board of Retirement v. Muriga, 427 U.S. 307 (1976); Vance v. Bradley, 440 U.S. 93(1979).

143. General Dynamics Land Systems v. Clines, 540 U.S. 581 (2004).

144. Smith v. City of Jackson, 544 U.S. 228 (2005).

145. Meacham et al. v. Knolls Atomic Power Laboratory, aka KAPL, Inc., et al., No. 06-1505 (2008). See also David Stout, "Supreme Court Eases Age Bias Suits for Workers," *New York Times*, June 20, 2008.

146. See Servicemembers Legal Defense Network, "A Guide to Don't Ask, Don't Tell," July 21, 2008. www.sldn.3cdn.net/43b1d9fec919b5918b_1zm6bxv9l.pdf; United States Government Accountability Office, "Military Personnel: Financial Costs and Loss of Critical Skills Due to DOD's Homosexual Conduct Policy Cannot Be Completely Estimated," GAO 05-299, February 2005.

147. Kyle Dropp and Jon Cohen, "Acceptance of Gay People in Military Grows Dramatically," *Washington Post*, July 19, 2008.

148. Quoted in Deb Price, "Gays: Not Special Rights, Just Equal Rights," *Des Moines Register*, November 8, 1995.

149. Bowers v. Hardwick, 478 U.S. 186 (1986); Boy Scouts of America v. Dale, 530 U.S. 640 (2000); Lawrence v. Texas, 539 U. S. 558 (2003).

150. National Gay and Lesbian Task Force, "Percentage of U.S. Population Covered by a State, County, and/or City Nondiscrimination Law and/or a Broad Family Recognition Law Over Time," May 8, 2007. www.thetaskforce.org/downloads/reports/fact_sheets/CoveredByNondiscrimLaws0507Color.pdf; Lydia Saad, "Americans Evenly Divided on Morality of Homosexuality," June 18, 2008. www.gallup.com/poll/108115/Americans-Evenly-Divided-Morality-Homosexuality.aspx.

151. Carroll J. Doherty, "How Initiatives Fared," *Congressional Quarterly Weekly Report*, November 7, 1992, 3595; Thomas Galvin, "States Use Ballot Propositions to Take the Initiative," *Congressional Quarterly Weekly Report*, October 31, 1992, 3506; and John Schrag, "In Oregon, the Debate That Will Not Die," *Washington Post National Weekly Edition*, January 8–14, 1996, 20.

152. Paul Carrier, "Voters Endorse Gay Rights Law; Reversing Previous Votes, Maine Becomes the Last New England State with a Law to Protect Gays against Bias," *Portland Press Herald*, November 9, 2005.

153. Romer v. Evans, 517 U.S. 620 (1996).

154. The Pew Forum on Religion & Public Life, "A Stable Majority: Most Americans Still Oppose Same-Sex Marriage," April 1, 2008. www.pewforum.org/docs/?DocID=290

155. The Florida case was Wilson v. Ake. See the list of cases on the Defense of Marriage Act (DOMA) Watch Web site: www.domawatch.org/index.php.

156. Craig v. Boren, 429 U.S. 190 (1976); Mississippi University for Women v. Hogan, 458 U.S. 718 (1982).

157. Craig v. Boren, 429 U.S. 197 (1976).

158. See, for example, Peter Passell, "Economic Scene," *New York Times*, January 11, 1996; "Short Guys Finish Last," *Economist*, December 23, 1995–January 5, 1996, 19–22.

159. Regents of the University of California v. Bakke, 438 U.S. 265 (1978); Grutter v. Bollinger, 539 U.S. 306 (2003); and Gratz v. Bollinger, 539 U.S. 244 (2003).

160. See United Steelworkers of America v. Weber, 443 U.S. 193 (1979); Sheet Metal Workers v. EEOC, 478 U.S. 421 (1986); Local Number 93, International Association of Firefighters, AFL-CIO, C.L.C. v. City of Cleveland, 478 U.S. 501 (1986).

161. Johnson v. Transportation Agency, Santa Clara County, 480 U.S. 616 (1987).

162. City of Richmond v. J.A. Croson Co., 488 U.S. 469 (1989).

163. Adarand Constructors v. Pena, 515 U.S. 200 (1995). See Holly Idelson, "Ruling Rocks Foundation of Affirmative Action," *Congressional Quarterly Weekly Report*, June 17, 1995, 1743–45.

164. Ann Devroy and Kevin Merida, "Drawing the Line on Affirmative Action," *Washington Post National Weekly Edition*, July 3–9, 1995.

165. Quoted in Steven A. Holmes, "White House to Suspend a Program for Minorities," *New York Times*, March 8, 1996.

166. See an excerpt of the list in "Affirmative Action in Action," *Wall Street Journal*, February 27, 1995; Holly Idelson, "A 30-Year Experiment," *Congressional Quarterly Weekly Report*, June 3, 1995, 1579.

167. Idelson, "A 30-Year Experiment," 1579.

168. Quoted in Holmes, "White House to Suspend a Program for Minorities."

169. Udayan Gupta, "Minority Firms Fear More Jobs Will Vanish as Mandates End," *Wall Street Journal*, April 12, 1995.

170. Paul M. Barrett, "Minority Contractors Find Gains Are Eroded by Courtroom Attacks," *Wall Street Journal*, December 7, 1994; Gupta, "Minority Firms Fear More Jobs Will Vanish."

171. Paul M. Barrett, "Federal Preferences for Minority Firms Illustrate Affirmative-Action Dispute," *Wall Street Journal*, March 14, 1995.

172. See Paul M. Barrett and Michael K. Frisby, "'Place, Not Race' Could Be Next Catch Phrase in Government's Affirmative-Action Programs," *Wall Street Journal*, October 19, 1995.

173. Daniel Golden, "Fudge Factor: Some High Schools Finagle to Cram Kids into Top 10% of Class," *Wall Street Journal*, May 15, 2000.

174. See University of California, Office of the President, Student Affairs, Admissions, CSG, "University of California Application Admissions and Enrollment of California Resident Freshmen for Fall 1989 through 2007," January 2008. www.ucop.edu/news/factsheets/Flowfrc_8907.pdf; Pamela Burdman, "UC Officials Roll Out Plans on Preferences," *San Francisco Chronicle*, December 14, 1995.

175. Joseph Williams and Matt Negrin, "Affirmative Action Foes Point to Obama, Say Candidate is Proof Effort is no Longer Needed," *Boston Globe*, March 18, 2008.

Part 2

Individuals and Groups in American Politics

6

Public Opinion

CHAPTER OUTLINE

In the summer of 2008, Senator Barack Hussein Obama faced an unusual political challenge. He had to convince the American public that he was, in fact, a Christian. His religion mattered in the upcoming presidential election because of anti-Islamic prejudice among some voters. Confusion about his religion could have cost him the election.

One might be surprised to learn that confusion about Obama's religion was a problem. Obama had routinely told audiences about his Christian faith. His United Church of Christ pastor in Chicago, the Reverend Jeremiah Wright, Jr., had caused an uproar with controversial statements about race relations, and Obama had responded by publicly breaking with his pastor and by delivering a nationally televised speech on race relations and religion. Nevertheless, a national poll in July showed that only 57 percent of Americans knew that Obama was a Christian, and 12 percent mistakenly thought he was a Muslim. As the wars in Iraq and Afghanistan continued to cost American lives, the public's confusion about Obama's religion coupled with prejudice could have been the difference in whether Obama won or lost.[1]

What Americans believe about Obama's religion is important because the fundamental principle of democracy is that the people rule. The people decide who will hold office, and through these officeholders, the people decide public policy. Knowing the basic facts about candidates and policies is critical for informed opinion and voting. To understand our elected officials and the policies they establish, we must begin by examining public opinion—what the people think about politics and political issues. Those opinions are the basic input to the system of political rules that produce public policy.

Although public opinion should guide public policy, converting opinion into policy is not an easy task. The problems extend beyond merely sorting out the conflicting opinions different members of the public express as to the best policies. The public often lacks knowledge about many issues that government officials must confront. In addition, most people do not think ideologically—that is, their opinions are not guided by a consistent underlying philosophy. The result is that public opinion on some issues is contradictory. For example, most Americans want a balanced federal budget, but they balk when they are asked to pay for it with either increased taxes or cuts in government services.

In this chapter, we will examine the public's understanding of politics. We will discuss how people acquire their opinions and how a relatively small number of people fit their opinions together into ideologies, or coherent philosophies about politics. Finally, we will examine the public's mix of opinions on a variety of issues—especially economic and social issues—to show where they are liberal, moderate, and conservative. By exploring all these elements of public opinion—knowledge, ideologies, and opinions—we will see how daunting a task it is for government officials to base public policies on public opinion.

Year	Item of Knowledge	Percent Who Know (%)
2007[a]	The Democrats held a majority in the House of Representatives	76
2004[b]	No weapons of mass destruction were ever found in Iraq	74
2007[a]	Dick Cheney was Vice President of the United States	69
2007[a]	The United States has a trade deficit	68
2007[a]	The name of their state's governor	66
2006[c]	Global warming has already started	58
2002[d]	Know about Kyoto Treaty to limit greenhouse gases	52
2007[a]	Nancy Pelosi was Speaker of the House of Representatives	49
2007[a]	Supreme Court Chief Justice John Roberts is a conservative	37
2007[a]	Vladimir Putin was president of Russia	36
2007[a]	The federal minimum wage is $7.25 an hour	34
2007[a]	Sunni is the other major Islamic branch besides Shia	32
2007[a]	Harry Reid was Democratic Majority Leader of the Senate	15

Table 6–1   The Public's Knowledge about Politics and Issues

Most Americans do not know much about politics or political issues.

Sources: [a]The Pew Research Center for the People & the Press, "Public Knowledge of Current Affairs Little Changed by News and Information Revolutions." April 15, 2007, available at www.people-press.org/report/319/public-knowledge-of-current-affairs-little-changed-by-news-and-information-revolutions; [b]Harris Poll, April 8–15, 2004, reported at pollingreport.com/iraq3.htm; [c]Gallup Poll. March 13–16, 2006, reported at www.pollingreport.com/enviro.htm; [d]Harris Poll, September 19–23, 2002 reported at pollingreport.com/enviro2.htm.

6-1 THE PEOPLE'S LIMITED KNOWLEDGE OF POLITICS

The public's limited knowledge about Obama is typical of its lack of knowledge about many aspects of politics. As Table 6–1 shows, only a few basic facts about politics are known to virtually all Americans. Huge numbers of people do not know that global warming has already started, what the minimum wage is, or even which party holds a majority in the two houses of Congress.[2] Knowledge about policy debates is even more limited. Consider, for example, the question of foreign aid. In a poll conducted in 2000, six out of ten Americans believed that the United States spent "too much" on foreign aid and the rest said they wanted to cut foreign aid programs. Yet the public had a vastly exaggerated sense of how much the United States actually spends on foreign aid. On average, those polled estimated that 24 percent of the federal budget went to foreign aid programs—more than twenty-four times greater than the actual amount of slightly less than 1 percent. This misperception about the extent of American assistance to other countries was held by all major age, race, income, and educational groups.[3]

The willingness of people to express opinions about a wide range of issues, even when their knowledge of those issues is sketchy, extends even to nonexistent events. For instance, in 1995, the *Washington Post* set out to determine how closely Americans follow the news. To do so, they asked people whether they thought that the 1975 Public Affairs Act should be repealed. Twenty-four percent said yes, whereas 19 percent responded it should not. The poll contained only one small hitch: The 1975 Public Affairs Act doesn't exist. Thus, 43 percent of those polled expressed an opinion about an imaginary law. As one of the people who oversaw the poll concluded, "The simple fact is that on a lot of big policy issues, there really isn't any informed public opinion."[4]

The explanation for the public's lack of knowledge about politics is not that people are fools. Rather, for most people, politics is unimportant. When national surveys ask people to identify their hopes and fears, few identify political problems. (To understand just how polling organizations survey public opinion, see Box 6–1.) Far more common are answers about people's health, jobs, families, and events or conditions that affect their daily lives more directly than politics.[5] Except for times of national crisis, most Americans do not pay much attention to what is going on in Washington or their state capitals. Moreover, politics ranks far behind movies, books, sports, and other leisure activities as a source of entertainment. Few people have any real incentive to follow or learn about politics.

Surveys about public interest in politics reveal the low level of importance most people assign to politics. For instance, in 2008—an historic year in which a black man and a white woman were the leading candidates for the Democratic nomination for president—only 46 percent of the respondents to a national survey said that they were following election news very closely and 48 percent said they mostly or completely agreed with the statement, "I'm generally bored by what goes on in Washington."[6] This lack of interest affects our democracy because the few who are interested and knowledgeable can exert disproportionate influence on decision makers.

6-1a The Distribution of Knowledge

Knowledge about politics is not uniformly distributed across the public. Some people know more and some know less. Who these people are matters because knowledge is a political resource that gives power to individuals and groups.

In general, people are likely to learn more about politics if they have the *opportunity* to learn, the *capacity* to learn, and an *interest* in learning.[7] One or more of these three elements show up in many demographic, social, and psychological characteristics related to political knowledge. The most prominent demographic traits associated with knowledge are high education, income, and occupation. Social characteristics such as being active in political or even nonpolitical organizations also produce more political knowledge. And psychological characteristics, especially interest in politics and feelings of political efficacy—the sense that one can have an impact on political decisions—lead to greater political knowledge as well.

POINT OF ORDER

Box 6–1 Public Opinion Polling Methods

Scholars learn a great deal of what they know about public opinion from public opinion surveys, or polls. The basic principles of surveys are quite simple. If the sample—the group of people who are asked questions—is representative of the entire population, if the sample is large enough, and if the questions are properly worded and ordered, then the answers are very likely to reflect the opinions of the entire population. The best, most representative type of sample is what statisticians call a *simple random sample.* To draw such a sample, one would need a complete list of people in the population (e.g., the United States). People would be randomly selected from the list, perhaps by writing everyone's name on separate pieces of paper and thoroughly mixing the pieces of paper in a huge bowl. If the bowl were mixed well enough that everyone had an equal chance of selection, we would have the perfect random sample. No such complete list exists, but pollsters have developed methods to get around this problem. Using census data and sophisticated sampling techniques, pollsters draw random samples of regions and then neighborhoods within the regions. An exact list of households (if the survey is conducted in person by interviewers in the respondents' homes) or telephone numbers (if the survey is conducted by telephone) is needed only at the end of the sampling process. Just as in a simple random sample, everyone has an equal chance of being selected for the survey. The result is a sample representative of the entire population. (Actually, the survey "population" for many polls includes only *noninstitutional, adult residents.* That is, they include all adults who live in the United States and who do not reside in "institutions" such as prisons; military housing; old-age homes; or college fraternities, sororities, and dormitories. Survey organizations exclude institutional populations to save money.)

To provide an accurate description of the population, a sample must also be large enough. It often surprises people that the size of the population does not matter, only the size of the sample. A survey of 1,000 respondents will work just as well to estimate public opinion in the United States (population 300 million) as in Normal, Illinois (population 45,386 in the last census). To see why this is so, try flipping a coin a number of times. After the first ten tosses, the percentage of heads may not be close to 50 percent. But after 100 tosses, the percentage of heads will be much closer to 50 percent, and after 1,000 tosses, the percentage will be very close. In fact, the chances are 95 percent that the number will fall between 46.9 percent and 53.1 percent. The 3.1 percent variation from 50 percent is called the sampling error.

Just as the sampling error decreases as you toss the coin an increasing number of times, the sampling error gets smaller as the sample size grows in a survey. In other words, the bigger the sample, the more accurate the result—no matter what the total population size. The sampling error on a sample of 500 is 4.4 percent. With 1,000 respondents, it falls to 3.1 percent. With a sample of 1,500, it falls to 2.5 percent. Typical commercial polls use samples of about 1,000 people.

PUBLIC OPINION POLLING METHODS

The final considerations in polling are question wording and question ordering. Slight changes in the way questions are asked can change the way people respond. For instance, a survey of two randomly selected samples found that 19 percent of those in the first sample favored "forbidding" public speeches against democracy, whereas 42 percent of those in the second sample favored "not allowing" such speeches. The polls produced very different answers to what were essentially identical questions because the questions differed in tone; *forbidding* sounds much harsher than

not allowing, even if the two phrases are synonymous. In a similar vein, mentioning a famous person when asking about a specific policy proposal can skew poll results. Questions about "cutting government spending" and "George W. Bush's plans for cutting government spending" will elicit different answers because the second version of the question taps into what people think about Bush personally as well as what they think about the issue of government spending. Because of the potential problem with question wording, pollsters try to write questions that use neutral wording and that focus on one policy or idea at a time.

Question order can also influence the way people answer survey questions. One lengthy poll asked respondents whether they favored increasing defense spending, cutting it, or keeping it at existing levels. Later in the survey, the pollsters repeated the question, this time immediately after asking whether people favored increasing, cutting, or maintaining spending on education. The second version of the question implied a trade-off between spending on education and spending on defense. As a result, the second version found support for cutting defense spending was 10 percentage points higher than the first, even though both questions were asked of the *same people in the same poll.*

Because of sampling error and the effects of question wording and question ordering, we must think of surveys as providing only rough indications of what the public thinks. Moreover, when evaluating polls, keep in mind that not all pollsters play by the rules of their profession. Interest groups can use poll results to influence government decisions, so some pollsters have an incentive to bias their results. For example, a story on animal rights in the *New York Times Magazine* reported that 51 percent of Americans think that "primates are entitled to the same rights as human children." In fact, the survey—which was paid for by the Doris Day Animal League and conducted by Zogby

POINT OF ORDER *(continued)*

International—actually asked respondents whether chimpanzees should be treated "like property," "similar to children," or "the same as adults." The leap from the survey finding that 51 percent of the public feels that chimpanzees should be treated like children, rather than property, to the claim that half the American public believes that primates and children should have equal rights was provided by the animal-rights activists. The survey results were misrepresented to help the activists' cause.

Sources: Floyd J. Fowler, Jr., *Survey Research Methods* (Newbury Park, CA: Sage Publications, 1993); Chris Mooney, "John Zogby's Creative Polls," *The American Prospect 7* (February 2003): 29–33; John Mueller, *Policy and Opinion in the Gulf War* (Chicago: University of Chicago Press, 1994), 2; Eric R. A. N. Smith and Peverill Squire, "The Effects of Prestige Names in Question Wording," *Public Opinion Quarterly* 54 (Spring 1990): 97–116.

Demographic Characteristics

The single most important trait related to knowledge about politics is demographic:—education.[8] Simply put, well-educated Americans are far more likely to be knowledgeable about politics than poorly educated Americans. Education combines all three elements of learning: Schools offer the opportunity to learn, and those who progress to higher levels of education must have both the capacity for and an interest in learning. Courses in high school and college on civics, government, and history play an important role in teaching students about politics, but education's effect is not limited to what students learn in classrooms. College life surrounds students with opportunities to learn about politics. Rallies, protests, and debates are common campus events that draw in even those students who are not studying politics. By the time they leave college, most students follow politics in daily newspapers or on the Internet. This habit creates a continuing source of information that lasts a lifetime.[9]

At the other end of the education spectrum lies the political wasteland of illiteracy and "basic skills." According to the Department of Education's 2003 Adult Literacy and Lifeskills Survey, 20 percent of adult Americans fell in the bottom literacy category. Although most were not illiterate in the sense of being completely unable to read or write, they lacked the basic skills necessary to follow even simple newspaper stories.[10] Because so much political information and debate are carried in newspapers and magazines written at a higher level (e.g., *Time* and *Newsweek* magazines are written at a high school senior reading level), people who are illiterate or who can read only at a basic skills level miss most of what is happening in politics.[11]

Occupation and income, which along with education constitute a person's **socioeconomic status**, also have substantial effects on political knowledge. People with white-collar jobs usually work in offices and deal with paperwork, which offers them more opportunities to learn than those in blue-collar jobs. People with higher incomes are also more likely than those with lower incomes to be targeted by political appeals.[12] Moreover, high-status jobs and incomes put people in contact with others who have more education and who are more likely to be interested in politics. Thus, those who have a good job or a high income also benefit from some

socioeconomic status

Social status as measured by one's education, income, and occupation.

of the indirect effects of education. These demographic characteristics are typical of people who know about political issues.[13]

Social Characteristics

People who are knowledgeable about politics also share certain social characteristics. In general, any activity that brings people into contact with others and provides opportunities to talk about politics increases learning. Consequently, people who join and become active in organizations, even if they are not political organizations, are likely to learn more about politics. Union members and participants in religious, civic, and other types of organizations, for instance, tend to become more knowledgeable.

Psychological Characteristics

The main psychological characteristics associated with people who know more about politics are interest in politics, a sense of political efficacy, and a tendency toward activism. Survey researchers measure interest with questions about whether respondents are interested in the current campaigns, whether they care who wins, and whether they follow politics. In every case, those who are more interested know more about politics.[14]

The second psychological trait associated with people who know more about politics, a sense of political efficacy, is a source both of interest and of knowledge. Efficacy is the belief that one can have some effect or influence on politics. Many people without a sense of political efficacy believe there is no point in bothering to learn about politics because they cannot influence any political decisions. Therefore, those who do not feel efficacious tend to know less than those who do. Polls measure sense of efficacy with questions such as whether respondents think that public officials care what they think.[15]

Finally, those who participate actively in politics know more than those who do not. Any kind of activity, from attending campaign rallies to working for candidates, gives people opportunities to learn. Whether people become active because of their interest in politics or because of apolitical reasons such as doing a favor for an activist friend, the result is a learning experience. At least in theory, people in a democracy should be knowledgeable about government and issues to govern themselves wisely. Because activists have a disproportionate influence over policy decisions and rules, it is fortunate that they also have a lot of knowledge about politics. In other words, those who exercise more influence in politics also know more about politics.

6-1b Sources of Knowledge

Aside from schools—which provide background information on government and politics—the principal sources of political information are the news media and the Internet, which provide information on current issues and political events. Since 1960, almost

90 percent of all Americans claim to have followed campaigns on television. A somewhat smaller percentage of people claim to have followed campaigns in newspapers, declining from about 80 percent in the early 1960s to 67 percent in 2004.[16] Studies of how Americans spend their time have found that the proportion of adult Americans who say that they "read a newspaper yesterday" declined from 71 percent in 1965 to 40 percent in 2006.[17] In addition, surveys show that people believe television news has improved and newspapers have gotten worse.[18] Thus, more and more people have come to think of television as their primary source of news.

The decline in newspaper reading and the growing dependence on television have disturbing implications because television offers much less information. As anyone who has compared the newspaper and television coverage of the same event can tell, newspaper coverage is far more thorough. Television news usually consists of a series of short reports on unrelated subjects—usually chosen for their action, drama, and splashy pictures. As we shall see in Chapter 8, many observers argue that television's need for exciting pictures leads television journalists to ignore important political issues and to concentrate on trivial aspects of politics such as campaign rallies, crowds, and the candidates' witty or embarrassing statements.[19] Defenders of television news counter that television can interest viewers in issues that otherwise would attract little attention—such as the plight of farmers struggling to combat a drought.[20] Moreover, although television news may be less informative than newspapers, regular followers of television news do learn from it.[21] Still, the decline in the reliance on newspapers as an information source seems to be reducing the public's overall level of knowledge about politics.

Another source of knowledge, which has received growing attention in the past decade, is the Internet. A staggering amount of information is available to anyone who is willing to spend time surfing the Web. Most newspapers are now published on the Web as well as in print, and all serious political candidates have their own Web sites. In the early days of the Internet, some observers predicted that the Web would revolutionize politics by making it easy for people to acquire political information and to contact political officials to express their views. These changes would force the political system to become more democratic. Politicians would have no choice but to respond to these more informed, connected citizens.[22]

Although the amount of effort needed to learn facts about politics certainly did decrease because of the Internet, the impact was far short of revolutionary. The development of the Internet changed politics, but it did not have a great impact on political knowledge. The central reason the Internet has had only a limited impact on what people know is that interest in politics has not increased. It is, indeed, easier to learn more about politics, but it is also easier to learn more about professional basketball, women's literature, Navajo jewelry, and every other imaginable topic. Just because the information is available does not mean that everyone will choose to look for it. First, people must be interested in a subject, and then they must decide to take the time to search actively for information about it. The people who do take the time to learn more about politics, of course, already know a good deal about politics. Interest and knowledge go hand in hand. So the result is that the well informed become even better informed, whereas others remain unaffected.[23]

Although the Internet did not revolutionize politics, it did have a substantial impact on people who use it regularly. One major study found that people who were "digital citizens"—that is, people who use the Internet daily—are far more likely than the rest of the public to be informed about politics, to be engaged in civic matters, and to participate in politics. As a consequence, they are also far more likely to be politically influential.[24]

6-1c People with Knowledge: Issue Publics

Despite the tremendous publicity surrounding issues such as Barack Obama's religion, global warming, or the religions of Iraq, the public's lack of knowledge about them can now be understood in context. Many people—even those who regularly watch television—know little about politics and policy issues, but others know a great deal. People who follow a particular issue closely, are well informed about it, and have strong opinions on the issue are called **attentive publics** or **issue publics**.[25]

A few people belong to many issue publics. They closely follow a wide range of issues. Other people pay attention to only one or two issues. And many people don't follow any issues at all. Some farmers, for instance, may follow farm policy; some auto workers may know a good deal about tariffs on Japanese cars; and some students at public universities may follow policies that set tuition increases. And some people take a special interest America's foreign policy, especially the wars in Iraq and Afghanistan.

In thinking about issue publics, one needs to recognize that only *some* members of groups that are affected by government policies pay attention to them. All farmers do not follow farm policy, nor do all students follow tuition policies. So an issue public does not include all the people affected by a policy, but only the far smaller number of people who care enough about the issue to follow it—whether or not it affects them personally.

Issue publics are especially important to elected officials because these people know and care a great deal about a narrow range of policy issues and because they are often willing to vote or spend their time and money to support their opinions in campaigns (see Chapter 7). Thus, pleasing issue publics is especially important to politicians seeking reelection.[26]

Issue publics, then, are small groups of Americans who tend to know more about politics and exert more influence over particular issues. Not surprisingly, members of issue publics have the characteristics associated with greater political knowledge. They

attentive publics

People who follow a particular issue closely, are well informed about it, and have strong opinions on it.

issue publics

People who follow a particular issue closely, are well informed about it, and have strong opinions on it.

People who follow a few select issues closely, as some students follow the issue of tuition hikes, are issue publics.

generally are highly educated, have high incomes and good jobs, are active in political or other organizations, and are interested in and feel efficacious about politics. The first three of these characteristics, which make up socioeconomic status, are critical. People with higher socioeconomic status are far more politically knowledgeable than people with lower socioeconomic status. As we shall see in Chapter 10, this knowledge gives them a substantial advantage in political disputes. When a conflict over policy arises and the government must decide how to manage the conflict, the greater knowledge people of high socioeconomic status have gives them a better chance to get what they want from government.

6-2 THE NATURE AND ACQUISITION OF OPINIONS AND VALUES

Democracy depends on more than people's knowledge of politics; it depends on their preferences about government policies. Those preferences, or **opinions** (which are sometimes also called **attitudes**), are based both on factual knowledge and on underlying **values**, or principles. For instance, the general value of tolerance leads many people to hold the opinion that Congress should pass laws protecting gays and lesbians against discrimination.[27]

Public opinion may or may not be based on an informed appraisal of the issues. As the *Washington Post* poll on repealing the fictional 1975 Public Affairs Act shows, people are willing to express opinions even if they are not knowledgeable about the issue in question. They develop their opinions from what they know about the issues, from their values, and from the advice they receive from other people.[28]

opinions
Preferences on specific issues.

attitudes
Preferences on specific issues.

values
Basic principles that lead people to form opinions on specific issues.

People do not acquire opinions in the same way they learn facts. The process by which one acquires values and develops opinions from society is called **socialization**. Throughout life, from early childhood to old age, people undergo socialization. They develop new opinions and change old ones. The most important sources of socialization are family, friends, school, and the media.[29]

socialization
The process by which people acquire values and opinions from their societies.

6-2a Family and Friends

Parents have substantial influence over their children's values and attitudes when they are young. Long before formal schooling begins, parents start teaching their children facts about the world and values to guide them in it. Moral and religious values often receive special attention, but parents teach other political and social values as well—from racial prejudices to political preferences.[30]

Most socialization is informal. In fact, parents and children are often not even aware of it. Children pick up on and learn from the casual comments of parents in conversations with other adults, their reactions to television news broadcasts, and a host of other cues. The emotional bonds between parents and children become a powerful teaching tool. Given the informal nature of these messages, it should not be surprising to find that the children of more politically interested and involved parents both learn more and are more likely themselves to become interested and involved in politics. If parents talk more about politics, their children are likely both to learn what their parents think and to learn that politics is interesting and important.[31]

As children grow older, their peers begin to influence their attitudes and opinions as well. The approval of friends grows in importance, especially during adolescence. For some, the initial values acquired from parents are strengthened; for others, they are weakened. The party loyalty of a child from a conservative family growing up in a liberal neighborhood can be the hidden prize in a contest of loyalties.[32]

Children may learn value judgments before they have any clear idea of the situations in which they apply. By fifth or sixth grade, for example, most children understand the party labels *Democrat* and *Republican,* and they respond with their party's candidate when questioned about their voting preferences in presidential elections. Yet few fifth and sixth graders understand much about the presidency, Congress, or the political issues at stake in the elections.[33] Their choices stem more from their desire to be like their parents and friends than from any detailed consideration of political issues.

By the time children reach young adulthood, many shift away from their parents' views. A comprehensive study of high school seniors and their parents compared the party loyalties of the two groups and found a high but far from perfect level of parent-child agreement.[34] Almost 59 percent of the parent-student pairs agreed, whereas only 7 percent took opposing stands—one

Democratic, the other Republican. Most disagreement consisted of a parent or child claiming to be an independent, while the other identified with a party. In a follow-up study of the same people eight years later, the researchers found agreement had declined to only 48 percent, but still only 8 percent had aligned with opposing parties.[35]

When the researchers examined the extent of parent-child agreement on a range of political issues such as racial integration, school prayer, and free speech, they found much lower levels of agreement. Moreover, their follow-up study showed that agreement declined further as the years passed. The implication is that it is far easier to teach basic values, such as party identification, than to pass on specific opinions about public policies. Whereas values are usually acquired through socialization, opinions on specific policies form in response to other influences such as individual reasoning, guidance from friends, or information from trusted political leaders. Whatever one's views, they are rarely carbon copies of those of one's parents.[36]

6-2b School

Schools are another source of cues for acquiring values and opinions. Many of these cues are intentionally built into the system to teach patriotism, respect for the law, and acceptance of the basic democratic and capitalist values of our political system—the daily pledge of allegiance and required history and civics classes, for instance. Indeed, teaching obedience and respect for authority are major goals of elementary schools. Yet these blunt efforts to socialize students are not always effective.[37] For example, in the case of the high school seniors and their parents that we previously discussed, the researchers looked at the differences between students who did and did not take high school civics classes. They found that the African American students who took the class had greater knowledge and expressed greater support for democratic values than those who had not taken it, but they did not find differences among any other groups. For most students, the civics classes did not have the intended effect.

Other political cues in school are less obvious, but no less important. Students often acquire the values of their teachers and peers, as a classic study of the power of socialization at Bennington College in the 1930s shows.[38] The faculty at Bennington was predominantly liberal, whereas the students came mostly from well-to-do, conservative families. The political preferences of the first-year students matched those of their parents fairly closely—both groups were conservative. But the preferences of the juniors and seniors who had been under the influence of their more senior peers and the Bennington faculty changed substantially. Unlike their parents, the juniors and seniors were predominantly liberal. At this stage, the school seemed more influential than parents in the students' lives.

6-2c The Media

Along with family, friends, and school, the mass media also socialize people, often from an early age. Many children begin watching television when they are only babies. During the winter months, elementary school children typically spend more hours watching television than attending school. By the time of high school graduation, the average graduate will have watched 15,000 hours of television and attended only 11,000 hours of class.[39] Heavy users of mass media tend both to know more about current events and to support basic American values such as freedom of speech and tolerance. They also tend to hold the moderate political beliefs that television typically portrays.[40]

The mass media are influential in many ways, not just through news shows. Movies and television in the 1950s promoted racial and ethnic stereotypes, reinforcing prejudices. By the 1990s and 2000s, many stereotypes had changed or been abandoned. Television programs and films now commonly present bigots as fools to be pitied or scorned. Moreover, television and films have become a force pushing the public—especially the young—toward more tolerance for gays and lesbians. Beginning in the 1980s, gay and lesbian characters in television shows and movies became more and more common, and the characters were treated with respect. In 1997, Ellen DeGeneres became the first leading character on a television show to come out of the closet. Others, including Rosie O'Donnell, followed. The message coming out of Hollywood was clear: Being gay or lesbian is an acceptable lifestyle.[41]

Yet despite the television industry's decision to embrace the norm of tolerance, some stereotypes persist. Minorities and women still appear more commonly in weaker supporting roles rather than leading roles. A 2000 study, for example, found that Hollywood prefers Hispanic actors who have Mestizo features and who do not speak English as their first language. The study also found that they were disproportionately cast as "benevolent servants" or "criminals."[42] Another recent study showed that more than 40 percent of all MTV videos (other than those containing only footage of rock concerts) portrayed women as "being less than a person, a two-dimensional image. This characterization includes 'the dumb blonde,' the sex object and the whimpering victim."[43]

People often acquire mistaken impressions from the entertainment media. As media critics often observe, far more murders are committed on television and in movies than in real life. These fictional murders have real effects on public opinion, however. Heavy television watchers exaggerate the crime rate in the country, fear crime more than those who watch television less, and respond with calls for more police, more prisons, and longer sentences for criminals.[44] Entertainment affects the public's perceptions of society, so it indirectly affects public policy through public opinion.

6-2d Lifetime Learning and Incremental Change

Socialization does not end when a person leaves high school or college; it continues slowly throughout one's life. New jobs, new friends, new neighborhoods, and new political issues can change people's values and attitudes.[45] Significant change, however, is uncommon. Most people's basic values and attitudes change little after they are past their college years.

The conditions that cause change can be seen in a follow-up to the Bennington study. Researchers tracked down the participants in the original study after more than twenty years.[46] They found a high level of stability in the former students' attitudes. In the 1960 election, thirty of the thirty-three most liberal students from the 1930s voted for the Democratic candidate, John Kennedy; twenty-two of the thirty-three most conservative students from the 1930s voted for the Republican, Richard Nixon. The most important factor in explaining the few who changed views during the intervening years seemed to be whether the former student had married a liberal or a conservative and the political views of her friends. Having a spouse and friends who supported one's views resulted in little change, but being surrounded by those who disagreed caused some women to bring their opinions in line with their friends. Thus, the four years at Bennington College had a powerful influence, but not one that could always withstand later influences.

Despite the finding of some change among Bennington students, the most comprehensive studies of attitude change among Americans have concluded that people's values and attitudes typically change little over time.[47] People's attitudes do indeed change in response to changing conditions and events. Rising gasoline prices, wars, and terrorist attacks, for example, cause people to change their opinions on some issues. But as we shall explain, on most issues, public opinion is fairly stable.

The Bennington students of the 1930s do not differ very much from today's students. All children learn their initial values and attitudes from their parents. Over time, these beliefs change as other influences enter their lives—friends, schools, and the mass media, among others. In the realm of politics, party identification is more stable than virtually any other attitude, but as the Bennington study shows, it, too, can change over the years. Socialization factors—family, friends, schools, and the media—play a large role in determining public opinion, and through public opinion, they influence public policy.

6-3 IDEOLOGIES

Most people have opinions about a wide range of issues. As we just discussed, people's opinions are based on their knowledge and their underlying values and are shaped by socialization.

Opinions, however, do not exist in isolation. They are related to other opinions. When opinions and values fit together into a general philosophy about government, we call them an *ideology.*

The term **ideology** has been defined in many ways, but the core of most definitions—and the one used here—is that an ideology is an elaborate set of interrelated beliefs with overarching, abstract principles that provide people with coherent philosophies about politics.[48] This means that an ideology is both a list of opinions (e.g., conservatives should oppose high tax rates on corporations and government regulation of businesses) and a principled explanation of why those opinions fit together (e.g., the principle of minimal government interference in the marketplace implies that the government should let businesses keep as much of their profits as possible and should avoid regulating them).

The role of ideologies is more than just to fit opinions together in an intellectually pleasing fashion. Ideologies focus conflict in society. Ideologies tell us not only what to think, but also when we should agree and disagree with our opponents. The ideology of Marxism, for example, tells us that class distinctions are the most important divisions in society and that divisions within classes—such as race or ethnicity—should be ignored.[49] By establishing this, Marxism guides its adherents in identifying conflicts and in choosing the correct side to take. Other ideologies, including those that dominate American politics, point toward other conflicts.

The two ideologies most widespread in America today—**liberalism** and **conservatism**—agree on the basic principles of democracy and capitalism. These principles are well known to most Americans. *Democracy* means people control their government through elections and assumes that all people should have the same legal and political rights. Some writers describe this principle as *equality. Capitalism* means private ownership of the means of production and the free pursuit of profit in the marketplace. Closely associated with the idea of capitalism is the principle of *freedom,* which is the absence of government interference in one's economic activity and one's personal liberty.[50] Democracy and capitalism, then, are roughly synonymous with equality and freedom.

Although the ideologies of liberalism and conservatism agree on our basic democratic-capitalist system, they disagree on the balance between the two principles. Democracy and capitalism conflict with each other in many situations. Consider campaign contributions as an example. A wealthy person can afford to give far more money to candidates and thus, insofar as money buys influence, can exert more influence than a poor person. Should the wealthy person be allowed the *freedom* to give a huge amount, or should contributions be limited to preserve political *equality* between the rich and poor? As we shall see in the discussions that follow, conservatives place great value on freedom, whereas liberals value equality more.

ideology
An elaborate set of interrelated beliefs with overarching, abstract principles that make people's political philosophies coherent.

liberalism
The political philosophy that government should play an expansive role in society (except in the area of personal morality) with the goal of protecting its weaker citizens and ensuring political and social equality for all citizens.

conservatism
The political philosophy that government should play a minimal role in society (except in the area of traditional moral values) with the goal of ensuring all its citizens economic freedom.

6-3a Liberalism

Modern-day liberalism differs significantly from the classical liberalism described in Chapter 2. Today, the central principle of liberalism is that the government should play an extensive role in society, protecting poorer and weaker citizens. In economic matters, liberals are willing to curtail economic freedom and restrain capitalism to increase political and economic equality. In short, liberals believe that government should take an active role in moving society toward *equality of outcomes,* as described in Chapter 5. In social matters, however, liberals favor a much smaller role for government, believing that the government should not restrict individual freedoms, even when the majority wants to do so. In foreign affairs, liberals believe that U.S. foreign policy should play down the use of military force and should focus instead on humanitarian and economic aid (see Box 6–2).

In terms of specific issues, liberalism implies that the government should take the following actions:

- Make the wealthy pay more in taxes, raise minimum wages, and pass other laws to redistribute wealth from those who have more to those who have less.

- Regulate businesses to protect unions, to ensure safe working conditions, to guard consumers, and to protect the environment.

- Guarantee minimum levels of health care, income, and housing for the poor, elderly, and people with disabilities—using government programs such as Medicare, Medicaid, welfare, and food stamps.

- Prevent discrimination against racial, religious, or ethnic minorities, gays and lesbians, people with disabilities, and people with extreme or unpopular ideas.

- Assist underdeveloped foreign nations with economic and humanitarian aid.

left
The liberal end of the political spectrum.

Not all liberals, or people who are to the **left** of center, agree with all these positions. People naturally choose their own opinions. But when a person agrees with most or all of the ideas on this list, we describe that person as a liberal.

6-3b Conservatism

The central principle of conservatism is that the government should play a minimal role in society, except to uphold traditional moral standards. In economic matters, conservatives oppose governmental limitations on businesses or individual behavior, preferring to let the free market determine economic outcomes. Although conservatives favor a welfare "social safety net," they favor lower benefits than liberals do, and they prefer that private charities assist the poor so that the government is involved as little as possible. More broadly, conservatives believe that government should be limited to ensuring *equality of opportunities* in

The People behind the Rules

Box 6–2   The Liberals: Senator Barbara Boxer and the Reverend Jesse Jackson

One way to learn about liberalism is to look at the records of two prominent liberals—Senator Barbara Boxer (D-MA) and the Rev. Jesse Jackson. Although both belong to the Democratic Party, they are to the left of most of their fellow Democrats.

BARBARA BOXER

Barbara Boxer got her start in politics working as a peace activist for Senator Eugene McCarthy's 1968 unsuccessful bid for the Democratic presidential nomination. She later moved to Marin County, just north of San Francisco, and while working as a journalist, ran for county supervisor in 1972 and lost. Four years later, she won the job and held it until she moved up by winning election to the U.S. House of Representatives in 1982. Ten years later, she was elected to the U.S. Senate from California. Throughout all of her campaigns, she emphasized women's rights, social and economic justice, and environmental issues.

Sen. Barbara Boxer (D-CA).

Source: © Chip Somodevilla/Getty Images.

Boxer is recognized as perhaps the most prominent advocate of women's rights in Congress. In 1991, when Supreme Court nominee Clarence Thomas was accused of sexual harassment by his former special assistant and adviser, Anita Hill, Boxer led a group of female members of the House who marched across to the Senate to demand that the Judiciary Committee—all of whose members were white males—take the charges seriously. Boxer has also been a prominent supporter of abortion rights, women's health issues, and laws helping to protect children from abuse.

On the question of women in Congress, Boxer wrote, "I do not believe in quotas. I do believe that the nation would be better served if there were more women in the Senate. I'll settle for 50 percent."

On health care, Boxer has worked to increase medical research funding to find cures for HIV/AIDS, tuberculosis, and autism, and to conduct embryonic stem cell research. She is a strong advocate of expanding the health insurance system and has called for working toward universal health coverage. She was one of the early congressional advocates of establishing a patients' bill of rights.

On economic issues, Boxer has voted for increasing the minimum wage at every opportunity, and against repealing the estate tax and other tax cuts proposed by the George W. Bush administration. She opposed North American Free Trade Agreement (NAFTA) on the grounds that it would cost American workers their jobs. More recently, she co-authored a bill to give American companies incentives to bring overseas profits back to the United States to create jobs in America.

On environmental issues, Boxer has consistently opposed allowing oil drilling in the Arctic National Wildlife Refuge. She also pushed legislation that would sharply reduce toxic emissions from older, coal-fired power plants and other legislation that would increase energy conservation.

On social issues, Boxer voted against the constitutional ban on same-sex marriage and in favor of prohibiting job discrimination based on sexual orientation and of expanding the definition of hate crimes to include sexual orientation.

In foreign issues, Boxer has taken a strong stand against the War in Iraq. In 2002, she voted against authorizing the use of force in Iraq, a vote which she later described on the Daily Show with Jon Stewart as "the best vote of my life." In 2005, she introduced legislation calling for a timeline for withdrawal of troops from Iraq; and in

2006, she joined the majority of her fellow Democrats in voting for a resolution that urged President Bush to begin withdrawing American troops from Iraq that year.

JESSE JACKSON

Jesse Jackson entered politics as the student body president of North Carolina Agricultural and Technical State University, where he led civil rights sit-ins, marches, and other demonstrations in the early 1960s. After graduation, he moved to Chicago, where he attended the Chicago Theological Seminary and was ordained as a Baptist minister in 1968. While in Chicago, Jackson met the Rev. Martin Luther King, Jr., and worked with him and the Southern Christian Leadership Conference (SCLC). In 1966, King appointed Jackson to head the Chicago chapter of Operation Breadbasket—a program through which Jackson worked to improve the economic position of African Americans and to eliminate housing segregation in Chicago.

Rev. Jesse Jackson.

Source: ©AFP/Getty Images

In 1971, Jackson left SCLC and founded the People United to Serve Humanity (PUSH). As the leader of PUSH, Jackson led a string of marches, protests, and boycotts to fight discrimination and to improve the social and economic status of African Americans. In 1984 and again in 1988, Jackson ran for the Democratic nomination for the presidency. During his campaigns, he called for cutting defense expenditures and spending the resulting savings on domestic programs such as education, health, housing, and jobs programs. He favored increasing the taxes on the wealthy and cutting taxes on the working class and poor. He opposed abortion in the 1970s, but by 1984 he had reversed himself, supporting free choice in abortion. In foreign affairs, he favored putting pressure on South Africa to end apartheid and pulling

American aid out of countries he considered right-wing dictatorships.

In the 1990s and 2000s, Jackson often found himself at odds with the moderate Clinton administration and the conservative Bush administration. Jackson opposed welfare reform, arguing that the lifetime limits on welfare would eventually result in families and children becoming homeless and malnourished. He pushed for even greater increases in the minimum wage to benefit the poor and working class. He worked against English-only laws and anti-immigration laws, arguing that they were discriminatory. Although he

never won public office, he continues to be a prominent voice on the American left.

Sources: Michael Barone and Richard E. Cohen, *The Almanac of American Politics 2008* (Washington, D.C.: National Journal, 2007); Michael Barone and Richard E. Cohen, *The Almanac of American Politics 2003* (Washington, D.C.: National Journal, 2003); Barbara Boxer with Nicole Boxer, *Strangers in the Senate* (Washington, D.C.: National Press Books, 1994); Ruth Conniff, "Barbara Boxer Interview." *The Progressive* July 2005; *Candidates '88* (Washington, D.C.: Congressional Quarterly Press, 1988); Allen D. Hertzke, *Echoes of Discontent: Jesse Jackson, Pat Robertson, and the Resurgence of Populism* (Washington, D.C.: CQ Press, 1993), chap. 3; "On the issues: Barbara Boxer," available at www.ontheissues.org/Senate/Barbara_Boxer.htm.

economic matters, not equality of *outcomes*. In social matters, however, conservatives favor a more expansive role for government, believing that majorities ought to be able to limit personal behavior on moral grounds. In foreign affairs, conservatives believe that the United States should use military aid, and if necessary, military force to promote its interests overseas; they place less priority on economic and humanitarian aid (see Box 6–3).

In terms of specific policies, conservatism implies that the government should take the following actions:

- Make tax rates flatter so that everyone pays the same or nearly the same percentage, regardless of total income.

- Oppose efforts to increase the minimum wage, to raise tariffs on imported goods, and to place more regulations on the way businesses operate.

- Reduce environmental regulations on businesses so that they can prosper.

- Limit social welfare benefits for the poor, elderly, and people with disabilities.

- Uphold "traditional" values by strengthening laws against pornography, by limiting or outlawing abortion, and by opposing laws protecting the rights of homosexuals.

- Pursue American foreign policy interests with military force if needed.

right

The conservative end of the political spectrum.

Not all conservatives, or people who are to the **right** of center, agree with this list of positions. But when people agree with most of these ideas, we describe them as conservative.

Looking at liberalism and conservatism together, we see both consensus and conflict. Both agree on the general principles of democracy and capitalism, although they disagree on the balance

The People behind the Rules

Box 6–3   The Conservatives: Senator Mitch McConnell and Rush Limbaugh

To learn about conservatism, consider the records of two prominent conservatives—Senator Mitch McConnell and Rush Limbaugh. McConnell and Limbaugh stand at the opposite end of the political spectrum from Boxer and Jackson, and both are to the right of most of their fellow Republicans.

MITCH MCCONNELL

Mitch McConnell's enthusiasm for politics appeared at an early age. He was elected student body president at the University of Louisville, then president of the Student Bar Association at the University of Kentucky College of Law. In his last year of law school, McConnell was an intern for Senator John Cooper (R-KY) in 1967. After finishing his law degree, McConnell worked as a Senate staffer, and then was appointed a Deputy Assistant Attorney General under President Gerald Ford. In 1984, he was elected to the Senate from Kentucky. In 2007, the Senate Republicans elected McConnell as their leader.

Source: © Getty Images.

Sen. Mitch McConnell (R-KY).

McConnell is best known as an opponent of campaign finance regulation in defense of free speech. He argued, "You must have money in politics, because it's the only way the candidates can get their messages across." McConnell waged a tough fight against limitations on campaign donations, but lost when the Bipartisan Campaign Reform Act passed in 2003. He immediately filed a lawsuit challenging the constitutionality of the law, but lost when the U.S. Supreme Court upheld it.

Throughout his career, McConnell has sought to pass laws that were consistent with his Christian fundamentalist beliefs. He opposes abortion and has voted to limit it in every way he can—for example, by banning abortions at American military bases and hospitals, and by making it illegal for minors to cross state lines to obtain abortions. He has also voted to ban embryonic stem cell research, human cloning, and same-sex marriage.

On economic issues, McConnell has sought to reduce taxes and the size of government. He voted to eliminate the "marriage penalty" and to reduce estate taxes and taxes on capital gains and dividends. He voted in favor of the moratorium on Internet sales taxes. He also supported legislation to require a supermajority to increase taxes of any kind.

On energy and environmental issues, McConnell has voted to open the Arctic National Wildlife Refuge to oil drilling; he has sought to eliminate the automobile fuel efficiency (CAFE) standards; he has supported subsidies for exploration by oil and gas companies and opposed funding for solar and wind power. He has generally voted against environmental laws whenever he believed they would harm business interests and interfere with free markets.

In foreign affairs, he has established himself as a leading supporter of President George W. Bush's handling of the wars in Iraq and Afghanistan. He initially voted to give President Bush the authority to attack Iraq in 2002, and he continues to resist efforts to withdraw American troops from Iraq. He has argued that if the United States does not stay in Iraq, "the terrorists would come after us where we live." McConnell also believes in giving the government broad powers to fight terrorism. He introduced the Protect America Act of 2007, which would allow the federal government to monitor telephone and electronic communications of people both inside and outside the country without obtaining a warrant from the courts.

RUSH LIMBAUGH

Rush Limbaugh got his start in radio as a music disc jockey in Pittsburgh in the 1970s. He worked as a disc jockey for a string of radio stations through the 1970s and then briefly directed promotions for the Kansas City Royals. He returned to radio in 1984 as a political commentator in Sacramento. Four years later, he moved to New York City and began his nationally syndicated *Rush Limbaugh Show* on WABC. By 2008, his show had 20 million listeners on more than 600 stations. His reputation grew along with his audience. In 1992, former President Ronald Reagan called him "the Number One voice for conservatism in our country." The *National Review,* a prominent conservative magazine, described him as the "The Leader of the Opposition" against President Bill Clinton.

Source: © Bill Pugliano/Getty Images.

Rush Limbaugh.

Limbaugh is a prominent critic of feminism and women's equality. He has drawn attention to his cause by describing outspoken feminists as "feminazis." In *The Way Things Ought to Be,* Limbaugh wrote, "I prefer to call the most obnoxious feminists what they really are: feminazis. . . . I often use it to describe women who are obsessed with perpetuating a modern-day holocaust: abortion."

Limbaugh routinely attacks environmentalists on his show, calling

The People behind the Rules   *(continued)*

them "environmental wackos." He disputes scientific claims that human activity is causing global warming, arguing that the scientific evidence is "bogus." His prescription for cleaning up the environment is "unfettered free enterprise," rather than environmental regulation.

On other issues, Limbaugh calls for increasing border security to prevent illegal immigrants from entering the country, and for systematically arresting and deporting illegal immigrants who are already here. He

strongly opposes any path to citizenship for illegal immigrants, arguing that it is a reward for breaking the law. He is a supporter of capital punishment, and he has prominently mocked people who are concerned about potential torture at Guantanamo Bay or the Abu Ghraib prison in Iraq.

Sources: Michael Barone, *The Almanac of American Politics 2008.* (Washington, D.C.: National Journal, 2007), 679–82; David Bauder, "Rush Limbaugh Returns from Rehab," *Newsday,* 18 November 2003; James Bowman, "The Leader of the Opposition, political commentator Rush Limbaugh," *National Review* 6 September 1993;

Diana Dwyre and Victoria Farrar-Myers, *Legislative Labyrinth: Congress and Campaign Finance Reform* (Washington, D.C.: CQ Press, 2001); Rush H. Limbaugh, *The Way Things Ought to Be* (New York: Pocket Books, 1992); Rush Limbaugh, "Idiot Bird Extinct, Future of World at Risk," available at www.rushlimbaugh.com/home/estack/idiot_bird_extinct.guest.html.html; Dick Meyer, "Rush: MPs Just 'Blowing Off Steam,'" CBS News, May 6, 2004, available at www.cbsnews.com/stories/2004/05/06/opinion/meyer/main616021.shtml; Zachary Roth and Cliff Schecter, "Meet the New Boss," *Washington Monthly,* October 2006; On the Issues: Mitch McConnell, available at www.ontheissues.org/Senate/Mitch_McConnell.htm

between those principles. The conflicts between the two ideologies center on economic, social, and foreign policies. On economic policies, conservatives favor the interests of the wealthy by emphasizing economic growth, whereas liberals favor the interests of the poor by supporting income redistribution. On social policies, conservatives favor traditional moral standards and want to allow the majority to impose standards on the minority, whereas liberals prefer to prevent the government from legislating moral or religious standards. In foreign affairs, conservatives focus on preparing for military threats, whereas liberals emphasize efforts to aid the poor of other nations.

6-3c Changes over Time

Ideologies are not fixed sets of ideas; they change over time in response to changes in society. Industrialization, urbanization, technological development, immigration, population growth, and other economic and social trends have all caused shifts in ideologies over time. Some of these modifications have been huge, others small.

At the end of the 1700s, when the United States was founded, most of the people were independent farmers with little need for government services. *Classical liberals* saw government as a potential threat to the individual rights and liberties of these citizens and thus sought to keep government small.[51] Yet with industrialization in the late 1800s and the struggle of workers to form labor unions, liberals began to see the government's potential as a protector of the rights of weaker citizens, rather than as a threat to them. By the 1900s, a new "reform liberalism" had begun to emerge with the belief that government intervention in the marketplace could do more good than harm.[52]

Less dramatic changes in ideologies occur over shorter spans of time as new issues arise and old issues evolve. When Medicare, the federal health-care program for the elderly, was debated in

Congress in 1964, conservatives denounced it as "socialized medicine." A spokesperson for the American Medical Association—a vehement opponent of Medicare—argued that Medicare would be a giant step down the path to socialism in the United States; he declared that "medical care for the aged is a foot in the door of a government takeover of all medicine."[53] Yet by the time that spokesperson, Ronald Reagan, was elected president sixteen years later, the one-time socialist threat had become a popular program that liberals and conservatives both supported. Indeed, Medicare became so popular that when Republican members of Congress tried to restructure the program in 1995—at least in part to contain its skyrocketing cost—polls showed that the American public was deeply critical of the proposed changes.[54] In this case, as in many others, new ideas became accepted and the nature of the political conflicts changed over time.

6-3d Sources of Ideologies

Ideologies have their roots in two types of soil: in abstract ideas about the roles of individuals and the government in society, and in real-life groups of people helped or harmed by the ideas. Ideologies do not exist in a vacuum. Rather, they serve as justifications for groups seeking power, money, and other benefits. As a group's circumstances change, the ideology most closely associated with the group may be altered to rationalize new claims on social benefits.

As an example of how ideologies bend to group interests, consider how some conservatives reacted to the energy crisis that struck California in 2000. In 1996, Republican Governor Pete Wilson led California in passing a law deregulating the electricity industry. The law, which allowed electricity producers to charge whatever price the market would bear, was based on conservative, free-market principles. The idea was that if prices rose, energy companies would build new power plants, which would meet the demand for energy and keep prices from rising too high. At first, the law seemed to be working fine. But in 2000, the supply of electricity could not keep up with the surging demand and prices skyrocketed. When northern California was hit with rolling blackouts, many Republicans abandoned their free-market principles and declared deregulation a mistake. They started efforts to regulate energy anew and called on the federal government to cap the price of electricity being sold in the West. The principle of free markets gave way to the demands of voters outraged at receiving high electric bills.[55]

Of course, conservatives are not alone in adjusting their principles to satisfy group interests. For example, most liberals prefer to spend less money on defense. Yet when cutting defense spending means cutting spending on weapons programs or military bases that employ large numbers of their constituents, liberal lawmakers often vote for more defense spending. So when we speak of liberalism and conservatism, we must explain not only the ideas that

Source: © Reuters/Corbis.

Ronald Reagan once denounced Medicare as "socialism"; twenty years later, as president, he praised it.

make up those ideologies, but also the social groups that will benefit or lose if those ideas prevail.

Ideologies form around economic, racial, ethnic, religious, and gender groups. Probably the most important set of groups that ideologies form around are economic groups. Conservatism offers a rationalization for the wealthy and business interests to have the freedom to gain an even larger share of society's wealth; liberalism offers a rationalization for redistributing wealth so that the poor and working class get a larger share—moving them toward equality.

Racial, ethnic, and religious groups are also significant sources of ideological cleavages. Not only do members of these groups often share similar economic situations, but they also share similar cultural and religious values. Together with providing a sense of group identity, these values can lead a group to demand social benefits from the government. They can range from tangible, economic benefits—such as those benefits affirmative action programs for minorities provide—to intangible benefits—such as laws symbolizing the cultural superiority of a group (e.g., English-only laws, which establish English as the only language in which official government business can be conducted).[56]

The temperance movement to ban alcoholic beverages in the United States is a good example of the politics of cultural superiority.[57] Although some Protestant churches had objected to drinking since before the American Revolution, the temperance movement gained its greatest strength in the early 1900s when huge numbers of Catholic immigrants arrived from countries such as Ireland, Italy, and Poland in which drinking was socially and religiously acceptable. As the growing immigrant Catholic population began to threaten the Yankee Protestants' political control in some areas, the Protestants responded with calls for laws banning the sale or consumption of alcoholic beverages—laws that would symbolize Protestant superiority. In 1919, the temperance forces won passage of the Eighteenth Amendment to the Constitution, which established Prohibition. Fourteen years later, the political tides had changed as more immigrants became naturalized citizens with voting rights, and the Twenty-First Amendment repealed Prohibition.

The fight over temperance is typical of many ideological conflicts between social groups. The conservatives—mostly Yankee Protestants—sought laws against drinking to uphold the traditional moral value of abstinence. The liberals—mostly ethnic European Catholics—sought to resist those laws. The battleground was government policy; the prize both sides sought was a rule.

Since the late 1960s, gender has become the basis for ideological divisions as well. As we saw in Chapter 5, the women's movement has identified and challenged a range of government policies and social practices in which men and women have been treated differently—from discrimination in education, jobs, and government benefits to private clubs and sexist language.[58] The movement also has sought to establish the principle of reproductive rights (e.g., the right to family planning and the right to choose abortion) and to establish government policies that aid women in other ways (e.g., creating government-subsidized child care and parental leave for birth or adoption). As the women's movement expanded, it quickly became an established aspect of liberalism (although the label *feminist* seems to have fallen out of fashion).[59] For their part, conservatives began to defend the "traditional" roles of women in families.[60]

6-3e The Process of Molding Ideologies

So far we have been discussing changes in ideologies without explaining who causes the changes. Ideologies are not modified by some vague process, of course, but by people. The politicians, journalists, political writers, and academics who debate political issues in speeches, newspaper columns, political magazines, and books are modifying ideologies with their arguments. No one person can declare the true liberal or conservative position on an issue, but as influential liberal or conservative leaders debate issues, a rough consensus emerges. When liberal leaders such as Senator Barbara Boxer (D-CA) argue for legislation establishing a right to parental leave from one's job after the birth of a child, and conservative leaders such as Senator Mitch McConnell (R-KY) oppose it, less prominent liberals and conservatives follow along. In this manner, ideologies evolve over time.

Only a small number of people participate in the process of molding ideologies. Most people—even most politicians, journalists, writers, and academics—are no more than consumers of the ideological packages the few create. The debates over what society should do about various problems and what "true" liberals or conservatives should think include few participants and many observers. The results of the debates—the packages of liberal and conservative positions—are passed down to the rest of the public through the news media, classrooms, and other forums. From these sources, depending on which leaders we trust, we learn whether we should favor or oppose new rules and policies.[61]

6-4 PUBLIC OPINION ON THE ISSUES

Describing public opinion is a difficult task because of the many confusing and seemingly contradictory views people hold. We can see this contradictory nature when we look at the way people's opinions fail to fit into sets of liberal, moderate, or conservative ideologies or when we compare Americans' opinions on abstract symbols with their opinions on concrete policies. In both cases, people seem to hold conflicting opinions, which shows that few Americans think ideologically. Although most Americans do not think ideologically, clear patterns do show up in their opinions. When we look at public opinion on clusters of related issues, we can see these patterns, which help us to understand public opinion and the demands people put on government.

6-4a Ideological Thinking by the Public

Although most politicians and political activists see politics in terms of ideological battles, only a relatively small portion of the mass public thinks in ideological terms—that is, thinks about politics in terms of overarching, abstract principles relating a broad set of beliefs about policies. Estimating how many people think ideologically is difficult, but clearly only a minority does. One study found that in 1980, only 42 percent of the population could even crudely define the terms *liberal* and *conservative*.[62] The proportion of the population that understands the terms apparently has not changed in decades.[63]

Studies of **attitude consistency** show similar results. Attitude consistency is the degree to which one's opinions on political issues are all roughly at the same point on the ideological spectrum. That is, if one holds all liberal opinions, all moderate opinions, or all conservative opinions, then one is consistent; but if one holds a mixture of liberal, moderate, and conservative positions at the same time, then one is inconsistent. Although holding an ideologically consistent set of opinions is not the same as ideological thinking, it is closely related.[64] Repeated studies show that most of the public holds some mix of liberal, moderate, and conservative opinions.[65] Our political leaders may think in ideological terms, but most of the people who vote for them do not.

The studies showing that few people think ideologically imply that the public only weakly understands the political debates that dominate the world of politicians and journalists. As we previously discussed, the public has a weak grasp of the many facts needed to understand debates about public policy. Here, we see that the public also has a weak understanding of the philosophies that help us evaluate the meaning of those facts.

6-4b Abstract Symbols versus Concrete Policies

The contradictory nature of the American public also becomes apparent when we consider the difference between people's support for conservative symbols and their support for liberal policies. As two leading political scientists put it, the American public is best described as "both ideologically 'conservative' *and* programmatically 'liberal.' That is, Americans are opposed to 'big government' and respond favorably to the myths and symbols of competitive capitalism, in the abstract. When it comes to assessing specific government programs or the behavior of actual business enterprises, however, they support government spending in a variety of domestic areas and are profoundly suspicious of big business."[66]

The mix of liberal and conservative opinions is not some quirk of survey research methods. Rather, it stems from the public's lack of interest and political knowledge. Relatively few people know enough or spend enough time thinking about politics to recognize the connections between abstract statements with which they agree (e.g., "free enterprise"—which implies less government

attitude consistency
The degree to which a person's political opinions all fall at about the same point on the liberal-conservative dimension.

intervention in the marketplace) and government programs that they like (e.g., the minimum wage and government regulations to protect the environment—both of which imply more government intervention). Most people neither recognize nor resolve the contradictions among their opinions.

A good place to begin looking at symbols is by examining the ideological labels Americans use, shown in Figure 6–1. According to a survey conducted in 2006, more adult Americans claimed to be conservative (34 percent) than liberal (27 percent), with the rest describing themselves as moderate. Over the past twenty-five years, the ideological mix of Americans has remained relatively stable. From 30 to 40 percent of Americans have thought of themselves as conservative, and from 23 to 30 percent have thought of themselves as liberal.

Many abstract statements of conservative values attract majority support. For instance, a poll taken in 1995 asked people whether

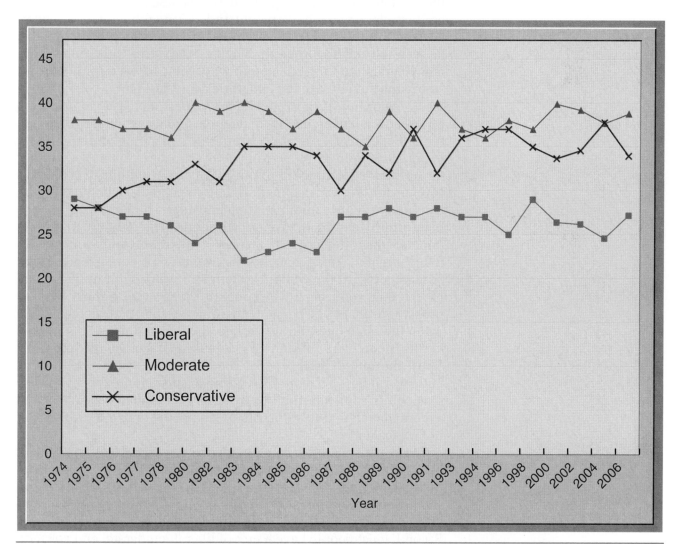

Figure 6–1   Percentage of Americans Who Identify Themselves as Politically Moderate, Conservative, or Liberal. Most Americans label themselves as moderate, but more people identify themselves as conservatives than as liberals—suggesting a more conservative electorate.

Source: *Data from surveys by National Opinion Research Center, General Social Survey, 1974–2006.*

they agreed with the Republican proposal to "create an 'opportunity society' in which the federal government assures all Americans of an equal chance to prosper based on each individual's merits" but does not "guarantee minimum living standards or provide social benefits for its citizens." Of those polled, 41 percent said they "somewhat agreed," and an additional 22 percent said they "agreed strongly."[67] In a 1999 poll, 55 percent of the respondents agreed that "regulation of business does more harm than good," whereas only 37 percent disagreed.[68] These figures would seem to indicate that the American public is predominantly conservative.

Turning to concrete policy issues, however, we see signs of a more liberal electorate. For more than two decades, Americans have been polled about various aspects of government spending. They are presented with a list of problems and asked whether "we're spending too much money on it, too little money, or about the right amount." As we previously discussed, conservatives generally prefer smaller government and less spending, whereas liberals tend to prefer larger government and more spending. This can be seen in campaign rhetoric when conservative candidates claim that liberals are "big spenders" who want to solve problems by "throwing money at them." Rhetoric aside, as Figure 6–2 shows, in 2006, majorities of those polled supported increases in spending on the environment, health, education, and crime. In the aftermath of the September 11 attacks, support for spending on the military increased significantly, peaking at 34 percent in 2004. Yet support for military spending fell to only 25 percent within two years as support for the war declined. Defense spending, which conservatives and the Bush administration consider a high priority, is not a high priority among the American public. The only programs less popular than defense were space exploration and foreign aid (which many Americans see as welfare for foreigners). Many observers regard the welfare system as a weak point of liberalism. Figure 6–2 confirms this claim; in 2006 more people favored reducing welfare (38 percent) than increasing it (25 percent). Yet when the same question was asked about spending for "assistance to the poor," the liberal, pro-spending majority reappeared.[69] Thus, the public believes that the welfare system works poorly, but nevertheless a majority is willing to spend more money to help the poor. In sum, questions on specific government programs paint a more liberal picture of the American people than questions about ideological labels.[70]

Faced with the conflicting evidence presented here, one might ask, "How should we describe the public? Is it liberal or conservative?" This question can be answered two ways—"neither" and "both." First, most people are neither very liberal nor very conservative. They are moderate, or lean only slightly to the left or right. Second, most people have a mix of liberal, moderate, and conservative opinions. Some of those opinions conflict. For instance, some people want to increase spending on virtually every government program, cut taxes, and balance the budget—all at the same time

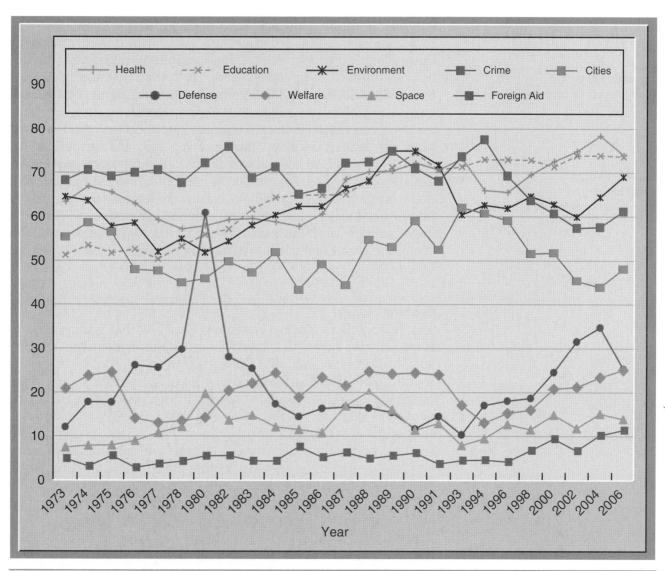

Figure 6–2   Percentage of Americans Who Support Increased Spending. Most Americans want to increase spending in most policy areas—suggesting a more liberal electorate.

Source: *Data from National Opinion Research Center, General Social Survey, 1974–2006.*

(which is a serious problem for those who must work out the federal budget, as Chapter 16 explains). Because they never address the problem of *how* to balance spending and taxes, they never have to sort out their opinions and decide which is most important. Their contradictory liberal and conservative opinions remain unresolved.

6-4c Public Opinion on Clusters of Related Issues

Although most people's opinions are not arranged in neat, ideologically consistent sets, people do think about political issues and their opinions make sense. When we focus on different types of issues and look for patterns, rather than contradictions, clear patterns distinguish economic issues from social issues.

economic issues
Issues relating to the distribution of income and wealth in society.

social issues
Issues based on moral or value judgments.

Public opinion analysts often distinguish between economic issues and social issues because the patterns of public opinion on these issues differ markedly.[71] **Economic issues** deal with the distribution of wealth in society—the tax system, welfare, Medicare, Social Security, regulation of businesses and unions, and similar issues. **Social issues** relate to religion, morals, and value judgments—civil rights, women's equality, abortion and birth control, stem cell research, drugs, pornography, sexual orientation, and related issues. Typically, those with higher incomes and educations tend to be conservative on economic issues (in part because this is to their economic benefit) and more liberal on social issues (because education fosters more tolerant attitudes). Those with lower incomes and educations tend to be the opposite—liberal on economic issues and conservative on social issues.

Economic Issues

The basic pattern among economic issues is that groups tend to favor policies that will benefit them economically. The wealthy tend to prefer tax cuts and flatter tax rates—so that taxes on the wealthy will drop—and reductions in government services—especially those such as welfare that go to the poor. In contrast, the poor tend to prefer tax increases and more progressive tax rates—so that the wealthy will pay more—and increases in government services, especially those that go to the poor. Economic self-interest also is apparent in the way many other groups view policies: Farmers tend to support federal crop subsidies; renters tend to favor rent control; business owners tend to favor reduction in government regulations unless the regulations protect their businesses.

A typical example of these patterns can be seen in the debate over the role the federal government ought to play in influencing the distribution of wealth in our country. As one might expect, income differences stand out in the data in Table 6–2. Whereas only 6 percent of people making more than $110,000 a year want strong action to reduce income differences, 26 percent of people making less than $20,000 a year want strong action. Educational groups also differ on this issue. Thirty-five percent of people who did not graduate from high school want the government to do something, but only 10 percent of college graduates and 20 percent of people with education beyond college do. African Americans favor government action more strongly than whites. There are also sharp differences of opinion between Democrats and liberals, who favor government action, and Republicans and conservatives, who oppose it. The gender and age differences are much smaller. Women prefer government action to reduce income inequality slightly more than men do, and the young prefer it more than the old.

Aside from noting the economic self-interest Table 6–2 reveals, we can make another useful observation. We can see that the opinions of various groups are not monolithic or uniform. Many of the

	Strongly Favor Government Action (%)	Strongly Oppose Government Action (%)
Nationwide		
Income	19	13
$110,000+	6	24
$75–109,999	15	21
$60–74,999	16	13
$40–59,999	22	13
$20–39,999	23	11
$0–19,999	26	10
Education		
College postgraduate	20	14
College graduate	10	20
Some college	30	13
High school	19	13
Less than high school	35	13
Race		
White	16	17
Black	46	8
Other	26	4
Sex		
Male	19	17
Female	22	12
Age		
18–29	24	9
30–49	20	15
50–64	21	17
65+	17	17
Party Identification		
Strong Republicans	3	35
Weak Republicans	4	15
Independent Republicans	15	24
Pure Independents	23	13
Independent Democrats	33	6
Weak Democrats	26	4
Strong Democrats	40	9

(Continued)

Ideology	Strongly Favor Government Action (%)	Strongly Oppose Government Action (%)
Extremely conservative	23	30
Conservative	16	23
Slightly conservative	13	16
Moderate	18	13
Slightly liberal	22	4
Liberal	34	6
Extremely liberal	53	5

Table 6–2   Support for Government Action to Reduce the Income Differences between the Wealthy and Poor
The wealthy, the well educated, whites, Republicans, and conservatives generally oppose government action to reduce income differences. The poor, the poorly educated, Democrats, and liberals are more likely to favor steps to reduce inequality.

Question: "Some people think that the government in Washington ought to reduce the income differences between the rich and the poor, perhaps by raising the taxes of wealthy families or by giving income assistance to the poor. Others think that the government should not concern itself with reducing this income difference between the rich and the poor. Here is a card with a scale from 1 to 7. Think of a score of 1 as meaning that the government ought to reduce the income differences between rich and poor, and a score of 7 meaning that the government should not concern itself with reducing income differences. What score between 1 and 7 comes closest to the way you feel?"
Note: The first column in the table ("Strongly Favor Government Action") shows the percent who said they placed themselves at "1" on the scale; the second column ("Strongly Oppose") shows the percent who said they placed themselves at "7" on the scale.
Source: National Opinion Research Center, General Social Survey, 2004.

wealthy supported taking action to increase income equality, whereas some of the poor opposed it. Opinions are mixed within every income group. This is a typical finding. When we describe public opinion about any group, we should always be careful to avoid exaggerating tendencies. When we say that the poor tend to be liberal on economic issues, we usually mean that more of the poor support liberal proposals compared with the wealthy. But this can still mean that both groups support or oppose the proposals.

Social Issues

The most important pattern among social issues is that the well educated tend to be liberal and the poorly educated tend to be conservative. This stems from the fact that education leads people to become more tolerant, and tolerance lies at the root of many social issues—tolerance for people of different races or ethnicities, tolerance for people with different religions or sexual orientations, and tolerance for people who make moral judgments different from one's own. Consequently, the well educated tend to take liberal positions on social issues, whereas the poorly educated tend to take conservative positions. Those with good educations are more likely to favor government intervention to prevent discrimination against racial, religious, or ethnic minorities, homosexuals, the handicapped, and people with extreme or unpopular ideas. By the same token, the well educated are less likely than the poorly educated to support government action to uphold "traditional" values at the expense of individual freedom.[72]

A typical example of the relationship between education and opinion on social issues appears in the public's opinions about whether homosexuals should be allowed to serve in the military, as Table 6–3 shows. In 2000, 84 percent of all adults with postgraduate degrees thought that homosexuals should be allowed to serve, but only 67 percent of those who had not attended college agreed. A similar pattern is evident among income groups—81 percent of those with the highest incomes believed homosexuals should be allowed to serve, but only 74 percent of those with the lowest incomes thought so.

Table 6–3 also reveals a second important pattern related to social issues. The young tend to be more liberal than the old. (Remember, however, that this is generally not true concerning economic issues—for example, recall the minimum wage poll results shown in Table 6–2). In the case of opinions about homosexuals in the military shown in Table 6–3, 90 percent of people twenty-five and younger favor allowing homosexuals to serve, but only 67 percent of people older than sixty-five agree.

The relationship between age and opinions on social issues has its roots in social change. At least since the 1950s, each generation has been more liberal and more tolerant than the previous generation. Many ideas about social issues that were unpopular fifty years ago—equality of the races, equality of the sexes, and the acceptability of homosexual relationships—have now gained a far larger measure of acceptance. As society changes from generation to generation, the young have usually led the way. In terms of public opinion, this means that at any one time, the young are typically more liberal than older people on social issues.[73]

One of the central areas of conflict in American society is another social issue—what role the government should play in guaranteeing civil rights for minorities and in working toward racial and ethnic equality. Should school children be bused to different schools to achieve racial balance? Should minorities receive special opportunities in school admissions or jobs to make up for past discrimination? Should the government make any effort to help lift more minorities into the middle class? As we discussed in Chapter 5, questions such as these have played a prominent role in American history.[74]

On virtually every civil rights issue, minorities differ sharply from whites. For example, when asked in 1991 whether they approved or disapproved of "marriage between blacks and whites," 70 percent of non-whites, but only 44 percent of whites, said they approved.[75] Similarly, a poll conducted in 2000 asked people whether they believed it was the federal government's responsibility to see to it that blacks get fair treatment in jobs. Eighty percent of non-whites, but only 46 percent of whites, said that it was the federal government's responsibility (see Table 6–4).

	Should Be Allowed (%)	Should Not Be Allowed (%)
Nationwide	76	24
Sex		
Men	66	34
Women	83	17
Age		
18–25	90	10
26–35	78	22
36–45	76	24
46–55	76	24
56–65	65	35
66+	66	34
Race		
White	78	22
Non-white	68	32
Education		
College postgraduate	84	16
College graduate	85	15
Some college	77	23
High school graduate	72	28
Less than high school	67	33
Income		
$75,000+	81	19
$50–74,999	75	25
$25–49,999	76	24
$0–24,999	74	26
Party Identification		
Republicans	65	35
Independents	77	23
Democrats	82	18
Ideology		
Liberal	87	13
Moderate	84	16
Conservative	68	32

Table 6–3   Attitudes toward Homosexuals Serving in the Military

The young, the well educated, and the wealthy are more likely to take the liberal stand of favoring rights for homosexuals; elderly people, the poorly educated, and the poor are more likely to take the conservative stand of opposing homosexual rights.

Question: "Do you think homosexuals should be allowed to serve in the United States Armed Forces or don't you think so?"

Source: Data from the CPS 2000 American National Election Study. In addition to finding racial patterns on civil rights opinions, we also see the same sort of age and education patterns that appear in other social issues. In the case of equal treatment in jobs, Table 6–4 shows that 71 percent of people twenty-five and under want the federal government to intervene, but only 45 percent of those over sixty-five agree. Similarly, those with postgraduate educations were more likely to favor federal action than those with fewer years of school.

	Government Should Ensure Equal Treatment (%)	Not Government's Responsibility (%)
Nationwide	54	46
Sex		
Men	54	46
Women	54	46
Age		
18–25	71	29
26–35	47	53
36–45	55	45
46–55	56	44
56–65	47	53
66+	45	55
Race		
White	46	54
Non-white	80	20
Education		
College postgraduate	63	37
College graduate	58	42
Some college	52	48
High school graduate	48	52
Less than high school	59	41
Income		
$75,000+	47	53
$50–74,999	62	38
$25–49,999	52	48
$0–24,999	55	45
Party Identification		
Republicans	36	64
Independents	53	47
Democrats	68	32
Ideology		
Liberal	66	34
Moderate	59	41
Conservative	35	65

Table 6–4   Support for a Federal Government Role Ensuring Job Equality

Question: "Some people feel that if black people are not getting fair treatment in jobs, the government in Washington ought to see to it that they do. Others feel that this is not the federal government's business. How do you feel? Should the government in Washington see to it that black people get fair treatment in jobs or is this not the federal government's business?"

Source: Data from the CPS 2000 American National Election Study.

Differences in perceptions of social conditions help explain these differences in opinion. To get a sense of how differently blacks and whites see race relations, consider the results of two Gallup polls conducted in 1999. The first survey asked, "Have you ever felt that you were stopped by the police just because of your race or ethnic background?" Only 6 percent of whites, but 42 percent of blacks, said yes.[76] The second survey asked blacks whether they felt they had experienced discrimination within the last thirty days. The group that felt the most discrimination was young black men between eighteen and thirty-four years old. Forty-five percent of them said they had experienced discrimination while shopping, 32 percent said they had experienced discrimination while dining out, and 23 percent said they had experienced discrimination at work.[77] These sharply differing perceptions help explain the different attitudes people have toward what the government should do about racial equality.

Given this context, Barack Obama's presidential campaign surprised many political observers. Early assessments of Obama's campaign agreed that his chances were slim. As recently as 2000, a CBS News Poll had shown that only 37 percent of the public said that America was "ready to elect a black president." By January, 2007, when Obama was beginning to campaign, that number had increased to only 54 percent.[78] Yet he captured the Democratic presidential nomination and won the presidency despite the fact that only two-thirds of the public said that they were "entirely comfortable" with an African American president.[79] One part of the explanation is that voters cared more about issues such as the economy and the wars in Iraq and Afghanistan than about Obama's race, but it may also be the case that more progress on racial attitudes has occurred than some observers recognized.

Our final example of a social issue is abortion. Since the Supreme Court ruled in *Roe v. Wade* (1973) that states could not make abortion illegal, abortion has been among the most divisive social issues in the nation.[80] Liberal political leaders tend to be **pro-choice** (i.e., favor a woman's right to choose abortion) and conservative leaders tend to be **pro-life** (i.e., favor making abortion illegal), yet a substantial amount of disagreement exists both among liberal political leaders and among conservative political leaders as well as in the population.[81] In other words, the liberal and conservative positions on abortion do not line up neatly with the liberal and conservative positions on other major issues.

Although abortion is not a typical social issue, as Table 6–5 shows, the college educated are still much more likely to say that abortion should always be legal than are those who did not attend college. Largely because the well educated have high incomes, a relationship also exists between income and opinion on abortion. In addition, Democrats and liberals are more likely to be pro-choice than are Republicans and conservatives.

As Table 6–5 also shows, the percentage of women who believe that abortion should always be legal is about the same as the percentage of men who think so. A few polls have found that women

pro-life

Favoring the policy of making abortion illegal.

pro-choice

Favoring the policy of allowing women to choose whether to have abortions.

	Never Permitted (%)	Rape, Incest, Danger to Woman (%)	Other Circumstances (%)	Always (%)
Nationwide	13	32	16	39
Sex				
Men	12	34	17	38
Women	14	30	15	41
Age				
18–25	16	35	13	37
26–35	9	32	18	42
36–45	13	22	17	47
46–55	11	29	16	45
56–65	14	39	11	36
66+	17	32	16	40
Race				
White	11	32	17	40
Non-white	22	30	12	40
Education				
College postgraduate	2	23	17	58
College graduate	7	29	14	50
Some college	12	34	17	38
High school graduate	16	32	16	36
Less than high school	21	34	14	30
Income				
$75,000+	6	32	15	47
$50–74,999	8	23	18	50
$25–49,999	10	30	14	47
$0–24,999	17	34	17	32
Party Identification				
Republicans	13	38	17	32
Independents	12	31	16	42
Democrats	14	27	13	46
Ideology				
Liberal	10	19	15	56
Moderate	8	32	20	40
Conservative	14	40	17	29

Table 6–5   Attitudes toward Abortion

The well educated, high-income earners, Democrats, and liberals are somewhat more in favor of legal abortion than the poorly educated, low-income earners, Republicans, and conservatives.

Question: "There has been some discussion about abortion during recent years. Which one of the opinions on this page best agrees with your view? (1) By law, abortion should never be permitted. (2) The law should permit abortion only in case of rape, incest, or when the woman's life is in danger. (3) The law should permit abortion for reasons other than rape, incest, or danger to the woman's life, but only after the need for the abortion has been clearly established. (4) By law, a woman should always be able to obtain an abortion as a matter of personal choice."

Source: *Data from the CPS 2000 American National Election Study.*

lean slightly toward a pro-choice position, but most have found no differences between men's and women's positions on abortion.[82] Although abortion is often described as a "women's issue," women and men have generally held similar views on the matter. However, men and women do typically differ on a range of other issues, including education, child care, parental leaves, and a wide range of social welfare benefits.

Taking a step back and looking broadly over the range of public opinion on issues, we see that when we analyze public opinion in terms of specific economic and social issues, making sense of it becomes easier. As we saw, people have contradictory opinions about some issues, but as we see here, that does not mean their opinions are random or chaotic.

Attitudes on economic issues are heavily influenced by economic self-interest—wealthier people tend to favor policies that benefit the wealthy; poorer people usually favor policies that benefit the poor. Attitudes on social issues are heavily influenced by education—well-educated people generally prefer more tolerant social policies, whereas poorly educated people usually prefer less tolerant social policies. Other patterns emerge as well. The young tend to be more liberal on social issues than the elderly, and whites tend to be more conservative on civil rights issues than non-whites. Together these patterns help us to describe public opinion and to understand the conflicting demands that the public makes on government officials.

6-4d Changes in Opinion over Time

For the most part, public opinion is fairly stable over time. Indeed, the key point to make about changes in public opinion is that there aren't many. The most thorough investigation of change in public opinion over time found a "remarkable degree of stability in Americans' collective policy preferences."[83] The study collected all the public opinion time series available from the major commercial and academic survey organizations from 1935 to 1990 and discovered that fewer than half of the opinions changed, and most of the changes were quite modest. Fewer than 7 percent of all public opinion items changed as much as 20 percentage points, and fewer than 2 percent changed as much as 30 percentage points (the size of the 1980 shift in opinion on defense spending in Figure 6–2).

When changes in opinion do occur, they tend to be modest, such as the 10 percentage point increase from 1974 to 2004 in people identifying themselves as politically conservative (see Figure 6–1). Large movements, such as the 30 percent jump in the number of people who thought that the government was spending too little on defense in 1980 (see Figure 6–2), are uncommon.

When public opinion does shift dramatically, it usually does so in response to dramatic events that capture the public's attention. For example, worries about the 1979 Iranian seizure of the American embassy in Tehran and the Soviet invasion of Afghanistan less than a month later, coupled with Ronald Reagan's 1980 presidential campaign calls for a bigger military, caused the surge of people clamoring for more money to be spent on defense.[84] Within two years, however, the American hostage crisis in Iran was over, the Soviet invasion was largely forgotten, and the public's willingness to spend more on the military returned to its original level.

The public's response to the war with Iraq from 2003 through 2006 offers another example of a rapidly changing public mood. As late as January 2003, only 57 percent of the public said they would favor having U.S. forces take military action against Iraq. Throughout January and February, as the United Nations and other western allies declined to join the United States in invading Iraq, and as President George W. Bush's rhetoric escalated, support for military intervention increased.[85] By April, as American and British troops entered Baghdad and Saddam Hussein's regime collapsed, 80 percent of the people said they supported President Bush's decision to go to war.[86] Five years later, however, the public had turned against the war. In July 2008, as the number of American soldiers killed in Iraq passed 4,000, the number of casualties exceeded 30,000, and the end of the war was still not in sight, a USA Today/Gallup poll found that 60 percent of Americans thought we had made a mistake going to war with Iraq.[87]

Happily, hostage crises and wars are not common events, so public opinion remains fairly stable on the whole. When changes do occur, they typically happen slowly, over long periods of time. We can describe these trends by once more breaking down issues into social and economic issues.

Since World War II, most changes in attitudes on *social* issues have headed in a liberal direction.[88] The public has moved to the left on a wide range of social issues—civil rights for minorities, equality for women, abortion, divorce, civil liberties, and gay and lesbian rights. Most of these changes in opinion have led to more liberal public policies.

Consider, as an example of change, opinions on civil rights issues, which have shifted relatively quickly during the past forty years. As recently as the 1960s, equal rights for minorities were controversial, but as Figure 6–3 shows, school integration is now almost universally accepted. Our society has also made progress toward more tolerant attitudes about open housing and interracial marriage; however, as Figure 6–3 shows, significant numbers of whites still support both forms of discrimination. Note that Figure 6–3 shows the results when people are asked whether they favor a *law* against interracial marriages, not whether they personally approve of interracial marriages, which is another matter. Forty-five percent of whites disapproved in 1995, but only 16 percent would support a law banning interracial marriage. In sum, support for racially intolerant laws has been steadily declining since the 1960s, but America is clearly a long way from being a nation without racial prejudice.[89]

Another social issue on which attitudes have been changing recently is the rights of gays and lesbians. In a series of surveys

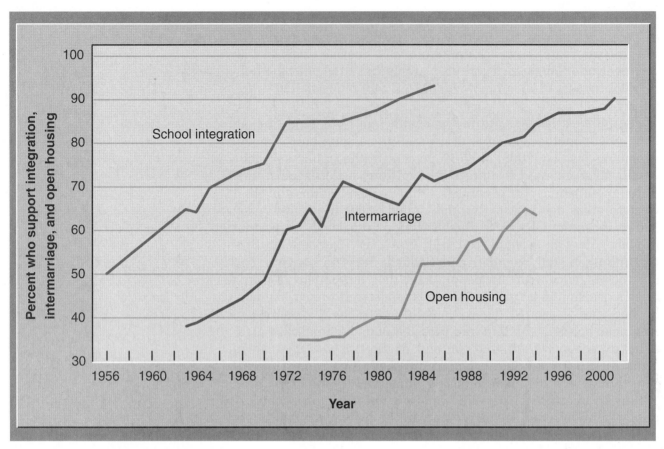

Figure 6–3   Percentage of White Respondents Who Supported School Integration, Intermarriage, and Open Housing.
Support for racial equality has been steadily growing, but many Americans still do not support complete
equality between the races.

Source: *Data from the NORC General Social Surveys. NORC data from 1956 to 1983 are from Howard Schuman, Charlotte Steeh, and Lawrence Bobo, Racial
Attitudes in America: Trends and Interpretations* (Cambridge: Harvard University Press, 1985), 74–75, 88–89.

conducted between 1973 and 1991, shown in Figure 6–4, the public's views were fairly stable. Seventy to 77 percent of the public said that sexual relations between adults of the same sex were always wrong. Starting in 1992, however, opinions began to change. By 2006, only 56 percent said they believed that gay and lesbian sexual relations were always wrong, whereas 32 percent said they were never wrong. Moreover, people seventy years and older are the most likely to condemn gay and lesbian sex. As younger generations with more accepting attitudes replace older generations, overall opinion toward homosexuality is likely to turn even more tolerant.

On economic issues, changes in public opinion have been mixed. Support for Social Security has been high since the 1930s and remains steady.[90] Most other *entitlement programs*—federal programs such as Medicare and veterans' benefits that provide direct benefits to individuals—have also remained highly popular. (See Chapter 16 for a discussion of entitlement programs.) From 1974 to 1980, a conservative trend caused support for big government, welfare, business regulation, environmental protection, and taxes to fall. From 1981 through the mid-1990s, those trends

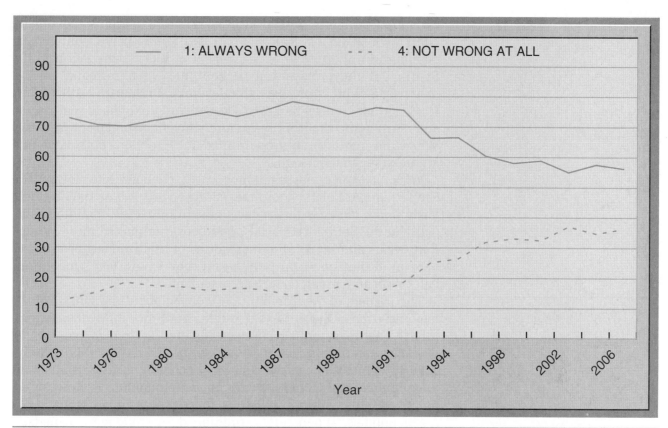

Figure 6–4   Percentage of Respondents Who Believe That Sexual Relations between Adults of the Same Sex Is "Always Wrong" or "Not Wrong at All."
Source: *Data from the NORC General Social Surveys, 1973–2006.*

reversed as public opinion on most economic issues began to move in a liberal direction. Since the mid-1990s, the direction of public opinion has been less clear. Opinion on some issues has moved in a more liberal direction, whereas opinion on other issues has moved in a more conservative direction.[91]

6-4e Causes of Change

Most movements in public opinion, like the changes in ideology previously discussed, can be traced to social or economic forces. The growth in support for women's equality, for instance, came about partly because of World War II. When the United States mobilized for war, many women entered the workforce to replace men who had joined the military. Although some women left the workforce when the war ended, many stayed. Moreover, many who worked during the war and then dropped out eventually returned to work. The growing number of working women became a major force underpinning the demands for equality.[92]

Social and economic forces alone may not be enough to produce changes in public attitudes. Often individuals or organizations play an important leadership role in bringing issues to the public's attention. For example, as we saw in Chapter 5, the growth in racial tolerance in the United States over the past fifty years depended critically on the leaders of the civil rights movement. Until the 1950s, most Americans largely ignored civil rights. Many people did not approve of the system of racial segregation in the South, but they allowed it to continue. In a series of sit-ins, marches, and other protests, the Reverend Dr. Martin Luther King, Jr., and other civil rights leaders forced the problems of segregation and racism onto the front pages and television screens of America. When the public finally confronted the problem, both laws and attitudes began to change.[93]

With racial attitudes, as in most cases, change came slowly. The Civil Rights Act of 1964 and the Voting Rights Act of 1965 brought fairly quick changes to the laws governing racial relations, especially in the South. Yet racial prejudices diminished more slowly. Forty years after the end of most forms of legalized segregation, 12 percent of the American public said they would feel "uncomfortable" with an African American president.

The framers of the Constitution worried about the whims of the majority—the possibility that public opinion could change rapidly.[94] That fear might have been justified 200 years ago, but, as we have seen in this section, it is not justified now. Public opinion is fairly stable. When sudden change occurs, it usually results from a dramatic event such as a war. Far more common is slow movement in public opinion, such as the changes in opinions about racial policies. When public opinion does shift, we can usually find the causes in social and economic changes in society and in the activities of political leaders.

SUMMARY

In a democracy, public opinion should guide the government's decisions. One might suppose that this means that the government should enact whatever policies the people want; that whenever a conflict arises, the government should do as the majority prefers. Yet our discussion of public opinion should make it clear that the matter is not so simple. The people's limited knowledge of politics, their inconsistent values and opinions, and their lack of a coherent ideology make it difficult for officeholders to gauge public opinion accurately.

Huge numbers of people do not know many basic facts about government and politics—from the fact that the United States must import oil to meet its energy needs to the name of the Chief Justice of the United States Supreme Court. Few people have any detailed understanding of the issues involved in congressional debates. Although almost everyone has some knowledge about some political issues, few have much detailed information. From the point of view of government officials, judging what the public would want if it knew the facts is extremely difficult.

To complicate matters, knowledge is not distributed equally in the population. The better educated, those with high incomes and high-status jobs, those who feel interested in and efficacious about politics, and those who are active in politics generally know a good deal more than the rest of the population and exert a disproportionate amount of influence.

People don't acquire opinions in the same way they learn facts about politics. People develop their values and opinions from those around them—from their families in early childhood and from friends, teachers, and coworkers in later life. The mass media—including both news and entertainment media—also play an important role in molding people's beliefs.

To see how people's values and opinions fit together, it helps to consider the role of ideology. The prevailing ideologies in the United States are liberalism—which emphasizes the government's role in protecting its weaker citizens—and conservatism—which calls for government to play a minimal role in society, except to protect traditional moral standards. Ideologies are not fixed. Rather, they evolve over time in response to changing social, demographic, and technological changes in society. As new issues arise and old issues change, political leaders debate them, and in doing so, bring about slow shifts in what we think of as liberalism and conservatism.

An evaluation of the public's political knowledge shows that, unlike most political leaders, ordinary people usually do not think in ideological terms. Many people cannot even describe the dominant ideologies of liberalism and conservatism. Rather than holding consistent sets of liberal, moderate, or conservative views, many people hold a range of opinions from liberal to conservative. Moreover, some people call themselves conservatives but actually favor liberal policies; for example, they think the government should cut back on regulations and let business alone (a conservative stand) but that the government should also increase regulations to protect workers' health and to prevent businesses from damaging the environment (a liberal stand). In short, the public often sends out vague or contradictory messages to government officials.

To sort out these opinions, it helps to break them down into specific economic and social issues. When we do this, we see the role of self-interest: The wealthy tend to be conservative on economic issues, whereas the poor tend to be liberal. On social issues, the well educated (who also tend to be upper income) tend to be liberal, whereas the poorly educated tend to be conservative.

Looking at the history of public opinion in the past fifty years, we find that the public has become far more liberal on social issues, whereas trends on economic issues have been mixed. On some economic issues, people are more liberal; in other areas, they have become more conservative.

The problem for government officials, then, is how to take public opinion into account. Doing so is difficult because the public so often sends mixed messages. Because public opinion can be hard to decipher in the precise terms needed for legislation and government decision making, we should perhaps think of it as only a rough guide to government policy. This vagueness allows political parties and interest groups to speak on behalf of the people and act as intermediaries between the people and their government.

KEY TERMS

attentive publics

attitude consistency

attitudes

conservatism

economic issues

ideology

issue publics

left

liberalism

opinions

pro-choice

pro-life

right

social issues

socialization

socioeconomic status

values

READINGS FOR FURTHER STUDY

Delli Carpini, Michael, and S. Keeter. *What Americans Know About Politics and Why It Matters* (New Haven, CT: Yale University Press, 1996). An important and comprehensive analysis of what Americans know about politics and a compelling argument that political knowledge is a powerful resource that helps knowledgeable Americans prevail in political conflicts.

Erikson, Robert S., and Kent L. Tedin. *American Public Opinion,* 7th ed., updated (New York: Pearson Longman, 2007). An outstanding textbook on American public opinion, which examines all the issues discussed in this chapter, but in far greater detail.

Graber, Doris. *Mass Media and American Politics,* 7th ed. (Washington, D.C.: CQ Press, 2006). An outstanding textbook examining the influence of the mass media on public opinion and elections in America.

Jennings, M. Kent, and Richard G. Niemi. *The Political Character of Adolescence: The Influence of Families and Schools* (Princeton, NJ: Princeton University Press, 1974). A classic study of the transmission of values and opinions from parents to their high-school-age children. Jennings and Niemi based their study on a nationwide survey of high school seniors and their parents conducted in 1965 and a follow-up survey conducted in 1973.

Mayer, William G. *The Changing American Mind: How and Why American Public Opinion Changed Between 1960 and 1988* (Ann Arbor: University of Michigan Press, 1992). A comprehensive history of American public opinion since 1960. Mayer not only documents trends in opinion, but he also systematically examines explanations for those trends and shows why public opinion changed.

McClosky, Herbert, and John Zaller. *The American Ethos* (Cambridge: Harvard University Press, 1984). A fascinating study of the two major traditions of American belief—capitalism and democracy. McClosky and Zaller blend a historical analysis of American beliefs and American culture with an analysis of modern survey data on what Americans and their political leaders think.

Mossberger, Karen, Caroline J. Tolbert, and Ramona S. McNeal. *Digital Citizenship* (Cambridge, MA: MIT Press, 2008). This study examines the impact of the Internet on economic opportunity, democratic participation, and social interaction. It demonstrates the profound effect of the Internet on the lives of the "digital citizens" who use the Internet regularly.

Page, Benjamin, and Robert Y. Shapiro. *The Rational Public* (Chicago: University of Chicago Press, 1992). An examination of public opinion on virtually every aspect of domestic and foreign policy from the 1930s to 1990. Page and Shapiro show how public opinion guides public policy, and they argue that public opinion is collectively rational—that it makes sense viewed in its entirety.

Smith, Eric R. A. N. *Energy, the Environment, and Public Opinion* (Lanham, MD: Rowman & Littlefield, 2002). A comprehensive study of public opinion toward energy issues, especially oil drilling and nuclear power. Smith reveals what the public thinks, how those views have changed over time, and what causes changes in environmental opinions.

REVIEW QUESTIONS

1. Public perceptions about American foreign aid expenditures demonstrate that
   a. people are generally knowledgeable about public affairs.
   b. people are generally not knowledgeable about public affairs.
   c. people understood that this accounts for 24 percent of the federal budget.
   d. both a and c.
2. The single most important trait related to knowledge about politics is
   a. age.
   b. gender.
   c. ethnicity.
   d. education.
3. The primary source of news for most Americans is
   a. the Internet.
   b. the daily newspaper.
   c. television.
   d. the news weekly.

4. Attentive publics or issue publics
   a. do not have much influence on the political process.
   b. typically include people without a high school diploma.
   c. typically include people with high incomes and good jobs.
   d. do not have high levels of political efficacy.
5. The Bennington study illustrated that
   a. parents help their children acquire their political values and opinions.
   b. educators influence the political values and opinions of their students.
   c. the average high school graduate spends more time in the classroom than viewing television.
   d. both a and b.
6. Which of the following is *true* about contemporary liberals?
   a. They believe that government should be proactive in moving society toward equality of outcomes.
   b. They tend to oppose raising the minimum wage.
   c. They tend to oppose an increase in government regulation of the environment.
   d. They tend to favor laws that limit or outlaw abortion.
7. Describe attitude consistency in the United States.
   a. People tend to think in ideological terms.
   b. People tend to think in nonideological terms.
   c. People tend to have a good understanding of different political philosophies.
   d. Ideology has little to do with social class.
8. The history of public opinion in America over the past fifty years demonstrates that the public has become more
   a. conservative on social issues and more liberal on economic issues.
   b. liberal on social issues and more conservative on economic issues.
   c. liberal on social issues and that longitudinal trends on economic issues have been mixed.
   d. liberal on both social and economic issues.
9. To gauge national adult public opinion within plus or minus 3.1 percent, _____ people need to be randomly surveyed.
   a. 250
   b. 1,000
   c. 10,000
   d. 250,000
10. For the most part, public opinion is
    a. almost always destined to become more conservative.
    b. fairly stable over time.
    c. fairly unstable over time.
    d. almost always destined to become more liberal.

NOTES

1. Jeff Zeleny, "Obama Urges U.S. to Grapple with Racial Issue," *New York Times*, March 19, 2008; Jeff Zeleny and Adam Nagourney, "An Angry Obama Renounces Ties to His Ex-Pastor," *New York Times*, April 30, 2008, A1; The Pew Research Center for the People & the Press, "McCain's Enthusiasm Gap, Obama's Unity Gap," July 10, 2008, available at www.people-press.org/reports/pdf/436.pdf.

2. Stephen Earl Bennett and Linda L. M. Bennett, "Out of Sight, Out of Mind: Americans' Knowledge of Party Control of the House of Representatives, 1960–1984," *Political Research Quarterly* 46 (March 1993): 67–80.

3. See Richard Morin, "Foreign Aid: Mired in Misunderstanding," *Washington Post National Weekly Edition*, March 20–26, 1995, 37.

4. Richard Morin, "What Informed Opinion?" *Washington Post National Weekly Edition*, April 10–16, 1995, 36.

5. Robert S. Erikson, Norman R. Luttbeg, and Kent L. Tedin, *American Public Opinion*, 4th ed. (New York: Macmillan, 1991), 1–2.

6. The Pew Research Center for the People & the Press, "McCain's Enthusiasm Gap, Obama's Unity Gap."

7. Giuseppe DiPalma and Herbert McClosky, "Personality and Conformity: The Learning of Political Attitudes," *American Political Science Review* 70 (December 1970): 1054–73.

8. Michael S. Delli Carpini and Scott Keeter, "Stability and Change in the U.S. Public's Knowledge of Politics," *Public Opinion Quarterly* 55 (Winter 1991): 583–612.

9. Maxwell E. McCombs and L. E. Mullins, "Consequences of Education: Media Exposure, Political Interest and Information-Seeking Orientations," *Mass Communication Review* 1 (August 1973): 27–31; Eric R. A. N. Smith, *The Unchanging American Voter* (Berkeley: University of California Press, 1989), 180–86; Karen Mossberger, Caroline J. Tolbert, and Ramona S. McNeal, *Digital Citizenship* (Cambridge, MA: MIT Press, 2008).

10. Irwin Kirsch, Ann Jungeblut, Lynn Jenkins, and Andrew Kolstad, *Adult Literacy in America: A First Look at Results of the National Adult Literacy Survey*, U.S. Department of Education, September 2003. See also National Center for Education Statistics, Department of Education, Adult Literacy and Lifeskills Survey, available at www.nces.ed.gov/Surveys/ALL/.

11. David B. Magleby, *Direct Legislation: Voting on Ballot Propositions in the United States* (Baltimore: Johns Hopkins University Press, 1984); Irwin Kirsch, Henry Braun, and Kentaro Yamamoto, *America's Perfect Storm: Three Forces Changing Our Nation's Future* (Princeton, NJ: Educational Testing Service, 2007).

12. Steven J. Rosenstone and John Mark Hansen, *Mobilization, Participation, and Democracy in America* (New York: Macmillan, 1993), 164–65.

13. Robert C. Luskin, "Explaining Political Sophistication," *Political Behavior* 12 (December 1990): 331–61.

14. See Smith, *The Unchanging American Voter*, 178–80, 196–210.

15. See Paul R. Abramson, *Political Attitudes in America* (San Francisco: Freeman, 1983).

16. Data from the *American National Election Studies* (Ann Arbor, MI: Inter-University Consortium for School and Political Research, various years).

17. The Pew Research Center for the People & the Press, "TV Viewership Declines," May 13, 1996, 64, available at www.people-press.org/report/127/tv-news-viewership-declines; The Pew Research Center for the People & the Press, "Online Papers Modestly Boost Newspaper Readership," July 30, 2006, available at www.people-press.org/report/282/online-papers-modestly-boost-newspaper-readership.

18. Robert T. Bower, *The Changing Television Audience in America* (New York: Columbia University Press, 1985); Smith, *The Unchanging American Voter*, 180–86.

19. Thomas E. Patterson, *Out of Order* (New York: Vintage, 1993).

20. W. Russell Neuman, Marion R. Just, and Ann N. Crigler, *Common Knowledge: News and the Construction of Political Meaning* (Chicago: University of Chicago Press, 1992), 78–95.

21. Larry M. Bartels, "Message Received: The Political Impact of Media Exposure," *American Political Science Review* 87 (June 1993): 267–85; Xinshu Zhao and Steven H. Chafee, "Campaign Advertisements versus Television News as Sources of Political Issue Information," *Public Opinion Quarterly* 59 (Spring 1995): 41–65.

22. Bruce A. Bimber, Doris Graber, W. Lance Bennett, Richard Davis, and Pippa Norris, "The Internet and Politics: Emerging Perspectives," in *The Academy and the Internet*, eds. Monroe Price and Helen Nissenbaum (New York: Peter Lang Publishing, 2004), 90–119.

23. Bruce A. Bimber and Richard Davis, *Campaigning Online: The Internet and U.S. Elections* (New York: Oxford University Press, 2003); Bruce Bimber, *Information and American Democracy: Technology in the Evolution of Political Power* (New York: Cambridge University Press, 2003); The Pew Research Center for the People & the Press, "Public Knowledge of Current Affairs Little Changed by News and Information Revolutions," April 15, 2007, available at www.people-press.org/report/319/public-knowledge-of-current-affairs-little-changed-by-news-and-information-revolutions.

24. Mossberger, Tolbert, and McNeal, *Digital Citizenship*.

25. V. O. Key, Jr., *Public Opinion and American Democracy* (New York: Knopf, 1961), 265, 282–85.

26. R. Douglas Arnold, *The Logic of Congressional Action* (New Haven, CT: Yale University Press, 1990), 64–68.

27. Stanley Feldman, "Structure and Consistency in Public Opinion: The Role of Core Beliefs and Values," *American Journal of Political Science*, 32 (May 1988): 416–40.

28. John R. Zaller, *The Nature and Origins of Mass Opinion* (New York: Cambridge University Press, 1992).

29. Richard Dawson, Kenneth Prewit, and Karen Dawson, *Political Socialization*, 2nd ed. (Boston: Little, Brown, 1977).

30. Christine B. Williams and Daniel R. Minns, "Agent Credibility and Receptivity Influences in Children's Political Learning," *Political Behavior* 8 (1986): 175–200.

31. Sandra K. Schwartz, "Preschoolers and Politics," in New *Directions in Political Socialization*, eds. David C. Schwartz and Sandra K. Schwartz (New York: Free Press, 1975).

32. Paul Allen Beck, "The Role of Agents in Political Socialization," in *Handbook of Political Socialization*, ed. Stanley A. Renshon (New York: Free Press, 1977).

33. Fred I. Greenstein, *Children and Politics* (New Haven, CT: Yale University Press, 1965), 55–84; Robert D. Hess and Judith V. Torney, *The Development of Political Attitudes in Children* (Chicago: Aldine, 1967).

34. M. Kent Jennings and Richard G. Niemi, *The Political Character of Adolescence: The Influence of Families and Schools* (Princeton, NJ: Princeton University Press, 1974), 39.

35. M. Kent Jennings and Richard G. Niemi, *Generations and Politics: A Panel Study of Young Adults and Their Parents* (Princeton, NJ: Princeton University Press, 1981), 91.

36. Donald Searing, Gerald Wright, and George Rabinowitz, "The Primacy Principle: Attitude Change and Political Socialization," *British Journal of Political Science* 6 (March 1976): 83–113.

37. Richard Merelman, "Democratic Politics and the Culture of American Education," *American Political Science Review* 74 (June 1980): 319–33.

38. Theodore M. Newcomb, *Personality and Social Change* (New York: Holt, Rinehart & Winston, 1943).

39. George Comstock, "Social and Cultural Impact of the Mass Media," in *What's News: The Media in American Society*, ed. Elie Abel (San Francisco: Institute for Contemporary Studies, 1981).

40. Doris A. Graber, *Mass Media and American Politics*, 3rd ed. (Washington, D.C.: CQ Press, 1989), 167–76.

41. Suzanna Danuta Walters, *All the Rage: The Story of Gay Visibility in America* (Chicago: University of Chicago Press, 2001); Steven Capsuto, *Alternate Channels: The Uncensored Story of Gay and Lesbian Images on Radio and Television* (New York: Ballantine Books, 2000); Rodger Streitmatter, *Sex Sells!: The Media's Journey from Repression to Obsession* (Cambridge, MA: Westview Press, 2004).

42. Harry P. Pachon, Louis DeSipio, Chon A. Noriega, and Rodolfo O. de la Garza, *Still Missing: Latinos In and Out of Hollywood* (Los Angeles: Tomas Rivera Policy Institute, 2000).

43. Richard C. Vincent, "Clio's Consciousness Raised? Portrayal of Women in Rock Videos, Reexamined," *Journalism Quarterly* 66 (Spring 1989): 155–60.

44. Linda Heath and John Petraitis, "Television Viewing and Fear of Crime: Where Is the Mean World?" *Basic and Applied Social Psychology* 8 (March/June 1987): 97–123.

45. William Mayer, *The Changing American Mind: How and Why American Public Opinion Changed Between 1960 and 1988* (Ann Arbor: University of Michigan Press, 1992), 165.

46. Theodore M. Newcomb, "Persistence and Regression of Changed Attitudes: Long-Range Studies," *Journal of Social Issues* 19 (October 1963): 3–14; see also Duane F. Alwin, Ronald Cohen, and Theodore Newcomb, *Political Attitudes over the Life Span: The Bennington Women after Fifty Years* (Madison: University of Wisconsin Press, 1991).

47. William Mayer, *The Changing American Mind*; Benjamin I. Page and Robert Y. Shapiro, *The Rational Public* (Chicago: University of Chicago Press, 1992).

48. See Herbert McClosky, "Consensus and Ideology in American Politics," *American Political Science Review* (June 1964): 361–82.

49. Kenneth R. Hoover, *Ideology and Political Life* (Monterey, CA: Brooks/Cole, 1987), 80–106.

50. This discussion of democracy and capitalism follows that of Herbert McClosky and John Zaller, *The American Ethos: Public Attitudes toward*

Capitalism and Democracy (Cambridge, MA: Harvard University Press, 1984). For an analysis of ideologies focused on the values of equality and freedom, see Kenneth M. Dolbeare and Linda J. Medcalf, *American Ideologies Today* (New York: Random House, 1988).

51. Hoover , *Ideology and Political Life*, 9–28.

52. Ibid., 60–72.

53. Bill Boyarsky, *Ronald Reagan: His Life and Rise to the Presidency* (New York: Random House, 1981), 79; see also James A. Morone, *The Democratic Wish* (New York: Basic Books, 1991), chap. 7.

54. See, for example, Richard Morin, "Medicare Changes Get a Jaundiced Look," *Washington Post National Weekly Edition*, July 10–16, 1995, 37.

55. Kim Murphy, "Energy Secretary Rejects Calls for Power Price Caps," *Los Angeles Times*, February 3, 2001, A1.

56. Jack Citrin, Beth Reingold, Evelyn Walters, and Donald P. Green, "The 'Official English' Movement and the Symbolic Politics of Language in the United States," *Western Political Quarterly* 43 (September 1990): 535–59; James Crawford, *Hold Your Tongue: Bilingualism and the Politics of "English Only"* (Reading, MA: Addison-Wesley, 1992).

57. See Joseph R. Gusfield, *Symbolic Crusade: Status Politics and the American Temperance Movement* (Urbana: University of Illinois Press, 1963).

58. Mary Lou Kendrigan, *Gender Differences: Their Impact on Public Policy* (Westport, CT: Greenwood, 1991).

59. See "What Women Think about the Feminist Label," *The Public Perspective* 3 (November/December 1991): 92–93.

60. Ethel Klein, *Gender Politics* (Cambridge, MA: Harvard University Press, 1984).

61. Philip E. Converse, "The Nature of Belief Systems in Mass Publics," in *Ideology and Discontent*, ed. David Apter (New York: Free Press, 1964), 211–12.

62. Luttbeg, Norman R., and Michael M. Gant, "The Failure of Liberal/Conservative Ideology as a Cognitive Structure," *Public Opinion Quarterly* 49: 85.

63. Smith, *The Unchanging American Voter*, 171–72.

64. Ibid., 105.

65. Stephen Bennett, "Consistency among the Public's Social Welfare Policy Attitudes," *American Journal of Political Science* 17 (August 1973): 544–70; Norman H. Nie with Kristi Andersen, "Mass Belief Systems Revisited: Political Change and Attitude Structure," *Journal of Politics* 36 (August 1974): 541–91; Gerald Pomper, "From Confusion to Clarity: Issues and American Voters: 1956–1968," *American Political Science Review* 66 (June 1972): 415–28.

66. Thomas Ferguson and Joel Rogers, *Right Turn: The Decline of the Democrats and the Future of American Politics* (New York: Hill and Wang, 1986), 12. For a similar description, see Lloyd A. Free and Hadley Cantril, *The Political Beliefs of Americans: A Study of Public Opinion* (New Brunswick, NJ: Rutgers University Press, 1967), 37.

67. "Portrait of a Skeptical Public," *Business Week*, November 20, 1995, 138.

68. Pew Center for the People & the Press, *Retropolitics, The Political Typology: Version 3.0* (Washington, D.C.: Pew Center for the People & the Press, 1999), 16.

69. These data are not shown. See Tom W. Smith, "That Which We Call Welfare by Any Other Name Would Smell Sweeter: An Analysis of the Impact of Question Wording on Response Patterns," *Public Opinion Quarterly* 51 (Spring 1987): 75–83. See also Stanley Feldman and John Zaller, "The

Political Culture of Ambivalence: Ideological Responses to the Welfare State," *American Journal of Political Science* 36 (February 1992): 268–307.

70. On spending preferences, see Theodore J. Eismeier, "Public Preferences about Government Spending: Partisan, Social, and Attitudinal Sources of Policy Differences," *Political Behavior* 4 (1982): 133–45; Arthur Sanders, "Rationality, Self-Interest, and Public Attitudes on Public Spending," *Social Science Quarterly* 69 (Summer 1988): 311–34.

71. Richard M. Scammon and Ben J. Wattenberg, *The Real Majority* (New York: Coward, McCann & Geoghegan, 1970), 35–44.

72. Paul M. Sniderman, Richard A. Brody, and Philip E. Tetlock, *Reasoning and Choice: Explorations in Political Psychology* (New York: Cambridge University Press, 1991), chap. 7; Samuel A. Stouffer, *Communism, Conformity and Civil Liberties: A Cross-Section of the Nation Speaks Its Mind* (Garden City, NY: Doubleday, 1955); see also John L. Sullivan, James Pierson, and George E. Marcus, *Political Tolerance and American Democracy* (Chicago: University of Chicago Press, 1982).

73. Paul R. Abramson, *Political Attitudes in America: Formation and Change* (San Francisco: Freeman, 1983), 241–59; see also Howard Schuman, Charlotte Steeh, and Lawrence Bobo, *Racial Attitudes in America: Trends and Interpretations* (Cambridge, MA: Harvard University Press, 1985), 163–92; Paul M. Sniderman, Richard A. Brody, and Philip E. Tetlock, *Reasoning and Choice: Explorations in Political Psychology* (New York: Cambridge University Press, 1991), 120–39; Sullivan, Pierson, and Marcus, *Political Tolerance and American Democracy*.

74. Thomas Byrne Edsall with Mary D. Edsall, *Chain Reaction: The Impact of Race, Rights, and Taxes on American Politics* (New York: Norton, 1991).

75. George Gallup, Jr. and Frank Newport, "For First Time, More Americans Approve of Interracial Marriage than Disapprove," *The Gallup Poll Monthly*, no. 311 (August 1991): 60.

76. "Gallup Poll Topics: Race Relations," The Gallup Poll, available at www.gallup.com/poll/indicators/indrace.asp.

77. "Social Audit: Black/White Relations in the U.S." The Gallup Poll, available at www.galluppoll.com/content/default.aspx?ci=9901.

78. CBS News Polls, February 6–10, 2000 and January 18–21, 2007, reported by www.PollingReport.com, available at www.pollingreport.com/politics.htm.

79. ABC News/Washington Post Poll, May 8–11, 2008, reported by www.PollingReport.com, available at www.pollingreport.com/politics.htm.

80. Elizabeth Adell Cook, Ted G. Jelen, and Clyde Wilcox, *Between Two Absolutes: Public Opinion and the Politics of Abortion* (Boulder, CO: Westview, 1992); Barbara Hinkson Craig and David M. O'Brien, *Abortion and American Politics* (Chatham, NJ: Chatham House, 1993).

81. Warren E. Miller and M. Kent Jennings, *Parties in Transition* (New York: Sage, 1986); Benjamin I. Page, Robert Y. Shapiro, Paul W. Gronke, and Robert M. Rosenberg, "Constituency, Party, and Representation in Congress," *Public Opinion Quarterly* 48 (Winter 1984): 741–56; Eric R. A. N. Smith, Richard Herrera, and Cheryl L. Herrera, "The Measurement Characteristics of Congressional Roll-Call Indexes," *Legislative Studies Quarterly* 15 (May 1990): 283–95.

82. See *Gallup Report*, no. 281, February 1989.

83. Benjamin I. Page, and Robert Y. Shapiro, *The Rational Public* (Chicago: University of Chicago Press, 1992), 45.

84. Larry M. Bartels, "Constituency Opinion and Congressional Policy Making: The Reagan Defense Buildup," *American Political Science Review* 85 (June 1991): 457–74. See also Arthur Sanders, *Victory* (Armonk, NY: Sharpe, 1992), 48–53.

85. ABC News Poll: January 16–20, 2003, reported by PollingReport.com, available at www.pollingreport.com/iraq3.htm.

86. USA Today/Gallup Poll, June 15–19, 2008, reported by PollingReport.com, available at www.pollingreport.com/iraq.htm. See also John Mueller, *Policy and Opinion in the Gulf War* (Chicago: University of Chicago Press, 1994), chap. 4.

87. CNN Poll: May 5–7, 2006, reported by PollingReport.com, available at www.pollingreport.com/iraq.htm.

88. Tom W. Smith "Liberal and Conservative Trends in the United States since World War II," *Public Opinion Quarterly* 54 (Winter 1990): 479–507, which is the source for the facts in this and the next two paragraphs.

89. Schuman, Steeh, and Bobo, *Racial Attitudes in America*, chap. 3; George Gallup, Jr., and Frank Newport, "For First Time, More Americans Approve of Interracial Marriage than Disapprove," *The Gallup Poll Monthly*, no. 311 (August 1991): 60. See Smith, "Liberal and Conservative Trends in the United States since World War II," which is the source for the facts in this and the next two paragraphs.

90. Jennifer Baggette, Robert Y. Shapiro, and Lawrence R. Jacobs, "The Polls: Social Security: An Update," *Public Opinion Quarterly* 59 (Fall 1995): 420–42.

91. Mayer, *The Changing American Mind*, 111–34.

92. Mary Lou Kendrigan, "Progressive Democrats and Support for Women's Issues," in *The Democrats Must Lead*, eds. James MacGregor Burns, William Crotty, Lois Lovelace Duke, and Lawrence D. Longley (Boulder, CO: Westview, 1992); Klein, *Gender Politics*, esp. 32–46.

93. Taylor Branch, *Parting the Waters: America in the King Years, 1954–63* (New York: Simon & Schuster, 1988); Dennis Chong, *Collective Action and the Civil Rights Movement* (Chicago: University of Chicago Press, 1991).

94. Alexander Hamilton, James Madison, and John Jay, *The Federalist Papers*, ed. Garry Wills (New York: Bantam Books 1982), nos. 63 and 71.

7

Voting and Participation

CHAPTER OUTLINE

The presidential election of 2008 was historic. The Republicans nominated Senator John McCain of Arizona, a former prisoner of war in Vietnam who—at 72 years of age—would have been the oldest man ever to win his first term in the White House. The Democrats put forward Senator Barack Obama of Illinois, the first African American to win a major party nomination—a nomination he won by narrowly defeating Senator Hillary Clinton, who would have been the first woman to win the nomination. To add to the mix, the two candidates offered sharply differing views about how to help the faltering economy, how to deal with high gasoline prices, how—or even whether—to get the United States out of the war in Iraq, and a host of other issues.

The campaign was fiercely fought. Hundreds of millions of dollars were spent, and tens of thousands of campaign workers tried to persuade voters to back their candidates. Yet on this historic Election Day, only 63 percent of eligible voters chose to vote.[1]

The central activity that characterizes democracy is voting. When we think of democracy, we think of elections. Yet most people do not participate in most elections. Some sit out elections and watch the results come in on television; some cannot even muster the interest to find out who won. At the same time, others become intensely involved—walking through neighborhoods to talk with potential voters, organizing rallies, raising money, and performing the dozens of other tasks that make up campaigning. Who chooses to participate and who chooses to sit at home greatly influence which candidates win and what policies become laws. As we shall see, both the characteristics of individual citizens and the rules of the political system determine who participates and who wins.

When people do go to the polls, their choices depend on many things. Some committed activists never know a moment's doubt about how they will vote. Other, less-interested citizens decide, sometimes at the last moment, on the basis of a few stray facts they have learned in the last weeks of the campaign.

In this chapter, we will examine voter participation, political activism, and voting choice. We will begin by looking at who votes and why, and then we will examine other forms of political participation, exploring why certain individuals choose to become activists. Finally, we will discuss why people choose to vote for particular candidates. Perhaps not surprisingly, we will see that people's voting decisions are based not only on the issues but also on party identification, the characteristics of the candidates, and the past performance of the incumbent president. Finally, we will look at the tendencies of various social groups to vote Democratic or Republican. Who votes and why, and how they vote, are crucial questions in a democracy—because those who join the conflict are usually the ultimate winners.

7-1 WHO VOTES?

More people vote than engage in any other kind of political activity. Even so, just 63 percent of all Americans who were eligible to vote chose to do so in the 2008 presidential election, and far fewer people voted in primaries and other elections. The opportunity to vote may characterize a democracy, but not all citizens take advantage of this opportunity.

Voter turnout, or the percentage of people who actually vote, depends on many factors. Here, we will use presidential election data to examine three of the most crucial: individual voter characteristics, registration laws, and campaign contacts. We will use data from the 2004 election because 2008 data are not available yet, but the patterns we will see have held across elections for decades.

voter turnout
The percentage of people who actually vote.

7-1a The Effect of Individual Voter Characteristics

People who vote, like those who are knowledgeable about politics, tend to have certain socioeconomic, demographic, and psychological characteristics. We will discuss each of these types of characteristics in turn.

Socioeconomic Characteristics

In the United States, the most important variable explaining whether one votes is a socioeconomic characteristic: *education.* As Table 7–1 shows, those with college educations report voting at almost twice the rate of high school dropouts. The reason is as follows:

> The personal qualities that raise the probability of voting are the skills that make learning about politics easier and more gratifying and reduce the difficulties of voting. Education increases one's capacity for understanding complex and intangible subjects such as politics, as well as encouraging the ethic of civic responsibility. Moreover, schools provide experience with a variety of bureaucratic problems, such as coping with requirements, filling out forms, and meeting deadlines.[2]

Family income and occupational status—which along with education make up socioeconomic status—also strongly influence voter turnout. As Table 7–1 shows, turnout rises sharply from low to middle income levels, and those with white-collar jobs vote at far higher rates than laborers. Although income and occupational status to some extent reflect the effect of education, both contribute independently to turnout. Having more money to spend on political interests and holding a high-status job draw people into social circles in which more people are interested in politics. Moreover, having the skills needed to participate (which are associated with white-collar jobs) makes participation easier.

Demographic Characteristics

Besides being affected by socioeconomic characteristics, voter turnout is also affected by demographic characteristics such as race, ethnicity, age, and gender. *Race* and *ethnicity* seem to make a substantial difference in turnout rates. In 2004, non-Hispanic whites reported voting at the highest rate, 80 percent, whereas African Americans, Hispanic Americans, and Asian Americans

Voter Characteristics			
Education	**Turnout (%)**	**Age**	**Turnout (%)**
0–8 years	51	18–25	60
9–11 years	54	26–35	74
High school graduate	71	36–45	75
Some college	80	46–55	84
College graduate	91	56–65	82
Higher degree	95	66+	80
Income	**Turnout (%)**	**Gender**	**Turnout (%)**
$0–8,999	64	Men	75
9,000–14,999	70	Women	78
15–24,999	71	**Strength of party identification**	**Turnout (%)**
25–34,999	83	Strong identifiers	89
35–49,999	83	Weak identifiers	78
50–69,999	87	Leaning independents	71
70–89,999	91	Pure independents	49
90,000+	90	**Efficacy**	**Turnout (%)**
Occupation	**Turnout (%)**	Low	73
Professional	92	Medium	72
Managers/technical	84	High	87
Sales/clerical	82	**Interest in campaign**	**Turnout (%)**
Service	58	Very much	89
Skilled labor	74	Somewhat	71
Unskilled labor	42	Not much	33
Race/Ethnicity	**Turnout (%)**	**Read Newspapers about Campaign**	**Turnout (%)**
White	80	Read	87
African American	70	Did not read	73
Hispanic American	63	**Region**	**Turnout (%)**
Asian/Indian	74	Northeast	76
		North central	82
		South	70
		West	81

Table 7–1 Percentage of Self-Reported Turnout in the 2004 Election

The people most likely to vote are the well educated, the wealthy, those with high-status occupations, whites, the elderly, strong party identifiers, those with a high sense of political efficacy and high interest in campaigns, those who read about campaigns in newspapers, and those who live outside the South and border states.

Note: *Turnout is self-reported. People often claim to have voted when, in fact, they have not; therefore, these turnout percentages are inflated.*

Source: *Data from the 2004 American National Election Survey.*

voted at lower rates. However, if we take socioeconomic status into account by comparing non-Hispanic whites, African Americans, Hispanic Americans, and Asian Americans with similar levels of education and income (e.g., low-education whites versus low-education African Americans or high-education whites versus high-education African Americans), race and ethnicity make only small differences in turnout rates.[3] The lower average educations and incomes of these racial and ethnic groups reduce the likelihood that members of these groups will vote, and hence, limit their political power at election time (see Chapter 3).

Turnout also depends on one's *age.* As people grow older, they gain knowledge and other resources that make participation easier. They learn more about the parties and candidates, and they become more attached to them over time. People also gain the social contacts that make participation easier as they age. Community ties such as homeownership, marriage, and children develop, and with those ties greater interest in politics and higher voter turnout develop as well. By the time people are in their eighties, some begin to lose the ability to participate. But poor health and other problems cause only a slight drop in turnout among the elderly. They remain far more likely to vote than those under thirty.[4]

Social commentators occasionally complain about the low turnout rate of the young. They criticize the young for being lazy and apolitical. When they do so, however, they forget that in every generation, the young are the least likely to vote. Even in the heady days of the 1960s when young faces filled the civil rights and anti-Vietnam War marches, the young were the least likely to turn out to vote on Election Day. Young people of today, therefore, behave quite like the generations before.

A final demographic characteristic worth mentioning is *gender*—not because men or women vote at very different rates in the twenty-first century, but because they used to do so in the past. When women first won the **franchise**, or right to vote, in 1920, the voting rate among women was substantially lower than among men.[5] Many women in 1920 had been socialized to believe that politics was men's business and that they should stay out of it. As recently as the 1950s, women were still about 10 percent less likely to vote than men.[6] Beginning in the late 1960s, however, the women's movement changed the role of women in politics. The movement sought to change both the way society treated women and the way in which women were socialized to think of themselves. The result was that women, especially younger women—who were socialized after the women's movement began—started to vote at the same rate as men. In fact, since 1984, white women have often voted at a higher rate than white men in presidential elections.[7]

franchise
The right to vote.

Psychological Characteristics

In addition to socioeconomic and demographic characteristics, psychological characteristics such as party identification, sense of political efficacy, group consciousness, and interest in politics all contribute to voter turnout. *Strength of **party identification***

party identification
The psychological feeling of belonging to a particular political party, which influences voting behavior.

political efficacy
The feeling that one can have an effect on politics and political decision makers.

group consciousness
Identification with one's social group (for instance, African-American consciousness).

significantly influences turnout. People who identify strongly with one of the political parties are more likely to show up at the polls on Election Day than weak identifiers or independents because strong identifiers generally both know and care more about politics. (We will explain party identification in more detail)

A strong sense of **political efficacy**—the feeling that one can have an effect on politics and political decision makers—also motivates people to vote.[8] As we explained in Chapter 6, people who believe they cannot affect government have less incentive to learn about politics and are, therefore, less knowledgeable than those who feel they can. Lacking a strong sense of efficacy, by the same token, makes one less likely to vote. Those who believe that elected officials do not care what they think view voting and other types of political participation as wasted efforts.

Another psychological characteristic that explains participation is **group consciousness.** Several studies have found that African Americans and women who identify strongly with their race or gender and whose racial and gender identities are important to them are more likely to participate.[9]

Finally, people who are *interested in politics* and who follow politics in newspapers and magazines are also more likely to vote than those who are not interested and who do not follow politics in the print media. This generalization does not hold true for those who follow politics on television, apparently because so many people watch television casually, with little real interest, and because television news does not convey much solid information about politics. Those who read about politics learn a good deal; those who only watch television do not.[10] The difference shows up in voter turnout.

Another attitude that deserves mention is *trust in government,* even though it seems to have little or no influence on turnout. A fairly popular notion is that people don't vote because they don't trust government leaders, they are cynical about politics and politicians, and they feel alienated. Indeed, survey measures of trust in government indicated a decline during the 1960s and 1970s—paralleling the decline in voter turnout. For instance, the following question has been asked regularly in national surveys since the 1950s: "How much of the time do you think you can trust the government in Washington to do what is right—just about always, most of the time, or only some of the time?" In 1964, 76 percent of the respondents said "just about always" or "most of the time." By 1980, only 25 percent gave such trusting responses. Although the public gained confidence in government during the 1980s, raising the confidence level to 35 percent, that gain did not last. Trust actually hit a low point in 1994 at 23 percent and then rose to 44 percent in 2000—well below the levels of the 1950s and 1960s.[11] When political scientists examined the data carefully, however, they discovered that trust in government has little or no impact on turnout.[12] People don't refrain from voting just because they do not like or trust politicians. If they believe their votes can affect politicians and policies, they vote despite their low opinions of officeholders and candidates.

All these characteristics paint a picture of the American most likely to vote: well educated with a high-status job and a high income; white and over thirty years old; a strong party identifier with a strong sense of political efficacy, a sense of group consciousness, and a high interest in politics. People with these traits are the most likely to vote, but they are hardly typical American citizens (see Chapter 3). Our system of rules gives every citizen the right to vote, but many people decline to exercise that right. When they decline, they allow those who do vote to determine who will be elected to public office.

7-1b The Effect of Registration Laws

The characteristics of individual voters are not the only influences on decisions about whether or not to vote. Registration and voting laws also affect turnout by changing the costs of voting from state to state. The more difficult and time consuming it is to vote, the less likely people are to do so. Moreover, by manipulating voting laws, legislators can influence how many people—and, more importantly, which people—vote. Ultimately, these rules can greatly affect which policies the government adopts and who wins political conflicts.

Registration laws dramatically demonstrate the important effects rules have on outcomes. These effects can be seen most clearly when one compares turnout in the United States with turnout in other industrial democracies. As Figure 7–1 shows, of twenty-one industrial democracies, only Switzerland had a lower turnout rate than the United States in the 1990s; most of the other countries had turnout rates 20 to 30 percentage points higher. Some of the difference is actually the result of the way in which we count voter turnout in the United States. Because there is no master list of all eligible citizens, government reports normally divide the number of voters by the Census Bureau estimate of the voting age population to calculate the turnout rate. This practice underestimates actual turnout because the voting age population includes people who live in the United States but are not citizens, patients at mental institutions, and people convicted of felonies who have had their voting rights taken away. When these people are taken into account, U.S. voter turnout is actually a few percentage points higher than officially reported. Nevertheless, it remains far below the turnout levels in other democracies.[13]

Two rules account for the low voter turnout rate in the United States. First, almost all other industrial democracies have automatic voter registration. That is, the government automatically registers voters; individual citizens are not responsible for initiating the registration process. In fact, "the United States is the only country where the entire burden of registration falls on the individual rather than the government."[14] A second rule that affects voter turnout is that many industrial democracies have some system of compulsory voting; they penalize their citizens for failure to vote (although in most cases, the penalties are never enforced).

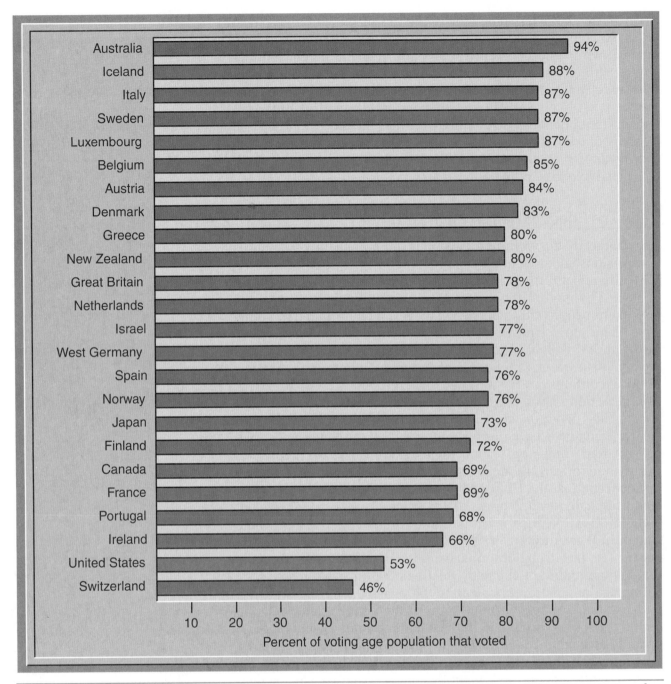

Figure 7–1   Ranking of Countries by Turnout in the 1990s. The United States has one of the lowest turnout rates of
any industrial democracy.

Source: *Data from Russell J. Dalton, Citizen Politics,* 2nd ed. (Chatham, NJ: Chatham House, 1996), 45.

Together, these two rules raise turnout in most of these countries
to levels far higher than in the United States.

Automatic registration and compulsory voting also affect who
votes. For example, the pattern of higher turnout among those of
high socioeconomic status does not appear in countries with automatic registration and compulsory voting.[15] People with low
incomes and poor educations vote at rates similar to those with
high incomes and good educations. The class bias in turnout van-
ishes. In short, the rules exert a powerful influence on who votes.

Looking now at turnout within the United States, we can see that registering to vote seems to be the major obstacle for most Americans. In states with lenient registration laws, voting participation is high; in states with tougher laws, participation is lower. The most important aspect of the law is the **closing date**, or the last day before the election when one can register to vote in the upcoming election.[16] States with Election Day registration have substantially higher turnout than those that close off registration thirty days before the election. Other laws that contribute to higher turnout rates in some states include those requiring voter registration offices to be open at least forty hours each week and on weekends or evenings, and those allowing absentee registration (e.g., registration by postcard).

In general, southern states have the toughest voter registration laws in the nation. Their restrictive voting policies are a legacy of the post-Civil War drive to disenfranchise African Americans and to reduce the political clout of poor whites.[17] Before the Twenty-Fourth Amendment to the Constitution abolished **poll taxes** (which required citizens to pay a tax if they chose to vote) in 1964 and the Voting Rights Act of 1965 eliminated **literacy tests** and other barriers thrown up to prevent voting (see Box 7–1), turnout in some southern states lagged below 10 percent. Although turnout increased enormously following the successes of the civil rights movement of the mid-1960s, turnout in the South remains slightly below the national average, as Table 7–1 shows.

With the passage of the National Voter Registration Act in 1993, Congress took another step toward easing voter registration laws. Known commonly as the Motor Voter Act, the law requires all states to offer people the opportunity to register by mail or when they go to motor vehicle bureaus, welfare agencies, disability offices, or military recruitment centers.[18] As with most reforms of voting and election rules, partisan controversy surrounded almost every aspect of the motor voter bill. Republicans in the Senate resisted the provisions of the bill requiring states to provide voter registration forms at agencies that assist people with disabilities or that deal with welfare clients. Democrats fought back, hoping to increase the turnout of groups that they expected would vote for them. In the end, the Democrats won.[19]

What has been the effect of the Motor Voter Act? It has clearly led to a dramatic surge in voter registration. An estimated 11 million new voters signed up under the law in 1995. Georgia alone added more than 500,000 new voters, a 19 percent increase.[20] At the polls, however, the Motor Voter Act has apparently made a much smaller difference. Despite early predictions that the law would substantially increase voting, turnout in both 1996 and 2000 was lower than in 1992. Although making registration easier may have caused some people to vote who otherwise would not have, the drop in voter interest following the 1992 campaign washed away any potential turnout gains. In the long run, however, voting analysts expect the law to have some positive effect, possibly increasing turnout by as much as 9 percent.[21] That boost

closing date
The last day before the election when one can register to vote—usually described in number of days before Election Day.

poll taxes
Before 1964, the taxes that people paid in some states if they chose to vote.

literacy tests
Tests of ability to read and write, used in the South to prevent people from voting.

POINT OF ORDER

Box 7–1   The Voting Rights Act of 1965

Source: © Reuters/Corbis.

As recently as the 1960s, voter registration laws prevented many nonwhites from voting. The Voting Rights Act of 1965 swept away most of these discriminatory rules.

Today, virtually all Americans take the right to register and vote for granted. Yet as recently as the early 1960s, that right was not extended to huge numbers of Americans in the South. The rules governing registration and voting can have a huge impact on voter turnout. Seldom has that been more clearly demonstrated than in the case of the Voting Rights Act of 1965.

Because of restrictive voter registration laws in southern states, which was a legacy of the Civil War, registration and voter turnout in the South have always been lower than in other parts of the country. All southern states discriminated against African Americans, and some sought to lessen the electoral impact of poor whites as well. In 1960—after civil rights workers spent almost a decade in massive efforts to register African Americans—the average percentage of southern whites registered to vote was 61.1 percent, whereas the average

percentage of African Americans was only 29.1 percent. The state with the widest racial gap was Mississippi, where 63.9 percent of all voting age whites were registered, but only 5.2 percent of African Americans were registered.

The Voting Rights Act of 1965 radically changed the rules by directly involving the federal government in local voter registration and by establishing an extensive set of regulations. The act swept away a wide range of requirements and tests that some states used to prevent African Americans from voting—including tests of literacy, educational attainment, knowledge, and good moral character. In one of the most important sections of the act, Congress allowed the federal courts to appoint federal observers and examiners empowered to register voters. In effect, the federal government took on the oversight of registration and voting in southern elections and in other scattered areas across the nation that had shown patterns of racial or ethnic discrimination.

Perhaps the section of the Voting Rights Act that best reflects the problem Congress faced is the "preclearance" section. Congress feared that if one method of discrimination were made illegal, southern states would immediately replace it with another. To prevent this, Congress required states and counties with records of blatant discrimination to submit proposed changes in registration and voting laws to the U.S. Attorney General or to the Federal District Court for the District of Columbia, which must give permission

or "clearance" before the changes could take effect. To gain clearance, the jurisdiction proposing the change would have to prove that there was no discriminatory intent behind the change and that there would be no discriminatory impact.

The Voting Rights Act had an immediate effect. By 1968, registration and turnout in the South jumped sharply, and it continued to rise in the following years (at a time when turnout outside of the South was falling). By 2004, the racial gap in registration still existed, but the gap was far smaller than it had been before passage of the Voting Rights Act—only a few percentage points.

The struggle minorities must face for voting rights is by no means over. Although most barriers to registration and voting have been torn down, some remain. More important, more subtle methods exist to limit the political influence of minorities in elections. Thus, every election year, the battle over minority political power continues in courtrooms across the nation. These disputes flare up because, as the effects of the Voting Rights Act of 1965 show, the rules do matter.

Sources: "Assessing the Effects of the U.S. Voting Rights Act," *Publius* 16 (Fall 1986); Paul Allen Beck and Frank J. Sorauf, *Party Politics in America,* 7th ed. (New York: HarperCollins, 1992), 211; Chandler Davidson, ed., *Minority Vote Dilution* (Washington, D.C.: Howard University Press, 1984); Steven F. Lawson, *In Pursuit of Power: Southern Blacks and Electoral Politics, 1965–1982* (New York: Columbia University Press, 1982); Harold W. Stanley and Richard G. Niemi, *Vital Statistics on American Politics,* 5th ed. (Washington, D.C.: CQ Press, 1995), 79; *Statistical Abstract of the United States, 1980,* 101st ed. (Washington, D.C.: U.S. Bureau of the Census, 1980), 514; and *Statistical Abstract of the United States, 2004–2005,* 124th ed. (Washington, D.C.: U.S. Bureau of the Census, 2004), 256.

would still leave U.S. turnout well below that of most other industrial democracies, but as George W. Bush's Florida victory in 2000 demonstrated, even a few votes can make a critical difference.

7-1c The Effect of Campaign Contacts

A staple of American campaigns since the early days of the Republic has been the drive to persuade citizens to vote (see Box 7–2). For some people, simply being asked to vote—even if the person

The People behind the Rules

Box 7-2   The Politics of Voter Turnout: William Marcy "Boss" Tweed and Willie Velasquez

The means by which parties, campaign organizations, and other groups register voters and get them out to the polls have changed enormously since the nineteenth century. In the mid-1800s, few laws regulated the behavior of parties and campaigns, and those that did often went unenforced. Most parts of the country did not even require voters to register until the late 1800s. Now all states but North Dakota require voter registration and carefully regulate registration and turnout efforts.

WILLIAM MARCY "BOSS" TWEED

New York City's Tammany Hall, led by William Marcy "Boss" Tweed after the Civil War, was notorious among big city party machines. New York had a voter registration law, but Tweed had little trouble getting around it. A U.S. House of Representatives report on the 1868 election described Tweed's practice of organized "repeating," or sending people to vote more than once:

On the 30th and 31st of October, when only two days intervened until the day of the election, gangs or bodies of men hired for the purpose, assembled at these [Tammany Hall] headquarters where they were furnished with names and numbers [of voters], and under a leader or captain, they went out in ones and twos and threes and tens and dozens, in nearly every part of the city, registering many times each, and when the day of election came these repeaters, supplied abundantly with intoxicating drinks, and changing coats, hats, or caps, as occasion required to avoid recognition or detection, commenced the work of "voting early and often," and this was carried on by these vagabonds until, wearied and drunken, night closed on the stupendous fraud which their depravity had perpetrated.

The practice of repeating helped Boss Tweed and his cronies to dominate politics in New York City during the 1860s and 1870s.

WILLIE VELASQUEZ

By 1992, the Tammany Halls and repeat voters had all but disappeared. Today's voter registration and turnout organizations are often more like the Southwest Voter Registration Education Project (SVREP). Founded by Willie Velasquez in 1974, SVREP registered people by sending thousands of volunteers door to door armed with clipboards and voter registration forms. First in Texas and then all across the Southwest, Velasquez organized Hispanic Americans and persuaded them that the path to political power was through registration and voting. SVREP's slogan said it all: "*Su voto es su voz*"—Your vote is your voice.

Over the years, Velasquez led more than 1,000 registration drives and filed dozens of lawsuits under the Voting Rights Act to defend the interests of Hispanic Americans. Unlike Tweed, whose goal was personal wealth and political power, Velasquez sought to increase the power of the people. He believed that voting power could accomplish that:

If your streets and drainage are bad, register and vote. If you don't like the way the schools are educating your kids, register and vote. If City Hall doesn't pay attention to you, register and vote.

Velasquez died in 1988 at the age of forty-four. In the words of Michael Dukakis, then Governor of Massachusetts and the 1988 Democratic presidential candidate, Willie Velasquez "changed the world."

Sources: Richard Avena, "One Last Vote for Willie Velasquez," *Los Angeles Times*, June 18, 1988; David Lauter, "Dukakis Eulogizes Latino Political Leader," *Los Angeles Times*, June 19, 1988; U.S. House of Representatives, Report No. 41, 1868, 40, quoted in M. R. Werner, *Tammany Hall* (New York: Greenwood Press, 1928, reprinted 1968), 138.

asking is a stranger—is enough to bring them out to the polls on Election Day. The result is that every election brings with it voter registration and get-out-the-vote drives.

Efforts to mobilize voters come from many directions. Most large campaigns use registration and get-out-the-vote drives as one part of their overall strategy, taking advantage of the fact that it is usually easier and more efficient to gain votes by increasing the turnout among a candidate's supporters than by converting a candidate's opponents.[22] Campaigns, therefore, often put huge amounts of money into their registration and get-out-the-vote drives, targeting people they think are likely to support their candidate. The Republican and Democratic efforts were one of the reasons why turnout rose in 2004.[23]

Nonpartisan interest groups also work to increase turnout for their own purposes. Unions, civil rights groups, churches, and others seek to increase voting among their members to increase their influence with politicians or to try to get the politicians they favor elected.

Efforts to mobilize voters come in many forms. Some efforts rely on expensive mass mail campaigns and telephone banks. Other efforts rely on volunteer labor provided by people such as college students, who walk door to door in their communities, encouraging their party's or group's supporters to vote. Although these activities may seem small in scale, they actually make a substantial difference in voter turnout and sometimes determine who wins the elections. Figure 7–2 reproduces a typical set of instructions that a campaign—in this case a Democratic campaign—gives to workers who are charged with trying to get out the vote.

One electoral innovation that may relieve political parties and interest groups of some of the burden of turning out voters on Election Day is to allow people to mail in their ballots. Over the years, some local governments have experimented with voting by mail. In 1996, Oregon filled a vacant U.S. Senate seat by holding the nation's first mail-in congressional election. Ballots were mailed to all the state's voters, and they had three weeks to mail the ballots back or drop them off at specified locations. When the ballots were finally counted, voter turnout exceeded 65 percent of registered voters, a record for a special election in Oregon. Moreover, the mail-in vote cost the state of Oregon about $1 million less than a traditional election in which voters go to the polls.[24] The success of Oregon's mail-in Senate election persuaded Oregon voters to pass a statewide initiative permanently establishing a Vote-by-Mail system in 1998. That success has led to calls for use of mail-in voting in other states as well. Critics of voting by mail, however, oppose any move away from the tradition of filling out a ballot in secret in a polling booth. They argue that mail-in voting will lead to a rise in voting fraud because people will forge ballots and try to coerce their family and friends into voting for particular candidates.[25] Although it is too soon to tell which side will win the argument over voting by mail, many states are considering the idea and some have used vote-by-mail methods in special elections.

Overall, social scientists know a great deal about voter turnout in any given year. The 2004 turnout patterns look very similar to those seen in previous elections, and no doubt these patterns will continue to hold in the future. Although people from all parts of society vote, those who have better educations, better jobs, and higher incomes, who are white and middle-aged or older, who strongly identify with a political party and feel a strong sense of political efficacy, who identify with a group, and who are interested in and read about politics in newspapers are more likely to vote than those who do not have these characteristics. People who live in states with lenient registration requirements are more likely to vote than those who live in states with tough requirements. Finally, people contacted through political campaigns or voter registration and get-out-the-vote drives are more likely to vote than those not contacted.

INSTRUCTIONS TO PRECINCT WORKERS

Precinct work is the single most important aspect of a political campaign. Its purpose is to inform the voters about the candidates and the issues in the upcoming election and to record favorable voters so that they can be reminded to vote on Election Day-April 15.

Go to all voters on your precinct list except Republicans or American independents. Introduce yourself and ask for the voter by name. Indicate that you are campaigning for the BCA candidates. Talk to the voter. If the voter is favorable, mark a (+) next to his/her name; if the voter is unfavorable, mark a (-) next to her/his name; if the voter is undecided, mark a (0). Check to see if all the other voters in the household feel the same way.

If the voters support our candidates, ask them if they will help with the campaign, put up a poster, etc. If voters will help or if they want more literature please write down their names and addresses with the appropriate comments on the "Comment Sheet."

If the voter is not home mark a (NH) next to her/his name and leave some literature on the door knob or under the door. DO NOT LEAVE LITERATURE IN THE MAILBOX-IT IS ILLEGAL! At a later date go back to the voters who were not home or were undecided.

If the voter has moved mark an (M) next to his/her name. Try to get the voter's new address and telephone number (by asking the present occupants, etc.) so we can tell the voter where her/his polling place is on election day. Write the voter's new address and telephone, if known, on the precinct list. Return the "comment" sheets to the office on a weekly basis, so we can take care of them.

If you have any questions, need help finishing your precinct or need more literature, bumper strips, buttons, etc., contact the campaign office.

Figure 7–2   Instructions to Precinct Workers. A typical set of instructions for precinct canvassers seeking to get out the vote on Election Day.

All these patterns of voter characteristics, registration laws, and campaign contacts hold true in every year for which data are available. Yet these findings do not explain changes in turnout over time. Explaining why turnout has decreased over the years is difficult.

7-1d The Puzzling Decline of Voter Turnout

In a democracy, it would be ideal if every eligible citizen voted. The United States, sadly, does not even approach that ideal. Turnout was generally 75 to 80 percent in the late 1800s, but it fell in the first two decades of the 1900s. It then bounced back to hit a high of almost 63 percent in 1960. Since then, turnout has generally been lower, although the 2004 election saw turnout rise to almost 60 percent again (see Figure 7–3).

The decline in voter turnout used to puzzle political scientists because they expected the rising level of education since the end of the nineteenth century and the easing of voter registration laws since the 1960s to lead to an increase in voter participation, contrary to what actually happened.[26] Several explanations for the decline have been proposed, some of which are controversial.

Analyses of the decline focus on two periods—the years immediately after 1896 and the post-1960 decline. Two competing explanations for the drop in voting participation after 1896 have been proposed. One side claims that economic tensions between

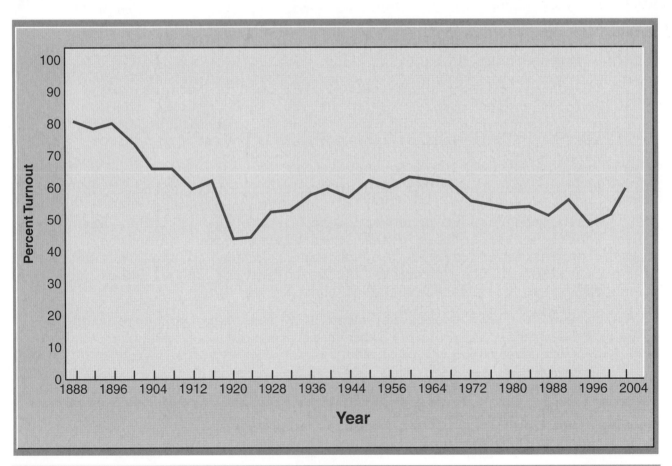

Figure 7–3   Voter Turnout, 1888–2004. Turnout declined sharply from 1896 to1920, increased until 1960, and then began another uneven decline. In 1996, only 49 percent of the eligible electorate voted. In 2004, however, turnout shot up to 59.6 percent.

Sources: *Source for turnout through 1996: Richard M. Scammon, Alice V. McGillivray, and Rhodes Cook, eds., America Votes 22 A Handbook of Contemporary American Election Statistics* (Washington, D.C.: Congressional Quarterly, 1998). Source for turnout in 2000: *Statistical Abstract of the United States, 2002,* 122d ed. (Washington, D.C.: U.S. Bureau of the Census, 2002), 255; Curtis Gans, "President Bush, Mobilization Drives Propel Turnout to Post-1968 High; Kerry, Democratic Weakness Shown," November 4, 2004, available at www.american.edu/ia/cdem/csae/pdfs/csae041104.pdf.

industrialists and workers rose during the late 1800s and came to a head during the depression of 1893 to 1896. Even though the Democrats turned their backs on their own party's president, Grover Cleveland, and gave the nomination to the populist William Jennings Bryan, the Democrats were crushed at the polls. Republican William McKinley won the presidency by putting together a business-worker coalition that survived and prospered for the next thirty years. The success of this coalition forced the Democratic Party to favor business interests as well in their pursuit of office, and resulted in both parties putting forth "corporate-conservative" platforms that offered little to the working class. Lacking any real choices between the parties, so the argument goes, many people dropped out of politics and stopped voting.[27]

The other argument about the decline of voter turnout after 1896 claims that turnout declined not because the parties shifted toward business interests but because of changes in voting laws.[28] Scholars who accept this argument point to three key changes: the introduction of the **Australian ballot** (ca. 1889–1896), the passage of laws requiring people to register to vote (ca. 1890–1920), and the passage of the Nineteenth Amendment to the Constitution (1920). With the introduction of the Australian ballot, state governments took over the task of printing ballots from political parties. This allowed people to cast secret votes for the first time. The passage of registration laws meant that voters could no longer simply show up at the polls on Election Day. Instead, to be eligible to vote, they first had to register with the local government, usually well in advance. The Nineteenth Amendment gave women the right to vote.

Many scholars believe that these three changes in voting laws led to lower turnout rates. The Australian ballot lowered voter turnout because corrupt party bosses could no longer force people to go to the polls and vote for them. The bosses could still force people to go to the polls, but because of the secret ballots, the bosses could no longer ensure that voters would vote for them. The result was that, instead of using threats to win elections, the party bosses had to use persuasion. Forcing unwilling voters to turn out on Election Day was no longer effective (see Chapter 9). Voter registration laws reduced turnout because they made it difficult for people to vote more than once on Election Day. And the Nineteenth Amendment lowered overall turnout because it extended the franchise to women, who as a group did not vote as often as men did. As we mentioned previously, before the 1920s, most women had been socialized to believe that politics was men's business; consequently, even when they had the right to vote, many women chose not to do so. This meant that while the number of eligible voters roughly doubled, the percentage of eligible people who actually voted decreased.

Like most rule changes, the reforms of the registration and voting laws between the 1880s and 1920 were anything but neutral. Some people pushed for the reforms for good government reasons—they wanted to eliminate corruption and they believed that women should be treated equally.[29] Other people wanted the reforms

Australian ballot

A government-printed ballot (as opposed to one distributed by political parties) that allows people to vote in secret.

because of the effects the reforms were expected to have on who voted and on who would win elections. Among the reforms' most prominent backers were upper-class Yankee Protestants who wanted to reduce turnout among the poor—especially those of Irish and Italian ethnicity, who were building majorities in many Northeastern cities. In addition to reducing corruption, the new voter registration requirements made it difficult for large numbers of the poor, many of whom were illiterate, to register, thus giving an advantage to the upper classes.[30] Similarly, women from upper-class Protestant households were far more likely than women from poor, European ethnic households to think that politics was women's business as well as men's. When women won the right to vote, upper-class women voted at a far higher rate than lower-class women, again giving the advantage to the upper class.[31] Finally, voter registration was welcomed in the South as a means to prevent African Americans—and in some states, poor whites—from voting (see Section 7-1b).[32] In short, registration and voting rules were regarded as powerful weapons in political conflicts across the nation.

The debate about the reduction in turnout after 1960 differs from the debate about the earlier drop because survey researchers left a record covering the later period.[33] Analyses of survey data have identified several population trends that account for part of the drop in turnout after 1960—decreases in the average age of the population, in the electorate's strength of party identification, in the electorate's sense of political efficacy, and in the number of people who regularly read newspapers. In other words, after 1960, a larger and larger portion of the electorate consisted of people less likely to vote.[34]

In addition to changes in the population, a change in the rules caused turnout to drop. The Twenty-Sixth Amendment to the Constitution, ratified in 1971, gave the right to vote to eighteen-, nineteen-, and twenty-year-olds. This rule change, like the one in 1920, added a very low turnout group to the electorate, and therefore lowered the overall turnout rate, beginning with the 1972 presidential election.

Still, these changes, even taken together, do not fully explain the decline in voting participation. The last piece of the puzzle, which scholars only recently identified, is the decline in party and candidate efforts to recruit campaign volunteers to contact voters and persuade them to vote. Because parties have turned away from grassroots organizations and toward television and direct mail campaigning, voter turnout has fallen.[35] Old-fashioned, door-to-door campaigning may not seem an obvious way to get votes in the days of Internet campaigning, but it remains one of the most effective get-out-the vote methods ever developed. Candidates who successfully recruit enough campaign workers win elections by getting their voters out to the polls.

7-1e Does Turnout Matter?

Does higher or lower turnout in an election affect who wins? Many politicians and journalists believe that elections with high turnout favor Democratic candidates, whereas elections with low turnout favor Republicans. The reasoning is that people of high socioeconomic status, who tend to vote Republican, generally turn out to vote in almost all elections, but people of low socioeconomic status turn out only for some elections. It would follow that as turnout increases, the additional voters would more likely be Democrats. When the question was finally studied, however, that argument turned out to be flawed.

A classic study of voter turnout conducted in the 1970s found that if all states relaxed their voter registration laws to match those in the most lenient states in 1972 (the year of the data used in the study), turnout would increase about 9 percent.[36] Although the turnout among low socioeconomic voters would go up more than the turnout for those with high status, all socioeconomic groups would show overall increases in turnout. In addition, people with few years of school, low incomes, and low-status jobs are not, as some assume, all Democratic voters (as we shall see in Section 7-3e). Many would vote for Republicans, just as many high socioeconomic voters would vote for Democrats. When all the numbers were added up, the study estimated that the result of the hypothetical 9 percent increase in turnout would actually yield a Democratic advantage of less than one-half of 1 percent—a difference so small the authors could not be sure it was real. Most other studies that followed came to the same conclusion. A modest increase in turnout of 10 or 15 percent would be unlikely to make any difference in who wins.[37]

To the delight of Republicans and despair of Democrats, that prediction was borne out in the 2004 presidential election. Throughout the summer and early fall, newspapers regularly ran stories reporting a surge in voter registration. Because the newly registered voters included a high proportion of young adults—a group that leaned toward Senator John Kerry, according to the polls—Democrats hoped that the polls showing a narrow George W. Bush lead would be wrong and that Kerry would take the White House. On Election Day, turnout was up—but it rose among both Democrats and Republicans. The higher turnout did not help Kerry.[38]

Although most studies suggest that a 10 to 15 percent increase in voter turnout probably would not affect many election outcomes, scholars are unsure about what would happen if the United States ever experienced a huge increase in voter turnout. What if turnout were 80 or 90 percent—as it is in many European nations—instead of 50 or 60 percent, as it is in presidential elections in the United States?[39] We know that the Voting Rights Act of 1965, which raised turnout enormously in the South, had a substantial impact on who won office and what policies they favored.[40] So we cannot be sure that other dramatic changes would not ensue if a surge in turnout occurred in the United States.

Although general swings in the turnout rate do not seem to give either party an advantage, both major parties spend a great deal of time and money registering voters and getting them to the polls on Election Day. These efforts work not because higher or lower turnout will benefit one of the parties, but because the parties target particular groups they know will vote for them in overwhelming numbers.

Republicans register voters only in Republican-leaning communities, while Democrats focus their efforts only in areas where they expect people to vote for their candidates. When the parties run their get-out-the-vote drives, they call only on voters already registered with their parties. Thus, each party targets its own supporters. To spur on their efforts, they only have to remember the election of 2000—an election in which Bush won Florida by less than one one-thousandth of a percent, and with it, won the presidency.[41]

We have now learned that individual voter characteristics, registration laws and rules, and campaign contacts all have a pronounced effect on who chooses to vote. But voting is not the only way to participate; people can participate actively in the American political system in many other ways.

7-2 POLITICAL ACTIVISTS

Even though voting is the most common way to try to influence who wins elections or what policies the government will adopt, it is not the only way to exert influence. Other forms of political activism are more influential than voting because political activists can often swing many votes beyond their own. Still, despite the potential to have a tremendous impact on who gets elected and what they do once in office, few people participate beyond voting.

7-2a Who Becomes an Activist?

Most Americans do not qualify as political activists, people whose involvement in politics goes beyond the mere act of voting. As Figure 7–4 shows, only small numbers of people report having worked in campaigns, attended rallies or political meetings, or donated money. This is true even though casually attending a political rally or even making a minor gesture such as placing a bumper sticker on one's car makes one an activist by these standards. The only widespread form of political activity other than voting is talking with other people and trying to persuade them how to vote, but that is generally not on behalf of any organized political effort in most cases. Clearly, the number of hard-core political activists in the United States is quite small.

In general, the best way to explain the causes of activism is to focus on three factors: a person's resources, his or her psychological engagement in politics, and his or her access to networks of people for recruitment into political activity. This approach is called the **civic voluntarism model**.[42] The principal resources are time, money, and civic skills. Having sufficient free time and discretionary money for donations obviously allows people to participate more easily. Having appropriate civic skills is equally as important. The ability to speak in public or to organize a meeting is useful in politics, as it is in other spheres of life. Indeed, skills learned in parent-teacher associations (PTAs), churches, or other nonpolitical organizations transfer over into politics quite well.

civic voluntarism model

A theory claiming that political activism can be explained by the time, money, and civic skills that people have.

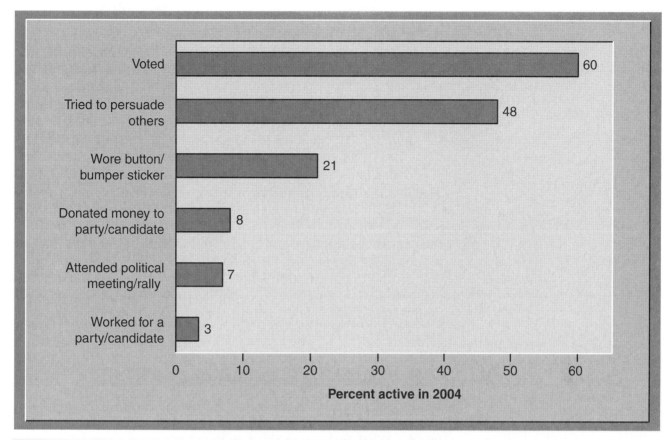

Figure 7-4   Participation in Politics. Voting is the most common form of participation. Many people also talk about politics, trying to persuade others how to vote. Quite a few wear campaign buttons, put bumper stickers on their cars, or put up yard signs. Very few participate in any other specific way.

Source: *Data from the 2004 American National Election Study.*

Those skills make participation easier, and people with those skills are often targeted for recruitment into politics.

Psychological engagement in politics refers to a group of related predispositions. Are people interested in politics? Do they feel a civic obligation to participate? Do they have a sense of political efficacy—that is, the feeling that politicians will pay attention to them? Are they committed to particular issues or social groups with political agendas? People who feel politically engaged in these ways are far more likely to become active than those who do not.

Finally, belonging to and participating in organizations offers people opportunities to be recruited to join in political efforts. When people are asked to participate in politics—whether at work, at home, in union meetings, in churches or synagogues, or in clubs—they often agree to do so. The wider the network of contacts people have, the more likely they are to be asked, and the more likely they are to become active. This applies not only to political activism, but also to running for office. A key reason why far more men than women are in political office is that men are far more likely to be asked to run. Recruitment by party leaders, elected officials, and political activists makes a difference in who wins office.[43]

Source: © *Reuters NewMedia, Inc. /CORBIS.*

Protests—once considered unconventional—are now a standard form of political participation.

The net result of these factors is that political activism tends to be more common among upper than among lower socioeconomic status citizens. They have more discretionary income and often broader networks of contacts, which lead them into participation. Nevertheless, having a low income or a weak education is not necessarily an impediment to participation. A good deal of political participation involves skills that almost everyone has or can easily acquire by joining churches, PTAs, clubs, or neighborhood associations. In particular, college students—who generally have low incomes—have both good educations and enough free time to participate if they choose. That is why so many campaign offices are staffed with young workers.

Although relatively few people participate in politics in any way other than voting, activists are highly influential. They staff the campaigns, register the voters, and perform all the other tasks that produce our elected officials. Moreover, because they participate in the demonstrations and write the letters that public officials read when they try to decipher public opinion, they affect many decisions. In short, activists may be few in number, but they are not small in influence in our political system.

7-3 HOW VOTERS MAKE CHOICES

Who turns out to vote obviously helps determine who wins. But once people are in the voting booths, how do they make up their minds? What influences their choices? Newspaper and television election coverage offers many answers—the candidates' television ads, their campaign strategies, their personalities, their spouses' personalities, their behavior during the Vietnam War, their stands on the issues, their experiences, their physical appearances, and a dozen other factors.

To some extent, all these answers are right. But to arrive at a useful explanation or theory of voting behavior, we must reduce this long list to a few major causes. The list most political scientists use consists of party identification, candidate characteristics, and issues. The most important of these three factors, and the one least often discussed by the news media, is party identification.

7-3a Party Identification

People identify with political parties in the same way they identify with religions or ethnicities. Party identification is more than an emotional or psychological attachment; it is a way in which people think of themselves and an influence on how they behave.

As we discussed in Chapter 6, children begin to learn about politics from their parents early in life. Children begin identifying with political parties when they are as young as eight to ten years old.[44] In fact, children often identify with political parties before they understand what parties or elections are. Their parents socialize them to accept the political labels. At least in the early years, party preference is not a reasoned choice. Although many children break away from their parents in later years, the early learning has a powerful influence.

To understand the role party identification plays in our lives, we must start by examining the way it is measured. Political scientists measure party identification with the following questions:

"Generally speaking, do you usually think of yourself as a Republican, a Democrat, an Independent, or what?"

If the respondent answers "Democrat" or "Republican," the next question is:

"Would you call yourself a strong Democrat [Republican] or a not-so-strong Democrat [Republican]?"

If the respondent answers "Independent," he or she is asked:

"Do you think of yourself as closer to the Republican Party or the Democratic Party?"

From these questions, we can construct a scale ranging from "Strong Republican" to "Strong Democrat" and a residual category of people who identify with minor parties or who have no interest in politics or parties whatsoever.

As Table 7–2 shows, in 2004, 48 percent of all Americans identified themselves as some kind of Democrat, whereas 40 percent

	Strong Democrats (%)	Weak Democrats (%)	Independent Democrats (%)	Pure Independents (%)	Independent Republicans (%)	Weak Republicans (%)	Strong Republicans (%)	Apolitical (%)
1952	22	25	10	6	7	14	14	3
1956	21	23	6	9	8	14	15	4
1960	20	25	6	10	7	14	16	3
1964	27	25	9	8	6	14	11	1
1968	20	25	10	11	9	15	10	1
1972	15	26	11	13	11	13	10	1
1976	15	25	12	15	10	14	9	1
1980	18	23	11	13	10	14	9	2
1984	17	20	11	11	12	15	12	2
1988	18	18	12	11	13	14	14	2
1992	18	17	14	12	12	15	11	1
1994	15	18	13	10	12	15	16	1
1996	18	20	13	8	11	16	13	*
2000	19	15	15	12	13	12	13	1
2004	16	15	17	10	12	12	16	1

Table 7–2 Percentage of People Who Identify with a Party, 1952–2004
The distribution of party identification has remained fairly stable over time, with Democratic identifiers outnumbering Republican identifiers.

Note: *Rows may not add up to 100% because of rounding error.*
* Less than one-half percent.
Source: *Data from the 1952–2004 SRC/CPS American National Election Studies.*

Percentage Who Voted for the Democratic Presidential Candidate														
	1952 (%)	1956 (%)	1960 (%)	1964 (%)	1968 (%)	1972 (%)	1976 (%)	1980 (%)	1984 (%)	1988 (%)	1992 (%)	1996 (%)	2000 (%)	2000* (%)	2004 (%)
Strong Democrats	82	85	90	94	80	66	88	83	87	93	93	95	97	0	98
Weak Democrats	61	62	71	81	54	44	72	53	63	67	69	83	85	1	85
Independent Democrats	59	65	86	89	50	58	70	41	76	88	71	76	71	8	83
Pure Independents	17	15	49	75	22	25	41	21	22	32	41	38	43	5	57
Independent Republicans	7	7	13	25	4	12	14	11	5	14	11	25	13	7	14
Weak Republicans	5	7	11	40	9	9	21	5	6	16	15	19	16	2	10
Strong Republicans	2	1	2	9	3	2	3	4	2	2	2	4	2	1	3

Table 7–3   Party Identification and Vote for Democratic Presidential Candidates, 1952–2004

People who identify with parties usually vote for their party's presidential candidate, but Republicans are generally more loyal to their nominee than democrats are.

Source: *Data from the 1952–2004 SRC/CPS American National Election Studies.*

* Voted for Ralph Nader

identified themselves as Republicans. Although the Democrats have an advantage, we shall see in the following discussion why this advantage does not always guarantee victory at the polls.

The most obvious effect of party identification is on voting choice. People who think of themselves as Democrats generally vote for Democratic candidates, whereas those who think of themselves as Republicans generally choose Republican candidates. Table 7–3 shows the impressive loyalty rates of strong identifiers. In 2004, 98 percent of the strong Democrats voted for Senator Kerry, whereas only 3 percent of the strong Republicans voted for him. Typically, Republicans are slightly more loyal to their candidates than Democrats are to theirs. The higher loyalty rate of Republican identifiers over the years is a major advantage for Republican candidates because it helps offset the greater number of Democratic identifiers.

Table 7–3 reveals another curious fact: People who say they are independent, but who lean toward one of the major parties, behave just like partisan voters. In fact, in eight of the fourteen presidential elections from 1952 to 2004, independent Democrats were more likely to vote for the Democratic candidate than those who said they were weak Democrats. Independent Republicans were more loyal than weak Republicans about half the time. So although people may call themselves independents, if they say they lean toward one of the parties, they are, for practical purposes, partisan voters. As one voter admitted in 1996, "I have never aligned with a party, but I have generally voted Republican all my life."[45]

As one might suspect, Table 7–3 also shows that people who label themselves independents are usually the strongest supporters of independent or minor party presidential candidates. In 2000, Ralph Nader drew more support from people who thought of themselves as independents than from either Democrats or Republicans. He received his weakest support from strong Democrats and strong Republicans—people already satisfied with their parties.

A less obvious, but no less important, aspect of party identification is its role as a perceptual screen that helps people interpret the world of politics.[46] Much of what we learn about politics from the mass media is ambiguous. Will President Bush's proposed energy reform package work? Would the United States have been better off invading Iraq or allowing United Nations arms inspectors to continue their work? Was President Bush honest with Americans when he claimed that he was invading Iraq to protect the United States from Saddam Hussein's weapons of mass destruction (WMD)? Answering such questions is difficult because many people lack the necessary knowledge and because many value judgments are required. Party identification provides guidance in these matters by identifying which political leaders to trust and which to doubt. As a result, people who identify with different parties "see" things differently. To see how party identification functions as a perceptual screen, consider people's assessments of the allegation that President Bush and his administration intentionally exaggerated the evidence that Iraq had weapons of mass destruction. As Figure 7–5 shows, people's opinions tended to match their party identifications. Although Republicans and Democrats heard similar news accounts about Iraq and WMD, 78 percent of the Democrats believed that President Bush exaggerated, but only 24 percent of the Republicans saw it that way.

The fact that people view evidence through partisan eyes and find their own party's leaders more believable than the other party's leaders influences more than candidate evaluations. Party identification also influences what positions people favor on the issues.[47] As we discussed in Chapter 6, people generally don't know much about politics—especially about complicated policy matters. When people have to decide where they stand on complex questions such as Social Security reform or how tax cuts will affect the economy, they have little choice but to look to someone for guidance. Consequently, although people do not blindly follow their party's leaders, they do look to them for advice on political issues.

Party identification's influence on voter evaluations of the candidates and voter policy preferences is important because those factors also affect voting choices. Thus, party identification has both a direct effect on voting and many indirect effects—swaying what we think of the candidates' stands on the issues, for instance, which in turn influences how we vote. For these reasons, party identification is the most important cause of voting choices. We must note, however, that even though most voters see the candidate through

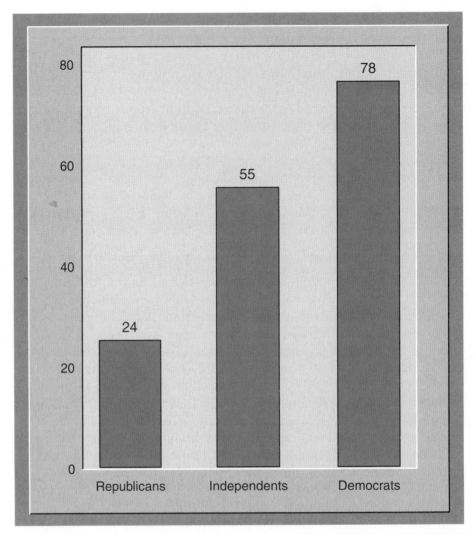

Figure 7-5   Partisan Perceptions of Whether the Bush Administration Told the Truth about Iraq. The question asked was: "Before the war began, do you think the George W. Bush administration did or did not intentionally exaggerate its evidence that Iraq had weapons of mass destruction?" The numbers indicate the percentages who believed that President Bush intentionally exaggerated evidence that Iraq had weapons of mass destruction.

Source: *Data from Washington Post/ABC News Poll, February 10–11, 2004. © 2004 Washington Post. All Rights Reserved.*

partisan eyes, party identification only influences how people evaluate the candidates; it does not strictly predict the voters' perceptions.

7-3b Candidate Characteristics

The candidates' personalities, experiences, past records, and even their physical appearances make up another set of voting influences called **candidate characteristics.** Relying on some candidate characteristics in deciding how to vote makes perfect sense. Whether the candidate has experience in elective office; how well

candidate characteristics
The candidate's character, personality, experiences, past record, and physical appearance.

he or she handled previous jobs; and whether the candidate seems intelligent, honest, and trustworthy are important considerations. A voter might reasonably choose an experienced candidate he or she disagrees with on some issues over a less-experienced candidate with whom he or she agrees on all the issues, or a voter might choose someone who stands by his convictions over someone who flip-flops. In the 2008 Republican primaries, for instance, Senator McCain's experience in Vietnam helped persuade Republicans that he could handle the war in Iraq, whereas stories about Governor Mitt Romney's flip-flops on issues such as gay rights, abortion, and stem cell research helped kill his campaign.[48]

Although some candidate characteristics are clearly related to job performance, others are not. Prejudices and stereotypes influence some voters' choices. As a result, they may vote for or—more commonly—against a candidate who is African American, Hispanic American, female, or Jewish.[49] Some people actually openly admit their biases. For example, a May 2008 ABC News/Washington Post polls asked a national sample, "If you honestly assessed yourself, thinking in general about an African-American president of the United States, is that something you'd be entirely comfortable with, somewhat comfortable, somewhat uncomfortable or entirely uncomfortable?" Only 66 percent said "entirely comfortable," whereas another 22 percent said "somewhat comfortable." When the same question was asked about "a woman president of the United States," 62 percent said "entirely comfortable" and 22 percent said "somewhat comfortable."[50] Figuring out how much influence those prejudices had in the 2008 primary and general elections is complicated because some voters who admitted prejudice against an African American or a woman did, nevertheless, vote for Obama or Clinton because of other issues such as the economy or the war in Iraq. In addition, some people who denied they were prejudiced may have voted against Obama or Clinton because of their prejudices. Moreover, both Obama and Clinton clearly gained some votes because of people who voted for them because of their race or gender. A look at the exit polls from primary elections clearly shows that Obama won an overwhelming majority of African Americans, whereas Clinton won a huge majority of women.[51]

On balance, however, researchers find that prejudices generally work against Jews, African Americans, and Hispanics. Whether they work for or against women is not clear.[52] Overall, racial, religious, and gender prejudices no longer dominate American elections, but they still play a large enough role to affect the outcomes of some elections.[53]

More subtle prejudices also affect voter choice. Many political observers believe that being overweight or short puts a candidate at a disadvantage. Other characteristics or experiences can give candidates advantages—heroism of some kind has launched the careers of many politicians. Senator McCain's record as a decorated Vietnam War hero and prisoner of war certainly helped him in his bid for the Republican nomination in 2000, just as Senator Kerry's Vietnam decorations helped him in 2004.

Source: © Getty Images.

Both Barak Obama and Hilary Clinton faced voter prejudices when they ran for the 2008 Democratic nomination for president.

Although it is hard to figure out why being an athlete or child of a politician can be considered a qualification for office, Congress boasts quite a few. In 2004, Congress had a Hall-of-Fame pitcher (Senator Jim Bunning, R-KY), the former holder of the world record in the mile (Rep. Jim Ryun, R-KA), a former First Lady (Senator Hillary Clinton, D-NY), one widow of a former rock star (Rep. Mary Bono, R-CA), and several sons of well-known politicians (Senator Evan Bayh, D-IN; Rep. Jesse Jackson, Jr., D-IL; Rep. John Sununu, R-NH; Rep. Mark Udall, D-CO; and Rep. Patrick Kennedy, D-RI), among others.[54] Clearly, then, candidate characteristics influence voting behavior.

7-3c Issues

Issues lie at the heart of democratic elections. Through elections, we control what policies our government will follow in the coming years. Yet as we saw in Chapter 6, few people know much about the details of public policy. This lack of knowledge does not eliminate the role of issues in elections, but it does affect the types of issues politicians and journalists emphasize during campaigns and the roles these issues play.

Issues influence voting decisions in two ways, retrospectively and prospectively. In **retrospective issue voting**, the voter decides how to vote on the basis of past policy *outcomes*. That is, the voter considers recent history and decides whether the incumbent has performed well enough to be retained in office. In this case, a voter might ask, Has the unemployment rate or the crime rate been too high in the last couple of years?[55] Unemployment and crime rates, of course, are not policies but the results of

retrospective issue voting
Deciding how to vote on the basis of past policy outcomes.

policies. In retrospective voting, the choice depends on outcomes such as those. In **prospective issue voting**, the voter decides how to vote on the basis of what policies the candidates promise to pursue when elected. That is, the voter chooses between alternative sets *of future government policies.* In this case, a voter might ask, Should we allow women to have the option of abortion, or should we make abortion illegal? Or in the case of crime, a voter might ask: Is the candidate's proposal to increase sentences for violent crimes the best policy to reduce crime?[56] When voting prospectively, voters must assume that the candidates will carry out their promises about policies.

prospective issue voting
Deciding how to vote on the basis of a candidate's likely future policies.

Retrospective Issue Voting

An important aspect of retrospective voting is that it does not require voters to understand the specific details of public policy. They may need to know only a few generalities about how well the economy or the Iraq War has been doing recently to form judgments about how well the president has been handling his job. From these judgments about past performance, people can develop expectations about how well the president will perform in the future.

When retrospectively evaluating an incumbent president's performance in office, most voters focus on the economy and consider the president's past performance as a good predictor of future performance. If the economy has been doing well, voters tend to reward the incumbent with reelection; if the economy has been weak, voters tend to throw out the incumbent and vote in the opposition party's candidate. In other words, voters act as the "rational god of vengeance and of reward."[57] Because of this behavior, political scientists have been able to develop models that can predict presidential elections fairly accurately on the basis of economic indicators such as change in gross domestic product, the unemployment rate, and the inflation rate.[58] We can see why these models work by looking at the results of the 2008 exit polls. Senator McCain won the votes of 72 percent of voters who thought the economy was "excellent" or "good," whereas Senator Obama won the votes of 54 percent of those who thought it was "not good" or "poor." McCain's problem was that 93 percent of the voters thought that the economy was not good or poor.[59]

The conventional wisdom regarding retrospective voting is that people "vote their pocket-books" by rewarding or punishing incumbents for the voters' personal economic situations. Yet when researchers began investigating the question, they found that most people seem to be **socio-tropic voters.** That is, they seem to be influenced far more by their community's or the nation's economic condition than by their own economic situations. The evidence for this pattern of behavior is that public opinion survey questions about personal economic situations poorly predict how people will vote, but questions about the respondents' perceptions of the nation's economic situation predict voting choices fairly well.[60] In other words, when people lose their jobs or suffer financial

socio-tropic voters
People who vote on the basis of their community's economic interests, rather than their personal economic interests.

hardships, they do not necessarily blame the incumbent administration in the White House. However, when the unemployment
rate goes up and people in their communities begin to lose their
jobs, many voters do blame the incumbent administration.

The 2008 presidential election was not just about the economy,
of course; it was also a referendum on the war in Iraq. Throughout
the campaign, Senator McCain emphasized his ability to lead the
nation during wartime. He argued that American efforts were successful; Senator Obama argued that they were not and called for
pulling U.S. troops out of Iraq. Here, too, we see evidence of retrospective voting. The exit polls showed that 86 percent of voters
who approved of the conduct of the war supported Senator
McCain, whereas only 22 percent of those who thought the war
was going "badly" supported him.[61]

Prospective Issue Voting

It might seem reasonable that prospective issue voting—voting on
the basis of policies a candidate promises to pursue in the future—
should be a dominant factor in voting decisions. Yet one of the earliest and most disturbing findings about voting behavior was that
prospective issues do not actually have much influence on voting
decisions. That is, whether voters agree or disagree with candidates on public policy choices seems to make only a small difference in how they vote.

In a major study conducted in the 1950s, several researchers
proposed that three conditions must be met for issues to influence
voting decisions.[62] For an issue to play any role in a voter's choice,
the voter must (1) be aware of the issue and have an opinion on it,
(2) have some idea about what the government is currently doing
on that issue, and (3) see a difference between the policies the two
candidates propose in response to the issue. Although these conditions may seem easy to satisfy, we should remember that few
people in the American public are well informed about politics
and public policy (see Chapter 6). This lack of knowledge helps
explain why the researchers found that only one-fourth to one-third
of the electorate met the three conditions necessary to characterize
voters as engaging in prospective issue voting.

More recent studies paint a somewhat better—but still not
glowing—picture of the electorate.[63] To help judge the presence of
prospective issue voting, researchers use a series of issue questions
in which survey respondents are presented with a scale (see the
example in Figure 7–6). The respondents are asked to say which
point on the scale best reflects their views and which points best
reflect the views of the two presidential candidates. The researchers then suggest the following criteria for issue voting. An issue
can influence someone's vote if (1) the voter can place himself or
herself on the scale, (2) the voter can place both candidates on the
scale, (3) the voter sees a difference between the candidates, and
(4) the voter correctly places the Democratic candidate to the left
of the Republican candidate. Although these criteria differ from

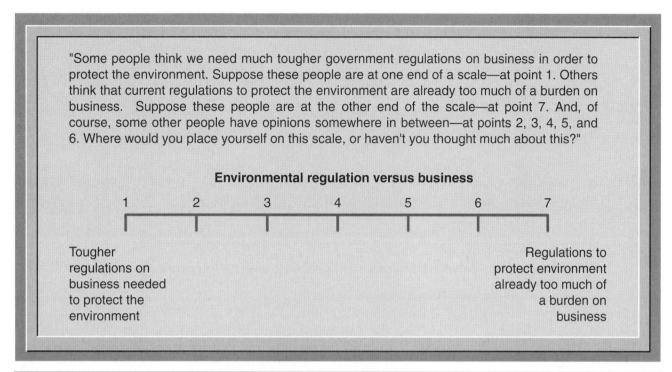

"Some people think we need much tougher government regulations on business in order to protect the environment. Suppose these people are at one end of a scale—at point 1. Others think that current regulations to protect the environment are already too much of a burden on business. Suppose these people are at the other end of the scale—at point 7. And, of course, some other people have opinions somewhere in between—at points 2, 3, 4, 5, and 6. Where would you place yourself on this scale, or haven't you thought much about this?"

Environmental regulation versus business

1   2   3   4   5   6   7

Tougher regulations on business needed to protect the environment

Regulations to protect environment already too much of a burden on business

Figure 7-6   A Seven-Point Issue Scale. Issue scales, such as this environmental regulation versus business scale, help us understand the influence issues have on voting decisions.
Source: *Codebook, 2004 American National Election Study.* Ann Arbor, MI: University of Michigan, Center for Political Studies, 2005.

those used in the study conducted in the 1950s, they spring from the same basic ideas. For an issue to matter at the polls, the voter must care about it enough to offer an opinion and must correctly distinguish differences between the two candidates on the issue.

Table 7–4 presents the data researchers compiled using this method for the 2004 election. For the first issue, whether to prefer diplomacy or military force in foreign policy, 87 percent of the voters in the national sample had opinions about the best foreign policy approach, and 81 percent thought they understood the positions of the presidential candidates—Kerry and Bush. Seventy-eight percent thought Kerry and Bush disagreed, and 74 percent correctly *realized* that Kerry favored diplomacy more than Bush did. Therefore, if this issue had any effect on people's voting decisions, it could only be among these 74 percent of the voters.

The question of whether diplomacy or military force works better is not typical of most political issues. The 2004 presidential election was regarded by many people as a referendum on the wars in Afghanistan and Iraq. Four out of five voters correctly realized where the candidates stood on the use of force in foreign policy. On many other issues, however, far fewer voters met the criteria for issue voting. Table 7–4 shows, for instance, that only 27 percent of the public recognized that Senator Kerry was more likely than President Bush to favor the environment if there were a jobs-versus-environment trade-off.

| Percentage of Sample Who: | | | |
| Issue scale | Placed Both | | |
	Self on scale (%)	Candidates on scale (%)	Saw difference between candidates (%)	Placed Kerry to left of Bush (%)
Diplomacy versus military force	93	88	85	81
Increase or cut both spending and services	86	76	66	53
Women equal versus women at home	95	77	45	35
Jobs vs. environment	83	66	52	27

Table 7–4   Four Criteria for Issue Voting, 2004
In most presidential elections, about half the public fails to meet the four necessary conditions for issue voting.
Source: *Data from the 2004 American National Election Study.*

easy issues
Simple issues that allow voters to make quick, emotional decisions without much information.

hard issues
Complicated issues that require voters to have information about the policy and to spend time considering their choices.

Over the last half-dozen presidential elections, about half the people on average met the criteria for issue voting on the major issues of each election. We may think that everyone knows and cares about major political issues, but, in fact, many people either don't know or don't care.

Although most prospective issues do not seem to have much effect on voting decisions, some do. To examine which issues are more or less likely to influence voting outcomes, it helps to divide issues into two categories: easy and hard.[64] Simple or **easy issues**—those that allow voters to give quick, emotional responses to symbols—usually dominate election debates. For example, issues such as fighting terrorism or abortion don't require much thought for many people—virtually everyone supports fighting terrorism and many voters have well-established pro-choice or pro-life stands on abortion. Candidates can therefore package these issues in thirty-second television spots or sound bites in speeches for the nightly news. **Hard issues**—those that are complicated and require some knowledge of the subject and some thought before coming to a conclusion—do not play much part in voters' decisions. Issues such as how to provide health care to all Americans; what, if anything, we should do to fight global warming; or how best to support Georgia and the other emerging democracies of eastern Europe cannot readily be reduced to campaign slogans or sound bites for television. They rely too much on the voters' knowledge of the issues and willingness to consider the problems carefully. The few who do follow these issues, of course, have a disproportionately large influence on the decisions officeholders make.

7-3d Changes over Time

Party identification, candidate characteristics, and issues all influence voters' choices in elections, but the relative importance of each factor changes from one election to the next. Calls to party unity have dominated some past presidential elections, issueless appeals to vote for the more "trustworthy" or "experienced" candidate have dominated others, and strident debates about public policy have characterized still other campaigns.

Several factors may change the nature of voter decisions over time. Dramatic events or conditions, such as wars or deep recessions, can focus the nation's attention on particular issues, reducing the impact of party identification or candidate characteristics. In other times, however, the candidates and the journalists who cover them decide the nature of the campaigns. When campaigns stress issues and ideological conflicts, the voters mirror the candidates by giving issues more weight in their voting choices. Alternatively, when campaigns focus on character or scandal, the voters pay less attention to issues.[65]

The ability of voters to pass the issue voting tests, described in Table 7–4, reflects the strategic choices candidates and journalists make about what to emphasize in campaigns. For instance, in the 2004 presidential election, the candidates' views on how to deal with the war in Iraq and its aftermath dominated the news. By contrast, in the 2000 presidential election—one characterized by George W. Bush's focus on his character, Al Gore's focus on his experience, and the shadows of Bill Clinton's scandals—fewer people knew enough about the issues to meet the issue voting criteria than in any other recent election. The people may want the candidates to talk about the issues, but the decision is up to the candidates and the journalists who cover them. If the candidates avoid the issues or the journalists choose not to discuss them, the people can do little to change things. They must then revert to making decisions based on other factors—party identification and the characteristics of the candidates.

7-3e Voting and Social Groups

A final way to look at voting is to examine which candidates and parties different social groups favor. These voting patterns largely reflect the groups that make up the Democratic and Republican parties (see Chapter 9). That is, in terms of our previous discussion, people's party identifications vary from one social group to another.

To illustrate the social composition of the Democratic and Republican parties, Table 7–5 presents a portrait of the electorate in the 2008 presidential election. (Minor party voters have been excluded because they rarely exceeded 1 percent in any category.) The outlines of the party coalitions are clear here, but we also see that all groups split their votes between Democrats and Republicans. Stereotypes such as "all the rich vote Republican" or "all the poor are Democrats" are wild exaggerations.

Beginning at the top of the table, we see that Democrats win a majority of the votes of the poor, whereas Republicans win a majority of the votes of the wealthy. Obama beat McCain 73 percent to 25 percent among those with incomes less than $15,000; by

Percentage of all voters (%)	Group	Percentage Voting for	
		Obama (%)	McCain (%)
Family income			
6	Less than $15,000	73	25
12	$15,000–29,999	60	37
19	$30,000–49,999	55	43
21	$50,000–74,999	48	49
15	$75,000–99,999	51	48
14	$100,000–149,999	48	51
6	$150,000–199,999	48	50
6	$200,000 or more	52	46
Education			
4	No high school	63	35
20	High school graduate	52	46
31	Some college	51	47
28	College graduate	50	48
17	Post-graduate education	58	40
Union member in household			
21	Yes	59	39
79	No	51	47
Race/ethnicity			
74	White	43	55
13	African American	95	4
9	Hispanic American	67	31
2	Asian American	62	35
Age			
18	18–29	66	32
29	30–44	52	46
37	45–64	50	49
16	65 and older	45	53
Gender			
47	Men	49	48
53	Women	56	43

Percentage of all voters (%)	Group	Percentage Voting for	
		Obama (%)	McCain (%)
Sexual orientation			
4	Gay, lesbian, or bisexual	70	27
96	Other	53	45
Size of city			
30	Urban	63	35
49	Suburban	50	48
21	Rural	45	53
Religion			
54	Protestant	45	54
27	Catholic	54	45
2	Jewish	78	21
6	Other	73	22
12	None	75	23
Church attendance			
12	More than weekly	43	55
27	Weekly	43	55
15	Monthly	53	46
28	A few times a year	59	39
16	Never	67	30
Ideology			
22	Liberals	89	10
44	Moderates	60	39
34	Conservatives	20	78

Table 7–5   Voting by Social Groups in the 2008 Presidential Election

Groups favoring the Democratic Party include the poor, people with either few years of formal education or with postgraduate degrees, union members, African Americans, Asian Americans, Hispanic Americans, women, people who live in big cities, Catholics, Jews, people who are not religious, people who rarely or never attend church, and liberals. Groups favoring the Republican Party include the wealthy, college graduates, non-union members, whites, men, people who live in rural areas, Protestants, people who are regular churchgoers, and conservatives.

Note: *Each row may not total 100 percent because of excluded minor-party voters and rounding error.*

Source: *Data from National Election Pool exit polls by Edison/Mitofsky. Reported at www.cnn.com/ELECTION/2008/results/polls/#val=USP00p1.*

contrast, McCain beat Obama 52 percent to 46 percent among those with incomes higher than $200,000.

The pattern of voting by education is more complex than that of voting by income. Obama won majorities in every group, but he did best among people with the least education and the most education. McCain fared best among people with middle levels of education—high school graduates through college graduates. This coalition of the middle (Republicans) against the top and bottom (Democrats) appeared in the 1960s and has regularly appeared ever since.[66]

Union members and their families tend to vote Democratic, whereas people without union affiliations tend to vote Republican. This pattern has consistently appeared since the New Deal in the 1930s.

Along racial and ethnic lines, whites tend to support Republicans, whereas African Americans, Hispanic Americans, and Asian Americans tend to support Democrats. Although Asian Americans had been in the Republican camp in the past, by 2000 they had moved toward the Democrats. They stayed with the Democrats in 2008. Young voters gave Obama a two-to-one majority, whereas older voters leaned toward McCain.

Women tend to vote more Democrat than men do. In the 2008 election, women were 7 percent more likely to vote for Obama than were men. Political observers have labeled this difference in voting between men and women the **gender gap.** The gender gap has never been very large—averaging 7 or 8 percent in most surveys.[67] Although the gender gap is a small percentage, its political impact is huge; had only men been allowed to vote, Obama might not have won the 2008 election.

In addition to gender, sexual orientation also made a difference in 2008. The small percentage of voters who identified themselves as gay, lesbian, or bisexual leaned heavily toward the Democratic candidate. Although many observers believe this is a long-standing pattern, we cannot be sure because 2004 was the first year that a question about sexual orientation was asked in the exit polls.

The size of the community in which voters resided also made a large difference. Obama won a substantial majority in big cities, tied McCain in suburbs, and lost in rural areas. This urban-rural split can be seen in Figure 7–7a, which shows which candidate won each county. Most of the map in Figure 7–7a is red, indicating that Republicans won majorities in most counties in the 2008 presidential election. The oddly shaped "cartogram" in Figure 7–7b shows why the election was so close. The cartogram is a map in which the counties have been rescaled according to their population. For example, Dade County, Florida (in the southeastern corner of the state) covers a small area in Figure 7–7a but a huge area in the cartogram in Figure 7–7b because so many people live in Miami. Here, we see that Obama may have won majorities only in big cities, but because so many people live in big cities, the election was close.

By religion, Protestants tend to vote Republican, whereas Catholics lean toward the Democratic Party and Jewish voters are strongly Democratic. In addition, people who attend churches, temples, or mosques frequently are more likely to vote Republican than those who attend infrequently or never.

Finally, those who identify themselves as liberals are far more likely to vote for Democratic candidates than are those who identify themselves as conservatives. Conversely, of course,

gender gap

The difference between men's and women's voting rates for either a Democratic or Republican candidate.

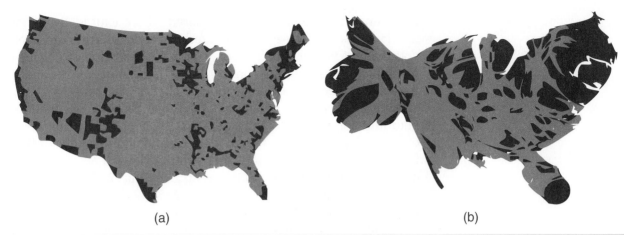

(a)   (b)

Figure 7-7   The Urban-Rural Split between Obama and McCain, 2008. *A,* The breakdown by county, with red being
Republican and blue being Democratic. *B,* A cartogram of the election, with the counties scaled according
to population.

Source: © 2008 Mark E. J. Newman. Available at www.personal.umich.edu/~mejn/election/2008/.

conservatives are more likely than liberals to vote Republican. Although voting patterns change somewhat from one election to the next, the results in Table 7–5 are typical of most post-1930s presidential elections. People who are upper income, well-educated, nonunion, white, Protestants, and who attend church regularly and think of themselves as conservatives tend to support Republican candidates. Lower income, poorly educated people who are union members, African American, Asian American, or Hispanic American, who are Catholic or Jewish, who attend church infrequently or never, and who think of themselves as liberals tend to support Democratic candidates. Since the late 1970s, women have also been more likely than men to support Democratic candidates. These groups make up the party coalitions of the 2000s.

SUMMARY

Although the rules of the political system in the United States allow almost everyone eighteen and older the opportunity to vote and participate, they do not guarantee that these people will choose to do so. There is no guarantee that "the will of the people" will be reflected in the election winners or the policies they set for our nation. Who votes or becomes politically active and how those people make their choices have a great impact on which candidates win and which policies become laws.

Slightly more than half of eligible voters turn out in presidential elections; even fewer vote in other elections. People with high incomes, good educations, and high-status jobs—that is, people of high socioeconomic status—are more likely to vote than those with low incomes, poor educations, and low-status jobs. Whites are likely to vote at higher rates than are African Americans, Hispanic Americans, or Asian Americans, but these differences are caused by socioeconomic status. Middle-aged and elderly Americans are more likely to vote than the young. Finally, strong party identification, strong feelings of political efficacy, group consciousness, interest in politics, and reading about politics make people more likely to participate.

Although voting is a personal act, the decision about whether to vote and for whom to vote depends on more than the personal characteristics of the voters; it also depends on the rules of the political system. Voting and registration laws can substantially change the turnout rate. States with laws that make it more difficult or time consuming to register and vote have lower turnout rates than states with more lenient laws.

Aside from personal characteristics and rules, the behavior of campaigns and party organizations also influences turnout. Contacts from campaigns or voter registration and get-out-the-vote drives help bring people to the polls. As we shall see in Chapter 9, the rules governing the behavior of political parties also affect these campaign efforts.

Voter turnout has declined since the turn of the century. The debate about the drop in turnout early in the century centers on whether changes in the parties' positions on the issues or changes in the rules governing registration and voting caused the decline. The post-1960 decline seems to be attributable to voters' personal characteristics, voting rules, and party strategy. Personal characteristics of voters have contributed to the decline because the average age of the population has fallen, and people identify less with political parties, feel less efficacious about politics, and are less likely to read newspapers than they were before 1960. Changes in rules have also contributed to the post-1960 decline—more young voters became eligible to vote with the passage of the Twenty-Sixth Amendment to the Constitution, which added a relatively low turnout group to the electorate. Finally, parties and campaigns have put less effort into contacting and mobilizing voters over the past few decades.

The causes of activism are best described in terms of people's resources (e.g., time, money, and civic skills), their psychological engagement in politics (in terms of interest, sense of political efficacy, and enthusiasm for issues or social group commitments), and their involvement with networks of people who might recruit them into political activity. Few people are politically active in any way beyond voting, but those who are active have influence far beyond their numbers.

Three broad sets of forces influence people's voting decisions— party identification, candidate characteristics, and issues. Of these, party identification is the most influential and issues the least. When looking at the role of issues in elections, one must distinguish between retrospective voting and prospective voting. People who vote retrospectively look back at recent conditions in the nation and assess them, whereas those who vote prospectively look forward and vote on the basis of candidate promises and what policies they want the government to follow in the future. When people do vote prospectively, they tend to do so on the basis of easy issues, which allow voters to give quick, emotional responses. Hard issues, which require some knowledge of the subject and careful thought, generally do not have much effect in elections.

Voting choice depends not only on the individual's preferences, but also on the strategic choices the candidates and journalists make about whether to emphasize party labels, particular candidate characteristics, or particular issues. Therefore, even if individuals' preferences were fixed, the ways in which candidates present different aspects of their personalities and different issues can alter the choices voters face and therefore change the outcomes.

In short, who wins elections depends on many factors—on who votes; on whether the rules in a given state encourage or discourage voting; on whether campaigns, parties, or other groups make an effort to contact voters; on people's preferences about party labels, candidate characteristics, and issues; and on the strategies and behavior of the candidates and journalists who cover them. An election outcome depends on much more than the personal preferences of the citizens. The people, the politicians, the journalists, and the rules under which they compete all play roles in determining who prevails in any given election.

KEY TERMS

Australian ballot	literacy tests
candidate characteristics	party identification
civic voluntarism model	political efficacy
closing date	poll taxes
easy issues	prospective issue voting
franchise	retrospective issue voting
gender gap	socio-tropic voters
group consciousness	voter turnout
hard issues	

READINGS FOR FURTHER STUDY

Abramson, Paul R., John H. Aldrich, and David W. Rohde. *Change and Continuity in the 2004 and 2006 Elections* (Washington, D.C.: CQ Press, 2007). This is a sophisticated but easily readable analysis of who turns out to vote and how they make up their minds. This study examines the central questions of voting analysis from the most important theoretical perspectives.

Dalton, Richard J. *The Good Citizen: How a Younger Generation is Reshaping American Politics* (Washington, D.C.: CQ Press, 2008). Dalton describes what a "good citizen" is, and then proceeds to show that young Americans are more engaged, active, and civic-minded than generations that came previously. He shows that the conventional wisdom, which downplays the contributions of the young, is mistaken.

Keith, Bruce E., David B. Magleby, Candice J. Nelson, Elizabeth Orr, Mark C. Westyle, and Raymond E. Wolfinger. *The Myth of the Independent Voter* (Berkeley: University of California Press, 1992). A penetrating study of the behavior of people who call themselves political independents. Keith and his colleagues argue that the rise of independents was mythical and that most people still behave as if they are partisans.

Piven, Frances Fox, and Richard A. Cloward. *Why Americans Don't Vote* (New York: Pantheon, 1988). An investigation of why the turnout rate has dropped so sharply since the nineteenth century. Piven and Cloward argue persuasively that manipulation of registration laws is to blame.

Rosenstone, Steven J., and John Mark Hansen. *Mobilization, Participation, and Democracy in America* (New York: Macmillan, 1993). A path-breaking study of why people vote and participate in other ways in our political system. The study reveals the key role parties and campaigns play when they choose whether to mobilize voters and activists.

Semiatin, Richard J. *Campaigning on the Cutting Edge* (Washington, D.C.: CQ Press, 2008). This edited volume offers a set of chapters describing current campaign methods from fundraising through handling the media and mobilizing voters. It offers an outstanding look at how modern elections are run in the 2000s.

Tate, Katherine. *From Protest to Politics: The New Black Voters in American Elections,* enlarged edition (Cambridge: Harvard University Press, 1994). An in-depth examination of African American political behavior in the 1984, 1988, and 1992 elections, with special attention to the impact the Reverend Jesse Jackson's campaigns had on the Democratic presidential nominations.

Westlye, Mark C. *Senate Elections and Campaign Intensity* (Baltimore: Johns Hopkins University Press, 1991). A comprehensive and systematic study of modern Senate elections. Westlye draws on a wealth of survey and election data to show why we choose our senators.

Wolfinger, Raymond E., and Steven J. Rosenstone. *Who Votes?* (New Haven, CT: Yale University Press, 1980). In this classic study of who turns out to vote, Wolfinger and Rosenstone use census data to examine the demographic and social characteristics of voters.

REVIEW QUESTIONS

1. What is the *most* important variable that explains whether or not a person votes?
   a. political efficacy
   b. race and ethnicity
   c. age
   d. education

2. Compared with most other countries in the world, the United States
   a. has a high level of voter turnout.
   b. is about in the middle in terms of voter turnout.
   c. has a lower level of voter turnout.
   d. typically has a voter turnout rate exceeding 70 percent.

3. States with election-day registration have _____ turnout than states that close off registration thirty days before the election.
   a. a higher
   b. a lower
   c. basically the same
   d. none of the above

4. The 1965 Voting Rights Act helped
   a. to increase registration and voter turnout by minorities.
   b. to force the Ku Klux Klan to dissolve.
   c. to increase discrimination against minorities in the South.
   d. precinct workers assist voters on election day.

5. Who of the following is most likely to be a political activist?
   a. fifty-five-year-old corporate lawyer
   b. twenty-five-year-old unemployed factory worker
   c. nineteen-year-old student
   d. forty-six-year-old janitor

6. Which of the following is an "easy" issue?
   a. health care
   b. budget deficit
   c. abortion
   d. immigration

7. When it comes to issue voting,
   a. most Americans have a good understanding of the issues.
   b. hard issues tend to dominate election debates.
   c. prospective issue voting is a dominant factor in voting decisions.
   d. most Americans tend to look at the past, not the future.

8. Most of the people who participate in politics do so by
   a. donating money to a political candidate.
   b. attending political rallies.
   c. working for a political campaign.
   d. voting.

9. Which of the following influences voting decisions the most?
   a. issues
   b. candidate characteristics
   c. party identification
   d. political climate

10. The Twenty-Fourth Amendment abolished
    a. slavery.
    b. poll taxes.
    c. literacy tests.
    d. grandfather clauses.

NOTES

1. Curtis Gans, "African-Americans, Anger, Fear and Youth Propel Turnout to Highest Level Since 1960." Center for Study of the American Electorate, American University, December 17, 2008, available at www.american.edu/ia/cdem/csae/pdfs/2008pdfoffinaledited.pdf.

2. Raymond E. Wolfinger and Steven Rosenstone, *Who Votes?* (New Haven, CT: Yale University Press, 1980), 102.

3. Steven J. Rosenstone and John Mark Hansen, *Mobilization, Participation, and Democracy in America* (New York: Macmillan, 1993), 130–31.

4. Ibid., 136–41.

5. Walter Dean Burnham, "Theory and Voting Research: Some Reflections on Converse's 'Change in the American Electorate,'" *American Political Science Review* 68 (September 1974): 1002–23.

6. Angus Campbell, Philip E. Converse, Warren E. Miller, and Donald E. Stokes, *The American Voter* (Chicago: University of Chicago Press, 1960), 483–89.

7. Paul R. Abramson, John H. Aldrich, and David W. Rohde, *Change and Continuity in the 2000 Elections* (Washington, D.C.: CQ Press, 2002), 78.

8. See Paul R. Abramson, *Political Attitudes in America* (San Francisco: Freeman, 1983).

9. Arthur H. Miller, Patricia Gurin, Gerald Gurin, and Oksana Malanchuk, "Group Consciousness and Participation," *American Journal of Political Science* 25 (August 1981): 494–511; Richard D. Shingles, "Black Consciousness and Political Participation: The Missing Link," *American Political Science Review* 75 (March 1981): 76–91.

10. Eric R. A. N. Smith, *The Unchanging American Voter* (Berkeley: University of California Press, 1989), chap. 4. Although watching television does not cause turnout, it can focus people's attention on particular issues and help them learn about some types of politics. See W. Russell Neuman, Marion R. Just, and Ann N. Ciglar, *Common Knowledge* (Chicago: University of Chicago Press, 1992).

11. M. Margaret Conway, *Political Participation in the United States*, 2nd ed. (Washington, D.C.: CQ Press, 1991), 49–50. The 1994 and 2000 data are from the 1994 and 2000 American National Election Studies.

12. Jack Citrin, "The Alienated Voter," *Taxing and Spending* (October 1978): 1–7; Rosenstone and Hansen, *Mobilization, Participation, and Democracy*, 147–50; Stephen D. Shaffer, "A Multivariate Explanation of Decreasing Turnout in Presidential Elections, 1960–1976," *American Journal of Political Science* 25 (February 1981): 68–95.

13. Wolfinger and Rosenstone, *Who Votes?* 115–18; Michael P. McDonald and Samuel Popkin, "The Myth of the Vanishing Voter," *American Political Science Review* 95 (2001): 963–74.

14. David Glass, Peverill Squire, and Raymond Wolfinger, "Voter Turnout: An International Comparison," *Public Opinion* 6 (December/January 1984): 49–55. See also Russell J. Dalton, *Citizen Politics*, 2nd ed. (Chatham, NJ: Chatham House, 1996), chap. 3.

15. Sidney Verba and Norman H. Nie, *Participation in America* (New York: Harper & Row, 1972), chap. 20.

16. Wolfinger and Rosenstone, *Who Votes?* 77–78; Glenn Mitchell II and Christopher Wlezien, "The Impact of Legal Constraints on Voter Registration, Turnout, and the Composition of the American Electorate," *Political Behavior* 17

(June 1995): 179–202; Jack Citrin, Eric Schickler and John Sides, "What if Everyone Voted? Simulating the Impact of Increased Turnout in Senate Elections," *American Journal of Political Science* 47 (January 2003): 75–90.

17. V. O. Key, Jr., *Southern Politics* (New York: Random House, 1949).

18. Michael Ross, "Landmark Voter Bill OKd; GOP Filibuster Fails," *Los Angeles Times*, May 12, 1993.

19. See Richard Sammon, "Deal May Speed Up 'Motor Voter,'" *Congressional Quarterly Weekly Report*, May 1, 1993, 1080; Richard Sammon, "House OKs 'Motor Voter' for Final Senate Vote," *Congressional Quarterly Weekly Report*, May 8, 1993, 1144; Richard Sammon, "Senate Kills Filibuster Threat, Clears 'Motor Voter' Bill," *Congressional Quarterly Weekly Report*, May 15, 1993, 1221; David G. Savage, "High Court Backs Law to Spur Voter Registration," *Los Angeles Times*, January 23, 1996.

20. John Harwood, "In a Surprise for Everyone, Motor-Voter Law Is Providing a Boost for GOP, Not Democrats," *Wall Street Journal*, June 11, 1996.

21. Barbara Vobejda, "Just Under Half of Possible Voters Went to the Polls," *Washington Post*, November 7, 1996; Benjamin Highton and Raymond E. Wolfinger, "Estimating the Effects of the National Voter Registration Act of 1993," *Political Behavior* 20 (June 1998): 79–104; Stephen Knack, "Does 'Motor Voter' Work? Evidence from State-Level Data," *Journal of Politics* 57 (August 1995): 796–811; Staci L. Rhine, "Registration Reform and Turnout Change in the American States," *American Politics Quarterly* 24 (October 1994): 409–26.

22. Rosenstone and Hansen, *Mobilization, Participation, and Democracy*, chap. 6.

23. Committee for the Study of the American Electorate, "President Bush, Mobilization Drives Propel Turnout to Post-1968 High; Kerry, Democratic Weakness Shown," November 4, 2004, available at www.fairvote.org/reports/CSAE2004electionreport.pdf.

24. Timothy Egan, "Oregon's Mail-in Senate Vote Buoys Clinton and Democrats," *New York Times*, February 1, 1996; Jeffrey A. Karp and Susan A. Banducci, "Going Postal: How All Mail Elections Influence Turnout," *Political Behavior* 22 (September 2000): 223–39; Secretary of State, Oregon, "Online Voters Guide," available at www.sos.state.or.us/elections/nov72000/guide/cover.htm.

25. See, for example, Brad Cain, "U.S. Senate Primary in Oregon a Test of Mail Voting," *Seattle Times*, October 8, 1995.

26. Richard A. Brody, "The Puzzle of Political Participation in America," *The New American Political System*, ed. Anthony King (Washington, D.C.: American Enterprise Institute, 1978), 287–334.

27. See Walter Dean Burnham, "The Changing Shape of the American Political Universe," *American Political Science Review* 59 (March 1965): 7–28; Walter D. Burnham, *Critical Elections and the Mainsprings of American Politics* (New York: Norton, 1970); Burnham, "Theory and Voting Research," 1002–23.

28. See Philip E. Converse, "Change in the American Electorate," in *The Human Meaning of Social Change*, eds. Angus Campbell and Philip E. Converse (New York: Russell Sage Foundation, 1972); Philip E. Converse, "Comment on Burnham's 'Theory and Voting Research,'" *American Political Science Review* 68 (September 1974): 1024–27; Jerrold G. Rusk, "Comment: The American Electoral Universe: Speculation and Evidence," *American Political Science Review* 68 (September 1974): 1028–49.

29. Richard Hofstadter, *The Age of Reform* (New York: Vintage Books, 1955).

30. Frances Fox Piven and Richard A. Cloward, *Why Americans Don't Vote* (New York: Pantheon, 1988), chap. 3.

31. Ibid., chap. 2; Paul Kleppner, *Who Voted? The Dynamics of Electoral Turnout* (New York: Praeger, 1982); Burnham, "Theory and Voting Research," 1002–23.

32. Piven and Cloward, *Why Americans Don't Vote*, chap. 3; Morgan J. Kousser, *The Shaping of Southern Politics: Suffrage Restrictions and the Establishment of the One-Party South* (New Haven, CT: Yale University Press, 1974); C. Vann Woodward, *Origins of the New South: 1877–1913* (Baton Rouge: Louisiana State University Press, 1951).

33. Widespread scientific survey research did not begin until the mid-1930s. George Gallup conducted the best-known early work. See George H. Gallup, *The Gallup Poll: Public Opinion 1935–1971* (New York: Random House, 1972).

34. Ruy A. Teixeira, *The Disappearing American Voter* (Washington, D.C.: Brookings Institution, 1992).

35. Rosenstone and Hansen, *Mobilization, Participation, and Democracy*, chap. 7.

36. Wolfinger and Rosenstone, *Who Votes?* chap. 4.

37. Stephen Earl Bennett and David Resnick, "The Implications of Nonvoting for Democracy in the United States," *American Journal of Political Science* 34 (August 1990): 771–802; Mitchell and Wlezien, "The Impact of Legal Constraints on Voter Registration, Turnout, and the Composition of the American Electorate"; but see Benjamin Radcliff, "Turnout and the Democratic Vote," *American Politics Quarterly* 22 (July 1994): 277–96.

38. Alan Brinkley, "What's Next?" *American Prospect* 12 (December 2004): 18–23; Curtis Gans, "President Bush, Mobilization Drives Propel Turnout to Post-1968 High; Kerry, Democratic Weakness Shown," Committee for the Study of the American Electorate, November 4, 2004, available at www.american.edu/ia/cdem/csae/pdfs/csae041104.pdf.

39. On European turnout, see Russell J. Dalton, *Citizen Politics*, 2nd ed. (Chatham, NJ: Chatham House, 1996) and Glass, Squire, and Wolfinger, "Voter Turnout," 49–55.

40. See Steven F. Lawson, *In Pursuit of Power: Southern Blacks and Electoral Politics, 1965–1982* (New York: Columbia University Press, 1982).

41. Florida Department of State, Division of Elections, available at www.election.dos.state.fl.us/online/index.shtml.

42. Sidney Verba, Kay L. Schlozman, and Henry E. Brady, *Voice and Equality: Civic Voluntarism in American Politics* (Cambridge, MA: Harvard University Press, 1995), part III.

43. Jennifer L. Lawless and Richard L. Fox, *It Takes a Candidate: Why Women Don't Run for Public Office* (Cambridge: Cambridge University Press, 2005), chap. 5.

44. Robert D. Hess and Judith V. Torney, *The Development of Political Attitudes in Children* (Chicago: Aldine, 1967), 96.

45. Quoted in Dan Balz, "A Little Too Social for Suburbia," *Washington Post National Weekly Edition*, May 27–June 2, 1996, 13; see also Bruce E. Keith, David B. Magleby, Candice J. Nelson, Elizabeth Orr, Mark C. Westyle, and Raymond E. Wolfinger, *The Myth of the Independent Voter* (Berkeley: University of California Press, 1992), chap. 4.

46. See Campbell, Converse, Miller, and Stokes, *The American Voter*, chap. 3; Abramson, *Political Attitudes*, chap. 5; Larry A. Bartels, "Beyond the

Running Tally: Partisan Bias in Political Perception," *Political Behavior* 24 (June 2002): 117–50.

47. Gregory B. Markus and Philip E. Converse, "A Dynamic Simultaneous Equation Model of Electoral Choice," *American Political Science Review* 73 (December 1979): 1055–70.

48. Evan Thomas, "What These Eyes Have Seen," *Newsweek* (February 11, 2008): 24–31; Michael Finnegan, "Turnabouts by Romney are Fair Game," *Los Angeles Times*, February 1, 2007, a16; Michael Luo, "Romney Faces Another 'Flip-Flop' Question: Has He Changed on Stem Cells?" *New York Times*, national edition, June 15, 2007, A16.

49. Susan E. Howell, "Racism, Cynicism, Economics, and David Duke," *American Politics Quarterly* 22 (April 1994): 190–207.

50. ABC News/Washington Post Poll, May 8–11, 2008, reported by PollingReport.Com, available at www.pollingreport.com/politics.htm (accessed July 14, 2008).

51. Pew Research Center for the People & the Press, "McCain's Enthusiasm Gap, Obama's Unity Gap," July 10, 2008, www.people-press.org/reports/pdf/436.pdf

52. Eric R. A. N. Smith and Richard Fox, "The Electoral Fortunes of Women Candidates for Congress," *Political Research Quarterly* 54 (March 2001): 205–21.

53. See Thomas Byrne Edsall with Mary D. Edsall, *Chain Reaction: The Impact of Race, Rights, and Taxes on American Politics* (New York: Norton, 1991); Nicholas P. Lovrich, Jr., Charles H. Sheldon, and Erik Wasmann, "The Racial Factor in Nonpartisan Judicial Elections: A Research Note," *Western Political Quarterly* 41 (December 1988): 807–16.

54. On the subject of amateurs in politics, see David T. Canon, *Actors, Athletes, and Astronauts: Political Amateurs in the United States Congress* (Chicago: University of Chicago Press, 1990).

55. Abramson, Aldrich, and Rohde, *Change and Continuity in the 2000 Elections*, chap. 7; Morris P. Fiorina, *Retrospective Voting in American National Elections* (New Haven, CT: Yale University Press, 1981).

56. Abramson, Aldrich, and Rohde, *Change and Continuity in the 2000 Elections*, chap. 6.

57. V. O. Key, Jr., *Politics, Parties, and Pressure Groups*, 5th ed. (New York: Crowell, 1964), 568.

58. Michael S. Lewis-Beck and Tom W. Rice, *Forecasting Elections* (Washington, D.C.: CQ Press, 1992).

59. Data from the CNN 2008 Exit Poll, available at www.cnn.com/ELECTION/2008/results/polls/#val=USP00p1.

60. See D. Roderick Kiewiet, *Macroeconomics and Micropolitics* (Chicago: University of Chicago Press, 1983); Donald R. Kinder and D. Roderick Kiewiet, "Economic Discontent and Political Behavior," *American Journal of Political Science* 23 (August 1979): 495–527; Donald R. Kinder and D. Roderick Kiewiet, "Sociotropic Politics: The American Case," *British Journal of Political Science* 11 (April 1981): 129–61. For an alternate view, see Steven J. Rosenstone, John Mark Hansen, and Donald R. Kinder, "Measuring Change in Personal Economic Well-Being," *Public Opinion Quarterly* 50 (Summer 1986): 176–92.

61. Data from the CNN 2008 Exit Poll, available at www.cnn.com/ELECTION/2008/results/polls/#val=USP00p1.

62. Campbell, Converse, Miller, and Stokes, *The American Voter*, 168–87.

63. Abramson, Aldrich, and Rohde, *Change and Continuity in the 2000 Elections.*

64. See Edward G. Carmines and James A. Stimson, "Two Faces of Issue Voting," *American Political Science Review* 74 (March 1980): 78–91.

65. See Abramson, Aldrich, and Rohde, *Change and Continuity in the 2000 Elections*, 135–42; William H. Flanigan and Nancy H. Zingale, *Political Behavior of the American Electorate*, 6th ed. (Dubuque, IA: Brown, 1988), 132–40.

66. Carll Everett Ladd, Jr., with Charles D. Hadley, *Transformations of the American Party System: Political Coalitions from the New Deal to the 1970s* (New York: Norton, 1975).

67. Barbara G. Farah and Ethel Klein, "Public Opinion Trends," in Gerald M. Pomper, Ross K. Baker, Walter D. Burnham, and Barbara G. Farah, *The Election of 1988: Reports and Interpretations* (Chatham, NJ: Chatham House, 1989), 121–25; Ethel Klein, *Gender Politics* (Cambridge, MA: Harvard University Press, 1984), chap. 9; Susan Welch and Lee Sigelman, "A Black Gender Gap," *Social Science Quarterly* 70 (March 1989): 120–33; Susan Welch and Lee Sigelman, "A Gender Gap among Hispanics? A Comparison with Blacks and Anglos," *Western Political Quarterly* 45 (March 1992): 181–99.

8

The News Media

CHAPTER OUTLINE

The campaign for the Democratic presidential nomination had not gone as expected. Rather than grabbing a commanding lead in the early primaries and caucuses, Senator Hillary Clinton trailed Senator Barack Obama. Many of her campaign advisers blamed the news media. In their view, journalists were rooting for Obama rather than reporting on him. A mock debate on *Saturday Night Live* captured the flavor of their complaint: It showed reporters asking Clinton tough questions while offering to make Obama more comfortable by getting him a pillow. Shortly after the satirical skit aired, Clinton and Obama squared off for real in a debate in Cleveland. When Brian Williams, the anchor for NBC's *Nightly News* and the debate's moderator, asked Clinton a question about trade policy, she showed her irritation at what she thought was unfair treatment. "Maybe we should ask Barack if he's comfortable and needs another pillow," she responded. "I just find it kind of curious that I keep getting the first question on all of these issues."[1]

Complaints about how the media cover politics have a long history in the United States. Thomas Jefferson suggested that newspaper editors should divide their papers "into four chapters, heading the 1st, Truths. 2d, Probabilities. 3d, Possibilities. 4th, Lies."[2] Harry Truman pitied "the great body of my fellow citizens, who, reading newspapers, live and die in the belief that they have known something of what has been passing in the world in their time."[3] George H. W. Bush complained during the 1992 campaign that journalists ignored his accomplishments and exaggerated his failures: "When the Berlin Wall fell, I half expected to see a headline: WALL FALLS, THREE BORDER GUARDS LOSE JOBS. And underneath, it probably says, CLINTON BLAMES BUSH."[4] Bill Clinton, however, did not think the news media gave him a free ride. He complained that he had "not gotten one damn bit of credit from the knee-jerk liberal press."[5] George W. Bush was overheard during a campaign stop referring to a reporter he thought had treated him unfairly as a "major-league asshole from the *New York Times.*"[6]

Although not new, complaints about the news media are nonetheless troubling. By all accounts, the success of American democracy rests on the existence of a free press. After all, the media are responsible for finding out what government is doing and reporting that information to the public; without a free press, the people could not govern themselves because they would have no way to monitor the actions of government and to decide whether they like what it is doing. As James Madison put it: "A popular Government without popular information, or the means of acquiring it, is but a Prologue to a Farce or a Tragedy; or, perhaps both."[7] Yet our very dependence on newspapers, radio, and television for information gives the media the potential to influence public opinion and government behavior.

The existence of a free press, then, creates a tension: Democracy demands a free and vigorous news media, yet such a news media may abuse its power. How can the rules of our political system support freedom of the press while restraining the media's potential to shape the course of political debate? The answer is that the same structural rules that ensure freedom of the news media to report on issues also ensure that the news media do not possess unbridled power. Just as the First Amendment declares that Congress shall make no law abridging the freedom of the press, it also guarantees every American citizen the right to speak freely. As a result of this guarantee, the United States enjoys an enormous array of different media voices, ranging from liberal magazines such as *The Nation* to conservative television shows such as *The O'Reilly Factor*. The great diversity in media voices makes it less likely that any one media outlet will determine what Americans think.

In this chapter, we explore the news media's role in American politics. We will begin by asking whether the media influence political debate in the United States. We will see that the answer is complex; what the news media report often reflects what the American people are thinking and what government is doing, rather than the reverse. In the second section of the chapter, we will review the changing nature of the news business. We will see that the rules of American politics give the news media great freedom to define their role in the political arena and that, as a result, their role has changed greatly over the past two centuries. In the third section, we will analyze the rules that both guarantee and limit the freedoms the media have to report the news. In the fourth section, we will look at the media's tremendous power to define what is news, and we will explore how the media follow self-imposed rules to keep this power in check. Finally, we will evaluate several complaints that the news media have abused their power and harmed the democratic process in the United States.

8-1 DO THE NEWS MEDIA MATTER?

The authors of the Constitution believed that democracy could not flourish without a free press. In their view, the press—the term *news media* was invented in the twentieth century to include radio and television—is essential to enable the people to watch over government. Thomas Jefferson, who, as we have seen, could be quite critical of the press, went so far as to write: "Were it left to me to decide whether we should have a government without newspapers, or newspapers without a government, I should not hesitate a moment to prefer the latter."[8]

To what extent do the media actually matter in American politics? Are they neutral channels of information, or do they shape the course of political debate? As we saw in Chapter 6, the media are but one factor influencing people's deep-seated beliefs about politics. Moreover, in most instances, the media appear to have only a small impact on fundamental beliefs such as a person's political affiliation and faith in government.[9] People's deep-seated beliefs about politics seem to be more heavily influenced by their families, friends, and schooling.

political agenda
The list of issues that people think are important
and that government officials are actively debating.

If the news media lack the power to dictate the fundamental beliefs of the American public, they nonetheless have a significant, though complex, influence on the course of American politics. To see why, we need to examine how the news media affect public opinion on specific issues, shape the **political agenda**, and influence what government does.

8-1a The News Media and Public Opinion

Most Americans believe the news media exert considerable influence over public opinion in the United States.[10] That belief seems perfectly reasonable. After all, most of our knowledge about what government does, both at home and abroad, comes from reading the newspaper, watching television, or listening to the radio.

Yet in practice, it is difficult to determine the impact of the news media on public opinion. One difficulty comes in trying to disentangle the effect of media coverage from the effect of the event itself. For example, did Barack Obama succeed in winning the White House because he received favorable media coverage or because he ran a better campaign than John McCain? Another difficulty stems from the enormous array of media voices in the United States. Are public attitudes toward Republican plans to cut taxes shaped more by an editorial in the *Wall Street Journal,* a story on ABC's *World News Tonight,* or a satirical skit on Comedy Central's *The Daily Show with Jon Stewart?* (A 2007 poll found that Americans ranked Stewart, the fake news anchor, as their fourth most admired journalist, the same ranking they gave real news anchors like Brian Williams of NBC News and Anderson Cooper of CNN.)[11]

A third difficulty in assessing the impact of the news media is the fact that people choose which media voices, if any, they will listen to. For example, conservatives make up a disproportionate share of

Source: © Reuters / Corbis.

President George W. Bush sometimes expressed his frustration with the media. Because we depend on the media for information, they have the potential to influence our opinions as well as the behavior of the government.

the audience for the cable channel Fox News, which prides itself on providing more conservative (or less liberal) coverage of the news than its competitors do. Because people are free to listen to Fox News or to change the station, the news media may not influence opinion even when they advocate a specific point of view.

In grappling with these problems, researchers have found that news coverage has, at most, a small effect on public opinion on specific issues.[12] A major reason for the news media's limited influence on public opinion is **selective perception**: People often see the same events differently because they have different beliefs and personal experiences. For example, public opinion polls show that Democrats and Republicans disagree sharply on how well Barack Obama has handled his job as president, on the wisdom of when to withdraw troops from Iraq, and on the importance of balancing the federal budget. Given the importance of selective perception, it is not surprising that researchers have found that the news media are most likely to influence opinion when a person knows little about an issue or has no strong beliefs concerning it.

selective perception
A phenomenon in which people perceive the same event differently because they have different beliefs and personal experiences.

8-1b The News Media and the Political Agenda

Even though stories that appear in the news media have at most a moderate effect on what Americans think, they have considerable influence over what Americans think about. Researchers have found that the news media play a major role in shaping the political agenda, which is the list of issues that people think are important and that government officials are actively debating. For example, if the news media run a series of stories on the problems that people with disabilities face in their everyday lives, more people will think about the obstacles society creates, worry about how to remove those obstacles, and communicate their concerns to public officials. In many ways, it makes sense that the news media choose the stories that affect which issues become important to people and government. After all, we depend on the news media to tell us what is happening in the world around us.

Television has the greatest impact on which issues the public thinks about because it is so widely watched. The more people are exposed to television news coverage on a given issue, the more likely they are to believe the issue is an important national problem. This suggests that "By attending to some problems and ignoring others, television news shapes the American public's political priorities."[13] Moreover, "the more removed the viewer is from the world of public affairs, the stronger the agenda-setting power of television news."[14]

Although newspaper, radio, and television coverage affects the political agenda, the agenda-setting power of the news media should not be exaggerated. The studies on agenda setting show only that people's opinions about the importance of an issue vary with the amount of news coverage; these studies do not show that the media consciously manipulate the political agenda. Why the news media cover some stories and not others is an important question we will examine in Section 8-4a. Here, it is sufficient to point out that, in many instances, the media follow rather than lead the public when it comes to choosing news stories. In 2008, for example, the future of electric-powered cars and public transportation became a hot topic in the nation's newspapers and on radio and television news shows. The media's interest in high-mileage automobiles and mass transit was not the result of a conspiracy on the part of journalists; instead, it reflected the public's interest in ways to deal with the skyrocketing price of gasoline.

8-1c The News Media and Government

If the news media do influence public opinion and the political agenda, do they also influence what government does and does not do? The answer, once again, is complex. On the one hand, the news media's coverage of an issue can put tremendous pressure on government officials to act. When Hurricane Katrina struck New Orleans in 2005, for example, President George W. Bush initially praised Washington's response to the disaster. After the airways filled with horrific videos of residents left behind without food, water, shelter, or police protection, Bush reversed course. He replaced the official in charge of federal response efforts and directed more government resources to the stricken Gulf Coast. News coverage can have a similar effect on Congress.[15] As Rep. Howard Berman (D-CA) notes, Congress is "a very big institution and it's very hard to get everybody's attention on something which isn't on the front pages every day."[16]

Yet the relationship between the news media and government is not a one-way street. Because news coverage has the potential to influence both public opinion and the political agenda, officials at all levels of government actively try to influence news coverage. Presidents have the greatest power to influence which stories the media cover because they are the single most important political figure in the United States.[17] Simply by giving a speech, a president can pluck an issue from obscurity and put it in the national spotlight. Indeed, the ability of the president to influence the political agenda is a major source of presidential power, as we shall see in Chapter 12.

Presidents, members of Congress, and other government officials also devote considerable effort to **spin control**—the practice of trying to persuade journalists to cover news stories in ways that put policies one likes in the most favorable light. (People outside government who want to influence public policy, such as leaders of interest groups and political parties, also try to "spin" stories.) Efforts to spin stories may rely on so-called third parties, people who are technically independent of the people or groups trying to generate favorable press coverage but who are either loyal or beholden to them. For instance, George W. Bush's administration regularly gave special access and briefings to retired military officers who worked as expert analysts for television and radio networks. Many of the retired officers also worked for military

spin control

The practice of trying to persuade journalists to cover news stories in ways that put policies one likes in the most favorable light.

contractors whose financial success depended on remaining in the Pentagon's good graces. The administration expected that the analysts would make its case to the American public.[18] An effort to spin a story using third parties can be effective precisely because even a reasonably informed reader or viewer may assume that the analyst is providing a neutral viewpoint on the story at hand.

Because government officials work so hard to influence news coverage, the news media's influence is often less powerful than the public supposes. Rather than setting a lead for government to follow, in many instances, the news media are actually following the lead government sets.

As you can see, the role of the news media in American politics is complex. Americans clearly depend on newspapers, radio, and television to keep them informed about what government is doing and not doing. And which stories the news media choose to cover, as well as how they cover the news, can significantly affect both public opinion and government behavior, and therefore public policy. Yet the relationship between the news media and the American people and government is a two-way street. In many instances, the news media's reports reflect what the American people are already thinking and what the government is already doing, rather than the reverse.

8-2 THE CHANGING FACE OF THE NEWS MEDIA

Although the authors of the Constitution believed that a free press is essential to the success of democracy, the nature of the news business has changed dramatically over the past two centuries. The most obvious change has been in technology. In April 1775, for example, local militia in Massachusetts clashed with British soldiers at Lexington and Concord, but people in Savannah, Georgia, did not read of the first battles of the American Revolution for another five weeks.[19] In contrast, in March 2003, American warplanes attacked Baghdad. Halfway around the world, the American public watched the start of the Iraq War live on television.

Although technological developments have produced the most obvious changes in the media over the past 200 years, the news media have changed in other ways as well. In this section, we discuss three such changes: (1) changes in the conventions of journalism, (2) changes in the sources from which the public obtains its news, and (3) changes in the pattern of media ownership. All these changes illustrate the immense freedom the media have to define their role in the American political system.

8-2a Changes in Journalistic Conventions

The newspapers Thomas Jefferson criticized differ greatly from the ones we read today. Then, newspapers were a *partisan press;* that is, they had formal ties to political parties or other political interests. A typical paper sold for six cents, at a time when the average worker earned less than a dollar a day. The high cost of a paper confined circulation to the wealthy. Even then, sales did not cover costs, so most newspapers required subsidies to continue operating. The subsidies typically came from business and political groups. In return for providing a subsidy, these groups expected that news reports and editorials would be slanted to promote their interests. The link between party and press accounts for the sometimes vicious edge found in the partisan press. The targets of a newspaper's ire might find themselves denounced as "serpents," "guileful betrayers," "an abandoned liar," or "an ill-looking devil."[20]

The 1830s ushered in the era of the *penny press.* With each paper selling for only one cent, the penny press revolutionized journalism. First and most important, the penny press relied on mass circulation to succeed, thereby expanding the number of Americans who read. Second, the penny press emphasized human interest stories rather than business and political news in its bid to attract readers. Third, the penny press covered its costs by relying on advertising and sales rather than on subsidies from business and political groups. Thus, the penny press had no formal party ties. It was not, however, nonpartisan. Penny papers frequently favored one party or another, but unlike the partisan press, the penny press did not see exerting political influence as its primary purpose.[21]

The 1890s saw the rise of **yellow journalism**. Taking its name from *The Yellow Kid,* a comic strip popular at the time, the yellow press emphasized sensational and even lurid news coverage. Its leading practitioners were Joseph Pulitzer (for whom the Pulitzer Prize is named) and William Randolph Hearst (see Box 8–1). The yellow press often crossed the line that separates reporting the news from making the news. When Cubans rebelled against Spanish rule in 1895, for example, the yellow press ran a stream of stories urging American intervention. When the United States finally declared war against Spain in 1898, one of the papers Hearst owned, the *New York Journal,* gleefully asked on its front page, "How do you like the *Journal's* war?"[22]

Besides yellow journalism, the turn of the century saw the rise of a type of investigative reporting called **muckraking**. The name originated with President Theodore Roosevelt, who criticized some journalists for raking muck (or manure) in what he considered their excessive zeal to expose the unsavory aspects of government and business. Muckrakers, however, took the name as a badge of honor. They saw themselves as crusading against injustice, raking away the muck to expose wrongdoing. Ida M. Tarbell revealed the unfair business practices that John D. Rockefeller used to build the Standard Oil Company, and Lincoln Steffens uncovered political corruption in several major cities. Muckrakers published mostly in magazines such as *Collier's, Cosmopolitan, Ladies Home Journal,* and the *Saturday Evening Post.*

yellow journalism
A form of journalism, popular at the end of the nineteenth century, that emphasized sensational and sometimes lurid news coverage.

muckraking
An early form of investigative journalism popular at the beginning of the twentieth century.

The People behind the Rules

Box 8–1   William Randolph Hearst and Rupert Murdoch

The media may exert power over public opinion, but who controls the media? Two of the most powerful and colorful figures in news media history are William Randolph Hearst and Rupert Murdoch.

WILLIAM RANDOLPH HEARST

William Randolph Hearst was born in 1863 to a California family that had made its fortune in mining and ranching. He entered the newspaper business at the age of twenty-two when he returned home to San Francisco to work on the family newspaper, the *Examiner,* after being expelled from Harvard for decorating chamber pots with the likenesses of faculty members. In 1887, Hearst was given control of the paper, and the twenty-four-year-old quickly showed he had a knack for the newspaper business. He encouraged his reporters to sensationalize their stories, and the *Examiner*'s circulation (and profits) soared.

Source: © Bettmann/Corbis.

William Randolph Hearst.

In 1895, Hearst used the profits from the *Examiner* as well as funds from his family's fortune to buy a New York paper called the *Morning Journal.* As with the *Examiner,* Hearst directed the *Journal*'s reporters to emphasize stories about sex and crime. Once again, the *Journal*'s circulation quickly

skyrocketed, and many other newspapers began to imitate its yellow journalism.

The *Journal* also used its pages to champion what it saw as the people's interests. Many of the paper's crusades targeted issues of local concern, such as municipal corruption. Others focused on national concerns. For example, the *Journal* worked hard to whip up public sentiment for a war with Spain over Cuba, and it was widely rumored (though never proved) that Hearst cabled the *Journal*'s correspondent in Havana: "You furnish the pictures, and I'll furnish the war." The *Journal* also pushed what many at the time considered to be a radical political agenda: a graduated income tax, direct election of senators, and destruction of business trusts. The often venomous tone the *Journal* used to attack its opponents further cemented Hearst's reputation as a rabble-rouser.

With the fame he earned as the *Journal*'s publisher, Hearst turned his sights to political office. In 1902, he was elected to the House of Representatives from New York City and served two terms. In 1904, he failed in his attempt to win the Democratic presidential nomination, and the next year, ballot fraud cost him the New York mayoral race. In 1906, he ran for governor of New York but was defeated in a bitter race by Charles Evans Hughes (who would later become Chief Justice of the United States). Hearst subsequently ran independent campaigns for the White House and the mayor's office, but his efforts excited few voters.

Despite Hearst's failures as a politician, his newspaper empire grew steadily. At its peak in 1935, Hearst papers appeared in nineteen cities and accounted for nearly 14 percent of all newspapers sold on weekdays and 25 percent of those sold on Sunday. The newspaper chain Hearst left behind at his death in 1951 remains one of the largest in the country.

RUPERT MURDOCH

Like William Randolph Hearst, Rupert Murdoch was born into a family that owned a newspaper. And although he does not share Hearst's interest in running for elective office, he has shown an equal talent for building a media empire.

Source: © Chip Somodevilla/Getty Images.

Rupert Murdoch.

Murdoch was born in Australia in 1931. He attended elite private schools in Australia and then went to Oxford University in England for college. After his father's death in 1953, Murdoch returned home to help run the family business. Over the next fifteen years Murdoch turned the firm into the dominant media company in Australia. He bought existing newspapers, started new magazines, and launched Australia's first national newspaper, appropriately titled *The Australian.*

In 1968, Murdoch turned his sights to Great Britain. He bought the *News of the World,* which had once been the most popular English-language newspaper in the world. The following year he bought the *Sun.* Taking a page out of Hearst's playbook, the *Sun* quickly began to emphasize sensational stories about sex and crime. In 1981, Murdoch bought Britain's most prestigious paper, the *Times of London.*

In 1973, Murdoch made his first foray into the American newspaper business by buying the *San Antonio*

The People behind the Rules   *(continued)*

Express-News. He followed this purchase by launching the supermarket tabloid the *Star.* He then bought the *New York Post,* a paper that had been founded by Alexander Hamilton in 1801. The *Post* quickly adopted the sensationalist approach to the news that Murdoch used at the *Sun.* That style is perhaps best captured in one of the *Post's* most famous front-page headlines: "Headless Body in Topless Bar."

Murdoch also moved into the electronic media. He started a British-based satellite television network. In 1985, he became an American citizen so he could buy the television stations that eventually became the Fox network. (U.S. law bars foreign citizens from owning a U.S. television station).

In 1996, Murdoch started the Fox News Channel. It eventually passed CNN to become the most popular cable news channel in the United States.

Murdoch's empire building has made him a wealthy man. In 2008, *Fortune Magazine* ranked him as the 109th richest person in the world, with a net worth of more than $8 billion. His influence may be even greater. *Fortune* ranked him as the second most powerful person in business.

Murdoch has also created a lot of enemies with his empire building. Many of his critics in the United States complain that his newspapers and television channels slant the news to favor conservative causes. Other critics worry less about his political leanings and more that his preference for

sensationalism debases news coverage. This criticism was behind the opposition to his ultimately successful effort in 2008 to buy the *Wall Street Journal*—perhaps America's most serious newspaper.

None of these criticisms faze Murdoch. "You can't be an outsider and be successful over 30 years," he once explained, "without leaving a certain amount of scar tissue around the place."

Sources: Edwin Emery, *The Press and America: An Interpretative History of the Mass Media,* 3rd ed. (Englewood Cliffs, NJ: Prentice Hall, 1972; Mark Bowden, "Mr. Murdoch Goes to War," *Atlantic Monthly* (July/August 2008): 106–14; William Shawcross, "Rupert Murdoch," *Time* (October 25, 1999): 37. Available at www.mindfully.org/Reform/Murdoch-Media-Empire25oct99.htm.

objective press

A form of journalism that developed in the 1920s and which continues to predominate today. It emphasizes that journalists should strive to keep their opinions out of their coverage of the news.

Neither the muckrakers nor the yellow press believed their job was to be objective. But after World War I, objectivity emerged as the touchstone of American journalism. In 1923, the American Society of Newspaper Editors drew up a code of ethics, called the Canons of Journalism, that outlined the principles of an **objective press**. At its core, objectivity holds that journalists should "Tell the News Straight!"; opinions should appear only on the editorial page and not in news reports.

Although the idea of objectivity sounds lofty, the development of an objective press came about largely for economic reasons. To appeal to the mass audiences needed to attract the advertising dollars so vital to profits, newspapers (and subsequently radio and television) had to present the news so that it appealed to people with divergent views on the issues of the day. That could be done only by removing as much overt bias as possible from news coverage. As we shall see in Section 8-5a, the news media often fall short of pure objectivity. Nonetheless, for journalists today, objectivity remains the standard.

8-2b Changes in Readership and Viewership

The second half of the twentieth century has seen an information explosion. The United States has more than 1,700 television stations, 11,000 radio stations, 1,400 daily newspapers, and 13,000 journals and magazines.[23] Americans do not want for news and information, although, as we saw in Chapter 6, Americans are not necessarily better informed than they used to be.

The explosion of media outlets, however, obscures four important changes within the news business: (1) the declining number of daily newspapers, (2) the rise of **cable television**, (3) the rise of political talk shows on radio and television, and (4) the rapid growth of the Internet.

The Decline of Newspapers

The number of daily newspapers has declined since the middle of the twentieth century. The United States today has 300 fewer newspapers than it did five decades ago.[24] In 1950, most cities had several daily papers; today, very few do.[25] Many newspapers died because more and more people stopped reading them. At the end of World War II, newspaper market penetration was 135 percent, meaning that more newspapers were sold in the United States than there were households. Now newspaper market penetration stands around 45 percent.[26] As the number of newspapers has declined, overall daily newspaper circulation has fallen as well. Ten million fewer newspapers were sold in 2006 than in 1970, even though the population of the United States increased by nearly 100 million over the same period.[27] Newspaper reading has fallen across all age groups, but the newspaper industry has a particular problem with young adults. In the 1960s, 60 percent of Americans between the ages of eighteen and twenty-nine read a newspaper regularly. In 2006, only 24 percent did.[28]

The public's declining interest in newspapers largely results from the rise of television. Although few Americans owned televisions in 1950, 99 percent of all American households own one today.[29] As Table 8–1 shows, most Americans get their news from television rather than from newspapers or radio, although reliance on the Internet as a source of news is growing. The tremendous importance of television as a news source raises serious questions about the quality of the information people have about the world around them. As we discussed in Chapter 6, newspapers generally cover news events much more thoroughly than television does.

The Rise of Cable Television

Despite the increased popularity of television, so-called **broadcast television**, stations that transmit their programming over the airwaves without charge, faces problems of its own. One problem is tight budgets. The three leading broadcast television networks—ABC, CBS, and NBC—were originally independent companies that did not expect their news shows to turn a profit. Then in the mid-1980s, all three networks were bought by major corporations that placed tremendous emphasis on generating profits, which forced news shows to cut their budgets substantially.[30] Foreign news coverage was especially hard hit as the networks closed many of their overseas news bureaus, never to reopen. The networks today rely heavily on independent "stringers" rather than full-time correspondents for most of their foreign news coverage.[31] For example, in the early 1980s, "CBS News ran fourteen major foreign bureaus, [and] ten mini foreign bureaus." In 2005, it had only ten foreign correspondents: one in Tokyo, "five in a hub office in London,

cable television
Television programming not originally transmitted over the air, as with broadcast television, but rather carried via coaxial or fiber-optic cable into the homes of people who pay a monthly fee.

broadcast television
Television stations that make their programming available over the airwaves without charge. Most local cable companies include broadcast television channels as part of their basic package of services.

	1993	1996	1998	2000	2002	2004	2006	2008
Listened/Read Yesterday								
Newspaper	58*	50	48	47	41	42	40	34
Radio News	47**	44	49	43	41	40	35	35
Regularly Watch								
Nightly network news	60	42	38	30	32	34	28	29
Local TV news	77	65	64	56	57	59	54	52
Network morning news shows	—	—	23	20	22	22	23	22
Cable TV News	—	—	—	—	33	38	34	39
Online for News Three or More More Days a Week								
	—	2**	13	23	25	29	31	37

Table 8–1   Trends in Regular News Consumption (in Percent)

Notes: *The question was asked in 1994.
      **The question was asked in 1995.

Source: The Pew Research Center for the People & the Press, "Audience Segments in a Changing News Environment: Key News Audiences Now Blend Online and Traditional Sources," August 17, 2008, p. 3, available at www.people-press.org/reports/pdf/444.pdf (accessed August 2008).

three in Tel Aviv, one in Rome. It has no permanent bureau in the Arab or Muslim world, in Africa or South America."[32] At the same time, the audience for the evening news has been steadily declining. As Table 8–1 shows, the percentage of Americans who report regularly watching any of the three network television evening newscasts has fallen by half since the early 1990s, although these news shows still draw a combined audience of nearly 25 million people.[33] The declining audience makes network newscasts less attractive to advertisers, and in turn, makes it harder for the newscasts to turn a profit.

The problems network news departments face stem from increased competition from cable television, programming not originally transmitted over the airwaves, as with broadcast television, but carried via cable into the homes of people who pay a monthly fee. With the advent of cable television, Americans now have many more choices of what to watch than they did even a decade ago. Cable television offers more than old movies and sit-com reruns—it also offers an array of new sources of news and information. Cable's first major contributor to news was the Cable News Network—or CNN. Originally derided as "Chicken Noodle News," Ted Turner's brainchild was so successful that several other cable news networks soon emerged. One competitor, Fox News, which was started by newspaper baron Rupert Murdoch (see Box 8–1), is now the most popular cable news channel. Besides CNN and Fox News, cable television provides (among other channels) CNN Headline News, C-SPAN I and C-SPAN II (which cover the House and Senate), CNBC, MSNBC, and local access channels. For the minority of Americans who follow the news closely, television offers a smorgasbord of choices.

Source: © Mark E. Gibson/Corbis.

Originally derived as "Chicken Noodle News," CNN has become a major source of news and information for millions of Americans.

The increase in the percentage of people who get their news almost exclusively from television may simply mean, as Chapters 6 and 7 pointed out, that the American public is less well informed. Even though information bombards modern citizens, most Americans do not pay close attention to political issues. And those who obtain their political knowledge from television learn from short stories with quick, splashy visual images—not from in-depth analysis.

The Rise of Talk Radio

Although most Americans report getting their news from television, **talk radio** is an important force in American politics. Political talk radio exploded in popularity in the late 1980s. The number of radio stations featuring political talk shows rose from fewer than 250 in the mid-1980s to more than 1,000 in the mid-1990s.[34] Today, there are nearly 1,400 talk radio stations.[35] Rush Limbaugh, the most popular political talk-show host, broadcasts five times a week on nearly 600 radio stations across the country and draws a weekly audience estimated at more than 14 million listeners. Sean Hannity, the second most popular talk radio host, draws more than 13 million listeners weekly, and Michael Savage, the third most popular talk radio host, draws at least 8 million listeners weekly.[36] Nearly 50 million Americans listen to talk radio each week.[37]

Fans of talk radio argue that it serves an important function in our democracy by enabling Americans to hold in-depth discussions of pressing political issues. Critics complain that talk radio is more likely to distort than to clarify issues because talk-show hosts need controversy to attract an audience. Critics also complain that radio talk shows favor conservative causes. Approximately 75 to 80 percent of radio talk-show hosts with an identifiable ideology are conservative, and by a more than 2-to-1 margin, listeners say that talk shows are more critical of Democrats than Republicans.[38]

Not surprisingly, the Republican Party aggressively courts conservative talk-show hosts. Party officials regularly provide them

talk radio

Political talk shows on radio. Since the early 1990s, talk radio has emerged as an important force in American politics.

with talking points and send people to appear as on-air guests. For example, when the prospects for Republican candidates in the congressional midterm elections dimmed in October 2006, President George W. Bush invited leading conservative talk-show hosts to the Oval Office to hear an extended defense of his policies. Days later, an even larger number of radio hosts was invited to broadcast their shows from the White House grounds, where cabinet officials were made available for interviews. Tony Snow, the president's press secretary and himself a former conservative radio host, explained why the White House was so friendly to his former colleagues this way: "You want to make sure that your friends are friendly."[39]

Liberal talk radio shows have not enjoyed much commercial success. Backers of Air America Radio hoped to reverse that trend. The liberal radio network debuted in 2004. It struggled financially from the start and almost went out of business after only six weeks on the air. After two years, it was heard on only ninety-two stations nationwide and in only thirty-three states. With fewer than 2.5 million listeners a week, Air America Radio's financial problems grew. In 2006, it filed for bankruptcy. An investor stepped in to save the company. But at the start of 2008, Air America Radio was heard on only sixty-two radio stations nationwide. Its most popular radio personality, Thom Hartmann, drew fewer than 2 million weekly listeners.[40]

Analysts disagree over whether the audience for talk radio mirrors the distribution of party affiliations in the country as a whole. Some surveys show that the talk radio audience tilts heavily toward Republicans. Other surveys suggest the audience is spread relatively evenly among Republicans, Democrats, and Independents. Leaving this issue aside, analysts agree that the audience for talk radio is not representative of the country in important ways. Members of the talk-radio audience are more likely to be male (56 percent compared with 48 percent of the adult public as a whole); more likely to be under the age of 50 (65 percent compared with 59 percent of the adult public as a whole); more likely to be college educated (38 percent compared with 16 percent); and more likely to be doing well financially (57 percent earn more than $50,000 per year as compared with only 46 percent of the general public).[41] To the extent that talk radio influences elections and government policy, then, it reflects the concerns of an atypical group of Americans.

The Rapid Growth of the Internet

The Internet is a relatively new technology that may be dramatically changing the way Americans learn about political issues and communicate their political views. Although the Internet barely existed two decades ago, today more than 80 percent of American adults have access to it either at home or at work.[42]

The news media have sought to exploit the Internet's potential. Most media outlets maintain Web sites that feature some or all of their news articles and video reports. Most media outlets allow visitors to view their Web sites for free. Some media outlets like the *Wall Street Journal* require people to pay to view the material on their sites. Many media Web sites allow people to register for e-mail alerts that inform them of breaking news or the posting of a story on a topic of particular interest. In the future, the Internet may enable people to obtain entire newspapers and television news shows customized to feature only articles on subjects that interest them. Nearly four in ten American adults now say they go online regularly to get news.[43]

It was considered revolutionary in 1995 when the House of Representatives made it possible for Americans to get copies of pending legislation through the Internet. What was once revolutionary is now commonplace because government agencies, elected officials, candidates for public office, and political interest groups now routinely use the Internet as a tool of education and persuasion. The federal and state governments have put much of their activities online. (What appears on those Web pages changes as administrations do. When George W. Bush's presidency ended, a click of a mouse replaced his materials on the White House Web page with those of President Barack Obama.) Likewise, candidates for major public office routinely set up Web sites where Americans can obtain information about their stands on various issues, read biographies of their lives, and even sign up to work for and donate to a campaign.

The Internet has also enabled individuals to comment on the news—and even to shape it—through *Weblogs*. Often referred to more simply as "blogs," these Web sites contain periodic postings, usually in reverse chronological order, devoted to specific subjects. Some are the work of single authors, whereas others have multiple authors. Many blogs allow visitors to post their own comments; others are noninteractive. Blogs devoted to politics and government typically feature links to news articles, usually accompanied by commentary. The linked nature of blogs helps speed the spread of information across the Internet. Blogs, for instance, were credited in 2004 with revealing that CBS News had relied on forged documents in a story claiming that George W. Bush had used political pressure to get out of his Air National Guard service in 1973. CBS retracted the story under stinging criticism, and Dan Rather was forced to retire as the anchor for the *CBS Evening News* after nearly a quarter of a century on the job. The fact that blogs had helped topple a media giant prompted one blogger to write: "You cannot lie and forge and expect to hide from the Blog World—CBS and the rest of the 'big' name news organizations—get use[d] to it. We bloggers are not going away."[44]

It remains to be seen whether the *blogosphere*, as the community of blogs is known, will root out all lies and misstatements in the news media. More generally, the exact impact of the Internet on American politics stirs much debate. Optimists contend that the Internet will improve the quality of political debate by making it easier for Americans to learn about issues that matter to them and to communicate their views to public officials. Pessimists worry, however, that many Americans, and particularly poor Americans, will not have access to the Internet, and those who do will be buried under a mound of information they are not prepared to evaluate.

8-2c Changes in Media Ownership

The changes in what Americans read and watch have been accompanied by changes in the patterns of media ownership. Today, the news media are big business. The nine most influential national news organizations—ABC, CBS, NBC, the *New York Times, the Washington Post,* the *Wall Street Journal,* the *Los Angeles Times, Newsweek,* and *Time*—are all owned by corporations that rank among the 500 largest in the United States. Even more striking than the size of many media companies is the trend toward greater concentration in ownership. In 1981, forty-six corporations controlled a majority of the business in newspapers, radio, television, magazines, books, and movies. Nine years later, the number had shrunk to twenty.[45] Today the number is fewer than a dozen.

The trend toward increased concentration of ownership is most evident with newspapers. Between 1960 and 2004, newspaper chains—that is, companies that own more than two daily newspapers in different cities—increased their share of total daily newspaper circulation from 46 to 67 percent.[46] In 2008, for instance, the Gannett Company owned *USA Today* as well as eighty-four other dailies, and the McClatchy Company owned thirty daily newspapers, including the *Fort Worth Star-Telegram,* the *Miami Herald,* and the *Sacramento Bee.*[47]

Ownership of radio and television stations is less concentrated than newspaper ownership. The reason is that for many years, government policy deliberately sought to prevent concentrated "ownership" of the airwaves. Because the laws of physics limit the number of broadcast channels, and because of the belief that the public is best served by having a variety of broadcast voices, the federal government began limiting ownership of television and radio stations in the 1940s. For many years, broadcast companies were subject to a seven-seven-seven rule on cross-ownership—a single company could own at most seven AM, seven FM, and seven television stations. In the early 1980s, the rule was changed to twelve–twelve– twelve, with no more than two of each in the nation's largest media markets. And in 1992, the limit on radio stations was raised to twenty AM and twenty FM outlets. The rules on media ownership were loosened on the grounds that the success of cable television and the development of other technologies for delivering television to America's homes had reduced the possibility that a few broadcasters could dominate the nation's airwaves.

In 1996, the push to deregulate the telecommunications industry culminated in the passage of the Telecommunications Competition and Deregulation Act.[48] The new law eliminated many of the restrictions on media ownership. Most important, it freed companies to own as many local television stations as they want as long as the combined audiences of their stations did not exceed 35 percent of the American public. The bill also eliminated the national limit on the ownership of radio stations and loosened the rules restricting ownership of multiple stations in the same city.

In 2003, the Bush administration moved to further relax the rules on media ownership. Among other steps, it proposed raising the national cap on television ownership to 45 percent. Opponents of the new rules sued the government in federal court. They won an early victory, thereby putting implementation of the rules on hold pending resolution of the lawsuit. Meanwhile, Congress sided with the critics on the specific issue of the national television cap. After considerable political wrangling, the White House and Congress agreed to a compromise—a 39 percent cap. The agreement had only a modest practical effect because CBS and Fox had already reached the 39 percent ceiling through mergers and acquisitions, and ABC and NBC were only slightly below the cap.[49]

Even with the existing limits on ownership, a single broadcast company can influence what many Americans see and hear. In 2008, for instance, Gannett owned twenty-three television stations, reaching more than 20 million American households.[50] Figures like these understate the reach of media companies. Through the affiliated stations that make up each broadcast network, for instance, ABC, CBS, and NBC reach virtually the entire country with their news and entertainment programming. CNN reaches roughly 80 percent of all American households. Indeed, the five largest media conglomerates—Viacom (which owns CBS and MTV among other channels), General Electric (NBC, MSNBC, and Bravo), Disney (ABC, ESPN), News Corp. (Fox, FX, Fox News), and Time Warner (CNN, TNT)—control approximately 75 percent of broadcast and cable prime-time viewing.[51] This demonstrates the tremendous potential of a single company to influence the political views of huge numbers of people.

Although most radio and television stations are owned by companies seeking to make a profit, noncommercial or public broadcasting also exists. The Public Broadcasting System had 355 participating television stations in 2008, and National Public Radio counted more than 860 independently managed radio stations in its network.[52] In place of advertising revenue, public broadcasting depends on government funding, foundation and corporation grants, and viewer and listener donations. The Corporation for Public Broadcasting, an independent federal agency, oversees public broadcasting. To insulate programming decisions from political pressure, the corporation handles only administrative issues, but its ability to withhold funding from programs it dislikes gives the corporation some say in programming decisions.[53] This is a good example of how rules that empower the news media may also restrict their power.

Is the increased concentration of media ownership a matter of concern? Some observers argue that it is. They fear that as more and more media outlets are owned by a handful of large corporations, the diversity of news coverage and editorial opinion will diminish. The result will be a homogenized news media that restricts rather than promotes robust debate on the issues the country faces. The ultimate fear is that the number of independent media companies will shrink so far that the checks on media power will erode, and the few large companies that remain in business will have extraordinary influence over what Americans think.

Whether the increased concentration of media ownership has in fact homogenized news coverage and diminished editorial diversity is unclear. Efforts to study the question have produced mixed results.[54] Yet despite the increased concentration of media ownership, three key factors tend to promote news and editorial diversity in the United States. First, as we have just seen, the federal government regulates ownership of the electronic media with an eye toward preserving a diverse array of broadcast voices. Second, the expansion of cable television and the Internet increasingly exposes Americans to new sources of information. Third, media companies are in business to make money, and they do so by meeting the needs of their audience. If a substantial number of Americans should become dissatisfied with existing news coverage, some company is likely to try to provide coverage more to its liking.

8-3 FREEDOM OF THE PRESS

Thomas Jefferson wrote that "Our liberty depends on freedom of the press, and that cannot be limited without being lost."[55] The American press today enjoys the freedom that Jefferson believed was so vital to liberty. Unlike journalists in many African and Asian countries, journalists in the United States do not need a government license to work. Unlike journalists in China and North Korea, they do not need to clear their stories with a government censor. And unlike journalists in Great Britain, they seldom need to worry that government officials may limit their right to report on a story. For journalists in the United States, freedom from government censorship and harassment rests in the blanket declaration of the First Amendment: "Congress shall make no law-abridging the freedom...of the press." This rule underpins our cherished notions of the news media's right to report and the people's right to know.

At first glance, the rule set forth in the First Amendment might seem to give the news media unbridled power. After all, it suggests that the media are not only free to decide which issues are important, but free to report on them in any way they please. Yet very real constraints limit the power of the media. As we saw in Chapter 4, the courts have long recognized limits to "freedom of the press." Newspapers, radio, and television must all observe libel and obscenity laws. Journalists also must overcome a variety of obstacles to gather the news. And because the number of broadcast channels is limited, radio and television must follow regulations that do not apply to the print press.

8-3a Limits to Press Freedom

Several legal checks restrict the freedom of the media to report the news, including libel laws, obscenity laws, and prior restraint. The most common legal check by far is libel law. As Chapter 4 discussed, the media cannot legally write or broadcast a story that unjustly injures a person's reputation. The media are also barred from publishing or showing obscene materials, though as a practical matter, obscenity laws seldom affect news coverage. A third possible legal check on the news media is prior restraint. As we saw in our discussion of the Pentagon Papers and *Business Week* cases in Chapter 4, however, the circumstances under which the courts will bar the media in advance from reporting a story are extremely limited.

Besides these legal checks, the media find that several other factors constrain their ability to report the news, including government secrecy, government pressure, and limited access to news stories. After World War II, the federal government created a system for classifying government documents—some 20 million documents are now marked secret each year. Less than half a million of them involve national security matters. Most involve politically or personally sensitive material such as policy proposals and background checks on government personnel.[56] Because much of the classification system was created through executive orders issued by presidents rather than by laws passed by Congress, the media violate no laws when they obtain and publish government secrets. The one exception involves publishing classified information about intelligence operations, which is forbidden by law.

Concerns about excessive secrecy led Congress to pass the **Freedom of Information Act** in 1966. The act created a system through which anyone can petition the government to declassify documents. In practice, the act has displeased many. On the one hand, some in government argue that it leads to the publication of information that should remain secret. Many journalists, on the other hand, argue that the government declassifies information grudgingly, continuing to impede their ability to gather the news.

In addition to confronting government secrecy, the news media also find that government pressure to some degree constrains their ability to report the news. In some circumstances, the government may threaten to prosecute reporters for violating espionage laws, as the Ronald Reagan administration did on several occasions.[57] More commonly, government officials pressure the media by ostracizing journalists they dislike. Journalists depend heavily on access to officials for their stories, so when they lose access, they lose stories. Many reporters claimed that senior officials in George W. Bush's administration withheld access to punish journalists who wrote stories they did not like. As one *New York Times* reporter put it, "the Bush administration is quite willing at a brass tacks level to threaten reporters with a lack of access, with reprisals in a very overt way."[58] Of course, officials do not actually have to deny access to put pressure on journalists. The mere possibility

Freedom of Information Act
An act of Congress passed in 1966 that created a system through which anyone can petition the government to declassify secret documents.

that an important government official may respond to a critical story by refusing to return phone calls may be sufficient to temper the zeal of some reporters.

Another way government officials try to pressure the news media is by accusing reporters of bias or error. Officials hope that journalists will respond to such charges by leaning over backward to be fair. George W. Bush's first press secretary was "quite famous for calling reporters at the slightest provocation if there's something in their work that he doesn't like and complaining about it, not because he thinks it will change what happened in that story, but because he thinks the next time a reporter sits down to write a story, he or she will have that in mind and be aware of it."[59] Thus, complaining about the media is, as one adviser to President George H. W. Bush put it, rather like a coach "playing the referees" in the hope of winning by intimidation.[60]

Along with facing government secrecy and pressure, the media sometimes meet constraints when the government physically denies them access to news stories. This happens most often with regard to American military operations. Many military officials who served in Vietnam believe that news coverage undermined public support for that war. So they have been determined to prevent journalists covering a future war from having the same freedom to report that journalists enjoyed in Vietnam (as well as in World War II and Korea). When the United States invaded Grenada in 1983, the Defense Department declined to include journalists with the invasion force. The military even prevented journalists from reaching Grenada on their own, going as far as to send a fighter plane on a mock bombing run of a boat journalists chartered.[61]

Not surprisingly, journalists cried censorship. The Defense Department responded to the complaints by creating a system of **pool reporting**, a procedure under which military officers escort small groups of selected reporters through the war zone. The pool system figured prominently during the 1991 Gulf War as Saudi society and geography made it easy to limit media access to the front. Many journalists criticized the pool system, though, arguing that it prevented them from covering the news.[62] During the Afghanistan War, the Pentagon blocked journalists from accompanying American troops into combat, citing concerns for operational security. During the Iraq War, however, the Defense Department responded to media complaints and reversed course. It agreed to "embed" journalists in American military units. The reporters lived with their units and, in a few tragic instances, died with them. More than 500 journalists participated in the **embedding** program. They and the Pentagon both seemed pleased with the results.[63]

The restrictions on news reporting—libel laws, obscenity laws, prior restraint, government secrecy and pressure, and limited access to stories—might seem to put a considerable damper on the ability of the media to report the news. Yet in practice, only a tiny minority of news stories run afoul of any of these restrictions. Instead, as the First Amendment promises, journalists in the

pool reporting
A system the Defense Department instituted in the 1980s for reporting from a combat zone during wartime. With pool reporting, military officials escort small groups of reporters when they interview American troops.

embedding
A program under which the Defense Department allowed journalists to travel with the U.S. military during the Iraq War.

United States have a great deal of freedom to report on the vast majority of news stories.

8-3b The Electronic Media

The electronic media—that is, television and radio—must deal with numerous regulations that do not apply to the print press. Two factors explain the rationale for additional constraints on the electronic media. One is the so-called scarcity argument. The number of broadcast channels is limited, which in turn limits competition among electronic media. In contrast, anyone offended by newspaper coverage can in theory start a new newspaper. The other argument is that the airwaves belong to the public and not to any individual or corporation; hence, more government control is warranted.

The agency that oversees the electronic media is the **Federal Communications Commission (FCC)**, an independent federal regulatory agency headed by a five-member commission. The president appoints the members of the panel, only three of whom can belong to the same political party and none of whom may have a financial interest in any Commission-related business. The FCC's job is to regulate the electronic media in "the public interest, convenience, or necessity." Since its creation in 1934, the FCC's jurisdiction has grown to include AM and FM radio, broadcast television, cable television, commercial satellites, CBs, and cellular telephones.

Federal Communications Commission (FCC)
An independent federal agency that regulates interstate and international communication by radio, television, telephone, telegraph, cable, and satellite.

The FCC has four main tasks. One is to develop and administer the rules on cross-ownership in the media industry. The FCC, for instance, was the federal agency responsible for proposing the rule that would raise the cap on ownership of television stations to 45 percent of the national audience. Another FCC task is to set technical standards for the communications industry. For example, the FCC chose the technical standard for high-definition television, a new technology used to make televisions that produce much crisper and clearer images. By setting such technical standards, the FCC ensures that telephones and televisions bought in one region will work throughout the country.

The third task the FCC performs is to license television and radio stations to use the public airwaves. (Individual cities and towns control the charters for cable television.) Radio and television stations must renew their licenses every five to seven years. The FCC denies renewal applications only when stations violate its regulations—which, it turns out, seldom occurs.[64] Because radio and television stations can be worth tens and even hundreds of millions of dollars, station owners have a strong incentive to heed the wishes of the FCC.

The fourth task of the FCC is to set and administer broadcast standards. The standards define things such as how frequently stations must identify themselves and what words and images they can use on air (decency standards). For instance, in 2004, the FCC fined Viacom, the media conglomerate that produced Howard

Stern's radio show, \$3.5 million for the "shock jock's" indecent comments on air. Most FCC fines, however, are much smaller—many are only a few thousand dollars. Despite the small size of the fines—especially in comparison to the revenues media companies generate—the FEC hopes that the stigma of being fined will prompt stations to abide by the decency standards. Many media companies, however, have begun to contest FCC fines as being arbitrary and capricious. In 2008, CBS persuaded a federal judge on just those grounds to throw out a \$550,000 fine that the FCC had leveled against it because singer Janet Jackson's right breast was bared in a "wardrobe malfunction" during half-time of the 2004 Super Bowl. In other cases, ABC's affiliates sued to overturn \$1.2 million in fines that were imposed because they aired a glimpse of an actress's backside in a 2003 episode of *NYPD Blue,* and Fox refused to pay a \$91,000 fine (which it had bargained down from \$1.2 million) for airing a 2003 episode of "Married by America" that featured whipped-cream-covered strippers.[65]

A more important broadcast regulation for politics is the **equal-time provision**, which requires radio and television stations to provide all candidates for the same public office with access to the airwaves under the same conditions. Thus, a station cannot give free air time, say, to one candidate for Congress and deny it to another.[66] The equal-time provision does not, however, apply to news coverage. Congress passed the law requiring the FCC to monitor compliance with the equal-time provision because it wanted to ensure a level playing field for political debate in the United States.

Another broadcast standard that regulated how the electronic media handled political issues for almost forty years was the **fairness doctrine**, which required stations to provide "reasonable opportunities for the expression of opposing views on controversial issues of public importance." Like the equal-time provision, the fairness doctrine did not apply to news coverage, but unlike the equal-time provision, it was an FCC-created rule rather than a law Congress passed. The FCC created the fairness doctrine in 1949 to prevent stations from using their public affairs programming to advance a particular party or candidate.

Critics of the fairness doctrine complained that it was never applied to unpopular points of view, that many stations shied away from political issues entirely to avoid violating the doctrine, and that it violated the First Amendment. On the last point, the Supreme Court disagreed. Although the Court has struck down laws requiring newspapers to provide equal space for opposing points of view, it ruled that the shortage of broadcast channels justified the fairness doctrine.[67] As a practical matter, however, the issue is moot. In 1987, the FCC repealed the fairness doctrine on the grounds that the growth of cable television made it unnecessary. Efforts over the years by some members of Congress to enact the fairness doctrine into law have failed.

Although radio and television are subject to greater federal regulation than newspapers, they still enjoy tremendous freedom to

equal-time provision

A federal law that stipulates that if a radio or television station gives or sells air time to a candidate for political office, it must provide all candidates for public office with access to the airwaves under the same conditions.

fairness doctrine

A regulation the FCC adopted in 1949 and repealed in 1987. It required broadcasters to provide "reasonable opportunities for the expression of opposing views on controversial issues of public importance."

choose what they will broadcast. Unlike governments in many other democracies, the federal government cannot dictate the content of radio and television programs. Indeed, although the FCC can require the electronic media to follow certain broadcast standards, the legislation that created the agency specifically forbids it from censoring individual programs or otherwise interfering with the right to free speech. Of course, as critics of the fairness doctrine suggest, federal regulations may indirectly influence programming content. But even here, the effect of government regulations on programming content is unintended and, in all likelihood, quite minor.

8-4 REPORTING THE NEWS

How do the media decide what is news? And after they decide which stories to cover, how do they determine how to tell a story? The answers to these two questions are critical precisely because we depend on newspapers, radio, and television to tell us what is happening in the world. As we discussed in Section 8-1b, whether the media decide to cover an issue or ignore it plays an enormous role in shaping the political agenda. Moreover, the way the media cover a story has an enormous potential to influence the public's views on an issue.

8-4a What Is News?

What constitutes "news" is a subjective matter. Every day, thousands of events happen that could be news—the president begins a ten-day trip to Asia, Congress debates a crime bill, or the mayor announces the city budget. The news media cannot, however, cover every possible story. Each newspaper, magazine, and newscast has a limited *news hole,* the amount of space left for news stories after it takes all advertisements, commercials, and features into account. Network television news has an exceptionally tight news hole, only twenty-two minutes. (Commercials take up the other eight.) Because space is limited, journalists must choose which stories they will cover and which they will not.

How do journalists select the news? Three specific selection criteria stand out: conflict, proximity, and timeliness.[68]

Conflict

Journalists gravitate toward conflict. Wars, fires, heated debates, scandals—these stories dominate the news. The reason for the bias toward conflict is simple: Journalists see their job as ferreting out bad news. As one longtime network correspondent put it, the reporter's job is "to find out who did botch what, where, when, why, and how, and what's on the front burner for possible botching tomorrow."[69] Defining news as conflict means that the media tend to cover the failures of government rather than its successes, which helps to explain why presidents often complain that the news media treat their administration unfairly. The news media's emphasis on failure can breed an adversarial relationship between journalists and politicians.

Proximity

The news media select stories that are likely to affect the lives of their audience. As one scholar describes it, "Newspaper and wire service reporters quite early in their professional lives absorb the rough rule of thumb that, in terms of reader interest, '10,000 deaths in Nepal equals 100 deaths in Wales equals 10 deaths in West Virginia equals one death next door.'"[70] Thus, a newspaper in a farm state such as Kansas is far more likely to cover the new government policy on farm subsidies than its counterpart in a big city such as New York. In turn, what Kansans identify as pressing public policy issues may differ sharply from what New Yorkers do. The divergence of interest and proximity will be an increasingly important factor in shaping news coverage as the population in the United States becomes more diverse and technological advances make it possible to increase the number of media outlets.

Timeliness

The media prefer to cover the new and the unusual. As an old saying in journalism puts it, "It's only news when man bites dog." The corollary to this is that routine events lose their attractiveness as news. This reality is coldly illustrated by a comment that a television executive made after news coverage of a famine in Ethiopia faded even though the famine persisted. "What I'm about to say sounds very cruel, but when you hear that we have another famine story from Ethiopia there is a tendency to assume that it's just more of a story that seems to be eternal."[71] In short, the media came to see the story as old hat, so it stopped covering it.

Other Influences on News Selection

In addition to conflict, proximity, and timeliness, two other factors also influence the selection of specific news stories. First, journalists select news stories with an eye to what their colleagues are reporting—that is, **pack journalism** often governs news reporting.[72] "Reporters feel pressure not necessarily to get the exclusive or the scoop but to get the story everyone else is covering. In their cost-benefit calculations, they worry more about the embarrassment of having missed a story than the satisfaction of having beaten everyone else to the punch."[73] The key agenda setters are the *New York Times* and the *Washington Post.* As a veteran reporter for both the Associated Press and *Newsweek,* put it, if the *Times* and *Post* decide something is "not news, it's very hard to convince your editors at AP and even at *Newsweek* that it is news. Because they don't see it in the morning papers that they read. So they think, is this a guy who is off on his own tangent, following something that really isn't a story, that's going to get us in trouble?"[74] Although pack journalism is commonplace, it has a distinct weakness: Because reporters travel in groups and watch the same events, they are far more

pack journalism
The tendency of journalists to cover stories because other journalists are covering them and to ignore stories that other journalists aren't covering.

susceptible to manipulation at the hands of government officials than if they worked on their own.

Second, television adds another factor in deciding what is news, namely, the availability of exciting, splashy video. Because viewers want to see more than Katie Couric or Charles Gibson reading out loud, whether a story gets on the air may depend less on its intrinsic newsworthiness than on whether it comes with dramatic video images. A CBS executive explained the problem by comparing television's zeal for covering natural disasters, such as erupting volcanoes, with its aversion to covering complicated issues, such as the debt problems affecting the world's poorer countries. "The volcano wasn't there yesterday and is there today—that's television news. But with a low-level simmering sort of issue like the debt, it just doesn't work. People the next morning say, 'Gee, did you see the footage of that volcano last night on the news?' But nobody gets up in the morning and says, 'Gee, did you hear about that debt in Brazil?'"[75]

Absent from the list of criteria the media use to select news stories is the importance of a story. Many journalists argue, however, that their focus on conflict, proximity, and timeliness generally produces the most important stories of the day. However, as the waning coverage of the Ethiopian famine attests, some stories of great significance may fail to meet the media's definition of news.

Despite the fact that news is the product of subjective choice, journalists agree to a great extent on what constitutes the news of the day. This is seen most clearly on the evening news on ABC, CBS, and NBC. Studies find that on a typical night, roughly half the stories on each newscast are the same.[76] The networks agree even more on the most important story of the day. One study found that 91 percent of the time, two of the three networks lead their evening newscast with the same story, and 43 percent of the time, all three lead with the same story.[77]

What stories do the media cover? The answer obviously varies among media outlets. By far the most popular topics on network television news are domestic politics and the domestic economy. Coverage of international news declined in the 1990s as public interest in events abroad fell.[78] Foreign coverage soared in the wake of the September 11 attacks because Americans became gripped by events overseas. It dwindled with the end of the Afghanistan War, only to spike again with the Iraq War. The network newscasts also devote relatively little time to sports and science. Moreover, they present roughly the same mix of stories. This reconfirms the point that journalists agree to a surprising extent on what constitutes news.[79]

8-4b Telling the Story

The power of the news media rests in two areas: defining the issues by deciding what qualifies as news and then deciding how to report on those issues. We have just discussed the rules that journalists use to decide what constitutes news. Once they determine an event is news, what rules do journalists follow in telling the story to their audience?

It is tempting to answer that journalists tell their stories by holding up a mirror to reality. But although journalists can strive to be impartial, they cannot be mirrors. Telling a story requires answering dozens of questions. Should the story on the local school board meeting lead off with the discussion of teacher salaries or the debate on overcrowded classrooms? Should the story run on page one or page ten? Does the story merit a photo? If so, should the shot be of a single member of the school board or all of them? Because people can disagree over the "right" answers to these questions, purely objective news coverage is unattainable.

How do journalists square the impossibility of pure objectivity with the desire to tell the news impartially? They do so by following rules designed to minimize subjective reporting. Although government enacts rules such as libel law to ensure fair reporting, journalists set their own rules for reporting objectively. Four basic rules stand out:[80]

Rule 1: Keep personal preferences out of the story. From their first day in journalism school, reporters learn that reporting and advocacy do not mix. Journalists are not supposed to inject their personal feelings into a story.

Rule 2: Avoid using obviously value-laden words. The words used to describe a person or an event have tremendous power to color how readers and viewers see the world. People who would vote for a "conservative" candidate might oppose a "reactionary" one. Troops that "slaughter" their foes are viewed differently than troops that "kill" their foes. To avoid slanting a story, reporters shy away from words such as *reactionary* and *slaughter* that convey clear value judgments.

Rule 3: Get both sides of the story. Journalists assume that news stories have two sides (no more and no less). So when they cover a story, they seek the views of each side. Thus, when the Supreme Court rules on an abortion case, reporters interview leaders of both the pro-choice and pro-life movements for their reactions. Journalists are not, however, supposed to decide which side is right. That decision belongs to the audience.

Rule 4: Rely on "responsible" sources for information. Journalists define responsible sources as people who occupy positions of authority. Positions of authority mean first and foremost government officials. Both local and national media rely heavily on government sources for news. When reporters seek sources outside government, they speak mainly to experts rather than to average people. Thus, a story on the health of the auto industry is more likely to feature interviews with General Motors executives and industry analysts than with unemployed auto workers.

Journalists themselves admit they sometimes fail to follow the four basic rules of objective journalism. This happens most often when a consensus exists in society on an issue.[81] For instance, journalistic detachment frequently disappears when journalists cover American military actions abroad.[82] During the Iraq War, the news media did not pretend to be neutral about who they wanted to win. Likewise, reporters frequently use value-laden words when describing criminals and communists. Most Americans consider these individuals societal outcasts; hence, they do not receive evenhanded treatment.

Yet even scrupulous attention to the rules does not guarantee objective or even fair reporting. Journalists can suppress their personal opinions but still (inadvertently or willfully) slant the story by whom they quote and what they show. During the Iraq War, for example, embedded journalists gave Americans a close-up view of combat. Many of their early stories focused on how Iraqis loyal to Saddam Hussein were slowing the American military advance. Senior American military officers complained that the embedded journalists' "soda-straw view" of the world exaggerated the difficulties American troops initially encountered on the battlefield. The fact that Baghdad fell in less than four weeks suggests they were right. In a sense, then, the stories were accurate but misleading.

By the same token, avoiding value-laden terms does not end the problem of word usage. Many words carry more subtle value judgments. As the press critic A. J. Liebling once noted, when the media cover labor disputes and strikes, they describe management as making "offers," whereas labor unions make "demands."[83] In the same fashion, whether journalists use the term *conservative* or *right-wing* or *liberal* or *left-wing* may shape how voters assess political figures.

The injunction to get both sides of the story also creates problems. With some stories, attempts to balance one view against another distorts the issue. As famed CBS newsman Edward R. Murrow once complained, strict adherence to the command to present both sides of the story would require journalists to balance the views of Jesus Christ with those of Judas Iscariot.[84]

The reliance on responsible sources creates still other problems. One is that journalists often have no story if responsible sources will not talk about an issue. Reporters regularly complained that it was harder to cover George W. Bush's White House than Bill Clinton's because Bush's staff was far more disciplined and generally refused to talk about issues that might lead to unflattering stories. The other problem is that responsible sources inevitably bias news coverage toward the views of political and economic elites. As one researcher argues, the beliefs and desires of the poor and the powerless generally don't interest the media "until their activities produce social or moral disorder news."[85]

Thus, although journalists may try to be fair and objective, they are forced to make many subjective decisions when they report the news. Deciding what is a news story and exactly how to tell it gives the media, whether they seek it or not, great potential influence over public opinion and public policy. It is precisely the potential power of the news media to set the political agenda for government and to influence the terms of debate that has prompted many to complain about how journalists carry out their jobs.

8-5 EVALUATING THE NEWS MEDIA

We noted in Section 8-1 that the success of American democracy rests on the existence of a free press. Without it, the American people would be unable to monitor much of what the government does and to decide whether they like the policies their elected officials are pursuing. Yet dependence on the news media for information about government creates a potential problem: The press may abuse its power by distorting the information it provides. If the news media fail to report accurately or if they ignore some stories in favor of others, the results could compromise the democratic process in the United States.

How well, then, do the media perform their job of reporting the news? The answers to that question vary. Virtually everyone at one time or another takes offense at how the media cover the news. Indeed, much criticism of the news media comes from journalists. Far more than any other profession, journalists publicly discuss their job performance. Magazines such as *American Journalism Review* and *Columbia Journalism Review* debate whether journalists have performed their jobs well. Many newspapers devote space on their editorial pages each week to an ombudsperson, a person whose job is to evaluate the work of the paper. The news media are especially susceptible to criticism because, as we have seen, reporting a story requires journalists to make so many subjective choices.

In this section, we review six common complaints about the news media: (1) They are ideologically biased; (2) they are excessively cynical; (3) they increasingly treat news as entertainment; (4) they do a poor job of covering elections; (5) they do a poor job of reporting election results; and (6) they complicate the task of governing by reporting stories based on **leaks** of confidential government information. Each of these complaints raises questions about whether the news media are harming the democratic process in the United States.

leak
Confidential government information surreptitiously given to journalists.

8-5a Ideological Bias

Polls show that roughly half of all Americans believe the news media are ideologically biased.[86] Although there are some complaints that the media favor conservative causes, most complaints accuse journalists of a liberal bias. Republicans have been especially persistent in lambasting reporters for "liberal-left" journalism, but as we saw in the introduction to this chapter, even some Democrats have accused the media of tilting toward the left.

At first glance, the claim that the media promote liberal causes and undermine conservative ones might seem odd. After all, three times in the 1980s and again in 2000 and 2004, the American public elected a conservative candidate president; conservative hosts, as we have seen, dominate talk radio; and Bill Clinton certainly received considerable negative news coverage.[87] Moreover, by historical standards, modern journalism is the epitome of impartiality. No major newspaper stamped the word *fraud* on the forehead of each picture of George W. Bush as one New York paper did to Rutherford B. Hayes. Nor would the media today run an editorial declaring that "if bad institutions and bad men can be got rid of only by killing, then the killing must be done," as a Hearst paper did when William McKinley was president.[88] (McKinley was assassinated five months after the editorial, though the two events were not connected.)

Despite anecdotal evidence to the contrary, claims that the media favor liberal causes persist. To assess such claims, many scholars have turned to survey research.[89] They have found that journalists are far more likely to consider themselves liberal than does the public, although roughly equal percentages of both groups see themselves as conservative. And although journalists share many of the public's views on economic issues, they are far more liberal on social issues. Journalists are also more liberal than other college-educated professionals they might be expected to resemble. (Nearly 90 percent of journalists are college educated, compared with only 16 percent of the public.)[90] Finally, Washington-based journalists are more liberal than their colleagues elsewhere in the country.[91]

Do these surveys mean that the media favor liberal views in their reporting? No. Surveys tell us nothing about what journalists write. And the gap between what journalists think and what they write may be large. After all, the journalistic conventions we discussed in Section 8-4b are designed specifically to minimize the impact of a journalist's beliefs, whether liberal or conservative, on how the news is reported.

The emphasis placed on survey data also mistakenly assumes that the news reflects the work of lone journalists. Most reporting is a team effort, however. Group journalism is most pronounced in television. A report on the nightly news involves the work of many people besides the correspondent: research assistants, the sound and camera crews, the field producer, the managing editor, and the anchor. Newspaper reporters likewise must deal with bureau chiefs, copy editors, and managing editors. This teamwork helps temper individual opinions that might otherwise be more noticeable.

Journalists also have bosses—many of whom are conservative. Corporate executives generally hire reporters who avoid advocacy in their reporting.[92] Indeed, the fact that corporate executives hire and fire reporters raises the possibility that media coverage will have a conservative rather than a liberal bent as journalists curry favor with the people who set their salaries. Media organizations like Fox News make no bones about their conservative orientation. And although the nation's newspapers feature a mix of liberal and conservative columnists on their op-ed pages, newspaper editorials lean conservative. They are much more likely to endorse Republicans for president.[93] As you can see, then, journalistic conventions, team reporting, and corporate ownership all help limit partisan bias in the news media.

Because survey research cannot evaluate the possibility of media bias, some scholars sift through actual news stories looking for signs of bias. Such studies should be treated with great caution, however. Definitions of "positive" and "negative" coverage are inherently subjective. Measuring bias is especially difficult when it comes to elections. Most studies implicitly assume that each candidate should receive the same treatment from the news media. Such an assumption is unreasonable. Some candidates receive more negative news coverage because they run poor campaigns or fail to address the problems the public cares about. In short, politicians sometimes get critical news coverage because they deserve it.

In all, charges that the news media are ideologically biased are impossible to disprove. Examples of unfair reporting will always be available because the very nature of reporting requires journalists to make dozens of decisions that reasonable people may disagree with. Indeed, as longtime NBC News anchor Tom Brokaw pointed out, the subjectivity inherent in reporting the news means that "Bias, like beauty, is most often in the eye of the beholder."[94]

8-5b Cynicism

Talk of the possible ideological bias of the news media obscures a more pervasive bias in news coverage: the tendency to focus on the failures of government and to ignore its successes. As we saw in Section 8-4a, most journalists believe their job is to ferret out bad news. Indeed, journalists turn the old adage "no news is good news" on its head; in most news rooms, "good news is no news."[95]

Journalists defend their preoccupation with failures and misdeeds by arguing that the media's role is to act as a watchdog that monitors the actions of government. As one journalist puts it: "Our function in a democracy is to hold up to the public things that they have the ability to change, through their votes or pressures on public officials. We don't need to tell people that their roads are okay, because they don't need to do anything about that."[96] To carry out this watchdog role, journalists must inevitably be skeptical of what government does.

To many observers, however, the news media have gone beyond acting as a watchdog and have become an attack dog that assumes the worst about government officials and institutions. When Newt Gingrich was Speaker of the House, he complained that the news media were "pathologically negative and cynical."[97] Some scholars agree. One study argued that "the press is contemptuous of politicians, whether liberal or conservative," and another concluded that the greatest impact of the news media lies in their "encouragement of cynicism."[98] Implicit in these criticisms is the fear that cynical news coverage will erode the public's faith in the country's democratic institutions.

Have the news media crossed the line that separates healthy skepticism from debilitating cynicism? As with charges of ideological bias, this is a difficult question to answer. One reason is that cynicism often lies in the eyes of the beholder. For example, Democrats might view a story questioning President Obama's plans to withdraw U.S. troops from Iraq as cynical, whereas Republicans might see the same story as a solid piece of reporting. At the same time, journalists often have good reason to be cynical. Politicians have been known to change positions on an issue to curry favor with voters, and government agencies have been guilty of incompetence and duplicity.

The difficulty in agreeing on what constitutes excessive cynicism may help to explain why opinion polls show mixed results on the topic. One poll found that 54 percent of the journalists surveyed agreed that "the press is too cynical." However, two-thirds of these journalists disagreed with the statements that "the press is too adversarial" and "the press is too focused on reporting the misdeeds and personal failings of public figures." To further complicate matters, the poll found that a majority of Americans thinks that journalists are no more cynical than they are.[99]

If the degree of cynicism in news coverage is open to debate, virtually everyone agrees that the news media are more adversarial toward government officials and institutions today than they were several decades ago. When Franklin Delano Roosevelt was president, for example, journalists respected his wish not to be photographed using crutches or a wheelchair. As a result, many Americans had no idea of the extent of Roosevelt's physical disabilities. Most observers attribute the rise of adversarial news coverage to the Watergate scandal of the early 1970s. As Ben Bradlee, the *Washington Post* executive editor who helped to break the Watergate story, puts it: "Journalism was forever changed by the assumption—by most journalists—after Watergate that government officials generally and instinctively lied when confronted by embarrassing events."[100]

Some critics would like to see the news media return to being more deferential. Americans got a taste of what that would be like after September 11, 2001, when journalists for a time became noticeably less adversarial when questioning White House officials. After the American military failed to find weapons of mass destruction in Iraq, reporters heard from a different set of critics. They argued that the media had deferred too much to the Bush administration.[101] More than a few reporters agreed. Christiane Amanpour, a longtime foreign correspondent for CNN, said after the Iraq War ended, "I think the press was muzzled, and I think the press self-muzzled. I'm sorry to say but certainly television, and perhaps to a certain extent my station, was intimidated by the administration and its foot soldiers at Fox News."[102] Likewise, the *New York Times, Washington Post,* and other newspapers reviewed their coverage in the months leading up to the war and concluded that they had not given sufficient credence to claims that the Bush administration had exaggerated Iraq's weaponry. In particular, the newspapers noted that they put administration claims in headlines on the front page and buried questions about those claims deep inside the paper.[103]

President Bush's supporters scoffed at the notion that the news media gave him a free pass on Iraq. "The White House press corps sees its role as taking the opposite side of whomever they cover," insisted Bush's first press secretary, Ari Fleisher.[104] (His successor, Scott McClellan disagreed, calling reporters "complicit enablers" for the president's push to war. He made that charge, however, only after he left the administration.)[105]

Although the argument about whether the news media was a watchdog or a lapdog on Iraq will likely continue for some time, it is clear that deferential news reporting has its own risks. For example, McCarthyism became such a destructive force in American politics in the early 1950s in part because few journalists dared to challenge Sen. Joseph McCarthy's (R-WI) false claims that many federal government officials were communists or communist sympathizers.

8-5c News as Entertainment

Media frenzies over Britney Spears's parenting skills and Lindsay Lohan's party habits illustrate a third complaint with news coverage: the tendency to treat news as entertainment. This tendency stems from the fact that the news media in the United States are privately owned. They make money by running advertisements, and the amount they can charge for advertising depends on the size of the audience they attract. However, as the rise of cable television heated up the competition, newspapers, radio, and broadcast television saw their audiences diminish and their profits fall. Many media outlets have responded to the profit squeeze by favoring stories that emphasize the emotional, the novel, and the sensational.

Of course, sensational news coverage is hardly new (see Box 8–2). But in recent years, more and more news stories have tended toward the interesting rather than the important. Bill Moyers, a prize-winning television commentator, complains: "Our center of gravity shifted from the standards and practices of the news business to show business. Pretty soon...tax policy had to compete with stories about three-legged sheep, and the three-legged sheep won."[106]

The trend away from "hard" news is perhaps most visible in local television news, where the operating maxim often is "If it bleeds, it leads."[107] Beginning in the 1990s, though, network television also showed a greater appetite for "soft" news. The nightly newscasts regularly devoted their final few minutes to human interest stories, and stories on show business became common.[108] Many newspapers, in the meantime, tried to attract new readers by increasing their sports coverage, adding lifestyle sections, and making news stories shorter.[109] That trend changed abruptly with September 11, 2001. Television and newspapers shifted gears and tackled hard news about terrorism and Afghanistan. A year after the attacks, though, the news media were back to covering contestants on *American Idol*.[110]

Media executives defend the move away from hard news on the grounds that they are giving the public what it wants. If the public demanded more in-depth coverage of Middle East politics or banking regulations, they argue, they would gladly provide it.[111] This argument has considerable merit. Fewer Americans watch CNN than ESPN on an average day, and the audience for C-SPAN lags behind that of Country Music Television, the Cartoon Network, and Comedy Central. Indeed, to repeat a previous point, the audience for the cable news networks has been flat in recent years, whereas newspaper circulation and network television ratings continue to decline.[112]

POINT OF ORDER

Box 8–2 The Changing Rules of News Coverage

The media have come under fire during the past several years for sensationalizing the news. Critics complain that television news increasingly emphasizes stories about sex, crime, and scandal. Critics also have denounced the media's growing interest in what politicians do in their bedrooms. Whereas journalists in the 1960s closed their eyes to John F. Kennedy's philandering, the marital infidelities of Bill Clinton, John Edwards, New York Governor Elliot Spitzer, and other politicians have been the subject of intense media scrutiny.

For all the handwringing over tabloid television and voyeuristic

Source: © AP Photo/World Wide Photos.

Tabloid journalism focuses on the sensational, as when President Bill Clinton's relationship with Monica Lewinsky became public.

journalism, sensationalist news coverage is nothing new in American society; rather it has waxed and waned in accordance with America's changing social mores. The first newspaper published in the United States, *Publick Occurrences, Both Foreign and Domestic,* reported in its first issue in 1690 that a local man had hanged himself and that the king of France was sleeping with his daughter-in-law. Given that *Publick Occurrences* was published in the Puritan-dominated Massachusetts Bay Colony, it is perhaps not surprising that the paper was barred from publishing a second edition.

Sex and scandal featured prominently in the 1828 race for the presidency. Newspapers that favored the candidacy of Andrew Jackson printed stories alleging that President John Quincy Adams had procured a young woman for the Russian czar while he was American ambassador to Russia and that he had engaged in premarital sex. Newspapers that supported Adams's reelection returned fire with stories such as: "General Jackson's mother was a COMMON PROSTITUTE, brought to the country by the British soldiers. She afterward married a MULATTO MAN, with whom she had several children, of which number General JACKSON IS ONE!" Many newspapers also accused Jackson of living with his wife while she was still married to her first husband.

Sensationalist news coverage flourished during the heyday of yellow

journalism. Many newspapers regularly gave prominent coverage to the lurid and the sensational. Stories with headlines such as "Real American Monsters and Dragons," "The Mysterious Murder of Bessie Little," and "Startling Confession of a Wholesale Murderer Who Begs to Be Hanged" were typical of the fare that William Randolph Hearst offered his readers. And newspaper editors knew at the turn of the century what Madison Avenue would discover decades later: sex sells. In describing the illustrations that would accompany a story about Halley's comet, a staff member for Joseph Pulitzer's paper the *Sunday World* suggested that "if you can work a pretty girl into the decoration, so much the better."

Because the American news media are privately owned and therefore need to turn a profit, they inevitably will emphasize the novel over the important whenever there is a public demand for it. When social mores become more lax, as they have in the United States, the news media will relax their rules on what constitutes an acceptable news story. Conversely, should social mores in the United States become more conservative, the media no doubt will push the rules of news coverage back in the direction of hard news.

Sources: Edwin Emery, *The Press and America: An Interpretative History of the Mass Media,* 3rd ed. (Englewood Cliffs, NJ: Prentice Hall, 1972), 355, 359; Todd Gitlin, "Media Lemmings Run Amok!" *Washington Journalism Review* (April 1992): 32; Mitchell Stephens, *A History of News: From the Drum to the Satellite* (New York: Penguin Books, 1988), 187–88.

Whether the decline of hard news in noncrisis periods is due to a pandering news media or an apathetic public, the trend is troubling. By emphasizing the interesting over the important, the media can distort the public's perception of the country's problems. In turn, one must wonder how well a democracy can function if its citizens are ill-informed.

8-5d On the Campaign Trail

To judge by the postmortems of recent presidential campaigns, the news media do a poor job of covering elections. Critics single out

horse-race journalism

News coverage of elections that focuses on which candidate is leading in the polls rather than on the substantive issues in the campaign.

photo opportunities

Events that political candidates and government officials stage to allow newspaper photographers and television news crews to take flattering images.

sound bite

A short excerpt from a person's speech or conversation that appears on radio or television news.

three mistakes in particular. The first is that the media devote too much time to **horse-race journalism**, stories that focus on who's ahead in the race rather than on the issues in the campaign. Critics complain that by portraying elections as contests between individuals rather than as clashes of ideas—in essence, treating elections as sporting events—horse-race journalism does little to inform voters about whether any candidate is proposing viable solutions to the problems they consider important.

A second common criticism of campaign coverage is that journalists allow the candidates to manipulate them. Candidates often stage **photo opportunities** (or "photo ops" for short), which are carefully planned events designed to attract flattering news coverage. For example, a candidate may give a speech in front of the Statue of Liberty in the hope that when voters see pictures or videos of the event, they will think of the candidate as a patriot. Although these events may contain little hard news, journalists nonetheless cover them, turning many news reports into what amounts to unpaid political advertising. At the same time, the fear of being charged with bias leads many journalists to strive to give both political parties equal treatment, even when equal treatment is not justified.

A third common criticism of election coverage is that the news media seldom let the candidates speak at length about their views. The average length of a **sound bite** on the network evening news four decades ago ran 43 seconds. Today sound bites generally run fewer than 10 seconds.[113] Sound bites shrank for several reasons. Video replaced film, which made it easier to cut up speeches in time for the evening news. Correspondents seeking to avoid manipulation by the candidates increasingly substituted their own analysis for canned speeches. And the conviction among television executives that the public has a dwindling attention span spawned a general trend within television news toward shorter, faster-moving stories.[114] Critics worry that shrinking sound bites deny voters the opportunity to hear the candidates explain their policy proposals and instead encourage politicians to speak in slogans.

Many newspapers and television news shows have responded to these three criticisms by increasing the space they allot to stories on the issues, limiting their coverage of photo opportunities, and running extended excerpts of each candidate's basic campaign speech. Whether these and other reportorial changes have improved the coverage of campaigns, however, is debatable. In a 1988 survey, 68 percent of Americans gave the news media a grade of C or lower

Although journalists frequently debate the ethics of reporting stories that delve into the private lives of government officials, the need to attract an audience often leads them to put aside their ethical qualms.

for the way they covered that year's campaign. When Americans were asked to grade coverage of the 2004 campaign, 67 percent gave it a grade of C or lower. The public apparently has not noticed the news media's efforts to improve their campaign coverage.[115]

As newspapers and television news shows struggle to respond to complaints about how they cover elections, these media may be becoming less relevant to the election process. Candidates traditionally relied heavily on attracting news coverage in their efforts to reach the voters. In recent years, however, candidates anxious to avoid inquisitive journalists have been turning to radio and television talk shows as a way to bypass the press and speak directly to voters. During the 2008 presidential campaign, for example, Barack Obama appeared on *Oprah, The Daily Show with Jon Stewart, The Late Show with David Letterman,* and *The Tonight Show with Jay Leno* among other television shows. John McCain not only appeared on *The Daily Show* and *The Tonight Show,* he announced his 2008 presidential bid on *Letterman.*

Does talk-show campaigning serve the public interest? Many Americans, angry at what they see as the arrogance of the news media, applaud the willingness of candidates to go over the heads of the press corps and talk directly to voters. And many candidates argue that appearing in nonconventional forums helps them reach voters who feel alienated from politics. Some journalists concur. Tim Russert, the long-time moderator of NBC's *Meet the Press,* argued that talk shows "generated an enormous amount of interest by people who normally weren't turned on by the political process."[116]

Most journalists, however, denounce talk-show campaigning as a new form of political manipulation. They argue that talk-show hosts lack the training and aggressiveness needed to push candidates to explain their positions, a fact that candidates exploit to their advantage. When Oprah Winfrey had George W. Bush on her show in 2000, for example, she questioned him about his favorite sandwich (peanut butter and jelly on white bread), his favorite historical figure (British Prime Minister Winston Churchill), his favorite activity (running), and his favorite dream (taking the oath of office as president).[117]

Whether one believes that talk-show campaigning shows democracy at its best or worst, future candidates will continue to use nontraditional formats for two reasons. First, candidates want media coverage to show them in the best possible light, and journalists are trained to ask the sorts of questions candidates hate to answer. Second, because more and more Americans don't watch the evening news shows, candidates find them less useful for reaching voters. So candidates have turned their sights to radio and television talk shows, the place where much of the audience, and much of the voting public, has gone.

8-5e Reporting Election Results

The electronic media's mishandling of the 2000 Election Night results added to the public's dissatisfaction with journalists. The mistakes began early. At 7:50 p.m. Eastern time, the networks projected Al Gore the winner of Florida's 25 electoral votes, based on exit polls that asked voters as they left the ballot booth how they had voted. There were only two problems. First, although the polls close at 7 p.m. in Florida, the state's panhandle is on Central time. So, some Floridians were still voting when the networks called the race in the state. Second, the early projection for Gore was wrong. Over the next two hours, the actual vote count trended heavily toward George W. Bush. Around 10 p.m., red-faced news anchors were forced to pluck Florida out of the Gore victory column. The state was now "too close to call."

The mistakes didn't end there. As it moved past midnight in the East and polls began closing in the West, it became clear that whoever won Florida would be the next president. At 2:16 a.m., Fox News called Florida, and the presidency, for Bush. The other networks followed suit within minutes. Gore called Bush to concede. There was only one problem: Bush's lead was shrinking. A 50,000-vote Bush lead at 2 a.m. shriveled to a 200-vote lead less than two hours later, and votes were still trickling in. Gore called Bush to retract his concession. By 4 a.m., the networks reversed themselves a second time. Florida, and with it the presidency, was once again "too close to call."

The networks apologized for their Election Night blunders. "We don't just have egg on our face," said NBC's Tom Brokaw, "we have an omelet."[118] Computers got much of the blame. The computer program that the networks used to project the winner slightly exaggerated how well Al Gore would do in Florida and underestimated how many absentee ballots (which exit polls don't measure) would be cast. More mundane mistakes compounded these problems. At one point, the workers tabulating the exit polls inadvertently punched in the wrong numbers. At another point, several counties reported the wrong counts of actual votes. In any other election, these miscues would have been inconsequential. Given the closeness of the 2000 presidential election, however, they were pivotal.[119]

The Election Night blunders certainly gave the American public another reason to complain about the news media. But did they affect the outcome of the race? Republicans argued that calling Florida early for Gore cost Bush critical votes in Florida and elsewhere in the country because some Republicans decided not to vote when they knew who had "won."[120]

The merits of this claim, though, are debatable. Few Floridians were watching television, debating whether to vote, ten minutes before the polls closed. Nor is it clear why Democrats wouldn't be just as likely as Republicans to stay home. After all, their vote would not affect the outcome either. Moreover, most people do not go to the polls solely to vote for president. They vote in other races as well. The Florida call did not affect these races. Finally, the early call in Florida had a precedent. In 1980 President Jimmy Carter conceded the election to Ronald Reagan before the polls out West had closed. Analyses of that vote suggest that Carter's announcement had a negligible effect on the election.[121]

Democrats had their own complaints about Election Night 2000. They argued that the networks' decision to call the election for Bush encouraged many Americans to believe he had been elected president.[122] This belief, Democrats argued, complicated their efforts to get an accurate vote count because many people saw Gore as trying to take away something that was rightfully Bush's. Making the disputed call harder for Democrats to swallow was the identity of the man at Fox News who started the network stampede for Bush at 2:16 in the morning: John Ellis. He was Bush's first cousin.[123]

As with Republican complaints, the significance of the problems Democrats pointed to is debatable. Americans might have insisted on a complete recount, and Republicans might have been more open to one, if the networks had not called the race for Bush. Then again, nothing may have changed. As for Bush's cousin calling races, it was unusual, if not a violation of journalistic ethics. Even if Ellis had been silent, though, the only difference might have been that another network would have been the first to call the race for Bush.[124]

The Election Night 2000 fiasco prompted calls for change. The networks all revamped their Election Night reporting. Among other steps, they joined forces with CNN and the Associated Press to create the National Election Pool to conduct new, and presumably better, exit polls. That did not turn out to be the case. By late afternoon on Election Day 2004, these exit polls, along with one conducted by the *Los Angeles Times,* showed John Kerry cruising to victory. Neither the networks nor CNN called any races based on these results, though at least one prominent polling organization, Zogby International, used them to project Kerry as the winner with 311 electoral votes. (Kerry actually won 252, compared with Bush's 286.) Nonetheless, the early returns colored how the news media covered the voting. Republicans who watched the early returns could be forgiven for concluding that Bush was headed toward a crushing defeat, just as Democrats could be excused for assuming that Kerry had pulled off a major upset. Moreover, news about the early exit poll results quickly spread across the Internet, leading many people to conclude that the election was over before all the votes were cast.

Whether the exit poll information affected voter turnout is open to debate. We do not know whether information, either correct or erroneous, about how one side is faring actually affects voter decisions in a significant way. Equally important, the reasons the exit polls skewed in favor of Senator Kerry will be debated for years. Some analyses suggested that an unintended bias may have occurred because legal barriers designed to prevent people for electioneering—that is, pressuring people as they enter the polls—may have kept the pollsters from getting representative samples. It may also have been that Democrats were more eager than Republicans to tell pollsters how they voted.[125]

Regardless of why the exit polls were wrong, renewed efforts to change how the media cover elections are likely. Some critics call for new laws to make it more difficult for the networks to conduct exit polls and thereby harder to project election winners. Others propose a uniform closing time for all polling places. Whether there will be political support for these and other changes is doubtful. (Proposals for a uniform poll closing time run into a practical problem: If polls close at 8 p.m. in Hawaii, they would have to remain open until 1 a.m. on the East Coast.) Moreover, any effort to rein in the networks runs up against a fundamental rule: the First Amendment's guarantee of freedom of the press.

8-5f Reporting Leaks

In 2006, the *New York Times* and several other newspapers broke a story of a secret program run by the Central Intelligence Agency (CIA) that sought to track terrorists by scouring a vast international database of banking transactions. The stories were based on a leak—that is, confidential government information given surreptitiously to journalists. In this case, the people who leaked the story were executive branch officials who doubted the legality of the program and believed that it violated the privacy of American citizens. The incident brought to the fore yet again complaints that the news media's willingness to report stories based on leaks threatens the democratic process in the United States.

Those who complain about the news media's reliance on leaks sometimes contend that leaks jeopardize national security. President Bush called the stories about the secret CIA program "disgraceful," and Vice President Dick Cheney said the *Times* had "made the job of defending against further terrorist attacks more difficult."[126] Some critics argued that the *Times* had broken American law, which in some circumstances makes it illegal to knowingly reveal classified information. However, very few stories based on leaks involve true national security issues. The vast majority instead deal with more mundane matters of governing, such as who the president will nominate for a vacant seat on the Supreme Court or whether the secretary of state supports the president's proposal for national missile defense. Many government officials find such leaks maddening because an ill-timed leak can make it much harder for them to accomplish their policy goals and can put their agencies or themselves in an unflattering light. For example, a president would find it much harder to convince Congress to pass a health-care reform bill if it became public knowledge that White House economic advisers had concluded the reform proposal was too expensive.

Although complaints about leaks are commonplace, they should be taken with a grain of salt. After all, the reason the news media can write so many stories based on leaks is that many government officials are willing to leak confidential information.[127] Indeed, many of the most vociferous complaints about leaks come from officials who are leakers themselves.[128] The willingness to leak stories extends to the highest levels of government. For instance, in 2002 President George W. Bush authorized Vice President Dick

Cheney and an aide to leak the classified National Intelligence Estimate on Iraq to reporters. The decision was part of the administration's effort to convince the public of the need to remove Saddam Hussein from power.[129]

As Bush's decision suggests, officials leak stories to the news media because leaks can advance their personal and policy goals. Officials recognize that news coverage can move an issue onto the political agenda, help mobilize public opposition to new policy proposals, or damage a colleague they dislike.[130] In short, leaking stories can influence *what* the news media cover and *how* they cover it, and help leakers advance their own careers or derail the careers of others.

As leaking has become common practice in American politics, some journalists worry that leaks do more to damage the news media than government.[131] Leaks transform the media from observers into participants as officials try to use journalists as conduits for shaping policy. Worse yet, the need to cultivate a source may encourage journalists to treat leakers favorably and perhaps even to drop a potential story for fear of antagonizing a prized source of inside information. For example, many critics believe that the willingness of journalists to rely on White House leaks helped propel the country to war in Iraq. Major newspapers ran stories about Baghdad's pursuit of weapons of mass destruction based on information that Bush administration officials had leaked to them. The information later proved misleading or false.[132]

Yet despite the disadvantages, leaks are also one of the most powerful tools journalists have for getting at the heart of a story and keeping the American public informed. The Watergate scandal of the early 1970s, which forced Richard Nixon to resign the presidency, is a prime example. Investigative reporters Bob Woodward and Carl Bernstein were able to break the Watergate story only because a source known as "Deep Throat" leaked vital information about the Nixon administration's illegal activities.[133] (In 2005, it was revealed that Deep Throat was the number two official at the Federal Bureau of Investigation.) By reporting leaks, then, the news media can promote democracy by providing a powerful check on government power.

8-6 THE NEWS MEDIA AND DEMOCRACY

What are we to conclude about how well the media perform their job of reporting the news? Although criticisms of the news media are frequently exaggerated, even journalists agree they are far from perfect in doing their jobs. Bias can infect their stories; they may at times be too cynical; hard news increasingly must compete with soft news for print space and air time; coverage of election campaigns often emphasizes the contest at the expense of content; and government officials may selectively leak information to manipulate news coverage. Yet the freedom all Americans have to criticize what they see as poor reporting encourages the news media to improve their performance and helps check the abuse of media power. Thus, despite their occasional errors and excesses, the news media remain a vital component of the American democratic process.

SUMMARY

Freedom of the press is essential to the health of a democracy. Without a lively news media, we would not be able to monitor the actions of government. Yet our very dependence on newspapers, radio, and television for information gives the news media great power to influence public opinion and government behavior. Although the media in no way dictate what we think, they do influence politics in the United States. The media have some effect on the way we view political issues, and they have a substantial impact on the political agenda. Nonetheless, the power of the media should not be exaggerated. What the news media report often reflects what Americans are thinking and what government is doing, rather than the reverse.

Although the authors of the Constitution believed that a free press is essential to the success of democracy, the nature of the news business has changed dramatically over the past two centuries. Partisan journalism has given way to objective reporting, television has surpassed newspapers as the preeminent source of news, and news has become big business. All these changes illustrate the immense freedom the media have to define their role in the American political system.

To encourage vigorous reporting, American law extends great freedom to journalists. Unlike many other countries, the United States does not censor the media or require journalists to apply for licenses. The one exception to limited regulation is the electronic media. Because of the small number of broadcast channels, the government limits ownership of radio and television stations and sets some rules for public affairs programming. In the main, though, these regulations have relatively little effect on the content that the electronic news media broadcast.

The choices journalists make determine which events become news. Reporters generally define news as events that are conflictual, relevant, and timely. When they report the news, journalists try to tell the story straight, although pure objectivity is impossible.

Because reporting requires journalists to make subjective choices, criticism of the news media is inevitable. Many people claim that the media favor liberal causes, but convincing evidence of a persistent liberal bias in the media is hard to come by. A more pervasive bias in news coverage is the tendency of the news media to focus on the failures of government rather than its successes. Many critics complain that the news media have become so focused on misdeeds that news coverage has become cynical.

Another criticism of the news media is their growing tendency to treat news as entertainment. As greater competition has squeezed media profits in recent years, newspapers, radio, and television have increasingly come to favor soft news over hard news.

The news media also have been criticized for doing a poor job of covering elections. Critics complain that journalists engage in horse-race journalism, allow campaign staffs to manipulate them, and chop candidates' speeches into shorter and shorter sound bites. The news media have tried to improve their coverage of elections, but the public says it sees little improvement. Moreover, the traditional news media are finding themselves pushed to the margins of the political debate as candidates make increased use of talk shows and other nontraditional venues to reach voters.

The electronic media have also come under fire for their premature and incorrect calls in recent presidential elections. Some members of Congress hope to pass legislation restricting the ability of broadcast and cable networks to project election results, but these efforts are likely to run afoul of the First Amendment.

Finally, the news media have been criticized for reporting stories based on leaks of confidential government information. On closer inspection, however, the issue is more complicated than the criticisms suggest. Government officials frequently leak information to draw attention to an issue, to send a message to others in government, to derail a policy they oppose, or to damage a colleague they dislike. Although journalists worry that government officials selectively leak information to influence news coverage, they also know that leaks are one of the most powerful tools they have for getting at the heart of a story and keeping the American public informed.

KEY TERMS

broadcast television

cable television

embedding

equal-time provision

fairness doctrine

Federal Communications
    Commission (FCC)

Freedom of Information Act

horse-race journalism

leaks

muckraking

objective press

pack journalism

photo opportunities

political agenda

pool reporting

selective perception

sound bite

spin control

talk radio

yellow journalism

READINGS FOR FURTHER STUDY

Alterman, Eric. *What Liberal Media? The Truth About Bias and the News* (New York: Basic Books, 2003). A journalist argues that the news media not only lack a liberal slant, they in fact have a conservative bias.

Carter, T. Barton, Marc A. Franklin, and Jay B. Wright. *The First Amendment and the Fifth Estate: Regulation of the Electronic Mass Media,* 7th ed. (Mineola, NY: Foundation Press, 2008). A comprehensive overview of the legal regulations affecting the electronic media.

Fenton, Tom. *Bad News: The Decline of Reporting, the Business of News, and the Danger to Us All* (New York: Regan Books, 2005). A veteran CBS News correspondent accuses the networks of having dumbed down the news and driven away viewers.

Goldberg, Bernard. *Bias: A CBS Insider Exposes How the Media Distort the News* (New York: Regnery, 2002). A veteran CBS reporter argues that a liberal bias pervades the mainstream media.

Graber, Doris A. *Mass Media and American Politics,* 7th ed. (Washington, D.C.: CQ Press, 2005). Graber examines how the mass media affect the way political campaigns are run and how the voters view candidates and campaign issues.

Jamieson, Kathleen Hall, and Paul Waldman. *The Press Effect: Politicians, Journalists, and the Stories that Shape the Political World* (New York: Oxford University Press, 2002). An analysis of the role of the campaigns and the press in casting the 2000 general election as a contest between Pinocchio and Dumbo.

Massing, Michael, and Orville Schell. *Now They Tell Us: The American Press and Iraq* (New York: New York Review of Books, 2004). An analysis arguing that the contrast between the press's feistiness after the end of the Iraq War and its meekness before it points to entrenched and disturbing features of American journalism.

Mindich, David T. Z. *Tuned Out: Why Americans Under 40 Don't Follow the News* (New York: Oxford University Press, 2005). A media critic and former CNN editor explores why younger Americans are far less likely than older Americans to follow traditional news sources.

REVIEW QUESTIONS

1. Why did Congress pass the Freedom of Information Act in 1966?
   a. to enhance democratic accountability
   b. to reduce secrecy by the executive branch of government
   c. to comply with a ruling by the Supreme Court
   d. both a and b

2. Which of the following is *true* about the media coverage of election night 2000?
   a. The media exit polling in Florida was flawed.
   b. The networks wanted to maximize their profits.
   c. The networks stopped covering the race at midnight.
   d. All of the above.

3. The news media play a major role in shaping
   a. the political agenda.
   b. public policy making.
   c. public opinion.
   d. the outcome of elections.

4. Newspapers during Thomas Jefferson's era were
   a. heavily partisan.
   b. affordable only to the wealthy.
   c. dependent upon business and political groups.
   d. all of the above.

5. The penny press
   a. began during the 1920s.
   b. revolutionized journalism.
   c. was dependent upon the political parties for money.
   d. none of the above.

6. The rise of yellow journalism occurred during the
   a. 1830s.
   b. 1890s.
   c. civil rights movement.
   d. presidential election of 1988.

7. Objectivity emerged as the touchstone of American journalism after
   a. the Revolutionary War.
   b. the Civil War.
   c. World War I.
   d. World War II.

8. The equal-time provision
   a. helps provide "reasonable opportunities for the expression of opposing views on controversial issues of public importance."
   b. was struck down by the Supreme Court.
   c. is not necessary because all campaigns are funded equally.
   d. ensures that all candidates for public office have access to the airwaves under the same conditions.

9. In news reporting, which of the following statements concerning bias is *most* accurate?
   a. National journalists have a liberal bias in their reporting.
   b. National journalists have a conservative bias in their reporting.
   c. The media often treat news as entertainment.
   d. National journalists have a bias against Republican presidents.

10. What is a significant ramification of the shrinking sound bite?
    a. Americans know more about public affairs.
    b. Americans know more about where each presidential candidate stands on the issues.
    c. Americans seldom hear presidential candidates speak at length about their views.
    d. None of the above.

NOTES

1. Quoted in "Transcript: Democratic Debate in Cleveland," *New York Times*, February 26, 2008. Available at www.nytimes.com/2008/02/26/us/politics/26text-debate.html?pagewanted=all (accessed August 2008).

2. Thomas Jefferson, "To John Norvell," in *The Writings of Thomas Jefferson* (New York: G. P. Putnam, 1898), vol. ix, 224.

3. Quoted in Daniel P. Moynihan, "The Presidency and the Press," *Commentary* (March 1971): 41.

4. Quoted in Christopher Hanson, "Media Bashing," *Columbia Journalism Review* (November/December 1992): 52.

5. Quoted in Jann S. Wenner and William Greider, "The Rolling Stone Interview: President Clinton," *Rolling Stone* (December 9, 1993): 81.

6. Quoted in Mike Allen, "Bush Appeals for 'Plain-Spoken Folks' in Office," *Washington Post*, September 5, 2000.

7. James Madison, "Letter to W. T. Barry," in *The Writings of James Madison*, vol. 9, 1819–1836, ed. Gaillard Hunt (New York: G. P. Putnam, 1910), 103.

8. Thomas Jefferson, "To Edward Carrington," *Writings*, vol. iv, 360.

9. Among others, see Bernard Berelson, Paul Lazarsfeld, and William McPhee, *Voting* (Chicago: University of Chicago Press, 1954); Leo Bogart, *Press and Public: Who Reads What, When, Where and Why in American Newspapers* (Hillsdale, NJ: Lawrence Erlbaum Associates, 1981); Paul Lazarsfeld, Bernard Berelson, and Hazel Gaudet, *The People's Choice* (New York: Columbia University Press, 1948); Suzanne Pingree, "Children's Cognitive Processes in Constructing Social Reality," *Journalism Quarterly* 60 (Autumn 1983): 415–22.

10. Laurance Parisot, "Attitudes about the Media: A Five-Country Comparison," *Public Opinion* 10 (January-February 1988): 60; *The Year in Figures* (Washington, D.C.: Times Mirror Center for the People and the Press, 1995), 1.

11. Michiko Kakutani, "Is This the Most Trusted Man in America?" *New York Times*, August 17, 2008.

12. Benjamin I. Page, Robert Y. Shapiro, and Glenn R. Dempsey, "What Moves Public Opinion?" *American Political Science Review* 81 (March 1987): 23–43.

13. Shanto Iyengar and Donald R. Kinder, *News That Matters: Television and American Public Opinion* (Chicago: University of Chicago Press, 1987), 33.

14. Ibid., 60.

15. On the news media and Congress, see Timothy E. Cook, *Making Laws and Making News: Media Strategies in the U.S. House of Representatives* (Washington, D.C.: Brookings Institution, 1989); Stephen Hess, *Live from Capitol Hill! Studies of Congress and the Media* (Washington, D.C.: Brookings Institution, 1991); Stephen Hess, *The Ultimate Insiders: U.S. Senators in the National Media* (Washington, D.C.: Brookings Institution, 1986); Thomas E. Mann and Norman J. Ornstein, eds., *Congress, the Press and the Public* (Washington, D.C.: AEI/Brookings Institution, 1994).

16. Quoted in Pamela Fessler, "Congress' Record on Saddam: Decade of Talk, Not Action," *Congressional Quarterly Weekly Report*, April 27, 1991, 1068.

17. For discussions of the news media and the presidency, see, among others, Michael Baruch Grossman and Martha Joynt Kumar, *Portraying the President: The White House and the News Media* (Baltimore, MD: Johns Hopkins University Press, 1981); Samuel Kernell, *Going Public: New Strategies of Presidential Leadership*, 2nd ed. (Washington, D.C.: CQ Press, 1992); Fred Smoller, *The Six O'Clock Presidency: A Theory of Press Relations in the Age of Television* (New York: Praeger, 1990); John Tebbel and Sarah Miles Watts, *The Press and the Presidency: From George Washington to Ronald Reagan* (New York: Oxford University Press, 1985).

18. David Barstow, "Courting Ex-Officers Tied to Military Contractors," *New York Times*, April 20, 2008.

19. Mitchell Stephens, A *History of News: From the Drum to the Satellite* (New York: Penguin Books, 1988), 222.

20. Edwin Emery, *The Press and America: An Interpretative History of the Mass Media*, 3rd ed. (Englewood Cliffs, NJ: Prentice Hall, 1972), 118; Stephens, *A History of News*, 187–88.

21. See Emery, *The Press and America*, chap. 11; Michael Schudson, *Discovering the News: A Social History of American Newspapers* (New York: Basic Books, 1978), chap. 1.

22. Emery, *The Press and America*, 373.

23. *Statistical Abstract of the United States: 2008*, 127th ed. (Washington, D.C.: U.S. Bureau of the Census, 2007), 703, 705. Available at www.census.gov/compendia/statab/ (accessed August 2008).

24. *Statistical Abstract of the United States, 1970*, 91st ed. (Washington, D.C.: U.S. Bureau of the Census, 1970), 499; *Statistical Abstract of the United States: 2008*, 705.

25. Mark Hertsgaard, *On Bended Knee: The Press and the Reagan Presidency* (New York: Schocken Books, 1989), 78; D. Colin Phillips and Christopher Phillips, "Memo from the Publishers," *Editor and Publisher International Yearbook, 1999* (New York: Editor and Publisher, 1999).

26. Alex S. Jones, "Rethinking Newspapers," *New York Times*, January 1, 1991; *Statistical Abstract of the United States: 2008*, 52, 705.

27. *Statistical Abstract of the United States: 2008*, 7, 705.

28. Richard Harwood, "Rotten News for Everyone," *Washington Post*, September 1, 1991; Pew Research Center for the People & the Press, "Maturing Internet News Audience—Broader Than Deep," July 30, 2006, p. 9. Available at people-press.org/reports/pdf/282.pdf

29. *Statistical Abstract of the United States*, 2008, 704.

30. Ken Auletta, *Three Blind Mice: How the TV Networks Lost Their Way* (New York: Random House, 1991).

31. See Tom Fenton, *Bad News: The Decline of Reporting, the Business of News, and the Danger to Us All* (New York: Regan Books, 2005).

32. Ken Auletta, "Sign-Off," *New Yorker* (March 7, 2005): 52.

33. John Consoli, "New Context," *Brandweek* (May 29, 2000): U10; Brooks Barnes, "NBC's News Show Widens Its Lead in Rating Battle," *Wall Street Journal*, November 17, 2004, B3.

34. Howard Kurtz, "There's Anger in the Air," *Washington Post National Weekly Edition*, October 31–November 6, 1994, 8.

35. Project for Excellence in Journalism, *The State of the News Media 2008—Talk Radio,*" available at www.stateofthenewsmedia.com/2008/narrative_radio_talk_radio.php?cat=6&media=10.

36. "Rush Stations," RushLimbaugh.com, available at www.rushlimbaugh.com/home/menu/rush.guest.html; "The Top Talk Radio Audience," *Talkers Magazine*, available at www.talkers.com/main/index.php?option=com_content&task=view&id=17&Itemid=34.

37. Project for Excellence in Journalism, *State of the News Media 2008.*

38. Julia Angwin and Sarah McBride, "Radio's Bush-Bashing Air American Is Back in Fighting Form," *Wall Street Journal,* January 20, 2005.

39. Jim Rutenberg, "As Talk Radio Wavers, Bush Moves to Firm Up Support," *New York Times,* October 17, 2006.

40. Project for Excellence in Journalism, *State of the News Media 2008*; "Top Talk Radio Audience."

41. Project for Excellence in Journalism, *State of the News Media 2008.*

42. *Statistical Abstract of the United States: 2008,* 718.

43. Pew Research Center, "Maturing Internet News Audience."

44. "Blogs for Bush," available at www.blogsforbush.com/mt/archives/001985.html.

45. Ben H. Bagdikian, *The Media Monopoly,* 3rd ed. (Boston: Beacon Press, 1990), 21.

46. Hertsgaard, *On Bended Knee,* 78; Kubas Consultants, "Newspaper Industry Trends and Implications for Suppliers," October 5, 2004 available at www.npes.org/research/newspapers.pdf

47. "Company Profile," available at www.gannett.com/about/company_profile.htm; "About," available at www.mcclatchy.com/100/story/179.html.

48. See Dan Carney, "Congress Fires Its First Shot in Information Revolution," *Congressional Quarterly Weekly Report,* February 3, 1996, 289–94; Dan Carney, "From Televisions to Telephones...Highlights of the New Laws," *Congressional Quarterly Weekly Report,* February 3, 1996, 290–91.

49. Jeremy Pelofsky, "FCC's Powell Sees Long Road for Media Rules," December 2, 2004. Available at www.webcenters.compuserve.com/compuserve/tv/feature.jsp?story=APcensorship20044.

50. "Company Profile," available at www.gannett.com/about/company_profile.htm.

51. Center for Creative Voices in the Media, "Media Concentration," available at www.creativevoices.us/key.php?PHPSESSID=023575d35e2c62ba84b356ac78db57bc.

52. "About PBS: Welcome," available at www.pbs.org/aboutpbs/; "About NPR," available at www.npr.org/about/.

53. Doris A. Graber, *Mass Media and American Politics,* 4th ed. (Washington, D.C.: CQ Press, 1994), 39–40.

54. John C. Busterna and Kathleen A. Hansen, "Presidential Endorsement Patterns by Chain-Owned Papers, 1976–1984," *Journalism Quarterly* 67 (Fall 1990): 286–94.

55. Quoted in Robert Kurz, "Congress and the Media: Forces in the Struggle over Foreign Policy," in *The Media and Foreign Policy,* ed. Simon Serfaty (New York: St. Martin's, 1990), 77.

56. Elie Abel, *Leaking: Who Does It? Who Benefits? At What Cost?* (New York: Priority Press, 1987), 44. See also Daniel Patrick Moynihan, *Secrecy: The American Experience* (New Haven, CT: Yale University Press, 1998).

57. Jay Peterzell, "Can the CIA Spook the Press?" *Columbia Journalism Review* (July/August 1986): 18–19.

58. "Transcript of Bush Conference II," Princeton University Woodrow Wilson School, April 25, 2003, 16, available at www.wws.princeton.edu/bushconf/ Transcript%204-25-03.pdf. For discussions of George W. Bush's media strategy more generally, see Ken Auletta, "Fortress Bush," *New Yorker* (January 19, 2004): 52–65, and Ari Fleischer, *Taking Heat: The President, the Press, and My Years in the White House* (New York: William Morrow, 2005).

59. "Transcript of Bush Conference II," 17–18.

60. Quoted in Hanson, "Media Bashing," 54.

61. Peter Stoler, *The War Against the Press: Politics, Pressure and Intimidation in the 80's* (New York: Dodd, Mead, 1986), 4–5.

62. Jason DeParle, "17 News Executives Criticize U.S. for 'Censorship' of Gulf Coverage," *New York Times*, July 3, 1991. See also W. Lance Bennett and David L. Paletz, eds., *Taken by Storm: The Media, Public Opinion, and U.S. Foreign Policy in the Gulf War* (Chicago: University of Chicago Press, 1994); Hedrick Smith, ed., *The Media and the Gulf War: The Press and Democracy in Wartime* (Washington, D.C.: Seven Locks Press, 1992); *The Media at War: The Press and the Persian Gulf Conflict* (New York: Gannett Foundation, 1991).

63. Among others, see Reuters Correspondents, *Under Fire: Untold Stories from the Front Line of the Iraq War* (Upper Saddle River, NJ: Reuters Prentice Hall, 2004); Karl Zinsmeister, *Boots on the Ground: A Month with the 82nd Airborne in the Battle for Iraq* (New York: Truman Talley Books, 2003).

64. Paul Farhi, "TV Shows Come and Go, But Licenses Live On," *Washington Post National Weekly Edition*, October 23–29, 1995, 18.

65. Frank Ahrens, "Fox Refuses to Pay FCC Indecency Fine," *Washington Post*, March 25, 2008, available at www.washingtonpost.com/wp-dyn/content/ article/2008/03/24/AR2008032402969.html; John Eggerton, "ABC Stations Challenge FCC Fine, Not Authority," *Broadcasting & Cable*, June 21, 2008, available at www.broadcastingcable.com/article/CA6572207.html.

66. Graber, *Mass Media and American Politics*, 114–15.

67. Miami Herald Publishing Co. v. Tornillo, 418 U.S. 241 (1974); Red Lion Broadcasting Co. v. FCC, 395 U.S. 367 (1969).

68. Graber, *Mass Media and American Politics*, 83–86.

69. Sam Donaldson, *Hold On, Mr. President!* (New York: Fawcett Crest, 1987), 6.

70. Edwin Diamond, *The Tin Kazoo* (Cambridge: Massachusetts Institute of Technology Press, 1975), 94.

71. Peter J. Boyer, "Famine in Ethiopia: The TV Accident That Exploded," *Washington Journalism Review* (January 1985): 20.

72. Timothy Crouse, *The Boys on the Bus* (New York: Ballantine Books, 1974), 7.

73. Cook, *Making Laws and Making News*, 47.

74. Hertsgaard, *On Bended Knee*, 314. See also Nick Kotz, "What the *Times* and *Post* Are Missing," *Washington Monthly* (March 1977): 45–49; Timothy Noah, "The Pentagon Press: Prisoners of Respectability," *Washington Monthly* (September 1983): 44; Larry Speakes with Robert Pack, *Speaking Out: The Reagan Presidency from Inside the White House* (New York: Avon Books, 1989), 282.

75. Quoted in Lawrence Weschler, "The Media's One and Only Freedom Story," *Columbia Journalism Review* (March/April 1990): 31.

76. Gerald C. Stone and Elinor Grusin, "Network TV as the Bad News Bearer," *Journalism Quarterly* 61 (Autumn 1984): 517–23; Joseph R. Dominick, "Business Coverage in Network Newscasts," *Journalism Quarterly* 58 (Spring 1981): 179–85.

77. Joe S. Foote and Michael E. Steele, "Degree of Conformity in Lead Stories in Early Evening Network TV Newscasts," *Journalism Quarterly* 63 (Spring 1986): 19–23.

78. Antony J. Blinken, "Is Anybody Out There Listening?" in *Economic Strategy and National Security: A Next Generation Approach*, ed. Patrick J. DeSouza (Boulder, CO: Westview, 2000), 81.

79. Daniel Riffe, et al., "Gatekeeping and the Network News Mix," *Journalism Quarterly* 63 (Summer 1986): 315–21.

80. Stephens, *A History of the News*, 266–68.

81. See Daniel C. Hallin, "The Media, the War in Vietnam, and Political Support: A Critique of the Thesis of an Oppositional Media," *Journal of Politics* 46 (February 1984): 21.

82. Herbert J. Gans, *Deciding What's News: A Study of CBS Evening News, NBC Nightly News, Newsweek and Time* (New York: Vintage Books, 1980), 31–38.

83. Quoted in Stephen Bates, *If No News, Send Rumors: Anecdotes of American Journalism* (New York: Henry Holt, 1989), 61.

84. David Halberstam, *The Powers That Be* (New York: Knopf, 1979), 39.

85. Gans, *Deciding What's News*, 81.

86. Frank Newport, "Number of Americans Who Feel News Coverage Is Inaccurate Increases Sharply," *Gallup News Service*, December 8, 2000.

87. See Christopher Georges, "Bad News Bearers," *Washington Monthly* (July/August 1993): 28–34; Todd Gitlin, "Whiplash," *American Journalism Review* (April 1993): 35–36; William Glaberson, "The Capitol Press vs. the President: Fair Coverage or Unreined Adversity?" *New York Times*, June 17, 1993; Tom Rosenstiel, *Strange Bedfellows: How Television and the Presidential Candidates Changed American Politics, 1992* (New York: Hyperion, 1993).

88. Emery, *The Press and America*, 269,389.

89. See L. Brent Bozell III and Brent H. Baker, eds., *And That's the Way It Isn't: A Reference Guide to Media Bias* (Alexandria, VA: Media Research Center, 1990); S. Robert Lichter and Stanley Rothman, "Media and Business Elites," *Public Opinion* (October/November 1981): 42–46, 59–60; S. Robert Lichter, Stanley Rothman, and Linda S. Richter, *The Media Elite: America's New "Powerbrokers"* (New York: Adler and Adler, 1986); William Schneider and I. A. Lewis, "Views on the News," *Public Opinion* 8 (August/September 1985): 6–11, 58–59; G. Cleveland Wilhoit and David H. Weaver, *The American Journalist: A Portrait of U.S. News People and Their Work* (Bloomington: Indiana University Press, 1986).

90. Schneider and Lewis, "Views on the News," 6.

91. See Christopher Georges, "Dole Joins in Republican Attacks on the Press, While Party Expands Use of Alternative Media," *Wall Street Journal*, May 29, 1996; Elaine S. Povich, *Partners and Adversaries: The Contentious Connection Between Congress and the Media* (Arlington, VA: Freedom Forum, 1996).

92. Edward J. Epstein, *News from Nowhere* (New York: Random House, 1973), 137, 207.

93. Busterna and Hansen, "Presidential Endorsement Patterns," 286–94.

94. Quoted in Graeme Browning, "Too Close for Comfort?" *National Journal*, October 3, 1992, 2247.

95. Gloria Borger, "Cynicism and Tankophobia," *U.S. News & World Report* (June 5, 1995): 34.

96. *The People, the Press, and Their Leaders 1995* (Washington, D.C.: Times Mirror Center for the People & the Press, 1995), 9.

97. Quoted in Borger, "Cynicism and Tankophobia," 34.

98. Thomas E. Patterson, *Out of Order* (New York: Vintage, 1994), 245; Larry Sabato, *Feeding Frenzy: How Attack Journalism Has Transformed American Politics* (New York: Free Press, 1991), 207.

99. *The People, the Press*, 112–13.

100. Ben Bradlee, *A Good Life: Newspapering and Other Adventures* (New York: Simon & Schuster, 1995), 406.

101. See Michael Massing, *Now They Tell Us* (New York: New York Review of Books, 2004).

102. Quoted in Auletta, "Fortress Bush," 62.

103. See "From the Editors: The *Times* and Iraq," *New York Times*, May 26, 2004; and Howard Kurtz, "The Post on WMDs: An Inside Story," *Washington Post*, August 12, 2004.

104. Quoted in Auletta, "Fortress Bush," p. 62.

105. Quoted in Brian Stetler, "Was Press a War 'Enabler'? 2 Offer a Nod from Inside," *New York Times*, May 30, 2008.

106. Peter J. Boyer, *Who Killed CBS? The Undoing of America's Number One News Network* (New York: Random House, 1988), 308.

107. Robert Krolick, "Reuven Frank and Ed Bliss on TV News," *Washington Journalism Review* (July/August 1991): 43; see also Rick Marin with Peter Katel, "Miami's Crime Time Live," *Newsweek* (June 20, 1994): 71–72.

108. Walter Goodman, "Nightly News Looks Beyond the Headlines," *New York Times*, July 7, 1991.

109. Bogart, *Press and Public*, 200–204.

110. See James M. Lindsay, "The Unloved Trumpet: The News Media Report on the War on Terrorism," in *American Politics after September 11*, 2nd ed., ed. James M. Lindsay (Cincinnati, OH: Atomic Dog Publishing, 2002).

111. See, for example, Robert Entman, *Democracy without Citizens: Media and the Decay of American Politics* (New York: Oxford University Press, 1989), 103–8.

112. Mark Jurkowitz, "Broadcast TV News Losing Viewers to Internet, Study Says," *Boston Globe*, June 12, 2000.

113. Erika Falk and Sean Aday, "Are Voluntary Standards Working? Candidate Discourse on Network Evening News Programs," December 20, 2000, available at www.annen-bergpublicpolicycenter.org/03politicalcommunication/freetime/2000-voluntary%20standards%20report.pdf. See also "Local TV News Gives Cold Shoulder to Political Candidates," October 16, 2002, available at www.learcenter.org/html/about/index.php?cm=/lclna101602.

114. See John Tierney, "Sound Bites Become Smaller Mouthfuls," *New York Times*, January 23, 1992.

115. Pew Research Center for the People & the Press, "Voters Liked Campaign 2004, But Too Much Mud-Slinging," November 11, 2004, 3, available at www.people-press.org/reports/display.php3?ReportID=233.

116. Quoted in Elizabeth Kolbert, "Bypassing the Press Helps Candidates; Does It Also Serve the Public Interest?" *New York Times*, November 8, 1992.

117. Dan Balz, "Dreaming of a Resurgence," *Washington Post*, September 20, 2000.

118. Quoted in Steven Luxenberg, "Is TV to Blame?" *Washington Post*, November 12, 2000.

119. Felicity Barringer, "CBS Plans Changes in Election Night Reporting," *New York Times*, January 5, 2001; Howard Kurtz, "Errors Plagued Election Night Polling Service," *Washington Post*, December 22, 2000; Howard Kurtz, "Exit Wound: Polls Led Networks Astray," *Washington Post*, November 9, 2000; Lisa de Moraes, "Next Time, Fox News May Not Elect to Use VNS," *Washington Post*, November 30, 2000.

120. Kurtz, "Errors Plagued Election Night Polling Service."

121. Percy H. Tannenbaum and Leslie J. Kostrich with Eric R. A. N. Smith and Michael Berg, *Turned-On TV/Turned Off Voters: Policy Options for Election Projections* (Beverly Hills, CA: Sage, 1983).

122. Kurtz, "Errors Plagued Election Night Polling Service"; Luxenberg, "Is TV to Blame?"

123. Jane Mayer, "George W.'s Cousin," *New Yorker* (November 20, 2000): 36, 38.

124. Ibid; de Moraes, "Next Time, Fox May Not Elect to Use VNS."

125. Jim Rutenberg, "Report Says Problems Led to Skewed Survey Data," *New York Times*, November 5, 2004.

126. Sheryl Gay Stolberg, "Bush Says Report on Bank Data Was Disgraceful," *New York Times*, June 27, 2006, p. A1.

127. Martin Linsky, *Impact: How the Press Affects Federal Policymaking* (New York: Norton, 1986), 238.

128. See, for example, "Two Leaks, But by Whom?" *Newsweek* (July 27, 1987): 16.

129. Johanna Neuman, "McClellan Blames Bush, Not Aides, for Disillusionment," *Los Angeles Times*, May 29, 2008. Available at www.latimes.com/news/nationworld/nation/la-na-mcclellan30-2008may30,0,6516974.story.

130. Linsky, *Impact*, 238.

131. James J. Kilpatrick, "'Trust-Me' Journalism: An Identifiable Source Is Fed Up," *Washington Journalism Review* (January/February 1988): 43–45; William H. Lewis, "The Cloning of the American Press," *Washington Quarterly* 2 (Spring 1979): 31–38; Roger Morris, "Eight Days in April: The Press Flattens Carter with the Neutron Bomb," *Columbia Journalism Review* (November/December 1978) 25–30.

132. See, for example, Charles Layton, "Miller Brouhaha," *American Journalism Review*, August/September 2003, available at www.ajr.org/Article .asp?id=3057.

133. See Bob Woodward and Carl Bernstein, *All the President's Men* (New York: Simon & Schuster, 1974).

9

Political Parties

CHAPTER OUTLINE

On the evening of November 4, 2008, Senator Barack Obama, Senator John McCain, and hundreds of candidates for the U.S. Senate, House, and state and local offices eagerly listened to election returns. The candidates knew that the presidential race would be close, and many expected to be watching the returns until the wee hours of the next morning. The television networks announced the historic victory of President Obama the minute the polls closed on the west coast. Many other candidates, however, did not learn the results of their efforts until late that night, or in some cases, days or even weeks later.

Despite President Obama's early victory, his interest in the election results continued throughout the night. He cared about the results of more than just his own race because every time a Democratic candidate won a race for a seat in the House or Senate, a governorship or any one of many other offices, it strengthened his hand for governing the nation. Obama wasn't running alone; he was running as part of a Democratic team.

Who were all those candidates, and how did they come to run together under the same party label? In what sense were they a team? And why do two teams, the Democrats and Republicans, dominate American politics?

Parties were not written into the Constitution. Indeed, they were never even considered when the Founders debated the Constitution. Instead, politicians created parties to help them achieve their goals—winning elections and making public policy. For these reasons, the nature of parties changes over time and differs from one part of the country to another. Parties change because the people who make them up and who seek office respond to public preferences and to the rules and laws that govern competition for elected office—both of which vary over time and from place to place. To serve as a means for the people to control government decisions, the parties must respond to public opinion. Yet to serve as vehicles for politicians to win elections, they must respond to the rules of the system as well.

In this chapter, we will examine what political parties are and what functions they perform for the political system—from contesting elections to organizing the government and providing a means for people to hold their elected officials accountable. We will discuss why our nation has two centrist parties rather than a multiparty system. We will sketch out America's electoral history so that we can examine how parties have behaved over the past 200 years, and we will describe the current state of party organizations—including the roles they play in elections today.

9-1 WHAT IS A POLITICAL PARTY?

People have many images of political parties: the hoopla of presidential nominating conventions, smoke-filled backrooms full of politicians, and local party workers canvassing their neighbors for votes. All these images reflect different aspects of the truth.

The core of a political party's purpose, and the basis on which most scholars define parties, is their role as *electoral organizations.* A **political party** is a coalition of people seeking to control the government by contesting elections and winning office. A party differs from a single candidate's campaign because a party runs an entire slate of candidates for a wide range of offices rather than just one campaign for one office. A party also differs from an interest group because a party seeks to win offices rather than to influence those in office to win benefits from the government.

Party coalitions form around the basic **political cleavages**, or divisions, in society. For instance, on economic issues, today's Democratic politicians are mostly liberal—they represent the working class, the poor, and most minority groups in political conflicts. Today's Republican politicians are generally economic conservatives—they represent the wealthy and business interests. Thus, the two major parties offer opposing views on economic issues.

Of course, not all Democrats are liberal on economic issues, and not all Republicans are conservative. The overlap stems largely from the fact that economic differences are not the only important political cleavage in American society. A second basic cleavage divides people on social issues. As we saw in Chapter 6, Democrats tend to be liberal and Republicans tend to be conservative, but people's positions on social and economic issues do not always fall neatly along party lines; to some extent, these cleavages are cross-cutting. This means that within each party, we find some politicians who are liberal on economic issues and conservative on social issues, and vice versa. For example, we find both prochoice Republicans and pro-life Democrats. Because the cleavages do not form one perfect dividing line, most Democratic politicians are liberal and most Republican politicians are conservative, but both parties contain a mixture. So, although the parties offer voters a choice, the choice may not always be clear.[1]

political party
A coalition of people seeking to control the government by contesting elections and winning office.

political cleavages
Divisions in society around which parties organize.

Source: © Tom Sloan/AFP/Getty Images.

President George W. Bush at a White House press conference the day after the November 2006 election, explaining that the Republicans received a "thumping" at the polls.

To contest elections, the Democrats and the Republicans have developed a network of party organizations, from their national committees in Washington, D.C., to state committees and down to county committees and local clubs. In some towns and cities, parties are even organized at the neighborhood level. In addition, both parties have formed a number of affiliated organizations for special purposes such as raising money for congressional candidates and training campaign managers. These organizations work to recruit and nominate the candidates who run under the party's banner, to help the candidates win office after they are nominated, and to manage the party's affairs between elections.

9-1a Party Functions

A useful way to think about political parties and to see how they provide a means for the people to control their government is to consider the functions parties may perform in our political system. We say *may* perform because parties do not always perform these functions, and when they do, they may not perform them fully. At different times and different places in the country, parties have taken on different roles and behaved differently. The degree to which parties perform various functions depends on what party leaders and activists think will help them win elections and control the government. That is, party leaders look at the rules governing campaigns and elections as well as other factors such as current campaign technology, public preferences on the issues, and voter loyalties when they decide how best to organize their parties.[2] In other words, parties are changeable. They adapt to circumstances. So when we generalize about what functions parties perform, we must qualify our statements by noting that parties do not *always* do these things.

Broadly speaking, the parties link the people and the government by providing *organization* and *information.* The organization is easy to see—party headquarters, committees, campaigns, nominations, and so forth provide it. The information is less obvious, but no less vital. Parties provide information because the parties organize around basic political cleavages. The party labels, therefore, inform voters and other candidates roughly where candidates stand on the issues. When a voter knows little about the candidates up for election (which is unfortunately all too common, as we saw in Chapter 6), party labels provide essential cues about which side the candidates are likely to take on issues. If a voter knows only the candidates' names and party labels, for instance, the voter can make a fair guess that the Democrat will favor more spending on jobs programs or environmental protection and the Republican will favor less. Similarly, party labels provide information to activists and other politicians about whether given politicians are likely allies.

A look at seven specific functions that the parties usually perform shows how they help the political system work by organizing and providing information.

The mule is the symbol of the Democratic Party. The elephant is the symbol of the Republican Party—often called the "Grand Old Party" or "GOP" for short.

First, parties *recruit candidates* to run for office. In some cases, party leaders seek out potential candidates, urge them to run, and offer them support. Both the Democrats and the Republicans recruited Dwight Eisenhower, the enormously popular general who commanded the Allied forces during World War II, to run for president in 1952.[3] Far more commonly, *self-starting candidates* seek out party leaders (among others) and ask for their support. In either case, the party leaders help bring together candidates and campaign donors, activists to work in the campaigns, and the people with the technical skills needed in campaigns—campaign managers, fund-raisers, pollsters, public relations specialists, and others.

Recruiting candidates may seem to be a minor task, but it can have a huge impact on what the parties look like and where they stand on the issues. A path-breaking study of representation in public office found that a major reason why men outnumber women in Congress and other elected offices is that men are far more likely to be asked to run (see Chapter 7).[4] Encouragement from party leaders, elected officials, and political activists affects both who runs, and because women are more liberal than men on many issues, what the political beliefs of elected officials are.

Second, parties *nominate candidates.* Through party primaries, caucuses, conventions, or other means, parties bestow the right to run using the party labels. In doing so, they reduce the field of candidates to only a few—and usually to only two serious competitors, the Democratic and Republican nominees. In eliminating most of the candidates, nominations simplify the choices for voters and give them a more manageable task—learning about only two candidates instead of a pack of them.

The most common method of nominating candidates today is the **direct primary**—an election in which voters and not party leaders directly choose a party's nominees for office. The three different types of primaries vary according to who is allowed to vote. **Closed primaries**, used in about forty states, require voters to indicate their party affiliations before Election Day, when they register to vote. **Open primaries** allow voters to choose which party primary they will vote in on Election Day, when they arrive at the polls. **Blanket primaries** permit voters to cast their ballots for candidates from any party, casting one vote for each office. In all types of primaries, the winner of the primary becomes the party's nominee and goes on to run in the general election against the nominees of other parties.

An alternative nomination method is the **caucus/convention system**, in which registered party members attend a party caucus, or meeting, to choose a nominee. If the election were for a large district such as a state, the party would hold a number of local caucuses. Each caucus would then choose representatives, or delegates, to express their views and vote on their behalf at a statewide convention. In either case, people who consider themselves members of the party and who care enough to show up at the caucuses (which are far more time consuming than merely voting) make the

direct primary

An election in which voters and not party leaders directly choose a party's nominees for political office.

closed primaries

Direct primaries in which voters must register their party affiliations before Election Day.

open primaries

Direct primaries in which voters may choose which party primary they will vote in on Election Day.

blanket primaries

Direct primaries in which voters may cast ballots for candidates of any party but may vote only once for each office.

caucus/convention system

A nomination method in which registered party members attend a party caucus, or meeting, to choose a nominee. In large districts, local caucuses send delegates to represent them at a convention.

nominations. Because relatively few people normally turn out for party caucuses, party activists have greater control over the nomination process than they would with primaries. Their control has a cost, however, because critics can accuse the party of having "undemocratic" nomination methods. Most states now use direct primaries to select party nominees.

Third, parties *mobilize voters.* Through party identification, parties develop emotional bonds with voters and use these bonds to encourage voting (see Chapter 7). In a more practical vein, parties organize voter registration and get-out-the-vote drives all across the country. They are by no means the only groups to do this. Candidate campaign organizations and interest groups also run registration and get-out-the-vote drives, but parties often lead these activities.

Fourth, parties *contest elections.* They play a role in providing the candidates, the money, the managers, and the army of campaign workers that make up the campaigns. For most party activists, this is a party's core purpose—the campaigns.

Fifth, parties *form governments.* Once elected, officials organize governments along party lines. Presidents and governors normally choose from their own party ranks for appointments (see Chapters 12 and 15). Members of Congress and state legislatures also choose their leaders and fill their committees on the basis of party loyalties (see Chapter 11). Forming governments along party lines makes sense because each party consists of politicians representing voters who generally take the same side on the basic cleavages dividing society—the cleavages around which the parties formed.

Sixth, parties *coordinate policy across independent units of government.* Few problems can be dealt with effectively by a single branch of government; rather, most require the cooperation of the president, Congress, and state and local governments. Party loyalties often provide the basis for building the coalitions needed to develop public policies, to enact them with legislation or executive action, and to implement them. The cleavages underlying the party coalitions bolster that loyalty.

Seventh, parties *provide accountability.* The party labels offer easy cues for voting decisions because they identify which side politicians are likely to take on particular issues. Moreover, voters who like recent government policies or performance can express their approval by voting for members of the party that controls the White House or the statehouse. Those who dislike recent policies or performance can vote to "throw the rascals out." The party labels make it easy for voters to identify whom to reward or punish.

Politicians, of course, did not set up political parties for the purpose of providing accountability. The politicians who invented parties thought that parties would help them win elections and control government. Accountability turned out to be a by-product— but a crucial one for our system of government.[5]

To see why parties are crucial to democracy, consider the following thought experiment. What would we do if we had no political parties? For starters, there would be more candidates for each political office. Instead of choosing between Obama and McCain as the only candidates with a serious chance to win, we might have been given a choice of a dozen or more candidates running for the presidency in 2008. There were, after all, a dozen prominent candidates for the Democratic and Republican nominations in 2008, and earlier presidential contests have seen even more candidates. With so many candidates and without the party label to help voters figure out where the candidates stood on the issues, the choice for voters would be much harder. To worsen the situation, every four years would bring a new set of candidates. Because the major parties have existed throughout our lives, we can learn about them slowly over time. Without parties, however, we would have to learn about a new set of candidates for every election. The result would be many confused voters. That is why most political scientists agree with E. E. Schattschneider's famous claim: "Political parties created democracy, and...democracy is unthinkable save in terms of parties."[6]

As you can see, the seven functions that political parties serve extend well beyond just winning elections. Although the primary role of political parties is to act as electoral organizations, they also play a role in government—organizing it and forming the coalitions around which policy disputes are fought. In addition, they play a role in the electorate—organizing voters into large, informal coalitions of party identifiers and offering comprehensible choices to the voters.

By performing these functions, political parties form a critical link between the people and their government. They provide the organization and information that make understanding government, following politics, and choosing among competing candidates manageable tasks. Without parties, the chaotic free-for-all of elections would be difficult or impossible for ordinary citizens to understand.

9-2 CHARACTERISTICS OF U.S. POLITICAL PARTIES

Two of the fundamental characteristics of our political system are that we have a **two-party system** and that the dominant parties are centrist, or close to the political center. Since the development of political parties shortly after the founding of the nation, two major political parties have normally dominated American politics. During a brief period from 1816 to 1824, only one party was strong enough to contest the presidency seriously, and significant minor party challenges and independent presidential candidacies have cropped up from time to time (e.g., George Wallace's American Independent Party in 1968, Ross Perot's Reform Party campaigns for the presidency in 1992 and 1996, and Ralph Nader's pivotal 2000 and 2004 campaigns for the presidency), but for the most part, only two parties have had a realistic chance to win the presidency or

two-party system
A political system in which two major parties dominate.

centrist parties

Parties close to the political center.

any substantial number of seats in Congress. Since the formation of the Republican Party in 1854, those two parties have been the Democrats (who were organized in the early 1800s) and the Republicans.

Our two major parties have always tended to take stands close to the political center; that is, we have **centrist parties**. Democrats and Republicans certainly disagree about a wide range of issues, but their disagreements are narrower than disagreements among parties in many other democratic nations.[7] For instance, several western European nations have communist and socialist parties, which favor far larger government roles in regulating business and economic relations in society. In the United States, by contrast, even the most liberal Democrats favor capitalism and would reject the more extreme, heavy-handed government interference in the marketplace that occurs in some other countries.[8] On the other end of the political spectrum, some western European countries have fascist or monarchist parties, which favor limiting who can participate in elections (usually on racial or ethnic grounds). In the United States, even the most conservative Republicans favor democracy and reject any proposal restricting the right to vote. So by standards of democracies around the world, the differences between the dominant American parties are relatively small; they tend to take stands not too far from one another.

9-2a The Spatial Theory of Elections

The *spatial theory of elections* helps us to understand why the United States has two centrist parties.[9] The spatial model was developed to explain how politicians and voters would behave if they were acting rationally to achieve their goals. It shows how different sets of rules create different incentives and consequently cause politicians and voters to behave differently. Under American election rules, politicians are more likely to achieve their goals if they join one of two centrist parties; under other types of election rules used in other nations, many parties can thrive. Different rules produce different outcomes.

To focus on the effects of rules, the spatial model simplifies the real world and attempts to identify the essential characteristics of our political system that influence politicians and voters. As a description, therefore, the model does poorly; it doesn't take into account many of the complexities of particular elections. As a tool to help us understand how our system works, however, the model is useful.

The spatial theory assumes first that all political issues can be represented by a single left-right scale and that all parties, politicians, and voters can be placed on this scale. The scale shown in Figure 9–1, for instance, ranges from 0—an extreme liberal—to 100—an extreme conservative. On this scale, a liberal such as Senator Barbara Boxer (D-CA) might be placed at 10, whereas a conservative such as Senator Mitch McConnell (R-KY) might be placed at 95. (See Boxes 6–2 and 6–3 for profiles of Boxer and

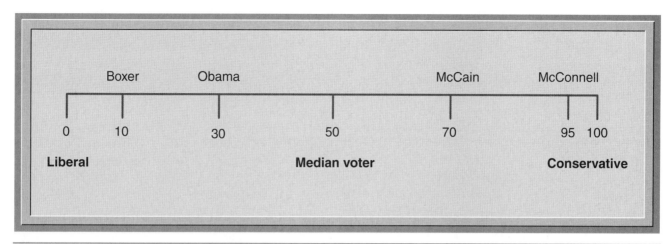

Figure 9-1 The Spatial Model of Elections. The *median voter hypothesis* predicts that candidates will move toward the median, or political center, because that position gives them the greatest chance of winning.

McConnell.) The more moderate 2008 Democratic and Republican presidential candidates, Senators Obama and McCain, would be closer to the center. The second assumption of the spatial model is that the voters know exactly where they and the candidates stand on the issue scale. That is, the model simplifies the real world by assuming that voters have "perfect information" about what politicians would do if they were elected. Third, the theory assumes that all people vote, choosing the candidate whose views are closest to theirs.

From these assumptions, the spatial model derives a conclusion known as the **median voter hypothesis**—namely, that the best possible position for a politician who cares only about winning elections is the center. The "center" is the position of the median voter, that is, the individual voter who has exactly half of all other voters to his or her left, and the remaining half of all voters to his or her right. On the scale in Figure 9–1, the center is the midpoint of the scale, 50.

The logic behind the median voter hypothesis can be seen in Figure 9–1. Consider first what would happen if the two parties chose Boxer and McConnell as candidates. Because every voter votes for the candidate closest to him or her on the scale, the voters to the left of Boxer would vote for Boxer, and those to the right of McConnell would vote for McConnell. The midpoint between Boxer (at 10 on the scale) and McConnell (at 95) is 52.5, so everyone to the left of 52.5 would vote for Boxer, and everyone to the right of 52.5 would vote for McConnell. So Boxer, with the 50 percent of the voters to the left of 50 on the scale, plus the additional voters between 50 and 52.5, would have a majority and win the election.

Now suppose that the Republicans nominated Senator McCain instead of Mitch McConnell. The midpoint between McCain (at 70 on the scale) and Boxer is to the left of center—at 40, which would yield a Republican victory. Because McCain is closer to the center, he would gain the half of the votes to the right of center and some to the left of center because he would still be the closer candidate

median voter hypothesis
The theory that the best possible position for a politician who cares only about winning elections is the center—that is, in the position of the median voter.

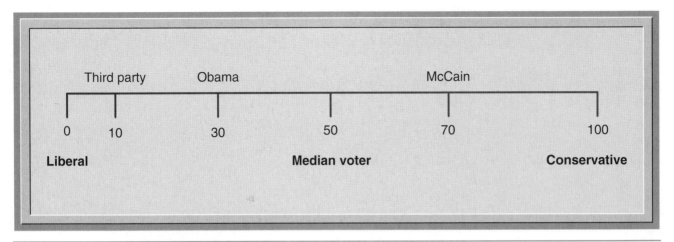

Figure 9–2   A Third-Party Challenge. The spatial model of elections predicts that minor-party challenges will probably lose and will hurt the major-party candidate who is closest to the minor party.

for voters from 40 to 50 on the scale. Those on the extreme right might prefer McConnell to McCain, but offered the choice between McCain and Boxer, they would vote for McCain.

The major point the spatial model and median voter hypothesis makes is that, given American election rules, the candidate closer to the center should win the election if the voters care only about issues (i.e., if they ignore candidate character, race, gender, and other nonissue considerations). Therefore, if the parties care only about winning elections (as they do in the simplified world of the spatial model), they should nominate candidates as close to the center, or median voter, as possible. This, according to the median voter hypothesis, is the reason the Democrats and Republicans are centrist political parties.

To see why we have only two major political parties, consider the public's reaction to a minor-party challenge. Figure 9–2 shows a hypothetical challenge from a left-wing party. If people vote for the candidate who is closest to them on the political spectrum, the challenge will draw off a substantial number of liberal votes, which would otherwise go to the Democrat, and thus make it extremely difficult for the Democratic nominee to beat even a conservative Republican. Therefore, minor-party challenges from the left or right are not only unlikely to win, but they are also likely to harm the party closest to them on the political spectrum and help the party that is further away (and with which they have the sharpest policy differences). In this way, minor parties in the United States are usually self-defeating.

Ralph Nader's presidential bid under the Green Party banner in 2000 provides a striking example of the consequences of minor-party challenges (see Box 9–1). Running far to the left of Al Gore, Nader sought to focus the nation's attention on corporate influence in the United States and to build a movement to reduce that influence. Although he drew few votes nationwide, he won enough to deliver victory to Governor George W. Bush. In Florida alone, Nader won more than 97,000 votes. Exit polls showed that fewer

POINT OF ORDER

Box 9–1 Minor Parties and the Federal Election Campaign Act

Ralph Nader's 2000 presidential campaign will no doubt be remembered because it took enough votes away from Al Gore to deliver the victory to George W. Bush. Yet that was not Nader's primary goal. Nader did not set out to defeat Gore, although at times during his campaign he suggested that having Bush in the White House would aid his cause in the long run. Nor did Nader set out to win the presidency. He openly admitted that he had no chance of winning. Instead, Nader set out to start a movement, and he wanted federal tax dollars to help him.

The 1971 Federal Election Campaign Act (FECA) and its 1974 amendments were passed by Congress to reduce the influence of money in presidential campaigns and prevent corruption. To achieve that goal, Congress set up a system to provide matching funds for small campaign contributions during the primaries when many candidates sought their

Green Party candidate Ralph Nader campaigned for matching funds as much as for the presidency.

party's nomination and to pay for the entire cost of the campaigns for major-party candidates after they were nominated. (See Chapter 12 for details.) The underlying idea was that if the major-party candidates did not need to raise campaign money, they would not be indebted to interest groups or wealthy donors.

Eventually, a series of Supreme Court decisions and congressional amendments to FECA opened new ways for special interests and wealthy donors to donate money, so presidential candidates continued to raise money and critics continued to call for campaign finance reforms. Nevertheless, the original FECA laws offering federal funding for campaigns remained in place. Ralph Nader's Green Party campaign sought to capture some of that money.

When Congress established a program for funding presidential candidates, a key question that faced them was this: Which political parties should get the money? Congress certainly intended that most or all of the money should go to the two major parties—the Democrats and Republicans. After all, they did not want to give tax dollars to the Communist Party, the American Nazi Party, or for that matter, the Birthday Party. However, Congress recognized that it would be unconstitutional to write a law saying that only two specific political parties would be funded. So how should they deal with minor parties?

The solution Congress devised was to give full funding to any political party that received at least 30 percent of the presidential vote and partial

funding to any party that received at least 5 percent of the vote. The 30 percent threshold virtually guaranteed that the Democrats and Republicans would always receive full funding. The 5 percent minimum threshold guaranteed that minor parties on the political fringes, such as the Communist Party, would never get any support from the government. It did, however, leave open the possibility that some minor parties would qualify for federal funding. That was Nader's goal.

In the end, Nader fell short, receiving only 2.7 percent of the vote. It was the strongest performance by any minor party in 2000, but it was not strong enough. Had Nader achieved his 5 percent goal, he would have received a check for more than $7 million from the Federal Election Commission to help pay his 2000 campaign expenses. Of course, any money left after paying off campaign debts could be spent on future elections. Moreover, the FECA also provides that any party that qualifies by receiving at least 5 percent of the vote in one presidential election automatically receives funding for the next presidential election as well. So achieving the 5 percent goal in 2000 would mean receiving an additional $7 million for the Green Party's 2004 campaign. If the goal is to build a political movement, that kind of campaign cash can be a real boost.

Sources: Sam Hananel, "Democrats Quick to Label Nader a Spoiler as He Runs for President Again," February 23, 2004; Andrea Stone, "Despite Charges of Being 'Spoiler,' Nader Unapologetic for Campaign," *USA Today*, November 3, 2004, 15a; "Report: Gore Won Popular Vote by 539,897," *Washington Post*, December 21, 2000, A9.

than half of Nader voters said they would have voted for Gore if Nader had not run. Nevertheless, the additional votes from Nader would have been far more than enough to deliver both Florida and the presidency to Gore had Nader not run.[10] As a consequence, Nader's candidacy helped to elect the candidate with whom he had the greatest differences.

Given Nader's impact on the 2000 election, it was no surprise that Republican activists flocked to support him in 2004. Their reasoning was simple. If they could get Nader on the ballot in the November election and provide him with funds to campaign, he would attract Democratic votes away from Senator John Kerry and help President Bush win reelection. As a result, Republican organizations in Arizona, Florida, Michigan, Oregon, and Wisconsin worked to qualify Nader for the ballot, and roughly 10 percent of Nader's major campaign donors were longtime Republican donors. Citizens for a Sound Economy, an organization led by former Republican House Majority Leader Dick Armey, even ran phone banks for Nader. None of these people, of course, actually wanted Nader to win. They only wanted to use him to defeat Kerry.[11] Unlike the race in 2000, Nader did not win enough votes to affect the 2004 outcome. The election was close, but George W. Bush would have won even without Nader's help. Nevertheless, looking at an example such as 2000, it is small wonder that serious minor-party challenges from the left or right are uncommon.

When minor party challengers do enter a race, they justify their campaigns by pointing to issues that they want the major parties to address. In his 2008 Libertarian Party campaign, for example, former representative Bob Barr (R-GA) explained that he was running because he was frustrated that Republican politicians have abandoned their party's core values of small government and limited spending. He wanted to raise these and other issues that Senators Obama and McCain were ignoring.[12]

9-2b The U.S. Two-Party System versus Multiparty Systems

Although the United States has two dominant, centrist parties, many other democracies around the world have more than two, some of which are not centrist. The difference is largely the result of the institutions, laws, and rules that govern different nations.

The United States has a **single-member, plurality electoral system**. In such a system, Congress and state legislatures are divided into geographic districts; the House of Representatives, for instance, has 435 districts. Each district elects a single member as its representative, and the winner in each district is the candidate who receives a plurality of the vote—that is, more votes than any other candidate.

Many democratic nations, unlike the United States, have a **proportional representation system** (or PR system). In such systems, each party puts forward a list of its nominees for the nation or for a large area such as a state or province, and citizens vote for the list as a whole. This means that each legislator is elected by and represents the entire nation or state rather than an individual district. In PR systems, the party wins seats in the legislature in proportion to the number of votes it receives. For instance, if a party receives 20 percent of the vote, it wins 20 percent of the seats in the legislature.[13]

The spatial model yields different predictions for single-member, plurality systems and proportional representation systems. In the United States and other single-member, plurality systems—as

single-member, plurality electoral system

A system in which each district elects a single member as its representative; the winner in each district is the candidate who receives a plurality of the vote.

proportional representation system

A system in which legislators are elected at large and each party wins legislative seats in proportion to the number of votes it receives.

we explained in Section 9-2a—a minor-party challenge virtually always ends in defeat. Consequently, nations with these rules almost always develop two-party systems. This generalization is often called **Duverger's Law**, after the person who first observed it.[14]

In a PR system, however, minor parties can prosper. Consider the hypothetical example in Figure 9–2. In a PR system, both the Democrats and the new left-wing party would win seats in the legislature. Typically, they would then work together to seek their common goals. So proportional representation election rules often produce multiparty systems. In practical terms, if the United States had a PR system, the Green Party would have won a few seats in Congress, and Nader would have been the leader of a small party that worked with the Democrats to form a coalition in support of their legislative goals. In our system, however, Nader and the Democrats are bitter enemies because Nader's success put George W. Bush in the White House.

Comparing the single-member, plurality and proportional representation systems helps us to see how rules and institutional structures create incentives for politicians and citizens to behave in different ways to obtain their goals. Under American rules, politicians who want to become president join one of the major parties; in PR systems, politicians seeking to lead their nations often have a wider choice of parties to join and may even do better by forming their own political parties.

9-2c The Spatial Model and Party Change over Time

Not only can the spatial model help us explain individual elections, it can help us explain how the parties evolved over time as well. To show this, we will discuss two examples—the politics of civil rights during the 1950s and 1960s, and the responses of the Republican and Democratic parties to their presidential election defeats in 1992 and 2004. As we shall show, the spatial model offers useful insights into the long-term change in electoral fortunes of the parties.

The Politics of Civil Rights
We have been speaking of parties taking and changing positions almost as if parties were individuals who could announce what they believe. Parties do take official positions in documents such as the Democratic and Republican **party platforms** (i.e., the statements of beliefs that presidential nominating conventions issue every four years), but there is more to party positions than that.[15] Most people see the positions of presidents, presidential candidates, and party leaders as representing the positions of the party as well. To see how party positions change in the real world, consider how the Democratic and Republican parties changed their views during the 1950s and 1960s on the issue of civil rights.[16]

In the 1950s, both the Democratic and Republican parties took moderate, centrist stands on issues related to civil rights for

Duverger's Law
The generalization that if a nation has a single-member, plurality electoral system, it will develop a two-party system.

party platforms
Official statements of beliefs, values, and policy positions that national party conventions issue.

African Americans. Of the two parties, the Republicans were slightly more supportive of civil rights, as they had been since they were founded in the 1850s as the antislavery party. The Democrats, by contrast, sought to avoid taking any firm stands on civil rights—a pro-civil rights stand would offend southern whites, who delivered the South to the Democrats in every presidential election; an anti-civil rights stand would offend northerners, who favored at least some progress toward integration.[17]

The parties' positions could be seen in their 1956 platforms. On the subject of the Supreme Court's decision in the historic *Brown v. Board of Education* case, which declared government laws mandating segregation in public schools to be unconstitutional (see Chapter 5), the 1956 Democratic platform said almost nothing. It observed only that "recent decisions of the Supreme Court of the United States relating to segregation in publicly supported schools and elsewhere have brought consequences of vast importance to our Nation as a whole and especially to communities directly affected."[18] The Republican platform supported the Court's decision, saying, "The Republican Party accepts the decision of the U.S. Supreme Court that racial discrimination in publicly supported schools must be progressively eliminated."[19]

In the 1960 election, pushed by an escalating series of boycotts, sit-ins, marches, and mass demonstrations in favor of civil rights, both parties moved toward greater support for equality for African Americans. The Democratic candidate, Senator John F. Kennedy, was regarded as slightly more supportive of civil rights because of a symbolic telephone call he had made to Coretta Scott King while her husband, civil rights leader the Reverend Dr. Martin Luther King, Jr., was being held prisoner in an Atlanta jail.[20] Solid differences between the two parties' platforms, though, were hard to find.

By 1963, President Kennedy had still not taken action, so civil rights leaders turned up the pressure with more and larger marches and demonstrations.[21] Many of these protests resulted in violent police retaliation, especially in Birmingham, Alabama—where police attacked peaceful marchers with fire hoses, police dogs, and clubs. By June, President Kennedy decided that he had no choice but to act. In a nationwide address, he called for an end to segregation and for serious legislation against it, and shortly after, sent a tough civil rights bill to Congress.[22] Four months later, with the bill still struggling in Congress, President Kennedy was assassinated. His successor, Vice President Lyndon Johnson, although a southerner and a former opponent of civil rights, threw his full weight behind the bill and refused to compromise. The Civil Rights Act of 1964, which passed the following June, was even more comprehensive than the bill Kennedy originally had proposed.[23]

The electoral impact of the Democratic Party's turn in favor of civil rights was shattering. The solid South had voted Democratic for nearly 100 years. That ended in the 1964 presidential election when the Republican candidate, Senator Barry Goldwater of Arizona—an opponent of the Civil Rights Act—won five states in the Deep South. African Americans, for their part, swung toward the Democrats, giving Johnson more than 90 percent of their vote.[24]

By the 1968 election, the positions of the Democratic and Republican parties had clearly changed. The Democratic presidential candidate, Vice President Hubert Humphrey, was a longtime leader in the civil rights struggle and had been the Senate floor manager for the Civil Rights Act of 1964.[25] The Republican presidential candidate was Richard Nixon. Although Nixon had been a moderate on civil rights in 1960, he turned to a "southern strategy" of wooing the white South in 1968 by moving toward a "go slow" position on desegregation and by choosing Governor Spiro Agnew of Maryland—an opponent of busing for school desegregation—as his vice presidential running mate. The campaigns reinforced the differences. The Democrats and Republicans had split—one party pushing for faster movement on civil rights, the other party urging slower action.[26]

Since the 1968 election, white southern voters have moved even more toward the Republican Party.[27] When the Democrats and Republicans agreed on civil rights and chose to leave the South alone, the South stayed with the Democrats. Once the parties differed and offered a clear choice, however, many southern whites chose to switch parties and vote Republican.[28]

This example of the politics of civil rights shows how the spatial model explains change over time. Parties do not usually take clear, unambiguous positions on issues. Rather, the views of presidential candidates and other party leaders, together with the statements in their parties' platforms and the legislation they support, make up party positions. Because party leaders disagree among themselves and sometimes disagree with their party's platform, few precise party positions exist. Similarly, the voters have no "perfect information" about party positions. Yet out of the sound and fury of day-to-day politics, positions can be seen and voters do respond to them. When the Democrats moved away from the political center on civil rights, they attracted voters who supported their stand and lost voters who opposed it—exactly as the model predicts. Thus, we see that the abstractions of the spatial model correspond to the real behavior of politicians and voters.

The Politics of Presidential Election Defeat

The implications of the rules are not lost on politicians. Although few politicians may know the spatial theory of elections, most recognize the incentives built into the system. For example, when Republicans lost control of the White House in 1992, party leaders and political pundits filled newspaper opinion columns and political magazines with articles debating what should be done to improve their party's chances in the next election. Should they move toward the center or take a more conservative stand and try to persuade voters to agree with them? A group of prominent Republican moderates formed the Moderate Majority Coalition in an effort to pull the Republican Party back toward the center. Meanwhile, Rep. Newt Gingrich (R-GA) and other conservative leaders fought to maintain their conservative position.[29] The Gingrich faction won in 1996, nominating the conservative Senator Bob Dole (R-KS), who was defeated by President Bill Clinton. Four years later, they nominated another conservative, George W. Bush. Despite the fact that Bush was further from the center than his Democratic opponent, he pulled out a victory with the help of Ralph Nader.

Four years later, after a second Bush victory, the Democrats were doing the soul searching. Some prominent liberals argued that the party should take a page from the Republican playbook and adopt a more confrontational, aggressive style. Others, such as moderate California Senator Dianne Feinstein, argued that the party must moderate its approach and move toward the center.[30] Both sides accepted the framework of the spatial model. They differed only in their views about whether voters could be persuaded to change their minds and move to the political left.

In both of our examples—in the historic shift of the Democratic and Republican parties on civil rights stretching out over a decade, and in the months of soul searching after a presidential election defeat—we see the spatial model at work. The details may be messy, but one central point stands out: Rules guide the behavior of politicians and voters. Because the rules of our single-member, plurality electoral system favor centrist parties, the parties debate their direction and periodically pull back toward the center. Similarly, minor parties may rise briefly, but they do not survive because their very existence makes it more difficult to achieve the policy goals they seek.

Before concluding our discussion of spatial models, we must comment on their limitations. Social scientists develop models that are useful simplifications of reality to help us understand it, not to be accurate descriptions of reality. Spatial models in particular are intended to help us understand the influence of election laws and the candidates' stands on the issues. To focus on the effects of laws and policy stands, the model simplifies reality by assuming that nothing else matters to voters. The model ignores candidates' races, genders, personalities, experiences, along with the government's performance in managing the economy, scandals, wars, and a host of other variables. Yet as we saw in Chapter 7, these variables do affect voters' choices. In short, the model is a poor description of some aspects of reality, and as a consequence, it does not always explain or predict correctly. Despite some lapses, however, the model helps us to understand the influence rules have on the behavior of politicians and voters.

9-3 THE HISTORY OF U.S. PARTIES AND ELECTIONS

The electoral history of the United States is a story of continuity and change. Some things have remained the same over time—the basic rules that produced our two-party system, for instance. Other things have changed—from the people and their occupations to the basic political cleavages that divide our society. In looking at the history of parties and elections in the United States, we need to sort out patterns over time so that we can describe it with enough economy to gain useful insights.

The history of elections in the United States consists of periods in which each election looks largely like the others, separated by elections of heightened conflict in which the basic party coalitions abruptly shift. Because of these patterns, historians often divide the history of elections in the United States into five—or some would argue, six—periods, or *party systems.*

9-3a The First Party System (1796–1824)

The Constitution does not mention political parties. In fact, the Founders did not foresee the development of political parties. They recognized the idea of social groups with common interests, *or factions,* as they called them at the time, but they failed to see the rise of parties.[31] Instead, shortly after the first Congress was elected, its members invented political parties because the parties helped them achieve their goals under the newly written rules of the Constitution.

The first political parties formed around a conflict arising from the framing of the Constitution—how powerful should the federal government be? The Federalist Party, led by John Adams and Alexander Hamilton, sought a strong federal government that would benefit the predominantly northern capitalist interests. The Democrat-Republican Party, led by Thomas Jefferson and James Madison, sought a weak federal government so that the agrarian interests to the south and west could prosper more. The first party coalitions thus formed around regional, *or sectional,* economic interests.

Although we refer to the Federalists and the Democrat-Republicans as political parties, they were not parties in the modern sense. They began as congressional factions in Washington. As parties, they had little existence outside the capital in their early years. Not everyone was allowed to vote in the early Republic, and without universal white male suffrage, politicians had little need to build party organizations across the nation.[32]

The Federalist Party did not last long. Following John Adams's defeat in his reelection campaign in 1800, the Federalists became the minority party. Their opposition to the War of 1812 and support for unpopular policies forced the Federalists into virtual collapse. After 1816, they left the field to the Democrat-Republicans, failing even to nominate a presidential candidate. This led to a brief period of one-party dominance by the Democrat-Republicans known (somewhat inaccurately) as the Era of Good Feelings.

9-3b The Second Party System (1828–1856)

In 1828, Andrew Jackson captured the presidency by transforming the Democrat-Republican Party into the first mass political party.[33] (The party quickly came to be known as the Democratic Party, the name it still holds.) Jackson, along with his ally (and successor as president) Martin Van Buren, took advantage of the recently passed state laws expanding the right to vote and worked to develop a truly national party. They established and subsidized a chain of newspapers to push their party. They toured the nation helping to set up state and local party organizations to support Jackson's campaign and get out the vote on Election Day.[34] Their strategy of using party organization to draw people into voting and participation brought about a fundamental change in our system of democracy. The rules had changed.[35] No longer were politics and elections left to small handfuls of elites. Participation in politics surged because Jackson's party used the new convention system to select its nominees and to adopt its platform.[36]

Jackson's success with the Democratic Party spurred the rise of the Whig Party. Like Jackson and the Democrats, the Whigs adapted to the laws extending the right to vote by building a coalition of northern industrialists and wealthy southern planters who opposed Jackson's western emphasis and his policies supporting the "common man." Although the Whigs won some presidential elections, their most prominent leaders—Daniel Webster and Henry Clay—never made it to the White House.

9-3c The Third Party System (1860–1892)

Throughout the early and middle 1800s, the morality of slavery became an increasingly contentious issue. Although both parties were divided over slavery, the Whig coalition of northerners—who mostly favored abolition—and southerners—who wanted to keep slavery—was especially divided. In 1854, the Republican party formed to offer the voters a clear antislavery choice, and the Whigs collapsed shortly afterward, not even nominating a presidential candidate in 1856.[37] In 1860, the Republican nominee, Abraham Lincoln, captured the White House, crystallizing political cleavages around the slavery issue and setting the nation on the path to the Civil War. The political system had successfully offered the voters a clear choice, but the losers were not willing to live with electoral defeat.

The Union victory in 1865 and the following twelve years of Reconstruction—the period during which the Union Army occupied the South—left white southerners united behind the Democratic Party. Outside the South, the sectional economic cleavages of the Jackson era remained, but the North shifted toward the Republicans. From the end of Reconstruction in 1877 until 1892, the Democrats and Republicans fought a series of close, competitive elections in which neither party managed to dominate. Among those close elections were two—the elections of 1876 and 1888—in which the candidate receiving the most popular votes lost the election in the electoral college. (Chapter 12 explains how this could happen.)

9-3d The Fourth Party System (1896–1928)

In 1893, with Democrat Grover Cleveland in the White House, a massive economic depression hit the nation. The stock market collapsed, banks failed, and unemployment soared. In 1896, while the country was still reeling from economic problems, the Democrats nominated William Jennings Bryan, who ran on a populist platform attacking big business and calling for the free coinage of silver. The economic effect of using silver, in addition to gold, as the basis for the money supply would be to expand the money supply and fuel inflation. This would benefit farmers and other debtors at the expense of the northeastern bankers and industrialists, the principal money lenders of the day. The Republicans countered by nominating William McKinley, who blamed the Democrats for the country's economic problems and defended business, the gold standard, and eastern interests against the "radical" westerners. Given the stark choice between opposing economic policies, the voters chose McKinley by a landslide.[38]

Following their crushing defeat, the Democrats were in disarray. They nominated Bryan twice more—in 1900 and 1908—but they slowly moved away from Bryan's populism toward what they thought was the political center, closer to the pro-business Republicans. The Republicans also moved toward the Democrats, led by President Theodore Roosevelt and other members of their progressive faction.[39] Nevertheless, for the next thirty-two years, Republican control of the White House was broken only by the two terms of Woodrow Wilson. Wilson first won the presidency in 1912 in a three-way race against the Republican incumbent—President William Howard Taft—and the former Republican president, Theodore Roosevelt.[40]

Throughout most of this period, Republicans held both houses of Congress, and with the exception of losing to Wilson, won the White House by lopsided margins. The closely fought elections of the post-Civil War years gave way to a solid Republican majority.

9-3e The Fifth Party System (1932–1980s)

As with the fourth party system, an economic collapse ushered in the fifth party system. The stock market crash of 1929 and the Great Depression that followed wreaked havoc, driving the unemployment rate up to 25 percent.[41] President Herbert Hoover's laissez-faire policies of limited government intervention in the economy did little to give people confidence in the Republican Party's ability to manage the nation's affairs. In the 1930 midterm elections, the Democrats picked up forty-nine seats in the House and eight in the Senate. Two years later, as the Depression raged on, the Democratic candidate, Franklin Delano Roosevelt (FDR), won the White House.

Once in office, FDR immediately launched a path-breaking series of reforms to turn the economy around—relief and jobs programs for the unemployed, aid for the elderly, agricultural price

New Deal coalition

The Democratic Party coalition that formed in 1932. It got its name from President Franklin Delano Roosevelt's New Deal policies.

supports for farmers, banking regulation, and other efforts.[42] As Chapters 2 and 17 discuss, these New Deal programs fundamentally altered relations between the federal government and state governments and established a new standard for federal government intervention in the economy. The political center had shifted to the left.[43]

In the elections that followed, further reforms cemented the new Democratic Party majority, labeled the **New Deal coalition**. Unlike previous party coalitions, which had been based on economic divisions between sections of the country, the New Deal coalition was an economic coalition that cut across regional lines. The poor, the working class, and union members in every part of the nation turned toward the Democrats, whereas the upper middle class and the wealthy moved toward the Republican Party. Only the South withstood the forces of realignment, remaining solidly Democratic during the Roosevelt years. Despite the economic appeal of the Republican Party to wealthier southerners, few shifted their allegiance away from the Democrats.[44]

Bolstered by the greater numbers of the working class, the Democrats began to dominate elections, as the Republicans had in previous years. Their domination lasted until the 1960s, when their grasp began to weaken. The changes to come, however, were unlike those leading up to the 1930s. Before we turn to the fall of the New Deal coalition, then, let us discuss the earlier shifts in party coalitions in more detail.

9-3f Critical Elections and Party Realignment Theory

critical elections

Elections that disrupt party coalitions and create new ones in a party realignment.

The party systems we just described were separated by **critical elections** in which normal politics was disrupted and the basic party coalitions changed. The parties fought these elections—in 1828, 1860, 1896, and 1932—with unusual intensity. The parties became more ideologically polarized, voter turnout increased, and large blocks of voters switched parties.[45] The result in each case was that the balance between the two parties shifted or—in the case of 1860—an entirely new party arose. Scholars describe these shifts as **party realignments**, in which the basic cleavages dividing the parties change.[46]

party realignments

Long-term shifts in the electoral balance between the major parties.

Two important theories explain what causes the parties to realign. One theory argues that social, economic, and demographic forces build tensions within the political system and that the parties fail to respond to these tensions.[47] The period of rapid industrialization in America after the Civil War, for instance, also saw the number of farmers decline and urban areas undergo rapid growth. The two major parties ignored the new problems of urban areas and continued to woo the diminishing number of farmers. The recession of 1893 triggered a sudden shift in party coalitions, and the parties suddenly began addressing the unfulfilled needs of the new urban, industrial sector in the United States.

The other major theory of party realignment contends that a major new issue arises that cuts across existing party lines.[48] If party leaders handle the issue well, the parties can adapt. If party leaders straddle the issue and allow public passions to become inflamed, the issue may force a realignment. According to this theory, the rising tide of antislavery sentiment was just such an issue in the 1840s and 1850s. The Whig Party attempted to avoid confronting it, hoping to preserve its coalition of northerners and southerners. By the mid-1850s, however, this response became unacceptable to many northerners, who abandoned the party. Some of them joined together in 1854 to form a new, antislavery political party—the Republicans.

Both theories of party realignment focus on the role parties play as linkages between the people and the government. The parties offer voters choices on the direction of public policy. Yet as years pass, social and economic changes occur and new issues arise. If the parties fail to adapt to the changes and to offer new choices on what the voters think are the most important issues, a realignment occurs. Thus, realignments are part of the process by which parties adjust to the changing demands people put on the government.[49]

9-3g From Realignment to Dealignment?

When scholars recognized that party realignments followed a historical pattern, they began to look for evidence of a new, post-1932 realignment. Because previous realignments had occurred roughly once every thirty-five to forty years, scholars began to look for evidence that a sixth party system had begun to emerge in the 1960s. What they found, however, was quite different. Although the party coalitions did begin to change in the 1960s, the changes did not fit the pattern of a traditional realignment. Instead, a new pattern appeared.

To understand what scholars found when they began looking for evidence of a sixth party system, recall that the fifth party system began in 1932 with the New Deal realignment. For the next thirty years, a Democratic majority dominated American politics. Most voters identified themselves as Democrats, and Democrats controlled Congress for all but a few years. The only Republican to win the White House was Dwight Eisenhower.

In the 1960s, as theories about realignment theory would predict, the Democrats began to lose their dominant position in American politics. Many voters blamed them for failing to solve the nation's problems. As a result, the Democratic Party saw its commanding lead in party identification begin to slip. Yet unlike the realignments of the past, people did not switch their allegiances to the other party. In fact, the number of Republican identifiers began to slip as well, although not as sharply. Instead, people increasingly began to identify themselves as independents, as Figure 9–3 shows. At the same time, they increasingly practiced ticket splitting, or voting for the presidential candidate of one party and the congressional or senatorial candidates of the other party (as Figure 9–3 also shows). People found it easier to vote for candidates of both parties in the same election, and party loyalties seemed to be weakening.

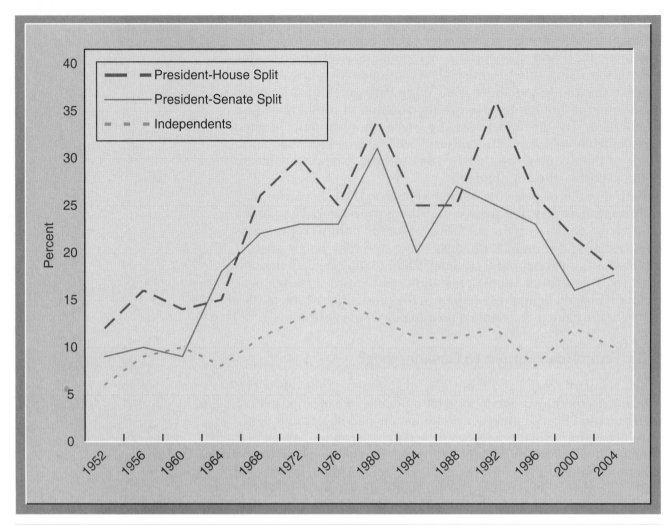

Figure 9–3   Signs of Party Dealignment. The increases in split-ticket voting and the number of people identifying
themselves as independents indicate that party labels may matter less to people than they did in the past.
Source: *Data are from SRC/CPS American National Election Studies.*

party dealignment

A trend in which voter loyalties to the two
major parties weaken.

Some observers see the rise in the number of people identifying
themselves as independents and the rise in split-ticket voting as
signs that, rather than realigning, voters have been *dealigning,* or
distancing themselves from the two major parties. Put another
way, these observers argue that since the late 1960s, the United
States has been experiencing a period of **party dealignment** in
which voters have become less partisan than they were in the
past.[50] Many Americans are no longer loyal to either the Democratic or Republican parties.

The evidence for dealignment, however, is ambiguous and subject to different interpretations. For example, although the number
of people identifying themselves as independents rose in the
1960s and early 1970s, most of the new independents were
actually independent in name only. Many people told survey
interviewers they were independents but "leaned" toward one of
the two major parties. As we saw in Chapter 7, these so-called
independents still voted as if they identified with one of the two
major parties.[51]

In the same vein, dealignment is only one possible explanation for the rise in split-ticket voting. Some scholars argue that party loyalties have not weakened since the 1960s; rather, incumbents have become harder to beat. These scholars argue that presidential and congressional candidates make different appeals based on different sorts of issues. Presidential candidates always address major issues such as what to do in Iraq and about high gasoline prices. In contrast, congressional candidates normally try to focus on their constituent services and the government benefits they have brought home to their districts. Because voters respond on the basis of different considerations when they vote for different offices, they end up splitting their ballots.[52] Again, the evidence for dealignment is ambiguous. Perhaps the electorate is dealigning, but perhaps other reasons explain ticket splitting.

To further complicate the debate over party dealignment, some evidence suggests that a party realignment is in fact occurring. Voters in the South and Rocky Mountain West are moving toward the Republican Party, whereas voters in the Northeast and Midwest are moving toward the Democratic Party.[53] One result of these trends is that split-ticket voting declined in recent elections. Whether we are witnessing party dealignment or party realignment, it is clear that the New Deal party system that began in 1932 has changed enormously—so much so that many scholars argue that the New Deal party system is dead and that a new system has begun to form.[54]

9-3h The Sixth Party System and the Uncertain Future

Since Ronald Reagan won the presidency in 1980, there have been signs that the trend toward dealignment, if there was such a trend, has stopped and that a sixth party system in which the two major parties are fairly evenly balanced has developed.

During the 1980s, the growth in the number of independents stalled, and the number of Republican identifiers increased. From 1981 through 1986, the Republicans held a majority in the Senate, for the first time since the 1950s. It seemed that a Republican realignment was finally happening. Yet by the end of the 1980s, that trend had weakened. The Democrats recaptured the Senate in 1986 and the White House in the 1992 election. In addition, the growth of Republican Party identifiers leveled off by the mid-1980s. Then, in 1994, the Republicans surged ahead again, capturing majorities in both the House and the Senate for the first time in forty years.[55] Bill Clinton was easily reelected in 1996, but the Republicans held on to their congressional majorities.

In 2000, George W. Bush took the White House for the Republicans. He actually lost the popular vote in 2000, and he won in 2004 only by a narrow 51 to 48 percent margin. The Republicans held both houses of Congress after the 2000 and 2004 elections, yet their margins of victory were far smaller than the majorities that the Democrats won in the 1960s and 1970s. In 2006, the Democrats regained control of Congress, but they, too, had narrow majorities. In 2008, Barack Obama won the White House and the Democrats gained a substantial number of seats in both houses. Yet they did it with the help Republican voters who crossed over party lines because of the weak economy, the high price of gasoline, and the War in Iraq—all of which most voters blamed on President Bush and his Republican allies. These voters still thought of themselves as Republicans. They had only temporarily switched sides, and consequently, they were not voters on whom the Democrats could depend in the future. No dominant party had emerged. In the short term, therefore, it seems likely that the United States will see more close elections in which both parties have a good chance at victory.

Looking at the election results since 1980, we can see that a slow, quiet realignment occurred during the last two decades of the century. Previous realignments have always come with crises that quickly reshaped people's party loyalties. The Civil War, the stock market crash and depression of 1893, and the Great Depression that began in 1929 all had rapid effects on the political landscape. No such crisis occurred in the last forty years, but the political landscape has certainly changed. Forty years ago, the Democrats held a huge advantage in party identification and voting for the president and Congress. By the 1980s that advantage had been effectively eliminated. The Democrats still held an edge in party identification, but because so many Democrats and independents vote for Republican candidates, the two parties are evenly matched. Although pinning an exact date on the transformation is difficult, we can safely say that some time in the 1980s, the United States entered a sixth party system.

9-4 MODERN PARTY ORGANIZATION

Because parties exist primarily to contest elections, their formal organizations parallel the different levels of government (see Figure 9–4). At the top of the party hierarchy are the national party conventions, made up of the delegates who nominate the party's presidential ticket and write the party's platform and rules. Beneath the conventions are the national party committees, which manage the national party affairs between conventions. Also at this level are the Senate and House campaign committees, which are the congressional fund-raising organizations that are independent of the national committees. The next rung down the ladder consists of the state party conventions and state party central committees. Below the state committees, in turn, are county central committees and in some areas legislative district committees, ward organizations, local party clubs, and precinct captains.

Although each party's organizational chart looks like a formal hierarchy, power and authority are not vested at the top, as they are in most organizations. Each party organization can make decisions independently on most questions and usually does not have to obey the decisions of the organization above it in the hierarchy.

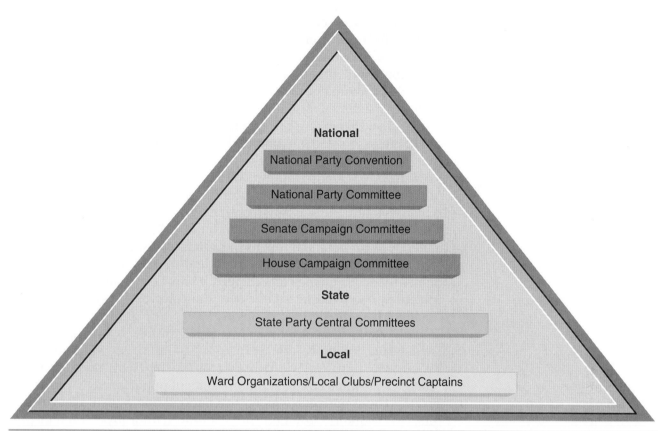

Figure 9–4 The Party Organization Hierarchy. Both the Democrats and the Republicans have hierarchically organized parties, but the organizations at the top do not have much control over the organizations below them.

Perhaps the best way to understand party organizations is to think of them as being similar to the government under the Articles of Confederation (see Chapter 2). The party organizations are loose confederations that agree to cooperate to achieve a common goal, yet cooperation is largely voluntary.

In many respects, the party organizations with the most independent power are those at the city and county levels. We shall, therefore, begin our examination of party organization at the bottom of the hierarchy.

9-4a Local Organizations

In the nineteenth century, the most important form of local party organization was the **party machine**. A machine is an organization built on the use of selective, material incentives for participation (see Chapter 10). **Selective benefits** are those that the party machine can give to its supporters and deny to others (e.g., a contract for city services), as opposed to collective benefits, which everyone gets; **material benefits** have real monetary value (e.g., a job) as opposed to nonmaterial benefits (e.g., a candidate's statement praising hard-working immigrants in her district). Of course, machines also use collective benefits that go to party supporters and opponents alike, such as public works like roads or airports,

party machine
A party organization built on the use of selective, material incentives for participation.

selective benefits
Any benefit given to a member of a group but denied to nonmembers.

material benefits
Goods and services with real, monetary value.

and nonmaterial benefits, such as statements of religious belief, to fortify their position, but these are not the keys to their success. Machines maintain power by doling out jobs, contracts, regulatory decisions, and other selective, material benefits in exchange for donations, campaign work, and support at the polls.

Party machines do not simply trade jobs for votes or buy votes with bribes. There are not enough jobs or money to do so. Instead, machines use selective, material benefits to raise an army of campaign workers who go door-to-door talking with voters and trying to persuade them to vote for the machine candidates.[56] Machines also use the campaign money they raise in all the other usual campaign methods. In the nineteenth century, this often meant giving precinct captains "walking-around money" so that they could buy small gifts for voters as tokens of friendship. Since the spread of radio and television, however, more and more machine money has gone into mass media campaigns.[57] Like other forms of party organization, party machines adapt to the rules of the system and the changes in campaign technology.

The best-known party machine since the 1950s was run by Chicago Mayor Richard J. Daley (see Box 9–2). At its height of power from 1955 until Daley's death in 1976, the Cook County Democratic Committee controlled thousands of public and private sector jobs.[58] These **patronage jobs** were handed out to loyal party workers. The workers provided the machine with a loyal force of precinct captains, who would get to know every voter in their precincts and try to persuade them to vote for the machine's candidates. This one-two punch—a loyal force of precinct captains and a steady supply of small gifts and favors—made the Daley machine unbeatable.

Although some weakened machines still survive in large northeastern and midwestern cities, most machines collapsed as the result of a series of Progressive Era reforms that swept the country from 1890 to 1920. In areas where support for progressives was strong, such as California, these reforms completely destroyed party machines and even weakened other types of parties. In other areas, such as Chicago, only some watered-down reforms passed, and machine politics survived.

Reforms that Affected Local Party Machines

The first blow to the party machines came just before the dawn of the Progressive Era—the introduction of the Australian idea of a government-printed, secret ballot, known as the **Australian ballot**. Used first in Massachusetts in 1888, the reform quickly spread across the nation.[59] As we discussed in Chapter 7, when people voted under the old system, they got their ballots from the local party and put them into ballot boxes in full view of the party's election watchers; consequently, the party could reward those who supported it and punish those who did not. The use of the Australian ballot, which allowed voters to enter a voting booth and vote in private, ended that system of reward and punishment and forced parties to persuade voters rather than threaten them.[60]

patronage jobs

Jobs given as a reward for loyal party service.

Australian ballot

A government-printed ballot (as opposed to one distributed by political parties) that allows people to vote in secret.

The People behind the Rules

Box 9–2   The Mayor and the Reformer: Richard J. Daley and Michael Shakman

When Chicago Mayor Richard J. Daley died, many journalists said the Chicago Democratic machine died with him. The machine died (or at least survives only on life support), but Daley's death was not the cause. If anyone killed the machine, it was a political reformer who helped change the rules—Michael Shakman.

RICHARD J. DALEY

Daley was born May 15, 1902, in the Bridgeport section of Chicago, the neighborhood in which he was to live his entire life. He graduated from a Catholic high school, worked briefly in the stockyards, and then at age twenty-one took a position as a precinct captain for Democratic ward boss Joe McDonough. Along with that position in the party machine came a patronage job as clerk for the City Council. Daley rose both in the machine and in government jobs until 1955, when he was elected Mayor of Chicago—a job he would hold until his death in 1976.

As Mayor and Chair of the Cook County Democratic Committee, Daley presided over a local party machine that completely dominated Chicago politics. Not only did the machine hold all the local elective offices, it controlled 35,000 government patronage jobs plus an additional 10,000 jobs in the private sector. Daley used the people in those jobs and the time and money they donated to the party to maintain his control. Although both Democratic and Republican reformers periodically challenged him in elections, none ever came close to winning.

Daley did not win merely because of his campaign workers and cash. He also won because he delivered good government—by Chicago standards. Chicago was, as its motto proclaimed, the city that worked. Under Daley's rule, government was efficient, in part because Daley could quickly resolve disputes between contending bureaucrats. Gridlock was never a problem. Moreover, Daley helped deliver federal subsidies for an enormous array of government development projects—including new expressways, a vastly expanded airport, and a revitalized downtown ("the Loop"). The rewards of having Daley as mayor were highly visible.

MICHAEL SHAKMAN

In 1969, Shakman was a young attorney and University of Chicago graduate with an abiding interest in politics. When the state of Illinois decided it was time to revise its outdated constitution, Shakman sought election as one of Chicago's delegates to the state's constitutional convention. When the election was held, however, he lost to a candidate supported by Mayor Daley's political machine. Rather than accept defeat, Shakman decided to challenge the Daley machine in court.

The premise of Shakman's legal challenge was simple, and to many observers, naive: Political patronage is illegal. Shakman pointed out that the precinct captains who had worked the neighborhoods on Election Day encouraging local residents to vote for his opponent were all city workers paid with city tax dollars to campaign. This gave machine candidates a nearly unbeatable edge over their opponents, who could not force city workers to help with their campaigns. In short, political patronage as it was practiced in Chicago virtually guaranteed that machine candidates would win political office.

Shakman eventually won two legal battles that devastated the patronage system on which the Chicago machine was built. In *Shakman v. the Democratic Organization of Cook County* (1972), a federal district court initially ruled that hiring city or county employees based on tests of political loyalty was acceptable only if the employees had policy-making positions or some confidential political role. Working for the party could not be a requirement for holding jobs such as garbage collector, building inspector, street cleaner, or clerk. In 1976, the district court extended its previous ruling to prevent firing government employees in Cook County for failure to perform political favors for a party or candidate.

A federal appeals court partially overturned the Shakman decisions but not before the newly elected, reform-minded Mayor Harold Washington accepted a consent decree in 1983 that made the Shakman decisions binding on the City of Chicago.

The Shakman decisions had a stunning effect on the Chicago machine. When Mayor Daley died in 1976, his machine controlled an estimated 35,000 government patronage jobs. When Harold Washington won the election for mayor in 1983, he had only 800 patronage jobs at his disposal to distribute to party loyalists.

A much weakened patronage system survives in Chicago, where Daley's son now serves as mayor. Few city jobs may be handed out as patronage, but some other government jobs in Cook County can be handed out in return for political favors. In addition, the machine still controls or influences many private sector jobs, although a 1996 Supreme Court decision weakened the ability of the party to use public contracts for patronage purposes. Yet without the huge supply of city jobs, the machine began to break up. Only a shadow of its past strength remains.

Sources: Anne Freedman, "Doing Battle with the Patronage Army: Politics, Courts, and Personnel Administration in Chicago," *Public Administration Review* 48 (September/October 1988): 847–59; Alton Miller, *Harold Washington: The Mayor, The Man* (Chicago: Bonus Books, 1989), 99–100; *O'Hare Truck Service, Inc., et al., v. City of Northlake et al.,* (1996) 95–191; Milton Rakove, *Don't Make No Waves. . .Don't Back No Losers* (Bloomington: Indiana University Press, 1975); Mike Royko, *Boss: Richard J. Daley of Chicago* (New York: Signet, 1971).

merit civil service system

A system of hiring government employees on the basis of merit, or the competence of the individual to do the job, rather than the individual's political loyalties.

The next critical reform was the direct primary, which a few states adopted in the 1890s and which was extended in some states to presidential nominations between 1904 and 1912. Under the old system, party committees—often dominated by bosses—selected nominees. In the primary system, voters in party primary elections choose the candidates they want to represent their party as nominees in the general election. When the party bosses lost the power to nominate candidates, they lost much of their ability to influence the behavior of elected officials as well. In some cases, voters chose anti-machine nominees; in other cases, the machine's own nominees turned away from their patrons. In both cases, political power shifted from local party organizations to elected officials. The bosses lost power and the candidates became the dominant players.[61]

Along with the Australian ballot and the direct primary, a third critical reform was the spread of the **merit civil service system**, under which government employees were hired on the basis of merit alone. Under the old patronage, or *spoils,* system, city and county employees were hired for political reasons and could be fired by party bosses if they became disloyal. The bosses justified the practice, in the candid words of William Marcy, a prominent nineteenth-century American politician, because "To the victor belong the spoils."[62] In the merit system, by contrast, employees are hired on the basis of merit—often determined by competitive examinations—and are protected from being fired for political reasons (see Chapter 13). Without control over the supply of jobs to use as selective, material benefits, many party machines collapsed.

The merit system was not a new idea. The federal government began hiring on merit as a result of the Pendleton Act of 1883, which Congress passed after a rejected job seeker expressed his disappointment by assassinating President James Garfield. From the 1890s through 1920, many states expanded civil service protection of employees so that they could not be fired for political reasons. Whenever jobs were converted from patronage to merit, the party machines lost power.[63]

The progressive reforms did not pass everywhere. Some states, such as California, swept away party machines and made it as difficult as possible for the surviving party organizations to have any influence.[64] Other states, such as Illinois, passed only a few of the reforms, so that machines survived.[65] The remaining machines are in what the map in Figure 9–5 describes as strong party states; they are mostly in the north central states and in the east.

Other Consequences of Local Reforms

The changes in rules that caused local party machines to collapse in many areas often went much further. Some progressive reformers sought not only to prevent corruption, but to destroy parties, which they considered inherently corrupt.[66] Additional reforms—formalizing party structure, requiring party leaders to be elected in primaries, inhibiting cooperation among campaigns and among

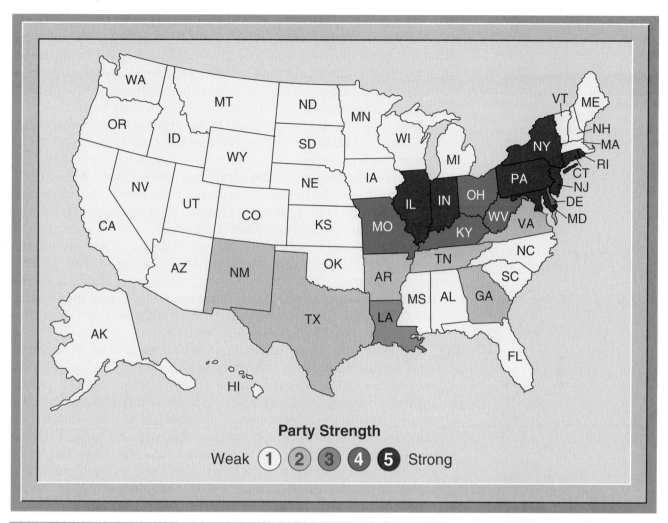

Party Strength

Weak ① ② ③ ④ ❺ Strong

Figure 9–5   Party Strength in America. Over time, the strongest political parties have been in the Northeast and Midwest; the weakest parties have been in the West and in the Plains states.

Source: *David R. Mayhew, Placing Parties in American Politics.* Copyright 1986 by Princeton University Press. Reprinted by permission of Princeton University Press.

different party organizations—enormously weakened parties. The result was that in progressive states, parties became weak and ineffective. Not only could parties not dominate politics, they were also less influential than many interest groups.

The weakening of party organizations had two major consequences: It encouraged the rise of private clubs of partisans and promoted a shift to candidate-centered campaigns. The private clubs of partisans began to organize to perform the tasks officially regulated parties were not allowed to do—for instance, endorse candidates in the primaries. The club movement spread rapidly in the 1950s so that in some progressive states, such as California, a network of clubs developed to parallel the official party organizations.[67] In California, for instance, the California Democratic Council developed as a coalition of local clubs. These local clubs have regular meetings and engage in many of the activities of old-fashioned parties (except nominating candidates), but they can do so with almost no government regulation or interference.

candidate-centered campaigns
Campaigns in which candidates set up campaign
organizations, raise money, and campaign
independently of other candidates in their party.

The second consequence of weakening parties was the rise of **candidate-centered campaigns**. Instead of relying on the local party organizations to run a slate of candidates (which happened in traditional strong parties), individual candidates set up their own campaign organizations, raised their own money, and campaigned independently of other candidates in their party.[68]

Two other causes, in addition to the decline of party organizations brought about by the progressive reforms, contributed to the rise of candidate-centered campaigns: the spread of radio and television and the passage of the campaign finance laws of the 1970s. The spread of radio in the 1930s, and far more importantly, television in the 1960s (described in Chapter 8), had a major impact on campaigns and parties. Candidates who had relied on party organizations to contact voters no longer had to do so. Television offered a way to speak directly to voters without enlisting an army of campaign workers to walk door-to-door. Increasingly throughout the 1960s, candidates began to put more time, effort, and money into developing mass media campaigns.[69] Traditional party organizations simply became less relevant.

The new rules for campaign finance also influenced what candidates for national office did when seeking office. Before the passage of the 1971 Federal Election Campaign Act (FECA) and its 1974 amendments, candidates could raise as much money as they wanted by soliciting donations of any size, but the new FECA laws restricted the size of donations for campaigns to federal offices (see Chapter 12). The most important limitations were that individuals could contribute no more than $1,000 to each candidate per election and that political action committees (PACs), could contribute no more than $5,000. Following the federal government's lead, a number of states passed similar laws limiting donations in state elections.[70] The consequence was that instead of relying on a relatively small number of wealthy patrons, candidates now had to engage in mass fund-raising.[71] Aided by computers and the new technology of mass mailing, candidates set up their own fundraising operations and thus became even more independent of political parties. In short, new rules and new technology combined to enable candidates to run independent campaigns.

With the club movement and the rise of candidate-centered campaigns, political parties in most areas of the country have been reduced to weak organizations that only assist the candidates with their campaigns. Candidates now commonly draw on the party organizations, on loose networks of local political activists, and on interest groups to staff and fund their campaigns. Because party organizations lack the strength to determine who wins the nomination and the election, they play only a supportive role to the candidates.

Although party organizations no longer dominate campaigns, they still matter. A 1979–1980 survey of the 7,300 county-level party organizations in the United States showed a high level of activity. Most of them engaged in a wide range of activities—

organizing fundraising and campaign events such as rallies, raising money for their own operations, donating money to the campaign organizations of their parties' candidates, distributing campaign literature, operating phone banks, organizing door-to-door canvassing, and conducting other campaign efforts.[72] No one has conducted a national survey of local party organizations since the 1979–1980 effort, but it is clear from smaller studies and anecdotal accounts that local party organizations are even more active now than they were twenty-five years ago. Nevertheless, their primary roles are still to support candidate-centered campaigns.

Almost all local party organization activity focuses narrowly on campaigns and occurs during the campaign season. The campaigns are the exciting part of politics for party activists. When the campaigns start, the activists arrive; when the campaigns end, they turn to other pursuits.[73] As a result, during the off-season, parties are barely noticeable.

The history of local parties since 1900, then, is one of declining influence, but it is also one of adapting to new rules and new technology. From the Progressive Era reforms to the FECA laws, the rules governing parties and campaigns have changed enormously. Similarly, the advent of radio, television, and the computer, which made modern mass fundraising possible, have also had a huge impact. Yet the parties have responded to these changes so that they can continue pursuing their goals—winning elections and controlling government.

9-4b State Organizations

State party organizations, like their local counterparts, usually lack political power. Every state has a Democratic and Republican state party organization, usually consisting of a state party chair, a party central committee, and a staff. Members of the central committee may be chosen in several ways. Most commonly, they are elected in primaries or sent as representatives of lower-level party organizations.

Although state party organizations sit above local organizations in the party hierarchy, they generally have little control over them. Many state organizations, in fact, have little control over anything.

State parties lack power for the same reasons that local organizations often lack power: State party leaders do not control or even have much influence over nominations and elections. In almost all states, voters choose their party's nominees in primary elections. The state party leaders cannot give the nominations to whomever they want. Moreover, the candidates for the nominations build their own campaign organizations and raise money independently of the state parties. The state parties can donate money or other resources, but for many years, few have had enough money to make much of a difference. A survey of state party leaders in the late 1970s showed that the average state party budget was only $341,000 and that state parties averaged only 7.7 staff members during election years.[74] State party funding grew substantially in the years that followed, mostly because the national party organizations gave the state parties money. The additional funds allowed the state organizations to hire more professional staff and do more to help their candidates win. Yet the money from the national parties was not enough to give the state parties control over candidates.[75]

Because they do not have legal control over nominations or the resources to have real power, state party organizations generally content themselves with providing services to candidates. They raise and distribute small amounts of money; they run voter registration and get-out-the-vote drives; they do public opinion polling and offer a variety of other useful services.

In a few cases in which state party organizations play a role beyond being a service bureau, they do so because others provide the political muscle. In some states, for instance, when a party controls the governorship, the governor appoints the state party chair, who acts as a political agent of the governor. A typical job for such a chair is to handle the governor's patronage appointments.[76] The state party committees and the state chair rarely have much independent political power.

9-4c National Organizations

At the top of each party's hierarchy are the national party conventions and the national party committees—the Democratic National Committee and the Republican National Committee. In addition, each party's members in the House and Senate have campaign committees to raise funds and help with campaigns for themselves. In short, it's somewhat crowded at the top.

Each major party has a national convention every four years to nominate its presidential and vice presidential candidates, to write its party platform, and to make changes in the party rules (the presidential selection process leading up to these conventions is discussed in Chapter 12). Between the national conventions, the national committees and party chairs conduct party business. When they were originally created in the 1850s, the national committees' only role was to organize the presidential conventions and to help coordinate the presidential campaign in the fall. Aside from helping with presidential campaigns, the national organizations did almost nothing. Over time, the committees gained other responsibilities and became involved in state and local races, but they remain focused on national politics.

The national party committees, like state party committees, do not have much power (although, as we shall see, their power has been growing recently). They neither control the presidential nomination nor have much influence on that or any other election. Thus, like the state party organizations, the national party organizations have few resources and are limited in what they can do.

During the 1950s and 1960s, the national committees barely had enough money to survive.[77] At the end of the 1970s, however, the national parties began to rebuild. Paradoxically, the parties' resurgence stems largely from the same factors that forced individual candidates to become less dependent on local political parties—the advent of computer-based, mass-mail technology and changes in federal campaign finance law. The development of mass mail allowed parties to raise money in the same way candidates did.[78] Then, in the 1980s and 1990s, a series of Supreme Court decisions opened the door on campaign spending. Parties could raise and spend unlimited amounts of "soft" money on campaigns, spending that was not coordinated with the campaigns. In other words, if the party committees did not talk with the candidates about how the money would be spent, they were free to spend as much as they pleased. The result was that parties raised more money and became more powerful. They did not, however, gain enough power to control candidates. Candidate-centered campaigns remained the norm in American elections.

In 2002, Congress changed the rules again by passing the Bipartisan Campaign Reform Act, which banned the use of soft money. The law (sometimes also called the McCain–Feingold Act after its Senate sponsors) was intended to prevent parties and issue advocacy groups from raising and spending huge amounts of money, which the law's supporters believed was corrupting politics. Individual donation limits were raised, but soft-money donations to parties were banned, and issue-advocacy groups were prevented from running advertising campaigns less than thirty days before a primary election or sixty days before a general election. Some parts of the Bipartisan Campaign Reform Act worked as the authors intended. Political parties can still raise money, but their ability to do so is sharply limited, and they will certainly have far less money than they did in the 1990s.[79] Other parts of the act did not work as planned. The Federal Election Commission ruled that so-called "527 groups"—groups that were organized under section 527 of the Internal Revenue Code—were not covered by the Act. As a result, 527 groups spent enormous sums during the 2004 elections. Despite the 527-group loophole, the Bipartisan Campaign Reform Act was a major blow against political parties. (See Chapter 11 for further discussion of campaign finance laws.)

The parties used the money to build professional staffs offering a wide range of services—registration and get-out-the-vote drives, polling, issue research, candidate schools, and campaign management schools. In addition, they gave limited cash donations to candidates and spent their own money on television and mass-mail ads.[80] Their newfound resources and success allowed them to branch out and exert more influence in elections around the country. They have even entered state politics, attempting to build up state and local party organizations with the ultimate goal of electing more of their candidates to national office. As for the four congressional fundraising committees, they have parlayed their

Tim Kaine, Democratic National Committee Chairman.

money and contacts into what may be described as a "national-party-as-intermediary" role—recruiting candidates for Congress and bringing together donors and candidates with good prospects for victory.[81] Thus, they, too, have gained in stature since the 1970s. In general, all the national party organizations have gained influence over the past three decades.

9-4d Relationships among Party Organizations

Looking over the full range of party organizations, from local to national, we see a set of independent organizations and groups of candidates cooperating with each other to achieve a set of common goals. The cooperation in almost all cases is voluntary. Although we may loosely speak of the national parties as being above the state and local parties in the party hierarchy, the national party organizations have little real control over local party organizations. Their cooperation stems from the belief that if they work together, they will more likely achieve the party's goals of winning elections and controlling government.

What parties do has changed over time and differs even now from one part of the country to another. Parties have responded not only to voters' preferences, but also to changes in rules and in campaign technology. In short, party history is the history of flexible organizations adapting to their times.

SUMMARY

Politicians organized political parties to achieve practical political goals. They set up parties primarily to help them win elections, and to a lesser extent, to help them govern and pursue policy goals once elected. Despite the immediate practical nature of these goals, parties serve other specific purposes. They recruit and nominate candidates, they mobilize voters, they contest elections, and they form governments and coordinate policy across independent units of government. By performing these tasks, parties help hold elected officials accountable for their actions. They perform a vital function for democracy.

The United States has a two-party system in which the election rules and laws encourage both parties to take stands near the political center. As the spatial theory of elections shows, in a single-member, plurality electoral system such as ours, politicians are more likely to win elections if they form two large, centrist parties. In a proportional representation system—more common in other democracies—there is much less incentive for large, centrist parties to form.

The history of American elections can best be described as consisting of six electoral periods—1796–1824, 1828–1856, 1860–1892, 1896–1928, 1932–1980s, and the 1980s to the present. With the exception of the recent, incremental realignment, the periods

Michael Steele, Chairman of the Republican National Committee

were separated by elections of sharp conflict in which the coalitions making up the two parties realigned and in which new issues arose. The most recent critical election occurred in 1932, when the Republican dominance from the turn of the twentieth century on crumbled, a Democratic majority emerged, and the parties began to differ primarily along economic lines. Since the 1960s, however, this New Deal coalition has frayed, and most observers suggest that we are now in a sixth party system, which began during the 1980s.

Parties operate at the local, state, and national level. To be useful to politicians, parties had to adapt to local conditions over the years—especially to laws regulating party organization. When mass political parties first organized, no laws limited their behavior. Relying on patronage and other selective, material benefits, party machines grew to dominate politics in most parts of the nation. Then, in a series of reforms enacted during the Progressive Era, state legislatures instituted the use of the Australian ballot, established direct primaries, limited patronage, and otherwise restricted the power of machines. Parties changed their behavior, losing power but continuing to do whatever they could to help party members win office. With the passage of laws in the 1970s limiting the size of campaign donations and the development of mass-mail technology, parties again adapted—this time shaping a role for themselves in coordinating fund-raising and other supportive activities among party donors, activists, and candidates across the country.

Although parties have changed enormously over the years, they still seek to win elections and thus still serve as links helping voters hold politicians accountable. To do so, they have adapted to two dynamics in the political system: changing voter preferences and changes in rules and campaign technologies.

KEY TERMS

Australian ballot

Blanket primaries

candidate-centered campaigns

caucus/convention system

centrist parties

Closed primaries

critical elections

direct primary

Duverger's Law

material benefits

median voter hypothesis

merit civil service system

New Deal coalition

Open primaries

party dealignment

party machine

party platforms

party realignments

patronage jobs

political cleavages

political party

proportional representation
  system

Selective benefits

single-member, plurality
  electoral system

two-partysystem

READINGS FOR FURTHER STUDY

Aldrich, John H. *Why Parties? The Origin and Transformation of Party Politics in America* (Chicago: University of Chicago Press, 1995). An examination of the histories of U.S. political parties from the 1790s to the Civil War and of modern parties after World War II. Aldrich shows why parties perform three essential tasks in our democracy: limiting the number of candidates for office, mobilizing voters, and maintaining the majorities necessary to attain policy goals once in office.

Canon, David T. *Actors, Athletes, and Astronauts: Political Amateurs in the United States Congress* (Chicago: University of Chicago Press, 1990). A definitive study of amateur politicians—people with no previous political experience—in elections and Congress. Canon examines why amateurs run for office, why they win, and how they behave once elected.

Corrado, Anthony, Thomas E. Mann, Daniel Ortiz, and Trevor Potter. *The New Campaign Finance Sourcebook* (Washington, D.C.: Brookings Institution, 2004). A comprehensive summary of campaign finance law in the United States. Corrado and his colleagues offer a series of short essays summarizing all the important areas of law and present excerpts from all the key court decisions.

Downs, Anthony. *An Economic Theory of Democracy* (New York: Harper & Row, 1957). The classic analysis of parties and elections that introduced the spatial model of elections. With minimal use of formal mathematics, Downs offers an abstract way of understanding how election rules affect government decisions and public policy.

Green, John C., and Daniel J. Coffey, eds. *The State of the Parties,* 5th ed. (Lanham, MD: Rowman and Littlefield, 2007). A collection of essays describing modern political parties from the local to the national level. The chapters include analyses of both the two major parties and minor parties.

Hershey, Marjorie Randon. *Party Politics in America,* 12th ed. (New York: Longman, 2007). An outstanding textbook on American political parties, covering virtually every aspect of their history, their organization, and their relationship with the people and the government.

Hofstadter, Richard. *The Age of Reform: From Bryan to FDR* (New York: Vintage Books, 1955). A classic study of political reform from 1890 to 1940. Hofstadter examines and explains the sweep of reform from the Progressive Era through Franklin Roosevelt's New Deal.

Lawless, Jennifer L., and Richard L. Fox. *It Takes a Candidate: Why Women Don't Run for Public Office* (Cambridge: Cambridge University Press, 2005). A path-breaking study that revealed the key factors explaining why women are underrepresented in political office in the United States.

Rakove, Milton. *Don't Make No Waves…Don't Back No Losers* (Bloomington: Indiana University Press, 1975). An insider's look at the Cook County Democratic machine of Chicago Mayor Richard Daley. Rakove, a political scientist and party worker in Chicago, both describes the machine and explains how it survived and prospered well into the 1970s.

Rosenstone, Steven J., Roy L. Behr, and Edward H. Lazarus. *Third Parties in America,* 2nd ed. (Princeton, NJ: Princeton University Press, 1996). The definitive study of minor parties. In the first part of the book, the authors provide a sweeping history of minor parties in the nineteenth and twentieth centuries up through Ross Perot's 1992 challenge. In the second part of the book, the authors present a theoretical analysis explaining the rise and fall of minor-party challenges to the Democrats and Republicans.

Sundquist, James L. *Dynamics of the Party System,* rev. ed. (Washington, D.C.: Brookings Institution, 1983). A study of party history and the politics of realignment. Sundquist blends an electoral history of the United States with a groundbreaking theoretical analysis of why party coalitions rise and fall.

REVIEW QUESTIONS

1. Closed primaries
   a. allow voters to choose on Election Day the party primary in which they will vote.
   b. permit voters to jump back and forth among the parties while they vote.
   c. require voters to indicate their party affiliations before Election Day.
   d. are used only by the Republican Party.
2. In proportional electoral systems, legislatures are
   a. elected at large.
   b. divided into districts.
   c. selected according to Duverger's Law.
   d. selected according to the winner-take-all principle.
3. In proportional electoral systems,
   a. minor parties hardly ever exist.
   b. minor parties can prosper.
   c. minor-party candidates hardly ever win seats in the national legislature.
   d. none of the above.
4. The Republican Party was originally founded as the
   a. party of big business.
   b. party of working-class Americans.
   c. antislavery party.
   d. party of Thomas Jefferson.
5. The Federalist Party
   a. was very strong until the Civil War.
   b. was supportive of a weak federal government.
   c. was founded by James Madison.
   d. did not last long.

6. *Reconstruction* describes
    a. the Colonies after the Revolutionary War.
    b. the period during which the South was occupied by Union forces.
    c. the merging of the Federalist and the Whig Parties.
    d. the New Deal era.
7. The last realigning election in the United States occurred in
    a. 1860.
    b. 1896.
    c. 1932.
    d. 1968.
8. Which of the following did *not* occur during the Progressive Era?
    a. spoils system
    b. Australian ballot
    c. direct primary
    d. merit system
9. Which of the following is an accurate description of political party organization?
    a. Power and authority are vested at the top of the party's organizational hierarchy.
    b. Parties are strong and centralized organizations.
    c. Party organizations are loose confederations that agree to cooperate to achieve common goals.
    d. Parties no longer have formal organizational structures.
10. Political campaigns are said to be candidate-centered when
    a. several candidates run for the same office.
    b. the candidates set up their own campaign organizations, raise their own money, and run independently of other candidates in their own party.
    c. the parties allow the candidates to be the focus of media attention, but the party organizations run the campaigns.
    d. candidates of the same party who are running for different offices work together by pooling their campaign funds and running as a slate.

NOTES

1. Cheryl Lynn Herrera, Richard Herrera, and Eric R. A. N. Smith, "Public Opinion and Congressional Representation," *Public Opinion Quarterly* 56 (Summer 1992): 185–205; Byron E. Shafer and William J. M. Claggett, *The Two Majorities: The Issue Context of Modern American Politics* (Baltimore: Johns Hopkins University Press, 1995), chap. 6.
2. Joseph A. Schlesinger, *Political Parties and the Winning of Office* (Ann Arbor: University of Michigan Press, 1991).
3. Michael Barone, *Our Country: The Shaping of America from Roosevelt to Reagan* (New York: Free Press, 1990), 247–48, 317.
4. Jennifer L. Lawless and Richard L. Fox, *It Takes a Candidate: Why Women Don't Run for Public Office* (Cambridge: Cambridge University Press, 2005), chap. 5.

5. John H. Aldrich, *Why Parties? The Origin and Transformation of Party Politics in America* (Chicago: University of Chicago Press, 1995).

6. E. E. Schattschneider, *Party Government* (New York: Farrar and Rinehart, 1942), 1.

7. G. Bingham Powell, Jr., *Contemporary Democracies* (Cambridge, MA: Harvard University Press, 1982).

8. Herbert McClosky and John Zaller, *The American Ethos: Public Attitudes toward Capitalism and Democracy* (Cambridge, MA: Harvard University Press, 1984).

9. The spatial model was first elaborated in Anthony Downs, *An Economic Theory of Democracy* (New York: Harper & Row, 1957). For an excellent introduction to contemporary work on the spatial theory, see James M. Enelow and Melvin J. Hinich, *The Spatial Theory of Voting* (New York: Cambridge University Press, 1984).

10. "Score One for the Raider," *Newsweek* (November 20, 2000): 25.

11. Holly Bailey, "Try to Guess Who's Backing Nader," *Newsweek* (July 19, 2004): 6.

12. Julie Bosman, "A Candidate Runs to a G.O.P. Chorus of Don't," *Los Angeles Times*, 28 June 2008, A1.

13. This is a generic description of a proportional system. The systems of individual nations differ in many details. See Rein Taagepera and Matthew Soberg Shugart, *Seats and Votes: The Effects and Determinants of Electoral Systems* (New Haven, CT: Yale University Press, 1989).

14. Maurice Duverger, *Political Parties* (New York: Wiley, 1959); see also William H. Riker, "The Two-Party System and Duverger's Law: An Essay on the History of Political Science," *American Political Science Review* 76 (December 1982): 753–66.

15. Donald Bruce Johnson and Kirk H. Porter, *National Party Platforms 1840–1972* (Urbana: University of Illinois Press, 1973); see also Gerald M. Pomper with Susan S. Lederman, *Elections in America: Control and Influence in Democratic Politics*, 2nd ed. (New York: Longman, 1980).

16. This description of the politics of civil rights is largely taken from Edward G. Carmines and James A. Stimson, *Issue Evolution: Race and the Transformation of American Politics* (Princeton, NJ: Princeton University Press, 1989), 35–58.

17. John Frederick Martin, *Civil Rights and the Crisis of Liberalism* (New York: St. Martin's, 1979); James A. Morone, *The Democratic Wish: Popular Participation and the Limits of American Government* (New York: Basic Books, 1990).

18. Johnson and Porter, *National Party Platforms*, 542.

19. Ibid., 554.

20. See Tom Wicker, *One of Us: Richard Nixon and the American Dream* (New York: Random House, 1991), 238–42.

21. Taylor Branch, *Parting the Waters: America in the King Years, 1954–1963* (New York: Simon & Schuster, 1988); Dennis Chong, *Collective Action and the Civil Rights Movement* (Chicago: University of Chicago Press, 1991).

22. Arthur M. Schlesinger, Jr., *A Thousand Days: John F. Kennedy in the White House* (Greenwich, CT: Fawcett, 1965).

23. Charles Whalen and Barbara Whalen, *The Longest Debate: A Legislative History of the 1964 Civil Rights Act* (New York: New American Library, 1985).

24. James L. Sundquist, *Dynamics of the Party System*, rev. ed. (Washington, D.C.: Brookings Institution, 1983).

25. Hubert H. Humphrey, *The Education of a Private Man* (Minneapolis: University of Minnesota Press, 1991), 203.

26. Wicker, *One of Us*, 336–86.

27. Robert Axelrod, "Presidential Election Coalitions in 1984," *American Political Science Review* 80 (March 1986): 281–84; Earl Black and Merle Black, *Politics and Society in the South* (Cambridge, MA: Harvard University Press, 1987).

28. Everett Carll Ladd, Jr., with Charles D. Hadley, *Transformations of the American Party System*, 2nd ed. (New York: Norton, 1978).

29. John W. Mashek, "Moderates Rally to Fight GOP's Religious Right," *Santa Barbara News-Press*, January 2, 1993.

30. Janet Hook and Richard Simon, "GOP Plans Major Push in Congress," *Los Angeles Times*, November 4, 2004, A13.

31. See Alexander Hamilton, James Madison, and John Jay, *The Federalist Papers*, ed. Garry Wills (New York: Bantam Books, 1982), esp. no. 10.

32. William Nisbet Chambers, *Political Parties in a New Nation* (New York: Oxford University Press, 1963).

33. Lee Benson, *The Concept of Jacksonian Democracy* (Princeton, NJ: Princeton University Press, 1961).

34. Robert V. Remini, *The Election of Andrew Jackson* (Philadelphia: Lippincott, 1963), 51–120.

35. Richard P. McCormick, *The Presidential Game: The Origins of American Presidential Politics* (New York: Oxford University Press, 1982).

36. Remini, *The Election of Andrew Jackson*, 184–91.

37. Everett Carll Ladd, Jr., *American Political Parties: Social Change and Political Response* (New York: Norton, 1963).

38. Sundquist, *Dynamics of the Party System*, 134–69.

39. Ibid., 170–81; Gabriel Kolko, *The Triumph of Conservatism: A Reinterpretation of American History, 1900–1916* (Chicago: Quadrangle Books, 1963).

40. Steven J. Rosenstone, Roy L. Behr, and Edward H. Lazarus, *Third Parties in America: Citizen Response to Major Party Failure* (Princeton, NJ: Princeton University Press, 1984), 85–88.

41. Sherman J. Maisel, *Macro-Economics* (New York: Norton, 1982).

42. Arthur M. Schlesinger, Jr., *The Coming of the New Deal* (Boston: Houghton-Mifflin, 1958).

43. Barone, *Our Country*, chap. 12.

44. Kristi Anderson, *The Creation of a Democratic Majority, 1928–1936* (Chicago: University of Chicago Press, 1979); Sundquist, *Dynamics of the Party System*, 198–239.

45. See Walter Dean Burnham, *Critical Elections and the Mainsprings of American Politics* (New York: Norton, 1970).

46. V. O. Key, Jr., "A Theory of Critical Elections," *Journal of Politics* 17 (February 1955): 3–18.

47. Burnham, *Critical Elections and the Mainsprings of American Politics*, esp. 9–10.

48. Sundquist, *Dynamics of the Party System*, 1–49, 298–331.

49. For another insightful theoretical interpretation, see Jerome M. Clubb, William H. Flanigan, and Nancy H. Zingale, *Partisan Realignment: Voters, Parties and Government in American History* (Beverly Hills: Sage, 1980).

50. See Martin P. Wattenberg, *The Decline of American Political Parties, 1952–1992* (Cambridge, MA: Harvard University Press, 1994); Martin P. Wattenberg, *The Rise of Candidate-Centered Politics* (Cambridge, MA: Harvard University Press, 1991).

51. See Bruce E. Keith, David B. Magleby, Candice J. Nelson, Elizabeth Orr, Mark C. Westyle, and Raymond E. Wolfinger, *The Myth of the Independent Voter* (Berkeley: University of California Press, 1992).

52. See Gary C. Jacobson, *The Electoral Origins of Divided Government: Competition in U.S. House Elections, 1946–1988* (Boulder, CO: Westview, 1990).

53. Eric R. A. N. Smith and Peverill Squire, "State and National Politics in the Mountain West," in *The Politics of Realignment*, ed. Peter F. Galderisi, Michael S. Lyons, Randy T. Simmons, and John G. Francis. (Boulder, CO: Westview, 1987), 33–54; see also the data on regional voting in Harold W. Stanley and Richard G. Niemi, *Vital Statistics on American Politics*, 5th ed. (Washington, D.C.: CQ Press, 1995), 129.

54. See John E. Chubb and Paul E. Peterson, "Realignment and Institutionalization," in *The New Direction in American Politics*, eds. John E. Chubb and Paul E. Peterson (Washington, D.C.: Brookings Institution, 1985), 1–30; and Thomas E. Cavanaugh and James L. Sundquist, "The New Two-Party System," in *The New Direction in American Politics*, eds. John E. Chubb and Paul E. Peterson (Washington, D.C.: Brookings Institution, 1985), 33–67.

55. See Alan L. Abramowitz, "The End of the Democratic Era? 1994 and the Future of Congressional Election Research," *Political Research Quarterly* 48 (December 1995): 873–89; Alfred J. Tuchfarber et al., "Interpreting the 1994 Election Results: A Direct Test of Competing Explanations," paper delivered at the American Association for Public Opinion Research, May 18–21, 1995, Fort Lauderdale, FL.

56. Edward C. Banfield and James Q. Wilson, *City Politics* (New York: Vintage, 1963), 116–21.

57. For a novel use of walking-around money, see Thomas B. Rosenstiel, "Consultant Rivalry Led to Lie, Rollins Says," *Los Angeles Times*, November 21, 1993; "'Walking-Around Money': A Dubious Tradition," *Newsweek* (November 22, 1993): 33.

58. Paul Allen Beck, *Party Politics in America*, 8th ed. (New York: Longman, 1997). For an excellent description of the Daley machine, see Milton Rakove, *Don't Make No Waves…Don't Back No Losers* (Bloomington: Indiana University Press, 1975).

59. Austin Ranney, *Curing the Mischiefs of Faction: Party Reform in America* (Berkeley: University of California Press, 1975), 79–80.

60. Jerrold G. Rusk, "The Effect of the Australian Ballot Reform on Split Ticket Voting: 1876–1908," *American Political Science Review* 70 (December 1970): 1220–38; see also Francis Fox Piven and Richard A. Cloward, *Why Americans Don't Vote* (New York: Pantheon Books, 1988), 73–74.

61. Joseph A. Schlesinger, "The New American Political Party," *American Political Science Review* 79 (December 1985): 1152–69.

62. *Bartlett's Familiar Quotations*, 16th ed., ed. Justin Kaplan (Boston: Little, Brown, 1992), 398.

63. Sean M. Theriault, "Patronage, the Pendleton Act, and the Power of the People," *Journal of Politics* 65 (February 2003): 50–68.

64. Spencer C. Olin, Jr., *California Politics, 1846–1920: The Emerging Corporate State* (San Francisco: Boyd and Fraser, 1981), chap. 5.

65. James Gimpel, "Reform-Resistant and Reform-Adopting Machines: The Electoral Foundations of Urban Politics: 1910–1930," *Political Research Quarterly* 46 (June 1993): 371–82; Raymond E. Wolfinger, *The Politics of Progress* (Englewood Cliffs, NJ: Prentice Hall, 1974), 87–92.

66. Richard Hofstadter, *The Age of Reform* (New York: Vintage, 1955).

67. James Q Wilson, *The Amateur Democrat* (Chicago: University of Chicago Press, 1962).

68. See Robert Agranoff, ed., *The New Style in Election Campaigns* (Boston: Holbrook, 1972).

69. Stephen A. Salmore and Barbara G. Salmore, *Candidates, Parties, and Campaigns: Electoral Politics in America* (Washington, D.C.: CQ Press, 1985), 19–61.

70. Herbert E. Alexander, *Financing Politics: Money, Elections and Political Reform*, 3rd ed. (Washington, D.C.: CQ Press, 1984), chap. 7.

71. Herbert E. Alexander, *Financing Politics*, 4th ed. (Washington, D.C.: CQ Press, 1992).

72. Cornelius P. Cotter, James L. Gibson, John F. Bibby, and Robert J. Huckshorn, *Party Organizations in American Politics* (New York: Praeger, 1984), 41–59.

73. Steven J. Rosenstone and John Mark Hansen, *Mobilization, Participation, and Democracy in America* (New York: Macmillan, 1993).

74. John F. Bibby and Thomas M. Holbrook, "Parties and Elections," in *Politics in the American State: A Comparative Analysis*, eds. Virginia Gray and Herbert Jacob (Washington, D.C.: CQ Press, 1996).

75. Peter L. Francia, Paul S. Herrnson, John P. Frendreis, and Alan R. Gitelson, "The Battle for the Legislature: Party Campaigning in State House and State Senate Elections," in *The State of the Parties*, eds. John C. Green and Rick Farmer (New York: Rowman and Littlefield, 2003), 171–89.

76. Robert J. Huckshorn, "The Role Orientations of State Party Chairmen," in *The Party Symbol*, ed. William Crotty (San Francisco: Freeman, 1980), 50–62.

77. Cornelius P. Cotter and Bernard C. Hennessy, *Politics without Power: The National Party Committees* (New York: Atherton, 1964).

78. Larry J. Sabato, *The Party's Just Begun* (Glenview, IL: Scott, Foresman/Little, Brown, 1988); David Ryden, "The Good, the Bad, and the Ugly: The Judicial Shaping of Party Activities" in *The State of the Parties: The Changing Role of Contemporary American Parties*, 3rd ed., eds. John C. Green and Daniel M. Shea (Lanham, MD: Rowman and Littlefield, 1994), 50–65; Noah J. Goodhart, "The New Party Machine: Information Technology in State Political Parties," in *The State of the Parties: The Changing Role of Contemporary American Parties*, 3rd ed., eds. John C. Green and Daniel M. Shea (Lanham, MD: Rowman and Littlefield, 1994), 120–34; Marianne Holt, "The Surge in Party Money in Competitive 1998 Congressional Elections," in *Outside Money*, ed. David B. Magleby (Lanham, MD: Rowman and Littlefield, 2000), 17–40.

79. Anthony Corrado, Thomas E. Mann, Daniel Ortiz, and Trevor Potter, *The New Campaign Finance Sourcebook* (Washington, D.C.: Brookings Institution, 2004); www.opensecrets.org/.

80. Laura Berkowitz and Steve Lilienthal, "A Tale of Two Parties: National Party Committee Policy Initiatives," in *The State of the Parties: The Changing Role of Contemporary American Parties*, eds. Daniel M. Shea and John C. Green (Lanham, MD: Rowman and Littlefield, 1994); Anthony Corrado, "The

Politics of Cohesion: The Role of the National Party Committees in the 1992 Election," in *The State of the Parties: The Changing Role of Contemporary American Parties*, eds. Daniel M. Shea and John C. Green (Lanham, MD: Rowman and Littlefield, 1994).

81. Diana Dwyre, "Party Strategy and Political Reality: The Distribution of Congressional Campaign Committee Resources," in *The State of the Parties: The Changing Role of Contemporary American Parties*, eds. Daniel M. Shea and John C. Green (Lanham, MD: Rowman and Littlefield, 1994); Paul S. Herrnson, *Party Campaigning in the 1980s* (Cambridge, MA: Harvard University Press, 1988).

10

Interest Groups

CHAPTER OUTLINE

The rise of the Internet has enabled many Americans to indulge in their passion for gambling. In 2006, Americans bet an estimated $6 billion online, more than four times the amount they wagered just five years earlier. One of the most popular forms of online gambling is poker. Upward of 25 million Americans go online to play games of 7 Card Stud, Omaha Hi/Lo, and Texas Hold 'Em. The explosion in online gambling has taken place even though American law bars online gambling companies from being based in the United States. The roughly 2,500 Internet gaming sites now operating get around the law by setting up their businesses in foreign countries.[1]

The explosion in online gambling has not been popular with everyone. Religious and conservative groups have long opposed the expansion of gambling and pushed legislation to ban it. They see it as an immoral activity that undermines society. As James Dobson, the founder of Focus on the Family, a leading group devoted to defending traditional values, puts it, "Clearly, gambling is a destroyer that ruins lives and wrecks families."[2] Conservative and religious groups argue that online gambling is especially dangerous: Players can gamble twenty-four hours a day from home; children can play because bettors are not required to verify their age; and betting by credit card rather than with cash can lull players into running up huge debts. Critics also argue that online gambling sites provide a means by which drug traffickers and terrorists can launder money.

To rein in online gambling, groups such as Focus on the Family, the Christian Coalition, the Family Research Council, and the Traditional Values Coalition turned to the federal government for help. They asked Congress to pass legislation making it illegal for banks and credit card companies to make payments to online gambling sites. In pushing for this legislation, antigambling groups got help from professional sports leagues and the horse racing industry. Major League Baseball (MLB) and the National Football League (NFL) both supported anti-online gambling legislation, provided that online fantasy leagues were exempted. (Both MLB and the NFL run fantasy leagues and receive royalties from other fantasy sites.) The National Thoroughbred Racing Association and other groups representing the horse racing industry agreed to support the legislation provided that Internet betting on horse racing was allowed.[3]

Proponents of online gambling countered that it is a harmless form of entertainment. "We don't think poker is a 'shadowy enterprise,' whether it is played at your home or on the Internet," said the spokesman for the Poker Players Alliance, a membership association created to fight efforts to curb online gambling.[4] Online gambling companies argued that the solution was not to ban online gambling but to regulate and tax it. "Prohibition would not stop online gambling, it would send it underground and leave the vulnerable unprotected," argued the chief executive officer of BetOn-Sports, one of the largest online gambling companies.[5] Banks and credit card companies complained that the bill would be difficult to enforce. And some trade experts argued that it would violate international trade agreements the United States had signed.

Despite these arguments, the proponents of restricting online gambling prevailed. In 2006, Congress passed, as a part of a broader piece of legislation, a provision banning most forms of Internet gambling. Antigambling groups hailed the new law, whereas gamblers condemned it. The law's immediate impact, however, was unclear. Many of the largest gaming companies moved quickly to bar people in the United States from accessing their sites. But others continued to operate. And as the Treasury Department undertook the arduous task of trying to enforce the new law, conservative and religious groups pledged to push their fight against gambling further. "We think this is the first step toward a larger bill that will come soon completely banning Internet gambling," said the director of communications for the Christian Coalition.[6] Meanwhile, proponents of online gambling and their allies on Capitol Hill pushed for legislation that would make many forms of Internet gambling legal once again and provide for government regulation of the industry.

The battle over Internet gambling vividly illustrates how interest groups can influence public policy. Indeed, interest groups are so much a part of American politics that the United States has been called "the interest group society."[7] Yet for more than 200 years, people have worried that interest groups distort public policy to serve narrow, selfish ends. In "Federalist No. 10," James Madison warned that, left unchecked, "factions"—the term *interest groups* appeared in a later era—would harm the public good.[8] Madison's fear echoes today in the many complaints that government is beholden to special interests.

Interest groups, like the other groups we are examining in this part of the book, both shape and are shaped by the rules of our political system. In previous chapters, we showed how the structural rules of American government favor the individual; they allow any person or group to challenge the political system. The large number of interest groups in the United States is the result of these rules. And, just as important, interest groups have a strong hand in shaping what the government does; after all, they exist primarily to ensure that government policy favors their causes.

Do interest groups help or harm democracy in the United States? Do they enable the public to obtain what it wants from government, or do they block the wishes of the American people? Is the success of groups opposed to Internet gambling typical of interest group politics or unusual? These are the questions we will explore in this chapter. We begin by discussing the role interest groups play in American politics. We go on to chart the growth of interest group activity since the end of World War II, to survey the increasingly diverse array of interest groups, and to analyze how interest groups form. We also review the strategies interest groups use to influence public policy and explain why some groups succeed and others fail. We conclude the chapter by assessing the vices and virtues of interest group politics and evaluating the effect interest groups have on American democracy.

10-1 DEFINING INTEREST GROUPS

interest group

An organized group of people who share some goals and try to influence public policy.

"An **interest group** is an organized body of individuals who share some goals and who try to influence public policy."[9] The key phrase here is "to influence public policy." There are thousands of different organizations in the United States. Most pursue some private or social purpose, as is the case with the college or university you attend. These organizations become interest groups only when they deliberately try to affect local, state, or federal government policies. Thus, when colleges and universities seek to influence public policy, say, by urging Congress to spend more money on basic scientific research, they become interest groups.

To further understand the concept of interest groups, one needs to answer two questions: First, what distinguishes an interest group from a political party? Second, what roles do interest groups play in American politics?

10-1a Interest Groups versus Political Parties

Because political parties and interest groups are both organized to influence public policy, you might wonder how the two differ. The answer lies in the difference between *aggregating* and *articulating* interests. As we saw in Chapter 9, political parties nominate candidates who run under the party banner in elections for government office. To win these elections, political parties typically try to combine, or aggregate, numerous different interests and viewpoints into a single policy platform they hope will appeal to a broad range of voters. In contrast, most interest groups focus their attention on articulating a specific interest or viewpoint, such as gun control, lower taxes, or health-care reform. As a result, most interest groups worry less about a politician's ideology or party affiliation than about whether he or she favors policies the group supports.[10]

Although political parties and interest groups are distinct entities, their fates are closely linked. Many interest groups are deeply involved in electoral politics, and some ally themselves with a political party. Labor unions, for example, traditionally support Democratic candidates, whereas the Christian Coalition helps the Republican Party recruit candidates for office. More generally, interest groups can address issues that political parties do not or cannot. Some issues simply are too narrow to be a high priority for either of the major political parties. Other issues are the subject of major disagreement within a party, which effectively prevents the party from advancing the interest in question. In either of these instances, an interest group can offer a useful alternative to a political party as a means of influencing public policy.

10-1b The Roles of Interest Groups

In seeking to influence public policy, interest groups try to protect existing rules or to establish new ones that benefit their particular interests. They exert their influence by performing five main functions: They represent the interests of their members to the government, enable people to participate in politics, educate government officials and the public about issues, build support for new policies, and monitor how the government administers programs.

Representation

Interest groups work first and foremost to see that public policy reflects the interests of their members. The Human Rights Campaign Fund works to advance the cause of gay and lesbian rights, the National Association of the Deaf Legal Defense Fund fights on behalf of the hearing impaired, and the Tobacco Institute promotes the interests of cigarette companies. Because the federal government has the power to set (or revise) the rules governing nearly every aspect of American society, almost every major interest group maintains an active presence in Washington, D.C. Interest groups also press their causes in state capitols and at city hall as well, as we will discuss at greater length in Chapter 15.

Political Participation

Interest groups also enable people to participate in politics. Most people lack the time, training, or desire to run for and hold public office, or as we saw in Chapter 7, to participate in politics in other ways. For many Americans, then, interest groups offer a more convenient and less time-consuming way to shape public policy. Moreover, by uniting people who share a common cause, interest groups take advantage of the fact that there is strength in numbers.

Education

Interest groups devote considerable effort to education. They clearly want to educate government officials. But interest groups also work to explain government policy to their members and the broader public. When George W. Bush nominated Samuel Alito, a conservative judge believed to be a staunch opponent of abortion, to the Supreme Court, pro-life and pro-choice groups sent spokespersons to news shows across the country, took out newspaper advertisements, and launched direct-mail campaigns giving their assessments of the nomination. The groups hoped their efforts would shape public opinion and thereby influence the chances that the Senate would confirm Alito's nomination.

Agenda Building

By educating their members, government officials, and the general public, interest groups help to push new issues onto the political agenda, which is the list of issues government officials are actively debating. For example, throughout the 1990s, conservative scholars and activists strived to persuade whoever would listen that rather than paying into Social Security working Americans should be allowed to invest at least some of their payroll taxes in private investment accounts to help pay for their retirement years. These efforts paid off. Many congressional Republicans, and more than a few Democrats, signed on to the idea. President George W. Bush made Social Security privatization one of his top priorities for his second term in office. (Congress ultimately declined to adopt the idea.)

Program Monitoring

Because it matters not only which laws are passed but also how those laws are implemented, many interest groups monitor how the government administers programs. Sometimes the law even requires federal agencies to work with interest groups. To ensure that the administration takes American economic interests into account during international trade talks, for example, Congress requires American negotiators to consult with labor, industry, farm, and consumer groups. If interest groups believe an agency is violating the intent of a law, they may alert sympathetic members of Congress, mobilize their membership, or even sue the government.

As you can see, interest groups play several important roles in American politics. By representing their members, participating in the political system, educating the general public, promoting their own agenda, and monitoring government programs, interest groups help shape the rules that define policy outcomes. Although interest groups matter, this does not mean they always help produce good public policy. Some citizens may not see their interests represented, groups may mislead the public about what the government is doing, and well-organized factions may distort public policy to benefit their own interests. In Section 10-7, we return to the question of the pros and cons of interest group politics.

10-2 THE GROWTH OF INTEREST GROUPS

With so many radio talk shows attacking "special interests," you might think that interest groups are a new phenomenon in American politics. They aren't. In 1773, a group of Bostonians banded together as the Sons of Liberty and protested the tax policies of the British crown by throwing the Boston Tea Party. Some sixty years later, the French writer Alexis de Tocqueville observed that interest groups, or what he called associations, were an integral part of American politics. "Americans of all ages, all stations in life, and all types of disposition, are forever forming associations."[11]

Almost all the associations Tocqueville witnessed in his travels around the United States were groups with a limited geographical reach. One of the first interest groups organized on a national level was the American Anti-Slavery Society, founded in 1833. The number of national interest groups grew after the Civil War. The

American Woman Suffrage Association and the National Woman Suffrage Association were both founded in 1869 to see that women won the right to vote (see Chapter 5). The Grange was formed in the 1860s to promote the interests of farmers whose ability to get crops and livestock to market was threatened by the monopolistic practices of the railroads. The Woman's Christian Temperance Union was founded in 1874 to persuade Congress and state legislatures to prohibit the manufacture and sale of liquor.

Interest groups, then, are well ingrained in American politics. What is new about them today is their sheer number. By one count, roughly 600 interest groups were based in Washington in 1942; by the mid-1990s, there were more than 7,000.[12] Even this number was a rough guess. No one knows the exact number of interest groups today because they come in so many different shapes and sizes.

What accounts for the rapid growth in interest groups? The answer lies in a complex mix of factors. Americans have become increasingly better educated, and as a result, are more apt to recognize the benefits of joining an interest group. The civil rights and antiwar protests of the 1960s demonstrated the power of interest group politics and provided examples for new groups to emulate. Improvements in computer and communications technology have made it far easier for groups to target supporters with mailings and phone calls soliciting contributions. And the emergence of issues that cut across party lines, such as consumer rights and the environment, has encouraged people to look to interest groups for action.

The legacy of the 1960s, improvements in technology, and the rise of new issues have all led people to place more demands on the government. And as Congress and the White House have acted to meet these demands, government itself has stimulated the growth of interest groups. When the government intervenes in (or withdraws from) the economy and society, it affects the interests of many people. If people feel harmed by government action, they are likely to band together. Thus, when defense spending dropped sharply after the Vietnam War, numerous interest groups sprang up to argue for greater defense spending. In turn, when the Ronald Reagan administration initiated a massive military buildup in the early 1980s, the number of peace and arms control groups jumped sharply. At the same time, the government may directly create interest groups. Many of the Great Society programs of the 1960s required the federal government to create and work with local groups. If the number of interest groups in the United States today is any indication, we are indeed an interest group society.

10-3 THE DIVERSITY OF ORGANIZED INTERESTS

The astounding number of interest groups in the United States is matched by their incredible diversity. As we discussed in Chapter 3, American society has become increasingly diverse, and this diversity has spawned a huge number of groups that flood government with conflicting demands and expectations. No simple typology fully captures the wide array of interest groups in the United States. Yet most interest groups fall into one of three categories: economic interest groups, citizen groups, and government interest groups.

10-3a Economic Interest Groups

The vast majority of interest groups work to advance the economic interests of their members. The four main types of economic interest groups are business groups, labor unions, agricultural organizations, and professional associations.

Business Groups

Business groups are the most common interest group. How common depends on how one counts. If we count only formally organized interest groups, then business accounts for 25 percent of the interest groups in Washington.[13] If, however, we also count lobbyists and law firms hired to represent business interests, business interests constitute up to 70 percent of all the interest groups that knock on Washington's doors.[14]

Businesses promote their interests using three distinct types of organizations. The organization with the broadest membership is the peak business association. Peak associations attempt, when possible, to speak for the business community as a whole. The most important peak business associations in the United States are the U.S. Chamber of Commerce, the National Association of Manufacturers (NAM), and the Business Roundtable. The Chamber represents an amalgam of local chambers of commerce and other groups, NAM represents more than 10,000 manufacturing firms, and the Business Roundtable represents the country's 200 largest corporations.

Many businesses also try to advance their economic interests through trade associations. These organizations represent companies in the same line of business. General Motors, Ford, and Chrysler, for example, all belong to the Alliance of Automobile Manufacturers, and McGraw-Hill, Random House, and Simon & Schuster all belong to the Association of American Publishers. As a rule, trade associations focus on issues that affect their particular industry.

Finally, many businesses try to influence public policy directly. Most large firms have offices in Washington that handle relations with the federal government. Firms without an office in the nation's capital often hire a Washington law firm or lobbyist to represent their interests.

Organized Labor

The most important voice in organized labor is the American Federation of Labor-Congress of Industrial Organizations (AFL-CIO), which is essentially a union of unions. Its member unions include the American Federation of State, County, and Municipal Employees (1.4 million members); the American Federation of Teachers (1.4 million); and the United Auto Workers (1.1 million). However, not all unions belong to the AFL-CIO. In 2005, the Service Employees International Union (1.8 million members), the International Brotherhood of Teamsters (1.4 million members), and the United Food and Commercial Workers Union (1.3 million members) left the AFL-CIO and joined with several other unions to form the Change to Win Coalition because of disagreements over the AFL-CIO's leadership and strategy. The powerful National Education Association, which represents 2.7 million schoolteachers, remains independent of both the AFL-CIO and the Change to Win Coalition.

Unions try to influence government policy on a wide range of issues. Besides issues of obvious interest to workers such as the minimum wage and safety regulations, many unions address broader political issues such as civil rights or health care. Yet the ability of unions to influence government policy has waned in recent decades. As we discussed in Chapter 3, union membership dropped sharply in the 1980s, before picking up slightly in the 1990s. Union influence was further undermined when union officials failed to persuade their members to vote for the candidates the unions endorsed. In 2008, for example, 38 percent of labor households voted for John McCain, even though most unions endorsed Barack Obama.[15]

Agricultural Groups

General farm interest groups are one kind of agricultural interest group.[16] The biggest and most influential general farm interest group is the American Farm Bureau Federation. It represents the interests of large farms, and it tends to favor the Republican Party and conservative causes.[17] Less consequential for policy making are the American Agricultural Movement, the National Farmers Organization, and the National Farmers Union. These groups represent the interests of small farmers, and they tend to ally with the Democratic Party and liberal causes.

In recent years, general farm interest groups have seen their influence eroded by groups organized around specific commodities. Almost every crop and livestock has a corresponding interest group. Corn farmers join the National Corn Growers Association, rice farmers join the American Rice Growers Cooperative Association, and hog farmers join the National Swine Growers Association. Farm-oriented businesses such as pesticide manufacturers and farm-implement dealers also have their own organizations.

Professional Associations

Professional associations resemble labor unions. The main difference is that professional associations involve higher-status occupations that generally require extended formal training and even government licensing. The two best-known professional associations are the American Bar Association (ABA), the largest organization of lawyers, and the American Medical Association (AMA). Although the ABA and the AMA garner the most headlines, almost every profession has its own association. Optometrists join the American Optometric Association; real estate agents, the National Association of Realtors; and pharmacists, the National Association of Retail Druggists. Still, not all professionals join the association that claims to represent them. For example, less than a third of doctors in the United States actually belong to the AMA.[18]

Besides groups organized along professional lines, some professional associations are organized to advance the interests of women and minorities in their membership. Examples include the American Association of University Women, the National Association of Black Accountants, and the National Association of Women Lawyers.

10-3b Citizen Groups

citizen groups
Interest groups, also known as public interest groups, dedicated to promoting a vision of good public policy rather than the economic interests of their members.

The civil rights and antiwar movements of the 1960s spurred the rise of **citizen groups.** Unlike economic interest groups, citizen groups mobilize to promote their visions of the public good rather than their own economic interests.[19] Because citizen groups seek to advance what they perceive to be the public good, they are often called public interest groups. This latter label is problematic: Conservatives seldom hail the American Civil Liberties Union (ACLU) for advancing the public interest, and many liberals do not praise the work of the National Rifle Association (NRA). Moreover, people's visions of the public good often coincide with their economic interests. For example, students tend to think that low-cost, high-quality public education is in the public interest.

Citizen groups exist for almost every issue. Some groups favor broad political agendas. Americans for Democratic Action and People for the American Way support a wide array of liberal policy positions; the American Conservative Union and the Eagle Forum push a variety of conservative policies. Other citizen groups are known as *single-issue groups* because they target specific issues, such as civil rights (National Association for the Advancement of Colored People [NAACP]), the environment (Greenpeace), good government (Common Cause), and women's issues (National Organization for Women [NOW]), to name just a few. Many distinct single-issue groups may exist on a given issue, with each taking a different emphasis and approach. For example, Greenpeace frequently takes a confrontational approach in dealing with the business community, whereas the World Wildlife Fund generally tries to work with the business community in fashioning solutions to environmental problems.

Although most citizen groups are secular in orientation, some interest groups are associated with the many religions people practice in the United States. Religious groups active in politics include the National Council of Churches, the U.S. Catholic Conference, and the American Jewish Congress.

Source: © Paul Richards/AFP/Getty Images. Reproduced by permission.

The National Association for the Advancement of Colored People (NAACP) is the nation's largest and most prominent civil rights interest group.

10-3c Government Interest Groups

The federal government funds and regulates many of the programs state and local governments run. Given the preeminence of the federal government, state and local governments have their own interest groups. Most states and many large cities have a liaison office in Washington, and many also hire Washington law firms to represent them. State and local governments also have their own associations. Issues that affect the interests of state and local governments are likely to attract the attention of groups such as the National Governor's Association, the National Association of Counties, and the National League of Cities.

Foreign governments provide another set of government interest groups. Most embassies devote much energy to representing their country's interests to Congress and the executive branch. Foreign governments also hire lobbyists and public relations firms to advance their interests.[20] For example, after September 11, 2001, the government of Saudi Arabia hired American public relations firms to refute accusations that it encouraged terrorism. Among other things, the firms ran ads on American television showing Saudi leaders meeting with American officials in an effort to improve Saudi Arabia's image in the United States.[21]

10-3d Coalitions and Divisions

To influence public policy, interest groups seek to join forces with other groups that share their position on an issue. The coalitions that arise around such mutual interests often bear out the saying that politics makes strange bedfellows. The battle over banning

Internet gambling is a case in point. Groups like Focus on the Family do not normally coordinate legislative strategy with organizations like Major League Baseball.

Although some issues produce coalitions composed of interest groups that do not normally work together, other issues may divide groups that usually are allies. For instance, the AMA and most other medical organizations staunchly oppose proposals to limit the fees physicians and hospitals can charge their patients. Two of the largest associations of medical specialists, however, the 126,000-member American College of Physicians (which represents doctors of internal medicine) and the 94,000-member American Academy of Family Physicians (which represents family practitioners) both support limits on doctor and hospital fees.[22] Interest groups with similar orientations sometimes divide on public policy issues because they see their interests and the likely impact of government policy differently.

If like-minded interest groups are not always united on the issues, neither are the members of an individual interest group. Many groups suffer from cross-cutting cleavages (differences that cut across group lines) as individual members embrace different interests. For example, in recent years, members of the National Association of Evangelicals, an umbrella organization of evangelical churches representing an estimated 30 million worshipers, have debated whether the organization should lobby for action to halt climate change. Those in favor argue that the Bible commands them to be good stewards of the environment. Those opposed argue that human-induced climate change is unproven and that addressing the issue will distract the organization from its traditional work opposing abortion and defending family values.[23]

The division within the National Association of Evangelicals over climate change is not surprising. As a rule, the larger the organization and the more diverse its membership, the more prone it is to cross-cutting cleavages. Members may rank the organization's priorities differently, harbor different visions of its future, or disagree over what strategies will advance the organization's goals. Moreover, the larger an interest group, the more likely that its members will belong to other interest groups with competing goals. The number and diversity of interest groups in the United States today reflect, as Chapter 3 pointed out, an almost limitless potential for cross-cutting cleavages to arise as different groups—and even different individuals within groups—vie to sway policy rules and outcomes in their favor.

10-4 INTEREST GROUP FORMATION AND MAINTENANCE

The tremendous number and diversity of interest groups in the United States reflect the enormous influence government has on our lives. Many organizations formed for purposes unrelated to politics become involved in interest group politics because government policy directly affects their interests. People form businesses, for example, to make products and money, yet the profound influence the government has on the economy leads businesses almost inevitably into interest group politics. Likewise, colleges and universities are founded as educational institutions and not as interest groups. Yet because government decisions on matters such as student loans and scientific research affect higher education, many colleges and universities have joined the fray of interest group politics.

Although many interest groups are organizations that formed for reasons unrelated to politics, other interest groups form for the specific purpose of influencing government policy. The process of forming a new interest group can be quite difficult; in many instances, interest groups often fail to materialize. In particular, the interests of minorities, women, and the poor are less well represented in the United States than are the interests of the wealthy and powerful. The discrepancies in interest group formation raise two critical questions: When do interest groups form? And who in American society gets their interests represented?

10-4a Obstacles to Interest Group Formation

Los Angeles County faced a problem: Too many taco trucks were operating on its streets. Residents complained that the mobile eateries were disrupting traffic, creating eyesores, and competing unfairly against local restaurants. So the Los Angeles Board of Supervisors passed an ordinance requiring the taco trucks to move every hour or risk fines or even jail time. The supervisors expected praise for their decision. Instead, they found themselves under fire. Food lovers, neighborhood workers on the run, and residents who liked being able to get good food quickly were outraged. They created a Web site at SaveOurTacoTrucks.org with the motto: "Carne Asada Is Not a Crime." They soon amassed 5,000 online signatures calling for the repeal of the ordinance.[24]

SaveOurTacoTrucks.org illustrates one way interest groups form—as a spontaneous response to changes that threaten the interests of some people. When people respond to proposed changes by spontaneously forming an interest group, political scientists explain the group's formation in terms of *disturbance theory*.[25] In the case of SaveOurTacoTrucks.org, the disturbance that propelled the creation of a new interest group came from a new government law. The disturbance can come from almost any source, however, including changes in social norms or even the actions of an existing interest group. For example, the group Frontier of Freedom, which seeks to limit government regulation of private property, formed to counter the work of environmental groups such as the Environmental Defense Fund and the Sierra Club.[26]

Although a threat to the status quo may trigger the creation of interest groups, in many instances it does not. For example, the flap over taco trucks caught the Los Angeles Board of Supervisors by

collective goods dilemma
A dilemma created when people can obtain the benefits of interest group activity without paying any of the costs associated with it. In this situation, the interest group may not form because everyone has an incentive to let someone else pay the costs of group formation.

free riders
People or groups who benefit from the efforts of others without bearing any of the costs.

surprise because their previous decisions on issues like urban renewal and road construction had not stirred a similar backlash. And relatively few college students banded together to fight the younger Bush administration's push to tighten restrictions on college loan programs, even though the new rules were expected to reduce the number of students eligible for federal Pell Grants as well as the amount they could borrow and to make state and university financial aid harder to get.

What we need to explain, then, is not only why interest groups form, but also why they sometimes do *not*. To explain the failure to organize, political scientists often point to the **collective goods dilemma**.[27] When an interest group shapes public policy, it usually produces a collective good—a benefit available to members and nonmembers alike. Thus, if the Center for Auto Safety convinces government officials to require automakers to build safer cars, it cannot dictate that only its members get to drive the safer cars. Yet if an interest group cannot deny benefits to nonmembers, rational people have an incentive to be **free riders**—that is, to gain the benefits of the group's work without bearing any of the costs (e.g., dues, meetings, and marches). Here's where the collective goods dilemma comes in: If everyone chooses to be a free rider, then the interest group will not form and no one will get any benefits. To return to the example of auto safety, if everyone acts rationally and refrains from paying dues and organizing meetings, groups such as the Center for Auto Safety will not form and the benefits that come from their activity will be lost.

10-4b Overcoming Obstacles to Interest Group Formation

Given the abundance of interest groups in the United States, we know that some groups do solve the collective goods dilemma. How do they do it? Most political scientists answer the question by highlighting the importance of political entrepreneurs—leaders who by dint of personal conviction or ambition will bear the cost of organizing others.[28] The driving forces behind SaveOurTaco-Trucks.org, for example, were Chris Rutherford and Aaron Sonderleiter, two twenty-something teachers who loved taco trucks.[29] On the national level, the most prominent interest group entrepreneur is Ralph Nader, who many view as the founder of the consumer movement.

In trying to organize an interest group, entrepreneurs may turn to patrons for help in raising the money needed for the group to operate. Who are these patrons? They may be wealthy private citizens, corporations, nonprofit foundations, or existing interest groups. The government itself may even act as a patron. For example, "The National Rifle Association was launched in close consultation with the Department of the Army in the nineteenth century to encourage familiarity with firearms among citizens who might be called to fight in future wars, and the American Legion was begun during World War I with government support to encourage patriotism and popular support for the war effort."[30] More recently, federal grants were crucial to the creation of the American Public Transit Association and the American Council on Education, among other interest groups.[31]

If an interest group is blessed with wealthy patrons or a small budget, it may be able to survive without recruiting members.[32] Most interest groups eventually try to recruit members, however. In general, people receive three types of benefits—material, solidary, and expressive—from joining an interest group.[33] **Material benefits** are actual goods and services that come from belonging to a group. Many states, for example, have so-called closed-shop rules, which means that people must belong to a union to get and keep certain jobs. Perhaps more commonly, interest groups try to entice members by offering material benefits not directly connected to the policy work of the group. The NRA's $35 annual membership fee entitles members to a magazine subscription and hotel and rental car discounts. Membership also makes one eligible to apply for a low-interest credit card and inexpensive insurance policies.

People also join interest groups because membership provides them with **solidary benefits**, the enjoyment that comes from being associated with a group of similarly minded people. Solidary benefits are strongest in organizations built around a shared experience, such as nationality, religion, or race.

Besides material and solidary benefits, people derive **expressive benefits** from group membership. Also known as purposive benefits, expressive benefits are the feelings of satisfaction people derive from working for a cause they believe is just and right. Many people join groups such as the Eagle Forum, Greenpeace, or Common Cause because they support the group's goals.

All three types of interest group benefits—material, solidary, and expressive—are what political scientists call **selective benefits.** That is, they are benefits received by people who join the group and denied to people who do not join. As we previously discussed, rational people may choose to be free riders if they can share in the collective good an interest group provides without having to join the group and pay some of the costs. Selective benefits go only to group members, however. Some people who would choose to be free riders will join the group so they can get the selective benefits and share in the collective benefit.[34] For example, people who want to see the environment protected might not join the Sierra Club without some additional enticement, such as *Sierra Magazine* and the low-cost vacation tours of wilderness areas the Sierra Club offers to its members.

Of course, the precise mix of material, solidary, and expressive benefits that leads people to join interest groups varies from person to person. You might join the NRA primarily to receive the magazine and only secondarily because you endorse the NRA's opposition to gun control. Your next-door neighbor's reasons might be the reverse. The mix of material, solidary, and expressive benefits that interest group membership provides also varies from

Material benefits
Goods and services with real, monetary value.

solidary benefits
The emotional and psychological enjoyment that comes from belonging to an interest group whose members share common interests and goals.

expressive benefits
The feelings of satisfaction people derive from working for an interest group cause they believe is just and right. Also known as purposive benefits.

selective benefits
Any benefit given to a member of a group but denied to nonmembers.

group to group. For example, an organization such as Veterans of Foreign Wars probably provides greater solidary benefits than a group such as the American Association of Retired Persons.

10-4c Interest Group Maintenance

After interest groups become established, they must worry about retaining members.[35] Maintaining membership can often be difficult. Members may lose interest in the group. As we noted previously, organized labor saw its membership decline in the 1980s. Citizen groups face an even more difficult task in retaining members because they must appeal to ideology rather than to more immediate concerns such as jobs. For instance, since the heyday of the civil rights movement ended in the mid-1970s, most civil rights groups have struggled to retain members. The NAACP has seen its membership fall by as much as 70 percent, and the Southern Christian Leadership Conference—the Rev. Dr. Martin Luther King, Jr.'s old organization—exists in name only.[36]

Interest groups seek to retain members by continuing to provide material, solidary, and expressive benefits. Yet groups may tinker with the mix of benefits over time to attract and retain members. A group may add new material incentives to make membership more appealing, or it may seize on current events to reemphasize the expressive benefits that come with membership. For instance, after Barack Obama won the Democratic presidential nomination in 2008, the NRA used his support for gun control to make its case that the right to own guns was threatened. In addition to changing the mix of membership benefits, groups may increase or decrease their reliance on patrons. As member contributions dropped with the warming of U.S.-Soviet relations in the late 1980s, for example, the Union of Concerned Scientists, a major arms control group, asked wealthy donors and private foundations to make up the shortfall.[37]

In extreme cases, changing events may force an interest group to redefine its mission to retain and attract members. With the passing of the Cold War, for example, the Project on Military Procurement became the Project on Government Procurement. Physicians for Social Responsibility, meanwhile, shifted its attention from the medical consequences of nuclear war to the medical consequences of environmental destruction, and several other groups shifted their attention from nuclear arms control issues to setting limits on the sale of conventional weapons to foreign countries.[38]

10-4d Interest Group Bias

Despite their great number, interest groups do not represent the interests of all people equally. Studies show time and again that the affluent and better educated are far more likely to belong to interest groups than are the poor and less educated.[39] Most political scientists attribute the discrepancy to differing expectations about the benefits of organizing: The wealthy and the educated have more faith that the political system will respond to their demands. This is not to say that the poor cannot organize. The late Cesar Chavez successfully organized farm workers despite their low wages, and in most cases, limited formal education. The success of the United Farm Workers notwithstanding, interest groups are least likely to represent the interests of people on the margins of society.

Although the rules of American politics allow virtually anyone to form an interest group, it is difficult to form and maintain an effective group. In practice, interest groups that have the backing of educated and well-to-do Americans are the most likely to survive. The bias of interest groups toward the affluent raises troubling questions about the nature of American democracy. Rich and poor Americans do not compete on a level playing field when it comes to interest group politics. How this disparity translates in terms of actual influence over government policy needs to be understood. First, however, we need to examine the strategies that interest groups use in their efforts to influence public policy.

10-5 INTEREST GROUP STRATEGIES

We said in the introduction to this chapter that interest groups seek to influence public policy. But just how do they do so? The strategies that interest groups pursue fall into four distinct categories: creating a political action committee, lobbying government officials, mobilizing public opinion, and litigating.

10-5a Creating Political Action Committees

In the early 1970s, Congress passed several laws designed to clean up the financing of federal election campaigns—in essence, to prevent an elite few from "buying" the loyalty of elected federal officials. A cornerstone of the new legislation was a provision allowing interest groups to set up **political action committees (PACs)**, which are organizations that solicit campaign contributions from group members and channel those funds to an election campaign. (The law had previously limited the use of PACs mostly to labor unions.) PACs now constitute the primary avenue by which interest groups contribute money to federal election campaigns.

political action committees (PACs)
Organizations that solicit contributions from members of interest groups and channel those contributions to election campaigns.

Federal campaign finance law prohibits PACs from giving more than $5,000 per election to any candidate seeking a federal office. Under the law, primary, general, run-off, and special elections are all considered separate elections. The rules governing PACs do not, however, apply to campaigns for state and local office. (The laws regulating campaign finance vary widely from state to state; many states allow interest groups to give directly to political campaigns without creating a PAC or making the detailed spending disclosures required by federal law. As a result, our knowledge about how much money interest groups contribute to state and local elections is limited.)[40]

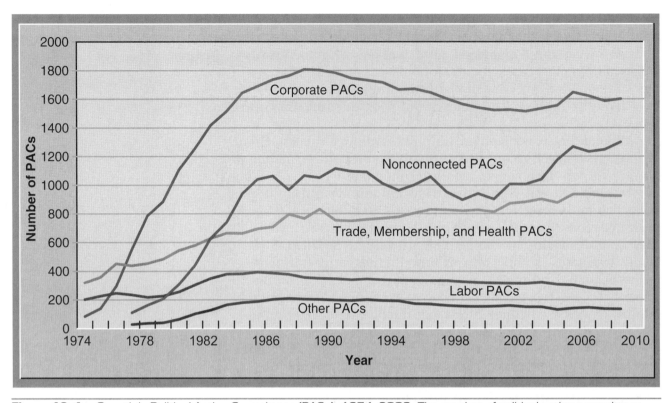

Figure 10–1 Growth in Political Action Committees (PACs), 1974–2008. The number of political action committees exploded in the 1970s and leveled off in the 1980s. Today there are roughly 4,200 PACs.

Source: *Data from Federal Election Commission, "FEC Records Slight Increase in the Number of PACs," January 17, 2008, available at www.fec.gov/press/press2008/20080117paccount.shtml.*

The number of PACs exploded in the 1970s before topping out in the 1980s at around 4,200. The number of PACs declined slightly during the 1990s before rising again to about 4,200 in 2008. As you can see in Figure 10–1, the most common type of PAC is a corporate PAC. The second most common is the nonconnected PAC, which is independent, at least in legal terms, from established interest groups. One nonconnected PAC is EMILY's List—the acronym stands for "early money is like yeast"—which gives money to Democratic women candidates who support abortion rights. Another nonconnected PAC, MoveOn.org Political Action favors progressive political candidates. Like EMILY's List and MoveOn.org, most (but not all) nonconnected PACs try to promote particular ideological positions rather than economic interests. Table 10–1 lists some PACs and their parent interest groups.

Over time, PAC spending has increased. During the 2005–2006 election cycle, for example, PACs spent $1.1 billion, which is twenty times more than they spent during the election cycle thirty years earlier and $212 million more than they spent during the 2003–2004 election cycle.[41] Figure 10–2 shows how much money different kinds of PACs spent during the 2005–2006 election cycle. Corporate and nonconnected PACs generally spend the most. Although the total amount of PAC money is considerable, most individual PACs spend relatively little. Many spend less than $100,000 during an election cycle. Some PACs, however, spend far more. During the 2005–2006 election cycle, for example, fifty

PAC Name	Associated Corporation or Interest Group
ATE PAC	Asplundh Tree Expert Company
BAKEPAC	Independent Bakers Association
BANKPAC	American Bankers Association
BEEF-PAC	Texas Cattle Feeders Association
BREADPAC	American Bakers Association
BUSPAC	American Bus Association
COLT PAC	American Horse Council, Inc.
COTTON PAC	California Cotton Growers Association
EGGPAC	United Egg Association
FOOD PAC	Food Marketing Institute
PEACH-PAC	California Peach Canning Association
PENNEYPAC	JC Penney Company CC
PORK PAC	National Pork Producers Council
POTATO PAC	National Potato Council
POWER PAC	American Public Power Association
PUMP PAC	American Concrete Pumping Association
PURDUE PAC	Purdue Pharma Inc.
RAMS PAC	American Sheep Industry Association
ROBIN PAC	Reinforcing Our Beliefs in North Carolina PAC
SKINPAC	American Academy of Dermatology Association
WIN PAC	Women's Pro-Israel National PAC

Table 10–1   Select Political Action Committees

Many different interest groups have formed political action committees.

Source: *Federal Election Commission, "Pacronyms," January 2008, available at www.fec.gov/ pubrec/pacronyms/pacronyms.pdf.*

PACs accounted for 33 percent of all PAC expenditures. MoveOn. org spent $28.1 million; EMILY's List spent $26.5 million; and the NRA of America Political Victory Fund spent $11.2 million.[42]

Who gets PAC money? A major portion of PAC money, perhaps as much as 50 percent for the average PAC, goes simply to pay the administrative expenses incurred in running the PAC and raising funds. After administrative expenses, the next biggest PAC expenditure is donations to political campaigns. During the 2005–2006 election cycle, contributions to candidates for federal office accounted for 35 percent of PAC spending.[43]

Who gets PAC contributions? The vast bulk goes to candidates for Congress, even during presidential election years. During the 2003–2004 election cycle, for example, PACs contributed $308 million to congressional candidates. In contrast, presidential candidates received only $3 million.[44] The reason PACs favor candidates for Congress over candidates for the presidency is

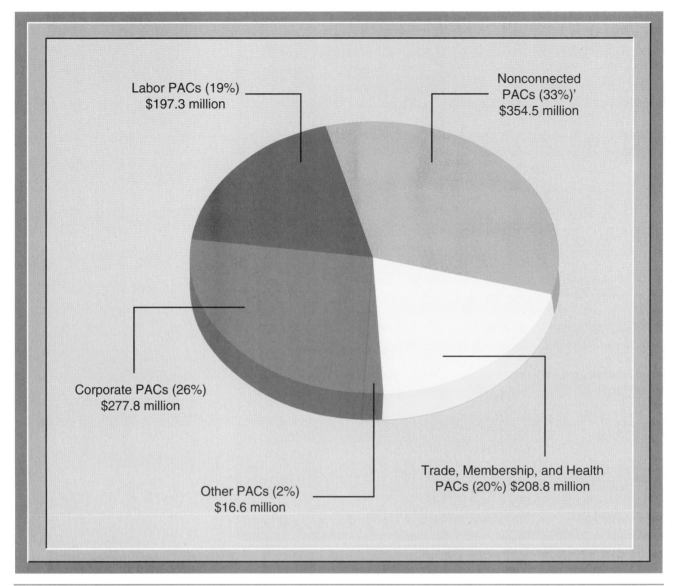

Labor PACs (19%)
$197.3 million

Nonconnected
PACs (33%)'
$354.5 million

Corporate PACs (26%)
$277.8 million

Other PACs (2%)
$16.6 million

Trade, Membership, and Health
PACs (20%) $208.8 million

Figure 10–2   Spending by Political Action Committees (PACs), 2005–2006. During the 2005–2006 election cycle, nonconnected PACs spent the most, followed in order by corporate PACs; PACs representing trade, membership, and health associations; and labor PACs.

Source: *Federal Election Commission, "PAC Activity Continues Climb in 2006," October 5, 2007, available at www.fec.gov/press/press2007/20071009pac/20071009pac.shtml.*

simple: The law enabling presidential candidates to receive public financing for their campaigns severely limits their ability to accept PAC contributions.

In addition to paying administrative expenses and contributing directly to political campaigns, PACs spend a small portion of their money on so-called *independent expenditures.* With an independent expenditure, a PAC promotes or attacks a candidate for office without formally coordinating its efforts with any political party or candidate. Take the 2008 Democratic presidential primary campaign, for example. The American Federation of State, County, and Municipal Employees PAC spent $2.3 million, and EMILY's List spent $1.3 million to help Hillary Clinton win the Democratic nomination. Meanwhile, the Service Employee's International

Union PAC spent $9 million and MoveOn.org spent $755,000 to help Barack Obama win.[45] PAC spending on independent expenditures is much higher during presidential election years than during congressional midterm years. The reason is simple: Presidential election years give PACs the opportunity to influence who sits in the White House as well as who controls both houses of Congress.

As you can see, the vast bulk of PAC money actually spent on political campaigns is spent on elections to Congress. When it comes to contributing to congressional campaigns, spending patterns vary among PACs. Corporate and trade association PACs largely ignore party labels; they care more about backing someone who will win the election and support their views than they do about helping the Democratic or Republican parties. Labor PACs and ideological PACs, however, pay attention to party labels. It is easy to see why. Many of the issues important to labor PACs and ideological PACs divide Democrats from Republicans. It would hardly make sense, for example, for a labor PAC to contribute to the reelection campaigns of Republicans who favor laws making it harder to unionize. Nor would it make sense for a group such as the National Conservative Political Action Committee to help *reelect* a liberal senator such as Edward Kennedy.

Although some PACs ignore party labels, all PACs pay close attention to whether a candidate is likely to win. Because of the high reelection rates in Congress, PACs favor incumbents. During the 2005–2006 election cycle, for instance, PACs gave nearly eight times more money to incumbents than they did to challengers.[46] And party leaders and committee chairs—especially those chairing the energy and tax committees—receive far more PAC contributions than average members of Congress.[47]

Of course, because PACs favor incumbent legislators, the party that benefits most from PAC contributions changes when partisan control of Congress changes. This is precisely what happened following the 1994 elections, when Republicans regained control of both houses of Congress for the first time in forty years. As Figure 10–3 shows, during the 1993–1994 election cycle, when Democrats were still the majority on Capitol Hill, they received nearly two-thirds of all PAC contributions to congressional candidates. During the 1995–1996 election cycle, however, the donation pattern was the reverse; Republican candidates received a majority of PAC contributions. Republicans maintained that funding edge over Democrats for the next decade. During the 2005–2006 election cycle, for example, 56 percent of PAC contributions went to Republican candidates. During the first nine months of 2007, however, PACs favored Democratic candidates, steering 57 percent of contributions their way. Again, the change occurred not because PACs suddenly decided that they liked the policies of the Democratic Party more than those of the Republican Party—although some of them may well have—but because, beginning in January 2007, more incumbents and all committee chairs were Democrats.

PACs are also often quick to switch sides if someone they back loses. During the 2000 primary and general election campaigns,

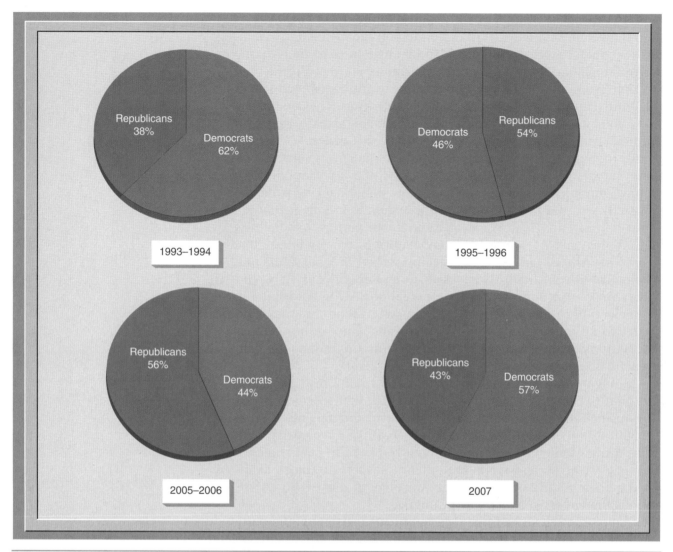

Figure 10–3   Changes in Political Action Committee (PAC) Contributions to Congress. PACs gave more money to
Democrats when the Democratic Party controlled Congress; they favored Republicans when the
Republican Party controlled Congress.

Sources: Data from Campaign Finance Institute, "PAC Fundraising Swings Democratic Over the First Nine Months Of 2007," November 8, 2007, available at
www.cfinst.org/pr/prRelease.aspx?ReleaseID=167; Federal Election Commission, "PAC Activity Continues Climb in 2006," October 5, 2007, available at
www.fec.gov/press/press2007/20071009pac/20071009pac.shtml; Harold W. Stanley and Richard G. Niemi, *Vital Statistics on American Politics,
2005–2006* (Washington, D.C.: CQ Press, 2006), 110.

for example, the PAC for General Dynamics, a major weapons
manufacturer, gave $10,000 to ten-term Democratic Rep. Sam
Gejdenson (D-CT). But Gejdenson lost to the Republican candidate, Rob Simmons. The General Dynamics PAC did not miss a
beat. Ten days after the polls closed, it wrote Simmons a $5,000
check. "He is representing a district where we have a major business," said a General Dynamics spokesperson. "A lot of our
employees are his constituents. Accordingly, we have an interest
in seeing Congressman Simmons succeed."[48]

What do PACs get for their campaign contributions? Much of
the popular debate over campaign financing suggests that PACs
are in the business of buying votes. Yet the testimony of PAC officials and political candidates, as well as a good deal of research by

political scientists, indicates that the impact of PAC money is greatly exaggerated.[49] As one PAC official puts it:

> You certainly aren't going to be able to buy anybody for $500 or $1,000 or $10,000. It's a joke. Occasionally something will happen where everybody in one industry will be for one specific solution to a problem, and they may then pour money to one guy. And he suddenly looks out and says, "I haven't got $7,000 from this group, I've got $70,000." That might get his attention: "I've got to support what they want." But that's a rarity.[50]

The reality of how difficult it is for PACs to buy votes is illustrated by the outcome of the 2006 debate over so-called net neutrality. Republican congressional leaders wanted to pass a bill that would have allowed telecommunications companies to charge different rates for different Internet users. The telecommunications companies, which had given money to many members of Congress, supported the bill enthusiastically. But a coalition of bloggers used the power of the Internet to mobilize public sentiment against the bill. It went down to defeat.[51]

Why does PAC money do a poor job of buying votes? There are several reasons. One is the $5,000 limit on contributions. The immense cost of political campaigns, which can exceed $5 million in a Senate race and $1 million in a House race, means that individual PACs provide a tiny percentage of a candidate's funding. Hence, candidates frequently can afford to ignore a contributor's wishes. Another reason that PAC money does a poor job of buying votes is that contributions from competing PACs frequently cancel each other out. Members who get contributions from both sides in a debate will inevitably disappoint one of set of contributors. A third reason PAC money does a poor job of buying votes is that most elected officials find it politically risky to abandon their policy preferences for the sake of a campaign contribution. Officials who change their position on an issue after receiving a PAC contribution make themselves an obvious target for political attack in the next election. Finally, PAC contributions are not the only factors members consider when deciding how to vote. As the 2006 net neutrality debate shows, angry voters can trump well-heeled lobbyists.

If PAC money generally does not buy votes, why do PACs continue to contribute to political campaigns? The answer is simple: to ensure access to elected officials.[52] Access clearly matters when you want to influence public policy; after all, persuading elected officials to adopt policies you favor is difficult if you cannot get your foot inside the door. PACs that fail to make campaign contributions worry they will find themselves on the outside looking in when matters of public policy relevant to their interests are being discussed. As one PAC official explains it: "You know, some congressman has got X number of ergs of energy, and here's a person or a company who wants to come see him and give him a thousand dollars, and here's another one who wants to just stop by and say hello. And he has only time to see one. Which one? So the PAC's an attention getter."[53]

The links between campaign contributions and access to elected officials is why so many PACs change which party they favor when partisan control of Congress changes. Wal-Mart, for instance, gave 98 percent of its political contributions to Republican candidates in 1996. In 2008, with all signs pointing to the Democrats solidifying their control on Congress and potentially winning the White House, Wal-Mart gave 46 percent of its political contributions to Democrats. The firm feared that Congress was poised to pass legislation that would make it easier for workers to unionize, something the big box retailer had fought for decades. The firm wanted to make sure that it was part of the conversation on any union bill that might be written.[54] As the Wal-Mart example suggests, the power in the relationship between PAC and elected officials does not always favor the PAC. One professional campaign fund-raiser notes, "Some members will get on the phone and be threatening: 'If you don't come [to my fund-raiser], I'll never vote for you again.' I'd like to think that doesn't happen, but I know it does, on both sides of the aisle."[55]

The fact that PAC contributions buy more access than votes suggests that the popular concern about PACs corrupting American politics is overstated. Instead of politicians being beholden to PACs, to some extent, PACs are beholden to politicians. If a group fails to contribute to campaigns, it risks losing access to elected officials. Thus, for interest groups, PAC contributions are to some degree an insurance policy (or, less charitably, protection money).

10-5b Lobbying the Government

With PACs, interest groups try to influence public policy by influencing who wins elected office. But interest groups do not stop there; they also try to influence what elected officials do after they are in office. Interest groups do this through **lobbying**—that is, attempting to influence governmental decisions, especially the voting decisions legislators make on proposed legislation. The phrase *to lobby* originated in seventeenth-century England, where people wishing to influence the government buttonholed members of Parliament in a large lobby off the floor of the House of Commons to plead their case. Not surprisingly, people who make their living trying to influence public policy are known as **lobbyists.**

Who are lobbyists? Some are staff members of the interest group they represent; others are "hired guns" who work for a law firm or a public relations firm the interest group retains (see Box 10–1). Although lobbying is traditionally a male-dominated profession, more and more women are becoming lobbyists. In recent years, women served as the chief lobbyists for more than forty major firms—including Coca-Cola, Ford, General Electric, and Hershey Foods. Women head up many prominent lobbying firms.[56] Most lobbyists are well paid—with the best earning hundreds of thousands and even more a year (although lobbyists for citizen groups typically earn far less). The allure of high pay explains why so many legislators, their aides, and even their family members

lobbying
Trying to influence governmental decisions, especially the voting decisions legislators make on proposed legislation.

lobbyists
People who make their living trying to influence public policy.

The People behind the Rules

Box 10-1   Tommy Boggs and Nancy Dorn

Professional lobbyists work the halls of the Capitol to promote the interests of the groups they represent. Two of the most successful lobbyists in recent years are Tommy Boggs and Nancy Dorn.

THOMAS HALE BOGGS, JR.

Corporations and business groups that want a lobbyist who knows the corridors of power in Washington turn to Tommy Boggs. Known around the nation's capital as a top gun among lobbyists, his firm, Patton Boggs, employs four hundred lawyers and billed $42 million in lobbying fees alone in 2007. Its roster of clients reads like a who's who of the corporate, professional, and academic worlds: the Association of Trial Lawyers of America, Clemson University, Mars, Microsoft, the National Geographic Society, New York Life, the University of Washington, and Wal-Mart among others.

Politics comes naturally to Boggs. His father, Hale Boggs, served as majority leader in the House of Representatives. His mother, Lindy Boggs, became a member of Congress on her husband's death and served for twenty years. And one of Tommy's sisters, Cokie Roberts, has been a correspondent for both National Public Radio and ABC News.

Early on, it looked as if Tommy Boggs would follow in his father's footsteps. After graduating from Georgetown University in 1961, he worked for the Joint Economic Committee of Congress and earned a law degree at Georgetown. In 1970, Boggs launched his own bid for Congress, running for a House seat

from Maryland. He did not, however, enjoy his parents' electoral touch. He lost decisively to a two-term incumbent.

Despite never winning elected office, Boggs remains a power in Washington politics. As one of Washington's "superlobbyists," he has been in the thick of numerous legislative battles. Yet the corporations and groups that hire Boggs are by no means guaranteed victory. Like all Washington lobbyists, he has both wins and losses to his credit. As one Washington observer puts it: "What you buy with Tommy Boggs is access. Very few people are gonna say they won't see him. You buy acumen. This is somebody who understands how the process works."

NANCY DORN

A lobbyist like Tommy Boggs works for clients who hire his firm. But some lobbyists work directly for a company or advocacy group. One of the best corporate lobbyists is Nancy Dorn, vice president for corporate government relations at General Electric (GE).

If anyone in Washington has the background to be a lobbyist, it is Dorn. She first arrived in the nation's capital in 1981 after graduating from Baylor University. She quickly landed a job working for a member of Congress from Texas. After six years on the Hill, she moved to the Reagan administration where she worked first as a Deputy Assistant Secretary for Legislative Affairs in the State Department and then as a Special Assistant to the President.

She stayed on at the White House to work for President George H. W. Bush.

In 1991, he named her Assistant Secretary of the Army for Civil Works, a position that oversees the Army Corps of Engineers. She was the youngest person and the first woman to hold the job.

When Bill Clinton took the oath of office in 1993, Dorn joined a lobbying firm. In 2000, she returned to government to work as national security adviser to House Speaker Dennis J. Hastert (R-IL). When Republicans retook control of the White House in 2001, she joined George W. Bush's administration. She worked first as an assistant to Vice President Dick Cheney and then as deputy director of the Office of Management and Budget. In 2003, she left government to work for GE.

GE, one the biggest companies in the world, is also one of the biggest spenders when it comes to lobbying. In 2007, it spent $26 million on lobbying. Dorn has been a big part of GE's ability to persuade lawmakers to see things its way. She has repeatedly been named one of the most influential lobbyists and women in Washington. The nation's capital, she says, is a good place for "alpha females."

Sources: Leslie Milk, "100 Most Powerful Women," *Washingtonian Magazine*, June 2006, available at www.washingtonian.com/print/articles/11/155/1670.html; OpenSecrets.org/Center for Responsive Politics, "Patton Boggs, LLP," available at www.opensecrets.org/lobby/firmsum.php?year=2007&lname=Patton+Boggs+LLP; Hedrick Smith, *The Power Game: How Washington Works* (New York: Random House, 1988), 234–35; "Top Corporate Lobbyists in D.C.," The Hill.Com, April 24, 2008, available at www.thehill.com/business–lobby/top-corporate-lobbyists-in-d.c.-2008-04-24.html.

become lobbyists after they leave Congress rather than returning to their home districts and states. Indeed, one study found that 43 percent of the 198 lawmakers who left Congress between 1988 and 2005 registered as lobbyists once they returned to private life.[57] Yet whether lobbyists come from Capitol Hill or elsewhere, all successful lobbyists share one trait: knowledge of the way government works.

direct lobbying
Trying to influence public policy through direct contact with government officials.

When lobbyists personally contact government officials to plead their case, they are engaging in **direct lobbying.** Interest groups devote much of their time to direct lobbying of members of Congress. The key to successful lobbying on Capitol Hill is information.[58] A journalist who spent a year observing the Senate writes, "more than 99 percent of lobbying effort is spent not on parties, weekend hosting, and passing plain white envelopes, but trying to persuade minds through facts and reason."[59] A successful lobbyist makes the same point even more bluntly: "Information is the currency of Capitol Hill, not dollars. And not friends."[60]

Information is the currency lobbyists use because members of Congress are forced to make decisions on far more issues than any person—even one with aides—can master. Members and their staff are so busy they may even rely on lobbyists to help them do their jobs. To quote one congressional staffer:

> My boss demands a speech and a statement for the *Congressional Record* for every bill we introduce or co-sponsor—and we have a lot of bills. I just can't do it all myself. The better lobbyists, when they have a proposal they are pushing, bring it to me along with a couple of speeches, a *Record* insert, and a fact sheet.[61]

Or as Senator Christopher Bond (R-MO) put it, "As lobbyists have expertise, we welcome whoever has good information."[62]

Because members need information, lobbyists might be tempted to play fast and loose with the truth. Yet although lobbyists often minimize facts that hurt their case and may well exaggerate their political strength, they generally avoid intentionally misleading members of Congress.[63] The reason is that the long-term costs of lying far outweigh the short-term benefits. Lobbyists can do their jobs only as long as members trust their word. That trust will evaporate if members discover a lobbyist has lied to them.

Lobbyists devote much of their time to working with members of Congress who support their cause as well as with those who are undecided. Not surprisingly, lobbyists generally avoid wasting their time trying to lobby members who take the opposite side of the issue. In working with their legislative allies, lobbyists often become deeply involved in activities such as planning hearings, drafting legislation, and plotting strategy. When the Republicans controlled the House and Senate, the congressional leadership ran a "Values Action Team" that held weekly meetings to coordinate strategy between Republican lawmakers and antiabortion and social-conservative groups such as Alliance for Marriage, Concerned Women for America, and Focus on the Family.[64]

Although lobbying is commonly associated with Congress, interest groups also lobby the executive branch. Lobbyists would prefer to speak directly to the president and cabinet officials. For most lobbyists, however, such meetings are difficult to arrange; presidents and cabinet officials are far less accessible than members of Congress. The bulk of executive branch lobbying focuses instead on senior aides in the White House and at the various federal agencies. Every president since Gerald Ford has maintained an Office of Public Liaison to keep open lines of communication with major interest groups, particularly those that support the president.[65] Like members of Congress, administrations work closely with groups that share their policy preferences.

As with Congress, the main tool interest groups use to lobby the executive branch is information. To gain an advantage in dealing with federal agencies, interest groups frequently hire former executive branch officials as lobbyists. Groups hope to benefit from the knowledge former officials have about how an agency works as well as from their friendships with agency employees. Much debate surrounds the propriety of hiring former executive branch officials as lobbyists. Critics worry that officials may favor certain interest groups to get well-paid jobs as lobbyists, and after they become lobbyists, exploit their insider knowledge to benefit their employer. To limit influence peddling of this sort, federal law prohibits executive branch officials and members of Congress from lobbying on matters they worked on while in government for one year after leaving office.[66]

Although lobbyists work to influence government, the reverse may be increasingly true. Historically, most lobbying firms hired both Republican and Democratic operatives so that they could have access to both parties. When Republicans took control of Congress after the 1994 elections, however, they sought to change that. Under the banner of the "K Street Project"—named after the street a few blocks north of the White House where many lobbyists have their offices—they pressed lobbying firms to hire only loyal Republicans for top jobs. Each week, Republican congressional leaders met with Republican activists and lobbyists to review lists of available jobs and to decide on appropriate candidates. Meanwhile, Republican activists tracked the party affiliation, Hill experience, and political giving of every lobbyist. Firms that ran afoul of the Republican leadership knew they risked being frozen out of policy discussions that affected their interests or those of their clients. Many lobbying firms saw that as a risk they could not afford to take, especially when Republican gained control of the White House as well as Congress after the 2000 election.

Democrats criticized the K Street Project. Their main complaint was that it steered campaign contributions to Republicans, thereby tipping the electoral playing field in their favor. Critics with no partisan interests at stake worried that lobbying jobs had become a powerful form of political patronage. A top government post might pay $140,000. In comparison, a top lobbying job could pay $500,000 or more. The prospect of such a financial windfall could have encouraged potential and actual lobbyists to be inordinately responsive to the Republican Party.

Few Republicans sympathized with the critics' complaints. "K Street is still only 30 percent Republican," said Representative Jennifer Dunn (R-WA), who interviewed with more than a dozen lobbying firms when she retired from Congress in 2005. "So there's a lot more work to do to make it even."[67] Others were even less apologetic. Former House Majority Leader Tom DeLay (R-TX), whose nickname is "the Hammer," was the driving force behind the K Street Project. He once told the *Washington Post,* "If you want to play in our revolution, you have to live by our rules."[68]

Democrats said they would not institute their version of the K Street Project when they took control of Congress after the 2006 election. "If we're ever going to have real change here" on Capitol Hill, said Democratic House leader Nancy Pelosi (D-CA) before the election, "we must kill the K Street Project."[69] But some Democrats thought that turnabout was fair play. Senator Bob Menendez (D-NJ) told lobbying firms in 2008 that if they didn't start sending friendlier faces up to Congress, they might find it "a little difficult at the end of the day for them to achieve the success they want" and that "they haven't come to terms with what happened two Novembers ago."[70] Republicans were quick to accuse Democratic leaders of hypocrisy.

10-5c Mobilizing Public Opinion

Efforts to lobby the government are sometimes called *inside strategies* because they rely on gaining access to government officials. But interest groups can also try to influence public policy through so-called *outside strategies,* which are efforts designed to put pressure on government officials by mobilizing public opinion on the group's behalf.[71] The outside strategies that interest groups use to mobilize public opinion include education campaigns, grass-roots lobbying, and civil disobedience. All three outside strategies rely on one simple idea: Government officials listen to what voters have to say.

Education Campaigns

One way interest groups try to mobilize public opinion is by educating the public about issues. Groups often find that one of the biggest obstacles to achieving their policy goals is the public's general ignorance of the issues. In turn, groups calculate that if they can raise public awareness about an issue, voters might demand government action. Thus, the Children's Defense Fund has sought to build political support for increased spending on social programs by educating Americans about the extent and consequences of childhood poverty in the United States.

One popular educational technique is the media campaign, which encompasses a broad array of activities. At one end of the spectrum lie efforts to shape the way the news media cover stories. Interest groups frequently send news organizations suggestions on stories to cover as well as information on stories they are covering. At the other end of the spectrum lies **advocacy advertising**, or the practice of buying newspaper, television, and radio advertisements that directly promote a group's views. Major defense companies, for example, routinely sponsor Sunday morning network talk shows and run commercials extolling the importance of a strong defense. As a rule, the great expense of advocacy advertising

advocacy advertising
Newspaper, television, and radio advertisements that promote an interest group's political views.

limits its use on a sustained basis to interest groups with deep financial pockets—which usually means big corporations.

Interest groups also try to educate the public by publishing research studies. Groups hope that people will read the studies themselves, or more likely, read or hear about the studies in the news media. For example, the liberal Center on Budget and Policy Priorities released several studies purporting to show that President Bush's tax cuts primarily benefited wealthy Americans, did little to stimulate the economy, and drove up the federal budget deficit. The conservative Tax Foundation released competing studies purporting to show that the tax cuts created jobs and benefited most Americans. Both groups hoped their studies would influence the congressional debate on tax policy.[72] A third way interest groups try to educate voters is by rating members of Congress in terms of how often each votes "correctly" on issues a group deems important. Most groups score members on a scale of 0 to 100, with 0 denoting a legislator staunchly opposed to the cause of the interest group and 100 denoting a legislator staunchly in favor. As you might imagine, liberal groups give Democrats high scores and Republicans low scores, whereas conservative groups do just the opposite.

Grass-Roots Lobbying

With **grass-roots lobbying**, interest groups go beyond education and actively try to mobilize their memberships and the broader public into action to influence policy. A common type of grass-roots lobbying is the petition drive, a technique in which people gather the signatures of registered voters to put a candidate or issue on the ballot. (The rules governing how many signatures are needed to put a candidate or issue on the ballot vary from state to state.) Other common types of grass-roots lobbying are letter writing and phone calling. These rather old lobbying techniques have enjoyed a renaissance in recent years with the growth of radio and television talk shows; many groups have found that talk shows are an effective way to mobilize voters to action. Interest groups calculate, with good reason, that members of Congress and executive branch officials will pay more attention to the letters and phone calls of a thousand voters than they will to the efforts of a dozen lobbyists.

Grass-roots lobbying may also involve protest marches and demonstrations as groups try to show Congress and the White House that their cause enjoys broad public support. Some protests come with a dash of political theater as groups try to maximize media coverage and thereby increase pressure on government officials. Peace groups often sponsor "die-ins" to illustrate the dangers of war, farmers occasionally drive their tractors to Washington in "tractorcades" to highlight their anger at agricultural policy, and pro-life advocates sometimes erect miniature cemeteries to dramatize their view that abortion is murder. Groups resort to political theater because they know, as we saw in Chapter 8, that dramatic

grass-roots lobbying
Trying to influence public policy indirectly by mobilizing an interest group's membership and the broader public to contact elected officials.

visual images attract the attention of the news media, especially television news.

Another type of grass-roots lobbying revolves around get-out-the-vote activities, a campaign strategy we discussed in Chapter 7. Several groups work on registering people to vote. One of the best known is the Rev. Jesse Jackson's Rainbow Coalition, which seeks to register minority voters. But organized labor runs the most extensive get-out-the-vote campaigns. Not only do labor unions run voter registration campaigns, but they also devote considerable time and effort to convincing union members and supporters to support the candidates the union endorses. When Election Day rolls around, many unions open phone banks so they can call labor supporters and encourage them to vote. In some instances, unions even arrange to drive voters to the polls.

A new type of grass-roots lobbying that has emerged in recent years with the spread of the Internet is **netroots lobbying.** The term refers to using blogs, wikis (Web sites where anyone can add or modify the content), and social networking sites to pressure elected officials on political issues. Although many Internet-savvy, liberal and progressive groups consciously use the term *netroots* to describe their activities, conservatives have been equally adept at using the Internet to advance political causes and pressure elected officials. For instance, conservative bloggers have been credited with fueling public opposition to immigration reform and bringing to light video of Barack Obama's pastor giving incendiary sermons.

Because grass-roots lobbying can be so effective in shaping government policy, wealthy interest groups (which usually means business groups) increasingly have sought to create synthetic grass-roots movements. Such **Astroturf lobbying** encourages individuals to contact their elected officials by making it very easy to do. Thus, groups send out preaddressed postcards with messages to members of Congress already printed on them, telephone potential supporters and connect them automatically to congressional offices, and advertise 800 numbers people can call if they want a letter to go to Congress in their name. For instance, in 2008 AngryRenter.com appeared on the Internet. The Web site criticized proposals for the federal government to help homeowners hurt by the severe downturn in the American mortgage market, proposals the Web site contended asked renters to pay taxes to bail out irresponsible homeowners. The Web site encouraged visitors to sign an online petition demanding that Congress say no to a bailout. Most of the nearly 50,000 people who signed the petition probably thought that AngryRenter had been put together by renters. Not only were the graphics amateurish, the Web site proclaimed "We are millions of renters standing up for our rights!" However, the Web site actually was put up by FreedomWorks, a conservative advocacy group led by former House Majority Leader Dick Armey and former Republican presidential candidate and publishing magnate Steve Forbes. Neither man was a renter. Forbes owned a mansion in New York and château in France. Armey

netroots lobbying
Using blogs, wikis and social networking sites on the Internet to pressure elected officials on political issues.

astroturf lobbying
Efforts, usually led by interest groups with deep financial pockets, to create synthetic grass-roots movements by aggressively encouraging voters to contact their elected officials about specific issues.

and Forbes were ideologically opposed to government intervention in the economy and believed that many renters shared their view.[73]

Astroturf lobbying obviously carries great potential for abuse. Just how great became clear when the Competitive Long Distance Coalition, a group seeking to block passage of a telecommunications bill, hired a firm to generate letters from consumers. It turned out, however, that "as many as half of the telegrams that deluged House members were sent without the signatories' approval."[74]

Because Astroturf lobbying can backfire if it is exposed, interest groups looking to mobilize the public on their behalf usually prefer broad-based education campaigns. The rationale is that if voters know a problem exists, they will demand government action. However, interest groups do not necessarily go out of their way to let voters know they are behind an education campaign. For example, in 2004, residents of Madison County, Illinois, suddenly had a new newspaper to read. The paper played up stories about questionable lawsuits against businesses, like one filed by a woman asking for $15,000 in damages after breaking her nose at a haunted house. What Madison County residents probably did not know was that the newspaper was owned by the U.S. Chamber of Commerce—its name was not listed on the paper's masthead. The Chamber of Commerce launched the newspaper as part of its multimillion dollar campaign to build support for restricting lawsuits against businesses. Madison County's courthouses led the nation in the number of lawsuits filed against businesses.[75]

Business organizations are not the only interest groups blurring the lines between media and advocacy. The Nuclear Threat Initiative (NTI), co-founded by Ted Turner and former Senator Sam Nunn, produced *Last Best Chance,* a forty-five-minute movie about terrorists who have stolen a nuclear bomb. The movie starred professional actors—its fictional American president was played by Fred Thompson, a former senator who played the role of district attorney on NBC's *Law & Order* and ran unsuccessfully for the Republican presidential nomination in 2008. NTI's hope was that the movie would raise public awareness about the threat posed by the spread of nuclear weapons. Unless viewers carefully watched the credits, they probably would not know that the movie was developed by an interest group looking to change government policy.

The U.S. Chamber of Commerce, NTI, and other interest groups that have bought media outlets or mimicked traditional media formats defend the practice as a legitimate way to spread their views. "We have as much right to be at the table delivering news and information to the American public as anyone else does," argues the executive director of the NRA, which runs an Internet radio news show and which has considered buying its own radio stations.[76] Critics, however, see dangers in the practice. "People judge communication by its source," notes one media expert, "so when you deny people full knowledge of the source of information they are losing something important about evaluating the message."[77] At the same time, ownership of a media outlet might enable interest groups to get around campaign finance laws, which is one of the reasons the idea appeals to some interest groups.[78] Despite these fears, the rules of the American political system, and in particular the First Amendment, make it difficult if not impossible to maintain a bright line between advocacy groups and the media.

Civil Disobedience

In some circumstances, interest groups break the law to pressure legislators into changing it. Rev. Dr. Martin Luther King forcefully advocated the practice of civil disobedience during the civil rights protests of the 1960s. More recently, the pro-life group Operation Rescue has used civil disobedience as a tactic. The group has blocked the entrances to abortion clinics in several cities, despite court orders to the contrary. Another practitioner of civil disobedience is the environmental group Earth First! that has illegally blocked logging of the forests.

Groups that practice civil disobedience hope that breaking the law will draw attention to what they see as unjust government policy. The success of the tactic depends first on having members who will risk going to jail and paying heavy fines. In most organizations, the number of such dedicated members is small. The success of civil disobedience also depends on the public's perception that the harm the group causes by breaking the law is not excessive. Law enforcement officials have denounced members of the Earth Liberation Front, which opposes urban sprawl, as "eco-terrorists" because they protest the "rape" of the environment by setting fires in new resorts and housing developments.[79] Finally, civil disobedience works only if groups can sustain their protests over time. If not, the public quickly forgets the sacrifice of the protesters.

Source: © Tim Sloan / AFP / Getty Images.

Some interest groups practice civil disobedience in the hope that by breaking the law they will draw attention to what they see as unjust government policy.

10-5d Litigating

Interest groups often influence public policy by going to court.[80] Sometimes groups seek test cases so they can challenge the constitutionality of existing laws. As Chapter 5 noted, the NAACP has long pushed the cause of civil rights by finding people who have been discriminated against and then helping them challenge that discriminatory behavior in court. Other lawsuits seek to compel the government to enforce existing laws. In recent years, for example, environmental groups have initiated litigation to see that corporations scrupulously obey laws such as the Clean Air Act and the Endangered Species Act.

Besides seeking test cases and initiating their own litigation, interest groups can join lawsuits others file. Individuals or groups who wish to air their views in a lawsuit may petition the court for the right to file an *amicus curiae* (friend of the court) *brief* that argues why the court should rule in favor of one of the parties to the case. Amicus curiae briefs are most commonly filed in lawsuits that involve matters of great public interest such as civil rights and liberties. For example, more than fifty amicus curiae briefs were filed in *Hamdan v. Rumsfeld*, a 2006 case in which the Supreme Court ruled that the military commissions President George W. Bush had created to try suspected members of Al Qaeda were unconstitutional because they had not been authorized by Congress. Some of the briefs were filed by organizations such as the American Civil Liberties Union (ACLU), the American Jewish Committee, and the Bar Association of New York City. Others were filed by individuals, including a former secretary of state, several former attorneys general, two senators, more than three hundred European parliamentarians, and a diverse array of law school professors.

amicus curiae brief
Literally, friend of the court. A brief filed with the court by a person or group who is not directly involved in the legal action but who has views on the matter.

In sum, interest groups can pursue a variety of strategies in their efforts to ensure that the government considers their interests. Indeed, most interest groups use a combination of tactics—forming PACs, lobbying the government, mobilizing public opinion, and even going to court—to try to influence public policy. As we shall see, however, some groups are more successful in their efforts than others.

10-6 INTEREST GROUP INFLUENCE

What makes one interest group more influential than another? The answer to this question is a mix of external and internal factors.

10-6a External Factors

The ability of any interest group to influence public policy depends in part on external factors that lie beyond its immediate control. Who sits in the Oval Office, which party controls Congress, who chairs the relevant congressional committee, which way public opinion is moving, and even how world events are breaking all help determine whether a group gets its way. For example, environmental groups are having more success pushing for action on climate change with Democrat Barack Obama sitting in the White House than they did when Republican George W. Bush resided at 1600 Pennsylvania Avenue.

The ability of an interest group to influence public policy also depends on whether other interest groups oppose its views. As we noted previously, the formation of one interest group can prompt another group to form in opposition. The result is that interest groups on opposite sides of a policy debate expend considerable energies countering—and often negating—each other's efforts. But as we also noted, there is no guarantee that opposing interest groups will form. When opposition fails to materialize, an interest group is better able to push its cause. Edward J. Derwinski, a former Secretary of Veterans Affairs, explained the tremendous success veterans groups have had in protecting veterans programs from budget cuts: "There is no anti-veterans group. It's just a one way street. Now we're not talking about a hell of a big army, but it's unopposed."[81] When an interest group is unopposed, members of Congress and executive branch officials face less pressure to resist the group's demands. Moreover, if no opposition exists to rebut the group's claims, government officials may come to see the policies the group advocates as good public policy.

10-6b Internal Factors

If the ability of an interest group to influence public policy depends partly on factors beyond its immediate control, the internal characteristics of a group also affect its ability to influence policy. Four internal factors in particular affect interest group success: the size and commitment of a group's membership, the political skills of its leaders, its financial resources, and its objectives. Groups need not score high along all four of these dimensions to be successful. But few groups are likely to be influential without at least some strength in these areas.

Membership
All else being equal, government officials are most likely to listen to interest groups that represent large numbers of voters. But size tells only part of the story. College-age Americans, for example, wield little clout in Washington despite their rather sizable numbers. The reason can be gleaned from the comment Senator Wyche Fowler (D-GA) once made in dismissing a request by student lobbyists for a meeting: "Students don't vote. Do you expect me to come in here and kiss your ass?"[82] The commitment of a group's members matters as much as sheer numbers. For instance, conservative and religious groups succeeded in their bid to restrict online gambling not because they represented a major chunk of the American public, but (in part) because they were cohesive and highly motivated.

Maintaining such cohesion and motivation can be difficult for some interest groups, especially those such as peak business associations and trade associations that are composed of many different groups or companies, each of which may have divergent interests. For example, the U.S. Chamber of Commerce is finding it harder to speak with one voice on climate change issues. Many of its members oppose efforts to regulate the emission of heat-trapping gases as costly and unnecessary. But several of the Chamber's biggest and most important members—including General Electric, Dow Chemical, and Alcoa—take an opposite stance. They see working with environmental groups to push for government regulation as good for business.[83]

Leadership

A skillful leadership greatly enhances the work of any interest group. The most effective interest group leaders combine two special skills. First, they understand the nuances of decision making in Washington and know how to represent the group's interest to government officials, the media, and the public. An interest group can waste its political capital if its leaders misjudge the mood on Capitol Hill, alienate the news media, or fail to mobilize public opinion on its behalf. Second, effective interest group leaders know how to manage their organizations. Decisions about how to recruit new members, how to deal with disputes within the group, and which issues to emphasize all affect the stability, and ultimately the success, of an interest group.

Financial Resources

As it does with many things in life, money matters in interest group politics. A large financial war chest enables a group to contribute to political campaigns, to host lavish parties for government officials, to hire the best lobbyists, to run nationwide media campaigns, and to buy the most advanced equipment for direct-mail operations. For example, deep financial pockets make it possible for business and advocacy groups to engage in Astroturf lobbying.

By the same token, lack of money need not condemn an interest group to irrelevance. Many consumer and environmental groups, for example, cannot compete dollar-for-dollar with business and trade groups. These citizen groups compensate for their financial disadvantage by honing their skills at generating so-called free media. They become adept at using research studies, publicity stunts, and protest marches to attract media coverage of their causes. Whether they can overcome their lack of deep pockets and push their political agenda depends on the other factors shaping interest group influence.

Objectives

What an interest group hopes to do also affects its ability to influence public policy. As a general rule, interest groups find it easier to block changes in policy than to lobby for new policies. The reason interest groups find it easier to block changes in policy can be found in Chapter 2: The rules of the American political system favor the status quo. To block new legislation, an interest group often needs only to persuade a few key members of Congress or officials in the executive branch. Yet if a group wants to change a law, it faces the more arduous task of convincing a majority of both houses of Congress as well as the president.

Interest groups also find it easier to get what they want on issues that have a narrow rather than a broad impact on society. The reason is that the greater the number of people affected by the policy change an interest group wants enacted, the more likely that other groups will mobilize to fight the change. For example, in 2006 the city of Thousand Oaks, California, persuaded Congress to appropriate $100,000 to help construct a "community aquatics complex" on the campus of California Lutheran University. You might wonder why the federal government would help a town whose median household income was 40 percent above the national average to build a swimming pool. But the fact the pool affected few people outside of Thousand Oaks made it unlikely the appropriation would attract attention, let alone opposition. [84]In contrast, pro-choice groups have failed to persuade Congress to pass legislation that would guarantee a woman's right to an abortion. Right-to-life groups vehemently oppose abortion, and they have lobbied furiously to make an abortion harder, if not impossible, to get.

In sum, external factors and internal group characteristics such as membership, leadership, financial resources, and objectives all help determine whether an interest group will succeed in its quest to shape a particular rule or policy outcome. We mentioned before that these factors often combine to favor more affluent and educated groups. Let's look now at the effect this may have on our democracy.

10-7 THE BALANCE SHEET ON INTEREST GROUPS

Where does the balance sheet on interest groups stand? Do they advance democratic dialogue? Or do they benefit political elites at the expense of the average citizen? To answer these questions, we need to review the love/hate relationship Americans have with interest groups, discuss the many calls for reforming interest group politics, and review the contributions interests groups make to American democracy.

10-7a A Love/Hate Relationship

We previously noted that the existence of interest groups has always raised troubling questions for American democracy. It seems that everyone denounces the harmful influence of special interests. For example, polls repeatedly find that most Americans believe that lobbyists wield too much influence over government policy.[85]

Yet as Tocqueville and many others have pointed out, joining interest groups seems to be in our blood. By one count, seven out of ten Americans belong to at least one organization that lobbies the government.[86] Of course, most Americans do not recognize the extent of their own involvement in interest group politics: "The typical person giving to the American Cancer Society doesn't think he's giving to a lobbying group. But that's lobbying too."[87] Indeed, if you buy the *Consumer Reports* magazine published by Consumer's Union (which lobbies on banking, insurance, and product safety laws), join the Boy Scouts or Girl Scouts (which lobby to protect tax deductions for charitable contributions), or contribute to the American Foundation of the Blind (which lobbies on behalf of people with disabilities), you become involved in interest group politics.

Moreover, although most Americans dislike interest groups in the abstract, they give specific interest groups high marks. Millions of Americans, for example, not only like the Consumer's Union, the Boy Scouts and Girl Scouts, and the American Federation for the Blind, they give them money each year. Even groups that many Americans dislike can have widespread and ardent supporters. Thus, although you might think that the American Civil Liberties Union and Planned Parenthood—or the National Rifle Association and the Christian Coalition—are pushing for policies that harm the country, millions of your fellow citizens disagree. Disagreement over the virtues of various interest groups means that attempts to distinguish between "good" and "bad" interest groups won't work. Americans are simply too diverse in terms of matters such as race, class, age, gender, religion, occupation, and ideology to produce a

Source: © Reuters/Corbis.

Many organizations in the United States are involved in interest group politics. The Girl Scouts, for instance, lobby to protect tax deductions for charitable contributions. Disagreements over the merits of what these groups are seeking to achieve make it impossible to distinguish between "good" and "bad" interest groups

consensus on which groups promote the public good. America's love/hate relationship with interest groups explains why President Harry Truman once answered a question about whether he would use lobbyists to push his legislative program through Congress by saying: "We probably wouldn't call those people lobbyists. We would call them citizens appearing in the public interest."[88]

What, then, can we conclude about interest group politics? The one thing on which almost all observers agree is that the interest group "chorus sings with a strong upper-class accent"; that is, the wealthy and the powerful are better represented than the poor and the powerless.[89] This is not to say that corporations or trade associations always get their way. They don't. But in politics the saying that "the squeaky wheel gets the grease" holds true more often than not. No matter how meritorious their claims or how just their cause, people who are not organized are at a disadvantage when it comes to ensuring that their views are heard.

10-7b Calls for Reform

Complaints that interest group politics favors the wealthy and the powerful—and particularly the interests of the business community—have prompted numerous calls for reform. Reformers understand a point we have made time and again in this book: Changing the rules of the political process can change the outcomes of that process.

Some changes have been made over the years to the rules governing interest groups. For instance, in the 1970s, Congress initiated public financing of presidential campaigns. In 1995, Congress enacted several different reforms that affected its own relations with interest groups. The Senate adopted rules that forbid senators from accepting any gift worth more than $50 from a lobbyist.[90] The House went even further; it adopted rules barring representatives from accepting gifts from anyone other than family members or friends.[91] Congress also passed a law that imposed tougher disclosure requirements on groups that lobby the federal government, as Box 10–2 discusses at greater length.[92]

In 2002, Congress went beyond limiting gift giving and toughening disclosure requirements for lobbyists by passing the **Bipartisan Campaign Reform Act (BRCA).** Better known as **McCain-Feingold** after its two Senate sponsors, the law is both complex and controversial. One controversial provision bars interest groups from circumventing limits on contributions to candidates for federal office by giving to the national political parties to run campaign ads. Another bars interest groups from running independent ads promoting or attacking federal candidates close to an election.[93]

Efforts such as McCain-Feingold that seek to reform interest group politics risk violating the basic rules of American politics—most notably, the right, enshrined in the First Amendment, of individuals and groups to petition the government and speak freely about political issues during campaigns. Indeed, the Supreme Court effectively gutted the first effort to regulate lobbyists, the

Bipartisan Campaign Reform Act (BCRA)
Also known as McCain-Feingold. A law passed in 2002 that restricts the ability of interest groups to donate funds to national political parties and bars interest groups from running ads promoting or attacking federal candidates close to an election.

McCain-Feingold
Also known as the Bipartisan Campaign Reform Act (BCRA). A law passed in 2002 that restricts the ability of interest groups to donate funds to national political parties and bars interest groups from running ads promoting or attacking federal candidates close to an election.

POINT OF ORDER

Box 10–2 Limiting the Influence of Interest Groups: The Lobbying Disclosure Act of 1995 and the Honest Leadership and Open Government Act of 2007

Americans have long been suspicious of their elected officials. They believe that too often laws are made "behind closed doors" with the public interest "sold out" in deals cut with "special interests." Books with titles such as *The Best Congress Money Can Buy* and *The Government Racket*, as well as television news exposes of well-heeled interest groups paying for members of Congress to attend "conferences" at plush resorts, testify to and feed those suspicions.

Reformers have sought to reduce the influence of special interests by changing the rules of political decision making. Over the past four decades, several such rules changes have been enacted. For example, the use of direct primaries has expanded to promote broader public participation in the presidential nomination process (see

Chapters 9 and 12). Likewise, Congress has opened up the deliberations of its committees to greater public scrutiny, and it has passed laws requiring candidates for federal office to disclose the identity of contributors to their election campaigns (see Chapter 12). In each of these instances, reformers were seeking to reduce the influence of special interests by exposing various aspects of the governing process to public view.

None of these changes, though, cut to the heart of the public's fears about interest group lobbying—who influences government officials? Congress took one step toward giving the public a better view of the lobbying process when it passed the Lobbying Disclosure Act of 1995. This law tried to accomplish many of the goals first set out, but not achieved, by the 1946 Federal Regulation of Lobbying Act. The Lobbying Disclosure Act law did so first by greatly broadening who is considered to be a lobbyist. It also required individuals who receive more than $5,000 in a six-month period for their lobbying efforts, as well as organizations that spend more than $20,000 on lobbying in a six-month period, to file reports with Congress.

(Tax-exempt organizations such as church groups are exempt from the filing requirement.) These reports must identify the lobbyist's clients, the issues lobbied, specific bills lobbied, and the executive agencies and houses of Congress lobbied; the reports must also estimate how much each lobbying campaign cost. The reports do not have to identify the specific individuals that lobbyists contacted. Lobbyists who fail to file the required report may be fined.

The Lobbying Disclosure Act change gave Americans information about lobbying activities. It did not, however, end lobbying abuses. By 2006, Congress was caught up in a new lobbying scandal. A prominent Republican lobbyist pled guilty to giving gifts and campaign donations to legislators in return for their support for legislation that helped his clients. The scandal forced two leading House Republicans to resign, and one pled guilty to criminal charges.

The new Democratic majority that took control of Capitol Hill after the 2006 elections responded by passing the Honest Leadership and Open Government Act of 2007. The law's proponents hailed it as the most sweeping reform legislation to pass Congress since Watergate. Among the law's many provisions it mandated that the reports required by the Lobbying Disclosure Act be filed quarterly rather than semi-annually; increased the penalties under the Lobbying Disclosure Act from $50,000 to $200,000; banned almost all gifts, including meals, from lobbyists to members of Congress; and required lobbyists to provide information about when they give so-called bundled donations, the practice by which lobbyists gather contributions from friends and associates and give the funds to a candidate.

Did the Honest Leadership and Open Government Act change things on Capitol Hill? Yes, though not as much as the law's supporters hoped. Lobbyists scrambled to comply with the law's disclosure requirements. But a standoff between President George W. Bush and Congress over filling

The Lobbying Disclosure Act of 1995 requires lobbyists to disclose more about their efforts to influence government policy.

POINT OF ORDER   *(continued)*

vacancies on the Federal Election Commission put the provisions regarding bundling on hold. The commission could not develop the regulations needed to implement that part of the law because it did not have enough commissioners to act. Meanwhile, lobbyists who studied the rules barring gifts and meals began to find ways to get around them.

The law did force the ethics committees in the House and Senate to specify exactly which contacts with

lobbyists are acceptable and which are not. Lawmakers and their staff cannot let lobbyists pick up the check for dinner. They can, however, eat food and drinks of nominal value that lobbyists offer at a reception or business meeting. So celery sticks and punch at a holiday reception are okay, but a hot dog is not because it is deemed to constitute a meal. The Senate Ethics Committee did make things easier for its members who like to appear on the Sunday morning

television news programs. They may accept a cup of coffee from their hosts—something otherwise forbidden because the networks employ lobbyists.

Sources: Adam Clymer, "Congress Passes Bill to Disclose Lobbyists' Roles," *New York Times,* November 30, 1995; Common Cause, "The Honest Leadership and Open Government Act of 2007," available at www.commoncause.org/site/pp.asp?c=dkLNK1MQIwG&b=3895141; Robert Pear, "Ethics Law Isn't Without Loopholes," *New York Times,* April 20, 2008; Elizabeth Williamson, "Reports on Lobbyists Hit Snag," *Wall Street Journal,* April 22, 2008.

527 groups

Tax-exempt organizations that engage in political activities, often funded with unlimited contributions. Most 527s try to influence federal elections through voter mobilization efforts and issue ads that praise or attack a candidate's record. These groups must publicly identify their contributors and expenditures.

Federal Regulation of Lobbying Act of 1946, on First Amendment grounds.[94] For that reason, BRCA's opponents almost immediately sought relief in the courtroom. They initially won in a lower federal district court. But in 2003, a closely divided Supreme Court upheld McCain-Feingold's main provisions.[95]

Although McCain-Feingold passed constitutional muster, it did not necessarily produce all the benefits its proponents expected. History is littered with examples of reform legislation that produced unintended (and undesirable) consequences as laws designed to fix one problem created others. PACs, for example, were created to clean up campaign financing, but many reformers now attack them as a form of legalized corruption.

McCain-Feingold was no exception to the law of unintended consequences. The law spurred increased activity by so-called **527 groups**, organizations that get their names from the section of the U.S. tax code that governs their operation and that exist only to influence who wins or lose elections for public office. (Section 527 groups are legally distinct from PACs. They are not regulated by the Federal Election Commission, they are not subject to the same contribution limits, and unlike PACs, they cannot explicitly advocate the election or defeat of any candidate for federal office. Still, the two share some similarities, so much so that 527 groups are sometimes referred to as "stealth" or "soft" PACs.) During the 2004 campaign, many 527 groups poured their money into issue ads that promoted general policy positions but that did not explicitly support or oppose a particular candidate. The most controversial of these efforts were sponsored by the Swift Boat Veterans for Truth, which ran ads questioning Senator John Kerry's Vietnam service, and MoveOn.org Voter Fund, which ran ads attacking President Bush. (MoveOn.org Voter Fund is legally distinct from MoveOn.org PAC.) Critics of 527 groups accused them of coordinating their attack ads with the campaigns of their preferred candidates, which, if true, would violate federal campaign laws. Critics also accused the groups of making inaccurate and misleading claims to advance their cause.

Dissatisfaction over the actions of section 527 organizations and more general disputes about the proper role of money in American politics mean that Congress is likely to revisit McCain-Feingold in the future. As Supreme Court Justices John Paul Stevens and Sandra Day O'Connor wrote in the majority opinion that found McCain-Feingold constitutional, "We are under no illusion that [McCain-Feingold] will be the last congressional statement on the matter. Money, like water, will always find an outlet. What problems arise, and how Congress will respond, are concerns for another day."[96]

The question of restricting lobbyists' ties to Congress resurfaced in the national debate in 2006. Former high-level Republican lobbyist Jack Abramoff pled guilty to illegally giving gifts and making campaign donations to members of Congress in return for supporting legislation that would benefit his clients. The scandal forced Majority Leader Tom DeLay (R-TX) and Representative Bob Ney (R-OH) to resign their congressional seats; Ney eventually pled guilty to criminal charges related to the scandal. With the midterm elections looming, both Democratic and Republican lawmakers endorsed lobbying reform. The two parties disagreed on what changes were necessary, however, and efforts to enact reform legislation before the 2006 election stalled. As Box 10–2 discusses, the new Democratic-controlled Congress passed new restrictions on the activities of lobbyists.

10-7c The Contributions of Interest Groups

Although interest groups may at times stir cynicism about politics, it is worth remembering that they also play a positive role in American politics. As we previously mentioned, interest groups help represent the views and interests of the American people to the government, and they enable people to participate in politics. Interest groups also educate Americans about the issues facing our society, push new issues onto the political agenda, and help people monitor the actions of government.

The positive contributions of interest group politics are evident in two of the most important political changes in the United States in the twentieth century: universal suffrage and the cause of civil rights. Ninety years ago, women could not vote in federal and most state elections. Fifty years ago, Jim Crow laws effectively disenfranchised most African Americans. These injustices have now been remedied, largely because of the efforts of dedicated interest groups such as the National American Woman Suffrage Association and the NAACP.

Thus, despite frequent complaints that special interests are too powerful in American politics, limiting the freedom of interest groups to petition the government probably would do the democratic process in the United States more harm than good. Interest groups give ordinary citizens access to government and allow them to communicate their values and expectations. The Constitution—the set of rules for our political system—makes it clear this is an essential and cherished right.

SUMMARY

Interest groups are organizations dedicated to influencing public policy. Although interest group politics is as old as the American republic, in recent years, the number of interest groups has exploded. Most interest groups work to advance the economic interests of their members. But other groups try to promote their visions of good public policy, and still others represent the interests of state, local, and foreign governments.

Interest groups frequently form when change threatens the interests of a group of people. But just as often, people fail to organize because of the collective goods dilemma—that is, the incentive people have to leave it up to someone else to organize the group. In practice, the collective goods dilemma is usually solved by political entrepreneurs who, because of personal conviction or ambition, bear the cost of organizing other people. To recruit followers, political entrepreneurs try to provide a mix of material, solidary, and expressive benefits to members.

To influence public policy, interest groups contribute to political campaigns, lobby members of Congress and the executive branch, mobilize public opinion, and litigate. The ability of any interest group to influence public policy depends in part on external factors beyond its immediate control. But the success of a group also depends on internal factors, including the size and commitment of its membership, the political skills of its leaders, its financial resources, and its policy objectives.

The prevalence of interest groups in the United States has fueled claims that special interests have taken the government away from the people. But distinguishing good interest groups from bad ones is impossible. Americans don't agree on which interests should be promoted and which shunned. And although it is clear that the interests of the rich and the powerful are more faithfully represented, interest groups have historically been an important vehicle for remedying the injustices done to the poor and oppressed.

KEY TERMS

advocacy advertising

amicus curiae brief

Astroturf lobbying

Bipartisan Campaign Reform
   Act (BRCA)

citizen groups

collective goods dilemma

direct lobbying

expressive benefits

free riders

grass-roots lobbying

interest group

lobbying

lobbyists

material benefits

McCain-Feingold

netroots lobbying

political action committees
   (PACs)

selective benefits

solidary benefits

527 groups

READINGS FOR FURTHER STUDY

Ainsworth, Scott. *Analyzing Interest Groups: Group Influence on People and Politics* (New York: Norton, 2003). A political scientist combines formal theory with more traditional historical analyses to examine how interest groups function.

Cigler, Allan J., and Burdett A. Loomis, eds. *Interest Group Politics,* 7th ed. (Washington, D.C.: CQ Press, 2007). A collection of essays that examines a wide variety of issues in interest group politics.

Frank, Thomas. *The Wrecking Crew: How Conservatives Rule* (New York: Metropolitan Books, 2008). A liberal journalist argues that political conservatives have built a powerful lobbying operation that has deliberately rendered the federal government ineffective.

Herrnson, Paul S., Ronald G. Shaiko, and Clyde Wilcox, eds. *The Interest Group Connection: Electioneering, Lobbying, and Policymaking in Washington,* 2nd ed. (Washington, D.C.: CQ Press, 2005). A collection of essays that examine how interest groups operate in Washington, D.C.

Olson, Mancur, Jr. *The Logic of Collective Action: Public Goods and the Theory of Groups* (Cambridge, MA: Harvard University Press, 1965). A classic work in which an economist examines the incentives for and obstacles to interest group formation.

Smith, Bradley A. *Unfree Speech: The Folly of Campaign Finance Reform* (Princeton, NJ: Princeton University Press, 2003). A law professor and former Federal Election Commission member argues that most of what Americans know, or think they know, about campaign finance reform is wrong.

Stone, Peter H. *Heist: Superlobbyist Jack Abramoff, His Republican Allies, and the Buying of Washington* (New York: Farrar, Strauss, and Giroux, 2006). A writer for the *National Journal* explores the Abramoff lobbying scandal.

REVIEW QUESTIONS

1. _____ said that "Americans of all ages, all stations in life, and all types of disposition, are forever forming associations."
   a. James Madison
   b. John C. Calhoun
   c. Alexis de Tocqueville
   d. King George III
2. Interest groups
   a. began to organize after the War of 1812.
   b. began to organize over the slavery issue.
   c. began to organize over the suffrage issue.
   d. have always been an integral part of American politics.
3. Which type of interest group is most common?
   a. organized labor
   b. business

    c. agriculture

    d. professional associations

4. Most people join interest groups for

    a. material benefits.

    b. solidary benefits.

    c. expressive benefits.

    d. irrational reasons.

5. What is the main tool that interest groups use in their lobbying efforts?

    a. information

    b. money

    c. civil disobedience

    d. litigation

6. *Amicus curiae* briefs are most commonly filed in lawsuits involving

    a. mundane issues.

    b. criminal charges.

    c. matters of great public interest.

    d. none of the above.

7. Interest groups have a strong

    a. upper-class bias.

    b. working-class bias.

    c. bias in favor of racial minorities.

    d. bias in favor of welfare recipients.

8. The Bipartisan Campaign Reform Act, also known as McCain-Feingold,

    a. requires lobbyists to disclose all contacts they have with members of Congress during campaign season.

    b. sets up a system of public financing of campaigns for federal office.

    c. lifts all spending limits on contributions to federal campaigns.

    d. bars interest groups from running ads promoting or attacking candidates for federal office close to an election.

9. Interest groups

    a. harm the American political system, just as James Madison warned in "Federalist No. 10."

    b. play a vital role in democracies.

    c. are too powerful and should be strictly regulated by the government.

    d. do not allow citizens access to the government.

10. Which of the following accounts for the rapid growth in the number of interest groups?

    a. the legacy of the 1960s

    b. improvements in technology

    c. rise of new issues

    d. all of the above

NOTES

1. Shailagh Murray and James V. Grimaldi, "House Passes Bill to Restrict Internet Poker," *Washington Post*, July 12, 2006; Jim Puzzanghera, "Congress to Deal with Online Gambling," *Seattle Times*, July 11, 2006.

2. Quoted in Emily Dagostino, "Religious Opposition to Gambling Is Waning," available at www.medillnewsdc.com/gambling/gambling_religion.shtml.

3. Dan Katz, "National Football League Involved in Anti-Gambling Bill," available at www.pokersourceonline.com/news.asp?poker=456; Kate Phillips, "Interest Groups Lining Up to Lobby on Web Gambling," *New York Times*, July 4, 2006; Nancy Zuckerbrod, "Bill Passed to Limit Internet Gambling," Associated Press, July 12, 2006, available at www.cbsnews.com/stories/2006/07/12/ap/politics/mainD8IQB60O0.shtml.

4. Quoted in Aaron Todd, "Congress Passes Unlawful Internet Gambling Enforcement Act," *Casinso City Times*, October 2, 2006, available at www.aarontodd.casinocitytimes.com/articles/30109.html.

5. Quoted in "Should Online Gambling Be Banned?" *Wall Street Journal* Online, April 4, 2006, available at www.online.wsj.com/public/article/SB114375000762012631-14PeR-y_IGy_Ax75SChM_gejdynE_20070403.html?mod=tff_main_tff_top.

6. Quoted in Todd, "Congress Passes Unlawful Internet Gambling Enforcement Act."

7. Jeffrey M. Berry, *The Interest Group Society*, 2nd ed. (Glenview, IL: Scott, Foresman/Little, Brown, 1989).

8. James Madison, "Federalist No. 10," in *The Federalist Papers*, ed. Garry Wills (New York: Bantam Books, 1982), 42–49.

9. Berry, *The Interest Group Society*, 4.

10. See Jack L. Walker, Jr., *Mobilizing Interest Groups in America: Patrons, Professions, and Social Movements* (Ann Arbor: University of Michigan Press, 1991), 20–23.

11. Alexis de Tocqueville, *Democracy in America*, ed. J. P. Mayer (New York: Anchor Books, 1969), 513.

12. Robert H. Salisbury, "Washington Lobbyists: A Collective Portrait," in *Interest Group Politics*, 2nd ed., ed. Allan J. Cigler and Burdett A. Loomis (Washington, D.C.: CQ Press, 1986), 148–49; David Segal, "A Nation of Lobbyists," *Washington Post National Weekly Edition*, July 17–23, 1995, 11.

13. Philip A. Mundo, *Interest Groups: Cases and Characteristics* (Chicago: Nelson-Hall, 1992), 9.

14. John T. Tierney and Kay Lehman Schlozman, "Congress and Organized Interests," in *Congressional Politics*, ed. Christopher J. Deering (Chicago: Dorsey Press, 1989), 198.

15. CNN.com, "Election Center 2008: Exit Polls," available at http://www.cnn.com/ELECTION/2008/results/polls/#val=USP00p3

16. On the agricultural lobby, see William P. Browne, *Private Interests, Public Policy, and American Agriculture* (Lawrence: University of Kansas Press, 1988); and John Mark Hansen, *Gaining Access: Congress and the Farm Lobby, 1919–1981* (Chicago: University of Chicago Press, 1991).

17. See Reed McManus, "Down on the Farm Bureau," *Sierra* (November/December 1994): 32–34.

18. Roger Bybee, "The Doctors' Revolt," *American Prospect*, July 1, 2008, available at www.prospect.org/cs/articles?article=the_doctors_revolt.

19. See Jeffrey Berry, *Lobbying for the People: The Political Behavior of Public Interest Groups* (Princeton, NJ: Princeton University Press, 1977).

20. For evidence on the effectiveness of public relations campaigns, see Robert B. Albritton and Jarol B. Manheim, "News of Rhodesia: The Impact of a Public Relations Campaign," *Journalism Quarterly* 56 (Winter 1983): 622–28; Jarol B. Manheim and Robert B. Albritton, "Changing National Images: International Public Relations and Media Agenda Setting," *American Political Science Review* 78 (September 1984): 641–57.

21. "Saudi Arabia Launches P.R. Campaign in U.S.," May 1, 2002, available at www.foxnews.com/story/0,2933,51584,00.html.

22. American Academy of Family Physicians, "AAFP Policies," available at www.aafp.org/online/en/home/policy/policies.html; American College of Physicians, "Where We Stand," available at www.acponline.org/advocacy/?hp.

23. Jeffrey Schmalz, "Gay Politics Goes Mainstream," *New York Times Magazine* (October 11, 1992): 21.

24. Jennifer Steinhauer, "In Taco Truck Battle, Mild Angelenos Turn Hot," *New York Times*, May 3, 2008.

25. See David B. Truman, *The Governmental Process: Political Interests and Public Opinion* (New York: Knopf, 1951), chap. 3–4.

26. Timothy Noah, "New Single-Issue Pressure Groups Sprout Up on the Right to Support the Republican Agenda," *Wall Street Journal*, May 31, 1995.

27. The classic statement of the collective goods dilemma is Mancur Olson, *The Logic of Collective Action* (Cambridge, MA: Harvard University Press, 1965).

28. Robert H. Salisbury, "An Exchange Theory of Interest Groups," *Midwest Journal of Political Science* 13 (February 1969): 1–32.

29. Jean-Paul Renaud, "On a Taco Truck Bandwagon," *Los Angeles Times*, May 1, 2008. Available at www.articles.latimes.com/2008/may/01/local/me-tacos1.

30. Walker, *Mobilizing Interest Groups*, 31.

31. Jack L. Walker, "The Origins and Maintenance of Interest Groups in America," 77 (June 1983): 401.

32. Berry, *Lobbying for the People*, 28.

33. Peter Clark and James Q. Wilson, "Incentive Systems: A Theory of Organizations," *Administrative Science Quarterly* 6 (September 1961): 129–66; Terry M. Moe, *The Organization of Interests: Incentives and the Internal Dynamics of Political Interest Groups* (Chicago: University of Chicago Press, 1980); James Q. Wilson, *Political Organizations* (New York: Basic Books, 1973).

34. Olson, *The Logic of Collective Action*, chap. 1.

35. On the problem of interest group maintenance, see David C. King and Jack L. Walker, Jr., "The Origins and Maintenance of Groups," in *Mobilizing Interest Groups in America: Patrons, Professions, and Social Movements*, ed. Jack L. Walker, Jr. (Ann Arbor: University of Michigan Press, 1991), 75–102; Lawrence S. Rothenberg, "Organizational Maintenance and the Retention Decision in Groups," *American Political Science Review* 82 (December 1988): 1129–52.

36. George E. Curry, "NAACP Finds New Life in Truth in Numbers," *New American Media*, July 29, 2006, available at news.newamericamedia.org/news/view_article.html?article_id=f8ad4909fa7ef4ed3e4fbbeb83fc924d.

37. Steven A. Holmes, "For the Civil Rights Movement, A New Reason for Living," *New York Times*, July 9, 1995.

38. David C. Morrison, "Sounding a Call to Arms for the 1990s," *National Journal* (November 13, 1993): 2728–30.

39. Kay Lehman Schlozman and John T. Tierney, *Organized Interests and American Democracy* (New York: Harper & Row, 1986).

40. On PAC contributions to state and local elections, see Herbert E. Alexander and Anthony Corrado, *Financing the 1992 Election* (Armonk, NY: Sharpe, 1995), chap. 1; Ruth S. Jones, "Financing State Elections," in *Money and Politics in the United States*, ed. Michael J. Malbin (Chatham, NJ: Chatham House, 1984); Ruth S. Jones, "State and Federal Legislative Campaigns: Same Song, Different Verse," *Election Politics* 3 (Summer 1986): 8–12; Frank J. Sorauf, *Money in American Elections* (Glenview, IL: Scott, Foresman/Little, Brown, 1988), chap. 9.

41. Harold W. Stanley and Richard G. Niemi, *Vital Statistics on American Politics, 2005–2006* (Washington, D.C.: CQ Press, 2006), 103; Federal Election Commission, "PAC Activity Continues Climb in 2006," October 5, 2007, available at www.fec.gov/press/press2007/20071009pac/20071009pac.shtml.

42. Federal Election Commission, "Top 50 PACs by Disbursements, January 1, 2005–December 31, 2006," available at www.fec.gov/press/press2007/2007 1009pac/top50pacdisbursements2006.pdf.

43. Federal Election Commission, "PAC Activity Continues Climb."

44. Federal Election Commission, "PAC Contributions 2003–2004 through December 31, 2004," available at www.fec.gov/press/press2005/20050412pac/contrib2004.pdf.

45. See Federal Election Commission, "Independent Expenditures Supporting/Opposing 2008 Presidential Campaigns by Candidate, Through July 30, 2008," available at www.fec.gov/press/press2008/2008indexp/2008iebycandidate.pdf.

46. Federal Election Commission, "PAC Activity Continues Climb."

47. "FEC Reports House PAC Funds," *Congressional Quarterly Weekly Report*, March 20, 1993, 696.

48. Quoted in "Political Committees Spread Money to Winners They Didn't Support," CNN.com, January 4, 2001.

49. For statistical studies of the effect of PAC contributions on congressional voting, see Janet M. Grenzke, "PACs and the Congressional Supermarket: The Currency Is Complex," *American Journal of Political Science* 33 (February 1989): 1–24; John R. Wright, "PACs, Contributions, and Roll Calls," *American Political Science Review* 79 (June 1985): 400–14; John R. Wright, "Contributions, Lobbying, and Committee Voting in the U.S. House of Representatives," *American Political Science Review* 84 (June 1990): 417–38.

50. Quoted in Dan Clawson, Alan Neustadtl, and Denise Scott, *Money Talks: Corporate PACs and Political Influence* (New York: Basic Books, 1992), 90.

51. Bill Myers, "The King of K St.: Tommy Boggs Faces a New Challenge," Examiner.Com, July 27, 2008, available at www.examiner.com/a-1508248~The_King_of_K_St__Tommy_Boggs_faces_a_new_challenge.html.

52. See, for example, Richard L. Hall and Frank W. Wayman, "Buying Time: Moneyed Interests and the Mobilization of Bias in Congressional Committees," *American Political Science Review* 84 (September 1990): 797–820; Laura Langbein, "Money and Access: Some Empirical Evidence," *Journal of Politics* 48 (November 1986): 1052–62; Laura Langbein and Mark Lotwis, "The Political Efficacy of Lobbying and Money: Gun Control in the U.S. House, 1986," *Legislative Studies Quarterly* 15 (August 1990): 413–40.

53. Quoted in Clawson, Neustadtl, and Scott, *Money Talks*, 1.

54. Ann Zimmerman and Kris Maher, "Walmart Warns of Democratic Win," *Wall Street Journal*, August 1, 2008.

55. Quoted in Phil Kuntz, "The Money Chase," *Wall Street Journal*, October 23, 1995.

56. Jill Abramson, "Women Are Now Key Players in Lobbying Game, for Big Companies or Heading Their Own Firms," *Wall Street Journal*, August 2, 1995.

57. Public Citizen, Congressional Revolving Doors: The Journey from Congress to K Street, July 2005, 1. Available at www.lobbyinginfo.org/documents/RevolveDoor.pdf.

58. See John R. Wright, *Interest Groups and Congress: Lobbying, Contributions, and Influence* (Boston: Allyn & Bacon, 1996).

59. Bernard Asbell, *The Senate Nobody Knows* (Baltimore: Johns Hopkins University Press, 1981), 370–71.

60. Quoted in Michael Wines, "A New Maxim for Lobbyists: What You Know, Not Whom," *New York Times*, November 3, 1993.

61. Quoted in Schlozman and Tierney, *Organized Interests*, 85.

62. Quoted in Terry Ganey, "Bond & Bacon," *Columbia Daily Tribune*, June 8, 2008.

63. On the strategic use of information by lobbyists, see Wright, *Interest Groups and Congress*, 4, 95–113.

64. Ibid., 38–49.

65. See Mark A. Peterson, "The Presidency and Organized Interests: White House Patterns of Interest Group Liaison," *American Political Science Review* 86 (September 1992): 612–26; John Orman, "The President and Interest Group Access," *Presidential Studies Quarterly* 18 (Fall 1988): 787–91; Joseph A. Pika, "Opening Doors for Kindred Souls: The White House Office of Public Liaison," in *Interest Group Politics*, 3rd ed., eds. Allan J. Cigler and Burdett A. Loomis (Washington, D.C.: CQ Press, 1991), 277–78.

66. Wines, "A New Maxim for Lobbyists."

67. Quoted in Center for Media & Democracy, "K Street Project," available at www.disinfopedia.org/wiki.phtml?title=K_Street_Project.

68. Quoted in Nicholas Confessore, "Welcome to the Machine: How the GOP Disciplined K Street and Made Bush Supreme," *Washington Monthly*, July/August 2003, available at www.washingtonmonthly.com/features/2003/0307.confessore.html.

69. William Schneider, "K Street's Capitol Connection," *National Journal*, January 24, 2006, available at www.theatlantic.com/doc/200601u/nj_schneider_2006-01-24.

70. Quoted in Kimberly A. Strassel, "The K Street Project, Part Blue," *Wall Street Journal*, July 25, 2008, available at online.wsj.com/article/SB121694153870182785.html?mod=todays_columnists; Jonah Goldber, "K Street Traffic Runs Both Ways," July 18, 2008, available at www.article.nationalreview.com/q=ZGYxNmZjNDhiYzYxMWZkOTAzN2RmZTcwOTI1ZTkzODg=.

71. On ways interest groups decide between inside and outside strategies, see Thomas L. Gais and Jack L. Walker, Jr., "Pathways to Influence in American Politics," in *Mobilizing Interest Groups in America: Patrons, Professions, and Social Movements*, ed. Jack L. Walker, Jr. (Ann Arbor: University of Michigan Press, 1991), 103–21.

72. The studies done by the Center for Budget and Policy Priorities are available at www.cbpp.org/. Those done by the Tax Foundation are available at www.tax-foundation.org/.

73. Michael M. Phillips, "Mortgage Bailout Infuriates Tenants (and Steve Forbes), *Wall Street Journal*, May 16, 2008.

74. Kirk Victor, "Astroturf Lobbying Takes a Hit," *National Journal*, September 23, 1995, 2359–60.

75. Jeffrey A. Birnbaum, "Advocacy Groups Blur Media Lines," *Washington Post*, December 6, 2004.

76. Ibid.

77. Ibid.

78. John R. Lott, Jr., "The NRA's Announcement," *Washington Times*, December 21, 2003, available at www.washtimes.com/op-ed/20031221-100044-6378r.htm.

79. Frank Ahrens, "An Elemental Clash of Earth and Fire," *Washington Post*, January 13, 2001.

80. Kim Lane Scheppele and Jack L. Walker, Jr., "The Litigation Strategies of Interest Groups," in *Mobilizing Interest Groups in America: Patrons, Professions, and Social Movements*, ed. Jack L. Walker, Jr. (Ann Arbor: University of Michigan Press, 1991), 157—83.

81. Quoted in Bill McAllister, "VA Hospitals Refuse to Sound Retreat," *Washington Post National Weekly Edition*, May 29–June 4, 1995, 31.

82. Quoted in Katherine McCarron, "Holding Lawmakers' Feet to the Fire," *National Journal*, October 17, 1992, 2379.

83. Elizabeth Williamson, "Climate Issues Divide U.S. Chamber of Commerce, Big Members," *Wall Street Journal*, April 17, 2008.

84. *2006 Pig Book Summary* (Washington, D.C.: Citizens against Government Waste, 2006), 48, available at www.cagw.org/site/DocServer/2006PigBook Summary.pdfdocID=1541.

85. *Harris Poll 1994*, no. 73, November 17, 1994, 3.

86. David Segal, "A Nation of Lobbyists," *Washington Post National Weekly Edition*, July 17–23, 1995, 11.

87. Ibid.

88. Quoted in William Safire, *Safire's Political Dictionary* (New York: Random House, 1978), 384.

89. E. E. Schattschneider, *The Semi-Sovereign People* (New York: Holt, Rinehart and Winston, 1960), 35.

90. Jonathan D. Salant and Richard Sammon, "Senate Bans Lavish Gifts from Interest Groups," *Congressional Quarterly Weekly Report*, July 29, 1995, 2237–38.

91. Jonathan D. Salant, "House Votes to Toughen Gift Restrictions," *Congressional Quarterly Weekly Report*, November 18, 1995, 3516–19.

92. See Adam Clymer, "Congress Passes Bill to Disclose Lobbyists' Roles," *New York Times*, November 30, 1995; Jonathan D. Salant, "Bill Would Open Windows on Lobbying Efforts," *Congressional Quarterly Weekly Report*, December 2, 1995, 3631–33.

93. For a history and analysis of the Bipartisan Campaign Reform Act, see Anthony Corrado, Thomas E. Mann, and Trevor Potter, eds., *Inside the Campaign Finance Battle: Court Testimony on the New Reforms* (Washington, D.C.: Brookings Institution, 2003).

94. *United States v. Harris*, 347 U.S. 612 (1954).

95. *McConnell v. Federal Election Commission*, 540 U.S. 93 (2003). Available at www.supct.law.cornell.edu/supct/search/display.html?terms=children&url=/supct/html/02-1674.ZS.html.

96. Quoted in Online Newshour, "Politics 101: Campaign Finance Reform," available at www.pbs.org/newshour/vote2004/politics101/politics101_cfreform.html.

Part 3

The Institutions of American Politics

11
Congress

CHAPTER OUTLINE

In July 2008, Senate Republican leaders wanted to kill a Medicare bill that the Democrats favored. The measure had already passed the House by an overwhelming 355 to 59 vote. The problem facing Senate Republican leadership was that they did not have the necessary number of votes to defeat the bill outright. The Democrats were the majority party in the Senate, and a few Republicans had decided to support the bill. Unable to win a straight up-or-down vote, the Republican leadership resorted to one of the Senate's time-honored parliamentary devices—the filibuster. It is a maneuver that allows opponents to prevent the full Senate from voting on measures they oppose.

To bring the filibuster to a halt, the Democratic leadership had to persuade the Senate to vote to invoke cloture, a different parliamentary maneuver that essentially forces a vote on a bill. Under Senate rules, cloture can be invoked only with the support of sixty senators. In late June, the Democrats had come close to breaking the filibuster when fifty-nine senators voted in support of cloture. As the Democratic leadership prepared for a second cloture vote on July 9, it looked as if they would once again fall a vote short of victory. But Majority Leader Harry Reid (D-NV) had an ace up his sleeve. Unbeknownst to all but a handful of Democrats, Reid had arranged for Senator Ted Kennedy (D-MA), who was undergoing chemotherapy following surgery for a cancerous brain tumor, to return to Washington to cast the needed vote. Kennedy's surprise appearance on the Senate floor shocked Republicans (and many Democrats as well). Knowing that the ailing senator's vote tipped the scales in the Democrats' favor, nine GOP senators switched from voting against invoking cloture to voting in favor of it, ending the filibuster with a vote of 69 to 30. The Senate then approved the Medicare bill by unanimous consent.[1]

The story of the 2008 Medicare bill did not end, however, with the breaking of the Senate filibuster. Under the Constitution, the president can veto legislation passed by Congress. President George W. Bush, unhappy because in his view, the Medicare bill was "fiscally irresponsible" and full of "short-term budget gimmicks," vetoed it.[2] The veto set the stage for a second confrontation. Congress could now attempt to override the president's veto. If the House and Senate each passed the bill a second time by the two-thirds margin that the Constitution required, the bill would become law.

The White House hoped that some Senate Republicans would switch their votes out of party loyalty and support the president's veto, but the Medicare bill had some surprising and powerful supporters. The American Medical Association (AMA), usually a GOP friend, supported the measure because it would rescind a 10.6 percent cut in Medicare payments to doctors serving elderly patients. The AMA started running television and radio advertisements in the home states of ten Republican senators who opposed the bill to pressure them to change their vote.

The House voted on the veto override first. To no one's surprise, it opted to overturn the president's decision on a 383 to 41 vote.

This was nearly 100 votes more than the required two-thirds majority (291 votes). The bill, however, had a smaller cushion of support in the Senate. The cloture vote had passed with 69 votes, and Democratic Senate leaders would need to keep 67 of those votes—two-thirds of the 100 member Senate—to override President Bush's veto. Although Senator Kennedy did not participate, the Senate voted 70 to 26 to follow the House's lead. The 2008 Medicare bill passed—the fourth time a measure had become law over President Bush's objection.[3]

This story about the Medicare bill reminds us that today's Congress is the product of both the original rules the Founders set down in the Constitution and decisions made over the past 200 years. In this chapter, we begin by examining the basic structure of Congress set forth in the Constitution. We then look at how the rules and norms of Congress have evolved since the House and Senate first met in 1789. Next, we turn to congressional elections—how members get to Congress and how they stay there. We explore service in Congress, focusing on who serves, Congress as a job, and Congress as an organization. We conclude by reviewing the law-making process and discussing the issue of legislative representation. The Founders created rules designed to make Congress representative of the public. What exactly does this mean? Are the rules successful? And is the Congress of the twenty-first century the representative body the Founders envisioned?

11-1 THE STRUCTURE OF CONGRESS

We have argued throughout this book that rules influence politics. Nowhere is this lesson more obvious than in Congress. The Constitution established the fundamental structure of Congress, and in doing so, largely determined the specific character of both the House and the Senate.

11-1a Bicameralism

When the delegates to the Constitutional Convention began to debate what the new national legislature would look like, they could have considered a wide range of possible structures. However, most of the delegates agreed from the start that Congress would be a two-chamber or **bicameral legislature** that would operate independently of the other two branches of government. In choosing a bicameral structure for Congress, the delegates were adopting what was then the most common structure for a legislature; the English Parliament and eleven of the thirteen state legislatures were bicameral.[4]

One difference that distinguishes Congress from most other bicameral legislatures in the world is that both chambers wield substantial power. Although the House and Senate each have a few distinct responsibilities, for the most part, they share law-making power. This shared power poses both advantages and

bicameral legislature
A legislature with two houses—such as the House and the Senate.

disadvantages. On the one hand, it increases the number of voices that are heard when policy proposals are being considered. On the other hand, bicameralism with two powerful houses makes lawmaking more difficult. No bill can be sent to the president to sign into law unless both the House and the Senate have passed it. This rule makes the American legislative process conservative—not in terms of the partisan or ideological substance of the legislation passed, but in terms of making it difficult to change existing laws. In creating a bicameral legislature with two powerful houses, the Founders purposely dispersed power to prevent one body of government from dominating all others. Although the bicameral structure of Congress does preclude a concentration of power in one house, it also contributes to the "gridlock," or inability to move forward quickly and decisively, that often seems to characterize today's federal legislative process.

11-1b The House of Representatives

Although the Founders made the House and the Senate equals in lawmaking, they structured the two chambers to have different virtues. The Founders wanted the House to be sensitive to public opinion, and the rules governing election to the House reflect this goal. The Constitution requires all representatives to stand for election every two years, which creates the opportunity for a rapid change or **turnover** in House membership if the public so desires. The Constitution also requires that all vacancies that arise during a two-year term must be filled through elections. Unlike the Senate, where vacancies are usually filled initially by appointment, the House can claim that every one of its members was elected by the voters.

The Constitution further ensures that the House will reflect public sentiment by requiring that the number of representatives in each state be proportional to the population. This means that states with larger populations have more representatives than states with smaller populations, although every state is guaranteed at least one representative.

The Constitution stipulated that the ratio of representatives to the population would be 1 for every 30,000 people, and it established the initial size of the House of Representatives at sixty-five members. To accommodate a growing population, the Constitution further stipulated that the number of seats a state was entitled to would change every ten years on the basis of the results of the national census. As the country added states and the population continued to increase, Congress responded by creating new House seats. After the first census in 1790, for example, the House expanded to 106 members. By 1860, the House had 243 members.

The rules Congress used to apportion seats changed over time.[5] By 1830, Congress had junked the prescribed constitutional ratio of constituents per representative, allowing bigger districts. (If the 1 to 30,000 ratio were still in effect, the House now would have 10,000 members.) In 1911, Congress decided to cap the number of

turnover
Change in membership of Congress between elections.

Source: © Bettmann/Corbis.

Members of the House have unassigned seating. With 435 members, the House floor can become quite crowded and noisy. Usually, personal staff members are not allowed on the floor.

House seats at 435, a number it reached in 1913 after New Mexico and Arizona entered the Union. The cap meant that in the future, those 435 seats would have to be redistributed or reapportioned among the states as the population grew or new states joined the Union. Congress bickered for nineteen years over a formula for **reapportionment** before finally adopting a new process in 1929, which it revised again in 1950. Since then, population changes have forced significant redistributions in seats among the states. For example, in 1911, California and Iowa each had eleven seats in the House. Following the 2000 redistricting, however, California had fifty-three seats to Iowa's five.

The Constitution specifies several other rules for the House, although none of them affects the character of the institution. All representatives must be at least twenty-five years of age and must have been U.S. citizens for at least seven years. (Among House members in 2009 were Anh "Joseph" Cao, R-LA, who was born in Vietnam; Ciro Rodriguez, D-TX, an immigrant from Mexico; and Ileana Ros-Lehtinen, R-FL, a native of Cuba.) The only residency requirement is that representatives must be inhabitants of the state where they are elected; it is only by tradition that we expect them to live in the district they represent. And not surprisingly, given the role that taxes played in triggering the American Revolutionary War, the Constitution states that all tax bills must originate in the House.

reapportionment

The redistribution of seats in the House of Representatives among the states, which occurs every ten years following the census, so that the size of each state's delegation is proportional to its share of the total population.

11-1c The Senate

In contrast to the rules that establish the structure of the House, the rules creating the Senate were designed to establish a more mature body: Members must be at least thirty years old and must

Source: © Bettmann/Corbis.

Senators have assigned desks. Their staff members can come to the floor.

have been citizens for at least nine years. As Chapter 2 discussed, the Connecticut Compromise gave each state two senators. The Founders also took two steps to insulate senators from the shifting tides of public opinion. First, they gave senators six-year terms, with only one-third of the Senate up for reelection in any election year. As a result, rapid turnover is far less likely in the Senate than in the House. Second, the Founders stipulated that state legislatures rather than voters elect senators. Eventually, this method of electing senators became more and more unpopular. The adoption of the Seventeenth Amendment in 1913 finally mandated the direct, public election of senators. (By then, a majority of states had instituted binding advisory elections that directed the state legislature whom to elect to the Senate.)[6] Unlike vacancies in the House, vacancies in the Senate can be filled by appointment rather than by election (with the governor of the affected state making the choice). These structural rules attempt to achieve a balance by making the Senate more distanced from public opinion while maintaining the House's sensitivity to it.

11-2 THE EVOLUTION OF CONGRESS

As we noted previously, although the Constitution specifies the basic structure of Congress, it says little about what rules should govern the day-to-day operation of the House and Senate. Article I stipulates that "The House of Representatives shall choose their Speaker and other Officers," that "the Vice President of the United States shall be President of the Senate," and that "the Senate shall choose the other Officers, and also a President pro tempore." Beyond these general guidelines, however, the Constitution says that "each House may determine the Rules of its Proceedings." Because members of Congress are free to adopt the sorts of rules and structures they want, norms and procedures in Congress have changed enormously over the past 200 years as the interests of members themselves have changed. Moreover, because of the differences in size between the House and Senate, the two chambers have developed very different sets of rules governing their proceedings.

11-2a Changing Attitudes toward Service in Congress

For close to a half-century, service in the House was deemed to be more prestigious than that in the Senate.[7] Overall, however, service in Congress was not thought to be of great importance for much of the nineteenth century. The real action was at the state level. Only slightly more than half of the original members of the House in 1789 returned to office in 1791, and similar turnover rates continued until well after the Civil War.[8] The situation in the Senate was worse. The Senate's first members "fled the Capitol . . . almost as fast as humanly possible."[9] Only two of the original twenty-six senators held their seats for more than six years—most left long before.

Several reasons explain the substantial turnover in congressional membership in the first half of the nineteenth century. Because many of the issues Congress was deciding were less important than those decided elsewhere, members who left voluntarily often did so to take another political office, usually at the state level.[10] For instance, during the first half of the nineteenth century, several speakers of the House gave up their posts to take what are by today's standards far less influential government jobs: receiver-general of the Pennsylvania Land Office, Virginia state treasurer, and lieutenant governor of Kentucky, to name a few examples.[11]

Another reason members left was the practice of rotation, an informal version of term limits. In many House districts, particularly in the North, representatives served just one or, more commonly, two terms and then retired so someone else could serve. Abraham Lincoln, for example, represented Illinois in the House for only one term because his district used the rotation rule.[12]

High congressional turnover also resulted from the lack of incentives for long service. Because congressional pay was low, members put their financial futures at risk by serving in Congress.[13] Moreover, life in Washington was not attractive, even to those who might have found congressional service satisfying. The then-new city was built on a drained swamp, and it lacked most of the amenities common to older cities. For several decades, members of Congress left their families at home and lived in boarding houses or hotels during their stays in Washington. Before the advent of railroads, travel to and from the capitol was difficult for most members. Finally, the summer weather was miserable— Congress did not meet year-round until well into the twentieth century, after the Capitol was air conditioned.[14]

High turnover had important consequences for both the House and Senate. Length of service in Congress meant almost nothing. For example, Henry Clay first came to Congress in 1812 and was immediately elected speaker of the House (see Box 11–1). He

The People behind the Rules

Box 11–1　The Political Careers of Henry Clay and Nancy Pelosi

One of the biggest changes in Congress over the past two centuries has been the path members take to attain positions of power. Two speakers of the House demonstrate the dramatic changes: Henry Clay, who served as speaker in three different short stints during the early 1800s, and Nancy Pelosi, who became speaker in 2006 after twenty years of relatively slow movement up the rungs of power in the House.

HENRY CLAY

Clay is one of the most important figures in American history. Known as the Great Compromiser, Clay dedicated much of his political career in the years preceding the Civil War to preventing the impending split between North and South. To this end, he was in large part responsible for the Missouri Compromise of 1820 and the Compromise of 1850. Clay's service to the country was extensive and varied. To our modern eyes, the leaps his career took—from senator to speaker of the Kentucky House of Representatives to senator again to speaker of the House of Representatives to secretary of state—are incredible. No modern politician could expect to hopscotch among such a variety of powerful posts. In 1806, Clay was appointed to fill the last two years of an unexpired

Senate term despite the fact that he was only twenty-nine, one year shy of meeting the constitutional requirement that senators be at least thirty years of age. (Clay was seated because none of his fellow senators challenged his right to the seat.) The next year, he returned home to Kentucky, where he served for two years as speaker in the Kentucky House of Representatives. He returned to Washington in 1809 when he was appointed to fill the last two years of another unexpired Senate term. In 1811, Clay was elected to the House and almost immediately became speaker. He resigned the speakership in 1814 to become a member of the American delegation that was negotiating a treaty to end the War of 1812 with Great Britain.

Clay returned to the House after completing the Treaty of Ghent, and he was again elected speaker. He left the House again in 1821, returned two years later, and served once more as speaker. After running unsuccessfully for president, Clay left the House in 1825, never to return. He served as Secretary of State under President John Quincy Adams. Later, Clay had two more tours of duty in the Senate, and he ran unsuccessfully for president two more times. He said of his failed bids for the White House, "I would rather be right than be President."

NANCY PELOSI

Pelosi is the first woman to serve as speaker of the House. Her rise to the speakership was far from inevitable. She was born into a political family; her father served in the House and as mayor of Baltimore. After graduating from Trinity College in Washington, D.C., she married and moved to San Francisco, her husband's hometown. While her husband built a successful business career, Pelosi raised their five children. She was active in Democratic Party affairs, but she held off running for office until her youngest child was a senior in high school. When a House seat in San Francisco unexpectedly became open in 1987, the forty-seven-

Source: © Chip Somodevilla/AFP/Getty Images.

Nancy Pelosi.

year-old Pelosi won the Democratic nomination by a small margin, and—not surprisingly given the partisan make-up of the district—the general election in a landslide. She has never had a competitive race since her first primary contest.

Once in the House, Pelosi slowly worked her way into positions of importance. In 1991, she was given a seat on the powerful Appropriations Committee. Two years later she was entrusted with a position on the Select Permanent Committee on Intelligence. She played a prominent role on a number of issues before the House during the 1990s. She led the opposition to granting China permanent normal trading relations because of Beijing's record on human rights. She also secured bipartisan support for increased funding for people suffering from acquired immune deficiency syndrome (AIDS).

In 2001, House Democrats elected Pelosi minority party whip, making her the first woman to hold a major leadership position in Congress. When Richard Gephardt (D-MO) chose to step down as minority party leader down following Democratic losses in the 2002 midterm elections, Pelosi won an easy contest to replace him. As party leader she was instrumental in positioning the Democrats to regain the majority. When the voters turned the

Source: © North Wind Picture Archives

Henry Clay.

The People behind the Rules *(continued)*

House back over to the Democrats in the 2006 midterm elections, Pelosi reaped the rewards. Her Democratic Party colleagues unanimously voted to make her the next speaker.

In January 2007, Pelosi was formally elected Speaker of the House, becoming the highest female elected officeholder in American history. It took Pelosi twenty years of service to

work her way up to the position of speaker—a position Clay reached almost immediately on his election to the House at the age of thirty-four.

subsequently left Congress and then returned, again claiming the post of speaker. Such a career pattern is unheard of in the modern Congress. More typical is the career path of the current speaker of the House Nancy Pelosi (D-CA), which was marked by twenty years of continuous service and slow movement up the leadership ladder.[15]

High turnover also affected how members of Congress conducted themselves. Because they intended to serve only a short time, members had little to fear if their behavior offended their colleagues, and the decorum of Congress suffered for it. Conduct on the floor of the House, for example, included bringing hunting dogs to lie alongside one member's desk; verbal debates degenerating into threats of bodily harm; fisticuffs; beatings with canes; and even one fight in which a gun was fired.[16]

Members of Congress began to view their service as a career sometime during the second half of the nineteenth century. Many reasons can be offered to explain the shift. The most important is that changes in the economic and social fabric of the country, especially those produced by industrialization, urbanization, and immigration, created new political interests that only the federal government could satisfy. This, in turn, pushed Congress toward the center of decision making, and it made being a member of Congress more interesting and important than it had been.

11-2b Change in the House

The House has undergone many changes since it first met in 1789. We can break down these changes into four distinct periods: the nineteenth century, the early twentieth century, the 1970s and 1980s, and the 1990s and after.

The Nineteenth Century

The shift toward viewing membership in Congress as a career affected both the House and the Senate, although it affected the House in particular. The most visible change involved member decorum. In the latter half of the nineteenth century, civility replaced outrageous behavior as strict rules and norms were developed to govern how members conducted themselves on the floor of the House and in committee meetings. For example, even in the midst of the most heated debate, members are now barred from

standing committee

A permanent committee in Congress with jurisdiction over a specific policy area. Such a committee has tremendous say over the details of legislation within its jurisdiction.

denigrating their opponents. Although such rules often lead to excessive (and stilted) civility, they serve a practical purpose: They limit rancorous exchanges and thereby make every member's service more tolerable.

The shift toward viewing congressional service as a career also has changed the balance of power within the House. Until the beginning of the twentieth century, the speaker dominated the work of the House. The bulk of the speaker's power stemmed from the committee system.

By 1820, the House had created a system of permanent, or standing, committees to help manage its workload. Each **standing committee** was given jurisdiction over a specific policy area, and it had an almost unlimited right to determine whether a bill within its jurisdiction would be put to a vote by the whole House. For example, in 1802, the House established the Ways and Means Committee to oversee the government's tax system. Any bill changing the tax structure had to pass through Ways and Means, giving that committee virtual control over tax policy.

Members served on a committee at the discretion of the speaker. The speaker also had the power to assign bills to committee and to determine the rules under which the full membership of the House would debate and vote on bills. Members gained influence through their relationship with the speaker; length of service in the House did not matter. Members who were in the speaker's good graces received positions of power, whereas those who were not found themselves serving on minor committees.

The Early Twentieth Century

The speaker's domination of the House continued as long as members had no desire to make congressional service a career. As members began to serve longer, however, they chafed at the speaker's immense power. In 1910 rank-and-file members revolted and enacted new rules that stripped the office of the speakership of much of its authority. They gave the power to make committee assignments to special groups in each party. Under the **seniority rule**, which is actually an informal norm rather than a written rule, the member of the majority party with the longest continuous service on a committee became the chair of the committee. Although the importance of seniority had been increasing since after the Civil War, it did not become absolute until around 1916.[17] Members accepted the seniority rule because it meant they would acquire positions of power such as the chair of a committee if they served long enough.

From the revolt of 1910 until the early 1970s, power in the House was concentrated in the hands of committee chairs and other senior members. On most issues, members deferred to the committees. Members were expected to focus on the issues before their committees and to avoid meddling in the affairs of other committees. Junior members were expected to serve an apprenticeship while they learned the substance of the issues before their committees. Only

seniority rule

The congressional norm of making the member of the majority party with the longest continuous service on a committee the chair of that committee.

as they gained seniority did they earn the opportunity to shape legislation.

Change in the 1970s and 1980s

Dissatisfaction with the power of committee chairs grew in the 1950s and 1960s. Democrats from northern and western states bridled at the disproportionate number of committee chairs southern Democrats held. The southerners held so many committee chairs because they had been elected at young ages, had never faced serious challenges in their one-party states, and as a result, had gained substantial seniority.[18] The immense power of the southern committee chairs would not have been a major problem if these members shared the views of other Democrats. They were much more conservative, however, and they used their committee positions to stifle the policy preferences of more liberal Democrats, especially in the area of civil rights.

In the early 1970s, northern Democrats gained the upper hand within their party because of their own increased seniority and because many elderly southerners retired. The northern Democrats used their power to make significant changes in the rules of the House. Most importantly, they took power away from committee chairs and gave it to the chairs of the **subcommittees**, the smaller units of a standing committee that oversee one part of the committee's jurisdiction. Now more than eighty-four subcommittee chairs—many of them junior members—enjoy considerable influence. As former representative Morris Udall (D-AZ) joked, "We've got so many committees and subcommittees now that if you can't remember somebody's name, you just say 'Hi, Mr. Chairman.'"[19]

The reform movement of the 1970s also targeted the seniority system. Over the years, many committee chairs had used their powers to impose their preferences on other committee members. To curtail such abuses, the Democratic **caucus**, which consists of all the Democratic members in the House, agreed in 1974 to elect committee chairs by secret ballot. (Because the Democrats were the majority party in the House, they had the responsibility for establishing the rules for selecting chairs.) In the first vote under the new rules, Democrats unseated three southern committee chairs who were legendary for their autocratic ways, but the vote did not mark a rejection of the seniority system itself. The caucus replaced two of the chairs with the next most senior member; the other new chair was fourth in seniority. After 1975, the caucus replaced very few chairs. The chairs knew, however, that they could be removed if they did not maintain the support of the caucus. And members realized that seniority did not guarantee that they would get to chair a committee.

The reform movement of the 1970s decentralized power in the House. Committee chairs accustomed to wielding extensive power found themselves having to share authority with subcommittee chairs. At the same time, committees no longer could write legislation and expect the full House to approve it without change.

subcommittees
The smaller units of a standing committee that oversee one part of the committee's jurisdiction.

caucus
A closed meeting of members of a political party to discuss matters of public policy and political strategy, and in some cases, to select candidates for office.

Individual members began to take advantage of the rules of the House to try to change or amend legislation once it came to the floor for a vote. From the mid-1970s to the mid-1980s, the number of amendments offered on the floor, and the number accepted, increased dramatically.[20] Thus, junior members had improved their prospects for influencing legislation, even in areas outside their committee jurisdictions.

The trend toward decentralization had important consequences for the House as an organization. Members found it more difficult to develop and agree on major legislation. Recognizing this problem, in the mid-1970s they adopted several changes designed to recentralize some powers in the hands of the party leadership. The speaker regained some, but by no means all, of the powers lost decades earlier. Under the new rules, the speaker had more say in committee assignments and more authority regarding the flow of legislation between committees and the floor.[21]

The nation's difficult budget situation in the 1980s accelerated the recentralization of power in the hands of the majority party leadership, and it increased the importance of the committees that oversaw taxes and spending. As the federal government's budget deficits grew, money for new programs became very tight, and the most important political battles were fought over legislation that determined how government money would be spent. Power over those bills was concentrated in the hands of relatively few people—party leaders such as the speaker and the members of the committees with the most input on budget bills. To some extent, members serving on other committees were left out of the process in which many important policy decisions were made.[22]

Under the Democrats, the trend toward recentralization was tempered by the legacy of the reforms of the 1970s. Strains of decentralization and recentralization coexisted somewhat uncomfortably together. Power continued to be diffused among many members, with subcommittees remaining important actors in the process and individual members continuing to amend legislation on the floor.[23] Senior members still exercised the most influence in the House, but junior members were deeply involved in lawmaking.[24] At the same time, the majority party leadership was stronger than at any time since the early part of the century. Budget constraints gave majority party leaders the opportunity to shape policy with input from relatively few members, although the reforms made the leadership dependent on the members for power; that is, the leaders were allowed to make decisions only as long as the membership was willing to accept the final package. Members were often willing to reject deals the leadership brought to the floor.[25] Moreover, members had more opportunities to remove leaders. Thus, the rules created a situation in which leaders had more power to shape policies than they had before, but rank-and-file members ultimately retained the ability to reject or constrain the decisions the leaders made.

Change in the 1990s and After

In 1995, the Republicans took control of the House for the first time in forty years, and with their new majority status came the responsibility of deciding what powers a Republican speaker would have. They ultimately decided to make relatively few changes to the formal powers of the speaker. One formal change they did make was to limit the speaker to four consecutive terms in office, a change that in the long run would tend to reduce the power of the speaker.

Despite these term limits and the lack of formal rules changes, Speaker Newt Gingrich quickly assumed powers unrivaled by any speaker since the turn of the century. For example, Gingrich made committee assignments, and he violated the unwritten seniority rule in naming the chairs of several committees and subcommittees. He forced all returning Republicans on the important Appropriations Committee to sign letters of loyalty to the party's programs. He also centralized important decision-making powers in his hands. On one occasion, he forced a committee chair to reverse a hard-won position on a major telecommunications bill before the full House voted on it. On another occasion, he moved negotiations on the controversial 1995 farm bill from the Agriculture Committee to his office. The House plan to reform Medicare was developed by an ad hoc task force working for the speaker, not by the committees that oversee the issue.[26]

As power flowed to the speaker's office, it ebbed away from committee and subcommittee chairs. For the most part, committee and subcommittee chairs accepted their diminished status. In 1995, for example, Rep. Henry Hyde (R-IL), the chair of the Judiciary Committee, had to push his party's term-limits measure through his committee even though he strongly opposed it. He observed, "There has not been time to implement items of my personal agenda. But they are small potatoes. I'm fully in accord with the priorities of this leadership."[27]

Speaker Gingrich succeeded in taking power away from committee and subcommittee chairs in the absence of any major change in the formal powers of the speaker's office because he had the loyal support of most House Republicans, and especially of first-term Republicans. As one former House member noted, "There is personal loyalty to him [Gingrich] that is without precedent in recent history."[28] But because Gingrich's expanded authority rested on personal loyalty rather than on the formal powers of the speaker's office, his powers faded over the rest of his tenure. His fellow Republicans became disillusioned with his leadership, and he quit the post after Democrats picked up seats in the 1998 elections. His successor, Dennis Hastert, initially operated more in the mold of previous speakers, giving somewhat greater deference to committee chairs than Gingrich had and restoring many committee prerogatives and powers. By the end of the decade, leadership in the House looked much the same as it did at the beginning of the decade. As Hastert became more entrenched in the speakership, he began to centralize power in the leadership's hands, choosing committee chairs and making important committee assignments. In 2003, the Republicans abolished the speakership term limit they had imposed a few years earlier, arguably making the speaker stronger. Thus, by 2006, the majority party in the House was dominated by its leadership, and for one of the rare times in American history, a congressional party was arguably disciplined.

One unanswered question for the Democrats after winning the majority in the 2006 elections was whether Speaker Pelosi would exercise as much power as Gingrich and Hastert had. Quickly it became apparent that she would. No term limits were imposed on Pelosi's service as speaker, but she kept the Republican six-year limit on committee chairs. Like her immediate GOP predecessors, Speaker Pelosi asserted considerable influence on committee appointments. She interviewed committee chair candidates, and although she ended up following seniority in naming them, it was by her choice to do so. Finally, Pelosi managed to make committee chairs follow her direction. At one point, for example, she created a select committee on environmental issues as a way of pressuring the chair of the Commerce Committee to become more aggressive in pursuing higher fuel economy standards for cars.[29]

11-2c Change in the Senate

The Senate has undergone less visible change than the House. Although it has grown in size from 26 to 100 members, the Senate continues to operate under rules that reflect its original small size. Senators have considerable freedom to debate policy proposals and to block legislation they dislike, and many senators have exploited these freedoms to see that their policy views are taken into account. As a result, individual senators have much greater influence over legislation than their counterparts in the House do.

Despite the tremendous continuity in its procedures, the Senate has seen some change over the past several decades. In the 1940s and 1950s, the Senate was often characterized as an elite men's club where a handful of senior members dominated decision making.[30] Junior members endured lengthy apprenticeships before earning the opportunity to participate, and they were expected to concentrate on a handful of policy areas.[31] During a committee meeting in the early 1960s, for example, one junior senator interrupted the discussion among the committee's senior members to ask the chair "if he would mind talking louder so we could hear what decisions were being made."[32]

In the 1970s, the Senate adopted several new rules that encouraged decentralization. Informal changes played an even bigger role, though, as new, more individualist senators refused to enter into apprenticeships while more senior members managed the business of the Senate. As a result, power in the Senate is now dispersed into the hands of many members. Even first-term senators can play key roles in policy making.[33] For example, Senator Lindsey Graham (R-SC) was only forty-seven years old when he was elected to the Senate in 2002 and took the leadership role in trying to assemble a bipartisan compromise on Social Security reform in 2005, even though he was a first-term senator and did not serve on the committee that would review the legislation.[34] Such boldness would never have been expected or tolerated from a junior senator a generation prior.

Nonetheless, the formal rules in the Senate do not change as often or as much as they do in the House. The reason is that each chamber has different rules governing how much support is needed to change any rule. In the House, which has all its seats up for election every two years and which sees itself as a new body at the beginning of each Congress, a simple majority is all that is needed to change a rule, which means that the majority party can dictate the rules as long as its members agree on them. In the Senate, which has only a third of its seats come up for election every two years and accordingly sees itself as a continuing body, two-thirds of the senators must approve any rule changes. Thus, unless the majority party in the Senate holds sixty-seven seats, or can gain the consent of the minority party, the rules will not change.

As noted at the beginning of this chapter, however, in recent years Republican leaders in the Senate suggested that they might challenge the notion that the Senate is a continuing body, and thereby substitute a majority vote requirement to pass rules changes in place of the traditional two-thirds vote.[35] But, although the threat of the nuclear option lingered, no attempt to change Senate rules by a simple majority vote was made.

11-3 GETTING THERE AND STAYING THERE—CONGRESSIONAL ELECTIONS

The Framers of the Constitution understood that the way elected officials gain office influences their behavior once there. For example, the Framers chose direct election and two-year terms to make representatives responsive to public opinion. In contrast, they chose six-year terms and election by state legislatures to insulate senators from the heat of public demands. Today, of course, members of both the House and the Senate are directly elected. The difference in term lengths, and for most senators, differences in the number of people they represent influence the way representatives and senators win election and the way they behave once in office.

11-3a Incumbents and Reelection

One overriding fact affects congressional elections: Incumbents who choose to run for reelection almost always win. Moreover, they usually win by large margins. As Figure 11–1 shows, the electoral success of incumbents is particularly striking for members of the House. Since 1946, representatives who run for reelection have

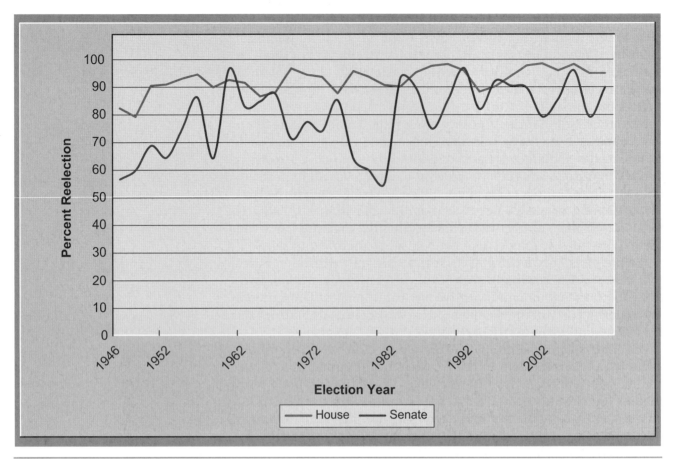

Figure 11-1 Percent of Incumbents Reelected, 1994–2008. Representatives have a higher reelection rate than senators, but both usually win.

Source: *Data for 1952–1994 from Norman J. Ornstein, Thomas E. Mann, and Michael J. Malbin,* Vital Statistics on Congress 1999–2000 *(Washington, D.C.: AEI Press, 2000), 57–58; data for 2000 2002, 2004, and 2006 and 2008 calculated by authors.*

won 93 percent of the time, whereas senators have won roughly 79 percent of the time. In 2008, more than 95 percent of the representatives who ran for reelection won, as did 90 percent of the senators. (As a rule, incumbents fare well at the ballot box in most democracies. A study of national legislatures in eight other industrialized democracies in the 1990s found that incumbent reelection rates averaged 75 percent, ranging from a low of 61 percent in Canada and France to a high of 89 percent in New Zealand.)[36]

Although the reelection rate for congressional incumbents is quite high, Congress still sees substantial turnover in its membership (although far less than the Founders envisioned). In 2007, for example, the average representative had been in the House for five terms (10.1 years), whereas the average senator had been in the Senate for just over two terms (12.8 years).[37] How can substantial turnover coexist with high reelection rates? The answer is that each year, many incumbents decide against running for reelection. Some retire because of age or a desire to pursue other activities, some seek election to a higher office, and some decide they cannot win reelection.

Why do incumbents who run for reelection fare so well? And why do representatives fare better than senators? To answer these two questions, we will examine the setting in which elections take place, the advantages incumbents have, and the disadvantages that challengers face. We will also consider why incumbents lose.

The Election Setting

One way to answer both questions—why incumbents fare so well when they run for reelection and why representatives running for reelection fare better than senators—is to look at the setting in which elections take place. Especially important is the way in which congressional districts are drawn and the greater homogeneity of congressional districts when compared with states.

Redistricting and Gerrymandering One possible explanation for why so many incumbents win reelection is that the maps of congressional districts are drawn to favor incumbents. Of course, such an explanation says nothing about why so many senators win reelection; after all, they represent states whose boundaries do not change. It might explain the electoral success of incumbents in the House, though. In theory at least, district boundaries could be drawn in ways that promote the electoral prospects of incumbent representatives.

The Constitution does not stipulate how states should draw their House districts. All members now are elected from so-called **single-member districts**, which means that the voters living in a defined geographic area known as a district elect just one representative. In the past, however, some members were elected from at-large districts, where everyone in the state voted for the representative. In 1842, Congress passed legislation requiring single-member districts, and in 1872, it also passed legislation requiring districts to be of roughly equal population. But these rules were not enforced on the states.[38] (Indeed, Congress outlawed multimember districts again in 1967.)

Until the early 1960s, state legislatures, which oversee redistricting, were not compelled to redraw district lines to take shifting populations into account. The result was that, in many states, voters were distributed unevenly across the districts, with some districts containing up to four times as many people as other districts. Typically, rural and Republican interests were overrepresented in such plans and urban and Democratic interests underrepresented.

In the early 1960s, the Supreme Court ruled that House districts must have roughly equal numbers of people, and it ordered states to redistrict on the basis of one person, one vote.[39] The Court did not define the fairest way to draw congressional districts, however; indeed, the Court could not specify objective guidelines for redistricting. Figure 11–2 shows why. Imagine that a state has eight members of the majority political party *(M)* for every four members of the minority political party *(Mi)*. How would you divide the state into four congressional districts? In the first plan, the district lines are drawn so that the *M*'s have a majority in each of the four districts. In the second plan, the *Mi*'s are heavily concentrated in one district, giving them the opportunity to control that single

single-member districts
A legislative district in which only one legislator is elected.

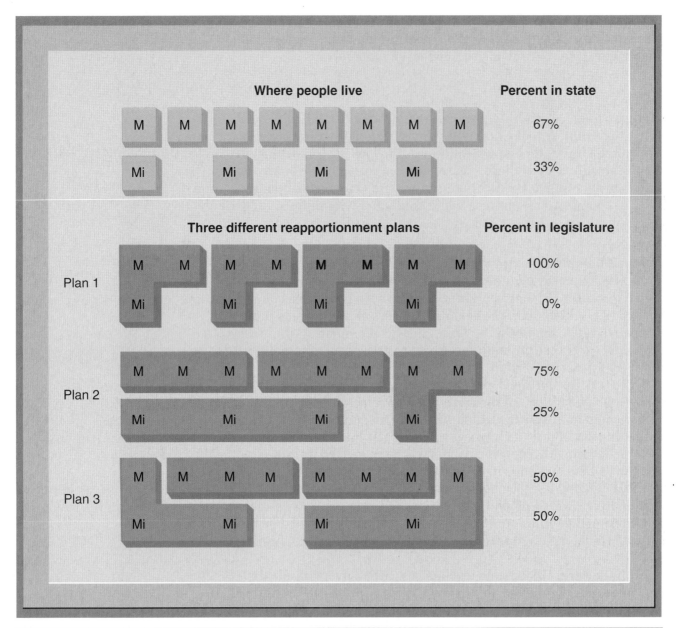

Figure 11–2   Hypothetical Redistricting. Even with the same distribution of majority and minority party members, different districting plans can produce quite different results.

district. In the third plan, *Mi*'s control half the districts, giving them a chance to elect two of the four representatives, despite making up just a third of the population.

Figure 11–2 illustrates two important points. First, the way district boundaries are drawn matters. Substitute ethnic, racial, or socioeconomic groups for our imaginary political parties *M* and *Mi* and you can see how redistricting can determine the composition of the House of Representatives. Second, district lines are not neutral. No matter who draws them or what their intentions are, any set of lines will help one group and hurt another. There is no ideal set of districts in Figure 11–2, no boundaries that guarantee perfect representation.

The fact that district lines are not neutral raises the possibility of **gerrymandering**—drawing district boundaries to favor one political party over another. (Gerrymandering gets its name from a redistricting plan drawn up by the political associates of Elbridge Gerry, a governor of Massachusetts in the early 1800s. Opponents of the plan drew a head and wings on the outline of one district—see Figure 11–3—and said that it looked like a salamander. One wit among them observed that it looked more like a gerrymander.) The Supreme Court ruled in 1986 that gerrymandering violates the Constitution, although the Court did not say how to determine a gerrymander. The Court revisited the issue in cases in 2004 and 2006 and came close to saying that it could never determine when a gerrymander occurred, but each time five justices held out the possibility that at some point in the future such a standard could be defined.[40] As with obscenity, the Court knows a gerrymander when it sees one, but it cannot specify exactly what it is. So parties retain the ability to draw district lines to their advantage.

Does the drawing of district lines explain the reelection success of incumbents? Although it is clear that incumbents may gain some advantages from redistricting, their reelection success is not a result of the way their districts are drawn.[41] Incumbents in districts in which lines are redrawn fare no better or worse than their colleagues in unchanged districts.[42] Also, over the ten years that district boundaries are in effect, parties that gerrymander sometimes gain more seats than they deserve based on their percentage of the vote, but in other cases, they do worse.[43]

Although redistricting does not explain high reelection rates among incumbents, considerable concern remains that district boundaries may be drawn in ways that minimize the chances that minorities will be elected to Congress. Based on Congress's 1982 amendments to the Voting Rights Act of 1965, the Supreme Court has thrown out such redistricting plans. As a result, many state legislatures have sought to maximize the chance of minority representation in the House by concentrating particular minority groups in single districts, or so-called majority-minority districts.[44] In 2008, for example, the first district in Illinois, on Chicago's south side, was 66 percent African American. Nearby districts included the second district, which was 62 percent African American; the third district, which was 78 percent white; and the fourth district, which was 75 percent Hispanic American. One effect of concentrating minorities in a district is that, as we will see, the number of minorities elected to Congress has increased appreciably. But, in an ironic twist, because most African Americans, and to a lesser extent, Hispanic Americans support the Democratic Party, concentrating them in a few districts has resulted in fewer Democrats and more Republicans being elected to the House.[45]

How far can states go to create districts that make the election of minorities likely? The answer is that race cannot be a predominant factor in the drawing of district lines. In a 1993 case involving a congressional district in North Carolina, the Supreme Court ruled that the use of extreme measures to ensure the election of

gerrymandering
Drawing congressional district boundaries to favor one party over the other.

Figure 11–3   The Original Gerrymander—Massachusetts, 1812. The practice of drawing district lines for partisan political advantage has a long history in American politics.

minorities amounts to racial gerrymandering and may violate the rights of white voters to equal protection under the law.[46] Although the Court's ruling in that case only established that white voters had the right to sue North Carolina, the tenor of the decision indicated that the redistricting plan would not pass constitutional muster. In a 1995 case involving a district in Georgia, the other shoe dropped. The Court ruled that use of race as a "predominant factor" in drawing district lines would be presumed unconstitutional.[47] In 1996, the Court tossed out several districts in Texas as well as the disputed North Carolina district. In these cases, the Court held open the possibility that states might be allowed to create districts in which members of minority groups were the majority, but it ruled that race cannot be the predominant factor in drawing district lines and that districts must be geographically compact and not bizarrely shaped. The Court then held in a 1999 decision that judges must delve deeply into the reasons behind the creation of a legislative district's lines before it can be thrown out. This suggests that the shape of a district and its demographic composition may not be sufficient evidence to declare it unconstitutional. Finally, in a 2003 case from Georgia, the Court loosened the legal expectation that minority voting interests could be protected only by the creation of majority-minority districts, finding instead that the drawing of districts with even just 25 percent minorities might still allow such groups to exert influence over their elected representatives. Still, in a 2006 case from Texas, the Court tossed out part of that state's congressional redistricting plan because it reduced the number of districts from which Hispanic Americans were likely to be elected.[48]

Districts versus States Redistricting may not explain why so many representatives win reelection, but the number of congressional districts does help explain why House incumbents fare better than Senate incumbents. Races for the House usually involve smaller and more homogeneous groups of voters than Senate elections. (The exceptions to this generalization are the seven states that have a single representative—Alaska, Delaware, Montana, North Dakota, South Dakota, Vermont, and Wyoming. And it is true that as House districts have increased in population size in the decades since the number of members was capped at 435, representatives have become increasingly less accessible to their constituents and have seen their approval ratings drop.)[49] Put simply, as the number of voters increases, so does their economic, ideological, and social diversity. The increased diversity makes it harder for Senate candidates to maintain a winning coalition of voters.

Table 11–1 uses the population characteristics from four California congressional districts to illustrate the tremendous diversity of many states. Notice how much the districts vary in terms of the percentage of households with children, median house values, and ethnic and racial makeup, even though the number of people living in each district is almost the same. The districts also have different economies. The first district encompasses the redwood

	State of California	First district	Twentieth district	Thirtieth district	Thirty-fifth district
2001 Population	33,871,648	639,087	639,088	639,088	639,088
Percent urban population	95%	76%	91%	98%	100%
Median household income	$47,493	$38,918	$26,800	$60,713	$32,156
Percent in poverty	14%	15%	32%	9%	26%
Percent blue collar	21%	21%	27%	7%	28%
Percent Hispanic American	32%	18%	63%	8%	47%
Percent African American	6%	1%	7%	3%	34%
Percent Asian American	11%	4%	6%	9%	6%

Table 11–1 Comparisons of State and Selected District Demographics: California, 2008

Senators usually face more diverse constituencies than representatives do.

Source: *Data from Michael Barone and Richard E. Cohen,* The Almanac of American Politics 2004 *(Washington, D.C.: National Journal, 2003), 166, 1515.*

forests and northern coast of California plus Napa County. Its economy depends heavily on fishing, logging, tourism, and wineries. The twentieth district lies in the Central Valley, an area in which large farms grow alfalfa, cotton, melons, sugar beets, walnuts, and a host of other crops. The thirtieth and thirty-fifth districts are both in Los Angeles, but they represent different communities. The thirtieth encompasses some wealthy areas, including Malibu and Beverly Hills, and it is home to the entertainment industry. In contrast, the thirty-fifth district includes some of the poorest neighborhoods in Los Angeles. An assessment of all 435 House districts on economics, health, and education levels in 2008 ranked California's thirtieth district the fifth best off in the nation. The other California districts in Table 11–1 did not fare as well. The first district was ranked 187, the thirty-fifth district was ranked 342, and the twentieth district placed 435, dead last. The local newspaper, the *Fresno Bee,* headlined its story on the twentieth district's ranking, "Worse than Appalachia."[50]

If people often do not have much in common with people living in other districts in the state, they usually have much in common with others living in the same district. They often hold similar kinds of jobs, cherish the same cultural heritage, and share the same political values. The relative homogeneity of congressional districts—and some districts are far more homogeneous than others—makes it easier for representatives to identify the interests of the district and to characterize their work in Washington in ways that appeal to voters. In turn, knowing what appeals to constituents helps members get reelected.

Now imagine the problem that confronts California's two senators. Not only must they develop a platform that appeals to the different voters living in the four districts shown in Table 11–1, but to the voters living in the state's other forty-nine districts as well! Crafting and communicating a political message that appeals to loggers in northern California, to farmers in the Central Valley, to movie stars in Beverly Hills, and to the poor of inner-city Los Angeles is difficult. California's senators run the risk that taking a stance on almost any issue will alienate some voters. In sum, larger and more diverse constituencies account, in part, for the lower reelection rate of senators.

The Incumbents' Advantages

A second set of explanations for the high incumbent reelection rate argues that simply being in office gives incumbents many opportunities to make themselves better known to and better liked by their constituents. The way members of Congress present themselves to the voters in their district or state is known as their **home style**.[51] Members adopt home styles that suit their personalities and the districts they represent. Although a representative from Manhattan may adopt a style different from that of his or her colleague from Salt Lake City, the two share the same goal: to present themselves as accessible and trustworthy. Members go to great lengths to convince voters that they share the same values and that they are making the same decisions the voters would if they sat in Congress.

Members of Congress have many tools with which to shape their home style. They can trumpet their legislative successes, use the resources of their office to reach out to voters, and raise funds to run political advertisements that burnish their image. If members develop an effective home style, they will enter every election with advantages that any challenger finds difficult to match.

The Advantages of Responsibility The responsibility of being an elected official carries with it several advantages. First of all, members of Congress have many opportunities to steer federal money into their districts and states. When members secure government funds to build a new bridge, to finance a research project at the local university, or to build a tank at a nearby defense plant, they can claim credit for improving the lives of their constituents.[52] For example, when Plainfield, Massachusetts, received federal money to buy new breathing apparatuses for its fire department, Rep. James McGovern (D-MA) not only announced the grant, but his picture also accompanied a story about it in the local paper.[53] As the federal budget tightens, members of Congress have even started to take credit for cutting funding. A press release for Rep. Paul Ryan (R-WI), for example, trumpeted "Ryan Wins Overwhelming Bipartisan Support to Stop Wasteful CDC Spending," an action he thought would be popular with his supporters.[54]

A second advantage that members of Congress gain from occupying a position of responsibility is that voters want to know their views on the major issues of the day. This allows members to stake out policy positions that please their constituents.[55] In some instances, members disregard their own personal views and adopt

home style
The way in which members of Congress present themselves to their constituents in the district.

the most politically advantageous position. In other instances, though, members take positions by framing their personal views to appeal to the maximum number of voters. For example, one representative wrote to his constituents to tell them: "I have worked hard on issues such as tax fairness, cutting federal red tape, creating jobs, making college education more affordable, improving our roads and airports, sensibly managing our resources, and at the same time eliminating government waste."[56] It is hard to imagine anyone taking the opposing side on any of these issues. Voting also gives members of Congress an opportunity to put themselves on record in support of politically popular positions.

In addition to claiming credit and taking positions, members of Congress take advantage of their position of responsibility by calling attention to their activities—in effect, advertising themselves.[57] Much of what happens in Congress is newsworthy, especially for local media. As a result, most members of Congress have press secretaries, and almost every congressional office issues press releases heralding the member's efforts to represent the voters back home.[58] The House, Senate, and both national party headquarters also have satellite facilities to tape the comments of members of Congress and send them to television stations back home.[59] Local media are eager to relay congressional press and video releases—sometimes edited, sometimes not—to the voters because their audiences want to know what is happening and because many of them need news items to fill their papers or airtime. Members also have begun to exploit new advertising opportunities by blogging and podcasting.[60]

Resources of the Office Along with the advantage that comes from being able to claim responsibility for government benefits, incumbents gain an advantage from the resources of their office. One such resource is the clout needed to help constituents deal with the federal bureaucracy. Servicing the needs of constituents is part of the representational duties of a member of Congress. **Constituent service** also makes good electoral sense. Most people speak fondly of members who persuade the Social Security Administration to reissue a lost check or who cut through the red tape blocking a cousin's effort to immigrate to the United States. During one of Senator Edward Kennedy's (D-MA) successful reelection efforts, for example, one lifelong Republican confessed, "My mother would die if she were alive to see [me vote for Kennedy, but] I don't care. He did me a very big favor. I had trouble getting my Medicare check and he took care of it for me."[61] Because constituent service can generate considerable goodwill at a relatively low cost, members have made sure that their office budgets are large enough to allow them to hire staffs to help constituents solve problems they may have with the federal government.

A second resource that comes with a seat in Congress is the **franking privilege**, the right to send official mail for free. With the franking privilege, members of Congress can bypass the local media and reach voters directly. Although members almost always

constituent service
Favors members of Congress do for constituents—usually in the form of help in dealing with the federal bureaucracy.

franking privilege
The right of a member of Congress to send official mail without paying postage.

PAGE 4 CONGRESSMAN DAVE NAGLE

CONSTITUENT SERVICE GUIDE

Information for Help With Federal Programs

When you have a specific need or problem with the Federal government, sometimes it can be difficult to find the right office or person who can help you.

Listed here are some of the programs, services, and federal agencies that my office can help you with.

- Social Security
- Federal Student Loans
- Farm Services
- Federal Employment
- Government Contracts
- Medicare and Medicaid
- Small Business Administration
- Civil Services
- Housing
- Consumer Programs
- Disability Eligibility
- Retirement Eligibility
- Food and Nutrition Programs
- Immigration and Naturalization Service

In your inquiry, please include your full name and address, telephone number, and Social Security number

Special Requests

ACADEMY APPOINTMENTS—Each year, Congressman Nagle nominates a number of qualified students to appointment at the four National Service Academies.

Please contact Toni Harn in the Waterloo office if you wish to apply for one of these academies.

WASHINGTON TOURS—Our office can arrange tours of various federal office buildings including the White House, the FBI Building, and the Supreme Court. These tours come in a very limited number and are offered on a first-come, first-served basis. So please, if your family or group is coming to Washington, let us know as early as possible.

PUBLIC APPEARANCES—I really enjoy speaking to community, civic, and school groups throughout our District. It helps keep you up to date and is a great opportunity for me to stay in touch with you.

If you would like me to address your group, please contact my Waterloo office and we'll do everything possible to work it out.

INTERNSHIPS—Internships are available in the District and Washington offices for college or high school students who would like to volunteer their time in the summer to learn about and participate in the workings of a Congressional office. Interns work with the staff performing routine office functions as well as other special projects. For more information please contact one of the offices.

U.S. FLAGS—Several sizes of American flags are available for purchase from my Washington office only. If you would like your flag flown over the Capitol Building on a specific date, please let us know. These orders take six weeks to fill.

Wilson Offices Here To Help

SAN FRANCISCO
450 Golden Gate Avenue
San Francisco, California 94102

LOS ANGELES
11000 Wilshire Boulevard
Suite 11221
Los Angeles, California 90024

SAN DIEGO
880 Front Street
Room 6-S-9
San Diego, California 92188

FRESNO
1130 O Street
Room 4015
Fresno, California 93721

WASHINGTON
Hart Senate Office Building
Suite 720
Washington, D.C. 20510

Caseworkers Can Help You To Cut Through Federal Red Tape

When artificial heart recipient William Schroeder took the opportunity of a get-well phone call from President Reagan to request that the President cut through the red tape Schroeder was encountering at the Social Security office, it was an example of the frustration Americans often feel when dealing with the federal bureaucracy.

Elected officials like myself can help you in such cases. I have a staff of trained individuals -- known as caseworkers -- who know how to negotiate the complicated twists and turns of federal regulations. Although my caseworkers are headquartered in my San Francisco office, all of my offices do casework.

Here's an example of how a case proceeds. You may recall reading about the six-month old French donkey that two San Diego veterinarians brought into the country in December only to be told by the U.S. Department of Agriculture that they could not prove that the animal was free of disease.

The vets argued the tests U.S.D.A. had used on the donkey were designed for horses and therefore worthless on donkeys. But in a classic Catch-22, U.S.D.A. ordered the donkey destroyed.

It took many of my staff members working on the case to save the donkey's life. But Sonnette -- French for "Little Bell" -- is safe now. Eventually she'll be bred as part of an effort to repopulate her nearly-extinct species.

My caseworkers aren't miracle workers -- they can only help solve problems with the federal government. But if you have such a problem, and you don't know where to turn, they may be able to help.

Pete Wilson
U.S.S.

UNITED STATES SENATE
WASHINGTON, D.C. 20510

PUBLIC DOCUMENT

OFFICIAL BUSINESS

BLK. RT.

Return Postage Guaranteed
ATTENTION POSTMASTER — OCR — PLEASE DO NOT MARK ON OR ABOVE THE LABEL.

8044

U.S. VOTER
MAIN STREET
ANYTOWN USA 12345-6789

Figure 11–4 Constituent Newsletters. Portions of newsletters from then-Rep. Dave Nagle *(top)* and then-Senator Pete Wilson *(bottom)*. Representatives and senators are eager to perform constituent services. Their newsletters drum up business, telling people what services members of Congress can perform and how to contact them.

Source: *Courtesy of Dave Nagle, Waterloo, Iowa*.

respond to letters from their constituents, the most prominent use of the franking privilege is the constituent newsletter (see Figure 11–4). Newsletters are mass mailings that members use to tell their constituents what they are doing in Washington and to alert voters to the array of constituent services they provide. Predictably, newsletters portray the members who send them in a favorable light.[62]

Members have long believed that the frank is an important political resource. Former Speaker of the House Sam Rayburn (D-TX) reportedly told incoming members, "There are three rules for getting reelected: one is to use the frank, two is to use the frank, and three is to use the frank."[63] For many years members heeded Rayburn's advice, and the amount of money spent on franked mail and the number of pieces of franked mail climbed over time. More franked mail was sent in election years than nonelection years. In recent years, however, Congress has imposed substantial limits on the use of mass mailings, and the amount of mail sent has declined dramatically.

In addition to having the staff needed to provide constituent services and the right to send official mail for free, members of Congress have ample travel budgets for visiting their district or state. And most members return home frequently, where they are in great demand as speakers. Take, for example, the activities of Rep. Eliot Engel (D-NY). Most weekends he attends as many as twenty events, working from 9:00 a.m. to 10:00 p.m. He holds "lobby days" when he sets up shop in the high-rise apartment buildings where his constituents live, meeting and greeting them as they come and go. According to one observer, "If there's a senior citizens' center he hasn't visited, it's in another state."[64]

Direct meetings with voters give members of Congress the opportunity to hear the concerns of their constituents firsthand. Such meetings between members and voters are what we expect in a democracy, but the meetings also give members valuable opportunities to make the case that they are doing a good job back in Washington. These meetings are made all the more valuable because most of them occur in nonpartisan forums such as senior centers. In these forums, members can emphasize their personal qualities. Thus, providing constituent services, sending franked mail, and taking opportunities to appear in the district give incumbents real advantages on Election Day.

Campaign Money Along with the advantages that come from occupying a position of responsibility and from having access to federal resources, incumbents have an advantage over their opponents when it comes to raising campaign funds. Money matters in elections because it pays for campaign workers, pollsters, offices, and advertising, among other things. And incumbents raise and spend large sums of money. In 2006, for example, Republican House incumbents raised an average of $1,513,148 per race, whereas the average Democratic House incumbent raised $983,625. The mean challenger raised only around $510,000. Senators usually spend even more because they generally represent more voters; the twenty-six incumbents who ran in 2006 spent an average of more than $9.4 million, with Senator Hillary Clinton (D-NY) leading the way at more than $34 million in a winning effort.[65]

Since the passage of the Federal Election Campaign Act in 1971, individuals, political action committees (PACs), and political parties have been limited in the amount of money they can contribute to a candidate for Congress. In 2007 and 2008, individuals could contribute only $2,300 per election—a primary election counts as one election, the general election another—and PACs, as Chapter 10 discussed, could contribute no more than $5,000 per election. Political parties operate under even more complex rules but are limited to $5,000 contributions for House candidates and $39,900 for Senate candidates per election. (A 1996 Supreme Court decision allows parties to spend unlimited sums independently of the candidates' campaigns.)[66]

Candidates may spend as much of their own money as they wish on their campaigns, and every election sees a few candidates who finance their campaigns out of their own bank accounts. Some, such as Bob Corker in Tennessee, who spent more than $4 million of his own money on his 2006 race for the Senate, are successful. Others, such as Ned Lamont, who put almost $17 million into his 2006 race for a Senate seat from Connecticut, lose. For the vast majority of candidates, though, the limits on fund-raising matter. As Figure 11–5 shows, congressional candidates receive contributions from several sources, but the single largest source of campaign contributions is individual contributors. Because most individuals contribute much less than the $2,300 maximum, incumbents looking to raise several hundred thousand dollars for a House race or several million dollars for a Senate race must tap a large number of sources.

Incumbency makes the task of raising campaign funds much easier than it otherwise would be. A series of successful runs for office enables incumbents to build a large network of contributors. More important, the very fact that incumbents hold office makes them attractive to many contributors, especially PACs. This is not surprising. As we saw in Chapter 10, interest groups want the opportunity to influence people in power, and they believe that campaign contributions buy them access. Given the reelection success

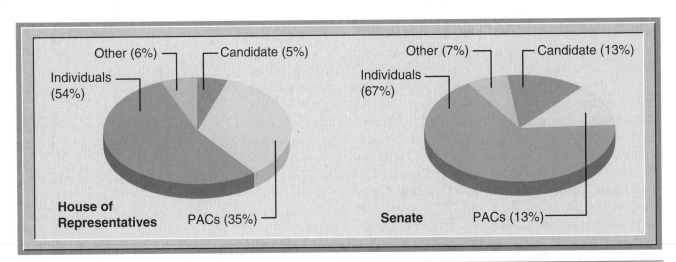

Figure 11–5   Sources of Funds for Congressional Candidates, 2006. Most campaign money comes from individuals, not political action committees (PACs) or parties. Senators rely less on PACs and more on individuals for campaign funds than representatives do.

Source: *Data from Campaign Finance Institute, available at www.cfinst.org/data/pdf/VitalStats_t8.pdf.*

that members of Congress enjoy, it makes sense for PACs to contribute to incumbents. Thus, in the 2006 elections, House and Senate incumbents received more than $279 million in contributions from PACs, whereas their challengers took in just over $31 million.[67] Indeed, PACs gave more money to open-seat candidates than they did to challengers, even though there were many more challengers.

Although House and Senate incumbents almost always raise the money they need to finance their campaigns, the limits on the size of individual campaign contributions mean that they must devote considerable time and energy to raising money for reelection. Because of this, Rep. Ginny Brown-Waite (R-FL) jokingly refers to herself as a "hooker," observing, "I have to go up to total strangers, ask them for money and then get them to expect me to be there when they need me."[68] In a more serious vein, Senator Evan Bayh (D-IN) recently lamented the "exploding costs of campaigns," noting that when his father, Birch Bayh (D-IN), served in the Senate several decades earlier, senators "didn't even think about their elections in the first four years of their terms." Today, the reality is very different. A first-term senator, John Thune (R-SD), admits,

> We're in the world of 24/7 virtual politics. In my case, it's almost like a permanent campaign. Everyone realizes you don't want to be flat-footed. The best way to arm yourself is to raise money.... You don't want to give any hope to a prospective opponent.[69]

To fully understand Senator Thune's reasoning, consider the effort any senator must make over the course of his or her six-year term. If an incumbent needs $30 million for his or her reelection effort—a likely target for incumbents from large states—that means he or she must raise more than $13,699 a day, *every day for six years.* That effort requires an enormous amount of time on the phone and attending fund-raising events, asking potential contributors for money—time that could be spent carrying out legislative duties.[70] Not surprisingly, in a 2005 survey of members of Congress, fund-raising was far and away their least favorite aspect of the job.[71]

The Ultimate Advantage of Office: Name Recognition The advantages of responsibility, the resources of the office, and access to campaign contributions all combine to make members of Congress well known and better liked by their constituents. Although only around 40 percent of voters can *recall* the name of their representative, and 60 percent can name a senator, name *recognition* is much higher; it stands at more than 90 percent for representatives and close to 95 percent for senators.[72] Name recognition matters because voters who enter the polling booth are more likely to vote for a name they recognize on the ballot. And while being known does not guarantee being liked, both public opinion surveys and election results suggest that voters like their legislators.

The popularity of individual members of Congress might seem remarkable given that public opinion polls show that the public

Source: © Courtesy of Steve McBride, Independence Daily Reporter, Kansas.

Although Americans generally hold Congress in low regard, they like their own representatives and senators. Thus, most incumbents are reelected, even when voters claim they want to "throw the bums out."

holds Congress as a whole in low regard.[73] The explanation for this apparent contradiction is that voters distinguish between their legislator and the larger institution. Thus, although voters may disparage Congress, they do not see the people they elect as part of the problem. The problem lies instead with the people everyone else elects. The willingness of many people to hold individual legislators in high regard while disparaging legislators as a group is not unusual; most people draw the same distinction between individual bureaucrats they work with and the federal bureaucracy, and between their own doctors and the medical profession.[74] As astute politicians, many members try to take advantage of the distinction people draw between individuals and institutions by attacking Congress in their run for office.

The Challengers' Disadvantages

We know that congressional incumbents bring enormous advantages into a campaign, but what about their opponents? If a challenger can counter the incumbent's advantages, then a competitive race should ensue. If, however, a challenger enters the campaign at a disadvantage, the incumbent is likely to win. As we have mentioned, in most elections, the incumbents win and win big. Why are challengers unable to counter the advantages the incumbent enjoys?

The answer is that the candidates most likely to unseat an incumbent often decide it is too risky to run. To see why, it is important to recognize that some people make stronger candidates than others. The strongest candidates for Congress usually are people who already have been elected to political office.[75] By winning an election to, say, the city council or state legislature, potential challengers learn how to run a political campaign, establish some name recognition, develop lists of campaign contributors, and perhaps, exploit the resources of their office to their advantage. Of course, some people without electoral office experience make good candidates because of their celebrity or personal appeal. Even celebrities are often unwilling to run. When Michigan Republicans tried to recruit Bill Laimbeer, a former Detroit Piston's center known for his rough-and-tumble style of play, to run for Congress in 1998, he declined, saying that politics was "too ugly of a sport, dog eat dog." Federal Bureau of Investigation whistle-blower Colleen Rowley rejected Democratic pleas to run for the House from Minnesota in 2004, just a year after she had been named one of *Time Magazine's* Persons of the Year, because, "I only sold 16 boxes of Girl Scout cookies. I was the lowest in the whole troop. I don't have much salesmanship in me."[76] Consequently, most strong challengers come from the ranks of the politically experienced.

If holding political office makes someone a stronger candidate for Congress, it also raises the costs of a failed campaign. In most situations, challengers must give up their current office (by not seeking reelection) to run for Congress. Many potential candidates decide that the risk of losing their current position is too great given the usually dismal prospects for winning a congressional campaign.[77] As a result, few House incumbents face strong challengers. Indeed, in the average election year, the prospects of unseating a House incumbent are so dim that in roughly one out of every seven districts no one bothers to run.[78] Senators usually face more competitive opposition, but many of them also face weak challengers.[79]

Does it matter if a better challenger runs? In a word, yes. Challengers who appear to have a good shot at winning a race find it easier to raise campaign contributions. For example, most PACs contribute only to the campaigns of challengers who have a credible shot at winning, but the standard that PACs use to determine credibility is money raised! As one challenger observed after he lost a bid for a House seat: "The PACs, seeing no 'viability' (their word for a snowball's chance in hell) in my election, weren't about to invest in my race. I faced the American campaign Catch 22: I couldn't raise money until I showed momentum, I couldn't show momentum until I raised money."[80]

Again, an inability to raise funds diminishes the chances of victory. Studies show that the more money challengers spend, the better they do.[81] Money does not guarantee victory, of course, but without an ample campaign treasury, challengers find it hard to reach voters. Most House races are uncompetitive precisely because the challenger lacks the money needed to counter the incumbent's advantages. On average, challengers in Senate races have an easier time raising money, and as a result, they tend to have closer contests.

Voters and Election Outcomes

If challengers face an uphill battle in trying to win a seat in Congress, why do incumbents ever lose? One set of answers points to the way incumbents behave. Some members of Congress succumb

midterm elections
The congressional elections that take place midway through a president's four-year term.

to "Potomac Fever" and lose touch with the interests of their constituents. In the 2004 elections, for example, long-time Representative Phil Crane (R-IL) was one of the few incumbents to lose, in large part because his challenger, Melissa Bean, convinced voters that the incumbent cared more about taking foreign junkets than about tending to his constituents' concerns.[82] Senators are somewhat more vulnerable to the charge they are out of step with the people back home because they are more likely to face well-funded challengers who can buy the political advertising needed to make the charge stick. Some incumbents also put their seats in Congress in jeopardy through personal impropriety. For example, many of the House incumbents who lost in the 1992 elections had been tarred by the so-called Rubbergate scandal in which some members repeatedly overdrew their checking accounts at the now-defunct House bank.[83] More recently, in 2006 several incumbents lost because of ethical lapses. In Pennsylvania, for example, veteran Republican representatives Curt Weldon and Don Sherwood were defeated because the former got caught in dubious financial dealings and the latter was entangled in a sordid romantic affair.

The second set of explanations for why some incumbents lose despite their tremendous advantages looks beyond individual behavior and points instead to national political forces. Some incumbents who belong to the president's political party almost always lose their congressional seats in the **midterm elections**, the elections held at the midpoint of the president's four-year term. (The party holding the White House did, however, pick up seats in 1998 and 2002.) These losses partly reflect the fact that voting in midterm elections constitutes a referendum on the president's performance rather than the member's.[84] For example, the Democrats' stunning success in the 2006 midterm elections was attributed in part to public dissatisfaction with President Bush. On rare occasions, parties may be able to overcome the voters' usual focus on local problems and candidates by seeking to nationalize the election, as the Democrats attempted to do with the Iraq War in 2006. Incumbent defeats in midterm elections also reflect strategic behavior on the part of challengers. Stronger challengers from the party not holding the White House enter midterm elections because they think it improves their odds for election, particularly when the president is riding low in the public opinion polls.[85]

If incumbents belonging to the president's political party face tougher going during midterm elections, incumbents benefit during presidential elections if their political party has a strong presidential candidate. Indeed, candidates who win big in the presidential race may significantly increase the vote for the party's congressional candidates. In recent presidential elections, however, the strength of this *presidential coattail effect* has diminished. This is not necessarily because the impact of the presidential vote has lessened, but rather because congressional incumbents now win by such large margins. Incumbents who regularly win with 65 percent of the vote have little to fear from an opposition party's presidential coattail effect of four or five points.[86]

The president's shrinking political coattails have been accompanied by the rise of **divided government**, when one party controls the White House and the other is the majority in at least one house of Congress. Although divided government has occurred throughout American history, it has become, as Chapter 9 points out, much more common in the past few decades. Bill Clinton's victory in 1992 marked the first time in twelve years that the voters put both the White House and Congress in the hands of one political party, but two years later, divided government returned as voters gave control of Congress to the Republicans. The 2000 and 2004 elections again unified government as Republicans took control of all three branches of government for the first time since 1953–1954. In 2006, however, the voters gave the Democrats control of both houses of Congress, producing divided government once more. Two years later voters gave the Democrats unified control of Congress and the White House. One possible explanation for divided government is that voters consciously put the presidency and Congress in different hands to encourage the two parties to compromise on policy differences.[87] Although such calculated behavior runs contrary to what we know about American voters, some survey evidence indicates that voters like divided control of government.[88]

Another explanation for the rise of divided government is that voters hold contrasting ideas about what they want from the two offices. On the one hand, voters want a president who will hold the line on taxes and cut government spending, yet on the other hand, they expect their member of Congress to bring government resources home.[89] This line of reasoning would predict Republican control of the White House and Democratic dominance in Congress—especially in the House—the trend experienced from the late 1960s until the mid-1990s. Election results from 1994 to 2004 raised serious doubts about this explanation, but the 2006 elections produced the predicted outcome, whereas the outcome in 2008 again contradicts it.

To sum up, the election setting, incumbents' advantages, challengers' disadvantages, and voter behavior all tend to favor incumbents' reelection, especially in House races. Nonetheless, because so many incumbents decide against running for reelection, Congress still sees substantial turnover in its membership (although far less than the Founders envisioned).

divided government
The type of government experienced when the president is of one party and the other party has a majority in at least one house of Congress.

11-4 SERVING IN CONGRESS

As we have just seen, seats in Congress are the targets of intense competition. Incumbents fight to stay in office, and challengers search for ways to unseat them. When the dust from the electoral competition finally settles, what kinds of people end up serving in Congress? And what is the job of being a member of Congress like?

11-4a Who Serves?

What sort of people succeed in getting elected to Congress? Does Congress represent a cross section of the American public? If not, what are the consequences for representative government?

When the first Congress convened in 1789, all its members were white males. Even at the beginning of the twenty-first century, white males continue to predominate. Although Congress now counts among its members women, African Americans, Asian Americans, Hispanic Americans, and American Indians, the number of women and minorities has grown slowly, as Figure 11–6 shows. For female members, the biggest change relates to the way they have acquired their seats in Congress. Until the past several decades, most women serving in Congress took their seats by replacing their dead husbands. Now, as Box 11–2 discusses, most are elected on their own.[90] As more women occupy elected offices at the state and local level, more women are in a position to run for Congress, and as more women run, more are elected.[91] As for African Americans, their relatively small gains in Congress have come in large part because of the Supreme Court's rulings on the laws governing redistricting.[92] With few exceptions, African Americans, Hispanic Americans, and Asian Americans are elected from districts with significant numbers of minority voters.[93]

Because white males predominate, neither the House nor the Senate is descriptively representative in the sense that the percentage of female and minority members reflects their percentage in the general population. Yet the lack of *descriptive representation*

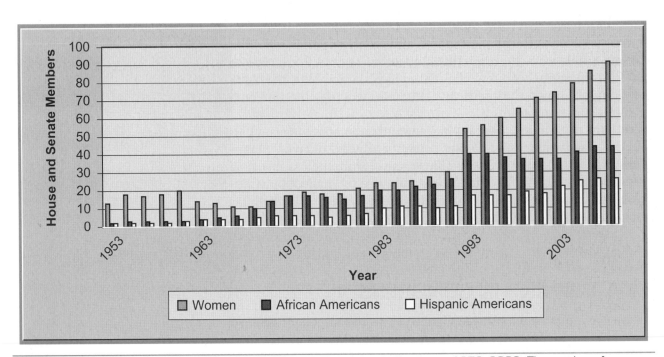

Figure 11–6 Women, African Americans, and Hispanic Americans in Congress, 1953–2009. The number of women and African Americans in Congress has grown rapidly in the past few years, but they are still underrepresented compared with their numbers in the American public.

Source: *Data for 1953–1998 from Norman J. Ornstein, Thomas E. Mann, and Michael J. Malbin,* Vital Statistics on Congress 1999–2000 *(Washington, D.C.: AEI Press, 2000), 60–61; data for 2001, 2003, 2005, and 2007 and 2009 calculated by authors.*

The People behind the Rules

Box 11–2 Changing Paths to the Senate: The Careers of Margaret Chase Smith and Olympia Snowe

In 1994, Olympia Snowe became the second woman elected to the Senate from the state of Maine. A comparison of Snowe's path to the Senate with that of Maine's first female senator, Margaret Chase Smith, illustrates important changes in the routes available to women seeking high political office in the United States.

MARGARET CHASE SMITH

Smith was born in 1897 to a family of modest means in Skowhegan, Maine. She never attended college, and after graduating from high school she worked as a telephone operator, a circulation manager for a weekly newspaper, a grade school teacher, and an executive at a woolen mill. In 1932, she married Clyde Smith, a newspaper owner and an activist in the Republican Party. In 1937, Mr. Smith was elected to the House of Representatives. When he became gravely ill in 1940, he asked his constituents to continue his policies by electing his wife to succeed him, something they did in the special election following his death. Thus, Margaret became one of only nine women serving in the House at that time.

In 1948, Smith ran for the Senate, easily defeating three male rivals in the Republican primary and another man

Margaret Chase Smith.

in the general election. When she was sworn into office, she was the only woman serving in the Senate, a distinction she held for many years. Her service was marked by a strong independent streak. In the early 1950s, she joined with a small group of other Republican senators to criticize their colleague, Senator Joseph McCarthy (R-WI), who had made sensationalistic charges of communist influence in the U.S. government. Smith challenged McCarthy's claims, saying "I don't want to see the Republican Party ride to political victory on the four horsemen of calumny—fear, ignorance, bigotry, and smear."

In 1952 and again in 1968, Smith was mentioned as a possible vice presidential candidate. She ran for the presidency in 1964, and she received several votes at that year's Republican National Convention. She finally lost her Senate seat in 1974. Smith ran that last campaign as she had her other races, hiring no campaign staff, putting out no advertising, and appearing in the state only for weekend receptions. Although questions were raised during the 1974 campaign about Smith's advanced age, she lived in good health until her death in 1995.

OLYMPIA SNOWE

Snowe was born in 1947 in Augusta, Maine, and she was orphaned as a child. She graduated from the University of Maine in 1969 and soon took a job as a legislative staffer for Rep. William Cohen (R-ME). Snowe first won elected office in 1973 when, like Smith before her, she was elected to take the seat of her deceased husband—in this case, a state representative who died in an auto accident. After four years in Maine's lower house, Snowe was elected to the state senate. After two years in that post, she was elected to the House of Representatives, taking the seat of her former boss, William Cohen, who was elected to the Senate. During her eight

Olympia Snowe.

terms in the House, Snowe established herself as leading Republican moderate. She voted with the more conservative element of the Republican Party on many economic issues, but she took more liberal positions on issues such as abortion and the environment. In 1989, Snowe married John McKernan, the governor of Maine and once one of her colleagues in the House of Representatives. In 1990, McKernan's unpopularity with the people of Maine almost cost Snowe her seat in the House. She won reelection again in 1992, and then raised and spent more than $2 million to beat a strong opponent for Maine's open Senate seat in 1994. When she was sworn in as senator in 1995, she became one of eight women serving in the Senate. She was reelected in 2000 and again in 2006.

As a senator, Snowe has followed the same moderate course she charted as a representative. She joined with other Republican moderates to temper the policies favored by their conservative colleagues on social issues, but at the same time agreed with conservatives on the need to balance the federal budget and to shrink the size of the federal government.

The People behind the Rules   *(continued)*

The careers of Senators Smith and Snowe resemble one another in some respects. Both sought elective office after their husbands died, and both were moderate Republicans who often found themselves taking positions outside their party's mainstream. In other ways, however, their careers are quite different. The social prejudices of Smith's era strongly discouraged women from standing for election, and it is unlikely that she would have won a seat in Congress if her husband had not died in office. In contrast, Snowe, like many other women of her generation, worked her way up through the political ranks. And although the number of women serving in Congress with Senator Snowe does not reflect their share of the population, many more populate Capitol Hill today than in the days of Senator Smith. Indeed, in 1996, Maine voters elected Republican Susan Collins to their other Senate seat, and reelected her in 2002 and 2008.

Sources: Michael Barone, Grant Ujifusa, and Douglas Matthews, *The Almanac of American Politics 1976* (New York: Dutton, 1975), 344; Michael Barone and Grant Ujifusa, *The Almanac of American Politics 1982* (Washington, D.C.: Barone and Company, 1981), 452–57; Michael Barone and Grant Ujifusa, *The Almanac of American Politics 1996* (Washington, D.C.: National Journal, 1995), 592–5; David S. Cloud, "GOP Moderates Refusing to Get in Line," *Congressional Quarterly Weekly Report*, September 30, 1995, 2963–65; Richard Severo, "Margaret Chase Smith Is Dead at 97; Maine Republican Made History Twice," *New York Times*, May 30, 1995; Patricia Ward, *Politics of Conscience: A Biography of Margaret Chase Smith* (Westport, CT: Praeger, 1995).

in Congress may not have significant consequences for *policy or political representation.*[94] A Congress that is descriptively representative might very well vote the same way on the same issues as it does now. For example, Table 11–2 compares the voting records of Senator Barbara Boxer (D-CA) and Senator Kay Bailey Hutchison (R-TX). The two differ in a predictable way on a number of important social, economic, and defense issues; Boxer votes like other Democrats, whereas Hutchison usually sides with her Republican colleagues. In 2006, for example, Boxer voted with a majority of Democrats to raise the federal minimum wage, while Hutchison, like most Republicans, opposed the increase. The fact that both are women does not mean that they vote alike. (Some evidence suggests, however, that the priorities of women legislators differ from those of men. Several studies of members of Congress have found that regardless of their political affiliation, women legislators tend to place greater importance on health, welfare, and education issues and less importance on business issues than men do.)[95]

Regardless of their race, gender, or ethnicity, members of Congress tend to vote in ways consistent with the desires of their constituents, particularly on highly salient issues. Thus, although it is true that almost every African American member of the House is a liberal, it is not race that dictates his or her behavior. Most of these members represent liberal districts. When their constituents are more conservative, they tend to be more conservative as well. In 2006, for example, Rep. Sheila Jackson Lee (D-TX) introduced a lenient immigration reform bill, but only nine of her forty-two colleagues in the Congressional Black Caucus signed on as cosponsors. Jackson's measure failed to garner much support in large part because her colleagues represented districts that preferred tougher immigration legislation.[96]

Other demographic characteristics also poorly predict the views of members of Congress. For example, Speaker Pelosi's net worth is estimated to be between $35 million and $156 million, yet she has consistently been among the most liberal members of the House. In contrast, among the most conservative Republican

Vote	Boxer	Hutchison
Ban Drilling in Arctic National Wildlife Refuge (D 40-3; R 7-48; I 1-0)[a]	For	Against
Raise Minimum Wage (D 43-0; R 8-46; I 1-0)	For	Against
Confirm Samuel Alito (D 4-40; R 54-1; I (0-1)	Against	For
Bar Same Sex Marriage (D 2-40; R 47-7; I 0-1)	Against	For
Urge Iraq Withdrawal (D 37-6; R 1-54; I 1-0)	For	Against
ADA rating 2006[b]	95	5
ACU rating 2006[c]	8	84

Table 11–2   Comparisons of the 2005–2006 Voting Records of Senator Barbara Boxer (D-CA) and Senator Kay Bailey Hutchison (R-TX)
Democrats tend to vote like other Democrats, and Republicans tend to vote like other Republicans.

Source: *Reprinted with permission from The Almanac of American Politics, 2004. © 2009 by National Journal Group, Inc. All Rights Reserved.*

[a]The parentheses contain the vote within each party, with the yes vote listed first.

[b]Americans for Democratic Action, a liberal group, which gives higher ratings to members of Congress who vote for liberal legislation.

[c]American Conservative Union, a conservative group, which gives higher ratings to members of Congress who vote for conservative legislation.

members of Congress in recent years were Speaker Gingrich, House Majority Leader Dick Armey, and House Ways and Means Committee Chair Bill Thomas. All were college professors in the social sciences or humanities before entering politics.

Like occupation, personal wealth, or other cross-cutting cleavages, religion cuts many ways. About 29 percent of all members of Congress are Catholic, roughly the same percentage as in the general population. Like Catholics in the general population, Catholics in Congress are found on either side of any controversial issue, including abortion and stem cell research. Descriptive representation, then, is not identical to policy or political representation. Although white males dominate Congress, they and their female and minority colleagues seem to vote according to their constituents' views much of the time.

11-4b Congress as a Job

Many people have sought a seat in Congress. They campaign at great cost in terms of time, energy, and money, and in the end, only a small handful succeed. For those who do, what are the advantages and disadvantages to the job?

Serving in Congress is a full-time job with significant attractions. It is prestigious, and members enjoy immense personal satisfaction from being considered important. In addition, the Constitution requires that members be paid for their service. Congressional pay has always been a politically sensitive issue. Originally, members were paid $6 a day. In 1816, members raised their pay to $1,500 a session to cover what they claimed was the growing cost of serving in Congress. A public furor ensued, and in 1817, members voted to rescind the raise. Thus, early on, the trend on congressional salaries was set: Members vote to raise their pay only when they are willing to withstand the inevitable public anger.[97]

In 2009, members of Congress earned $174,000. In the early 1990s, public outrage over what many saw as a conflict of interest forced Congress to outlaw *honoraria*—money members earned for giving speeches, usually to interest groups—as part of a political deal to raise member pay to its current level. Members continue to enjoy other benefits besides their substantial salary, though. The pension plan is generous. Members retiring under the current system received an average annual benefit of almost $36,000 in addition to Social Security and whatever they have accumulated in the government's Thrift Savings Plan.[98] (All members of Congress have been required to pay Social Security payroll taxes since 1984.) Members can buy life insurance at a low cost, and they pay nothing for health care. They can use a wide array of facilities in and around the Capitol, including a fully staffed medical clinic, restaurants, gyms, barber shops, and a stationery store, usually for less than the general public would pay for the same services.[99]

Although the rewards of congressional service sound appealing, the job has its disadvantages. One representative from Florida recently admitted, "Very candidly, this isn't the greatest job I've had."[100] The average member of Congress devotes an enormous amount of time to the job; one estimate has representatives working more than twelve hours a day.[101] As Figure 11–7 shows, members spend time attending committee and subcommittee meetings, participating in floor debates, working with staff, meeting with constituents and lobbyists, raising campaign funds, traveling to and from the district, and engaging in a host of other activities.

The time members of Congress devote to their job forces most of them to sacrifice other interests. The strain on their personal lives is apparent. When J. C. Watts (R-OK) served in the House, he observed, "This is a very tough business on family . . . you miss a lot of Little League, a lot of dance recitals."[102] It is particularly hard for women with young children. Speaking of being both a mother and a member of the House, one representative said, "You can do both jobs well, but you can't do it the same as everyone else in America."[103] Indeed, at a candidate forum Rep. Debbie Wasserman Schultz (D-FL) found herself taking notes with a peach crayon she pulled out of her purse.[104] Congressional spouses also pay a price. After her husband was elected to the House in 2006, one wife grumbled, "We don't really do anything together, . . . But he's so busy even when he is back here. I understand he has to see people. It's just that the schedule sometimes has been a bit of a problem." She later negotiated "one date night a month," with her husband.[105] In a harsher vein, the divorced wife of a representative bitterly claimed, "I think Washington corrupts people. [My former spouse] was a wonderful husband and father, the best I ever saw,

Sample Daily Schedule for Congressman James Leach—Wednesday, June 7, 2006 – Schedule in Washington, D.C.

9:00 A.M. – 10:00 A.M.
GOP Conference
HC-5 of the Capitol

10:00 A.M. – 10:30 A.M.
Meeting with the Under Secretary for Rural
Development, Tom Dorr
Representatives Leach's Office

10:30 A.M. – 12:30 P.M.
Congressman Leach to chair Asia and the
Pacific Subcommittee Hearing entitled
"North Korea Brinkmanship: Is U.S. Policy up
to the Challenge?"
2200 Rayburn
Note: Assistant Secretary of State Chris Hill to testify

12:00 P.M. – 1:00 P.M.
Tuesday Group Lunch
HC-6 of the Capitol

1:30 P.M. – 2:00 P.M.
Meeting with University of Iowa student
government representatives
Representative Leach's Office
Note: To discuss student education issues
and student financial aid

2:00 P.M. – 2:30 P.M.
Meeting with the Foreign Minister of Pakistan,
H.E. Khurshid M. Kasuri
Representative Leach's Office
Note: To discuss recent developments in
U.S. – Pakistan relations

2:30 P.M. – 3:00 P.M.
Meeting with six high school students from
Wayne County
Representative Leach's Office
Note: The students are participating in a program
called Citizenship Washington Focus

3:00 P.M. – 3:30 P.M.
Meeting with constituents from the American
Diabetes Association
Representative Leach's Office
Note: The Donald Family from Cedar Rapids will
be in to discuss funding for diabetes research

3:30 P.M. – 4:00 P.M.
Meeting with constituents from the Associated
Builders and Contractors of Iowa
Representative Leach's Office
Note: Several representatives from Frye Builders in
Muscatine will be in attendance

4:00 P.M. – 4:30 P.M.
Meeting with Paul Tagliabue, Commissioner of
the NFL
Representative Leach's Office
Note: To discuss HR 4411, the Unlawful Internet
Gambling Enforcement Act of 2006

5:00 P.M. – 6:00 P.M.
House Wednesday Group Hosted by Congress-
man Jim Kolbe
H-122 of the Capitol

6:00 P.M. – 8:00 P.M.
Greater Des Moines Partnership Opening
Reception
Hirshhorn Museum and Sculpture Garden

Sample Daily Schedule for Congressman James Leach—Saturday, June 10, 2006 – Schedule in the District

7:30 A.M. – 8:30 A.M.
Congressman Leach to speak at the Linn
County Medical Society Annual Legislative
Breakfast
Mercy Medical Center, Cedar Rapids

9:00 A.M. – 10:00 A.M.
Congressman Leach to attend the reopening
celebration of the Old Capitol Museum
The University of Iowa Pentacrest

11:30 A.M. – 12:00 P.M.
Congressman Leach to meet with members of
National Association of Retired Federal
Employees
Burlington Steamboat Center, Burlington

1:30 P.M. – 2:30 P.M.
Congressman Leach to speak on United States
policy on South Korea, North Korea, and Korean
Peninsula and what he saw during his visit to
Pyongyang, N. Korea
All Nations Baptist Church in Iowa City
Note: 200 people will attend this event, including
members of the Korean Consulate and reporters
from Radio Free Asia

3:00 P.M. – 5:00 P.M.
Congressman Leach to attend the Mormon
Handcart Pioneer Festival
Mormon Handcart Park in Iowa City

6:54 P.M. – 11:44 P.M.
United Flight #7742
   Departs Cedar Rapids at 6:54 p.m;
   Arrives O'Hare at 8 p.m
Flight #628
   Departs O'Hare at 9 p.m
   Arrives National 11:44 p.m.

Figure 11–7 A Daily Schedule for a Member of Congress. Members of Congress have full schedules, both in their districts and in Washington, D.C.
Source: *Courtesy of Representative James Leach, Davenport, Iowa .*

until he went there. I told him I was trying to get him out of the dark side, all that power and greed and people kissing up to them all the time. Now he is one of them. All they care about is getting reelected."[106] Indeed, the job can become so consuming that routine activities of life are ignored. Veteran Senator John McCain (R-AZ), for example, confessed that he has to ask his wife or his aides to get him online so that he can read newspapers.[107] Concerted efforts to make Congress more "family friendly" in recent years failed, leaving one member to complain, "Keeping us up here eats at families. Marriages suffer."[108]

There are other costs as well. Although members of Congress are well paid relative to the general population, they make far less than most people who hold positions of similar importance. In 2007, for example, the chief executive officers of 200 major American corporations averaged $8.8 million in total compensation.[109] (Members of Congress even make lower salaries than some people holding positions of less importance. For example, New York Yankees' third baseman Alex Rodriguez makes $179,000 for *every regular season game he plays, $5,000 more than a member of Congress gets as an annual salary*.) Most members would make more money if they went to work in the private sector. Moreover, members suffer because they have to pay to live both in Washington and back home. The financial strain can be real. For example, in 2005 Senator Rick Santorum (R-PA), a married father of six children, claimed, "We live paycheck to paycheck." He even admitted that his parents helped out. "They're by no means wealthy—they're two retired V.A. employees—but they'll send a check every now and then."[110] Many members try to cut expenses by sharing apartments in Washington with other members of Congress or by living with family or friends when they return home. For more than twenty years, Rep. George Miller (D-CA) has rented out space in his Washington, D.C., townhouse to colleagues. In 2007, he and Senator Dick Durbin (D-IL) had upstairs bedrooms, while Senator Charles Schumer (D-NY) and Rep. Bill Delahunt (D-MA) slept on beds in the living room.[111] Some members opt not to rent or buy housing in Washington. Rep. Joe Donnelly (D-IN), for example, stays with an aunt in Virginia, and Rep. Lee Terry (R-NE) sleeps on the sofa in his Capitol Hill office, having previously used an air mattress until it sprang a leak.[112]

The tremendous demands of congressional service prompt some members to leave Congress. Yet, for most, the reasons to stay outweigh the reasons to leave. As one representative reflected, "The demands of a congressional career can tend to crowd out other facets of a person's life . . . [but] I'm not complaining. I recognized the trade-offs, and I accepted them willingly. I would do so again."[113]

11-4c Congress and Ethics

Americans have always held the ethics of their elected representatives in low regard. In 1897, Mark Twain wrote, "It could probably be shown by facts and figures that there is no distinctly native

American criminal class except Congress."[114] In recent years, talk of corruption on Capitol Hill has reached a fevered pitch. But have members of Congress become more corrupt?

The best evidence suggests the answer is no. Cases of individual corruption—such as the 2005 conviction of Rep. Randy "Duke" Cunningham (R-CA) and the 2006 conviction of Rep. Bob Ney (R-OH) for accepting bribes in exchange for their performance of official duties—are far fewer now than in the past. (Indeed, Congress used to be so lax about such concerns that bribing a member was not declared illegal until 1853.)[115] Starting in the 1970s, Congress imposed strict legal and ethical regulations on itself, regulations that constitute perhaps the most stringent rules governing any legislative body in the world.[116] In 1995, for example, the House of Representatives adopted strict rules barring members from accepting free meals, gifts, or trips from anyone but family and close friends. (The Senate adopted less severe gift rules in the same year.) In 2003, as the memory of previous ethical problems faded, the House loosened some of its restrictions. In 2005 and 2006, as members of Congress again became enmeshed in scandals, both the House and Senate sought to tighten ethics rules, if only just a little bit.[117] However, when public pressure for reform waned by 2008, Congress began to relax the rules again, if only at the margins.[118]

In recent years, questions have been raised about the jobs members of Congress take after they leave office. A 2006 study revealed that 318 former members were currently employed as lobbyists in Washington.[119] In 2004, for example, Rep. Billy Tauzin (R-LA) stepped down as chair of the House Energy and Commerce Committee, the panel that, among other things, regulates the pharmaceutical industry. A few months later he took a highly paid position as the head of the Pharmaceutical Research and Manufacturers of America, the trade association representing the interests of drug makers.[120] The ethical concern with this sort of behavior is that members of Congress will take actions in office intended to make themselves attractive to wealthy interests that might later employ them. There is some evidence suggesting that this happens.[121]

11-5 CONGRESS AS AN ORGANIZATION

Congress consists of 535 individuals. Each of its members assumes office as an equal. As we previously discussed, the Constitution imposes almost no organization or structure on either house. What we could have, then, is an organization of 535 individually elected members, each pursuing his or her own policy agenda, with no mechanism in place to impose order and manage the conflicts that inevitably arise. Yet Congress has rules and structures that enable (or force) it to make decisions. How has order been imposed where chaos might reign?

The answer is political parties. Their very existence makes it possible to create the system of party leaders, committees, and staff that form the organizational heart of the modern Congress.

11-5a Political Parties in Congress

As we discussed in Chapter 9, the Framers of the Constitution had no use for political parties. Yet voting blocs emerged quite quickly in Congress.[122] The reason for their formation is simple: Organization begat organization. When members of Congress who favored the policies of George Washington's administration began working together, opponents countered with their own organization. As these organizations evolved into political parties, they simplified and structured decision making in Congress. In particular, they enabled members to unite in the pursuit of common goals.

Political parties have become so ingrained in congressional politics over the past 200 years that it is hard to envision how Congress could operate without them. Do not misconstrue the role of political parties in Congress. Only rarely do they control congressional decision making or develop and impose policy agendas on their members. When members of Congress find that their political interests or policy preferences diverge from those of their party, they usually go their own way. Thus, in Congress we can talk about *conditional party government*, wherein the majority party acts cohesively and under the leadership's direction only when substantial policy agreement exists among its members on important issues.[123]

Members of Congress can ignore the wishes of their political party because they know they do not owe their election to the party. As we discussed in Chapter 9, political parties in the United States are weak and decentralized organizations that work only when their members share common interests. Only in a few states do political parties control who is nominated as their candidate. In most states, individuals launch their candidacy, raise money, campaign, and win the nomination without the help or advice of what passes for the party organization. In short, parties lack clout because they cannot take away the jobs of maverick members.

What role, then, do political parties play in Congress? Parties matter because they provide the basic stuff of organization, the glue that binds some members together and allows the imposition of leadership and structure. Every leadership position in both the House and Senate is filled through the parties. Members get their committee assignments through their party. Even the few members elected as something other than a Democrat or a Republican are assigned committee seats by one of the parties.

11-5b Party Leadership in Congress

Most organizations can function effectively only with leadership. Congress is no exception; both House and Senate have developed leadership structures to help them conduct business. Because the majority and minority parties in the House organize their leadership differently, and because of differences between the House and Senate, we discuss majority and minority party leadership in each chamber separately.

Majority Leadership in the House

Despite the lack of constitutional guidance, both the House and the Senate have adopted similar leadership structures. The House's speaker is the only major difference between the two bodies. Although the full House membership formally elects the speaker, in reality, the members of the majority party decide before each two-year session of Congress which of their members will be given the job. On an organizational vote such as this, members cast their ballots along straight party lines, which means that the candidate of the majority party wins. During most of the twentieth century, speakers were senior members, but not the *most* senior members, and they tended to come from the moderate ranks of their party. Speakers hold office until they retire or their party loses the majority. Recent speakers have, however, deviated from that pattern. Jim Wright (D-TX), resigned the speakership in 1989 after he was accused of unethical behavior.[124] His successor, Tom Foley, became the first speaker in more than 100 years to be defeated for reelection in his home district when he lost in the 1994 elections. The Republican who replaced Foley, Gingrich, resigned from both the speakership and the House after his party failed to gain seats in the 1998 midterm election.

The rules of the House give the speaker substantial formal authority. As we discussed previously, these powers have changed over time; recent speakers have had more authority than speakers in the mid-twentieth century had, but less than speakers in the nineteenth century had. The speaker's power comes from being the chief parliamentary officer of the House, which enables the speaker to exercise great control over the referral of legislation to committee, the scheduling of legislative debate, and the recognition of members during floor debate. Because of these duties, the speaker rarely takes part in debates or votes.[125]

The speaker is also the leader of the majority party in the House, and this role gives the speaker other powers. Under the Republicans, for example, the speaker chaired the party's Steering Committee, which is the group that assigns Republican members to committees and named the chairs of committees and subcommittees. The speaker cast five of the thirty-three votes on the Steering Committee. As a result, the speaker had considerable say over committee assignments and decisions that strongly influence the course of each member's career. And the speaker appointed all the Republican members of the Rules Committee and the House Administration Committee. (The GOP minority leader retained those powers in 2007). Under the Democrats, Speaker Pelosi also controls much of the appointment process, although her choices are voted on by the party's Steering and Policy Committee, a body she chairs and her loyalists dominate.[126]

In addition to the formal powers of the office, the speaker has informal powers. Foremost among these is the ability to bestow (or withhold) favors. For example, speakers are responsible for making a small number of patronage appointments in the House, and they can help members raise campaign funds. Speakers can use these and other favors to win support from members of their own party or even, on occasion, members of the opposition.

A second informal power of the speaker is information. Speakers (and all other congressional leaders) sit at the center of the information flow in Congress. This information varies greatly, from the scheduling of floor debates to the policy preferences of individual members. In a real sense, speakers (and their staff) collect intelligence; they know more about what is going on in the institution than anyone else does, and they use that information to their advantage.

The speaker is joined in the formal leadership structure by the majority leader and majority whip. Both positions are elected by the majority caucus. The majority leader assists the speaker on scheduling matters and helps to develop the leadership's position on major issues. The majority leader also speaks for the party on the floor of the House. The whip sits at the center of a two-way information flow. (The term *whip* comes from the English term *whipper-in*, the person in a hunt who keeps the hounds together in pursuit of the fox.) The whip is the leadership's chief vote counter, the person who monitors the mood of members before a vote to see which way it is apt to go. In turn, the whip keeps members abreast of the legislative schedule and informs them about the party leadership's preferences. The whip works with a large group of assistant whips, usually organized along regional lines.

Although the speaker, majority leader, and majority whip wield tremendous influence, they lack the power needed to ram their own policy agendas through the House. As a result, most majority party leaders work to facilitate the development and passage of legislation that a majority of their party supports. Indeed, Speaker Hastert's promise to bring to a vote only legislation supported by a majority of his caucus—or a majority of the majority—became institutionalized as the "Hastert Doctrine."[127] Majority party leaders accomplish their party's goals by making legislation that enjoys support from their members a priority, marshaling support for it, and bringing it to the floor for a vote under favorable conditions. Ambivalence or outright opposition on the part of the leadership does not automatically kill a bill, but it does diminish the chances for its passage.[128] In working to pass legislation favored by their party, majority party leaders know that if their party unites, the bill will pass.

In practice, however, majority party leaders lack the tools needed to compel party discipline; in other words, they cannot always depend on every member of the party to follow their lead. As one representative described the difficulties that majority party leaders face in trying to lead: "It's like herding cats and everybody has their own idea about how to save Western civilization."[129]

The case of Rep. Mark Neumann (R-WI) illustrates the limits of party leadership power.[130] Neumann first came to Congress in 1995 as a strong supporter of Gingrich. The new speaker rewarded

Neumann by giving him a seat on the powerful Appropriations Committee as well as on its prestigious National Security Subcommittee, plum assignments for a first-term member. For the most part, Neumann proved to be a strong supporter of the Republican leadership. On some issues, however, he criticized the leadership for compromising on the principles set forth in the Contract with America. When the leadership watered down several provisions in the defense appropriations bill, Neumann helped defeat the bill on the floor of the House.

Neumann's opposition to the defense appropriations bill infuriated the chair of the Appropriations Committee. With the consent of Speaker Gingrich, he punished Neumann by taking away his seat on the National Security Subcommittee and reassigning him to a less prestigious appropriations subcommittee. Neumann's fellow first-term members, however, quickly rallied to his support. Meeting with Speaker Gingrich, one first-term member asserted: "This was an attempt to deal with Mr. Neumann that was also an attempt to send a message to the freshmen. We weren't sent here to kow-tow to anybody. We were sent here to vote our conscience."[131] Within hours, Neumann's situation improved. He was not restored to his seat on the National Security Subcommittee—the leadership could not back down from that decision. Instead, he was given a prized slot on the Budget Committee in addition to his already influential appropriations post. The lesson of the Neumann incident is clear: Even the most powerful leadership that the House had seen in a century was limited in the punishment it could inflict on even the most junior members of its party.

This is not to claim, however, the party leaders are powerless. From time to time, they do flex their muscles to enforce discipline. In early 2006, for example, two members of the House Republican whip operation were removed from their positions after they voted against the leadership's position on an important procedural vote. And a few weeks later, the House Majority Leader, John Boehner (R-OH), threatened to remove Republican members from highly prized committee assignments if they failed to vote as the leadership wanted on a controversial budget measure. The leaders are constrained by the knowledge that they retain their positions only with the support of a majority of their caucus.[132]

Minority Leadership in the House

The minority leader and minority whip lead the minority party. The minority leader faces problems different from those of the majority party leader. The minority party cannot prevail in House voting unless it is unified *and* can attract enough support from members of the majority party to become the functional majority, as happened with the appearance of the **Conservative Coalition**, an alliance of Republicans and southern Democrats that formed from time to time from the 1940s to the 1990s.[133] Operating from

Conservative Coalition
The Conservative Coalition appears when a majority of southern Democrats votes with a majority of Republicans against a majority of northern Democrats.

this position of weakness puts minority leaders in a bind. They can choose one of three strategies: to cooperate with, compete with, or obstruct majority party proposals.[134]

If the minority party cooperates with the majority, it gains some input into policy, but at the cost of being identified with the policies of the majority party. The minority party is unlikely to get credit if the policies succeed, and it cannot attack the majority party if the policies fail. Because the minority party hopes someday to become the majority party, cooperating with the majority party may produce short-term advantages but long-term disadvantages.

Electoral incentives, then, discourage cooperation with the majority party, and with it, the minority party's chance to influence policy. In choosing not to cooperate with the majority party, the minority party may decide to develop a competing policy program of its own. Although such a program will lack the votes needed to pass in the House, the minority party calculates that voters at the next election will find its program preferable to the one the majority party is offering. The minority party also might forgo developing its own policies and decide instead to focus on blocking legislation that the majority party favors. Such an obstructionist strategy has the advantage of preventing the majority party's preferences from becoming policy, but at a cost of preventing the minority party from developing an alternative program to take to the voters.

Minority party leaders in the House have pursued a mix of cooperative, competitive, and obstructionist strategies over the past five decades. And chronic tension exists among minority party members over which strategy is most effective. In 1989, for example, House Republicans elected Gingrich as the new whip largely because he favored a militant opposition to the Democrats quite unlike the cooperative approach associated with minority leader Robert Michel.[135] When the Democrats became the minority party in 1995, they, too, had to grapple with these problems. In some instances they cooperated with the majority; in others, they offered competing proposals or simply worked to obstruct the majority's will.[136] They quickly learned the opportunities and limitations of being in the minority. As one of their members observed, "The luxury of being in the minority is the freedom to change and think of new ways of doing things. You cannot do it the old [majority party] way and always worry about getting 218 votes. The fact is, like it or not, we don't have 218 votes."[137]

Leadership in the Senate

Under the Constitution, the vice president of the United States serves as the president, or presiding officer, of the Senate. The vice president usually appears in the Senate only on ceremonial occasions or when needed to break a tie on an important bill. The Constitution created the position of president pro tempore to preside over the Senate in the vice president's absence. The most senior majority party member is named the president pro tempore, but the post is largely honorific. Presiding over the Senate is a tedious chore, usually assigned to junior members of the majority party as a sort of hazing.

For more than a century, the Senate did without official party leaders. The Democrats named their first official party leader in 1920, and the Republicans followed suit in 1925.[138] The position assumed the importance we now attach to it during the 1950s, when Senators Lyndon Johnson (D-TX) and Robert A. Taft (R-OH) were party leaders.[139] Both men used their stints as majority leader to increase the power and status of the position. Now the majority leader is almost always considered the most important person in the Senate. Like the other leaders in the House and Senate, the majority leader gets far more national media attention than most members and becomes not only a spokesperson for the party, but also a recognized national political figure.[140]

The nature of the Senate does not, however, allow its leaders to exercise the same level of power their counterparts in the House enjoy. The Senate's rules make it hard for leaders in the Senate to get anyone to follow them. For example, the majority leader is in charge of the schedule, but even this power is at the mercy of virtually every member of the Senate. The objection of even the most junior minority party senator is often sufficient to disrupt the majority leader's plans. Thus, as one congressional observer notes, "The Senate has become a band of 100 individual operators.... There's very little a leader can do to impose his will on the members any more."[141] As a result, the power of Senate leaders rests largely on their own personal qualities and ambitions. Johnson, for example, epitomized the energetic leader. His power over the Senate stemmed from his unchallenged knowledge of the needs and wants of his fellow senators as well as his forceful and occasionally overbearing personal style. His successor as majority leader, Senator Mike Mansfield (D-MT), offered a stark contrast. Mansfield was a quiet person, much less driven by the need to pursue his own policy agenda. Yet, most observers considered Mansfield an effective leader as well. Effective leaders, in both the House and Senate, play the important role of managing conflict, keeping some semblance of order, and keeping the difficult business of lawmaking running smoothly.

11-5c Committees

To observe that committees are where Congress does its work is trite but true. Committees were created as a labor-saving device, allowing each chamber to handle its workload by assigning a few members to concentrate on particular areas, leaving others to deal with different problems. Virtually all legislation is reviewed by a committee before it is considered for debate and a vote on the floor of either house. Most bills are introduced and then sent immediately to a committee, and most never make it out of committee—which, in effect, kills them. The ability of committees to determine which bills go to the floor gives them considerable power.

conference committee

An *ad hoc* committee of House and Senate members formed to resolve the differences in a bill that passes each body with different provisions.

select committees

Congressional committees that typically are created for only specific lengths of time and that lack authority to report legislation.

Certainly, the place committees occupy in the legislative process makes them powerful. That is, being a "gatekeeper" on legislation that is introduced gives them an extraordinary opportunity to decide whether the legislation will be pursued. Committee power is also enhanced by the fact that the committee members who review a particular piece of legislation dominate a **conference committee** on it.[142] (A conference committee is an ad hoc committee of House and Senate members formed to resolve the differences in a bill that passes each body with different provisions.) Committee power rests on another source, as well—information. Members can acquire expertise on the issues that come before their committees. Knowledge about a particular subject gives committee members an advantage over their noncommittee colleagues who do not understand the ins and outs of the issue. Thus, noncommittee members may defer to their committee colleagues with the expertise.[143]

The House and the Senate have essentially the same workload, yet the House has 435 members to handle it, whereas the Senate has only 100 members. The House divides its work among twenty standing committees, whereas the Senate has sixteen standing committees. Standing committees continue from session to session and are charged with examining and reporting legislation to the full House or Senate. Both the House and the Senate also have special and **select committees**, almost all of which are created for only specific lengths of time and which lack authority to report legislation. Several joint House-Senate committees oversee administrative matters and conduct research.

House committees have more members than Senate committees, but the average representative serves on far fewer committees than the typical senator: just under two in the House to over three in the Senate. The number of subcommittee assignments reflects the same difference: Representatives serve on an average of four subcommittees, senators on nine subcommittees.[144]

Because representatives serve on fewer committees, they focus their attention on a smaller number of issues than senators do. Representatives generally concentrate on the areas under their committees' jurisdictions, and over time, most become experts on their subjects. Senators tend to be spread very thin by the many demands on their time. Their far-flung committee assignments enable them to have a say on a wide range of issues, but out of necessity, they tend to be generalists rather than specialists.

The 2007 committee assignments of Senator Claire McCaskill (D-MO) and Rep. Ike Skelton (D-MO) illustrate the difference between the Senate generalist and the House specialist. Senator McCaskill served on the Armed Services Committee; the Commerce, Science, and Transportation Committee; the Homeland Security and Governmental Affairs Committee; the Committee on Indian Affairs; and the Special Committee on Aging. She sat on eleven subcommittees. These positions gave McCaskill a platform from which to address a wide array of issues. Over the course of her brief career, she has been active on a wide range of issues, including agriculture, education, energy, homeland security, and immigration. In contrast, Rep. Skelton served on the Armed Services Committee, which he chaired. Like McCaskill, Skelton is an active legislator, but most of his efforts are confined to legislation involving defense issues, on which he is considered an expert.

Committee assignments matter more to representatives than to senators. Representatives find their influence is generally confined to those areas their committee assignments cover. As a result, which committees they sit on greatly affects the legislative activities they pursue. Not surprisingly, representatives seek slots on committees that help them reach their political goals, regardless of whether those goals are to protect the interests of their constituents, promote particular policies, or become influential in the House.[145] Thus, the roster of the Agriculture Committee is heavily weighted with members from farming districts, and the Resources Committee, which oversees the use of federally owned lands, is dominated by representatives from western states, where most federal land is located. Because committees such as Agriculture and Resources tend to attract members who represent particular economic interests, the decisions those committees reach may be biased in favor of those interests.[146] Committees with broader jurisdictions, however, tend not to become captured by specific interests.

The party groups that make committee assignments in the House—which the Democrats call the Steering and Policy Committee and Republicans call simply the Steering Committee—take member preferences into consideration. (The ratio of majority to minority party members on almost every committee reflects the ratio in the full House or Senate.) They also weigh party interests by balancing state, regional, and ideological concerns. Members assigned to the most powerful committees in the House—Appropriations; Energy and Commerce; Financial Services (for Democrats); Rules; and Ways and Means—are limited to that single post.[147] Other members usually serve on one major and one minor committee.

Representatives usually keep their initial committee assignments because their influence increases as they accumulate seniority on a committee. The only members who change assignments are those willing to sacrifice their seniority on a less important committee to gain a position on one of the most powerful committees. Because seniority usually determines who becomes chair, members may wait many years before they can assume the top committee post. But in 1995, at the behest of Speaker Gingrich, Republicans ignored seniority in selecting the chairs of three powerful committees. These decisions did not, however, signal the end of seniority. The men who jumped the line were hardly junior members. The chairs of the other committees all went to the Republican with the most seniority, a pattern followed in every case in succeeding years.

In 2001, however, the six-year term limit on committee chairs that House Republicans imposed after their takeover in 1994 first took effect. The chairs of all but four committees were vacated, leading to battles among senior Republicans to take them. In the end, seniority was violated on a number of important committees, but as in 1995, the members selected as chairs had all been in the House for many years, and strict seniority prevailed on most other committees. Indeed, several veteran members moved from the chair of one committee to the chair of another committee. In 2003, the GOP leadership again overrode seniority, skipping over the most senior Republicans on the Government Reform and Resources committees and giving the chairs to more junior members. However, the seniority rule was observed in other committees. By 2005, the increasing power of the party leadership and the weakening of the seniority system could no longer be denied. That year Speaker Hastert not only removed the chair of the Veterans Affairs Committee from his leadership post, but also from the committee altogether. The new chair, who promised to be more supportive of the leadership's spending preferences than his predecessor had been, leapfrogged over two more senior members to get the position. Thus, under their current system, Republicans picked a member with considerable seniority, but not necessarily the most senior member, to become a committee chair. The person selected also tended to have raised a considerable sum of campaign money that was shared with Republican House colleagues.[148] When the Democrats took control again following the 2006 election, Speaker Pelosi chose to follow seniority in naming chairs. As it happened, that allowed her to have women and minority members to hold committee chairs in proportion to their numbers in the party.[149] Speaker Pelosi still enjoys the flexibility to ignore seniority in naming future chairs.

In the Senate, senators are allowed to serve on only one of the "Big Four" or "Super A" committees—Appropriations, Armed Services, Finance (the counterpart to Ways and Means), and Foreign Relations. And they may serve on only two of the longer list of "A" committees.[150] Starting in 2005, Republicans gave their leader the power to fill half the "A" committee slots available to the party as a tool for enhancing party discipline.[151] Party rules prevent senators from hoarding leadership positions. Consequently, almost every majority party senator chairs either a committee or a subcommittee. Senators are much more likely than representatives to change committee assignments because many senators like to move to committees overseeing issues they find of current interest.

11-5d Staff

Congress employs a large number of people to assist members in their work. Each representative receives a set sum of money with which to hire personal staff, whereas senators receive an amount based on the number of people they represent. Both representatives and senators hire people to track legislation and research issues, and almost all have press secretaries. Many personal staff are assigned to handle constituent problems. More than 44 percent of the personal staff of House members and more than 33 percent of Senate staff members work in district or state offices rather than in Washington, D.C.[152]

In addition to the staff that work directly for members of Congress, some people work for committees. In most cases, the committee staff are experts on some aspect of the committee's business. Members also rely on three congressional support agencies for information. The Congressional Research Service performs extensive research on subjects members request and is considered an important source of information.[153] The Government Accountability Office and the Congressional Budget Office provide members and committees with the expertise necessary to keep track of the extensive activities of the federal government.

The number of personal, committee, and support staff in Congress has grown tremendously since the early 1970s, so much so that some observers now complain that the staff constitute a fourth branch of government. In 1995, however, Republicans fulfilled one of their pledges in the Contract with America by reducing the number of congressional staff members. In addition, the Republicans abolished the Office of Technology Assessment, a congressional support agency that reported to Congress on scientific matters. The Republicans also eliminated funds for legislative service organizations such as the Congressional Black Caucus, the Congressional Hispanic Caucus, and the Congressional Human Rights Caucus, which provide staff to enable members to work together on issues of common interest. (Some of these organizations carried on, using members' personal staff.)[154]

The growth of congressional staff has come largely in response to the growing size of the federal government and the desire of members of Congress to counter the executive branch's vast advantage in information and expertise. And although some personal staff work primarily to promote their member's electoral prospects, most congressional staff work to provide members with information they can use to increase their influence in the policymaking process. Staff thereby extend the members' reach, allowing them to be active on more issues than they could be otherwise. On many issues, staff members are important actors in the decision-making process. A recent study of the 2005 highway bill, for example, emphasized "the influential role often played by staffers in shaping congressional legislation and marshalling it through the legislative process, especially at critical junctures."[155] At times their considerable influence makes some members uncomfortable. Indeed, during a lengthy Senate Judiciary Committee hearing focused on the many complex details of an immigration bill, so many staff members were whispering information into their senators' ears that committee chair Arlen Specter compared his colleagues to Charlie McCarthy, a famous ventriloquist's dummy.[156]

11-6 THE BUSINESS OF CONGRESS

Congress is the country's supreme lawmaking body, but what is the legislative process—the set of rules that turns a policy proposal into a law? How do members of Congress decide whether to support the legislation they are asked to vote on? And what steps do members of Congress take to ensure that the laws they pass work as intended? In the following sections, we consider each of these questions in turn.

11-6a The Legislative Process

The legislative process formally begins when a member of Congress introduces a bill.[157] Only members can introduce a bill. Anyone else who wants Congress to consider a piece of legislation—even the president—must have a representative or senator do it for him or her. A bill may be introduced either in one chamber alone or in both chambers simultaneously, and it is generally considered first in committee and then on the floor. The same version of the bill must pass both the House and the Senate before it can go to the president for his signature. As Figure 11–8 shows, the process a bill follows is essentially the same in both houses, with the important exception of an additional hurdle, the Rules Committee, in the House.

Policy Initiation

Ideas for bills come from many sources, including the White House, executive agencies, interest groups, industry, and even professors. Members of Congress and their aides sometimes develop policy proposals on their own, but more often than not, members borrow ideas others have generated. In short, members usually act as policy entrepreneurs rather than policy innovators.

As soon as members begin the process of translating an idea into a bill, they begin to look for support. One way is by coming up with a catchy name for the bill, such as the Sober Truth of Preventing Underage Drinking Act of 2004, more easily remembered by its acronym, STOP Underage Drinking.[158] And before submitting a measure, the sponsor usually circulates a "dear colleague" letter informing other members about the legislation and why it is needed. The sponsor hopes to convince other members to become co-sponsors, thereby increasing the chances the bill will become law.[159] By the time most bills are introduced into Congress, they have a number of members listed as co-sponsors.

The Committee Process

Once a bill is introduced—dropped into a wooden hopper in the front of the House or handed to a clerk in the Senate—it is assigned a number, preceded by "H.R." for House bills and "S." for Senate bills. From time to time, members reserve numbers for special purposes. For example, one former representative, H. R. Gross, always

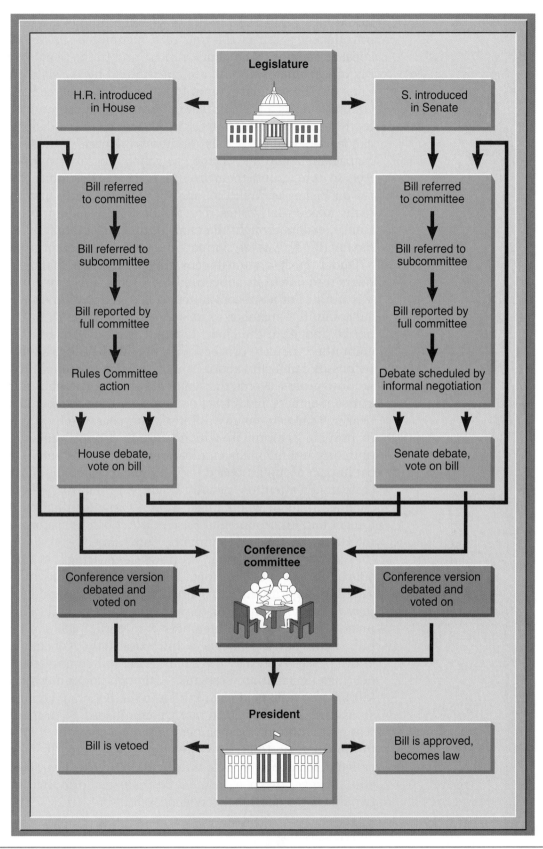

Figure 11–8 How a Bill Becomes a Law. A bill must overcome many obstacles before it is signed into law. Most bills never make it out of committee.

Source: *William F. Hildenbrand and Robert B. Dove, Enactment of a Law: Procedural Steps in the Legislative Process* (Washington, D.C.: Government Printing Office, 1982), 233.

introduced a bill H.R. 144 (144 of something is a gross).[160] Once introduced, a bill is referred to a committee. In the House, the speaker decides where a bill will go, and in the Senate, the presiding officer does, but both are constrained by the defined jurisdictions of the various committees and other precedents. Which committee gets a bill can matter because some committees may be more receptive than others. In 1995, for example, House Republican leaders rewrote legislation involving parts of the Coastal Zone Management and the Marine Protection, Research, and Sanctuaries Acts so as to reroute them around the House Resources Subcommittee on Fisheries, Wildlife, and Oceans, the body that would normally tackle such issues. The reason for this extraordinary action? House leaders thought the chair of that subcommittee, Rep. James Saxton (R-NJ), was too sympathetic to environmental groups.[161]

Under most circumstances, the committee that gets the bill refers it to one of its subcommittees. Most bills never pass beyond this point. For a subcommittee to take any action on a bill, some subcommittee member must express interest in it. Even that may not be enough if the chair does not want to pursue it. If the subcommittee wants to proceed with the bill, hearings are held so that witnesses can testify about its merits. Most subcommittee hearings are low-profile events that generate little participation from committee members and attract no attention from the media. Although hearings can serve many different purposes, the most important is to provide a forum in which affected groups can express their opinions and members can learn about the substantive and political impact of the proposed legislation. Occasionally, hearings generate media attention, usually because a celebrity gives testimony, such as in 2008, when singer Sheryl Crow testified on the Breast Cancer and Environmental Research Act before a subcommittee of the House Energy and Commerce Committee.[162]

A markup session usually follows the hearings. At this meeting, subcommittee members decide what changes the bill needs to secure a majority vote to send it to the full committee. Members may make no changes or they may rewrite the bill. Participation matters at the markup; members who participate can influence a bill significantly.[163] Once a bill passes the subcommittee, the entire process can play out again in the full committee, with more hearings and markup sessions. Although committees can and do kill bills by refusing to send them to the floor, subcommittee decisions carry great weight in many committees.[164] For many years, it was quite difficult for members to force a committee to send a bill to the floor. In 1993, however, the House voted to make the so-called discharge process less difficult to invoke. Over the next decade, however, even with the rules changes, only two of seventy-two discharge petitions were successful.[165]

The House Floor

Once a committee passes a bill and sends it to the floor, usually with a recommendation to pass, the House and Senate follow different procedures. In the House, bills are put on one of five legislative calendars, which make up an archaic and complex system that bears no relationship to the calendar used in everyday life. Most bills of any significance do not have to wait for the workings of the legislative calendars to bring them to the floor. Instead, the Rules Committee issues a special rule that takes them off the calendar and sends them to the floor.

The Rules Committee exists only in the House. (The Senate Rules and Administration Committee serves a different purpose.) The House Rules Committee regulates the flow of legislation to the floor and sets the conditions under which the full House will consider a bill. Unlike the membership of most other committees, the Rules Committee membership is stacked heavily in the majority party's favor. As we mentioned previously, the speaker selects the members of the majority party who serve on the Rules Committee, which makes the committee sensitive to the wishes of the majority party leadership. As a result, majority party leaders can use the Rules Committee to determine when and under what conditions the full House will consider a bill.

Before the House considers a bill, it first votes on the rule the Rules Committee proposes. The rule itself can be quite simple or, as Figure 11–9 shows, extremely complex. It almost always limits the amount of time a bill can be debated. The rule may also limit the number and type of amendments members can offer. Some bills come to the floor under a closed rule, meaning no amendments may be offered, while others come to the floor under a restricted rule, which means members can offer only certain amendments. The Rules Committee can also write an open rule, which permits members to offer any amendment.

Sometimes the Rules Committee crafts rules designed to provide members of the majority party with political cover on tough votes. The King-of-the-Hill rule, for example, states that the last amendment passed in a given sequence is the one that takes effect. The majority party finds the King-of-the-Hill rule helpful when the minority party is proposing amendments that members find politically difficult to oppose. Under the rule, the House votes on the opposition's amendments first, which allows members of the majority party to go on record in favor of them. The amendment the majority party leadership prefers comes up for a vote last, and supersedes and replaces the earlier amendments as long as it wins a majority of votes. In 1995, the new Republican majority created a Queen-of-the-Hill rule, which stipulates that the amendment garnering the most votes wins.[166]

As the King-of-the-Hill and Queen-of-the-Hill rules suggest, the vote on a rule often determines what kind of bill will emerge from the floor debate. Once a rule is adopted, the House dissolves itself into the Committee of the Whole, a parliamentary device that makes it easier to consider amendments. (The Committee of the Whole is made up of every member of the House.) Once amendments are disposed of, the Committee of the Whole dissolves and members vote on the bill. The House may follow many different voting procedures. Some procedures, such as voice votes, allow

H. Res. 416

Resolved, That at any time after the adoption of this resolution the Speaker may, pursuant to clause 1 (b) of rule XXIII, declare the House resolved into the Committee of the Whole House on the state of the Union for consideration of the bill (H.R. 4296) to make unlawful the transfer or possession of assault weapons. The first reading of the bill shall be dispensed with. All points of order against consideration of the bill are waived. General debate shall be confined to the bill and shall not exceed two hours equally divided and controlled by the chairman and ranking minority member of the Committee on the Judiciary. After general debate the bill shall be considered for amendment under the five-minute rule. The amendment in the nature of a substitute recommended by the Committee on the Judiciary now printed in the bill shall be considered as read. All points of order against the committee amendment in the nature of a substitute are waived. No amendment to the committee amendment in the nature of a substitute and no other amendment to the bill shall be in order. At the conclusion of consideration of the bill for amendment the Committee shall rise and report the bill to the House with such amendment as may have been adopted. The previous question shall be considered as ordered on the bill and any amendment thereto to final passage without intervening motion except one nation to recommit with or without instructions.

Figure 11–9   Example of a House Rule. Rules govern how a bill will be considered on the floor, determining how long debate will last and how many and what types of amendments will be offered.
Source: *Congressional Record, May 5, 1994, H3064.*

members to vote without making their position on the issue public. Since its inception in 1973, however, electronic voting has become the most common voting procedure. Members put something akin to a personal credit card into one of forty voting stations distributed around the House floor, and their vote registers on several scoreboards. Electronic voting has resulted in far more recorded votes; thus, it has increased member accountability to interest groups and the public.

The Senate Floor

Bills are brought to the Senate floor at the discretion of the majority leader, who works most of the time with the consent of the full Senate. When a bill makes it to the floor, debate is unlimited. A member can talk for as long as he or she desires or is physically able. The tactic of preventing a vote on a bill by talking it to death is known as a **filibuster**. A filibuster can be stopped only when at least sixty senators vote to invoke **cloture**, a procedure that limits the length of a debate. (The late Senator Strom Thurmond of South Carolina holds the record for a one-person filibuster. In 1957, he spoke for twenty-four hours and eighteen minutes straight in a failed effort to block a vote on a civil rights bill.) Only about half of all filibusters actually block a bill or convince sponsors to revise their proposal, but that figure is sufficient to encourage members to undertake them.[167]

Many bills, particularly the most important pieces of legislation, come to the Senate floor covered by a *unanimous consent agreement.* The majority leader negotiates these agreements, which can go into effect only if no senator objects. Unanimous consent agreements can be used, among other things, to limit debate and the number and type of amendments senators can offer. Thus, unanimous consent agreements allow the Senate to streamline its deliberative procedures. Still, as Box 11–3 shows, individual senators can impede the Senate's consideration of bills in ways their House counterparts cannot.[168]

The voting procedures in the Senate also differ from those used in the House. Most votes in the Senate are roll-call votes in which a clerk reads the names of each member and the senators respond by stating their position. Not surprisingly, the Senate is almost always in session for many more days than the more regimented House.

The Conference Committee

When the House and Senate pass different versions of the same bill, a conference committee usually meets to resolve the differences. The power to appoint the conference committee formally rests with the speaker of the House and the presiding officer of the Senate. In practice, however, the conferees are almost always chosen by the chairs and ranking members of the committees that sent the bill to the floor. (A ranking member is the minority party member with the most seniority on the committee. He or she acts as the minority party leader on the committee.)

Conference committees range in size from very small to very large; one conference in 1981 had more than 250 members. The conference committee is free to revise the bill, almost to the point of completely rewriting it, as happened with the landmark Tax Reform Act of 1986.[169] Once a conference committee reaches agreement, both chambers must approve it without any changes for the agreement to be sent to the president. If members do try to change the bill the conference committee reported, they risk forcing the appointment of a new conference committee or killing the bill entirely.

filibuster
The tactic of stalling a bill in the Senate by talking endlessly about the bill in order to win changes in it or kill it.

cloture
The procedure to stop a filibuster, which requires a supermajority of sixty votes.

POINT OF ORDER

Box 11–3   The Byrd Rule and Senate Voting on the Budget

Because rules structure how legislatures make decisions, rules can determine which side wins and which side loses in a conflict. One example of the power rules have to determine winners and losers is the operation of the Byrd Rule in the Senate during the epic budget fight in 1995.

In 1985, then-Senate Majority Leader Robert Byrd (D-WV) pushed through a new rule that governed how the Senate handled budget bills. In most circumstances, the Senate operates with unlimited debate, and only a unanimous consent agreement or a cloture vote can curtail it. One exception is consideration of budget bills (formally known as reconciliation measures), on which a twenty-hour limit on debate is imposed. The limit exists so that budget bills cannot be held hostage to a filibuster. Because filibusters are not allowed, senators have an incentive to attach extraneous (or nongermane) amendments to budget bills, knowing that their colleagues can do relatively little to stop them. The Byrd Rule, as it came to be known, was instituted to make it more difficult for individual senators to attach extraneous provisions to budget bills. In 1990, the Byrd Rule was made law by amending it into the Congressional Budget Act of 1974.

The exact details of the Byrd Rule are fairly complex; the Senate has developed more than a dozen different criteria for determining when a provision of a budget bill is

extraneous. The general thrust of these criteria is that the provisions of a budget bill are germane only if they are aimed at reducing the federal government's budget deficit. Provisions that increase the budget deficit and provisions that do not have a substantial impact on government revenues and spending are deemed extraneous. Thus, if a provision were added to a budget bill to expand the scope of the student loan program, the provision would be extraneous because it would increase government spending and, hence, the deficit. In a similar vein, a provision in a budget bill that made abortion illegal would also be extraneous, this time because deficit reduction is not the primary purpose of the provision.

If a provision of a budget bill is extraneous under the Byrd Rule, any senator may raise a point of order against it on the floor. Under the rules of the Senate, the offending provision is thereby struck from the bill. The point of order can be waived, and the provision reinstated in the bill, only if *three-fifths* of the senators agree to do so. Because the Byrd Rule can be waived only with the support of sixty senators, it is difficult to add extraneous provisions to budget bills. Of what relevance is the Byrd Rule? As the 1995 budget battle unfolded, House Republicans sought to include many of their significant policy proposals in one massive budget bill. They calculated that President Bill Clinton would have a harder time vetoing Republican policy proposals if those proposals were attached to a bill appropriating the money needed to run the federal government. What the House Republicans forgot, however, was that Senate Democrats could defeat their strategy by invoking the Byrd Rule once the bill came to the Senate. In November 1995, for example, Rep. John Doolittle (R-CA) commented, "We're just now becoming aware there is a major problem" because of the Byrd Rule.

And it was a major problem for the Republicans, who only had fifty-three votes in the Senate, or seven votes fewer than they needed to waive a point of order. Senate Democrats invoked the Byrd Rule and stripped

one extraneous provision after another from the budget bill. Gone were provisions that would have transferred federal land to California for use as a low-level radioactive waste dump, imposed a five-year limit on welfare, increased the eligibility age for Medicare recipients from sixty-five to sixty-seven years of age, and sold a government oil reserve, among a host of other things.

The damage was not confined to the votes in the Senate. In the conference committee called to reconcile the Senate and House versions of the budget bill, other provisions were deleted because Republican leaders realized that Senate Democrats could use the Byrd Rule to challenge them when the bill returned to the Senate floor for a final vote. Of course, Republicans had the option of resurrecting the deleted provisions by introducing them as individual bills, but they lost the tactical advantage they had hoped to gain by attaching them to budget measures.

The Byrd Rule was imposed to prevent senators from adding extraneous measures to budget bills and thereby abusing the budget process. When the Republicans were in the majority, they used it to their advantage. In 1995, with the tables turned, Democrats exploited the rule to their benefit. And the rule continues to be employed. From 1996 to 2004 it was applied forty-two times. Indeed, the rule now is so ingrained in the process that budget provisions that might be subject to it are referred to as being "Byrdable."

Sources: Christopher Georges, "Byrd Procedural Rule Is Threatening to Derail Substantial Portions of the Republican Agenda," *Wall Street Journal*, November 8, 1995; Christopher Georges and Greg Hitt, "GOP Conferees Reach Accord on Medicare Bill," *Wall Street Journal*, November 9, 1995; George Hager, "Reconciliation Now a Major Tool," *Congressional Quarterly Weekly Report*, October 28, 1995, 3286; Robert Keith, "The Budget Reconciliation Process: The Senate's 'Byrd Rule,'" updated April 7, 2005; Walter J. Oleszek, *Congressional Procedures and the Policy Process*, 6th ed. (Washington, D.C.: CQ Press, 2004), 67–68; Alissa J. Rubin, "Senate's Last-Minute Changes Kept Floor Activity Lively," *Congressional Quarterly Weekly Report*, November 4, 1995, 3360; Sheryl Gay Stolberg, "Issues and Egos Contend in Congress's Rush to Leave," *New York Times*, December 24, 2005; Charles Tiefer, *Congressional Practice and Procedure* (Westport, CT: Greenwood Press, 1989), 89–91.

Robert Byrd.

Source: © Courtesy of Brian Duffy, Des Moines Register.

Even members of Congress who do not support military spending in general are likely to fight to protect their districts from the economic damage the closing of a local military base causes.

11-6b Decision Making

The number of subcommittee, committee, and floor votes cast each session reaches well into the thousands. How do members decide how to vote?

Voting Cues

In many instances, the question of how to vote is easy for members of Congress to answer. They know how to vote on issues on which they are experts, say, because their committee held hearings on the bill or because they have a personal interest in the legislation. Members also know how to vote on the few issues on which their constituents have intense and uniform preferences. Given the political power of the agricultural lobby, for example, most members from farm states or districts do not have to read the details of a bill to know they will vote against any effort to cut crop subsidies. And often Congress votes on symbolic resolutions or on politically attractive issues that almost everyone can support. In 2008, for example, the House voted 415–0 for a resolution "Congratulating and recognizing Mr. Juan Antonio "Chi-Chi" Rodriguez for his continued success on and off the golf course, for his generosity and devotion to charity, and for his exemplary dedication to the intellectual and moral growth of thousands of low-income and disadvantaged youth in our country."

Yet on many votes, members know little about the issue at stake, their constituents lack well-formed opinions, and the legislation is substantive rather than symbolic. What do members do then? In these circumstances, members look elsewhere for guidance, or cues, on how to vote. Voting cues come from a wide variety of sources besides personal ideology and constituent opinion: party leaders, members of the committee that reported the bill, members from the same state, and friends. Members use the views of others to help them make up their own minds because they cannot possibly master all the issues they are asked to vote on. Put simply, voting cues are decision-making shortcuts that members hope will enable them to avoid making bad policy and bad political decisions.

One common voting cue is party, as undecided members look to see how others in their political party intend to vote. Party members tend to vote alike not because their leaders can discipline them but because they tend to represent similar sorts of people with similar preferences. Some issues can become highly partisan, with a majority of congressional Democrats taking one side of an issue and a majority of congressional Republicans taking the other side. On important votes, party leaders communicate their preferences clearly: Whips and their assistants may stand at the chamber doors signaling thumbs up or thumbs down. Members have great flexibility in deciding how to vote, and they rarely vote with their party on every issue.

Many bills do not excite partisan passions. Most look something like a bill to "bypass laws that require that meat products for use in schools be inspected at the point of processing by federal officials."[170] Sponsored by a Kansas representative on behalf of Pizza Hut, Inc., the bill sought to allow commercial pizza companies to sell pizzas in school cafeterias. Few members were experts on the specific issues the bill raised (i.e., market access, food safety, and childhood nutrition); few constituents cared, or even knew, about the bill; and neither political party had a position on pizza in schools. Most members had to look to other voting cues, such as their assessment of the sponsor of the legislation and the views of their colleagues, in deciding how to vote. As the late Representative Hyde observed, voting is usually "an exercise in mutual trust. I've been here twenty-one years, and you can't tell me that when they wave those continuing resolutions around at 2 a.m. that are 1,200 pages long, that they have been read by anybody. You have to do it that way. Otherwise, we'd have to stop what we were doing for two weeks just to read."[171]

Personal versus Constituent Preferences

Members of Congress are sent to Washington to represent the interests of their constituents, but they also have their own personal policy preferences. Sometimes the two conflict. Take the example of Rep. Adam Putnam (R-FL). He is a staunch opponent of allowing drilling for oil and natural gas off the Florida coast, despite his position as a proponent of drilling in the Arctic National Wildlife Refuge and other efforts to increase national energy production. Putnam's contradictory behavior shocks no one in Washington because Florida's economy depends heavily on tourism and many

Floridians oppose drilling off their coast because of the possibility of oil spills.

Although a member's personal preferences sometimes conflict with those of his or her constituents, they more often coincide. The reason lies in the nature of the recruitment process for Congress. The need to reside in a district for much of one's life to build a coalition of supporters and to win an election makes it likely that members will share the policy views of many of their constituents.[172]

Members of Congress constantly calculate possible trade-offs between their personal agendas and their understanding of what their constituents want.[173] Sometimes constituent apathy, division, or agreement leaves members free to vote as they see fit. At other times, members swallow their preferences to avoid alienating their constituents. How much electoral risk a member will tolerate in pursuit of his or her policy preferences varies with the individual.

11-6c Policy Oversight

The business of Congress does not end with voting on bills. Congress is also responsible for **policy oversight**, or seeing that the legislation it passes is implemented, that the expected results come about, and whether new laws are needed. Policy oversight is important because the complexity of many issues and the limited time members can devote to any single issue generally force Congress to pass legislation that is short on details. As a result, the bureaucracy has discretion to use its expertise to fill in the necessary details. And as we will discuss at greater length in Chapter 13, bureaucrats can use their discretion in ways contrary to what members of Congress had in mind when they passed the legislation.

As important as policy oversight is, it is a daunting endeavor. The federal bureaucracy is enormous; it spends more than $3.5 trillion dollars each year, employs millions of people, and administers thousands of programs. Members of Congress could not monitor a tenth of what the federal government does even if they and their staffs ignored all their other responsibilities. Moreover, the complexity of many issues makes it difficult for members to assess the effectiveness of government programs. For example, after the Gulf War, military experts disagreed over whether American weapons had performed as successfully on the battlefield as the Department of Defense claimed. Few members have the expertise needed to evaluate such disputes.

Given the abundance of programs to oversee, how do members of Congress decide which ones to examine? In general, they take two different approaches to the task of policy oversight: the police-patrol approach and the fire-alarm approach. **Police-patrol oversight** takes place when members hold hearings and request information on the off chance they might uncover something wrong.[174] For example, when the various committees in Congress conduct their annual budget reviews, they usually ask how government monies have been spent and request evidence that programs have accomplished their goals.

policy oversight
Efforts by Congress to see that the legislation it passes is implemented, that the expected results have come about, and whether new laws are needed.

police-patrol oversight
Congressional oversight hearings designed to take a wide-ranging look for possible problems.

Because executive agencies heed the wishes of Congress most of the time, police-patrol oversight may not uncover instances in which an executive branch agency has defied the will of Congress. The real merit of police-patrol oversight lies in its deterrent value; agencies that fear a congressional inquiry will abide by the wishes of Congress. Indeed, members of Congress often use police-patrol oversight to send signals to executive agencies about how they expect agencies to behave.[175] For instance, in 2003 the Defense Department planned to open a futures market in which anonymous investors would bet money on forecasts of terrorist events. When information on the proposed market became public, senators from both parties expressed outrage, calling the idea "grotesque" and "absurd." Shortly thereafter, Senator John Warner (R-VA), the chair of the Senate Armed Services Committee, met with the program's director, and they "mutually agreed that this thing should be stopped."[176]

Police-patrol oversight has one distinct disadvantage from the viewpoint of a member of Congress: Systematically examining the executive branch may provide no chance to curry favor with the voters. If a police patrol fails to uncover any abuses, members have nothing to show their constituents for their efforts. If it does uncover a problem, the abuse may not harm or interest constituents; hence, no opportunity exists for members to garner credit.

fire-alarm oversight
Congressional oversight hearings designed to investigate a problem after it has become highly visible.

To compensate for the disadvantages of police-patrol oversight, members of Congress also engage in **fire-alarm oversight**, investigating problems after they become highly visible. In fire-alarm oversight, members rely on constituents, the media, or some other aggrieved party to sound the alarm about a problem. For example, when the Equal Employment Opportunity Commission (EEOC) proposed guidelines in 1994 to stem religious harassment in the workplace, a diverse coalition of groups, including the American Civil Liberties Union and the Christian Coalition, argued that they violated the First Amendment. Congress immediately intervened and voted to urge the EEOC to rework the proposal. In response to the overwhelming signal Congress sent, the EEOC withdrew the proposal in short order.[177] The advantage of fire-alarm oversight in the eyes of members is that it enables them to focus on issues that matter to voters, thereby increasing their chances of winning points with the voters. As you might imagine, the disadvantage to fire-alarm oversight is that members might hear the alarm only after great damage has occurred.

11-7 CONGRESS AND THE IDEA OF REPRESENTATION

By proposing and refining legislation, making decisions to support or oppose a bill, and overseeing the effects of past legislation, Congress fulfills its duty to make laws and rules to govern the nation. In the process of governing, Congress has another obligation—to represent the will of the people. What exactly does representation entail? This seemingly simple question has long divided political philosophers. The *delegate theory of representation* holds that members should vote according to the preferences of their constituents. In contrast, the *trustee theory of representation* contends that voters have entrusted members with the responsibility of deciding what constitutes good public policy. Both theories raise thorny questions. If members act as delegates, which constituents should they look to when deciding how to vote? The majority on each issue? Members of their political party? People who donated to their campaign? Conversely, if members disregard constituent opinion, as the trustee theory says they may, does Congress cease to be a representative body?

Whichever theory of representation you find more appealing, in practice, members of Congress are both free to vote as they please and constrained by constituent opinion. The voters back home know little about the day-to-day activities of Congress, which gives members a tremendous amount of freedom in deciding how to act. Members even have considerable freedom to ignore the wishes of the interest groups that donate to their campaigns. Although interest groups carefully follow congressional business, they can ill afford to destroy their long-term relationship with a member because he or she votes against them on a specific issue.

Yet for all the freedom that members of Congress have in planning their legislative activities, they know that ultimately their position in Congress depends on maintaining constituent support. According to the rules, representatives must stand for election every two years, and senators every six years. Members who stray too far from the wishes of their constituents will quickly become former members of Congress.

Representation, then, hinges on elections. Citizens have a powerful weapon: They can replace a member of Congress with someone who better reflects their preferences. Of course, voters may find it hard to gather the information they need to evaluate how the current member measures up. Not only does it take time and effort to learn what members have done during their term in office, but members also frequently use parliamentary procedures

Voting in Congress can be complex, and sometimes, members can be on both sides of an issue.

such as the King-of-the-Hill rule to take both sides of controversial issues. Nonetheless, as long as members must worry about what voters think, representation is maintained. The rules largely work, and the representative body the Founders envisioned—although the details have changed—still exists.

SUMMARY

The Framers of the Constitution established Congress as a bicameral legislature that operates independently of the executive and judicial branches of government. Although the House and Senate are equals in lawmaking, the Framers structured them to have different virtues. To ensure the House would be sensitive to public opinion, the Framers stipulated that representatives would stand for election every two years, thereby creating the opportunity for rapid turnover in House membership. In contrast, the Framers gave senators six-year terms to give them some distance from the whims of the voters. Having two powerful houses makes it difficult to make things happen. Simply stated, "a bicameral body of 535 [is not] designed to be fast on its 1,070 feet."[178]

Although the Constitution specifies the basic structure of Congress, the House and Senate have the authority to decide what rules will govern their day-to-day operations. As a result, congressional norms and procedures have changed as the interests of members themselves have changed. The House has seen the most change, with authority at first concentrated in the office of the speaker, then dispersed to the committees, and eventually to the subcommittees. More recently, power in the House has begun to be recentralized in the hands of the majority party leadership. Generally, the Senate continues to operate under many of its original rules. Despite the tremendous continuity in its procedures, the Senate has decentralized its authority to some degree since the early 1970s.

The change in congressional rules and norms has been accompanied by a change in congressional elections: Unlike incumbents in past elections, incumbents who now run for reelection almost always win. Some explanations for the success incumbents enjoy point to the setting in which congressional elections occur. Although the relative homogeneity of most congressional districts helps explain why House incumbents usually fare better than Senate incumbents, the way district lines are drawn does not appear to explain the success of House incumbents. Better explanations for their electoral success point to the advantages members of Congress enjoy because they are officeholders and the disadvantages challengers face in mounting a campaign.

Members of Congress come from all parts of American society, but white males continue to predominate. The absence of descriptive representation in Congress may not have significant repercussions for political representation. Gender, race, ethnicity, and other demographic attributes do not appear to determine how members of Congress vote. Instead, members' votes tend to reflect the views of their constituents.

Serving in Congress is a full-time job with significant attractions. It is prestigious, it pays more than $169,000 per year, and it comes with many perks. But congressional service has its price. Members devote many hours to the job, and most members are forced to sacrifice other interests. Yet the number of members who run for reelection suggests that most members find the costs of the job tolerable.

Members of Congress assume their offices as equals, and chaos is one possible result when 535 equals each pursue their own interests. Yet Congress has managed to avoid chaos because of the existence of political parties. Although parties do not control congressional decision making, they do provide the basic stuff of organization, the glue that binds members together and allows for the imposition of leadership. Without political parties, the House and Senate would have a more difficult time maintaining the system of leaders, committees, and staff that form the organizational heart of Congress.

The organizational structure of Congress is designed to enable the institution to fulfill its role as the nation's supreme lawmaking body. To turn a policy proposal into a law, members must navigate a bill through subcommittee, committee, floor, and finally, conference committee deliberations. When deciding how to vote, members consider their own views, constituent opinion, and a host of other voting cues. The job of a member of Congress does not end with the passage of legislation. Members are also responsible for overseeing the executive branch to ensure that laws are implemented and that the expected results are achieved.

Does Congress represent the American public? In practice, members of Congress are both free to vote as they please and constrained by constituent opinion. The voters back home generally know little about the day-to-day activities of Congress, and interest groups often cannot afford to punish members who vote contrary to their wishes. Yet for all the freedom members have, they know that ultimately their seat in Congress depends on maintaining the support of constituents. Thus, as long as members face the prospect of competitive elections, representation is maintained, and the voters have the last word.

KEY TERMS

bicameral legislature	home style
caucus	midterm elections
cloture	police-patrol oversight
conference committee	policy oversight
Conservative Coalition	reapportionment
constituent service	select committees
divided government	seniority rule
filibuster	single-member districts
fire-alarm oversight	standing committee
franking privilege	subcommittees
gerrymandering	turnover

READINGS FOR FURTHER STUDY

Binder, Sarah A. *Stalemate: Causes and Consequences of Legislative Gridlock* (Washington, D.C.: Brookings Institution, 2003). A thorough examination of the legislative process highlighting the importance of party and bicameralism.

Dodd, Lawrence C., and Bruce I. Oppenheimer eds., *Congress Reconsidered*, 8th ed. (Washington, D.C.: CQ Press, 2005). A collection of articles by political scientists describing and analyzing the modern Congress.

Fowler, Linda L. *Candidates, Congress, and the American Democracy* (Ann Arbor: University of Michigan Press, 1993). A leading scholar's first-rate review of congressional elections.

Mayhew, David R. *Congress: The Electoral Connection* (New Haven, CT: Yale University Press, 1974). A path-breaking analysis of Congress that begins by asking the reader to imagine what Congress would be like if members cared only about reelection.

McGrath, Dennis J., and Dane Smith. *Professor Wellstone Goes to Washington* (Minneapolis: University of Minnesota Press, 1995). An interesting campaign diary by two reporters who followed the late Paul Wellstone's atypical Senate campaign.

Panagopoulos, Costas, and Joshua Schank. *All Roads Lead to Congress: The $300 Billion Fight Over Highway Funding* (Washington, D.C.: CQ Press, 2008). An insightful review of the contentious and convoluted process that produced the most recent federal highway bill.

Polsby, Nelson W. *How Congress Evolves* (New York: Oxford University Press, 2004). An engaging account of linking changes in the American South to the evolution of the House over the past half century.

Sulkin, Tracy. *Issue Politics in Congress* (New York: Cambridge University Press, 2005). An important analysis that links issues raised in congressional campaigns to subsequent behavior in office.

Zelizer, Julian E. *On Capitol Hill: The Struggle to Reform Congress and Its Consequences, 1948–2000* (New York: Cambridge University Press, 2004). A historian's fascinating account of how Congress changed in the post-World War II era.

REVIEW QUESTIONS

1. The use of franked mail by members of Congress in recent years has
   a. increased dramatically.
   b. decreased dramatically.
   c. stayed constant.
   d. been abolished by law.
2. What rule change that altered how committee chairs are selected in the House of Representatives went into effect in 2001?
   a. A six-year term limit is imposed on committee chairpersonships.

b. Members have the right to vote on who can become committee chairs.

c. Members bid on chairpersonships by seniority.

d. The speaker selects all committee chairs

3. Power became decentralized from committee chairs to many members in the House in the

   a. 1860s.

   b. 1890s.

   c. 1920s.

   d. 1970s.

4. What is the approximate reelection percentage rate of incumbents in the House of Representatives?

   a. 25

   b. 50

   c. 70

   d. 90

5. Election results suggest that voters

   a. like their legislators in Congress.

   b. like the opponents to their legislators in Congress.

   c. believe that Congress is doing a good job.

   d. believe that Congress should be changed to a unicameral legislature.

6. Most of the work done in Congress is done

   a. in the committees.

   b. on the floors of the House and Senate.

   c. by political party leaders.

   d. in the conference committees.

7. Compared with their Senate counterparts, House members

   a. serve on more committees.

   b. tend to be policy generalists.

   c. tend to be policy specialists.

   d. have a four-year term.

8. Which of the following committees is charged with the task of resolving legislative differences between House and Senate versions of the same bill?

   a. Standing

   b. Select

   c. Special

   d. Conference

9. Congress typically passes _____ legislation.

   a. specific

   b. broad

   c. radical

   d. socialist

10. In the original Constitution, which of the following institutions was most democratic?

    a. Supreme Court

    b. presidency

    c. House of Representatives

    d. Senate

NOTES

1. Carl Hulse and Robert Pear, "Kennedy Returns to Help Pass Medicare Bill," *New York Times*, July 10, 2008.

2. David Stout, "Congress Overrides Bush's Veto on Medicare," *New York Times*, July 16, 2008.

3. Stout, "Congress Overrides Bush's Veto on Medicare."

4. Peverill Squire and Keith E. Hamm, *101 Chambers: Congress, State Legislatures, and the Future of Legislative Studies* (Columbus: Ohio State University Press, 2005), 29.

5. See David Butler and Bruce Cain, *Congressional Redistricting: Comparative and Theoretical Perspectives* (New York: Macmillan, 1992), 17–23.

6. George E. Mowry, *The Era of Theodore Roosevelt and the Birth of Modern America* (New York: Harper & Row Torchbooks, 1958), 80, 264.

7. Elaine K. Swift, "Reconstitutive Change in the U.S. Congress: The Early Senate, 1789–1841," *Legislative Studies Quarterly* 14 (May 1989): 175–203.

8. Nelson W. Polsby, "The Institutionalization of the U.S. House of Representatives," *American Political Science Review* 62 (March 1968): 144–68.

9. H. Douglas Price, "Congress and the Evolution of Legislative 'Professionalism,'" in *Congress in Change*, ed. Norman J. Ornstein (New York: Praeger, 1975), 5.

10. James Sterling Young, *The Washington Community 1800–1828* (New York: Harcourt, Brace & World, 1966), 57.

11. Polsby, "The Institutionalization of the U.S. House of Representatives," 144–68.

12. Samuel Kernell, "Toward Understanding 19th Century Congressional Careers: Ambition, Competition, and Rotation," *American Journal of Political Science* 21 (November 1977): 669–93.

13. Young, *The Washington Community*, 52–53.

14. Nelson W. Polsby, "The Washington Community, 1960–1980," in *The New Congress*, ed. Thomas E. Mann and Norman J. Ornstein (Washington, D.C.: American Enterprise Institute, 1981), 30.

15. David T. Canon, "The Institutionalization of Leadership in the U.S. Congress," *Legislative Studies Quarterly* 14 (August 1989): 415–43.

16. Polsby, "The Institutionalization of the U.S. House of Representatives," 144–68.

17. Nelson W. Polsby, Miriam Gallaher, and Barry Spencer Rundquist, "The Growth of the Seniority System in the U.S. House of Representatives," *American Political Science Review* 63 (September 1969): 787–807.

18. Raymond E. Wolfinger and Joan Heifetz Hollinger, "Safe Seats, Seniority, and Power in Congress," in *Readings on Congress*, ed. Raymond E. Wolfinger (Englewood Cliffs, NJ: Prentice Hall, 1971).

19. Quoted in Roger H. Davidson and Walter J. Oleszek, *Congress and Its Members*, 3rd ed. (Washington, D.C.: CQ Press, 1990), 218.

20. Steven S. Smith, *Call to Order* (Washington, D.C.: Brookings Institution, 1989).

21. Lawrence C. Dodd and Bruce I. Oppenheimer, "Consolidating Power in the House: The Rise of the New Oligarchy," in *Congress Reconsidered*, 4th ed., ed. Lawrence C. Dodd and Bruce I. Oppenheimer (Washington, D.C.: CQ Press, 1989).

22. See Lawrence C. Dodd and Bruce I. Oppenheimer, "Maintaining Order in the House: The Struggle of Institutional Equilibrium," in *Congress Reconsidered*, 5th ed., ed. Lawrence C. Dodd and Bruce I. Oppenheimer (Washington, D.C.: CQ Press, 1993); Paul J. Quirk, "Structure and Performance: An Evaluation," in *The Postreform Congress*, ed. Roger H. Davidson (New York: St. Martin's, 1992).

23. Steven S. Smith and Christopher J. Deering, *Committees in Congress*, 2nd ed. (Washington, D.C.: CQ Press, 1990).

24. John R. Hibbing, *Congressional Careers: Contours of Life in the U.S. House of Representatives* (Chapel Hill: University of North Carolina Press, 1991).

25. John B. Gilmour, "Summits and Stalemates: Bipartisan Negotiations in the Postreform Era," in *The Postreform Congress*, ed. Roger H. Davidson (New York: St. Martin's, 1992); Quirk, "Structure and Performance," 311–12.

26. Jackie Koszczuk, "Gingrich Puts More Power into Speaker's Hands," *Congressional Quarterly Weekly Report*, October 7, 1995, 3049–53; David Rogers, "GOP's Rare Year Owes Much to How Gingrich Disciplined the House," *Wall Street Journal*, December 18, 1995.

27. Koszczuk, "Gingrich Puts More Power into Speaker's Hands," 3052.

28. David S. Cloud, "GOP, to Its Own Great Delight, Enacts House Rules Changes," *Congressional Quarterly Weekly Report*, January 7, 1995, 15; Koszczuk, "Gingrich Puts More Power into Speaker's Hands," 3053.

29. See Sarah Lueck, "Willing to Buck Traditions, Pelosi Rules the House," *Wall Street Journal*, May 8, 2008; Roger H. Davidson, Walter J. Oleszek, and Frances E. Lee, *Congress and Its Members*, 11th ed. (Washington, DC: CQ Press, 2008), 213–14.

30. See William S. White, *Citadel* (New York: Harper & Row, 1956).

31. Donald R. Matthews, *U.S. Senators and Their World* (New York: Vintage, 1960).

32. James M. Lindsay, *Congress and Nuclear Weapons* (Baltimore: Johns Hopkins University Press, 1991), 29.

33. Barbara Sinclair, *The Transformation of the U.S. Senate* (Baltimore: Johns Hopkins University Press, 1989).

34. William M. Welch, "Senator Takes Lead to Find Social Security Compromise," *USA Today*, February 11, 2005.

35. Alexander Bolton, "Frist Aims Nuke at the Dems," *The Hill*, January 19, 2005; Walter J. Oleszek, *Congressional Procedures and the Policy Process*, 3rd ed. (Washington, D.C.: CQ Press, 1989), 223.

36. Albert Somit and Andrea Roemmele, "The Victorious Legislative Incumbent as a Threat to Democracy: A Nine Nation Study," *Extension of Remarks*, July 1995, 9–11.

37. These data are from Mildred Amer, "Membership in the 110th Congress: A Profile," CRS Report for Congress, RS22555, December 15, 2006.

38. Butler and Cain, *Congressional Redistricting*, 24–26; George B. Galloway, *History of the House of Representatives* (New York: Crowell, 1961), 22–25.

39. In *Baker v. Carr* in 1962 (369 U.S. 186), the Supreme Court intervened for the first time in a dispute over the way legislative districts were drawn. In a 1963 decision, *Gray v. Sanders* (372 U.S. 368), the Court established the "one voter, one vote" principle in state judicial elections. A 1964 decision, *Wesberry v. Sanders* (376 U.S. 1), extended the one voter, one vote principle to U.S. House elections.

40. See *Davis v. Bandemer*, 478 U.S. 109 (1986), *Vieth v. Jubelirer*, 541 U. S. 267 (2004), and *League of United Latin American Citizens v. Perry*, 548 U.S. 399 (2006).

41. Butler and Cain, *Congressional Redistricting*, 11–13.

42. Albert D. Cover and David R. Mayhew, "Congressional Dynamics and the Decline of Competitive Congressional Elections," in *Congress Reconsidered*, 2nd ed., ed. Lawrence C. Dodd and Bruce I. Oppenheimer (Washington, D.C.: CQ Press, 1981), 72–73; John A. Ferejohn, "On the Decline of Competition in Congressional Elections," *American Political Science Review* 71 (March 1977): 166–76; Gary C. Jacobson, *The Electoral Origins of Divided Government: Competition in U.S. House Elections, 1946–1988* (Boulder, CO: Westview, 1990), 94–96.

43. Peverill Squire, "The Partisan Consequences of Congressional Redistricting," *American Politics Quarterly* (April 1995) 23: 229–40; Peverill Squire, "The Results of Partisan Redistricting in Seven U.S. States during the 1970s," *Legislative Studies Quarterly* 10 (May 1985): 259–66.

44. *Thornburg v. Gingles*, 478 U.S. 30 (1986).

45. Kevin A. Hill, "Does the Creation of Majority Black Districts Aid Republicans? An Analysis of the 1992 Congressional Elections in Eight Southern States," *Journal of Politics* 57 (May 1995): 384–401.

46. *Shaw v. Reno*, 509 U.S. 630 (1993).

47. *Miller v. Johnson*, 515 U.S. 900 (1995).

48. *Bush v. Vera*, 517 U.S. 952 (1996); *Shaw v. Hunt*, 517 US 899 (1996); *Hunt v. Cromartie*, 526 U.S. 541 (1999); *Georgia v. Ashcroft*, 539 U.S. 461 (2003); and *League of United Latin American Citizens v. Perry*, No. 05-204 (2006).

49. Brian Frederick, "Constituency Population and Representation in the U.S. House," *American Politics Research* 36 (May 2008):358–81.

50. Michael Doyle, "Worse than Appalachia," *Fresno Bee*, July 16, 2008. The House district rankings are from Sarah Burd-Sharps, Kristen Lewis, and Eduardo Borges Martins, *The Measure of America: American Human Development Report, 2008–2009* (New York: Columbia University Press, 2008).

51. Richard F. Fenno, Jr., *Home Style* (Boston: Little, Brown, 1978). See also Glen R. Parker, *Homeward Bound: Explaining Changes in Congressional Behavior* (Pittsburgh, PA: University of Pittsburgh Press, 1986).

52. David Mayhew, *Congress: The Electoral Connection* (New Haven, CT: Yale University Press, 1974).

53. See Rep. McGovern's press release, "U.S. Rep. Jim McGovern, Sens. Edward M. Kennedy and John Kerry Announce $132,525 for Plainville Fire Department, December 13, 2007," available at www.mcgovern.house.gov/?section id=15&parentid=4&sectiontree=4,15&itemid=98; and Jim Hand, "Federal Grant Boosts Plainfield's Firefighters," *Sun Chronicle*, August 8, 2008.

54. See Ryan's press release, July 19, 2007, available at: www.house.gov/ryan/press_releases/2007pressreleases/71907CDC.htm.

55. Mayhew, *Congress*, 61–73.

56. Quoted in David Yepsen, "Troopers Are in a Tough Spot," *Des Moines Register*, November 4, 1991.

57. Mayhew, *Congress*, 49–52.

58. See Timothy E. Cook, *Making Laws and Making News: Media Strategies in the U.S. House of Representatives* (Washington, D.C.: Brookings Institution, 1989); Stephen Hess, *Live From Capitol Hill! Studies of Congress and the Media* (Washington, D.C.: Brookings Institution, 1991).

59. See Mary Collins, "News of the Congress by the Congress," in *American Politics*, 2nd ed., ed. Allan J. Cigler and Burdett A. Loomis (Boston: Houghton Mifflin, 1992); Teresa Riordan, "Beam Me Up, Scotty," in *American Politics*, ed. Allan J. Cigler and Burdett A. Loomis (Boston: Houghton Mifflin, 1989); Steven Thomma, "Congress' Perks Add Up Quickly," *Des Moines Register*, October 20, 1991.

60. Daniel Lipinski and Gregory Neddenriep, "Using 'New' Media to Get 'Old' Media Coverage," *The Harvard International Journal of Press/Politics* 9 (Winter 2004): 7–21; Andrea Stone, "Blogs—the Hill's Version of Talk Radio," *USA TODAY*, June 1, 2006; Daniel Terdiman, "Congress Catches on to the Value of Blogs," news.com, January 26, 2006.

61. Ceci Connolly, "Leaving Very Little to Chance, Kennedy Pushes His Clout," *Congressional Quarterly Weekly Report*, September 17, 1994, 2593.

62. Diana Evans Yiannakis, "House Members' Communication Styles: Newsletters and Press Releases," *Journal of Politics* 44 (November 1982): 1049–71.

63. Rep. Morris Udall (D-AZ) quoted in William Boot, "Hustling the Folks Back Home," *Columbia Journalism Review* (November/December 1987): 24.

64. Christopher Georges, "Rep. Engel Triumphs by Being Dull in D.C. But Active at Home," *Wall Street Journal*, June 11, 1996.

65. Data gathered by the authors from Campaign Finance Institute, available at www.cfinst.org/data/VitalStats.aspx, and the Almanac of American Politics, available at www.nationaljournal.com/almanac/2008/charts.php

66. *Colorado Republican Federal Campaign Committee et al. v. Federal Election Commission*, 518 U.S. 604 (1996).

67. Calculated by the authors from Campaign Finance Institute data, available at www.cfinst.org/data/pdf/VitalStats_t8.pdf.

68. Quoted in Jeff DuFour, "Under the Dome," *The Hill*, October 4, 2005.

69. The quotes are from Erin P. Billings and Lauren W. Whittington, "Up in '10, Wasting No Time; Senators Quicken Fundraising Pace," *Roll Call*, April 18, 2007.

70. See, for example, John Harwood, "For California Senator, Fund Raising Becomes Overwhelming Burden," *Wall Street Journal*, March 2, 1994.

71. Richard E. Cohen and Peter Bell, "Congressional Insiders Poll: Q. What's Your Least Favorite Aspect of Your Job?" *National Journal*, November 12, 2005.

72. See Lyn Ragsdale, "Do Voters Matter? Democracy in Congressional Elections," in *Congressional Politics*, ed. Christopher J. Deering (Chicago: Dorsey Press, 1989).

73. Kelly D. Patterson and David B. Magleby, "Trends: Public Support for Congress," *Public Opinion Quarterly* 56 (Winter 1992): 539–51; Samuel C. Patterson and Gregory A. Caldeira, "Standing up for Congress: Variations in Public Esteem since the 1960s," *Legislative Studies Quarterly* 15 (February 1990): 25–47.

74. See "AMA Campaign Aims to Boost Doctor's Image," *Des Moines Register*, August 13, 1991; Robert L. Kahn, Barbara A. Gutek, Eugenia Barton, and Daniel Katz, "Americans Love Their Bureaucrats," in *Bureaucratic Power in National Policy Making*, 4th ed., ed. Francis E. Rourke (Boston: Little, Brown, 1986).

75. Jacobson, *The Electoral Origins of Divided Government*, chap. 4; Peverill Squire, "Challengers in U.S. Senate Elections," *Legislative Studies Quarterly* 14 (November 1989): 531–47.

76. Greg Gordon, "Rowley Decides against Making Run for Congress," *Star Tribune*, November 26, 2003; Jeff Gordon, "Looking at Who's In and Who's Out in the World of Sport," *St. Louis Post-Dispatch*, January 9, 1998. Generally, see David T. Canon, *Actors, Athletes, and Astronauts: Political Amateurs in the United States Congress* (Chicago: University of Chicago Press, 1990).

77. See Linda L. Fowler and Robert D. McClure, *Political Ambition: Who Decides to Run for Congress* (New Haven, CT: Yale University Press, 1989).

78. Peverill Squire, "Competition and Uncontested Seats in U.S. House Elections," *Legislative Studies Quarterly* 14 (May 1989): 281–95.

79. Squire, "Challengers," 531–47; Mark C. Westlye, *Senate Elections and Campaign Intensity* (Baltimore: Johns Hopkins University Press, 1991).

80. Mark G. Michaelsen, "My Life as a Congressional Candidate," in *The Quest for National Office*, ed. Stephen J. Wayne and Clyde Wilcox (New York: St. Martin's, 1992).

81. Gary C. Jacobson, *Money in Congressional Elections* (New Haven, CT: Yale University Press, 1980).

82. On the Crane/Bean race, see *Chicago Tribune*, "Time for Crane to Retire," October 11, 2004; Shamus Toomey, Lori Rackl, and Dan Rozek, "Bean Ends Crane's 3-Decade Reign," *Chicago Sun-Times*, November 3, 2004. On the general point, see Gary C. Jacobson, *The Politics of Congressional Elections*, 6th ed. (New York: Longman, 2004), 48–49.

83. Susan A. Banducci and Jeffrey A. Karp, "Electoral Consequences of Scandal and Reapportionment in the 1992 House Elections," *American Politics Quarterly* 22 (January 1994): 223–26; Gary C. Jacobson, "Checking Out: The Effects of Bank Overdrafts on the 1992 House Elections," *American Journal of Political Science* 38 (August 1994): 601–24.

84. James E. Campbell, "The Presidential Surge and Its Midterm Decline in Congressional Elections," *Journal of Politics* 53 (May 1991): 477–87.

85. Jacobson, *The Politics of Congressional Elections*, 164–69.

86. Randall L. Calvert and John A. Ferejohn, "Coattail Voting in Recent Presidential Elections," *American Political Science Review* 77 (June 1983): 407–19.

87. Morris P. Fiorina, *Divided Government* (New York: Macmillan, 1992).

88. See Rich Jaroslovsky, "Washington Wire," *Wall Street Journal*, January 21, 1994.

89. R. Michael Alvarez and Matthew M. Schousen, "Policy Moderation or Conflicting Expectations?" *American Politics Quarterly* 21 (October 1993): 410–38; Jacobson, *The Electoral Origins of Divided Government*, 112–20.

90. See Irwin N. Gertzog, *Congressional Women: Their Recruitment, Treatment, and Behavior* (New York: Praeger, 1984), 13–31.

91. Barbara C. Burrell, *A Woman's Place Is in the House: Campaigning for Congress in the Feminist Era* (Ann Arbor: University of Michigan Press, 1994), 131–50.

92. See Carol M. Swain, *Black Faces, Black Interests: The Representation of African Americans in Congress* (Cambridge, MA: Harvard University Press, 1993).

93. Bernard Grofman and Lisa Handley, "Minority Population and Black and Hispanic Congressional Success in the 1970s and 1980s," *American Politics Quarterly* 17 (October 1989): 436–45.

94. See, for example, Rodney E. Hero and Caroline J. Tolbert, "Latinos and Substantive Representation in the U.S. House of Representatives: Direct,

Indirect, or Nonexistent?" *American Journal of Political Science* 39 (August 1995): 640–52.

95. See Burrell, *A Woman's Place*, 151–74; Michele L. Swers, *The Difference Women Make: The Policy Impact of Women in Congress* (Chicago: University of Chicago Press, 2002); Sue Thomas, *How Women Legislate* (New York: Oxford University Press, 1994), chap. 3; Arturo Vega and Juanita M. Firestone, "The Effects of Gender on Congressional Behavior and the Substantive Representation of Women," *Legislative Studies Quarterly* 20 (May 1995): 213–22.

96. Drake Bennett, "Fence Sitters; Democrats are Having a Grand Old Time Watching the Republican Rumble Over Immigration," *Boston Globe*, April 9, 2006.

97. See Louis Fisher, "History of Pay Adjustments for Members of Congress," in *The Rewards of Public Service*, ed. Robert W. Hartman and Arnold R. Weber (Washington, D.C.: Brookings Institution, 1980).

98. See Patrick J. Purcell, "Retirement Benefits for Members of Congress," updated February 9, 2007; Mary William Walsh, "What If a Pension Shift Hit Lawmakers, Too?" *New York Times*, March 9, 2003.

99. See Peter J. Sepp, "Congressional Perks: How the Trappings of Office Trap Taxpayers," NTUF Policy Paper 131, November 1, 2000; Jane Norman, "Lawmakers' Health Perks Include Clinic in Capitol," *Des Moines Register*, October 6, 2007; "Congress' Perks," *Des Moines Register*, October 3, 1991.

100. Jessica Holzer, "Very Candidly, This Isn't the Greatest Job I've Had," *The Hill*, May 24, 2007.

101. Thomas J. O'Donnell, "Controlling Legislative Time," in *The House at Work*, ed. Joseph Cooper and G. Calvin Mackenzie (Austin: University of Texas Press, 1981); David E. Price, *The Congressional Experience*, 2nd ed. (Boulder, CO: Westview, 2000), 60–63.

102. Quoted in Amy Keller, "The Life of a Lawmaker," *Roll Call*, July 27, 2000.

103. Lyndsey Layton, "Mom's in the House, With Kids at Home," *Washington Post*, July 19, 2007.

104. Layton, "Mom's in the House, With Kids at Home."

105. Michael Leahy, "House Rules," *Washington Post*, June 10, 2007.

106. Albert Eisele, "Rep. LaTourette's Wife Says He Wants a Divorce after Admitting to D.C. Affair," *The Hill*, October 28, 2003.

107. Adam Nagourney and Michael Cooper, "McCain's Conservative Model? Roosevelt (Theodore That Is)," *New York Times*, July 13, 2008.

108. Rep. Jack Kingston (R-GA), quoted in Lyndsey Layton, "Culture Shock on Capitol Hill: House to Work 5 Days a Week, *Washington Post*, December 6, 2006.

109. "The Boss's Pay: The WSJ/Hay Group 2007 CEO Compensation Survey," *Wall Street Journal*, April 14, 2008.

110. Quoted in Michael Sokolove, "The Believer," *New York Times Magazine*, May 22, 2005.

111. Mark Leibovich, "Taking Power, Sharing Cereal," *New York Times*, January 18, 2007; Johanna Neuman, "At This 'Animal House,' the Party is Democratic," *Los Angeles Times*, July 25, 2005.

112. Jeff Dufour and Patrick Galvin, "Yeas and Nays: Friday, Jan. 12," *Washington Examiner*, January 12, 2007; Joseph Morton, "D.C. Lodgings Vary for Nebraskans," *Omaha World-Herald*, January 22, 2007; Betsy Rothstein, "Rep. Terry Resorts to Sleeping on Office Sofa," *The Hill*, July 18, 2007.

113. Rep. Donald Pease (D-OH), quoted in George Will, "Hating Government's Losses," *Iowa City Press-Citizen*, November 18, 1991.

114. Quoted in John L. Moore, *Speaking of Washington* (Washington, D.C.: Congressional Quarterly, 1993), 147.

115. Dennis F. Thompson, *Ethics in Congress: From Individual to Institutional Corruption* (Washington, D.C.: Brookings Institution, 1995), 2.

116. Ibid., 3.

117. Gail Russell Chaddock, "Ethics Reform Stalling in Congress," *Christian Science Monitor*, March 24, 2006; Jim Drinkard, "House Passes Lobbying Bill by Narrow 217-213 vote; Negotiators Must Work Out Variances from Senate Version," *USA TODAY*, May 4, 2006; Juliet Eilperin, "House GOP Softens Its Ethics Rules," *Washington Post*, January 8, 2003; Phil Kuntz, "House Vote Bars Members' Acceptance of Almost All Free Meals, Gifts, Trips," *Wall Street Journal*, November 17, 1995.

118. Elizabeth Williamson, "Congress Relaxes New Rules on Lobbyist Disclosures," *Wall Street Journal*, July 18, 2008.

119. Jim Snyder, "318 Ex-Lawmakers are Now Lobbyists, Report Says," *The Hill*, May 16, 2006.

120. William M. Welch, "Tauzin Switches Sides From Drug Industry Overseer to Lobbyist," *USA TODAY*, December 16, 2004.

121. Adolfo Santos, *Do Members of Congress Reward Their Future Employers?* (Lanham, MD: University Press of America, 2006).

122. Sarah A. Binder, "Partisanship and Procedural Choice: Institutional Change in the Early Congress, 1789–1823," *Journal of Politics* 57 (November 1995): 1093–1118; John F. Hoadley, "The Emergence of Political Parties in Congress, 1789–1803," *American Political Science Review* 74 (September 1980): 757–79.

123. David W. Rohde, *Parties and Leaders in the Postreform House* (Chicago: University of Chicago Press, 1991), 31–34.

124. See John M. Barry, *The Ambition and the Power* (New York: Penguin, 1989).

125. See the list of speaker powers in Valerie Heitshusen, "Party Leaders in the House: Election, Duties, and Responsibilities," CRS Report for Congress, RS20881, updated December 8, 2006.

126. Judy Schneider, "House Standing Committee Chairs and Ranking Minority Members: Rules Governing Selection Procedures, CRS Report for Congress, RS21165, updated December 27, 2006.

127. David S. Broder, "Immigration Deal? Don't Bet on It," *Washington Post*, May 28, 2006; "The Speaker Who Would Be Maitre D'," *New York Times*, December 2, 2004.

128. Barbara Sinclair, "The Emergence of Strong Leadership in the 1980s House of Representatives," *Journal of Politics* 54 (August 1992): 657–84.

129. Rep. Joe Scarborough (R-FL), quoted in "GOP Can't Sell Plan to Return Workers," *Des Moines Register*, January 5, 1996.

130. Donna Cassata, "GOP Leaders Walk a Fine Line to Keep Freshmen on Board," *Congressional Quarterly Weekly Report*, October 14, 1995, 3122–23; Kenneth Pins, "GOP Isn't Afraid to Flex Its Muscle to Ensure Unity," *Des Moines Register*, October 1, 1995; David Rogers, "GOP Disciplines Member of House Over 'Wrong' Vote," *Wall Street Journal*, October 12, 1995.

131. Cassata, "GOP Leaders Walk a Fine Line," 3122.

132. See Alexander Bolton, "Boehner Issues Threat," *The Hill*, May 18, 2006; Susan Davis, "Whip Cracks on Members of Blunt's Team," *Congress Daily AM*, March 31, 2006; Patrick O'Connor, "Chairmen Defy GOP Leadership," *The Hill*, December 14, 2005.

133. See Mary Alice Nye, "Conservative Coalition Support in the House of Representatives: 1963–1988," *Legislative Studies Quarterly* 17 (May 1993): 255–70.

134. See Charles O. Jones, *The Minority Party in Congress* (Boston: Little, Brown, 1970); Rohde, *Parties and Leaders in the Postreform House*, 127–32.

135. Dodd and Oppenheimer, "Maintaining Order in the House," 60–62.

136. Jennifer Babson, "Democrats Refine the Tactics of Minority Party Power," *Congressional Quarterly Weekly Report*, July 15, 1995, 2037; David S. Cloud with Julianna Grunwald, "Democrats Find Their Footing in Minority Party Trenches," *Congressional Quarterly Weekly Report*, July 1, 1995, 1893–96; Carroll J. Doherty, "Uproar over Democrat's Switch Snarls House Foreign Aid Bill," *Congressional Quarterly Weekly Report*, July 1, 1995, 1936–38.

137. Quoted in Albert R. Hunt, "A Voice for the Minority," *Wall Street Journal*, June 15, 1995.

138. "Senate Firsts," *Senate History* 14 (Fall 1991): 6–7.

139. See Roger H. Davidson, "The Senate: If Everyone Leads, Who Follows?" in *Congress Reconsidered*, 4th ed., ed. Lawrence C. Dodd and Bruce I. Oppenheimer (Washington, D.C.: CQ Press, 1989).

140. James H. Kuklinski and Lee Sigelman, "When Objectivity Is Not Objective: Network Television Coverage of U.S. Senators and the 'Paradox of Objectivity,'" *Journal of Politics* 54 (August 1992): 810–33; Peverill Squire, "Who Gets National News Coverage in the U.S. Senate?" *American Politics Quarterly* 16 (April 1988): 139–56.

141. Norman Ornstein, quoted in Graeme Browning, "Freelancers," *National Journal*, September 24, 1995, 2203.

142. Kenneth A. Shepsle and Barry R. Weingast, "The Institutional Foundations of Committee Power," *American Political Science Review* 81 (March 1987): 85–104; Kenneth A. Shepsle and Barry R. Weingast, "Why Are Congressional Committees Powerful?" *American Political Science Review* 81 (September 1987): 935–45.

143. Keith Krehbiel, *Information and Legislative Organization* (Ann Arbor: University of Michigan Press, 1991), 254–56.

144. Norman J. Ornstein, Thomas E. Mann, and Michael Malbin, *Vital Statistics on Congress, 2001–2002* (Washington, D.C.: AEI Press, 2002), 121.

145. Richard F. Fenno, Jr., *Congressmen in Committees* (Boston: Little, Brown, 1973).

146. Richard L. Hall and Bernard Grofman, "The Committee Assignment Process and the Conditional Nature of Committee Bias," *American Political Science Review* 84 (December 1990): 1149–66.

147. Judy Schneider, "House Committees: Categories and Rules for Committee Assignments," 98–151, updated February 25, 2005; Judy Schneider, "House Committees: Assignment Process," CRS Report for Congress, 98–367, updated May 10, 2007.

148. Christopher J. Deering and Paul J. Wahlbeck, "U.S. House Committee Chair Selection," *American Politics Research* 34 (March 2006): 223–42.

149. Rebecca Kimitch, "CQ Guide to the Committees: Democrats Opt to Spread the Power," *CQ Weekly*, April 16, 2007, 1080–83.

150. Judy Schneider, "Committee Assignment Process in the U.S. Senate: Democratic and Republican Party Procedures," updated November 3, 2006.

151. Ornstein, Mann, and Malbin, *Vital Statistics on Congress, 2001–2002*, 129.

152. See The Policy Council's "2006 Lobby Effectiveness Survey."

153. Geoff Earle, "Frist Gains New Powers: Majority Leader Will Control Half of 'A' Panel Seats," *The Hill*, November 18, 2004.

154. Jonathan D. Salant, "LSOs Are No Longer Separate, But Work's Almost Equal," *Congressional Quarterly Weekly Report*, May 27, 1995, 14.

155. Costas Panagopoulos, and Joshua Schank, *All Roads Lead to Congress: The $300 Billion Fight Over Highway Funding* (Washington, D.C.: CQ Press, 2008), 193. More generally see Christine DeGregorio and Kevin Snider, "Leadership Appeal in the U.S. House of Representatives: Comparing Officeholders and Aides," *Legislative Studies Quarterly* 20 (November 1995): 491–511.

156. John Harwood, "Washington Wire," *Wall Street Journal*, March 10, 2006.

157. For an extended discussion of the legislative process, see Oleszek, *Congressional Procedures and the Policy Process*.

158. Chrissie Long, "Lawmakers Turn to Catchy Names for Bills," *The Hill*, April 21, 2005.

159. Glen S. Krutz, "Issues and Institutions: 'Winnowing' in the U.S. Congress," *American Journal of Political Science* 49 (April 2005): 313–26; R. Eric Petersen, "Dear Colleague Letters: A Brief Overview," updated January 4, 2005.

160. Smith, *Call to Order*, 155.

161. Alan Greenblatt, "Two Members, Two Approaches to Competing Demands," *Congressional Quarterly Weekly Report*, June 17, 1995, 1705.

162. See Crow's testimony, available at www.energycommerce.house.gov/cmte_mtgs/110-he-hrg.052108.Crow-testimony.pdf; more generally see Jube Shriver, Jr., "Celebrities Capitalize on Star Power in D.C.," *Los Angeles Times*, January 22, 2006.

163. C. Lawrence Evans, "Influence in Congressional Committees: Participation, Manipulation, and Anticipation," in *Congressional Politics*, ed. Christopher J. Deering (Chicago: Dorsey Press, 1989); Richard L. Hall, "Committee Decision Making in the Postreform Congress," in *Congress Reconsidered*, 4th ed., ed. Lawrence C. Dodd and Bruce I. Oppenheimer (Washington, D.C.: CQ Press, 1989).

164. Richard L. Hall and C. Lawrence Evans, "The Power of Subcommittees," *Journal of Politics* 52 (May 1990): 335–55.

165. See Richard S. Beth, "The Discharge Rule in the House: Recent Use in Historical Context," updated April 17, 2003, 16; "Discharge Petitions Get GOP Attention," *Congressional Quarterly Weekly Report*, October 2, 1993, 2618; Phil Kuntz, "Anti-Secrecy Drive Putting Democrats on the Defensive," *Congressional Quarterly Weekly Report*, September 11, 1993, 2369–70.

166. Oleszek, *Congressional Procedures*, 149–50.

167. Sinclair, *The Transformation of the U.S. Senate*, 136.

168. Smith, *Call to Order*, 98–119.

169. Ibid., 202–3; Timothy J. Conlan, Margaret T. Wrightson, and David R. Beam, *Taxing Choices: The Politics of Tax Reform* (Washington, D.C.: CQ Press, 1990), 190–91.

170. George Anthan, "Congress Gives Pizza Firms a Slice of the School Lunch Pie," *Des Moines Register*, November 28, 1991.

171. Brigid Schulte, "Fine Print Is Often Missed," *Des Moines Register*, October 27, 1995.

172. Lindsay, *Congress and Nuclear Weapons*, 140.

173. See R. Douglas Arnold, *The Logic of Congressional Action* (New Haven, CT: Yale University Press, 1990); William T. Bianco, *Trust: Representatives and Constituents* (Ann Arbor: University of Michigan Press, 1994).

174. Mathew D. McCubbins and Thomas Schwartz, "Congressional Oversight Overlooked: Police Patrols Versus Fire Alarms," *American Journal of Political Science* 28 (February 1984): 165–79. For evidence on the frequency of police-patrol oversight, see Joel D. Aberbach, *Keeping a Watchful Eye* (Washington, D.C.: Brookings Institution, 1990), 93–104.

175. John A. Ferejohn and Charles R. Shipan, "Congressional Influence on Administrative Agencies: A Case Study of Telecommunications Policy," in *Congress Reconsidered*, 4th ed., ed. Lawrence C. Dodd and Bruce I. Oppenheimer (Washington, D.C.: CQ Press, 1989).

176. See Carl Hulse, "Pentagon Abandons Plan for Futures Market on Terror," *New York Times*, July 29, 2003, and Carl Hulse, "Swiftly, Plan for Terrorism Futures Market Slips into Dustbin," *New York Times*, July 30, 2003.

177. See Jennifer Babson, "House Approves Crime Funds, Rejects Peacekeeping Cuts," *Congressional Quarterly Weekly Report*, July 2, 1994, 1809; Joseph E. Broadhus, "The EEOC and the House," *Liberty*, November/December 1994, 16–17; Jon Healy, "Airport Funding Measure Heads to President," *Congressional Quarterly Weekly Report*, August 13, 1995, 2330; Jon Healy, "Airport Program Renewal OK'd," *Congressional Quarterly Weekly Report*, June 18, 1995, 1593.

178. Nelson W. Polsby, *Congress and the Presidency*, 4th ed. (Englewood Cliffs, NJ: Prentice Hall, 1986), 14.

12

The Presidency

CHAPTER OUTLINE

Barack Obama's victory in November 2008 culminated a historic presidential election, bringing the first African American to the highest office in the land. "Change," the theme of Obama's campaign, could also be used to describe what had taken place in the White House in the weeks preceding the inauguration. As Obama took the oath of office on the steps of the Capitol, the offices in the West Wing of the White House sat vacant and quiet. Filing cabinets that only days before had been crammed with documents addressing the nation's most pressing issues lay empty. Desks were devoid of the memos that had directed the work of hundreds of presidential assistants. Telephones that had once hummed with the daily press of presidential business sat silent. Computers had been stripped of their hard drives. This quiet was just a prelude to the impending deluge of change. Within hours, President Obama's aides moved into the White House and began to fill it with his papers and priorities. A new president had arrived to make his personal mark on the office of the presidency and on American history itself.

The physical transition that takes place as one president leaves the White House and another moves in illustrates the impact that each president has on the office of the presidency. Virtually all signs of the old president disappear as the White House is reshaped by its new occupant. Everything from who receives which job assignment to which policy receives top priority depends on the wishes of the president.

If the presidency changes in many ways with each new occupant of the White House, in many ways it also stays the same, structured by rules set forth in the Constitution and shaped by statutory laws and informal expectations that have built up over the course of more than 200 years. These rules ensure a peaceful transfer of power from one president to the next. They define, among other things, the length of the president's term, the number of days presidents have to exercise a veto, and the extent of their authority to make appointments and treaties. These rules create order, structure, and continuity as new presidents assume office.

In this chapter, we examine how the rules of American politics shape the presidency and how presidents shape the rules. We will see the dynamic interplay of the presidency on paper, as the rules set forth in the Constitution define the office, and the presidency in practice, as presidents interpret and reshape the rules to achieve their objectives. We begin by tracing the development of the presidency from its colonial roots to the appearance of the modern presidency in the 1930s. We go on to describe the political and institutional underpinnings of the office of the presidency by first reviewing the presidential selection process and then by examining the workings of the presidency as an institution. We will see how changes in political and institutional rules have molded the presidency into a highly individual and influential office. Finally, we will look at the modern presidency and its interactions with the rest of the political system. We will see that although the presidency has gained power over two centuries of American history, that power remains limited.

12-1 THE DEVELOPMENT OF THE PRESIDENCY

The presidency has evolved in response to many influences, including both the structural rules outlined in the Constitution and the way presidents have interpreted those rules over the past 200 years. These two influences have combined to mold the modern presidency.

12-1a The Presidency on Paper: Constitutional Rules

The constitutional rules that govern the presidency give the president power, but they also constrain that power. From the writing of the Constitution up to the present day, Americans have expressed ambivalence about the presidency. On the one hand, we recognize the need for a strong leader with the authority to make swift executive decisions. On the other hand, we are cautious about vesting too much power in any one individual or branch of government.

As we saw in Chapter 2, a deep distrust of executive power shaped the writing of the Articles of Confederation. The oppressive rule of King George III and his colonial governors convinced the authors of the Articles of Confederation to create a national government that had a legislature but no independent executive. By doing without an executive leader, the authors of the Articles of Confederation hoped to prevent the emergence of an American tyrant.

By the mid-1780s, however, the national government's fragmented approach to foreign affairs and other matters convinced many Americans that the decision to do without an executive was a mistake. They believed that the national government needed an independent executive who could implement a cohesive national policy. Thus, when the Constitutional Convention met in 1787 to write the Constitution, one of the foremost topics of discussion was the creation of a new national executive.

Although most of the delegates accepted the need for an executive in principle, their initial proposals envisioned a presidency with modest powers (see Box 12–1). In the end, delegates who favored a stronger presidency largely succeeded in pressing their point. The final provisions written into the Constitution created an office of the presidency with three primary characteristics: (1) legal and political independence from the other two branches of government, (2) shared powers with other institutions, and (3) vaguely defined powers.

Legal and Political Independence

The Constitution gives the office of the presidency a strong institutional and political foundation. In keeping with the doctrine of the separation of powers, the Founders established the presidency as a separate and independent branch of government. As we shall see,

POINT OF ORDER

Box 12–1 Alternative Arrangements for the Presidency Considered at the Constitutional Convention

Can you imagine a national government in which the presidency consists of a three-member team appointed by Congress for a single seven-year term? Strange as such an arrangement sounds, it is one of the possibilities that might have emerged from the Constitutional Convention in 1787. The Founders wanted executive leadership, but they were unsure how to design an office that provided energy and direction without the potential for tyranny. As a result, they considered a variety of arrangements for the presidency.

To understand the complexity and consequences of the choices the Founders faced, consider some of the questions they had to grapple with.

SHOULD A SINGLE PERSON OR A GROUP OF PEOPLE OCCUPY THE PRESIDENCY?

The Virginia Plan said nothing about the composition of the presidency, whereas the New Jersey Plan proposed creating a plural executive. The delegates to the Constitutional Convention eventually concluded that a plural executive would sap the executive of energy and accountability without making tyranny any less likely. As a result, they chose to assign the presidency to a single person rather than to an executive team.

WHO CHOOSES THE PRESIDENT?

Some delegates to the Constitutional Convention suggested that Congress should elect the president; others said the president should be elected by the people. Both proposals, and especially the suggestion for direct popular elections, stirred strong opposition. Critics of the plan allowing Congress to choose the president argued that it would deny the presidency the political independence it needed to succeed. Critics of the plan allowing the people to elect the president warned about the prospect of mob rule. Divided over how to elect the president, the delegates set up a committee to study the matter. The committee returned with a compromise proposal in which neither Congress nor the people chose the president. Their solution was the electoral college. If the committee had not devised the electoral college proposal, it is likely that the fears most delegates had about mob rule would have led the Convention to give Congress the authority to elect the president. Such an outcome, no doubt, would have seriously weakened the presidency.

ONE LONG TERM OR MANY SHORT TERMS?

Closely tied to the issue of who should choose the president were the questions of how long presidents should be allowed to serve in office and whether they should be eligible for reelection. The Founders wanted presidents to be able to stand for reelection because they judged that the

prospect of facing reelection would encourage presidents to discharge their duties faithfully. If Congress selected the president, allowing presidents to stand for reelection would be counterproductive; Congress simply would have too much influence over an incumbent president. As long as Congress was the leading choice to elect presidents, the delegates favored giving the president a long term of office with no possibility for reelection. Once the Convention adopted the proposal for the electoral college, however, the delegates moved quickly to give presidents a four-year term of office and to allow them to run for reelection.

Over the course of our nation's history, seventeen incumbents have been reelected. The prospect of single terms for George Washington, Thomas Jefferson, Andrew Jackson, Woodrow Wilson, Franklin Roosevelt, and Ronald Reagan underlines the significance of the choices the Founders made at the Constitutional Convention. A single-term presidency would have produced much different dynamics in the relations presidents have with the rest of government and with the American people. Once again, we see that the choices the Founders made about the structural rules of American politics carried consequences—in short, the rules mattered.

Source: Sidney M. Milkis and Michael Nelson, *The American Presidency: Origins and Development, 1776-2002*, 4th ed. (Washington, D.C.: CQ Press, 2003), chap. 2.

the Constitution gives the presidency certain powers that its constitutional coequals, Congress and the Supreme Court, cannot challenge. In a legal sense, then, neither Congress nor the Supreme Court directly controls or supervises the president.

However, the Founders knew that legal independence was not sufficient to ensure the presidency's autonomy. If the Constitution made it easy for either Congress or the Supreme Court to change the rules governing how presidents are elected or how long they may serve, they could place considerable political pressure on presidents. This political pressure could undermine the presidency's autonomy despite the office's *legal* independence. So the Constitution also gives the presidency substantial political independence. It limits the ability of the other two branches to select or remove presidents, or to alter the length of their term in office.

The Constitution does this in two ways. First, it gives neither Congress nor the Supreme Court a significant role in the presidential selection process. Congress has only two roles: (1) It formally counts (or certifies) each state's electoral votes, and (2) the House of Representatives elects the president and the Senate elects the vice president if no candidate receives a majority of the electoral college vote. Although a few Democrats challenged the validity of Florida's electoral votes as a symbolic gesture when the results of the 2000 election were certified, Congress has rejected electoral votes only once in American history. This happened in the 1876 election. Electoral votes from several southern states for the Democratic candidate, Samuel Tilden, were challenged and ultimately overturned, resulting in the election of the Republican candidate, Rutherford B. Hayes. Only twice in American history have the results of the electoral college vote forced Congress to choose the president and vice president. In 1800, the House selected Thomas Jefferson, and in 1824, it selected John Quincy Adams. As for the Supreme Court, the Constitution gives it no specific role in the presidential selection process. Until it intervened in Florida's election controversy following the 2000 election, the Court had never become directly involved in selecting a president.

Second, the rules the Constitution created for removing presidents from office, coupled with how we have come to interpret those rules over the years, make it difficult for Congress and the Supreme Court to force a president from office. The Constitution says that Congress can remove a president from office if the House of Representatives impeaches (that is, formally accuses) the president and the Senate then convicts him or her of "Treason, Bribery, or other High Crimes and Misdemeanors." The Constitution permits a simple majority in the House to impeach a president but requires a two-thirds vote in the Senate to convict. (The Chief Justice of the Supreme Court presides over the Senate trial.)

The **impeachment** power gives Congress a potentially powerful tool for disciplining presidents, and the ambiguity of the constitutional requirement that presidents commit "other High Crimes and Misdemeanors" gives it considerable discretion in deciding what constitutes sufficiently serious charges. In practice, though, Congress's ability to remove the president is fairly limited because the two-thirds majority requirement in the Senate is difficult to achieve. As long as a president can rely on the support of the senators of his or her own party, conviction is unlikely. Moreover, Congress's incentive to remove a president is limited because it does not have the power to select the next president. The Constitution requires the vice president to assume the presidency, and the vice president is likely to hold views similar to those of the president. These two legal limits on Congress's use of impeachment have led to an informal tradition that impeachment be used only under

impeachment
Formally charging a government official with having committed "Treason, Bribery, or other High Crimes and Misdemeanors." Officials convicted of such charges are removed from office.

extraordinary circumstances in which Congress believes the president has violated fundamental principles of government rather than when it simply disagrees with him or her on questions of policy or politics.

As a result of these limitations, Congress has tried to impeach a president on only three occasions in our nation's history. None of the presidents were convicted. President Andrew Johnson was impeached but not convicted in 1864. The House Judiciary Committee approved articles of impeachment against President Richard Nixon in 1974, but he resigned before the full House or Senate could act. In 1998, the House impeached Bill Clinton, but the Senate acquitted him the next year.

Congress's failure to remove Clinton from office shows why impeachment attempts are so rare. The House of Representatives impeached President Clinton on two grounds. First, it accused him of lying under oath about his relationship with one-time White House intern Monica Lewinsky. Second, it claimed that he obstructed justice in a variety of legal proceedings. Most Americans disapproved of Clinton's marital infidelity. However, his job approval ratings remained high, and congressional Democrats continued to support him. As a result, the House voted to impeach him without the support of any Democrats. When the issue went to the Senate, neither charge got more than fifty votes, or any Democrats' support. This enabled Clinton and his supporters to characterize the process as partisan and political, thereby minimizing its effects on his presidency.

The final source of political independence for the presidency comes from its four-year term of office and the provision that presidents can stand for reelection. As originally written, the Constitution placed no limit on the number of terms a president could serve. The combination of a long term in office and unlimited opportunities for reelection made it harder for Congress to defeat presidential initiatives simply by stalling until the president's term in office ended. As Chapter 1 discussed, following Franklin Roosevelt's record four terms as president, Congress passed and the states ratified the Twenty-Second Amendment, which states that "no person shall be elected to the office of the President more than twice." Even with this term limit, presidents still have up to eight years to press for adoption of their legislative and administrative goals. And because the Constitution gives presidents political, as well as legal, independence, the presidency is an office with which the other two branches have to contend.

Shared Powers

Although the doctrine of separation of powers influenced how the delegates to the Constitution wrote the structural rules governing the office of the presidency, the doctrine of checks and balances did as well. Once again, the Founders' fear of executive tyranny led them to check the president's ability to act by dispersing powers between the presidency and the other two branches of government, allowing the other branches to review or even reverse some of the president's actions. As we saw in Chapters 2 and 11, for example, presidents can sign treaties and nominate people to federal judgeships and senior posts in the executive branch, but no treaty becomes operative and no appointment becomes permanent until the Senate agrees. Likewise, as we saw in Chapter 4, and will see again in Chapter 14, the federal courts can declare a president's actions unconstitutional. In short, the Constitution constrains as well as empowers the president.

Vague Definition of Authority

Although the Founders feared executive tyranny and sought to prevent its emergence by creating a political system based on checks and balances, they defined the scope of the president's powers only vaguely.[1] As Chapter 2 discussed, the delegates to the Constitutional Convention disagreed on the proper scope of presidential authority. Some wanted to bestow substantial powers on the president, whereas others feared that creating a powerful presidency would promote tyranny. In the end, the delegates agreed to finesse their differences by making the precise boundaries of presidential power ambiguous. Yet, as we shall see shortly, this ambiguity created opportunities for presidents to reinterpret and expand the powers of their office in ways that most of the delegates to the Constitutional Convention never intended.

To be sure, Article II of the Constitution does list several specific or **enumerated powers** of the presidency. We have already mentioned the president's treaty and appointment powers, and as we saw in Chapter 11, Article I specifically empowers the president to veto congressional legislation, either directly or by refusing to sign a bill passed during the last ten days of a session of Congress. (This second type of veto is called a **pocket veto.**) The Constitution also stipulates that presidents are vested with "the executive Power"; that they may direct the head of an executive department to provide them with advice; that they have the power to pardon people suspected or convicted of federal crimes; that they may recommend legislation to Congress; that they may call Congress into special session if "extraordinary Occasions" warrant it; that they may order the adjournment of Congress if members cannot agree among themselves on when to adjourn; that they have the authority to receive ambassadors; and that they have the power to "take Care that the Laws be faithfully executed."

Although this list of enumerated powers may seem lengthy, it is relatively short compared with the list of powers the Constitution specifically assigns to Congress in Article I. Instead of being based solely on enumerated powers, much of the authority of the presidency stems from its **implied powers**, that is, powers the presidency is assumed to have because they are necessary for executing the enumerated powers of the office. Many of the implied powers of the presidency come from the Constitution's statement that "the executive Power shall be vested in a President of the United States of America." Other implied powers of the presidency stem from the fact that the Constitution names the president as the commander in

enumerated powers
Powers explicitly identified in the text of the Constitution.

pocket veto
The power of the president to veto a bill passed during the last ten days of a session of Congress simply by failing to sign it.

implied powers
Governmental powers not enumerated in the Constitution; authority the government is assumed to have in order to carry out its enumerated powers.

chief of the armed forces of the United States. The Founders used the title "commander in chief simply to designate a post at the top of the military chain of command rather than to denote an independent source of political power."[2] For most of U.S. history, however, and especially since World War II, presidents have argued that the commander-in-chief clause gives them wide powers in foreign policy. Because so much of presidential authority is implied rather than enumerated, presidents have been able to expand the powers of their office over the past 200 years.

Although the delegates to the Constitutional Convention created rules that make the presidency a powerful and independent branch of government, they also hedged the president's power with checks the other two branches hold. Perhaps most important, they only vaguely defined the powers of the presidency. These three characteristics of the structural rules governing the presidency have two important consequences for American politics. First, they set the stage for continual, although usually healthy, conflict among the three coequal branches of government. Second, they make the acts of individual presidents especially important. Because the president has considerable power and independence, and because the Constitution does not specifically spell out all the powers of the presidency, the structural rules of American politics allow presidents to define the implied powers of the presidency through their actions while in office.

12-1b The Presidency in Practice: Applying the Rules

In addition to being shaped by the rules set forth in the Constitution, the office of the presidency has been shaped by the decisions and behavior of the forty-three men who have been president.[3] Over the course of the past 200 years, various presidents have established new rules by asserting the existence of implied duties and powers, and these precedents have been incorporated into our view of the presidency. In essence, past presidents have shaped and reinterpreted the rules that govern the office of the presidency today, just as today's presidents are shaping the rules of the presidency for the future.

As the first president, George Washington established many important precedents.[4] With the help of Secretary of the Treasury Alexander Hamilton, he led Congress by proposing and lobbying for the passage of a legislative program. He fended off congressional intrusions into the presidency by establishing the principle of confidentiality between a president and his advisers, by limiting the Senate's role in appointing executive officers to providing consent rather than advice, and by denying Congress a role in establishing formal diplomatic relations with foreign countries. He established the presidency as the leader of the executive branch by closely supervising the executive departments. Finally, Washington enhanced the legitimacy of the presidency by stepping down after two terms. By relinquishing his position, he helped allay fears of executive tyranny and created an informal limit on how many terms future presidents might serve. After all, who deserved to serve longer than Washington?

Thomas Jefferson created a role for the president as a party leader.[5] As we saw in Chapter 9, political parties had emerged in the nation's early years to coordinate the actions of like-minded politicians. As president, Jefferson used his claim to be party leader to push his fellow party members in Congress to support his policy initiatives. It subsequently became the norm for presidents to assume the role of party leader and to demand that their fellow party members in Congress be loyal to the administration's policy initiatives.

Andrew Jackson was the first president to lead a mass-based political party, and he persuaded the public to accept the president as the voice of the people.[6] During the first four decades under the Constitution, people saw Congress as speaking for them, while they saw presidents as necessary but threatening; presidents provided much needed leadership, but many feared they might become tyrants. Jackson's election in 1828 was the first time that virtually all white males over the age of twenty-one were eligible to vote. (In previous elections, most states had limited voter eligibility by requiring voters to own property.) Jackson used the expanded electorate to buttress his claim that the presidency's national constituency made it the true voice of the people. In contrast, he characterized Congress as a collection of localized special interests that did not act in the best interest of the nation. Jackson's view of the president's role in American politics provides a key justification for the leadership role that most twentieth-century presidents have assumed.

Abraham Lincoln's handling of the Civil War marked a high point in the exercise of presidential power during the nineteenth century. Lincoln took several steps that he knew exceeded his authority, as when he ordered the secretary of the navy at the start of the war in April 1861 to take funds from the Treasury to buy military goods. Because Congress had not authorized the purchase— it was not in session and therefore unable to give the required approval—Lincoln's order usurped Congress's power of the purse. Although the Supreme Court declared after the Civil War ended that some of Lincoln's wartime decisions were unconstitutional, Lincoln showed that, under the right circumstances, presidents can take virtually any action they deem necessary, without regard to legal or constitutional boundaries.[7]

Presidential power, however, ebbs and flows. For nearly forty years after Lincoln was assassinated, the United States was led by a succession of weak presidents who were dominated by Congress. Theodore Roosevelt and Woodrow Wilson revived the activist role of the presidency in the first two decades of the twentieth century. Roosevelt's expansive view of the president's powers enabled him to take the initiative on a wide range of foreign and domestic issues. Wilson reclaimed the president's roles as party leader and voice of the nation, and he used both roles to persuade Congress to pass a large legislative agenda.[8] When the United States entered World War I, Congress gave him wide-ranging powers over the economy.[9]

12-1c The Advent of the "Modern" Presidency

The role and structure of the presidency changed dramatically during Franklin Delano Roosevelt's (FDR's) presidency. The changes were so great that most scholars credit FDR with ushering in the era of the "modern" presidency.[10] Since FDR, presidents have been expected to be active, preeminent national leaders representing the interests of the nation as a whole and providing leadership in a variety of roles.

The Impact of Franklin Delano Roosevelt

Why was FDR's presidency so pivotal? Before he took office, presidents were not expected to lead the nation, that is, to actively promote and implement new policy. They might try to lead if they had the personality to do so and the political climate was favorable, but they were not expected to be active, preeminent national leaders. When FDR was sworn into office in 1933, however, the country was in the depths of the Great Depression. Public faith in government was ebbing, and people were willing to accept strong, even authoritarian leadership. Roosevelt responded with a take-charge style and an extensive legislative agenda that restored the public's trust in the federal government. In the early days of his presidency, he delivered many major speeches, held press conferences twice a week, and persuaded Congress to pass more than a dozen major laws.[11] From 1941 to 1945, he led the United States in fighting World War II.

By the time of FDR's death in April 1945, he had established the presidency as the preeminent source of national leadership. Members of Congress, officials in the federal bureaucracy, and the American public began to expect strong policy leadership from the president. As a result, all of FDR's successors from Harry S Truman through George W. Bush either have felt compelled to follow the example he set of active, national leadership or have known they would be measured against it.

Institutionalized Leadership: The Presidency's Many Roles

The expectations institutionalized during FDR's presidency, the duties the Constitution defines, and the precedents presidential practices have established have combined to create leadership roles that we expect presidents to play in their relations with other political actors.[12] Although presidents play many such roles, six stand out.

First, the president is the nation's chief of state. This role consists of the ceremonial and largely nonpolitical duties that presidents perform on behalf of the nation as a whole, such as lighting the national Christmas tree, throwing out the first ball at the start of the baseball season, or awarding medals to citizens for their achievements.

Second, the president is the nation's chief legislator. In this role, presidents offer guidance and set priorities for Congress by proposing and pursuing a legislative agenda and by using the veto power to block bills they oppose. Presidents who fail to offer Congress a substantial agenda open themselves to criticism from their own party, from members of Congress, and from the news media.

Third, the president is the nation's chief executive. Presidents appoint (subject to Senate confirmation) the leaders of federal agencies and attempt to direct their actions through executive orders. As Chapter 13 shows, Congress and the presidency share responsibility for overseeing the work of the bureaucracy, but most people hold presidents responsible for the federal bureaucracy, expecting them to correct ineffective or abusive agency actions.

Fourth, the president is the nation's opinion leader. The public expects the president to identify and propose solutions to the problems the country faces. Theodore Roosevelt spoke of this role when he described the presidency as a bully pulpit from which presidents could shape the public's priorities, offer proposals to address those priorities, and mobilize the public on their behalf.

Fifth, the president is the nation's chief diplomat, representing the United States to the rest of the world. The Founders' belief in the need for a leader to fulfill this role helped motivate them to create the presidency as an independent office. Presidents negotiate treaties, send and receive ambassadors, and are expected to speak out on the nation's behalf when foreign policy crises arise.

Finally, the president is the nation's commander in chief. This role is written into the Constitution itself. Over the years, presidents have used their position as commander in chief to justify actions they have taken, often without congressional approval, to protect the nation's security from foreign military threats.

The historical development of the presidency demonstrates how the institution (as defined in the rules of the Constitution and laws passed by Congress) and individual presidents (as each reshapes the rules and expectations of the office) interact to create our expectations for the modern presidency. Had the rules defining the office been different—had the Constitution more sharply limited presidential power, for example, or had FDR been a more passive president—then our expectations of presidential roles and the behavior of individual presidents might be quite different as well.

12-2 SELECTING A PRESIDENT

The process by which Americans select a president has changed dramatically over the course of our nation's history. Just as constitutional rules and precedents have helped push the president to a position of preeminence as a national leader, the changing rules for selecting a president have placed increasing importance on individual candidates and their skills as political leaders.

The process of selecting a president takes place in three stages. First, candidates secure their party's nomination; next, they run in the general election; and finally, the results of the general election are used to allocate votes in the electoral college, which determines which candidate wins. The rules governing each of the three

Source: © CORBIS

Franklin Delano Roosevelt moved quickly and decisively in his efforts to lead the nation out of the Great Depression. His many speeches to Congress and the American people, combined with his extensive legislative agenda, stamped the presidency as the preeminent source of leadership. He established the era of the "modern" presidency. His successors have all felt compelled to follow in his footsteps as a leader.

stages have long been points of contention, and in the case of the nomination and general election stages, have undergone major changes. These changes, in turn, have significantly influenced both the election process itself and how presidents have behaved once in office.

12-2a The Nomination Process

The task of selecting presidential nominees for the nation's first two elections in 1789 and 1792 was simple: Everyone expected Washington to be president. When Washington declined to run for a third term in 1796, an informal process produced John Adams, Washington's vice president, and Thomas Jefferson, Washington's first secretary of state, as the two leading nominees. Since 1800, however, the business of nominating candidates has fallen to political parties. And over the course of our nation's history, political parties have used three different sets of nomination rules and procedures to choose their candidates: (1) congressional caucuses, (2) party conventions, and (3) direct primary elections.

Congressional Caucuses

Congress controlled the presidential nominating process from 1800 through 1824. The two major parties of the time, the Democrat-Republicans and the Federalists, each organized a **caucus**, or an informal meeting, in which their members in Congress selected a nominee. This procedure was later dubbed "King Caucus" by critics because it undermined the constitutional principle that the executive branch should be independent of the legislative branch. Because King Caucus meant that members of Congress decided who would be nominated as president, it also meant they could deny a president the chance to run for reelection. The threat of

caucus

A closed meeting of members of a political party to discuss matters of public policy and political strategy, and in some cases, to select candidates for office.

being denied renomination weakened the presidency and made Congress more dominant during the first two decades of the nineteenth century.[13]

Party Conventions

In 1824, the congressional caucus system broke down when candidates who lacked the votes needed to win in the Democrat-Republican Party caucus decided to attack the process as undemocratic. A national system to replace King Caucus did not emerge for another eight years. In the interim, nominations were determined on an ad hoc basis at the state and local levels. In 1824 and 1828, for example, Andrew Jackson was nominated for president by the legislature in his home state of Tennessee. By 1832, when Jackson was running for reelection, the two major groups contending for the presidency settled on a new nomination process—namely, party conventions, although each did so for a different reason.

The anti-Jackson group, the Whigs, understood that their prospects for beating "King Andrew," as they derisively called him, were slim. Everyone who opposed Jackson had to rally behind one candidate. To achieve that unity, they decided to hold a national convention, or party meeting, an innovation the small Anti-Masonic party had first used in 1830.[14] They met in Baltimore in December 1831 and named Henry Clay as their candidate.

President Jackson's advisers also decided to hold a national convention in 1832, but for a different reason. As Box 12–2 discusses in greater detail, Jackson's main adviser, Martin Van Buren, and others wanted to dump Vice President John C. Calhoun from the ticket because of fundamental disagreements on major issues. They thought a national convention would be the best way to remove Calhoun because Jackson's people would control the convention and could produce whatever outcome they wanted. Jackson's Democrat-Republican Party met in Baltimore five months after the Whigs. Delegates were allowed to vote only on the vice presidential nomination, and they cast their ballots for Martin Van Buren.[15] Thus, the rules governing the nomination process changed in the early part of the nineteenth century because political elites wanted to change them, not because the American public demanded it.

As the convention system took hold, each state party organization developed a process for choosing delegates to its party's national convention. State party delegates were chosen in a series of party conventions, with each convention choosing delegates to attend the convention at the next level. Local, county, and then state-level conventions took place, with state convention delegates choosing delegates to the national party convention. The national delegates from all the states then met together at a national convention to choose the party's presidential nominee (see Figure 12–1).

Because state party leaders typically dominated the local, county, and state conventions, they wielded enormous power under the state convention system. State party leaders would pick loyal delegates who could be counted on to follow their lead. At the national convention, the candidates would acquire delegates by

The People behind the Rules

Box 12–2   Martin Van Buren: Living and Dying by the Two-Thirds Rule

Martin Van Buren is an obscure name to most Americans. At best, he is remembered as the answer to a trivia question: Who was the last sitting vice president to be elected president before George H. W. Bush in 1988? But Van Buren played an important role in the development of the American political system—he is credited with developing a political theory justifying political parties in general and the two-party system in particular. His experience with the two-thirds rule highlights how rules affect who gets to serve in office.

Van Buren was born in 1782, making him the first person born in the United States to serve as president. He worked his way through the political ranks in his native New York, serving as state senator, attorney general, senator, and governor. Along the way his political skills earned him the nickname "the little magician." (Van Buren was only five feet, six inches tall.)

In 1828, Van Buren was a leading Northern supporter of Andrew Jackson's campaign for the presidency. After winning the presidency, Jackson rewarded Van Buren by naming him secretary of state. He quickly became one of the president's closest advisers, but he was forced to resign his position before the end of Jackson's first term because of what became known as the Petticoat Wars. The controversy erupted when Secretary of War John Eaton married a woman with an allegedly promiscuous past. Despite pressure from President Jackson—a widower whose own late wife had been the subject of scandalous rumors—the wives of other cabinet officials refused to socialize with Mrs. Eaton. Van Buren was the only cabinet member to support the Eatons, a position that increased the bad blood between him and Vice President John C. Calhoun. Van Buren feared the controversy was hurting the president, and he and Eaton eventually resigned their posts. President Jackson

subsequently nominated Van Buren to be ambassador to England. The Senate refused to confirm Van Buren's nomination, however, when Vice President Calhoun broke a tie vote by casting his ballot against him. Despite these setbacks, Van Buren continued to have the president's ear, and when Jackson ran for reelection in 1832, he was able to exact revenge against Calhoun.

Van Buren and others had little trouble convincing President Jackson, who had had a previous falling out with his vice president, to drop Calhoun from the ticket. Doing so was easier said than done, however, because Calhoun enjoyed considerable support in the Democrat-Republican Party. Van Buren and another Jackson adviser found the solution to their problem in what was then a new phenomenon in American politics, the national party convention. They arranged for the Democrat-Republican Party to hold its first national convention. At the convention, Van Buren pushed for the adoption of a two-thirds rule, which required that all nominees had to win the backing of two-thirds of the convention delegates. The convention then renominated Jackson by acclamation. But the real question was, who would be the vice presidential nominee? As Van Buren had calculated, Calhoun failed to muster the necessary two-thirds vote. With Calhoun's nomination defeated, Van Buren himself won the vice presidential nomination. The Jackson-Van Buren ticket won easily in the general election.

When Jackson announced he would not seek a third term as president in 1836, Van Buren was in line to be the Democrat-Republican Party's presidential nominee. Jackson strongly endorsed him, and no one else became a candidate for the party's nomination. Once again, a national party convention determined the party's nominees. At the convention there was considerable debate over the wisdom

of using the two-thirds rule. After prodding from Van Buren and after the Virginia delegation switched its vote, the convention decided to retain the two-thirds rule. Van Buren was easily nominated, and he won the general election.

Although Van Buren proved to be an unpopular president—he became known as Martin Van Ruin when the Panic of 1837 plunged the country into a severe economic recession—he was renominated in 1840 without opposition. (The 1840 convention also formally changed the party's name from Democrat-Republican to Democratic.) Van Buren was not, however, reelected. Despite the loss, he continued to be a major figure in the Democratic Party, and he entered the 1844 election as the leading candidate for the Democratic nomination. At the national convention, Van Buren won a majority of the votes, but he failed to muster the required two-thirds. Ultimately, the delegates turned to James Polk, the speaker of the House (and to this day, the only man to move from that position to the White House). How did Van Buren respond to his loss? The man who had instituted and strongly supported the two-thirds rule now denounced it as undemocratic. (In a final irony, Van Buren, the man who developed a political theory justifying the two-party system in the United States, finished his political career in 1848 as the presidential candidate of a third party, the Free Soil Party.)

The two-thirds rule made and broke Martin Van Buren's presidential aspirations. Before the Democratic Party abolished the two-thirds rule in 1936, one other prominent Democrat won the support of a majority of his party delegates only to lose the party's nomination because he failed to reach the magic two-thirds mark. (The unfortunate candidate was Speaker of the House Champ Clark of Missouri, who in 1912 lost the nomination to Governor Woodrow Wilson of New Jersey.) Over the years, the two-thirds

The People behind the Rules   *(continued)*

rule was justified as a device to ensure that the Democratic Party's presidential nominees enjoyed broad, national support. But as with all rules, it helped some candidates and hurt others. Van Buren happened to feel the effects of the two-thirds rule from both sides.

Sources: Paul T. David, Ralph M. Goldman, and Richard C. Bain, *The Politics of National Party Conventions* (Washington, D.C.: Brookings Institution, 1960), 17–20; Richard Hofstadter, *The Idea of a Party System* (Berkeley: University of California Press, 1969), 226–54; John L. Moore, *Speaking of Washington* (Washington, D.C.: Congressional Quarterly, 1993), 240–41; Robert B. Morris, ed., *Encyclopedia of American History* (New York: Harper & Brothers, 1953), 169–74; and Austin Ranney, *Curing the Mischiefs of Faction* (Berkeley: University of California Press, 1975), 71–72.

courting state party leaders, extracting their support in exchange for promising to reward the states with favors and benefits. The bargaining was usually protracted, and quite often the convention would vote several times before one candidate acquired the votes needed to win the nomination. (Indeed, in 1924, the Democratic Party needed 103 ballots to select its presidential nominee.)[16] But in the end, the eventual nominee had the endorsement of many state party organizations. In return, state party leaders had considerable influence over who their party nominated for president.

Direct Primary Elections

The next major change in the rules shifted control of the presidential selection process from state party conventions to direct primary elections in which voters themselves determined which delegates would attend the national party convention. This shift placed increased emphasis on the candidates and their ability to win the support of the public and decreased emphasis on the parties.

Early in the twentieth century, the **Progressive movement** sought to reform the presidential selection process and reduce the influence of state party leaders by persuading states to change their rules for selecting candidates. Progressives urged the states to use primary elections to choose delegates to the national conventions, thereby giving the public a more direct say in choosing party nominees. But after an initial surge in adoptions, most states reverted

Progressive movement
An early twentieth-century political movement that sought to advance the public interest by reducing the power of political parties in the selection of candidates and the administration of government.

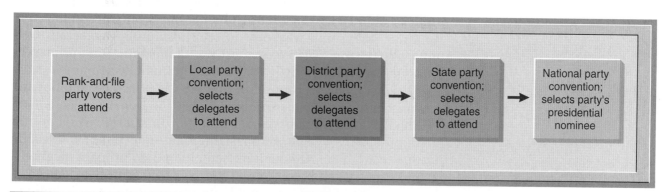

Figure 12–1   The Party Convention Presidential Nominations System. The many stages of the party convention nominating system enabled party organizations to select delegates to state and national nominating conventions. This gave the parties, rather than the voters, the power to nominate candidates. As a result, prospective candidates had to be responsive to the party organization's wishes and demands.

to the use of conventions by the 1920s, and most of the states that used primaries did not select their delegates on the basis of the results of those elections. So, for example, a candidate might win 60 percent of the votes in a state's Democratic primary but receive only a small percentage of that state's delegates because the delegates were selected through a different process.

Consequently, through the 1968 election, serious presidential candidates did not rely on primaries as the fundamental way to win delegates. Nonetheless, two factors made primaries attractive to some candidates. First, primaries offered lesser-known candidates who lacked party leaders' support a way to draw public attention and win delegates. Second, primaries gave candidates a way to show party leaders they had popular support and were thus worthy of the party's support. For example, John F. Kennedy used the 1960 West Virginia primary to prove to Democratic Party leaders that conservative Protestants would support a Roman Catholic, thereby making himself a more viable candidate.[17]

Although the Constitution gives states the power to set their own delegate selection rules, the national parties can set guidelines that the states must follow to ensure that their delegates are seated at the national convention. The most important set of guidelines were adopted by the national Democratic Party following the tumultuous 1968 presidential election. These rule changes gave the states a strong incentive to adopt primaries. In 1968, Democrats were deeply divided over the Vietnam War. The Lyndon Johnson administration was committed to continuing the war, whereas most liberals wanted to end U.S. involvement. Senator Eugene McCarthy (D-MN) opposed the war and challenged Johnson for the nomination in the New Hampshire primary, which then, as now, is the nation's first primary. (The Iowa caucuses, which since 1972 have been held before New Hampshire's primary, hold the distinction of being the nation's first significant nomination event. In caucuses, party members meet face-to-face to discuss their candidate preferences; as a result, these meetings require more time and effort than voting in a primary.) When Johnson failed to beat McCarthy by a large margin, he withdrew from the presidential race.

With Johnson out of the race, the Democratic Party organization rallied behind Vice President Hubert Humphrey, who promised to continue Johnson's war policies. In response, Democrats who opposed the war began to contest the Democratic state primaries. Senator Robert Kennedy (D-NY) emerged from the primaries as the leading challenger to Humphrey, but he was assassinated following his win in the California primary. When the Democrats convened in Chicago for their national convention, Humphrey, who had run a traditional campaign emphasizing state conventions, was the leading candidate. Although he had entered no primary elections, Humphrey still had won more than half of the primary delegates because most of them were not bound to any candidate.[18] Following heated debate over the merits of the nominating process inside the convention hall, and despite protests on the streets outside, the Democrats nominated Humphrey as their presidential candidate.

Many Democrats believed that Humphrey's nomination lacked legitimacy because he had not faced the voters in the primaries and because the delegates to the Democratic National Convention in Chicago did not reflect the diversity of the party's membership. These dissatisfactions, coupled with Humphrey's loss to Nixon, led the national Democratic Party to adopt two major sets of rule changes in its nominating process. The first set sought to increase the participation of women, minorities, young adults, and other groups that had been underrepresented at the national conventions. The second set of proposed rule changes sought to ensure that delegates to the party's national convention were allocated in proportion to the support each candidate had among the party's rank and file. Many state party organizations decided that binding primary elections in which delegates were pledged to support the candidates that the electorate voted for were the easiest way to satisfy both sets of rules and so avoid having their delegates challenged at the national convention.[19] As state legislatures adopted presidential primaries because of the changes in Democratic Party rules, the Republican Party was swept along, and a number of changes were forced on it as well.[20] Consequently, primaries have become the main method both parties use to choose delegates.

Binding primaries have changed the nature of the presidential nomination process in five ways: They have elevated the importance of early nominating events, encouraged candidates to start their campaigns months and even years ahead of the election, prompted the states to hold their primary races earlier, increased the importance of raising campaign funds, and most importantly, weakened the influence of state party organizations. Primaries elevate the importance of the early contests because of the **bandwagon effect**: Candidates who do well early find it easier to raise campaign funds, receive media coverage, and gain additional public support. Conversely, candidates who do poorly early on, or who sit out the early contests altogether, usually lose the ability to raise campaign funds, attract media attention, or hold their public support.[21] This creates a self-reinforcing **winnowing effect** that dooms candidates who perform poorly in the early contests to eventual defeat. Although a few candidates with extraordinary financial resources can withstand missteps early in the campaign, most are quickly eliminated from the contest. Three examples illustrate how candidates with strong financial backing can stay in the race, and sometimes even win the nomination. In 1996, then-Senator Robert Dole (R-KS) did worse than expected in winning the caucuses in Iowa and lost the New Hampshire primary. In 2000, then-Governor George W. Bush of Texas also lost New Hampshire and several other early primaries. Both candidates had already amassed large campaign war chests that enabled them to weather the early setbacks and go on to win the Republican nomination. In 2008, Senator Hillary Clinton (D-NY) fell behind early to Barack Obama (D-IL) but still managed to raise (and lend herself) the millions of dollars needed to continue her eventually losing

bandwagon effect
Candidates who do well in early primary elections find it easier to raise campaign funds, receive media coverage, and gain additional public support.

winnowing effect
Candidates who do poorly in early primary elections usually lose the ability to raise campaign funds, attract media attention, or hold their public support, which dooms them to eventful defeat.

campaign. The 2008 experiences of the other contenders from both parties are more typical of candidates who do poorly early on. Heading into the January 2008 caucuses in Iowa, Democratic senators Joe Biden of Delaware and Chris Dodd of Connecticut, along with 2004 vice presidential candidate John Edwards and New Mexico Governor Bill Richardson, could all stake legitimate claims to the Democratic nomination. Within one month, only Clinton and Obama remained. The Republican Party's candidates went through a similarly rigorous winnowing process. Former New York mayor Rudy Giuliani, former Massachusetts governor Mitt Romney, former Arkansas governor Mike Huckabee, and former Senator Fred Thompson from Tennessee all were viewed as serious contenders in January, but all but Huckabee had departed the field by early February, and by then even Huckabee's candidacy was no longer viewed as a serious threat to Senator John McCain from Arizona. Thus, for most candidates, the lesson is simple: succeed early, or not at all.

To win primaries, candidates need the voters' support. To win that support, they need strong name recognition. As we saw in Chapter 6, voters are ill-informed about political affairs. This forces candidates to spend many months campaigning to acquire the name recognition needed to do well in the early nominating contests. Until the 1970s, presidential candidates seldom announced their candidacies more than a few months before the first primary. In 1968, for example, no Republican candidate announced his candidacy more than a year before the general election. Because a poor showing in an early primary can now force a candidate out of the race, most candidates today formally enter the race and campaign extensively more than a year before the first primary, often after informally testing the political waters even earlier. For example, in contrast to the race in 1968, during the 2004 campaign, nine Democrats announced their plans to run for president more than eighteen months before the general election.[22]

Informal campaigning begins even earlier. Less than six months after the 1992 election, senators Dole and Phil Gramm (R-TX) had visited Iowa and New Hampshire to talk to the voters and to meet with state party leaders.[23] Dole scheduled a brief vacation in New Hampshire in August 1993; the "vacation" consisted of "four days of nonstop [political] events."[24] At the 2004 Republican National Convention, potential candidates looking ahead to 2008 lavished attention on the Iowa delegation. They spoke at an Iowa reception and hosted receptions for Iowans.[25] Even before the 2006 midterm elections, one close observer of the 2008 nomination contests had identified at least six Democrats and nine Republicans who were actively preparing for their parties' 2008 nominations.[26] Candidates test the political waters in this fashion because they want to get their campaigns up and running and to gain name recognition among the voters and party leaders.

In addition to elevating the importance of early primary elections and encouraging candidates to start their campaigns months or even years before the first primary election in New

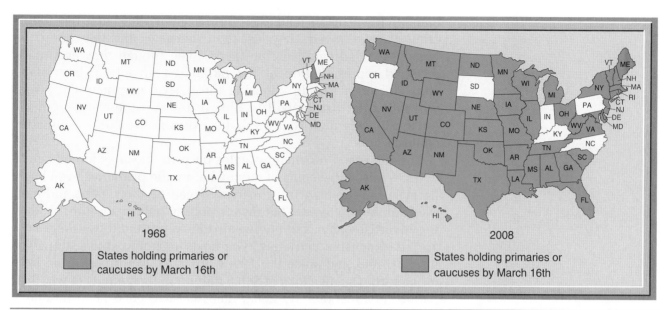

Figure 12-2 Frontloading the Presidential Nomination Process. Most states now hold their primaries or caucuses by mid-March. This development, called frontloading, means candidates must start campaigning very early to stand a chance of winning their party's nomination.

Hampshire, the increased importance of primary elections has prompted many states to hold their primaries earlier in the election year. This process, known as **frontloading**, is illustrated in Figure 12–2. In 1968, New Hampshire was the only state to hold its primary on or before March 16. In contrast, in 2008, forty-four states held at least one of their presidential primaries or caucuses on or before March 16, including the four most populous states: California, New York, Texas, and Florida. The desire to hold the first primary or caucus has created conflicts. States move up the dates of their contests so their voters play a more prominent role in determining whom each party selects as its nominee. In most years, states that hold late presidential primaries discover that their elections are essentially irrelevant because a candidate has already won a majority of the delegates to the national convention by the time their vote is held. The Democrats' 2008 nominating contest, in which Senators Clinton and Obama competed to the very last contests (New Mexico and Montana on June 3) was the exception to that rule. To control these frontloading pressures, in 2008 the Democratic Party inserted the more demographically diverse states of Nevada and South Carolina earlier in the delegate selection process, while preventing any other states from leapfrogging Iowa and New Hampshire as the traditional first nominating events. Under the new rules, Iowa held the first caucus and five days later, Nevada held its caucuses. Then New Hampshire held the first direct primary, followed closely by South Carolina. Only then were the other states allowed to schedule their nominating contests. When Florida

frontloading

The decision states make to move their primaries and caucuses to earlier dates to increase their impact on the nomination process.

and Michigan each held their primaries earlier than the Democratic Party allowed, they lost their delegates and the candidates largely avoided campaigning there. Even though they eventually received representation at the national convention, both states were denied a role in choosing the party's nominee. Only time will tell if the parties will be able to restrain the states from following Florida and Michigan's lead during the 2012 nominating contests.

The increased reliance by states on primaries has forced candidates to raise large sums of money before the primaries even begin because candidates win primaries by getting their name and message out to the voters. That means polling public opinion, producing advertisements, and buying airtime to present those ads. Those are all expensive activities. The costs of nominating campaigns have skyrocketed since the 1960s. In 1976, candidates from both major parties spent a total of $66.8 million in their efforts to win their parties' nominations. By 2008, that total exceeded $830 million.[27] The most common reason candidates give for dropping out of the race for their party's nomination is that they do not have enough money to conduct an effective campaign. Thus, the lesson remains—successful fund-raising is a necessary part of a successful campaign for a party nomination.

The final and most significant consequence of the increased importance of primaries is the weakening of state party organizations. Under the convention system, state party organizations chose delegates to the national party convention. In the primary system, however, voters in the primaries do the choosing. By shifting control of the nomination process from state party officials to voters, the primary system undermined the party-oriented character of nomination and general election campaigns, thereby freeing presidential candidates from party influence.[28]

As we have discussed, the rules governing the presidential nomination process have changed greatly over the past two centuries. The power to decide who will be a party's next presidential nominee has shifted from congressional caucuses to state party conventions to primary elections. In turn, control over the nominating process has shifted from Congress to the state party organizations, and finally, to the voting public. These rule changes also have shifted the burden of securing a nomination from party leaders to the candidates. Although party leaders acting together once had the power to decide who would be the next nominee, individual candidates are now in a better position to secure their own nominations, with or without the support of party leaders.

12-2b The General Election

After the Democratic and Republican parties each have selected a nominee, the next stage in the presidential selection process is the general election. During this stage, the nominees from each party, plus any independent or third-party candidates, take the contest before the entire American public. Just as rule changes in the nomination process have weakened the role political parties play and given individual candidates more influence, changes in the conduct of the general election have strengthened the candidate's role and weakened the role of party leaders.[29] Two of these changes are the emergence of radio and television and new and evolving campaign finance laws.

The Emergence of Radio and Television

Radio and television have radically altered the way presidential campaigns are run. They have had two important effects on the election process. First, they allow each candidate to address voters directly in their homes, increasing the visibility of the candidate and decreasing the candidate's reliance on the party organization to get the message to the voters. Second, the broadcast media have made elections more expensive because campaigns now must craft effective commercials. Presidential candidates today spend about one-half of their campaign funds on activities related to television.[30] Because parties have neither the expertise nor the financial resources candidates need to make use of the media, candidates must build their own resources. This again increases the candidate's role in the election process.

Campaign Finance Laws

With the increased use of television advertising in the 1960s, the costs of campaigning for president in the general election grew dramatically. The increasing importance of money in presidential campaigns has led to five significant changes in the rules regulating how candidates finance their campaigns: (1) the Federal Election Campaign Act (FECA) of 1971, (2) the 1974 amendments to FECA, (3) the Supreme Court's 1976 decision in *Buckley v. Valeo*, (4) the 1979 amendments to FECA, and (5) the Bipartisan Campaign Reform Act (BCRA).

The Federal Election Campaign Act of 1971 The first serious attempt at campaign finance reform occurred in 1971, with the passage of FECA. (Chapter 11 discusses how FECA applies to congressional campaigns.) FECA allowed presidential candidates to contribute no more than $50,000 to their own campaigns. It also placed limits on how much they could spend on media advertising, and it required candidates to disclose the names of anyone who contributed more than $100 to their campaigns. However, the original version of FECA did not limit the size of individual contributions or the total amount candidates could spend on their campaigns.

The 1972 presidential election campaign convinced many people that the original version of FECA did not go far enough in reforming campaign finance and that it was necessary to limit both the size of campaign contributions and the total amount of campaign spending. During the 1972 campaign, Democratic candidate George McGovern raised $30 million in campaign funds, more than any other previous candidate for president. Nonetheless, his campaign treasury was dwarfed by the $61.4 million incumbent President Nixon raised. The controversy surrounding Nixon's fund-raising techniques was heightened by the Watergate scandal, which began when police in Washington, D.C., caught low-level employees from Nixon's campaign trying to plant listening devices in the offices of the Democratic National Committee at the Watergate building. Further investigation uncovered that Nixon's reelection campaign had secretly received large campaign contributions from wealthy contributors. The Watergate scandal persuaded Congress to amend FECA in 1974.

The 1974 Amendments to Federal Election Campaign Act The 1974 amendments to FECA created three sets of rules designed to reduce the impact of campaign contributions on presidential elections.[31] The first set of rules created a voluntary system for public financing of presidential campaigns. (This innovation had its roots in a 1971 law that permitted people to direct one dollar of their income taxes to the Presidential Election Campaign Fund.) Under this system, candidates who participate in the system receive public funds at two stages: (1) during the nominating campaign, when candidates who meet certain eligibility requirements receive government contributions that match the first $250 of each private contribution; and (2) during the general election, when candidates whose parties meet a different set of eligibility requirements— which traditionally means the nominees of the Democratic and Republican parties but in 1996 and 2000 included the Reform Party's candidates as well—can finance their campaigns entirely with federal funds.

The second set of rules in the 1974 amendments imposed mandatory limits on the size of the contributions that candidates could accept, as well as the amount that candidates could contribute to their own campaigns. Individual contributors could give no more than $1,000 per candidate per contest up to a maximum of $25,000 per year, and political action committees (PACs) could contribute up to only $5,000 per candidate per election. The 1974 changes retained the requirement that candidates could contribute no more than $50,000 of their own money to their campaign.

The third set of rules in the 1974 amendments limited the amount of money that candidates who choose to receive public financing can spend during both the nomination process and the general election. These limits are increased before each election to reflect the effects of inflation and growth in the number of eligible voters. In 2008, spending by candidates who participated in the system was limited to $42.05 million for the nomination stage and $84.1 million for the general election. The Federal Election Commission was created to administer these rules.[32]

Recent developments suggest that this voluntary system has become irrelevant. In 2000, George W. Bush decided not to take public financing during the nomination process. Although he was still subject to the mandatory limits on the size of campaign contributions, he did not have to observe any spending limits. Bush believed he could raise substantially more money on his own than he would receive from the government, and by not taking public financing, he could spend what he raised as he saw fit. Bush's strategy paid off. By January 2000, he had raised more than $67 million, four times more than what his chief opponent, Senator McCain, had collected. By July 2000, Bush had raised nearly $96 million, compared with McCain's $58 million. In 2004, Bush, Senator John Kerry (D-MA), and former Vermont Governor Howard Dean, the early Democratic frontrunner, all opted out of the public finance system during the nomination process. Bush held a sizable early lead in fund-raising and Kerry raised large amounts in the latter months of the campaign. By July 2004, Bush had raised almost $228 million and Kerry had raised more than $186 million, both of which were several times larger than what the public finance system permitted.[33] This trend culminated in 2008, when John Edwards was the only candidate who won any delegates in either party's contest to accept public financing.

Despite their success in the nominating stage, both Bush and Kerry chose to participate in the public financing system for the 2004 general election, receiving the same $73 million to spend. In 2008, the general election public financing system was also threatened with irrelevance when Obama decided to forego public money and to raise hundreds of millions of dollars in contributions instead. Although McCain decided to accept the $84.1 million, unless the spending limits are greatly increased, he will probably go down in history as the last major party candidate to accept public funding.

***Buckley v. Valeo* (1976)** The third important change in campaign finance laws occurred in 1976, when the Supreme Court handed down its decision in the case of *Buckley v. Valeo*. The *Buckley* case undermined the impact of the FECA reforms by invalidating two of their key provisions. First, the Court distinguished between contributions to a candidate's campaign and independent expenditures made on behalf of a candidate. The Court ruled that the government can limit contributions but that it cannot regulate **independent expenditures**—that is, money that groups or individuals spend on behalf of a candidate without formal contact with that candidate. In the eyes of the Court, limits on independent expenditures infringe impermissibly on the right of free speech.

Since the Supreme Court handed down its decision in *Buckley v. Valeo*, independent expenditures have become a significant part of the campaign process. Between 1980 and 1992, groups spent $49.8 million on independent expenditures, with more than $40 million of that amount going to support Republican candidates. Although independent expenditures declined in the 1990s, they surged again in 2004 following the abolition of "soft money" by the Bipartisan Campaign Reform Act. Preliminary results show that groups like MoveOn.org, which supported Kerry, and Swiftboat Veterans for Truth, which supported Bush, spent tens of millions of dollars on the election.[34]

independent expenditures
Funds raised and spent without contact with the supported candidate.

Many independent expenditure campaigns have proven quite effective. During the 1988 presidential campaign, for example, supporters of George H. W. Bush ran an independent television ad campaign asserting that Bush's opponent, Michael Dukakis, was soft on crime. The ad told how Willie Horton, an African American convicted of murder, had raped a Maryland woman while on release from a Massachusetts prison as part of a prison furlough program that operated during Dukakis's governorship. The Horton ad misleadingly raised the volatile issues of race and crime, implying that Dukakis was responsible for Horton's release and that Horton's actions were typical of participants in the furlough program.[35] The false implication damaged Dukakis's electoral chances, but he could not meaningfully confront his accusers because they were not formally linked to Bush's campaign. In 2004, Kerry's attempt to use his experience in Vietnam to bolster his image as a strong leader was blunted by Swift Vets' ads that challenged the validity of the wounds and medals Kerry received during his service.

The second key FECA provision that *Buckley v. Valeo* invalidated was the limit on the amount of money candidates can contribute to their own campaigns. The Supreme Court ruled that any law that limits self-contributions in all circumstances amounts to an unconstitutional restriction on a candidate's right to free speech. The Court did rule, however, that the federal government can limit how much money candidates contribute to their own campaigns if the candidate agrees to accept public funding. In this situation, the Court argued, limits on self-contributions are constitutional because public funding is designed to ensure that candidates can speak out.

As a result of *Buckley v. Valeo*, candidates who choose not to accept public funding do not have to abide by FECA's limits on total spending. They can contribute as much of their personal wealth to their campaigns as they want. This has recently proven useful to several candidates. In 2004, Kerry used his own financial resources to sustain his campaign before the Iowa caucuses and New Hampshire primary. In 2008, Romney and Clinton contributed or loaned millions of their own dollars to their campaigns as they fought, unsuccessfully, for their respective party's nomination.

The 1979 Federal Election Campaign Act Amendments Like the *Buckley* decision, the 1979 FECA amendments undermined the limits the 1974 amendments placed on campaign spending. The amendments were intended to expand the role political parties play in elections by allowing them to collect and spend unlimited sums of **soft money**, which are expenditures designed to increase voter participation by strengthening party organizations, registering voters, and getting out the vote on Election Day. The parties spent soft money on behalf of candidates for many offices at the federal, state, and local levels. Soft money became especially important in the presidential contest. In 1980 and 1984, Republicans raised more than $15 million in each election, whereas Democrats raised only $10 million total in the two elections together. In 1988,

soft money
Expenditures political parties make during an election for any activity that serves the purpose of increasing voter turnout.

Democrats outspent Republicans $23 million to $22 million, and in 1992, they outspent Republicans $22.1 million to $15.6 million. In 1996, candidates found ways to use soft money to indirectly advertise for their campaigns, and soft money expenditures by both parties more than doubled, to $48.2 million by Republicans and $54.1 million by Democrats.[36] In 2000, both parties' soft money spending doubled again, to more than $100 million each.[37] This dramatic increase led to calls to reform campaign finance laws. The result was the Bipartisan Campaign Reform Act.

The Bipartisan Campaign Reform Act The **Bipartisan Campaign Reform Act (BCRA)**—also known as McCain-Feingold—ended soft money expenditures by the parties. It prohibited independent expenditures by PACs in the weeks before an election. BCRA also doubled the size of contributions of individuals to candidates for federal offices from $1,000 to $2,000, with subsequent increases tied to increases in inflation. The law took effect immediately following the 2002 congressional midterm elections and was intended to block the influx of private funds into the campaign. Although BCRA eliminated soft money and regulated PACs, alternative channels for spending money on elections emerged. Organizations known as **527 groups** (named for the section of the Internal Revenue code creating these groups) like MoveOn.org and Swiftboat Veterans for Truth quickly formed and spent millions of dollars to support the candidacies of Kerry and Bush in 2004. Spending by these types of groups appears to have been especially useful in rallying the candidates' core supporters with hard-edged attacks on their opponents.[38] After the election, Congress and the courts encouraged the Federal Election Commission to limit 527 groups' spending, but it refused. As a result, these groups raised and spent funds at an even faster rate in the 2008 election.[39]

Candidate-Centered Campaigns

As a result of the changes in both the nominating and general election stages, individual candidates increasingly control their own campaigns so that we now have candidate-centered campaigns.[40] Each candidate constructs his or her own organization of personal loyalists and hired experts whose main duty is to win the election. This loyalty often weakens cooperation with the party. For example, in 1972, Nixon created his own campaign organization, the Committee to Re-Elect the President (CREEP); the Republican Party had no role in organizing, financing, or conducting his campaign. Likewise, in 1976, Jimmy Carter campaigned for president by running against the Washington establishment, implicitly criticizing members of his own party. More commonly, candidates do work with their parties, but on their own terms. Candidates run their campaigns and use state and national party organizations as resources. Some candidates make a concerted effort to attend to their party's needs. Ronald Reagan in 1984 and the elder Bush in 1988 attended to the wishes of the Republican Party and, as a result, received their party's help in raising funds and organizing

Bipartisan Campaign Reform Act (BCRA)
Also known as McCain-Feingold. A law passed in 2002 that restricts the ability of interest groups to donate funds to national political parties and bars interest groups from running ads promoting or attacking federal candidates close to an election.

527 groups
Tax-exempt organizations that engage in political activities, often funded with unlimited contributions. Most 527s try to influence federal elections through voter mobilization efforts and issue ads that praise or attack a candidate's record. These groups must publicly identify their contributors and expenditures.

grass-roots activities.[41] Thus, candidates choose the extent to which they work with their party and direct the party's activities when they do. In essence, the candidates themselves decide the extent to which they will coordinate their campaign activities with those of their party.

12-2c The Electoral College

The general election stage ends when the public casts its votes on Election Day. But, as the 2000 election dramatically demonstrated, the popular vote is not the final step in selecting a president. Instead, following the nomination and general election stages, the contest moves to the **electoral college**. In this final stage of the selection process, the results of the popular vote are used to choose electors who will vote in the electoral college. The votes of these electors actually determine who will be president. The rules governing the electoral college significantly affect the way the candidates conduct their campaigns, the winner's margin of victory, and even who wins.[42]

The Constitution sets forth most of the rules governing the electoral college. Each state casts electoral votes equal to the number of its senators and representatives. Thus, in the 2008 election, California, which has two senators and fifty-three representatives, cast fifty-five electoral votes, whereas Montana, which has two senators and one representative, cast three. Although the District of Columbia has no senators or representatives, since the ratification of the Twenty-Third Amendment in 1961, it has been entitled to cast three electoral votes. In all, the electoral college has a total of 538 electoral votes. Figure 12–3 shows the relative weight each state had in the electoral college during the 2008 election.

The Constitution permits each state to decide how to allocate its electors among the competing candidates. Every state but Maine and Nebraska uses the **unit rule**, which means that the candidate with the most popular votes in a state—that is, a plurality—receives *all* of that state's electoral college votes. To win in the electoral college, the Constitution requires that a candidate receive a majority of the electoral votes to win, which is currently 270 votes out of 538. In the absence of a majority, the newly elected House of Representatives elects the president from the top three finishers, with each state delegation casting one vote, and the newly elected Senate elects the vice president from the top two finishers, with each senator casting one vote.

The states use of the unit rule and the constitutional requirement that presidents must win a majority of the votes in the electoral college provide excellent examples of how rules affect outcomes. The unit rule has two important consequences for presidential elections. First, it gives candidates a reason to devote their attention to the most populous states in which they have a reasonable chance of winning because the most populous states are the most valuable. To see why, consider the following comparison. The candidate who wins the general election in California receives

electoral college

The body of electors, whose composition is determined by the results of the general election, that chooses the president and vice president. To win in the electoral college, candidates must secure a majority of the electoral vote.

unit rule

A winner-take-all system which requires that the candidate with the most popular votes receive all of that state's electoral votes.

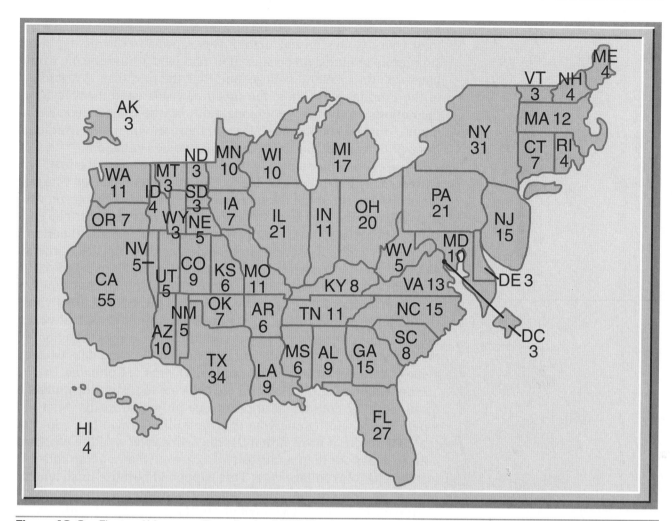

Figure 12-3 Electoral Votes per State for the 2008 Election. This map of the United States demonstrates the relative importance of large-population states such as California and Texas in the electoral college.

every one of California's fifty-five electoral votes, even if he wins the general election by only one vote. In contrast, if his opponent wins the general election in Montana, she receives only three electoral votes, even if everyone in Montana voted for her. As you can see, the use of the unit rule gives presidential candidates good reasons to focus their efforts on states with large populations.

However, the candidates also consider whether they have a reasonable chance of winning those states. For example, even though New York cast thirty-three electoral votes in 2000, Bush ignored it in the last weeks of the campaign because it was clear that Al Gore would win the state. Although Bush knew he could make the New York contest closer by spending more time and money there, he also knew that a narrow loss is no better than a crushing defeat when it comes to electoral college math. By the same token, it is important not to take victory in a state for granted. Gore was criticized for not spending more time in his home state of Tennessee. He apparently believed he would win his home state and so did not give it as much attention as other states where the outcome was in doubt. On Election Day in 2000, however, more Tennesseans voted for Bush than for Gore, so Bush won all eleven of the state's electoral votes. Gore's miscalculation was especially distressing to his supporters in hindsight because if he had won Tennessee, he would have won the electoral college (and thus the presidency) regardless of the Florida vote. Thus, the unit rule leads candidates to focus their efforts on the most populous states in which the outcome is in doubt. The least populous states and those in which one candidate has a prohibitive advantage tend to receive less attention.

The second consequence of the unit rule stems from the first: The winner-take-all requirement can lead to an electoral college vote that looks different from the popular vote. In most cases, the person who wins the popular vote wins by an even larger margin in the electoral college. For example, Appendix H reveals that Reagan's 10 percentage point victory over Carter in the popular vote translated into an electoral college landslide, with Reagan winning 91 percent of the electoral votes. Similarly, in 1992 and 1996, Clinton failed to win a simple majority of the popular vote, but still won substantial victories in the electoral college. At the extreme, a candidate could sweep the electoral college vote despite winning the general election by only fifty-one votes, provided, of course, that the candidate wins by a one-vote margin in every state and the District of Columbia.

The tendency of the electoral college vote to distort the outcome of the popular vote might appear to be only a curiosity. After all, whether you win by one vote or by a million, a win is a win. Yet the 2000 election proved that the distorting effects of the electoral college are more than a curiosity. Gore won the popular vote but lost the electoral college vote. This happened because Bush tended to win his states by narrower margins than the margins by which Gore won his states. It is a tribute to the high regard with which the American people hold the country's electoral rules that they accepted Bush's election as valid even though he was not the winner of the popular vote. And the 2000 election is not the only time that the popular vote winner lost the electoral college vote. Samuel Tilden lost to Rutherford B. Hayes in this way in 1876, and Grover Cleveland repeated the trick in his loss to Benjamin Harrison in 1888.[43] Thus, the unit rule can have a undemocratic effect on the outcome of presidential elections.

Like the unit rule, the rule requiring candidates to win a majority of the electoral college vote also can have an undemocratic effect. If no candidate wins a majority, the decision of who should be president is put in the hands of the House of Representatives. As long as only two candidates have a chance of winning electoral votes, the only way the election can end up in the House is if there is a tie in the electoral college—and that has never happened. So if only two candidates receive votes, one is virtually certain to receive a majority. Occasionally, a third-party candidate may be able to win electoral votes in a few states. This can prevent either of the two major candidates from securing a majority, as happened to Jackson in 1824. Jackson won a plurality of the popular and electoral votes, but with three other candidates in the race, he failed to win a majority in the electoral college. The election went to the House of Representatives, which chose John Quincy Adams, who had finished second in both the popular and electoral college vote. The country has narrowly avoided a similar outcome several times more recently. For example, in 1960, a shift of less than 5,000 votes in both Illinois and Missouri would have deprived both Kennedy and Nixon of electoral college majorities (fifteen electoral votes were cast for Senator Harry Byrd of Virginia that year), and a shift of less than 7,000 votes in both Delaware and Ohio in 1976 would have tied Carter and Ford in electoral votes, again throwing the election to the House of Representatives.[44]

For years, the possibility that the winner of the popular vote could still lose the race for the presidency has triggered calls to adopt some form of direct popular election. The 2000 election added urgency to these demands. Changing the rules governing presidential elections would dramatically alter the dynamics of presidential politics and could lead to a cure worse than the disease. To understand why, remember that moving to a direct popular election would eliminate the use of the unit rule. In turn, eliminating the unit rule would encourage candidates with limited regional or national appeals to run for president because they no longer would have to worry about winning a plurality of the popular vote in a large number of states. With more candidates in the race, the popular vote would likely be spread across a larger number of candidates, which would make it far less likely that the winning candidate would receive a majority or even a large plurality of the popular vote. Indeed, direct popular elections would even make it possible to elect a president the vast majority of the American public opposed. And a direct popular election that produced a close vote like what we had in the 2000 election would trigger recounts not in one state but in fifty. Because direct presidential elections contain the potential for such undesirable consequences, they are not likely to be adopted.

12-2d Consequences for Governing

The many changes in the nomination, general election, and electoral college stages of the presidential selection process have encouraged modern presidents to move away from their parties and to create more personalized presidencies. Other developments in American politics have also weakened parties. As Chapter 7 showed, voters often split their tickets between the two major parties, and as Chapter 11 discussed, members of Congress also run candidate-centered campaigns in which they downplay their party affiliation.

With weakened political parties, modern presidents cannot rely on their parties to create a single governing coalition that will support them across the broad spectrum of problems facing the nation. Instead, modern presidents must create new coalitions to support each issue on their agenda. This shift in the nature of the president's leadership role has had major implications for the way presidents structure and run their presidencies.

12-3 THE PRESIDENCY AS AN INSTITUTION

Tremendous changes have affected the presidency as an institution. As we previously discussed, the rules that bring the candidate to the fore during the election process also bring the president to prominence in the governing process. As the presidency has increased and political parties decreased in strength and significance, modern presidents have relied less on their parties and more on their staffs to accomplish their goals in office. This change has had several consequences for the power of the president, the organizational structure of the presidency, and the way in which presidents work to secure their personal and policy goals.

12-3a The Powers of the Presidency

As we noted previously, the Constitution defines the powers of the presidency for the most part only in vague terms. In practice, this vagueness has permitted a dynamic and flexible interpretation of presidential powers. In the modern era, presidents have become increasingly visible, influential, and active national leaders. As a result, modern presidents have consistently sought to exploit the ambiguous nature of their power by claiming that ever more powers are implied in the Constitution. We can trace the growth in presidential power by examining first the sources and then three models of presidential power.

Sources of Presidential Power

The power of the presidency is grounded in one or more of three sources: the Constitution, statutory laws passed by Congress, and precedents set by earlier presidents. As we mentioned previously, the specific constitutional powers assigned to the president include the veto power, the treaty power, and the appointment power. These powers give the president considerable say in the policies of the federal government. Take, for example, the veto power. Between 1789 and 2006, Congress overrode only 107 of 1485 regular vetoes, a success rate of roughly 7 percent. Presidents also used the pocket veto to block passage of an additional 1,066 bills.[45] Thus, in 1995, President Clinton was able to block congressional Republicans from enacting their plans to cut taxes and restructure Medicare because they could not garner enough votes to override his vetoes. Because presidents can almost always make their vetoes stick, the threat of a presidential veto often is sufficient to convince Congress to make its legislation reflect the preferences of the White House.

A second source of presidential power is statutory law—that is, legislation passed by Congress. When passing legislation, Congress frequently includes provisions that give presidents some discretion in deciding how to implement the law. For instance, during Harry Truman's presidency, more than 1,100 different laws gave

Source: © Reuters/Corbis.

Bill Clinton vetoed the Republicans' Medicare reform bill in 1995 with a pen Lyndon Johnson used to sign Medicare into law.

him some degree of discretionary authority.[46] Congress delegates such discretion because it often lacks the time and expertise needed to write all the details of legislation and because experience has shown that giving the executive branch some flexibility to carry out the spirit of a law often serves the public interest best.

One example of how statutory law can enhance presidential power is the president's *reprogramming authority,* or the power to redirect government spending. The Constitution gives the power of the purse to Congress, but most appropriations bills give the president limited authority to reprogram funds as circumstances warrant. Congress gives the president this power because it cannot anticipate all the events that may influence how money should be spent over the course of a year. Most reprogramming decisions are routine, and they enable the federal government to spend more wisely. At times, however, presidents use their reprogramming power to pursue their own policy objectives. For example, when Nixon sent troops into Cambodia in 1970, he initially funded the operation by reprogramming foreign aid appropriations intended for other countries.[47] In 1991, George H. W. Bush accelerated $9.7 billion in government spending to try to stimulate the economy as part of his reelection campaign.[48] In these ways, presidents can shape congressional priorities to better match their personal preferences.

Statutory law may also enable presidents to take more complete advantage of their constitutional powers. For instance, the Constitution allows presidents to "recommend to [Congress's] consideration such measures as he shall judge necessary and expedient." For more than a century, however, the president lacked the institutional apparatus needed to use that authority fully, particularly when it came to federal spending. Federal agencies simply made their legislative and budgetary requests directly to Congress,

central legislative clearance

The power the Budget and Accounting Act of 1921 granted to the president to create a package of legislative proposals and budgets for congressional consideration.

without presidential involvement. In 1921, however, Congress passed the Budget and Accounting Act, which gave presidents the authority and the staff needed to review, revise, and assemble the budget requests of federal agencies into a comprehensive budget and to review and revise each agency's legislative proposals before they were submitted to Congress. This process is now referred to as the power of **central legislative clearance**. Presidents use this power to shape Congress's legislative agenda by presenting it with a comprehensive package of bills and budget proposals each year.

In addition to the Constitution and statutory law, presidential power is grounded in custom and precedent. When Congress, the courts, and the public accept as legitimate presidential actions those that were previously thought to lie beyond the proper scope of presidential authority, the power of the presidency is enhanced. As William Howard Taft, the only man to serve both as president and Chief Justice of the United States, once put it: "So strong is the influence of custom that it seems almost to amend the Constitution."[49] In general, precedents redefine the scope of the implied powers of the presidency, that is, the powers the presidency is assumed to have but that are not specifically mentioned in the Constitution.

The evolution of the president's dismissal power, or the ability to fire or retain federal appointees, illustrates how precedent can serve as a source of power.[50] The Constitution says nothing about the president's power to dismiss executive appointees, and throughout the nineteenth century, presidents and Congress argued over whether the Senate's consent was needed to fire an executive officer, as it is to appoint one. Indeed, when President Andrew Johnson was impeached in 1868, one of the articles of impeachment charged him with dismissing his secretary of war without Senate approval. (Johnson was not removed from office because the Senate fell one vote short of convicting him.) Not until the early twentieth century, however, did presidential arguments that the power to dismiss was separate from the power to appoint gain general acceptance.[51]

President George W. Bush was especially vigorous in his efforts to establish new precedents and expand existing precedents that strengthen the powers of his office.[52] In some cases Congress and the courts accepted his claims; in others they did not. For example, as we saw in the introduction to Chapter 2, he asserted the authority to hold foreign prisoners indefinitely without allowing them access to lawyers or the courts. The Supreme Court has rejected that claim.[53] He has also broadened the use of **presidential signing statements**, which his predecessors used to explain their understanding of the laws they were signing, to exempt the presidency from having to obey certain provisions within those laws.[54] Although the underlying principle behind signing statements is well established, President Bush's interpretation has not yet been either definitively challenged or endorsed. Most recently, President Bush authorized surveillance of communications involving U.S. citizens without warrants or congressional oversight, in part

presidential signing statements

A statement issued by the President about a bill, in conjunction with signing that bill into law.

claiming that "the President's well-recognized inherent constitutional authority as Commander-in-Chief" empowers him to do so.[55] The laws that Congress subsequently enacted to define and limit this power granted the presidency much of the power that Bush had initially sought. None of these powers are explicitly defined in either the Constitution or laws. In each case, President Bush has inferred the power's existence from broad statements in the Constitution or laws. How Congress and the Supreme Court respond to these and other claims of authority will determine the extent to which the presidency's precedent-based powers continue to expand.

Models of Presidential Power

Examining the sources of presidential power is one way to see the gradual changes in rules that have expanded the powers of the presidency. Another is to look at what presidents have understood their powers to be. Past presidents have adhered to three competing conceptions of presidential power: the Restricted, Prerogative, and Stewardship Models.

The most limited conception of presidential power is identified with President Taft and is known as the *Restricted Model.* Taft claimed that presidents are permitted to exercise only those powers explicitly granted to them by the Constitution or statutory law, or that could be clearly implied from those sources. According to the Restricted Model, presidents can propose and veto legislation because the Constitution explicitly authorizes the president to do both. The president should not, however, lobby Congress on legislation because the Constitution makes no provision for it. Presidents who adhere to the Restricted Model of presidential power tend to be passive and reactive.

The most expansive conception of presidential power is identified with Lincoln and is known as the *Prerogative Model.* Lincoln held that when the existence or integrity of the nation is at stake, presidents may take any action, without regard to constitutionality or legality, to protect it. Adhering to that precept, he violated the Constitution to achieve the higher goal of maintaining the Union. Some presidents since Lincoln have made recourse to prerogative powers on occasion, especially in foreign policy, but no subsequent president has used it as a general model for his presidency.[56]

Between these two extremes lies the *Stewardship Model,* which is associated with President Theodore Roosevelt. The Stewardship Model turns Taft's Restricted Model on its head. Roosevelt claimed that because presidents alone represent the entire nation, they have a duty to act as stewards of the national interest. In that role, they can take any action not explicitly prohibited by law or the Constitution. Presidents following the Stewardship Model actively seek power and use it to lead the country.

Although most nineteenth-century presidents adhered to the Restricted Model, modern presidents have all conceived of their power in terms of the Stewardship Model. This influences the way they interpret and reshape the rules of the presidency because they

believe they have the power to take any action not expressly prohibited by the Constitution or statutory law. In turn, conceiving of
presidential power in terms of the Stewardship Model helps presidents who can no longer rely extensively on their political parties
to help them accomplish their goals. A more expansive view of the
inherent power of the presidency gives them the influence and
flexibility they need to create new coalitions of supporters for their
programs.

12-3b The Organizational Structure of the Presidency

The organizational structure of the presidency has changed dramatically over the past two centuries. From 1789 to today, the
office has grown in size, complexity, and power as the presidency
has become a more active and powerful position.

Historical Development

Historically, the presidency was a small and personal office. Presidents relied on family and friends to serve as staff; those who
agreed to help did so without pay or were paid by the president
himself. For example, Washington hired his nephew to be his personal secretary, and Jackson created a "kitchen cabinet" of close
political friends who advised him on policy and politics. Congress
appropriated funds to hire some presidential aides in 1857 and
gradually appropriated more money for White House staff over the
next sixty years. Still, presidential staffs remained small and informal until 1939.[57]

As the presidency grew in prominence and power, the presidential staff grew in number and complexity as well. Once again,
FDR's presidency marks the turning point in defining the modern
presidency. As FDR enacted his New Deal programs, the executive
branch became more active and the federal bureaucracy grew. The
president's administrative duties expanded as well. To handle his
growing administrative burden and to help coordinate the various
agencies and staff that reported to him, FDR used authority Congress had given him to create the Executive Office of the President
(EOP) in 1939. The EOP is an "umbrella" organization that
includes several influential agencies that perform key functions
for the president.

The EOP grew steadily from FDR's presidency through the
1960s. Staff support expanded as presidents were expected to provide leadership in more policy areas. At its peak during the Nixon
administration, the EOP employed nearly 6,000 people spread
across twenty agencies.[58] In the aftermath of the Vietnam War and
the Watergate scandal, however, congressional criticism and public mistrust of a too-powerful presidency led Presidents Gerald
Ford and Carter to reduce the EOP to roughly its present size—
eleven staff agencies, which together employ about 1,500 workers.
Nonetheless, presidents will create new EOP agencies when they
feel the need. Most recently, President Obama has expanded the

presidency by creating several "czars" who oversee policies such as health care, the economy, and energy.

Key Agencies of the Contemporary Executive Office of the President

Although each of the eleven agencies in the EOP is important to the workings of the presidency, four merit special attention: the White House Office, the Office of Management and Budget, the National Security Council, and the Office of the Vice President.

In many respects, the most important agency in the EOP is the White House Office. It employs more than 400 people whose primary task is to meet the immediate personal and policy needs of the president. The people who work for the White House Office include the president's primary advisers on policy and political matters, administrators who manage the internal operation of the White House and supervise the workings of the rest of the bureaucracy, and aides who conduct relations with important actors such as Congress, the mass media, and special interest groups. As you might imagine, presidents try to staff the White House Office with loyal aides who will carry out their wishes.

The White House Office also includes the Office of the First Lady. Traditionally, the president's wife served as the nation's hostess, welcoming guests to the White House. She stayed away from politically controversial issues. Many first ladies in the modern era have pursued government policies that particularly interested them and enjoyed broad public support: Lady Bird Johnson advocated beautifying America's highways, Nancy Reagan urged Americans to "Just Say No" to drugs, and Barbara Bush helped promote literacy. On occasion, first ladies have played more prominent political roles. Eleanor Roosevelt, for example, was a leading figure in publicizing the civil rights movement during the 1930s.[59] Carter openly acknowledged that his wife, Rosalynn, was one of his most important advisers, and she was the first presidential spouse to regularly attend cabinet meetings.[60] Hillary Rodham Clinton undertook a political role unprecedented in its prominence when President Clinton put her in charge of drafting a proposal to overhaul the nation's health-care system. When Congress refused to pass legislation enacting the reforms she had helped to craft, Mrs. Clinton retreated from the political spotlight and assumed the more traditional roles of the first lady. (White House aides called this resumption of a more traditional role "the *Redbook* strategy" because they were trying to appeal to *Redbook* magazine's audience, the average American woman.)[61] Nonetheless, Mrs. Clinton clearly extended the boundaries of the role of the first lady. She also broke new ground for former first ladies when New Yorkers elected her to the Senate, making her the first former first lady to ever seek or achieve elective office after leaving the White House. Laura Bush was a more conventional first lady. It remains to be seen whether Michelle Obama and her successors (be they first ladies or first gentlemen) will ever play so prominent a role as Mrs. Clinton.

Source: © Reuters/Corbis.

Laura Bush fulfilled the role of First Lady in a traditional manner, serving as the nation's official host for important state events and speaking out on behalf of widely accepted public goals, such as public education.

The Office of Management and Budget (OMB) helps the president draft the annual federal budget request and oversee the work of the federal bureaucracy. The OMB was created by the Budget and Accounting Act of 1921 as the Bureau of the Budget (BOB), and it became part of the EOP in 1939. In 1970, President Nixon expanded the size and functions and changed the name of the agency. The OMB's career civil servants review the budgetary and legislative requests each federal agency makes to Congress to ensure that they conform to the president's priorities. The OMB also helps presidents direct the bureaucracy by making sure that laws and presidential directives are implemented according to the president's wishes.

The National Security Council (NSC), created in 1947, consists of the secretaries of state and defense, the vice president, and the president. The NSC provides a forum for discussing foreign policy options. It is supported by a staff of policy experts appointed by the president. Since the Kennedy presidency, the NSC staff has been an important source of foreign policy advice and advocacy.

The Office of the Vice President serves the needs of the vice president. The importance of the vice presidency has changed dramatically over the past 200 years. John Adams, our first vice president, called the vice presidency "the most insignificant office that ever the invention of man contrived or his imagination conceived."[62] Most nineteenth-century vice presidents were undistinguished politicians whose sole role was to attract votes during the general election. Vice presidents gained a measure of prominence in the early twentieth century as they began to participate in cabinet meetings, serve as emissaries to foreign governments, and act as liaisons with Congress. Nonetheless, as late as the 1930s, FDR's first vice president, John Nance Garner, observed that the vice presidency "isn't worth a pitcher of warm spit."[63]

The Office of the Vice President has gained in stature in recent years as presidents have entrusted their vice presidents with more important duties. Nelson Rockefeller (under Ford), Walter Mondale (under Carter), George H.W. Bush (under Reagan), and Dan Quayle (under the elder Bush) all served as advisers to the president on a range of policy and political questions.

Gore built on the recent tradition of an active vice presidency by playing important roles for President Clinton in both domestic and foreign policy. Gore led a task force that restructured and revitalized the federal bureaucracy and was a key liaison to the environmental community. In foreign affairs, Gore helped strengthen U.S. relations with Russia and South Africa.[64] The prominent roles that the younger Bush gave to Vice President Dick Cheney in energy policy and the war on terrorism exceed those assigned to Gore and demonstrate that the vice presidency has become one of the most important presidential offices. Ultimately, however, a vice president exercises no more power than the current president is willing to delegate. Only time will tell if future presidents rely on their vice presidents to the extent that Bush has.

In sum, the organizational structure of the presidency was relatively small and stable for more than 150 years. Since the mid-twentieth century, however, it has grown in both size and complexity. As the presidency has evolved from a small, personal office into a conglomerate of support agencies under the umbrella of the EOP, presidents have found themselves able to rely on a larger number of people and agencies to accomplish their goals. In turn, this expansion has changed the way presidents work.

12-3c The Workings of the Presidency

A third way the presidency as an institution has changed since the mid-twentieth century, along with the changes in the powers of the presidency and the organizational structure of the presidency, is the way in which the office works. The workings of the presidency are influenced by both internal and external factors. These factors, like the structural rules set forth in the Constitution, combine both to empower and constrain the president.

Internal factors that affect the workings of the presidency include the functions the agencies of the EOP perform for the president, the president's style of managing those agencies, and the president's conception of the role staff should play. Internal factors tend to give presidents the ability to run their presidencies as they wish. External factors include the expectations that others have for the president and what they believe he or she should accomplish. External factors tend to constrain the president.

Internal Factors—Functions of Executive Office of the President Agencies

The agencies that make up the EOP advise presidents on public policy, help presidents conduct relations with others in and out of government, and assist presidents as they look ahead to reelection.

Each agency in the EOP has a specific role to play in advising and supporting the president on public policy. For example, the

Source: © Reuters/Corbis.

Over the past quarter century, vice presidents have played an increasingly important role as advisers and surrogates for their president. Vice President Dick Cheney continued this trend by serving as a central player in the George W. Bush administration.

NSC recommends foreign policy options, the Council of Economic Advisers helps formulate economic policy, and the Office of Policy Development advises presidents on a wide range of domestic policies.

Some agencies in the EOP also act as liaisons to Congress and interest groups, helping presidents build political support for their policy initiatives. This is especially true of various units of the White House Office. For example, every president since Dwight Eisenhower has used the Office of Legislative Affairs to develop support on Capitol Hill for his legislative agenda. Likewise, every president since Ford has used the Office of Public Liaison to improve his relations with interest groups. And the Office of Strategic Planning and Communications helps presidents present a dignified, professional image and present persuasive messages to the public through the national press corps.

In addition to advising the president on public policy and acting as liaisons with groups in and out of government, agencies in the EOP also act to advance the president's prospects for reelection. Again, this is especially true of the White House Office, which, since the 1970s, has developed into a shadow campaign organization. The reason is that after presidents enter office, they usually transfer their key campaign aides into important positions in the White House. These aides advise the president both on policy and electoral matters. When the time for reelection nears, these aides often move out of the White House staff and back into the president's reelection campaign staff. •

One example of the dual policy and electoral roles played by units in the White House Office is illustrated by the Office of Public Liaison. Not only does it work to enlist the support of interest groups for the president's legislative agenda, but it also tries to keep the president's fences mended as the White House looks to the next election. White House opinion pollsters also play dual policy and electoral roles. They measure the public's reactions to the president's proposals to determine how best to mobilize support for the administration's legislative agenda. They also routinely survey the public to determine which issues will have the most appeal in the next election and to determine the president's political standing with the voters.[65] Clinton relied more heavily on public opinion analysts than did any of his predecessors, commissioning three to four polls each month to assist him in achieving both his policy and political goals.[66]

Thus, the functions the agencies of the EOP perform have evolved over time. In particular, the liaison and reelection functions of EOP agencies have both become more prominent as political parties have weakened. The White House and other EOP agencies have stepped in to fill the role parties once played in helping presidents both lead the government and win reelection.

Internal Factors—Presidential Management Styles

Modern presidents have developed different management styles, which range from an informal "spokes of the wheel" style to a highly structured "pyramid" style. No president employs a pure version of either style. Rather, each president draws on features of both, but tends to place relatively greater emphasis on one or the other.[67]

As Figure 12–4 shows, in a wheel style of management, the White House has few layers of hierarchy, and the president is accessible to many different assistants. Presidents who use the wheel style of management prefer to take a hands-on approach to the presidency. They are less likely to appoint a strong chief of staff to oversee the White House's administration, preferring to assume that task themselves. They frequently change staff assignments, and they may fail to clearly divide responsibility among their aides. FDR, Kennedy, Carter, and Clinton (see Box 12–3) all tended toward the wheel style of management, although each also adjusted his style over the course of his administration and from issue to issue.

In contrast to the wheel style, the pyramid style of management creates a fairly formal and hierarchical command structure within the office of the presidency. As Figure 12–6 shows, a White House organized according to the pyramidal style has several layers of authority and more formal and rigid staff assignments, with clear lines of authority and duties. One staff member is typically designated as chief of staff and given authority to oversee other White House aides. Presidents who resort to the pyramid style of management generally limit their contact to a small number of senior staff. Eisenhower, Nixon, Reagan (see Box 12–3), and the elder Bush all tended toward the pyramid style of management to varying

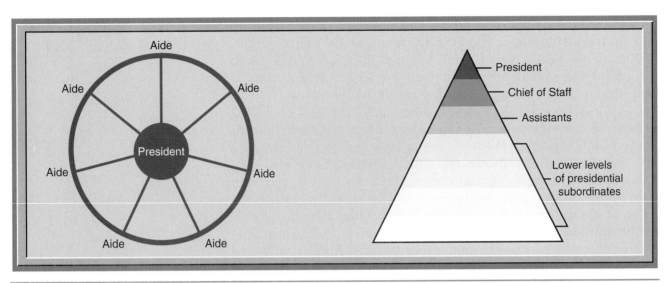

Figure 12-4   The Spokes of the Wheel and Pyramid Styles of Presidential Management. Although no president employs a fairly structured pyramid approach to management, Bill Clinton embraced the more free-flowing spokes of the wheel style. For example, whereas George W. Bush used experiences, party membership, and length of time in office. For example, whereas George W. Bush used a fairly structured pyramid approach to management, Bill Clinton embraced the more free-flowing spokes of the wheel style.

degrees; the most recent former president, the younger Bush, tended toward this style as well.

Each management style has advantages and disadvantages. Proponents of the wheel approach claim that it enables presidents to receive more complete and accurate information about what their administrations are doing. By communicating with many different aides, including those who hold only midlevel appointments, presidents are more likely to know what is happening both inside and outside government. Yet the wheel style places enormous demands on a president's time because no one else in the White House is empowered to make key decisions. And the more time presidents spend on internal White House matters, the less time they have to make important political and policy decisions. Thus, the wheel style forces presidents to pay a high price for being well informed.

The advantages and disadvantages of the pyramid approach tend to be exactly the opposite. The strength of the pyramid style is that it places relatively few administrative demands on the president. Those duties are assigned to the chief of staff. Moreover, the clear chain of command limits disputes over who has authority to make decisions. The pyramid style's weakness is that it can leave presidents insulated from political reality because they depend on a small number of aides for information. No one wants to be the bearer of bad tidings, especially if it puts one's self or one's boss in a bad light, so as the number of people with access to the president declines, and the number of layers through which information must pass increases, it becomes more likely that bad news will never make it to the president's desk. As a result, presidents who rely on the pyramid style of management may develop a distorted understanding of what Americans and their elected representatives in Congress are thinking.[68]

The People behind the Rules

Box 12–3   Contrasting Management Styles: Reagan and Clinton

All presidents today must not only lead the nation, but they also must oversee and coordinate the activities of the roughly 500 members of the White House staff. Yet different presidents bring different management styles to the Oval Office. To see just how different presidential management styles can be, compare how Ronald Reagan and Bill Clinton approached the task of running the White House.

RONALD REAGAN

Reagan directed his administration by voicing general goals and letting his subordinates work out the details. During his first term, he employed a well-organized staff structure based on a "Troika" of key aides: Michael Deaver, James Baker, and Edwin Meese. These three assistants then managed the workings of the rest of the White House. In Reagan's second term, his style of management became even more formal and pyramidal, as he appointed Donald Regan chief of staff to replace the Troika. Regan ran the White House in a highly structured fashion, staffing the office with carefully chosen subordinates rather than peers who could challenge his authority. President Reagan left day-to-day operational decisions to Regan.

Reagan's supporters praised his ability to delegate authority; his detractors denigrated his detachment. Both were right. Praise for his hands-off style produced, for example, an article in the business magazine *Fortune* headlined "What Managers Can Learn from Manager Reagan." But hosannas turned to ridicule when it became known in late 1986 that members of his National Security Council staff had secretly (and illegally) traded weapons with Iran to secure the release of Americans held hostage in Lebanon and then (again, illegally) used some of the profits to aid the Contra rebels in Nicaragua. Reagan defended himself against resounding public and congressional criticism of the Iran-Contra Affair by claiming he was unaware of what his most senior aides were doing.

BILL CLINTON

Clinton took a hands-on, wheel-style approach to managing his presidency. He provided ambiguous job descriptions to his top aides, and he often kept in touch with lower-level White House aides by dropping in on them in their offices to discuss policy. Clinton's hands-on approach was reflected in how his first chief of staff,

Mack McLarty, operated. Rather than relying on the pyramidal structure Regan favored, McLarty employed an "inclusive, nonhierarchical" approach. He did not require that the flow of information to the president go exclusively through his office, and he permitted as many as eight advisers direct access to Clinton (compared with three or four during Reagan's terms). Clinton's second chief of staff, Leon Panetta, imposed more structure on the Clinton White House.

Clinton's management style met with a fair degree of success. His administration convinced Congress to approve both a major deficit reduction bill and the North American Free Trade Agreement. Clinton's management style also drew sharp criticism. Critics complained that too many aides had a say in policy making and that the lines of decision-making authority were too blurred; as a result, they claimed the Clinton White House took too long to develop domestic policy initiatives and was too slow to respond to events overseas.

Sources: Stephen Hess, *Organizing the Presidency,* 2nd ed. (Washington, D.C.: Brookings Institution, 1988), chap. 9; and Burt Solomon, "A Modish Management Style Means. . .Slip-Sliding around the West Wing," *National Journal,* October 30, 1993, 2006–07.

Why do presidents develop a preferred management style? Each president's management style depends on his prior political experiences, his political party affiliation, the size and complexity of the EOP during his administration, and how long the president has served in office.

Prior political experience leads presidents to favor one style over the other. Most Republican presidents have had executive backgrounds in large organizations: Eisenhower in the Army, Nixon as vice president, Reagan as governor of California, the elder Bush in a variety of executive branch offices, including the vice presidency, and the younger Bush as governor of Texas. As a result, Republicans tend to be more comfortable with the pyramid style. Only Ford, as a long-time member of the House, had a predominantly legislative background, and he was the most wheel-oriented Republican president. In contrast, most Democrats have had political careers that predispose them toward the wheel style.

Truman, Kennedy, and Johnson spent most of their careers in the Senate, which has a decidedly nonpyramidal structure. Although Carter and Clinton served as governors, both served in smaller states and did not need large staffs.

Party is important because presidents tend to model themselves on predecessors from their party. Modern Democratic presidents have tended to emulate FDR's wheel style. In contrast, Republicans have tended to model their presidencies on Eisenhower's formal, pyramidal approach.

The size and complexity of the presidency has led presidents elected since the 1960s to rely more on the pyramid style than previous presidents did. As the presidency has grown larger and more complex, the wheel style's high administrative costs have made it less attractive.

Finally, presidents tend to shift their management styles toward the pyramid approach as their administrations progress. Early on, presidents promise open administrations, assuring the cabinet, Congress, and the public access to the president, which fits the wheel model. Moreover, the first tasks facing a president concern policy formulation: What to do and how to do it? These factors lead presidents to seek input and to tolerate debate and dissent, attitudes that lend themselves to the wheel style. However, as they move further into their terms, presidents find their task shifts to implementing policies. This is easier to accomplish with the pyramid style's formal chain of command.

Internal Factors—The Role of Staff

Closely related to a president's management style is his or her concept of the role the presidential staff should play. This is another area in which the presidency has gained influence since the mid-twentieth century, as presidents have rewritten the informal rules that govern their use of staff. In general, presidents have abandoned the idea of hiring objective, neutral staff in favor of hiring staff members who are politically loyal.

When the EOP was first created, most of the agencies were staffed according to the principle of **neutral competence**, which holds that staff members should be permanent career civil servants whose task is to provide competent and objective advice to every president rather than to advocate each president's policy preferences.[69] The exception to this rule was staff that presidents appointed to work in the White House Office. These temporary employees were expected to serve the political interests of the president who appointed them. According to the principle of neutral competence, then, most presidential staff members were committed to the presidency as an institution, but not necessarily to the policy goals of a particular president. Obviously, the norm of neutral competence limited what the president's staff was willing to do for him.

Most presidents grow dissatisfied with staff members who fail to respond to their immediate political needs. As a result, they have tried to weaken the norm of neutral competence and to politicize most agencies in the EOP. For example, during the 1960s, Johnson

neutral competence

The belief that staff members (usually career civil servants) should be able to work competently for any president, regardless of partisan affiliation or policy preferences and without advocating the policies of individual presidents.

Source: © Getty Images.

President Obama relies heavily on personal assistants and staff members who are committed to ensuring the success of his presidency.

pressured the Bureau of the Budget (now known as the OMB) to abandon its neutral perspective and advocate his policies, whereas Nixon and Carter imposed new layers of political appointees on the OMB to gain greater control of its operation.[70] David Stockman, Reagan's first director of the OMB, ordered the agency to alter its projections of government spending and revenue to support Reagan's claim that he could raise defense spending, cut domestic spending, lower taxes, and still balance the budget.[71]

Presidents also have politicized the workings of the key presidential agency on foreign policy, the staff of the NSC. Kennedy ended the practice of filling positions on the NSC staff with career officers from the departments of defense and state, and instead appointed outside experts who shared his views on foreign policy. Nixon gave Henry Kissinger, his national security adviser and the head of the NSC staff, enormous powers to conduct foreign policy, relegating the State Department to a peripheral caretaker role. Members of the NSC staff assumed a key role in implementing foreign policy on behalf of Reagan in the mid-1980s. Members of Reagan's NSC staff secretly (and in violation of U.S. law) sold weapons to Iran in a bid to secure the release of several Americans held hostage in Lebanon. Some of the proceeds from these secret sales were then routed to the Contra rebels in Nicaragua, an act that violated legislation restricting U.S. aid to the Contras. The resulting scandal, known as the Iran-Contra Affair, rocked the Reagan administration and damaged Reagan's reputation. Secretary of State Condoleezza Rice was the younger Bush's national security adviser during his first term. In that role, she strongly advocated on behalf of Bush's war on terror in general and war in Iraq in particular. Her actions as national security adviser demonstrated that personal loyalty and responsiveness continue to be imperative characteristics of the NSC.

The politicization of the institution of the presidency is one of the most important trends of the modern era.[72] As the OMB and Iran-Contra examples show, presidents who have loyal staffs dedicated to serving their personal aims are far better positioned to pursue their goals than presidents whose staffs adhere to the norm of neutral competence. In short, by politicizing the EOP, recent presidents have increased their personal power.

As the Founders feared, and episodes such as Iran-Contra confirm, too much personal power encourages presidents to abuse their authority. Remember that our constitutional rules give Congress and the courts the ability to check presidential power. Less formal rules also constrain the presidency and keep it in check. These rules spring from the expectations of people and forces external to the presidency.

External Influences—The Expectations of Others

We have reviewed the effects of internal factors, such as styles of presidential management and conceptions of staff roles, on the power and workings of the presidency. The last factor that influences the power and workings of the presidency is the expectations of outside political actors. When these expectations are so ingrained that new presidents and presidential staffs instinctively meet them, we can say that these expectations have been *institutionalized*—that is, they have become a part of the institution and are unlikely to change even when new presidents take office or when they hire new staffs. Institutionalized expectations, then, are essentially informal rules.

The importance of institutionalized expectations is seen in the widely accepted belief that presidents should propose legislation for Congress to consider and thereby set the nation's political agenda. As we previously discussed, this expectation dates back to the aggressive legislative agenda FDR put forward to combat the Great Depression. Since FDR, presidents with limited legislative agendas have paid a heavy price in the form of criticism from Congress, the news media, and the public. For example, Eisenhower took office in 1953 without a specific legislative agenda in mind. When it became clear he had few legislative proposals to submit to Congress, even his fellow Republicans joined in the chorus of criticism. Within a year, Eisenhower had generated an agenda of proposals for Congress to consider.[73] Likewise, the elder Bush was criticized during his bid for reelection in 1992 for having offered Congress and the American public little in the way of a domestic legislative agenda.

A second example of how external expectations become institutionalized, and thereby constrain presidential behavior, can be found in the president's annual State of the Union message. The Constitution requires the president "from time to time to give to the Congress Information of the State of the Union," but it does not stipulate how the president is to deliver the message. Every president from Jefferson through Taft presented the State of the Union message to Congress in the form of a letter. Wilson, however, revived the practice of Washington and John Adams and delivered the State of the Union address in a speech before a joint session of Congress. The practice of delivering the State of the Union address in a speech to Congress is now so ingrained that it is unthinkable that a president would return to the practice of delivering it in a letter.[74] Indeed, Congress, the media, interest groups, and the public now expect the president to use the State of the Union speech to spell out a vision for the country's future.

As the examples of presidential proposals to Congress and speeches on the State of the Union show, institutionalized expectations constrain the discretion of the presidency. The expectations of Congress, the news media, and the public all impose political accountability on the White House and direct the president's efforts toward some activities and away from others. Without institutionalized expectations and the criticisms that arise when they are violated, fewer checks would limit the power of the presidency and presidents would have greater opportunity, as the Founders feared, to abuse their power.

As you can see, then, the workings of the presidency have become increasingly complex as the presidency has grown in size, structure, and power. Within this more complex environment, presidents still try to use the factors they can control—such as defining the functions of an agency, establishing a management style, and influencing the role that staff members play—to enhance their power. At the same time, factors outside the presidents' control—such as the expectations and unwritten rules created by others in the American political system—curb their power and help prevent presidents and their staffs from abusing it. Over time, there is a constant push and pull as presidents push for power, and other political actors rein presidential power back in.

12-3d Assessing the Presidency as an Institution

Just as changes in the rules governing the presidential selection process have increased the power and personal nature of the presidency, changes in the institution of the presidency have also tended to make the modern presidency a more individualized and influential office.

For the most part, the changes that have taken place in the presidency as an institution have increased the power of the president. By adopting the Stewardship Model of presidential authority and boldly acting in ways not expressly prohibited by the Constitution or statutory law, modern presidents have increased their power. The organizational structure of the presidency has become much larger and more complex, and as a result, presidents have had more staff to help them pursue their goals. Finally, the workings of the presidency reflect a more powerful and personalized modern institution. Because modern presidents have loyal staffs to help them win support and advance their more aggressive personal and policy goals, they are more likely to achieve these goals.

Still, despite the empowerment of the modern presidency, several forces constrain presidential power, including constitutional rules, statutory laws, the courts, and informal rules embodied in the expectations of the public and other political actors. Although modern presidents reach—and sometimes overreach—for power, and the flexible rules of the American political system allow them to do so, the rules also work to rectify past abuses of presidential power and to prevent future abuses.

The office of the presidency, then, is a dynamic, continually changing institution, marked by a tension between empowerment and constraint. Although the office of the presidency has gained influence over the past 200 years and especially since FDR's administration, the balance of power is by no means set in stone. Each new president has the opportunity to test the limits of presidential authority, just as other political actors are free to challenge the president's authority. Because presidents do not operate in a vacuum but must instead deal with other government officials, interest groups, and the broader public, we need to look at the place the presidency occupies within the American political system.

12-4 THE PRESIDENCY IN AMERICAN POLITICS

Thus far in our discussion of the presidency, we have focused on the office of the presidency itself. Now that we have seen how the presidency has evolved, how the rules of the presidential selection process have changed, and how rules and circumstances have changed the institution of the presidency, let's draw back and examine the presidency against the broader background of the rest of the American political system. We can see how the modern presidency fits into the larger political system by focusing on the political context within which presidents operate, the strategies they use to achieve their goals, and their relations with other political actors.

12-4a The Political Context: Permanent Crisis

Modern presidents operate within a political context that has been called a "permanent crisis."[75] As the presidency has gained power and prominence since FDR's administration, the American public has come to look to the president to address pressing national problems, and it expects the president to produce quick, effective, and even painless solutions. At the same time, presidents face constraints that make it difficult to find and implement solutions. Not only might Congress and the American public balk at following the president's lead, but time and institutional constraints also frequently hamper presidential efforts to address national problems.

Conflicting Expectations of Leadership: Initiative and Responsiveness

One of the most important developments of the modern era has been the emergence of the presidency as the primary focus of American society's expectations for leadership. Whenever a problem claims the country's attention, we expect the president to find a solution. Congress, the federal bureaucracy, interest groups, and the public all look to the president to set the course for the nation.

Although Americans look to the White House for leadership, we are by no means obligated to follow the president's lead. Indeed, one of the most serious obstacles presidents face is that people urge them to lead but often refuse to follow. Although we want presidents to produce bold and timely initiatives, we also expect them to protect our interests when devising solutions to the nation's problems. For example, when Clinton took office, a majority of the public believed that the nation's health-care system was in crisis—costs were skyrocketing, and millions of Americans had no health insurance. Many on Capitol Hill and elsewhere urged the president to find a solution. The president made health-care reform the centerpiece of his legislative agenda, and he placed the first lady in charge of developing a reform proposal. After the president made his proposal public, however, dozens of groups attacked it and members of Congress offered competing plans. Despite the administration's intensive efforts, Congress refused to pass his health-care proposal.[76] As Clinton's experience shows, presidents at times find it quite difficult to meet the conflicting expectations others place on them.

Time Constraints

Not only must presidents address a host of important issues, but they must also do so within a relatively brief period of time. Presidents cannot afford the luxury of making long-term plans. Rather, they must move quickly to generate concrete results that meet the expectations of Congress, the bureaucracy, interest groups, and most importantly, the American voters. This combination of insistent demands and limited time creates the sense of permanent crisis in the White House.

Modern presidents want to hit the ground running when they first enter office.[77] They usually (but not always) enjoy a "honeymoon" period for the first several months of their term as Congress, the press, and the public defer somewhat to their leadership. Yet after the first **One Hundred Days**—a benchmark chosen largely because at that point in FDR's first term Congress had passed a substantial portion of his New Deal legislation—presidents typically find Congress, journalists, and the public judging their presidency. As presidents enter their second year in office, they face even greater pressure to enact their legislative program. The reason is that the president's party usually loses seats in Congress in the midterm elections—an average in the modern era of twenty-four in the House and one and a half in the Senate—and as a result, Congress generally becomes even less willing to follow

One Hundred Days

A benchmark period for assessing a new president's performance, based on the first three months of Franklin Roosevelt's presidency, when he gained passage of more than a dozen major bills as part of his New Deal agenda.

the president's lead. The year 2002 was the exception to the rule. It was the first midterm election since FDR's presidency in which a first-term president's party gained seats in the House of Representatives and the only time a president's party gained control of the Senate. By the fourth year of a president's first term, both the president and Congress are looking to the next election, further diminishing their incentives to cooperate. Should a president be reelected, the fifth and sixth years may provide an echo of the opportunities of the first two. For example, in 2005, the first year of his second term, President Bush tried but failed to reform the Social Security system. He then spent much of 2006 persuading Congress to make permanent the tax cuts that it enacted in 2003. The last two years of a president's second term are usually spent as a "**lame duck**," defending past achievements from the attacks of Congress while the political system begins to anticipate the selection of a new president. In short, even when presidents succeed in serving for eight years, the political winds are often unfavorable much of the time.[78]

lame duck
An officeholder whose political power is weakened because his or her term is coming to an end.

Institutional Constraints

Presidents contending with the public's demands for action and the limits that time imposes must also contend with the institutional constraints the Constitution imposes. Although we have emphasized throughout this chapter the gradually growing scope of presidential authority, we must always view this power against the larger backdrop of our constitutional rules. Only in certain limited circumstances can presidents act independently to accomplish their aims. Our system of shared powers means that presidents must gain the cooperation of others—Congress, the bureaucracy, and interest groups—if they are to succeed in translating their vision of good public policy into reality.

Cooperation is often not forthcoming because presidents frequently have goals and perspectives different from those of members of Congress, bureaucrats, and interest groups. Presidents possess a uniquely national orientation. Their national electoral constituency forces them to address problems from a national perspective. In contrast, each member of Congress sees problems in terms of their impact on his or her local constituency; agencies see issues through the prism of their particular mission; and interest groups advocate their specific needs and wishes without regard to national agendas. For example, President Bush's domestic agenda for 2005 included immigration reform proposals that would benefit the national economy by making it easier for undocumented workers to obtain "guest worker" status. Congressional Republicans, worried about the growing presence of illegal immigrants within their particular states and districts, resisted those proposals.[79] Only presidents must contend with the wide range of issues seeking space in the set of national priorities. To meet the demands placed on them as a national leader confronted by these many constraints, modern presidents have developed strategies for advancing their political agendas.

12-4b Presidential Strategies

Scholars have identified two strategies that presidents use in their efforts to provide national leadership: bargaining and going public.

The Bargaining Strategy

Presidents try to influence other political actors by bargaining for their support. To make this **bargaining strategy** effective, presidents must be good negotiators skilled at interpersonal relations and able to construct supportive coalitions with leaders in Congress, the federal bureaucracy, and interest groups. A president who can persuade political actors with conflicting aims and desires to support his or her programs is more likely to succeed than one who cannot. Often, part of the persuasive process means promising groups some benefit or favor in return for their support, or threatening to use presidential powers (such as the veto power) if they try to pass legislation the administration opposes.[80]

Presidents are more likely to succeed in their bargaining strategy when they possess a reputation for being an effective leader. Presidents acquire such a reputation when their past behavior instills confidence among their supporters and fear among their opponents. Congress, the bureaucracy, interest groups, and the public are much more likely to follow the lead of a president with a string of policy successes than the lead of a president with a string of policy failures. Put another way, success tends to breed success for the White House. Presidents are also helped in their bargaining when they are personally popular with the public because popular support enhances the legitimacy of their claim to national leadership.[81] Presidents can use high public approval ratings to argue that they have the public's confidence and support, and thus, that Congress should follow their lead.

bargaining strategy
Direct negotiations the White House conducts with other political actors, such as members of Congress and leaders of interest groups, that attempt to reach mutually beneficial agreements.

The Going Public Strategy

As we saw in previous chapters, by the 1970s, congressional authority had become fragmented among dozens of subcommittees and the number of interest groups had exploded. Because these changes made it harder to build coalitions to support legislation, presidents have begun to try to win support for their policies by using a **going public strategy**—that is, by appealing directly to the American people.[82] Of special importance to the going public strategy is mass communications technology. To build support for their policies, presidents frequently give televised addresses to the nation, hold news conferences, or grant interviews to journalists. Presidents also pursue the going public strategy by traveling around the country giving speeches to major organizations and by meeting with representatives of groups the policies in question are likely to affect. Figure 12–5 describes the trend toward an increased number of presidential public appearances. By going public, presidents hope to mobilize public support, which in turn will put pressure on Congress to pass their proposals.

going public strategy
Direct presidential appeals to the public for support. Presidents use public support to pressure other political actors to accept their policies.

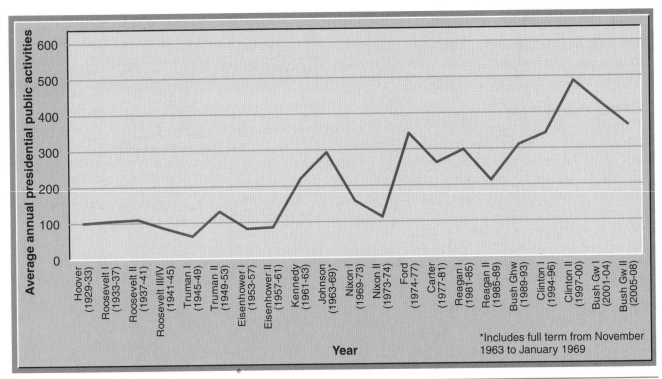

Figure 12–5   Annual Average Presidential Public Activities, by Term, 1929–2008. Presidents have increasingly turned
to the public to support their agendas. As a result, the number of presidential public appearances has
grown through the era of the modern presidency.

Source: Congressional Quarterly by Lyn Ragsdale. Copyright 1998 by Congressional Quarterly, Inc. Reproduced with permission of Congressional Quarterly,
Inc. via Copyright Clearance Center. 1998–2006: The Gallup Organization.

Of course, presidents may combine the bargaining and going
public strategies, appealing to the public for support while bargaining with key leaders in Congress and among interest groups.
Reagan, for example, relied heavily on public support to build momentum for his program of tax and budget cuts in 1981, but he also
bargained with members of Congress to build majorities in both
houses.[83] The younger Bush also combined the bargaining and
going public strategies in his effort to persuade Congress to enact
tax cuts in 2003. Bush visited the home states of key senators to
mobilize their constituents to generate pressure on those senators
to support his tax cuts. At the same time, he and his aides negotiated with Senate leaders to write a compromise version of the bill.

12-4c Presidential Relationships

Presidents work with many groups both in and out of government
to achieve their goals. To achieve their goals and retain their stature as national leaders, presidents must maintain good relations
with Congress, the American public, and the bureaucracy.

Presidents and Congress
As we discussed previously, modern presidents are expected to
play the role of chief legislator by presenting a package of legislative proposals to Congress. This power to propose legislation is

one of the presidency's most important powers because it helps presidents set Congress's legislative agenda. Presidents use both bargaining and going public strategies to form coalitions and win congressional support. Whether Congress enacts a president's proposals, however, depends heavily on the relationship between the president and Congress.

The most important influence on a president's relationship with Congress is whether the president's party is the majority party in Congress. This is important for two reasons. First, as we saw in Chapter 11, members of Congress are more likely to vote with members of their own party and against members of the opposition party. Even though presidents cannot count on total party loyalty, when the president's party is the majority party, the president's legislative agenda is more likely to win congressional support.[84] Second, when the president's party is the majority party in Congress, it controls the legislative process. As we also saw in Chapter 11, control of the legislative process gives the majority party a decided advantage in passing the legislation it favors. In contrast, when **divided government** exists—that is, when the opposition party controls at least one house of Congress—presidential proposals are much less likely to make their way through Congress. In addition, presidents faced with divided government must spend more of their time opposing the agenda of the opposition party, usually a difficult and time-consuming task.[85]

The contrast between Clinton's first two years in office, during which he worked with a Democratic majority in Congress, and his second two years, when he confronted a Republican majority, illustrates why presidents prefer to avoid divided government. Although Clinton lost his bid to revamp the nation's health-care system, he still recommended and Congress enacted a wide range of bills during his first two years in office. By early 1995, however, he was nearly a forgotten man as Speaker of the House Gingrich and the new Republican majority in Congress took center stage. Even though Clinton subsequently assumed greater prominence by vetoing Republican legislation and forcing congressional Republicans to negotiate with him, he clearly lost the aura of leadership and initiative that marked his first two years. The younger Bush was particularly weakened during his last two years in office, when he found himself simultaneously a lame duck and operating in a divided government.

Although members of Congress frequently criticize and oppose presidential proposals, most presidents still secure passage of a substantial portion of their agenda.[86] We cannot assess with certainty how much influence presidents exert on the legislative process on Capitol Hill, but no one doubts that every president will continue to act as a key agenda setter and chief lobbyist for bills sent to Congress.

divided government
The type of government experienced when the president is of one party and the other party has a majority in at least one house of Congress.

Presidents and the Public

Because the public eye has focused increasingly on the president as national leader since FDR's administration, presidents must develop good relations with the public. Advances in modern mass

Source: © Chip Somodevilla/Getty Images.

Presidents must communicate and negotiate with the leaders of Congress to fulfill their role in the legislative process.

communications have enabled today's presidents to appeal directly to the public, and presidents regularly use their ready access to the news media to try to shape the public's interpretation of important events.[87] Presidents also have created elaborate structures within the office of the presidency to help them deal with the public. All presidents now employ public opinion polling experts to recognize and interpret the public's views, and they also employ speech writers and media consultants to help them cultivate the proper image with the public.[88]

Despite concerted efforts to maintain popularity with the American public, Figure 12–6 shows that most presidents experience declining popularity over the course of their four-year terms. Two factors help contribute to this pattern of decline. First, presidents begin their terms with an exaggerated sense of public support. The public, including many who voted for the other candidate, rallies around a new president, giving the president the benefit of the doubt and hoping for the best. This behavior contributes to the honeymoon effect described previously and quickly disappears when the president begins to act on the promises made during the campaign. A second reason for decline is an "expectations gap" that develops as the president's term proceeds.[89] During the campaign, candidates overpromise to attract votes. Once in office, the winners decide that they either should not or cannot deliver on their promises, and so they fail to meet the expectations of those who supported them. President Clinton, for instance, promised during the 1992 campaign to end a blockade that prevented Haitian refugees from entering the United States. When he was in office, he decided he had been in error and continued the blockade.[90] Clinton was also unable to end the ban on gays in the military or reform health care as he had promised to do during the 1992 campaign.[91]

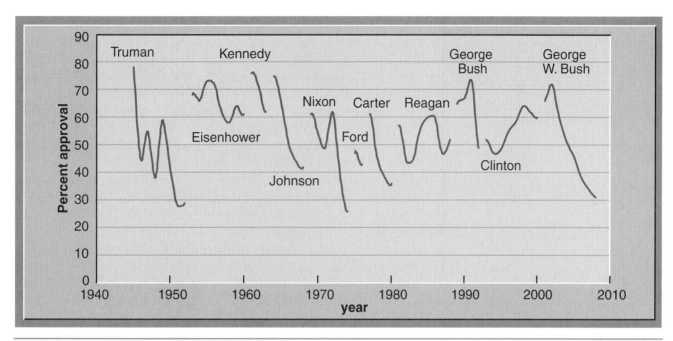

Figure 12-6 Annual Average Presidential Approval Rating, 1945–2008. Most presidents experience declining levels of public approval over the course of their term due to artificially high initial levels of support and high public expectations that most presidents fail to fulfill. This gives presidents an incentive to accomplish their goals early in their terms.

Source: *The Gallup Organization, available at http://www.gallup.com/poll/116677/Presidential-Approval-Ratings-Gallup-Historical-Statistics-Trends.aspx.*

Important events, especially those that provoke concerns about the nation's security, can lead the public to believe there is a national crisis, which often disrupts this pattern. Whenever events create the perception of a national crisis, presidential approval tends to rise. This "rally effect" occurs regardless of the president's behavior. For example, even though President Kennedy set into motion the failed Bay of Pigs invasion of Cuba, his public approval ratings following the failure increased. In Figure 12–6, the increases in public support for the elder President Bush between 1989 and 1991 and for the younger President Bush between 2001 and 2002 are due largely to the public rallying to the presidents' support in response to the Gulf War and the terrorist attacks on September 11, 2001, respectively.

Presidents care so much about their public image because, as we have seen, greater popularity often means greater influence on Capitol Hill. To be sure, popularity does not guarantee that presidents will get their way in Congress.[92] For example, even though Bush was quite popular following the war in Iraq, he could not persuade Congress to enact his $720 billion tax cut proposal. Although public popularity does not always translate into political power, presidents who have little public support lose much of their ability to lead Congress, the federal bureaucracy, and the American people.

Presidents and the Federal Bureaucracy

Presidents must not only cultivate good relations with Congress and the public, they must also persuade the federal bureaucracy to support and implement their programs. Although we often think of the president as the "head" or director of the federal bureaucracy, in reality, the president cannot command the obedience of agencies in the executive branch. As we shall discuss at greater length in Chapter 13, presidents must share their authority over the federal bureaucracy with Congress and the courts. As a result, presidents must bargain with and persuade agencies to do their bidding, all the while competing with the conflicting demands Congress, the courts, and interest groups place on the bureaucracy.

Presidents use a number of resources to influence the behavior of the federal bureaucracy.[93] First, presidents are responsible for appointing the heads of federal agencies, and they usually try to appoint people who share their political preferences. Second, presidents influence agencies through their budget-making power. Because presidents can recommend that Congress cut or increase spending for an agency, every agency has an incentive to heed the wishes of the White House. Third, presidents have some authority to reorganize the structures and duties of federal agencies. Finally, presidents can issue an **executive order** that directs a federal agency to take some specific action. Although Congress has the power to block each of these four moves, presidents usually can force a federal agency to obey their wishes if they are willing to devote time and effort to the issue.

In practice, however, presidents usually find that the overwhelming nature of their workload prevents them from concentrating their attention on a single federal agency for any sustained period of time. And as presidential interest in an agency wanes, that agency's responsiveness to presidential wishes erodes.[94] Moreover, when confronted with criticism that it has failed to comply with the preferences of the White House, a federal agency typically can blame its failure on its need to respond to political pressure from other political actors such as Congress and interest group clienteles. In short, presidents must compete for control of the federal bureaucracy.

As we have seen, then, modern presidents frequently cannot exercise their powers independently of the rest of government; all their actions take place in a political system characterized by shared powers and conflicting priorities. The expectations we place on modern presidents—to take bold initiatives but respond to our desires, to act quickly and decisively, and to work within the rules and boundaries laid down in the Constitution—create a permanent atmosphere of crisis. Presidents respond by adopting strategies that help them manage political conflict and meet the expectations of national leadership; they bargain with other actors in the political system, and they appeal to the public to mobilize support for their programs. To make these strategies effective, presidents must maintain positive relationships with Congress, the federal bureaucracy, and the public.

Thus, although changing rules and norms have empowered the presidency and brought the president prominence as a national leader, they have also limited the way presidents perform their

executive order

A presidential directive to an agency of the federal government that tells the agency to take some specified action.

roles. The ambivalence of the Founders is still present today; the presidency is shaped by rules that infuse it with power yet constrain its ability to act.

SUMMARY

The United States has a president because early Americans discovered through their experience with the Articles of Confederation that the federal government could not function well without one. Yet in recognizing the need for a president, the Founders worried about vesting too much power in any one individual or branch of government. As a result, the structural rules set forth in the Constitution try to balance the need for executive leadership with protections against tyranny. Thus, although the Constitution gives the president specific or enumerated powers to act, the Founders also checked the ability of presidents to act by sharing many of these powers with the other two branches of government.

Yet the president's role in American politics has been defined not only by the structural rules of the office, but also by the actions of the forty-one men who have served in the White House. In keeping with the expectations of the Founders, most eighteenth- and nineteenth-century presidents were fairly passive executives, reacting to Congress rather than leading it. All that changed when FDR assumed office in 1933. FDR established the modern presidency with his forceful national leadership during the Great Depression and World War II. All of FDR's successors have felt compelled to fill the role of national leader.

Just as the president's role in American politics has changed over the 200 years, so has the presidential selection process. Initially, the parties in Congress controlled the nomination stage, but by the 1830s, state parties had gained the upper hand and selected candidates at their national conventions. In the 1970s, the increased use of primaries diminished the parties' role, giving greater control to the candidates themselves and the people who voted in the primary elections. The general election process has also changed significantly. The rise of television has given candidates even more control over their campaigns, and campaign finance laws have failed to limit the growth in campaign spending. The one aspect of the presidential selection process that has not changed is the electoral college. As has been the case for two centuries, the use of the unit rule in the states and the use of majority rule in the electoral college determine how the outcome of the popular vote will translate into votes in the electoral college, and as a result, which candidate wins the presidency.

The institution of the presidency has also changed in three important ways since Washington was president. First, the powers of the presidency have grown. Because the Constitution defines the powers of the presidency in relatively vague terms, presidents have been able to interpret the rules in ways that expand their authority. Second, as the federal government has grown larger and more complex, the expectations for presidential leadership have grown as well and the institution of the presidency has evolved from a small, informal organization into the EOP, a larger, more formal organization employing some 1,500 people. Third, the way presidents work in office has changed. The growing size and complexity of the presidency has forced presidents into a more hierarchical, pyramidal style of management, and whereas presidents once expected staff members in the EOP to provide neutral competence, they now expect those staff members to work on behalf of their programs. Although these developments have tended to enhance presidential power, a rising tide of expectations about what presidents are supposed to accomplish has tended to constrain presidential power.

In discharging their responsibilities and attempting to fulfill the expectations of Congress and the public, presidents operate within a political context that has been described as permanent crisis. Because the presidency has gained power and prominence since the days of FDR, the American public now looks to the White House for answers to pressing national problems. The increase in presidential power and the public's high expectations for the president have not changed one fundamental structural reality about American politics: Presidents still share many of the powers of government with Congress, the bureaucracy, and the courts. Presidents can bargain with members of Congress and appeal directly to the public to support their programs, but they cannot compel obedience from Capitol Hill or even federal agencies. In the end, presidents often must rely on their powers of persuasion to accomplish their policy goals.

KEY TERMS

bandwagon effect

bargaining strategy

Bipartisan Campaign Reform Act (BCRA)

caucus

central legislative clearance

divided government

electoral college

enumerated powers

executive order

frontloading

going public strategy

impeachment

implied powers

independent expenditures

lame duck

neutral competence

One Hundred Days

pocket veto

presidential signing statements

Progressive movement

soft money

unit rule

winnowing effect

527 groups

READINGS FOR FURTHER STUDY

Howell, William G. *Power without Persuasion: The Politics of Direct Presidential Action* (Princeton, NJ: Princeton University Press, 2003). A thorough, systematic, yet readable analysis of the way presidents use executive orders to achieve their goals as an alternative to persuasion.

Kernell, Samuel. *Going Public: New Strategies of Presidential Leadership,* 3rd ed. (Washington, D.C.: CQ Press, 1997). The most authoritative revision of the Neustadt model of presidential influence. Kernell argues that presidents increasingly rely on public support rather than personal bargaining to achieve their goals in government.

Light, Paul C. *The President's Agenda: Domestic Policy Choice from Kennedy to Clinton,* 3rd ed. (Baltimore: The Johns Hopkins University Press, 1999). Light identifies the factors that affect how much presidents try to accomplish and how successful they will be in enacting domestic policy legislation.

Milkis, Sidney M., and Michael, Nelson. *The American Presidency: Origins and Development, 1776–2002,* 4th ed. (Washington, D.C.: CQ Press, 2003). A concise yet remarkably complete review of the historical development of the presidency from Washington to Clinton.

Neustadt, Richard. *Presidential Power and the Modern Presidents* (New York: Free Press, 1990). The definitive starting point for any discussion of the modern presidency. A must-read for any serious student of the institution.

Polsby, Nelson W., Aaron Wildavsky, and David A. Hopkins. *Presidential Elections,* 12th ed. (Rowman & Littlefield Publishers, 2007). The authoritative treatment of presidential elections in the modern era. It encompasses virtually every facet of elections and the way they have evolved over the past forty years.

Woodward, Robert. *Plan of Attack* (New York: Simon & Shuster, 2004). Woodward provides an insider's description of the decisions and events leading up to Bush's decision to attack Iraq in 2003.

Woodward, Robert. *State of Denial* (New York: Simon & Shuster, 2006). Woodward continues his insider's account of the Bush administration's attempts to secure democracy within Iraq.

REVIEW QUESTIONS

1. Which of the following constitutes an important change in the financing of presidential elections?
   a. Candidates in 2008 spent less than in 2004 because new communication technologies like the Internet reduced the costs of advertising.
   b. The Bipartisan Campaign Reform Act doubled the amount of money candidates receive from the federal government in exchange for not accepting private contributions during the primaries.

    c. The Bipartisan Campaign Reform Act eliminated "soft money" expenditures by the political parties.

    d. "Fat cats" have become more important to financing candidates' general election campaigns as public financing has diminished.

2. During his second term, President Clinton was
    a. impeached but not convicted.
    b. convicted but not censured.
    c. censured but not impeached.
    d. none of the above.

3. Which president established the era of the "modern presidency"?
    a. Theodore Roosevelt
    b. Woodrow Wilson
    c. Franklin D. Roosevelt
    d. John F. Kennedy

4. Who controlled the presidential nominating process from 1800 to 1824?
    a. the general public
    b. King Caucus
    c. party conventions
    d. the Progressives

5. The Progressives sought to
    a. reform the political process and reduce the influence of state party leaders.
    b. eliminate the use of primary elections.
    c. implement the spoils system.
    d. do away with voter registration.

6. Under the Constitution, what happens if no candidate receives a majority in the electoral college?
    a. The winner of the popular vote becomes president.
    b. The president is selected in the Senate.
    c. The president is selected in the House.
    d. The president is selected by the Supreme Court.

7. The stewardship model is associated with
    a. George Washington.
    b. Abraham Lincoln.
    c. Theodore Roosevelt.
    d. William Howard Taft.

8. Presidential staff remained small and informal until
    a. 1812.
    b. 1865.
    c. 1896.
    d. 1939.

9. The National Security Council includes the president,
    a. vice president, secretary of state, and secretary of defense.
    b. secretary of state, secretary of defense, and secretary of commerce.
    c. attorney general, director of the Central Intelligence Agency, and director of the Office of Management and Budget.
    d. vice president, secretary of treasury, and secretary of state.

10. Who is (are) the primary agenda setter(s) in the United States?
    a. congressional leaders
    b. lobbyists
    c. executive bureaucrats
    d. the president

NOTES

1. James L. Sundquist, *The Decline and Resurgence of Congress* (Washington, D.C.: Brookings Institution, 1981), chap. 2.

2. See David Gray Adler, "The Constitution and Presidential Warmaking," *Political Science Quarterly* 103 (Spring 1988): 8–13; Alexander Hamilton, "Federalist No. 69," in *The Federalist Papers*, ed. Garry Wills (New York: Bantam Books, 1982); Louis Henkin, *Foreign Affairs and the Constitution* (Mineola, NY: Foundation Press, 1972), 50–51; Arthur M. Schlesinger, Jr., *The Imperial Presidency* (Boston: Houghton Mifflin, 1989), 6, 61–2.

3. Some scholars argue that the president's personality is the single most important determinant of how a presidency works. See, for example, James D. Barber, *The Presidential Character: Predicting Performance in the White House*, 4th ed. (Englewood Cliffs, NJ: Prentice Hall, 1992).

4. Wilfred Binkley, *The Powers of the President* (Garden City, NY: Doubleday, Doran, 1937), chap. 2.

5. James Sterling Young, *The Washington Community 1800–1828* (New York: Harcourt, Brace & World, 1966), 160–80.

6. Leonard D. White, *The Jacksonians: A Study in Administrative History, 1829–1861* (New York: Macmillan, 1954), 22–25.

7. Binkley, *The Powers of the President*, 120–30.

8. George B. Galloway with Sidney Wise, *History of the House of Representatives*, 2nd ed. (New York: Crowell, 1976), 315–17.

9. Sidney M. Milkis and Michael Nelson, *The American Presidency: Origins and Development, 1776–1998*, 3rd ed. (Washington, D.C.: CQ Press, 1999), 234–35.

10. Fred Greenstein, "Change and Continuity in the Modern Presidency," in *The New American Political System*, ed. Anthony King (Washington, D.C.: American Enterprise Institute, 1978), 45–85; Nelson W. Polsby ed., *The Modern Presidency* (New York: Random House, 1973).

11. William E. Leuchtenburg, *Franklin D. Roosevelt and the New Deal* (New York: Harper & Row, 1963), chap. 3; Nelson W. Polsby, "Some Landmarks in Modern Presidential-Congressional Relations," in *Both Ends of the Avenue*, ed. Anthony King (Washington, D.C.: American Enterprise Institute, 1983).

12. Clinton Rossiter, *The American Presidency* (New York: Harcourt, Brace, 1960), chap. 1.

13. Austin Ranney, *Curing the Mischief of Faction* (Berkeley: University of California Press, 1975), 171–74.

14. Ibid., 68.

15. Ibid., 69.

16. Robert K. Murray, *The 103rd Ballot* (New York: Harper & Row, 1976).

17. Nelson W. Polsby, *Consequences of Party Reform* (New York: Oxford University Press, 1983), 9–16.

18. James Lengle and Byron Shafer, "Primary Rules, Political Power, and Social Change," *American Political Science Review* 70 (March 1976): 25–40.

19. Polsby, *Consequences of Party Reform*, 56.

20. Ibid., 53–54.

21. See the discussion in Nelson W. Polsby, "The Iowa Caucuses in a Front-Loaded System: A Few Historical Lessons," in *The Iowa Caucuses and the Presidential Nominating Process*, ed. Peverill Squire (Boulder, CO: Westview, 1989).

22. Dan Balz, "Democrats Head to S.C. for First Debate: Nine Presidential Hopefuls Try to Gain Visibility, Draw Distinctions in '04 Field," *Washington Post*, May 3, 2003, A5.

23. "OK, Phil, Take Off the Snowshoes," *National Journal*, April 10, 1993, 857;

24. "Don't Expect Many Postcards," *National Journal*, August 7, 1993, 1959.

25. Rod Boshart, "Emerging GOP Field Quietly Lays Groundwork for 2008," *The Cedar Rapids (IA) Gazette*, September 4, 2004.

26. Chris Cillizza, "Chris Dodd's White House Surprise," available at www.washingtonpost.com, May 23, 2006, and www.blog.washingtonpost.com/thefix/2006/05/chris_dodd_for_president.html; Chris Cillizza, "The Friday Line: Another Early Look at the 2008 Race," available at www.washingtonpost.com, May 5, 2006, and www.blog.washingtonpost.com/thefix/2006/05/the_friday_line_another_early.html.

27. Center for Responsive Politics, "Presidential Fundraising and Spending, 1976-2008," available at www.opensecrets.org/pres08/totals.php?cycle=2008.

28. Polsby, *Consequences of Party Reform*, 66.

29. Lester G. Seligman and Cary R. Covington, *The Coalitional Presidency* (Chicago: Dorsey Press, 1989), chap. 3.

30. Anthony Corrado, "Financing the 2000 Elections," in *The Election of 2000*, ed. Gerald M. Pomper (New York: Chatham House Publishers, 2001).

31. For a detailed discussion of FECA and its amendments, see Nelson W. Polsby and Aaron Wildavsky, *Presidential Elections: Strategies and Structures of American Politics*, 9th ed. (Chatham, NJ: Chatham House, 1996), chap. 3.

32. Federal Election Commission, "Presidential Spending Limits for 2008," available at www.fec.gov/pages/brochures/pubfund_limits_2008.shtml.

33. Information on fund-raising by all candidates for both the 2000 and 2004 nomination election cycles is presented by the Campaign Finance Institute at its Web site available at www.cfinst.org/pr/pdf/June_Table1.pdf.

34. Herbert E. Alexander and Anthony Corrado, *Financing the 1992 Election* (Armonk, NY: Sharpe, 1995), 244; Stephen J. Wayne, *The Road to the White House 1996*, (New York: St. Martin's Press, 1997), 51; Herbert E. Alexander, "Spending in the 1996 Elections," in *Financing the 1996 Election*, ed. John C. Green (Armonk, NY: M. E. Sharpe, 1999), 22; Stephen J. Wayne, *The Quest for the 2004 Nomination and Beyond* (Belmont, CA: Thomson Wadsworth, 2005), 10.

35. Kathleen Hall Jamieson, *Dirty Politics* (New York: Oxford University Press, 1992), 17–25.

36. Alexander and Corrado, *Financing the 1992 Election*, 110; Alexander, "Spending in the 1996 Elections," 22.

37. Corrado, "Financing the 2000 Elections," 119.

38. An excellent summary and analysis of BCRA can be found at the Campaign Finance Institute's Web site available at www.cfinst.org/eguide/index.html; Thomas B. Edsall and James V. Grimaldi, "New Routes for Money to Sway Voters: 501c Groups Escape Disclosure Rules," *Washington Post*, September 29, 2004, A1.

39. Thomas B. Edsall, "FEC Adopts Hands-Off Stance on '527' Spending," *Washington Post*, June 1, 2006, A4; Steven Weissman and Margaret Sammon, "CFI Analysis: Fast Start for Soft Money Groups in 2008 Election," April 3, 2008 (Washington D.C.: The Campaign Finance Institute).

40. Martin Wattenberg, *The Rise of Candidate-Centered Politics: Presidential Elections of the 1980s* (Cambridge, MA: Harvard University Press, 1991).

41. Wayne, *The Road to the White House 1996*, 193.

42. For an excellent discussion of the details and "what ifs" that enshroud the electoral college, see Walter Berns ed., *After the People Vote: A Guide to the Electoral College*, rev. ed. (Washington, D.C.: American Enterprise Institute, 1992).

43. Norman J. Ornstein, "Three Disputed Elections," in *After the People Vote: A Guide to the Electoral College*, rev. ed., ed. Walter Berns (Washington, D.C.: American Enterprise Institute, 1992).

44. Michael L. Goldstein, *Guide to the 1996 Presidential Election*, (Washington, D.C.: CQ Press, 1995), 74.

45. "Table 6-9 Presidential Vetoes, 1789–2006, and Signing Statements, 1929–2006," CQ Electronic Library, CQ's Vital Statistics on American Politics Online Edition, vsap07_tab6-9, www.library.cqpress.com/vsap/document.php?id=vsap07_tab6-9&type=toc&num=10.

46. Louis Fisher, *Constitutional Conflicts Between Congress and the President*, 3rd ed. (Lawrence: University of Kansas Press, 1991), 86, 93.

47. Louis Fisher, *Presidential Spending Power* (Princeton, NJ: Princeton University Press, 1975), 107.

48. Robert Pear, "Bush Orders Quicker Expenditure of $9.7 Billion to Aid Economy," *New York Times*, December 6, 1991.

49. Quoted in Louis Fisher, *President and Congress* (Princeton, NJ: Princeton University Press, 1972), 36.

50. See Fisher, *Constitutional Conflicts Between Congress and the President*, chap. 2–3.

51. *Myers v. United States*, 272 U.S. 52 (1926); *Humphrey's Executor v. United States*, 295 U.S. 602 (1935).

52. Scott Shane, "Behind Power, One Principle as Bush Pushes Prerogatives," *The New York Times*, December 17, 2005, A1.

53. Peter Baker and Jim VandeHei, "Clash is Latest Chapter in Bush Effort to Widen Executive Power," *Washington Post*, December 21, 2005, A1; David Von Drehle, "Executive Branch Reined In," *Washington Post*, June 29, 2004, A1.

54. Christopher S. Kelley, "The Significance of the Presidential Signing Statement," in *Executing the Constitution: Putting the President Back into the Constitution*, ed. Christopher S. Kelley (Albany: State University of New York Press, 2006).

55. U.S. Department of Justice, "Legal Authorities Supporting the Activities of the National Security Agency Described by the President," January 19, 2006, 1.

56. Schlesinger, *Imperial Presidency*, esp. chap. 5–8.

57. John Hart, *The Presidential Branch* (New York: Pergamon Press, 1987), chap. 2.

58. U.S. Congress, Committee on Post Office and Civil Service, "Presidential Staffing—A Brief Overview," (Washington, D.C.: U.S. Government Printing Office, 1978); Harold W. Stanley and Richard G. Niemi, *Vital Statistics on American Politics*, 2003–2004 (Washington, D.C.: CQ Press, 2003), 254–55.

59. Leuchtenburg, *Franklin D. Roosevelt and the New Deal*, 192.

60. Jimmy Carter, *Keeping Faith: Memoirs of a President* (New York: Bantam Books, 1983), 32–33.

61. Kenneth T. Walsh and Bruce B. Auster, "Taking the Offensive," *U.S. News & World Report*, January 29, 1996, 34.

62. Quoted in Paul C. Light, *Vice Presidential Power: Advice and Influence in the White House* (Baltimore: Johns Hopkins University Press, 1984), 13. For a review of some of the most amusing disparagements of the vice presidency, see Paul F. Boller, Jr., *Congressional Anecdotes* (New York: Oxford University Press, 1991), 223–29.

63. Quoted in Milkis and Nelson, *The American Presidency*, 407. Milkis and Nelson observe that Garner actually referred to "a bodily fluid other than spit" (420).

64. Matthew Cooper and Sander Thoenes, "Leave It to Al and Victor," *U.S. News & World Report*, June 26, 1995, 43; Donald G. McNeil, Jr., "Gore Visit Signals New Status for Pretoria," *New York Times*, December 4, 1995.

65. Paul Brace and Barbara Hinckley, *Follow the Leader: Opinion Polls and the Modern Presidents* (New York: Basic Books, 1992).

66. James M. Perry, "Clinton Relies Heavily on White House Pollster to Take Words Right Out of the Public's Mouth," *Wall Street Journal*, March 23, 1994.

67. Alexander George, *Presidential Decision making in Foreign Policy: The Effective Use of Information and Advice* (Boulder, CO: Westview, 1980); Richard T. Johnson, "Presidential Style," in *Perspectives on the Presidency*, ed. Aaron Wildavsky (Boston: Little, Brown, 1975).

68. George E. Reedy, *The Twilight of the Presidency* (New York: World Publishing, 1970).

69. Hugh Heclo, "OMB and the Presidency: The Problem of 'Neutral Competence,'" *Public Interest* 38 (Winter 1975): 80–98.

70. Larry Berman, *The Office of Management and Budget and the Presidency, 1921–1979* (Princeton, NJ: Princeton University Press, 1979).

71. William Greider, "The Education of David Stockman," *Atlantic Monthly*, December 1981, 32.

72. Terry M. Moe, "The Politicized Presidency," in *The New Direction in American Politics*, ed. John E. Chubb and Paul E. Peterson (Washington, D.C.: Brookings Institution, 1985).

73. Richard E. Neustadt, "Presidency and Legislation: Planning the President's Program," *American Political Science Review* 49 (December 1955): 980–1021; Richard E. Neustadt, "Presidency and Legislation: The Growth of Central Clearance," *American Political Science Review* 48 (September 1954): 641–71.

74. Jeffrey K. Tulis, *The Rhetorical Presidency* (Princeton, NJ: Princeton University Press, 1987), chap. 5.

75. Richard E. Neustadt, "The Presidency at Mid-century," in *The Presidency*, ed. Aaron Wildavsky (Boston: Little, Brown, 1969), 199.

76. David Stoesz, *Small Change: Domestic Policy under the Clinton Presidency* (White Plains, NY: Longman, 1996), chap. 2.

77. See James P. Pfiffner, *The Strategic Presidency: Hitting the Ground Running* (Chicago: Dorsey Press, 1988).

78. Stephen Hess, *Organizing the Presidency*, 2nd ed. (Washington, D.C.: Brookings Institution, 1988).

79. Jim VandeHei and Charles Babington, "More Aggressive Congress Could Hinder Bush's Plans," *The Washington Post*, December 20, 2004, A04.

80. Richard E. Neustadt, *Presidential Power and the Modern President* (New York: Free Press, 1990), chap. 3.

81. Tulis, *The Rhetorical Presidency*, chap. 5.

82. Samuel Kernell, *Going Public: New Strategies of Presidential Leadership*, 2nd. ed. (Washington, D.C.: CQ Press, 1992).

83. Barbara Kellerman, *The Political Presidency: Practice of Leadership from Kennedy through Reagan* (New York: Oxford University Press, 1984); Kernell, *Going Public*, chap. 5.

84. Jon R. Bond and Richard Fleisher, *The President in the Legislative Arena* (Chicago: University of Chicago Press, 1990).

85. Cary R. Covington, J. Mark Wrighton, and Rhonda Kinney, "A 'Presidency-Augmented' Model of Presidential Success on House Roll Call Votes," *American Journal of Political Science* 39 (November 1995): 1001–24.

86. Mark A. Peterson, *Legislating Together: The White House and Capitol Hill from Eisenhower to Reagan* (Cambridge, MA: Harvard University Press, 1990).

87. John A. Maltese, *Spin Control: The White House Office of Communications and the Management of Presidential News* (Chapel Hill: University of North Carolina Press, 1992).

88. Lyn Ragsdale, "The Politics of Presidential Speechmaking, 1949–1980," *American Political Science Review* 78 (December 1984): 971–84.

89. See Richard W. Waterman ed., *The Presidency Reconsidered* (Itasca, IL: F. E. Peacock, 1993).

90. Jennifer S. Thomas, "A Haitian Chronology," *Congressional Quarterly Weekly Report*, October 23, 1993, 2898.

91. Christine C. Lawrence, "Ban on Homosexuals to End in Two Steps, Frank Says," *Congressional Quarterly Weekly Report*, January 23, 1993, 187.

92. Bond and Fleisher, *The President in the Legislative Arena*, chap. 7.

93. See Robert Maranto, *Politics and Bureaucracy in the Modern Presidency* (Westport, CT: Greenwood, 1993); Richard W. Waterman, *Presidential Influence and the Administrative State* (Knoxville: University of Tennessee Press, 1989).

94. Ronald Randall, "Presidential Power versus Bureaucratic Intransigence: The Influence of the Nixon Administration on Welfare Policy," *American Political Science Review* 73 (September 1979): 795–810; B. Dan Wood, "Principals, Bureaucrats, and Responsiveness in Clean Air Enforcements," *American Political Science Review* 82 (March 1988): 213–34.

13

The Federal Bureaucracy

CHAPTER OUTLINE

Since the 1960s, the Food and Drug Administration (FDA) has required pharmaceutical companies to demonstrate both the safety and effectiveness of any new drug before doctors can prescribe it. The agency walks a fine line between being too cautious and keeping beneficial drugs off the market and being too aggressive and allowing dangerous drugs to slip through the approval process. During the 1960s and 1970s, the public preferred that the FDA "go slow." It would rather the FDA make sure drugs are safe and effective than have unsafe or ineffective drugs make it through the system undetected.[1] As a result, drug testing usually took several years to complete.

In the 1980s, the FDA faced political pressure to speed up its testing procedures. As acquired immunodeficiency syndrome (AIDS) became a health crisis, interest groups representing people with AIDS claimed that the FDA was depriving patients of the potentially beneficial, even lifesaving, effects of many drugs still in the testing process. Ronald Reagan and Republicans in Congress had pledged to reduce government regulation of industry, so they encouraged the FDA to streamline its regulatory process. Finally, the pharmaceutical industry joined the fray, seeking to get new drugs to market faster so they could start generating revenues sooner.[2]

The FDA initially resisted pressure to speed up the drug approval process, but in the end, it gave patients with life-threatening diseases greater access to experimental drugs and dramatically shortened the time required to test new drugs. Consequently, the length of time required to test drugs plummeted. In 1987, testing the average new drug took almost three years. By 1992, that average had fallen to nineteen months. In 1992, the pharmaceutical industry offered to give the FDA millions of dollars if the agency agreed to spend a specified level of those funds on processing new drug approvals. The government accepted the offer, enacting the Prescription Drug User Fee Act (PDUFA). As private funding flowed into the FDA, public funding ebbed, and the agency's efforts to ensure that approved drugs were in fact safe suffered the largest budget cuts. A new set of expectations and budgetary priorities had emerged, and the FDA responded with a change in its rules and its culture. Drugs began to be approved following shorter and more streamlined procedures, and fewer efforts were made to ensure the safety of approved drugs. At least five FDA safety reviewers who recommended against the approval of new drugs were punished or discouraged from making that recommendation. As a result, by 2003, the average approval time fell to fourteen months, and the average approval time for "priority" drugs fell to only six months.[3]

In the late 1990s, people began to wonder whether the FDA had gone too far and was failing to protect the public from unsafe drugs. In 1997, a new diabetes pill, Rezulin, was approved for sale. By 2000, it was suspected as a cause in sixty-three deaths. The clinical tests had not been sufficiently extensive to uncover the degree of risk to patients, and its manufacturer pulled it from the market.[4] Even greater problems in the FDA's monitoring of approved drugs were acknowledged in 2004, when it removed Vioxx, a drug previously deemed safe and effective for the treatment of arthritis, because it doubled patients' risks of heart attacks. Studies showed that a more rigorous analysis of risks should have led to a decision to remove Vioxx three years previous, in 2001.[5] As medical and consumer rights communities increased their demands for a return to a more cautious drug approval regimen, the FDA again adjusted its procedures. Now, the FDA has created a program for evaluating the safety of new drugs eighteen months after their introduction. The FDA also permits its own drug reviewers to slow down the drug approval process, which has already begun to generate criticism for its effects on the profitability of the pharmaceuticals industry.[6]

In our study of political institutions, we have repeatedly made the point that institutions both shape and are shaped by the rules of American politics. As the FDA's inability to satisfy all the competing interests over the testing of experimental drugs demonstrates, the federal **bureaucracy** is no exception. The FDA's experience highlights three important lessons about the place of the federal bureaucracy in American politics. The first is that the bureaucracy helps shape the nation's policy rules, and those rules have biases. Federal agencies administer government policy, and their decisions greatly affect our lives. For example, when the FDA took a cautious approach to drug testing, it denied the public potentially helpful treatments. When the FDA sped up its drug testing procedures, however, it may have exposed citizens to potentially dangerous drugs. The stakes in this situation are unusually high, but the central role that agencies' rules play in the lives of Americans is common. Most of the direct contact Americans have with the federal government is with the bureaucracy rather than Congress or the president. When Americans mail their income tax returns to the Internal Revenue Service, receive a check from the Social Security Administration (SSA), or visit a national park maintained by the National Park Service, they are dealing with federal agencies, and they are affected by the policy rules those agencies create.

If the FDA's experience reminds us that the federal bureaucracy helps determine the rules that affect our everyday lives, it also teaches us a second lesson about the bureaucracy: The rules of American politics affect the bureaucracy. In our system, the president, Congress, the courts, interest groups, and the public all possess political power. Because the rules empower citizens to protest, interest groups to lobby, and the president and Congress to set new rules, the FDA responded to the combined efforts of activists, presidents, members of Congress, and the pharmaceutical industry. The bureaucracy's powers are limited by the constitutional rules that disperse power among other groups. The FDA's change in drug testing policies, in turn, produced new pressures on the agency to further modify its rules.

By no means, however, is the bureaucracy simply a mindless tool in the hands of Congress, the president, or the courts. These other political actors may sketch the broad outlines of government

bureaucracy

In general usage, the set of government agencies that carries out government policies. The bureaucracy is characterized by formalized structures, specialized duties, a hierarchical system of authority, routine recordkeeping, and a permanent staff.

policy, but the bureaucracy fills in the details. And because it has the discretion to make and implement rules—to decide who wins or loses in conflicts over government policies and services—the bureaucracy possesses political power. This leads us to the third lesson the FDA example has to offer: The bureaucracy is a political institution. Political pressures—from AIDS activists, a president who pledges to cut bureaucratic red tape, an industry with a vested interest in reshaping an agency's priorities, and patients' rights groups—affect the bureaucracy, and the bureaucracy's actions affect the political environment. To understand the federal bureaucracy, then, it is crucial to understand its political nature.

We begin our study of the role of the federal bureaucracy in American politics by defining the characteristics that distinguish a bureaucracy from other forms of political organization. We go on to examine the structure and tasks of the federal bureaucracy, showing how the agencies in the federal bureaucracy make and implement rules. We then discuss the evolution of the bureaucracy—how changes in society and in the rules of government have shaped the size, functions, and hiring practices of the federal bureaucracy over the course of American history. Finally, we discuss the political character of the federal bureaucracy, focusing on its goals, its political resources, and the constraints others place on its power. We analyze some of the typical patterns of cooperation that develop among federal agencies, the congressional committees they report to, and the interest groups they affect.

We conclude the chapter by asking a question: Can we "reinvent" the federal bureaucracy to meet the demands of the twenty-first century? An increasingly diverse society presents government with an increasingly diverse—and often conflicting—list of demands. Whether the bureaucracy can successfully manage and respond to the growing expectations of the American public depends on the rules government sets for the bureaucracy and the bureaucracy's ability to shape effective new rules for the future.

13-1 WHAT IS BUREAUCRACY?

bureaucrats

A term used generally to identify people who work within a large, formal organization. More specifically, it refers to career civil service employees of the government.

Americans often have unkind things to say about government bureaucracy. They tend to see it as "overstaffed, inflexible, unresponsive, and power-hungry, all at once," and they see its employees, known as **bureaucrats**, as "lazy, snarling, or both."[7] Jokes about bureaucratic ineptitude are a staple on late-night television talk shows, as comedians such as Jay Leno and David Letterman draw huge laughs lampooning bureaucrats for such misadventures as taking fourteen pages to lay out the recipe for making fruitcake.[8] And Americans regularly complain that the federal bureaucracy wastes their tax dollars and drowns the country in a sea of bureaucratic red tape.[9]

Yet for all the jokes and complaints about bureaucratic ineptitude, bureaucracy is an inescapable part of modern government. The United States is simply too large and the issues too complex for Congress and the president to run the country themselves. They must create other agencies to administer the policy decisions they reach—to carry out the rules.

What precisely distinguishes a bureaucracy from other forms of political organization? The great German sociologist Max Weber (1864–1920) defined the ideal, or model, bureaucracy as an organization that possesses five distinctive characteristics:[10]

1. *Specialization*—The organization has a well-defined division of labor. Jobs are divided up and assigned to subsidiary groups within the organization that have expertise in that particular task.

2. *Hierarchy*—The organization has a clear chain of command in which workers are arranged in order of rank or authority.

3. *Formality*—The organization has a formal set of rules and procedures to ensure that it performs its duties in a consistent manner.

4. *Recordkeeping*—The organization retains written records of its decisions and actions.

5. *Professionalization*—The organization is staffed with full-time career workers who are paid a regular salary and hired and promoted on the basis of their competence.

The many agencies that make up the federal bureaucracy generally exhibit most of the characteristics Weber identified as typical of the ideal bureaucracy. Virtually all federal agencies are permanent organizations in which workers are assigned to different levels in the organizational hierarchy on the basis of the authority they wield. Almost all federal agencies follow well-developed rules and procedures in performing their specialized tasks, and they are required by law to keep detailed records of their actions. Finally, most federal employees today are permanent, career-oriented people who are, in principle, hired, compensated, and promoted on the basis of merit.

13-2 THE STRUCTURE AND TASKS OF THE FEDERAL BUREAUCRACY

Although the agencies that make up the federal bureaucracy generally share the five characteristic features that Weber identified with bureaucracy, they vary widely in terms of their organizational forms and duties. Some federal agencies are huge and actually are composed of hundreds of subsidiary agencies, bureaus, and offices; others are so small that they have few subunits. Whereas some federal agencies are responsible for national security matters, others deal with health, economic, or safety issues. Despite these differences, all federal agencies perform three general tasks: They administer the rules of public policy, develop new rules as the need arises, and determine when their rules have been broken or their procedures ignored.

EXECUTIVE DEPARTMENTS

State, Treasury, Defense, Justice, Interior, Agriculture, Commerce, Labor, Health and Human Services, Housing and Urban Development, Transportation, Energy, Education, Veterans Affairs, Homeland Security

INDEPENDENT AGENCIES*

Environmental Protection Agency, Federal Emergency Management Agency, General Services Administration, National Aeronautics & Space Administration, Office of Personnel Management, Peace Corps, Small Business Administration, Central Intelligence Agency, National Archives and Records Administration, Merit Systems Protection Board

INDEPENDENT REGULATORY COMMISSIONS*

Federal Communications Commission, Federal Maritime Commission, Federal Reserve System, Federal Trade Commission, National Labor Relations Board, Securities and Exchange Commission, Consumer Product Safety Commission, Commodity Futures Trading Commission, Nuclear Regulatory Commission, Federal Election Commission, Equal Employment Opportunity Commission, Occupational Health and Safety Review Commission

GOVERNMENT CORPORATIONS*

Federal Deposit Insurance Corporation, Export-Import Bank of the United States, Tennessee Valley Authority, Inter-American Foundation, Corporation for National and Community Service, National Railroad Passenger Corporation (Amtrak)

*Principal examples of agencies within this category

Figure 13–1   Organization of the National Bureaucracy. This description of the principal agencies of the federal bureaucracy illustrates the wide range of activities the federal government is involved in.

Sources: *Adapted and updated from Harold Seidman and Robert Gilmour,* Politics, Position and Power, *4th ed. (New York: Oxford University Press, 1986), 254–57;* The United States Government Manual, 2005/06, *available at www.gpoaccess.gov/gmanual/browse-gm-05.html.*

13-2a Types of Federal Agencies

The agencies that make up the federal bureaucracy vary widely in organizational structure, size, and responsibility. Figure 13–1 gives examples of the four main kinds of organizations within the federal bureaucracy: executive departments, independent regulatory commissions, government corporations, and independent agencies.

Executive Departments

Executive departments are the primary form of organization in the federal bureaucracy. In 2009, the United States had fifteen executive departments in all. Executive departments were the first bureaucratic organizations Congress created, and they continue to carry out most of the federal government's responsibilities. Executive departments are hierarchically organized, and they are headed by a single individual, usually known as the secretary. Thus, the person in charge of the Defense Department is known as the secretary of defense, and the person in charge of the State Department is known as the secretary of state. The secretaries of defense and state, like the secretaries of all other executive departments, are appointed by the president with the **advice and consent** of the Senate, which means that a majority of the Senate must approve, or confirm, the president's choice. The president also has the power to fire the secretary of an executive department, and as we saw in Chapter 12, the Senate has no say over whether to remove the secretary of an executive department from his or her post.

The secretaries of the fifteen executive departments in the federal bureaucracy, along with other key government officials, make up the **cabinet**, a group that, in theory, advises the president on all aspects of public policy. In practice, however, most presidents make little use of the cabinet as a source of advice, preferring instead to rely on the White House staff. Although the cabinet tends to have little impact on presidential decision making, the fact that an executive department has cabinet-level status is important. Being a member of the cabinet gives secretaries greater stature in Washington politics, stature they can use as a political resource to advance the interests of their departments.[11]

As a result of their great size, executive departments consist of dozens and even hundreds of subsidiary agencies, bureaus, and offices, each of which handles some small part of the department's responsibilities. To give you a sense of what these subsidiary agencies do and how they fit into the overall organization of a department, Figure 13–2 presents the organizational chart for the Department of the Treasury. As you can see from the figure, which is actually a simplified view of how the department is organized, the secretary of the treasury oversees a wide array of different agencies, bureaus, and offices, including the U.S. Mint; the Bureau of Alcohol, Tobacco, and Firearms; the Secret Service; the Office of the Comptroller of the Currency; and the Internal Revenue Service. In turn, the responsibilities of the many subsidiary agencies in the Department of the Treasury span the policy spectrum, ranging from domestic matters such as tax policy and corporate finance to foreign policy matters such as international monetary policy and trade and investment policy.

Independent Regulatory Commissions

Independent regulatory commissions constitute the second major type of organization within the federal bureaucracy. Whereas some executive departments date back to 1789, the first independent regulatory commission, the Interstate Commerce Commission (ICC), was not established until 1887. (Chapter 17 discusses the history of the ICC, which was abolished in 1996.) All independent

advice and consent
The requirement that the president gain the Senate's approval of appointees to a variety of government positions, as per the provision in Article II of the Constitution.

cabinet
An informal designation that refers to the collective body of individuals appointed by the president to head the executive departments. The cabinet can, but rarely does, function as an advisory body to the president.

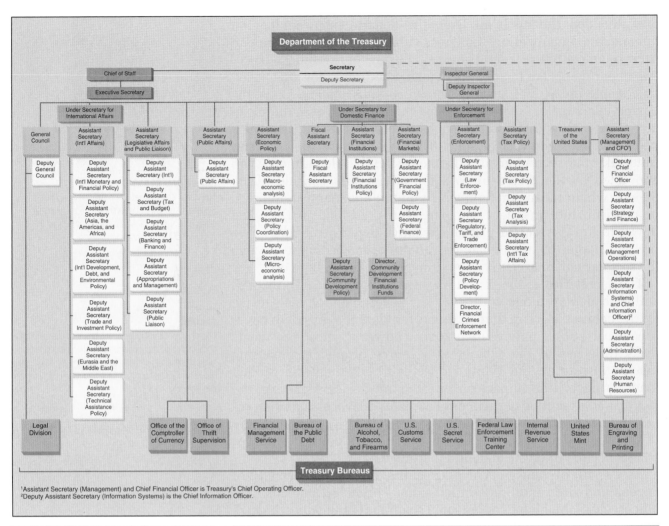

Figure 13-2   The Department of the Treasury: An Organizational Chart. This simplified depiction of the primary components of the Treasury Department illustrates the breadth of duties as well as the internal complexity that characterizes most departments.

Source: United States Government Manual, 2000/01 (Washington, D.C.: U.S. Government Printing Office, 2000), 343.

regulatory commissions are charged with performing the same basic function: promoting the public interest by writing and enforcing rules that regulate the operations of some sector of private industry. For example, the Consumer Products Safety Commission works to ensure that companies produce goods that are not likely to harm consumers, and the Nuclear Regulatory Commission regulates the nation's nuclear power plants.

Independent regulatory commissions differ dramatically from executive departments in terms of size, leadership structure, and political independence from the president. To begin with, independent regulatory commissions are much smaller than most executive departments; whereas the Defense Department has more than 670,000 employees, the Federal Trade Commission has barely 1,000.[12] Independent regulatory commissions also differ from executive departments in that they are headed by a commission, usually consisting of three to eleven people, rather than by a single secretary. The chair of a commission is the first among equals,

Source: © White House photo by Eric Draper

The president's cabinet consists of the secretaries of the government's fifteen executive departments and other designated officials. Although the cabinet seldom serves as an important source of advice, its individual members are often close confidants of the president. The prestige of cabinet rank also assists cabinet members in their political conflicts.

lacking the authority the secretaries of executive departments enjoy. Finally, as the name implies, independent regulatory commissions enjoy greater political independence from the president than executive departments do. The reason has to do with the nature of each commissioner's appointment. Like the secretaries of the executive departments, commissioners are appointed by the president and confirmed by the Senate. Instead of serving at the pleasure of the president, however, commissioners serve fixed terms that are staggered over time. As a result, when new presidents take office, they confront independent regulatory commissions headed by people previous presidents appointed, and they can appoint new commissioners only when vacancies open up.

Government Corporations

In addition to executive departments and independent regulatory commissions, a third type of bureaucratic organization is the *government corporation*. Government corporations are, in essence, government-owned companies that sell services or products to the public to generate their own revenues. For example, the Postal Service pays for its operations by selling stamps and charging for other postal services. Therefore, it has worked hard to produce stamps, such as those of Elvis Presley and Marilyn Monroe, that customers will retain rather than use because the Postal Service pockets more money from the sale of stamps that are never used for postage.[13] The Tennessee Valley Authority pays for its operations by charging its customers for the electricity generated by the dams and nuclear power plants it operates. And the Federal Deposit Insurance Corporation (FDIC) charges banks a fee in return

The Postal Service promotes stamp collecting as a hobby because stamps purchased and placed in a collection book make much more money for the Postal Service than stamps placed on an envelope and mailed.

rule administration
The core function of the bureaucracy—to carry out the decisions of Congress, the president, or the courts.

for insuring customer deposits against a possible banking collapse. Some government corporations are headed by single individuals, whereas others have plural leadership.

In principle, government corporations are self-supporting agencies; they sell their services at prices that enable them to break even each year. When a government corporation fails to generate enough revenue to cover its expenses, however, the federal government will supplement the corporation's income. Thus, when the Federal Savings and Loan Insurance Corporation (FSLIC) exhausted its financial reserves after many of the savings-and-loan companies it insured went bankrupt in the 1980s, Congress bailed it out by giving it more money and merging it with the larger and more financially stable FDIC.

Independent Agencies

The category *of independent agencies* encompasses all other types of federal agencies. Independent agencies are not part of any executive department, and their leaders usually lack the cabinet-level status of department secretaries. Some independent agencies, such as the National Aeronautics and Space Administration (NASA), are headed by individuals, whereas others, such as the Merit System Protection Board, are headed by a commission. Some, such as the Small Business Administration (SBA), provide a service; others, such as the Environmental Protection Agency (EPA), perform a regulatory function. With the exception of the Central Intelligence Agency (CIA), independent agencies do not enjoy the same sort of political prestige as executive departments. The relative lack of political prestige has important implications for the well-being of independent agencies. As we shall see, the more power an agency possesses, the better it can fulfill its mission and ensure its own survival. Cabinet-rank status contributes to the deference that others accord an agency, and so to its ability to achieve its own goals.

13-2b The Tasks of the Federal Bureaucracy

Despite major differences in organization, structure, and political accountability, all agencies in the federal bureaucracy perform three key tasks: rule administration, rule making, and rule adjudication.

Rule administration involves carrying out, or administering, the public policy decisions Congress, the president, or the courts make. For example, the EPA administers laws Congress passes to clean up the nation's air and water. Likewise, when the president declares a state eligible for disaster relief in the wake of a flood, earthquake, or hurricane, the Emergency Preparedness and Response Directorate of the Department of Homeland Security (DHS; formerly the Federal Emergency Management Agency) administers federal relief programs. As you can see, rule administration is the most basic function of any agency; after all, Congress and the president create bureaucratic agencies because they themselves lack the time and resources needed to implement the public policy decisions they make.

To administer public policy, agencies often must engage in two other kinds of activities: rule making and rule adjudication. In **rule making**, a federal agency drafts regulations—that is, rules that govern the operation of government programs. The federal bureaucracy writes new regulations and revises old ones because Congress frequently passes laws long on broad guidelines but short on details. As we saw in Chapter 11, in many instances Congress gives federal agencies the authority to flesh out the details of legislation because the issues are too complex and members too pressed for time to provide the specifics themselves. Of course, the discretion agencies have to translate the spirit of a congressional mandate into detailed rules gives bureaucrats tremendous influence over the substance of public policy. As we will see, this freedom of interpretation on occasion enables bureaucrats to frustrate the will of Congress.

How extensive is rule making among federal agencies? We can glean some idea from Figure 13–3, which shows the number of

rule making
Formulating the rules for carrying out the programs a bureaucratic agency administers.

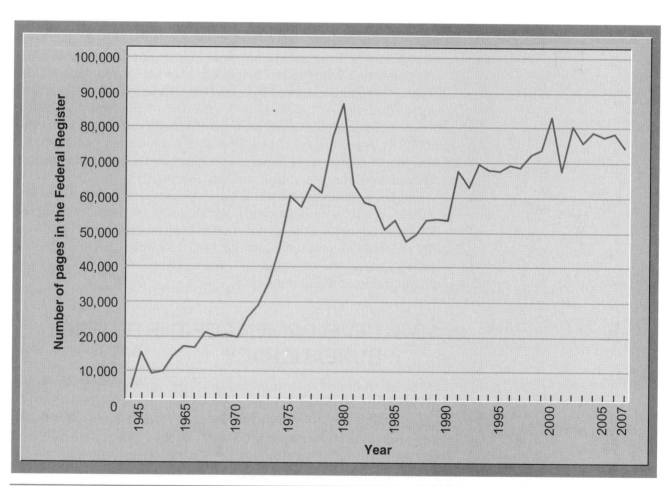

Figure 13–3   Measuring Agency Activity, 1940–2007. The 1970s saw a dramatic rise in the amount of rule-making government agencies engaged in as the federal government's role in providing all kinds of services grew. Rule making declined markedly in the first half of the 1980s in response to Ronald Reagan's efforts to reduce government activity. After resuming its climb through the 1990s, it stabilized under George W. Bush.

Sources: "Table 6-14 Number of Pages in Federal Register, 1940–2006," CQ Electronic Library, CQ's Vital Statistics on American Politics Online Edition, vsap07_tab6-14. Originally published in Harold W. Stanley and Richard G. Niemi, Vital Statistics on American Politics 2007–2008 (Washington, D.C.: CQ Press, 2008). See also www.library.cqpress.com/vsap/vsap07_tab6-14 and successive editions of The Federal Register, available at www.origin. www.gpoaccess.gov/fr/.

pages published each year in a government document known as the *Federal Register*. By law, a federal agency's rule cannot go into effect until thirty days after its publication in the *Federal Register*, so the annual length of the *Register* provides a crude measure of the amount of rule making that takes place. As you can see, bureaucratic rule making rose sharply from the 1940s, when Franklin Delano Roosevelt (FDR) was president, through the late 1970s, when Jimmy Carter was president. The amount of rule making dropped during Reagan's presidency because administration officials sought to halt, if not reverse, government regulation of the economy. In 1991, with the elder George Bush in the White House, the amount of rule making rose once again, and it continued to increase during Bill Clinton's administration. Under George W. Bush, rule making activity stabilized.

In addition to making rules, many federal agencies are responsible for determining whether the rules they administer and formulate have been broken, a process known as **rule adjudication**. Whereas federal agencies operate as Congress does when they make rules, they operate as the courts do when they adjudicate rules. These judges, who exercise great independence because they cannot be fired except for gross misconduct, review evidence and determine whether the defendants violated any relevant rules or laws. For example, the National Labor Relations Board employs administrative law judges to hear complaints that unions or businesses have violated provisions of the National Labor Relations Act.[14] Rule adjudication has grown in importance over the past fifty years because more federal agencies have gained the responsibility of regulating economic activity in the private sector.

The federal bureaucracy is a huge conglomerate of diverse, specialized agencies charged with carrying out government policies. All these agencies administer, make, and enforce rules, but how did the bureaucracy become the large, complex institution it is today? This is the question we will answer next as we trace the development of the bureaucracy.

rule adjudication
Determining whether an agency's rules have been violated.

13-3 DEVELOPMENT OF THE FEDERAL BUREAUCRACY

On a visit to almost any American city, you can find visible evidence of the reach of the federal bureaucracy: post offices, military recruiting stations, Social Security offices, agricultural extension offices, and offices for a mind-numbing array of other federal bureaus and agencies. To staff the far-flung federal bureaucracy, the federal government employs just over 2.6 million civilian employees.[15] Yet the federal government was not always such a massive presence in American life. When Thomas Jefferson sat in the White House, the federal government employed only about 2,700 civilians.[16]

The tremendous growth in the size of the federal bureaucracy raises several important questions: What is the constitutional status of the bureaucracy? How rapidly did it grow, and is it still growing today? And how have the functions of the bureaucracy and the rules used to hire bureaucrats changed over the past two centuries?

13-3a Constitutional Foundations

Chapters 11 and 12 noted that the Constitution specifies the basic structure of both Congress and the presidency. This is not true for the federal bureaucracy. Rather than stipulating the creation of specific federal agencies, the Constitution gave both Congress and the president authority to devise and operate a bureaucracy that would meet the changing needs of a growing country. Congress has the power to create new agencies—which, by implication, means it can abolish or reorganize existing ones—and it decides how much money each agency can spend in a given year. The president has the power to appoint (subject to Senate confirmation) the heads of federal agencies. The Constitution also directs the president to "take care that the laws be faithfully executed," a provision that authorizes the president to order the federal bureaucracy to carry out government policy.

As you can see, the federal bureaucracy is something of a constitutional hybrid. It bridges the gap between the legislative and executive branches of government: It is created by Congress, under the direction of the president, and accountable to both. Of course, agencies vary in the degree to which they respond to the wishes of Congress or the president. Secretaries of the executive departments tend to be more responsive to the White House because they serve at the pleasure of the president. In contrast, the commissioners of independent regulatory commissions serve fixed terms that place them beyond the president's direct control.

13-3b The Growth of the Federal Bureaucracy

Because the Constitution does not specify the structure of the federal bureaucracy, one of the major tasks the first Congress had to accomplish when it met in 1789 was to create agencies for the new government. In doing so, the first Congress created a simple bureaucratic structure consisting of three executive departments: the Department of State, the Department of War, and the Department of the Treasury. The first Congress also created the positions of attorney general and postmaster general. The attorney general is the federal government's chief legal official and a member of the president's cabinet. (The attorney general was put in charge of the Justice Department when that agency was created in 1870.) The postmaster general was placed in charge of the Department of the Post Office, which had been created under the Articles of Confederation. The postmaster general was added to the cabinet when Andrew Jackson became president and was dropped from the cabinet when the post was abolished in 1971 as part of a reorganization of the Postal Service.

By the standards of 2009, the early federal bureaucracy was extremely small. In 1816, the federal government employed fewer than 5,000 civilian workers. As Figure 13–4 shows, that number grew slowly throughout the nineteenth century and the first three decades of the twentieth century. Then the total number of federal civilian employees skyrocketed, increasing more than fourfold between 1931 and 1951. The number of federal employees grew so rapidly in the 1930s and 1940s because of the Great Depression and World War II. These events provided the impetus to rewrite many of the rules of American government. For example, to help restart the stalled American economy, FDR and Congress enacted a series of programs known as the New Deal that greatly expanded the federal government's role in American society. And once Japan attacked Pearl Harbor in December 1941, the federal government needed to hire many more people to run the war effort; indeed, the federal workforce expanded to 3.8 million workers in 1945 before falling back to 1.9 million in 1950. In the decades since then, the number of federal civilian employees has grown much more slowly and has actually declined since the 1990s.

Figure 13–4 shows the *absolute* number of federal civilian employees, but what does change in the size of the federal workforce look like when we take into account the growing size of the

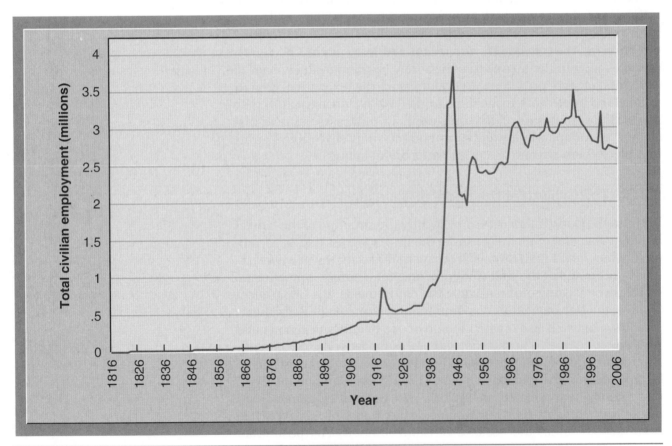

Figure 13–4   Total Number of Federal Civilian Government Employees, 1816–2006. Our perception of the federal government's size is affected by what aspect of the government we look at. This figure shows that total federal employment grew fairly steadily until the 1990s, apart from the abrupt spike that accompanied World War II.

Sources: *1816–1998: Harold W. Stanley and Richard G. Niemi*, Vital Statistics on American Politics, 1999–2000 *(Washington, D.C.: CQ Press, 2000), 259; 1999–2006: "Table 6-12 Number of Civilian Federal Government Employees and Percentage under Merit Civil Service, 1816–2006," CQ Electronic Library, CQ's Vital Statistics on American Politics Online Edition, vsap07_tab6-12. Originally published in Harold W. Stanley and Richard G. Niemi*, Vital Statistics on American Politics 2007–2008 *(Washington, D.C.: CQ Press, 2008).*

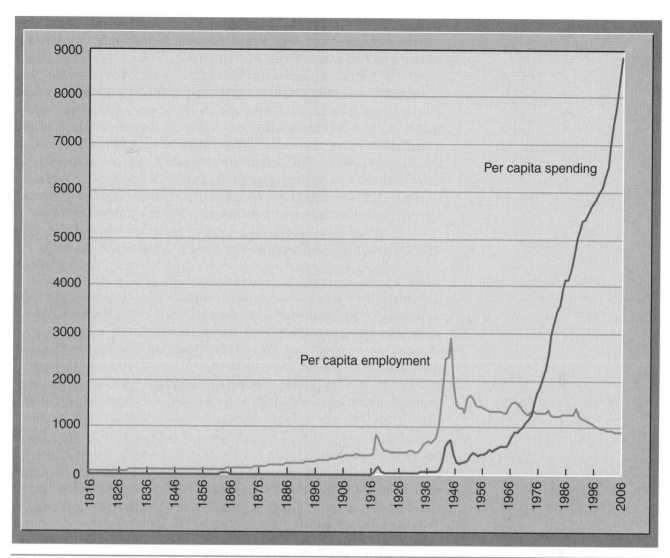

Figure 13-5   Growth of the Federal Government, 1816–2006. In contrast with Figure 13–4, Figure 13–5 shows that per capita federal employment has actually declined since the 1950s. The figure also shows that the federal government spends more money every year, but it does so while employing proportionately fewer people.

Sources: *Data from Historical Statistics of the United States: Colonial Times to 1970 (Washington, D.C.: U.S. Bureau of the Census, 1975), pp. 14, 1114–15;* Harold W. Stanley and Richard G. Niemi, Vital Statistics on American Politics, 1999–2000, *(Washington, D.C.: CQ Press, 2000), 259, 392; Table 6-12 Number of Civilian Federal Government Employees and Percentage under Merit Civil Service, 1816–2006." CQ Electronic Library, CQ's Vital Statistics on American Politics Online Edition, vsap07_tab6-12. Originally published in Harold W. Stanley and Richard G. Niemi, Vital Statistics on American Politics 2007–2008 (Washington, DC: CQ Press, 2008); U.S. Census Bureau, The 2008 Statistical Abstract, The National Data Book, available at www.census.gov/ compendia/statab/tables/08s0006.pdf.*

American population? After all, one reason a bureaucracy might hire more workers is to meet the needs of a growing population. To answer the question, Figure 13–5 shows the number of federal civilian employees per every 100,000 Americans for the years 1816 to 2006. As you can see, Figure 13–5 tells much the same story as Figure 13–4 for the years 1820 through 1951: The size of the federal workforce grew in both absolute and relative terms, with peak employment reached during World War II. The big difference between Figures 13–4 and 13–5 lies in the decades since 1951. Although the absolute number of federal civilian workers increased less than 10 percent between 1951 and 2006, the number of federal civilian workers per 100,000 Americans actually *fell* by almost 43 percent. In sum, in 2006, the federal bureaucracy was serving the needs of the American public with relatively fewer workers than it was five decades previous.

Although the number of federal civilian employees has declined in recent years, after change in the size of the population is taken into account, Figure 13–5 also shows that per capita spending by federal agencies increased dramatically in the second half of the twentieth century and continues to grow at an even faster pace in the first decade of the twenty-first century. To understand why federal agency spending rose so sharply, we need to look at how Congress and the president changed the rules to expand the number of functions the federal bureaucracy is called on to perform.

13-3c The Expanding Functions of the Federal Bureaucracy

The history of the federal government is a history of expanding duties and responsibilities. As Americans have come to demand more services from the federal government, federal agencies have assumed more functions. These functions fall into four categories: national maintenance, clientele service, private sector regulation, and income redistribution. In many instances, a single agency performs more than one of these functions. In a similar vein, in many cases more than one federal agency may carry out the same function.

National Maintenance

Early in American history, the functions of the federal government were limited largely to carrying out a small number of tasks essential to maintaining the country: collecting tax revenue (the job of the Treasury Department), defending the country against external threats (the War Department), conducting relations with other countries (the State Department), enforcing federal laws (the attorney general), and promoting internal communications (the Post Office).

As long as the federal government limited itself to these core duties, growth in the size of the federal bureaucracy was driven largely by growth in the size of the country itself. For example, the Post Office accounted for most of the early growth in the number of federal employees because it added more workers to deliver the mail to a growing population and an expanding national border.[17] The acquisition of new territories also drove bureaucratic growth; Congress created the Interior Department in 1849 to manage the western territories. The threat of terrorism following the September 11, 2001, attacks led to the creation in 2003 of the nation's most recent agency dedicated to national maintenance: the DHS. It is large, with over 150,000 employees and a 2008 budget estimated at more than $40 billion. Because DHS consolidated twenty-two existing agencies into a single department, it did not dramatically expand the size of the government's workforce or budget.[18]

Clientele Services

Midway through the nineteenth century, organized interest groups began demanding that the federal government go beyond its traditional national maintenance functions to serve the particular needs of their members. Washington responded to the demands by creating new agencies designed to provide these groups, or clients, with services. In the 1850s, for example, farming interests began lobbying for greater federal involvement in agricultural policy, and Congress responded in 1862 by creating the Department of Agriculture. During the 1880s, labor organizations followed the example the farm groups set and demanded the creation of a department designed to serve their interests. Congress responded in 1884 by creating the Bureau of Labor. Pressures from business interests led Congress (over the objections of labor groups) to create a combined Department of Commerce and Labor in 1903. Finally, at the insistence of the American Federation of Labor, Congress established separate Departments of Commerce and Labor in 1913.

Part of the growth in both federal employment and spending since the 1930s can be traced to the expansion of the **clientele** services the federal government provides to American citizens. The New Deal launched the country on an era of government activism intended to stimulate the economy and provide for the public's general welfare. In 1953, Congress created the Department of Health, Education, and Welfare (renamed the Department of Health and Human Services in 1979) to administer the nation's health, education, and income assistance programs. In the 1960s, the federal bureaucracy expanded again in response to the passage of the Great Society programs, President Lyndon Johnson's effort to reduce economic and racial inequality in the United States. Many new agencies were created or expanded into executive departments. Thus, in 1965, the Housing and Home Finance Agency was elevated in status and renamed the Department of Housing and Urban Development. A year later, Congress merged programs and activities from eight separate departments into the Department of Transportation. Over the next three decades, three more executive departments were created: the Department of Energy in 1977, the Department of Education in 1979, and the Department of Veterans Affairs in 1989.

The creation of new federal agencies designed to serve the needs of specific segments of American society accounts for much of the growth in the total number of federal civilian employees between 1950 and 2006. The growth in the number of federal agencies also accounts for the even more spectacular growth in federal spending. As we discuss at greater length in Chapters 15 and 16, most federal spending takes the form of grants to state and local governments and direct payments to individuals. By increasing its grants to state and local governments and its direct payments to individuals, the federal government expanded the services it could provide without having to hire more employees.

clientele
The recipients of the services a government agency's programs provide.

Regulation of the Private Sector

In addition to maintaining the basic needs of the country and serving the needs of specific segments of American society, the federal bureaucracy has grown because it has acquired the responsibility of regulating the American economy. The federal government first moved into the regulatory arena in 1887 when it created the ICC to end the predatory business practices of the railroad industry. (The ICC's jurisdiction eventually expanded to include trucking, bus lines, water carriers, oil pipelines, and express delivery agencies before it was abolished in 1996.) In 1913, Congress created the Federal Reserve Board to regulate the activities of commercial banks, and in 1914, it created the Federal Trade Commission to regulate the trade practices of businesses. The regulatory responsibilities of the federal government expanded yet again during the administration of FDR. In 1934, Congress created the Federal Communications Commission (see Chapter 8) to regulate the emerging field of electronic communications and the Securities and Exchange Commission to regulate the operation of the stock market.

As Chapter 17 discusses at greater length, the regulatory agencies created before 1960 were responsible largely for regulating economic matters, such as the price of goods and services, the amount of competition in the marketplace, and the kinds of information sellers must disclose to buyers. During the 1960s, however, Congress expanded the focus of government regulation to include social regulation, rules that emphasize "the conditions under which goods and services are produced, and the physical characteristics of products that are manufactured."[19] Toward that broader end, Congress created agencies to protect the environment, employees in the workplace, and consumers. The EPA and the Occupational Safety and Health Administration (OSHA) were created in 1970, and the Consumer Products Safety Commission in 1972. These agencies have broad mandates that extend beyond the traditional practice of regulating particular industries. The EPA, for example, can regulate pollution from all sources, including industrial plants, automobiles, landfill sites, animal feed lots, and all places where pollution appears (i.e., soil, air, and water.) The wide-ranging nature of the mandate Congress gave the EPA means the agency has extensive influence across a wide segment of American society. The broadening scope of the government's regulatory duties helps account for the pattern of growth in the volume of regulations the government issued in the 1970s, as shown in Figure 13–3.

Income Redistribution

The fourth function of the federal bureaucracy, and the one most recent in origin, involves the redistribution of income. Redistribution refers to government efforts to shift resources, either directly or indirectly, between classes of people in society, from richer to poorer or vice versa. In the wake of the Great Depression, the federal government increasingly assumed a role in maintaining the economic and social welfare of the American people. As a result, income redistribution became an important part of government policy and yet another factor contributing to the expansion of the federal bureaucracy.

Chapters 16 and 17 discuss in considerable detail the ways in which the federal government redistributes income among American citizens. Here, it is sufficient to make two points. First, most of the redistributive efforts of federal agencies involve direct payments to individuals. For example, the Social Security system, established in 1935, makes cash payments to elderly Americans as well as to dependent children of deceased workers and to Americans with disabilities. Likewise, Aid to Families with Dependent Children (AFDC), established as part of the same legislation that created Social Security, provided cash benefits to needy families. As the number of people eligible for programs such as Social Security and AFDC has increased, the budgets of the federal agencies that make the transfer payments have grown as well. The federal government made a decisive turn away from redistributive policies in 1996, however, when President Clinton and the Republican majority in Congress replaced AFDC with the Temporary Assistance for Needy Families program (TANF). TANF gives specific amounts of money in the form of block grants to states and limits the length of time that individuals can participate in the program. The states decide who is eligible for aid. This has reduced the numbers of people receiving aid by 60 percent in less than ten years.[20] (Chapter 17 discusses the TANF program in more detail.)

The second point about the federal government's attempts to redistribute income is that although some programs transfer money from the rich to the poor, as AFDC did and TANF now does, some transfer money to the wealthy. For example, many federal programs make direct payments to wealthy individuals and firms. Much of the money the Department of Agriculture pays to keep farmers in business goes to wealthy corporate farmers. Likewise, the SSA mails the largest Social Security checks to elderly Americans who had the highest incomes during their working years, regardless of whether they are currently rich or poor. Thus, income redistribution is not a one-way street. Both the wealthy and the poor can benefit from government policies if the government deems their well-being a proper goal of government policy. It all depends on the rules.

13-3d Changes in the Federal Bureaucracy's Personnel System

The past two centuries have seen dramatic changes in the size of the federal bureaucracy and in the sorts of functions it is expected to undertake. The past two centuries also have seen dramatic changes in the bureaucracy's personnel system and the rules that govern the hiring and firing of federal employees. The question of who works for the federal bureaucracy is important because bureaucrats are responsible for implementing public policy, and so they greatly shape the actions of the federal government. In the United States, the rules used to hire and fire federal employees have changed in response to changes in the nation's political climate. In turn, these changes have affected the way in which the federal bureaucracy performs its work.

Government by Gentlemen

From the time the nation was founded until 1829, the federal bureaucracy consisted of political appointees recruited primarily from the elite classes in American society, and service in the bureaucracy was viewed as a high calling. The pool of eligible appointees was limited for the most part to white males who had demonstrated their loyalty to the party in power, who possessed high social standing and an advanced education, and who had relatives who were government officials. Both the Federalist and the Democrat-Republican parties followed this pattern, sometimes called "government by gentlemen" because the "business of governing was prestigious, and it was anointed with high moral imperatives of integrity and honor."[21]

The Spoils System

The era of "government by gentlemen" gave way in 1829 to the **spoils system**, the practice of hiring and firing federal workers on the basis of party loyalty and support in election campaigns. The spoils system was implemented by Andrew Jackson, the first president to be elected with election rules that allowed nearly all adult white males to vote, and it got its name when Senator William Marcy defended Jackson's practice of appointing his political supporters to government jobs by arguing that "to the victor belong the spoils of the enemy."[22] Jackson wanted to make the federal bureaucracy more responsive to presidential leadership, and he believed that most government jobs required little more than common sense. As a result, he made party loyalty the primary consideration in hiring people to work for the federal government.

Under the spoils system, the spoils—that is, government jobs—went to the victor in an election. The result of this winner-take-all approach was that a great deal of turnover occurred in government jobs each time a new administration came to the White House. Members of the defeated political party would lose their government jobs, and members of the victorious political party would replace them. The ability of presidents to reward their followers with government jobs is known as **patronage**. Presidents often found patronage quite helpful for building political support for their proposals. For example, Abraham Lincoln used his patronage powers to secure political support for his policies on the Civil War.[23]

The spoils system held sway from Jackson's presidency until the 1880s. Although nineteenth-century presidents found patronage useful for winning political support and ensuring that bureaucrats responded to their wishes, the spoils system bred cynicism among the American public about the integrity of federal employees. Many federal employees began to see their jobs not only as rewards, but also as a means of self-enrichment. Political corruption grew rampant. By the 1870s, a growing public awareness of government corruption, along with a mistrust of the way ethnic groups such as Irish Americans had used patronage to gain political power in large cities, led to increased calls for a new personnel

spoils system
The method used to hire and fire government employees during most of the 1800s. Government employees of the new president's choosing would replace those a previous president had appointed. Government jobs were the "spoils" (or rewards) of the electoral "wars." This system was also known as patronage.

patronage
The practice of rewarding partisan supporters with government jobs. Also known as the spoils system.

system based on merit rather than political ties. The push for reform gained momentum in 1881 when a disgruntled job seeker assassinated President James Garfield. Two years later, Congress passed the Pendleton Act of 1883, which held that people should be hired on the basis of their qualifications rather than their political connections.

The Civil Service System

The Pendleton Act established the third type of personnel system for the federal bureaucracy and the one that remains in effect today: **civil service**. In a civil service system, the rules for hiring workers stress the competence of the job applicant rather than his or her political affiliation. In other words, civil service puts a premium on *what* you know, rather than *who* you know. At first, the federal civil service system encompassed only 10 percent of the federal workforce, and people who held these jobs became known as civil servants. Over the years, however, the number of federal jobs subject to the rules of civil service was gradually enlarged. In 2007, nearly 80 percent of all civilian bureaucratic employees fell under some part of the civil service system, with over 50 percent participating in what is known as the General Schedule Classification System, and almost 30 percent working under the Postal Service System.[24] The president, however, retains the power to appoint people to jobs in the highest levels of the federal bureaucracy, subject to Senate confirmation in most instances.

In addition to expanding to encompass most federal jobs, the civil service system has changed in other ways as well. One major change has been the effort to recruit more women and minorities. Historically, both groups were grossly underrepresented in the federal bureaucracy. In the early 1970s, Congress took steps to remedy the problem by requiring the federal government to follow affirmative action guidelines in making hiring decisions (see Box 13–1). As a result of this change in hiring rules, the proportion of government jobs going to women and minorities grew significantly in the 1970s and 1980s. By 2005, women made up about 44 percent of the federal workforce and minorities 32 percent—both roughly comparable to their proportions of the general population.[25] Women and minorities continue, however, to be underrepresented at the highest levels of the civil service.[26] Thus, although some progress has been made, the objectives of the affirmative action policy have yet to be fully achieved.

The Civil Service Reform Act of 1978 further revised the operations of the civil service system. Among the many changes that the law mandated, two are especially important. First, the act reorganized the agencies that oversee the civil service system. Before the passage of the Civil Service Reform Act, the Civil Service Commission had the dual tasks of advising presidents on personnel policy and protecting civil servants from the political interference of elected officials. In practice, these two responsibilities often came into conflict because many presidents wanted to influence the behavior of career bureaucrats. Carter proposed to remedy the

civil service

The method by which most government employees have been hired, promoted, and fired since the 1880s. Personnel decisions are based on merit, or the competence of the individual to do the job, rather than the individual's political loyalties.

POINT OF ORDER

Box 13–1   Who Gets the Job? The Effects of Veterans' Preference and Affirmative Action Rules on Government Hiring

The criteria used to hire career federal civil servants provide a clear example of the way government rules distribute benefits. With the passage of the Pendleton Act in 1883, the government made merit (the ability to do the job) the primary standard for making hiring decisions. Under this system, job applicants are tested and scored on a 100-point scale that measures their ability to perform different types of jobs. If merit were the only consideration the federal government used in hiring new workers, then it would hire the people with the highest scores. Over the years, however, Congress has modified the merit system to provide special benefits to specific groups of Americans.

One group that benefits from the modified merit system is military veterans. The federal civil service system adds a bonus of between five and fifteen points to the test scores of all applicants who have served on active military duty. The number of bonus points increases if the veteran has war-related disabilities or served in the Vietnam War. Spouses, widows, widowers, and mothers of military veterans also may have bonus points added to their test scores under certain circumstances. Other sections of the American public that benefit from the modifications to the merit system are women and minorities. The federal government is an affirmative action

employer. This means that when a federal agency is filling a position and all candidates have roughly equal merit, women and minority candidates receive strong consideration or even preference based on their gender or ethnic background. The rules direct the federal agency to try to hire women and minority candidates. To meet the federal government's affirmative action employment targets, federal agencies must set numerical goals for the employment of women and minorities, and they must establish timetables for achieving those goals.

Veterans' preferences and affirmative action have affected the composition of the federal workforce. Not counting postal workers, one-fourth of all federal employees are military veterans. In contrast, veterans make up only 10.6 percent of the civilian labor force in the United States. Women make up about 45 percent and minorities 30 percent of federal employees. In contrast, in 1970, before the hiring preferences were established, women made up only 33 percent of the federal workforce and minorities only 20 percent.

Veterans' preferences and affirmative action are controversial policies because they make exceptions to the conventional notion of merit. Proponents argue that these policies advance goals that are important to the country. They argue that the veterans' preference rewards people who have served the country and thereby encourages other Americans to serve in the military. Along the same line, affirmative action tries to correct past discrimination and ensure that the people who work in the federal

bureaucracy mirror the American public.

Opponents challenge veterans' preferences and affirmative action on the grounds that the two policies run contrary to the idea of merit hiring. Critics recognize the value of the veterans' preference in helping veterans find jobs when they first leave the military but oppose allowing veterans who have already obtained gainful employment to use it. Many attempts have been made to limit the use of the veterans' preference, but politically powerful veterans' organizations have lobbied hard to protect a rule that benefits so many of their members. As for affirmative action, it is criticized for rewarding people who themselves have not experienced discrimination. As we saw in Chapter 5, some opponents even label the policy as reverse discrimination because it consciously denies equal treatment to white males. The controversy over affirmative action has generated many attempts in both Congress and the courts to expand as well as limit its scope.

Veterans' preferences and affirmative action show that even the seemingly technical rules governing who the federal government hires have a tremendous effect on which groups of Americans benefit from government policy. As a result, many groups try to change the rules of government in ways that will benefit their members.

Sources: Donald F. Kettl and James W. Fesler, *The Politics of the Administrative Process*, 3rd ed. (Washington, D.C.: CQ Press, 2005), 175–6; Michael E. Milakovich and George J. Gordon, *Public Administration in America*, 9th ed. (New York: St. Martin's, 2007); *Statistical Abstract of the United States* (Washington, D.C.: U.S. Bureau of the Census, various years).

conflict-of-interest problem by abolishing the Civil Service Commission and dividing its duties between two new agencies. Congress then enacted Carter's proposal, which created the Office of Personnel Management to advise the president on personnel matters and the Merit System Protection Board to administer the civil service system.

The Civil Service Reform Act also created the Senior Executive Service (SES), which consists of civil servants who have reached the highest ranks of their careers. The purpose of the SES is to enable the most senior career civil servants to move into high-level policy-making positions in the federal government that are traditionally reserved for political appointees. Individuals who join the SES retain the basic protections of the civil service system, but the president can shift them from one job to another on the basis of his or her personal policy preferences. For example, a Republican president can replace a liberal member of the SES who holds a senior post in the Interior Department with a conservative member of the SES. The liberal member of SES must then receive a commensurate job elsewhere in the federal bureaucracy. Thus, the SES helps civil servants by giving them opportunities to undertake more challenging work, and it helps presidents by enabling them to fill important government jobs with people who share their policy preferences.

The formation of the DHS created another opportunity to make revisions designed to improve agency responsiveness to the president. At the younger President Bush's insistence, Congress stripped many of the protections that the civil service system and unionization had created from federal civilian employees. Bush claimed that homeland security was so important that the department's personnel must be more accountable and responsive to presidential leadership than most civil servants. Now, after a period of court challenges and negotiations with public employee unions, Congress enacted a modified version of a pay-for-performance system for the Defense Department. Although department officials did not gain as much control over the personnel system as Bush preferred, the laws show that the Bush administration had not finished its efforts to make the bureaucracy more susceptible to presidential leadership.[27]

Thus far, we have painted the bureaucracy as a huge institution that is accountable to both Congress and the president and that provides an expanding set of government services to the American public. We have seen how the bureaucracy shapes rules and how rules and other changes affect the bureaucracy. Now let's look at how the bureaucracy performs its tasks, focusing particularly on the third lesson about the bureaucracy we are discussing in this chapter: the fact that the bureaucracy is a political institution.

13-4 THE POLITICS OF THE FEDERAL BUREAUCRACY

Americans historically have believed that the federal bureaucracy is and should be nonpolitical.[28] Yet as we noted in the introduction to this chapter, federal agencies are fundamentally political organizations. They do not simply implement the decisions of Congress and the president; they also make rules and policies. And just as the laws Congress passes and the president signs benefit some Americans and hurt others, so do the rules and policies the federal bureaucracy develops. Thus, to understand the role federal agencies play in American politics, it is important to understand the inherently political nature of their jobs, the goals they try to accomplish, the source of their political power, the constraints that limit their power, and the alliances they can form with other actors in the policy-making process.

13-4a The Political Character of the Federal Bureaucracy

An enduring feature of the American public's attitude toward government bureaucracy is the belief that bureaucracies are, and should be, politically neutral organizations that carry out the administrative tasks elected officials assigned to them. In this view, Congress and the president should *formulate* policy and the bureaucracy should *implement* it. From this perspective, then, bureaucratic administration is simply a mechanistic process for implementing the wishes of elected officials efficiently and effectively.[29]

The American expectation that government bureaucracy should be politically neutral has greatly affected the development of the federal bureaucracy. For example, the push in the 1870s and 1880s to create a civil service system sprang from the desire to hire workers who could perform skilled tasks and who would be protected from the political pressures their presidentially appointed superiors imposed. The move to create independent regulatory commissions stemmed from the similar belief that bureaucracies should be politically neutral organizations. Proponents believed that providing members of a commission with fixed and staggered terms in office would minimize the possibilities for political interference and thereby enable the commissioners to act in the best interests of the American public.

Although the notion of bureaucratic neutrality is appealing, close examination of the administrative tasks of federal agencies shows that bureaucracies are inherently political institutions. To begin with, implementing the decisions of Congress, the president, and the courts requires that federal agencies do much more than mechanically put the wishes of others into effect. Because Congress, the president, and the courts lack the time needed to specify all the details of public policy, as well as the clairvoyance needed to anticipate all possible future developments, bureaucracies by necessity must try to translate broad principles and goals into concrete programs. The power to give meaning to what may be no more than a general principle gives bureaucrats a range of discretion as they decide how to fulfill their duties. As we shall see, agencies use their power to administer policy and shape policy rules to pursue their own interests and their own visions of good public policy as well as to respond to the demands of other political actors.

The work of the federal bureaucracy is also political because Congress and the president seldom speak with a single, coherent voice. Both want to direct the actions of the bureaucracy, but neither can unilaterally command its obedience. Instead, they must compete for its allegiance. Federal agencies can turn this competition to their advantage because they can play Congress and the president against each other. For example, if the Defense Department favors the president's proposal to spend more than Congress wants on defenses against nuclear missiles, it can produce studies showing the wisdom of the president's idea. In contrast, if the Defense Department opposes the president's decision to remove U.S. troops from South Korea, it can give Congress studies showing that the president's proposal will increase the chances of war in Asia. In short, the fact that federal agencies serve two masters gives them some freedom to shape public policy to advance their own interests and their own vision of good public policy.

In sum, the work of the federal bureaucracy is inherently political. The changes in how the Interior Department manages public lands under leaders with divergent policy goals attests to this (see Box 13–2). Federal agencies do not mechanically implement orders they receive from elected officials or the courts. Rather, because the process of implementing policy almost by necessity gives them discretion, and because they are responsible to both Congress and the president, federal agencies have some freedom to shape their own rules and pursue their own political goals.

13-4b The Goals of the Federal Bureaucracy

Government agencies have two types of goals: *mission goals* and *survival goals.* Mission goals are the policy objectives that justify the creation and existence of an agency. The Department of Transportation, for example, was created to promote the development of the nation's transportation systems. Most employees in an agency see its mission goals as a matter of good public policy. Thus, employees for the Department of Transportation generally believe that the federal government should do its best to build and maintain interstate highways, improve the nation's airports, and encourage mass transit use.

Survival goals refer to the desire bureaucrats have to see the agency they work for grow and prosper. Civil servants typically are career-oriented individuals whose personal advancement hinges on the success of their agency, which is usually defined in terms of whether the agency's budget, workforce, jurisdiction, and power are growing. No matter what an agency's original mission goals, it invariably seeks to survive and prosper once it exists. Indeed, "executive agencies often come to regard preserving their own organizational well-being as the most important of all public goods."[30] Thus, agency officials may work to keep their agency alive even when others believe its mission goals have become obsolete. For example, in 1995, congressional Republicans proposed abolishing the Commerce Department, which is home to agencies such as the Census Bureau, the National Weather Service, and the Patent and Trademark Office. Republicans argued that most of the department's functions were unnecessary, duplicated by other agencies, or best performed by the private sector or other federal

The People behind the Rules

Box 13-2   Managing Public Lands: Bruce Babbitt and Gale Norton

Bureaucracies are political institutions, and changes in the political climate affect federal agencies. A change in the leadership of a federal agency can profoundly affect how the agency operates, as a comparison of the record of the Department of the Interior under Secretary Bruce Babbitt (1993–2001) and its actions under recently retired Secretary Gale Norton (2001–2006) suggests. The Interior Department, created in 1849 to manage federally owned land, must weigh and manage conflicting demands. Environmental groups want to preserve public land and ensure the health of the ecosystem. Ranching, mining, logging, and oil businesses want to develop the land's economic potential. Although both Babbitt and Norton grew up in the West—Babbitt in Arizona and Norton in Colorado—the Interior Department weighed these competing demands quite differently during Norton's tenure than was the case during Babbitt's term in office.

BRUCE BABBITT

Babbitt made a name for himself as a strong advocate for the environment during his thirty years of public service before his appointment as secretary of the interior. He served as attorney general and then as governor of Arizona. In 1988, he ran for the Democratic presidential nomination. Although he failed in his bid to be president of the United States, he subsequently became president of the League of Conservation Voters, a

leading environmental group. In 1993, Bill Clinton named Babbitt secretary of the interior.

Although strongly identified with the environmental movement, Babbitt kept the channels of communication open to both environmentalists and private industry. Under Babbitt, the Interior Department placed more emphasis on protecting public lands than on developing them. After three years in office, Babbitt had forged a number of compromises that, although not satisfying his environmental supporters or silencing his business community critics, were viewed as progress after twelve years of Republican control of the department. After several false starts, he revised regulations for cattle grazing on federal lands, developed a plan to require the sugar industry to begin paying for cleanup of the damage it inflicted on the Everglades, and devised a solution (since superseded by the courts and Congress) to the dispute between logging interests and environmentalists over the logging of public lands that provide a habitat for the endangered spotted owl. Thus, Babbitt showed during his tenure as secretary of the interior that whoever heads the department sets the tone for its operations.

GALE NORTON

Norton advocated a market-based, pro-business environmental policy and is perhaps best known as a protégé of

Ronald Reagan's controversial secretary of the interior, James Watt. Norton joined Watt's Mountain States Legal Foundation after graduating from law school in 1979, and she served as Watt's associate solicitor during the Reagan presidency. In that capacity, she worked (unsuccessfully) to open up the Alaskan National Wildlife Refuge to exploration by oil and gas companies. She left government to practice law in the late 1980s, and she was elected Colorado Attorney General in 1990 and 1994.

On returning to government service as secretary of the interior, Norton continued her efforts to open federally owned lands to gas and oil exploration, timber-cutting operations, cattle grazing, recreation (e.g., snowmobiling), and other uses that have previously been limited or barred. She believed federal policies should give great weight and deference to the views of local interests and state governments and that the rights of private property owners should receive greater consideration in decisions concerning public lands. She was actively involved in building congressional support for the George W. Bush administration's unsuccessful effort to open the Alaskan National Wildlife Refuge to oil exploration and development. Her views represent a major break from Babbitt's. Although Norton's supporters view her as a consensus-building leader, environmentalists consider her a "James Watt in a skirt," who is leading the Interior Department in new directions that undermine long-standing protections of the environment.

Sources: William Booth, "For Norton, a Party Mission," *Washington Post,* January 8, 2001; Margaret Kriz, "Cabinet Scorecard: Interior Secretary Babbitt," *National Journal,* November 6, 1993, 2640–41; Margaret Kriz, "Environment: A New Look at Land Use," nationaljournal.com, January 26, 2001; Margaret Kriz, "Quick Draw," *National Journal,* November 13, 1993, 2711–16; National Journal *The Hotline,* "BUSH: Trying To Shift Enviro Issues Away From Nat'l Debate?" March 4, 2002; National Journal *The Hotline,* "ENERGY: Carpe Drill 'em," April 10, 2002; Timothy Noah, "Babbitt, Once the Darling of Environmentalists, Discovers Some Decisions Are Costing Him Allies," *Wall Street Journal,* May 3, 1994.

Source: © Wally McNamee/Corbis.

Bruce Babbitt.

Source: © Reuters/Corbis.

Gale Norton.

agencies. They also estimated that abolishing Commerce would save the federal government $8 billion over five years. Rather than meekly accepting the Republican proposal, Commerce Department officials argued that the agency performed vital services, and they eventually succeeded in keeping it in business. (Congressional Republicans succeeded in sharply cutting the Commerce Department's budget for the next year, but it has now recovered and grown substantially in the past ten years.)[31]

The desire that agencies have to grow and prosper almost inevitably brings them into conflict with other political actors, be they Congress, the president, other federal agencies, state and local governments, or interest groups. The reason is that when one agency grows in power, other agencies and interests almost invariably lose power. In the early 1980s, for example, defense spending rose rapidly because the Reagan administration launched a major buildup of U.S. military forces. Concerned that defense spending was taking too much away from spending on social programs, liberal members of Congress and their interest group allies fought to cut funding for the Defense Department and to increase funding for domestic agencies. Thus, when an agency grows in size and power, it almost always makes some enemies. To protect themselves against potential enemies, agencies try to develop their own independent bases of power.

13-4c The Political Resources of the Federal Bureaucracy

Power is "the lifeblood" of government agencies.[32] Agencies want political power because their view of good public policy may differ substantially from the views other government agencies, elected officials, and the public hold. They also want power to ensure their own survival. Agencies that have their own power bases can protect themselves from opponents and perhaps even expand their influence over public policy. They develop these power bases by exercising discretion in their policy areas, establishing strong client support, and developing policy expertise.

Administrative Discretion

Agencies establish their political power in part through their rule-making responsibilities. As we saw in the introduction to this chapter, agencies exercise discretion in deciding how to administer policy. They can use that discretion to implement policies to reflect their view of good public policy and to benefit their self-interest. For example, the fact that the EPA is responsible for generating many of the rules needed to carry out the nation's clean air laws gives it considerable power to influence the health of the American economy as well as the health of individual Americans. Similarly, the fact that the Justice Department is responsible for deciding when evidence is sufficient to prosecute someone for breaking a federal law gives the department tremendous power on matters involving the federal criminal justice system.

expertise
Specialized knowledge acquired through work experience or training and education.

In addition to the power that comes from discretion in implementing public policy, the two main sources of power for a government agency are the support of its clientele and its specialized knowledge, or **expertise**.[33] Because agencies differ in terms of clients and expertise, they also differ in terms of the amount of political power they wield.

Clientele Support

Whenever a government agency provides a service or regulates behavior, it seeks to help a targeted segment of society. Those intended beneficiaries compose the agency's clientele. In most instances, an agency's clientele consists of organized interest groups, although congressional committees or subcommittees may be part of an agency's clientele as well.

The power an agency exercises depends heavily on the power of its clientele. An agency supported by large, well-organized, and well-funded interest groups is likely to fare much better in achieving its goals than an agency that lacks such support. As we discussed in Chapter 10, such groups can help an agency by pressuring Congress and the president to give it bigger budgets, greater powers, or new duties. Because interest groups make campaign contributions and mobilize voters, both members of Congress and the president have an incentive to listen to interest group pleas on behalf of a federal agency.

The Defense Department and the State Department illustrate the two extremes when it comes to clientele support. A wide array of groups benefits from the operations of the Defense Department, including the companies that manufacture weapons and other products for the armed services, the people who work for defense contractors, the cities and towns located near military bases, and the more than 1.4 million people who serve on active duty. Because these clients represent a sizable segment of the American public, the Defense Department exercises tremendous political power. (Were it not for the power of its clients, the Defense Department's budget no doubt would have decreased far more sharply following the end of the Cold War than it did.) In contrast, the State Department is a classic case of an agency without a politically significant clientele. Few groups benefit directly from the work of the State Department, so few groups advocate its interests before Congress or the president. Not surprisingly, federal spending on foreign economic aid—which the State Department and its subordinate agencies oversee—was estimated to amount to less than one-half of one percent of all federal spending in 2008.[34]

Agencies do not have to stand idly by waiting for their clientele groups to act on their behalf. In many instances, agencies try to improve their political positions by helping to organize their clients into politically significant groups. For example, the Labor Department advocated the expansion of labor unions, at least in part because workers are much more powerful when they are formally organized into unions than when they act as individuals. Similarly, federal agencies often give grants to state or local governments, and they encourage the recipients to organize into groups. These groups can then urge Congress and the president to give the granting agency more funds and greater say in the distribution of grants.[35] Thus, agencies benefit from serving powerful clienteles, and they have an incentive to try to strengthen their clienteles.

If a clientele is especially powerful, an agency may come to depend so heavily on it that it loses much of its autonomy and becomes a "captive agency."[36] Sometimes the clientele that captures an agency is the intended beneficiary of the agency's activities. For example, the Department of Agriculture is quite sensitive to the wishes of agricultural interest groups because they form the core of the department's power base. In other situations, an agency may be captured by other groups, as is often the case with independent regulatory commissions. The reason independent regulatory commissions are created is to regulate business practices within some industry and thereby produce benefits for the general public. Yet the public is an unorganized and unmotivated client, so it exerts relatively little influence on behalf of a commission. In contrast, an industry is often well organized and strongly motivated to oppose any actions that might hurt its profitability. As a result of this imbalance, independent regulatory commissions frequently are captured by the industries they regulate. This leads to regulations that often serve the interests of the industry rather than those of the broader public.

Agency Expertise

In addition to gaining political power from administrative discretion and the support of clientele groups, agencies gain power from the expertise their employees develop. As civil servants undergo special training and education, and as they acquire hands-on experience from years on the job, they may develop specialized knowledge that few people outside the agency can match. An agency can then use its employees' expertise to argue that it "knows best" and that members of Congress and the president should adopt the policies it prefers. Because most members of Congress and most occupants of the Oval Office are likely to lack the same level of expertise, they may be inclined to accept the agency's recommendations. As a result, agencies can use their expertise to see that the government follows their policy preferences.

The political value of expertise depends on two critical factors: the extent to which an agency's employees are the only ones who possess expertise on the issue in question and the size of the knowledge gap between the experts and nonexperts. The experience of the SSA illustrates the value of holding a monopoly, or exclusive possession, on expertise. In the 1930s and 1940s, the SSA persuaded Congress to adopt the policies it preferred because Congress lacked the economic expertise needed to challenge the analyses the SSA produced. By the 1960s, however, congressional committees had developed their own staffs of economic experts, which enabled Congress to make independent judgments about the merits of the SSA's recommendations.[37]

The effect a large knowledge gap has on the political power of an agency is clear in the different experiences of NASA and the State Department. When NASA advised Congress during the 1960s on the best way to implement President John F. Kennedy's goal of reaching the moon, most members did not have access to independent scientific advice and were inclined to accept the advice of NASA's scientists. NASA gained considerable prestige and power as a result. In contrast, White House officials and many members of Congress believe they know as much about diplomacy and foreign policy as the foreign service officers in the State Department. As a result, they do not hesitate to challenge or dispute the advice the department offers or to second-guess its actions. Unable to convince other government officials that it possesses a special expertise, the State Department finds itself seriously constrained in deciding how to conduct diplomatic relations.

Differences in Agency Power

Agencies differ widely in their ability to achieve their mission and survival goals.[38] Agencies with politically strong clienteles and formidable levels of expertise have much greater say over the course of public policy than agencies with weak clienteles or expertise perceived to be common knowledge. Thus, although some agencies are recognized as powerful players in the federal government and have more influence in creating rules, others must act much more deferentially.

13-4d Political Constraints on the Federal Bureaucracy

Although government agencies seek political power to ensure their survival and to promote their policy preferences, they are by no means all powerful. Because the rules of American politics disperse and balance power, no individual or institution possesses unrestrained power over the system. The bureaucracy, like other institutions, exercises power, but always within constraints. Congress, the president, interest groups, other federal agencies, and the courts all may challenge an agency's decisions. Such challenges make an agency accountable for its actions and encourage it to do more than simply respond to its own preferences, its self-interest, or the interests of its clientele.

Congress

The Constitution gives Congress important powers over the bureaucracy, including the authority to create (and therefore abolish or modify) agencies, to determine their structure and responsibilities, and to appropriate funds for their use. These are truly "life and death" powers from the agencies' viewpoint, and as a result, Congress wields enormous influence over the workings of the federal bureaucracy.

Congress exercises its bureaucratic powers primarily through its committees and subcommittees. Each committee oversees the operation of agencies that fall within its jurisdiction and makes recommendations regarding the operation and funding of those agencies to the parent body—the House or the Senate. Committees oversee agencies by a variety of means. The most common methods include direct communications between committee staff and the agency, hearings held to oversee or reauthorize agency programs, and evaluations of agency programs performed by congressional support agencies such as the Government Accountability Office.[39]

Congress's decision to assign oversight responsibilities to its committees has significantly affected its relations with the bureaucracy. Committees tend to be controlled by members whose constituents are also the clienteles of the agencies the committees are charged with overseeing.[40] For example, legislators from farm states are more likely to serve on the agriculture committees, and legislators with military bases in their districts are more likely to serve on the armed services committees. These committee members have a greater incentive to cooperate with the agency they oversee than members whose constituents have little or no stake in the operations of the agency. As a result, the committees charged with overseeing a federal agency often are more inclined to help that agency than the House or Senate as a whole is.

The President

Presidents often find themselves in conflict with the federal bureaucracy over the resources the agencies should receive and the manner in which agencies should administer policy. Because the nation cannot afford to give each federal agency all the money it wants, presidents must set spending and policy priorities, a process that makes some agencies winners and others losers. Agencies that win are those whose budgets increase and whose policy proposals move to the top of the president's political agenda. The agencies that lose are those forced to make do with smaller budgets and whose policy proposals are ignored or opposed by the White House.

Of course, when presidents seek to set spending and policy priorities for the federal bureaucracy, they must compete with the more specialized policy aspirations of agencies and their clienteles. And often presidents get bloodied in the resulting political battle. Take, for example, Clinton's promise during the 1992 presidential election campaign to end the ban on allowing gays and lesbians to serve openly in the armed forces. After he was inaugurated in January 1993, Clinton found his proposal denounced by members of the military, their allies on Capitol Hill, and conservative interest groups. Thus, despite his position as commander in chief, Clinton eventually was forced to accept a substitute policy on gays and lesbians that effectively gutted his campaign promise.

Although the battle over gays and lesbians in the military reminds us that presidents do not always get their way in battles with the federal bureaucracy, they do win more often than not. The reason is that the rules of American politics give presidents several powers they can use to enforce their spending and policy priorities. First, the Constitution charges the president with seeing that the laws are faithfully executed. This power permits presidents to oversee the work of federal agencies. Second, presidents appoint (subject to Senate confirmation) the leadership of most agencies. Presidents who use the appointment power effectively can influence how agencies implement policy.[41] For example, after more than a decade of relaxed enforcement of various regulatory policies under agencies headed by Republican appointees, President Clinton appointed individuals with a more activist orientation to agencies such as the OSHA, the FDA, and the Consumer Product Safety Commission. These agencies, in turn, were much more aggressive and vigilant in enforcing regulations affecting the industries within their jurisdictions. The younger President Bush appointed officials who have returned to the less assertive enforcement practices of previous Republican presidents. For example, between 1999 and 2003, the number of employers prosecuted by the Immigration and Naturalization Service for unlawfully employing immigrants dropped from 182 to 4, and fines declined from $3.6 million to $212,000. A similar pattern exists at the FDA. Between 2000 and 2005, it cut the number of warning letters to companies under its jurisdiction by 54 percent and the number of seizures of unsatisfactory products by 44 percent.[42]

In addition to using their oversight and appointment powers, presidents can constrain the power of the federal bureaucracy by exercising their right to propose budgets and legislation to Congress. Although Congress is ultimately responsible for appropriating all government expenditures, presidential budget proposals are usually the starting point for most debates on federal spending and public policy because presidents have the power to both propose budgets to Congress and to veto appropriations bills with which they disagree. The burden then rests with an agency and its allies on Capitol Hill to build a majority coalition that will change the president's budget, a task that often proves difficult. Thus, when Ronald Reagan proposed lower budgets for the EPA in the early years of his administration, Congress largely followed his lead. As a result, the agency was forced to reduce its research and enforcement activities, an outcome that pleased a president who thought that environmental regulations were unduly hampering the growth of the American economy.[43]

The fourth way presidents can influence the behavior of the federal bureaucracy is by reorganizing the structures of individual agencies. Reorganization can strengthen or weaken an agency. In 1970, for example, Richard Nixon sought to demonstrate his personal commitment to the environment and to strengthen the government's ability to protect the environment by consolidating the government's many environmental programs under the leadership of the newly formed EPA.[44] In contrast, in 1971 Nixon sought to undermine the government's core welfare program, AFDC. Political support for AFDC was weak, but the program was administered by the Department of Health, Education, and Welfare (HEW) along with several other assistance programs that enjoyed strong political support. Nixon moved the more politically popular assistance programs into another part of HEW and then imposed spending cuts and other changes on AFDC that he hoped would reduce the welfare rolls.[45]

Finally, presidents can use the Office of Management and Budget (OMB) to curb the power of the federal bureaucracy. As we discussed previously, agencies issue rules as part of their task in administering government policies. Since the 1970s, these rules have had to be cleared by OMB before they can be issued. If the president objects to a proposed rule, the OMB can block its implementation or force the agency to rewrite it to the president's liking.[46] The sharp decline in the rule-making activities of the federal bureaucracy in the 1980s, as Figure 13–3 depicts, was owed largely to President Reagan's adroit use of the OMB clearance process to block the imposition of new rules he disliked.

Interest Groups

One of the most potent checks on the power of the federal bureaucracy comes from the opposition of interest groups whose interests have been harmed by the actions of an agency. Few agencies pursue policies that harm no one. For example, in 1995, the FDA proposed rules to limit the sale of cigarettes to minors. Even though most people agree that minors should be discouraged from smoking, the FDA's proposal triggered a torrent of protests from tobacco companies, advertising agencies, magazine publishers, sponsors of sporting events, and even some charitable groups that receive contributions from tobacco companies.[47] In general, the more important an issue is to the groups that oppose it, and the more powerful those opponents are, the less likely an agency is to get its own way.

Groups that believe they have been or are about to be harmed by a federal agency may look to the president for help.[48] In the early 1970s, many companies found that the cost of adhering to new EPA regulations was squeezing their profit margins. The companies responded by urging President Nixon to intervene on their behalf and convince the agency to relax its regulations. The elder Bush's administration actually formalized the process of responding to complaints from the business community about burdensome government regulation when it created the White House Council on Competitiveness. Under the leadership of Vice President Dan Quayle, the Council advocated business interests, forcing federal agencies to revise regulations that it believed damaged American economic competitiveness.[49]

Groups that oppose an agency's actions may also turn to Congress for help. The ongoing conflict between business and labor over the extent to which workers need protection from repetitive motion injuries illustrates this strategy. In 1995, OSHA proposed regulations to protect workers from repetitive motion injuries. Employees in occupations such as meatpacking and computer programming are prone to such injuries because they have jobs that require them to make the same movements over and over all day long. Business groups, including the National Association of Manufacturers and the National Federation of Independent Business, denied that employees suffered repetitive motion injuries on the job. They appealed to the Republican majorities in Congress to block the proposed regulations. In the face of this pressure, OSHA withdrew its proposed regulations.[50] Labor unions then appealed to President Clinton for help. During his last days in office, he issued executive orders designed to protect workers from repetitive motion injuries. Business groups returned to Congress and persuaded it to pass a bill rescinding Clinton's directives. When newly elected president George W. Bush signed the bill into law, the rules ceased to exist.

Other Agencies

In addition to the constraints Congress, the president, and interest groups impose, the aspirations of agencies with overlapping or competing jurisdictions also constrain the power of an agency to act as it sees fit. Although agencies occasionally cooperate with one another, they much more commonly view one another as potential competitors for clients and resources. As a result, agencies engage in "bureaucratic imperialism" as they try to establish themselves as the lead organization in a contested policy area.[51]

A good example of the way federal agencies fight one another can be found in the events leading up to the Cuban Missile Crisis of 1962. The crisis arose when the United States discovered that the Soviet Union was installing nuclear missiles in Cuba, a discovery that brought the two superpowers to the brink of war. (War was averted when Soviet leaders eventually agreed to remove the missiles from Cuba.) The discovery of the missiles was delayed for ten crucial days while the State Department, the CIA, and the Air Force squabbled over a proposal to send a U-2 spy plane to take aerial photographs of what they believed were missile launch sites. The State Department opposed the plan, arguing that the United States would find itself in a diplomatic crisis if the Cuban military shot down the plane. The CIA and the Air Force both supported the proposed flight, but they disagreed over who should run the operation. The CIA wanted its pilots to fly the mission because the flight involved covert intelligence gathering, whereas the Air Force insisted that, given the high risk that the plane might be shot down, a uniformed military officer should make the flight. After ten days of haggling, an Air Force officer, flying a CIA-owned U-2 plane, made the flight, which took the pictures that provided definitive evidence that the Soviets were preparing to install nuclear missiles in Cuba.[52]

Bureaucratic arguments are by no means limited to agencies in the foreign policy bureaucracy. Domestic agencies engage in jurisdictional disputes as well.

For example, the failure of World Trade Center towers to withstand the September 11, 2001, terrorist attacks led two government agencies to take opposing positions on how to improve the safety of skyscrapers. On one side of the debate, the National Institute of Standards and Technology (NIST), an agency of the Commerce Department, recommended in 2005 that the building codes for skyscrapers be strengthened. According to the NIST, improved fireproofing and additional emergency stairwells would save many lives in the event of another attack. Taken in isolation, the goal of saving lives seems unassailable. The other side of the argument was taken up by General Services Administration (GSA), an independent agency that helps manage and supply other agencies. In 2008, the GSA objected that the costs of the proposed changes would be too high. The agencies continue to dispute one another's claims and advocate for their own positions.[53]

The Courts

A final check on the power of the federal bureaucracy comes from the federal courts. They are often the last refuge for groups that oppose an agency's decisions. The courts can overturn the decisions of federal agencies because the rules of American politics authorize federal judges to review the legality of decisions the government makes.

As we shall see in Chapter 14, the federal judiciary is much less sensitive to political pressure than the other two branches of government. Because federal judges generally do not need to satisfy politically influential interests, they are free to base their decisions on their interpretations of the law rather than on the wishes of the majority or the pleadings of a powerful interest group. The politically insulated nature of legal deliberations makes the courts an attractive access point for groups that have failed to persuade Congress and the president to overturn an agency's decisions. In court, what matters more than political power is whether a group can mount a compelling legal argument that an agency has exceeded its authority or otherwise violated the law.

Instances in which the federal courts limit or overturn the actions of federal agencies abound. A classic example came during the 1980s when environmental groups failed to persuade the Interior Department to stop companies from clear-cutting old forests on federal property in Oregon. Interior Department officials instead favored the interests of the logging industry, which wanted to cut the very old trees because the timber from these old-growth forests commanded higher prices in the market. Unable to persuade the Interior Department to change its policy, environmental groups turned to the federal courts. They asked the courts to bar further logging in the old-growth forests on the grounds that clear-cutting endangered the habitat of the spotted owl, which was protected under the provisions of the Endangered Species Act. Successive federal courts agreed, and they issued injunctions barring further logging. Although President Clinton and Congress subsequently became involved in trying to resolve the issue, the courts remain a potent tool for environmentalists as they struggle to protect these forests.[54]

As you can see, the agencies that make up the federal bureaucracy are political institutions. Their ability to exercise discretion and the often contradictory instructions coming from Congress and the White House enable them to inject their preferences into public policy. To promote their mission and survival goals, agencies seek to gain power by expanding their clientele and by taking advantage of their specialized expertise. Of course, not all federal agencies are equally successful in acquiring political power, and none is free to act entirely as it sees fit. Congress, the president, interest groups, other federal agencies, and the courts all can challenge an agency's decisions. Indeed, because federal agencies constantly interact with these other political actors, particularly congressional committees and interest groups, a predictable pattern of interaction known as the "iron triangle" often results.

13-4e Alliances and the Federal Bureaucracy

Federal agencies are key actors in the policy-making process. As we have just seen, however, they do not act alone. Other political actors also try to influence public policy. At times, these other actors constrain what agencies want to accomplish, but they can also share the same goals with federal agencies. As a result, in some instances they form informal alliances with federal agencies. In essence, they join forces with the bureaucracy to achieve common ends. The exact nature of these alliance patterns has changed over time.

Traditional Alliance Patterns: Iron Triangles

Many observers of the federal bureaucracy have noticed that federal agencies, congressional committees, and interest groups sometimes form a three-way alliance of mutual cooperation. These alliances have earned a variety of names, including policy subgovernments, policy whirlpools, cozy triangles, and **iron triangles**. Despite the different names, all the terms highlight the same common theme: Federal agencies, congressional committees, and interest groups work together to shape public policies within their realm of influence to their mutual advantage.[55]

Figure 13–6 illustrates the pattern of mutual interests that holds together the iron triangle. Each participant in an iron triangle provides benefits to the other participants and in turn receives benefits. Political interest groups get Congress to pass laws that reflect their views, and they get the bureaucracy to carry out those laws in a favorable manner. In return, they help members of Congress win reelection, research policy issues, and formulate draft legislation. The groups help federal agencies by lobbying Congress on the agency's behalf. Members of congressional committees participate in iron triangles to advance their chances for reelection and to gain allies for their legislative proposals. In exchange, they provide the votes needed to enact the proposals an interest group favors, and they protect the agency from criticism and push to expand its

iron triangles
The alliance of a government agency, congressional committee or subcommittee, and political interest group for the purpose of directing government policy within the agency's jurisdiction to the mutual benefit of the three partners.

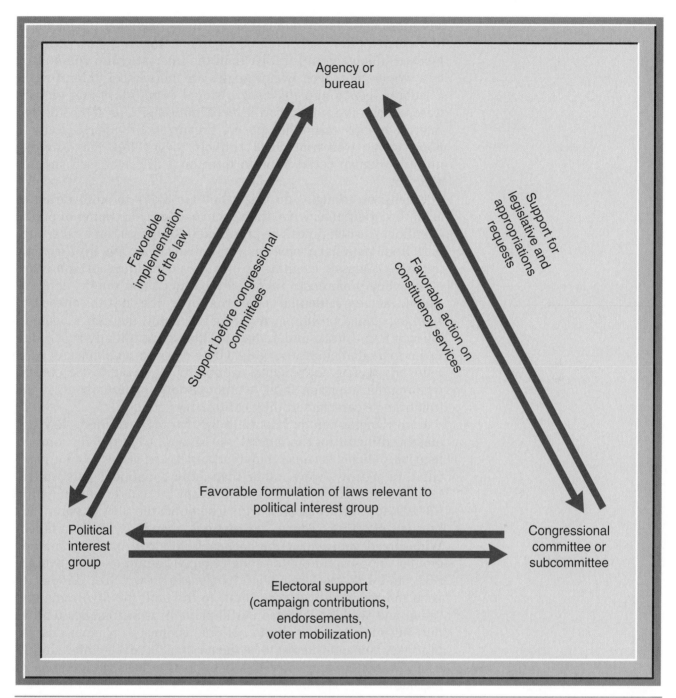

Agency or
bureau

Favorable
implementation
of the law

Support before congressional
committees

Favorable action on
constituency services

Support for
legislative and
appropriations
requests

Favorable formulation of laws relevant to
political interest group

Political
interest
group

Congressional
committee or
subcommittee

Electoral support
(campaign contributions,
endorsements,
voter mobilization)

Figure 13–6   The Workings of an Iron Triangle. The durability of an iron triangle depends on the extent to which each participant is able to benefit from and help the other two and outside groups refrain from getting involved.

duties and budget. Federal agencies receive support for their budgetary and legislative requests from interest groups (who constitute their clientele) as well as from the relevant congressional committees. In exchange, the agencies implement the law in ways that aid the interest group and help members perform constituency service and other activities.[56]

Iron triangles operate most effectively when they form around narrowly defined policy issues. Thus, they typically involve specialized subunits of an agency rather than entire departments, the members of a subcommittee rather than the parent committee, and narrowly focused interest groups rather than the interest group community as a whole. Moreover, iron triangles are most likely to form when a federal agency and the congressional committees that oversee it face a cohesive and powerful set of interest groups. If the affected interest groups are either poorly organized or bitterly divided, however, an iron triangle is unlikely to develop. For example, no iron triangle could hope to form on a divisive issue such as abortion.

When iron triangles do exist, they are likely to be thwarted in achieving their aims when their issue becomes the center of public attention. At such times, the president or Congress can muster support from national majorities for policies that the iron triangle opposes. A classic example of outsiders overriding an iron triangle's policy preferences involved tobacco. When public, congressional, and presidential concerns over the health effects of smoking gained prominence during the 1960s, the iron triangle in tobacco found itself under attack. Although it initially succeeded in fending off attempts to regulate both cigarette smoking and cigarette advertising, opponents eventually won out.[57] Of course, when public attention shifts to other issues, the participants in the iron triangle can reassert their control over policy.

Iron triangles can be important for two reasons. First, they can make it difficult for the federal government to formulate comprehensive policies because they tend to look at issues from a parochial, or narrow, view rather than from a national perspective. Consider, for example, Reagan's attempt in 1985 to eliminate the SBA. Despite repeated efforts to close down the SBA as part of his broader effort to reduce government spending, Reagan failed. Widespread support for the agency from small business interest groups, opposition from the congressional committees that oversee SBA, and a discreet campaign by Reagan's own SBA director to keep the agency alive meant that, in the end, the SBA remained "alive and well."[58] Because participants in iron triangles tend to put self-interest ahead of the national interest—or, more charitably, take their self-interest to be the national interest—they complicate presidential and congressional efforts to pass comprehensive legislation.

Second, iron triangles shape public policy rules to benefit their members at the expense of the general public. The reason stems from the way in which participants in an iron triangle evaluate the benefits and costs of a legislative proposal. They are quite sensitive to how much they stand to benefit from a program they support, and they will identify every possible benefit and use the information to justify the program. In contrast, participants in an iron triangle have every reason to ignore the costs of a program because the American taxpayer usually bears those costs. To take one example, farmers, members of the agriculture committees in Congress, and the Department of Agriculture pay close attention to what they stand to gain from the government's policy of crop subsidies. They worry less about how much those subsidies will add to the federal budget because the cost of the subsidies is spread across the entire American public.

The ability of iron triangles to obstruct national legislation and benefit narrow interests appears to be highly undemocratic.[59] Yet iron triangles flow directly from the decision the Founders made at the Constitutional Convention to decentralize political authority in the United States. As we discussed in Chapter 2, the Founders believed that the best way to protect minority rights from a tyranny of the majority was to structure the rules of politics so that small groups would have opportunities to block or promote legislation on which they held strong preferences. Iron triangles provide minorities with just such an opportunity. Of course, as we have seen, the majority also has the opportunity to override the decisions that iron triangles make, but only if the majority becomes concerned with the issue.

New Alliance Patterns: The Rise of Issue Networks

In recent years, iron triangles have become less of a force in American politics. Fewer iron triangles exist, and those that do are less important in making public policy. The reason for the decline in iron triangles lies in broader changes in American society and politics.[60]

Beginning in the 1970s, the political forces that promoted the rise of iron triangles began to give way. The most important change was a development we discussed in Chapter 10, namely, the tremendous rise in the number of organized interest groups. As interest groups multiplied in the 1970s and 1980s, so did the competition for the attention of congressional committees and federal agencies. Because iron triangles operate most effectively when a federal agency and the congressional committees that oversee it face a cohesive interest group community, the appearance of new interest groups with competing policy agendas caused many iron triangles to collapse. The result was to make policy making, and the federal agencies themselves, more responsive to broader segments of the American public.

Iron triangles have often been replaced by less structured policy-making arrangements that are more open to participation. These structures have been called **issue networks** or "hollow core" policy-making processes.[61] These arrangements permit the involvement of a wider range of participants, both in and out of government, who may take opposing positions on the issues involved. The policy-making activities discussed in the introduction to this chapter exemplify the workings of issue networks. No ongoing iron triangle is at work in determining the process by which drugs are certified by the FDA. Rather, participants get involved only when they felt their interests were at stake. Thus, for example, AIDS activists were heavily involved in the process during the 1980s and were not as involved during the 1990s. The shift from iron triangles to issue networks has resulted in more conflictual interactions and less predictable policy decisions.

issue networks

A loose collection of groups or people in and out of government who interact on a policy issue on the basis of their interest and knowledge rather than just on the basis of economic interests.

13-5 FORMING AND REFORMING THE FEDERAL BUREAUCRACY: THE PURSUIT OF COMPETING VALUES

The younger President Bush sought important changes in the federal bureaucracy. Like many Americans, he believed it was not effectively performing its missions. According to political scientist Herbert Kaufman, many of our criticisms arise because we expect the bureaucracy to achieve three competing values: representativeness, politically neutral competence, and executive leadership. Representativeness embodies the desire that the federal workforce exhibit demographic characteristics valued by the American people. Politically neutral competence seeks efficient and economical government action, free from the wasteful effects of political pressure. Executive leadership reflects the desire that the bureaucracy's actions conform to the political values of its elected executive officers.[62] The problem with attempts to reform the bureaucracy is, as we saw in Chapter 1, that rules are biased: They inevitably help some and harm others. Thus, when a group enacts a rules change designed to accomplish one value, it often weakens the bureaucracy's ability to achieve values that others may prefer. For example, rules that promote a workforce's representativeness can undermine its competence. Rules that create a politically neutral bureaucracy can weaken the executive's ability to lead it. These unavoidable conflicts creating controversy have led to frequent attempts at reform because the values emphasized by reformers change over time. Thus, President Bush's initiatives, which sought a more efficient bureaucracy and stronger executive leadership, are part of a long and ongoing history of reform.

At several times in our history, we have reformed government rules in the pursuit of bureaucratic representativeness. In the 1830s, public support for employing "the common man" in government led Jackson to challenge the Founders' aristocratic system with the patronage system. Turnover in public employment increased, and average citizens found it easier to obtain government jobs. But, as we saw previously, the spoils system also undermined neutral competence and efficiency, leading to widespread corruption. After World War II, the people wanted to ensure that veterans were included in the federal workforce and so Congress created the policy of veterans' preference. Veterans are now advantaged in the government's hiring processes and dominate the upper levels of the civil service system. In the 1960s, the public's belief that disadvantaged groups needed to be represented in government led to affirmative action programs that have increased the numbers of minorities and women in government (see Box 13–1).

Politically neutral competence promotes efficiency and economy in government. Everyone wants the government to do more with less, so this value has generated many reforms. In the 1880s, Progressives passed laws that created the civil service system and independent regulatory commissions. The civil service system was designed to hire employees on the basis of merit while protecting them from politically motivated dismissals. Independent regulatory commissions were supposed to regulate industries without concern for the political consequences of their decisions. Both reforms were motivated by the belief that removing politics from the administrative process would enable the bureaucracy to do its job more efficiently and effectively. However, the civil service reforms also tended to reduce the representativeness of the bureaucracy and make it less responsive to executive leadership. The commissions further reduced the presidents' control of the bureaucracy. The enduring attraction of politically neutral competence is reflected in the frequency with which it has motivated reforms. During the twentieth century alone, presidents created more than a dozen commissions charged with finding ways to streamline the workings of government. The bureaucracy has implemented hundreds of recommendations.[63] In 1993, for example, President Clinton created the National Performance Review to find ways to cut spending and employment. This "Reinventing Government" initiative produced billions of dollars in savings and in six years helped cut more than 300,000 jobs from the federal workforce.[64]

The younger President Bush is not alone in emphasizing the value of executive leadership. Presidents and other politicians supported the patronage system not only because it opened the federal workforce up to a wider range of workers, but because it also gave them more influence over who worked for the government. That made federal workers more susceptible to executive leadership. In 1978, President Carter persuaded Congress to pass the Civil Service Reform Act, which created the SES. This law gives presidents more control over decisions about which civil servants to place in important policy-making positions in the bureaucracy. This enables them to benefit from the expertise of sympathetic civil servant and avoid the resistance of bureaucrats who oppose their policies.

The younger President Bush undertook several initiatives designed to strengthen his control over the bureaucracy. First, he directed the OMB to encourage government agencies to "privatize" as many as one-half of all federal civilian jobs. He argued that this change would reduce the government's personnel costs because private employees can be paid lower wages and provided less generous benefits, thus improving the government's efficiency. In response, the government has contracted out dramatically more work to the private sector, rising from $207 billion to almost $400 billion during the first six years of the Bush presidency. Although little evidence supports Bush's claim that privatization saves money, it does strip the job protections that the civil service system provides, making the composition of the workforce more responsive to the president wishes.[65] Second, President Bush has pushed a plan to limit automatic, seniority-based pay increases for civil servants and replace them with a pay system that bases pay raises on judgments about job performance. Again, President Bush argued that this "pay for performance" initiative will make the workforce more efficient and effective. Critics worry about undue political influence because the individuals who judge the workers' performance are appointed by the president. Those appointees could use their power over pay increases to bend the behavior of civil servants to the president's will, thus blurring the distinction between doing a job "well" and doing a job the way the president wishes.[66] Thus, another effect of this reform would be to strengthen executive leadership. Finally, during negotiations over the creation of the DHS, President Bush demanded that employees not receive many of the civil service protections that workers in other agencies enjoyed. This would enable him to more easily hire and fire civil servants. Bush argued that DHS's mission was too important to allow rules to protect incompetent workers. Senate Democrats resisted, but Bush ultimately prevailed. The Department of Defense (DOD) subsequently undertook similar changes in its civil service rules. These rule changes would improve the president's ability to dismiss civil servants who disagree with the president's policies and replace them with individuals who are more willing to follow orders regardless of their own professional judgment. This would have risked reducing politically neutral competence in exchange for increasing responsiveness to executive leadership. However, appeals courts have rejected both the "pay for performance" and the DHS and DOD reforms because they violated employee rights, and in 2008, Congress enacted legislation restoring most of the employee rights that existed before Bush undertook his initiatives.[67]

As we have seen, the younger President Bush's reform initiatives were not the first to be proposed, and they will not be the last. Indeed, President Obama has already begun to try and reverse the privatization of DOD employment by replacing 39,000 contracted employees with civil servants.[68] As long as changes in the rules create advantages for some groups and disadvantages for others, presidents and Congress will continue to struggle for control over the rules that organize the bureaucracy.

SUMMARY

The rules set forth in the Constitution define the organizational and political context in which the federal bureaucracy must operate. Most importantly, the Constitution assigns the power to oversee federal agencies to both Congress and the president. Whereas the rules authorize Congress to create and fund agencies, they authorize presidents to appoint senior agency officials (subject to Senate confirmation) and to see that agencies faithfully enact laws. Paradoxically, serving two political masters means that the federal bureaucracy is not entirely under the total control of either. The constitutional rules that divide control of the bureaucracy between Congress and the presidency give federal agencies some freedom to follow their own public policy preferences.

The federal bureaucracy has developed over time in response to political pressures and rule changes. As the public made more demands on the federal government, Congress created new agencies and added more employees and additional duties to existing agencies. At the same time, the rules governing who works in the federal bureaucracy and under what conditions also have changed in response to changing political pressures. For much of the nineteenth century, political loyalty was the primary criterion for hiring federal workers, but the American public increasingly came to view this practice as corrupt and inappropriate. Beginning in the 1880s, the federal bureaucracy moved away from the spoils system and toward a new set of rules—a civil service system in which merit rather than political or party loyalty is the primary standard for hiring new workers.

Although many Americans believe that federal agencies should be apolitical organizations that simply administer the decisions of Congress and the president, the administrative tasks of the federal bureaucracy are inherently political. Congress and the president lack the time needed to specify all the details of public policy, and they often give contradictory directions. As a result, federal agencies have some freedom to decide how to fulfill their responsibilities. To that end, each agency's performance is colored by its defined mission and by its desire to survive and grow as an organization.

To carry out their mission and survival goals, agencies seek to acquire power. The two most important sources of agency power are the support of well-organized clientele groups and the agency's own expertise. Agencies that serve politically powerful clients and that have highly valued expertise are well positioned to achieve their goals. This is not to say, of course, that these agencies can act as they see fit. All federal agencies operate within constraints that Congress, the president, interest groups, competing agencies, and the courts impose. The rules of American politics disperse power, which gives the bureaucracy some influence but also imposes constraints.

To enhance their influence in policy making, many federal agencies take part in a coalition known as an iron triangle, a three-way alliance of mutual cooperation that involves an agency, the congressional committees that oversee it, and interest groups affected by the agency's decisions. The participants work together to enact policies that benefit the interest group, help members of the committees get reelected, and enable the agency to grow and prosper. Iron triangles are most likely to succeed when their activities generate little public attention and the affected interest groups are unified in their views. In the 1970s and 1980s, however, the political environment became increasingly hostile to iron triangles. As the number of interest groups multiplied, many agencies found themselves involved in issue networks, facing a host of new interest groups with competing policy agendas. The appearance of interest group competition made policy making, and the federal agencies themselves, more responsive to a broader segment of the American public.

Despite these developments, Americans continue to complain about the federal bureaucracy. The younger President Bush's reform initiatives are only the most recent example of attempts to reform the bureaucracy in pursuit of various values. Americans place a diverse set of demands on the federal government, with the result that the federal bureaucracy faces complex and often contradictory goals. The rules of American politics that allow a diversity of voices to define the goals of government also make it difficult for government to respond with a unified, cohesive set of public policy rules.

KEY TERMS

advice and consent	iron triangles
bureaucracy	issue networks
bureaucrats	patronage
cabinet	rule adjudication
civil service	rule administration
clientele	rule making
expertise	spoils system

READINGS FOR FURTHER STUDY

Kerwin, Cornelius M. *Rulemaking: How Government Agencies Write Law and Make Policy,* 3rd ed. (Washington, D.C.: CQ Press, 2003). A detailed review illustrated with case studies showing how agencies make rules and how politics shapes the rule-making process.

Kettl, Donald F. *System under Stress: Homeland Security and American Politics,* 2nd ed. (Washington, D.C.: CQ Press, 2006). A thorough analysis of the difficulties and problems that arose as the national government undertook the massive reorganization of agencies in the aftermath of the terrorist attacks on September 11, 2001.

Kettl, Donald F., and James W. Fesler. *The Politics of the Administrative Process,* 4th ed. (Washington, D.C.: CQ Press, 2008). A thorough review and analysis of the tasks, processes, characteristics, and problems of the bureaucracy.

Neiman, Max. *Defending Government: Why Big Government Works* (Upper Saddle River, NJ: Prentice-Hall, 2000). A forceful defense of the bureaucracy against stereotypical criticisms, which demonstrates that bureaucratic behavior is generally acceptable and responsible.

Quarles, John. *Cleaning Up America: An Insider's View of the Environmental Protection Agency* (Boston: Houghton Mifflin, 1976). An engaging account of the origins and early years of the Environmental Protection Agency. Illustrates the many political pressures agencies confront in fulfilling their administrative duties.

Rourke, Francis E. *Bureaucracy, Politics and Public Policy,* 3rd ed. (Boston: Little, Brown, 1984). An excellent introduction to the broad topic of politics in the bureaucracy. Discusses both the goals and resources of the bureaucracy, as well as the constraints it operates within.

Seidman, Harold. *Politics, Position, and Power: The Dynamics of Federal Organization,* 5th ed. (New York: Oxford University Press, 1997). A classic and comprehensive discussion of the functions and politics of the bureaucracy. A challenging book with commensurate rewards.

Wilson, James Q. *Bureaucracy: What Government Agencies Do and Why They Do It,* 2nd ed. (New York: Basic Books, 1991). Wilson analyzes why some government agencies work well and others do not.

REVIEW QUESTIONS

1. Who defined the ideal bureaucracy?
   a. Max Weber
   b. James Watt
   c. Woodrow Wilson
   d. Norton Long
2. Every type of government agency administers
   a. the president's policy objectives.
   b. Congress's policy objectives.
   c. rules.
   d. the will of the majority.
3. The most basic function of any agency is rule
   a. adjudication.
   b. administration.
   c. making.
   d. violation.
4. The number of federal civilian employees per capita has _____ since 1951.
   a. increased dramatically
   b. increased slightly
   c. stayed about the same
   d. decreased
5. Who has benefited from income redistribution?
   a. poor people
   b. rich people
   c. corporate farmers
   d. all of the above
6. What event prompted the passage of the Pendleton Act?
   a. the Civil War
   b. the Great Depression
   c. World War II
   d. the assassination of James Garfield
7. Iron triangles are most effective when they form around _____ issues.
   a. broad policy
   b. narrow policy
   c. philosophical
   d. partisan

8. Agencies can use their _____ to ensure that their policy preferences are followed.
   a. mission goals
   b. survival goals
   c. legal constraints
   d. expertise

9. Plans to make the bureaucracy more efficient
   a. date back to President Theodore Roosevelt.
   b. rarely draw bipartisan support.
   c. have been successful over the last three decades.
   d. date back to President Ronald Reagan.

10. The younger President Bush's attempts to reform the bureaucracy have emphasized the goal of
    a. representativeness.
    b. political neutral competence.
    c. executive leadership.
    d. expertise.

NOTES

1. Christopher H. Foreman, Jr., "The Fast Track: Federal Agencies and the Political Demand for AIDS Drugs," *Brookings Review* 9 (Spring 1991): 30–37.

2. "FDA's Critics Renew Efforts to Kill Agency," *Des Moines Register*, January 30, 1995.

3. Gardiner Harris, "At F.D.A., Strong Drug Ties and Less Monitoring," *New York Times*, December 6, 2004; David Brown, "Congress Seeks to Balance Drug Safety, Quick Approval," *Washington Post*, July 5, 2007, A04; Gardiner Harris, "Potentially Incompatible Goals at F.D.A.," *New York Times*, June 11, 2007.

4. LeadLawyer.com, "Liver Failure, Even Death, Linked to Rezulin," available at www.leadla-wyer.com; Joseph P. Shapiro, "A Pill Turned Bitter," *U.S. News & World Report*, December 11, 2000.

5. David Brown, "Congress Seeks to Balance Drug Safety, Quick Approval," *Washington Post*, July 5, 2007, A04.

6. Gardiner Harris, "F.D.A. Widens Safety Reviews on New Drugs," *New York Times*, January 31, 2007; Adam Feuerstein, "FDA Backlog Leaves Biotech Stocks in Limbo," The Street.com, March 25, 2008, available at www.thestreet.com/print/story/10409034.html.

7. Charles T. Goodsell, *The Case for Bureaucracy*, 3rd ed. (Chatham, NJ: Chatham House, 1994), 2.

8. See Murray Weidenbaum, "The Pentagon Fruitcake Rules," *New York Times*, January 5, 1992.

9. Despite diffuse public hostility toward "the bureaucracy," surveys show that most citizens are pleased with their personal contacts with government agencies. For a synopsis of these surveys, see Goodsell, *The Case for Bureaucracy*, chap. 2.

10. This definition is adapted from Michael E. Milakovich and George J. Gordon, *Public Administration in America*, 9th ed. (New York: St. Martin's, 2007), 156.

11. Harold Seidman and Robert Gilmour, *Politics, Position, and Power: From the Positive to the Regulatory State*, 4th ed. (New York: Oxford University Press, 1986), 261–65; Shirley Anne Warshaw, *Powersharing: White House–Cabinet Relations in the Modern Presidency* (Albany, NY: SUNY Press, 1996), chap. 1.

12. "Table 481. Federal Civilian Employment by Branch and Agency: 1990 to 2007" from the *Statistical Abstract of the United States 2009: The National Data Book* (Washington, D.C.: Census Bureau, 2009), available at www.census.gov/compendia/statab/tables/09s0481.pdf.

13. Linda Lee, "Dagwood, Meet the Mailman," *New York Times*, November 6, 1995.

14. Terry M. Moe, "Control and Feedback in Economic Regulation: The Case of the NLRB," *American Political Science Review* 79 (December 1985): 109–16.

15. "Table 481. Federal Civilian Employment by Branch and Agency: 1990 to 2007," from the *Statistical Abstract of the United States 2009: The National Data Book* (Washington, D.C.: Census Bureau, 2009), available at www.census.gov/compendia/statab/tables/09s0481.pdf.

16. Michael Nelson, "The Irony of American Bureaucracy," in *Bureaucratic Power in National Policy Making*, 4th ed., ed. Francis E. Rourke (Boston: Little, Brown, 1986), 163–87.

17. James Q. Wilson, "The Rise of the Bureaucratic Society," *Public Interest* 41 (Fall 1975): 77–103.

18. DHS's employment history can be found in "Table 481. Federal Civilian Employment by Branch and Agency: 1990 to 2007" while its budget history can be found in "Table 454. Federal Budget Outlays by Agency: 1990 to 2008." Both tables are available in the *Statistical Abstract of the United States 2009: The National Data Book* (Washington, D.C.: Census Bureau, 2009), the tables are available at www.census.gov/compendia/statab/tables/09s0481.pdf and www.census.gov/compendia/statab/tables/09s0454.pdf, respectively.

19. William Lilley III and James C. Miller III, "The New 'Social Regulation,'" *Public Interest* 47 (Spring 1977): 49–61.

20. Robert Pear, "New Rules Force States to Curb Welfare Rolls," *New York Times*, June 28, 2008, available at www.nytimes.com/2006/06/28/washington/28welfare.html.

21. Frederick C. Mosher, *Democracy and the Public Service*, 2nd ed. (New York: Oxford University Press, 1982), 58, 60.

22. Jay M. Shafritz, *The Dorsey Dictionary of American Government and Politics* (Chicago: Dorsey, 1988), 511.

23. N. Joseph Cayer, *Managing Human Resources: An Introduction to Public Personnel Administration* (New York: St. Martin's, 1980), 21.

24. "Table 479. Full-Time Federal Civilian Employment—Employees and Average Pay by Pay System: 2000 to 2007," *Statistical Abstract of the United States 2009: The National Data Book* (Washington, D.C.: Census Bureau, 2009), available at www.census.gov/compendia/statab/tables/09s0479.pdf.

25. "Table 482. Federal Employees—Summary Characteristics: 1990 to 2005," *Statistical Abstract of the United States 2009: The National Data Book* (Washington, D.C.: Census Bureau, 2009), available at www.census.gov/compendia/statab/tables/09s0482.pdf.

26. Milakovich and Gordon, *Public Administration in America*, 343.

27. For information on the Department of Homeland Security, see Stephen Barr, "Work Begins on Rules for New Department—and Perhaps All of Government," *Washington Post*, April 2, 2003, B2. For information on the Defense Department's pay-for-performance plan, see Brittany R. Ballenstedt, "Bush Signs Bill That Sends Unions Back to Bargaining Table at Defense," GovernmentExecutive.com, January 28, 2008, available at www.govexec.com/story_page.cfm?articleid=39147&dcn=specialreports_NSPS.

28. Mosher, *Democracy and the Public Service*, 6–8; James Q. Wilson, "The Bureaucracy Problem," *Public Interest* 6 (Winter 1967): 3–9.

29. Frank J. Goodnow, *Politics and Administration: A Study in Government* (New York: Russell and Russell, 1900), 17–26; Woodrow Wilson, "The Study of Administration," *Political Science Quarterly 2* (June 1887): 197–222. Both discussions are reprinted in *Classics of Public Administration*, 5th ed., ed. Jay M. Shafritz, Albert C. Hyde, and Sandra J. Parkes (Belmont, CA: Wadsworth/Thomson Learning, 2004).

30. Francis Rourke, *Bureaucracy, Politics, and Public Policy*, 3rd ed. (Boston: Little, Brown, 1984), 3.

31. Donna Cassata, "Freshmen 'Have to Get' Commerce," *Congressional Quarterly Weekly Report*, July 29, 1995, 2273; Annie Tin, "House Unveils Plan to Abolish Department of Commerce," *Congressional Quarterly Weekly Report*, May 27, 1995, 1502. You can trace the Commerce Department's recent budgetary history at www.census.gov/prod/2005pubs/06statab/fedgov.pdf, 462.

32. Norton E. Long, "Power and Administration," *Public Administration Review* 9 (Autumn 1949): 257.

33. Rourke, *Bureaucracy, Politics, and Public Policy*, chaps. 2–3.

34. "Table 455. Federal Outlays by Detailed Function: 1990 to 2008," *Statistical Abstract of the United States 2009: The National Data Book* (Washington, D.C.: Census Bureau, 2009), available at www.census.gov/compendia/statab/tables/09s0455.pdf.

35. Samuel H. Beer, "Bureaucracies as Constituencies: The Adoption of General Revenue Sharing," in *Bureaucratic Power in National Policy Making*, 4th ed., ed. Francis E. Rourke (Boston: Little, Brown, 1986), 45–56.

36. Rourke, *Bureaucracy, Politics, and Public Policy*, 58.

37. Martha Derthick, "The Art of Cooptation: Advisory Councils in Social Security," in *Bureaucratic Power in National Policy Making*, 4th ed., ed. Francis E. Rourke (Boston: Little, Brown, 1986), 361–79.

38. See, for example, Kenneth Meier, "Measuring Organizational Power: Resources and Autonomy of Government Agencies," *Administration and Society* 12 (November 1980): 357–75.

39. Joel D. Aberbach, *Keeping a Watchful Eye: The Politics of Congressional Oversight* (Washington, D.C.: Brookings Institution, 1990), 132.

40. Christopher J. Deering and Steven S. Smith, *Committees in Congress*, 3rd ed. (Washington, D.C.: CQ Press, 1997), chap. 3.

41. Richard P. Nathan, *The Administrative Presidency* (New York: Macmillan, 1986).

42. For stories about the behavior of Clinton's appointees, see Laurie McGinley, "Clinton's Regulators Zero In on Companies with Renewed Fervor," *Wall Street Journal*, October 19, 1994. For stories about the behavior of Bush's appointees, see Spencer S. Hsu and Kari Lydersen, "Illegal Hiring is Rarely Penalized," *Washington Post*, June 19, 2006, A01; and Gardiner Harris, "Top Democrat Finds F.D.A.'s Efforts Have Plunged," *New York Times*, June 27, 2006.

43. B. Dan Wood, "Principals, Bureaucrats, and Responsiveness in Clean Air Enforcements," *American Political Science Review* 82 (March 1988): 213–34.

44. John Quarles, *Cleaning Up America: An Insider's View of the Environmental Protection Agency* (Boston: Houghton Mifflin, 1976), chap. 2.

45. Ronald Randall, "Presidential Power versus Bureaucratic Intransigence: The Influence of the Nixon Administration on Welfare Policy," *American Political Science Review* 73 (September 1979): 795–810.

46. Elizabeth Sanders, "The Presidency and the Bureaucratic State," in *The Presidency and the Political System*, 3rd ed., ed. Michael Nelson (Washington, D.C.: CQ Press, 1990), 409–42.

47. Timothy Noah, "Tobacco-Marketing Rules Anger Many Non-Tobacco Industries," *Wall Street Journal*, October 17, 1995.

48. E. E. Schattschneider, *The Semi-Sovereign People* (New York: Holt, Rinehart and Winston, 1961).

49. Philip J. Hilts, "In Debate on Quayle's Competitiveness Council, the Issue Is Control," *New York Times*, December 16, 1991.

50. Steven Lohr, "Administration Balks at New Job Standards on Repetitive Strain," *New York Times*, June 12, 1995.

51. Matthew Holden, Jr., "'Imperialism' in Bureaucracy," *American Political Science Review* 60 (December 1966): 943–61.

52. Graham T. Allison, *Essence of Decision: Explaining the Cuban Missile Crisis* (Boston: Little, Brown, 1971), 121–23.

53. Eric Lipton, "Agency Fights Building Code Born of 9/11," *New York Times*, September 8, 2008.

54. Margaret Kriz, "Timber!" *National Journal*, February 3, 1996, 252–57.

55. Douglass Cater, *Power in Washington* (New York: Vintage Books, 1964); J. Leiper Freeman, *The Political Process* (New York: Random House, 1965); Arthur Maass, *Muddy Waters: The Army Engineers and the Nation's Rivers* (Cambridge, MA: Harvard University Press, 1951); Daniel McCool, "Subgovernments as Determinants of Political Viability," *Political Science Quarterly* 105 (Summer 1990): 269–93.

56. Morris P. Fiorina, *Congress: Keystone of the Washington Establishment*, 2nd ed. (New Haven, CT: Yale University Press, 1989), 37–47.

57. A. Lee Fritschler, *Smoking and Politics*, 3rd ed. (Englewood Cliffs, NJ: Prentice-Hall, Inc., 1983), 142.

58. Randall B. Ripley and Grace A. Franklin, *Policy Implementation and Bureaucracy*, 2nd ed. (Chicago: Dorsey Press, 1986), 40–41.

59. See Theodore J. Lowi, *The End of Liberalism*, 2nd ed. (New York: Norton, 1979).

60. Allan J. Cigler and Burdett A. Loomis, "Organized Interests and the Search for Certainty," in *Interest Group Politics*, 3rd ed. (Washington, D.C.: CQ Press, 1991), 388–89; Tom L. Gais, Mark A. Peterson, and Jack L. Walker, "Interest Groups, Iron Triangles, and Representative Institutions in American National Government," *British Journal of Political Science* 14 (April 1984): 161–85.

61. Hugh Heclo, "Issue Networks and the Executive Establishment," in *The New American Political System* (Washington, D.C.: American Enterprise Institute, 1978); John P. Heinz, Edward O. Laumann, Robert L. Nelson, and Robert H. Salisbury, *The Hollow Core: Private Interests in National Policy Making* (Cambridge, MA: Harvard University Press, 1993).

62. Herbert Kaufman, "Administrative Decentralization and Political Power," *Public Administration Review* 29 (January/February 1969): 3–15.

63. Brian Balogh, Joanna Grisinger, and Philip Zelikow, "Chart 1: Milestones in Twentieth-Century Executive Reorganization," in *Making Democracy Work: A Brief History of Executive Reorganization* (Charlottesville, VA: The Miller Center, University of Virginia, 2002).

64. Donald F. Kettl, "Building Lasting Reform: Enduring Questions, Missing Answers," in *Inside the Reinvention Machine*, ed. Donald F. Kettl and John J. DiIulio, Jr. (Washington, D.C.: Brookings Institution, 1995), 16–7, 22, 74; "Testimony of Jacob J. Lew," Director, Office of Management and Budget,

before the Committee on Rules, United States House of Representatives. Re: Budget Reform, March 10, 2000, available at www.whitehouse.gov/omb/legislative/testimony/20000310.13946.html.

65. Edward Walsh, "OMB Details 'Outsourcing' Revisions," *Washington Post*, May 30, 2003; Office of Management and Budget, "Circular No. A-76 (Revised), November 14, 2002; Scott Shane and Ron Nixon, "In Washington, Contractors Take On Biggest Role Ever," *New York Times*, February 4, 2007; Paul Krugman, "Victors and Spoils," *New York Times*, November 19, 2002.

66. Stephen Barr, "Big, Bold Plan Headed at Defense Bureaucracy," *Washington Post*, April 27, 2003.

67. Dana Milbank, "Two Fights Could Produce a Big Winner," *Washington Post*, October 8, 2002; Barr, "Work Begins on Rules for New Department"; Stephen Barr, "A Symbolic Setback to Linking Pay with Performance," *Washington Post*, February 26, 2007; Ballenstedt, "Bush Signs Bill That Sends Unions Back to Bargaining Table at Defense."

68. Dana Hedgpeth, "Contracting Boom Could Fizzle Out," *Washington Post*, April, 2009.

14

The Courts

On December 5, 2001, Hedrick Humphries was fired as an associate manager of a Cracker Barrel restaurant in Bradley, Illinois. Humphries, an African American, had held his position for three years. During most of that time his supervisors had given him good evaluations and pay raises. He did not, however, get along well with his white general manager, who Humphries claimed had said, among other things, that he was "at Cracker Barrel for the white people" and was "going to take care of the white people." Humphries followed company procedures to complain to higher management about these and similar comments and about the dismissal of an African American employee for behavior for which white employees were not punished. Shortly after bringing these problems to management's attention, Humphries was fired because he had failed to secure the restaurant's safe, a charge Humphries denied.[1]

Humphries contested his dismissal, claiming that Cracker Barrel had retaliated after he brought racial discrimination claims to their attention. He first filed a complaint with the federal Equal Employment Opportunities Commission (EEOC), which, after investigating the grievance, issued Humphries a right-to-sue letter, permitting him to take his case to federal court. Humphries subsequently brought suit against Cracker Barrel under both Title VII of the Civil Rights Act of 1964 and section 1981 of the federal code. Section 1981 was derived from the Civil Rights Act of 1866, and says in part, "All persons within the jurisdiction of the United States shall have the same right in every State and Territory to make and enforce contracts, to sue, be parties, give evidence, and to the full and equal benefit of all laws and proceedings for the security of persons and property as is enjoyed by white citizens…" The district court tossed out the Title VII claim on procedural grounds and held that Humphries had not presented sufficient evidence to pursue his Section 1981 claim. However, the Court of Appeals for the Seventh Circuit overturned the district court's decision, finding that Humphries could bring suit against Cracker Barrel for retaliation based on Section 1981. Cracker Barrel (under its corporate name, CBOCS West) then appealed the circuit court's decision to the Supreme Court.

On May 27, 2008, the Supreme Court held on a 7 to 2 vote that section 1981 allows employees who complain about racial discrimination to sue their employers for retaliation. The majority opinion, written by Justice Stephen Breyer, relied heavily on previous Court decisions to justify an expansive reading of Section 1981 to include retaliation claims. The majority opinion asserted, "We agree with CBOCS that the statute's language does not expressly refer to the claim of an individual (black or white) who suffers retaliation because he has tried to help a different individual, suffering direct racial discrimination, secure his [section] 1981 rights. But that fact alone is not sufficient to carry the day. After all, this Court has long held that the statutory text of [section] 1981's sister statute, [section] 1982, provides protection from retaliation for reasons related to the *enforcement* of the express statutory right." The dissenting opinion, written by Clarence Thomas, the only African American justice, lambasted the majority, claiming that "the Court's holding has no basis in the text of [section] 1981" and that consequently they were perpetuating a mistaken reading of the law.[2] The majority's decision was widely interpreted as offering considerable protection to workers who bring retaliation claims for racial discrimination.[3]

The Supreme Court's ruling in *CBOCS West, Inc. v. Humphries* highlights an important lesson about democracy in the United States: Every day, judges make decisions, large and small, that affect the way Americans live. Yet although Americans have the right to choose who represents them in Congress and who will serve in the White House, they have no direct say in who sits on the Supreme Court or any other federal court, and in a number of states, they have only limited say over who serves on state courts. How does a judiciary that often lies beyond the direct control of the public fit into the concept of a democracy?

The answer lies in the nature and purpose of the court system in the United States. All democracies need a formal system that allows individuals, groups, and government agencies to challenge people they believe have violated the rules and infringed on their rights. Without such a system, political might will triumph over individual rights, and societal conflict will likely escalate into violence. Thus, although the courts have few democratic qualities, they are an integral part of our democracy because they can protect the rights of individuals and restrain the government from overstepping or abusing its power.

In this chapter, we examine the role the courts play in our democracy. We begin by looking at what the Constitution says—and does not say—about the federal courts, and we examine the way Congress has structured the federal judiciary. We then discuss how the federal courts have become important policy makers by exercising their power to decide the legality of government actions, how justices are picked for the Supreme Court, and how they decide cases when they reach the bench. We also analyze the work of the lower federal courts. We conclude the chapter by examining the state courts, which handle the vast majority of legal cases in the United States. Although state courts mirror some of the basic attributes of the federal judiciary, they also differ in important ways from the federal courts.

14-1 THE FEDERAL COURTS

The federal court system is a joint creation of the Constitution and Congress. The Constitution established the federal judiciary as one of the three branches of government, but it says remarkably little about what the federal court system should look like. Instead, the Founders delegated to Congress the task of designing a court system that would fit the needs of the new country. Over the next 220 years, Congress fulfilled its constitutional duty by passing legislation that created (and abolished) federal courts as the needs of an ever-changing country demanded.

14-1a The Constitution and the Federal Courts

The delegates to the Constitutional Convention firmly believed that the success of American democracy depended on the creation of a court system independent of the executive and legislative branches of government. To this end, Article III of the Constitution created the federal judiciary as a separate branch of government.

Although the Founders believed deeply in the idea of an independent judiciary, they spent relatively little time discussing it, and they provided little guidance on how to organize the federal courts. Article III says "the judicial power of the United States shall be vested in one supreme Court," and it lists the subjects on which the federal courts can rule (although Congress is authorized to make exceptions to the list). Article II gives the president the right to appoint federal judges with the advice and consent of the Senate, and it gives Congress the right to remove judges and other government officials through the impeachment process. Overall, however, the Constitution is silent on the question of how to organize the federal courts. Indeed, although the Constitution specifically creates the Supreme Court, it says nothing about how many justices should serve on it.

Instead of providing a blueprint for the federal court system, the Constitution charged Congress with designing one. The Founders delegated the task to Congress because they disagreed over how many federal courts the country needed. Some argued that all court cases should originate in state courts, thereby negating the need for any federal courts other than the Supreme Court.[4] Rather than allowing the Constitutional Convention to flounder over a dispute on how to organize the judiciary, the Founders authorized Congress to decide the matter.

14-1b Congress and the Federal Courts

Over the past 220 years, Congress has passed many laws affecting the organization of the federal judiciary. The first was the Judiciary Act of 1789. One key provision of the act stipulated that the Supreme Court would consist of a chief justice and five associate justices. The act also settled the question of how many federal courts there should be by creating a federal court system consisting of the Supreme Court, circuit courts, and district courts.

Although the Judiciary Act of 1789 set important precedents, it has been modified many times. For example, the Supreme Court initially was created with six seats. Congress changed the number of Supreme Court justices more than half a dozen times during the nineteenth century, resulting in the Court having as few as five members at one point and as many as ten members at another. The current number of nine justices was set in 1869. Since then, there have been several attempts to make the Court larger. The most famous was the so-called court-packing scheme of 1937 in which President Franklin Roosevelt asked Congress to pass a law requiring the appointment of one additional justice for each sitting justice over the age of seventy. This would have immediately increased the size of the Court to fifteen members. Roosevelt hoped that a larger Court stacked with his appointees would be more sympathetic to his New Deal programs, but ultimately his plan failed to secure congressional support, and the number of justices remained at nine.[5]

Likewise, over time Congress has changed elements of the court system. In the Court of Appeals Act of 1891, Congress created powerful courts of appeals; the original circuit courts withered and were finally abolished in 1911. Since 1911, the Supreme Court, appeals courts, and district courts have remained the three basic levels in the federal judiciary.[6] And as the American population has grown, Congress has responded by adding to the number of appeals and district courts.

Legal scholars refer to the Supreme Court, appeals courts, and district courts as **constitutional courts** because Article III of the Constitution provides for their creation and because that Article's safeguards against removal from the bench and salary cuts apply to the judges appointed to them. In addition to its responsibility for organizing the constitutional courts, Congress can also establish **legislative courts**, so called because their legal basis stems not from Article III but from a clause in Article I allowing Congress "to constitute tribunals." Legislative courts are usually designed to deal with specific issues or to administer specific congressional statutes. In 1988, for example, Congress established the Court of Veterans Appeals to review the decisions the Department of Veterans Affairs makes. Legislative courts enjoy less independence than constitutional courts. Judges on the Court of Veterans Appeals, for example, serve for fifteen-year terms, whereas constitutional judges serve for life.[7] Other legislative courts include the U.S. Court of Military Appeals, the Court of International Trade, and the U.S. Tax Court. Although legislative courts can be important in specific circumstances, the constitutional courts handle most federal litigation, and they are the focus of our attention in this chapter.

constitutional courts

The three-tiered system of federal district courts, courts of appeals (originally circuit courts), and the Supreme Court. Article III of the Constitution provides for the creation of these courts.

legislative courts

Various administrative courts and tribunals that Congress establishes, as Article I of the Constitution provides.

14-2 THE FEDERAL COURT SYSTEM

Figure 14–1 shows the three tiers in the current configuration of the federal court system. The Supreme Court sits atop the federal judiciary. Almost all the cases it takes are on appeal from other courts. The decisions the Supreme Court makes are final unless Congress and the president go to extraordinary lengths—such as passing new laws or proposing constitutional amendments—to overturn them, or the Court chooses to reverse itself. Although the Court can decide broad issues, such as the constitutionality of laws, many of its holdings (or rulings) are decided on narrow

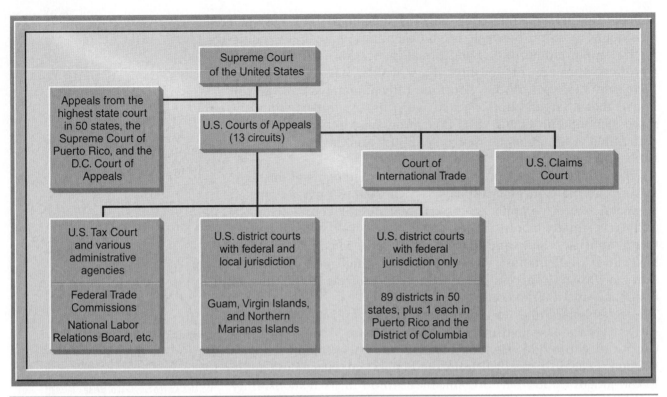

Figure 14–1   The U.S. Federal Court System. The federal court system has three tiers: district courts, courts of appeals, and the Supreme Court.

Source: *Harold W. Stanley and Richard G. Niemi*, Vital Statistics on American Politics, 2001–2002, *3rd ed. (Washington, D.C., CQ Press, 2001),* 265. Copyright © 1992 CQ Press. Reprinted by permission.

grounds. Thus, only a few of its decisions each year gain much public attention; many are of interest to relatively few people.

Beneath the Supreme Court are the thirteen courts of appeals. As Figure 14–2 shows, twelve of the courts of appeals have a geographical jurisdiction. Congress created the Thirteenth Court of Appeals in 1982. Called the Court of Appeals for the Federal Circuit, it fields cases dealing with specialized subjects such as patents, copyrights, and trademarks. The courts of appeals form the middle tier of the federal judiciary, and they hear appeals of decisions that the district courts and some federal administrative agencies make.

The lowest tier in the federal court system comprises the ninety-four district courts (eighty-nine districts in fifty states, with each state having at least one district, plus one each in the District of Columbia, Puerto Rico, Guam, the Virgin Islands, and the Northern Marianas Islands). The district courts are almost always the courts of original jurisdiction, meaning they are the first court to hear a case. In a district court, a single judge presides over a trial to determine guilt or innocence in federal (but not state) criminal cases or to assess responsibilities or fault in federal civil cases. District courts handle more than 325,000 cases each year.[8]

Most of the cases that reach the Supreme Court were heard first in one of the ninety-four federal district courts and then in one of

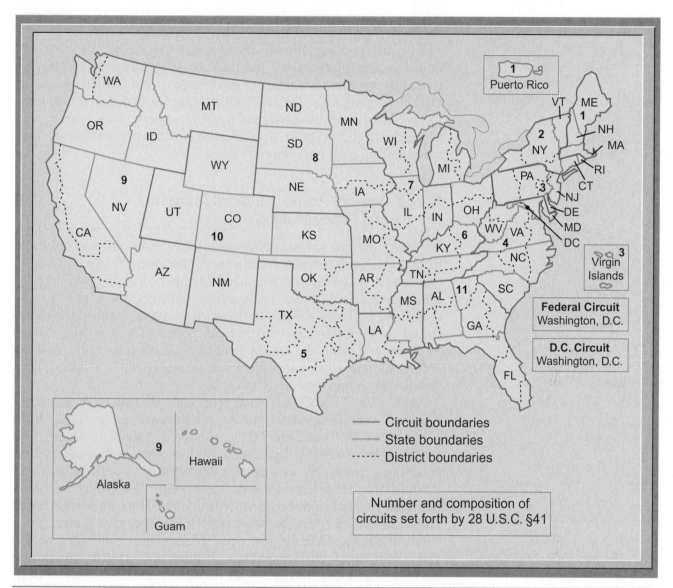

Figure 14–2 The Thirteen Federal Judicial Circuits and Ninety-Four U.S. District Courts. The courts of appeals and the district courts are organized geographically.

Source: *Harold W. Stanley and Richard G. Niemi*, Vital Statistics on American Politics, 2001–2002, *3rd ed. (Washington, D.C., CQ Press, 2001), 266. Copyright © 1992 CQ Press. Reprinted by permission.*

the thirteen appeals courts. The vast majority of legal cases, however, never make it to a federal appeals court, let alone the Supreme Court. Only about 10 percent of cases in district court are appealed to courts of appeals. In turn, only a small percentage of the cases the courts of appeals decide are appealed to and taken up by the Supreme Court. Legal cases also can make it onto the docket of the Supreme Court through other routes. For example, the decisions of each state's highest court can be appealed directly to the Supreme Court when a substantial federal question is involved, as can other cases that Congress may specify. Nonetheless, the most common route is federal district court to federal appeals court to Supreme Court.

14-2a The Federal Courts as Policy Makers

The Founders envisioned the federal courts as independent bodies, applying the laws and policies established by the legislative and executive branches of government. Yet the federal courts almost immediately became policy makers when the Supreme Court established the power of judicial review. This power gives the federal courts great influence over the way our democracy operates and over our everyday lives.

14-2b Judicial Review, Judicial Activism, and Policy Making

By sketching the federal court system in broad outlines only, the Constitution left unclear what powers the federal judiciary would exercise. As a result, the federal courts spent the first two decades after the Constitutional Convention defining their role in the American political system. In these years, the federal courts established two key rules of the American political system: The rulings of the federal judiciary are superior to those of state courts, and the federal judiciary has the authority to overturn the decisions of both the executive and legislative branches of government.

Article VI of the Constitution stipulates that the U.S. Constitution is to be held superior to state constitutions and laws. The Judiciary Act of 1789 confirmed the supremacy of the federal judiciary by giving the Supreme Court the right to review and overturn state court decisions on laws or treaties that conflicted with federal law. And in the 1796 case of *Ware v. Hylton*, the Supreme Court declared a state law to be unconstitutional.[9] Thus, almost immediately, the federal courts asserted superiority over state courts.

Although the Constitution does declare the supremacy of the U.S. Constitution over state laws, it does not explicitly empower the Supreme Court to review and overturn the decisions of Congress and the president. Instead, Chief Justice John Marshall claimed that right for the Supreme Court in the 1803 case *Marbury v. Madison*.

Marbury v. Madison
The Supreme Court decision in 1803 that established the principle of judicial review.

The case stemmed from a dispute between members of the Federalist Party and the Democrat-Republican Party. On March 2, 1801, President John Adams, a Federalist, appointed William Marbury to be a justice of the peace in Washington, D.C. The next day, Adams's last in office, the proper appointment papers were filled out and signed, but acting Secretary of State John Marshall (who had just recently been named Chief Justice of the Supreme Court) failed to deliver the papers before the stroke of midnight, when Adams's term of office expired. Subsequently, Adams's Democrat-Republican successor, Thomas Jefferson, ordered his secretary of state, James Madison, not to give Marbury the papers.

Marbury filed suit with the Supreme Court, asking it to issue a writ of *mandamus* ("we command") to Madison; that is, he wanted a Court order forcing Madison to give him his appointment papers. Marbury could request a writ of mandamus because a section of the Judiciary Act of 1789 provided for it. The Court did not make a decision on the case until February 1803, in its first meeting since December 1801. The Court's opinion, written by Chief Justice Marshall, was a legal and political masterpiece. In it, Marshall, an ardent Federalist, scolded President Jefferson for not giving Marbury his rightful position. Marshall went on to say that the Court did not have the power to force the president to deliver the appointment papers because the Court found the section of the Judiciary Act giving them that power to be an unconstitutional extension of the Court's jurisdiction. Thus, the Court claimed the right to declare a law unconstitutional by nullifying a law Congress had passed to increase the Court's power.[10]

The Supreme Court's ruling in *Marbury v. Madison* established the doctrine of **judicial review**. This doctrine, a bedrock principle of American jurisprudence, allows the Supreme Court, none of whose members must stand for election, to declare the acts of the president and Congress unconstitutional, and thus null and void. Federal district courts and courts of appeals also may rule that legislation is unconstitutional, and their rulings are binding unless a higher court reverses them.

judicial review

The doctrine allowing the Supreme Court to review and overturn decisions made by Congress and the president.

President Thomas Jefferson and members of Congress recognized at the time that Chief Justice Marshall was claiming a new power for the Supreme Court. Yet neither Jefferson nor Congress moved to kill the doctrine of judicial review. The White House and Capitol Hill agreed to accept the new doctrine partly because both Jefferson and a majority in Congress agreed with the substantive decision that the Court had reached in *Marbury,* if not with the reasoning it used. A second reason that the White House and Capitol Hill accepted judicial review was the persuasiveness of Marshall's skillfully written opinion. Although the Constitution did not explicitly grant the power of judicial review, Marshall argued convincingly that it did so implicitly.[11]

A third reason Congress and the president accepted the doctrine of judicial review was that the Supreme Court used its newfound power sparingly. Indeed, the Court did not declare another act of Congress unconstitutional for more than fifty years. (The second instance came in *Dred Scott v. Sandford*, the tragic 1857 case that helped set the stage for the Civil War.) As Figure 14–3 shows, in recent years, the Supreme Court has become more willing to overturn federal, state, and local laws, although judicial review is still a rather rare event. Even so, judicial review remains a powerful weapon. The threat that the Supreme Court may overturn a law often influences how Congress, state legislatures, and city councils draft legislation.

The power the federal courts have to decide which laws are and are not constitutional raises concerns. Many observers worry that judicial review has evolved into **judicial activism** because federal judges may overturn laws to impose their policy preferences on the public rather than to uphold the Constitution. A problem arises, however, when it comes to distinguishing between judicial review, which is acceptable, and judicial activism, which, to many

judicial activism

The vigorous use of judicial review to overturn laws and make public policy from the federal bench.

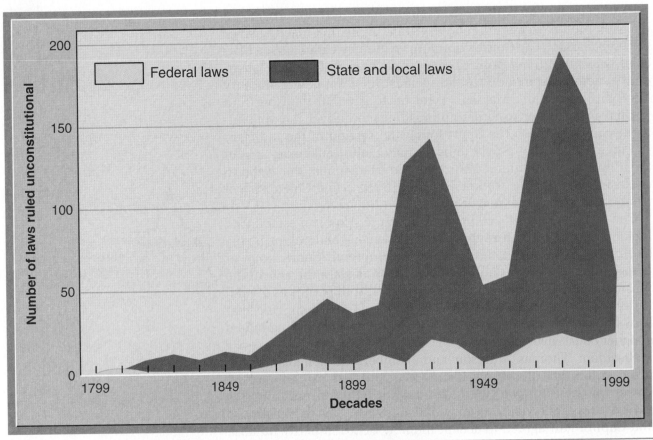

Figure 14–3   Laws Declared Unconstitutional, 1799–1999. The number of state and federal laws the Supreme Court has declared unconstitutional each decade has increased over time.

Source: *Data from Harold W. Stanley and Richard G. Niemi,* Vital Statistics on American Politics, 2001–2002 *(Washington, D.C.: CQ Press, 2001), 288.*

people, is not. In most instances, the distinction lies in the eye of the beholder.

To see how difficult it is to distinguish between judicial review and judicial activism, consider the criticisms leveled against the Supreme Court since the 1950s. Under the leadership of Earl Warren, Chief Justice of the United States from 1953 to 1969, the Court handed down many liberal decisions. Liberals applauded the Court for upholding the meaning of the Constitution, while conservatives accused the justices of ignoring it. In the 1980s, however, the tables were turned when Ronald Reagan and George H. W. Bush's appointees pushed the Court in a conservative direction. Liberals began to criticize the Court's activism, particularly in the areas of personal and civil rights. Conservatives, on the other hand, lauded the Court for adhering to the essential meaning of the Constitution. One study of the Court from 1994 to 2005 found that Justices Thomas and Anthony Kennedy, appointed by Republican presidents, were the most likely to vote to strike down a law passed by Congress, while Justices Ruth Bader Ginsburg and Breyer, nominated by President Bill Clinton, a Democrat, were the least likely to vote to overturn a law passed by Congress.[12] Another study of the same time period concluded that the conservative justices were more likely to invalidate federal laws and to overturn legal precedents, while the liberal justices were more apt to declare state laws unconstitutional.[13]

Concerns about judicial activism are neither trivial nor academic. Since the 1950s, the Supreme Court has rendered decisions that have dramatically changed American life. It has overturned state laws prohibiting abortions and the sale of birth control devices. It has fundamentally restructured the criminal justice system by directing the police to follow strict procedures when investigating crimes and by requiring that poor defendants receive a lawyer. On all sorts of issues, from legislative redistricting to environmental issues to free speech to prayer in the public schools, the Court has changed the way government operates and the way Americans live. Clearly, judicial review might give judges bent on judicial activism powers inconsistent with common notions of democracy because judges are free to impose their views on the public through the legal system.

14-2c Limitations on the Courts

Despite the doctrine of judicial review and the potential for judicial activism, the federal judiciary does not exercise unlimited power. Four factors curb the power of the courts: the reactive nature of the courts, their inability to enforce their rulings, the ability of the president and Congress to draft new laws, and public opinion.

American courts are by their nature reactive. In our legal system, courts can rule only on cases brought before them; they cannot seek out cases to decide or issue rulings on hypothetical cases. (They can, however, shift the focus of a case from the issues the litigants want to discuss to matters the justices find more compelling. For example, the famed case of *Mapp v. Ohio* [1961] initially involved obscenity issues. Yet, because the police had seized the obscene materials without a search warrant, the Court used the case to rule that evidence obtained from an illegal police search must be excluded from a trial.[14] There is evidence that the Court answers questions not raised by the parties with some frequency.)[15] For example, if Supreme Court justices want to change previous abortion decisions, they must wait until a relevant case is appealed to them; they cannot go out and drum up business. In contrast, the president and Congress are both free to initiate policy. In addition, decisions the courts reach tend to be on small, specific points, producing policy changes that are narrowly focused rather than expansive.[16] The courts tend to take small steps, not large ones, in changing policy.

The second limitation on the power of the courts is that they depend on other government agencies to enforce their decisions. Once, when President Andrew Jackson did not like a decision written by Chief Justice John Marshall, he was reported to have said, "John Marshall has made his decision; now let him enforce it." Such sentiments are not necessarily idle threats. As we saw in Chapter 5, many southern states initially refused to obey the

Supreme Court's ruling in *Brown v. the Board of Education* that they desegregate their schools. Indeed, a federal lawsuit filed in February 1956 to desegregate the public schools in East Baton Rouge, Louisiana, was only settled in June 2003, after a forty-seven-year battle. Similarly, four decades after the Court declared prayer in the public schools to be unconstitutional, resistance to the decision, and attempts to evade or ignore it continue throughout the country.[17] The refusal to obey court decisions also arises on far less prominent matters. For example, in 1989, the Supreme Court ruled that states cannot exempt religious periodicals or books from sales taxes.[18] In Rhode Island, however, shopkeepers continued to exempt bibles and other "canonized scriptures" from the sales tax because a 1982 state law required them to do. Even after the state division of taxes notified all Rhode Island bookstores in 1992 that the exemption was now illegal, many stores continued to exempt religious books. Even more striking is that Rhode Island's legislative leaders failed to support the repeal of the unconstitutional religious exemption from the state statutes when some legislators introduced legislation that would have done just that. And Rhode Island was not alone in its defiance. Indeed, in 2006 several other states, among them Georgia and Florida, still had laws on the books exempting religious publications from their state sales tax.[19]

In addition to being limited by the reactive nature of the legal system and a lack of enforcement power, the power of the courts is limited by the ability of Congress and the states to write new laws. Sometimes Congress responds to Supreme Court decisions by proposing amendments to the Constitution. When the Supreme Court overturned a federal law lowering the voting age to eighteen in 1970, Congress and the states nullified the Court's decision by adopting the Twenty-Sixth Amendment a year later.[20] The Eleventh, Fourteenth, and Sixteenth Amendments also were adopted to overcome Supreme Court decisions.[21] In other cases in which the courts find a law is flawed, Congress may simply rework the offending provision. As we will discuss at greater length in Chapter 16, the Supreme Court in 1985 overturned Gramm–Rudman, a bill designed to cut the federal budget deficit because it contained a provision that violated the separation of powers. Congress responded by rewriting the offending provision to comply with the Court's objections.[22] After the Court's controversial 2005 decision in *Kelo v. New London*, which allowed states to use their eminent domain power to obtain land for use by private developers, state legislatures responded vigorously in opposition. By 2007, thirty-one states had passed laws, five more states had adopted constitutional amendments, and three other states had passed both a law and adopted a constitutional amendment, all essentially inhibiting the state's use of its eminent domain powers for private purposes.[23]

Not all attempts to overturn the Court's decisions succeed.[24] Members of Congress have submitted many proposed constitutional amendments to overturn the ban on official school prayer. None has passed. And when the Court ruled in 1989 that the First

Amendment protected an individual's right to burn the flag, outraged members of Congress tried (and failed) to amend the Constitution to outlaw flag burning. And occasionally, even if Congress responds, the Court can still hold its position. After the Court handed down a 1990 decision making it easier for states to restrict religious practices, Congress and the president responded in 1993 with the Religious Freedom Restoration Act, returning the standard the courts were to use to the stricter interpretation used before the 1990 decision. But, in a 1997 decision, *City of Bourne (Texas) v. Flores*, the Court ruled the restoration act unconstitutional, returning the standard to the one the Court had set in its 1990 decision. In the Court's opinion, Justice Kennedy asserted, "The power to interpret the Constitution in a case or controversy remains in the judiciary."[25] In 2000, however, Congress passed the Religious Land Use and Institutionalized Persons Act, intended to apply their preferred standard in some narrowly defined situations. In 2005, the act was declared constitutional by the U.S. Supreme Court in the case of *Cutter v. Wilkinson*. The courts of appeals had split on the measure, with four circuits finding it to be constitutional and one circuit finding it unconstitutional.[26]

The final limitation on the power of the courts is public opinion. The Founders designed the courts to be isolated from public and political sentiments. As Justice Felix Frankfurter observed, though, "The Court's authority—possessed of neither the purse nor the sword—ultimately rests on sustained public confidence."[27] Although the public hardly follows the courts in any detail—on average, only 30 percent of Americans say they follow important Supreme Court cases closely—public opinion of the Court does change in response to its decisions.[28] For example, when the Warren Court handed down a series of unpopular decisions protecting the rights of people accused of crimes, public confidence in the courts dropped. Similarly, following the Court's decision in *Bush v. Gore* deciding the 2000 presidential election, around 30 percent of Americans said they had lost confidence in the Court.[29]

The risk the Supreme Court faces is that a series of unpopular rulings will anger the public and move Congress to pass laws that restrict the independence of the judiciary. And the justices recognize the risk they run. During their deliberations on the abortion-rights case *Planned Parenthood of Southeastern Pennsylvania v. Casey* (1992), the justices were acutely aware of the need to maintain the legitimacy of the Court in the public eye (see Box 14–2). Yet throughout its history, the Court rarely has been out of step with the mainstream of public opinion for an extended period of time, although it is quicker to respond on some issues, such as criminal procedure, than it is on others, such as civil rights.[30] Indeed, with the exception of a liberal period under Chief Justice Earl Warren, the Court has tended toward moderate decisions. The reason for this congruence is not that justices respond to current political passions, although they sometimes may, but rather that, as we will see, the political process by which judges are appointed to the bench keeps the courts in touch with public sentiment.

14-3 THE SUPREME COURT AS A POLITICAL INSTITUTION

Supreme Court justices wield considerable power. Acting collectively, they have the power to set the course the law will follow, even to the extent of overruling the preferences of the president and Congress. Like all federal judges, the justices attain their seats on the Supreme Court through a highly politicized process. How does politics affect the selection of justices? Does a politicized process ensure a more democratic system, or undercut it? Obviously, who serves—and how they get to the bench—matters.

14-3a The Characteristics of the Court

To understand how the Supreme Court operates, it is necessary first to explain the basic characteristics of the Court: who serves, the typical career path of a justice, the special powers of the chief justice, the average length of service on the Court, and the rewards of service.

Who Serves?

Since the Court's inception, slightly more than 100 people have served as justices. As is the case with presidents and members of Congress, almost all the justices have been white Protestants, and all but two have been men. Several Catholics have served,

Source: © Collection of the Supreme Court of the United States./Steve Petteway

2006 U.S. Supreme Court Justices. *Seated left to right:* Justice Anthony M. Kennedy; Justice John Paul Stevens; Chief Justice John G. Roberts, Jr.; Justice Antonin Scalia; Justice David H. Souter. *Standing left to right:* Justice Stephen G. Breyer, Justice Clarence Thomas, Justice Ruth Bader Ginsburg, Justice Samuel Anthony Alito, Jr.

although little attention was paid to their religion. Controversy did surround the nomination of the first Jewish justice, Louis Brandeis, in 1916. (Indeed, one of the other justices refused to talk to Brandeis for the first three years he served on the Court and even refused to sit next to him when the Court had its picture taken.) The first African American justice, Thurgood Marshall, was not appointed until 1967. On his retirement in 1991, he was succeeded by another African American, Clarence Thomas. The first woman justice, Sandra Day O'Connor, was named only in 1981. In 1993, Ruth Bader Ginsburg joined her. When O'Connor retired in 2006, she was replaced by Samuel Alito, leaving Justice Ginsburg as the only female on the Court. No other minorities or women have served on the Supreme Court.

How They Arrive at the Court

Although each Supreme Court justice has followed a different career path, they all share one common trait: They all have been lawyers. (The Constitution does not require justices to be lawyers, nor does it establish a minimum age as it does for Congress and the presidency.) Most justices have served previously as judges at either the state or federal level. Even William Howard Taft, the president who later became chief justice, served as a state and federal judge early in his career. If anything, previous judicial experience has become even more important in recent decades. Every justice since William Rehnquist and Lewis Powell in 1971 has had judicial experience. But some notable members of the Court have not served on the bench before joining the Supreme Court. For example, Earl Warren was the governor of California and had been the 1948 Republican nominee for vice president when President Dwight Eisenhower appointed him chief justice in 1953.

The Chief Justice

The chief justice is considered first among equals on the Supreme Court, but the job's importance and standing has evolved over time. The Constitution mentions the position only in passing; Article I, Section 3 requires that the chief justice preside over any impeachment trial of a president. As mentioned previously, the Judiciary Act of 1789 specified a chief justice, along with five associate justices. Since the mid-1860s, the official title of the post of chief justice has been "Chief Justice of the United States," further distinguishing it from the positions of the associate justices, who are justices "of the Supreme Court."[31] Like the other justices, the chief justice is nominated by the president and confirmed by the Senate. Even sitting members of the Court must be reconfirmed if they are elevated to chief justice. The chief justice typically is the most publicly prominent member of the Court. The chief justice, for instance, usually administers the oath of office to the president and speaks for the federal courts to Congress and the public. The chief justice plays this latter role because he—so far every chief justice has been a man—is responsible for carrying out numerous administrative tasks, such as chairing the organizations that over-see the management of the federal courts.

Chief justices can influence the direction of the Supreme Court in several ways. The chief justice presides at the public hearing in which the lawyers in a case present their oral arguments, chairs the conference where the justices decide each case, determines who will write the opinion of the Court when he is part of the majority, and initiates the discuss list.[32] This last power is important. The discuss list contains those cases appealed to the Court that the chief justice believes are important enough to warrant further discussion. Only about 20 to 30 percent of all cases appealed to the Supreme Court make it onto the discuss list. The other justices may add to the discuss list the chief justice starts, but they may not subtract from it. Thus, the chief justice always has the opportunity to convince his colleagues to hear a case he thinks warrants attention.[33] Because of the leadership role chief justices play, Supreme Court eras are usually associated with a particular chief justice, such as the Warren Court (1953–1969) or the Rehnquist Court (1986–2005).

Length of Service

Justices can serve for life—and most serve until they die or retire from public life. Service on the Supreme Court has not always been attractive. One of George Washington's original appointees declined the offer, preferring instead to take a state office. Another served just two years and never attended any sessions before he resigned to become the chief justice of the South Carolina State Supreme Court. Among Washington's original appointees, most served only a few years, and only one served as long as ten.

A seat on the Supreme Court became more appealing, and members began to serve longer, after the Court established itself as an important part of the American political system. William O. Douglas had the longest career of any Supreme Court justice, serving from 1939 to 1975, a period that spanned seven presidencies. Lengthy service on the Court is now the norm—the last ten justices to die or retire from office served an average of twenty-six years each. In 2009, Justice John Paul Stevens was in his thirty-fourth year on the Court. Such long tenures explain why presidents regard a Supreme Court nomination as one of the most important decisions they will make—the justices they appoint are likely to be on the bench long after the president has left the White House (see Figure 14–4).

Rewards of Service

The attraction of a seat on the Supreme Court today is easy to see. Becoming a justice represents the pinnacle of a legal career, even though the $208,100 salary in 2008 was much lower than any of the justices could expect to make in private practice. (The chief justice earned slightly more—$217,400. In 2003, his last full year in private practice, Chief Justice John Roberts earned slightly more than $1 million.)[34] Each justice is allowed to select his or her own law

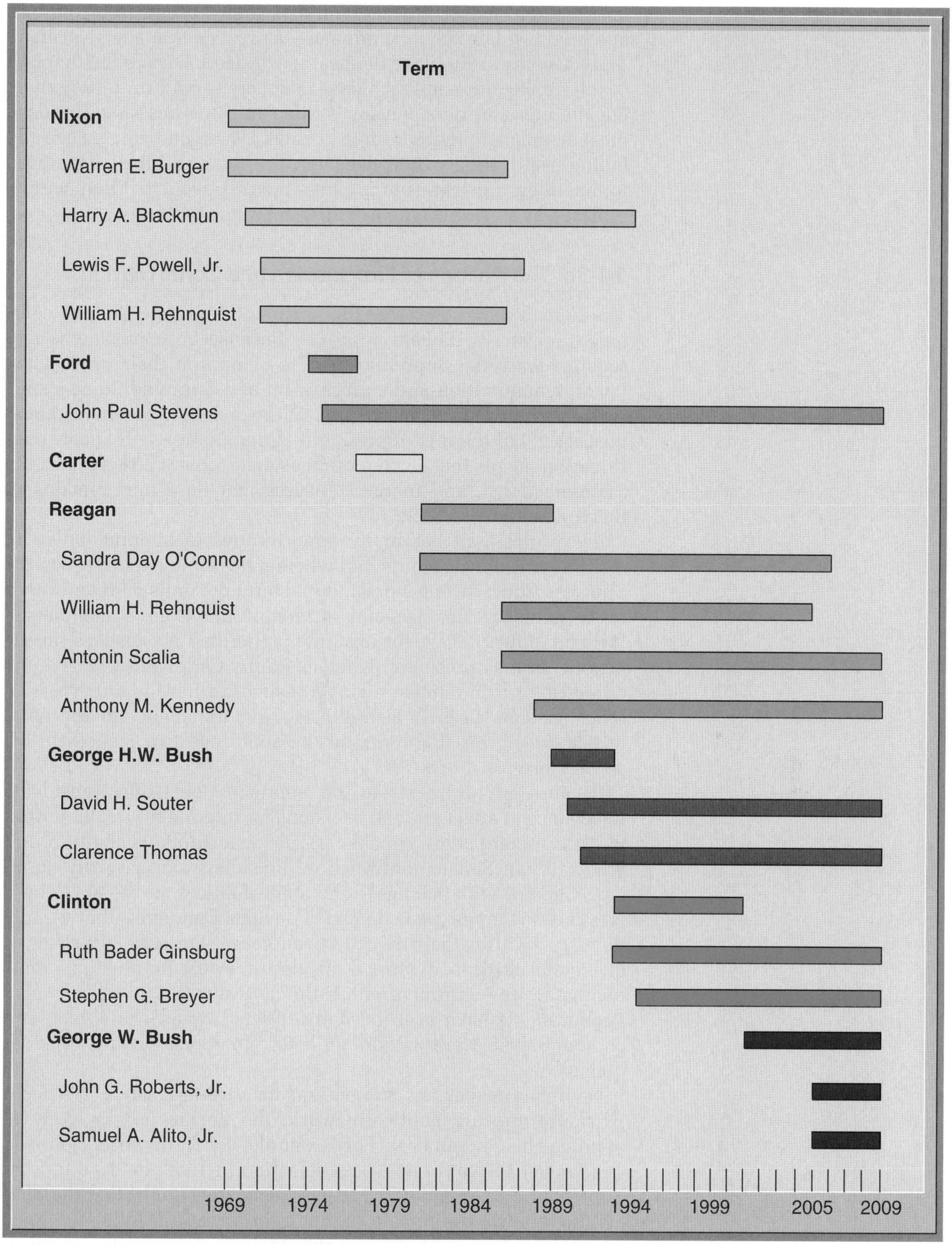

Figure 14–4 Presidential Legacies on the Supreme Court, 2008. Presidents can influence Supreme Court decision making long after they have left the Oval Office.

clerks—almost every justice employs four, chosen from the best and brightest law school graduates—a practice that allows even elderly justices to shoulder the heavy workload. During the first half of the nineteenth century, many members served until they died, but the creation of a pension system in 1869 has since induced most members to retire from the bench. Usually advancing age and failing health trigger their decision, but some members have tried to time their departures to improve the prospects that they will be replaced by someone with a similar approach to the law.[35]

14-3b The Politics of Nomination and Confirmation

The Constitution states that the president nominates federal court judges subject to Senate approval. Because both presidents and senators want the Supreme Court to champion their view of the law, the nomination and confirmation of a Supreme Court justice is an inherently political process. At times the process may appear unseemly, but the mix of presidential nomination and Senate confirmation means that elected officials determine who serves on the Supreme Court, and in turn, ensures that the Court remains in touch with the electorate.

Every president has many opportunities to appoint judges to district and appeals courts, but whether a vacancy opens up on the Supreme Court during a presidential term depends on many variables, including the age and tenure of the Court's members.[36] William Howard Taft, for example, appointed six justices during his one term as president, whereas Jimmy Carter did not have the opportunity to nominate a single justice during his four years in office. George W. Bush also did not have the chance to appoint a justice during his first term, but he appointed two justices in his second term.

Because appointments to the Supreme Court offer presidents the chance to affect judicial decisions far into the future, they want to choose competent, capable people who think as they do *and* who can win Senate confirmation. Presidents occasionally nominate a justice who belongs to the other political party—as Richard Nixon did when he picked Lewis Powell, a Democrat—but usually they stay within their own partisan camp. Perhaps surprisingly, given the partisan overtones of almost every nomination, most nominees are confirmed with little controversy. However, twelve appointments have been formally rejected by a Senate vote, and another eleven were withdrawn before the Senate could consider them.[37]

Nominations become contentious for several reasons.[38] When a president appears politically weak, the Senate is less likely to approve his nominees. For example, after Lyndon Johnson announced he would not seek reelection in 1968, he tried to fill a Supreme Court vacancy. Although Democrats controlled the Senate, Republicans were able to block confirmation of his nominee, arguing that the next president should make the selection. A president's nominees may also run into trouble when his party is the

Supreme Court confirmations have become contentious since the Senate rejected Robert Bork's nomination.

minority party in the Senate. Richard Nixon, for example, saw the Democratic-controlled Senate reject his nominations of Clement Haynsworth and G. Harrold Carswell in 1969 and 1970, and a Democratic-controlled Senate rejected Ronald Reagan's nomination of Robert Bork in 1987.

Supreme Court nominations also can become controversial if the nominee is perceived to lack the necessary credentials for the post or has exhibited behavior some people regard as improper. For example, Carswell's credentials for a seat on the Supreme Court were so weak that one Republican senator was forced to defend him by arguing that, "There are a lot of mediocre judges and people and lawyers and they are entitled to a little representation [on the Court], aren't they?"[39] Douglas Ginsburg, who Reagan nominated to the Supreme Court in 1987, was forced to withdraw from consideration because he admitted using marijuana while he was a law professor. Many Democrats disliked Clarence Thomas's legal and political views, but his nomination was not seriously threatened until a former subordinate, Anita Hill, accused him of sexual harassment. More recently, President George W. Bush had to withdraw his nomination of Harriet Miers when many people, including some prominent members of the Republican Party, raised doubts about her qualifications.[40]

Besides becoming controversial because the president is politically weak or because of shortcomings in the credentials or character of the nominee, a Supreme Court nomination may become contentious if a nominee's legal and political views clash with those of powerful members of the Senate. In the past few decades, only the nomination of Bork was contested wholly on the nominee's views, although ideological differences are usually what drive senators to try to defeat a nomination. (Senators prefer to attack a nominee's credentials or character rather than his or her political views because doing so protects them from charges that they are making the Supreme Court a partisan political issue.) Bork's legal views came under attack because he had taken controversial positions on a wide range of social and legal issues in his distinguished career as a Yale law professor and as a court of appeals judge. Worried that his confirmation would give conservative justices a majority on the Court, liberal senators used Bork's writings to argue that his beliefs were out of step with those of a majority of Americans.

Although Bork's nomination was defeated, and Reagan's second choice, Ginsburg, withdrew, President Reagan succeeded in appointing a conservative when the Senate confirmed his third choice, Anthony Kennedy. Similarly, even after the Senate rejected Nixon's nominees, Haynsworth and Carswell, it confirmed his third choice, Harry Blackmun. The lesson is simple: Although it may take some perseverance, presidents can almost always appoint a Supreme Court justice who they believe shares their legal views. In recent years the nomination contest has become more contentious, with presidents subjected to more pressures as they decide on a nominee and all steps of the process taking longer as supporters and opponents gather information and map political strategies.[41]

14-3c Presidential Legacies on the Supreme Court

Do justices vote the way the president who selected them wants? Not necessarily. Among the justices serving on the Court in 2009, Reagan's two appointees (Antonin Scalia and Kennedy) and George W. Bush's two choices (Roberts and Alito) were clearly conservative, as we would expect. Similarly, President George H. W. Bush's selections reflected his more muddled ideological disposition: One was a moderate (David Souter) and the other a hardline conservative (Thomas). President Clinton's choices seemed consistent with his preferences: a moderate (Breyer) and a liberal (Ginsburg). But among the generally liberal members of the Court was Stevens, who was named to the bench by Gerald Ford, a conservative Republican. Overall, presidents are usually happy with their selections, but the voting behavior of some justices clearly comes as a surprise.

Although observers frequently generalize about a justice's conservative or liberal leanings, on particular issues, a justice may take positions that contradict his or her usual behavior. Justice Sandra Day O'Connor, for example, was generally conservative during her tenure, but on cases involving sex discrimination in the workplace, she sometimes sided with the Supreme Court's liberals—perhaps because of her own experience with sex discrimination. Justices Kennedy and Scalia surprised their conservative supporters when they agreed with the Court's majority that flag burning is a constitutionally protected form of speech.

A justice's legal views also may change over the course of his or her career.[42] Former Justice Blackmun, for example, was thought to be so conservative when he first joined the Supreme Court that he and the conservative Chief Justice Warren Burger—a lifelong friend from Minneapolis and another Nixon appointee—were referred to as the "Minnesota Twins."[43] Over time, their voting records diverged widely, with Blackmun championing many liberal positions. Similarly, there is evidence that Justice O'Connor became less conservative over the course of her twenty-five years on the Court.[44] In sum, a judge's ideology can be complex and variable, making it tricky to reduce it to a simple label such as liberal or conservative. Thus, even when presidents get the people they want on the bench, there is no guarantee the results will be what they wanted.[45]

14-4 DECISION MAKING AT THE SUPREME COURT

When justices take their seat on the Supreme Court, they are assuming one of the most powerful posts in American politics. The immense responsibility that the justices bear for deciding the course of American law raises four key questions: What procedures does the Court follow when deciding whether to hear a case? How do individual justices decide which way to rule on a case? How does the Court communicate its opinion in a case to the public? And do some groups in American society enjoy an advantage over others when it comes to arguing their positions before the Supreme Court?

14-4a Hearing a Case

The Supreme Court meets annually in one regular session, starting on the first Monday in October. The term lasts until the Court has finished the business before it or has decided to lay over to the next session any undecided cases. In most years, that means the Court is in session until June or July. The Court meets in a special session when it must decide a case that cannot wait for the regular term.

Cases may reach the Supreme Court by several routes. In a few rare situations, most notably in disputes between states or between a state and the federal government, the Supreme Court has original jurisdiction, meaning it is the first court to hear the case. Another unusual route to the Supreme Court is certification, when an appeals court requests a review to settle a question of law. The majority of cases presented to the Supreme Court are appeals of court of appeals decisions, and most of the rest come directly from state supreme courts when an important federal issue is at stake. Technically, most appeals ask for a **writ of certiorari**, an order the Supreme Court issues requiring a lower court to send the records of a case to it for review.

Since 1988, when Congress changed some of the rules governing how cases reach the Supreme Court, the justices have had almost complete control over which cases they will hear. The Court is

writ of certiorari
A Supreme Court order for a lower court to send it the records of a case—the first step in reviewing a lower court case.

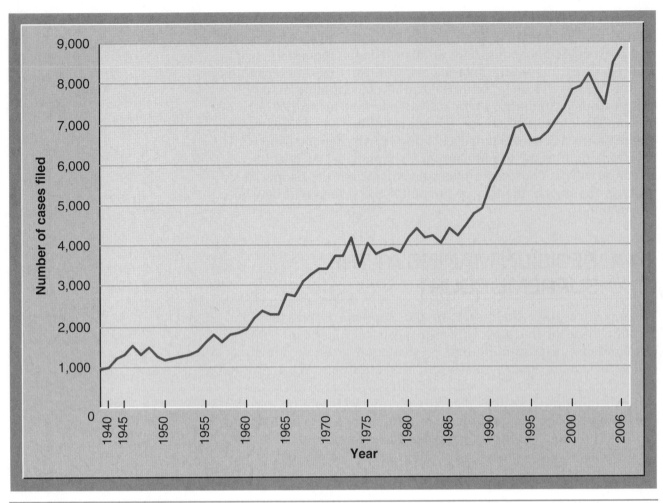

Figure 14–5   Cases Filed in the Supreme Court, 1938–2006. More and more cases are being appealed to the Supreme Court.

Source: Statistical Abstract of the United States 1999, p. 227, and The Supreme Court of the United States, "2007 Year-End Report on the Federal Judiciary," January 1, 2008, and earlier year-end reports. www.supremecourtus.gov/publicinfo/year-end/2007year-endreport.pdf

asked to hear far more cases each year than it has the capacity to handle, and as Figure 14–5 shows, the number of cases appealed to the Supreme Court has escalated since the 1950s. Despite the growing number of appeals, the number of cases the Court decides has declined, as Figure 14–6 shows. From the mid-1970s to the early 1990s, the Court issued an average of slightly more than 140 signed decisions each year, but since then it has issued far fewer decisions.[46] With a few exceptions, the Court can pick and choose the cases it wishes to decide. No one is sure why the Court is deciding fewer cases in recent years. It may be that because of the ideological split on the Court, neither the liberal justices nor the conservative justices wish to take a case they are not sure their side will win. It may also be that the Court is being given fewer important legal issues to resolve, in part because Congress is writing fewer major laws than in the past and because the federal government, whose appeals the Court usually takes, is winning more often in district court and appeals court cases.[47]

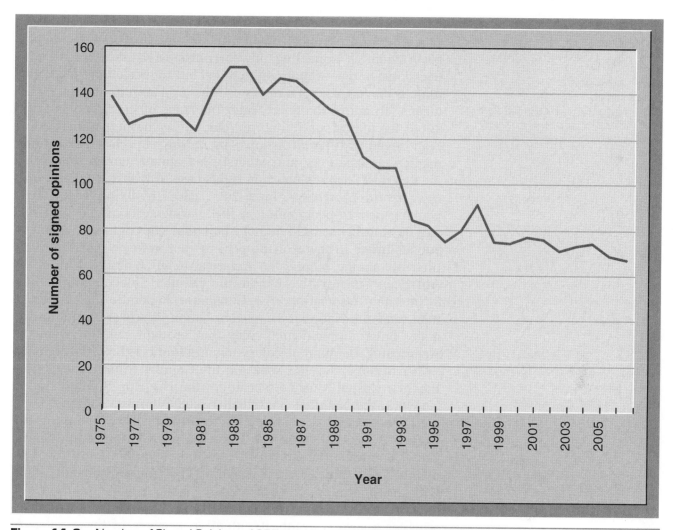

Figure 14–6 Number of Signed Opinions, 1975–2006. In recent years the Supreme Court has decided far fewer cases than it did in the 1970s and 1980s.

Sources: *Various editions of the* Statistical Abstract of the United States *and the Chief Justice's Year-End Report on the Federal Judiciary for various years.*

All the cases appealed to the Supreme Court are first reviewed to determine if they raise legal issues the Court needs to address. Most of the cases the Court is asked to hear fail to make it past an initial screening the justices' law clerks perform. The 20 to 30 percent of the cases deemed important enough for consideration by the chief justice or any one of the associate justices are placed on the discuss list.[48] The discuss list is brought before a conference that only the nine justices attend. The decision on which cases to accept is based on the **Rule of Four**: If at least four justices want to hear a case, it goes on the schedule. The Rule of Four is used to manage the demands on the Court's time by focusing the attention of the justices on the most important cases.[49]

Which cases are heard?[50] Procedural considerations eliminate some from consideration. These considerations include whether there is an issue to be adjudicated (a case may be moot by the time it reaches the Supreme Court) and whether the person or group bringing the suit has a legal right, or standing, to do so. Other

Rule of Four

The Supreme Court rule that at least four justices must decide that a case merits a review before it goes on the Court's schedule.

amicus curiae

Literally, friend of the court. A brief filed with the court by a person or group who is not directly involved in the legal action but who has views on the matter.

variables also matter in deciding whether the Court will hear a case. The Court is most likely to hear cases in which the federal government is appealing, lower courts have issued conflicting decisions, or one or more uninvolved but interested parties, called *amicus curiae,* ask for a review.[51] The term amicus curiae literally means "friend of the court," and the rules of the Supreme Court allow for almost unlimited amicus curiae participation.[52] More than seventy different groups, including church organizations, medical associations, and others, filed amicus curiae briefs with the Court in the 1989 abortion-rights case of *Webster v. Reproductive Health Services.*[53] In a 2005 case involving a suit over whether peer-to-peer computer file-sharing systems such as Grokster or Morpheus could be held liable for copyright infringement, amicus briefs in favor of the peer-to-peer systems' position were filed by, among others, the American Civil Liberties Union, the American Conservative Union, the Cellular Telecommunications & Internet Association, the Consumer Federation of America, Intel, and the National Taxpayers Union. Taking the side of the major entertainment companies that brought the suit were the American Federation of Television and Radio Artists; the commissioner of Major League Baseball; the Country Music Association, Inc.; the Gospel Music Association; the Hip-Hop Summit Action Network; the National Basketball Association; the National Football League; and a coalition of recording artists including the Eagles, Brooks & Dunn, the Dixie Chicks, Bonnie Raitt, Sheryl Crow, Babyface, the Grateful Dead, Jimmy Buffet, Patti Loveless, Stevie Nicks, and Gavin Rossdale. (The Court ultimately sided with the entertainment companies.)[54] The presence or absence of amicus briefs may give the Court an important signal as to whether a case warrants its attention because of the number of people and groups affected by it in some significant way. Amicus briefs may also be important because of the information they impart about the legal underpinnings of the case.[55] If the Court refuses to take up a case, the last decision reached on the case becomes final.

Once the Supreme Court accepts a case, it is usually scheduled for an oral argument, typically at least three months later. (The Court disposes of some cases by issuing *per curiam*—unsigned—opinions and memorandums.) A few weeks before the hearing, the lawyers for each side submit their written arguments, or briefs. The oral argument allows the lawyers for each side to present their case before the Court. Although oral argument on a single case often continued for days in the nineteenth century, today each side is limited to only thirty minutes. During a lawyer's presentation, the justices often interrupt to ask questions. Indeed, on one recent occasion a lawyer's argument on behalf of a convict on death row had barely begun when the justices raised questions that instigated a discussion among themselves. When the red light on the lawyer's lectern flashed, signaling the end of the allotted thirty minutes, Chief Justice Rehnquist said, "Thank you Ms. Foster…I think you did very well in the four minutes the court allowed you."[56] These short hearings may have much less effect than the written briefs do on a justice's final decision, but some justices find the oral arguments useful in highlighting the important issues the briefs raise, and evidence suggests that a strong presentation can influence a justice's thinking.[57]

14-4b Individual Decision Making

How do individual justices make decisions? Decisions usually rest on a combination of precedent and the justice's personal judicial beliefs.[58] In some sense, each case argued before the Court has distinctive elements; otherwise, there would be no reason for the members of the Court to want to decide it. Almost every case is similar to some other case or cases the Court has decided before. For example, the Court has taken up numerous cases involving free speech. Each case raises certain core issues. Yet each case also presents a new twist on the issue, which gives the Court another opportunity to fine-tune the law on First Amendment rights.

The question that confronts each justice on each case is how bound is he or she to the line of argument previous Supreme Court decisions laid out on this issue? What is the role of **stare decisis**, or precedent—the idea that current decisions should be based on past judgments? The answer to this question is somewhat elusive. On occasion, members of the Court will agree on the relevant precedent and employ it without controversy. In a few situations, the Court will choose to reverse itself and overturn a precedent. As noted in Chapter 4, in recent years the Court has reversed its positions on applying the death penalty to sixteen- and seventeen-year-olds, on the constitutionality of same-sex sodomy laws, and on the legality of partial-birth abortion bans.[59] As the dialogue in Box 14–1 demonstrates, however, explicitly overturning a precedent has a potential political cost to the Court. Justices worry that if they overturn too many decisions, the public will conclude that the Court swims with the political tide rather than adheres to legal principles.

More typical is a case in which precedents are less obvious or lead in different directions. A liberal justice and a conservative justice may agree on the basic facts of a case but rely on different precedents or legal reasoning to reach conflicting decisions. Because the relevance of past cases is often open to dispute, each justice is invariably influenced by his or her past experiences, judicial philosophy, and political beliefs when making legal decisions.[60] It would be hard to imagine, for example, that Thurgood Marshall's experiences as an African American living in a segregated society did not influence the decisions he later reached as a Supreme Court justice.

The Supreme Court's decision in *Reynolds v. Sims* (1964) shows not only how justices can bring their view of the world to bear on a decision, but also how serving on the bench can change that view. The Court decided in *Reynolds* that state legislatures must apportion their legislative districts strictly on the basis of population.

stare decisis
The doctrine that previous Supreme Court decisions should be allowed to stand.

POINT OF ORDER

Box 14–1 Precedent, Public Opinion, and the Supreme Court's Legitimacy

It is sometimes difficult for Supreme Court justices to determine how much weight to give to precedent and when to overturn a previous Supreme Court decision. A particularly clear example of the justices grappling with this issue occurred in 1992, when the Supreme Court issued a much anticipated decision on the constitutionality of a Pennsylvania law that imposed strict regulations on abortion. Abortion-rights supporters argued that the law clearly sought to make it more difficult for women to obtain an abortion, whereas abortion-rights opponents argued that the law was needed to protect the well-being of women having abortions. In any event, the act did not outlaw abortions. Abortion-rights supporters hoped the Supreme Court would strike down Pennsylvania's law as unconstitutional, whereas abortion-rights opponents hoped the Court would use the case to overturn the 1973 decision in *Roe v. Wade* (which established a constitutional right to abortion) and declare abortion unconstitutional.

The decision the Supreme Court handed down in *Planned Parenthood of Southeastern Pennsylvania v. Casey* left both sides disappointed. The majority opinion was a rare collaborative effort written by Justices Sandra Day O'Connor, Anthony Kennedy, and David Souter. Chief Justice William Rehnquist authored one of the dissents. Among the issues they debated was stare decisis—that is, the role precedent, or previous decisions, should play in reaching the current decision. The justices also touched on the question of the Court's legitimacy and public opinion. The following excerpts illustrate the role precedent played in the arguments of the justices.

JUSTICES O'CONNOR, KENNEDY, AND SOUTER

The root of American governmental power is revealed most clearly in the instance of the power conferred by the Constitution upon the Judiciary of the United States and specifically on this Court. As Americans of each succeeding generation are rightly told, the Court cannot buy support for its decisions by spending money and, except to a minor degree, it cannot independently coerce obedience to its decrees. The Court's power lies, rather, in its legitimacy, a product of substance and perception that shows itself in the people's acceptance of the Judiciary as fit to determine what the Nation's law means and to declare what it demands....

Source: © AP/Wide World Photos

Former Justice Sandra Day O'Connor.

Source: © AP/Wide World Photos

Justice Anthony Kennedy.

Source: © Reuters New Media, Inc./CORBIS

Justice David Souter.

The Court must take care to speak and act in ways that allow people to accept its decisions on the terms the Court claims for them, as grounded truly in principle, not as compromises with social and political pressures having, as such, no bearing on the principled choices that the Court is obliged to make. Thus, the Court's legitimacy depends on making legally principled decisions under circumstances in which their principled character is sufficiently plausible to be accepted by the Nation.

The need for principled action to be perceived as such is implicated to some degree whenever this, or any other appellate court, overrules a prior case. This is not to say, of course, that this Court cannot give a perfectly satisfactory explanation in most cases. People understand that some of the Constitution's language is hard to fathom and that the Court's Justices are sometimes able to perceive significant facts or to understand principles of law that eluded their predecessors and that justify departures from existing decisions. However upsetting it may be to those most directly affected when one judicially derived rule replaces another, the country can accept some correction of error without necessarily questioning the legitimacy of the Court.

There is....a point beyond which frequent overruling would overtax the country's belief in the Court's good faith. Despite the variety of reasons that may inform and justify a decision to overrule, we cannot forget that such a decision is usually perceived (and perceived correctly) as, at the least, a statement that a prior decision was wrong. There is a limit to the amount of error that can plausibly be imputed to prior courts. If that limit should be exceeded, disturbance of prior rulings would be taken as evidence that justifiable reexamination of principle had given way to drives for particular results in the short term. The legitimacy of the Court would fade with the frequency of its vacillation....

The Court's duty in the present case is clear. In 1973, it confronted the already-divisive issue of governmental power to limit personal choice to undergo abortion.... Whether or not a new social consensus is developing on that issue, its divisiveness is no less today than in 1973, and pressure to overrule the decision, like the pressure to retain it, has grown only more intense. A decision to overrule *Roe's*

essential holding under the existing circumstances would address error, if error existed, at the cost of both the profound and unnecessary damage to the Court's legitimacy, and to the Nation's commitment to the rule of law.

CHIEF JUSTICE REHNQUIST
We believe that *Roe* was wrongly decided, and that it can and should be overruled consistently with our

Source: © AFP/Getty Images

Former Chief Justice William Rehnquist.

traditional approach to *stare decisis* in constitutional cases.... The joint opinion of Justices O'Connor, Kennedy, and Souter cannot bring itself to say that *Roe* was correct as an original matter, but the authors are of the view that "the immediate question is not the soundness of *Roe's* resolution of the issue, but the precedential force that must be accorded to its ruling...." Our constitutional watch does not cease merely because we have spoken before on an issue; when it becomes clear that a prior constitutional interpretation is unsound we are obliged to reexamine the question....

The Judicial Branch derives its legitimacy, not from following public opinion, but from deciding by its best lights whether legislative enactments of the popular branches of Government comport with the Constitution....

Source: *Planned Parenthood of Southeastern Pennsylvania v. Casey,* 505 U.S. 833 (1992).

Before the *Reynolds* decision, several states, including California, had one house in which seats were apportioned as they are in the U.S. Senate, with no assurance that equal numbers of people lived in each district. This way of allocating legislative seats effectively gave certain groups in the state more political clout. In *Reynolds,* the Court held that seats in both houses of a state legislature must be apportioned as they are in the U.S. House of Representatives, with each state divided into districts of equal population so that every citizen of the state is equally represented.

The author of the *Reynolds* decision was Chief Justice Earl Warren. When he was governor of California, Warren had led a successful fight to defeat a state ballot proposition that would have apportioned the state senate on the basis of population. As Chief Justice, he assigned himself the *Reynolds* decision, in part to atone for his past partisan sins:

My own state was one of the most malapportioned in the nation...The last attempt [to change the apportionment system] was made in 1948 when I was governor. I joined ... in opposing it. It was frankly a matter of political expediency.

I thought little more about this until *Baker v. Carr* came to the Supreme Court.... I concluded that it was a matter for the courts to decide when I...remembered my California experience. I then decided that rather than merely join the opinion of one of the other Justices, after having taken the political stand I had in California, I should now squarely face up to the question from a judicial viewpoint. Accordingly, I assigned the state malapportionment cases to myself, knowing that this would create much comment in California.[61]

14-4c Supreme Court Opinions

A few days after the Supreme Court hears a case, the nine justices meet alone—with no clerks, stenographers, or other staff present—to discuss the case, along with others they have recently heard. The conference begins as the chief justice offers his analysis of the case and says how he will vote to decide it. The discussion then proceeds in order from the most senior member of the Court (based on length of Court service) to the most junior.[62] In most cases, after the most junior member of the Court has spoken, the chief justice announces a tally of the vote. If the chief justice is in the majority, he assigns himself or one of the justices who voted with him to draft the Court's **majority opinion**, the written document that announces to the public the Court's decision on a case and the reasoning the Court used to arrive at that decision. If the chief justice sides with the minority, the most senior justice in the majority determines who will write the opinion.

majority opinion
The document announcing and usually explaining the Supreme Court's decision in a case.

Majority Opinions

The selection of a justice to write the majority opinion is an important decision. Different justices are likely to write different opinions. Chief justices often assign themselves important cases. Even if they assign a major case to another justice, that choice may determine what sort of decision is written. The last several chief justices have waited until roughly two weeks after a conference before making assignments on cases in which they were in the majority. Such a delay allows the chief justice to accumulate assignments, then distribute them to make the workload more or less even among his colleagues, yet also maintain his flexibility in assigning important decisions.[63]

Once a justice drafts a majority opinion, it is circulated among the other eight justices. Each justice is free to offer suggestions and criticisms. Indeed, the vote taken in the conference is not binding. On occasion, justices change their position on a case after the conference because they find the draft opinion persuasive or because they disagree with it. In a 1989 civil rights case, for example, Justice Kennedy initially sided with the Supreme Court's liberals, but later changed his mind and agreed with the conservatives, swinging the Court's majority with him. Indeed, Kennedy often waits to see how the argument in a decision develops before he commits to it, a practice that has led some law clerks to call him "Flipper" behind his back.[64] All the Court's members realize that a decision becomes final only when five or more members of the Court agree to sign the majority opinion.

The importance of the majority opinion extends beyond simply announcing which side won. By presenting the reasoning behind the decision it reached, the Court majority sends a signal to lower courts, lawyers, potential litigants, and others about how they are likely to treat similar cases in the future. The opinion, then, is important for what it says and for what it does not say. In a sense, it is the best road map available for figuring out how the law is evolving.

Concurring and Dissenting Opinions

On occasion, a justice will agree with the decision in a case but not with the reasoning used to reach it. In this situation, a justice may write a **concurring opinion**, which lays out how he or she would have preferred the Supreme Court to have arrived at its decision. Justices who disagree with the decision may write a **dissenting opinion**, which explains why they disagreed with the Court's ruling. Dissents are usually more than just sour grapes. They can lay the groundwork for future decisions. During the first decades of the twentieth century, for example, Justice Oliver Wendell Holmes wrote a series of dissents that favored laws giving the federal government more control over commerce. In 1938, the Court finally adopted Holmes's reasoning.[65] Indeed, dissents have become so important over the past few decades that, since the 1970s, the senior justice on the losing side assigns responsibility for writing one, just as the senior justice in the majority assigns the Court's opinion.[66]

Concurring and dissenting opinions perform a valuable function because they state the terms of disagreement clearly and explicitly, but they have become commonplace only since the 1940s. They became more common in large part because Chief Justice Harlan Stone (1941–1946) encouraged his colleagues to engage in open and vigorous argument and because several justices who joined the Supreme Court in the 1940s were less committed to the established norms of doing business.[67] The increase in the number of dissents and concurrences can make it difficult to understand the Court's decision. Listing off the large number of dissents and concurrences in a 2005 decision, Chief Justice Rehnquist announced wryly, "I didn't know we had that many people on the court."[68] The tendency to air differences has occasionally led the Court to issue decisions in which a majority agrees on the outcome but not on the reasoning behind it. Thus, in the 2008 case in which the Court found Kentucky's use of lethal injection in applying the death penalty to be constitutional, the justices wrote five concurring opinions in addition to the majority opinion. Consequently, Justice Thomas admitted in his concurrence, "Today's decision is sure to engender more litigation," because, "Needless to say, we have left the States with nothing resembling a bright-line rule."[69] In such situations, a final ruling giving guidance on the law in that issue is deferred to another time when the members of the Court can come to agreement.

concurring opinion

A statement from one or more Supreme Court justices agreeing with a decision in a case but giving an alternative explanation for it.

dissenting opinion

A statement from one or more Supreme Court justices explaining why they disagree with a decision in a case.

Voting Patterns

In recent years, a substantial percentage of cases in each session have been decided by unanimous votes, as were just under 30 percent of the decisions in the 2007–2008 term. However, the decisions in many other cases hinge on a single vote. During the 2007–2008 term, 16 percent of the Court's sixty-seven signed decisions came down to a 5–4 decision, with Justice Kennedy usually being considered the key vote—and often writing the Court majority's opinion.[70] Thus, with a significant number of close cases, Justice Kennedy is often the critical swing vote, able to decide the direction of the majority decision. Other justices are somewhat more predictable. Conservative Justices Scalia and Thomas agreed with each other just under 93 percent of the time between 1995 and 2002, whereas Clinton's more liberal appointees, Breyer and Ginsburg, ended up on the same side in about 90 percent of the nonunanimous cases. In contrast, Justices Stevens and Thomas disagreed on 44 percent of the cases. And Justice Stevens was the one most often found in dissent.[71]

14-4d Who Wins before the Supreme Court?

Who wins before the Supreme Court? It is reasonable to expect that litigants who appear before the Supreme Court on a regular basis have an advantage over those who do not. After all, groups that regularly argue cases before the Court are likely to have resources and expertise that others lack.

The federal government is the most frequent litigant before the Supreme Court. The federal government is represented in Supreme Court cases by the solicitor general, who is appointed by the president. The solicitor general decides which cases the government should ask the Court to review and with the assistance of staff members, prepares the government's position on the cases the Court accepts. The solicitor general tends to appeal cases only when the government stands a good chance of winning.[72] Not surprisingly, the federal government won 66 percent of the cases it was involved in between 1985 and 1997, virtually the same percentage it won over the previous three decades.[73] Regardless of whether the opposing litigant is a state government, a corporation, a labor union, or an individual, the Supreme Court usually rules in favor of the federal government. Several arcane legal rules that incline the Court to favor the positions the federal government takes aid the federal government's enviable winning percentage. In addition, the solicitor general usually brings only strong cases before the court; likely losers are not pursued.

In ruling so often in favor of the federal government, the justices are not merely repaying favors to their employer. Supreme Court justices, like all federal judges, enjoy considerable independence. The Constitution makes it difficult for Congress or the president to remove a justice, and it bars Congress and the president from punishing justices by cutting their pay. Thus, when a special prosecutor probing the Watergate scandal asked the Supreme Court to order President Nixon to hand over tapes of conversations recorded in the Oval Office, the justices—three of whom Nixon had nominated—voted unanimously to grant the request. (Justice Rehnquist, the fourth Nixon appointee on the Court at that time, did not participate in the decision because he had been a member of the Justice Department during the Nixon administration.) The Court's decision led to Nixon's resignation.

Aside from the federal government, no other litigants appear to have an advantage when arguing before the Supreme Court. Perhaps surprisingly, corporations and other litigants that can afford high-powered and expensive legal counsel do not fare appreciably better than poor Americans. The ability to pay for legal counsel is not a determining factor in part because "even poor defendants with interesting cases can attract skilled and experienced counsel and the financial support of powerful interest groups."[74] Moreover, when deciding a case, the justices look past the resources of particular litigants to the merits of their cases. Although the resource differences between rich and poor matter at lower levels of the court system where access to legal expertise is much more uneven, they do not have much impact at the top.[75]

14-5 THE LOWER FEDERAL COURTS

As we noted previously, Congress, using the power the Constitution gives it, created two lower federal courts: district courts and the courts of appeals. Like Supreme Court justices, judges in the lower federal courts are appointed in a political process. As we shall see, this process may actually help make the lower federal court system more democratic because elected officials who represent the areas where the judges will serve strongly influence the selection of federal judges.

14-5a District Courts

The district courts, which hold trials and establish the facts of a case, are the starting and ending point of most federal cases. Most federal cases are civil rather than criminal cases: In 2007, of all federal district court cases, 257,507, or 79 percent, were civil cases. More than half of all district court cases involve statutory actions, petitions from prisoners, civil rights violations, labor laws, and personal injury cases. Most of the rest involve enforcement of contracts and various liability claims. Relatively few federal cases involve crimes; most criminal cases involve state laws and state courts.[76]

District court judges exercise less discretion than appellate judges or Supreme Court justices. Much of their job is to apply the law as Congress and the Supreme Court have defined it. But district judges still have some opportunities to exercise discretion as they apply the law, particularly in new areas where the law is not well developed.[77]

14-5b Courts of Appeal

Courts of appeal decide cases appealed to them from the district courts. Unlike district courts, they do not determine the facts of a case. Instead, they focus on legal issues that a case tried in district or state court might raise, such as whether a trial was conducted fairly or whether a judge applied the law correctly. Usually, a panel of three appeals court judges hears an appeal and renders a judgment. As a rule, judges on the appeals courts have more flexibility than district court judges to interpret and extend the law.

14-5c Nomination and Confirmation

senatorial courtesy
The practice a president follows in choosing a nominee for a district or appeals court judgeship. The president selects a nominee from a list supplied by the senior senator of the president's party from the state or region where the vacancy occurs.

Like Supreme Court justices, district and appeals court judges are nominated by the president and confirmed by the Senate. However, members of the Senate have much greater say in the selection of nominees for the lower federal courts than they do for the Supreme Court. In most circumstances, the president selects nominees for district and appeals courts by following the tradition known as **senatorial courtesy:** The president asks a senior senator in his party from the state or region where the vacancy occurs to supply a list of possible nominees. If there is no senator of his party from the state or region, the president will ask a member of his party from the House or a state party leader to supply the list. If the president declines to nominate any of the suggested choices, another list will be prepared. Although presidents have more freedom to nominate whoever they want for appeals courts than for district courts, they generally refrain from nominating a candidate who lacks the support of party members from the affected state or region. For example, when President Clinton's nominee for a federal district court judgeship in Missouri in 1999 failed to get the support of that state's two Republican senators, the nomination failed on the floor of the Senate on a party-line vote. Even Republican senators who had supported the judge's nomination in committee voted no when Missouri's two senators did.[78]

Partisan politics clearly influences the naming of federal judges. Take, for example, a vacancy that arose on the Eighth Circuit Court of Appeals in 1991. The Eighth Circuit includes seven midwestern states. President George H. W. Bush's rumored choice for the post was a district court judge from Arkansas. After Senator Charles Grassley (R-IA) complained, Bush appointed a district court judge from Iowa. According to Grassley, "We just implored them to look at it from a political standpoint, that Iowa having a Republican senator, Arkansas not having Republican senators, they were going to be relying on Chuck Grassley to a greater extent for help. They weren't going to get it out of Democratic senators from Arkansas."[79]

Although the president and members of Congress reap clear political benefits from choosing judges on political grounds, it is less obvious how the selection process benefits the judicial system.

Yet injecting politics into the selection process actually helps make the judicial system more democratic. Allowing elected officials from the state or region to influence who is named to the bench makes federal judges more politically representative of the areas they serve in than they otherwise might be. Over time, presidents can shift the partisan character of the bench. President Reagan, for example, selected 78 court of appeals judges and 290 district court judges during his eight years in office, filling close to 50 percent of all federal judgeships.[80] These appointments gave the lower courts a discernible conservative bent, which was still evident in 2008, nineteen years after Reagan left office, because 9 percent of federal judges were his appointees.[81] As shown in Box 14–2, lifetime appointments can leave judges on the federal bench for a long time.

As Table 14–1 shows, presidents appoint judges from their own party. Although federal judges may be politically representative,

The People behind the Rules

Box 14–2   Milton Pollack and the Impact of Lifetime Appointments

Source: © Chrystyna Czajkowsky/AP Photo.

Milton Pollack.

At the height of the stock market scandals that rocked Wall Street in the early part of the current decade, Judge Milton Pollack handed down one of the first legal decisions on a case brought against a major brokerage house. He tossed out a lawsuit filed by unhappy investors who claimed brokers and analysts had misled them into buying bad stocks. In a scathing analysis, Judge Pollack ridiculed the investors' case, finding that they were "high risk speculators who now hope to twist securities law into a scheme of cost-free speculators insurance." He

declined to do their bidding, observing, "plaintiffs would have this court conclude that the federal securities laws were meant to underwrite, subsidize and encourage their rash speculation in joining a freewheeling casino that lured thousands obsessed with the fantasy of Olympian riches."

Although his words were harsh, Judge Pollack's decision was well written and his reasoning was deemed sound by the legal community. Indeed, the opinion was entirely in keeping with the judge's well-established reputation as an expert on securities law. Perhaps the most noteworthy thing about the decision, however, was that Judge Pollack was ninety-six years old when he wrote it.

Pollack was born in 1906. He graduated from Columbia Law School in 1929—the year of the great stock market crash. Pollack spent thirty-eight years in private practice, specializing in securities law, usually representing investors. He was nominated to be a District Court judge by President Lyndon Johnson in 1967. Pollack assumed senior status—meaning he was retired but available to handle cases when needed—in 1983. (About

15 percent of federal cases are overseen by judges holding senior status.) He continued to hear cases until his death in 2004, meaning his judicial career spanned from President Johnson to President George W. Bush.

Despite his long life and judicial service, Judge Pollack did not set any records. Joseph W. Woodrough was still serving as a senior Court of Appeals judge when he died at the age of 104 in 1977, having been on the federal bench for sixty-one years. And Giles S. Rich, another Court of Appeals judge, never retired and was still on active status at the time of his death at age ninety-five in 1999.

The careers of Judges Pollack, Woodrough, and Rich demonstrate the potential impact of lifetime appointments to the bench. Clearly, the decisions presidents and senators make about who serves on the federal judiciary can affect public policy long after they have left public life.

Sources: Ann Davis and Randall Smith, "Judge Pollack's Investor Lectures," Wall Street Journal, July 3, 2003; Landon Thomas, Jr., "Judges Reject Suits Blaming Analysts for Losses," New York Times, July 2, 2003. Data on senior judges and judicial careers are taken from the U.S Courts Web site, available at www.uscourts.gov/faq.html and the Federal Judicial Center Web site, available at www.fjc.gov/public/home.nsf/hisj.

	Ford (1974–1977)	Carter (1977–1981)	Reagan (1981–1989)	Bush (1989–1993)	Clinton (1993–2001)	Bush (2001–2007)
District Court Judges						
Partisanship						
Democrat	21%	93%	5%	5%	88%	7%
Republican	79%	4%	93%	89%	6%	85%
Independent	0%	3%	2%	6%	6%	8%
Race, Ethnicity						
White	89%	79%	92%	89%	75%	83%
African American	6%	14%	2%	7%	18%	6%
Hispanic American	2%	7%	5%	4%	6%	11%
Asian American	4%	1%	1%	0%	1%	1%
American Indian	—	—	—	—	0.3%	0%
Sex						
Female	2%	14%	8%	20%	29%	20%
Number of appointees	52	202	290	148	305	203

Table 14–1   Characteristics of Federal District Court Appointees (in percent)
Presidents usually appoint people from their own party to the federal bench.

Sources: Sheldon Goldman, "Bush's Judicial Legacy: The Final Imprint," Judicature 76 *(April/May 1993): 287, 293; Sheldon Goldman, Elliot Slotnick, Gerard Gryski, and Gary Zuk, "Clinton's Judges: Summing Up the Legacy," Judicature 84 (March–April 2001): 244; Sheldon Goldman, Elliot Slotnick, Gerard Gryski, Gary Zuk, and Sara Schiavoni, "W. Bush Remaking the Judiciary: Like Father Like Son?" Judicature 86 (May–June 2003): 304; Sheldon Goldman, Elliot Slotnick, Gerard Gryski, and Sara Schiavoni, "W. Bush's Judiciary: The First Term Record," Judicature 88 (May–June 2005): 269; Sheldon Goldman, Elliot Slotnick, Gerard Gryski, and Sara Schiavoni, "W. Bush's Judiciary During the 109th Congress," Judicature 90 (May–June 2007): 277.*

they are not demographically representative. Presidents tend to select white, middle-aged males. The federal bench started to become noticeably more diverse under Democratic President Jimmy Carter in the late 1970s. In the 1980s and early 1990s, Republican Presidents Reagan and George H. W. Bush appointed fewer African Americans—which is not surprising given that more African Americans identify with the Democratic Party than the Republican Party—but they did appoint a growing number of Hispanic Americans to the bench.[82] President George W. Bush has appointed more Hispanic Americans to the bench than any of his predecessors. The number of women appointed as federal judges also has grown over time. The highest proportions of women and minorities appointed to the federal bench, however, occurred during the Clinton administration.

14-6 STATE COURTS

Whether it is through a speeding ticket, a dispute over the terms of a contract, or an accusation of criminal wrongdoing, the interaction most Americans have with our country's legal system is with state, not federal, courts. In contrast to the 325,000 cases that federal district courts handle each year, state trial courts handle just over 100 million.[83] For this reason, most of what we think, hear, and read about in regard to the American legal system has to do with state laws, not federal laws. And as we will see, not only do state courts operate differently from the federal courts, but states also vary dramatically in the way they organize their court systems, in the methods they use to select judges, in their limits on the length of judicial service, and in the laws they have on the books.

14-6a Organization

State courts exhibit a wide variety of forms, structures, and names. Every state has a highest court, or court of last resort, although Texas and Oklahoma have two such courts, one for civil cases and the other for criminal cases. Most states refer to their highest court as the supreme court, and its role is usually similar to its federal namesake. (New York and Maryland call their highest courts the court of appeals, however, and to make matters more confusing, New York calls its lower courts supreme courts.) State courts of last resort are highly professionalized, and several enjoy the same level of pay, resources, and control of their agendas as the U.S. Supreme Court.[84]

One of the important roles state supreme courts play is to interpret state constitutions. In many cases, state constitutions provide civil rights protections that go beyond those afforded to citizens by the U.S. Constitution, a notion state courts have pursued more aggressively since the 1970s.[85] For example, in 1988, the U.S. Supreme Court held that federal law officials did not need a warrant to search a person's garbage.[86] But state courts in New Jersey and Washington subsequently held that their state constitutions required state law officials to obtain a warrant before rifling through a suspect's garbage. Indeed, the New Jersey Supreme Court also used the state constitution to expand the rights of their citizens beyond those given in the federal constitution in the areas of automobile searches, school finance, and exclusionary zoning.[87] And several state supreme courts have established a right to privacy based on their state constitution, thereby guaranteeing abortion rights.[88] Some state supreme courts become legal pathbreakers, establishing precedents that other states and the federal courts cite in later disputes.[89]

The other tiers of most state judicial systems differ somewhat from the federal system. Intermediate appeals courts, similar in purpose to the federal appeals courts, are found in thirty-nine states. Most states have trial courts of general jurisdiction where most cases are handled. Again, the names vary—California and several other states call theirs superior court, while elsewhere they are called circuit court, district court, or court of common pleas. Some states have several different types of major trial courts. In addition to the major trial courts, a majority of states have trial courts of limited jurisdiction, including family court, juvenile court, and even justices of the peace. A few states have unusual specialized courts. Vermont, for example, has an environmental court, while Colorado and Montana have water courts.

14-6b Judicial Selection

The method by which judges gain the bench varies from state to state and by level within some states. Most states do not follow the federal model of judicial selection. In Virginia, for example, the state legislature selects judges for the state supreme court, state appellate courts, circuit courts, and district courts. Voters in Wisconsin elect all state judges in nonpartisan elections, whereas voters in Pennsylvania elect all state judges in partisan elections.

Missouri and many other states use a mix of appointment and election to select judges. In Missouri, for example, a seven-member nonpartisan commission initially screens potential appellate court justices. The commission then submits the names of three candidates for a judgeship to the governor. The candidate the governor selects is appointed to the bench but must face the voters in the first general election after serving for a year. The nonpartisan ballot on which the judge's name appears allows voters to either confirm (retain) or reject the judge. If the judge is retained, he or she must again get voter approval to stay on the bench at the end of each twelve-year term.[90]

Many judicial reformers favor variants of this procedure, which is usually called the **Missouri Plan** (because it was first introduced in that state) or the **merit system**, because it supposedly reduces the role of partisan politics in the selection of judges. Judges covered by retention elections strongly favor them, in large part because such elections remove them from partisan politics.[91] Incumbent judges, however, do even better in retention elections than incumbent legislators in seeking reelection; less than 1 percent of judges are not retained.[92] In recent years, the Missouri Plan has become controversial in a few states that use it—Missouri among them—because some conservatives argue that the nomination process is not sufficiently transparent and is too easily manipulated for the benefit of the legal community.[93] Moreover, partisan elections may be more substantive on issues, and nonpartisan elections less insulated from party politics, than reformers anticipated.[94] There is little evidence, however, that any particular system produces better judges or influences the sorts of decisions the courts render.[95]

Do different selection processes produce different sorts of people on the bench? Overall, evidence on the relationship between selection processes and diversity on the bench is mixed. One study of African Americans serving as state court judges suggests that the relationship between the judicial selection system and minority representation is not clear. More African American judges are found in states using partisan and nonpartisan judicial elections than in states using some other system—which is not surprising

Missouri Plan

The system some states use to select judges, appointing them but requiring them to stand for periodic reelection. Also called the merit system.

merit system

Also called the Missouri Plan. The system some states use to select judges, appointing them but requiring them to stand for periodic reelection.

because most states with significant African American populations use elections. Even in these states, though, most African American judges initially gain the bench by appointment. Because most states with elective systems allow the governor to fill a vacancy between elections, most African American judges are appointed to the bench by the governor.[96] Minority judges facing retention election fare almost as well as their white colleagues, winning at a 96 percent rate.[97]

14-6c Length of Service

States differ from the federal government not only in how they select judges, but also in deciding how long judges may serve on the bench. Whereas federal judges are appointed for life, most state judges serve for specific terms. In addition, although federal judges can be removed only through impeachment and conviction, many states have a variety of other mechanisms for removing judges from the bench, including reelection defeat, recall, and action by a judicial disciplinary commission.

The federal system of appointing judges for life protects their independence from politics. States that use elections sacrifice judicial independence in favor of encouraging political responsiveness and judicial accountability. In many states, however, judges seeking reelection must "raise huge sums of money, often from special interest groups that have a tangible stake in the outcome of cases before the courts." The candidates for a seat on the Alabama Supreme Court in 2006 raised and spent more than $13.4 million. An analysis of all the judicial elections held that year revealed that nationally, state supreme court candidates raised a total of $34.4 million, with lawyers (21 percent) and business interests (44 percent) contributing almost two-thirds of that total.[98] Not surprisingly, most incumbent judges, like their legislative counterparts, win reelection, but in theory, at least, voters can remove state judges whose behavior or rulings displease them. Judicial elections and the fundraising that accompanies them, however, may undercut citizen support for the state legal system.[99]

14-6d State Laws

The laws that judges are asked to uphold vary, sometimes dramatically, across the fifty states. For example, in thirty-six states, a judge and jury may impose the death penalty on a person convicted of first-degree murder; in thirteen states, the maximum punishment is life in prison. The final state, New York, has a death penalty on the books, but that law was declared unconstitutional by a state court in 2004, and the legislature has yet to pass any fix for it. As Figure 14–7 shows, in 2008, twenty states had laws requiring motorcyclists to wear a helmet. In twenty-four states, only people under a certain age were required to wear helmets. Three states, Florida, Kentucky, and Texas, allowed only adults covered by medical insurance or with specific training to ride

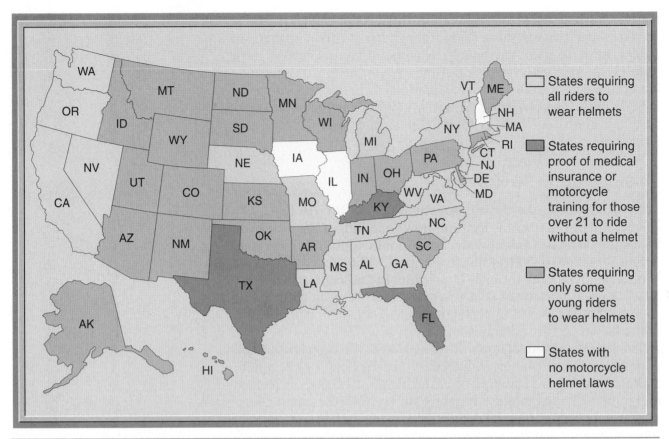

Figure 14–7   Motorcycle Helmet Laws, 2008.

Source: *Insurance Institute for Highway Safety as of August 2008.*

without a helmet. And three states permitted any motorcyclist to go without a helmet. Similar variations on other laws occur across the country: Acts that are illegal in some states (e.g., gambling or prostitution) are legal in others, and the penalties attached to a crime also vary from state to state. Although the federal Constitution and the Supreme Court's interpretation of it impose some uniformity on our legal system, significant differences across the states are still evident.

SUMMARY

Although the Founders were almost unanimous in their support for creating an independent federal judiciary, they left it to Congress to specify the details of the federal court system. Over the years, Congress has passed many laws regarding the structure and organization of the federal judiciary. The main thrust of these laws has been to create a three-tiered system of constitutional courts: district courts, courts of appeals, and the Supreme Court. Congress has also established legislative courts to deal with specific issues or to administer specific congressional statutes.

The Founders thought the federal courts would simply apply the laws and policies Congress and the president establish. Almost immediately, however, the federal courts became policy makers themselves. Early on, the Supreme Court asserted the doctrine of judicial review, the right of federal courts to declare both federal and state laws unconstitutional and therefore null and void. Although judicial review now constitutes a bedrock principle of the American legal system, some critics complain that federal judges use judicial review as an excuse for imposing their policy preferences on the public rather than for upholding the Constitution. Complaints about judicial activism notwithstanding, the power of the federal judiciary is limited by the reactive nature of the courts, their inability to enforce their rulings, the ability of the president and Congress to draft new laws, and the force of public opinion.

The Supreme Court is the nation's highest court. More than 100 justices have served on the Court. All have been lawyers, only two have been female, and only two have been African American. The chief justice is considered first among equals on the Supreme Court, and all nine justices are nominated by the president and confirmed by the Senate. Because the justices serve for life and have the power to shape American law for generations, the process of nomination and confirmation of a justice is inherently political. Senators are most likely to contest a nomination when a president is politically weak, when a nominee's credentials are questionable, or when his or her legal views clash with those of powerful senators.

The Supreme Court hears only a small portion of the cases appealed to it. If the Court decides to hear a case, it schedules an oral argument. To reach their decisions, the justices rely both on legal precedent and on their own experiences, judicial philosophies, and political beliefs. The justices render their decision in the form of a majority opinion that outlines the reasoning they used to reach their decision. Justices who agree with the conclusion the majority reached but not with the reasoning behind it may write concurring opinions. Justices who disagree with the majority opinion in its entirety may write dissenting opinions. The federal government wins a majority of the cases it argues before the Supreme Court; no other group in society enjoys the same success rate.

District courts and courts of appeals constitute the lower federal courts. Like Supreme Court justices, judges in the lower federal courts are appointed in a political process. In their case, elected officials representing the areas where the judges will serve strongly influence the selection of an appointee. The district courts form the lowest rung in the federal judiciary; they hold trials and establish the facts of a case. Courts of appeal focus on legal issues that a case tried in a district or state court might raise. Appeals court judges generally have more flexibility than district court judges to interpret and extend the law.

In addition to the federal judiciary, each state maintains its own separate court system. Most state courts operate differently from the federal courts, and states vary dramatically in the way they organize their court systems, in the methods they use to select judges, in their limits on the length of judicial service, and in the laws they have on the books.

As we have seen in this chapter, both federal and state courts lack many of the qualities we normally associate with democratic politics. Yet, at many levels, the court system appears responsive to political shifts in the public. The main reason for this responsiveness is that either voters (in many states) or their elected representatives (at the federal level) control the process by which judges gain the bench.

KEY TERMS

amicus curiae	majority opinion
concurring opinion	merit system
constitutional courts	Missouri Plan
dissenting opinion	Rule of Four
judicial activism	senatorial courtesy
judicial review	*stare decisis*
legislative courts	writ of certiorari
Marbury v. Madison	

READINGS FOR FURTHER STUDY

Breyer, Stephen. *Active Liberty: Interpreting Our Democratic Constitution* (New York: Knopf, 2005). A spirited defense by a Supreme Court justice of the idea that the Constitution is adaptable in its application to modern legal issues.

Carp, Robert A., and Ronald Stidham. *The Federal Courts,* 4th ed. (Washington, D.C.: CQ Press, 2001). A leading textbook on the organization and politics of the lower federal courts.

Epstein, Lee, and Jeffrey A. Segal. *Advice and Consent: The Politics of Judicial Appointments* (New York: Oxford University Press, 2005). Two leading judicial scholars provide a balanced analysis of the politicization of the judicial nomination process.

Greenburg, Jan Crawford. *Supreme Conflict: The Inside Story of the Struggle for Control of the United States Supreme Court* (New York: Penguin, 2007). An examination of the justices as jurists, focusing on the clash of legal philosophies.

Keck, Thomas M. *The Most Activist Supreme Court in History: The Road to Modern Judicial Conservatism* (Chicago: University of Chicago Press, 2004). A provocative analysis suggesting the Rehnquist Court was the most activist in modern American legal history.

O'Brien, David. *Storm Center: The Supreme Court in American Politics,* 7th ed. (New York: Norton, 2005). A useful historical analysis of the Supreme Court.

Rehnquist, William H. *The Supreme Court,* rev. ed. (New York: Knopf, 2002). A succinct and readable history of the Supreme Court by the late Chief Justice.

Scherer, Nancy. *Scoring Points: Politicians, Activists, and the Lower Federal Court Appointment Process* (Stanford, CA: Stanford University Press, 2005). An examination of the rise of a more politicized appointment and confirmation process for lower court judges over the last fifty years.

Segal, Jeffrey A., and Harold J. Spaeth. *The Supreme Court and the Attitudinal Model Revisited* (New York: Cambridge University Press, 2002). Two leading judicial scholars examine the relationship between the attitudes of justices and their decision-making behavior.

REVIEW QUESTIONS

1. In its decision in *CBOCS West, Inc. v. Humphries*, the Supreme Court held that
   a. racial discrimination in the workplace is constitutional.
   b. employers are free to retaliate against employees who complain about racial discrimination.
   c. The laws passed by Congress do not allow for retaliation claims.
   d. employees who complain about racial discrimination are allowed to sue their employers for retaliation.

2. Between 1995 and 2002, which justices were most likely to be found voting together?
   a. Stevens and Scalia
   b. Scalia and Thomas
   c. Thomas and Souter
   d. Kennedy and Breyer

3. In 2008, nineteen years after he left the White House, _____ percent of all federal judges had been appointed by President Ronald Reagan.
   a. 9
   b. 19
   c. 30
   d. 45

4. Which of the following has the constitutional power to create new federal courts?
   a. Supreme Court
   b. president
   c. Congress
   d. executive bureaucracy

5. At the present time, there are _____ courts of appeal and _____ district courts at the federal level.
   a. 7; 256
   b. 13; 94
   c. 21; 178
   d. 45; 512

6. The doctrine of judicial review was established by the Supreme Court in
   a. 1803.
   b. 1857.
   c. 1896.
   d. 1937.

7. Most cases arrive to the Supreme Court by
   a. a writ of certification.
   b. original jurisdiction.
   c. a writ of certiorari.
   d. a writ of errors.

8. If the chief justice sides with the minority, who assigns the task of writing the majority opinion?
   a. The chief justice still assigns the duty to one of the associate justices.
   b. The oldest justice in the majority decides who will write the opinion.
   c. The justices in the majority take a vote.
   d. The most senior justice in the majority assigns the task.

9. Most federal cases are
   a. criminal cases.
   b. civil cases.
   c. tax cases.
   d. administrative cases.

10. Whereas federal district courts handle approximately 325,000 cases each year, how many cases are typically handled by state trial courts?
    a. 500,000
    b. 1,000,000
    c. 20,000,000
    d. 100,000,000

NOTES

1. The facts of the case are taken from Humphries's legal brief, available at www.abanet.org/publiced/preview/briefs/pdfs/07-08/06-1431_Respondent.pdf, and from information on the On the Docket Web site, available at www.otd.oyez.org/cases/2007/cbocs-west-v-humphries.

2. *CBOCS West, Inc., v. Humphries,* No. 06-1431 (2008).

3. Robert Barnes and William Branigin, "Justices Uphold Retaliation Lawsuits," *Washington Post,* May 28, 2008; Linda Greenhouse, "Justices Say Law Bars Retaliation over Bias Claims," *New York Times,* May 28, 2008; Warren Richey, "Workers Can Sue Firms Over Retaliation, Supreme Court Rules," *Christian Science Monitor,* May 28, 2008.

4. C. Herman Prichett, *The American Constitution* (New York: McGraw-Hill, 1977), 17–18.

5. See Gregory A. Caldeira, "Public Opinion and the U.S. Supreme Court: FDR's Court-packing Plan," *American Political Science Review* 81 (December 1987): 1139–53.

6. See Robert A. Carp and Ronald Stidham, *The Federal Courts*, 2nd ed. (Washington, D.C.: CQ Press, 1991), 63; Thomas G. Walker and Lee Epstein, *The Supreme Court of the United States* (Washington, D.C.: CQ Press, 1993), 75.

7. See Robert A. Carp and Ronald Stidham, *Judicial Process in America* (Washington, D.C.: CQ Press, 1993), 47–49; Paul C. Light, *Forging Legislation* (New York: Norton, 1992), 177–78, 226–27.

8. *Statistical Abstract of the United States 2008*, available at www.census.gov/compendia/statab/tables/08s0327.pdf.

9. *Ware v. Hylton,* 3 Dall. 199 (1796).

10. *Marbury v. Madison,* 1 Cr. 137 (1803).

11. Robert G. McCloskey, *The American Supreme Court* (Chicago: University of Chicago Press, 1960), 40–44.

12. Paul Gewirtz and Chad Golder, "So Who Are the Activists?" *New York Times*, July 6, 2005. See also Thomas M Keck, *The Most Activist Supreme Court in History: The Road to Modern Judicial Conservatism* (Chicago: University of Chicago Press, 2004).

13. Lori Ringhand, "Judicial Activism: An Empirical Examination of Voting Behavior on the Rehnquist Natural Court," *Constitutional Commentary* 24 (Spring 2007): 43–87.

14. See the excellent discussion of *Mapp v. Ohio* in Fred W. Friendly and Martha J. H. Elliot, *The Constitution—That Delicate Balance* (New York: Random House, 1984), 128–42.

15. Kevin T. McGuire and Barbara Plamer, "Issue Fluidity on the U.S. Supreme Court," *American Political Science Review* 89 (September 1995): 691–702.

16. See Donald L. Horowitz, *The Courts and Social Policy* (Washington, D.C.: Brookings Institution, 1977).

17. Kevin T. McGuire, "Public Schools, Religious Establishments, and the U.S. Supreme Court," *American Politics Research* 37 (January 2009):50–74.

18. *Texas Monthly v. Bullock,* 489 U.S. 1 (1989).

19. Tom Mooney, "Breaks for Bibles," *Liberty*, March/April 1995, 22–25; Diana B. Henriques, "Religion-Based Tax Breaks: Housing to Paychecks to Books," *New York Times*, October 11, 2006.

20. *Oregon v. Mitchell,* 400 U.S. 112 (1970).

21. Joseph T. Keenan, *The Constitution of the United States: An Unfolding Story*, 2nd ed. (Chicago: Dorsey Press, 1988), 42–43.

22. Steven E. Schier, *A Decade of Deficits* (Albany: State University of New York Press, 1992), 119.

23. See National Conference of State Legislatures, "Legislative/Electoral Response to Kelo," November 7, 2007, available at www.ncsl.org/print/natres/mapslide.pdf; and *Kelo v. New London,* 545 U.S. 469 (2005).

24. Keenan, *The Constitution of the United States*, 43–49.

25. Peter Steinfels, "New Law Protects Religious Practices," *New York Times*, November 17, 1993; *City of Bourne (Texas) v. Flores,* 521 U.S. 507 (1997).

26. *Cutter v. Wilkinson,* 544 U.S. 709 (2005).

27. *Baker v. Carr,* 369 U.S. 186 (1962).

28. The survey data are from The Pew Research Center for the People & the Press, *The Times Mirror News Interest Index: 1989–1995* (Washington, D.C.: Pew Center). On the notion that opinion on the Supreme Court can be changed, see Valerie J. Hoekstra, "The Supreme Court and Opinion Change: An Experimental Study of the Court's Ability to Change Opinion," *American Politics Quarterly* 23 (January 1995): 109–29.

29. Gregory A. Caldeira, "Neither Purse Nor the Sword: Dynamics of Public Confidence in the U.S. Supreme Court," *American Political Science Review* 80 (December 1986): 1209–26. On public reaction to the Supreme Court's decision in *Bush v. Gore*, see the CNN/USA Today/Gallup Poll, December 13, 2000, and the ABC News/Washington Post Poll, December 14, 2000. www.pollingreport.com/wh2post.htm

30. Michael W. Link, "Tracking Public Mood in the Supreme Court: Cross-Time Analysis of Criminal Procedure and Civil Rights Cases," *Political Research Quarterly* 48 (March 1995): 61–78; William Mishler and Reginald S. Sheehan, "The Supreme Court as a Countermajoritarian Institution? The Impact of Public Opinion on Supreme Court Decisions," *American Political Science Review* 87 (March 1993): 87–101.

31. John L. Moore, *Speaking of Washington* (Washington, D.C.: Congressional Quarterly, 1993), 178.

32. Walker and Epstein, *The Supreme Court of the United States*, 130–31.

33. Gregory A. Caldeira and John R. Wright, "The Discuss List: Agenda Building in the Supreme Court," *Law and Society Review* 24 (1990): 807–36.

34. Linda Greenhouse, "Chief Justice Advocates Higher Pay for Judiciary," *New York Times*, January 1, 2007.

35. See Timothy M. Hagle, "Strategic Retirements: A Political Model of Turnover on the United States Supreme Court," *Political Behavior* 15 (March 1993): 25–48; Peverill Squire, "Politics and Personal Factors in Retirement from the United States Supreme Court," *Political Behavior* 10 (1988): 180–90.

36. Gary King, "Presidential Appointments to the Supreme Court," *American Politics Quarterly* 15 (July 1987): 373–86.

37. See the Senate list, "Supreme Court Nominations, present-1789," available at www.senate.gov/pagelayout/reference/nominations/Nominations.htm.

38. See Charles M. Cameron, Albert D. Cover, and Jeffrey A. Segal, "Senate Voting on Supreme Court Nominees: A Neoinstitutional Model," *American Political Science Review* 84 (June 1990): 525–34; Jeffrey A. Segal, "Senate Confirmation of Supreme Court Justices: Partisan and Institutional Politics," *Journal of Politics* 49 (November 1987): 998–1015.

39. Bob Woodward and Scott Armstrong, *The Brethren* (New York: Avon Books, 1979), 83.

40. On the importance of professional merit and qualifications, see Lee Epstein, René Lindstädt, Jeffrey A. Segal, and Chad Westerland, "The Changing Dynamics of Senate Voting on Supreme Court Nominees," *Journal of Politics* 68 (May 2006): 296–307; and Lee Epstein, Jeffrey A. Segal, Nancy Staudt, and René Lindstädt, "The Role of Qualifications in the Confirmation of Nominees to the U.S. Supreme Court," *Florida State University Law Review* 32 (Summer 2005): 1145–74.

41. Lee Epstein, and Jeffrey A. Segal, *Advice and Consent: The Politics of Judicial Appointments* (New York: Oxford University Press, 2005).

42. Lee Epstein, Andrew D. Martin, Kevin M. Quinn and Jeffrey A. Segal, "Ideological Drift Among Supreme Court Justices: Who, When, and How Important," *Northwestern University Law Review* 101 (No. 4 2007): 1483–1541; Thomas R. Hensley and Christopher E. Smith, "Membership Change and Voting Change: An Analysis of the Rehnquist Court's 1986–1991 Terms," *Political Research Quarterly* 48 (December 1995): 837–56.

43. Woodward and Armstrong, *The Brethren*, 139–40.

44. Andrew D. Martin, Kevin M. Quinn, and Lee Epstein, "The Median Justice on the United States Supreme Court," *North Carolina Law Review* 83 (June 2005): 1275–1320.

45. See, for example, Michael Comisky, "Can Presidents Pack the Supreme Court? A Micro-and Macro- Look at FDR," *Congress and the Presidency* 22 (Spring 1995): 19–33.

46. Charles Lane, "Caseload Reflects Court's Altered Role," *Washington Post*, February 2, 2004; Philip Allen Lacovara, "The Incredible Shrinking Court; If Their Productivity Were Measured by Private Sector Standards, the Supremes Might Receive Pink Slips," *The American Lawyer* (December 2003); W. John Moore, "Court Is in Recess," *National Journal*, October 30, 1993, 2587–90.

47. Linda Greenhouse, "Dwindling Docket Mystifies Supreme Court," *New York Times*, December 7, 2006.

48. Caldeira and Wright, "The Discuss List," 813.

49. David O'Brien, *Storm Center: The Supreme Court in American Politics*, 3rd ed. (New York: Norton, 1993), 247–56.

50. See Walker and Epstein, *The Supreme Court of the United States*, 81–94.

51. Gregory A. Caldeira and John R. Wright, "Organized Interests and Agenda Setting in the U.S. Supreme Court," *American Political Science Review* 82 (December 1988): 1109–27.

52. Gregory A. Caldeira and John R. Wright, "Amici Curiae before the Supreme Court: Who Participates, When, and How Much," *Journal of Politics* 52 (August 1990): 782–806.

53. Walker and Epstein, *The Supreme Court of the United States*, 136–37.

54. The case was *Metro-Goldwyn-Mayer Studios Inc. v. Grokster, Ltd.,* 545 U. S. 913 (2005). Legal briefs filed in the case can be found on the Electronic Frontier Foundation Web site, available at www.eff.org/IP/P2P/MGM_v_Grokster/.

55. Kevin T. McGuire and Gregory A. Caldeira, "Lawyers, Organized Interests, and the Law of Obscenity: Agenda Setting in the Supreme Court," *American Political Science Review* 87 (September 1993): 717–26; and Paul M. Collins Jr., "Friends of the Court: Examining the Influence of Amicus Curiae Participation in U.S. Supreme Court Litigation," *Law and Society Review* 38 (November 2004): 807–32.

56. Quoted in Paul M. Barrett, "Lawyers Arguing Cases Before Supreme Court Find Experience Can Be Less than Appealing," *Wall Street Journal*, January 17, 1994.

57. Barrett, "Lawyers Arguing Cases"; Timothy R. Johnson, Paul J. Wahlbeck, and James F. Spriggs, II, "The Influence of Oral Arguments on the U.S. Supreme Court," *American Political Science Review* 100 (February 2006): 99–113; Walker and Epstein, *The Supreme Court of the United States*, 106.

58. Tracey E. George and Lee Epstein, "On the Nature of Supreme Court Decision Making," *American Political Science Review* 86 (June 1992): 323–37.

59. The death penalty cases were *Stanford v. Kentucky,* 492 U.S. 361 (1989) and *Roper v. Simmons,* 543 U.S. 551 (2005). The same sex sodomy decisions were *Bowers v. Hardwick,* 478 U.S. 186 (1986); and *Lawrence v. Texas,* 539 U.S. 558 (2003).

60. Ward Farnsworth, "Signatures of Ideology: The Case of the Supreme Court's Criminal Docket," *Michigan Law Review* 104 (October 2005): 71–104; Jeffrey A. Segal and Albert D. Cover, "Ideological Values and the Votes of the U.S.

Supreme Court Justices," *American Political Science Review* 83 (June 1989): 557–65.

61. Earl Warren, *The Memoirs of Earl Warren* (Garden City, NY: Doubleday, 1977), 309–10.

62. See the letter from Chief Justice William Rehnquist in the *Law, Courts, and Judicial Process Section Newsletter* 7 (Fall 1989): 8.

63. O'Brien, *Storm Center*, 306–14.

64. Joan Biskupic, "The Quiet But Critical Fifth Vote," *Washington Post National Weekly Edition*, June 19–25, 1995.

65. McCloskey, *The American Supreme Court*, 185–86.

66. Beverly Blair Cook, "Justice Brennan and the Institutionalization of Dissent Assignment," *Judicature* 79 (July–August 1995): 17–23.

67. Thomas G. Walker, Lee Epstein, and William J. Dixon, "On the Mysterious Demise of Consensual Norms in the United States Supreme Court," *Journal of Politics* 50 (May 1988): 361–89.

68. Craig Gilbert, "Rehnquist Silent on His Plans," *Milwaukee Journal Sentinel*, June 27, 2005.

69. See *Baze v. Rees,* No. 07-5439 (2008).

70. Linda Greenhouse, "On Court That Defied Labeling, Kennedy Made the Boldest Mark," *New York Times*, June 29, 2008; Patrick D. Schmidt and David A. Yalof, "The 'Swing Voter' Revisited: Justice Anthony Kennedy and the First Amendment Right of Free Speech," *Political Research Quarterly* 57 (June 2004): 209–17.

71. Lawrence Sirovich, "A Pattern Analysis of the Second Rehnquist U.S. Supreme Court," *Proceedings of the National Academy of Sciences* 100 (June 24, 2003): 7432–35.

72. Christopher J. W. Zorn, "U.S. Government Litigation Strategies in the Federal Appellate Courts," *Political Research Quarterly* 55 (March 2002): 145–66.

73. Linda R. Cohen and Matthew L. Spitzer, "The Government Litigant Advantage: Implications for the Law," *Florida State University Law Review* 28 (Fall 2000): 391–425; Reginald S. Sheehan, William Mishler, and Donald R. Songer, "Ideology, Status, and the Differential Success of Direct Parties before the Supreme Court," *American Political Science Review* 86 (June 1992): 464–71.

74. Sheehan, Mishler, and Songer, "Ideology, Status, and the Differential Success of Direct Parties before the Supreme Court," 469.

75. Marc Galanter, "Why the 'Haves' Come out Ahead: Speculations on the Limits of Legal Change," *Law and Society Review* 9 (Fall 1974): 95–160.

76. These data are taken from Administrative Office of the United States Courts, "Judicial Business of the United States Courts 2007." www.uscourts.gov/judbus2007/contents.html

77. Carp and Stidham, *Judicial Process in America*, 45–46, 310–12; Richard Neely, *How Courts Govern America* (New Haven, CT: Yale University Press, 1981), 204–5.

78. Carp and Stidham, *The Federal Courts*, 102–4. The Missouri example is taken from Michael Grunwald, "Ashcroft's '99 Tactics in Spotlight," *Washington Post*, January 1, 2001.

79. Quoted in Frank Santiago, "Bush Chooses Hansen to Join Appeals Court," *Des Moines Register*, July 31, 1991.

80. See "Imprints on the Bench," *Congressional Quarterly Weekly Report*, January 19, 1991, 173.

81. Data from Alliance for Justice, www.judicialselectionproject.org/

82. Gerard S. Gryski, Gary Zuk, and Deborah J. Barrow, "A Bench That Looks Like America? Representation of African Americans and Latinos on the Federal Courts," *Journal of Politics* 56 (November 1994): 1076–86; Rorie L. Spill Solberg and Kathleen A. Bratton, "Diversifying the Federal Bench: Presidential Patterns," *Justice System Journal* 26 (No. 2 2005): 119–33.

83. National Center for State Courts, *Examining the Work of State Courts, 2006* (Willamsburg, VA: National Center for State Courts, 2007).

84. Peverill Squire, "Measuring the Professionalization of State Courts of Last Resort," *State Politics and Policy Quarterly* 8 (Fall 2008): 223–38.

85. Ronald K. L. Collins, Peter J. Galie, and John Kincaid, "State High Courts, State Constitutions, and Individual Rights Litigation Since 1980: A Judicial Survey," *Publius* 16 (1985): 141–61; G. Alan Tarr, "The New Judicial Federalism in Perspective," *Notre Dame Law Review* 72 (May 1997): 1097–118; and Robert F. Williams, "Introduction: The Third Stage of the New Judicial Federalism," *New York University Annual Survey of American Law* (2003) 59: 211–29.

86. *Greenwood v. California,* 486 U.S. 35 (1988).

87. See John Kincaid and Robert F. Williams, "The New Judicial Federalism: The States' Lead in Rights Protection," *Journal of State Government* 65 (April/June 1992): 50–52, Laura Mansnerus, "High Court in New Jersey Strictly Limits Auto Searches," *New York Times*, March 5, 2002, and G. Alan Tarr and Robert F. Williams, "Decidedly Co-Equal: The New Jersey Supreme Court," unpublished paper, Center for State Constitutional Studies, Rutgers-Camden.

88. Lawrence Baum, "Making Judicial Policies in the Political Arena," in *The State of the States*, 2nd ed., ed. Carl E. Van Horn (Washington, D.C.: CQ Press, 1993), 164–65.

89. Gregory A. Caldeira, "Legal Precedent: Structures of Communication between State Supreme Courts," *Social Networks* 10 (1988): 29–55; Gregory A. Caldeira, "The Transmission of Legal Precedent: A Study of State Supreme Courts," *American Political Science Review* 79 (March 1985): 178–93.

90. Richard J. Hardy and Joseph J. Carrier, "Missouri Courts, Judges, and Juries," in *Missouri Government and Politics*, rev. ed., eds. Richard J. Hardy, Richard R. Dohm, and David Leuthold (Columbia: University of Missouri Press, 1995), 173–87.

91. Larry T. Aspin and William K. Hall, "Retention Elections and Judicial Behavior," *Judicature* 77 (May–June 1994): 306–15.

92. Larry Aspin, "Judicial Retention Election Trends, 1964–2006," *Judicature* 90 (March–April 2007): 208–13; Larry Aspin, William K. Hall, Jean Bax, and Celeste Montoya, "Thirty Years of Judicial Retention Elections: An Update," *Social Science Journal* 37 (2000): 1–17; William K. Hall and Larry T. Aspin, "What Twenty Years of Judicial Retention Elections Have Told Us," *Judicature* 70 (April–May 1987): 340–47; Robert C. Luskin, Christopher N. Bratcher, Christopher G. Jordan, Tracy K. Renner, and Kris S. Seago, "How Minority Judges Fare in Retention Elections," *Judicature* 77 (May–June 1994): 316–21.

93. "House OKs Change to Missouri Plan," *Columbia Daily Tribune*, April 15, 2008; John Rodgers, "Wilder's Last Gasp on State Judges Falls Short," *Nashville City Paper*, May 27, 2008.

94. Melinda Gann Hall, "State Supreme Courts in American Democracy: Probing the Myths of Judicial Reform," *American Political Science Review* 95 (June 2001): 315–30.

95. Burton M. Atkins and Harry R. Glick, "Formal Judicial Recruitment and State Supreme Court Decisions," *American Politics Quarterly* 2 (October 1974): 427–49; Henry R. Glick, "The Politics of State-Court Reform," in *The Politics of Judicial Reform*, ed. Philip Dubois (Lexington, MA: Heath, 1982), 29–31. But see Damon Cann, "Beyond Accountability and Independence: Judicial Appointment and State Court Performance," *Judicature* 90 (March–April 2007): 226–32.

96. Malia Reddick, "Merit Selection: A Review of the Social Scientific Literature," *Dickinson Law Review* 106 (Spring 2002): 729–44; Barbara Luck Graham, "Judicial Recruitment and Racial Diversity on State Courts: An Overview," *Judicature* 74 (June–July 1990): 28–34.

97. Luskin, Bratcher, Jordan, Renner, and Seago, "How Minority Judges Fare," 316–21.

98. James Sample, Lauren Jones, Rachel Weiss, and Jesse Rutledge, "The New Politics of Judicial Elections 2006," *Justice at Stake Campaign*, May 17, 2007; Deborah Goldberg, Sarah Samis, Edwin Bender, and Rachel Weiss, "The New Politics of Judicial Elections 2004," *Justice at Stake Campaign*, June 2005; Samantha Sanchez, "A Costly Contest: Pennsylvania 2003 Supreme Court Race Tops All 2001–02 Judicial Races in Fundraising," *The Institute on Money in State Politics*, May 19, 2004. See also Marlene Arnold Nicholson and Norman Nicholson, "Funding Judicial Campaigns in Illinois," *Judicature* 77 (May–June 1994): 294–99; Amy E. Young, "Judicial Politics in the States," in *State Government: CQ's Guide to Current Issues and Activities 1991–92*, ed. Thad L. Beyle (Washington, D.C.: CQ Press, 1991); Robert F. Utter, "Justice, Money, and Sleaze," in *State Government: CQ's Guide to Current Issues and Activities 1992–93*, ed. Thad L. Beyle (Washington, D.C.: CQ Press, 1992).

99. Damon M. Cann, and Jeff Yates, "Homegrown Institutional Legitimacy," *American Politics Research* 36 (March 2008): 297–329.

Part 4

The Policy Process in American Politics

15

The Federal System and State Government

CHAPTER OUTLINE

In 2003, the state of Iowa faced the prospect of losing $4.7 million in federal highway construction funds each year for the following four years. Why? Because it was reluctant to give in to pressure from Washington to toughen its laws against drunken driving. In 2000, Congress passed legislation requiring states to make 0.08 blood alcohol the standard for drunken driving, penalizing states that failed to pass such a law by withholding a percentage of their federal highway construction funds. Members of Congress might have thought that tougher laws were needed, but some of their Iowa counterparts disagreed. As an Iowa state legislator who resisted the pressure from Washington said, "I think this is absolutely a totalitarian enactment. It's the federal government saying you shall do this and if you don't we're going to spank your bottom." One of his colleagues concurred, observing, "Anyone who thinks that .08 is being passed on its morals is fooling themselves. We are voting on money."[1]

Iowa was not alone in resisting the federal government's directive to toughen drunken driving laws. In 2003, ten other states also stood to lose some portion of their highway construction funds for failing to comply with the federal mandate. And South Carolina was even threatening to sue the federal government over the issue, but in Iowa, and in every other state, the federal government's threat worked. In 2003, Iowa adopted the 0.08 standard, and in 2005, Minnesota became the final state to put it into effect.[2]

The conflict over appropriate drunken driving laws illuminates two key points about American politics. The first is that the rules that govern the relationship between the federal government and state governments matter because they determine how much influence the federal government has over state and local policies. The second is that the rules within each state matter because they determine the policies that affect people's everyday lives. Because the federal government helps to finance many state and local programs, it has potentially tremendous influence over the policy choices state and local governments make. However, most of the laws Americans live under are made at the state and local levels, not at the federal level. Although the federal government can pressure cities and states to conform to its wishes, in many instances, state and local governments can make their own policy choices. Thus, a combination of federal and state rules determines the policies that serve, protect, and limit Americans in their everyday lives.

In this chapter, we examine both aspects of state politics—how state and local governments fit into the federal system and how governments within the states operate. We begin by looking at the changing relationship between the federal government and state and local government, discussing how federal aid has become a major source of revenue for state and local governments and has increased the influence of the federal government over state and local policies. We go on to explore how state governments operate, focusing especially on state budgeting, government institutions, interest groups, and the public's role in state politics. Finally, we look at local government. We conclude the chapter by discussing how citizens assess the relative performance of federal, state, and local government.

As the public's expectations of government evolve, the rules governing the relationship between the federal government and state governments change and the rules within each state change in response. As with other aspects of American politics, the rules matter because the rules determine who wins and loses in the competition for government programs and services.

15-1 RELATIONS AMONG FEDERAL, STATE, AND LOCAL GOVERNMENTS

We have said that the federal government helps pay the cost of many city and state programs, but how much aid does Washington provide? What rules structure the allocation of aid, and how do those rules affect the policy choices made in state capitals and mayors' offices around the country? What other tools does Washington use to influence cities and states? Answers to these questions will help us understand how state and local governments fit into the national political system.

15-1a Federal Aid to State and Local Governments

Federal aid to state and local governments dates back to our nation's origins. During the 1800s, the most important form of federal aid consisted of grants of land to the states to support the creation of colleges and universities; direct cash payments to cities and states were rare. All that changed, however, in the 1930s, with the shift from dual to fiscal federalism. Federal aid is now a major source of revenue for cities and states, which gives the federal government considerable influence over the policy choices that state and local governments make.

Dual Federalism

For the first 140 years of U.S. history, the federal government provided minuscule amounts of aid to state and local governments. As Table 15–1 shows, as late as World War I, federal grants constituted less than 1 percent of all state and local revenues. Federal aid was low because the idea of **dual federalism**, which held that the federal government and state governments should work in parallel without much interaction, governed the relations between Washington and the states. Because the doctrine of dual federalism meant no federal aid, state and local governments covered the cost of almost all their programs through their own taxes. In turn, Washington had relatively little input into the decisions cities and states made.

dual federalism

An interpretation of federalism that held that the national government was supreme within those areas specifically assigned to it in the Constitution, and the states were supreme in all other areas of public policy.

Fiscal Federalism

The tradition of dual federalism collapsed in the 1930s with the advent of President Franklin Roosevelt's New Deal programs. As

Year	Total federal grants-in-aid (in millions of dollars, $)	Federal grants as a percentage of state and local government expenditures (%)
1902	7	1.0
1913	12	1.0
1922	108	2.1
1932	232	3.0
1940	945	10.2
1950	2,486	10.9
1960	6,974	14.8
1970	24,065	20.1
1980	91,385	27.4
1990	135,325	18.9
2000	285,900	22.2
2007	443,800	22.6

Table 15–1   Patterns of Federal Aid to State and Local Governments
During the twentieth century, the federal government became an important source of revenue for state and local governments.

Source: *1902–1960:* Historical Statistics of the United States: Colonial Times to 1970, Part 2 *(Washington, D.C.: U.S. Bureau of the Census, 1975), 1125–28; 1970–1999: Total Federal Grants-in-Aid: Office of Management and Budget,* Budget of the United States Government, Fiscal Year 2001, Historical Tables *(Washington, D.C.: U.S. Government Printing Office, 2001), 205–6; Federal Grants as a Percentage of State and Local Government Expenditures: Office of Management and Budget,* Budget of the United States Government, Fiscal Year 2009, Analytical Perspectives *(Washington, D.C.: U.S. Government Printing Office, 2008), 113.*

fiscal federalism

The principle that the federal government should play a major role in financing some of the activities of state and local governments.

we discussed in Chapter 2, the New Deal ushered in the era of **fiscal federalism**, which holds that the federal government has a role to play in providing financial assistance to state and local governments. Until the mid-1960s, fiscal federalism had a strong element of cooperation between the levels of government because they often worked together to solve problems such as unemployment. In more recent years, fiscal federalism has taken on a less cooperative and more conflictual tone.

As Table 15–1 shows, the amount of federal aid to state and local governments has soared since the 1930s. By the time Dwight Eisenhower left the White House in 1961, the federal government provided $7 billion in aid to cities and states, or roughly 13 percent of all state and local expenditures. The trend toward increased federal aid to cities and states was boosted during the 1960s when President Lyndon Johnson and Congress sought to end poverty in the United States by enacting the Great Society programs—an ambitious and expensive set of programs designed to increase educational and job training opportunities for the poor while improving their general quality of life. By 1970, the federal government's share of state and local expenditures stood at 23 percent. Over the next decade, Congress further accelerated the trend toward increased federal aid by expanding the scope of assistance programs and relaxing the eligibility criteria so that most middle-class towns and cities could qualify. As a result, when Ronald Reagan took the oath of office in 1981, the federal government was providing more than $91 billion in aid, a thirteenfold increase in a span of twenty years, and federal assistance accounted for 30 percent of all state and local expenditures.

Rather than continue the trend of having Washington underwrite more and more of the cost of state and local government, President Reagan worked to eliminate federal aid programs. In doing so, he was motivated by his twin desires to reduce how much the federal government spent on domestic programs and to reduce the federal government's influence over state and local politics.[3] As a result, the rules changed, and the federal government's contribution to state and local expenditures fell to 19 percent by 1990. Under President Bill Clinton, however, federal aid grew rapidly; by 1996, its share of state and local spending reached 25 percent. Federal aid continued to grow even though Republicans controlled both houses of Congress during almost all of the time since the second half of the 1990s. In 2007, federal aid constituted less than 23 percent of state and local spending. Thus, it appears likely that federal aid will continue to be one of the major sources of funding for state and local expenditures in the twenty-first century.

Forms of Financial Assistance

Federal assistance may be divided into three general types: categorical grants, block grants, and revenue sharing. Since the 1930s, the backbone of federal aid to state and local governments has been **categorical grants-in-aid**—programs that Congress creates and national agencies administer to fund narrow, specific categories of activities, such as building highways or paying welfare recipients. Categorical grants may be project or formula-based, but either way, they give recipient governments little discretion in spending the money. *Project grants* are awarded on a competitive basis; a federal agency accepts applications from cities and states and then funds the projects it deems the most worthy. This procedure gives the granting agency great power to decide who gets a grant, leaving open the possibility of political favoritism. In contrast, *formula grants* automatically set the number of dollars a recipient government gets based on certain objective local conditions, such as the population and the unemployment rate. Formula grants are not immune to politics, however. Congressional battles over setting the formulas often include detailed discussions of which locales stand to win or lose, and many of the formulas are designed to ensure that money is spread across the country.[4] Although categorical grants are an attractive source of financing for state and local programs, they come with strings attached, particularly for the more numerous project grants. Recipients usually must follow detailed rules, written in Washington, that govern how the money can be spent.

categorical grants-in-aid

Grants of money from the federal government to pay for specific state and local government activities under strict federal guidelines.

block grants

Grants of money from the federal government that state and local governments may spend on any program serving the general purpose of the grant.

general revenue sharing

A program giving federal money to state and local governments with no restrictions on how it will be spent.

The number of categorical grant programs rose tenfold during the 1960s, and with this increase came numerous complaints that the grants were too difficult to administer and the rules too rigid to meet the needs of state and local governments.[5] In response to these criticisms, in the early 1970s, Congress instituted a system of **block grants**, allocating federal funds for broad policy purposes rather than for specific purposes, as categorical grants do. Because block grants come with fewer federal rules attached, state and local governments may spend the money on a variety of activities within the designated policy area. A city that receives a law enforcement block grant, for example, can use the money to purchase police cars, hire new police officers, improve its communications network, or perform any of a variety of other actions. As with categorical grants, block grants may be made on the basis of individual projects or general formulas.

In 1972, Congress supplemented categorical and block grants by instituting **general revenue sharing**, a program that allocated federal funds to state and local governments on the basis of a formula that took into account a community's needs and its willingness to tax its own citizens. Recipients were allowed to use the money as they saw fit. Because no federal rules dictated how the money was spent, revenue sharing marked a significant retreat by the federal government from its habit of trying to shape state and local government policy choices. Although some supporters of revenue sharing hoped it eventually would replace all categorical and block grants, the program ended in 1986 as part of the Reagan administration's effort to restrain the growth in federal aid to cities and states.

The Persistence of Categorical Grants

In 2008, the federal government provided roughly $467 billion in financial assistance to the nation's cities and states.[6] About 75 percent of federal aid was allocated through categorical grants, with the bulk allocated through about two dozen formula-based programs.[7] Categorical grants have persisted as the dominant form of aid despite repeated threats to do away with them. State and local governments complained about their complexity in the 1960s. Richard Nixon attempted to replace them with revenue sharing in the 1970s. Ronald Reagan repeatedly attempted to cut spending on these grants in the 1980s. Most recently, the Republican Congress sought to consolidate them into smaller numbers of block grants during the 1990s.

Why have categorical grants persisted? Federal officials like them for two reasons. First, categorical grants provide the federal government with a way to hold recipient governments financially accountable for their actions. Because cities and states must follow the detailed rules that come with a categorical grant, the federal government can track how the money is spent, ensuring effective and efficient spending. In contrast, block grants and revenue sharing limit the federal government's ability to monitor how aid is spent, raising the possibility that the state or local government will not spend the money as federal officials wish. Federal government officials thus have a strong interest in retaining categorical grants.

Second, categorical grants are attractive because they enable members of Congress to claim credit for directing federal dollars into their home districts. As we pointed out in Chapter 11, members find that claiming credit for federal programs that benefit their constituents can boost their prospects for reelection. Because categorical grants are tied to specific purposes, they provide members with opportunities to claim credit. With more general block grants and revenue sharing, however, members of Congress can claim no specific credit because state and local officials decide how to spend the money. As a result, until recently, there was little political support in Congress for expanding block grants or reviving revenue sharing.

When the Republicans took control of Congress in 1995 for the first time in forty years, they called for greatly expanding the use of block grants. They argued that state and local governments would be able to use federal aid more wisely and productively if they were freed from having to follow the detailed guidelines that come with categorical grants. They had some success in shifting federal aid to block grants. The share of federal aid going to states and localities through categorical grants declined from 90 percent in 1995 to 75 percent in 1999. In the end, however, categorical grants continue to be the primary type of federal aid.

Consequences of Financial Assistance

The rules governing the distribution of the immense amount of federal aid to state and local governments have had several consequences: increased federal power over the states, increased lobbying of the federal government by states and localities, and an increased emphasis on the importance of the federal census. First and foremost, increased federal aid gives the federal government tremendous leverage over the policy choices cities and states make. The federal government does not directly provide most domestic services; police and fire protection, education, sanitation, libraries, welfare, and most other public services are all programs that state and local governments pay for and administer. By providing or denying funds to cities and states, however, Washington can influence the kinds of services they provide.[8] Thus, the federal government can use its financial leverage to accomplish policy goals it could not otherwise achieve. As noted in the introduction to this chapter, Congress used a financial carrot to force states to adopt the 0.08 drunken driving standard. And it was not the first time the approach was employed. In 1984, Congress passed a law stating that states that did not raise their legal drinking age to twenty-one by 1986 would lose 5 percent of their national highway funds, with more severe cuts to follow in succeeding years. Despite grumbling from several states that the federal government was intruding into their affairs, they all knuckled under to the pressure and raised their legal drinking age.[9] Absent a big financial carrot, however, the federal government has less success in getting state governments to follow its preferences. In 2008, for example, twenty-two states opted not to participate in a federal grant program to promote sexual abstinence education in public schools, even though by doing so each was foregoing hundreds of thousands of dollars.[10]

A second consequence of the tremendous amount of federal aid that goes to cities and states is that state and local governments now actively lobby the federal government. During the era of dual federalism, state and local governments could afford to ignore much of what happened in Washington, D.C. When federal aid became a major source of revenue, however, state and local governments had a vested interest in seeing that aid programs minimized their administrative costs and maximized their administrative discretion. As Chapter 10 noted, state and local governments have their own interest groups, and most states and many large cities maintain their own liaison offices in Washington. Lobbying by cities and states contributed to the creation of block grants and revenue-sharing programs, and it is a major reason why the federal government often uses formula-based categorical grants.

The success that state and local governments have had in promoting formula-based grants has led to the third consequence of federal aid: the increased importance of the federal census. Cities and states like formula-based grants because every community that meets the eligibility criteria receives aid, which minimizes the chances that politically well-connected communities can manipulate the allocation process in their favor. No formula can end all controversy. Federal aid is largely allocated on the basis of population; therefore, whom the U.S. Census Bureau counts and doesn't count affects how aid is allocated. Following the 2000 Census, several cities and states argued that the Census had undercounted the number of people living in their communities, thereby costing them federal aid, and even in the case of Utah, a seat in the House of Representatives.[11]

15-1b Other Forms of Federal Influence

Along with financial aid, the federal government also influences state and local governments through two other means: mandates and the relationships that picket-fence federalism creates.

mandates
Laws Congress passes that require state and local governments to undertake specified actions.

Mandates
The federal government can influence state and local governments by issuing **mandates**—that is, laws Congress passes that require other levels of government to take specified actions.[12] Whereas financial aid constitutes a "carrot" the federal government can use to encourage cities and states to enact its policy priorities, mandates are the "stick." In some circumstances, Washington orders cities and states to abide by its regulations. For example, the federal government has ordered cities and states to avoid discriminating on

the basis of race, gender, or religion, and it can require them to meet clean air standards.

As you might imagine, Washington's use of mandates irritates many state and local officials. Their irritation has mounted in recent years because the federal government has continued to issue mandates even though a persistent federal budget deficit has prevented it from providing cities and states with the money they need to comply. The amount of money involved is significant. In 2008, for example, the National Conference of State Legislatures estimated the states were confronted with $131 billion in unfunded mandates from the federal government over the previous five years.[13]

Because cities and states are required to satisfy federal mandates whether Washington provides the money or not, they must make tough choices about whether to raise taxes or cut existing programs. For example, the Asbestos Hazard Emergency Response Act, which Congress passed in 1986, required schools to remove asbestos from their buildings at an estimated cost of $3.1 billion over thirty years. Although the federal government mandated the asbestos removal, it did not provide any money to reimburse other levels of government to cover the cost.[14] Washington left it up to cities and states to decide how they would pay for the cleanup.

Although federal mandates have been imposing costs on the states for years, unfunded mandates only burst onto the national political scene as a major issue in 1993. In that year, President Clinton ordered government agencies to reduce their reliance on unfunded mandates, and in 1995, Congress passed the Unfunded Mandate Reform Act of 1995. The Act, one of the first major pieces of the new Republican majority's agenda to be signed into law, changed the rules to make it harder for Congress to require state and local governments to undertake new programs without providing the money to fund them. Federal agencies have responded by enacting fewer unfunded mandates for state and local governments. According to the Congressional Budget Office, in 2007, 175 bills were signed into law, 14 of which included intergovernmental mandates. Only three of those mandates, however, crossed the $66 million threshold to trigger the Unfunded Mandate Act. Indeed, only eight bills enacted into law between 2003 and 2007 surpassed that threshold, but the National Conference of State Legislatures notes several ways for Congress to create unfunded mandates without violating the Unfunded Mandates Act. Congress can, for example, underfund a program, as they have routinely done with the Individuals with Disabilities Education Act, or threaten sanctions, as with the drunken driving standards. Moreover, some mandates, such as No Child Left Behind, an educational reform package that George W. Bush succeeded in having enacted into law in 2002, do not meet the definition of a mandate used in the Unfunded Mandates Act. And, of course, Congress did not make the 1995 law retroactive, so the states still have to bear the cost of previous unfunded mandates.[15]

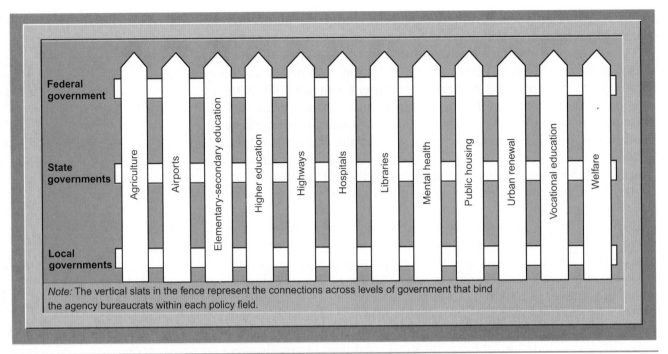

Figure 15-1   Picket-Fence Federalism. Strong working relationships often develop among federal, state, and local government officials working on the same issues.

Source: *George J. Gordon*, Public Administration in America, *3rd ed. (New York: St. Martin's Press, 1986); Deil S. Wright,* Understanding Intergovernmental Relations, *3rd ed. (Pacific Grove, CA: Brooks/Cole, 1988).*

picket-fence federalism

The tendency of federal, state, and local agencies concerned with the same issues to coordinate their efforts with each other and to be insulated from other government agencies that deal with different issues.

Picket-Fence Federalism

Along with mandates, the federal government influences cities and states through the close working relationship that many federal, state, and local agencies have with one another. Figure 15–1 illustrates this phenomenon, which has been called **picket-fence federalism**.[16] Federal, state, and local agencies that work together on an issue often discover they have common interests. At the same time, agencies at all three levels become insulated from agencies that deal with other issues; for example, a state highway commission might work more closely with its federal counterpart than with the state agencies that deal with public housing or higher education. This tendency for agencies at all three levels of government to coordinate their efforts on a shared issue creates the separate "pickets" shown in Figure 15–1. Because the federal agency on each picket channels federal funds to, and is usually larger and better staffed than, its state and local counterparts, it gains greater influence over the state and local agencies. In turn, the horizontal insulation of agencies from each other makes it more difficult for state and local officials to coordinate the work of the agencies they oversee. Some observers think that increased competition for scarce public funds within some issues areas—for example, between different groups pushing health programs for the elderly, young, people with AIDS, and many others—makes the picket-fence analogy less powerful today than it was in recent decades. The relationships that exist among federal, state, and local agencies can still be quite important.

The Founders envisioned a small federal government with relatively limited powers. But, as we noted in Chapter 2, the brevity and vagueness of the Constitution have allowed each generation to restructure the way the rules of American politics are played out. In the case of federalism, the federal government can exert power over state and local governments through aid programs, direct mandates, and the establishment of close working relationships with local and state agencies. Since the 1930s, the federal government has used its influence extensively, but more recent changes in policies and rules have again shifted some power back into the hands of state and local government.

15-1c The Changing Nature of Federalism

The rules that regulate the relationship between the federal government and state and local governments determine where political power lies in the United States. In the 1930s and again in the 1960s, Washington assumed a larger role in American political life as it increasingly came to underwrite the costs of state and local government. In the 1980s, however, that trend came to a halt as the Reagan and George H. W. Bush administrations succeeded in slowing the growth of federal aid and in shifting more of the cost of state and local government back onto the cities and states.

Although the retrenchment that took place in Washington in the 1980s created many headaches for state and local officials, especially when it came to finding new sources of revenue, it also increased their power. In seeking to curtail federal assistance to state and local governments, the Reagan and Bush administrations were motivated both by a desire to restrain federal spending and a desire to shift political power back to the cities and states. Moreover, the reluctance of both Ronald Reagan and George H. W. Bush to propose new domestic programs forced political activists to look at state governments in a new light. Proponents of many new programs found that they received a more cordial hearing in state capitals than in Washington. As a result, state and local governments have increased their say in policy decisions.[17] The changes in rules changed the centers of power and the targets of interest groups.

The dynamics of the federal system promise to change even more in future years. When Republicans took control of Congress in 1995, they vowed to take power away from the federal government and restore it to the states.[18] One obvious product of this movement was the bill forbidding unfunded mandates, which congressional Republicans were not content with simply limiting. They also set to work on a variety of fronts to take power from Washington and to give it to the state capitals.

One example of the Republican effort to shift power to the states occurred in 1996 when, in cooperation with President Clinton, Congress abolished the existing Aid to Families with Dependent Children (AFDC) welfare program. As Chapter 17 discusses in greater detail, this program was replaced with a block grant called

Temporary Assistance for Needy Families (TANF). This new welfare program delegates control over welfare policy to the states, granting them considerable flexibility in designing their own programs. Although the welfare reform bill gave control over much of welfare policy back to the states, the Republicans buried in the legislation a provision that tied some of the money in it to a requirement that the states establish abstinence-only educational programs.[19]

Indeed, it is important to note that while Republicans in Washington were in the majority, they did not always prefer to transfer power from the federal government to the states. The No Child Left Behind Act, for example, involves the federal government more deeply than ever in primary and secondary education policy, an area traditionally left to the states. The USA Patriot Act, passed in the aftermath of the terrorist attacks in 2001 and reauthorized in 2006, gave federal law enforcement officials new powers to supersede state and local law enforcement officials in the course of many criminal investigations and prosecutions. And on a host of other issues ranging from setting driver's license standards to control over the placement of liquid natural gas terminals, Republicans in Congress preferred to make decisions in Washington, rather than allowing the states to make them.

State officials are usually eager to see the balance of power in the federal system shift in their favor.[20] Pressuring Congress to fund any future mandates was just one step toward this goal. Some state legislatures are trying to prompt other changes. After Congress passed the Real ID bill in 2005 forcing states to change the way they issue driver's licenses, many states rebelled. Under the measure the federal government required the states to establish tough personal identity standards to obtain a driver's license. It also forced the states to make license information more easily accessible through electronic databases. Resistance to Real ID was driven by two concerns. Some state legislators and national organizations as diverse as the American Civil Liberties Union and the libertarian Cato Institute feared that Real ID created the equivalent of a national identification card, and thus they opposed it as an invasion of privacy. Other legislators disliked the billions of dollars required to pay for the program—costs the states would have to bear. By 2008, Alaska, Arizona, Idaho, Louisiana, Maine, Montana, New Hampshire, Oklahoma, South Carolina, and Washington had all passed legislation refusing to comply with Real ID.[21] Just before the deadline for Real ID requirements was to take effect on March 31, 2008, the federal government bowed to the pressure from the states and gave them several more years to comply with the new policy provisions, a time line that allows the Obama administration an opportunity to review the program.[22]

On other issues the states have been out ahead of the federal government over the past decade. In 2003, the federal government instituted a "do not call" list for people not wanting to be contacted by telemarketers, but only after thirty-nine states had already established them. Several states have been pushing to allow the reimportation of prescription drugs from Canada, something the federal government has been reluctant to do. And seven states (i.e., California, Connecticut, Illinois, Maryland, New Jersey, New York, and Ohio) have developed programs to fund embryonic stem cell research, pursuing a policy that the George W. Bush administration adamantly opposed.[23]

The efforts of state legislatures to take power back from the federal government remind us that the nature of federalism changes with time and events. Over the course of the twentieth century, the federal government increased its financial aid to state and local governments and thereby became more involved in state and local affairs. That involvement in turn sparked political conflict over the proper nature of the relationship between the federal government and state and local governments. Many people today want to rewrite the rules governing that relationship and restructure the nature of relations between Washington and the states.

15-2 STATE GOVERNMENT AND POLITICS

The first fourteen chapters of this book focused on how the federal government works rather than on how state governments work. The focus on the federal government is not as misplaced as it might seem because in many ways, state governments are smaller versions of the federal government. Although the Constitution requires only that states adopt a republican form of government, all fifty states have the same three distinct branches of government with similar checks and balances among them. By the same token, however, state capitals are not carbon copies of Washington. Nor are states all alike. In this section, we look at the states, examining key aspects of state government and politics: state constitutions, governors, legislatures, interest groups, and direct democracy.

15-2a State Constitutions

Like the U.S. Constitution, state constitutions establish the basic rules of the political system in each state. The changeable nature of these rules is even clearer at the state level than at the federal level. The U.S. Constitution has been amended only twenty-seven times since it was written in 1789. Few state constitutions have enjoyed similar stability. Only Massachusetts's constitution, which was adopted in 1780, is older than the U.S. Constitution. Most states have had several constitutions; Louisiana leads the way with eleven. (Its current constitution was adopted in 1974.) States also have been quite willing to amend their constitutions. By 2008, the Alabama constitution had been amended 799 times since it was adopted in 1901. (The Alabama constitution contains provisions specific to particular counties, and many of the amendments relate to matters only in a single county.) More than half the states have amended their current constitutions more than 100 times.[24]

State constitutions have been far less stable than the U.S. Constitution for two reasons. First, state constitutions are much more detailed and specific than the federal constitution. Alabama's constitution, for example, runs some 350,000 words long, which makes it by far the nation's longest. To put that figure in perspective, the U.S. Constitution contains roughly 7,500 words. All this detail makes state constitutions less flexible and more often in need of change. The second reason state constitutions have changed so frequently is that, unlike the U.S. Constitution, most state constitutions make it easy for dissatisfied groups to pass constitutional amendments.

The history of state constitution making reveals an interesting pattern. Constitutions adopted around the time the U.S. Constitution was ratified tended to emulate it; they were relatively brief and written in broad, general language. During the nineteenth and early twentieth centuries, longer, more detailed state constitutions became the norm. "The Arkansas Constitution of 1874, for example, contained articles regulating Municipal and Private Corporations,' 'Horticulture, Mining and Manufacturing,' and 'Railroads, Canals and Turnpikes.'"[25] Since the mid-twentieth century, however, states that have revised their constitutions have again written shorter and more flexible documents.[26]

15-2b Governors

Most Americans see their governor as an important political figure who affects their daily lives more than their elected officials in Washington do. Almost three-fourths of all Americans can recall the name of their governor, whereas only 40 to 50 percent can name one of their U.S. senators.[27] Gubernatorial races bring more people to the polls than senatorial races, and voters care more about the outcomes of gubernatorial than senatorial races.[28] And, as the careers of Jimmy Carter, Ronald Reagan, Bill Clinton, and George W. Bush attest, many governors become politicians of national stature.

Terms of Office
All but two states have shifted their governors to four-year terms of office. The move from one-, two-, and three-year terms to four-year terms was fueled by the desire to save the governor from perpetual campaigning. A longer term allows governors to learn their job and have a chance to pursue their policy agendas before they have to face the voters again.

Many states limit the number of terms their governors may serve. In Virginia, for example, the governor may serve only one four-year term. Limiting governors to one term of office brings with it a decided disadvantage: The governor finds it more difficult to fulfill his or her campaign pledges. The reason is that a one-term governor is soon considered a **lame duck**—an officeholder whose political power is weakened because his or her term is coming to an end. Because state legislators and other government officials

lame duck
An officeholder whose political power is weakened because his or her term is coming to an end.

Source: © 2009 Jeff Schultz / AlaskaStock.com

Alaska Governor Sarah Palin started her political career as the mayor of Wasilla, a town with a population of 7,000. In 2008, she was the Republican Party's candidate for vice president.

know that the governor cannot run for reelection, they have less incentive to cooperate with the governor's office. For this reason, a two-term limit is more common than a one-term limit. Indeed, thirty-five states emulate the Twenty-Second Amendment of the U.S. Constitution and limit their governor to two four-year terms.

Some states do not place any limits on how many terms a governor may serve, though among those that do not, several have an informal norm that limits service to two terms. A few midwestern states have had governors serve for more than two terms. In Iowa, for example, Robert Ray served as governor from 1969 to 1983 and was followed by Terry Branstad, who held the office from 1983 to 1999. Such lengthy service offers a governor the best chance to make a mark on the state.

Who Serves?

Almost all governors have been white males. A few minority members have held the office in states where their numbers are strong, notably Asian Americans in Hawaii and Hispanic Americans in New Mexico. Washington state voters elected Gary Locke, a Chinese American, governor in 1996, and he served two terms. In 2007, Bobby Jindal, whose parent immigrated from India, was elected governor of Louisiana. The only African Americans elected governor are Douglas Wilder of Virginia, who held office from 1990 to 1994, and Deval Patrick of Massachusetts, who was elected in 2006. No American Indians have served as governor, although in 1994, Idaho's Attorney General, Larry EchoHawk, a Pawnee, lost a close race for the office.

The first women to serve as governor followed their husbands' footsteps; indeed, some were just surrogates on the ballots. The first women were elected governor in 1924: Nellie Tayloe Ross in

Wyoming, who filled the term of her dead husband, and Miriam "Ma" Ferguson in Texas, who was on the ballot because her husband, a former governor, was ineligible to hold the office again. Ferguson was reelected in 1932. (Ma Ferguson's campaign slogan, "Two governors for the price of one," clearly signaled to voters what they would be getting if she were elected.) No woman was elected governor again until the 1960s, when Lurleen Wallace won in Alabama. Like Ma Ferguson, Wallace ran as a stand-in for her husband, George, whom the state constitution barred from running for reelection.[29]

In recent years, several women have been elected governor in their own right. The first woman elected governor whose husband had not been governor was Ella Grasso of Connecticut in 1974. Two years later, Dixie Lee Ray was elected governor in Washington. Since then, women have been elected governor in many other states, including Alaska, Arizona, Delaware, Hawaii, Kansas, Kentucky, Louisiana, Michigan, Montana, Nebraska, New Hampshire, New Jersey, North Carolina, Oregon, Texas, and Vermont.

Most governors come from either the Democratic or Republican parties. However, some independent or third-party candidates have been elected governor. For example, in 1990, voters in both Alaska and Connecticut chose independents, and the voters of Maine did likewise in 1994. In some cases, these independent candidates were previously elected to office as either a Democratic or a Republican but, for one reason or another, bolted their political party when they ran for governor. In other cases, the independent candidates have been wealthy individuals who had not held public office before becoming governor. The election of Jesse Ventura in Minnesota in 1998 represented a victory for the Reform Party but also resulted from his celebrity as a pro wrestler and actor. Indeed, when Ventura opted not to run for reelection in 2002, a Republican succeeded him in office, not the independent candidate who ran. Since then every governor in office was elected as either a Republican or a Democrat.

Formal and Informal Powers of the Office

Although the powers that governors exercise vary from state to state, almost every governor has formal powers a president would envy. And since the 1960s, these powers have generally increased.[30] This was not always the case. In the past, most governors operated under rules that limited their ability to lead their states.

Over the past several decades, however, governors in most states have gained new powers, making them powerful political leaders. The number of other statewide elected administrators has declined in recent years, but the states still vary considerably in the number of such posts. In North Dakota, for example, in addition to the governor, voters also elect the lieutenant governor, secretary of state, attorney general, treasurer, auditor, agricultural commissioner, commissioner of insurance, labor commissioner, tax commissioner, superintendent of public instruction, and three public service commissioners. In contrast, in Maine, New Hampshire, and

New Jersey, the governor is the only elected administrative official. In those states, executive power is much less fragmented than it is in North Dakota, where the governor has to contend with a host of competing elected administrators. Governors are at an advantage when they can appoint people to head administrative agencies because this power enables them to staff state government with loyal subordinates, people likely to follow the governor's lead.[31] There is, of course, no guarantee that independently elected officials will do so. In addition, appointments can give the governor considerable leverage when negotiating with legislators and others in the policy-making process because the governor can use appointments to reward political support.[32]

Many states have also changed their constitutions to give their governors greater say in the budget-making process, to allow them to fire selected state employees, and to enable them to initiate plans to reorganize the state bureaucracy. In addition, most states have given their governors more staff. In 1956, for example, governors' offices averaged eleven staff members; in 2008, the average was more than sixty-two.[33] The increase in staff has increased the governors' power by giving them greater access to information.

The most important formal power any executive has is the veto. Every state gives its governor the same veto power the president has: the ability to reject a bill in its entirety. (In 1996, North Carolina became the final state to give its governor a veto.) Most states go even further. Forty-three states permit a **line-item veto**, which authorizes the governor to delete some provisions from a bill while allowing the rest to become law. Governors in fourteen states enjoy extraordinary line-item veto power that allows them to veto selected words; in another three states, they can veto in a way that allows them to change words.[34] In Wisconsin, for example, the governor can veto words and even letters and digits in a bill. In the 1987–1989 budget bill, for example, Wisconsin Governor Tommy Thompson altered a provision that mandated courts to hold a juvenile for "not more than forty-eight hours" for certain offenses; by excising certain words and letters, he turned "forty-eight hours" into "ten days." Although legislators challenged this clear example of a change in the intent of legislation, the courts upheld the governor's right to do so.[35] Wisconsin voters reined in the governor's powers in 1990 by passing what was called the "Vanna White" amendment to the state constitution, a measure that prevents the governor from striking letters to make new words. In 2008, Wisconsin voters acted to further limit their governor's veto power, this time taking away the right to create a new sentence from fragments of two or more sentences, a tactic that had been referred to as a "Frankenstein veto."[36]

Eleven states give their governor the power to reduce spending provisions, and fifteen allow an **executive amendment**, a procedure by which the governor rejects a bill but returns it to the legislature with changes that would make it acceptable.[37] This is a powerful weapon. In Illinois, for example, the legislature eventually accepts most of the governor's suggested amendments on vetoed bills.[38]

line-item veto
The ability of an executive to delete or veto some provisions of a bill, while allowing the rest of the bill to become law.

executive amendment
A procedure allowing governors to reject a bill by returning it to the legislature with changes that would make it acceptable; the legislature must agree to the changes for the bill to become law.

In many states, governors use the veto power liberally, and the number of vetoed bills has increased in recent years.[39] In 1995, for example, Governor Gary Johnson of New Mexico set what may be a national record by vetoing 48 percent of the 424 bills sent to his desk. During Johnson's eight years in office, he vetoed 742 bills with only two overridden by the legislature, and he became known around the state as "Governor No."[40] Similarly, in 2007, Governor Martin O'Malley of Maryland rejected 22 percent of the 652 bills sent to him, and the legislature did not override a single veto.[41] Indeed, few legislatures override vetoes.[42] The state legislature with the least success in overriding vetoes may well be New York's; it failed to override a single veto between 1873 and 1976.[43]

Governors can make their vetoes stick for three reasons. First, in thirty-eight states, an override requires a two-thirds majority; in another six states, a three-fifths majority is needed. Most governors can muster the relatively few votes they need to sustain their vetoes. Second, many state legislatures pass most of their bills in the last few days of the legislative session, enabling the governor to veto their work after they have adjourned and cannot respond. Third, some legislators introduce bad bills at the behest of important constituents and push them through the legislature expecting the governor to veto them. In these situations, the legislator can claim credit for passing the bill, while letting the governor take the blame for not allowing it to become law.[44]

Governors also have informal powers that increase their influence, particularly over the actions of the legislature. They receive much more media attention than any other politician in the state.[45] This publicity advantage allows them to set the policy agenda, and if they are skillful, to frame public debate on the issues.[46] For example, South Carolina's governorship is considered among the least powerful in the country. Yet, when Richard Riley occupied the post from 1979 to 1987, he used his domination of the media to push through a series of important educational reforms.[47] Similarly, then-Governor Bill Clinton used the media to rally public support for his controversial education reform package in Arkansas in 1983.[48] Indeed, the ability to work well with the media and to use them to communicate policy decisions to the voters is a key characteristic of successful and popular governors.[49]

Gubernatorial Elections

Governors, like other incumbents in American elections, win much more often than they lose.[50] However, governors are reelected at a lower rate than are senators, representatives, or state legislators, and on average, governors get a lower percentage of the vote than other elected officials do. Voters hold governors responsible for problems in ways they do not hold other politicians accountable. For example, issues closely identified with governors, such as education, health, crime, and the environment, usually are more salient to voters than national issues, such as defense and foreign policy, that often occupy members of Congress. Because governors also get much more news coverage than other elected officials, they are more vulnerable to blame when things do not go well. Thus, it is not surprising that governors have more difficulty getting reelected.[51]

15-2c State Legislatures

Since the 1960s, state legislatures have changed dramatically. Member salaries have increased markedly, sessions have grown longer, and facilities and staff have greatly improved.[52] Because state legislatures have become more professional, their members are serving longer, and they have, by and large, increased both their influence over policy and their independence from the governor. At the same time, the mix of people who serve in state legislatures has changed, as have the rules governing how long state legislators may serve in office.

Organizational Arrangements

The fifty state legislatures vary along every imaginable dimension. They range in size from the twenty-member Alaska state senate to the 400-member New Hampshire House of Representatives. The forty state senators in California each represent roughly 911,000 people—making their districts not only substantially larger than the districts of members of the U.S. House of Representatives but also larger than the constituencies of U.S. senators from six states—while the average state representative in New Hampshire has slightly more than 3,000 constituents. State legislatures also differ in how much they pay their members, how much staff they provide, and in the number of days they meet each year.

Every state except one has a bicameral legislature. Most states call their lower house the *House of Representatives,* although a few call it the *Assembly* or *House of Delegates.* Every state calls its upper house the *Senate.* Most states designate two-year terms of office for state representatives (or members of the assembly or delegates, as the case might be) and four-year terms for state senators. In addition twelve states mandate two-year terms for members of both houses, and five states—most recently, North Dakota, which switched in 1996—give all of their legislators four-year terms.

Nebraska provides the lone exception to the rule of bicameral state legislatures; it has a one-house state legislature known as the *Unicameral.* In addition to being the only one-house legislature in the United States, the Unicameral is also the only legislature in the nation whose members are elected in nonpartisan elections. Nebraska's citizens voted to switch from a partisan bicameral legislature to a nonpartisan unicameral legislature in 1934, during the Great Depression. Voters hoped the switch would reduce the cost of running the legislature and make the legislative process more efficient. It is not clear, however, that the Unicameral functions better than other state legislatures.[53] For example, the Unicameral costs more to run per citizen than the larger two-house state legislature next door in Iowa. Still, proponents of unicameral legislatures have promoted the idea in Iowa, California, Minnesota,

Pennsylvania, South Dakota, and other states. (In 2005, voters in Puerto Rico endorsed a proposed constitutional amendment to create a unicameral legislature, but the courts later scuttled the reform effort).[54]

Professionalization

Most state legislatures have experienced dramatic changes in the past several decades. Until the 1960s, most governors exercised far more political power than their state's legislature did. State legislators were poorly paid, rarely received staff or even offices, and were often limited by law in the number of days they could meet in session; most were populated with farmers, lawyers, or businesspeople serving in the legislature part-time, outside their regular profession. Thus, most legislators did not serve for long, and they never acquired the sorts of expertise about issues and government operations that they needed to be a strong political force. Legislators were only able to respond to the governor's initiatives.

During the 1960s, state legislatures undertook a series of reforms, collectively referred to as *professionalization,* that greatly strengthened their power. The reforms came about in large part because of the efforts of Jesse Unruh, who turned the California Assembly into the model of a professional legislature during his tenure as Speaker of the Assembly, and the Citizens Conference on State Legislatures, a reform group that proposed guidelines for establishing more professional state legislatures. Many legislatures increased member pay to make service more attractive and affordable. They also expanded and improved staff resources and facilities, enabling legislators to counter the governor's traditional advantages in expertise and staff. And many legislatures lifted laws limiting how often the legislature could meet so that legislators could meet year round.

Reformers, then, have consciously sought to make state legislatures more professional—that is, more like the U.S. Congress. How successful have their efforts been? The answer varies from state to state.[55] The state legislatures in California, Michigan, and New York are the most professionalized. These three legislatures pay well, meet in unlimited sessions, and provide ample staff. A few legislatures, such as those in Massachusetts and Ohio, are substantially professionalized. Most others, however, are not, with the legislatures in New Hampshire, New Mexico, North Dakota, South Dakota, and Wyoming being the least professionalized. New Hampshire, for example, pays its state legislators only $100 per year, a salary that has not been changed since it was set in the state constitution in 1889. (In contrast, California legislators are paid $116,208 per year.)

Does this mean that the less professional legislatures are less effective? Not necessarily; the benefits of professionalization are not clear-cut. Legislators in more professionalized legislatures serve longer and come to know more about how government works. They also have more staff. With more information at their fingertips, legislators in professionalized legislatures are better able to generate their own policy initiatives. This in turn makes them less inclined to accept the governor's preferences. The public, however, is not impressed by professionalized legislatures; they give them lower approval ratings than they give less professionalized legislatures.[56]

Overall, partisanship—whether the same party controls both the legislature and governorship—still dominates the relationship between governor and legislature, regardless of professionalization.[57] States in which the same party holds the governorship and controls the state legislature have much smoother executive-legislative relations than states in which political control is divided. The public, however, gives state government higher approval ratings to states with split party control.[58]

Who Serves?

Historically, state legislators were overwhelmingly white males, many of whom were lawyers. Reformers argued in the 1960s that professionalization would redraw the face of each state legislature because it would make it easier for women and minorities to run for election. As the Citizens Conference on State Legislatures claimed: "Other things being equal, the diversity of legislatures will increase as it is economically possible for larger numbers of people to consider running for office."[59]

As reformers hoped, the number of women and minorities serving as state legislators has increased over the past few decades. In 2007, African Americans held 8.2 percent of all state legislative seats, and Hispanic Americans held 3.2 percent.[60] Few Asian Americans and American Indians serve in state legislatures.[61] However, members of minority groups are more often elected in the states where they constitute larger proportions of the population. In California, for example, Hispanic Americans are an increasingly important political bloc. In 1997, Cruz Bustamante became the first Hispanic American selected Speaker of the California Assembly. Among his successors in that post have been other Hispanic Americans, Antonio Villaraigosa and Fabian Nunez. In 2003, Albio Sires was elected Speaker of the New Jersey Assembly, becoming the country's first Cuban American to hold such a post.

The number of women in state legislatures is much higher now than thirty-five years ago: Just 4 percent of state legislators were women in 1969; in 2008, almost 24 percent were women.[62] One reason for the increase is that women are just as likely as men to win state legislative races.[63] Contrary to reformers' hopes, women tend to be found in larger numbers in less professionalized legislatures such as those in New Hampshire and Vermont. In recent years, however, they also have found success in somewhat more professionalized state legislatures in conservative states such as Arizona, Colorado, Kansas, and Nevada.[64] About 70 percent of female state legislators are elected as Democrats, the other 30 percent as Republicans.[65]

The influx of women, minorities, and other underrepresented groups into state legislatures (see Box 15–1) has made the legislatures more diverse and more attuned to issues that affect these groups, particularly where they form a substantial portion of the membership.[66] For example, African American women in state

The People behind the Rules

Box 15–1   The Changing Face of the State Legislature

State legislatures have long been the bastion of white males. That, however, is changing. Many more African Americans and Hispanic Americans serve in the legislature than even a decade ago. And members of other underrepresented groups are winning office. The number of openly gay and lesbian legislators, for example, has increased substantially in recent years. In 2008, seventy-eight openly gay, lesbian, and bisexual people served in thirty state legislatures around the country.

Another example of the increasing diversity of state legislatures is the number of foreign-born legislators. In recent years, state legislators have hailed from a wide array of foreign countries, including Austria, the Azores, the Bahamas, the Cape Verde Islands, Canada, China, Cuba, the Dominican Republic, France, Germany, Greece, Haiti, Hungary, India, Ireland, Italy, Jamaica, South Korea, Laos, Mexico, Norway, Nigeria, Pakistan, Panama, the Philippines, Poland, Portugal, Spain, Thailand, the United Kingdom, Venezuela, and Vietnam. Most came to the United States as children or young adults, became established in their communities, and then committed themselves to public service.

One example is Swati Dandekar of Marion, Iowa. Dandekar and her husband immigrated to the United States from India in the early 1970s, settling in a small town in eastern Iowa. While her husband pursued his business career, Dandekar, who holds two degrees from Indian universities, tended to their two sons and threw herself into community affairs. She served on the

local area Boy Scout council, was a member of the high school boosters club, and joined the Cedar Rapids Junior League. In 1996, she became an American citizen. That same year she was elected to the local school board, where she served for six years.

Swati Dandekar, a state senator in the Iowa Senate.

Source: © Photo courtesy Swati Dandekar Campaign Committee.

In 2002, Dandekar decided to run for the thirty-sixth district seat in the Iowa House of Representatives. As a Democrat, she faced an uphill battle because the district's demographics tilted toward the Republicans. The seat was open, meaning that with no incumbent, Dandekar had a shot at winning. The contest appeared to be tight when, just days before the election, her opponent blundered by making Dandekar's ethnicity a campaign issue. The Republican sent an e-mail to a conservative organization suggesting Dandekar should not represent the district

because, "Without having had the growing-up experience in Iowa, complete with the intrinsic basics of Midwest American life, how is this person adequately prepared to represent Midwest values and core beliefs, let alone understand and appreciate the constitutional rights guaranteed to us in writing by our Founding Fathers? (Not her Founding Fathers)." This was leaked to the local newspaper, creating a furor. Dandekar refused to make an issue out of it, opting instead to "stay above the fray." The state Republican Party, however, immediately disavowed its candidate's comments, and it cut off her funding and all other support. The state party chair commented, "Anyone who wants to represent the people of Iowa or the United States must understand the foundations of this great nation and the ideals on which it was built."

On election day Dandekar won a comfortable victory with 57 percent of the vote, becoming the first Asian Indian American woman to serve in a state legislature. In 2004 and 2006, she was reelected in less contentious races. In 2008, she won a seat in the state senate. Her presence in the legislature, like that of other legislators from underrepresented groups around the country, helps bring different experiences and different perspectives to the lawmaking process.

Sources: Todd Dvorak, "Comment Prompts GOP to Yank Support for Candidate," October 29, 2004; Gay and Lesbian Victory Fund, available at www.glli.org/out_officials; Diana Gordon, "Legislative Melting Pot," *State Legislatures Magazine* (July/August 2002), available at www.ncsl.org/programs/pubs/702pot.htm; and Lynn Okamoto, "Candidate's Comments Cost GOP Support," *Des Moines Register*, October 30, 2002.

legislatures tend to focus their policy agendas on education, health care, and economic development.[67] And unlike their counterparts several decades ago, women elected to state legislatures in recent years are just as politically experienced as men and are just as likely to see themselves as effective legislators.[68] Younger women with children, however, are still much less likely to serve in state legislatures than younger men who are fathers.[69]

The occupational backgrounds of state legislators have also changed. During the first half of the twentieth century, state legislatures were disproportionately populated by lawyers and farmers; each group represented more than 20 percent of the membership.[70] By 1999, the percentage of attorneys serving in state legislatures had dropped to 15 percent. The percentage of farmers holding legislative office has declined to 7 percent, largely because farmers are a decreasing percentage of the nation's population. Farmer-legislators are most common in North Carolina and North Dakota; fourteen state legislative chambers had no farmers as members.

A wide variety of other occupations is now represented in state legislatures. Most prominent among these are educators, business owners, and business employees. The percentage of homemakers, students, and retirees combined stands at around 9 percent. These groups are concentrated in the highly unprofessionalized New Hampshire and Vermont legislatures.[71]

As one might expect, given the successful attempts to professionalize state legislatures, the number of members who work as full-time legislators has grown sharply. Forty years ago, few legislators claimed to work full-time at the state house; now 14 percent do, and this figure probably is low.[72] In Michigan, for example, observers believe that two-thirds of the members are full-time legislators, but few of the members will publicly admit it because they fear that being labeled a professional politician will hurt their chances for reelection.[73] Those who admit to being full-time legislators are concentrated in the most professionalized legislatures, such as New York and Pennsylvania.[74]

Elections, Turnover, and Term Limits

State legislators win reelection at high rates and by wide margins.[75] Legislators in more professionalized bodies seem to enjoy slightly more success than average, but reelection rates are high in almost every state.[76] Nonetheless, turnover rates in some state legislatures are quite high, especially when compared with Congress.[77] In the Kansas state Senate, for example, turnover averaged 43 percent during the 1990s. Overall, during that decade an average of 25 percent of state legislators were in their first term, compared with 17 percent in the U.S. House over that same time period.[78] Turnover is related to professionalization; the more professionalized the legislature, the lower the turnover rate.[79]

In California and a few other states, turnover is high, even though the legislature is quite professionalized. One reason for the high turnover rate in California is that state legislators have relatively more opportunities to run for a seat in the U.S. House of Representatives. Recall that California has more seats in Congress than in its own state senate. As a result, ambitious politicians are willing to give up their seat in the statehouse for a chance to go to Capitol Hill.[80] In 1990, Californians voted to make their state one of the first to limit the number of terms a person may serve in the state legislature.

As Figure 15–2 shows, the push for term limits caught on in other parts of the country. In 1990, voters in Oklahoma and

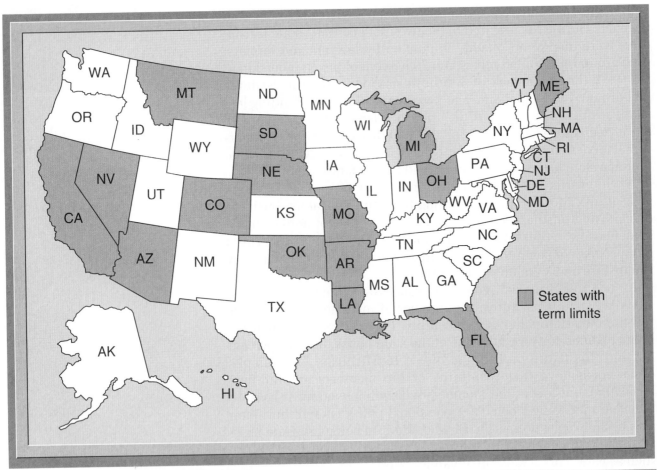

Figure 15-2   Term Limits and State Legislatures, 2005. Term limits for state legislators first surfaced as an important issue in 1990. Currently, they are in place in fifteen states.

Source: *National Conference of State Legislatures.*

Colorado joined with voters in California to impose term limits on their state legislators. Two years later, term-limit measures passed in all twelve states in which they appeared on the ballot, and Maine voters imposed limits on their legislators in 1993. Idaho and Nevada joined the list in 1994, as did Louisiana in 1995. Nebraska voters passed term limits for a fourth time in 2000; the Nebraska Supreme Court tossed out the first three measures that passed on legal technicalities. (Term-limit laws passed by the voters were overturned by the state supreme courts in Massachusetts in 1997, Washington in 1998, Oregon in 2002, and Wyoming in 2004.) In only two states, Utah in 1994 and Louisiana in 1995, did legislators place limits on themselves, but in Utah they were pressured by the threat that voters would use a ballot measure to impose term limits.[81] Term-limit measures vary across the states; the most stringent restrict a person from serving more than six years in office. Although critics have complained that term limits violate state constitutions, the limits have usually withstood challenge in the courts.[82]

The term-limit movement is pushed by several national organizations, with one organization, U.S. Term Limits, supplying much of the money. For example, in 2006, U.S. Term Limits gave $110,000 out of the $151,497 raised by supporters of an attempt to reinstitute term limits in Oregon, a pattern similar to that found in other states in previous years.[83] Some evidence indicates that voters responded to term-limit campaigns in part because of their dissatisfaction with the way government works.[84] The debate also had a partisan edge; some sophisticated voters see term limits as a device to dislodge the majority party in their state from office. This usually, but not always, meant Republicans were more likely to favor limits, whereas Democrats were less likely to support them, behavioral differences that have carried over to current debates on weakening term limits.[85] Similarly, it is not surprising, given their longtime status as the minority party in many states, that Republican legislators are far more likely than Democrats to support term limits.[86]

In recent years, the tide appears to have turned against the term-limit movement. Other than Nebraska, no state has adopted them since 1995. And in 2002, the heavily Republican state legislature in Idaho repealed the term limits voters had imposed eight years earlier (an option afforded to legislatures in a few states).[87] In the general elections that fall, Idaho voters upheld the legislators' decision to remove term limits, albeit by only the thinnest of margins. Utah's Republican-controlled legislature repealed term limits in 2003. Oregon voters declined to reimpose term limits in 2006. Term limits, however, still appear to have some appeal for voters. Ballot measures to soften or abolish term limits were defeated in California in 2002 and 2008, Arkansas and Montana in 2004, Maine in 2007, and South Dakota in 2008.

As we discussed in Chapter 1, term-limit proponents argue that dislodging incumbents will make legislatures more responsive to the average voter. However, term limits rob a legislature of continuity and expertise, although some evidence indicates that members of legislatures with term limits double their efforts to master legislative rules and public issues.[88] Depending on the length of service allowed, term limits may have scant effect on many of the less professionalized state legislatures where few legislators serve longer than the limits in any event.[89] The full effects of term limits will not be apparent until the new rules have pushed experienced legislators out the door, an effect felt first in California (see Box 15–2) and Maine in 1996, but not until 2008 in Nevada.

15-2d Interest Groups in State Politics

At the beginning of the twentieth century, politics in many states was dominated by a few large interest groups. In California, for example, the Southern Pacific Railroad wielded enormous political power, and Anaconda Copper exercised near total control of politics in Montana. Although the ability of a few private interests to dominate state government largely disappeared by the 1950s, interest group activity at the state level continued to be restricted to a handful of groups, usually those with a substantial interest in the state's economy. Most national interest groups, and especially

POINT OF ORDER

Box 15–2 Changing the Rules: The Effects of Legislative Term Limits on the California Assembly

In the early 1990s, term limits swept the nation. By 1996, eighteen states had imposed term limits on their state legislators—twenty-one if limits in Massachusetts, Nebraska, and Washington tossed out by their state supreme courts are counted. All these laws were passed before anyone had had any experience with the consequences of living under a term-limit law—the first-term legislators that the laws affected were in California and Maine, and they were only prevented from running again starting in 1996. Thus, an examination of the California Assembly, the lower of the two houses in the California state legislature, and a chamber whose members are now limited to six years in office, gives us a glimpse into the consequences of changing the rules and imposing term limits.

The California Assembly has traditionally been considered the model of a professional legislative body. Its members are well paid, work at the job full-time and have impressive staff resources. Yet in 1990, California voters approved a term-limit law and voted to cut the budget for running the Assembly and state senate by 40 percent. The message the voters seemed to be sending was, "We think that doing away with professional politicians and big government will result in better public policy."

What has happened in the California Assembly since the voters approved term limits and cut its budget? One result is hardly surprising: Members of the Assembly, who by and large are professional politicians, have looked for opportunities to move on to other, usually higher, offices. That is nothing new; members of the Assembly have always used it as a springboard. With term limits in place, however, the search for opportunities to leave has been hastened, and this has taken a toll on the operations of the Assembly. For example, in 1995, the Republican leader in the Assembly resigned from his post, in large part because he was being forced out of office by term limits and he wanted to concentrate on campaigning for a seat in the state senate. Indeed, by their final term, many members appear to be thinking less about their constituents and the pursuit of good public policy and more about currying favor with people and interests who can assist them in attaining higher office or help them find work when their days in the Assembly come to an end.

What about the people who have replaced members of the Assembly who left because of term limits? Contrary to the hopes of supporters, term limits do not appear to change the nature of the people elected to the Assembly or how they behave once in office. Analyses show that new members behave much like their more senior colleagues and former members. They, too, are professional politicians. Indeed, more of them now come from local government than in the past, and when they leave the Assembly, they run for other offices; and they raise their campaign money in the same ways and from the same people and interests as their predecessors—only in even greater amounts. Moreover, they are just as partisan in their voting behavior.

Newer members of the Assembly differ from the members they have replaced in one key respect—they have less knowledge about how to operate the institution. For instance, following the 1994 elections, the Assembly found itself embroiled in a bitter power struggle over who should be the next speaker. As the more senior members who understood the parliamentary rules shaped the terms of the debate, most first- and second-term members found themselves pushed to the sidelines. Since the limits kicked into effect in the 1996 election, the Assembly has had a few veterans— former members who returned or an occasional former state senator—to rely on for experience. Otherwise, the body's wise sages are in their third and final term. Many members and knowledgeable observers have noted that the Assembly is a less efficient lawmaking body than it used to be. In addition, committees and the expertise they represent are less important today than in the past.

Perhaps the most obvious change in the Assembly has been its instability at the top. The Assembly had the same speaker from 1981 to 1995. In the next thirteen years, nine different people held the post. Senior members of the Assembly now work to groom new leaders to take the places of those

Source: © AP/Wide World Photos

The California Assembly.

POINT OF ORDER *(continued)*

pushed out. Since the introduction of term limits, many first- and second-term members have been given important committee and leadership posts, a change from past practice when seniority played a bigger role in allocating top positions. Members of the Assembly have come to realize, though, that term limits place them in a bind when making decisions about leadership positions. If they select a third-term member for a top post, he or she will be forced out at the end of the session. If they choose a first- or second-term member, they risk getting a leader with little experience.

Finally, imposing term limits has encouraged a decline in civility within the Assembly. Members realize that because of term limits, they will not work with each other for long. This creates a scenario much like the nineteenth-century House of Representatives, where, as we saw in Chapter 11, rapid turnover meant that proper decorum and civil behavior were the exception rather than the rule. During the first sessions following the implementation of term limits, for example, members made obscene gestures and said rude and uncivil things to each other on the Assembly floor. Such childish behavior breeds

hard feelings and makes it difficult for people to work together. With term limits, members have little incentive to adopt rules and norms that promote decorum. (Term limits can, under certain circumstances, work to improve the political tone of a legislature. By 2001, for example, every member who had served in the Assembly during a bloody and divisive leadership battle in 1995 had been term-limited out.)

Overall, changing the rules by imposing term limits has changed the California Assembly. The lack of legislative seasoning has left the Assembly weak relative to the state senate (where members are limited to eight years and where many Assembly members move after they are term-limited out of the Assembly), and more importantly, to the governor. Observers who had expected experienced staff to compensate for inexperienced legislators were surprised to learn that turnover among staffers mirrored that of their employers, leaving few people around to provide institutional memory. Most reforms have unintended consequences and leave unfulfilled promises. Imposing term limits in the California Assembly is no exception.

Sources: Dan Bernstein, "Assembly Still Dealing with Freshman Jitters," *Sacramento Bee,* March 17, 1997; Kathleen A. Bratton and Kerry L. Haynie, "The Unintended Consequences of Term Limit Reform: The Influence of Gender and Race in State Legislative Leadership Selection," presented at the 2000 annual meeting of the Washington, D.C. American Political Science Association; Bruce E. Cain and Thad Kousser, *Adapting to Term Limits: Recent Experiences and New Directions* (San Francisco: Public Policy Institute of California, 2004); Stanley M. Caress, "Legislative Term Limits: Evidence from the States," presented at the 2000 annual meeting of the Washington, D.C. American Political Science Association; Ken DeBow, "Decline of the California Legislature: Why New Faces Won't Help," presented at the 1996 annual meeting of the San Francisco Western Political Science Association; Mark Gladstone, "State's Lower House Sinks a Bit Lower," *Los Angeles Times,* July 6, 1997; Patrick Hoge, "Term Limits Touch Off Battles within Parties: Facing Job's End, Some Targeting Colleagues' Posts," *Sacramento Bee,* January 25, 2000; Charles R. Kesler, "Reaping What Voters Sowed," *Los Angeles Times,* September 15, 1995; Raymond J. La Raja and Dorie Apollonio, "Term Limits and Campaign Contributions: Do Lame Ducks Suffer?" presented at the 1999 annual meeting of the Chicago Midwest Political Science Association; George Skelton, "Institutional Amnesia Does Have Its Good Points," *Los Angeles Times,* December 7, 2000; Peverill Squire, "The Theory of Legislative Institutionalization and the California Assembly," *Journal of Politics* 54 (November 1992): 1026–54; Bill Stall, "Brulte Resigns as GOP Leader in Assembly," *Los Angeles Times,* August 19, 1995; Mary Lynne Vellinga, "Assembly Member's Debate Turns Personal," *Sacramento Bee,* January 24, 1997; Dan Walters, "Villaraigosa's Rookie Errors," *Sacramento Bee,* April 20, 1998; and Jenifer Warren, "Term Limits Put Legislators on Fund-Raising Fast Track," *Los Angeles Times,* April 27, 1999.

business interest groups, focused their attention on lobbying Congress and the executive branch because they made most of the important policy decisions.

The preoccupation interest groups had with Washington, D.C., changed in the 1980s. As the Reagan administration sought to curtail federal assistance and to shift decision-making authority back to cities and states, interest groups began to pay more attention to what was happening in Albany, Austin, Jefferson City, Sacramento, Springfield, Tallahassee, and other state capitals.[90] Lobbying of state governments exploded. A 2006 survey counted more than 56,000 registered state lobbyists, who spent $1.3 billion lobbying in the forty-three states that track such spending.[91] That worked out to eleven lobbyists and $205,000 per state legislator. Indeed, because many interest groups now use the same techniques to lobby both federal and state governments, some observers argue that we are witnessing the "nationalization" of state politics. The American Association of Retired Persons (AARP), for example, had long focused on Washington, D.C., but because of the increasing importance of decisions being made at the state level, it had lobbying offices in seventeen states by 2000 and offices in all fifty states by the end of 2001.[92]

Interest group activity differs across the fifty states. Interest groups are more powerful in some states than in others, and which groups are active varies from state to state.[93] It is no surprise, for example, that the United Auto Workers is more active in Michigan than in Hawaii, or that the Farm Bureau has a stronger presence in Iowa than in New Jersey. We can make two important generalizations about interest groups and state politics; both relate to economics. First, the more diverse the state economy, the more diverse the types of interest groups active in the state. Second, the larger a state economy, the more interest groups in the state.[94]

Across the states, business groups tend to exercise more power than other groups.[95] The other most influential interest group in most state politics is the public school teachers lobby, which in most states means the local chapters of the National Education Association.[96] In Alabama, for example, teachers became politically active in the 1970s, and by 1987, 41 percent of state legislators were teachers, former teachers, or people married to teachers.[97] In addition, the Alabama Education Association has been able to register more lobbyists than any other interest in the state, and during the 2001–2002 election cycle, its political action committee (PAC) was the third largest contributor among all PACs in the state.[98]

Teachers have enjoyed substantial political success because they enjoy several organizing advantages.[99] First, teachers live in every town (and legislative district); thus, they can exert constituent pressure on all legislators. Second, as is true of most well-educated people, teachers are more disposed than the average American toward joining political groups. Third, state legislatures greatly influence education funding and directives. This means that teachers who work for public schools have a strong incentive to lobby state government. Indeed, in the first half of 2008, the California Teacher's Association spent $2.7 million on lobbying, making it the second biggest lobbying organization in the state.[100]

As a general rule, the states have taken a more aggressive role than the federal government in regulating interest group lobbying. All fifty states require lobbyists to register and to disclose who employs them. Most states also require lobbyists to file reports listing their business expenditures.[101] The strongest regulations tend to be enacted in states with more professionalized legislatures and in states with a lower tolerance for political corruption.[102]

States have also actively regulated campaign finance. All fifty states impose regulations of some sort on political action committees. Again, the regulations vary. Some states provide public funds for candidates in some or all state elections. Some states bar corporations, labor unions, and public utilities from contributing to campaigns, whereas others impose no contribution limits.[103] Each state has its own web of regulations governing the interaction of interest groups and public officials. Regardless of the details of those regulations, interest groups are paying increased attention to state governments.

15-2e The Public and Direct Democracy

Under the U.S. Constitution, Americans can pass formal judgment on the work of the federal government only by voting in congressional and presidential elections. In contrast, state constitutions provide an array of mechanisms that enable voters to record their views on the work of the state government. In many states, the rules allow voters to revise the state's constitution, overturn bills the state legislature passes, enact their own bills, and even vote to remove elected officials from office. Each of these mechanisms is a form of **direct democracy**.

Referenda and Initiatives

Two ways voters can directly control state policy are through referenda and initiatives. A **referendum** is a rules change, proposed by a legislature and put to a direct public vote, whereas an **initiative** is a voter-proposed change. Every state except Delaware requires that amendments to the state constitution be put to a vote in a statewide election known as a *constitutional referendum*.[104] Sixteen states also provide for a *constitutional initiative* in which citizens can put a proposed constitutional amendment on the ballot, usually after they have collected a set number of signatures on a petition. (The Massachusetts state constitution also provides for an indirect initiative, whereby the legislature may pass an acceptable version of the proposed amendment before it is put to the voters.) In every state except one, only a majority of voters must support a constitutional amendment for it to pass. The exception is New Hampshire, where a two-thirds majority is needed.

In twenty-four states, voters can demand a *citizen* or *popular referendum* in which a measure the state legislature has passed is placed on the ballot and made subject to voter approval. Like the rules on constitutional initiatives, the rules governing a popular referendum usually require sponsors of the measure to collect a set number of signatures on a petition. Twenty-two states also allow the legislature itself to put measures it has passed before the voters for approval in a *legislative referendum*. Both popular and legislative referenda give voters the opportunity to override the decisions of their elected representatives. In 2006, for example, South Dakota voters rejected a law banning abortions that had been passed by the state legislature.

In some states, citizens need not wait for the legislature to act. Voters in seventeen states may use a *direct initiative* to sidestep the state legislature and place a proposed piece of legislation directly before the voters. Direct initiatives enable citizens to tackle issues that state legislators may wish to avoid or are unable to settle. A recent example is term limits. With the exception of Louisiana and Utah, every state that has or did have a law limiting the number of terms legislators may serve enacted that law as the result of a direct initiative.

direct democracy
Mechanisms such as the initiative, referendum, and recall—powers that enable voters to use the ballot box to set government policy.

referendum
An election held allowing voters to accept or reject a proposed law or amendment passed by a legislative body.

initiative
A proposed law or amendment placed on the ballot by citizens, usually through a petition.

In recent years, the use of referenda and initiatives has increased. In 2008, 153 statewide measures appeared on ballots across the country. Voters in California passed a proposal to set minimum living space requirements for pregnant pigs, calves, and egg laying-hens. Massachusetts voters defeated a measure to abolish the state income tax, and voters in Missouri backed an initiative to require investor-owned utilities to generate more of their electricity from renewable sources. Yet the increased use of referenda and initiatives reflects more than greater political interest or unhappiness among the general public. National political activists have seized on direct democracy as a way to translate their policy preferences into law in individual states. (Recall how much out-of-state money flowed into term-limit campaigns.) As a result, a national group that can afford to round up the signatures needed to hold an initiative in a particular state can set the policy agenda in that state. Indeed, in 2006 more than $369 million was spent in California on influencing voter decisions on initiative campaigns, which was far more than the $128 million spent on the 100 state legislative races that year.[105]

For voters, referenda and initiatives pose a problem. Because interest groups rather than political parties usually push these measures, voters cannot use party affiliation to decide how to vote. Of course, voters can do their own research on an issue, but that takes time, and many referenda and initiatives involve issues of great interest to activists and far less interest to everyone else. Moreover, as Figure 15–3 illustrates, some referenda and initiatives are exceptionally detailed and complex, making it impossible for all but the most dedicated and well-informed voters to decipher them.

Because referenda and initiatives typically involve matters of little interest to the general public and because they can be so complex, most voters rely on advertising to gain information about what a referendum or initiative means. In short, they may use advertisements as a shortcut to becoming informed.[106] The information gleaned from political advertisements may be biased, however, especially if only one side can afford to make its case heard. Because reliable information can be scarce, surveys find that voters are much more likely to change their minds about a referendum or an initiative during the course of a campaign than they are to change their minds about a candidate.[107] Although referenda and initiatives may in theory be direct democracy in action, they are a vehicle that well-financed interest groups can use to maneuver the public into voting for the groups' policy preferences.

Although a well-financed interest group can help improve the chances that a ballot measure will pass, money by no means guarantees victory. Consider, for example, the fate of two measures that appeared on Arizona's ballot in 2006. Supporters of Proposition 201, which proposed to ban smoking in most public places, spent $1.8 million in a winning effort. Backers of Proposition 206, which also would have banned smoking in most public places aside from exempted bars and well ventilated areas of restaurants, spent $8.8 million (almost all of which was contributed by the R. J. Reynolds Tobacco Company) in a losing effort.[108]

Proposition 71: Text of Proposed Law

This initiative measure is submitted to the people in accordance with the provisions of Section 8 of Article 11 of the California Constitution.

This initiative measure expressly amends the California Constitution by adding an article thereto; and amends a section of the Government Code, and adds sections to the Health and Safety Code; therefore, new provisions proposed to be added are printed in italic type to indicate that they are new.

PROPOSED LAW

CALIFORNIA STEM CELL RESEARCH AND CURES INITIATIVE

SECTION 1. Title

This measure shall be known as the "California Stem Cell Research and Cures Act."

SEC. 2. Findings and Declarations

The people of California find and declare the following:

Millions of children and adults suffer from devastating diseases or injuries that are currently incurable, including cancer, diabetes, heart disease, Alzheimer's, Parkinson's, spinal cord injuries, blindness, Lou Gehrig's disease, HIV/AIDS, mental health disorders, multiple sclerosis, Huntington's disease, and more than 70 other diseases and injuries.

Recently medical science has discovered a new way to attack chronic diseases and injuries. The cure and treatment of these diseases can potentially be accomplished through the use of new regenerative medical therapies including a special type of human cells, called stem cells. These life-saving medical breakthroughs can only happen if adequate funding is made available to advance stem cell research, develop therapies, and conduct clinical trials.

About half of California's families have a child or adult who has suffered or will suffer from a serious, often critical or terminal, medical condition that could potentially be treated or cured with stem cell therapies. In these cases of chronic illness or when patients face a medical crisis, the health care system may simply not be able to meet the needs of patients or control spiraling costs, unless therapy focus switches away from maintenance and toward prevention and cures.

Unfortunately, the federal government is not providing adequate funding necessary for the urgent research and facilities needed to develop stem cell therapies to treat and cure diseases and serious injuries. This critical funding gap currently prevents the rapid advancement of research that could benefit millions of Californians.

The California Stem Cell Research and Cures Act will close this funding gap by establishing an institute which will issue bonds to support stem cell research, emphasizing pluripotent stem cell and progenitor cell research and other vital medical technologies, for the development of life-saving regenerative medical treatments and cures.

SEC. 3. Purpose and Intent

It is the intent of the people of California in enacting this measure to:

Authorize an average of $295 million per year in bonds over a 10-year period to fund stem cell research and dedicated facilities for scientists at California's universities and other advanced medical research facilities throughout the state.

Maximize the use of research funds by giving priority to stem cell research that has the greatest potential for therapies and cures, specifically focused on pluripotent stem cell and progenitor cell research among other vital research opportunities that cannot, or are unlikely to, receive timely or sufficient federal funding, unencumbered by limitations that would impede the research. Research shall be subject to accepted patient disclosure and patient consent standards.

Assure that the research is conducted safely and ethically by including provisions to require compliance with standards based on national models that protect patient safety, patient rights, and patient privacy.

Prohibit the use of bond proceeds of this initiative for funding for human reproductive cloning.

Improve the California health care system and reduce the long-term health care cost burden on California through the development of therapies that treat diseases and injuries with the ultimate goal to cure them.

Require strict fiscal and public accountability through mandatory independent audits, open meetings, public hearings, and annual reports to the public. Create an Independent Citizen's Oversight Committee composed of representatives of the University of California campuses with medical schools; other California universities and California medical research institutions; California disease advocacy groups; and California experts in the development of medical therapies.

Protect and benefit the California budget: by postponing general fund payments on the bonds for the first five years; by funding scientific and medical research that will significantly reduce state health care costs in the future; and by providing an opportunity for the state to benefit from royalties, patents, and licensing fees that result from the research.

Benefit the California economy by creating projects, jobs, and therapies that will generate millions of dollars in new tax revenues in our state.

Advance the biotech industry in California to world leadership, as an economic engine for California's future.

SEC. 4. Article XXXV is added to the California Constitution, to read:

Article XXXV. Medical Research

SECTION 1. There is hereby established the California Institute for Regenerative Medicine.

SEC. 2. The institute shall have the following purposes:

(a) To make grants and loans for stem cell research, for research facilities, and for other vital research opportunities to realize therapies, protocols, and/or medical procedures that will result in, as speedily as possible, the cure for, and/or substantial mitigation of, major diseases, injuries, and orphan diseases.

(b) To support all stages of the process of developing cures, from laboratory research through successful clinical trials.

(c) To establish the appropriate regulatory standards and oversight bodies for research and facilities development.

SEC. 3. No funds authorized for, or made available to, the institute shall be used for research involving human reproductive cloning.

SEC. 4. Funds authorized for, or made available to, the institute shall be continuously appropriated without regard to fiscal year, be available and used only for the purposes provided in this article, and shall not be subject to appropriation or transfer by the Legislature or the Governor for any other purpose.

SEC. 5. There is hereby established a right to conduct stem cell research which includes research involving adult stem cells, cord blood stem cells, pluripotent stem cells, and/or progenitor cells. Pluripotent stem cells are cells that are capable of self-renewal, and have broad potential to differentiate into multiple adult cell types. Pluripotent stem cells may be derived from somatic cell nuclear transfer or from surplus products of in vitro fertilization treatments when such products are donated under appropriate informed consent procedures. Progenitor cells are multipotent or precursor cells that are partially differentiated, but retain the ability to divide and give rise to differentiated cells.

SEC. 6. Notwithstanding any other provision of this Constitution or any law, the institute, which is established in state government, may utilize state issued tax-exempt and taxable bonds to fund its operations, medical and scientific research, including therapy development through clinical trials, and facilities.

SEC. 7. Notwithstanding any other provision of this Constitution, including Article VII, or any law, the institute and its employees are exempt from civil service.

SEC. 5. Chapter 3 (commencing with Section 125290.10) is added to Part 5 of

Figure 15–3 Example of a Ballot Initiative. Ballot initiatives can be quite complex, as suggested by this first of nine pages of text for the California Stem Cell Research and Cures Initiative put to the state's voters in 2004. The initiative was passed.

Source: *From Official Voter Information Guide, California General Election.*

Recall

Citizens in eighteen states have the right to vote to recall all or most state elected officials. Residents of Montana can go even further and recall appointed officials. Recall votes for state officials are not common. In October 2003, however, the process gained considerable attention when California voters, unhappy with the performance of Governor Gray Davis, whom they had reelected to office by a large margin just the year before, removed him in a special recall election. The same ballot that gave the voters the option to recall the governor also presented them a list of 135 candidates seeking to replace him. Most of the candidates were frivolous—among them were porn actress Mary Carey and former child actor Gary Coleman—but three—state Senator Tom McClintock, Lieutenant Governor Cruz Bustamante, and Arnold Schwarzenegger—ran serious, well-funded campaigns. Ultimately, the voters selected Schwarzenegger by a comfortable margin, catapulting him from Hollywood to Sacramento. Davis became the first governor to be recalled since North Dakota voters removed Governor Lynn Frasier from office in 1921.[109]

Recall elections are much more common at the local government level. At least thirty-six states allow recall of local government officials. California, which makes it relatively easy to initiate a recall election, has seen more of them than any other state. Attempts to remove local officials in recent years also took place in Alaska, Arizona, Colorado, Massachusetts, Michigan, Nevada, Oregon, Ohio, and Wisconsin. Recall efforts are typically motivated by unpopular personnel decisions, budget problems, or a loss of confidence in local officials. In 2003, for example, vote unhappiness with a decision by the Covina, California, city council to impose a 6 percent utility tax without voter approval prompted a recall effort that removed all five city councilors. (Ultimately, however, the recall effort was unable to change the fiscal realities faced by the city. The successor council, which included vocal opponents of the original utility tax increase, had to pass an even higher tax to prevent the layoff of numerous city employees and the closing of a library and a fire station.)[110]

15-2f Summing Up

State government institutions, interest groups, and the public are the forces that drive state politics. Although state governments are similar to the federal government in many ways, they are very different in others. Governors exercise more power in their states than presidents do over the federal system; state legislatures exercise less power than the Congress. The public can vote directly on some state and local policies, but not on national issues. And interest groups are more regulated—and often more influential—at the state level.

As state and local governments have gained influence, however, the public has looked to them for an increasing number of programs and services. The increased demand has placed new pressures on state government. Like their federal counterparts, state political leaders are focusing on their budgets as they grapple with determining the programs and services they can afford to provide.

15-3 STATE BUDGETS

States raise and spend money in many ways. Some rely heavily on income taxes, whereas others do not. A few can rely on taxes on drilling and mining, but most cannot. Some states have high taxes and provide many public services; others tax less and do less. In the next sections, we examine how states raise and spend money and how the differences among states affect their policy choices.

15-3a Raising Revenues

States impose three basic types of taxes: taxes on property, sales, and income. During the first decades of the twentieth century, property taxes were the major source of state tax revenue. In response to fiscal pressures the Great Depression generated, states imposed sales taxes and transferred the right to tax property to local governments. In the 1940s, states added taxes on individual and corporate incomes. Although the relative mix of sales and income taxes has changed over the past several decades, states have not added any major new types of taxes in recent decades. In recent years, however, they have turned increasingly to less traditional sources of revenue, including state lotteries and other forms of gambling.

Figure 15–4 shows the average breakdown for state tax collections in 2005–2006. As you can see, states rely heavily on two sources of revenue: a general sales tax and individual income taxes. Taxes on motor fuels, corporations, and alcohol and tobacco products generate smaller sums. Property taxes, the staple at the beginning of the twentieth century, now contribute little to state coffers—only 2 percent.[111]

Figure 15–4 presents the national average. Many states differ markedly from the average in terms of their sources of revenue. Alaska, for example, relies heavily on taxes on the drilling and mining of its oil and mineral riches, so much so that Alaskans pay neither a personal income tax nor a general sales tax. The result, as Table 15–2 shows, is that Alaskans bear the lowest overall state and local tax burden in the United States; that is, the average Alaskan pays less in state and local taxes than other Americans. Indeed, most of the states that do not tax personal income are among the lowest tax states in the country.

States also vary in their reliance on a general sales tax. In addition to Alaska, four other states—Delaware, Montana, New Hampshire, and Oregon—have no general sales tax. The sales tax rate varies from state to state (and even within states because many give their county and local governments the right to impose their own sales taxes). Almost all sales tax states exempt prescription drugs, and more than half also exempt food. Excluding food, prescription drugs, and other necessities of life makes the sales tax less regressive than it would otherwise be.[112] States without a sales tax must compensate for the lost revenue by relying more on other

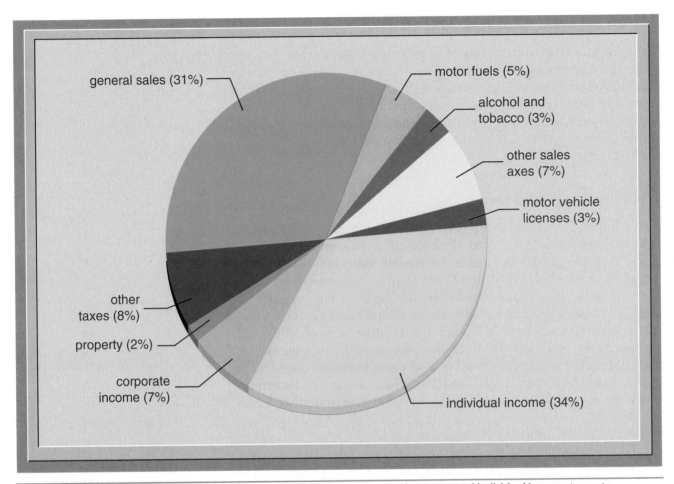

general sales (31%)

motor fuels (5%)

alcohol and tobacco (3%)

other sales axes (7%)

motor vehicle licenses (3%)

other taxes (8%)

property (2%)

corporate income (7%)

individual income (34%)

Figure 15-4   State Tax Sources, 2005–2006. States rely heavily on sales taxes and individual income taxes to generate most of their revenue.

Source: *Data from U.S. Bureau of the Census, "State Government Tax Collections: 2006." www.census.gov/govs/statetax/0600usstax.html.*

types of taxes. Oregon, for example, relies more on income taxes than any other state.[113]

Like sales tax rates, income tax rates vary from state to state. (Seven states—Alaska, Florida, Nevada, South Dakota, Texas, Washington, and Wyoming—have no individual income tax, and two others—New Hampshire and Tennessee—tax only interest income and dividends.) It is difficult to compare income tax rates across states because each state has different rules regarding the kinds of income and expenses that are exempt from taxes. For example, some states allow taxpayers to deduct the taxes they pay to the federal government from the income subject to state tax; others do not. Such deductions effectively lower the real tax rate. Attempts to compare tax rates are also difficult because most states have a progressive income tax in which the tax rate increases with income. Only six states have a flat tax rate in which everyone's income is taxed at the same rate.

Although it is difficult to compare income tax rates across states, general trends in income tax rates are clear. Spurred by a nationwide tax revolt that began in the late 1970s and was epitomized by

Rank	State	State and local taxes as a percentage of income (%)	Rank	State	State and local taxes as a percentage of income (%)
1	New Jersey	11.8	26	Oregon	9.4
2	New York	11.7	27	Michigan	9.4
3	Connecticut	11.1	28	Indiana	9.4
4	Maryland	10.8	29	West Virginia	9.3
5	Hawaii	10.6	30	Illinois	9.3
6	California	10.5	31	Iowa	9.3
7	Ohio	10.4	32	Missouri	9.2
8	Vermont	10.3	33	North Dakota	9.2
9	Wisconsin	10.2	34	Colorado	9.0
10	Rhode Island	10.2	35	Washington	8.9
11	Pennsylvania	10.2	36	Mississippi	8.9
12	Minnesota	10.2	37	South Carolina	8.8
13	Idaho	10.1	38	Alabama	8.6
14	Arkansas	10.0	39	New Mexico	8.6
15	Maine	10.0	40	Montana	8.6
16	Georgia	9.9	41	Arizona	8.5
17	Nebraska	9.8	42	Louisiana	8.4
18	Virginia	9.8	43	Texas	8.4
19	Oklahoma	9.8	44	Tennessee	8.3
20	North Carolina	9.8	45	South Dakota	7.9
21	Kansas	9.6	46	New Hampshire	7.6
22	Utah	9.6	47	Florida	7.4
23	Massachusetts	9.5	48	Wyoming	7.0
24	Delaware	9.5	49	Nevada	6.6
25	Kentucky	9.4	50	Alaska	6.4

Table 15–2   Average State and Local Tax Burdens by State, 2008
The overall state tax burden varies greatly from state to state.
Source: *Gerald Prante*, Tax Foundation, Special Report, *No. 163, August 2008.*

Ronald Reagan's election as president, many states tried to reduce their tax rates in the 1980s. As states saw their expenditures begin to outstrip their revenues in the early 1990s, the trend reversed; more states began to contemplate increasing their tax rates, especially the rates the wealthy pay.[114] Indeed, budget shortfalls have caused several states without an income tax to consider imposing one. Connecticut, for example, imposed a state income tax for the first time in 1991 after a bitter political battle.[115]

During the 1980s, the budgetary problems facing many states prompted them to look elsewhere for money. One revenue source that grew in importance was so-called sin taxes—taxes on alcohol and tobacco. (Some people support sin taxes less for their revenue-generating potential than because they may force people to drink and smoke less, thereby reducing health-care costs.) Again, the tax rates applied to alcohol and tobacco vary by state. The range on tobacco products is amazing: Up until 2005, tobacco-producing states such as Kentucky and North Carolina levied a tax of only a few cents per pack of cigarettes (three and five cents, respectively). That year both states raised their taxes to $0.30 per pack. In 2008, South Carolina had the lowest tax, at $0.07 per pack, whereas the tax in Alaska, Arizona, Connecticut, Hawaii, Maine, Maryland, Massachusetts, Michigan, New Jersey, New York, Rhode Island, and Washington was $2.00 or higher. (In New York City, which is allowed to assess a local tax on cigarettes, the combined city and state tax on a pack is $4.25.)[116] One constraint states face in setting tax rates on alcohol and tobacco (and other taxes as well) is the rates in nearby states. If taxes soar too high, people living near the state border may buy their cigarettes and alcohol in a neighboring state, denying their home state the revenue it hoped to generate.[117]

Because the public usually frowns on higher taxes, governors and legislators increasingly have looked to develop revenue sources that do not require taxes. One popular source of nontax revenue is a state lottery. New Hampshire instituted the first modern state lottery in 1964. By 2008, forty-two states, including all the major industrial states, and the District of Columbia had lotteries. Ticket sales in the United States totaled $52.6 billion in 2006, generating $17.1 billion in revenue for the states.[118] In some states, lottery revenues are dedicated to specific expenditures. For example, lottery revenues in California go to education; and in Kansas, 90 percent of the revenues go to economic development, the other 10 percent to prisons. In some states where lottery revenues have been earmarked for a special purpose, concerns have been raised that the money is used *in place of* regular tax funds in the budget, rather than adding to it, as voters thought would be the case.

Another source of state revenue that has gained in popularity is gambling, which generates money for the state from licenses and taxes on the profits. For many years, gambling was illegal in every state except Nevada (which legalized it in 1931), largely because powerful religious interests argued that it undermined public morality. In 1976, New Jersey legalized gambling in Atlantic City as part of an effort to revitalize the downtrodden seaside resort community. In 1989, Iowa responded to its budgetary woes by permitting gambling on riverboats plying the rivers along the state's borders. Riverboat gambling quickly became the rage as several other states along the Mississippi followed Iowa's lead. By 2007, twelve states had legalized commercial casino gambling, generating $5.8 billion in tax revenue; another $2.2 billion in tax revenue was produced by racetrack casinos in the eleven states that allow them. And twenty-eight states had agreements allowing American Indians to operate casinos on tribal lands. Gambling continues to expand. Only Hawaii and Utah do not allow any form of wagering.[119]

One possible explanation for why states have turned to legalized gambling is that state budget conditions forced governors and legislators to scramble to find politically palatable ways to generate more revenue. As the budget picture deteriorated for most states in 2007 and 2008, twenty-four states cut income taxes, but four states had to raise them. Similarly, whereas twenty-two states cut their sales tax, two states increased them. Corporate income taxes were raised in nine states and lowered in eight. Overall, state governments find themselves in financial difficulties even in relatively good economic times for several reasons. Many states have structural spending problems; even with higher revenue, they have laws on the books that automatically increase spending at a faster rate, particularly for education and Medicaid. And many states face looming budget crises because they have failed to fully fund state worker pension plans.[120]

Because of their dire financial circumstances, most states continue to explore new ways to increase their revenues. Most notably, a coalition of states belonging to the Streamlined Sales Tax Project is pushing Congress for the authority to impose sales taxes on Internet commerce; estimates on the amount of revenue states lose annually from uncollected taxes on Internet sales range upward of $18 billion. In late 2005, eighteen states belonging to the project initiated a voluntary program to help capture lost sales tax revenues on catalogue and online purchases.[121]

15-3b Budgeting

Most states make their budgetary decisions much as the federal government does. The main similarity is that the governor, like the president, has the right to make the initial budget proposal. (In eight states, the governor must share this power with others.)[122] Making the initial budget proposal is an important power because it enables the governor to set the parameters of the debate, in many cases reducing the legislature's role to making changes only at the margins.

State budgetary processes differ from the federal budget process, however, in two important respects. First, as we mentioned previously, most governors have a line-item veto that allows them to cut spending they dislike. Evidence exists, however, that governors are just as likely to use the line-item veto to shape spending to their partisan preferences as they are to use it to lower the overall budget.[123] In addition, state legislatures can structure line-item budgets in ways that make it difficult for governors to veto spending they oppose.[124] Thus, the power of the line-item veto as a tool to control spending may be overstated. Second, every state but one has a constitutional or statutory requirement that the state government balance its budget. Vermont is the one exception, but by tradition, it balances its budget.[125]

The balanced budget requirements so common in state government should not be taken literally. They do not prevent states from running a deficit, and they do not always bar states from accruing debt. In 2004, for example, state debts totaled $754 billion.[126] (Indeed, one reason state governments appear to have balanced budgets while the federal government does not is that states use different budget and accounting practices than the federal government does.) Deficits can occur because the budget is a forecast of how much money a state will have coming in and how much money it plans to spend. The forecast can be wrong for many reasons, particularly if the economy fails to perform as expected. Thirty-six states have laws that prohibit them from carrying deficits into the next fiscal year, so the government must take immediate steps to correct a budget shortfall when one becomes apparent. These corrective steps include giving the governor power to make budget cuts and using money set aside in **rainy day funds** to cover the deficit.[127]

rainy day funds
Surplus revenues a state government holds in reserve for budget emergencies and shortfalls.

Some states borrow to cover deficits, although sixteen states have strict constitutional controls on the borrowing process. Borrowing increases a state's long-term costs because it must repay not only the money it borrowed, but also the interest on the loan. States that run chronic deficits become poor credit risks and have to pay higher interest rates on the bonds they issue to raise money. As states ran into budgetary problems in the early 1990s and again in the early 2000s, all except a few saw their credit ratings drop.[128] States also issue bonds to cover expenditures to construct roads, schools, hospitals, sports facilities, college dormitories, and the like. States have a variety of different controls governing the issuance of such bonds, but state constitutional limits on debt do not appear to slow the growth of state debt.[129] Many bonds now issued do not guarantee repayment of the debt through taxes; instead, they pledge the revenues the facility being financed will generate.[130]

15-3c Spending

The spending priorities of states differ from those of the federal government. The federal government, for example, pays the full cost of defending the United States. States pay for the vast bulk of public spending on schools and prisons. As relations between Washington and the states have become increasingly complex over time, however, state spending priorities have changed.

As recently as the 1970s, education took far and away the biggest chunk of state funds, with roads and highways also claiming a respectable percentage of the budget. By the early 1990s, however, the composition of state budgets had changed, largely in response to federal mandates and increased public demands for other services. Education (i.e., primary, secondary, and higher education combined) remains the biggest single component in state budgets, but it has declined as a percentage of state spending. Roads and highways also get a smaller percentage of state funds. In turn, state spending on human services and health care has increased dramatically, as have the costs of running prisons and paying interest on state debts.[131] Corrections now gets more funding than higher education in five states (i.e., Connecticut, Delaware, Michigan, Oregon, and Vermont).[132] And starting in their fiscal year 1994 budgets, states for the first time spent more on Medicaid—the federal-state health program for low-income people—than on their colleges and universities.[133] In 2006–2007, for example, California spent $13.8 billion from its general fund on Medi-Cal (the state's Medicaid program), while spending $11.4 billion on higher education.[134]

Although every state faces much the same demand for spending, some difference in spending emphases are noticeable across the states. Many large, heavily urbanized states, for example, tend to spend more money per citizen on fighting crime than smaller, more rural states.[135] Wealthier states tend to spend more on welfare benefits for their citizens than do poorer states.[136] Expenditures for public education also vary, with East Coast states tending to spend more per pupil than do other states, particularly those in the South.[137]

Because states vary in the priorities and rules they set for raising revenues, budgeting, and spending, the resident of one state may enjoy more or different services than a similar individual in another state. This is also true within a single state, as local governments write their own rules and policies.

15-4 LOCAL GOVERNMENT

The U.S. Constitution says nothing about local government. Thus, unlike the federal government and state governments, cities and towns have no independent constitutional standing in the United States. Instead, the power to create local governments rests with state governments. Each state decides not only what types of local governments will exist within its borders, but also what their geographic boundaries will be and what powers they may exercise. One result is that local government comes in different forms and employs different structures. Despite this variety, local government in many respects constitutes the most representative level of government. And as the cost of running local government has risen in recent years, some local governments have responded by privatizing some of their public services.

15-4a Forms of Local Government

Local government comes in many forms. Most state constitutions provide for the creation of counties, which are charged with actually administering many state services much as states administer federally funded programs. In New England, towns perform the same functions as counties. Most Americans live in municipalities or cities. Unlike counties, cities are created by the specific action of the state. A city comes into legal existence only when the state incorporates it by granting it a charter that spells out its jurisdiction, powers, and duties.

In addition to counties, towns, and municipalities, states also create a wide variety of single-purpose governments. The most common are school districts and special fire or water districts. These districts deliver government services to an area that may cross city or county lines. For example, most metropolitan regions have a special district known as a public transit authority responsible for providing public transportation to the cities and towns in the region.[138]

The number of local governments in the United States has declined dramatically since World War II. The main reason for the decline has been the effort over the years by state and local governments to save money by consolidating school districts. In 1942, the states oversaw 155,067 different local governments, 70 percent of which were school districts. By 2007, however, the number of local governments had shrunk to 89,476, only 15 percent of which were school districts.[139]

15-4b Local Government Structures

Local governments are organized in a variety of ways.[140] Municipalities generally use one of three different governing structures: mayor-council, city commission, and council-manager. Each form of government has strengths and weaknesses. The most popular form of government, particularly in larger cities, is the *mayor-council form.* The mayor-council structure can have either a strong mayor or a weak mayor. A strong mayor system invests the mayor with the sort of executive leadership powers the president and governors enjoy. In a weak mayor system, the mayor is essentially the figurehead leader of a council, and the council performs all executive functions. Some people prefer the strong mayor system because it enhances the political accountability of the executive, a position echoing the arguments made about the presidency during the Constitutional Convention (see Box 12–1).

The *city commission form* of government fuses legislative and executive functions in one elected group. Commissioners make policy as a group, but each commissioner also heads a major department of government. Under this system, one commissioner is named mayor to preside over commission meetings. One concern with the city commission system is that elected officials do not always have the managerial skills needed to successfully lead their departments. Such complaints led voters in Cedar Rapids, Iowa, to pass a 2005 measure changing their form of city government to council-manager from city commission. Portland, Oregon, is the only large city in the United States that uses the city commission form of government.

The *council-manager form* of government is designed to place administrative power in the hands of a city manager. The city manager is a professional administrator the elected city council hires to implement the policies it sets. Under this system, it is not uncommon for the city manager to become a powerful force in set-ting city policy, contrary to the system's intention to separate administration from politics. Many observers credit this form of government with professionalizing city administration. In most counties, an elected body, usually called a board of supervisors or commissioners, governs. This board often shares power in the county with other elected officials, such as a sheriff, county attor-ney, and county clerk, but most executive power is vested in the board. Some counties use a council-administrator system, an arrangement similar to the council-manager form of city govern-ment. Still others come under a county council-elected executive arrangement. Under this system, executive power rests with an elected executive, whereas legislative power rests with the board. As with the various forms of city governments, the different county arrangements allow counties to place different emphases on politi-cal accountability and administrative professionalization and skill.

15-4c Local Government and Representation

Although the Constitution does not mention local governments, they play an important role in the lives of Americans. Local gov-ernments provide most basic public services, so the decisions made at City Hall greatly affect the level of police protection, the quality of public schooling, the price of public transportation, and hundreds of other issues, large and small. At the same time, people tend to view their local government as the most representative level of government. Local government does reflect America's eth-nic and racial diversity to a far greater extent than do the federal and state governments. Although few minority members have been elected governor or senator, many have served as mayor, council-person, or school board member. In 2001, for example, more than 8,400 of the 9,101 African Americans holding elected office in the United States served at the local level.[141]

15-4d The Costs of Local Government

The role of local government has become increasingly important as federal aid to cities and towns has risen. For example, in 1932, federal aid to local governments amounted to only $10 million. By 1981, that aid had grown to $21 billion, but by 1990, it had declined to $20 billion. In 2005–2006, federal aid had rebounded to $55 billion, a sum that represented 4 percent of the $1.4 trillion local governments raised. State governments provided some 30 percent of the money local governments had; the rest they raised on their own.[142]

Local governments rely heavily on property taxes for their self-generated revenue; other taxes contribute relatively little to local government treasuries. In 2005–2006, for example, property taxes accounted for 72 percent of all tax dollars local governments raised.[143] Heavy reliance on property taxes poses several problems for local governments. Property taxes are the main source of funding for primary public education, which leads to inequities in school finances between communities with high and low property values. For two decades, the federal and state courts have struggled to devise solutions to this problem.[144] In most situations, raising property taxes to generate more money is not an acceptable answer. It is unpopular, particularly among older, retired people who tend to have difficulty keeping up with increasing tax rates.[145] Voter rebellions against rising property taxes have prompted most states to impose limits on the ability of local governments to raise property taxes.[146]

15-4e Privatization of Government Services

Over the past three decades, many state and local governments have sought to save their taxpayers money by turning government services over to private companies. The **privatization** movement began in earnest in the 1970s when Phoenix, Arizona, hired private businesses to take over trash collection, a task its city workers had performed. Since then, many of the services local governments used to provide are now contracted out to private companies, as Figure 15–5 shows. Governments looking to

privatization

Turning government programs over to private companies to run or selling government assets to the private sector.

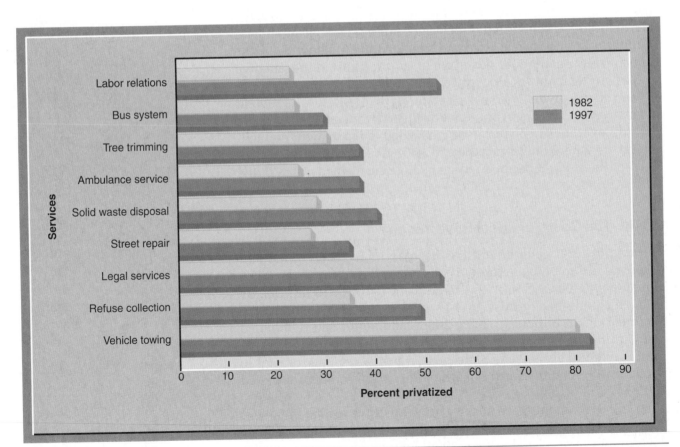

Figure 15–5 Privatization of Local Government. The percentage of local governments contracting out a variety of services has climbed steadily in recent years.

Source: *Data from Jeffrey D. Greene,* Cities and Privatization: *Prospects for the New Century* (Upper Saddle River, NJ: Prentice-Hall, 2002), 51.

save money have even started to turn to private companies to run public libraries.[147]

Indianapolis has been particularly aggressive about privatizing services. In 1995, the city had fewer employees on its payroll than it had twenty years earlier, and it had cut its budget by more than $100 million since 1992.[148] Indianapolis, though, has not pursued a simple-minded strategy of privatization. Instead, the administration introduced competition to the bureaucracy, allowing city departments to bid for contracts against private concerns. In many instances, city workers won the contracts, and the city ended up with better service at lower cost.[149]

Privatization has also begun to move beyond the provision of services to the private ownership of items such as highways. Indeed, in 1995, a privately owned, fourteen-mile long highway between Washington, D.C., and Dulles International Airport in Virginia opened, and in California, four new privately constructed and owned lanes were added to a busy highway. It may well be that private money will provide other public facilities that government cannot or is not willing to afford, with those who use the facilities paying the cost. In 2006, for example, Indiana leased the Indiana Toll Road to an Australian-Spanish business consortium; a year previously Chicago had leased the Chicago Skyway, a 7.8 mile toll road, to the same group. By 2008, twenty major transportation projects funded by public-private partnerships were in development across the country, and the Bush administration was calling for even more private funding of highways.[150]

Privatization is more likely to occur where local governments already operate under "good government" laws—particularly policies that promote merit systems rather than patronage in hiring government workers and that promote the use of purchasing standards.[151] The existence of good government laws usually signifies that a local community values efficiency and effectiveness over patronage. As a result, it normally has laws on the books that make it easier for government officials to contract services to the private sector.

Privatization is not a panacea for all government spending problems. In the 1990s, for example, many communities privatized their water systems when they faced significant expenses to cover the costs of required upgrades to their infrastructure. In recent years, many of them reinstituted public control over their water supplies. They did so because they calculated that they could supply water to their citizens at a lower cost and with better service.[152]

Overall, as local governments have acquired more revenue outside state control, they have become more independent in making and implementing policy. Indeed, they are far ahead of the federal government in promoting privatization. As a result of their independence, local governments are and will continue to be important participants in American politics.

15-5 WHO DELIVERS? PUBLIC OPINION AND LEVEL OF GOVERNMENT

Three levels of government serve Americans: federal, state, and local. Which level of government do people think gives them the most for their tax dollars? The answer has changed over time. During the 1970s, more people had confidence in how the federal government spent their money than in how their local and state governments did. From 1979 to 1999, however, public confidence in the federal government dropped. Today, about the same number think the federal or local government gives them the most for their money, with state government lagging behind.[153]

Republicans played to these changed attitudes toward the federal government when they took control of Congress in 1995. As part of their Contract with America, for example, they worked to shift responsibility for many government programs from Washington to the state capitals, an objective they have pursued since. By and large, Americans are sympathetic to that effort. In a 1997 survey, more people trusted the state government than federal government to control welfare policy, provide job training, control education programs for poor children, and to fight crime.[154] In that same poll, people had more confidence in the federal government when it came to providing services for immigrants and health care for the elderly and poor, and to protecting civil rights. A 2000 survey produced similar findings—with the public having more confidence in the federal government than state government in the areas of environmental protection and food safety. Finally, a 2006 survey revealed that Americans believe that federal elected officials are much more likely to be corrupt than are their local or state counterparts.[155]

When asked in 2007 which level of government they trust and have confidence in when it comes to handling problems, Americans expressed greater faith in local government than the federal or state governments. Only 61 percent said they had a great deal of confidence in the federal government to handle domestic problems, whereas 52 percent confessed they had little or no confidence. In contrast, 22 percent gave their local government high marks for dealing with problems and 29 percent gave negative marks. Confidence in state government fell in between that for the federal and local governments. The differences in opinion on the federal, state, and local government are not great, but they clearly suggest greater confidence in government the closer it is to them.[156] It is not, however, that people now think the world of their state and local governments; they just think much less of the national government than in the past.

SUMMARY

For much of American history, state and local governments had few dealings with the federal government. That changed in the 1930s when the New Deal prompted a sizable increase in federal assistance to cities and states. The Great Society programs of the 1960s carved out an even larger financial role for the federal government, allowing the federal government to exercise influence through aid programs, mandates, and picket-fence federalism. In the 1980s, however, Republican presidents Reagan and George H.W. Bush sought to shift the cost of governing as well as the authority to govern back onto cities and states. As a result, state and local governments have regained influence over many programs. And when Republicans controlled Congress between 1995 and 2007, they attempted to shift even more decision-making authority back to the states.

State governments in many ways resemble the federal government. They all have the same three distinct branches of government, and they all operate according to the same system of checks and balances. However, states do differ from the federal government and from each other. Each state has its own constitution, which sets forth the rules that shape politics in that state. In every state, the governor is the single most powerful political figure, and voters hold their governors to a higher standard of accountability than they do other politicians. State legislatures vary enormously in size, organization, and influence.

Since the early 1980s, interest groups have begun to pay more attention to state governments. Business groups constitute the most powerful category of interest groups. The single most powerful lobby, however, has been public school teachers. They have been successful because they live in every town and city, are eager to organize, and have strong incentives to lobby. States have been more aggressive than the federal government in regulating interest groups. All fifty states require lobbyists to disclose who they work for, and every state regulates political action committees.

One area interest groups have been active in is promoting ballot initiatives. Unlike the U.S. Constitution, many state constitutions promote direct democracy, mechanisms that allow voters to use the ballot booth to set the policy of state government. In many states, voters can revise the state constitution, overturn bills the state legislature passes, enact their own bills, and even vote to remove elected officials from office. Many interest groups have seized on these ballot initiatives as a way to translate their policy preferences into law.

States raise and spend money in many different ways. Sales taxes and income taxes are the two biggest sources of revenue in most states. As budgetary problems have increased over the in recent years, states have relied more and more on sin taxes on alcohol and tobacco and on revenues generated by lotteries and gambling. States need to keep revenue in line with spending because virtually every state has a law that requires a balanced budget. State spending looks much different from federal spending. Most state revenues are spent on education and prisons, which make up only a small portion of the federal budget.

Local governments are the offspring of state governments. They come in many different forms, with the states determining which forms may be used. In recent decades, local governments have become more independent of their parent states, with the federal government sending some financial aid directly to them. This has increased their independence and power. Local governments have been in the forefront of the privatization movement.

Public assessments of the effectiveness of federal, state, and local government have changed over time. In the 1970s, Americans were more likely to credit the federal government than state or local governments with spending their tax dollars wisely. Americans now think less of the federal government than they do their local and state governments.

KEY TERMS

block grants

categorical grants-in-aid

direct democracy

dual federalism

executive amendment

fiscal federalism

general revenue sharing

initiative

lame duck

line-item veto

mandates

picket-fence federalism

privatization

rainy day funds

referendum

READINGS FOR FURTHER STUDY

Altschuler, Bruce E. *Running in Place: A Campaign Journal* (Chicago: Nelson-Hall, 1996). A political scientist's interesting account of another political scientist's unsuccessful campaign for a seat in the New York Assembly.

Bouton, Jim. *My Life and Hard Times Trying to Save an Old Ballpark, plus PART II* (Guilford, CT: Lyons Press, 2005). An amusing and insightful account of the questionable local politics surrounding an attempt to save an old minor league ballpark.

Bryan, Frank M. *Real Democracy: The New England Town Meeting and How It Works* (Chicago: University of Chicago Press, 2003). An exhaustive and fascinating examination demonstrating how town meetings operate in Vermont.

Gray, Virginia, and Russell L. Hanson, eds. *Politics in the American States: A Comparative Analysis,* 9th ed. (Washington, D.C.: CQ Press, 2008). A collection of articles by political scientists examining several areas of state politics and public policies in some depth.

Moncrief, Gary F., Peverill Squire, and Malcolm E. Jewell. *Who Runs for the Legislature?* (Upper Saddle River, NJ: Prentice Hall, 2001). An important study of candidate recruitment for the state legislature based on a survey of candidates in eight states.

Rosenthal, Alan. *Heavy Lifting: The Job of the American Legislature* (Washington, D.C.: CQ Press, 2004). A comprehensive study of what state legislatures do and how they go about doing it.

Squire, Peverill, and Keith E. Hamm. *101 Chambers: Congress, State Legislatures, and the Future of Legislative Studies* (Columbus: Ohio State University Press, 2005). An instructive comparison of Congress and state legislatures over time and cross-sectionally, demonstrating similarities and differences in the institutions.

Wright, Ralph G. *Inside the Statehouse: Lessons from the Speaker* (Washington, D.C.: CQ Press, 2005). An entertaining account of state legislative politics written by a former speaker of the Vermont House of Representatives.

REVIEW QUESTIONS

1. In 1969, 4 percent of state legislators were women. In 2008, _____ percent of state legislators were women.
   a. 12
   b. 24
   c. 33
   d. 50

2. As of 2008, _____ only do not allow any form of gambling.
   a. Nevada and Indiana
   b. Idaho and South Carolina
   c. New York and Minnesota
   d. Hawaii and Utah

3. During the 1800s, what was the most common form of federal aid to the states?
   a. block grants
   b. categorical grants
   c. land
   d. revenue sharing

4. When did the tradition of dual federalism collapse?
   a. Civil War
   b. World War I
   c. New Deal
   d. World War II

5. During Ronald Reagan's presidency, the federal government's contribution to state and local revenues
   a. increased dramatically.
   b. increased by a small percentage.
   c. stayed about the same as when Jimmy Carter was president.
   d. decreased.

6. Which of the following is *not* true?
   a. State constitutions are typically much longer than the U.S. Constitution.
   b. State constitutions are more stable than the U.S. Constitution.

       c. State constitutions are easier to amend than the U.S. Constitution.

       d. Most states have had several constitutions.

7. _____ is the only state with a unicameral legislature.

       a. Maine

       b. Massachusetts

       c. Nebraska

       d. Colorado

8. Which of the following state legislatures are the *most* professionalized?

       a. New Hampshire, Vermont, and Connecticut

       b. Texas, Florida, and Virginia

       c. California, Michigan, and New York

       d. Wyoming, Washington, and West Virginia

9. Lobbyists for _____ are the *single* most influential interest group in state politics.

       a. the environmental movement

       b. farmers

       c. public schoolteachers

       d. civil liberties

10. Most of the revenue generated in states comes from

       a. sin taxes (taxes on alcohol and tobacco).

       b. taxes on corporations.

       c. taxes on motor fuels.

       d. sales taxes and individual income taxes.

NOTES

1. Rod Boshart, "Lower Level for OWI Gets Panel OK," *Iowa City Gazette*, January 23, 2003; Erin Madigan, "Drunken Driving Limits Threaten Highway Funds," Stateline.org, February 12, 2003.; www.stateline.org/live/ViewPage.action?siteNodeId=136&languageId=1&contentId=15157 David Pitt, "Tougher Drunken Driving Law Passes Legislature," Associated Press State and Local Wire, April 16, 2003.

2. Alexandra Zayas, "Last State to Act: DWI Now at .08," Minneapolis *Star Tribune*, July 31, 2005.

3. Richard P. Nathan, "The Role of the States in American Federalism," in *The State of the States*, 2nd ed., ed. Carl E. Van Horn (Washington, D.C.: CQ Press, 1993), 23–25.

4. Richard P. Nathan, "The Politics of Printouts: The Use of Official Numbers to Allocate Federal Grants-in-aid," in *American Intergovernmental Relations*, 2nd ed., ed. Lawrence J. O'Toole, Jr. (Washington, D.C.: CQ Press, 1993).

5. Kenneth Vines, "The Federal Setting in State Politics," in *Politics in the American States*, 3rd ed., eds. Herbert Jacobs and Kenneth Vines (Boston: Little Brown, 1976), 3–48.

6. Office of Management and Budget, *Budget of the United States Government, Fiscal Year 2007, Analytical Perspectives* (Washington, D.C.: U.S. Government Printing Office, 2006), 99.

7. Michael E. Milakovich and George J. Gordon, *Public Administration in America*, 7th ed. (Boston: Bedford/St. Martin's, 2001), 131.

8. See David C. Nice, *Federalism: The Politics of Intergovernmental Relations* (New York: St. Martin's, 1987), 51–54.

9. Russell L. Hanson, "Intergovernmental Relations," in *Politics in the American States: A Comparative Analysis*, 5th ed., eds. Virginia Gray, Herbert Jacob, and Robert B. Albritton (Glenview, IL: Scott, Foresman/Little, Brown, 1990), 61.

10. "Abstaining from Abstinence-Only," *Columbia Daily Tribune*, June 25, 2008.

11. Julie Cart, "Utah Sues Census to Prove That Missionaries Abroad Count Too," *Los Angeles Times*, March 8, 2001; Erin Texeira, "L.A. Sues in Effort to Get an Adjusted Census Count," *Los Angeles Times*, February 22, 2001.

12. Hanson, "Intergovernmental Relations," 60–62.

13. National Conference of State Legislatures, *Mandate Monitor*, April 8, 2008, 6 (no. 1).

14. David R. Beam and Timothy J. Conlan, "The Growth of Intergovernmental Mandates in an Era of Deregulation and Decentralization," *in American Intergovernmental Relations*, 2nd ed., ed. Lawrence J. O'Toole, Jr. (Washington, D.C.: CQ Press, 1993), 325–26.

15. Congressional Budget Office, "A Review of CBO's Activities in 2007 Under the Unfunded Mandates Reform Act," March 2008; See also Janet M. Kelly, "The Unfunded Mandate Reform Act: Working Well for No Good Reason," *Government Finance Review* 19 (February 2003): 28–31.

16. The term *picket fence federalism* was coined in Terry Sanford, *Storm over the States* (New York: McGraw-Hill, 1967), 80.

17. See Nathan, "The Role of the States in American Federalism," 17–19; Carl E. Van Horn, "The Quiet Revolution," in *The State of the States*, 2nd ed., ed. Carl E. Van Horn (Washington, D.C.: CQ Press, 1993).

18. Michael A. Pagano and Ann O'M. Bowman, "The State of Federalism, 1994–1995," *Publius* 25 (Summer 1995): 1–10.

19. Jim Abrams, "As Republicans Gain Power, Enthusiasm for States' Rights Wanes," *Detroit News*, January 3, 2004; Dan Froomkin, "Welfare's Changing Face," Washington Post.com, July 23, 1998, available at www.washingtonpost.com/wp-srv/politics/special/welfare/welfare.htm.

20. See, for example, Clifford J. Levy, "States Rally Round a Cry for Less," *New York Times*, February 11, 1996.

21. Data on state legislation gathered by the authors from National Conference of State Legislatures, REAL ID State Legislation Database. www.ncsl.org/standcomm/sctran/RealIDdb.cfm

22. See Ben Arnoldy, "States Fight as Real ID Deadline Nears," *Christian Science Monitor*, March 31, 2008; Eric Kelderman, "Real ID Showdown Averted," Stateline.org, April 4, 2008. www.stateline.org/live/details/story?contentId=297809

23. National Institute of Health, Stem Cell Research, State Initiatives for Stem Cell Research, available at www.stemcells.nih.gov/research/stateResearch.htm; Dennis Cauchon, "Fed-Up States Defy Washington," *USA Today*, December 8, 2003; Mark Kaufman, "Illinois Governor Launching Program to Reimport Drugs; Move May Force FDA's Hand," *Washington Post*, August 17, 2004.

24. These data are drawn from *The Book of the States 2008* (Lexington, KY: Council of State Governments, 2008), 10–11.

25. John J. Carroll and Arthur English, "Traditions of State Constitution Making," in *Politics in the American States and Communities*, ed. Jack R. Van Der Slik (Boston: Allyn & Bacon, 1996), 26.

26. Ibid., 30.

27. Richard Morin, "They're All Crooks—Whatever Their Names Are," *Washington Post National Weekly Edition*, May 29, 1989.

28. Richard W. Boyd, "The Effects of Primaries and Statewide Races on Voter Turnout," *Journal of Politics* 51 (August 1989): 713–39; Raymond E. Wolfinger and Steven J. Rosenstone, *Who Votes?* (New Haven, CT: Yale University Press, 1980); Gerald C. Wright, Jr., *Electoral Choice in America* (Chapel Hill, NC: Institute for Research in Social Science, 1974), 55.

29. Larry Sabato, *Goodbye to Good-Time Charlie* (Lexington, MA: Lexington Books, 1978), 21–22.

30. Thad L. Beyle, "Governors: Elections, Campaign Costs, Profiles, Forced Exits, and Power," in *The Book of the States 2004*, 154–55; Thomas M. Holbrook, "Institutional Strength and Gubernatorial Elections," *American Politics Quarterly* 21 (July 1993): 261–71.

31. Beyle, "Governors," 220–21; Sabato, *Goodbye to Good-Time Charlie*, 3–5, 71–74.

32. Alan Rosenthal, *Governors and Legislators: Contending Powers* (Washington, D.C.: CQ Press, 1990), 14–15.

33. Data for 2008 calculated from *The Book of the States 2008*, 183. See also Thad L. Beyle, "Being Governor," in *The State of the States*, 2nd ed., ed. Carl E. Van Horn (Washington, D.C.: CQ Press, 1993), 82.

34. The data on gubernatorial veto powers are taken from National Association of State Budget Officers, "Budget Processes in the States," Summer 2008. www.nasbo.org/Publications/PDFs/2008%20Budget%20Processes%20in%20the%20States.pdf

35. Rosenthal, *Governors and Legislators*, 161.

36. Monica Davey, "Wisconsin Voters Excise Editing From Governor's Veto Power," *New York Times*, April 3, 2008; Michael H. McCabe, "Wisconsin's 'Quirky' Veto Power," in *State Government 1992–93*, ed. Thad L. Beyle (Washington, D.C.: CQ Press, 1992).

37. Beyle, "Governors," 224–26; Rosenthal, *Governors and Legislators*, 9–13.

38. Jack R. Van Der Slik and Kent D. Redfield, *Lawmaking in Illinois* (Springfield, IL: Sangamon State University, 1986), 165–67.

39. Charles W. Wiggins, "Executive Vetoes and Legislative Overrides in the American States," *Journal of Politics* 42 (November 1980): 1110–17.

40. Peter Eichstaedt, "No, No, Two Hundred Times No," *State Legislatures*, July/August 1995; John Fund, "They Did It Their Way," *Opinion Journal*, January 2, 2003, available at www.opinionjournal.com/diary/prevweek.html.

41. Maryland data calculated from *The Book of the States 2008*, 130–31; Thad Beyle, "Governors: The Middlemen and Women in Our Political System," in *Politics in the American States*, 6th ed., eds. Virginia Gray and Herbert Jacob (Washington, D.C.: CQ Press, 1996), 234.

42. Wiggins, "Executive Vetoes and Legislative Overrides," 1110–17.

43. Joseph F. Zimmerman, *The Government and Politics of New York State* (New York: New York University Press, 1981), 200–204.

44. Alan Rosenthal, *Legislative Life* (New York: Harper & Row, 1981), 70.

45. Kim Fridkin Kahn, "Characteristics of Press Coverage in Senate and Gubernatorial Elections: Information Available to Voters," *Legislative Studies Quarterly* 20 (February 1995): 23–35; Peverill Squire, "Changing State Legislative Leadership Careers," in *Changing Patterns in State Legislative Careers*, eds. Gary F. Moncrief and Joel A. Thompson (Ann Arbor: University of Michigan Press, 1992), 179–80; Charles M. Tidmarch, Lisa J. Hyman, and Jill E. Sorkin, "Press Issue Agendas in the 1982 Congressional and Gubernatorial Election Campaigns," *Journal of Politics* 46 (November 1984): 1226–42.

46. E. Lee Bernick and Charles W. Wiggins, "Executive-Legislative Relations: The Governor's Role and Chief Legislator," in *Gubernatorial Leadership as State Policy*, eds. Eric B. Herzik and Brent W. Brown (New York: Greenwood, 1991), 75–76.

47. Richard C. Kearney, "How a 'Weak' Governor Can Be Strong: Dick Riley and Education Reform in South Carolina," in *State Government 1988–89*, ed. Thad L. Beyle (Washington, D.C.: CQ Press, 1988).

48. See Dan Durning, "Education Reform in Arkansas: The Governor's Role in Policy Making," in *Gubernatorial Leadership and State Policy*, eds. Eric B. Herzik and Brent W. Brown (New York: Greenwood Press, 1991).

49. Thad Beyle, "Enhancing Executive Leadership in the States," *State and Local Government Review* 27 (Winter 1995): 18–35.

50. Peverill Squire, "Challenger Profile and Gubernatorial Elections," *Western Political Quarterly* 45 (March 1992): 125–42; Mark E. Tompkins, "The Electoral Fortunes of Gubernatorial Incumbents: 1947–1981," *Journal of Politics* 46 (May 1984): 520–43.

51. Peverill Squire and Christina Fastnow, "Comparing Gubernatorial and Senatorial Elections," *Political Research Quarterly* 47 (September 1994): 703–20.

52. Alan Rosenthal, "The Legislative Institution: Transformed and at Risk," in *The State of the States*, ed. Carl E. Van Horn (Washington, D.C.: CQ Press, 1989).

53. Jack Rodgers, Robert Sittig, and Susan Welch, "The Legislature," in *Nebraska Government and Politics*, ed. Robert D. Miewald (Lincoln: University of Nebraska Press, 1984).

54. Robb Douglas, "Going Nebraska's Way," in *State Government 1993–94*, ed. Thad L. Beyle (Washington, D.C.: CQ Press, 1993); Bob Mercer, "Reforms Mulled for Legislature," *Rapid City (SD) Journal*, August 14, 1996; "A Tropical Unicameral? If Puerto Ricans are Still Mad at Lawmakers in Two Years, Nebraska could have Company in 1-House Club," *Omaha World-Herald*, July 24, 2005; Mario F. Cattabiani, "Toward a Smaller Harrisburg," *Philadelphia Inquirer*, May 9, 2007;

55. Peverill Squire, "Measuring Legislative Professionalism: The Squire Index Revisited," *State Politics and Policy Quarterly* 7 (Summer 2007): 211–27; Peverill Squire and Keith E. Hamm, *101 Chambers: Congress, State Legislatures, and the Future of Legislative Studies* (Columbus: Ohio State University Press, 2005), 79–95; Peverill Squire, "Uncontested Seats in State Legislative Elections," *Legislative Studies Quarterly* 25 (February 2000): 131–46; Peverill Squire, "Legislative Professionalization and Membership Diversity in State Legislatures," *Legislative Studies Quarterly* 17 (February 1992): 69–79.

56. Peverill Squire, "Professionalization and Public Opinion of State Legislatures," *Journal of Politics* 55 (May 1993): 479–91.

57. Rosenthal, *Governors and Legislators*, 202–3.

58. Peverill Squire, "Divided Government and Public Opinion in the States," *State and Local Government Review* 25 (Fall 1993): 150–54.

59. Citizens Conference on State Legislatures, *State Legislatures: An Evaluation of Their Effectiveness* (New York: Praeger, 1971), 24.

60. National Conference of State Legislatures, "Numbers of African American Legislators 2007" and "Latino Legislators 2007." www.ncsl.org/programs/legismgt/about/afrAmermain.htm; www.ncsl.org/programs/legismgt/about/Latino2007.htm

61. Victoria Van Son, *CQ's State Fact Finder: Rankings across America* (Washington, D.C.: Congressional Quarterly, 1993), 296–97.

62. Data from Center for American Women and Politics, "Women in State Legislatures 2008." www.cawp.rutgers.edu/fast_facts/levels_of_office/documents/stleg.pdf

63. Richard A. Seltzer, Jody Newman, and Melissa Vorhees Leighton, *Sex as a Political Variable: Women as Candidates and Voters in U.S. Elections* (Boulder, CO: Lynne Rienner, 1997).

64. Center for American Women and Politics, "Women in State Legislatures 2008." www.cawp.rutgers.edu/fast_facts/levels_of_office/documents/stleg.pdf See also Alan Ehrenhalt, *The United States of Ambition* (New York: Times Books, 1991), 197–207.

65. Center for American Women and Politics, "Women in State Legislatures 2008." www.cawp.rutgers.edu/fast_facts/levels_of_office/documents/stleg.pdf

66. See, for example, Chris T. Owens, "Black Substantive Representation in State Legislatures from 1971 to 1994," *Social Science Quarterly* 86 (December 2005): 779–91; Albert J. Nelson, *Emerging Influentials in State Legislatures: Women, Blacks, and Hispanics* (New York: Praeger, 1991); Beth Reingold, "Concepts of Representation among Female and Male State Legislators," *Legislative Studies Quarterly* 17 (November 1992): 509–37; Michelle Saint-Germain, "Do Their Differences Make a Difference? The Impact of Women in Public Policy in the Arizona Legislature," *Social Science Quarterly* 70 (December 1989): 956–68; Sue Thomas, "The Impact of Women on State Legislative Policies," *Journal of Politics* 53 (November 1991): 958–76; Sue Thomas and Susan Welch, "The Impact of Gender on Activities and Priorities of State Legislators," *Western Political Quarterly* 44 (June 1991): 445–56.

67. Edith J. Barrett, "The Policy Priorities of African American Women in State Legislatures," *Legislative Studies Quarterly* 20 (May 1995): 223–47.

68. Sue Thomas, *How Women Legislate* (New York: Oxford University Press, 1994).

69. Debra L. Dodson, "Women Officeholders: Continuity and Change across Two Decades," presented at the 1994 annual meeting of the Southern Political Science Association Meeting, Atlanta.

70. Squire and Hamm, *101 Chambers*, 134. See also Charles S. Hyneman, "Who Makes Our Laws?" *Political Science Quarterly* 55 (December 1940): 556–81; V. O. Key, Jr., *American State Politics* (New York: Knopf, 1956), 258–63; Samuel P. Orth, "Our State Legislatures," *Atlantic Monthly* (December 1904): 728–39; Belle Zeller, ed., *American State Legislatures* (New York: Crowell, 1954), 71.

71. Squire and Hamm, *101 Chambers*, 134; Eric Hirsch, *State Legislators' Occupations 1993 and 1995* (Denver: National Conference of State Legislators, 1996), 11.

72. Rosenthal, "The Legislative Institution," 99.

73. Squire and Hamm, *101 Chambers*, 134; Beth Bazar, *State Legislators' Occupations: A Decade of Change* (Denver: National Conference of State Legislatures, 1987), 4; Rosenthal, "The Legislative Institution," 72.

74. Squire and Hamm, *101 Chambers*, 134; Hirsch, *State Legislators' Occupations*, 42; see also Rosenthal, "The Legislative Institution," 71–72; Peverill Squire, "Career Opportunities and Membership Stability in Legislatures," *Legislative Studies Quarterly* 13 (February 1988): 65–82; Squire, "Legislative Professionalization," 74.

75. David Breaux and Malcolm Jewell, "Winning Big: The Incumbency Advantage in State Legislative Races," in *Changing Patterns in State Legislative Careers*, ed. Gary F. Moncrief and Joel A. Thompson (Ann Arbor: University of Michigan Press, 1992); Gary W. Cox and Scott Morgenstern, "The Increasing Advantage of Incumbency in the U.S. States," *Legislative Studies Quarterly* 18 (November 1993): 495–514; James C. Garand, "Electoral Marginality in State Legislative Elections, 1968–1986," *Legislative Studies Quarterly* 16 (February 1991): 7–28.

76. See, for example, Cox and Morgenstern, "The Increasing Advantage of Incumbency in the U.S. States," 500; Thomas M. Holbrook and Charles M. Tidmarch, "Sophomore Surge in State Legislative Elections, 1968–86," *Legislative Studies Quarterly* 16 (February 1991): 49–63; Ronald E. Weber, Harvey J. Tucker, and Paul Brace, "Vanishing Marginals in State Legislative Elections," *Legislative Studies Quarterly* 16 (February 1991): 29–47.

77. Gary F. Moncrief, Richard G. Niemi, and Lynda W. Powell, "Time, Term Limits, and Turnover: Trends in Membership Stability in U.S. State Legislatures," *Legislative Studies Quarterly* 29 (August 2004): 357–81; Richard G. Niemi and Laura R. Winsky, "Membership Turnover in U.S. State Legislatures: Trends and Effects of Districting," *Legislative Studies Quarterly* 12 (February 1987): 115–23; Kwang S. Shin and John S. Jackson, III, "Membership Turnover in U.S. State Legislatures: 1931–1976," *Legislative Studies Quarterly* 4 (February 1979): 95–114.

78. Squire and Hamm, *101 Chambers*, 143.

79. Squire, "Career Opportunities and Membership Stability," 71.

80. Ibid., 72; Peverill Squire, "Member Career Opportunities and the Internal Organization of Legislatures," *Journal of Politics* 50 (August 1988): 730.

81. Jack M. Treadway, "Adoption of Term Limits for State Legislatures," *Comparative State Politics* 16 (July 1995): 1–3; see also the data in U.S. Term Limits, "Coming to Terms with Term Limits: A Summary of State Term Limits Laws," *Term Limits Outlook Series* 3 (December 1994); U.S. Term Limits, "Louisiana Goes Big for Term Limits," December 30, 1995.

82. Thomas Galvin, "Limits Score a Perfect 14 for 14, But Court Challenges Loom," *Congressional Quarterly Weekly Report*, November 7, 1992, 3593–94; "Supreme Court Declines Review of State-Level Term Limits," *Congressional Quarterly Weekly Report*, March 14, 1992, 654.

83. "Term-Limits Supporters Make Run at the Ballot," *Corvallis Gazette-Times*, June 2, 2006. For previous years, see Margaret Engle, "Initiative Spending Brings Mixed Results," *Capital Eye*, December 15, 1994, 3–4.

84. Jeffrey A. Karp, "Support for Term Limits," *Public Opinion Quarterly* 59 (Fall 1995): 373–91; James D. King, "Term Limits in Wyoming," *Comparative State Politics* 14 (April 1993): 1–18.

85. Karp, "Support for Term Limits"; Janine Parry and Todd Donovan, "Leave the Rascals in? Explaining the Poor Prospects of Term Limit Extensions," *State Politics and Policy Quarterly* 8 (Fall 2008): 293–308.

86. Glenn Sussman, Nicholas Lovrich, Byron W. Daynes, and Jonathan P. West, "Term Limits and State Legislatures," *Extension of Remarks*, July 1994, 3.

87. See Daniel A. Smith, "Overturning Term Limits: The Legislature's Own Private Idaho?" *PS: Political Science and Politics* 36 (April 2003): 215–20.

88. Rebecca L. Noah, "The Limited Legislature: The Arizona Case," presented at the 1995 annual meeting of the Western Political Science Association, Portland, Oregon.

89. Gary F. Moncrief, Joel A. Thompson, Michael Haddon, and Robert Hoyer, "For Whom the Bell Tolls: Term Limits and State Legislatures," *Legislative Studies Quarterly* 17 (February 1992): 37–47; Cynthia Opheim, "The Effect of U.S. State Legislative Term Limits Revisited," *Legislative Studies Quarterly* 19 (February 1994): 49–59.

90. Alan Rosenthal, *The Third House: Lobbyists and Lobbying in the States* (Washington, D.C.: CQ Press, 1993), 3.

91. Leah Rush, "Influence: A Booming Business," The Center for Public Integrity, December 20, 2007. www.projects.publicintegrity.org/hiredguns/report. aspx?aid=957

92. Kenneth G. Hunter, Laura Ann Wilson, and Gregory G. Brunk, "Societal Complexity and Interest-Group Lobbying in the American States," *Journal of Politics* 53 (May 1991): 488–503; Clive S. Thomas and Ronald J. Hrebenar, "Nationalization of Interest Groups and Lobbying in the States," in *Interest Group Politics*, 3rd ed., ed. Allan J. Cigler and Burdett A. Loomis (Washington, D.C.: CQ Press, 1991); Blaine S. Walker, "AARP Out to Show Clout at State Level," Stateline.org, September 28, 2000, www.stateline.org/live/View Page.action?siteNodeId=136&languageId=1&contentId=14131 and AARP Web site, available at hwww.aarp.org/states/.

93. Clive S. Thomas and Ronald J. Hrebenar, "Understanding Interest Group Power: Lessons from Developments in the American States since the Mid-1980s," presented at the 1995 annual meeting of the Midwest Political Science Association, Chicago.

94. Virginia Gray and David Lowery, "The Diversity of State Interest Group Systems," *Political Research Quarterly* 46 (March 1993): 81–97.

95. Margery M. Ambrosius and Susan Welch, "State Legislators' Perceptions of Business and Labor Interests," *Legislative Studies Quarterly* 13 (May 1988): 199–209; Gray and Lowery, "The Diversity of State Interest Group Systems," 81–97; Clive S. Thomas and Ronald J. Hrebenar, "Interest Groups in the States," in *Politics in the American States*, 8th ed., ed. Virginia Gray, and Russell L. Hanson (Washington, D.C.: CQ Press, 2004), 119–20.

96. Thomas and Hrebenar, "Interest Groups in the States," 119–20.

97. Ehrenhalt, *The United States of Ambition*, 173.

98. The 2001–2002 data are from The Institute on Money in State Politics. See also John Archibald and Michael Sznajderman, "PACs Fill Campaign Coffers," *Birmingham News*, March 15, 1999; David L. Martin, "Alabama," in *Interest Group Politics in the Southern States*, ed. Ronald J. Hrebenar and Clive S. Thomas (Tuscaloosa: University of Alabama Press, 1992).

99. See, for example, the discussion in Tom Loftus, *The Art of Legislative Politics* (Washington, D.C.: CQ Press, 1994), 133–34.

100. Shane Goldmacher, "Lobbyists Report Spending $143 million in First Half of '08," *Sacramento Bee*, August 16, 2008.

101. Cynthia Opheim, "Explaining the Differences in State Lobbying Regulations," *Western Political Quarterly* 44 (June 1991): 405–21; The Center for Public Integrity, "How the Feds Stack Up: Not Good," May 15, 2003. www.projects.publicintegrity.org/hiredguns/report.aspx?aid=167

102. Opheim, "Explaining the Differences in State Lobbying Regulations," 405–21.

103. Frank J. Sorauf, *Money in American Elections* (Glenview, IL: Scott Foresman/Little, Brown, 1988), 284–90.

104. The numbers reported on initiatives and referendums are drawn from *The Book of the States 2000–2001* (Lexington, KY: Council of State Governments, 2000), 7, 233.

105. Calculated by authors from data provided by the National Institute for Money in State Politics, available at www.followthemoney.org/index.phtml.

106. Arthur Lupia, "Shortcuts Versus Encyclopedias: Information and Voting Behavior in California Insurance Reform Elections," *American Political Science Review* 88 (March 1994): 63–76.

107. David B. Magleby, "Taking the Initiative: Direct Legislation and Direct Democracy in the 1980s," *PS: Political Science & Politics* 21 (Summer 1988): 600–611.

108. Howard Fischer, "Defeated Smoking Curb Spent Nearly $14 Per Vote," *Arizona Daily Star*, December 8, 2006.

109. See Thad Kousser, "The California Governor's Recall," in *The Book of the States 2004*, 307–15. On state recall provisions, see *The Book of the States 2004*, 316–22.

110. Valerie Alvord, "Recall Ax Falling at Local Level," *USA Today*, June 29, 2003; Morgan E. Felchner, "Recall Elections: Democracy in Action or Populism Run Amok?" *Campaigns & Elections* 25 (June 2004): 30–32.

111. Data from U.S. Bureau of the Census, "State Government Tax Collections: 2005–06"; Susan B. Hansen, "The Politics of State Taxing and Spending," in *Politics in the American States*, 5th ed., ed. Virginia Gray, Herbert Jacob, and Robert B. Albritton (Glenview, IL: Scott, Foresman/Little, Brown, 1990), 339–40.

112. Richard F. Winters, "The Politics of Taxing and Spending," in *Politics in the American States*, 6th ed., ed. Virginia Gray and Herbert Jacob (Washington, D.C.: CQ Press, 1996), 332.

113. Ibid., 333; Federation of Tax Administrators, "2007 State Tax Collection by Source."

114. Sylvia Nasar, "Like U.S., State Governments Look to Affluent to Pay More Tax," *New York Times*, March 21, 1993.

115. Russell D. Murphy, "Connecticut: Lowell P. Weicker, Jr., a Maverick in the 'Land of Steady Habits,'" in *Governors and Hard Times*, ed. Thad Beyle (Washington, D.C.: CQ Press, 1992).

116. The data on tobacco taxes are taken from the Campaign for Tobacco-Free Kids, "State Cigarette Excise Tax Rates & Rankings," October 15, 2008. www.tobaccofreekids.org/research/factsheets/pdf/0097.pdf

117. Amir Efrati, "Cigarette-Tax Disparities Are a Boon for Border Towns," *Wall Street Journal*, March 2, 2007.

118. Data from North American Association of State and Provincial Lotteries, "Sales and Profits," available at www.naspl.org/index.cfm?fuseaction=content&PageID=3&PageCategory=3.

119. These data are drawn from the American Gaming Association, 2007 statistics. www.americangaming.org/assets/files/aga_2007_sos.pdf

120. Robert D. Behn and Elizabeth K. Keating, "The Fiscal Crisis of the States: Recession, Structural Spending Gap, and Political 'Disconnect,'" Taubman Center Policy Brief, April 27, 2005 *www.hks.harvard.edu/taubmancenter/ pdfs/fiscalcrisis.pdf*; Iris J. Lav, Elizabeth McNichol, and Robert Zahradnik, "Faulty Foundations: State Structural Budget Problems and How to Fix Them," Center on Budget and Policy Priorities, May 2005 www.cbpp.org/ 5-17-05sfp.pdf; National Governors Association and National Association of State Budget Officers, "The Fiscal Survey of States," December 2007 www.nga.org/Files/pdf/FSS0712.PDF; Government Accountability Office, "State and Local Government Retiree Benefits, GAO-08-223," January 2008. www.gao.gov/new.items/d08223.pdf

121. Brian Krebs, "States Hope to Revive Push for Online Sales Tax," *Washington Post*, December 16, 2004; Martha Stoddard, "States Team Up on Sales Taxes, 18 Will Encourage Retailers to Collect on Catalog and Online Purchases," *Omaha World-Herald*, October 1, 2005.

122. See *The Book of the States 2002* (Lexington, KY: Council of State Governments, 2002), 150–51. On state budgeting, see Edward J. Clynch and Thomas P. Lauth, eds., *Governors, Legislatures, and Budgets* (New York: Greenwood Press, 1991).

123. Glenn Abney and Thomas P. Lauth, "Governors and the Line-Item Veto," presented at the 1994 annual meeting of the Southern Political Science Association, Atlanta; Glenn Abney and Thomas P. Lauth, "The Line-Item Veto in the States: An Instrument for Fiscal Restraint or an Instrument of Partisanship?" *Public Administration Review* 45 (May/June 1985): 372–77.

124. Abney and Lauth, "Governors and the Line-Item Veto," 15–16; Pat Thompson and Steven R. Boyd, "Use of the Line-Item Veto in Texas, 1940–1990," *State and Local Government Review* 26 (Winter 1994): 38–45.

125. Rosenthal, *Governors and Legislators*, 132.

126. Data from U.S. Bureau of the Census, *Statistical Abstract of the United States, 2008*, available at www.census.gov/compendia/statab/tables/ 08s0440.pdf.

127. Henry J. Raimondo, "State Budgeting in the Nineties," in *The State of the States*, 2nd ed., ed. Carl E. Van Horn (Washington, D.C.: CQ Press, 1993), 34–35.

128. Dennis Cauchon, "States Choose Debt to Fill Gaps," *USA Today*, February 25, 2003; and Jason White, "Bond Rating Drop Another of States' Fiscal Woes," Stateline.org, July 31, 2003. www.stateline.org/live/ViewPage. action?siteNodeId=136&languageId=1&contentId=15334

129. James C. Clingermayer and B. Dan Wood, "Disentangling Patterns of State Debt Financing," *American Political Science Review* 89 (March 1995): 108–20.

130. Hansen, "The Politics of State Taxing," 338; D. Roderick Kiewiet and Kristin Szakaly, "Constitutional Restrictions on Borrowing: An Analysis of State Bonded Indebtedness," *Journal of Law, Economics and Organization* 12 (1996): 62–97.

131. David Merriman, "What Accounts for the Growth of State Government Budgets in the 1990s?" (Washington, D.C.: Urban Institute, 2000); Rudolph G. Penner, "A Brief History of State and Local Fiscal Policy," Urban Institute, October 1998 www.urban.org/UploadedPDF/anf27.pdf; Hansen, "The Politics of State Taxing," 361–63; Raimondo, "State Budgeting in the Nineties," 33.

132. The Pew Center on the States, "One in 100: Behind Bars in America 2008," February, 2008, 16. www.pewcenteronthestates.org/uploadedFiles/8015PCTS_Prison08_FINAL_2-1-1_FORWEB.pdf

133. Laurie McGinley, "States' Finances Are Improving, Survey Reports," *Wall Street Journal*, July 27, 1993.

134. State of California, *State Budget Highlights 2006–07*, 48, 103. www.dof.ca.gov/budget/historical/2006-07/documents/StateBudgetHighlights2006-07.pdf

135. Wesley G. Skogan, "Crime and Punishment," in *Politics in the American States*, 5th ed., ed. Virginia Gray, Herbert Jacob, and Robert B. Albritton (Glenview, IL: Scott, Foresman/Little, Brown, 1990), 386.

136. Mark Rom, "Transforming State Health and Welfare Programs," in *Politics in the American States*, 8th ed., ed. Virginia Gray and Russell L. Hanson (Washington, D.C.: CQ Press, 2004), 334.

137. Kenneth Wong, "The Politics of Education," in *Politics in the American States*, 8th ed., ed. Virginia Gray and Russell L. Hanson (Washington, D.C.: CQ Press, 2004), 375.

138. On the forces driving the development of single-purpose or special districts, see Nancy Burns, *The Formation of American Local Governments* (New York: Oxford University Press, 1994).

139. U.S. Census Bureau, *2007 Census of Governments*, available at www.census.gov/govs/www/cog2007.html.

140. Ann O. Bowman and Richard C. Kearney, *State and Local Government*, 2nd ed. (Boston: Houghton Mifflin), 312–20.

141. David A. Bositis, "Black Elected Officials: A Statistical Summary 2001," Joint Center for Political and Economic Studies, 2003, Table 1. www.jointcenter.org/publications1/publication-PDFs/BEO-pdfs/2001-BEO.pdf

142. Calculated by the authors from U.S. Bureau of the Census, "State Government Tax Collections: 2006." www.census.gov/govs/statetax/0600usstax.html.

143. Calculated by the authors from Ibid.

144. Lawrence Baum, "Making Judicial Policies in the Political Arena," in *The State of the States*, 2nd ed., ed. Carl E. Van Horn (Washington, D.C.: CQ Press, 1993), 163–64.

145. U.S. Advisory Commission on Intergovernmental Relations, "Public Attitudes on Government and Taxes," in *American Intergovernmental Relations*, 2nd ed., ed. Lawrence J. O'Toole, Jr. (Washington, D.C.: CQ Press, 1993), 109–10.

146. Dennis L. Dresang and James L. Gosling, *Politics, Policy, and Management in the American States* (New York: Longman, 1989), 41–42.

147. "Libraries Turn to Private Companies to Survive," *Cedar Rapids Gazette*, October 7, 2007.

148. John L. Chapman, "The Privatization of Public Services"; Ludwig von Mises Institute, February 21, 2008; Stephen Goldsmith, "Competing for Better Government," *New York Times*, December 7, 2001; Dirk Johnson, "City Services, It's Now 'Indy-a-First-Place,'" *New York Times*, March 2, 1995.

149. Chapman, "The Privatization of Public Services"; Johnson, "City Services, It's Now 'Indy-a-First-Place.'"

150. Christopher Conkey, "Bush Calls for New Highway Tolls, More Private Funding of Roads," *Wall Street Journal*, July 30, 2008; Amy Goldstein, "Strapped States Try New Route, Lease Toll Roads to Foreign Firms," *Washington Post*, June 14, 2006; Lianne Hart, "Texas Thinking Big on

Transportation," *Los Angeles Times*, January 4, 2005; Craig Karmin, "Leasing of Landmark Turnpike Puts State at Policy Crossroads," *Wall Street Journal*, August 26, 2008; Laura Meckler, "Making Public Highways Private," *Wall Street Journal*, April 18, 2006; Peter Samuel, "Should States Sell Their Toll Roads?" Reason Foundation, May 2005 www.reason.org/ps334.pdf; U.S. Department of Transportation, "Innovation Wave: An Update on the Burgeoning Private Sector Role in U.S. Highway and Transit Infrastructure," July 18, 2008 www.fhwa.dot.gov/reports/pppwave/ppp_innovation_wave.pdf; and David Wessell, "The American Way?" *Wall Street Journal*, October 2, 1995.

151. Robert Barro, "The Imperative to Privatize," *Wall Street Journal*, June 29, 1995.

152. Jim Carlton, "Calls Rise for Public Control of Water Supply," *Wall Street Journal*, June 17, 2008.

153. Richard L. Cole and John Kincaid, "Public Opinion on U.S. Federal and Intergovernmental Issues in 2006: Continuity and Change," *Publius* 36 (Summer 2006): 443–59.

154. "In Retrospect, Public Opinions 1997," The Pew Research Center for the People & the Press, 10. See also Richard Morin, "Power to the States," *Washington Post National Weekly Edition*, March 27–April 2, 1995, 37.

155. "In Retrospect, Public Opinions 1997," 10. The 2000 data are from NPR-Kaiser-Kennedy School Poll, "Attitudes toward Government," May 26–June 25, 2000. The 2006 data are from a Diageo/Hotline Poll, January 12 to 15, 2006. www.npr.org/programs/specials/poll/govt/gov.toplines.pdf

156. The data are from Jeffrey M. Jones, "Low Trust in Federal Government Rivals Watergate Era Levels," The Gallup Poll, September 26, 2007. www.gallup.com/poll/28795/Low-Trust-Federal-Government-Rivals-Watergate-Era-Levels.aspx

16

The Federal Budget

CHAPTER OUTLINE

When President George W. Bush submitted his 2009 budget to Congress in February 2008, he asserted, "I have set clear priorities that will help us meet our Nation's most pressing needs while addressing the long-term challenges ahead."[1]

In developing the budget, the president confronted the same reality every political leader faces: a budget constraint. His proposal called for spending just over $3.1 trillion ($3,100,000,000,000) during the 2009 fiscal year. Yet, even with that level of spending the government still could not afford to fully fund everything the president and Congress wanted to do. Nor could it afford to meet all of the public's expectations for education, health care, law enforcement, and many other programs. This means that the government must decide which programs it will fund and which it will not. These decisions are made during the budgetary process. And because dollars are policy, budgetary decisions represent the most important decisions the president and Congress make each year.

In this chapter, we examine the federal budget. We begin by discussing the dramatic growth in government spending over the past 220 years. We review government revenue sources and look at what the government spends its money on. We then explore why for many years federal spending exceeded federal revenues. We examine the rules of the budgetary process, focusing on efforts the president and Congress made over recent decades to bring government spending into line with government revenue, and we explain why most of these efforts failed. Then we explore how in recent years revenues came to exceed spending. Finally, we consider whether the process the federal government uses to set its budget makes sense.

16-1 BUDGETS, DEFICIT SPENDING, AND THE NATIONAL DEBT

For good or for ill, the budget of the federal government greatly affects the well-being of the American public. To put the current debate over government spending in context, we review the growth of the federal budget over the past 220 years, the rise of deficit spending from the early 1960s to the late 1990s, the brief period of surpluses around the turn of the century followed by a return to deficits since then, and the consequences of the increasingly large national debt.

16-1a The Growing Federal Budget

The size and composition of the federal budget have changed dramatically since the days of George Washington. During Washington's presidency, the federal government spent roughly $3 to $5 million annually. Several times in the 1790s, government spending exceeded government revenues, creating the first **budget deficits**.

budget deficits
The amount by which government spending exceeds government revenues in a single year.

(Deficits occur when the government spends more money than it brings in during a fiscal year.) To make up for the gap between spending and revenue, the government borrowed money (much as you might do to pay your tuition). The money that Washington's government borrowed, in turn, formed the first **national debt**. (The national debt is the total amount of money the government owes—that is, the accumulation of unpaid annual deficits.) Because the government did not immediately repay the money it borrowed, the national debt began to grow.

The budget deficits that occurred under George Washington and his immediate successors, however, tended to be small and infrequent. (One notable exception was in 1803, when the federal government had an $8 million budget, but borrowed $15 million to pay for the Louisiana Purchase, adding more than a million square miles of land to the country.)[2] Throughout the nineteenth century, government revenues usually equaled expenditures, thereby creating a **balanced budget**. In some years, government revenues actually exceeded expenditures, creating a **budget surplus**. Balanced budgets were expected, in part because many politicians saw them as a way to limit the growth and power of the federal government.[3] Indeed, in the nineteenth century, the federal government generally ran budget deficits only when the country was at war and faced an urgent need to increase military spending.

As presidents and Congresses struggled throughout the nineteenth century to keep government spending in line with government revenues, the size of the federal budget grew slowly. The federal budget did not exceed $1 billion in spending—or about 1 percent of what the government spent in 2006 on hurricane relief alone—until the close of the Civil War in 1865. After the Civil War, government spending dropped sharply. The federal budget did not exceed $1 billion again until 1917 with the country's entry into World War I.

The growth in federal spending picked up speed after World War I, and it accelerated further after World War II. The federal government's budget first broke the $100 billion mark in 1962, and it topped $1 trillion for the first time in 1987. The federal budget first exceeded $2 trillion in 2002. It surpassed $3 trillion in 2009.

What accounts for the rapid growth in federal spending over the past eighty years? The answer lies in the vast expansion of the federal government's role in American life. When the Great Depression prompted President Franklin Roosevelt to push through Congress the programs that made up the New Deal, the federal government assumed new responsibilities for stimulating the national economy and maintaining social welfare. After World War II, the newfound role of the United States as a superpower led the federal government to increase dramatically the size and cost of the military. And in the 1960s, President Lyndon Johnson championed the establishment of the Great Society, a set of programs that greatly expanded the federal government's role in reducing economic and racial inequality. As the federal government's responsibilities expanded in all these areas, it spent rapidly increasing sums to meet its new obligations.

national debt
The total amount of money the federal government owes to pay for accumulated deficits.

balanced budget
A federal budget in which spending and revenues are equal.

budget surplus
The amount by which government revenues exceed government spending in a single year.

16-1b The Rise and Fall of Deficit Spending

The growth in government spending brought a change in political attitudes toward deficit spending. The theories of British economist John Maynard Keynes, who argued that national governments should use deficit spending to stimulate the economy during a recession, influenced President Roosevelt and his advisers. The Roosevelt administration ran record budget deficits to end the Depression and to finance the cost of World War II. Despite Roosevelt's use of deficit spending, the expectation of a balanced federal budget remained strong. When the country returned to economic prosperity after the war, the federal government returned to the tradition of balancing its budget.

In the early 1960s, however, the inhibitions against deficit spending faded. During the Johnson administration, the budget began to balloon as new social programs such as Medicare—created in 1965 to help the elderly and people with disabilities pay for immediate (as opposed to long-term) health care—were created and the cost of the Vietnam War began to escalate. The president and Congress did not want to cut spending, and when they finally raised taxes, the revenue was insufficient to balance the budget.[4] As Figure 16–1 shows, budget deficits became commonplace. Congress and the president were unwilling or unable to raise enough revenue to pay for government spending or to cut spending to match revenues. With the exception of fiscal year 1969 (when a change in accounting rules produced a small surplus), the budget stayed in the red every year from 1961 through 1997. Then, after four years of surpluses, deficits returned again, starting in 2002.

Budget deficits became a potent political issue in American politics not only because they became chronic, but also because they grew tremendously in size. As Figure 16–1 shows, the size of the

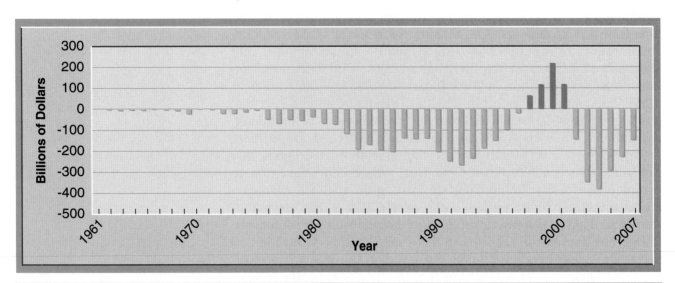

Figure 16–1   Budget Surplus and Deficit, 1961–2008. Budget deficits have been a chronic problem for many years, but particularly since 1980.

Source: *Data from Office of Management and Budget,* The Budget for Fiscal Year 2009, *Historical Tables, 22. www.whitehouse.gov/omb/budget/fy2009/pdf/hist.pdf*

budget deficit grew especially rapidly under Presidents Ronald Reagan and George H. W. Bush. In 1992, the budget deficit reached a record, totaling almost $300 billion (even higher by some accounting rules). The federal government ran up such large budget deficits even though its revenues were growing rapidly. The problem was that spending was growing even faster.

In 1993, President Bill Clinton and Congress (without any votes from Republican members) agreed on a package of spending cuts and tax increases designed to reduce the size of the budget deficit. The changes had some effect. The deficit gradually declined in the mid-1990s, falling to just $22 billion in 1997. At that time, President Clinton and the Republican-controlled Congress agreed on a balanced budget plan that greatly limited growth in government spending. That agreement, coupled with a strong economy, pushed the budget into a surplus in 1998 for the first time in twenty-eight years. The budget surpluses continued for the next three years.

By the end of 2001, however, government black ink was turning red. A combination of forces in 2000 and 2001 was responsible—an economic recession, a stock market crash, surging government spending on the war on terrorism as well as domestic programs, and a substantial cut in federal income taxes. Additional tax cuts in 2002 and 2003 combined with growing domestic spending and the cost of fighting wars in Afghanistan and Iraq only added to the size of the deficits. In 2004, the federal government ran a record $413 billion budget deficit. An improving economy led to increasingly smaller deficits through 2007. Then a confluence of events—the continuing overseas military conflicts, a crisis in the housing market, and a dramatically slowing economy—conspired to push the 2008 deficit back to the $400 billion level. The deficit for 2009 was forecast to be well over $1 trillion.

16-1c The National Debt

As Figure 16–2 shows, deficit spending over the past four decades led to an explosion in the size of the national debt. As we previously mentioned, the federal government first went into debt during George Washington's presidency. Nonetheless, it took from 1789 to 1981, or 192 years, for the national debt to reach $1 trillion. Over the next twelve years, the national debt quadrupled, reaching $4 trillion in 1993. Bill Clinton supplied another way to look at the rapid increase in the size of the debt during the Reagan and George H. W. Bush administrations in his address to a joint session of Congress early in 1993: "I well remember twelve years ago President Reagan stood at this podium and told you and the American people that if our debt were stacked in $1,000 bills, the stack would reach sixty-seven miles into space. Well, today that stack would reach 267 miles."[5] By the middle of 2008, the national debt stood at $9.6 trillion, and the stack of $1,000 bills would reach some 628 miles into space.

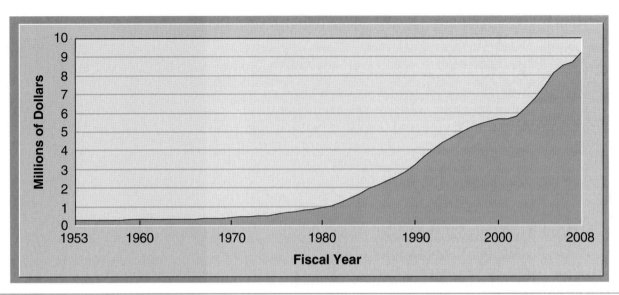

Figure 16-2   Growth in National Debt, 1953–2008. Because of chronic annual deficits, the total national debt has exploded over the last several decades.

Sources: *Data from Bureau of the Public Debt, available at www.treasurydirect.gov/govt/reports/pd/mspd/mspd.htm.*

We have said that the federal government finances its budget deficits by borrowing, but from who does it borrow money? Or to put the question another way, to whom does the government owe the debt? As of December 2007, American investors, including individuals, mutual funds, pension funds, and banks, held about 11 percent of the debt. The federal government held 52 percent in various trust funds required to invest in government securities, most importantly those for Social Security, Civil Service Retirement, Military Retirement, Medicare, and Unemployment Insurance. State and local governments held another 7 percent directly and in pension funds. Thus, most of the debt we owe to ourselves; foreigners hold 26 percent of the debt.[6] Foreign investors profit when they lend money to the U.S. government—as do American investors—thus deficit spending entails a transfer of American wealth to foreign citizens and governments. The sum of money paid in interest to foreign investors is growing and is likely to continue doing so in the future, potentially giving them considerable influence over the course of the American economy.[7]

The United States is not the only industrialized country suffering from debt problems. Although the absolute size of the American national debt swamps that of any other country, when debts are calculated in relative terms as a percentage of a nation's gross domestic product—essentially, the size of its economy—the United States fares better than many countries but worse than some others. For example, in 2009, Italy, and Japan had debts that were greater than the size of their entire annual gross domestic product, whereas the debt of the United States was roughly 70 percent of its gross domestic product. Among the major industrial democracies, the United Kingdom (52 percent of its gross domestic product), Germany (63 percent), and Canada (65 percent) had a lower national debt.[8]

16-1d The Consequences of a Large National Debt

Are budget deficits and a national debt matters for concern? To answer the question, it is important to recognize that debt itself is not inherently evil. Borrowing may make sense if the money is used to finance productive investment. For example, businesses borrow money to modernize their factories in the hope that modern plants will mean bigger profits, and many college students borrow money for college in the hope that a bachelor's degree will enable them to earn more in the future. (Indeed, businesses and private households in the United States are further in debt than the federal government.)[9] Thus, the country may benefit if the government borrows to build highways, train workers, develop new technologies, or otherwise improve the economy.

If debt is not inherently evil, neither is it always beneficial. During the debates in the last several decades over the wisdom of deficit spending, much of the discussion focused on two concerns. The first was that a rapidly growing national debt can retard economic growth. Whenever the federal government borrows money, it competes against other borrowers for loans, thereby raising interest rates higher than they otherwise would be. Higher interest rates may discourage firms from borrowing money to invest in the new factories and technologies needed to spur economic growth. Thus, some economists argue that the federal government can best stimulate the economy by living within its means. In 2002, the George W. Bush administration began to question whether deficits in fact lead to higher interest rates, and the record of low interest rates and large deficits during Bush's first term in office gave some credence to the doubts about the relationship.[10]

The second and more widespread concern was the fear that the government was running deficits less to finance productive investment than to pay for current consumption. (An example of the difference between investment and consumption is the difference between using money to pay your tuition—investment, which is likely to help you earn money—and using money to pay for a spring break trip—consumption, which means the money you used is gone.) Borrowing to finance programs such as health care, veterans' benefits, and military pensions, as opposed to investing in education or new technologies, will not make the country better prepared to pay tomorrow's bills. And, as we shall see, the cost of paying the interest on the borrowed money consumes a significant portion of the federal budget. In fiscal year 2007, interest payments alone totaled as much as the budgets of the Departments of Commerce, Education, Energy, Homeland Security, Housing and Urban Development, Interior, Justice, Labor, State, and Transportation; the budgets of the Army Corp of Engineers, the Environmental

Protection Agency, the National Science Foundation, and the operating expenses of the Congress, the Executive Office of the President, and the judicial branch *combined*.[11] Obviously, interest payments are money lost for other uses; these funds cannot be used to improve schools, repair highway bridges, find a cure for cancer, or clean up the environment.

16-2 WHERE DOES GOVERNMENT REVENUE COME FROM?

The rapid growth in the national debt during the 1980s and early 1990s made reducing the federal budget deficit a hot political topic. With the return of deficits in the new millennium, similar concerns once again surfaced. Many ideas were discussed to deal with the deficits, and they boiled down to a few options. A government can reduce a budget deficit by increasing revenues—which usually, but not always, means raising taxes—by cutting spending, or by some mix of the two. (Printing more money and reneging on the national debt are unacceptable alternatives for a number of reasons.) So where does government revenue come from? We will answer that question in Sections 16-2a and 16-2b. In Section 16-3, we will examine where government spending goes.

16-2a Government Revenue in Historical Perspective

The federal government's revenue sources have changed dramatically over the past 200 years. Until the early 1900s, the government obtained much of its revenue from customs duties (also called tariffs), which are taxes on imported goods. As Figure 16–3A shows, in 1900, nearly half of all government revenue came from customs duties. The other half came from excise taxes, mostly on alcohol

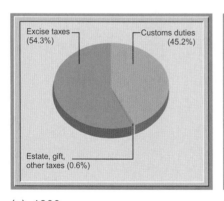

(a) 1900

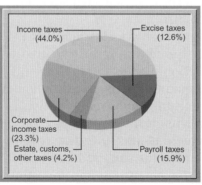

(b) 1960

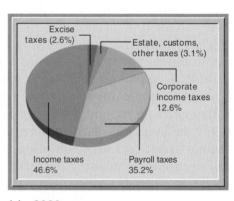

(c) 2009

Figure 16–3 Government Revenue Sources—1900, 1960, and 2009. *A,* In 1900, the federal government obtained most of its money from excise taxes and customs duties *B,* By 1960, the individual income tax was the largest source of revenue for the federal government. *C,* Today, although income taxes remain an important source of federal government revenue, payroll taxes are almost as important.

Sources: *Data from* Historical Statistics of the United States: Colonial Times to 1970 *(Washington, D.C.: U.S. Bureau of the Census, 1975), 1106; U.S. Bureau of the Census,* Statistical Abstract of the United States, 1980, *101st ed. (Washington, D.C.: U.S. Bureau of the Census, 1980), 260; and calculated by the authors from "The Budget for the Fiscal Year 2009, Historical Tables," 31. www.whitehouse.gov/omb/budget/fy2009/pdf/hist.pdf*

and tobacco products. A small portion of government revenue came from estate and gift taxes and a few other sources.

The federal government gained a new source of revenue in 1913 with the adoption of the Sixteenth Amendment to the Constitution. The amendment allowed the federal government to impose an income tax on individuals and corporations. Although the government had enacted an income tax during the Civil War (and allowed it to expire it in 1872) and again in 1894, the Supreme Court ruled in 1895 that the Constitution prohibited a federal income tax.[12] After ratification of the Sixteenth Amendment, Democrats and progressive Republicans quickly joined with newly elected President Woodrow Wilson in passing an income tax. (The Supreme Court ultimately upheld this tax.)[13]

Initially, the federal income tax affected few people.[14] Indeed, many members of Congress voted to impose a federal income tax because they knew that it would not affect most of their constituents. As one member of Congress from Kansas observed bluntly at the time the tax was debated, "I stand here as a representative of the Republican Party of the central West to pledge to you my word that the great western states will be found voting...for an income tax. Why? Because they will not pay it!"[15] Indeed, in 1913, only 358,000 Americans, or about 0.8 percent of the population, filed income tax returns.[16] And until World War II, tax rates remained low, and the average American paid little, if anything. By the early 1940s, income taxes had become the major source of federal revenue.

The federal government gained another source of revenue with the passage of the **Social Security Act of 1935**. The act imposed a payroll tax (often labeled FICA—for Federal Insurance Contribution Act—on a pay stub) on all wage earners to pay for Social Security and associated programs. As with the first income taxes, Americans initially paid only a small payroll tax. Over time, however, payroll tax rates and the amount of government revenue they provide have risen sharply.

Social Security Act of 1935

The act of Congress that created the Social Security tax (Federal Insurance Contribution Act—FICA) and Social Security programs.

The addition of income and payroll taxes led to a tremendous change in the composition of federal revenues in the middle part of the century. As Figure 16–3B shows, by 1960, almost half of all government revenue came from taxes on the incomes of individual Americans. Taxes on corporate incomes accounted for nearly one-fourth of all government revenue, and payroll taxes contributed another 16 percent. Meanwhile, customs duties, which were once the single largest source of government revenue, fell to less than 5 percent.

Since 1960, the federal government has refrained from adding new revenue sources, despite calls from some economists for a national sales tax or a value-added tax (a tax imposed on a product at each stage of production, as it increases in value). The federal government has, however, expanded the reach of existing taxes. Payroll taxes have increased to cover the costs of Medicare. The federal government also has extended excise taxes to include gasoline, tires, and a few other items in addition to alcohol and tobacco.

Although the federal government has not imposed any new types of taxes in recent decades, the mix of revenue sources has changed. As Figure 16–3*C* shows, in 2009, individual income taxes comprised virtually the same share of total revenue as in 1960. The share of government revenue coming from corporate income taxes dropped by roughly half, however, and the share generated by excise taxes fell by more than three-quarters. Meanwhile, the share of government revenue generated by payroll taxes more than doubled.

16-2b Income and Payroll Taxes

In 2009, the individual taxpayer provided, through income and payroll taxes, more than 80 percent of the federal government's revenue. Yet, some Americans earn a great deal of money each year, and some earn very little. How is the federal tax burden distributed across the American public? The answer depends on whether you are talking about individual income taxes or payroll taxes.

The income tax has always been intended to be a **progressive tax**—the more money a person makes, the higher the tax rate he or she pays. The highest tax rate has varied over time, from a low of 7 percent in 1913 (applied to annual incomes of $500,000 and higher) to 91 percent during most of the 1950s and 1960s (on annual incomes of $200,000 and higher).[17] These percentages are somewhat misleading, however. The federal tax code has always provided tax breaks (or, less charitably, loopholes) that allow people to declare some income exempt from taxation.

In the 1960s and 1980s, the federal government lowered income tax rates, especially the top rate, and eliminated many tax breaks. However, as part of President Clinton's first budget package, Congress raised the top tax rate from 31 to 36 percent. Individuals with more than $250,000 in taxable income also had to pay a 10 percent surtax—making their effective tax rate 39.6 percent. But most Americans were taxed at 15 percent. Moreover, people with low incomes were not required to pay any income tax. (Indeed, the Earned Income Tax Credit actually supplements the incomes of the working poor.)

The Bush administration pushed a major income tax cut bill through Congress in 2001. A new tax bracket of 10 percent was created for the first $6,000 of taxable income for an individual or $12,000 for a married couple. Lower rates for the other tax brackets were to be phased in by 2006. In 2003, however, the Bush administration wanted the scheduled rate reductions speeded up to help stimulate the sagging economy. Many Democrats countered that rate reductions for the wealthiest Americans should be postponed or cancelled because of the federal government's growing budget deficits. The president's position prevailed, and starting that year, the highest tax bracket was set at 35 percent.

progressive tax

A tax system in which those with high incomes pay a higher percentage of their income in taxes than those with low incomes.

The progressive character of the federal income tax is revealed when we examine who pays it. Taxpayers in 2007 who earned more than $1 million in adjusted gross income—only 0.3 percent of all taxpayers—received 12 percent of all income in the country but paid 24 percent of all income taxes. Those who made $50,000 or more, 38 percent of taxpayers, took in 79 percent of income but paid 99 percent of all income taxes. The bottom 62 percent of wage earners, those making less than $50,000 a year and who account for 21 percent of all income, produced only 1 percent of the federal government's income tax revenue. Thus, the more you make, the more you pay as a percentage of your income. Indeed, one study suggested that in 2005 the country's 400 highest income taxpayers combined paid 1.7 percent of all income taxes that year; slightly more than the total income taxes paid by the 90 million Americans with incomes under $50,000.[18]

The picture looks quite different when it comes to payroll taxes. Unlike income taxes, payroll taxes are not progressive; the same percentage is removed from every employee's check, and all employees must pay the tax, no matter how little they earn. The payroll tax also applies to employers, who must pay the federal government an amount equal to every employee's contribution. Like income taxes, payroll taxes started at low rates: In 1965, the rate was 3.625 percent and was applied only to the first $4,800 of income, making the highest payroll tax bill $174.[19] (Taking into account inflation, $174 in 1965 was equivalent to $1,215 in 2008.) Over time, however, rates increased. In 2008, the payroll tax rate for employees was 7.65 percent, which is split 6.20 percent for Social Security and 1.45 percent for Medicare. (Self-employed workers must pay the employer's share as well, thus doubling their payroll tax rate to 15.3 percent.) The Social Security portion of the tax applied to all wages up to a total of $102,000. As part of President Clinton's budget package in 1993, all wages were made subject to the Medicare portion of the payroll tax starting in 1994. Thus, a college professor earning $102,000 paid the same amount of money in Social Security tax in 2008 ($6,324) as multibillionaire Bill Gates. However, Mr. Gates paid more for the Medicare portion of the payroll tax because all of his income from wages—although not income from other sources—was subject to it. Because people earning above the payroll tax limit for Social Security spend a smaller percentage of their income on payroll taxes than people earning below the limit, the payroll tax is considered a **regressive tax**. Indeed, taxpayers earning more than $1 million pay 1.8 percent of all payroll taxes, whereas taxpayers earning less than $20,000 pay 4.7 percent.[20]

regressive tax
A tax system in which those with high incomes pay a lower percentage of their income in taxes than those with low incomes.

The federal government's reliance on individual Americans for most of its revenue has tremendous political ramifications. People know that the federal government takes a big bite out of their wages. Although Americans know what their total income tax bill is each year, most fail to appreciate how much they pay in payroll taxes. Americans are not generally asked to file annual returns on their payroll taxes, and the employer's matching contribution is money the employee never sees. Thus, although most Americans are correct to think that they pay more taxes to the federal government than they did in the past, they probably do not realize that payroll taxes are the source of the increased pain. Indeed, more than 86 percent of households with wage earners currently pay more in payroll taxes (counting their employer's contribution) than in income taxes.[21] Americans, however, shoulder a smaller tax burden than people in most other industrialized democracies (see Figure 16–4).

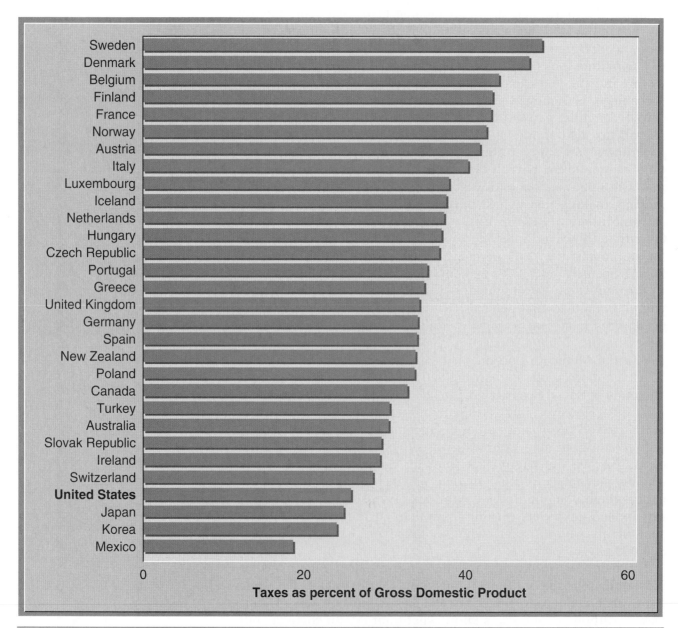

Figure 16–4   Comparing Tax Burdens: Tax Revenue as Percentage of Gross Domestic Product, 2004. Overall, Americans pay less in taxes than citizens in most other industrialized countries.

Source: *OECD, "Tax revenues on the rise in many OECD countries, OECD report shows," November 2006, Table A. www.oecd.org/dataoecd/8/4/37504406.pdf*

16-3 WHERE DOES GOVERNMENT SPENDING GO?

As we mentioned previously, the level of federal spending has grown dramatically since the mid-twentieth century. Whereas the federal government spent less than $10 billion in 1940, it spent more than $3.1 trillion dollars—that is, more than $3,107 billion, or more than 310 times as much—in 2009. The growth in federal spending has been accompanied by major changes in what the government spends money on. Today an overwhelming percentage of the federal budget goes to direct payments to individuals, to payments on the national debt, and to the military. The tasks we normally associate with the federal government—drug enforcement, air traffic control, national parks, medical research, and so forth—consume only a small portion of the budget.

16-3a The Changing Nature of Government Spending

One area where the changes in federal spending show up is defense. As Figure 16–5 shows, in 1940, the federal government spent less than 20 percent of its budget on defense. With the onset of the Cold War, however, spending priorities changed. Defense spending took a growing chunk of the federal budget in the 1950s and claimed roughly half of federal spending in 1960. In the four decades since then, however, the share of the budget devoted to defense has declined, so much so that in 2009, defense spending as a percentage of the budget was only slightly higher than in 1940. Of course, since 1940, the absolute level of defense spending has grown enormously (as is true for every category of federal spending). As Figure 16–5 shows, however, even with increased spending on defense early in the Reagan administration and during President George W. Bush's first term, growth in defense spending has lagged behind increased spending for other components of the federal budget.

Between 1940 and 1980, interest payments on the national debt were remarkably stable as a percentage of the national budget, which suggests that the debt was not growing more rapidly than either the population or the national economy. In the 1980s, however, the percentage of the budget devoted to interest payments nearly doubled, rising to almost 15 percent by 1990. To put that growth in perspective, interest payments in 1990 were twenty-three times the size of the *entire national budget* in 1940. By 2009, interest payments as a percentage of the budget had declined to the levels seen around 1980.

Although the past six decades have seen changes in the share of the federal budget devoted to defense and interest payments, the most dramatic spending shifts have been in two other categories: direct payments to individuals and all other spending. In 1940, shortly after Franklin Roosevelt and Congress established Social Security and several other social programs, payments to individuals

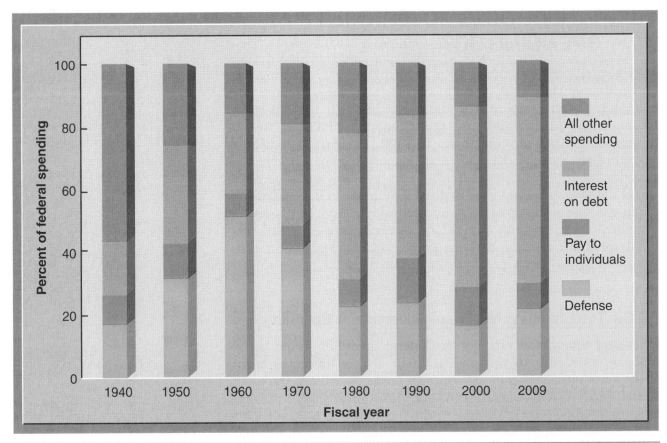

Figure 16–5   Percent of Federal Spending by Type, 1940–2009. Payments to individuals are a bigger part of federal government spending now than they were sixty-seven years ago, whereas defense spending takes roughly the same share.

Source: *Data from Office of Management and Budget,* The Budget for Fiscal Year 2009, *Historical Tables, 119–126. www.whitehouse.gov/omb/budget/ fy2009/pdf/hist.pdf*

consumed less than 20 percent of the budget. By 2009, that number had increased to 60 percent. In contrast, in 1940, roughly 55 percent of all federal dollars went to the services we associate with government: building roads, running parks, fighting crime, and so forth. However, by 2009, spending on all those programs constituted 10 percent of federal spending.

16-3b The Growth of Entitlement Programs

Figure 16–6 shows that the most rapidly growing segment of the federal budget is spending on human resources, mostly in the form of direct payments to individuals. Most of these benefits are paid through **entitlement programs**. The name comes from the fact that people who meet the program's eligibility requirements are legally entitled to its benefits. For example, in 2008 any person living on his or her own who earned less $1,107 a month and who had less than $2,000 in liquid assets, such as a bank account, was eligible to receive food stamps. Such a person would receive the food stamps even if the federal government had not budgeted enough money for the program.

entitlement programs

Programs, created by legislation, that require the government to pay a benefit directly to any individual who meets the eligibility requirements the law establishes.

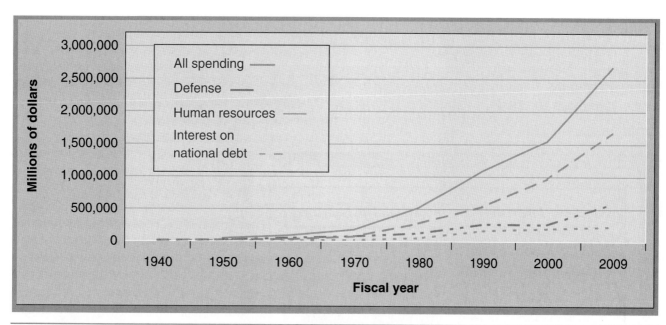

Figure 16-6 Changing Federal Spending, 1940–2009. Although all spending has increased over time, money going to human resources has increased much faster than that allotted to defense or to paying interest on the national debt.

Source: *Data from Office of Management and Budget,* The Budget for Fiscal Year 2009, *Historical Tables, 47–55. www.whitehouse.gov/omb/budget/fy2009/pdf/hist.pdf*

Social Security

The largest entitlement program by far is Social Security, which is actually two separate programs—the Old Age and Survivors Insurance program created in 1935 and the Disability Insurance program created in 1956. Social Security paid more than $613 billion in 2008 to some 50 million Americans. As we previously discussed, a payroll tax finances Social Security.

The money each recipient receives from Social Security is determined by a formula that takes into account that person's lifetime earnings. Since 1972, federal law has required that Social Security benefits be tied (or indexed) to the rate of inflation as measured by the Consumer Price Index-W (see Box 16–1). This means that when the cost of living rises, Social Security benefits rise, too. In 2008, for example, the annual **cost-of-living adjustment (COLA)** raised the monthly benefit 2.3 percent from the previous year, to an average of $1,079. For members of Congress, the law mandating COLAs was politically irresistible because it was popular with senior citizens who wanted their benefits protected from the ravages of inflation.[22] Social Security benefits also enjoy a partial exemption from income taxes, although President Clinton's first budget reduced the exemptions. In 2008, single individuals earning more than $34,000 annually and married couples earning more than $44,000 paid income taxes on 85 percent of their Social Security benefits. For these people, the other 15 percent of their Social Security income was exempt from taxes. (Individuals making between $25,000 and $34,000 and married couples making between $32,000 and $44,000 pay taxes on 50 percent of their

cost-of-living adjustment (COLA)
An increase in Social Security or other benefits designed to keep pace with inflation.

POINT OF ORDER

Box 16–1　Measuring Inflation and Its Consequences for the Budget

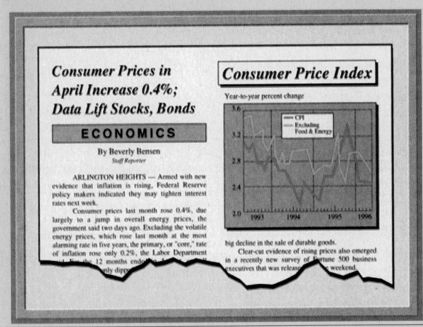

The federal government uses the Consumer Price Index (CPI) to adjust federal benefits such as Social Security to reflect changes in the cost of living. (Technically, the federal government ties the cost-of-living adjustment (COLA) for Social Security to the Consumer Price Index for Urban Wage Earners and Clerical Workers (CPI-W), which provides slightly more generous increases than the more widely reported measure covering all urban consumers (CPI-U). Switching the COLA to the CPI-U from the CPI-W is one proposal being floated to save the Social Security system billions of dollars over the next several decades.)

Each month, the Bureau of Labor Statistics publishes the Consumer Price Index (CPI)—a measure of inflation, or how much the cost of goods and services has increased. Few statistics are followed as closely as the CPI. For example, investors use the index to judge whether inflation is becoming a serious threat, and they adjust their behavior accordingly. The CPI also has a tremendous impact on the federal budget. Many federal benefits (most notably Social Security, Food Stamps, and federal and military pensions) as well as income tax brackets are indexed (or tied) to changes in the cost of living. Thus, when the Bureau of Labor Statistics reports that the CPI has gone up over the past year, the federal government must pay beneficiaries of Social

Security and other programs more benefits (which increases government spending), and it must move the upper limit of each tax bracket higher (which costs the government revenue). Because the CPI affects the federal budget in such a fundamental way, Congress and the president have begun to consider whether the rules used to determine the CPI should be rewritten.

The Bureau of Labor Statistics developed the CPI during World War I to figure cost-of-living adjustments for shipyard workers. A national CPI has been published regularly since 1921. Over the years, the Bureau has tinkered with its method for determining the CPI, but in general, its basic approach has remained the same: It tries to measure how the price of a

fixed "market basket" of goods and services an urban wage earner might purchase has changed overtime. Currently, the CPI "is based on prices of food, clothing, shelter, fuels, transportation fares, charges for doctors' and dentists' services, drugs, etc., purchased for day-to-day living." The Bureau collects prices on a monthly and bimonthly basis from eighty-seven areas around the country, sending out 400 data collectors who gather prices on 80,000 items and rents on 5,000 housing units. The Bureau then takes the data it collects, weights the various prices to reflect their importance in a typical consumer's budget, and averages them across the regions sampled.

Economists and statisticians have argued for many years about whether the CPI measures the inflation rate accurately. In the 1990s, a consensus emerged that the CPI overstated the actual inflation rate, but the experts disagreed over how much. For example, in the mid-1990s the Congressional Budget Office (CBO) suggested that the CPI exaggerated the actual inflation rate by 0.2 to 0.8 percent per year; Alan Greenspan, the chair of the Federal Reserve, argued that it exaggerated the actual inflation rate by 0.5 to 1.5 percent per year; and a blue-ribbon panel of economists that Congress commissioned to evaluate the CPI concluded that it exaggerated the actual inflation rate by 0.7 to 2 percent per year.

Experts agreed on why the CPI overstated inflation. First, the method used to calculate the CPI failed to take into account substitution effects, which occur when a consumer buys a cheaper generic product rather than its more expensive name-brand competitor, or switches to chicken when steak gets too expensive. Second, in the 1970s and 1980s shopping patterns in the United States changed. Many Americans switched from shopping in department stores (which the Bureau of Labor Statistics used in calculating the CPI) to shopping in lower-cost discount stores. Third, the method used to calculate the CPI failed

POINT OF ORDER (continued)

to incorporate new products into the market basket in a timely fashion. Fourth, the method used to calculate the CPI failed to capture improvements in product quality, such as the increasing capabilities of personal computers.

Does it matter if the CPI overstates the actual inflation rate? When it comes to the federal budget, the answer is yes. To see why, consider what would happen if the annual CPI between 1996 and 2005 had been 2 percent rather than 3 percent. Over that ten-year period, a 1 percentage point reduction per year would have saved the federal government a total of $634 billion! Moreover, because the method used to calculate the CPI exaggerated the actual inflation rate, "the overindexing [would] itself become the fourth-largest spending program in the budget by 2005," overtaking all other expenditures except Social Security, health care, and national defense. In short, a new and more accurate measure of the actual inflation rate would save the federal government money and help balance the federal budget.

Although experts agreed that the rules used to calculate the CPI needed to be changed, doing so was politically difficult. To see why, consider Social Security benefits. Take, for example, a married couple on Social Security who receives $14,160 in benefits. If the CPI were 3 percent per year for the next five years, their Social Security benefits—indexed to the CPI—would rise to $16,416. In contrast, if the CPI were to rise 2 percent per year over those same five years, the same married couple would end up receiving $15,635, or almost $800 less.

As you can see, correcting the rules used to calculate the CPI so that it did not overstate the actual inflation rate meant that people who received government benefits would receive less than they would under the existing method. And because many of these beneficiaries were the elderly—who, as we have noted before, are among the Americans most likely to vote—politicians approached the prospect of tinkering with the CPI with great trepidation.

In 1995, congressional Republicans embraced a proposal to revise the rules used to calculate the CPI as part of their plan to achieve a balanced federal budget. In doing so, however, they opted for a proposal to reduce the CPI by 0.2 percent, which is far smaller than the reduction most economists advocated. President Bill Clinton indicated that he was sympathetic to such a reduction, but he did not formally endorse it.

By 1996, neither Congress nor the president had agreed on legislation requiring the Bureau of Labor Statistics to change the rules it uses to calculate the CPI. Nonetheless, the Bureau announced some changes in the way it calculated the CPI starting in 1997. These revisions cut the reported inflation rate by between 0.1 percent and 0.3 percent, which is projected to save some $30 billion over seven years. In 1998, the Bureau of Labor Statistics substantially revised the CPI measure, a procedure it undertakes roughly every ten years. The changes were expected to further reduce inflation by another 0.2 percent.

Starting in 2000, the Bureau began calculating increases in prices using an approach that allowed for product

substitutions. (The idea behind product substitution is that when, for example, the price of beef increases, consumers will buy chicken instead.) This substitution measure lowers the calculated inflation rate. If this measure were tied to government programs instead of the current CPI measure, it would decrease Social Security cost of living adjustments by an estimated $70 billion over the next decade, while also raising income tax revenues (because of a link to tax brackets) by $83 billion over the same time span. Congress has expressed little interest in mandating a change in how the government measures inflation.

The Bureau continues to tinker with the measure, as it attempts to better capture the dynamics of American economic life. And, as always, the alterations it makes will have implications for the budget.

Sources: Timothy Aeppel, "An Inflation Debate Brews Over Intangibles at the Mall," *Wall Street Journal*, May 9, 2005; Bureau of Labor Statistics, "Overview of the 1998 Revision of the Consumer Price Index," Bureau of Labor Statistics, Testimony of Katharine G. Abraham, Commissioner of Labor Statistics, before the Subcommittee on Human Resources House Committee on Government Reform and Oversight, April 29, 1998; Bureau of Labor Statistics, "Understanding the Consumer Price Index: Answers to Some Questions," August 2004 www.bls.gov/cpi/cpifaq.pdf; David Fischer, "Conquering Inflation," *U.S. News and World Report*, (November 20, 1995): 77–79; Robert D. Hershey, Jr., "Panel Sees a Corrected Price Index as Deficit-Cutter," *New York Times*, September 15, 1995; Robert J. Samuelson, "What's in a Number?" *Newsweek* (October 23, 1995): 52; Herbert Stein, "The Consumer Price Index: Servant or Master?" *Wall Street Journal*, November 1, 1995; U.S. Bureau of the Census, *Statistical Abstract of the United States, 2000*, 120th ed. (Washington, D.C.: U.S. Bureau of the Census, 2000), 483–84; Jonathan Weisman, "Measuring the Economy May Not Be as Simple as 1, 2, 3," *Washington Post*, August 29, 2005; and David Wessel, "Why the CPI Fix Looks So Likely," *Wall Street Journal*, December 11, 1995.

Social Security benefits.) Less than a third of Social Security recipients pay any income tax on their benefits.[23]

Despite the size and importance of Social Security, most Americans do not understand how it works. For example, only 26 percent of the public knows that Social Security is one of the two most expensive items in the federal budget.[24] And 23 percent mistakenly think the money they pay (or paid) in Social Security taxes is set aside in a personal account for their retirement.[25] It is not. "Social Security, in fact, has always been an inter-generational chain letter. Throughout the program's history, today's workers have been paying the benefits for today's recipients."[26] (People today are better informed on this point than they were a decade ago.)[27]

The fact that Social Security is a pay-as-you-go system, in which current workers pay for the benefits paid to current retirees, is key to understanding both the popularity of Social Security and why many experts believe it must be fundamentally restructured. For the first several decades Social Security was in place, the number of workers far outnumbered the number of retirees. This simple demographic fact meant that for many years, the federal government could pay for Social Security by imposing only a small payroll tax on workers. And this meant, in turn, that Social Security benefits became quite generous relative to each beneficiary's contributions. (Ida May Fuller of Ludlow, Vermont, who received the first monthly Social Security check in 1940, paid only $24.75 in taxes and collected $22,888.92 in benefits, in part because she lived to be 100 years old.)[28] Until recently, retirees received all their Social Security contributions back *with interest* within about four years after retiring—and the average male lives 17 years after age 65 and the average female 20 years.[29] Indeed, to be consistent with life expectancy after retirement when the program was established in the mid-1930s, the current retirement age would have to be increased to age 71 or possibly even as high as age 74.[30]

Any program that asks for little in contributions but provides a lot in benefits is destined to be politically popular. Yet the changing demographics of the United States make it almost impossible to sustain the generosity of Social Security. As Chapter 3 discussed, the American population is aging. Whereas in 1950 there were 16.5 workers paying into Social Security for every retiree, in 2008, there were only 3.3, and experts predict that by 2035, there will be 2.1.[31] To make up for this shortfall, the federal government has gradually been forced to require workers to pay more in payroll taxes and (to a lesser degree) to accept lower benefits. As a result, many retirees in the near future will take longer to recoup their contributions, and many may end up taking out less than they contributed.[32] One analysis, for example, shows that "While a worker born in 1915 who retired at 65 in 1980 collected $71,390 *more* than he paid into Social Security, a worker born in 1975 can expect to collect $93,486 *less* than she contributed." Another study shows that a single worker born in 1930 with average earnings can expect to get back about 90 percent of the total payroll tax paid, plus interest, while the same kind of worker born in 1950 will end up with just 55 percent.[33] Many experts fear that workers now entering the workforce will be forced to pay high payroll taxes over the course of their careers and will receive relatively few benefits when they retire.[34]

Whatever misconceptions Americans may have about how Social Security works, the program remains extraordinarily popular.[35] In one 2005 survey, for example, 88 percent of respondents said they considered Social Security "very important"; in another 2005 survey, 79 percent said the program's impact on the country over the years had been "good" or "very good."[36] Its popularity explains why elected officials are loath to tamper with it, long referring to Social Security as the "third rail" of American politics: "Touch it and die."[37] Indeed, the political power of the senior citizen lobby helps explain why: In 2000, 34.8 percent of the federal budget went to programs for the elderly, while just 8.4 percent went to programs for children.[38] On a per capita basis, the elderly received $17,688 in benefits from the federal government, whereas children got just $2,106.[39] Political support to reform Social Security is emerging. Polls conducted in 2004 and 2005 found that more than half of Americans do not expect Social Security to have enough money to provide them full benefits. Indeed, 88 percent of people younger than age thirty think they will receive lower benefits or no benefits at all.[40] In 2007, 30 percent of Americans said that Social Security was in crisis, while another 33 percent said it was in serious trouble. Only 5 percent said it was not in any trouble.[41] So most people seem to understand that something needs to be done to maintain the program in the future.

Hoping to capitalize on such sentiments, President George W. Bush made Social Security reform the centerpiece of his second-term agenda. He used his 2005 State of the Union address to present the bare outlines of an ambitious plan to redirect some payroll taxes to what he termed "personal" accounts for workers younger than age fifty-five. The administration then launched a high profile "60 Stops in 60 Days" tour around the country to push the president's approach to reform. Democrats quickly attacked his proposal, calling it a scheme to "privatize" Social Security.[42] Public support for the president's plan evaporated as people came to understand that it would be expensive in the near term—costing between $1 trillion and $2 trillion to cover paying benefits to those retirees and older workers promised them while siphoning payroll taxes to establish personal accounts for younger workers—and it would also fail to solve Social Security's long-term solvency problems. By the fall of 2005, Republican leaders quietly backed away from the president's plan and other efforts to reform the program.[43] No other serious attempts to alter the Social Security program were made during the rest of the Bush administration.

Given the lack of public support for changing Social Security dramatically, elected officials are reluctant to tackle the problems that most informed observers agree confront the program. Unfortunately, little support has coalesced around any reform proposal. As a former member of Congress laments, "All you have to do is open your mouth and you're dead meat...If you say you might have to raise payroll taxes, the no-tax crowd jumps all over you. Say you might have to decrease benefits, and the AARP and the Democrats will kill you."[44] Given these political realities, nothing is apt to be done to reform the program in the near future.

Other Entitlement Programs

Even though Social Security is the largest entitlement program, many other entitlement programs also serve the American public. For example, Medicare served more than 44 million people, at a cost of $432 billion in 2007. Indeed, it is projected that by 2028 the cost of the Medicare program will exceed the cost of the Social Security program. Medicaid, also created in 1965 to help provide medical care for low-income people, cost $192 billion in 2007. An average of more than 26.5 million people used food stamps each month in 2007 at a total cost in excess of $31 billion.[45]

Although Social Security affects far more Americans than most entitlement programs, the others are also extremely popular. Medicare enjoys strong support among the elderly. Entitlement programs also draw political support from groups that benefit indirectly. For example, farmers and food companies support the Food Stamp program because it helps them sell more of their products. Every entitlement program has staunch supporters who resist cutting funding for their favorite program. This makes it difficult to limit entitlement programs and to restrain their growing appetite for federal funds.

16-3c Limiting Entitlement Programs

With the return of chronic budget deficits comes much talk about the need to cut the cost of entitlement programs. With the first baby boomers starting to retire at the end of the current decade, Social Security and Medicare systems are likely to come under increasing strain. Administration officials and members of Congress usually prefer to steer clear of talk about cutting entitlements. The reason is simple: They do not want to take the political heat for trying to reduce benefits.

The difficulty that Congress and the president have in cutting an entitlement program is amplified by their inability to control entitlements through the budgetary process. As we previously noted, federal law stipulates that everyone who meets the eligibility requirements for an entitlement program must receive its benefits. Thus, if unemployment rises, the government must provide unemployment benefits to everyone who qualifies, even if that means spending on unemployment benefits will exceed what was budgeted.

The only way Congress and the president can reduce the cost of an entitlement program is to rewrite the law that established it. They can then tighten eligibility requirements, reduce the benefits provided, or enact some mix of both. Changing the rules governing entitlement programs risks starting a political donnybrook, as President George W. Bush learned in 2005, when he proposed making significant changes to Social Security. Supporters of the program mobilized political support and easily rebuffed the proposed changes.

Because Congress and the president cannot use the budget process to limit entitlements, these programs are often referred to as **nondiscretionary spending**. Interest on the national debt also represents nondiscretionary spending because the government must

nondiscretionary spending
Federal spending on programs such as Social Security that cannot be controlled through the regular budget process.

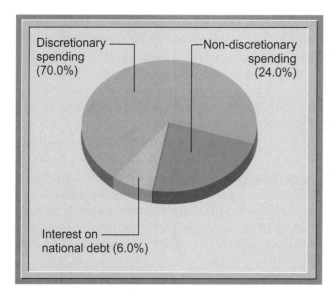

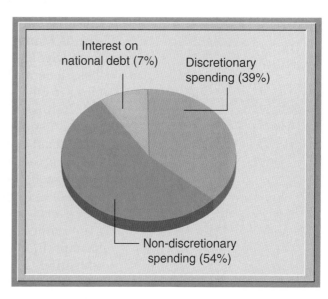

(a) 1962

(b) 2009

Figure 16-7 Discretionary Federal Spending, 1962 and 2009. *A*, Discretionary spending made up more than two-thirds of the federal budget in 1962. *B*, But it decreased to just over one-third of the federal budget in 2007.

Sources: *Data from Harold W. Stanley and Richard G. Niemi*, Vital Statistics on American Politics, 5th ed. *(Washington, D.C.: CQ Press, 1995), 391; and calculated from Congressional Budget Office, "Current Budget Projections," March 3, 2008. www.cbo.gov/budget/budproj.shtml*

make the interest payments. In contrast, expenditures on most other federal programs involve **discretionary spending** that can be controlled through the budgetary process. For example, the president and Congress can use the budgetary process to raise or lower spending on nuclear weapons, cancer research, and foreign aid.

The issue of discretionary spending is crucial because the share of the federal budget that can be controlled through the budgetary process has fallen sharply over the past four decades. As Figure 16-7*A* shows, in 1962, nondiscretionary spending on entitlements and interest payments on the debt consumed 30 percent of the budget, leaving 70 percent for discretionary spending. As Figure 16-7*B* shows, however, in 2009, the figures were reversed. The rising share of the budget devoted to nondiscretionary spending makes it far more difficult to reduce the budget deficit.

16-3d What about Pork?

To this point we have said nothing about government spending on **pork-barrel** projects—the portion of discretionary spending that funds programs, often of dubious value, designed to benefit individual congressional districts. (The term *pork barrel* refers to the nineteenth-century practice of packing salted pork in barrels; the term likens members of Congress to hungry diners reaching in for their share of the goodies.)[46] Critics of the 2008 budget identified a host of pet projects members of Congress championed for their constituencies, among them $49,000 for construction of a National Mule and Packers Museum in Bishop, California; $245,000 for building the Walter Clore Wine and Culinary Center in Prosser,

discretionary spending
Federal spending on programs that can be controlled through the regular budget process.

pork barrel
Legislation that appropriates government money for local projects of questionable value that may ingratiate a legislator with his or her constituents.

Washington; and $188,000 for the Lobster Institute at the University of Maine. Although these and other federal projects might seem frivolous, members of Congress can take credit for directing these federal dollars to their states and districts. Noting the large number of Alaska projects he got funding for in a transportation bill, Rep. Don Young (R-AK) bragged to his state's largest newspaper, "I stuffed [the bill] like a turkey."[47]

In recent years much of the discussion about pork-barrel politics has revolved around congressional earmarks. Definitions of what exactly constitutes an earmark differ, but they all revolve around a member of Congress inserting a provision in an appropriations bill that directs spending to a geographically specific project or program without any review of its merit. By any definition earmarks have proliferated over the last two decades.[48] Earmarks for higher education, for example, have increased significantly, reaching a total of 2,300 projects at 920 institutions, costing $2.25 billion in 2008.[49] These earmarks pay for programs such as a grant to study the Chinese stock market, which was given to the University of Missouri, Kansas City. They also pay for buildings. For example, between 1999 and 2008 the University of Missouri campus in Columbia received $69 million in earmarked funds to pay for campus construction, including $31 million for a Life Sciences Center named for the state's senior U.S. senator.[50]

What portion of the budget goes to pork-barrel projects? It is difficult to know precisely because one person's pork is another's essential government service. Thus, members of Congress vigorously defend their earmarks. For instance, Rep. Howard "Buck" McKeon (R-CA), the member who inserted the earmark for the National Mule and Packers Museum, argued, "One thing we forget is the people in Bishop pay taxes…they have gotten very little back from the federal government."[51] In a similar vein, Senator Ted Stevens (R-AK) told his constituents, "And if I don't earmark these monies for Alaska, your taxes aren't going to go down. The money will simply go to other states for their needs and ours will go unmet…. So I ask you, is it wrong for a village in rural Alaska to want help with providing running water when places like New York City get millions in federal funds for their water projects?"[52]

Perhaps the most prolific provider of pork over the years has been Senator Robert Byrd (D-WV). Senator Byrd considers his congressional activities "West Virginia's billion-dollar industry." By one account, he channeled more than $2.95 billion in federal money into his home state between 1991 and 2006.[53] At his behest, West Virginia has become home to a new Federal Bureau of Investigation Identification Center, the Treasury Department's Bureau of Public Debt, an Internal Revenue Service processing center, and a host of other public facilities. His justification of these endeavors to the voters back home echo those of his longtime colleague, Senator Stevens: "You, the federal taxpayers of this country, have invested $7 billion—that's billion with a B—for the mass transit system in Washington. Now that's pork. What I'm doing is spreading good seed that will bear fruit a hundredfold [in West Virginia]. Prosperity flows along concrete rivers."[54]

Even allowing for differences in definitions, earmarks and pork-barrel projects constitute a small part of federal spending. By one accounting, pork-barrel spending totaled $17.2 billion, or about 0.5 percent, of the federal budget in 2008.[55] A much bigger expense to the federal treasury is subsidies and tax breaks to corporations, or what critics call **corporate welfare**. Each year, the federal government provides money to corporations or agrees to reduce their taxes, ostensibly for the purpose of helping them remain competitive in the marketplace but sometimes only because they are politically well connected. For example, the Agricultural Marketing Service in the Department of Agriculture "funds the promotion of agricultural products such as cotton, various fruits and vegetables, eggs, and beef"; the Coal Research Initiative in the Department of Energy "funds joint public-private demonstration projects designed to assist private industry in developing coal that burns in a more environmentally friendly way"; and the Commercial Space Transportation program in the Department of Transportation is designed to "encourage private space launches and development of launch vehicles with taxpayer money."[56]

Just how much does corporate welfare—or what supporters prefer to call corporate support—cost the government each year? The exact number is hotly disputed. Estimates run from $60 billion to $175 billion.[57] Despite the different estimates, most everyone agrees that corporate subsidies and tax breaks cost the federal government far more money than pork-barrel projects such as the National Mule and Packers Museum.

Whatever the exact cost of corporate subsidies and tax breaks, college students might fairly ask why the federal government is spending millions to help farmers and private companies turn a profit when it is not fully funding Pell Grants. Yet, as we just saw with pork-barrel projects, what constitutes corporate welfare lies in the eye of the beholder. (This is why estimates of what the government spends on corporate welfare vary so widely.) The most strident critics of corporate welfare believe that any corporate subsidy or tax break is by definition wasteful because they believe the marketplace and not the government should determine all business decisions. In contrast, proponents of corporate subsidies and tax breaks argue that they stimulate economic growth and provide jobs for thousands of Americans. For instance, the timber industry argues that without the roughly $30 million the federal government provides each year to build roads in national forests, it would be too expensive in many parts of the country to log. Thus, if timber subsidies were reduced, timber companies would have to lay off workers, and these workers would ultimately have to turn to the government for unemployment and other benefits. (Whether such claims are true tend to be a matter of debate.)

The debate over the need for corporate subsidies and tax breaks may intensify in coming years for the simple reason that they

corporate welfare
Government subsidies or tax breaks of questionable value to private corporations.

represent a sizable government expense. Even so, corporate welfare is not likely to become a partisan issue—Democrats and Republicans take both sides of the debate. For instance, in 2008, members of both parties in Congress overrode President Bush's veto of the farm bill, which was loaded with millions of dollars in corporate welfare. That same year Democrats and Republicans alike voted to suspend the introduction of a competitive bidding process to pay for medical equipment under Medicare. Consequently, the federal government continued to pay higher than market prices for medical equipment, to the benefit of only the equipment manufacturers.[58] In his first budget plan, George W. Bush proposed to eliminate some programs identified as corporate welfare, but he met with little success. By his last year in office, his proposals to eliminate corporate welfare in the form of the Export-Import Bank and the Overseas Private Investment Corporation had gained almost no support in Congress.

16-4 WHO IS RESPONSIBLE FOR THE BUDGET?

Who is responsible for deciding how much the federal government spends and what it spends its money on? Both Congress and the president clearly play a role. The American public is responsible, too. When Congress and the president set the budget, they are responding to the will of the public. And the public is of two minds, on the one hand calling for more government services, and on the other hand calling for lower taxes. These contradictory demands are a recipe for budget problems.

16-4a Congress and the President

Since 1921, presidents have been charged with submitting a single budget to Congress. In recent years, Congress has stayed within the overall spending total the president has established.[59] In the thirty-one years between 1968 and 1998, for example, Congress appropriated less money than the president requested in twenty-five years and more money than the president requested in only six years.[60] From 1981 until 1998, no president came close to submitting a balanced budget. With the return of deficits, President George W. Bush again failed to propose balanced budgets.

The failure of Presidents Ronald Reagan, George H. W. Bush, Bill Clinton (except from 1998 to 2001), and George W. Bush to submit a balanced budget might make it seem that the president was to blame for America's chronic budget deficits. That oversimplifies the case. When presidents decide how much money to request, they often anticipate the preferences of Congress. For example, Reagan asked for more domestic spending than he would have preferred because he knew if he asked for less, Congress would have rejected his proposed budget and substituted a (higher) one of its own. And on occasion, Congress does ignore the president's preferences on how much the government should spend. Congress sometimes even underfunds programs that by law must be fully funded (by intentionally underestimating expected costs) and gives the money instead to other programs its members favor. Such tactics force the president to return to Capitol Hill to ask for a supplemental appropriation that will fund the required program in full.[61]

In sum, both the president and members of Congress were responsible for the persistence of budget deficits, and they are responsible for deciding what to do with any budget surplus. Although it is true that only Congress can appropriate federal monies, it is also true that a presidential veto usually can keep an appropriations bill from becoming law.

16-4b The American Public

Although the president and members of Congress are responsible for drawing up the federal budget, they do not operate in a vacuum. When they make budgetary decisions, they are usually doing what elected officials are supposed to do in a democracy—responding to the wishes of the public.

When the federal government ran large deficits in the early 1990s, public opinion surveys consistently showed that 70 to 85 percent of the American public wanted the federal budget balanced. When asked how the government should balance the budget, more than 80 percent of Americans opted for cutting spending, while fewer than 10 percent favored raising taxes. However, when asked which government programs should be cut, most Americans failed to identify programs they would be willing to trim. After the 1994 election that gave the Republicans control of both houses of Congress, 64 percent of Americans thought federal spending on education should increase; only 6 percent thought it should decrease. Majorities also thought the federal government should spend more to fight crime, provide health care, take care of the homeless, and conduct acquired immune deficiency syndrome (AIDS) research. Only defense spending aroused much support for a spending cut, and only 23 percent took that position. Otherwise, people either wanted to spend more or to keep funding at current levels for government programs.[62]

When the federal government ran surpluses at the end of the 1990s, the public had different sorts of questions to consider. Most revolved around what to do with the surplus. When given the choice, more Americans preferred to use it to strengthen Social Security, Medicare, and educational programs than to use it for tax cuts, as President Bush proposed in 2001 or to pay down the national debt as the Democrats proposed. Increases in spending on defense or foreign aid had relatively little support. When asked to choose between tax cuts and paying down the debt, more Americans opted for the former than for the latter. Once again, the American public sent confusing signals.

With the return of deficits in the current decade, confusion still reigns. In a 2006 survey, 55 percent of Americans said balancing the federal budget was a top priority, though when given three options to reduce the budget deficit—cutting domestic spending, cutting military spending, or raising taxes—a majority was opposed to each choice.[63] Along the same lines, in a 2008 poll a majority said they wanted a smaller government with fewer services, but at the same time 66 percent favored providing health care for all Americans rather than holding down taxes if that meant that more people would go without any coverage.[64]

Part of the explanation for the public's seemingly contradictory opinions is that most people do not have a good grasp of the federal budget. In a survey conducted in 1994, for example, 61 percent of people supported cutting entitlement programs to help eliminate the deficit. In that same survey, 66 percent opposed cuts in "programs such as Social Security, Medicare, Medicaid and farm subsidies," which are, of course, the biggest entitlement programs.[65] Similarly, in a poll taken in 2002, some 48 percent thought the United States spends too much on foreign aid; only 14 percent thought too little was being spent. Respondents were then asked what percentage of the budget they thought foreign aid constituted and what the appropriate level of spending should be. The median response on the first question was 25 percent; the median answer on the second was 10 percent. In reality, foreign aid constitutes less than 1 percent of the federal budget.[66] (Roughly 50 percent of the public mistakenly thinks foreign aid is one of the two largest components of the budget.)[67] Eliminating all foreign aid would make only a trivial dent in an annual budget of $3.1 trillion.

The public's lack of knowledge about the particulars of federal spending extends to the tax code as well. Although Americans generally oppose tax increases, they often fail to recognize how they benefit from exemptions in the tax code. Figure 16–8 shows the six tax breaks for individuals that cost the federal treasury the most in terms of lost revenue in 2009. The federal government lost the most money, some $169 billion, by not taxing employer-paid health benefits. The second most costly tax break is exempting pension contributions and their accrued interest from taxes, costing the government $122 billion. No taxes are levied on the interest homeowners pay on their mortgages, which cost the federal treasury another $101 billion. Most of these tax breaks advantage the wealthiest Americans. About 79 percent of the benefits of the home mortgage deduction, for example, go to the top 20 percent of income earners.[68] If the federal government eliminated the three biggest tax breaks, the savings would cover the cost of paying the interest on the national debt. The tax breaks listed in Figure 16–8 and many smaller ones also enjoy great public support, however. Elected officials who try to repeal these tax breaks risk defeat in the next election.

The public's attitudes toward spending and taxes mean that individual members of Congress have few political incentives to keep the budget in balance or to protect surpluses. Constituents want the budget balanced, but not if a balanced budget means

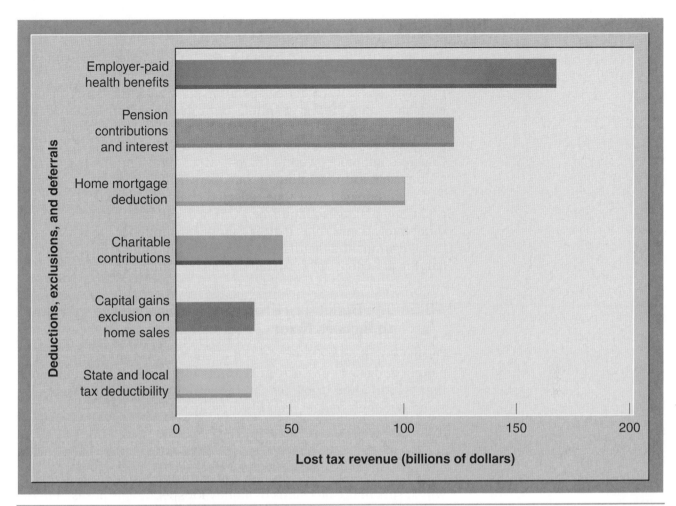

Figure 16-8   Top Tax Breaks, 2009. By giving tax breaks, the federal government gives up billions of dollars of revenue.

Source: *Computed by authors from Office of Management and Budget,* Budget of the United States Fiscal Year 2009, Analytical Perspectives, 288–91. www.whitehouse.gov/omb/budget/fy2009/apers.html

raising their taxes or cutting programs they like. As one anonymous member of Congress commented, "I think most of us are frustrated with the cynicism we find out there…It's frustrating to…have to face an angry mob of people who demand that the budget deficit and their taxes be reduced but who won't give up their favorite programs."[69] Members respond to the public's wishes by protecting the interests of their constituents. In 2003, for example, Rep. Jim Nussle (R-IA), confessed, "Even though I am the Budget Committee chairman, I am much more concerned about my constituents' family budgets and their small business budgets and their farm budgets than the federal budget."[70] The battle cry on Capitol Hill is, in the folksy words of Russell Long, a senator from Louisiana in the mid-twentieth century: "don't cut you and don't cut me, cut that fellow behind the tree." In this sense, what one member blasts as pork, another defends as good and necessary. Because no one agrees on whose programs should be cut, members find it easiest simply to provide the goods their constituents want and to let future generations decide how to pay for the national debt.

16-5 THE BUDGETARY PROCESS

The incentive the president and members of Congress have to provide voters with benefits and to protect them from taxes creates an inherent bias toward deficit spending. One way to control the government's appetite for spending is to design a budgetary process that imposes fiscal discipline on the president and members of Congress. As budget deficits grew in the 1970s, 1980s, and 1990s, Congress adopted several different procedural reforms that sought to impose fiscal discipline on members. Differences in the reforms that were pursued over time reflected changing notions of what the government's goals should be.[71] As we will see, however, procedural reforms and rule changes cannot substitute for the will to control government spending, although the amount of time Congress and the president devote to the subject has grown enormously.

16-5a The Budgetary Process from George Washington to Richard Nixon

During the nineteenth century, the federal government followed a simple budgetary process, in keeping with the low level of spending.[72] Individual agencies in the executive branch essentially submitted their budget requests directly to Congress, without soliciting the president's input. Congress at first appropriated funds in lump sums, giving agencies discretion in spending the money. When members of Congress grew distrustful of the executive branch, however, they shifted more toward *line-item budgeting,* which specifies exact sums of money for specific purposes.

As the budget grew in response to the country's growth, members of Congress changed the budgetary process to cope with their increased workload. Until the mid-1860s, the House Ways and Means Committee and the Senate Finance Committee handled both tax and appropriations bills. The growth of the budget forced both the House and the Senate to create Appropriations committees. This gave power over government revenues to one group of legislators (Ways and Means in the House and Finance in the Senate) and control over spending to a different group (the Appropriations committees in each chamber).

Although separating decisions about revenues from decisions about spending created the potential for budgetary confusion, the process worked relatively well throughout the rest of the nineteenth century. During World War I, however, the federal government ran large deficits, raising the national debt from $1 billion to $25 billion in less than three years. One response to the government's sudden surge of red ink was the **Budget and Accounting Act of 1921.** This act authorized presidents to coordinate the spending proposals of government agencies with their own priorities and to submit a single budget to Congress. To assist the president in dealing with the budget, Congress created the Bureau of the Budget (BOB). The BOB initially was part of the Treasury Department, but it moved into the newly created Executive Office of the President in 1939. President Nixon reorganized and renamed the agency the

Budget and Accounting Act of 1921
An act of Congress that created the Bureau of the Budget and allowed the president to review and coordinate the spending proposals of federal agencies and departments.

Office of Management and Budget (OMB) in 1970, but Congress explicitly retained the right to review and change the president's budget.

The budget process remained essentially unchanged from 1921 until 1974. The president submitted a budget and Congress considered it—a process often described as "the president proposes and Congress disposes." Although no formal mechanism reconciled revenue and spending, the Appropriations committees acted as the guardians of the federal treasury.[73] As one House Appropriations Committee chair observed, "You may think my business is to make appropriations, but it is not. It is to prevent their being made."[74] The norm in the House Appropriations Committee was to cut budget requests. This loosely coordinated budget process, based on mostly unwritten rules, tended to produce balanced budgets, in large part because the members of the House Appropriations Committee played the role of budgetary watchdogs.

The House Appropriations Committee's power to cut the budget, however, dissipated over time. This happened in part because of the rise in entitlement programs, which the House and Senate Appropriations committees do not control. Fundamentally, the House Appropriations Committee lost power because House members no longer wanted it to make difficult choices. As pressures for increased spending mounted, the House Appropriations Committee no longer had the power to guard the budget because it did not have the support it needed from the rest of the House to keep spending in line with revenues.[75]

16-5b Budgetary Reform in the 1970s

As we noted previously, budget deficits began to become the norm rather than the exception for government spending in the mid-1960s. When the deficit suddenly escalated in the early 1970s, rising from $8.6 billion in 1970 to $26.4 billion in 1972, many observers blamed the budgetary process. They argued that the process was too fragmented to produce a coherent, balanced budget.[76] At the same time, many members of Congress worried that the enormous size of the budget gave the president too much power. They argued that the president had a terrific informational advantage because of the OMB's expertise. Richard Nixon's behavior during his first years as president reinforced fears that the White House had too much power. The conservative Nixon impounded (refused to spend) funds a more liberal Congress appropriated; sometimes members of Congress learned about the impoundment of funds only by reading the newspaper.

Concerns over budget deficits and presidential impoundments combined to produce a significant reform of the budget process: the **Congressional Budget and Impoundment Control Act of 1974**. The Budget Act curtailed the president's ability to impound appropriated funds, and it created the **Congressional Budget Office (CBO)** to give Congress the same level of expertise that the OMB gave the president. The main purpose of the Budget Act was to impose collective responsibility on members of Congress themselves. Because the Ways and Means, Finance, and Appropriations

Office of Management and Budget (OMB)
The agency in charge of assisting the president in reviewing and coordinating budget requests to Congress from federal agencies and departments. Formerly the Bureau of the Budget.

Congressional Budget and Impoundment Control Act of 1974
An act of Congress that created the new budget process and the Congressional Budget Office and that curtailed the president's power to impound funds.

Congressional Budget Office (CBO)
A nonpartisan congressional agency in charge of assisting Congress in reviewing and coordinating budget requests to Congress.

committees had failed to reconcile revenue and spending, the Budget Act also established budget committees in both the House and Senate. These new committees were responsible for shepherding two budget resolutions, one preliminary and the other final, through Congress each year. The purpose of the budget resolutions was to set a limit on total government spending and then to make sure that the sum of the various spending bills did not exceed that limit. Figure 16–9 outlines the timetable that the Budget Act created for the budgetary process.

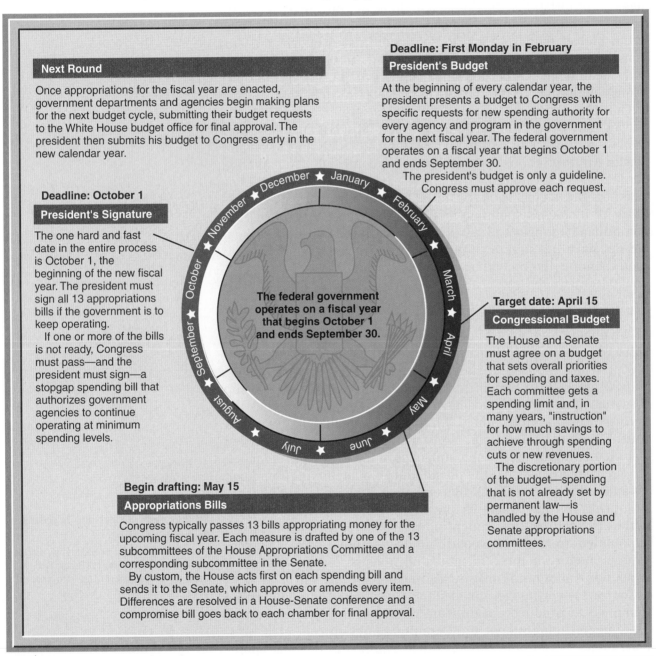

Next Round

Once appropriations for the fiscal year are enacted, government departments and agencies begin making plans for the next budget cycle, submitting their budget requests to the White House budget office for final approval. The president then submits his budget to Congress early in the new calendar year.

Deadline: First Monday in February
President's Budget

At the beginning of every calendar year, the president presents a budget to Congress with specific requests for new spending authority for every agency and program in the government for the next fiscal year. The federal government operates on a fiscal year that begins October 1 and ends September 30.

The president's budget is only a guideline. Congress must approve each request.

Deadline: October 1
President's Signature

The one hard and fast date in the entire process is October 1, the beginning of the new fiscal year. The president must sign all 13 appropriations bills if the government is to keep operating.

If one or more of the bills is not ready, Congress must pass—and the president must sign—a stopgap spending bill that authorizes government agencies to continue operating at minimum spending levels.

The federal government operates on a fiscal year that begins October 1 and ends September 30.

Target date: April 15
Congressional Budget

The House and Senate must agree on a budget that sets overall priorities for spending and taxes. Each committee gets a spending limit and, in many years, "instruction" for how much savings to achieve through spending cuts or new revenues.

The discretionary portion of the budget—spending that is not already set by permanent law—is handled by the House and Senate appropriations committees.

Begin drafting: May 15
Appropriations Bills

Congress typically passes 13 bills appropriating money for the upcoming fiscal year. Each measure is drafted by one of the 13 subcommittees of the House Appropriations Committee and a corresponding subcommittee in the Senate.

By custom, the House acts first on each spending bill and sends it to the Senate, which approves or amends every item. Differences are resolved in a House-Senate conference and a compromise bill goes back to each chamber for final approval.

Figure 16–9 The Budget Cycle. The basic budget cycle the federal government currently uses begins when the president submits a budget to Congress and ends when all thirteen appropriation bills are signed into law.

Source: Congressional Quarterly. Copyright © 1993 by Congressional Quarterly, Inc. Reproduced with permission of Congressional Quarterly, Inc. via Copyright Clearance Center.

A procedure that requires Congress to reconcile individual spending bills with an overall spending target sounds eminently sensible. In practice, however, the Budget Act of 1974 failed to work. Only three times between 1977 and 2007, for example, did Congress met the October 1 deadline the Budget Act established for assembling all pieces of the budget, and it has often had to resort to stop-gap measures called **continuing resolutions** to keep the government running.[77] Moreover, in 1983 Congress gave up entirely on trying to pass a second budget resolution.

Even more significant is the failure of the budget resolutions to cap spending. During the early 1980s, individual appropriations bills were not trimmed to meet the spending limits contained in the second resolution. Instead, Congress increased the spending limit to match whatever spending decisions it had adopted. Moreover, both spending resolutions were suspect because they usually contained favorable and unrealistic forecasts about the health of the economy.[78] Such "rosy scenarios" allowed members of Congress (and presidents as well) to inflate expected revenue and underestimate spending. The final failing of the reforms was the absence of any penalty if appropriations exceeded the spending limits adopted in the first resolution. With no mechanism for capturing excess spending, each succeeding deficit was tacked on to the national debt, with the results we have discussed.[79]

The failure of the Budget Act shows that changing the rules of the budgetary process will not work when no agreement exists in Washington on how to control government spending. Budget deficits grew despite the Budget Act not because of flaws in the legislation, but because Congress and the president disagreed over budgetary priorities. President Reagan, for instance, insisted on cutting domestic programs and opposed tax increases, while the Democratic majority on Capitol Hill favored protecting domestic programs and urged tax increases. When Reagan refused to raise taxes and Congress refused to cut domestic spending, budget deficits were inevitable, regardless of the provisions of the Budget Act.

continuing resolutions
Temporary laws Congress passes to keep the government running when Congress misses the deadline for passing the budget.

16-5c Budgetary Reform in the 1980s

By the early 1980s, the rapidly escalating size of the federal deficit had exposed the failings of the Budget Act of 1974. Members concerned about the size of the deficit began to cast about for changes in the rules of the budgetary process that would impose fiscal discipline on Congress. What members settled on was legislation known as Gramm-Rudman-Hollings, in honor of its sponsors, Senators Phil Gramm (R-TX), Warren Rudman (R-NH), and Ernest Hollings (D-SC).

Gramm-Rudman (as the reforms were commonly called) came in two versions. The first was rushed through a near-panicked Congress in the fall of 1985—it is one of the few bills to become law without having been reviewed by any congressional committee.[80] Many members of Congress voted for Gramm-Rudman because they wanted to do something to bring deficits under control, or at least, because they wanted to show their constituents they were tackling the problem. Most members knew, though, that the bill contained a fatal constitutional flaw. Indeed, the bill contained a clause requiring the federal courts to hear the case on an accelerated basis. When the Supreme Court ruled in July 1986 that the first Gramm-Rudman law was unconstitutional, Congress was again spared from making difficult budgetary choices. (The bill gave the head of the General Accounting Office—now known as the Government Accountability Office—a member of the legislative branch, power to impose across-the-board spending cuts on the federal government. The Supreme Court held that because such power properly rests with the executive branch, the bill violated the separation of powers.)[81] Continued concern over the deficit spurred Congress to pass another version of Gramm-Rudman in 1987, this one written to pass constitutional muster. (It allowed the head of the OMB, an executive agency, to impose the cuts.)

Like the Budget Act of 1974, both versions of Gramm-Rudman sought to impose collective responsibility on members of Congress. Both bills set annual deficit targets that over several years would produce a balanced budget. To ensure that the deficit reduction targets would be met, Gramm-Rudman stipulated that if Congress failed to produce a budget deficit less than or equal to the target for that year, then an automatic, "almost" across-the-board budget cut known as *sequestration* would be implemented. (The "almost" is important because some 70 percent of the budget, including programs such as Social Security, were exempt from the cuts.)[82] Supporters of Gramm-Rudman believed that members would put together budgets that met the deficit targets rather than risk maiming their favorite programs through the mandatory, across-the-board cuts sequestration required.

Unfortunately, despite the reformers' predictions, the federal budget deficit grew rather than shrank while Gramm-Rudman was in effect. Why did Gramm-Rudman fail to reduce the deficit? The answer is the same reason the Budget Act of 1974 failed: Congress and the president could not agree on budgetary priorities. Like the 1974 reforms, Gramm-Rudman was susceptible to manipulation. Members overestimated revenue and underestimated spending, and they used accounting tricks to meet the target limits. (Congress once went so far as to shift the date for charging the budget for military pay from October 1 to September 30. This shifted the pay date from one fiscal year—the one they were setting the budget for—to the current fiscal year, in which there was no sanction for overspending.) And like the 1974 reforms, Gramm-Rudman only required Congress to produce a budget forecasted to meet the deficit targets. After the members had voted to accept a particular forecast, they were no longer bound to meet it, and no penalties or spending cuts were imposed if the forecast proved faulty.

16-5d From Deficits to Surpluses: What Changed in the 1990s?

Gramm-Rudman's failure to stem the growing tide of red ink in the federal budget prompted concerned members of Congress to search for another remedy. In 1990 President George H. W. Bush and the Democratic leadership of Congress held extended negotiations over how to reduce the budget deficit. The negotiations became quite contentious, and at one point, the president allowed the government to run out of money, forcing many government operations to shut down for one weekend. Eventually, however, the president and Congress reached an agreement that was enacted into law as the Budget Enforcement Act (BEA) of 1990.[83]

An extremely complex law, the BEA changed the focus of budgeting by setting limits on expenditure growth and imposing sanctions for not meeting budgetary targets. In essence, the BEA divided the budget into three domains: defense, domestic policy, and international affairs. If spending exceeded the limit in any of the three domains, the excess had to come out of the next year's funds for that domain. Moreover, if members wanted to increase spending on a particular program, the BEA required them to find a way to pay for the new spending, either by raising taxes or by taking the money from another part of the same budget domain. So-called *firewalls* barred members for three years from cutting funds in one budget domain to spend more in another. (These provisions, known as PAYGO, were kept in place until 2002, when the Republican majority in Congress allowed them to lapse. In 2007, the new Democratic majority reinstated them, although without some of the more stringent penalties associated with the earlier PAYGO rules.)[84] Finally, the BEA required that any revenue beyond that projected had to be applied to bring down the deficit, and it required Congress to use better revenue and spending projections when setting the budget.

At the time it was passed, the BEA was projected to reduce budget deficits by some $490 billion over its five-year life span. But that meant only that the debt would be $490 billion less than it would have been without the BEA. Deficits (and an ever larger debt) would remain. The BEA set budget deficit targets that were much higher (and more realistic) than the Gramm-Rudman targets. In retrospect, as Table 16–1 shows, the BEA did help reduce the size of the deficit, even if it did not eliminate them.

	Budget Enforcement Act, 1990	Clinton budget, 1993	Budget deal, 1997
Five-year deficit reduction	$579 billion	$472 billion	$118 billions
Percent spending cuts (%)	63	38	100
Percent from tax increases (%)	0	37	62

Table 16–1   The Impact of the Three Budget Deals in the 1990s

Source: *Data from Robert Reischauer, reported in* Wall Street Journal, *"Tale of Three Budget Deals," August 2, 2000.*

When President Clinton took office in 1993, two key things happened. The first was apparent to everyone at the time. Clinton's first budget submission, which passed Congress with only Democratic votes, cut some government spending and raised taxes on the wealthy. The second key change became obvious only in retrospect. Starting in 1992, the American economy pulled out of recession. It then began what became the largest and longest economic expansion in American history. The budgetary consequences were immense. When the economy grows, fewer people are unemployed and drawing unemployment insurance or needing welfare. And when people are employed, they pay taxes. With the economy growing and the BEA and Clinton budgets in place, deficits started declining in size.

When Republicans took control of Congress following the 1994 election, they sought to make their own mark on the budget. In 1995 and 1996, they pushed for legislation to balance the federal budget by 2002. With cohesive majorities in both Houses—powered in large part by a sizable group of first-year members devoted to balancing the budget—congressional Republicans were well-positioned to push through their proposals. And with the 1994 election results and the promises in the Contract with America, Republicans could (and did) claim to have a mandate from the American people to balance the budget.

Devising a detailed budget plan their own members could agree on proved a daunting task for Republican congressional leaders. For one thing, balancing the budget without raising income taxes or payroll taxes requires substantial cuts in federal spending. Early in the budget process, House Majority Leader Dick Armey (R-TX) predicted, "Once members of Congress know exactly, chapter and verse, the pain that the government must live with in order to get to a balanced budget, their knees will buckle."[85] And once congressional Republicans announced their complete budgetary package, one first-term member commented, "If we had come out with this [detailed plan] as our Contract [with America], they [the public] wouldn't have voted us in."[86]

Republican efforts to balance the budget were further hampered by another of their campaign promises: a pledge to cut taxes. Most economists believe that tax cuts will reduce the amount of revenue the government takes in—although a few argue that cutting taxes so stimulates the economy that more tax revenues are generated despite the lower rates. The reality is, as former Reagan economics advisor Martin Feldstein observed, "It is not that you get more revenue by lowering taxes, it is that you don't lose as much."[87] Because congressional Republicans were committed to cutting taxes, they had to find even more money to cut from the federal budget than they would have had to otherwise. Despite having to overcome many obstacles, including the very real concern that many voters might not like the cuts, the Republicans eventually produced a massive bill that proposed to balance the federal budget over seven years. The bill cut spending for many domestic programs, kept defense spending at about the same level, and still provided some $245 billion in tax cuts.

Budgets have to be negotiated between presidents and Congress. By law, the president and Congress have until September 30 to agree on a budget for the next fiscal year. (A fiscal year is a twelve-month accounting period, which for the federal government runs from October 1 to September 30.) Congress and the president often fail to complete work on the budget by September 30, but they keep the government open by passing short-term continuing resolutions to keep things running until they reach a final agreement. In 1995, however, President Clinton and the Republican majority in Congress were too far apart in their views to reach a final agreement. When a continuing resolution expired in mid-November, the federal government lost its authority to spend money, and it had to shut down all nonessential services. A week later, a new continuing resolution was passed, but then the same pattern was repeated: The continuing resolution expired, and parts of the federal government shut down until Congress and the president agreed on a new continuing resolution.

When Congress and President Clinton finally reached agreement on a new budget in April 1996—seven months into the fiscal year—they imposed some substantial cuts in spending. For example, federal spending on transportation in 1996 was set at $12.5 billion, an 8.9 percent reduction from the previous year. Thus, for the first time in recent history, many federal programs had to make do with less money than they did the year before.[88] Moreover, the budget wrangling persuaded President Clinton to develop his own plan for balancing the budget. His proposed budget for fiscal year 1997, which he unveiled in February 1996, proposed spending less than previously planned on Medicare, Medicaid, and welfare and making significant cuts in discretionary programs. This budget proposal promised to produce a budget surplus by 2002. This plan marked a dramatic shift from the budget Clinton had proposed one year earlier, and it represented a victory for the Republican majority in Congress.[89]

In many ways, the Republican position on government spending was vindicated by the budget agreement reached between President Clinton and the Republican majority in Congress in 1997. The agreement covered five fiscal years—1998 to 2002—and achieved most of its budget savings by cutting Medicare costs through reduced payments to doctors and other health-care providers while also making more minor cuts in Medicaid. Ultimately, as Table 16–1 shows, the agreement helped further cut the deficit significantly.[90]

To almost everyone's surprise, the federal government ran a surplus in 1998, the first time it had done so in twenty-eight years. Surpluses continued for the next three years. What caused the abrupt turnaround? As Table 16–1 suggests, the cumulative effect of the BEA, the 1993 Clinton budget, and the 1997 balanced budget agreement was substantial. Collectively, they cut some $1.1 trillion from government spending over the decade, but the budget cuts alone did not produce the surplus. The impressive performance of the American economy also gets much of the credit. As the ranks of the employed swelled and the stock market soared, the government reaped far more in taxes than anyone had forecasted. With spending controlled and revenues exploding, the result was surpluses.

16-5e Surpluses or Deficits for Forever?

When President George W. Bush took office in 2001, the federal government's budget picture could not have been more different from the one in President Clinton had inherited in the early 1990s. Where only red ink spread as far as the eye could see in 1993, by 2001 the government ledger was deep in the black. Indeed, the CBO forecasted that the federal government would generate a total surplus of $5.6 trillion between 2002 and 2011. As is often the case, budget forecasts can be wrong. How believable such rosy forecasts are, then, matters a great deal to policy makers, as Box 16–2 discusses. Much of the American public, however, is skeptical of such forecasts. A 2001 poll found that seven in ten Americans dismissed the forecast of a $5.6 trillion budget surplus as "unrealistic"; skepticism that time proved correct.[91] Between 2002 and 2007, rather than running a huge surplus, the federal budget ran deficits totaling $1.7 trillion.

The public was right to be pessimistic because serious budgetary problems loom on the horizon. As Chapter 3 noted, we know for certain that the portion of the population age sixty-five and older will start climbing over the next decade. In addition, healthcare costs continue to increase. Thus, as the population ages, great strains will be placed on the Social Security and Medicare systems. Because of this, even forecasts based on the most favorable economic assumptions project that the federal budget will be plagued by deficits in the future unless both Social Security and Medicare are reformed. As Medicare is currently configured, it is forecasted to exhaust its trust fund by 2019, at which time tax revenues are expected to cover only 78 percent of anticipated costs. Social Security is in less immediate difficulty. It is predicted to exhaust its trust funds by 2042, with available tax revenues then able only to cover 78 percent of promised benefits.[92]

16-5f More Budget Reforms?

Many different budgetary reforms have been suggested over the past 200 years. Two much-discussed rule changes are the proposal to give the president a line-item veto and the proposal to amend the Constitution to require Congress to balance the budget. Both these proposals seek to make it more likely that the federal government will balance its budget each year. Other budget reform proposals seek to change the way the federal government raises revenue. Most prominent among these is the flat tax, which would dramatically restructure the current system for taxing income.

The People behind the Rules

Box 16–2 Estimating the Numbers: Who Is Robert Dennis and Why Do His Forecasts Matter

In January 2001, the Congressional Budget Office (CBO) issued a report titled "The Budget and Economic Outlook Fiscal Years 2002–2011." The report was one of two such analyses CBO issues each year. This report was of particular note because it forecast that the U.S. economy would continue its high rate of growth over the next decade. Because of that growth, tax revenues would continue to surge, generating an enormous projected surplus of more than $5.6 trillion over ten years. The projections could not have been any better for the new president, George W. Bush, because he had campaigned on a promise to cut income taxes. CBO's forecast greatly buttressed Bush's claim that the government had more than enough revenues to meet its needs, allowing for a substantial tax cut.

Forecasting how the economy is likely to perform over an extended period is risky business. The CBO employs more than 220 people, about 70 percent of whom hold advanced degrees in economics or public policy. The person charged with figuring out how the economy is likely to perform is Robert Dennis, the Assistant Director for Macroeconomic Analysis. Dennis, a native of England who studied at Oxford, is now an American citizen and a registered Democrat. He started working at the CBO on a summer internship in 1979 and stayed to work his way up through the ranks. The CBO's staff works hard to protect its nonpartisan reputation, and the

forecast Dennis and his team issued in January 2001, although more optimistic than previous forecasts they had made, was grounded in what they saw as objective evidence that private sector investments in computers and telecommunications equipment had dramatically increased worker productivity, and that those gains would continue into the future. Thus, although many politicians and economists disputed their analysis, there was little suggestion that the CBO had cooked the books to curry the new administration's favor.

But how credible are such forecasts? The CBO issues reports analyzing its own forecasting record. Erroneous forecasts are not hard to find. In early 1997, for example, the CBO predicted that the federal government would run a $147 billion deficit in 2000. In reality, the government ran a surplus of more than $230 billion—an error of almost $400 billion. And forecasts over ten years are even more likely to be wrong than those covering shorter periods. As the CBO's deputy director confessed in 2001, "Do we know what the country will look like in 2010? Hell, no. We don't even know if the glaciers will roll back over the continent by then."

Overall, the CBO's forecasting record may be reasonably good. In a recent assessment, the CBO reported that since "publishing its first macroeconomic forecast in 1976, the Congressional Budget Office. . .has compiled a forecasting track record

comparable in quality with that of the *Blue Chip* consensus [an average of private-sector forecasters] as well as that of the Administration." Moreover, the report noted that the mistakes CBO economists make are same ones made by other forecasters: "Comparing CBO's forecasts with those of the *Blue Chip* consensus suggests that when the agency's economic predictions missed by the largest margin, those inaccuracies probably reflected problems that all forecasters had in predicting turning points in the business cycle."

Budget projections matter because they become the basis on which members of Congress and others try to figure out how much money the government will have in years to come and how much money it is likely to need to spend. The government needs to be able to peer into the future to make informed decisions today. Dennis and others at the CBO help provide them with objective forecasts to use.

Sources: Congressional Budget Office, "CBO's Economic Forecasting Record," November 2006 www.cbo.gov/ftpdocs/76xx/doc7680/11-09-EconForecast.pdf; Congressional Budget Office, "The Budget and Economic Outlook, Fiscal Years 2002–2011," January 2001 www.cbo.gov/ftpdocs/27xx/doc2727/entire-report.pdf; Congressional Budget Office, "The Budget and Economic Outlook, Fiscal Years 2004–2013," January 2003 www.cbo.gov/ftpdocs/40xx/doc4032/EntireReport_WithErrata.pdf; Congressional Budget Office, "The Uncertainty of Budget Projections: A Discussion of Data and Methods," March 2007 www.cbo.gov/ftpdocs/78xx/doc7837/03-05-Uncertain.pdf; Bob Davis, "President Owes a Lot to Two Economists You Never Heard Of," *Wall Street Journal*, February 27, 2001.

The Line-Item Veto

Every president from Jimmy Carter to Bill Clinton asked for a **line-item veto**. (The notion goes back to the 1870s, when President Ulysses Grant called for such a veto.)[93] The Constitution states that presidents can veto only entire bills. If a bill they favor comes with provisions they dislike, they must decide whether it is better to sign a bill with some flaws or no bill at all. With a line-item veto,

line-item veto
The ability of an executive to delete or veto some provisions of a bill, while allowing the rest of the bill to become law.

presidents would have the authority to veto provisions they dislike while still accepting the bill. As Presidents Carter, Reagan, and Clinton—all former governors—noted, the line-item veto is common in state government; forty-three states give their governor a line-item veto.

Supporters argue that the line-item veto would enable the president to eliminate pork-barrel spending. Although this sounds sensible, the line-item veto comes with several flaws. To start with, as we have discussed, what constitutes pork lies in the eye of the beholder. Members of Congress (and their constituents) might disagree vehemently with the president about which programs are wasteful. Indeed, as we pointed out in Chapter 15, the experience of state government suggests that governors use their line-item vetoes to shape spending to their policy preferences as much as to reduce spending.[94] Members also fear that a president might use the threat of a line-item veto to coerce them into supporting other policy proposals the White House favors. For example, a president might threaten to eliminate funds for highway construction in Texas as a way to pressure the Texas congressional delegation into supporting a White House proposal to reform the health-care system.

Disagreement over what constitutes wasteful spending and fears of enhancing presidential power make it highly unlikely that Congress will pass a true line-item veto because doing so would require it to propose a constitutional amendment. Because proponents of the line-item veto know they don't have the votes they need to propose an amendment, they have instead offered a variety of bills that seek to create the functional equivalent of a line-item veto through ordinary legislation. (Although these bills would not create a true line-item veto, they are routinely if somewhat inaccurately referred to as line-item veto bills, a practice we adopt here. The differences between a true line-item veto and its legislative substitutes are complex and need not detain us here.) In 1995, House and Senate Republicans passed different (and incompatible) versions of the line-item veto.[95] A year later, however, at the behest of the Republican presidential nominee, then-Senator Robert Dole (R-KS), House and Senate Republicans agreed on a line-item veto bill, which Congress passed and President Clinton signed into law.

The line-item veto, technically known as enhanced rescission, went into effect on January 1, 1997. The law authorized the president to veto spending on specific items mentioned in an appropriations bill or in the congressional report that accompanies each appropriations bill. The law also authorized the president to veto any tax break that benefited fewer than 100 taxpayers. The president's line-item veto power applied only to dollar figures. The law did not allow a president to strike legislative prescriptions, that is, language Congress inserts in appropriations bills directing the executive branch how to spend the appropriations. (As Chapter 15 noted, some states give their governors such authority.) Thus, if Congress directs the government to spend $10 million on AIDS research, the president could ignore the directive and spend the money on something else. The president's only options were to approve the line-item spending figure or veto it. When the president vetoed a line item, Congress could pass a free-standing bill reinstating the spending. The president could then, however, exercise a constitutional veto, thereby requiring Congress to muster a two-thirds vote in both the House and Senate before the spending is reinstated.[96]

Supporters of the line-item veto argued that presidents would use it to strike wasteful government spending. Critics, however, argued that the law shifted too much power to the White House. Senator Byrd, a staunch supporter of congressional prerogatives, denounced the line-item veto as a plan that "James Madison and the framers would abhor."[97] In an unusual move, the Judicial Conference of the United States, the organization that represents federal judges, denounced the line-item veto as a threat to judicial independence because presidents could use it to punish judges or courts that make unpopular decisions. Moreover, the *threat* of a veto might influence how judges or courts decide cases.[98]

President Clinton used the line-item veto only sparingly in cutting the fiscal year 1998 budget. He vetoed some $869 million in spending and tax breaks. Congress overrode his veto of an appropriations measure containing thirty-eight military construction projects worth $287 million.[99] Even those small cuts out of a $1.6 trillion budget met with howls of protest from members of Congress who lost prized projects and provisions. Senator Byrd, for example, commented, "I have railed against this abomination, this gimmick, this legislative end-run around the Constitution.... I wonder how some members who did make the very unwise choice to support it are feeling now that their legislative initiatives have felt the line-item meat cleaver." Senator Ted Stevens (R-AK) proclaimed, "We're dealing with a raw abuse of power."[100]

The battle over the line-item veto ended abruptly. The president could not use it in the next budget cycle because the government started to generate a surplus, and under the law creating the line-item veto, it could be used only to reduce a deficit.[101] In June 1998, however, before the potential surplus became an issue, the Supreme Court ruled that the line-item veto was unconstitutional. Writing for the majority, Justice John Paul Stevens observed that the line-item veto law "gives the president the unilateral power to change the text of duly enacted statutes," and that "there is no provision in the Constitution that authorizes the president to enact, to amend or to repeal statutes."[102] Although some members of Congress wanted the president to exercise a line-item veto, many members supported the Court's decision.

In 2006, President George W. Bush revived the notion of a presidential line-item veto. Under his proposal, the president would identify spending on items he does not support, although signing the rest of a bill. Congress would then have ten days to vote on whether to fund the disputed items. A majority of each house, not the two-thirds margin required to override a veto, would be needed to pass the spending. Regardless of what appeared to be bipartisan support for the idea—Senator John Kerry (D-MA), Bush's opponent in the 2004 election, had already introduced similar legislation—it was unlikely that a majority of members of Congress would want to give any president such powers. Scholars also raised constitutional objections to the plan. In the end, Congress did not give President Bush a line-item veto.

Balanced Budget Amendments

Various constitutional amendments have been offered to require Congress and the president to balance the budget. A balanced budget amendment was the number one item on the Republican's Contract with America in 1994. One almost passed in 1997, falling just one vote short in the Senate. A problem with all such measures is that they do not specify how to balance the budget. Moreover, a budget that runs deficits measured in the hundreds of billions of dollars cannot be cut quickly without wreaking havoc on the American economy and society. As a result, most balanced budget amendments delay the requirement for balancing the budget until some time in the future. Finally, it is unlikely that a balanced budget amendment would prevent budget deficits, or that it could even be enforced.[103] Many states that have constitutional provisions requiring a balanced budget still have managed to build their own debts.

Despite the practical problems with a balanced budget amendment, it has great popular appeal. After all, it sounds sensible to require the government to live within its means. But the rub comes in deciding *how* to balance the budget. Indeed, public support for a balanced budget amendment fades when people are confronted with its possible consequences. For example, one survey found that 68 percent of those polled supported the idea of a balanced budget amendment in the abstract. When they were then told that balancing the federal budget would require cuts in Medicare, Medicaid, and veterans benefits, support for the balanced budget amendment fell to 33 percent.

The initial popularity of a balanced budget amendment with the average voter explains its continued popularity with many members of Congress. Politicians who support the balanced budget amendment can reap an immediate political benefit, leaving the hard choices needed to balance the budget to future years. When the government ran surpluses, much of the steam left the balanced budget amendment movement. But with the return of deficits, balanced budget amendments have again been proposed in Congress. But this time the politics surrounding the issue are different. In 2004, it was the Republican leadership in the House that prevented the proposed amendment from being brought up for a vote, and some conservative organizations actively opposed the measure.[104] Nonetheless, five different versions of a balanced budget amendment were introduced in Congress in 2007. None was given serious consideration.

The Flat Tax

Americans generally don't like to pay taxes. In 1949, 43 percent of Americans thought their federal income taxes were too high, a figure that reached 68 percent in 1999. Even after the Bush administration's various tax cuts, 52 percent still thought they were paying too much in 2008.[105] In another 2008 survey, 55 percent said they would like to see the amount of money Americans pay in income taxes decreased.[106] So proposals to cut taxes have considerable popular appeal.

One plan to cut taxes would enact a **flat tax**, which would replace the current progressive tax system with one in which everyone would pay the same percentage on their taxable income. Flat tax plans have been around for many years; for example, Nobel Prize-winning economist Milton Friedman floated the idea in 1962.[107] Over the last two decades, several members of Congress have introduced legislation to create a flat tax. But the idea of a flat tax did not inspire much public debate until 1996, when Malcolm S. "Steve" Forbes, Jr., made the idea the centerpiece of his unsuccessful bid to win the Republican nomination for president. (Surprisingly little notice is given to the fact that six states have a flat tax on income; whether the flat tax promotes more rapid economic growth in those states is a matter of debate.)[108]

Although all flat tax plans propose to tax income at a single rate, they differ in setting what the tax rate will be, determining what kinds of income are exempt from taxes and establishing which expenses are deductible when calculating taxable income. For example, the Forbes plan would have established a 17 percent rate on wages, but it would have made an initial amount of income from wages exempt from tax. (The amount of the exemption increased with family size.) And the Forbes plan would have made all income from dividends, interest, and capital gains exempt from taxes. (Capital gains are profits from the sale of assets such as stocks, bonds, and real estate.) The Forbes flat tax, then, would effectively have created two rates, zero for people who earn less than the exempted amount ($36,000 for a married couple with two children), and 17 percent on income over the exempted amount for everyone else.[109]

The details of any flat tax proposal are critical because they determine how much money the federal government will raise in revenue. As the tax rate falls and as exemptions become more liberal, the federal government takes in less revenue. To avoid making the federal budget deficit larger, many people argue that any new tax system should be **revenue neutral**; that is, it should neither increase nor decrease government revenue from current levels. By this standard, the Forbes flat tax proposal failed to pass muster. According to most independent analyses done at the time, the Forbes plan would have lowered federal revenues by more than $100 billion, precisely because it would cut almost everyone's tax bill. The result would have been a sharp jump in the size of the federal deficit at that time, unless Congress and the president agreed to make offsetting cuts in federal spending. To make

flat tax
Any income tax system in which taxable income is taxed at the same percentage rate regardless of the taxpayer's income.

revenue neutral
A quality of any tax reform plan that will neither increase nor decrease government revenue.

the Forbes flat tax plan revenue neutral given the size of the deficit the government was running, the tax rate would have had to have been increased from an attractive 17 percent to more than 20 percent. Yet raising the tax rate that high would have meant that the taxes of many middle-class Americans would have gone *up,* not down.[110]

Although the prospect of a smaller tax bill is one reason for the appeal of the flat tax, another is its simplicity. The Tax Code has become incredibly complex over time. In 1913, it filled 400 pages. By 2008, it was up to 67,506 pages![111] And at more than 7 million words, the Tax Code is more than ten times longer than the Bible. In 2001, Treasury Secretary Paul O'Neill received a joint letter from the American Bar Association tax section, the American Institute of Certified Public Accountants tax division, and the Tax Executives Institute, worrying that "the cost and complexity of administering the tax system...undermines the public's general confidence in government." It is estimated that in 2005 Americans spent $265 billion to comply with the income tax laws alone.[112]

Because a flat tax would eliminate the vast majority of exemptions and deductions in the Tax Code, supporters claim it will enable most taxpayers to file their income tax returns on a postcard. Not surprisingly, many people find the prospect of a greatly simplified tax appealing. Indeed, during his unsuccessful 1996 presidential campaign, Forbes got his biggest applause when he promised that his flat tax proposal would kill the present Tax Code, "drive a stake through its heart," and bury it.[113] As a practical matter, however, the switch to a flat tax would not change the tax filing process for most people. Just under 66 percent of Americans currently do not use the exemptions in the Tax Code; hence, they already file their taxes on a one- or two-page form.[114]

The appeal of the flat tax diminished somewhat during the battle over the 1996 Republican presidential nomination. To stop Forbes's surge in the public opinion polls, his Republican opponents pointed out that the two greatest strengths of his flat tax proposal—lower tax bills and simplified tax returns—were also its two biggest weaknesses. Not only would a 17 percent flat tax in all likelihood increase the size of the federal deficit, but simplifying tax returns means forcing Americans to give up cherished tax breaks such as the home mortgage interest deduction. After the national media had discussed the idea of a flat tax for several months, polls found that a majority of Americans preferred a progressive tax rate over a flat tax system. Only the wealthiest Americans gave the flat tax much support, a finding in keeping with analyses that suggest they would benefit the most from such plans.[115] Forbes ran another unsuccessful presidential campaign on the flat tax in 2000, and in 2005, he wrote a book, *The Flat Tax Revolution,* extolling the virtues of his plan. (The current plan is much the same as the one Forbes campaigned for in 1996, but now a married couple with two children would pay no taxes on their first $46,165 in income).[116] And several members of Congress, notably Senator Arlen Specter (R-PA), continue to push the idea, but with little success.

In recent years a different twist on a flat tax surfaced. Representative John Linder (R-GA) and others have touted replacing the income tax with a national sales tax of 23 percent, arguing that taxing consumption rather than income would promote economic growth.[117] Legislation proposing such a tax—called the "Fair Tax"—has been introduced in Congress.[118] In 2008, the measure had seventy-three co-sponsors in the House and five in the Senate, but it failed to advance. Opponents of the Fair Tax raise two major objections. First, they argue that the tax rate would have to be set higher than 23 percent to produce the same amount of revenue that the current system generates. Second, they argue that the Fair Tax would shift the tax burden from the wealthiest Americans and put it on the middle class and poor. To partially counter this objection, Fair Tax proponents propose giving "prebates"—monthly payments to cover the projected cost of the national sales tax—to the poor. Doing this would leave the wealthiest and poorest taxpayers better off but still leave those in the middle paying more in taxes.[119]

For the most part, the movement to radically change the federal tax system has generated little political momentum. Indeed, although President George W. Bush initially made tax reform a major priority in his second term, he did not propose adopting any form of a flat tax. And only a few unsuccessful candidates promoted the idea in the 2008 presidential nomination campaign.

16-6 IS THE BUDGET PROCESS IRRATIONAL?

A budget of $3.1 trillion is almost beyond comprehension. It is hard to fathom how to devise a rational way to budget such a large amount of money. Even if we could all agree on what constitutes worthwhile spending, just imagine how difficult it would be to ensure that the government spent every one of those $3.1 trillion wisely. The federal government has tried to allot small chunks of the budget using innovative techniques such as program-planning budgeting, management by objective, and zero-based budgeting, each of which requires agencies to justify funding for all of their programs. But each of these budgeting techniques failed, in large part because they overwhelmed the bureaucracy and Congress with work. No one had the time and expertise to conduct complete budgetary reviews on an annual basis.[120]

In general, although budgets almost always grow, they usually change only slightly from year to year. That is, the best predictor of how money will be spent in this year's budget is how it was spent in last year's budget. Although there may be a few significant shifts in spending, in a budget the size of the federal government's, adding a few billion for this program or taking a few billion from that program really makes changes only at the margins. Some people argue that such incremental budgeting is rational.[121] It simplifies budgeting decisions by focusing attention on a few programs, usually those that arouse some political controversy. But incremental budgeting also means that most spending continues on autopilot, with little or no evaluation of whether the money is being spent wisely.

In the end, budgeting is fundamentally a political, not a mechanical, process. Like all governments, the federal government makes budgetary decisions in response to political demands and to meet political realities. When deficits occur, as they have chronically since 1960, the reason is not irrational budgetary rules, but elected officials responding to contradictory constituent demands.

SUMMARY

Federal spending has grown enormously since George Washington was president. The federal government now spends $3.1 trillion or more every year. From the 1960s to the late 1990s, and again since 2002, the growth in spending outpaced the growth of revenue. As a result, the federal government regularly ran large budget deficits. These massive deficits led to a rapid increase in the size of the national debt. By 2009, the national debt was nine times greater than it was only twenty-five years earlier.

Reducing the size of the budget deficit will require the federal government to increase revenue, decrease spending, or both. The sources of government revenue have changed greatly since the beginning of the twentieth century. In 1900, the federal government got almost all its revenue from customs duties on imported goods and excise taxes on tobacco and alcohol. In contrast, in 2009, more than 80 percent of government revenue came from the income and payroll taxes individual Americans paid.

Government spending patterns have also changed dramatically over the past 100-plus years, and especially over the past 65 years. In 1940, nearly two-thirds of government spending went to programs we normally associate with government, such as road construction, medical research, national parks, and so forth; only 20 percent went to entitlement programs that made direct payments to individuals. In 2009, the numbers were almost exactly the reverse. The expansion of entitlement programs such as Social Security, Medicare, unemployment insurance, and the Food Stamp program has greatly complicated the task of balancing the budget. Not only are most entitlement programs popular, which discourages members of Congress from trying to cut benefits, but entitlements by their very nature cannot be controlled through the budgetary process. Reducing entitlement benefits requires Congress to rewrite the laws that created the programs in the first place.

Responsibility for the federal government's budget falls at the doorsteps of both Congress and the president. But responsibility also rests with the American public. When Congress and the president assemble budgets, they are responding to the public's contradictory demands for more government services and lower taxes. Congress passed several budgetary reforms designed to balance the budget, but none succeeded until a robust economy over many years and agreements between presidents and Congress to limit spending increases combined to push the budget into surplus. In the end, budgets are the result of political decisions, not budgetary processes.

KEY TERMS

balanced budget

Budget and Accounting Act of 1921

budget deficits

budget surplus

Congressional Budget and Impoundment Control Act of 1974

Congressional Budget Office (CBO)

continuing resolutions

corporate welfare

cost-of-living adjustment (COLA)

discretionary spending

entitlement programs

flat tax

line-item veto

national debt

nondiscretionary spending

Office of Management and Budget (OMB)

pork barrel

progressive tax

regressive tax

revenue neutral

Social Security Act of 1935

READINGS FOR FURTHER STUDY

Bank, Stephen A., Kirk J. Stark, and Joseph J. Thorndike, *War and Taxes* (Washington, D.C., Urban Institute Press, 2008). The authors document that the current conflict with Iraq is the first war to be waged by the federal government without asking citizens to make sacrifices through raising taxes, cutting domestic spending, or floating war bonds.

Gordon, John Steele. *Hamilton's Blessing: The Extraordinary Life and Times of Our National Debt* (New York: Walker, 1997). A readable account of the role the national debt has played in American history.

Graetz, Michael J., and Ian Shapiro. *Death by a Thousand Cuts: The Fight over Taxing Inherited Wealth* (Princeton, NJ: Princeton University Press, 2005). A fascinating account of the largely successful effort by conservatives to dismantle the inheritance tax, or what they cleverly labeled "the death tax."

LeLoup, Lance T. *Parties, Rules, and the Evolution of Congressional Budgeting* (Columbus: Ohio State University Press, 2005). A comprehensive examination of the way the congressional budget process has changed since the 1974 reforms.

Osborne, David, and Peter Hutchinson. *The Price of Government: Getting the Results We Need in an Age of Permanent Fiscal Crisis* (New York: Basic Books, 2004). A proposal to radically change the budget process by having government focus on "buying results for citizens."

Savage, James D. *Balanced Budgets and American Politics* (Ithaca, NY: Cornell University Press, 1988). An examination of balanced budgets and the changing arguments for and against them from colonial times to the Reagan years.

Steuerle, C. Eugene. *Contemporary U.S. Tax Policy* (Washington, D.C.: Urban Institute Press, 2004). A leading tax expert examines the evolution of the federal tax policies over the last quarter century.

Weisman, Steven R. *The Great Tax Wars* (New York: Simon & Schuster, 2002). An accessible examination of the battle to create the federal income tax in the early part of the twentieth century.

REVIEW QUESTIONS

1. What is the current status of the line-item veto at the national level?
   a. The president uses the line-item veto to cut some $1 billion out of the budget each year.
   b. The U.S. Supreme Court held the line-item veto to be unconstitutional.
   c. Congressional Republicans continue to push for a line-item veto to be given to the president.
   d. The president has the line-item veto, but rarely uses it.

2. Foreign aid currently constitutes about _____ percent of the federal budget in the United States.
   a. 1
   b. 10
   c. 15
   d. 25

3. The first federal budget deficits occurred in the
   a. 1790s.
   b. 1830s.
   c. 1930s.
   d. 1980s.

4. What accounts for the rapid growth in federal spending in the past seventy years?
   a. The role of the United States as a military superpower
   b. the increase in the federal government's role in American life

    c. President Franklin Delano Roosevelt's New Deal programs

    d. both a and b

5. What are the two most important sources of revenue for the federal government?

    a. corporate income taxes and social insurance taxes

    b. personal income taxes and social insurance taxes

    c. personal income taxes and excise taxes

    d. personal income taxes and corporate income taxes

6. The federal tax code in the United States is

    a. regressive.

    b. misleading because of loopholes.

    c. completely progressive.

    d. much higher than in most other industrialized countries.

7. _____ is (are) the largest entitlement program.

    a. Social Security

    b. Medicare

    c. Unemployment

    d. Food stamps

8. Spending on pork-barrel projects amounts to _____ percent of the federal budget.

    a. 25

    b. 15

    c. 5

    d. less than 1

9. The president was authorized to submit a single budget to Congress in

    a. 1860.

    b. 1892.

    c. 1921.

    d. 1967.

10. Continuing resolutions

    a. keep the government running.

    b. have been used frequently since 1975.

    c. give Congress more time to debate the budget.

    d. all of the above.

NOTES

1. See the "The Budget Message of the President," February 4, 2008. www.whitehouse.gov/omb/budget/fy2009/message.html

2. John Steele Gordon, "Our Debt to Hamilton," *Wall Street Journal*, March 12, 1997.

3. James D. Savage, *Balanced Budgets and American Politics* (Ithaca, NY: Cornell University Press, 1988).

4. Donald F. Kettl, *Deficit Politics* (New York: Macmillan, 1992), 21–22.

5. Quoted in "Clinton Outlines His Plan to Spur Economy," *Congressional Quarterly Weekly Report*, February 20, 1993, 399.

6. Calculated by the authors from *Treasury Bulletin*, June 2008, Table OFS-2.

7. Frederick Kempe, "Holdings of U.S. Debt Become Potential Weapon," *Wall Street Journal*, May 9, 2006.

8. *OECD Economic Outlook No. 83*, June 2008, Annex Table 32.

9. Robert Eisner, "We Don't Need Balanced Budgets," *Wall Street Journal*, January 11, 1995.

10. For the former position, see, for example, Paul W. McCracken, "Why Deficits Matter," *Wall Street Journal*, December 26, 1995. For the latter position, see, for example, Alan Reynolds, "Do Budget Deficits Raise Long-Term Interest Rates?" *Tax and Budget Bulletin* 1, February 2002, available at www.cato.org/pubs/tbb/tbb-0202.html. See also Greg Ip, "Why Today's Soaring Deficits Don't Inspire Fear," *Wall Street Journal*, July 12, 2004; and William G. Gale and Peter R. Orszag, "Economic Effects of Sustained Budget Deficits," *National Tax Journal* 56 (September 2003): 463–85.

11. Calculated by the authors from budget documents.

12. Barber B. Conable, Jr., *Congress and the Income Tax* (Norman, OK: University of Oklahoma Press, 1989), 34–37; John F. Witte, *The Politics and Development of the Federal Income Tax* (Madison: University of Wisconsin Press, 1985), 67–75. The court case was *Pollock v. Farmers' Loan and Trust Co.,* 157 U.S. 429, 158 U.S. 601 (1895).

13. *Brushaber v. Union Pacific Railroad Company,* 240 U.S. 1 (1916).

14. Witte, *The Politics and Development of the Federal Income Tax*, 78.

15. Rep. James Monroe Miller, quoted in David Brinkley, "The Long Road to Tax Reform," *Wall Street Journal*, September 18, 1995.

16. "Tax Report," *Wall Street Journal*, October 26, 1994.

17. See Joint Committee on Taxation, "Overview of Present Law and Economic Analysis Relating to Marginal Tax Rates and the President's Individual Income Tax Proposals," March 7, 2001, 7–8. www.house.gov/jct/x-6-01.pdf

18. Individual income tax percentages calculated by the authors from Urban-Brookings Tax Policy Center, "Current-Law Distributions of Federal Taxes by Cash Income Class, 2007," November 30, 2006. www.taxpolicycenter.org/numbers/displayatab.cfm?Docid=1390 The study of the 400 highest paid Americans is reported in Tom Herman, "There's Rich, and There's the 'Fortunate 400,'" *Wall Street Journal*, March 5, 2008.

19. U.S. Bureau of the Census, *Statistical Abstract of the United States, 1980*, 101st ed. (Washington, D.C.: U.S. Bureau of the Census, 1980), 339.

20. Payroll tax percentages calculated by the authors from Urban-Brookings Tax Policy Center, "Current-Law Distributions of Federal Taxes by Cash Income Class, 2007, November 30, 2006." www.taxpolicycenter.org/numbers/displayatab.cfm?Docid=1390

21. Len Burman and Greg Leiserson, "Two-Thirds of Tax Units Pay More Payroll Tax than Income Tax," Tax Policy Center, Urban Institute and Brookings Institution, April 9, 2007. www.urban.org/UploadedPDF/1001065_Tax_Units.pdf

22. R. Kent Weaver, *Automatic Government* (Washington, D.C.: Brookings Institution, 1988), 67–79.

23. See Social Security Administration, Social Security Online, Frequently Asked Questions, "Do I Have to Pay Income Tax on My Social Security Benefits?" www.ssa-custhelp.ssa.gov/cgi-bin/ssa.cfg/php/enduser/std_adp.php?p_faqid=493

24. Washington Post/Kaiser Family Foundation/Harvard University, "Survey on Social Security," February 2005. www.kff.org/newsmedia/washpost/upload/Survey-on-Social-Security-Toplines.pdf

25. Ibid. See also the excellent discussion in Paul Light, *Artful Work* (New York: Random House, 1985), esp. 63.

26. Kettl, *Deficit Politics*, 49.

27. Washington Post/Kaiser Family Foundation/Harvard University, "Survey on Social Security." www.kff.org/newsmedia/washpost/upload/Survey-on-Social-Security-Toplines.pdf

28. Social Security Administration, Brief History, available at www.ssa.gov/history/history6.html#idamay.

29. Kettl, *Deficit Politics*, 50.

30. Brian Blackstone, "Report Urges Raising Social Security Age," *Wall Street Journal*, August 20, 2008; John B. Shoven, Gopi Shah Goda, "Adjusting Government Policies for Age Inflation," *National Bureau of Economic Research Working Paper No. 14231*, August 2008.

31. The Board of Trustees, Federal Old-Age and Survivors Insurance and Federal Disability Insurance Trust Funds, "2008 Annual Report of the Board of Trustees of the Federal Old-Age and Survivors Insurance and Disability Insurance Trust Funds," April 10, 2008, table IV.B2 www.ssa.gov/OACT/TR/TR08/lr4b2.html; See also Eric R. Kingson and Edward D. Berkowitz, *Social Security and Medicare: A Policy Primer* (Westport, CT: Auburn House, 1993), 102–7.

32. Kingson and Berkowitz, *Social Security and Medicare*, 131; Peter G. Peterson, *Facing Up: How to Rescue the Economy from Crushing Debt and Restore the American Dream* (New York: Simon & Schuster, 1993), 108–9.

33. The first statistics are from Mark Schmidt, "Young and Overtaxed—A Prescription for Ruin," National Taxpayers Union and NTU Foundation, available at www.ntu.org/features/commentary/OPED0207generationaltaxes.php3. The second statistics are from Peter Passell, "Can Retirees' Safety Net Be Saved?" *New York Times*, February 18, 1996.

34. See, for example, Ann Reilly Dowd, "Needed: A New War on the Deficit," *Fortune* (November 14, 1994): 191–200.

35. "People, Opinions, and Polls," *The Public Perspective* 6 (February/March 1995), 23.

36. The first figure was taken from The Kaiser Family Foundation, "National Survey of the Public's Views about Medicaid," June 2005. The second figure was taken from The Pew Research Center for the People & the Press, "AARP, Greenspan Most Trusted on Social Security, Bush Failing in Social Security Push," March 2, 2005. www.people-press.org/reports/pdf/238.pdf

37. George Hager, "Seven Ways to Cut the Deficit . . . Easier Said than Done," *Congressional Quarterly Weekly Report*, May 2, 1992, 1144–45.

38. CBO Testimony, statement of Dan L. Crippen, Director, "Preparing for an Aging Population," before the Committee on the Budget, U.S. House of Representatives, July 27, 2000.

39. Ibid.

40. The 2004 data are from a CBS News/*New York Times* Poll, November 18–21, 2004, and a *Washington Post*/ABC News poll, December 16–19, 2004; the 2005 data are from a *Newsweek* Poll, February 3–4, 2005; all at www.pollingreport.com/social2.htm see also John Harwood and John D. McKinnon, "Public Doubts Bush's New Agenda," *Wall Street Journal*, December 16, 2004.

41. These figures are from a CBS News Poll, October 12–16, 2007. www.pollingreport.com/social.htm

42. On trying to define privatization, see Don Fullerton and Michael Geruso, "The Many Definitions of Social Security Privatization," *Economists' Voice* 3 (March 2006). Vol. 3: Iss. 4, Article 3. Available at: www.bepress.com/ev/vol3/iss4/art3

43. On the failure of President George W. Bush's plan, see George C. Edwards III, *Governing by Campaigning: the Politics of the Bush Presidency* (New York: Pearson Longman, 2007), 215–80; and Gary C. Jacobson, *A Divider, Not a Uniter* (New York: Pearson Longman, 2007), 206–17.

44. Larry Rohter, "Social Security Too Hot to Touch? Not in 2008," *New York Times*, August 14, 2008.

45. The Medicare and Medicaid numbers and figures are drawn from The Boards of Trustees of the Federal Hospital Insurance and Federal Supplementary Medical Insurance Trust Funds, "2008 Annual Report of the Boards of Trustees of the Federal Hospital Insurance and Federal Supplementary Medical Insurance Trust Funds," March 25, 2008; www.cms.hhs.gov/report strustfunds/downloads/tr2008.pdf and Congressional Budget Office, "Historical Budget Data," March 2008; www.cbo.gov/budget/historical.shtml The Food Stamp data are from U.S. Department of Agriculture, "Food Stamp Program Participation and Costs," November 28, 2008. www.fns.usda.gov/pd/SNAPsummary.htm

46. See William Safire, *Safire's New Political Dictionary* (New York: Random House, 1993), 596–97.

47. Quoted in Bret Schulte, "A Bridge (Way) Too Far," *U.S. News & World Report*, August 8, 2005. The 2008 budget examples are drawn from Citizens against Government Waste, *2008 Congressional Pig Book*. www.cagw.org/site/DocServer/CAGW-Pig_Book_08.pdf?docID=3001

48. See Citizens against Government Waste, "Pork Trends, 1991–2008," available at www.cagw.org/site/PageServer?pagename=reports_porkbarrelreport#trends; Congressional Research Service, "Earmarks in Appropriation Acts: FY1994, FY1996, FY1998, FY2000, FY2002, FY2004, FY2005," January 26, 2006. www.fas.org/sgp/crs/misc/m012606.pdf

49. Jeffrey Brainard and J.J. Hermes, "Colleges' Earmarks Grow, Amid Criticism," *Chronicle of Higher Education*, March 28, 2008.

50. Terry Ganey, "Bond & Bacon," *Columbia Daily Tribune*, June 8, 2008.

51. Quoted in Citizens against Government Waste, *2008 Congressional Pig Book*, 53.

52. Lisa Demer and Kyle Hopkins, "Friendly Crowd Welcomes Stevens," *Anchorage Daily News*, August 8, 2007.

53. See Citizens against Government Waste, "Byrd Droppings, Senator Robert C. Byrd's Pork Tally," available at www.cagw.org/site/PageServer?pagename=news_byrddroppings_porktally.

54. Quoted in Katharine Q. Seelye, "The Race that Invective Forgot," *New York Times*, November 4, 1994. See also Francis X. Cline, "How Do West Virginians Spell Pork? It's B-Y-R-D," *New York Times*, May 4, 2002.

55. Data from Citizens against Government Waste, *2008 Congressional Pig Book*.

56. Stephen Slivinski, "The Corporate Welfare State," *Cato Institute, Policy Analysis, No. 592*, May 14, 2007.

57. See Slivinski, "The Corporate Welfare State"; Citizens for Tax Justice, "Surge in Corporate Tax Welfare Drives Corporate Tax Payments Down to Near Record Low," April 17, 2002 www.ctj.org/html/corp0402.htm; Ed Feulner, "Corporate Gravy Train is Railroading Rest of the Country," *Chicago Sun-Times*, April 12, 2006; and Brian M. Reidl, "The Other Welfare Reform," *The Heritage Foundation*, February 4, 2003. www.heritage.org/press/commentary/ed020403.cfm

58. David Leonhardt, "High Costs, Courtesy of Congress," *New York Times*, June 25, 2008; "Farm Bill Chestnuts: Why Does Helping the Poor Have to be Held Hostage to Wasteful Subsidies," *Washington Post*, May 16, 2008; "Fat Farm Bill Gives Welfare to Well-Off," *St. Petersburg Times*, May 9, 2008.

59. Paul E. Peterson, "The New Politics of Deficits," in *The New Direction of American Politics*, eds. John E. Chubb and Paul E. Peterson (Washington, D.C.: Brookings Institution, 1985).

60. Norman J. Ornstein, Thomas E. Mann, and Michael J. Malbin, *Vital Statistics on Congress 1999–2000* (Washington, D.C.: Congressional Quarterly, 2000), 180.

61. Christopher B. Wlezien, "The Political Economy of Supplemental Appropriations," *Legislative Studies Quarterly* 18 (February 1993): 51–76; Christopher B. Wlezien, "The President, Congress, and Appropriations, 1951–1985," *American Politics Quarterly* 24 (January 1996): 43–67.

62. Times Mirror Center for the People & the Press, "Public Expects GOP Miracles," December 8, 1994, 34–35. www.people-press.org/reports/pdf/19941208.pdf

63. See Carroll Doherty, "Do Deficits Matter Anymore? Apparently Not to the Public," Pew Research Center, March 14, 2006. www.pewresearch.org/pubs/10/do-deficits-matter-anymore-apparently-not-to-the-public

64. Washington Post-ABC News Poll, June 12–15, 2008. See questions 34 and 36. www.washingtonpost.com/wp-srv/politics/documents/postpoll_061608.html

65. Ronald G. Shafer, "Washington Wire," *Wall Street Journal*, July 29, 1994.

66. These data come from a Worldviews 2002, "American Public Opinion & Foreign Policy," survey www.worldviews.org/detailreports/usreport/index.htm. See also Program on International Policy Attitudes, University of Maryland, survey, "Americans on Foreign Aid and World Hunger," conducted between November 1–6, 2000, and released on February 2, 2001. www.pipa.org/OnlineReports/ForeignAid/ForeignAid_Feb01/ForeignAid_Feb01_rpt.pdf

67. Washington Post/Kaiser Family Foundation/Harvard University, "Survey on Social Security." www.kff.org/newsmedia/washpost/upload/Survey-on-Social-Security-Toplines.pdf

68. James R. Hagerty, "Housing Sector Seeks No Tax Remodeling," *Wall Street Journal*, January 31, 2005.

69. This quote was contained in a report on a project by the Joyce Foundation. See Mike Feinsilber, "Congressional Members Want Public to Share Blame," *Iowa City Press-Citizen*, April 6, 1992.

70. James Q. Lynch, "Nussle: No Feud with Grassley," *The Gazette*, Cedar Rapids, April 25, 2003.

71. Janet M. Kelly, "A Century of Public Budgeting Reform," *Administration & Society* 37 (March 2005): 89–109.

72. Our discussion on the evolution of the budgetary process draws heavily on Aaron B. Wildavsky, *The New Politics of the Budgetary Process*, 2nd ed. (New York: HarperCollins, 1992).

73. Richard F. Fenno, Jr., *The Power of the Purse* (Boston: Little, Brown, 1966).

74. Speaker of the House Joe Cannon, quoted in ibid., 99.

75. John B. Gilmour, *Reconcilable Differences* (Berkeley: University of California Press, 1990), 28–35; Allen Schick, *Congress and Money* (Washington, D.C.: Urban Institute, 1980), 415–40.

76. See the discussion in Gilmour, *Reconcilable Differences*, chap. 1.

77. Sandy Streeter, "The Congressional Appropriations Process: An Introduction," CRS Report for Congress, 97-684, updated February 22, 2007. www.senate.gov/reference/resources/pdf/97-684.pdf

78. Steven E. Schier, *A Decade of Deficits* (Albany: State University of New York Press, 1992), 82.

79. Gilmour, *Reconcilable Differences*, 107–30.

80. Joseph White and Aaron B. Wildavsky, *The Deficit and the Public Interest* (Berkeley: University of California Press, 1989), 427.

81. *Bowsher v. Synar,* 478 U.S. 714 (1986).

82. See Kettl, *Deficit Politics*, 99.

83. James A. Thurber and Samantha L. Durst, "The 1990 Budget Enforcement Act: The Decline of Congressional Accountability," in *Congress Reconsidered*, 5th ed., eds. Lawrence C. Dodd and Bruce I. Oppenheimer (Washington, D.C.: CQ Press, 1993), 375–97.

84. Steven S. Smith, Jason M. Roberts, and Ryan J. Vander Wielen, *The American Congress*, 5th ed. (New York: Cambridge University Press, 2007), 382.

85. Quoted in Phil Kuntz, "Congressional Democrats Attack GOP over Balanced Budget Amendment," *Wall Street Journal*, January 9, 1995.

86. Rep. George Radanovich (R-CA), quoted in Jackie Calmes, "House GOP Freshmen, Unafraid of Sacred Cows, Face Moment of Truth in Balanced-Budget Talks," *Wall Street Journal*, May 11, 1995.

87. The Feldstein quote is from Louis Uchitelle, "A Political Comeback: Supply-Side Economics," *New York Times*, March 26, 2008. For evidence that tax cuts do not recoup the full amount of lost revenue, see CBO, "Analyzing the Economic and Budgetary Effects of a 10 Percent Cut in Income Tax Rates," December 1, 2005 www.cbo.gov/ftpdocs/69xx/doc6908/12-01-10Percent TaxCut.pdf; and N. Gregory Mankiw and Matthew Weinzierl, "Dynamic Scoring: A Back-of-the-Envelope Guide," Harvard University, December 12, 2005. www.papers.nber.org/papers/w11000

88. David Wessel, "Budget Battle Hides Congressional Victories That Reduce Spending," *Wall Street Journal*, November 27, 1995.

89. Jackie Calmes, "Clinton's Fiscal '97 Budget Reflects Major Shift toward Ending Deficits and 'Big Government,'" *Wall Street Journal*, February 6, 1996.

90. George Hager, "Clinton, GOP Congress Strike Historic Budget Agreement," *Congressional Quarterly Weekly Report*, May 3, 1997, 993–97; Lance LeLoup, *Parties, Rules, and the Evolution of Congressional Budgeting* (Columbus: Ohio State University Press, 2005), 176–77.

91. Richard Morin and Dana Milbank, "Poll Shows New Doubts on Economy," *Washington Post*, March 27, 2001.

92. Social Security and Medicare Boards of Trustees, "A Summary of the 2008 Annual Reports," Social Security Administration. www.ssa.gov/OACT/TRSUM/trsummary.html

93. Viveca Novak, "Defective Remedy," *National Journal*, March 27, 1993, 750.

94. Glenn Abney and Thomas P. Lauth, "The Line-Item Veto in the States: An Instrument for Fiscal Restraint or an Instrument of Partisanship?" *Public Administration Review* (May/June 1985): 372–77; Thomas P. Lauth and Catherine C. Reese, "The Line-Item Veto in Georgia: Fiscal Restraint or Inter-Branch Politics?" *Public Budgeting & Finance* 26 (2006): 1–19.

95. See, for example, Jackie Koszczuk, "Republicans' Hopes for 1996 Lie in Unfinished Business," *Congressional Quarterly Weekly Report*, January 6,

1996, 25; Andrew Taylor, "Line-Item Veto Compromise Passes Senate Easily, *Congressional Quarterly Weekly Report*, March 25, 1995, 855.

96. See Jerry Gray, "Compromise Bills Approved on Debt and Line-Item Veto," *New York Times*, March 29, 1996; Andrew Taylor, "Congress Hands President a Budgetary Scalpel," *Congressional Quarterly Weekly Report*, March 30, 1996, 864–67; Andrew Taylor, "Republicans Break Logjam on Line-Item Veto Bill," *Congressional Quarterly Weekly Report*, March 16, 1996, 687.

97. Quoted in Adam Clymer, "Legislation Pits Clinton vs. Democrats," *New York Times*, March 18, 1996.

98. Robert Pear, "A Judicial Group Condemns the Planned Line-Item Veto," *New York Times*, March 27, 1996.

99. Helen Dewar and Joan Biskupic, "Court Strikes Down Line-Item Veto," *Washington Post*, June 26, 1998.

100. Quoted in John Diamond, "Congress Upset over Line-Item Veto," October 10, 1997, available at allpolitics.com.

101. Tom Raum, "Balanced Budget May Doom Line-Item Veto," October 15, 1997, available at cnn.com.

102. *Clinton v. City of New York,* 524 U.S. 417 (1998); see also Philip G. Joyce, "The Federal Line Item Veto Experiment: After the Supreme Court Ruling, What's Next?" *Public Budgeting and Finance* 18 (Winter 1998): 3–21. Linda Feldmann, "More Power to the Pen: Bush Urges New Veto Tool," *Christian Science Monitor*, March 8, 2006; Michael A. Fletcher, "Bush Proposes Law to Give the President Line-Item Veto Power," *Washington Post*, March 7, 2006.

103. See, for example, Richard J. Tofel, "A Boon for the Constitutional Bar," *Wall Street Journal*, January 31, 1995.

104. Albert R. Hunt, "The Balanced Budget Amendment: A Contract with Evasion," *Wall Street Journal*, January 12, 1995. On 2004, see Jonathan Weisman, "GOP Drops Work on Balanced Budget," *Washington Post*, September 30, 2004, and Brian M. Riedl, "The Balanced Budget Amendment: The Wrong Answer to Runaway Spending," Web Memo, The Heritage Foundation, October 4, 2004. www.heritage.org/Research/budget/wm580.cfm

105. Gallup, "Gallup's Pulse of Democracy, Taxes and Tax Cuts," available at www.gallup.com/poll/1714/Taxes.aspx.

106. Ibid.

107. Milton Friedman, *Capitalism and Freedom* (Chicago: University of Chicago Press, 1962), 174–76.

108. John E. Berthoud, "State Lessons for the Flat Tax Debate," *Comparative State Politics* 17 (February 1996): 23–29; David E. Rosenbaum, "A Key Point by Forbes Proves Hard to Confirm," *New York Times*, February 3, 1996.

109. Alan Murray, "GOP Adherents Study Merits of a Flat Tax," *Wall Street Journal*, January 29, 1996.

110. Rosenbaum, "A Key Point by Forbes."

111. CCH, "Federal Tax Law Keeps Piling Up," 2008. www.cch.com/wbot2008/WBOT_TaxLawPileUp_(24)_f.pdf

112. J. Scott Moody, Wendy P. Warcholik, and Scott Hodge, "The Rising Cost of Complying with the Federal Income Tax, *Tax Foundation Special Report 138* (December 2005).

113. R. W. Apple, Jr., "Candidate of the Flat Tax Is a Bit of a Flat Campaigner," *New York Times*, February 12, 1996.

114. Calculated by authors from IRS, SOI Tax Stats - Individual Statistical Tables by Size of Adjusted Gross Income, All Returns: Adjusted Gross Income, Exemptions, Deductions, and Tax Items, "Table 1.2—All Returns: Adjusted Gross Income, Exemptions, Deductions, and Tax Items, by Size of Adjusted Gross Income and by Marital Status, Tax Year 2006." www.irs.gov/taxstats/indtaxstats/article/0,,id=134951,00.html

115. Albert R. Hunt, "The Flat-Tax Snow Job," *Wall Street Journal*, January 11, 1996; "Poll Finds Surprising Support for Tax System," *Cedar Rapids Gazette*, February 26, 1996; "The Flat Tax Is Losing Its Appeal Among U.S. Voters, Poll Finds," *Wall Street Journal*, March 8, 1996. More recently, see the similar results of the NBC News Poll, April 3–5, 2005. www.pollingreport.com/budget.htm

116. Steve Forbes, *The Flat Tax Revolution* Washington, D.C.: Regnery, 2005. See also Steve Forbes, "One Simple Rate," August 21, 2005, available at OpinionJournal.com.

117. Neal Boortz and John Linder, *The Fair Tax Book: Saying Goodbye to the Income Tax and the IRS* (New York: Regan, 2005); Neal Boortz and John Linder with Rob Woodall, *Fair Tax: Answering the Critics* (New York: Harper, 2008).

118. This count is taken from FairTax.org, available at www.fairtax.org/site/PageServer?pagename=news_cosponsor.

119. Jackie Calmes, "Income-Tax Foes Regroup," *Wall Street Journal*, August 20, 2007.

120. Wildavsky, *The New Politics of the Budgetary Process*, 436–40; Kettl, *Deficit Politics*, 76–91.

121. Wildavsky, *The New Politics of the Budgetary Process*, chap. 10.

17

Domestic Policy

CHAPTER OUTLINE

In 1996, President Bill Clinton declared in his State of the Union speech that "the era of big government is over."[1] The number of federal government employees did, in fact, shrink during Clinton's administration, and it continued to shrink under President George W. Bush's administration. In 1990, the number of federal civilian employees had reached an all-time high of 3,233,000—2.7 percent of the American workforce. By 2006, the number of federal, civilian employees had shrunk to only 2,700,000—or 1.9 percent of the workforce.[2] Yet the era of big government was anything but over. Neither President Clinton nor President Bush sought to eliminate any major federal program. They sought to trim them and make them more efficient but not to end them. Moreover, the twin problems of global warming and the eventual decline of world oil supplies on which the U.S. depends are creating the need for more government programs. The public has already begun to demand regulations to increase automobile fuel efficiency, to provide for more, cheaper energy, and to do something about the problems caused by global warming. The need for government continues.

Throughout the nineteenth century, the federal government played a very limited role in domestic policy. In the twentieth century, however, the federal government took on new responsibilities for managing the economy, regulating the practices of private businesses, and providing a social safety net for the American people. Although the American public does not like the idea of "big government," they do like a huge number of specific government programs—including programs that fight poverty; help young people earn college degrees; provide medical care to the young, the poor, and the elderly; guarantee safe working conditions; prevent hazardous products from reaching the marketplace; protect the environment; keep energy prices low; end discrimination in the workplace; and regulate the financial and stock markets so they do not collapse triggering recessions. So although the public may not like the *idea* of big government, they like big government *in practice.*

In this chapter, we examine the federal government's changing role in American life. We look at three broad tasks the federal government has assumed in domestic policy—managing the economy, regulating the practices of private business, and promoting social welfare. We begin by sketching out the growth of the government's tools for managing the economy, and then we assess the success of current efforts to guide the nation's economy toward a stable, prosperous future. In the second section, we first discuss the development and consequences of the federal government's efforts to regulate the competitive practices of business. We then review social regulation, analyzing in particular worker safety and health regulations and environmental regulations. In the third section, we discuss the historical development and current status of social welfare policy in the United States. We conclude our discussion of social welfare policy by reviewing the core issues in the debates over Social Security, welfare reform, and health care.

In all three of these areas—economic policy, regulatory policy, and social welfare policy—the rules change as the needs and views of the American public and their elected representatives change. In domestic policy, as in all areas of government, changes in the rules of politics cause some groups to gain and others to lose. Which is preferable: a smaller, more limited federal government or a larger one with more expansive responsibilities? The controversy rages on.

17-1 MANAGING THE ECONOMY

Most Americans now expect the federal government to manage the overall health of the national economy. They count on the government to promote the creation of new jobs, to keep inflation and interest rates low and stable, to maintain gasoline and other energy supplies at affordable prices, and to ensure that the economy grows at a steady rate. Although the idea that the federal government should manage the economy seems natural to us today, it is a relatively recent phenomenon. Indeed, at the beginning of the twentieth century, most people believed that the federal government should have no role in managing the economy. Thus, to understand the federal government's current role in managing the economy, we need to review how the government's role in economic management has changed over the course of the century as well as to discuss what tools the government has today to manage the nation's economy.

17-1a From Government Restraint to Government Intervention

At the opening of the twentieth century, the dominant economic wisdom was what we know today as *classical economics*. A fundamental principle of classical economics was that government should follow a ***laissez-faire*** approach to the national economy. Taken from the French expression "let it be," laissez-faire held that the government's only role in the economy was to ensure a stable supply of money; other than that, the government should leave the success or failure of private businesses up to the forces of the free market. This let-it-be approach to the economy applied even when economic growth faltered and unemployment rose. During economic hard times, classical economics held that the government should avoid intervening in the economy and simply allow the business cycle to run its course.

The last president associated with laissez-faire economic policies was Herbert Hoover, who was elected in 1928. During Hoover's first year in office, the stock market crashed and the Great Depression began. Although he wanted the government to take a more active role in leading the country out of its economic slump, Hoover lacked the popular and political support needed to institute major changes in the way the government managed the economy. As a result, much of his administration's work was limited to assuring Americans that better days were just around the corner

laissez-faire
An economic theory, dominant at the start of the twentieth century, that argued that the federal government's only role in the economy was to ensure a stable supply of money.

and urging them to help those in need. Hoover's let-it-be approach failed to solve the country's economic problems, and the economic picture worsened. Not surprisingly, Hoover lost the 1932 presidential race to his Democratic rival, Franklin Delano Roosevelt (FDR), and Hoover found himself labeled (somewhat misleadingly) by later generations of Americans as a president who believed strongly in a laissez-faire approach to business and society.[3]

When Roosevelt began his first term as president in 1933, he faced a daunting challenge. The Great Depression had led to the collapse of thousands upon thousands of banks, farms, and businesses, and unemployment soared to 25 percent. Yet FDR had something that Hoover had lacked, namely, the political support he needed to carve out a more active role for the federal government. As a result, FDR responded to the country's economic hardship by initiating a series of programs, known collectively as the New Deal, that sought to get the country back on its economic feet by expanding the federal government's power over the economy.[4] Ironically, many of these programs had their roots in proposals that the Hoover administration had originally developed.[5]

Roosevelt's New Deal programs slowly began to work. Unemployment edged down from 25 percent in 1933 to 14 percent in 1937. When the economy suddenly began to falter and unemployment shot up again in 1938; however, FDR took a new approach to the country's economic problems.

The approach Roosevelt adopted in 1938 was based on the idea that government spending can be used to rejuvenate the economy—in short, if the government spends more money, and even if it goes into debt to do so, the extra money will help get private businesses going again and put people back to work. Accordingly, FDR changed the rules. He persuaded Congress to put aside its traditional commitment to a balanced budget—even though he had endorsed the idea of balancing the budget during his first presidential campaign in 1932—and to launch an ambitious program of increased government spending. The federal government's deficit grew, but the hope was that the nation could spend its way out of the Depression. Although the United States never fully pulled out of the Depression until World War II—when deficit spending reached stunning heights—FDR established the federal government's role as manager of the economy and convinced American policy makers that they could use **fiscal policy**—that is, government taxing and spending decisions—as a management tool.[6] (For more details of the deficit during this period, see Chapter 16.)

fiscal policy
Using the federal government's control over taxes and spending to influence the condition of the national economy.

17-1b Managing the Economy by Taxing and Spending

Franklin Roosevelt's decision to use fiscal policy to combat the Great Depression was inspired by the work of John Maynard Keynes, a British economist whose work revolutionized the way governments attempt to manage their economies. In his seminal book, *The General Theory of Employment, Interest, and Money,* published in 1936, Keynes argued that capitalist economies do not always run at full throttle.[7] Instead, they experience periods of recession, or economic slowdown, and periods of growth. During recessions, both the supply of goods and services business produces and the demand for goods and services to purchase fall. Because businesses cannot sell their goods, they fire workers and produce fewer goods. Because fewer people have jobs, less money is available to buy goods. In the resulting cycle, unemployment rises and the country's **gross domestic product (GDP)**, or overall economic output, falls.

gross domestic product (GDP)
A measure of a country's total economic output in any given year.

Keynes believed that government can manage the economy and push it out of recession by employing certain policies—in effect, by changing the rules of fiscal policy according to the situation. To push a country out of recession, Keynes argued, a government should spend enough money to raise demand for goods and services, even if it must borrow money and run a budget deficit. This, in turn, would cause businesses to hire more people, which would give the new workers salaries to push demand up even further. In other words, Keynes said that deficit spending—spending more than the government is taking in—could pull nations out of recessions.

The other side of Keynes's theory was that the economy could run too fast. Businesses, seeking to expand production, could seek new workers by paying them more, thus bidding up the prices of workers and causing inflation. Similarly, consumers, seeking to purchase more goods than were available, could drive inflation by offering to pay more for goods. Eventually prices might spiral so high that people could no longer afford basic goods; the economy might then nose dive into a recession as people quit spending and businesses lose money and have to lay off workers. To prevent the economy from growing too rapidly and thereby creating unacceptable levels of inflation, Keynes argued that the government should cut its spending or raise taxes to soak up the excess demand and slow the economy down to a more stable level. That is, the government could use budget surpluses—taking in more tax revenues than it spends—to keep inflation in check.

Thus, in Keynes's view, the main tool for managing the national economy is simply the amount of the federal government's surplus or deficit spending: the decision to raise more in revenue than it spends (a surplus) or spend more money than it raises (a deficit). Keynes's theory, known as **Keynesian economics**, did not specify what governments should spend their money on or what taxes should be raised or cut; it specified only the overall amounts of deficit or surplus spending. Later work by Keynes and other economists refined and expanded on his original idea by identifying factors that influence the health of the economy. Nonetheless, for Keynesians, the main tool for managing the national economy remains the size of the budget deficit or surplus.

Keynesian economics
An economic theory, based on the work of British economist John Maynard Keynes, that contends that the national government can manage the economy by running budget surpluses and budget deficits.

By the end of World War II, Keynes's activist approach to government management of the economy was firmly rooted in American politics. When Congress passed the Employment Act of 1946, it officially declared that the federal government was responsible for assuring full employment, stable prices, and a strong economy.

counter-cyclical programs
Government programs that automatically increase spending when the economy slows down and unemployment rises, and decrease spending when the economy speeds up.

Although Keynesian economics gained wide acceptance among economists and politicians, it had a critical weakness. Slowing down an overheated economy by raising taxes and cutting services might work in economic theory, but in practice, persuading Congress to take such actions is politically difficult. Some government programs such as welfare, food stamps, and unemployment insurance are automatic, **counter-cyclical programs**. This means that when the economy slows down and unemployment rises, government spending on these programs automatically increases; when the economy speeds up and unemployment falls, government spending on these programs falls. Most efforts to slow the economy by cutting government spending or raising taxes require Congress to pass laws, however, which members of Congress find politically difficult. Once a "temporary" jobs program or a "temporary" business tax cut to boost the economy has done its work, advocates for the program defend it in Congress and the temporary program often becomes permanent. Thus, Keynes's advice to increase spending when the economy falters generally leads to bigger government and greater deficit spending because the corresponding spending cuts and tax increases are usually not enacted when the economy improves.

17-1c Managing the Economy by Controlling the Money Supply

Although Keynesian economics and a belief in the merits of fiscal policy guided the federal government's efforts to manage the national economy in the 1950s, 1960s, and 1970s, some economists argued that Keynes had fundamentally misunderstood how the economy works, and as a result, that his policy advice was misguided. These economists offered a competing economic theory which contends that changes in a nation's money supply—that is, in the amount of money in circulation—are the primary if not the sole determinant of its economic health. Because these economists emphasize the importance of the money supply, they are known as monetarists and their views as **monetary theory**.

monetary theory
An economic theory which contends that a nation's money supply, or the amount of money in circulation, is the primary if not sole determinant of the health of the national economy.

Unlike Keynesian economic theory, monetary theory was not suddenly presented to the world by a single, brilliant economist. Instead, the roots of monetary theory are found in the nineteenth-century debates over what the federal government should do regarding the money supply and setting up a central bank. During the nineteenth century, the United States was on a gold standard, which meant that people holding paper currency had the right to convert their currency into gold on demand. Because the supply of gold was limited, the 1800s saw heated debates over how much money should be minted and what the government should do to stabilize the value of money and prevent currency crises.[8] By the late 1800s, periodic currency crises were seriously disrupting the country's economic growth. This led to calls for Congress to create a powerful central bank that could stabilize the country's money supply.

In 1913, Congress finally responded by establishing the **Federal Reserve System**, often referred to by its nickname, the Fed.[9] By law, the Fed is an independent regulatory commission, which means that it operates with relatively little direct interference from either the rest of the executive branch or from Congress (see Chapter 13). The reason Congress made the Fed independent of the rest of government is simple: The sponsors of the law creating the Fed wanted to limit the ability of elected officials to manipulate the economy for political gain.

The structure of the Federal Reserve System has changed little since it was established. The Fed has four parts: (1) the Board of Governors; (2) the Federal Open Market Committee; (3) the twelve regional Federal Reserve Banks; and (4) the commercial banks that are members of the Fed, including all national banks and any state-chartered banks that choose to join. The president appoints the chair and vice-chair of the Fed (with the consent of the Senate); the commercial banks that are members of the system elect the directors of the Federal Reserve Banks. Thus, some Federal Reserve officials are appointed by the president with the Senate's approval, and some are elected by private businesses.

By the 1960s, leading monetary theorists such as Milton Friedman had developed sophisticated economic models showing how the Federal Reserve's management of the money supply influences the economy.[10] Friedman and his colleagues argued that to keep the national economy growing at a healthy pace, the government should expand the money supply at a steady rate that matches the growth rate of the economy. If the money supply expands too quickly, the excess money will drive down interest rates, which will make it cheaper for businesses and individuals to borrow money, which will encourage faster growth, which will fuel inflation. If the money supply expands too slowly, the lack of money will drive up interest rates, which will make it more expensive for companies and individuals to borrow money, which will slow down the economy and possibly even force it into a recession. Indeed, some monetary theorists argue that the Fed's refusal in the late 1920s to expand the money supply—a strategy that monetary theorists call a tight money policy—helped cause the Great Depression.[11]

The Fed controls the money supply that lies at the core of monetary theory in three main ways: (1) by setting the discount rate, (2) by deciding how many treasury securities to buy or sell, and (3) by changing the required reserve ratio. The *discount rate* is the interest rate the Fed charges its member banks when it lends them money. If the Fed wishes to reduce the money supply and slow down the economy, it can raise the discount rate, making it more expensive to borrow money. Similarly, if it wishes to increase the money supply, it can lower the discount rate. The Fed's Board of Governors is responsible for deciding where to peg the rate.

The second primary method the Fed uses to affect the country's money supply is buying and selling *treasury securities,* or government IOUs. When the Fed wishes to change the amount of money in circulation, it does not simply turn on or off the presses that

Federal Reserve System
An independent regulatory commission that Congress created in 1913 to oversee the nation's money supply.

print money. Instead, the Fed buys or sells treasury securities. When the Fed sells treasury securities, it takes money out of circulation and leaves the purchaser with a bond—a piece of paper promising to repay the purchaser principal plus interest over a set period of time, which may range from as short as three months to as long as thirty years. When the Fed buys treasury securities, it redeems bonds, or pays back its IOUs, and thereby puts more money into circulation. Thus, decisions about the sale of treasury securities can also affect the money supply and indirectly influence whether the economy speeds up or slows down. Decisions about buying and selling treasury securities are up to the Federal Open Market Committee, made up of the Board of Governors plus the five elected representatives of the Federal Reserve Banks.

The third method the Fed uses to affect the country's money supply is changing the *required reserve ratio.* By law, banks must hold a specified percentage of their deposits as required reserves— that is, money they cannot lend. When the Fed raises the required reserve ratio, banks must keep more of their deposits on hand; as a result, they have less money to lend, which reduces the money supply. Conversely, when the Fed lowers the reserve requirement, banks have more money to lend, which increases the money supply. Because changing the required reserve ratio can produce dramatic changes in the money supply and the economy, the Fed seldom uses this method.

Guiding the economy by controlling the money supply is extraordinarily complicated. Economists may agree about the general causes of economic prosperity, but they disagree about technical questions such as when to change the discount rate and how many treasury securities to buy or sell in any given month. The controls over the money supply are, after all, fairly crude. Moreover, virtually all economists recognize that to work, monetary policy must be coordinated with fiscal policy.[12] The money supply decisions the Fed makes and the budget decisions Congress and the president make both influence the economy in ways that interact with each other. No group can operate without considering the actions of the others.

Some observers liken the problem of guiding the economy with fiscal and monetary policy to steering an ocean liner. When the captain turns the rudder sharply to the right, it takes the ship a long time to change course. If the captain waits too long before turning the rudder back, the ship may continue turning to the right far longer than the captain wished.

In 2006, President Bush appointed Ben S. Bernanke as the new chair of the Fed. Along with the five other members of the Board of Governors, Bernanke is now setting the course for interest rates and monetary policy. His predecessor, Alan Greenspan, held the job from 1987 through the beginning of 2006. He is widely regarded as having been the best chair in the Fed's history. So far, Bernanke is off to a rough start because of the energy crisis, the home mortgage crisis, and the collapse of the financial markets in 2008. Whether or not he can help return the economy to good health remains to be seen.

Ben S. Bernanke, members of the Board of Governors, The Federal Reserve Board, USA.

17-1d Can the Government Manage the Economy?

Keynesian and monetarist theories have come under fire in recent years from economists who argue that the ability of the federal government to use fiscal and monetary policy to manage the economy is actually quite limited. In the early 1970s, Robert Lucas of the University of Chicago began to examine a question that Keynesian and monetarist theories left unaddressed—namely, how do firms and individuals react to changes in government policy? Using sophisticated mathematical models, Lucas posited what became known as the **Lucas critique**, the argument that if people act rationally, then their reactions to changes in government policy will often negate the intent of those changes. Moreover, the Lucas critique suggests that in some circumstances, firms and individuals will react to changes in fiscal and monetary policy in ways that will produce results opposite those that government officials intended.[13] (In 1995, Lucas won the Nobel Prize in economics for his critique.)

Lucas critique
An economic theory which contends that if people act rationally, then their reactions to changes in government policy will often negate the intent of those changes.

To understand the basic intuition behind the Lucas critique, consider what happens when the government decides to cut taxes. According to traditional Keynesian economics, this use of fiscal policy will stimulate the demand for goods and services, which in turn will encourage economic growth. The Lucas critique takes this line of thinking one step further, arguing that people know from past experience that government efforts to stimulate the economy will spur inflation and erode their earnings. Workers will therefore demand higher wages, and businesses will demand higher prices. The result will be higher inflation and continued unemployment, the exact opposite of what policy makers hoped to accomplish. Monetary policy can produce the same perverse outcome. When the Federal Reserve tries to slow economic growth to a more reasonable level by raising interest rates, it may well plunge the country into a recession as businesses and workers react to the higher rates by cutting back on their purchases of goods and services.

The Lucas critique suggests two simple, yet important, pieces of advice to government policy makers. First, the government cannot use fiscal and monetary policy to fine-tune the economy. Firms and individuals will react to government efforts to manipulate the economy in ways that may cancel out what policy makers hope to achieve. Second, the government's only role in the economy should be to maintain a steady growth in the money supply. Because Lucas and his colleagues are so skeptical of the ability of the federal government to manage the economy, their arguments have come to be called the "new classical economics." Much like the classical economists of the nineteenth century, the new classical economists argue that the government should not intervene in the economy; it should follow laissez-faire policies.[14]

In the mid-1980s, a group of economists who called themselves "new Keynesians" began to respond to the arguments of the new classical economists. They accepted much of the reasoning behind the Lucas critique, but they dissented on some key issues. In particular, they argued that the new classical economists were mistaken in their policy recommendations because their mathematical models assumed that wages and prices change quickly in response to changes in the economy. The new Keynesians argued that in the real world, wages can be "sticky"—in other words, they might not rise or fall quickly in response to changes in economic conditions.[15] Consequently, the new Keynesians argued that persistent unemployment could exist. Similarly, in some circumstances, prices might be sticky and not change rapidly in response to supply and demand. As a result, shortages and excess supplies of goods might develop. Because the new Keynesians believe that the actual economy does not work in precisely the fashion the mathematical models of the new classical economists predict, they argue that the government should intervene in the economy to deal with market failures such as high unemployment.[16]

In sum, economists continue to disagree over how the economy works and over what economic policies the government should follow. Whereas many economists believe that the government has a significant role to play in managing the economy, many others argue that its role is small at best. No resolution of their debates is in sight, but the rules or theories policy makers choose to put into play will affect the economy and create economic winners and losers.

17-1e The Current Status of Economic Stewardship

An old joke about economists suggests that if you bring twelve prominent economists together and ask their advice, you will get at least thirteen contradictory opinions. Yet the record suggests that although economists may disagree about minor matters, they have been right about the big ones. As Figure 17–1 shows, fiscal and monetary policy controls have successfully stabilized the American economy since World War II. Wide swings from boom to bust have largely disappeared.

Despite the general success of our economic policy, many areas of conflict remain. Politicians, economists, and citizens continue to disagree about issues such as how America's wealth should be distributed, how to spur the economy, and how to regulate the home mortgage industry.

The Distribution of Income and Wealth

Although discussions of the American economy frequently focus on topics such as unemployment, inflation, and economic growth, people care about more than just a few summary measures of the economy's success. They also care about how particular groups in American society are faring. One trend occurring over the past twenty-five years is that the distribution of resources in American society has changed dramatically—the rich are increasingly laying claim to more of the country's economic pie, while the poor are laying claim to less. In 1980, the highest paid 20 percent of American families earned 44.1 percent of all income, whereas the lowest paid 20 percent received only 4.2 percent of all income. By 2005, the top

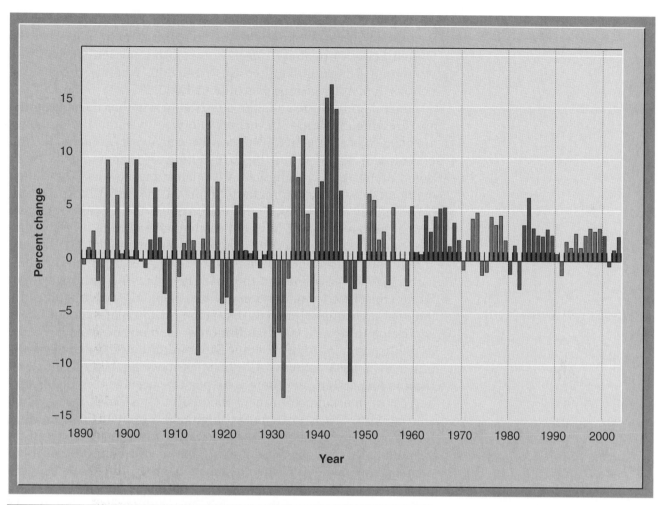

Figure 17-1 A Century of American Economic Growth. The volatility of annual changes in gross domestic product, after inflation has been factored out, has diminished since the mid-twentieth century. Most economists attribute the disappearance of wide swings from boom to bust to the successful use of fiscal and monetary policy.

Source: © *Louis Johnston and Samuel H. Williamson, "The Annual Real and Nominal GDP for the United States, 1789–Present" www.eh.net/hmit/gdp/.*

20 percent had increased its share to 50.4 percent of all income, whereas the share of the bottom 20 percent had dropped to 3.4 percent.[17] Nonetheless, the income gap between rich and poor in the United States remains much smaller than it was in the 1930s, and it is not radically larger than the gap in most other advanced industrialized democracies.[18]

America's wealth—which encompasses not only income but also assets such as real estate, stocks, bonds, and material goods—is even less equally distributed than its income. The richest 1 percent of all American households own about 33 percent of the nation's wealth. The top 5 percent control about 58 percent of the country's wealth. In contrast, the bottom 50 percent of the population owns only 3 percent of the nation's wealth. The concentration of wealth in the United States is greater than that in any European democracy. For example, the richest 1 percent of all British households holds 18 percent of the wealth in the United Kingdom, and the richest 1 percent of French households holds 26 percent of the wealth in France.[19] Moreover, the concentration of wealth in the United States is related to race. In 2004, the median net worth of white, non-Hispanic families was $140,700, whereas the median net worth of other groups was only $24,800.[20]

Much dispute surrounds the question of whether the substantial and growing disparities in income and wealth in the United States are good or bad. In general, conservative analysts minimize the importance of statistics on the distribution of income and wealth. Some argue that such figures are misleading because they often overlook how welfare programs improve the lot of the poor and because they say nothing about the turnover that occurs from year to year across different levels of income and wealth.[21] (For example, most young people look impoverished in statistics that measure income and wealth because they are just starting out on their careers. A few years down the road, they may be quite wealthy.) Some conservative analysts argue that inequality is inherent in a free-market economy such as that of the United States; hence, there is no such thing as a fair distribution of income and wealth. As the Republican majority of the Joint Economic Committee of Congress put it in a 1995 report: "All societies have unequal wealth and income dispersion, and there is no positive basis for criticizing any degree of market-determined inequality."[22] Some conservative analysts go so far as to argue that high levels of inequality are good for the economy if the rich are encouraged to invest their savings in economically productive ventures. This would help promote economic growth, which in theory should benefit individuals at every income level. In short, in *relative* terms, the poor might end up with a smaller share of the pie, but in *absolute* terms they would end up with more pie than they might otherwise have received.

Not surprisingly, liberal analysts take a much more pessimistic view of the consequences of rising inequality.[23] They cite data showing that the poor are increasingly likely to stay poor, and as a result, they worry that the United States, which historically has prided itself on being an egalitarian society, is becoming a nation of haves and have-nots.[24] Liberal analysts fear that one consequence of dividing the country into haves and have-nots will be slower economic growth. The poor will increasingly lack the incomes they need to consume goods and services, which will deprive businesses of potential customers. At the same time, liberal analysts worry that rising inequality will tear at the nation's social fabric. The rich will be even better able to shift political and economic decisions in their favor, thereby producing further inequality. In turn, the poor might become increasingly envious of the rich, sowing the seeds of class conflict and spawning social problems such as crime.

Supply-Side Economics

To some extent, the increased inequality in the distribution of income and wealth in the United States in the 1980s was the consequence of **supply-side economics**, an economic theory developed by an influential group of conservative economists led by George

supply-side economics

An economic theory which argues that if the government cuts taxes, reduces spending, and eliminates regulations, resources will be freed up to fuel the economy to produce even more goods and services.

Gilder and Arthur Laffer.[25] Proponents of supply-side economics believe that the government has become too large and that it is soaking up too much money from the private sector. They argue that if the government cuts taxes, reduces government spending, and eliminates many government regulations, resources will be freed up to fuel the economy to produce even more goods and services for everyone. In short, supply-siders argued that cutting taxes would increase the supply of goods and services to the benefit of all. (Because supply-side economics seeks to affect the economy by changing government spending and taxing decisions, it is a type of fiscal policy, although its underlying logic and policy recommendations differ sharply from those of Keynesian economics.)

President Ronald Reagan championed the idea of supply-side economics. In the first years of his administration, Reagan persuaded Congress to enact large cuts in income taxes. At the same time, the Reagan administration pushed Congress to slow the growth of federal spending, if not actually cut it. Because the tax cuts primarily benefited the rich—after all, they paid more income taxes to begin with—and because many of the spending cuts fell heavily on programs such as welfare and job training that go mostly to the poor and working class, one consequence was increased inequality in the distribution of income and wealth in the United States. As you might imagine, as it became clear that the distribution of income and wealth was becoming more unequal, supply-side economics became the subject of considerable controversy and was often derided by its critics as *Reaganomics* and *voodoo economics.*[26] (George H. W. Bush coined the term *voodoo economics* when he criticized Reagan's economic proposals during his unsuccessful bid to win the Republican presidential nomination in 1980.)

For their part, proponents of supply-side economics point out with pride that both inflation and unemployment fell sharply and the economy grew rapidly while President Reagan was in office. Whether supply-side economics was responsible for this good fortune is another matter. Monetarists argue that much of the credit for the healthy economy is owed to the Fed for administering a wise monetary policy. Keynesians frequently argue that in practice, supply-side economics looks a lot like Keynesian economics. The reason is that, although members of Congress were happy to cut taxes, they refused to accept the advice of supply-side economists and cut government spending on politically popular and expensive programs such as Social Security and Medicare. As we saw in Chapter 16, combining tax cuts with increased government spending produced massive budget deficits during the Reagan years. And as Keynesian economists had long argued, if government runs large budget deficits, it will stimulate economic growth.

Because of evidence of growing inequality in the distribution of income and wealth, and because of well-justified fears that Congress would not match politically popular tax cuts with politically unpopular spending cuts, proponents of supply-side economics won few battles in Washington from the mid-1980s through the end of the Clinton administration in 2000.[27] With the end of budget deficits during the Clinton years, tax cuts once again rose to the top of the Republican Party's political agenda. When the younger President Bush came to office, he promised large tax cuts, and he delivered. His first major tax bill slashed taxes by $1.35 trillion over ten years. He followed that move with smaller tax cuts in each of the next two years and wrapped up his first administration with a $136 billion corporate tax cut bill shortly before the 2004 election. Supply-side arguments featured prominently in Bush's efforts to persuade Congress and the American public to support his legislation. The bulk of the tax reductions went to the wealthiest Americans, which supply-siders argued was the best policy to help the overall economy.[28] A major item at the top of President Bush's agenda for his second term was extending the tax cuts and making them permanent. By 2008, he succeeded in extending them, but could not persuade Congress to make them permanent. Once again, supply-side economics was playing an influential role in Washington.

Industrial Policy

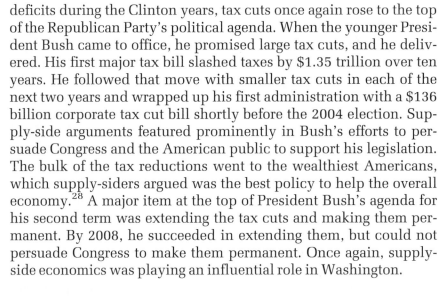

industrial policy
The policy of seeking to strengthen selected industries by targeting them for governmental aid rather than letting the forces of the free market determine their fates.

Since the early 1980s, some liberal economists have urged Congress and the president to develop an **industrial policy** to strengthen the American economy. These economists argue that the United States will prosper even more if the government helps specific industries rather than leaves their fate solely to the free market.[29] Government aid can come in a variety of forms, ranging from special tax incentives to government funds for research and development to exemptions from some types of government regulations. Whatever form the aid takes, the basic idea behind industrial policy is for the government to select an industry it believes can become a world leader with the proper help and encouragement, and then give it that help.

Many advanced industrialized nations have had considerable success with industrial policies. In the 1970s and 1980s, for example, the Japanese government transformed its automobile and high-technology industries into world leaders.[30] The United States, however, has generally shied away from an organized industrial policy, partly because of deep-seated philosophical objections to government intervention in the marketplace and partly because of practical doubts about the ability of the government to pick industries likely to be "winners." Moreover, enthusiasm for industrial policy faded in the 1990s when the Japanese economy entered a prolonged recession, whereas the American economy experienced an unprecedented boom.

Avoidance of industrial policies, however, seems to be changing. Attention has returned to industrial policies because of the threat of global warning, the recognition of unstable foreign oil supplies, and the expectation that in the next few decades world oil supplies may peak, causing oil prices to skyrocket.[31] Congress has already passed some laws intended to give domestic, alternative energy industries a boost—for example, the production tax credit for wind power and the investment tax credit for solar power. Some politicians are calling for far stronger industrial policies designed to boost wind, solar, nuclear, and other energy industries and to reduce American reliance on imported oil and gas.[32] The belief underlying these calls for an industrial policy is that if the problems of global warming and our reliance on imported oil are left up to the free market without any government intervention, the problems will not be solved, and the United States will suffer.

In steering our modern economy, the government uses both fiscal and monetary policy. Yet different people with different goals hold the controls. Congress and the president control the primary fiscal policy tool, the budget. They make decisions about the size of the surplus or deficit as well as decisions about supply-side economics and industrial policy, such as how big the government should be and whether it should favor particular industries. The independent Fed controls monetary policy. It makes decisions about the money supply by setting the discount rate and regulating the purchase and sale of treasury securities. Thus, although most Americans reward or blame the president for the performance of the economy, the president must share management of the economy with many other people in government.

The 2008 Financial Crisis

In 2007, two new weaknesses began to appear in the American economy—a bubble in the housing market, which will be explained later, and increasingly aggressive and risky investment behavior by banks and insurance companies. Neither problem was fully understood at the time, but by the following year, they would bring about a major financial crisis.

Housing prices had increased throughout the 1990s, but beginning in 2000, housing prices shot up far more rapidly than the rate of inflation. From the first quarter of 2000 through the beginning of 2007, the median price of a house increased 69 percent in the U.S., while the median family income increased only 0.4 percent. In some areas, the rise in prices was almost unbelievable. In California, the price of a median home rose 245 percent from 2000 to 2007. Within ten years, Californians had gone from paying four times their median family income for a typical home to paying over ten times the median income for that home.[33]

Speculation fueled the rapidly rising prices. People were bidding up the prices of homes because they hoped to sell them for a profit after prices rose even further. The television show "Flip this House" captured the spirit of the times. Each week, it presented stories of people who bought homes, fixed them up, and sold them for huge profits within 90 days. The speculation-driven, inflated prices were a "housing bubble."

Easy credit also fueled the rapidly rising home prices. To increase their profits, many banks took the risky step of lending money for home purchases to people who were poor credit risks—so-called "subprime borrowers."[34] In some cases, banks gave high-risk borrowers interest-only loans with "balloon payments" after a few years. These loans required that borrowers only pay the interest on the money they borrowed for the first few years, after which they had to pay both the interest and part of principal in one huge payment. In addition, some homeowners borrowed money, using their homes as collateral to guarantee the loans. The high housing prices allowed people to borrow a great deal on the equity in their homes—far more than they could afford to repay if their houses fell in value. As a result, many homeowners were financially vulnerable when the economy slowed down and housing prices fell.

A further problem that developed during these years was that minimally regulated banks and insurance companies began taking larger risks with their investments. In effect, they bet that the stock market, which had been rising since the 1991 recession, would continue to rise. Investment banks, unlike commercial retail banks in which people have checking and savings accounts, operate with minimal regulations. Similarly, although individual home, fire, and automobile insurance markets are strictly regulated, large insurance companies can issue policies to guarantee that people will not default on home loans or that a company's stock will not fall. In fact, they can issue policies to guarantee almost anything they like because, like investment banks, they are largely free of government limits and regulations.

Banks and insurance companies began creating and investing in *derivatives*—financial instruments whose value depends on the value of other financial instruments.[35] For example, a derivative might be a contract to purchase a company's stock at some time in the future or a contract to guarantee a package of home mortgage loans. Of course, stock prices rise and fall, and the value of a set of home mortgages might fall if the home owners default on their loans, so the actual value of derivatives is often extremely difficult to measure. As a result, a great deal of confusion developed over the value of both derivatives and the companies that owned them.

In 2007, the rise in housing prices slowed, and Congress recognized the potential for problems. To protect the banking industry, Congress passed the Federal Housing Finance Reform Act of 2007, which established the Federal Housing Finance Agency (FHFA) to regulate federal home loan banks—including Fannie Mae (formally, the Federal National Mortgage Association) and Freddie Mac (the Federal Home Loan Mortgage Corporation), the two government-chartered mortgage giants that owned or guaranteed half of the nation's $12 trillion in American home loans. In 2008, Treasury Secretary Henry Paulson persuaded Congress to expand federal authority to allow the FHFA to lend banks taxpayer money, to buy their stock, and even to force them into conservatorships (a type of bankruptcy) if necessary.[36]

In 2008, the home mortgage crisis struck with a vengeance. Housing prices fell, the unemployment rate rose, and borrowers found themselves unable to make their mortgage payments. As a result, banks were forced to foreclose on hundreds of thousands of homes. Some people even walked away from their homes when they realized that they owed more money on their homes than the homes were worth. Banks began to fail for the same reason. The people to whom they had lent money had defaulted on their mortgages and had left the banks with homes that were worth less than the money they had lent. A string of bankruptcies and business failures followed, beginning with the collapse of Bear Stearns—one of the nation's largest and oldest investment banks.[37]

By September 2008, Fannie Mae and Freddie Mac were heading toward bankruptcy. At that point, the federal government stepped in, placing both banks under federal control in conservatorships.[38] The investment banking giant Lehman Brothers filed for bankruptcy a week later, and the Federal Reserve Bank had to step in with an $85 billion bailout of the insurance giant American International Group two days after that. America's financial system was teetering on the brink of complete failure, and Congress had to act.[39]

The key problem that forced the government to act was that credit markets were drying up. Because of the failure of many of the nation's largest banks, there was not enough money to lend to businesses and governments that needed to borrow money to conduct ordinary business. For example, every fall the state of California sells revenue anticipation bonds to cover its expenses until tax revenue starts flowing after the April 15 income tax deadline. In October 2008, however, the state realized that when they offered to sell the bonds, there might not be enough buyers. The result, according to Governor Arnold Schwarzenegger, would be that the government would run out of money by the end of the month and would have to start shutting down.[40] The problem California faced was being faced by businesses and governments all across the nation. People needed to borrow money, but banks either did not have enough money to lend or were unwilling to lend what they had.

As the threat of financial collapse grew, Treasury Secretary Paulson proposed a $700 billion bailout plan. His plan was initially rejected by the House of Representatives, but within two weeks, congressional leaders, Secretary Paulson, and Federal Reserve Chair Bernanke had worked out a compromise plan that passed Congress and was immediately signed by President Bush.[41]

The plan was the biggest intervention into the market place since the Great Depression in the 1930s. The legislation provided for $700 billion for the Treasury to buy or insure securities based on bad mortgages. By purchasing the mortgage-based securities, the government was injecting badly needed money into the economy and preventing the nation's largest banks from failing. In exchange for purchasing the bad debt, the government would get an ownership share in the firms that sold the bad debt to the government. This was the guarantee for the taxpayers. In addition, the plan required the Treasury to modify troubled mortgages, which it purchased in the bailout, to help homeowners. In a gesture to an outraged public, the plan also limited the amount of compensation that the executives of the failed Wall Street firms could earn. Finally, the plan created a Financial Stability Oversight Board and a Special Inspector General to oversee the bailout and report to Congress and the public on what was being done.

The bailout plan with its new bureaucracy, expanded banking regulations, and bank takeovers represented a huge increase in federal authority over the banking and home loan industry. Ironically, the Bush administration, which had championed free market economics, oversaw the greatest expansion of federal regulation of markets in many decades. It is too soon to evaluate the effectiveness of the government's actions in the area, but it is clear that at least in the area of home mortgages, the era of big government has not ended.[42]

17-2 REGULATING BUSINESS

As Chapter 13 explains, regulation of the private sector is one of the four major functions of the federal bureaucracy. The government regulates private business to protect both consumers and other businesses from what the government decides are unfair business practices, to protect workers from unsafe or unhealthy working conditions, to protect consumers from unsafe products, to protect the environment from damage, and to protect a number of groups from discrimination. Although **regulatory policy** certainly affects the overall state of the economy, its primary aim is to manage these problems, not to affect the economy, as fiscal and monetary policies do.

Regulation first became an important federal activity more than a century ago, when Congress passed the Interstate Commerce Act of 1887. Since then, the federal government has become heavily involved in regulating the competitive practices of business. Beginning in the 1960s, it became involved in regulating the social effects of business activity as well.

The idea of regulation has always received a mixed response from the public. When public opinion surveys ask about government regulations on business in general, the public splits over whether they are desirable. When asked about specific regulations such as minimum wage laws, product safety laws, and environmental regulations, however, the public usually favors regulations.[43] For example, according to a 2008 public opinion poll conducted when gasoline prices were nearing a record high, 90 percent of the public favored increasing automobile fuel efficiency (CAFE) standards.[44] The tension between disliking regulation in the abstract and liking regulation in specific cases has fueled political conflict ever since the federal government began to regulate private business.[45] Those battles are still being fought. To understand them, we need to review some basic concepts and to discuss the federal government's role in economic and social regulation.

17-2a Basic Concepts and Categories

As Chapter 13 discusses, the federal government carries out its regulatory duties through its executive departments (e.g., the Department of Health and Human Services, which houses the Food and Drug Administration), its independent regulatory commissions (e.g., the Nuclear Regulatory Commission), and its independent

regulatory policy

Laws and government rules targeting private business for the purpose of (1) protecting consumers and other businesses from what the government deems unfair business practices, (2) protecting workers from unsafe or unhealthy working conditions, (3) protecting consumers from unsafe products, and (4) protecting a number of groups from discrimination.

agencies (e.g., the Environmental Protection Agency). These agencies regulate private sector activity in three ways: (1) through rule administration, which means the agencies implement the decisions of Congress, the president, or the courts; (2) through rule making, which means the agencies write their own regulations (because congressional, presidential, and judicial decisions are often long on broad guidelines but short on details); and (3) through rule adjudication, which means the agencies judge whether their regulations have been violated.

Regulatory efforts fall into two categories. First, **economic regulation** consists of rules affecting the competitive practices of businesses. Antitrust laws, which seek to prevent any single company or group of companies from suppressing competition, are an example of economic regulation. Second, **social regulation** consists of rules designed to protect Americans from dangers or unfair practices associated with how companies produce their products as well as from dangers associated with the products themselves. For example, regulations prevent the automobile industry from polluting the air, from practicing racial discrimination when they hire new employees, and from producing unsafe cars.

Economic and social regulation emerged at different times for different purposes, and they involve different patterns of governmental action. For these reasons, we will discuss each type of regulation separately.

economic regulation
Laws and governmental rules that affect the competitive practices of private business.

social regulation
Laws and governmental rules designed to protect Americans from dangers or unfair practices associated with the way private businesses produce their products or with the products themselves.

17-2b The Objectives of Economic Regulation

Economic regulations enable the government to influence the competitive practices of industry. In doing so, the government can strive to accomplish one of two goals.[46] First, it may seek to encourage economic competition by preventing monopolies from forming and by deterring unfair forms of business competition. In 2001, for example, Enron Corporation began to collapse amid revelations that it had hidden debts, exaggerated profits, and defrauded both employees and stockholders with a series of illegal accepting maneuvers. In late 2001, the Securities and Exchange Commission launched an investigation, which forced Enron into bankruptcy at the end of the year. Further revelations about document shredding and other illegal activities by Enron and its accounting firm, Arthur Andersen, led to an investigation and a series of criminal indictments and convictions by the Justice Department.

A second goal the government may strive to achieve is to use economic regulation to control the ability of firms to enter an industry or to control the prices they charge for their goods or services. The government typically steps in to control market entry or product pricing when competition in a given market is, for one reason or another, impractical or has undesirable side effects. For instance, Congress created the Interstate Commerce Commission (ICC) in 1887 because in many parts of the country, a single railroad company served the entire region. These companies faced no real competition—trucks and cargo planes had not been invented yet—so they could charge their customers exorbitant rates to ship goods. Because it did not make financial sense to create competition by constructing additional sets of rail lines, Congress instead directed the ICC to regulate how much railroads could charge their customers.[47] The same logic lies behind the regulation of other "natural" monopolies such as water, electricity, and other utilities.

Of course, politicians disagree about whether many conditions warrant regulation. Should Congress regulate cable television? Many people subscribe to cable services, but cable is hardly as economically essential as water, electricity, or transportation. When cable was first introduced, it was financially impractical for two or more cable companies to wire the same community, so cable companies had natural monopolies in their communities. As a result, Congress passed laws that regulated how much cable companies could charge their customers. Then the development of satellite dish technology presented an alternative to cable and weakened its monopoly. The anticipated development of cable services over ordinary telephone wires should further erode cable's domination of the market and open up even more competition. These trends prompted Congress to do away with essentially all the rules that regulate cable company pricing in 1996. As many experts predicted, in the short run at least, the price of cable TV rose.[48] Increased rates may make the deregulation of cable TV a matter ripe for political conflict.

17-2c The Evolution of Economic Regulation

The federal government has been enacting economic regulations for more than 100 years. During that time, regulatory policy has gone through three phases.[49] In the first phase, which lasted from the 1880s through the 1910s, the government first established a role for itself in regulating the economy. This began, as we have noted, when Congress established the ICC in 1887. Three other important laws passed during this first phase of government regulation of the economy were the Sherman Antitrust Act of 1890, the Clayton Antitrust Act of 1914, and the Federal Trade Commission Act of 1914. The Sherman Antitrust Act was designed to break up trusts, a form of business organization in which several large firms join together to dominate an industry and raise prices higher than they could charge in a competitive market. The Sherman Antitrust Act prohibited companies from fixing prices and creating monopolies. It did not, however, provide workable enforcement mechanisms. The Clayton Antitrust Act and the Federal Trade Commission Act were attempts to remedy the weaknesses of the Sherman Antitrust Act. As a result of the "trust-busting" efforts of the Federal Trade Commission (FTC) and the Antitrust Division of the Justice Department, trusts were eliminated by the 1930s.[50]

The second phase of economic regulatory activity began during Franklin Roosevelt's presidency. During this phase, Congress greatly expanded the federal government's role in regulating the economy. As part of the New Deal, Congress established a host of regulatory agencies, including the Federal Communications Commission in 1934 to regulate radio and television, the Securities and Exchange Commission in 1934 to oversee the stock market, and the Civil Aeronautics Board in 1938 to regulate the airline industry.[51]

By the early 1960s, the federal government had established four areas of economic regulatory policy: antitrust, financial institutions, transportation, and communications.[52] The very size of the federal government's regulatory role prompted considerable criticism. The reason stemmed from the fact that Congress typically passed regulatory legislation that listed only broad goals such as promoting justice and protecting the public interest. Congress left it up to individual regulatory agencies to translate these broad goals into specific rules for specific industries. The ambiguity of congressional directives and the immense political pressure regulated industries placed on the regulatory agencies triggered charges that the purpose of government regulation had been subverted—instead of protecting the public, regulations were protecting industries.[53]

These charges gave rise to the third and most recent phase of economic regulation: deregulation. This phase began in the 1970s and continues today. By the 1970s, many consumer advocates had concluded that government regulation too often ended up hurting the public it was intended to protect. They argued that regulated industries were able to maintain inflated prices because the regulating agencies stifled price competition and blocked new firms from entering the market. For example, critics accused the Civil Aeronautics Board of preventing airlines from competing on ticket prices.[54] In response to these criticisms, the federal government, beginning with the Jimmy Carter administration and continuing through the Clinton administration, deregulated (among others) the airline, trucking, savings and loan (S&L), and telecommunication industries. In the cases of the airline and trucking industries, Congress went so far as to abolish the Civil Aeronautics Board and the ICC, the nation's oldest regulatory agency.[55]

Proponents of deregulation argue that regulated industries are too often able to capture control of the bureaucrats who regulate them and manipulate regulations for their benefit rather than for the benefit of the public. Moreover, they contend, freeing markets from regulation stimulates competition and promotes both better products and lower prices.[56] In some cases, with airline deregulation perhaps the most notable example, deregulation has produced at least some of the benefits proponents claimed for it.[57] In other cases, however, deregulation has produced unintended consequences. For example, following the deregulation of the S&L industry, many S&Ls made risky loans and went bankrupt, leaving taxpayers responsible for their debts. The government spent billions of dollars to cover the losses that bankrupt S&Ls incurred.[58]

Thus, the nation has learned that although deregulation has succeeded in some areas, it may not always be the best solution to problems of competitiveness within industries. Deregulation can lead to industry behavior that damages the public interest—making industry the winner and the public the loser in the conflict over regulatory policy. As a result, some moves have been made in the past few years to bring back regulation for certain aspects of deregulated industries. Future developments in economic regulation will reflect an awareness of both the advantages and disadvantages of regulation and deregulation.

17-2d Social Regulation

Social regulation "affects the conditions under which goods and services are produced, and the physical characteristics of products that are manufactured."[59] In other words, the social regulation of business affects both working conditions and the safety and efficacy of the products themselves. As Table 17–1 shows, social regulation dates back to the 1930s. The push for social regulation rose sharply in the 1960s and 1970s, however, as the public came to demand that the federal government do something about problems such as hazardous working conditions, unsafe consumer products, pollution, and discrimination in the workplace.[60]

Social regulation differs from economic regulation in two important ways. First, whereas economic regulations usually are industry-specific, social regulations tend to cut across industries. Government regulations on work and product safety, the environment, and equal opportunity are social regulations that apply to all industries. Second, social regulations are usually grounded in specific, technical legislation rather than vague guidelines that require federal agencies to protect the public interest.

Agency	Year Established
Food and Drug Administration	1930
National Labor Relations Board	1935
Equal Employment Opportunity Commission	1964
Environmental Protection Agency	1970
Occupational Safety and Health Administration	1970
National Highway Traffic Safety Administration	1970
Consumer Product Safety Commission	1972
Nuclear Regulatory Commission	1975

Table 17–1   Principal Agencies Engaged in Social Regulation

The number of federal agencies responsible for social regulation grew sharply in the 1960s and 1970s as the American public demanded that the federal government do something about hazardous working conditions, unsafe consumer products, pollution, and discrimination in the workplace.

Social regulation runs the gamut from prohibiting employment discrimination to ensuring safety in the workplace to eliminating hazardous consumer products. The great diversity of social regulations makes it impossible to discuss each specific type. Instead, we will examine the evolution of and debates over two types of social regulation: policies protecting worker safety and health, and policies designed to protect the environment. (Chapter 5 discusses several of the laws Congress has passed to fight discrimination in the workplace.)

17-2e Protecting Worker Safety and Health

One of the best known and most controversial federal regulatory agencies is the Occupational Safety and Health Administration (OSHA). Congress established OSHA with the Occupational Safety and Health Act of 1970 and directed it to write and enforce rules to protect the health and safety of the American workforce. Congress took this action because the high rate of worker injuries and deaths was a serious problem for the economy and because labor unions and middle-class environmental and consumer activists were pressing for action.[61] The legal foundations for the act came from the provisions of Article I of the Constitution—that Congress should provide for the general welfare and that Congress has the power to regulate interstate and foreign commerce.

Congress set up OSHA as an agency with broad powers to identify safety and health risks in working conditions and in products and to write and enforce regulations to reduce those hazards. In 2008, OSHA had a staff of 2,186, including 1,100 inspectors, who visit job sites, conduct safety tests of consumer products, and otherwise seek to ensure the health and safety of the 115 million American workers at their 8.9 million work sites, along with the safety of the products they make.[62] Since 1972, OSHA has established safety and health standards for asbestos, lead, vinyl chloride, pesticides, and a host of other hazards. OSHA enforces its regulations by issuing warnings to or in some cases fining businesses that fail to comply with its rules.

Criticism of OSHA began almost as soon as it hired its first regulator. Business leaders complained that OSHA wrote maddeningly complicated rules that interfered with businesses, failed to make workers safer, and cost too much.[63] They cited examples such as rules specifying exactly what size the letters in "Emergency Exit" signs had to be, claiming that OSHA had become an example of an overbearing government bureaucracy at its worst.[64]

Labor leaders and consumer advocates, in contrast, defended OSHA. They pointed to specific cases, such as the Love Canal toxic waste dump in upstate New York, in which government regulations would have saved money and prevented illnesses had they been in place. Had the owners of Love Canal invested $4 million initially, they would have saved $27 million in eventual cleanup costs.[65] Far greater savings would have been achieved if businesses had paid attention much earlier to the dangers of asbestos.[66]

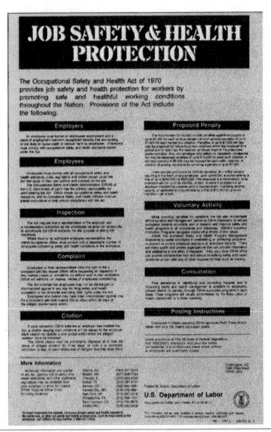

The Occupational Safety and Health Administration (OSHA) came under attack in the 1990s as lawmakers wrangled over its role as a governmental regulator over private business.

Defenders of OSHA also pointed to evidence that OSHA's regulations had reduced the rates of workplace injuries and illnesses. For example, between 1971, when Congress created OSHA, and 2003, the rate of workplace deaths was cut from 18 per 100,000 workers to only 3.5 per 100,000.[67] Although OSHA's supporters acknowledged that some of its regulations needed to be changed, they argued that, on the whole, the agency had succeeded in reducing health and safety risks to workers and consumers.

During the Reagan years, Congress cut OSHA's budget and staff, and the White House steered OSHA in a more business-friendly direction. OSHA complied, cutting many of its regulations, simplifying others, and reducing the penalties it charged for violations.[68] Business leaders cheered, while labor leaders and other critics of the Reagan administration charged that OSHA was allowing businesses to expose workers to unacceptable dangers.[69]

The Clinton administration initially sought to increase spending on OSHA, but in 1995, the agency came under attack once again. Led by Speaker Newt Gingrich, the new Republican majority on Capitol Hill moved to dismantle regulations that it claimed placed excessive burdens on private business.[70] The House, for example, passed a bill that (among other things) eliminated rules barring teenagers from using baler machines that crush cardboard cartons and from driving vehicles on the job, and it prohibited OSHA from doing anything to prevent repetitive-stress injuries in the workplace. The effort to weaken OSHA slowed in the late 1990s, but was reenergized under President George W. Bush after the 2000 election. Although Bush left the OSHA budget largely unchanged, he persuaded Congress to reduce the number of inspectors examining workplaces and to increase voluntary compliance programs to reduce workplace injuries.[71] Business advocates argued that these changes reduced unnecessary regulations, while health and safety advocates argued that they opened the door for more workplace injuries.

Public opinion polls provide ammunition for both sides in the OSHA dispute. On the anti-OSHA side, a majority of survey respondents in one national poll agreed that "Regulation of business does more harm than good." On the pro-OSHA side, surveys show that the public recognizes the economic costs of health and safety regulations and is willing to pay them.[72] At present, the fight over OHSA has died down, but given that the public seems to be open to arguments from both sides, and that government regulation of business lies at the core of liberal-conservative disputes, we are likely to see more fights over OSHA in the future.

17-2f Protecting the Environment

Since the 1960s, Congress has passed many laws designed to protect the environment. These laws have become a source of considerable political conflict because, like other types of social regulation, they create winners and losers. Although environmental activists argue that the government needs to do more to protect the environment, private businesses complain that environmental regulations have become too costly and are costing the United States too many jobs. The conflict between those who want to do more to protect the country from environmental threats and those who want to do more to protect business from excessive regulation will shape the rules of environmental policy for years to come.

The Evolution of Environmental Policy

Before the mid-1960s, federal policy on the environment reflected a conservationist approach; the government's efforts were aimed largely at setting aside public lands for recreational use. The environmental movement had yet to ignite, and Congress felt little pressure to take any action.[73] In 1962, however, urged on by Rachel Carson's disturbing book, *Silent Spring*—a book arguing that DDT and other pesticides were killing off birds and other species by the millions—the public began to pay attention to the dangers of a polluted environment.[74] Congress responded by passing the Water Quality Act of 1965, the Clean Water Restoration Act of 1966, and the Air Quality Act of 1967. These laws gave the Department of Health, Education, and Welfare (later to become the Department of Health and Human Services) the power to establish clean water standards, provided federal funds for sewage treatment plants, and required the states to establish air quality standards (including automobile emission standards) with the advice and consent of the federal government.[75] Although these laws began moving the federal government into environmental regulation, none of them was stringent enough, according to environmentalist activists.[76]

The environmental movement received a second jarring boost in 1969 when an offshore oil drilling platform owned by Union Oil Company of California blew out, dumping somewhere between 1 and 4 million gallons of oil into the Santa Barbara Channel along the California coast. The resulting publicity, including nightly television coverage of thousands of dead fish and oil-coated birds, pushed both Congress and President Richard Nixon into aggressively seeking to regulate businesses and protect the environment.[77]

The passage of the National Environmental Policy Act (NEPA) in 1969 reflected the federal government's new approach to the environment. NEPA took several important steps. First, it set forth the basic goals and responsibilities of the federal government in protecting the environment. Second, it established the Council on Environmental Quality within the Executive Office of the President to advise presidents on the environment. Finally, NEPA created the **environmental impact statement** process, which requires federal agencies to analyze the environmental impact of any significant action they may take. Environmental groups have used the federal government's many environmental impact statements to influence, delay, and even block actions federal agencies proposed.[78]

In 1970, President Nixon went further by consolidating the federal government's many environmental tasks into the Environmental Protection Agency (EPA), a new agency whose purpose was to protect the environment. Not to be outdone, Congress enacted new laws strengthening the Clean Air and Clean Water Acts, protecting wildlife, and extending environmental regulations into new areas. By the end of the 1970s, the EPA was left with a vast array of laws to administer, as Table 17–2 shows.[79]

Ronald Reagan, who was elected president in 1980, entered office with an entirely different view of environmental regulations: He saw them as undue burdens on business and major obstacles to economic growth. His appointees to agencies such as the EPA and the Interior Department shared his opposition to the government's environmental policies. Although the Reagan administration sought to dismantle many environmental regulations, it met with only mixed success.[80] It succeeded in cutting the budgets for environmental programs; government spending in constant dollars (i.e., adjusted for inflation) on natural resources and the environment fell dramatically between 1980 and 1981 and did not return to 1980 levels until 1993.[81] Yet by the end of Reagan's first term, Congress again began enacting legislation to protect the environment. Members of Congress were responding to opinion polls that showed public support for environmental protection rising throughout Reagan's presidency.[82]

George H. W. Bush ran for election in 1988 promising to be an "environmental president," and early in his term, he gained

environmental impact statement
A document federal agencies must issue that analyzes the environmental impact of any significant action they plan to take.

In the area of air quality, the EPA

■ Establishes national air quality standards.
■ Sets limits on the level of air pollutants emitted from stationary sources such as power plants, municipal incinerators, factories, and chemical plants.
■ Establishes emission standards for new motor vehicles.
■ Sets allowable levels for toxins like lead, benzene, and toluene in gasoline.
■ Establishes emissions standards for hazardous air pollutants such as beryllium, mercury, and asbestos.
■ Supervises states in their development of clean air plans.

In the area of water quality and protection, the EPA

■ Issues permits for the discharge of any pollutant into navigable waters.
■ Develops "effluent guidelines" to control discharge of specific water pollutants, including radiation.
■ Develops criteria that enable states to set water quality standards.
■ Administers grants program to states to subsidize the cost of building sewage treatment plants.
■ Regulates disposal of waste material, including sludge and low-level radioactive discards, into the oceans.
■ Cooperates with the Army Corps of Engineers to issue permits for dredging and filling of wetlands.
■ Sets national drinking water standards to ensure that drinking water is safe.
■ Regulates underground injection of wastes to protect purity of ground water.
■ With the Coast Guard, coordinates cleanup of oil and chemical spills into American waterways.

To control the disposal of hazardous waste, the EPA

■ Maintains inventory of existing hazardous waste dump sites.
■ Tracks more than 500 hazardous compounds from point of origin to final disposal site.
■ Sets standards for generators and transporters of hazardous wastes.
■ Issues permits for treatment, storage, and disposal facilities for hazardous wastes.
■ Assists states in developing hazardous waste control programs.
■ Maintains a multibillion-dollar fund ("Superfund") from industry fees and general tax revenues to provide for emergency cleanup of hazardous dumps when no responsible party can immediately be found.
■ Pursues identification of parties responsible for waste sites and eventual reimbursement of the federal government for Superfund money spent cleaning up these sites.

To regulate chemicals, including pesticides and radioactive waste, the EPA

■ Maintains inventory of chemical substances now in commercial use.
■ Regulates existing chemicals considered serious hazards to people and the environment, including fluorocarbons, polychlorinated biphenyls (PCBs), and asbestos.
■ Issues procedures for the proper safety testing of chemicals and orders them tested when necessary.
■ Requires the registration of insecticides, herbicides, or fungicides intended for sale in the United States.
■ Requires pesticide manufacturers to provide scientific evidence that their product will not injure humans, livestock, crops, or wildlife when used as directed.
■ Classifies pesticides for either general public use or restricted use by certified applicators.
■ Sets standards for certification of applicators of restricted-use pesticides. (Individual states may certify applicators through their own programs based on the federal standards.)
■ Cancels or suspends the registration of a product on the basis of actual or potential unreasonable risk to animals or the environment.
■ Issues a "stop sale, use, and removal" order when a pesticide already in circulation is in violation of the law.
■ Requires registration of pesticide-producing establishments.
■ Issues regulations concerning the labeling, storage, and disposal of pesticide containers.
■ Issues permits for pesticide research.
■ Monitors pesticide levels in the environment.
■ Monitors and regulates radiation in drinking water, oceans, rainfall, and air.
■ Conducts research on toxic substances, pesticides, air and water quality, hazardous wastes, radiation, and the causes and effects of acid rain.
■ Provides overall guidance to other federal agencies on radiation protection matters that affect public health.

In addition, the EPA

■ Sets noise levels acceptable for construction equipment, transportation equipment (except aircraft), all motors and engines, and electronic equipment.

Table 17–2   The Responsibilities of the Environmental Protection Agency
Congress has given the Environmental Protection Agency (EPA) responsibility for overseeing a vast array of environmental regulations.
Source: *Walter A. Rosenbaum*, Environmental Politics and Policy, *3rd ed. (Washington, D.C.: CQ Press, 1995), 116–17.*

political credit for taking a more protective approach toward the environment than Reagan had. In 1990, for example, Bush reversed Reagan's policy of opposing legislation to strengthen the 1972 Clean Air Act, and together with Congress, he hammered out the 1990 Clean Air Act.[83] As Bush prepared to run for reelection, however, he deemphasized environmental issues and instead sought to attract political support from the business community by helping it obtain regulatory relief. As a result, during the second half of his presidency, Bush repeatedly blocked and watered down regulations designed to protect the environment.[84]

Bill Clinton came to office promising to renew public efforts at environmental protection, but his administration moved slowly on most matters. His approach in most aspects of environmental policy was to move toward compromise, which generally yielded only slow changes in policy—especially after Republicans captured a majority in Congress in 1994.

The environmental policy that received the most attention during Clinton's presidency was global warming. During Clinton's years in office, global warming moved from a worrisome yet unproven hypothesis to a finding widely accepted by scientists who specialize in climate research.[85] In 1997, delegates from 166 nations met in Kyoto, Japan, to work out a treaty to limit the emission of carbon dioxide and other "greenhouse gases" that trap the sun's heat in the atmosphere and cause global warming. The resulting Kyoto Protocol called for reducing greenhouse gases to 5 percent below their 1990 level by the year 2012. Although Clinton supported the treaty, he never submitted it to the Senate for approval because he knew it did not have enough votes to pass.[86]

George W. Bush took a very different approach on environmental policy. Like President Reagan, Bush thought that environmental regulations unreasonably interfered with business practices. Bush moved to weaken environmental regulations in a wide range of areas—from oil drilling and logging in the national forests, to protecting clean air and clean water.[87] Throughout his eight years in office, he championed the cause of opening the Arctic National Wildlife Refuge to oil and gas drilling—an idea that Congress repeatedly rejected. Through most of his administration, he denied that global warming was real, was caused by human activity, and would harm human beings, despite the consensus on those issues that had developed among scientists.[88] When he finally admitted that global warming was real, he continued to argue that global warming was a minor problem that should be addressed only with voluntary steps, and he resisted all efforts to have the government do something about the problem.[89]

Political Conflicts in Environmental Protection

One can easily see why environmental regulation generates political conflict. When the government imposes a regulation, it benefits one group, often the public at large, and imposes costs on another group, perhaps a firm or an individual. For example, when the government requires auto manufacturers to make cars that get better gas mileage, the public at large benefits, but oil companies lose sales and auto manufacturers may also lose if they cannot build cars to compete with smaller, more efficient imported cars (see Box 17–1). As one might expect, individuals or firms that bear the cost of regulations usually oppose them.

Four other factors shape the course of political debate over environmental regulations. First, environmental regulations (and other social regulations as well) tend to produce diffuse benefits spread across society, while imposing focused costs that affect relatively few businesses or individuals. The benefits of environmental regulations are typically spread out across the United States, and many (if not most) Americans do not notice them. In contrast, the firm that must pay to clean up its toxic waste or the lumber company that cannot log timber for fear of harming the habitat of an endangered animal, such as the spotted owl, is acutely aware of the costs

POINT OF ORDER

Box 17–1 Corporate Average Fuel Economy Standards, Energy Supplies, and Global Warming

The regulations governing automobile fuel efficiency, or corporate average fuel economy (CAFE) standards, are among the most hotly contested of all government rules. They lie at the center of the controversy about how to address our nation's energy supply problems and global warming.

The CAFE standards have their origins in the Yom Kippur War. In October, 1973, Egypt and Syria launched a surprise attack on Israel. When the United States intervened by sending supplies to Israel, the Arab members of the Organization of Petroleum Exporting Countries (OPEC), responded with a boycott of oil shipments to the West. The price of oil shot up from three dollars a barrel to $11.65, and there were shortages of gasoline in the U.S. It was America's first energy crisis.

Congress responded by passing the Energy Policy Conservation Act of 1975, which established the CAFE standards and took other steps to reduce America's dependence on imported oil. The law required each automobile company to sell a mix of

cars, which attained a minimum average miles per gallon. The standard for new passenger cars started at 18 miles per gallon (mpg) in 1978 and rose to 27.5 mpg in 1985. The standard for light trucks—which included pickup trucks, vans, and sport utility vehicles (SUVs)—rose from 17.2 mpg in 1979 to 20.7 mpg. Failure to meet the standards triggered fines for every car a company sold.

The goal was to double the fuel efficiency of cars by 1985 and set the country on its way toward energy independence. The goal was met, although not quite by 1985. In 1974, the average American car got 12.9 miles per gallon; by 1987, that had increased to 26.2 miles per gallon. The National Academy of Sciences estimated that if the CAFE standards had not been established, the United States would be importing about 2.8 million barrels of oil per day more than the roughly 10 million barrels per day we import now. The policy had been a success.

By the mid-1980s, however, the price of oil had fallen sharply. People no longer worried about the price of gasoline, and they started buying larger, less fuel efficient cars, trucks, and SUVs. While the number of passenger cars on the road remained roughly constant in the 1990s, the number of light trucks increased from 48 million to 79 million. The result

was a decline in the actual mileage of the automobiles that Americans drove.

Since the mid-1980s, environmentalists have been pushing to raise the CAFE standards, which are far lower than those in other industrial democracies. Until 2007, they were effectively blocked by the automobile industry, which argued that increasing the fuel efficiency of the cars they made would cost their workers jobs and that making cars smaller would make them less safe.

The skyrocketing gas prices of 2007, however, finally led Congress and President George W. Bush to increase the CAFE standards. The Energy Independence and Security Act of 2007 increased the standards to 35 mpg by 2020. Environmentalists say more is needed to address both global warming and the huge cost of imported oil, so another round of increased fuel efficiency standards is possible. Nevertheless, the 2007 law should lead to a substantial reduction in how much oil Americans consume and how much we need to import.

Sources: Board on Energy and Environmental Systems, National Academy of Sciences, *Effectiveness and Impact of Corporate Average Fuel Economy (CAFE) Standards* (Washington, D.C.: National Academy Press, 2002); Eric R. A. N. Smith, *Energy, the Environment, and Public Opinion* (Lanham, MD: Rowman & Littlefield, 2002); U.S. Energy Information Administration, Department of Energy, "Supply and Disposition," available at www.tonto.eia.doe.gov/dnav/pet/hist/MCRIMUS1m.htm.

of regulation. Because benefits are diffuse while costs are concentrated, opponents of environmental regulation often have a greater incentive to fight against regulation than proponents have to fight for it.[90]

A second factor that affects the debate on environmental regulations is the fact that the benefits of some environmental regulations are hard to measure, but the costs are not.[91] For instance, it is difficult to measure the health benefits that come from having cleaner air or water. Medical researchers can see the benefits in terms of saved lives or reduced numbers of illnesses, but the general public cannot. Measuring the benefit to society of preserving an ancient forest or saving an endangered species is even more difficult. This "measurement" depends on the value one places on the forest or endangered species. In contrast, it is fairly easy to measure jobs and income lost because of environmental regulation. Because environmentalists sometimes find it impossible to produce definitive evidence that the benefits of regulation will exceed the costs, they sometimes find themselves at a disadvantage in the political arena.

A third factor that affects the debate is that measuring the magnitude of environmental problems can be difficult. This is becoming increasingly so as the government addresses the more obvious forms of pollution and begins to address so-called second-generation environmental issues such as global warming and ozone depletion. It is one thing to measure the presence and health effects of pollutants in the air; it is quite another to establish that industrial development is changing the climate in ways that will wreak environmental havoc on some parts of the world.[92] Climate-change scientists have reached a clear consensus that global warming is real; that it is caused by human activity; that if greenhouse gas emissions continue, global warming will continue as well; and that global warming will have enormous, harmful impacts on human society and the environment. Yet because many of the specifics are still poorly understood, defenders of the status quo can easily attack the scientists' lack of detailed knowledge.[93]

Finally, protecting the environment becomes increasingly costly as the standards of environmental quality rise. As government seeks to reduce pollution even more, the costs associated with marginal improvements grow. This raises the stakes for the individuals and firms that must pay for these improvements, and it gives them incentives to resist regulation even more strenuously.

Future Directions for Environmental Policy

When President Clinton proposed to "reinvent government," he made environmental regulation a prime target (see Chapter 13). Traditional regulatory policy emphasizes a *command-and-control approach* to the environment in which agencies draft regulations dictating how to protect the environment (commands) and then create mechanisms for forcing targeted polluters to comply (controls). The regulations are detailed, specifying both the amount of pollution that any source may produce and how the pollution must be reduced. These regulations are also universalistic, leaving little room for adaptations to local situations. Because of its inflexibility, the command-and-control approach to regulation has drawn complaints from environmentalists as well as from the business community.

Two frequently mentioned alternatives to the command-and-control approach are *market incentives* and *pollution prevention.* With a market-incentives approach, the government would abandon its efforts to develop uniform, nationwide regulations that specify how to eliminate pollution. Instead, it would establish an overall level of pollution allowable for different geographic areas, and it would issue a permit to each potential polluter within a region specifying how much pollution it may produce. Polluters would then be allowed to trade permits. If one firm can reduce its pollutants cheaply, say, by closing down an unneeded plant, it could then sell its permit to a firm that can reduce its pollutants only at great expense. In theory, creating a market in which firms can trade pollution permits will produce a greater reduction in pollution at less cost than is true with the command-and-control approach.[94]

In 1990, Congress directed the federal government to create a market for air pollution permits as part of the Clear Air Act. Separate emissions trading markets were set up in different parts of the country for different pollutants—sulfur dioxide, nitrous oxide, and others. The markets have now been operating long enough to show that they are fulfilling their promise. Air pollution continues to decline in the United States, and the cost of complying with air pollution laws has fallen as well. One study estimated that by 2010, the cost to businesses of complying with clean air laws will be less than half of what it would have been without the allowance trading system.[95]

The second alternative to the command-and-control approach is pollution prevention. Unlike command-and-control methods, which emphasize government intervention to correct an existing problem, pollution prevention emphasizes avoiding pollution in the first place. The pollution-prevention approach has wide support from business and the public, and the Pollution Prevention Act of 1990 added it as one of the EPA's policy options. The act requires the EPA to give priority to programs designed to help industry produce less pollution and waste. Hundreds of firms are voluntarily revising their production activities to conform with the law.[96] As with the market-incentive approach, it is still too soon to render a definitive judgment on the effectiveness of the pollution-prevention approach, but the early signs are promising.

The future of environmental policy remains unclear. In the 1960s and 1970s, politicians in both parties supported steps to reduce pollution and protect the environment. As a result, the Clean Air Act, the Clean Water Act, and other landmark pieces of environmental legislation passed. These laws worked. Air pollution, water pollution, and many other environmental threats have been significantly reduced.

The United States now faces another set of threats—a growing reliance on imported oil and gas to sustain our economy, the

Source: AP/Wide World Photos

Emission trading markets reduce pollution at a lower cost to businesses than command-and-control regulations.

possibility that the world oil supply may peak and supplies may begin to run out, and global warming, which is driven largely by the use of fossil fuels.[97] Yet now environmental policy is sharply partisan. Most Democrats in Washington advocate strengthening environmental protections and taking significant steps to limit global warming. Most Republicans advocate weakening environmental protections and moving slowly in response to global warming in order to prevent harming the economy. Whether the two sides can compromise and work out solutions that both minimize global warming and protect businesses remains to be seen.

The debate over environmental policy, like the debates over the wisdom of economic deregulation and the future of OSHA, reminds us that regulatory policy is a source of tremendous conflict in American politics. Although government regulations may benefit consumers, workers, and the environment, they also impose costs on businesses and limit their freedom of action. Not surprisingly, businesses that are the targets of government regulation usually oppose new regulations and try to have existing ones repealed. As views on the desirability of government regulation change over time, the rules of regulatory policy change as well.

17-3 PROMOTING SOCIAL WELFARE

The federal government runs a variety of programs designed to promote social welfare. To understand the broad range of social welfare policies in the United States, we need to discuss some basic concepts and categories, to trace the evolving role of the federal

The People behind the Rules

Box 17-2   People behind the Rules: Al Gore and Climate Change

Albert Gore, Jr., was born into a prominent Tennessee political family. His father, Albert Gore, Sr., had represented Tennessee in the U.S. House and Senate from 1938 to 1970. After graduating from Harvard and serving in the Army in Vietnam, Al Gore, Jr. briefly worked as a journalist, then ran for and won the House seat his father had held in 1976. As a member of the Science Committee and the Energy and Commerce Committee, Gore soon developed a reputation as someone who understood and cared about scientific issues. He pursued those interests in the Senate after winning election to that chamber in 1984.

Gore first heard about global warming in a lecture from Professor Roger Revelle when Gore was an undergraduate at Harvard. In 1981, he began a series of congressional hearings on climate change to learn more about it and explore the potential risks for America. By the mid-1980s, Gore had come to believe that climate change posed a serious threat to the nation and that immediate action was required. He began issuing dire warnings and pushing Washington for action.

Gore's first prominent call to action came in his book, *Earth in the Balance,* which he wrote to accompany his 1992 presidential bid. In it he wrote, "I have

come to believe that we must take bold and unequivocal action: we must make the rescue of the environment the central organizing principle for civilization." Gore lost his bid for the Democratic presidential nomination, but he clearly established himself as the leading environmentalist in Washington and a leader in the movement to take action on global warming.

As Vice President under Bill Clinton, Gore pushed for the United States to take stronger steps on global warming but largely failed. He directed the U.S. team in negotiating the Kyoto Protocol on climate change, which 170 nations signed in 1997; however, he was unable to persuade the Senate to ratify it. President Clinton symbolically signed the treaty, but no action was ever taken as a result.

After his loss in the 2000 presidential campaign, Gore turned his attention to the fight against climate change. He delivered lectures around the country in which he explained climate change and argued for policy steps to reduce its threat. In 2006, he published *An Inconvenient Truth: The Planetary Emergency of Global Warming and What We Can Do About It.* Later that year, he starred in the documentary version of the book, which won an Oscar. The following year, he shared the Nobel Peace Prize

with the Intergovernmental Panel on Climate Change (IPCC) for his work on global warming.

Gore's efforts to bring attention to the problem of global warming are a major reason for the passage of the Energy Independence and Security Act of 2007. That law raises automobile fuel economy standards so that by 2020, new cars sold in the United States should average at least 35 miles per gallon. In addition, other requirements increase the energy efficiency of appliances, buildings, and other products.

In the coming years, if more legislation does address climate change and energy efficiency, Gore's efforts will no doubt have played a major role. His work to bring attention to global warming has had a major impact on our country.

Sources: Michael Barone, *The Almanac of American Politics 1992* (Washington, D.C.: National Journal Press, 1991), 1144–48; CNN-All Politics, "Clinton Hails Global Warming Pact," December 11, 1997, available at www.cnn.com/ALLPOLITICS/1997/12/11/kyoto/; H.R. 6. Library of Congress-Thomas, available at www.thomas.gov/cgi-bin/bdquery/z?d110:h.r.00006; Al Gore, *Earth in the Balance: Forging a New Common Purpose* (New York: Houghton Mifflin, 1992); Al Gore, *An Inconvenient Truth: The Planetary Emergency of Global Warming and What We Can Do About It* (New York: Rodale Book, 2006); Spencer R. Weart, *The Discovery of Global Warming* (Cambridge, MA: Harvard University Press, 2003).

government in providing social welfare benefits, to review the current status of social welfare programs, and to identify the issues that will shape the future of social welfare policy. The rules we choose for social welfare policy may affect more Americans more dramatically and directly than any other type of domestic policy. They certainly create social "winners" and "losers"; who gains and who loses depends on the rules we adopt.

17-3a   Basic Concepts and Categories

Social welfare policy refers to government programs that provide goods and services to citizens to improve the quality of their lives. This broad definition includes many different types of programs.

social welfare policy
Government programs that provide goods and services to citizens to improve the quality of their lives.

Income Maintenance Programs

Low-Income Energy Assistance
Temporary Assistance for Needy Families (TANF)
Social Security
Supplemental Security Income (SSI)
Unemployment Compensation
Workers' Compensation

Nutrition Programs

Food stamps
Meals on Wheels
School breakfasts
School lunch
Special Supplemental Nutrition Program for Women, Infants, and Children

Health Programs

Medicare
Medicaid
Public health

Housing Programs

Low-income housing assistance
Low-rent public housing
Rural housing loans

Education Programs

Pell Grants
Head Start
Stafford loans
Federal Work-Study Program

Social Services programs

Community action
Community mental health
Job Training Partnership Act
Legal services
Social services for children and families
Social services for the elderly
Vocational rehabilitation

Table 17–3　Different Types of Social Welfare Policies
The federal government and state governments administer a wide range of social welfare programs.

Source: *From Diana M. Di Nitto, Social Welfare, 2nd ed. (Boston, MA: Allyn and Bacon, 1987). Copyright © 1987 by Pearson Education. Adapted by permission of the publisher.*

To show just how broad the notion of social welfare policy is, Table 17–3 lists a variety of social welfare programs that the federal government or state governments have enacted at one time or another.

Because the idea of social welfare policy encompasses everything from Social Security to vocational rehabilitation, how should we organize this broad array of programs? Table 17–3 offers one way to classify social welfare programs; namely, to organize them according to their substantive purpose. Some programs seek to ensure that individuals have adequate incomes, others seek to provide them with nutritious diets, and still others seek to protect their health, and so on.

A substantive approach, however, is not the only way to classify social welfare programs. A second approach differentiates policies that operate on the principle of **social insurance** from those based on **public assistance**. Social insurance programs (e.g., Social Security and Medicare) require those who will receive benefits to make contributions (pay taxes), and they distribute benefits without regard to the recipient's level of income. For example, to receive Social Security benefits when you retire, you must pay Social Security taxes while you are employed. After you retire, you *receive* benefits regardless of whether you are a millionaire or live in poverty. In contrast to social insurance programs, public assistance programs (e.g., Medicaid and food stamps) are funded out of general tax revenues. Their benefits go only to recipients who qualify through a **means test**, which shows that they are poor enough to be eligible for the program.

Finally, social welfare programs can be classified according to the strategy they use to improve recipients' quality of life.[98] One strategy is *alleviative;* it encompasses programs that attempt to soften—or alleviate—the hardships of poverty. Most public assistance programs are alleviative. A second strategy is *preventative;* this strategy encompasses programs that require individuals to take action today (e.g., making contributions to a social insurance program) to prevent themselves from falling into poverty later in life. A third strategy is *curative;* it encompasses programs such as Head Start and job training that seek to cure poverty by giving the poor the skills they need to lift themselves out of poverty.

The three different approaches to classifying social welfare programs are important because each highlights different ways the government can seek to maintain and improve the general welfare.

social insurance

Government programs, such as Social Security and Medicare, that require future beneficiaries to make contributions (otherwise known as taxes) and that distribute benefits without regard to the recipient's income.

public assistance

Government programs, such as Medicaid and food stamps, that are funded out of general tax revenues and that are designed to provide benefits only to low-income people.

means test

A requirement that people must fall below certain income and wealth requirements to qualify for government benefits.

Source: AP/Wide World Photos

Head Start is an example of a curative social welfare program. It seeks to cure poverty by giving poor children the strong educational foundation they need to succeed.

In addition, the differences among social welfare programs help explain why each enjoys a different level of political support, and the different approaches fuel disagreements over how the federal government should structure its social welfare programs. For example, some Americans favor social insurance programs but want cuts in public assistance programs; others support alleviative programs but not curative programs. As we shall see, the political support behind each of these types of programs influences which rules are adopted and who gains or loses under those rules.

17-3b The Evolution of Social Welfare Policy

Social welfare policy in the United States changed dramatically throughout the twentieth century. In the nineteenth century, most people believed caring for the poor was the responsibility of the private sector or local government, not the federal government. The only federal social welfare program in the nineteenth century was one that offered pensions to soldiers who fought for the Union in the Civil War. The Great Depression of the 1930s led the federal government to carve out a prominent role in guaranteeing the welfare of American citizens. That role expanded yet again in the 1960s as Washington sought to eradicate poverty and provide health care to the elderly and the poor.

Welfare as a Private Sector and Local Responsibility

For the first half of our nation's history, the norms (or informal rules) of American society worked to keep the federal government largely out of social welfare policy.[99] To begin with, the poor were often blamed for their own situation. Poverty was regarded as a product of a person's character: The able-bodied poor were lazy, shiftless, or spendthrifts, and therefore they did not deserve help. If people were in need, family members were expected to be the first source of assistance. Moreover, American society mostly viewed public assistance as a local rather than national responsibility. It was up to the community in which the poor lived to decide who was eligible for aid and to raise the resources needed to provide assistance—either through local churches and charities, or in some cases, through local governments.[100] Finally, aid was meager; when it was provided, it was less than the amount a person could earn working at a low-wage job.

When federal and state governments finally did begin to become involved in social welfare policy, they did so by narrowly targeting groups of "deserving poor," rather than by offering general forms of assistance. The first federal social program, for example, gave benefits to veterans of the Civil War who fought on the Union side. From the 1880s through the 1910s, Congress passed a series of laws granting and then expanding pensions for disabled and elderly veterans. Congress justified the pensions on the grounds that these soldiers had fought for the Union and deserved to be compensated. After 1910, states began to develop their own social welfare policies. Forty state governments set up programs to give money to widowed mothers living in poverty so that they could care for their children without working. In sum, before the 1930s, state and federal programs targeted specific groups of "deserving" poor people, rather than providing general assistance to those in poverty.[101]

At the same time that the American government slowly edged into the business of providing social welfare benefits to a few, narrow groups, many European nations were establishing broad social welfare programs for all of their poor and elderly. Germany, for example, created a system of old-age pensions in 1889, and most of the rest of Europe had similar programs in place by 1914.[102] In contrast, the United States did not adopt its nationwide system of old-age pensions, what we call Social Security, until 1935. Thus, providing broad social welfare services became a governmental responsibility in the United States several decades after it did in Europe.

Nationalizing Social Welfare: The Social Security Act of 1935

Although most states had enacted limited social welfare programs by the mid-1930s, the inadequacy of these programs became clear during the Great Depression. As Chapter 2 notes, the Great Depression deprived the states of the tax revenues they needed to fund public assistance. Moreover, with one out of every four American workers unemployed, the conventional stereotype of the poor as too lazy to work no longer held. Millions of people desperately sought work, but few jobs were available. People who had conscientiously saved for the proverbial rainy day found themselves with nothing to fall back on as banks across the country failed. Surely these people deserved help, yet because they were able-bodied adults, they did not fit in the traditional category of the deserving poor. The federal government, under the leadership of FDR, stepped in to fill the gap.

The Social Security Act of 1935 laid the foundation of the federal government's role in social welfare policy. This legislation created two types of federal social welfare programs: (1) social insurance programs for the elderly and the unemployed; and (2) public assistance programs to help the elderly, the blind, and dependent children.

Social Insurance Programs

The main social insurance program the Social Security Act created was the Old Age and Survivors program. (Recall that a social insurance program is a program that benefits all who contribute, regardless of income level.) In 1956, Congress added a new social insurance program, the Disability Insurance program. Taken together, these two programs constitute what we call Social Security—the oldest and largest social welfare program in the United States. The number of people receiving Social Security benefits has grown from 222,000 in 1940 to 48.4 million in 2005. Costs have also increased. In 1940, Social Security paid out just $32 million; in 2004, it paid out $520 billion.[103]

Social Security is the country's oldest and largest social welfare program. In 2004, Social Security paid out $520 billion in benefits to just over 48 million Americans.

As Chapter 16 discusses, Social Security is financed by a payroll tax (usually labeled FICA or OASDI on your pay stub); in other words, it comes out of your pay before you receive your paycheck. This tax is separate from any income tax you pay to federal, state, or local government. Each recipient receives an amount based on his or her lifetime earnings. Since 1972, federal law has required that Social Security benefits be indexed to the rate of inflation; when the cost of living rises, so do Social Security benefits. The increase in payments is called a cost-of-living adjustment (COLA).

In addition to creating the Old Age and Survivors Insurance program, the Social Security Act established a social insurance program that provides benefits to the unemployed. Employers pay special unemployment taxes on behalf of their employees. Should the employers lay off those workers, the workers are entitled to receive unemployment benefits. Unemployment insurance is a small program compared with Social Security; in 2006, the program paid only $30 billion.[104]

Public Assistance Programs

The second type of social welfare program the Social Security Act created was public assistance, which comes from general tax revenues and is granted only to those who qualify by income. The act established programs to assist the elderly (Old Age Assistance), the blind (Aid to the Blind), and children (Aid to Dependent Children). In 1950, Congress added a new public assistance program for people with disabilities (Aid to the Permanently and Totally Disabled). These public assistance programs are funded out of the federal government's general tax revenues.

For many years, the federal government left the job of administering (as opposed to financing) its public assistance programs to the states. Individual states set eligibility requirements and benefit levels as they saw fit. The states paid for the programs with grants they received from the federal government. Because states were free to run the programs as they saw fit, wide disparities developed among them in terms of benefits and eligibility requirements.[105] Some states offered meager benefits and severely restricted eligibility, whereas others were much more generous. In 1972, Congress standardized the benefits and eligibility requirements of the programs for the elderly, the blind, and people with disabilities by consolidating them into a single, federally administered program called Supplemental Security Income (SSI). The cost of SSI and its predecessor programs grew substantially over the last half of the twentieth century, rising from $495 million in 1940 to $37 billion in 2005.[106]

In the 1960s, Congress made mothers as well as children eligible for benefits and changed ADC's title to Aid to Families with Dependent Children (AFDC). This program was controversial from its inception. Liberals complained about AFDC because—unlike the programs for the elderly, the blind, and people with disabilities—it continued to operate as a separate program with different levels of support from one state to another. Some states paid relatively well, whereas others paid barely enough for welfare recipients to eat, let alone pay rent. In 1996, Mississippi's maximum AFDC grant was only $120 per month. Tennessee and Texas followed as the next lowest paying states at $185 and $188 per month, respectively. In contrast, Vermont paid up to $639 per month, Connecticut up to $636 per month, and California and Massachusetts paid as much as $565 per month.[107] Even these benefits were quite modest. Over all, the average benefit per family in 1996 was only $386 per month, or $4,633 per year, well below the poverty threshold of $16,036 per year.[108] Moreover, if you take inflation into account, AFDC benefits actually fell by 43 percent between 1970 and 1993.[109]

Conservatives complained about AFDC because it served too many people and cost too much. By 1996, AFDC served 12.6 million people at a cost of $23.7 billion per year.[110] Conservatives saw this as evidence that AFDC made its recipients dependent on the government and thereby trapped them in poverty. Critics also accused AFDC of undermining the two-parent family and allowing absent parents to avoid taking responsibility for their children.[111] Finally, critics complained that AFDC was riddled with fraud and waste. During the 1970s and 1980s, the federal government improved the management of AFDC, restricted eligibility, and made greater efforts to force deadbeat parents to support their children. In addition, many states cut the amounts of money AFDC recipients received each month.[112] The cumulative effect of these changes was to remove many thousands of families from the program, and as several studies suggest, allow millions of children to fall below the poverty line.[113] Still, complaints about AFDC remained.

In 1996, President Clinton, working with the Republican majority in Congress, abolished AFDC and replaced it with **Temporary Assistance for Needy Families (TANF)**. Under TANF, the federal

Temporary Assistance for Needy Families (TANF)

A public assistance program that provides government aid to low-income families with children for a limited amount of time.

government no longer gives money directly to welfare recipients. Instead, it awards block grants to the states, which have some flexibility in designing welfare policies. One key theme in TANF is the need to place welfare applicants in jobs as quickly as possible. Recipients are required to work or be enrolled in work-related activities such as training programs. Moreover, recipients can receive assistance for only two consecutive years, and for only five years in their lifetimes.[114] The focus on job placement and the limits on how long people can receive welfare constitute sharp breaks with the old AFDC system.

Because TANF has been operating only since 1997, because relatively few welfare recipients have come up against the five-year, lifetime limit on welfare, and because the United States has not yet faced a long recession, it is too soon to offer a final judgment on TANF's success. Nevertheless, the early assessment of most observers is that TANF has worked well.[115] The number of families receiving welfare declined sharply during the 1990s, falling from 5 million in 1994 to just 1.9 million in 2005.[116] The decline actually began before TANF was implemented. The booming economy during the Clinton years helped many people find jobs and get off welfare. Nevertheless, the TANF program's carrot-and-stick approach of helping welfare recipients find jobs and threatening them with an end to their welfare benefits clearly contributed to the decline in the number of people on welfare.

The number of families on welfare, however, is not the only measure of a program's success. Another measure is how the families who have left welfare are faring. Early studies indicate that conditions for most of those families have significantly improved, although conditions have deteriorated for some. The overwhelming majority of people who have moved off welfare are working and have higher incomes than they did when on welfare. The poorest 5 to 10 percent, however, seem to be sinking into worse situations. For example, the average income for the poorest 5 percent of single mothers fell from $6,900 to $6,400 after TANF was implemented.[117] Legal immigrants who have fallen into poverty have also suffered because the 1996 law cut their benefits from TANF, food stamps, Medicaid, and SSI. Perhaps the biggest unknown is what will happen if (or when) the United States experiences a lengthy recession. Some critics worry that TANF's time-limit rules might force thousands of families onto the streets. Because TANF was instituted at a time of great economic prosperity in the United States, no one knows whether it will be seen as a success in a different economic climate.

The War on Poverty

The Social Security Act of 1935 introduced the first major wave of social welfare policies in the United States. The second major wave came about during the presidency of Lyndon Johnson as part of his Great Society program. The public's attention had been drawn to the existence of widespread poverty by Michael Harrington's famous book, *The Other America*.[118] Johnson responded by using his surge of popularity following President John F. Kennedy's assassination to persuade Congress to undertake the War on Poverty.[119]

One legislative landmark in the War on Poverty was the passage of the Economic Opportunity Act of 1964. The act created the Office of Economic Opportunity (OEO), which was charged with administering a host of different social services programs. Among OEO's programs were the Job Corps, which provided job training for poor youths; the Neighborhood Youth Corps, which offered poor youths an opportunity to gain work experience; and Head Start, which provided educational opportunities for disadvantaged preschool children. Unlike the Social Security Act, which created programs that sought to alleviate or prevent poverty, the Equal Opportunity Act created programs that sought to "cure" poverty by helping the poor pull themselves out of poverty.[120]

The other major landmark in the War on Poverty was the passage of the Food Stamp Act of 1964, which created the **Food Stamp Program**. The Department of Agriculture administers this program, which provides benefits only to people who meet a means test. Participants receive electronic benefit transfer (EBT) cards (similar to a bank debit card) that they use to buy food. Originally, recipients purchased the stamps at a discounted price, but today they receive them free of charge. The Food Stamp Program cost relatively little in its early years, but its cost eventually ballooned as the pool of recipients expanded and the purchase requirement was eliminated. The cost of the program also responds quickly to changes in the economy. When unemployment rises during recessions, huge numbers of people apply for food stamps to help them through hard times. During the 1991 recession, for example, the number of people receiving food stamps jumped by 3 million to a total of almost 24 million at a cost of approximately $18 billion.[121]

Although the War on Poverty attracted considerable fanfare, its success in reducing poverty was limited. Many of the programs created under the Economic Opportunity Act lasted only a few years before they were eliminated, consolidated, or transferred to other departments and agencies. The OEO itself was abolished in 1975. A few of the more popular and successful programs, such as Head Start, remain in operation today.

Why were so many of the War on Poverty programs phased out? A major reason was their curative approach to poverty.[122] Because they worked to empower the poor, these programs often produced activist organizations that challenged established power centers in cities across the country. This strained relations between the War on Poverty agencies and more traditional social services providers.[123] At the same time, although the OEO may have helped to reduce poverty, it did not eliminate it, which made it hard to maintain congressional support for the programs. In contrast, the Food Stamp Program survived because it took the more traditional alleviative approach to poverty and because it had strong political support. Members of Congress from farm states support the Food Stamp Program because it helps the poor to purchase more food products, and members from poor regions support it because it

Food Stamp program

A public assistance program established in 1964 that provides stamps (or coupons) to low-income people to buy food.

feeds their constituents. In other words, both farm state residents and residents of poverty-stricken areas are winners under the rules that administer the Food Stamp Program.

Health Care

At the same time that the Johnson administration was launching its War on Poverty, it was also creating a new role for the federal government in financing health care for American citizens. Until the 1960s, the federal government had been hesitant to fund health services. Whereas public health insurance had become commonplace in Europe by the 1940s, Congress repeatedly rejected any form of national health assistance on the grounds that such programs would open the door to "socialized medicine."[124] Why do Americans mistrust the idea of a nationalized health-care system, which is so common in other industrialized democracies? Three reasons may be our historic skepticism of big government dating back to the days of the American Revolution, our tendency to look to the private sector to provide most goods and services, and massive public relations campaigns by the health-care industry to avoid nationalization.

Because the United States had a history of leaving most aspects of social welfare in private hands and because most Americans preferred to rely on private business rather than government to deliver goods and services, the federal government did not develop a publicly financed health-care system. Instead, it used its tax policies to support the development of a private health insurance system. Employers could deduct payments to employee health insurance programs as a part of the cost of doing business, and thus they did not pay taxes on those expenditures. At the same time, employees could exclude the value of their health insurance benefits at work from their income, thus making those benefits more attractive than comparable increases in taxable income. As a result, the United States developed a large private health insurance industry.

With the Democrats' landslide victory in the 1964 elections, supporters of national health care finally had an opportunity to enact a federally financed health-care program. Congress responded by passing the Medicare Act of 1965.[125] Much as the Social Security Act did, the Medicare Act created both a social insurance program (Medicare) and a public assistance program (Medicaid). Both programs target certain groups of Americans; neither provides the sort of universal health-care coverage most other advanced industrial democracies provide.

Medicare
A social insurance program that provides basic hospital insurance and supplementary insurance for doctors' bills and other health-care expenses for people over the age of sixty-five.

Medicare is a social insurance program that provides basic hospital insurance and supplementary insurance for doctors' bills and other health-care expenses for people over the age of sixty-five. Its benefits are not means-tested. Anyone receiving Social Security is also eligible for Medicare. Part A of Medicare is a compulsory program funded by payroll taxes. It pays for a share of the recipient's hospital costs. Part B of Medicare is a voluntary program. Participants may choose to buy insurance to pay their doctor bills. Participants pay about one-fourth of the cost of the Part B insurance; the federal government pays for the rest out of general tax revenues.[126]

Starting in 2006, the Medicare program was expanded to provide prescription drug coverage. Under the new program, Part D of Medicare, people who are eligible to receive Medicare can enroll in one of two private insurance plans, which are subsidized by the federal government. The program is controversial because of its cost to taxpayers, gaps in its coverage, and confusion about benefits. Nevertheless, it has given low-cost drug benefits to a huge number of people.[127]

Medicaid is a public assistance program that provides publicly subsidized health care—that is, health care paid for by the government. Participation is means-tested, with benefits available only to people with low incomes. The program consists of federal grants to the states that are funded out of general tax revenues. States match the federal government's contribution, establish their own eligibility requirements and benefit levels, and administer the program. Anyone eligible for TANF or SSI payments is eligible (i.e., meets the means or income test) for Medicaid. Most states model their programs on Medicare and make direct payments to doctors on behalf of the recipient.

Medicaid
A public assistance program that provides publicly subsidized health care to low-income Americans.

Table 17–4 shows how the costs of Medicare and Medicaid have grown. Clearly, the cost of both programs skyrocketed, making health care the federal government's fastest growing form of public assistance. This growth resulted from both the increasing cost of health care and the fact that Congress expanded Medicare and Medicaid eligibility, bringing new people into the programs. The question of how to rein in these costs is the subject of considerable debate.[128]

17-3c The Current Status of Social Welfare Policy

What is the current status of social welfare policy in the United States? There are at least four ways to answer this question: (1) by comparing social welfare policies in the United States with those in other advanced industrial democracies, (2) by analyzing how

Year	Medicare, in billions of current dollars ($)	Medicaid, in billions of current dollars ($)
1970	7.5	0.3
1980	35.0	25.8
1990	109.7	72.5
2000	219.0	208.0
2004	301.1	297.5

Table 17–4 Costs of Federal Medicare and Medicaid Programs

The costs of Medicare and Medicaid have risen sharply since 1970.

Sources: *1970 data from U.S. Bureau of the Census*, Statistical Abstract of the United States, 1995, *115th ed. (Washington, D.C.: U.S. Bureau of the Census, 1995), 113, 116; 1980–2000 data from U.S. Department of Health and Human Services, 2005 CMS Statistics, 25, table 26, available at www.cms.hhs.gov/MedicareMedicaidStatSupp/downloads/ 2005_CMS_Statistics.pdf.*

the share of the federal budget spent on social welfare programs has changed in recent years, (3) by examining what the federal government spends on different types of social welfare programs, and (4) by trying to measure the success of social welfare programs.

Social Welfare Policies in Other Advanced Industrial Democracies

By virtually any measure one chooses, the United States spends far less on social welfare and provides a lower level of services than European nations. For example, whereas the United States spends roughly 16 percent of its GDP on social welfare programs, most industrialized democracies spend from 18 to 28 percent of their GDP on social welfare programs.[129] Because European countries spend so much more on social welfare, their citizens receive greater government benefits. For example, unlike the United States, most European countries have national health-care programs in which the national government, rather than the individual citizen, pays for medical services.[130] The United States provides fewer public social welfare benefits than other advanced industrial democracies largely because of the American tradition of relying on the private sector for assistance.

Social Welfare versus Other Types of Government Spending

As we mentioned previously, the definition of social welfare policy is imprecise, so some controversy inevitably surrounds ways to measure spending on social welfare. A good (but by no means perfect) measure is the portion of the federal budget devoted to making payments to individuals. This number includes the social welfare payments to individuals we discussed in this chapter, other social welfare benefits such as veterans benefits, and federal government pensions. As we saw in Chapter 16, payments to individuals consumed less than 20 percent of the federal budget in 1940. Yet by 2005, this figure stood at roughly 60 percent.[131] Thus, social welfare constitutes an increasingly important priority in the federal government's budget. From a politician's perspective, the huge number of people receiving some kind of direct benefits from the government makes cutting those benefits politically hazardous.[132] As a result, Congress is reluctant to cut benefits, even though they constitute a huge and growing portion of the federal budget.

Spending on Different Types of Social Welfare Programs

What relative emphasis does the federal government place on different categories of social welfare programs? The answer can be found in Table 17–5, which compares how the federal government spent its social welfare dollars in 1970 and 2005.

As Table 17–5 shows, the federal government places its greatest emphasis on the preventative and alleviative strategies and the least emphasis on the curative strategy (see Section 17–3a). The preventative strategy approach includes our two largest social insurance programs—Social Security and Medicare. In 2005, those programs accounted for more than 80 percent of the federal

Year	Social insurance (%)	Health and medical (%)	Veterans programs (%)	Public aid (%)	Unemployment insurance (%)	Training and education (%)
1970	49.5	18.8	18.8	14.3	6.1	0.6
2005	37.8	45.4	2.5	10.9	2.2	1.1

Table 17–5   Distribution of Social Welfare Expenditures across Programs (as a Percentage of All Social Welfare Expenditures)

The federal government spends the biggest share of its social welfare expenditures on social insurance programs that take a preventative approach to the problem of social welfare. It spends the smallest share on programs such as job training and education that take a curative approach to social welfare.

Source: *Data from U.S. Bureau of the Census,* Statistical Abstract of the United States, 2008, *127th ed. (Washington, D.C.: U.S. Bureau of the Census, 2007), 346, table 522.*

government's social welfare expenditures. Spending on public aid, the primary example of the alleviative strategy, accounted for only 11 percent. That left little room for spending on service-oriented, curative strategy programs such as job training or education, which received only 1.1 percent. Moreover, as a comparison of spending in 1970 and 2005 makes clear, the emphasis on the preventative and alleviative strategies has increased over the past three decades.

What accounts for these spending patterns? First, social insurance programs have their own earmarked source of revenue—namely, payroll taxes. Second, social insurance payments are popular with Americans of all ages.[133] These programs are not means-tested, so everyone who meets age and other eligibility criteria receives a payment regardless of income. Third, Social Security and Medicare largely benefit the elderly, who also happen to be a politically powerful interest group. People age sixty and over make up 16 percent of the population, but they have the highest voter turnout rate of any age group (see Chapter 7). No politician wants to alienate such a powerful voting bloc. As a result, members of Congress find it politically difficult to enact legislation to restrict eligibility or lower benefits.

Measuring the Success of Social Welfare Programs

The success of the federal government's social welfare programs is a matter of sharp conflict. Conservatives claim that social welfare programs have failed; liberals claim that most of them work and that the rest need only moderate reform to work.[134] To a large extent, the question of success or failure turns on which measures one chooses to use.

Direct measures of the success of social welfare programs reveal a great deal of success in some areas and only mixed progress in others. Poverty has declined substantially in the United States, largely as the result of social welfare programs. It is, however, far from being eliminated.[135] As we saw in Chapter 3, 22 percent of the population lived in poverty in 1960, but by 1970—after the expansion of Social Security and the introduction of food stamps, AFDC, Medicare, and Medicaid—only 13 percent lived below the poverty line (see Figure 3–6).[136] After 1970, government social

Source: © Corbis Stock Market/Tom & Dee Ann McCarthy, 2000

Social welfare programs have had some successes. For example, following the creation in the 1960s of programs such as Medicaid and Food Stamps, the infant mortality rate in the United States dropped sharply.

welfare programs ceased to expand and the proportion of our population living in poverty leveled off. It then began to edge up again in the 1980s, but it remained well below the poverty level of the 1950s despite recessions during the Reagan and Bush administrations. During the Clinton administration from 1993 through 2000, the poverty rate fell to a historic low of 11.3 percent. Under the George W. Bush administration, poverty began edging up again as the American economy faltered. In 2005, 13.3 percent of the population had incomes under the poverty line.[137]

The decline and eventual leveling off of the overall poverty rate in the United States obscures important differences among different groups of Americans. As we saw in Chapter 3, the drop in poverty that the Great Society programs produced was especially rapid for the elderly. Before 1960, people over age sixty-five had a higher poverty rate than any other age group; by 2005, just 10.1 percent of those over sixty-five lived in poverty—below the national average of 13.3 percent.[138] One government study found that in 1984, the poverty rate would have been 55 percent among those over sixty-five if not for Social Security.[139] In contrast, the poverty rate among children has actually grown over the past three decades; in 1970, 14.9 percent of all children under the age of eighteen lived below the poverty line, whereas in 2005, the figure stood at 17.6 percent.[140]

The state of the nation's health has also improved as a result of social welfare programs. Measuring the health of a nation is difficult, but one widely used measure is the infant mortality rate (i.e., the percentage of children who die before their first birthdays). Following the introduction of Medicaid, which provides health care for the poor, and the AFDC and Food Stamp programs, which provide healthier diets, the infant mortality rate in the United States dropped quickly. In 1960, the rate stood at 26.0 per 1,000 live births; by 1975, it was only 16.1 per 1,000; and by 2004, it was 6.8 per 1,000.[141] Improved medicine certainly caused some of the decline in infant mortality, but the decline was sharpest among the poor—who directly benefit from social welfare programs. Consequently, experts agree that social welfare programs explain a large portion of the improvement in our nation's health.[142]

When one examines other possible effects of social welfare programs, the system seems less successful. The divorce rate, the percentage of children living in single-parent families, and the crime rate have all increased sharply since the 1960s. Some critics argue that the welfare system has caused these changes as unintended side effects. Perhaps most disturbing of all, some conservative critics contend that the old welfare system produced an underclass of people who were permanently trapped in poverty because of the incentives the welfare system offers.[143] Had AFDC not been abolished and replaced with TANF, they argue, government policy would continue to perpetuate a permanent welfare underclass. The extent to which the welfare system has caused these changes in our society is difficult to estimate, however, because divorce, single-parent households, and crime are increasing among both those who receive welfare and those who do not.[144]

17-3d The Future of Social Welfare Policy

Social welfare policy is an issue that unites as well as separates Democrats from Republicans. On the one hand, neither Democrats nor Republicans are eager to cut back the country's largest social welfare program, Social Security, even though most impartial analyses show that the program is headed for bankruptcy unless Congress makes fundamental changes to it.[145] On the other hand, Democrats and Republicans disagree sharply over what should be done in the important areas of welfare and health care. Whereas Democrats argue that the federal government should play a major role in lifting people out of poverty and ensuring that they have adequate medical care, Republicans argue for greater reliance on individual initiative and the workings of the marketplace.

Social Security

Social Security looms as a potential point of conflict between the generations in the years ahead. Two important questions lie at the core of the debate: (1) on whom should the federal government spend its money, and (2) what steps should be taken to prevent Social Security from going bankrupt?

As Chapter 16 discusses, the federal government spends more than four times more per capita on the elderly than on the young.[146] Three factors explain why this disparity in government spending exists. First, Social Security is a mandatory social insurance program for all workers, whereas programs for the young target only children in poor families. Second, because Social Security affects many more people, it enjoys greater political support and is less vulnerable to budget-cutting pressures. Third, the young, unlike the elderly, have no direct representation or access to power in government; hence, they aren't able to push for programs that affect their interests. One question facing the American public, therefore, is whether the federal government should continue to spend so heavily on Social Security for the elderly when far more children than senior citizens live in poverty. When the interests of the elderly and children conflict, how should the rules of social welfare be structured? Who should benefit? These are difficult questions that arouse considerable controversy.

The second issue surrounding Social Security concerns how to keep the program solvent.[147] As Chapter 16 notes, revenues from current payroll taxes pay for current Social Security benefits. The flaw with this pay-as-you-go system is that, over the years, the ratio of workers paying taxes to retirees drawing benefits has fallen. In 1950, for instance, there were 16.5 workers for every retiree; in 2000, there were 3.4; and experts project that by 2045, when most of today's college students start retiring—there will be only 2. If this trend continues unchanged, some time around 2017 the annual cost of Social Security will exceed the revenue from payroll taxes; and after the surpluses that have built up over the years are exhausted—roughly in 2041 unless something is done—Social Security will become insolvent.[148]

Proposals for keeping Social Security solvent traditionally have included increasing payroll taxes, cutting benefits, tightening eligibility standards for recipients, and tapping general tax revenues. None of these options is attractive. The public isn't interested in paying more or getting less. That is why during the acrimonious debates in the mid-1990s over shrinking the size of the federal government, both Democrats and Republicans insisted that they would not touch Social Security. Nonetheless, if the ratio of workers to retirees continues to decline, Congress and the president will eventually be forced to confront the contentious question of how to keep Social Security solvent.[149]

These political realities have spurred interest in nontraditional solutions to Social Security's funding woes. One proposal, which George W. Bush championed in the 2000s, would permit individuals to channel a portion of their Social Security taxes into individual retirement accounts. They could then invest this money in the stock market. The idea is that these investments would earn a higher rate of return than the standard Social Security program.

Yet this proposal and others like it have their own shortcomings. One is that payroll taxes that go into individual retirement accounts is revenue that cannot be used to pay the benefits of current retirees. So partially privatizing Social Security would intensify the program's funding problems, at least in the short term. Another problem is that stock market investments can underperform as well as outperform the expected return from the traditional Social Security program. Should the stock prices fall for a sustained period of time, as they did during 2001, people would see their retirement benefits dwindle. For these reasons, efforts to fix Social Security's funding problems raise considerable passions both in Washington and among the American public.

Although Social Security reform was at the top of President Bush's agenda following his reelection, his efforts to reform Social Security faded along with his falling popularity.[150] Congress never

acted on it. The problem of how to rescue Social Security, therefore, remains unsolved.

Welfare Policy

Welfare policy in the United States continues to reflect an uneasy
balance between the public's desire to help people in need and its
reluctance to give aid to the able-bodied or to those, such as
impoverished drug addicts, who the public believes are responsible for their own poverty.[151] Although the public expresses dissatisfaction with welfare, an overwhelming majority endorses the
idea that the government should provide a social safety net of welfare programs for the poor (although this support has eroded somewhat in recent years).[152] The widespread belief that welfare often
goes to people who are to blame for their poverty or who do not
actually need assistance fueled welfare reform in the 1990s.

The 1996 welfare reform law that abolished AFDC and created
TANF struck a new balance between these competing concerns.
Whether this is the proper balance, however, remains to be seen.
Welfare experts warn that recipients may not receive adequate job
training and that there may not be enough jobs for them—
especially when the American economy enters a recession. An
economic downturn could throw hundreds of thousands of people
out of work and leave them and their families without any government help.[153] If the experts' warnings prove true, then welfare
reform will likely return to the top of the nation's agenda.

Health Policy

The central issues in health-care policy are cost and access. The
government's health-care costs have grown much faster than the
cost of living. Spending on Medicaid leads the way, with an annual growth rate of 30 percent.[154] The cost of privately paid health
care has skyrocketed as well. As a result, health care is consuming
a large and growing share of the economy. In 1950, the United
States spent roughly 4 percent of its GDP on health care. By 1970,
that figure had risen to 7 percent, and by 2005 it had risen to 16
percent.[155] Although the booming economy of the late 1990s kept
pace with the growing cost of health care, once the boom ended in
2001, health-care costs began to rise once again.[156]

The other major issue in health-care policy is access to medical
care. Even though the United States has the world's largest private
health insurance industry as well as both Medicare and Medicaid,
the percentage of the population without any health insurance at
all has been growing since the 1980s, reaching 15.3 percent—or
45.7 million people—in 2007.[157] Most people who lack health insurance either are unemployed or work at low-paying jobs that do
not provide medical benefits. Because doctor visits can be expensive, people without insurance tend to seek medical care only
when their illnesses are more advanced and thus more expensive
to treat. Other consumers of medical care finance part of the cost
of treating the uninsured by paying higher bills and premiums as

doctors and hospitals pass their expenses on to patients who have insurance. Finally, despite the fact that the United States pays more per capita for medical care than any other major industrial nation, many objective measures of our nation's health (e.g., the infant mortality rate) indicate that the quality of our health care is among the lowest of the major industrial nations.[158]

In 1993, President Clinton attempted to deal with the problems of both cost and access by proposing to overhaul the health-care system in the United States.[159] He sought to create a system of universal health insurance, or insurance covering all Americans, that would combine the current system of private insurers and employment-based coverage with government administration. Clinton's proposal attracted criticism from both Democrats, many of whom favored creating a government-run national health insurance program, and Republicans, most of whom preferred to rely on the private sector to solve the cost and access problems. Congress failed to act on Clinton's proposal before the 1994 elections, and the subsequent Republican victory dealt the final death blow to his plan.

When the Republicans took control of Congress in 1995, they sought to enact their own plans for dealing with escalating health-care costs. As part of an ambitious effort to cut federal spending, the Republicans passed legislation that would have revamped both Medicare and Medicaid. The Republican plan would have reduced spending on Medicare, the federal government's health insurance for the elderly, by paying doctors and hospitals less for their services, by requiring more affluent beneficiaries to pay more for their Medicare coverage, and by encouraging elderly Americans to choose lower-cost forms of health insurance. As for Medicaid, the Republican plan would have cut spending on the public assistance program for the poor by giving state governments the authority to decide who would be covered and what benefits they would get.[160] Not surprisingly, Democrats denounced the Republican legislation as an effort to balance the budget on the backs of the poor and the elderly.[161] Ultimately, Republicans lacked the votes they needed to override President Clinton's veto, and their plan failed.

During President George W. Bush's eight years in office beginning in 2001, little attention was given to the twin problems of the rising cost of health care and declining health insurance coverage. Both Congress and President Bush focused on Social Security reform and largely ignored problems with health care other than the affordability of prescription drugs. However, in the 2008 presidential campaign, both Senators Barack Obama and John McCain made health insurance coverage one of their central issues, and both offered plans to cover far more Americans with health insurance. Adding urgency to the situation were warnings that the Medicare system was expected to fail by 2018 unless steps were taken by Congress to put it on a firm financial foundation. Like Social Security, Medicare is spending more money every year than it is getting in revenue. A key difference between the two programs, however, is that Medicare is expected to fail within the next decade.[162]

In health care, welfare, Social Security, and other aspects of social welfare policy, a tension exists that symbolizes the broader questions the United States faces in dealing with domestic policy: What responsibility does government have to address the problems of the people? What limitations should government face when intervening in these areas? Conflicts over domestic policy will continue as our society experiences changing pressures, and the rules of domestic policy will change as government responds.

SUMMARY

In this chapter, we have considered three types of domestic policy: management of the economy, regulatory policy, and social welfare policy. In all three areas, the rules change as the needs and views of the American people and their elected representatives change. And in domestic policy, as in all areas of government, changes in the rules cause some groups to gain and others to lose. This creates an ongoing question for Americans: To what extent should the federal government intervene in the lives of people? How active a role should the government take in setting domestic policy?

Traditionally, the federal government adopted laissez-faire domestic policy, allowing the economy, businesses, and individuals to manage without government interference. However, during the Great Depression of the 1930s, the federal government took on a new activist role. It now uses both fiscal tools (the budget) and monetary tools (the Fed's control over the money supply) to manage the economy. Although these policies have generally been successful, many conflicts over economic policy remain. Today's economic theorists split in advocating either more or less government intervention in the economy.

The federal government currently engages in economic and social regulation. With economic regulation, the government seeks to promote economic competition when possible and to counter the harmful effects of monopoly when not. Social regulation became a significant government activity in the 1960s and 1970s. It seeks to protect Americans from dangers or unfair practices associated with the way companies produce their products as well as from dangers associated with the products themselves.

The federal government's involvement in social welfare dates back to the New Deal. Today, it includes both social insurance programs to protect the elderly and public assistance programs to help the poor. The bulk of social welfare is provided through social insurance programs. Debates over the future of social insurance programs will be shaped by the strong support they enjoy and by their growing cost. In contrast, the future of most public assistance programs is clouded by public skepticism over their effectiveness in alleviating poverty and helping the poor to become self-sufficient. Debate also centers on the most effective type of public assistance programs—alleviative, preventative, or curative—and whether the federal government or the states should administer such programs.

As the United States faces the rapid changes and challenges of the twenty-first century, it will need to adapt. In domestic policy, as in other areas of government, this means constantly reexamining and changing our rules and policies to reflect changes in society and in the world. And so the political conflict goes on—the groups compete—and the ever-changing rules of domestic policy create new winners and losers in American society. Just who those winners and losers will be over the next few decades remains to be seen.

KEY TERMS

counter-cyclical programs

economic regulation

environmental impact
  statement

Federal Reserve System

fiscal policy

Food Stamp Program

gross domestic product (GDP)

industrial policy

Keynesian economics

Lucas critique

laissez-faire

means test

Medicaid

Medicare

monetary theory

public assistance

regulatory policy

social insurance

social regulation

Social welfare policy

supply-side economics

Temporary Assistance for
  Needy Families (TANF)

READINGS FOR FURTHER STUDY

Cook, Fay Lomax, and Edith J. Barrett. *Support for the American Welfare State: The Views of Congress and the Public* (New York: Columbia University Press, 1992). The authors argue that the "American welfare state is here to stay" because support for social welfare programs has deep roots with the American people and their elected representatives in Congress.

Gans, Herbert J. *The War against the Poor: The Underclass and Anti-Poverty Policy* (New York: Basic Books, 1995). A leading sociologist argues that pejorative labels have been used to relegate the poor to the margins of society.

Gautier, Catherine. *Oil, Water, and Climate.* (Cambridge: Cambridge University Press, 2008). A thorough assessment of the critical energy, water, climate and population problems facing our country and the world. Gautier's study explains the urgency of the problems and sets out the policy choices we face.

Greider, William. *Secrets of the Temple: How the Federal Reserve Runs the Country* (New York: Simon & Schuster, 1987). An absorbing account of how the Federal Reserve Bank manages the American economy.

Sawhill, Isabel, R. Kent Weaver, Ron Haskins, and Andrea Kane, eds., *Welfare Reform and Beyond: The Future of the Safety Net* (Washington, D.C.: Brookings Institution, 2002). A thorough discussion of the current state of welfare in the United States and review of problems that we still face.

Starr, Paul. *The Social Transformation of American Medicine* (New York: Basic Books, 1982). An award-winning book that shows why the United States developed a health-care system that relies so heavily on private businesses rather than the government.

Vig, Norman J., and Michael E. Kraft, *Environmental Policy: New Directions for the Twenty-First Century,* 6th ed. (Washington, D.C.: CQ Press, 2005). A comprehensive discussion of environmental politics and policy in the United States since 1960.

REVIEW QUESTIONS

1. The unemployment rate during the Great Depression was _____ percent.
    a. 5
    b. 15
    c. 25
    d. 50
2. President Franklin Delano Roosevelt's decision to use fiscal policy to combat the Great Depression was inspired by the work of
    a. John Maynard Keynes.
    b. Milton Friedman.
    c. Karl Marx.
    d. Alan Greenspan.
3. In 2004, the richest 1 percent owned about _____ percent of the wealth in the United States.
    a. 20
    b. 33
    c. 50
    d. 67
4. Which of the following is *not* supported by supply-side economic theorists?
    a. tax cuts for the wealthiest Americans
    b. decrease in government spending
    c. decrease in government regulation
    d. tax increases for the wealthiest Americans
5. Which of the following is *true* about the Kyoto Protocol?
    a. President Clinton signed the treaty.
    b. The Senate ratified the treaty.
    c. The Senate did not ratified the treaty.
    d. Both a and b.

6. Which of the following is *true* about the contemporary United States?
   a. Air pollution has declined.
   b. Air pollution has increased.
   c. President George W. Bush urged Congress to take action on global warming.
   d. Americans trust the Republicans to protect the environment more so than they do the Democrats.

7. The _____ introduced the first major wave of social welfare policies in the United States.
   a. Social Security Act of 1935
   b. Great Society
   c. War on Poverty
   d. Economic Opportunity Act of 1955

8. Which of the following was (were) created during President Lyndon Johnson's War on Poverty?
   a. Medicaid
   b. food stamps
   c. Medicare
   d. all of the above

9. According to the federal government in 2005, approximately what percent of Americans are living in poverty?
   a. 6
   b. 13
   c. 21
   d. 42

10. What are the central issues in health-care policy?
   a. cost and access
   b. cost and political ideology
   c. access and influence
   d. access and individualism

NOTES

1. "Prepared Text for the President's State of the Union Message," *New York Times,* January 24, 1996.

2. U.S. Bureau of the Census, *Statistical Abstract of the United States, 2008,* 126th ed. (Washington, D.C.: U.S. Bureau of the Census, 2007), 322, table 482.

3. William J. Barber, *From New Era to New Deal: Herbert Hoover, the Economists, and American Economic Policy, 1921–1933* (New York: Cambridge University Press, 1985); Michael S. Lewis-Beck and Peverill Squire, "The Transformation of the American State: The New Era-New Deal Test," *Journal of Politics* 53 (February 1991): 106–21; Albert U. Romasco, "Herbert Hoover's Policies for Dealing with the Great Depression: The End of the Old Order or the Beginning of the New?" in *The Hoover Presidency,* eds. Martin L. Fausold and George T. Mazuzan (Albany: State University of New York Press, 1974); Herbert Stein, *The Fiscal Revolution in America* (Chicago: University of Chicago Press, 1969).

4. Arthur M. Schlesinger, Jr., *The Coming of the New Deal* (Boston: Houghton Mifflin, 1958).

5. See David Burner, *Herbert Hoover: A Public Life* (New York: Knopf, 1979), 244.

6. Robert Lekachman, *The Age of Keynes* (New York: Vintage, 1966), chap. 5.

7. John Maynard Keynes, *The General Theory of Employment, Interest, and Money* (New York: Harcourt, Brace, 1965).

8. See John T. Woolley, *Monetary Politics: The Federal Reserve and the Politics of Monetary Policy* (Cambridge: Cambridge University Press, 1984), chap. 2.

9. James Livingston, *Origins of the Federal Reserve System: Money, Class, and Corporate Capitalism, 1890–1913* (Ithaca, NY: Cornell University Press, 1986).

10. Milton Friedman, "The Optimum Quantity of Money," in *The Optimum Quantity of Money and Other Essays* (Chicago: Aldine, 1971), 1–50; Milton Friedman and Anna G. Schwartz, A *Monetary History of the United States* (Chicago: University of Chicago Press, 1963); A. Robert Nobay and Harry G. Johnson, "Monetarism: A Historic-Theoretic Perspective," *Journal of Economic Literature* 15 (June 1977): 470–85; Thomas Mayer, ed., *The Structure of Monetarism* (New York: Norton, 1978).

11. Milton Friedman with Rose D. Friedman, *Capitalism and Freedom* (Chicago: University of Chicago Press, 1962), chap. 3.

12. Joseph A. Pechman, *Federal Tax Policy,* 5th ed. (Washington, D.C.: Brookings Institution, 1987), 8.

13. Robert E. Lucas, Jr., "Expectations and the Neutrality of Money," *Journal of Economic Theory* 4 (April 1972): 103–24; Robert E. Lucas, Jr., "An Equilibrium Model of the Business Cycle," *Journal of Political Economy* 83 (December 1975): 1113–14.

14. James K. Galbraith and William Darity, Jr., *Macroeconomics* (Boston: Houghton Mifflin, 1994), chaps. 8–9; Kevin D. Hoover, *The New Classical Macroeconomics* (Cambridge, MA: Basil Blackwell, 1988).

15. Robert Solow, "On Theories of Unemployment," *American Economic Review* 70 (March 1980): 1–11.

16. James K. Galbraith and William Darity, Jr., *Macroeconomics* (Boston: Houghton Mifflin, 1994), chap. 10; see also Arjo Klamer, *Conversations with Economists: New Classical Economists and Opponents Speak Out on the Current Controversy in Macroeconomics* (Totowa, NJ: Rowman & Allanheld, 1983).

17. *Statistical Abstract of the United States, 2008,* 450, table 675.

18. "Across the Great Divide," *Wall Street Journal,* October 2, 1995; Keith Bradsher, "Widest Gap in Incomes? Research Points to U.S.," *New York Times,* October 27, 1995; Steven A. Holmes, "Income Disparity between Poorest and Richest Rises," *New York Times,* June 20, 1996; Robert J. Samuelson, "The Wealth Statistic Myth," *Washington Post National Weekly Edition,* May 1–7, 1995, 5.

19. Arthur B. Kennickell, "A Rolling Tide: Changes in the Distribution of Wealth in the U.S., 1989–2001," Bard College: Levy Economics Institute, 2003, available at www.levy.org/vdoc.aspx?docid=73; Keith Bradsher, "Gap in Wealth in U.S. Called Widest in West," *New York Times,* April 17, 1995; Samuelson, "The Wealth Statistic Myth," 5; see also Keith Bradsher, "Rich Control More of U.S. Wealth, Study Says, as Debts Grow for Poor," *New York Times,* June 22, 1996.

20. *Statistical Abstract of the United States, 2008,* 463, table 699.

21. See, for example, Michael Novak, "What Wealth Gap?" *Wall Street Journal,* July 11, 1995; Samuelson, "The Wealth Statistic Myth," 5.

22. Quoted in Keith Bradsher, "America's Opportunity Gap," *New York Times,* June 4, 1995.

23. See, for example, Steven Rattner, "GOP Ignores Income Inequality," *Wall Street Journal,* May 23, 1995.

24. See the data cited in Bradsher, "America's Opportunity Gap."

25. George Gilder, *Wealth and Poverty* (New York: Basic Books, 1981); Jude Wanniski, *The Way the World Works* (New York: Basic Books, 1978).

26. See Kevin Philips, *The Politics of Rich and Poor: Wealth and the American Electorate in the Reagan Aftermath* (New York: Random House, 1990).

27. David A. Stockman, *The Triumph of Politics: Why the Reagan Revolution Failed* (New York: Harper & Row, 1986).

28. "On the Issues: The Economy, Taxes, and Trade," *New York Times* online, available at www.nytimes.com/ref/politics/campaign/issue_economy.html.

29. See, for example, Ira C. Magaziner and Robert B. Reich, *Minding America's Business: The Decline and Rise of the American Economy* (New York: Harcourt, Brace, Jovanovich, 1982); Lester C. Thurow, *The Zero-Sum Solution* (New York: Simon & Schuster, 1985).

30. See Giovanni Dosi, Laura D'Andrea Tyson, and John Zysman, "Trade, Technologies, and Development: A Framework for Discussing Japan," in *Politics and Productivity: How Japan's Development Strategy Works,* eds. Chalmers Johnson, Laura Tyson, and John Zysman (New York: Harper Business, 1989); Chalmers A. Johnson, *MITI and the Japanese Miracle: The Growth of Industrial Policy, 1925–1975* (Stanford, CA: Stanford University Press, 1982).

31. Kenneth S. Deffeyes, *Hubert's Peak: The Impending World Oil Shortage* (Princeton, NJ: Princeton University Press, 2001); Matthew R. Simmons, *Twilight in the Desert: The Coming Oil Shock and the World Economy* (New York: John Wiley, 2005); Vaclav Smil, *Energy at the Crossroads: Global Perspectives and Uncertainties* (Cambridge, MA: MIT Press, 2003).

32. John M. Broder, "Gore Calls for Energy Shift to Avoid a Global Crisis," *New York Times,* national edition, July 18, 2008, A17; Mary Ann Giordano and Larry Rohter, "McCain at Nuclear Plant Highlights Energy Issue," *New York Times,* national edition, August 6, 2008, A16.

33. Data are from the U.S. Census Bureau, Historical Income Tables – Families, available at www.census.gov/hhes/www/income/histinc/f07AR.html and the Office of Federal Housing Enterprise Oversight, Median Housing Price Index, available at www.ofheo.gov/hpi_download.aspx.

34. Peter Coy, "Why Subprime Lenders are in Trouble," *Business Week,* March 2, 2007, available at www.businessweek.com/bwdaily/dnflash/content/mar2007/db20070302_477856.htm.

35. Daniel Gross, "Stocks are *So* 20th Century," *Slate* May 22, 2006, available at www.slate.com/id/2142158/?nav=tap3; "A Beginner's Guide to Derivatives," *Money Week,* September 29, 2006, available at www.moneyweek.com/investment-advice/how-to-invest/a-beginners-guide-to-derivatives.aspx.

36. U.S. House of Representatives, "The 'U.S. Federal Housing Finance Reform Act of 2007 Summary,' available at www.house.gov/apps/list/press/financialsvcs_dem/hr1427summary030907.pdf; Peter Gosselin, "Fannie, Freddie takeover Possible," *New York Times,* September 7, 2008, a1.

37. Roddy Boyd, "The Last Days of Bear Stearns," CNNMoney.com, March 31, 2008, available at www.money.cnn.com/2008/03/28/magazines/fortune/boyd_bear.fortune/.

38. Henry M. Paulson, "Statement on Treasury and Federal Housing Finance Agency Action to Protect Financial Markets and Taxpayers," available at www.treasury.gov/press/releases/hp1129.htm; Peter Gosselin, "U.S. Seizes Mortgage Titans in Multibillion-Dollar Rescue," *Los Angeles Times*, September 8, 2008, a1; Stephen Labaton and Edmund Andrews, "In Rescue, U.S. Takes over Mortgage Finance Titans," *New York Times*, September 8, 2008, A1.

39. "Lehman Folds with Record $613 Billion Debt," *Marketwatch*, September 15, 2008, available at www.marketwatch.com/news/story/lehman-folds-613-billion-debt/story.aspx?guid={2FE5AC05-597A-4E71-A2D5-9B9FCC29 0520}; Edmund L. Andrews, "Fed in $85 Billion Bailout Plan of Faltering Insurance Giant," *New York Times*, September 17, 2008, A1.

40. Marc Lifsher and Evan Halper, "State may need to ask U.S. for $7-billion loan," *Los Angeles Times*, October 3, 2008, A1.

41. Mark Landler and Edmund L. Andrews, "Bailout Plan Wins Approval; Democrats Vow Tighter Rules," *New York Times* October 4, 2008, A1; Maura Reynolds and Tiffany Hsu, "Approval of Bailout Comes Amid Signs that a Steep Recession is Just Beginning," *Los Angeles Times*, October 4, 2008, A1.

42. We would like to thank Eric Sonquist, Chief Financial Officer of the UCSB Foundation and Director of Finance and Administration of Institutional Advancement for the University of California, Santa Barbara for his input and advice on this section.

43. William G. Mayer, *The Changing American Mind: How and Why American Public Opinion Changed Between 1960 and 1988* (Ann Arbor: University of Michigan Press, 1992), 100–102, 482–85.

44. Pew Research Center for the People & the Press, "Public Sends Mixed Signals on Energy Policy," March 6, 2008, available at www.people-press.org/report/400/public-sends-mixed-signals-on-energy-policy.

45. Benjamin I. Page and Robert Y. Shapiro, *The Rational Public: Fifty Years of Trends in Americans' Policy Preferences* (Chicago: University of Chicago Press, 1992), chap. 4.

46. James W. Fesler and Donald F. Kettl, *The Politics of the Administrative Process* (Chatham, NJ: Chatham House, 1991), 292–93.

47. Gabriel Kolko, *The Triumph of Capitalism: A Reinterpretation of American History, 1900–1916* (Chicago: Quadrangle Books, 1963).

48. Bryan Gruley and Albert R. Karr, "Telecom Vote Signals Competitive Free-for-All: Bill's Passage Represents Will of Both Parties," *Wall Street Journal,* February 2, 1996; Albert R. Karr, "Cable Rates Are Up an Average of 10.4% This Year," *Wall Street Journal,* August 29, 1996.

49. David P. Baron, *Business and Its Environment* (Englewood Cliffs, NJ: Prentice Hall, 1993), 252.

50. George C. Thompson and Gerald P. Brady, *Text, Cases and Materials on Antitrust Fundamentals* (St. Paul, MN: West, 1979).

51. William E. Leuchtenburg, *Franklin Roosevelt and the New Deal, 1932–1940* (New York: Harper & Row, 1963).

52. George J. Gordon and Michael E. Milakovich, *Public Administration in America,* 5th ed. (New York: St. Martin's, 1995), 408.

53. Martha Derthick and Paul J. Quirk, *The Politics of Deregulation* (Washington, D.C.: Brookings Institution, 1985).

54. Bradley Behrman, "Civil Aeronautics Board," in *The Politics of Regulation,* ed. James Q. Wilson (New York: Basic Books, 1980).

55. Larry N. Gerston, Cynthia Fraleigh, and Robert Schwab, *The Deregulated Society* (Pacific Grove, CA: Brooks/Cole, 1988); "President Signs Bill Terminating ICC," *Congressional Quarterly Weekly Report,* January 6, 1996, 58; David E. Sanger, "A U.S. Agency, Once Powerful, Is Dead at 108," *New York Times,* January 1, 1996; Richard W. Waterman, *Presidential Influence and the Administrative State* (Knoxville: University of Tennessee Press, 1989), chap. 4.

56. Murray Edelman, *The Symbolic Uses of Politics* (Urbana: University of Illinois Press, 1964); Theodore J. Lowi, *The End of Liberalism* (New York: Norton, 1969), chaps. 3–4; George J. Stigler, "The Theory of Economic Regulation," *Bell Journal of Economics and Management Science 2* (Spring 1971): 3–21.

57. Gerston, Fraleigh, and Schwab, *The Deregulated Society,* chap. 5.

58. Barry Bearak and Tom Furlong, "Toting Up Blame for S&L Crisis," *Los Angeles Times,* September 16, 1990; Steven Waldman et al., "The S&L Firestorm," *Newsweek* (July 23, 1990): 14–16.

59. William Lilley III and James C. Miller III, "The New 'Social Regulation,'" *Public Interest* 47 (Spring 1977): 49–61.

60. Gordon and Milakovich, *Public Administration in America,* 408–9.

61. Charles Noble, *Liberalism at Work: The Rise and Fall of OSHA* (Philadelphia: Temple University Press, 1986), chap. 3.

62. U.S. Department of Labor, Occupational Health and Safety Administration, "OSHA Facts," available at www.osha.gov/as/opa/oshafacts.html.

63. Wayne B. Gray, *Productivity versus OSHA and EPA Regulations* (Ann Arbor: University of Michigan Research Press, 1986).

64. W. Kip Viscusi, *Risk by Choice: Regulating Health and Safety in the Workplace* (Cambridge, MA: Harvard University Press, 1983).

65. David P. McCaffrey, *OSHA and the Politics of Health Regulation* (New York: Plenum Press, 1982), 168.

66. M. Green and N. Waitzman, *Business at War on the Law: An Analysis of the Benefits of Safety and Health Regulation* (Washington, D.C.: Corporate Accountability Research Group, 1979).

67. Noble, *Liberalism at Work,* 201–5; *Statistical Abstract of the United States, 2006,* 125th ed. (Washington, D.C.: U.S. Census Bureau, 2005), 433, table 640; *Statistical Abstract of the United States, 2008,* 420, table 635.

68. Noble, *Liberalism at Work,* chap. 7.

69. Don J. Lofgren, *Dangerous Premises: An Insider's View of OSHA Enforcement* (Ithaca, NY: ILR Press, 1989).

70. See, for example, Michael Weisskopf and David Maraniss, "Ruling Out OSHA," *Washington Post National Weekly Edition,* September 4–10, 1995, 6–7.

71. Robert Pear, "With or Without a Budget Pact, the G.O.P.'s Fiscal Squeeze Is On," *New York Times,* February 1, 1996; U.S. Department of Labor, Occupational Health and Safety Administration, "OSHA Facts."

72. Noble, *Liberalism at Work,* 124–26; Pew Center for the People & the Press, *Retropolitics, The Political Typology: Version 3.0* (Washington, D.C.: Pew Center for the People & the Press, 1999), 16.

73. On the public's attitude toward the environment before the 1960s, see Roderick Nash, *Wilderness and the American Mind* (New Haven, CT: Yale University Press, 1967).

74. Rachel Carson, *Silent Spring* (Boston: Houghton Mifflin, 1962).

75. Marc K. Landy, Marc J. Roberts, and Stephen R. Thomas, *The Environmental Protection Agency,* exp. ed. (New York: Oxford University Press, 1994), chap. 1.

76. See, for instance, the Ralph Nader group's report on the Air Quality Act in John C. Esposito et al., *Vanishing Air* (New York: Grossman, 1970).

77. Tom Wicker, *One of Us: Richard Nixon and the American Dream* (New York: Random House, 1991), 507–18; see also the "1969 Santa Barbara Oil Spill—Presentation Source Materials," available at www.geog.ucsb.edu/~jeff/sb_69oilspill/.

78. Walter A. Rosenbaum, *Environmental Politics and Policy,* 2nd ed. (Washington, D.C.: CQ Press, 1991), chap. 3.

79. Mayer, *The Changing American Mind,* 102–8.

80. Paul Portney, "Natural Resources and the Environment," in *The Reagan Record,* eds. John L. Palmer and Isabel V. Sawhill (Cambridge, MA: Ballinger, 1984), 141–75.

81. "Appendix 2: Federal Spending on Natural Resources and the Environment, Selected Fiscal Years, 1980 to 1993," in *Environmental Policy for the 1990s,* 2nd ed., eds. Norman J. Vig and Michael E. Kraft (Washington, D.C.: CQ Press, 1994), 403.

82. Christopher J. Bosso, "After the Movement: Environmental Activism in the 1990s," in *Environmental Policy for the 1990s,* 2nd ed., eds. Norman J. Vig and Michael E. Kraft (Washington, D.C.: CQ Press, 1994), 31–50; Mayer, *The Changing American Mind,* 102–8.

83. Richard E. Cohen, *Washington at Work: Back Rooms and Clean Air,* 2nd ed. (Boston: Allyn & Bacon, 1995).

84. Norman J. Vig, "Presidential Leadership and the Environment: From Reagan and Bush to Clinton," in *Environmental Policy for the 1990s,* 2nd ed., eds. Norman J. Vig and Michael E. Kraft (Washington, D.C.: CQ Press, 1994), 71–95.

85. Robert M. White, "Climate Change: Where Do We Go from Here?" *Issues in Science and Technology,* 14 (Spring 1998): 59–66; John M. Wallace and John R. Christy, "The Truth about Global Warming," *National Academies Op-Ed Service Guide,* February 4, 2000, available at www4.nationalacademies.org/onpi/oped.nsf/; S. George Philander, *Is the Temperature Rising?* (Princeton, NJ: Princeton University Press, 1998).

86. John Thor Dahlburg, "U.S. Is Feeling Heat in Climate Meeting Gridlock," *Los Angeles Times,* November 24, 2000; Sebastian Rotella, "U.S. Endorses Treaty on Global Warming," *Los Angeles Times,* November 13, 1998.

87. Elizabeth Shogren and Kenneth R. Weiss, "Environmental Officials See a Chance to Shape Regulations," *Los Angeles Times,* November 10, 2004, A12.

88. Naomi Oreskes, "The Scientific Consensus on Climate Change," *Science,* 306 (3 December 2004): 1686; American Association for the Advancement of Science, "Climate Change," available at www.ourplanet.com/aaas/pages/atmos02.html; National Academies of Science, "Joint Science Academies' Statement: Global Response to Climate Change," June 7, 2005, available at, www.nationalacademies.org/onpi/06072005.pdf.

89. James Kirkup, "Climate-change Talks Poisoned by US Self-interest," *The Scotsman,* December 10, 2005, 6.

90. For a discussion of how this logic plays out in Congress, see R. Douglas Arnold, *The Logic of Congressional Action* (New Haven, CT: Yale University Press, 1990), chap. 2.

91. Norman J. Vig and Michael E. Kraft, "Conclusion: The New Environmental Agenda," in *Environmental Policy for the 1990s,* 2nd ed., eds. Norman J. Vig and Michael E. Kraft (Washington, D.C.: CQ Press, 1994), 378–85.

92. H. W. Lewis, *Technological Risk* (New York: Norton, 1990), 266–79.

93. Naomi Oreskes, "The Scientific Consensus on Climate Change," *Science* 306 (3 December 2004): 1686; John T. Houghton, *Global Warming: The Complete Briefing,* 3rd ed. (New York: Cambridge University Press, 2004); John T. Houghton, ed., *Climate Change 2001: The Scientific Basis: Contribution of Working Group I to the Third Assessment Report of the Intergovernmental Panel on Climate Change* (New York: Cambridge University Press, 2001).

94. Baron, *Business and Its Environment,* 318–31.

95. Executive Office of the President, Council on Environmental Quality, *Environmental Quality: 25th Anniversary Report* (Washington, D.C.: GPO, 1995), 179–92.

96. Vig and Kraft, "Conclusion," 379–80.

97. Kenneth S. Deffeyes, *Hubbert's Peak: The Impending World Oil Shortage* (Princeton, NJ: Princeton University Press, 2001); Matthew R. Simmons, *Twilight in the Desert: The Coming Saudi Oil Shock and the World Economy* (New York: John Wiley, 2005).

98. Diana M. DiNitto and Thomas R. Dye, *Social Welfare Politics and Public Policy,* 2nd ed. (Englewood Cliffs, NJ: Prentice Hall, 1987), 189.

99. Charles E. Gilbert, "Welfare Policy," in *Handbook of Political Science,* vol. 6 (Menlo Park, CA: Addison-Wesley, 1975), 111–240.

100. Theda Skocpol, *Protecting Soldiers and Mothers: The Political Origins of Social Policy in the United States* (Cambridge, MA: Harvard University Press, 1992), chap. 1.

101. Ibid.

102. Congressional Quarterly, *Congress and the Nation, 1945–1964* (Washington, D.C.: Congressional Quarterly Service, 1965), 1225; Peter Flora and Jens Alber, "Modernization, Democratization and the Development of Welfare States in Western Europe," in *The Development of Welfare States in Europe and America,* eds. Peter Flora and Arnold J. Heidenheimer (New Brunswick, NJ: Transaction Press, 1981), 37–80.

103. U.S. Bureau of the Census, *Historical Statistics of the United States, Colonial Times to 1970,* bicentennial edition, part 2 (Washington, D.C.: Government Printing Office, 1975), 348–49; *Statistical Abstract of the United States, 2008,* 350–51, tables 528–29.

104. *Statistical Abstract of the United States, 2008,* 355, table 539.

105. Iris J. Lav, Edward Lazere, and Robert Greenstein, *The States and the Poor* (Washington, D.C.: Center on Budget and Policy Priorities, 1993).

106. *Statistical Abstract of the United States, 2008,* 358, table 545.

107. Harold W. Stanley and Richard G. Niemi, *Vital Statistics on American Politics, 1999–2000* (Washington, D.C.: CQ Press, 2000), 364–65.

108. Stanley and Niemi, *Vital Statistics,* 363.

109. "Welfare Rolls," *Congressional Quarterly Weekly Report,* January 22, 1994, 121.

110. U.S. Bureau of the Census, *Statistical Abstract of the United States, 2000,* (Washington, D.C.: U.S. Bureau of the Census, 1999), 389.

111. Mary Jo Bane, "Household Composition and Poverty," in *Fighting Poverty: What Works and What Doesn't,* eds. Sheldon H. Danziger and Daniel H. Weinberg (Cambridge, MA: Harvard University Press, 1986); William Julius Wilson and Kathryn M. Neckerman, "Poverty and Family Structure: The Widening Gap between Evidence and Public Policy Issues," in *Fighting Poverty: What Works and What Doesn't,* eds. Sheldon H. Danziger and Daniel H. Weinberg (Cambridge, MA: Harvard University Press, 1986).

112. George T. Martin, Jr., *Social Policy in the Welfare State* (Englewood Cliffs, NJ: Prentice Hall, 1990), 68–69; Lav, Lazere, and Greenstein, *The States and the Poor,* 11–33.

113. DiNitto and Dye, *Social Welfare Politics,* 126.

114. Mickey Kaus, "Clinton's Welfare Endgame," *Newsweek,* August 5, 1996; Sam Fulwood III, "Broad Reach of Welfare Reform Stirs Anxiety," *Los Angeles Times,* August 25, 1996, A1; Elizabeth Shogren, "Clinton's Signature Launches Historic Overhaul of Welfare," *Los Angeles Times,* August 23, 1996; Virginia Ellis and Mark Gladstone, "'It Will Be Much Tougher' in Era of Welfare Limits," *Los Angeles Times,* August 23, 1996, a1.

115. Isabel Sawhill, R. Kent Weaver, and Andrea Kane, "An Overview," in *Welfare Reform and Beyond: The Future of the Safety Net,* eds. Isabel Sawhill, R. Kent Weaver, Ron Haskins, and Andrea Kane (Washington, D.C.: Brookings Institution, 2002), 3–8.

116. *Statistical Abstract of the United States, 2008,* 358, table 546.

117. Christopher Jencks and Joseph Swingle, "Without a Net: Whom the New Welfare Law Helps and Hurts," *The American Prospect,* January 3, 2000, 37–41; U.S. General Accounting Office, "Welfare Reform: State Sanction Policies and Number of Families Affected," Report no. HEHS-00-44, 2000, available at www.gao.gov/; Kathryn Porter and Wendell Primus, "Recent Changes in the Impact of the Safety Net on Child Poverty" (Washington, D.C.: Center on Budget Policy and Priorities, 1999), available at www.cbpp.org/12-23-99wel.htm; Demetra Smith Nightingale, "Work Opportunities for People Leaving Welfare," in *Welfare Reform: The Next Act,* eds. Alan Weil and Kenneth Finegold (Washington, D.C.: Urban Institute Press, 2002), 103–20.

118. Michael Harrington, *The Other America* (Baltimore, MD: Penguin, 1962); see also the influential review of Harrington's book in Dwight McDonald, "Our Invisible Poor," *New Yorker,* January 19, 1963.

119. Michael Barone, *Our Country: The Shaping of America from Roosevelt to Reagan* (New York: Free Press, 1990), chap. 37; Lyndon Baines Johnson, *The Vantage Point: Perspectives of the Presidency 1963–1969* (New York: Popular Library, 1971), chap. 4.

120. Michael B. Katz, *The Undeserving Poor: From the War on Poverty to the War on Welfare* (New York: Pantheon, 1989), chap. 3.

121. Clarke E. Cochran, et al., *American Public Policy,* 4th ed. (New York: St. Martin's, 1993), 225.

122. Hugh Heclo, "The Political Foundations of Antipoverty Policy," in *Fighting Poverty: What Works and What Doesn't,* eds. Sheldon H. Danziger and Daniel H. Weinberg (Cambridge, MA: Harvard University Press, 1986), 312–40.

123. Frances Fox Piven and Richard A. Cloward, *Regulating the Poor: The Functions of Public Welfare,* updated ed. (New York: Vintage, 1993), chaps. 9–10; David Stoloff, "The Short Unhappy History of Community Action Programs," in *The Great Society Reader* (New York: Vintage, 1967), 231–39.

124. James A. Morone, *The Democratic Wish* (New York: Basic Books, 1991), chap. 7.

125. Johnson, *Vantage Point,* chap. 9.

126. Lawrence G. Brewster and Michael E. Brown, *The Public Agenda: Issues in American Politics,* 3rd ed. (New York: St. Martin's, 1994), 109.

127. Centers for Medicare and Medicaid Services, "Medicare and Modernization Act Update – Overview," available at www.cms.hhs.gov/PrescriptionDrug CovGenIn/01_Overview.asp; Ceci Connolly and Mike Allen, "Medicare Drug Benefit May Cost $1.2 Trillion," *Washington Post,* September 22, 2007; Amanda Gardner, "Medicare Prescription Drug Benefit Shows Mixed Results," *Washington Post,* April 22, 2008, A1; Rich Lowry, "The National Drug Scam," *National Review Online,* January 16, 2007; Lori Montgomery and Christopher Lee, "Success of Drug Plan Challenges Democrats," *Washington Post,* November 26, 2006, a1.

128. See, for example, Terry Savage, "Boomers could get buffeted in retirement," *Chicago Sun Times,* May 29, 2006; "Crisis du Jour or the Real Thing?" *American Enterprise Institute On-Line,* May 3, 2006, available at www.aei.org/ publications/filter.all,pubID.24319/pub_-detail.asp; Lois Weiss, "Greenspan: Medicare's Dangerous," *New York Post,* May 20, 2006, available at www. nypost.com/business/68840.htm.

129. Christopher Howard, "Is the American Welfare State Unusually Small?" *PS: Political Science and Politics* 36 (July 2003): 411–16.

130. See Joseph White, *Competing Solutions: American Health Care Proposals and International Experience* (Washington, D.C.: Brookings Institution, 1995).

131. U.S. Office of Management and Budget, *The Budget for Fiscal Year 2007,* Historical Tables, table 12.1, available at www.whitehouse.gov/omb/ budget/fy2007/

132. Ruth Rosen, "Which of Us Isn't Taking 'Welfare'?" *Los Angeles Times,* January 27, 1995; Steven Waldman, "Benefits 'R' Us," *Newsweek* (August 10, 1992): 56–58.

133. Lawrence R. Jacobs, Robert Y. Shapiro, and Eli C. Shulman, "The Polls: Medical Care in the United States—An Update," *Public Opinion Quarterly* 57 (Fall 1993): 394–427; Robert Y. Shapiro and Tom W. Smith, "The Polls: Social Security," *Public Opinion Quarterly* 9 (Winter 1985): 561–72; Robert Y. Shapiro and John T. Young, "The Polls: Medical Care in the United States," *Public Opinion Quarterly* 50 (Fall 1986): 418–28. For recent survey results on support for Social Security and various reform proposals, see the Social Security page of PollingReport.com, available at www.pollingreport.-com/social.htm.

134. For contrasting views, see Charles Murray, *Losing Ground: American Social Policy 1950–1980* (New York: Basic Books, 1984); John E. Schwarz, *America's Hidden Success: A Reassessment of Public Policy from Kennedy to Reagan,* rev. ed. (New York: Norton, 1983).

135. Theodore R. K. Marmor, Jerry L. Mashaw, and Philip L. Harvey, *America's Misunderstood Welfare State* (New York: HarperCollins, 1990), chap. 4.

136. *Statistical Abstract of the United States, 1995,* 115th ed. (Washington, D.C.: U.S. Bureau of the Census, 1994), 480.

137. *Statistical Abstract of the United States, 2008,* 457, table 687; Carmen DeNavas-Walt, Bernadette D. Proctor, and Robert J. Mills, U.S. Census Bureau, Current Population Reports, P60–226, *Income, Poverty, and Health*

Insurance Coverage in the United States: 2003 (Washington, D.C.: U.S. Government Printing Office, 2004).

138. U. S. Census Bureau, "Poverty in the United States: 1995," *Statistical Abstract of the United States, 2008,* 459, table 691.

139. Merton C. Bernstein and Joan Brodshaug Bernstein, *Social Security: The System That Works* (New York: Basic Books, 1988), 208.

140. DeNavas-Walt, Proctor, and Mills, U.S. Census Bureau, Current Population Reports, P60–226, *Income, Poverty, and Health Insurance Coverage in the United States: 2003,* 9; *Statistical Abstract of the United States, 2008,* 459, table 691.

141. *Statistical Abstract of the United States, 2008,* 81, table 108.

142. Maurice MacDonald, *Food Stamps and Income* (New York: Academic Press, 1977); U.S. Senate Committee on Agriculture, *Hunger in America: Ten Years Later* (Washington, D.C.: U.S. Government Printing Office, 1979).

143. Murray, *Losing Ground,* chaps. 12–13.

144. Ronald B. Mincy, "The Underclass: Concept, Controversy, and Evidence," in *Confronting Poverty: Prescriptions for Change,* eds. Sheldon H. Danzinger, Gary D. Sandefur, and Daniel H. Weinberg (New York: Russell Sage Foundation, 1994), chap. 5.

145. U.S. Social Security Administration, "The 2008 OASDA Trustees Report," available at www.ssa.gov/OACT/TR/TR08/trTOC.html.

146. CBO Testimony, statement of Dan L. Crippen, Director, "Preparing for an Aging Population," before the Committee on the Budget, U.S. House of Representatives, July 27, 2000.

147. See, for example, ibid.; Bipartisan Commission on Entitlement and Tax Reform, *Final Report to the President* (Washington, D.C.: U.S. Government Printing Office, 1995).

148. Social Security Administration, "The 2008 OASDA Trustees Report."

149. See B. Guy Peters, *American Public Policy: Promise and Performance,* 4th ed. (Chatham, NJ: Chatham House, 1996), chap. 10.

150. Amol Sharma, "Focusing on a Fresh Start," *Congressional Quarterly Weekly Report,* January 2, 2006.

151. The following discussion draws on Carl P. Chelf, *Controversial Issues in Social Welfare Policy: Government and the Pursuit of Happiness* (Newbury Park, CA: Sage, 1992), chaps. 1 and 6.

152. See R. Kent Weaver, Robert Y. Shapiro, and Lawrence R. Jacobs, "The Polls—Trends: Welfare," *Public Opinion Quarterly* 59 (Winter 1994): 606–27.

153. Alan Finder, "Welfare Clients Outnumber Jobs They Might Fill," *New York Times,* August 25, 1996; Jeffrey L. Katz, "After 60 Years, Most Control Is Passing to States," *Congressional Quarterly Weekly Report,* August 3, 1996, 2190–96; Jared Bernstein and Mark Greenberg, "Reforming Welfare Reform," *The American Prospect,* 12 (January 1–15, 2001): 10–16.

154. Brewster and Brown, *The Public Agenda,* 109.

155. *Statistical Abstract of the United States, 2008,* 97, table 123.

156. Brewster and Brown, *The Public Agenda,* 101; *Statistical Abstract of the United States, 2008,* 96, table 122.

157. U.S. Census Bureau, Historical Health Insurance Tables, available at www.census.gov/hhes/www/hlthins/historic/index.html.

158. Laurene A. Graig, *Health of Nations: An International Perspective on U.S. Health Care Reform,* 2nd ed. (Washington, D.C.: CQ Press, 1993), chap. 1.

159. Bill Clinton, *Health Security: The President's Report to the American People* (Washington, D.C.: U.S. Government Printing Office, 1993).

160. See, for example, Colette Fraley, "GOP Scores on Medicare, But Foes Aren't Done," *Congressional Quarterly Weekly Report,* November 18, 1995, 3535–38; Colette Fraley, "Historic House Medicare Vote Affirms GOP Determination," *Congressional Quarterly Weekly Report,* October 21, 1995, 3206–10; Colette Fraley, "Republicans Outline Medicare Plan...To Hit $270 Billion Budget Target," *Congressional Quarterly Weekly Report,* September 16, 1995, 2780–81; Colette Fraley, "Scaled-Back Medicaid Savings Plan Emerges from Conference," *Congressional Quarterly Weekly Report,* November 18, 1995, 3539; Alissa J. Rubin, "Spadework on Medicare Pays Off for GOP," *Congressional Quarterly Weekly Report,* September 23, 1995, 2895–97.

161. See, for example, Colette Fraley, "Democrats Say GOP Surgery on Medicare Goes Too Far," *Congressional Quarterly Weekly Report,* October 7, 1995, 3068–70.

162. Boards of Trustees, Federal Hospital Insurance and Federal Supplementary Medical Insurance Trust Funds, "2008 Annual Report," available at www.cms.hhs.gov/ReportsTrustFunds/downloads/tr2008.pdf.

18

Foreign Policy

CHAPTER OUTLINE

At 8:45 a.m. on September 11, 2001, a hijacked American Airlines plane flew into the north tower of the World Trade Center in New York City. Over the next ninety minutes, a second plane smashed into the south tower of the World Trade Center, a third hit the Pentagon, and a fourth crashed in a field in rural Pennsylvania. Nearly three thousand people died in the attacks, making September 11th one of the bloodiest days in American history. The surprise strike by the terrorist group Al Qaeda led to the American military bombing Afghanistan in October 2001 and helping opposition groups overthrow the Taliban government. In March 2003, the American military invaded Iraq and toppled the regime of Saddam Hussein as part of the George W. Bush administration's war on terrorism. The American occupation of Iraq proved difficult, however, and American troops soon found themselves fighting determined Iraqi insurgents. Meanwhile, American intelligence and law enforcement officers fanned out across the globe in search of Osama bin Laden and his followers.[1]

September 11th and the events it triggered provided a tragic reminder that what lies outside the borders of the United States can have a profound effect on the well-being of its people. For that reason, the federal government must be able to chart a wise course in foreign policy. When asked about foreign policy, most people naturally think of wars. But American involvement with the rest of the world extends far beyond military matters. Foreign policy encompasses all the decisions that govern the relations of the United States with the rest of the world. Climate change, drug trafficking, human rights, immigration, nuclear proliferation, and trade are just a few of the issues on the foreign-policy agenda. And as we have seen throughout this book, changes in priorities and needs mean changes in rules, and new rules mean new outcomes. Foreign policy presents an especially challenging arena because the potential for conflict and the need to manage that conflict extend beyond the boundaries of the United States to nations around the globe.

We begin the chapter with a brief history of American foreign policy, reviewing how the United States abandoned its traditional isolationism when it assumed the role of a global superpower after World War II. In the second section of the chapter, we analyze the differences between decision making on foreign policy and domestic policy, discussing how the inherent advantages of the presidency and changing interpretations of constitutional rules have increased the power of the executive branch at the expense of Congress when it comes to foreign policy. In the third section, we review the roles of the president, the foreign-policy bureaucracy, Congress, and the public in making foreign policy. And finally, we explore the challenges the United States faces in the post-Cold War era.

18-1 A BRIEF HISTORY OF AMERICAN FOREIGN POLICY

Americans are accustomed to thinking of the United States as a global power. Yet for most of its history, the United States played a small role in world politics. Before World War II, both Democratic and Republican administrations generally avoided becoming entangled in the affairs of other countries, and especially the affairs of Europe. Pearl Harbor changed all that. The twenty-first century may see yet another dramatic change in the direction of American foreign policy as Americans debate the role the United States should play in the world.

Because the choices and rules made in the past greatly influence the present, we briefly survey three periods in American diplomatic history: the isolationist era (1789–1941); the era of globalism (1942–1989); and the post-Cold War era (1990 to the present).

18-1a The Isolationist Era

For its first 150 years, the United States followed a policy of **isolationism**, avoiding what Thomas Jefferson called "entangling alliances" with other nations.[2] When war broke out in Europe in 1793, President George Washington had to decide whether the United States should side with France because the French had sided with the American colonists fifteen years earlier. Unwilling to plunge a young and weak country into war, Washington announced the United States would pursue a policy of neutrality. Three years later, Washington laid down a general guideline for American foreign policy in his Farewell Address: "The great rule of conduct for us in regard to foreign nations is, in extending our commercial relations to have with them as little *political* connection as possible."[3]

The young nation followed the advice of its first president to avoid formal political ties with other countries while pursuing business relationships abroad. The staying power of isolationism was the result of three factors. First, because the United States was a weak country with a small military, it made sense for the country to keep out of foreign wars. Second, the geographic isolation of the United States from the great powers of Europe saved it from being drawn inadvertently into conflicts with larger and more powerful countries. Third, for much of the nineteenth century, most of the energies of the United States were absorbed in settling the frontier—and conquering the American Indian population—and not in playing a major role on the world stage.

Although American foreign policy can be characterized as isolationist for the century and a half preceding World War II, this does not mean that the United States ignored the rest of the world during that time. The main thrust of isolationism was to avoid political and military obligations to other countries. The United States eagerly sought, however, to develop its overseas trade. To that end, presidents negotiated an array of treaties with other countries on matters such as commercial relations and navigation of the seas. Most Americans believed that international trade would help develop the American economy and promote international goodwill.

Along with avoiding political ties, isolationism primarily meant staying out of the affairs of Europe. Asia and particularly Latin America were another matter. Relatively early in American history, presidents began to distinguish between the "Old World" of Europe and the "New World" of the Western Hemisphere. In a message to Congress in

isolationism
A foreign policy built on the principle of avoiding formal military and political alliances with other countries.

Monroe Doctrine

A basic principle of U.S. foreign policy that dates back to a warning President James Monroe issued in 1823 that the United States would resist further European efforts to intervene in the affairs of the Western Hemisphere.

1823, President James Monroe announced that the United States would not interfere in the affairs of Europe, but he warned Europeans that the Americas were "henceforth not to be considered as subjects for future colonization" and that the United States would "consider any attempt on their part to extend their system to any portion of this hemisphere as dangerous to our peace and safety."[4] With this speech, which laid the foundation for what became known as the **Monroe Doctrine**, the United States promised to stay out of European affairs and warned Europe to stay out of Latin America.[5]

When Monroe declared the Americas off limits to further European colonization, the United States lacked the military power to back up its threat. Nor was the United States heavily involved in Latin America for most of the nineteenth century; no president formally invoked the Monroe Doctrine until 1895.[6] As the turn of the century approached, American involvement in Latin America, and Asia as well, began to grow.[7] In the Spanish-American War of 1898, for instance, the United States acquired control of Puerto Rico and the Philippines from Spain, and it used the war as an opportunity and a justification to annex the formerly independent Hawaiian Islands. (The Philippines received its independence in 1946.)

American involvement abroad was especially prominent in Latin America at the turn of the century. Whereas the Monroe Doctrine originally sought to bar outside interference in the affairs of Latin America, by 1900, presidents had begun to use it to justify American intervention in the region. In 1903, the American Navy intervened to help Panama secede from Colombia, an event that enabled the United States to build the Panama Canal and to gain control over the canal zone. And between 1904 and 1934, the United States sent eight expeditionary forces to Latin America and conducted five extended military occupations, including one in Nicaragua that lasted nineteen years.

If the first decades of the twentieth century saw increased American involvement in Asia and Latin America, they also witnessed the first major break with the tradition of staying aloof from European wars. When World War I began in Europe, President Woodrow Wilson urged Americans to be "neutral in thought as well as in action."[8] However, Germany's decision to wage submarine warfare against American shipping and its efforts to convince Mexico to attack the United States (and thereby reclaim New Mexico, Texas, and Arizona) combined to push the United States into the war.

With the end of World War I, the United States reverted to its tradition of isolationism. In 1919 and again in 1920, the Senate refused to approve the Treaty of Versailles, which was the treaty that President Wilson had helped to negotiate to end World War I. The major point of controversy was the treaty's provisions that created a League of Nations. Critics complained that membership in the League violated the American tradition of avoiding political alliances and that the League would draw the United States into conflicts in which it had no interests. Although supporters of the treaty formed a majority in the Senate, they lacked the two-thirds majority needed to prevail.[9]

With the rejection of the Treaty of Versailles, isolationist sentiment in the United States intensified. Throughout the 1920s and 1930s, isolationist forces in Congress, who counted their greatest strength among Republicans from the Midwest, fought efforts supporting a more internationalist foreign policy. Although many isolationists worried about the rise to power of Adolf Hitler in Germany and Benito Mussolini in Italy, they believed that American interests would be best served by staying out of the affairs of Europe. For most Americans, that belief died on December 7, 1941, when Japanese planes bombed the American fleet at Pearl Harbor.

18-1b The Global Era

When the Japanese attacked Pearl Harbor, a shocked nation abandoned its traditional isolationism and embraced the war against the Axis Powers. As the war came to a close, however, many Allied leaders feared that the United States would disengage itself from world affairs as it had after World War I, leaving Europe and Asia to fend for themselves. These fears proved groundless, however. By 1950, the United States had abandoned its traditional isolationism for a foreign policy based on **globalism**, which is the idea that the United States should be prepared to use military force around the globe to defend its political and economic interests.

The turning point in American policy came in 1947. Greek communists were waging a guerrilla war, and American officials feared that a communist victory in Greece would destabilize Europe. After consulting with congressional leaders, President Harry Truman proposed sending aid to Greece. In a speech to Congress defending the proposal, the president announced what became known as the **Truman Doctrine:** The United States must "support free peoples who are resisting attempted subjugation by armed minorities or by outside pressure."[10] For the first time, a president had defined American interests in global terms.

The **Marshall Plan**, named after then-Secretary of State George C. Marshall, soon followed the Truman Doctrine.[11] Under this program, the United States provided massive amounts of aid to help rebuild war-torn Europe. Between 1948 and 1952, the United States spent nearly 1.5 percent of its gross national product each year, or the equivalent of more than $100 billion today, on aid to Europe. To put these figures in perspective, in 2006 the United States spent $23.4 billion on official development assistance. That constituted only 0.18 percent of its gross national product, ranking the United States next-to-last among industrialized democracies in terms of the amount of aid it provided relative to its overall economy.[12]

By defining American interests in global terms, President Truman established what would become the overriding objective of American foreign policy for the next forty years: the **containment** of communist expansion. American officials especially feared Soviet expansionism. Although the United States and the Soviet Union had been allies during World War II, tensions between the two were so high by the late 1940s that people spoke of a **Cold War** (as

globalism
The idea that the United States should be prepared to use military force around the globe to defend its political and economic interests.

Truman Doctrine
A policy, announced by President Truman in 1947, that the United States would oppose communist attempts to overthrow or conquer noncommunist countries.

Marshall Plan
A multibillion-dollar U.S. aid program in the late 1940s and early 1950s that helped Western European countries rebuild their economies in the wake of World War II.

containment
A bedrock principle of U.S. foreign policy from the 1940s to the 1980s that emphasized the need to prevent communist countries, especially the Soviet Union, from expanding the territory they controlled.

Cold War
A phrase used to describe the high level of tension and distrust that characterized relations between the Soviet Union and the United States from the late 1940s until the early 1990s.

North Atlantic Treaty Organization (NATO)

A military alliance founded in 1949 for the purpose of defending Western Europe from attack. Members of NATO now include the United States, Canada, and twenty-six European countries.

distinct from a hot, or shooting, war). Fears of Soviet expansionism led the United States in 1949 to help create the **North Atlantic Treaty Organization (NATO)**, a military alliance designed to protect Western Europe against a Soviet invasion (see Figure 18–1). By making itself the guarantor of European security, the United States clearly cast off its traditional isolationism to assume a leading role in world politics.

The policy of containment was tested in June 1950, when communist North Korea invaded South Korea. Although the Truman administration had previously doubted the strategic importance of the Korean peninsula, the United States, acting with the approval

Figure 18–1   Cold War Military Alliances. During the Cold War, Europe was divided into three distinct political groups: the North Atlantic Treaty Organization, the Soviet bloc, and the neutral and nonaligned countries.

of the United Nations (UN), quickly came to South Korea's defense. After initially being almost driven off the Korean peninsula, American and South Korean forces came close to defeating the North Korean army. They were forced to retreat once again, however, and the war turned into a stalemate when the People's Republic of China intervened on behalf of North Korea in November 1950. (Chinese communists had triumphed in China's civil war a year earlier.) By the time both sides signed an armistice in 1953, more than 54,000 Americans had died.

The failure to win in Korea did not undermine the American commitment to containment. In Europe, the United States spent tremendous sums to deter a possible Soviet invasion. In the **Third World**, a term loosely defined to mean Asia, Africa, and Latin America, the United States continued to move aggressively against what it perceived as communist threats. It began to provide economic and military aid to anticommunist governments, and it encouraged them to form military alliances modeled after NATO. In some cases, the United States went so far as to help overthrow governments it perceived as too sympathetic to the Soviet Union.

Third World
A term loosely defined to mean the developing countries in Asia, Africa, and Latin America.

In pursuing the policy of containment in the 1950s and early 1960s, presidents enjoyed considerable congressional and public support. When presidents did come under fire on foreign policy, they usually were criticized for being too passive rather than too aggressive in dealing with the communist threat. John F. Kennedy, for example, campaigned for the White House in 1960, criticizing Dwight Eisenhower for allowing the Soviet Union to grab the lead in ballistic missile technology (a claim that turned out to be false). Kennedy later found himself criticized for being too soft in dealing with the Soviet Union.

The national consensus in favor of a policy of global containment crumbled in Vietnam.[13] Unlike the case with the war in Korea, the United States became involved in Vietnam slowly, over a period of years. The United States initially became involved in 1950, when the Truman administration responded to the communist victory in China by agreeing to pay part of the cost of French rule in Vietnam. (France, which had lost control of Vietnam to Japan during World War II, had subsequently tried to reestablish its colonial rule.) American officials hoped that the French would block Chinese expansionism in the region. When Vietnamese communist troops forced France to withdraw from Vietnam in 1954, the country split in two and the United States threw its support behind the noncommunist South. The first American military advisers went to South Vietnam during the Eisenhower administration to try to stem a communist insurgency. American combat troops did not arrive in South Vietnam in large numbers, however, until 1965. The number of American soldiers in South Vietnam steadily increased over the next three years, peaking at 540,000 in 1968.

The communist insurgency continued despite the American military buildup. As public criticism of the war began to surface in late 1967, the American commander in Vietnam claimed the situation had reached the "point where the end begins to come into view."[14]

Then in January 1968, communist forces launched a surprise attack called the Tet Offensive. Although the attackers were eventually routed, television scenes of fighting on the streets of the South Vietnamese capital convinced many Americans that the war could not be won at an acceptable cost. In the ensuing public uproar, President Lyndon Johnson decided not to run for reelection. His successor, Richard Nixon, spent much of his first term seeking to extricate the United States from Vietnam. The signing of the Paris Peace Accord in 1973 marked the end of American combat involvement in Vietnam. In all, more than 58,000 Americans died in the Vietnam War.

Vietnam drove a deep wedge into the American national consensus on the merits of globalism. For so-called hawks, the Vietnam War was, in the words of Ronald Reagan, a "noble cause." In this view, the war would have been won if it had enjoyed greater public support. For so-called doves, Vietnam attested to the folly of viewing Third World struggles through the prism of the American-Soviet rivalry. In this view, Vietnam was a war of national unification that had no significant impact on American interests. Although Americans disagreed over the lessons of Vietnam, the war succeeded in curtailing direct American military intervention in the Third World for a decade. Throughout the 1970s and into the 1980s, presidential efforts to intervene in places such as Angola, Lebanon, and Central America foundered over fears both in Congress and among the public of "another Vietnam."

Although Vietnam diminished the appetite of the United States for confronting communism outside Europe, containment of the Soviet Union remained the focal point of American foreign policy. The tone of American policy toward the Soviet Union, however, varied greatly during the 1970s and 1980s. President Nixon initiated a policy of **détente**, or more cordial relations, with Moscow. Detente governed American policy until 1979, when the Soviet invasion of Afghanistan plunged U.S.-Soviet relations into a deep chill. During the first Reagan administration (1981–1985), tensions between the United States and the Soviet Union reached levels not seen since the 1950s. Nonetheless, with the ascension of Mikhail Gorbachev to power in the Soviet Union in 1985, U.S.-Soviet relations gradually improved.

détente

A policy the Nixon administration followed to develop more cordial relations with the Soviet Union.

18-1c After the Cold War

The reforms Mikhail Gorbachev initiated in the Soviet Union unleashed a series of sweeping changes in Eastern Europe that eventually ended the Cold War and ushered in a new era in American foreign policy. In October 1989, the Soviet army stood silent as the Berlin Wall fell. Within six months, the communist governments in the Soviet bloc were swept from power, and within a year, East and West Germany were reunited, removing one of the last tangible legacies of World War II. Then, in August 1991, hard-line communists failed in their bid to seize control of the Soviet Union. After the failed coup, the Soviet Union splintered into more than a dozen separate countries.

The decline and eventual collapse of the Soviet Union changed the face of the international system. As the lone remaining superpower, the United States suddenly found itself with new freedom of maneuver in world politics. In December 1989, American troops invaded Panama and overthrew the government of General Manuel Noriega, who the United States accused of aiding the international cocaine trade. An even clearer example of the increased freedom of maneuver the United States enjoyed came in 1991, when President George H. W. Bush assembled and led a multinational coalition that liberated Kuwait from Iraqi occupation.[15] Although Panama and the Gulf War showed that the United States had thrown off some of its post-Vietnam reluctance to use force, they also revealed the limits of force as a foreign-policy tool. The flow of drugs through Panama actually increased after Noriega's removal, and Saddam Hussein remained the leader of Iraq.

The decline and eventual collapse of the Soviet Union prompted many calls for a new American foreign policy. People disagreed over how that policy and the rules that accompany it should look. President Bill Clinton proposed to replace the policy of containment with one of **enlargement**.[16] Under this policy, the United States would seek to promote the emergence of successful market democracies—that is, countries that, like the United States, combine a free market economy with a democratic political system. Clinton proposed to pursue the policy of enlargement through a variety of means: by promoting world trade, providing economic and technical aid to emerging democracies and market economies, and as a last resort, using military force to resist antidemocratic forces.

enlargement
The policy President Bill Clinton proposed as a substitute for containment. It called on the United States to promote the emergence of market democracies, that is, countries that combine a free market economic system with a democratic political system.

The policy of enlargement underlay President Clinton's decision in 1994 to threaten to invade Haiti if that country's military rulers did not return power to the democratically elected president they had overthrown. (When Haiti's military leaders did step down, an American peacekeeping force went to Haiti to oversee its return to democratic rule.) It also underlay Clinton's decision to send American troops to Bosnia in 1995 as part of a NATO peacekeeping mission. And in 1999, the United States led NATO as it bombed Serbia in a bid to force the government of Slobodan Milosevic to stop persecuting ethnic Albanians living in the Serbian province of Kosovo.[17] The bombing campaign eventually worked, and NATO peacekeeping troops entered Kosovo. In 2000, Serbian protesters toppled Milosevic's government and a new democratic government took power.

During the 2000 presidential campaign, George W. Bush accused Clinton of "sending our military on vague, aimless, and endless deployments" and promised "an immediate review of our overseas deployments—in dozens of countries."[18] At the same time, however, he agreed with Clinton that the United States should not embrace a policy of **neoisolationism** in which it disengaged from world affairs. Bush argued that the country had to resist the temptation to withdraw because that "approach abandons our allies, and our ideals . . . . The result, in the long run, would be a

neoisolationism
The idea that the United States should reduce its role in world affairs and return to a foreign policy similar to the one it pursued before World War II.

Source: © Spencer Platz/Getty Images. Reproduced by permission.

The attack on the World Trade Center in New York City on September 11, 2001, and the events it triggered provided a tragic reminder that what lies outside the borders of the United States can profoundly affect the well-being of its people.

Bush Doctrine
A policy, announced by President George W. Bush in 2001, stating that the United States would target terrorist groups and the states that aided them.

stagnant America and a savage world." Bush made few changes to American military deployments overseas before September 11th. After the terrorist attacks, he announced what came to be called the **Bush Doctrine**—the United States would target terrorist groups and the states that aided them. The Afghanistan and Iraq wars were examples of this doctrine in action.[19]

The American invasion of Iraq took less than a month to remove Saddam Hussein from power, and fewer than 150 American soldiers died. Only months after the Iraqi government fell, a powerful insurgency rocked the country. Over the next five years, more than 4,000 American soldiers, and many more Iraqis died. As was the case with Vietnam, public support in the United States for the war plummeted. In 2007, President Bush sent additional American troops to Iraq despite fierce political opposition. The so-called surge helped stem the violence in Iraq. Nonetheless, the question of when American troops could be withdrawn and at what rate was a hot topic during the 2008 presidential campaign. Meanwhile, an insurgency led by members of the former Taliban government gained ground in Afghanistan, raising the question of how to keep the pro-American government in Kabul in power.

18-2 FOREIGN POLICY VERSUS DOMESTIC POLICY

How does decision making on foreign policy differ from decision making on domestic policy? It is sometimes tempting to answer this question by invoking the concept of the **national interest**, the idea that a consensus exists about the role of the United States in

national interest
The idea that the United States has certain interests in international relations that most Americans agree on.

the world even though none exists about policies at home. Although Americans agree that American foreign policy should aim to promote peace and prosperity, the debates over issues, such as Iraq and free trade, show that Americans disagree, sometimes vehemently, over how best to achieve the nation's foreign-policy goals. Indeed, how people define the national interest varies with their party affiliation, ideological beliefs, socioeconomic background, and ethnicity. To put it simply, Americans disagree just as sharply over rules and policies for our relations abroad as they do over rules and policies at home.

Foreign policy, then, is subject to the same kinds of debate and division that characterize domestic policy. What distinguishes foreign policy from domestic policy is that presidents usually have more say over foreign policy. The president's greater success in shaping foreign policy is so marked that scholars sometimes speak of the United States as having **two presidencies**, a weak, embattled one at home and a strong, confident one abroad.[20] The strength of the president in foreign policy cannot be explained on the basis of a literal reading of the Constitution. Instead, the president's strength in foreign policy stems from four sources: the president's inherent advantages in foreign policy, precedents set by previous presidents, the rulings of the Supreme Court, and the behavior of Congress.

two presidencies

The argument that presidents have much greater influence over the content of foreign policy than the content of domestic policy.

18-2a The Constitution and Foreign Policy

Why do presidents have a greater say in making foreign policy than domestic policy? The Constitution itself does not provide an answer.[21] The framers of the Constitution, ever fearful of the potential for executive tyranny, gave the president relatively few specific (or enumerated) foreign-policy powers. Article 2, Section 2 of the Constitution designates the president as "Commander in Chief of the Army and Navy of the United States" and specifies that, subject to the approval of the Senate, the president has the power "to make Treaties" and "appoint Ambassadors." Although today most people believe the position of commander in chief confers special powers on the president, the framers of the Constitution saw the position as an office and not as an independent source of decision-making authority.[22]

In contrast to the few specific foreign-policy powers granted to the president, the Constitution explicitly allocates numerous foreign-policy powers to Congress. Article 1 assigns Congress the power "to provide for the common Defence," "to regulate Commerce with foreign Nations," "to define and punish Piracies and Felonies committed on the high Seas," "to declare war," "to raise and support Armies," "to provide and maintain a Navy," and "to make Rules for the Government and Regulation of the land and naval Forces." Article 2 specifies that the Senate must give its advice and consent to all treaties and ambassadorial appointments. And Congress's general power to approve government spending gives it potentially great influence over foreign policy.

18-2b The President's Inherent Advantages

If the rules set forth in the Constitution do not explain the president's tremendous influence over foreign policy, what does? One answer is the inherent advantages of the presidency, the informal powers that enable presidents to act swiftly and unilaterally in foreign affairs. Success in foreign policy, far more than in domestic policy, places a premium on speed, discretion, and flexibility. And as Alexander Hamilton put it in "Federalist No. 70," "decision, activity, secrecy, and dispatch will generally characterize the proceedings of one man, in a much more eminent degree, than the proceedings of any greater number."[23] The president's ability to initiate policy confers an additional advantage on the White House. In domestic affairs, presidential initiatives generally remain proposals *until* Congress assents. In foreign policy, however, presidential initiatives often become policy *unless* Congress acts to block them. Thus, if Congress ignores a president's proposal to raise taxes, the proposal dies. If Congress fails to act on the president's decision to terminate a treaty or to send troops abroad, the president's proposal prevails. The inherent advantages of the presidency are the greatest in crisis situations. When Americans are taken hostage in a foreign land or an American ally comes under attack, the president may be forced to make quick decisions. Often these decisions leave members of Congress with little choice politically but to follow the lead of the White House. Of course, Congress has the authority to overturn many presidential decisions in foreign policy, including decisions to send American troops into combat. Building a veto-proof majority in Congress is usually extremely difficult because of partisan, regional, and institutional divisions on Capitol Hill.

18-2c Precedent

The authority the president wields on foreign policy stems not only from the inherent advantages of the office but also from the way precedent, or past practice, has modified the rules set down in the Constitution. Presidents frequently cite precedents their predecessors have set to claim or justify new foreign-policy powers, as the evolution of the war power attests (see Box 18–1). Although the first presidents sometimes used force without congressional approval, none claimed an inherent right to order troops into combat. James Madison even vetoed a bill authorizing him to use the Navy to protect American merchant ships against pirates on the grounds that Congress could not delegate its war power. Madison's successors have not always shared his reluctance to take on that power. Presidents from Truman onward have argued that they have an inherent right as commander in chief to order troops into combat.[24] Thus, just as the Constitution has been interpreted and reinterpreted to meet the demands of an ever-changing domestic environment, presidents

POINT OF ORDER

Box 18–1   The War Power

The most weighty decision any country faces is the decision to go to war. The rules regarding the war power matter because wars bring about momentous changes in the lives of both individuals and nations. When a country goes to war, soldiers lose limbs and lives. Families lose loved ones. The economy reels or explodes in growth. The nation gains or loses credibility and respect on the world stage.

In the United States, the Constitution assigns the power to declare war to Congress. Congress has formally declared war four times: the War of 1812 (1812–1815), the Spanish-American War (1898), World War I (1917–1918), and World War II (1941–1945). In the case of the Mexican-American War (1846–1848), Congress technically did not declare war but rather passed a resolution recognizing that a state of war existed. The Civil War was undeclared because a declaration of war would have recognized the legitimacy of the Confederate government.

Although the Constitution assigns the war power to Congress, presidents have used their own authority to order American troops into combat or into situations where hostilities are imminent since the early days of the Republic. The exact number of such instances is unclear. In 1971, Senator Barry M. Goldwater (R-AZ) identified 192 instances in which the president used his own authority to send American troops into combat. Twelve years later, Ronald Reagan cited 125 precedents for his decision to send American troops to Lebanon.

Whatever the actual number of cases, until recently, presidents sent troops into actual or potential combat situations, on their own authority, only when the prospect for casualties was low. Most of the cases Senator Goldwater and President Reagan cited involved military action against brigands, pirates, and other stateless groups. When sustained combat was likely, presidents asked Congress for a formal declaration of war. Senator Goldwater implicitly acknowledged this distinction between levels of conflict when he noted that, of the 192 undeclared uses of force on his list, "nearly half involved actual fighting."

The willingness of presidents to order the use of force against sovereign states on their own authority grew after World War II. When North Korea invaded South Korea in June 1950, President Harry Truman decided against asking Congress to declare war because he thought his critics might filibuster the resolution and dilute its symbolic effect. After it was reported in August 1964 that North Vietnamese boats had attacked American ships in the Gulf of Tonkin, Congress passed a resolution approving President Lyndon Johnson's decision to use force to prevent further aggression. Although Johnson used the Gulf of Tonkin Resolution to justify his decision several months later to send combat troops to Vietnam, few members of Congress thought at the time that they were voting for war.

Vietnam convinced many in Congress that a change in the rules was necessary—specifically, a change that would check the president's war powers. The result was the passage in 1973 of the War Powers Resolution. This rather complicated law specifies, among other things, that the president can send troops into combat for no more than sixty days (ninety days in some circumstances) unless Congress authorizes the deployment.

The War Powers Resolution has proven a failure. Every president except Jimmy Carter and Bill Clinton has denied its constitutionality, and administrations have exploited ambiguities in the law to prevent the sixty-day clock from starting. President Reagan did sign a 1983 bill that gave him authority to keep American troops in Lebanon for eighteen months, but he repeated the claim that the War Powers Resolution is unconstitutional. The resolution did not figure in the invasions of Grenada and Panama, in the peacekeeping missions in Haiti and Bosnia, or in the bombing of Serbia.

When Iraq invaded Kuwait in August 1990, President George H. W. Bush sent American troops to Saudi Arabia. He, too, initially refused to invoke the War Powers Resolution. Public opinion, however, eventually forced him to seek Congress's approval, which he got. Three days after September 11th, a near-unanimous Congress authorized President George W. Bush "to use all necessary and appropriate force" against those responsible for the attacks. In October 2002, Congress granted his request for authority to invade Iraq. Although in each of these three cases the resolution Congress passed was technically not a declaration of war—the words "to declare war" appeared nowhere in them—most members regarded them as the functional equivalent of one.

Sources: Ronald D. Elving, "America's Most Frequent Fight Has Been the Undeclared War," *Congressional Quarterly Weekly Report,* January 5, 1991, 37–40; James M. Lindsay, *Congress and the Politics of U.S. Foreign Policy* (Baltimore, MD: Johns Hopkins University Press, 1994), 84–85, 147–53; Arthur M. Schlesinger, Jr., *The Imperial Presidency* (Boston: Houghton Mifflin, 1989).

Source: © Department of Defense

Going to war is the most difficult decision a nation has to make.

have used the flexibility of constitutional rules to their advantage in foreign policy.

18-2d Supreme Court Rulings

The Supreme Court has ratified the president's expanded authority in foreign affairs through its interpretation of the rules set forth in the Constitution.[25] Perhaps the most notable Court ruling is the 1936 case *U.S. v. Curtiss-Wright Export Corporation*. In this case, the Court held that, unlike presidential powers in domestic affairs, the president's foreign-policy powers go beyond what the Constitution mentions. Although subsequent Supreme Court opinions disavowed the idea of extra-constitutional powers, presidents continue to cite *Curtiss-Wright* when claiming extensive foreign-policy powers for themselves. Another Supreme Court case that expanded the president's powers in foreign policy was *United States v. Belmont*. In this 1937 ruling, the Court held that although treaties must be approved by two-thirds of the Senate, presidents can make equally binding international commitments by signing **executive agreements**, which do not necessarily require Senate approval. The Court's decision in *Belmont* restructured the constitutional rules and diminished the effectiveness of the Senate's treaty power (see Box 18–2).

The Supreme Court has also enhanced presidential power by declining to hear most lawsuits challenging the president's authority in foreign affairs. The federal courts routinely dismiss such cases on the grounds that the contested issues are not ripe for judicial decision, that they raise political and not legal questions, or that members of Congress do not have a legal right (or "standing") to sue. In 1999, for example, twenty-six members of the House of Representatives sued President Clinton for ordering the bombing of Serbia without first obtaining congressional authorization. Two lower federal courts dismissed the lawsuit, however, on the grounds that the legislators did not have legal standing. The Supreme Court refused to hear the appeal.[26] The courts dismiss many cases challenging presidential authority in foreign affairs because they believe that foreign policy raises issues that lie beyond their competence. The courts also fear that hearing such lawsuits will draw them into political conflict with the other two branches of government.[27]

The Supreme Court does not always rule in the president's favor, however. In the 2006 case *Hamdan v. Rumsfeld*, the Court ruled against the Bush administration's claim that it had the authority to try suspected foreign terrorists before special military commissions. The Court instead held that the commissions were not authorized by federal statute and violated international law. Most observers interpreted the ruling as undercutting many of the arguments that the Bush administration had made after September 11th justifying an expansive reading of presidential power.

executive agreements

International agreements that, unlike treaties, do not require the approval of two-thirds of the Senate to become binding on the United States.

POINT OF ORDER

Box 18–2 Executive Agreements

In 1967, President Lyndon Johnson asked the Senate to approve a treaty the United States had signed with Thailand on the subject of double taxation. Although the president deferred to the Senate's treaty power on this rather minor (and obscure) issue, he felt no similar need to seek Senate approval when he subsequently decided to commit the United States to defend Thailand against communist aggression and send 40,000 troops to the Southeast Asian country. Johnson's ability to make a major international commitment to Thailand without securing the consent of the Senate illustrates one of the reasons presidents have gained considerable power over foreign policy in the past half century: the rise of the executive agreement.

The United States has two tools for making binding commitments to other countries: treaties and executive agreements. Article 2 of the Constitution stipulates the rule governing treaties: They must win the approval of two-thirds of the Senate before they can take effect. If a treaty falls even one vote short of the magic two-thirds number, it is dead. Between 1789 and 2004, the Senate voted down 22 treaties (out of the more than 1,800 signed), and it blocked more than 120 others by refusing to consider them. The most recent treaty to go down to

defeat was the Comprehensive Test Ban Treaty. It would have barred the United States and other countries from ever testing nuclear weapons again. Despite President Bill Clinton's strong support for the treaty, a majority of the Republican-controlled Senate voted against it in 1999.

An executive agreement carries the same force of law as a treaty, but the rules of American politics do not require that two-thirds of the Senate approve it. Indeed, most executive agreements require no congressional approval at all. For reasons concerning statute, tradition, and political pragmatism, some executive agreements do require the approval of a majority of both the House and Senate. Under American law, for instance, all trade agreements are handled as executive agreements and must be submitted to Congress for simple majority approval. Even when an executive agreement requires congressional approval, presidents prefer it to a treaty because they usually find it easier to round up majority support in both chambers than two-thirds support in the Senate.

Every president since George Washington has used executive agreements. As the following table shows, however, in recent decades, executive agreements have replaced treaties as the primary tool by which the United States makes commitments to other countries: Not only did the use of executive agreements skyrocket after

1940, but presidents also became more inclined to use them to make major commitments to other countries. The Yalta and Potsdam Agreements, which governed the division of Europe after the end of World War II, were both executive agreements, as were the Offensive Arms Pact of the Strategic Arms Limitation Talks (SALT I) and the Paris Peace Accord ending American involvement in Vietnam. Until Congress passed a law in 1972 requiring the White House to notify Capitol Hill of all executive agreements, presidents frequently kept the commitments they had made through executive agreements secret from members of Congress.

What distinguishes an executive agreement from a treaty? No one knows for sure. As the historian Arthur Schlesinger, Jr., writes,

> When Senator Gillette of Iowa asked the State Department in 1954 to make everything perfectly clear, the Department (or so Gillette informed the Senate) replied "that a treaty was something they had to send to the Senate to get approval by two-thirds vote. An executive agreement was something they did not have to send to the Senate." This reminded Gillette of the time when as a boy on the farm he asked the hired man how to tell the difference between male and female pigeons. The answer was: "You put corn in front of the pigeon. If he picks it up, it is a he; if she picks it up, it is a she."

Although no one knows what precisely distinguishes an executive agreement from a treaty, it is clear that presidents use executive agreements to enhance their foreign-policy powers at the expense of Congress.

Sources: Ellen C. Collier, "U.S. Senate Rejection of Treaties: A Brief Survey of Past Instances," Congressional Research Service, Report No. 87–305F, March 30, 1987, 2–3; Congressional Record, 90th Cong., 1st sess., 1967, 113, pt 15:20717; James M. McCormick, American Foreign Policy and Process, 2nd ed. (Itasca, IL: F. E. Peacock, 1992), 276; Arthur M. Schlesinger, Jr., The Imperial Presidency (Boston: Houghton Mifflin, 1989), 104; Harold W. Stanley and Richard G. Niemi, Vital Statistics on American Politics, 2005–2006 (Washington, D.C.: CQ Press, 2006), 339.

Years	Number of treaties	Number of executive agreements	Executive agreements as a percentage of all international agreements (%)
1789–1839	60	27	31
1840–1889	215	238	57
1890–1932	431	804	65
1933–1968	455	5,423	92
1969–2004	671	9,971	94

Table 18–1

18-2e The Behavior of Congress

Besides inherent advantages, precedent, and the rulings of the Supreme Court, the president's strength in foreign policy stems from the behavior of members of Congress. Partisan and institutional divisions on Capitol Hill mean that without widespread agreement among members—something that is often missing on foreign policy—Congress will not act. Congressional influence is also complicated by a belief held by many on Capitol Hill (and among the public) that strong presidential leadership is essential for a successful foreign policy.[28] Thus, immediately after September 11th many members of Congress naturally rallied around President Bush.

In addition to divisions on Capitol Hill and beliefs about the necessity of strong presidential leadership, many members defer to the president on foreign policy because of electoral considerations. Members of Congress want to avoid stands on policy matters that leave them open to blame, and thus, to punishment at the polls. So when the public supports the president, legislators are likely to as well. For example, members of Congress usually feel comfortable challenging and criticizing suggestions that American troops might be sent to another country. Once the president decides to send American troops, however, many members fear they will be labeled unpatriotic if they attack the decision.

The influence of electoral considerations on the behavior of Congress helps explain the surge of congressional activism on foreign policy after Vietnam as well as the return to congressional deference after September 11th. The first two decades after World War II were marked by extensive (although by no means total) congressional deference to the president on foreign policy.[29] That deference was partly the result of agreement on the substance of policy. It also stemmed from legislative fears that the public would see challenges to the president as unpatriotic. Once Vietnam shattered the nation's consensus on the merits of globalism, however, the public became much more tolerant of legislative challenges to presidential authority, and congressional activity increased. With the end of the Cold War, Congress became even more involved in foreign policy.[30] With the attacks on the World Trade Center and the Pentagon, congressional activism once again ebbed. Again, the surge in deference was motivated partly by principle and partly by lawmakers' justifiable fear that their criticisms could be labeled unpatriotic. Then in 2004, as the Iraqi insurgency took root and President Bush's once sky-high public approval ratings fell, congressional foreign-policy activism returned.

Because of the inherent advantages of being a single person with executive authority, precedents previous occupants of the Oval Office have set, the rulings of the Supreme Court, the institutional disadvantages of Congress, and the reticence of its members to challenge foreign-policy decisions in many instances, the president wields much more power over foreign than domestic policy. Nevertheless, the president does not dictate the content of American foreign policy. As we shall see in the next section, other government officials and institutions also contribute to making foreign policy.

18-3 WHO MAKES AMERICAN FOREIGN POLICY?

We have noted that both the president and Congress claim significant powers in American foreign policy. However, influence over the course of foreign-policy decision making in the United States is not equally distributed between the two branches of government or across government institutions. Instead, it can be thought of as a series of concentric circles involving the White House, the foreign-policy bureaucracy, Congress, and the public (see Figure 18–2). At the heart of the decision-making process are the president and the White House staff. Next in importance are the agencies that make up the foreign-policy bureaucracy. By virtue of their expertise and responsibilities, these agencies wield tremendous influence over both the formulation and implementation of foreign policy. Congress occupies the third circle. It influences foreign policy by passing legislation and shaping public opinion. Furthest from the center of power is the public. Because it does not play a role in the day-to-day affairs of governing, the public shapes policy largely by placing constraints on which policies the government can pursue.

Of course, Figure 18–2 should not be taken literally. Presidential strength on foreign policy is not preordained. Through inattention or incompetence, presidents may see other actors eclipse their influence over specific foreign policies. For example, intense congressional criticism following the deaths of eighteen American soldiers in Somalia in October 1993 eventually forced the Clinton administration to withdraw all American peacekeepers from the African country. Likewise, Clinton initially ruled out even considering the possibility of using American combat troops to fight the Kosovo War because he believed (incorrectly if polls are to be trusted) that the public would oppose the idea. Nonetheless, the general pattern of influence outlined in Figure 18–2 holds. Each set of institutions plays a role in formulating the rules that guide foreign policy.

18-3a The White House

The president is the single most important actor in foreign policy. As we have discussed, presidents draw their powers from the Constitution, from the inherent advantages of the office, and from the fact that Congress and the public look first to the White House for leadership on foreign policy. And although no single individual can match the resources and expertise of the bureaucracy, presidents gain considerable influence from their power to appoint agency heads and to decide whose advice they will heed. This

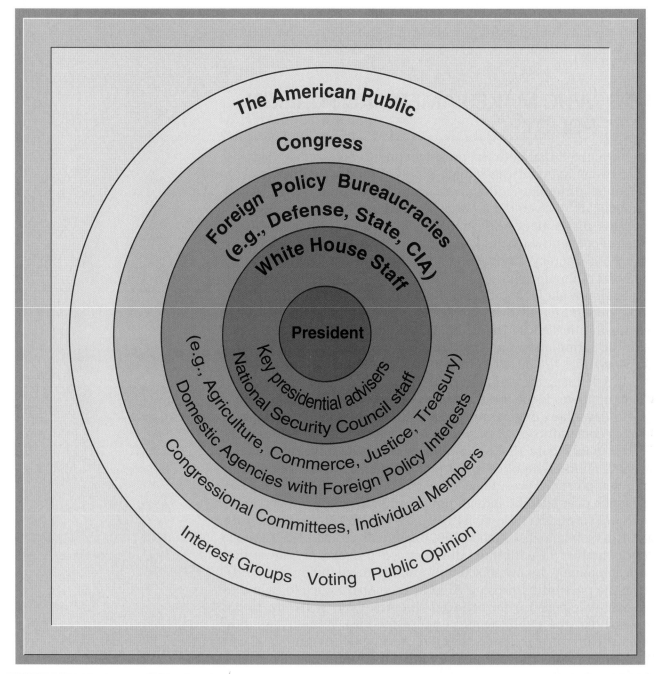

Figure 18–2   The Concentric Circles of Power in Foreign-Policy Decision Making. Presidents and their advisers lie at the heart of foreign-policy decision making in the United States, whereas the American public is furthest from the center of power.

latter power is crucial. Take the case of Colin Powell, who was widely regarded both at home and abroad as the most distinguished member of George W. Bush's cabinet when he agreed to serve as secretary of state. Powell lost more bureaucratic battles than he won during his four years on the job because he usually could not persuade the president to follow his advice. It was not surprising, then, that Bush did not ask Powell to stay on for the second term.[31]

One way the president is able to wield considerable power in foreign policy is through the National Security Council (NSC), a body created by the passage of the National Security Act of 1947.[32] This law, which has been amended over the years, designates the president, the vice president, the secretary of state, and the secretary of defense as the statutory members of the NSC. Presidents may invite other Cabinet officers to participate in NSC meetings as nonstatutory members. The National Security Act also designates the director of National Intelligence and the chair of the Joint Chiefs of Staff as advisers to the NSC. (The Joint Chiefs of Staff is composed of the uniformed heads of the Army, Navy, Air Force, and Marines.) A staff of foreign policy analysts supports the work of the NSC. The head of this staff is commonly known as the national security adviser, although his or her formal title is assistant to the president for national security affairs.

The NSC staff was originally intended to be small and to act primarily to coordinate the activities of the foreign-policy bureaucracy rather than to make policy. Over time, however, the NSC staff grew to become a major player in policy formation. The national security adviser first came to play a substantial policy-making role during the Kennedy administration.[33] Then Henry Kissinger used the position to dominate foreign policy in the Nixon administration.[34] Although no subsequent national security adviser has wielded as much power as Kissinger, they have, to varying degrees, all been independent sources of policy ideas.

Presidents rely heavily on the national security adviser and the NSC staff for several reasons.[35] First, many of the people who work in the foreign-policy bureaucracy are career bureaucrats who owe their loyalty to the agency they serve. In contrast, presidents and their national security advisers choose who will serve on the NSC staff, and not too surprisingly, they tend to pick people who will be staunch advocates of the president's foreign-policy wishes. Second, the president relies on the NSC staff because of its physical proximity. The national security adviser is based in the White House—rather than across town or across the Potomac River, as the secretaries of state and defense are—and thus can develop a close relationship with the president. Third, presidents find that the small size of the NSC staff makes it easier to control.

18-3b The Foreign-Policy Bureaucracy

Although presidents are powerful on foreign policy, their influence has limits. American foreign policy is also shaped by the agencies that make up the foreign-policy bureaucracy: the State Department, the Defense Department, the intelligence community, and a number of other federal agencies. All these agencies perform two roles: They offer expert advice to the president on foreign-policy issues, and they implement the foreign-policy decisions the president and Congress make.

As a repository of expertise, the foreign-policy bureaucracy plays a major role in formulating policy proposals. This role enables agencies to influence policy by determining which proposals reach the president's desk and how those proposals are framed. The foreign-policy bureaucracy also influences policy because it implements presidential directives.[36] Most presidents at one time or another have shared the frustration Franklin Delano Roosevelt felt when dealing with the U.S. Navy: "To change anything in the Navy is like punching a featherbed. You punch it with your right and you punch it with your left until you are finally exhausted, and then you find the damn bed just as it was before you started punching."[37] The foreign-policy bureaucracy often succeeds in derailing initiatives it dislikes because presidents frequently lack the time needed to monitor compliance with their directives.

In seeking to shape the content of American foreign policy, the agencies that make up the foreign-policy bureaucracy regularly compete with each other for power.[38] The State Department, the Defense Department, and the intelligence community jealously guard their turf and fight for presidential attention. Sometimes the competition for power even extends into an agency's suborganizations as they compete to see which will control the actions of the parent agency. These struggles among and within agencies influence the course of American foreign policy.

The State Department

The State Department was originally founded to conduct and monitor all American diplomatic relations with other countries. As the oldest cabinet-level bureaucracy, the State Department has grown as the role of the United States in world affairs has increased. Whereas the first secretary of state, Thomas Jefferson, oversaw the work of five employees and two embassies, today the secretary of state oversees roughly 30,000 employees working both in Washington and at some 250 embassies, missions, consulates, and other offices abroad. In a typical year, the State Department's offices abroad will send more than 2.5 million cables (essentially secure telegrams) back to Washington. Still, with an annual budget of roughly $10 billion, the State Department remains one of the smallest cabinet-level bureaucracies.

Who works at the State Department? Roughly 8,000 of its employees belong to the Civil Service like most federal workers. Another 10,000 are foreign nationals who hold support jobs such as driver and cook at American embassies overseas. The core of the State Department is the foreign service, the roughly 14,500 career diplomats who are known formally as **foreign service officers** (see Box 18–3). They are chosen through a highly competitive written examination and a series of oral interviews that test them on geography, history, culture, people skills, and even food and drink. Not surprisingly, the products of this selection process see themselves as the foreign-policy elite of the United States. Presidents and members of Congress are often suspicious of foreign service

foreign service officers
Career professional diplomats who work for the Department of State.

The People behind the Rules

Box 18-3   The (Very Slowly) Changing Face of the Foreign Service

The State Department bears primary responsibility for conducting American foreign policy. At the heart of the State Department is the Foreign Service and its 14,500 foreign service officers. Chosen through rigorous competitive examinations that are separate from the Civil Service system we discussed in Chapter 13, foreign service officers form an elite corps of professional diplomats who hold key positions within the State Department and who also represent the United States in its many embassies, missions, consulates, and other offices abroad. Yet as they work to represent American interests overseas, foreign service officers themselves are not representative of the American people.

For much of the history of the Foreign Service, its officers were overwhelmingly white and almost exclusively male. Studies show that in the 1950s, foreign service officers were far more likely than other government employees or members of the

American public to come from families whose fathers held prestigious occupations. The tremendous homogeneity of foreign service officers in terms of race, gender, and background helped promote the popular stereotype of foreign service officers as "upper-class men from the Northeast with degrees from Ivy League colleges."

In 1980, Congress passed legislation that, among other things, required the Foreign Service to be "representative of the American people." Despite the push for greater diversity, the demographic makeup of the Foreign Service has been slow to change. For example, in 2006, the percentage of female foreign service officers stood at 45 percent, up from 16.4 percent in 1980, but still short of the percentage of women in American society. The results for members of minority groups were even less impressive. The percentage of African American foreign service officers rose from

5.5 to only 6.2 percent between 1980 and 2006, the percentage of Hispanic Americans rose from 2.4 to 6.6 percent, the percentage of Asian Americans from 1 to 6.2 percent, and the percentage of American Indians from 0.2 to 0.35 percent.

Thus, the Foreign Service has recruited more women and minorities, but it still falls short of mirroring the diversity of American society. As one observer puts it, "If the Foreign Service is no longer a smug men's club, it is more like one than any other part of the U.S. government."

Sources: Barry Rubin, *Secrets of State: The State Department and the Struggle over U.S. Foreign Policy* (New York: Oxford University Press, 1985); United States Department of State, *Multi-Year Affirmative Action Plan, FY 1990–92*, April 30, 1991; U.S. Department of State, Personnel Inventory Report, June 30, 1996, 67; U.S. Department of State, Office of Civil Rights, "2006 Foreign Service Officers: Total Workforce Distribution by Sex and Race/Ethnicity," undated; W. Lloyd Warner, Paul P. Van Riper, Norman H. Martin, and Orvis F. Collins, *The American Federal Executive* (New Haven, CT: Yale University Press, 1963).

officers, however, believing them to be more interested in placating foreign governments than in advocating American interests.

Although the State Department traditionally has portrayed itself as playing the lead role in foreign policy, in practice its influence has been eclipsed by other agencies.[39] The decline of the State Department has been the result of several factors. First, the prominence of military issues during the Cold War naturally played to the strengths of other agencies, most notably the Defense Department. Second, the State Department's small size and lack of a vocal domestic constituency make it easier to push aside in the bureaucratic battles that attend policy making. Third, most presidents have distrusted the State Department as too cautious, too sensitive to the interests of other countries, and too quick to overlook the president's political interests at home.[40] As a result of all these factors, the State Department now plays a much less influential role in formulating foreign policy than it did in the past. Former Secretary of State Colin Powell was not able to use his personal prestige to reverse the department's decline. Condoleezza Rice had more success asserting her views as secretary of state, but that reflected her closeness to President Bush rather than a reassertion of the State Department's strength as an institution.

The Defense Department

One agency that contributed to and benefited from the State Department's declining influence is the Defense Department, otherwise known as the Pentagon after the shape of the building that houses it. The Defense Department, as its name implies, is responsible for defending the United States against foreign threats. The Defense Department is a relatively new agency, created when the National Security Act of 1947 merged the War Department and the Department of the Navy. The Defense Department is now the largest federal bureaucracy. In 2008, its budget was more than $600 billion, and it employed more than 675,000 civilian workers, or roughly one-fourth of all federal civilian employees.

In many respects, the Defense Department is a collection of agencies rather than one cohesive bureaucracy.[41] The uniformed military consists of the four services—the Army, Navy, Air Force, and Marines—each of which has its own history, uniforms, and even battle songs. (The Coast Guard is part of the Homeland Security Department during peacetime and reports to the Navy during wartime.) The Defense Department also includes the Office of the Secretary of Defense (OSD), the civilian component of the Pentagon that supports and advises the secretary of defense. Inter- and intraservice rivalries, as well as tensions between the services and OSD, have long bedeviled decision making on defense policy. The ability of the secretary of defense to lead the various organizations that make up the Defense Department is limited. As former Secretary of Defense James Schlesinger writes, the responsibilities of the secretary of defense are "not matched by the powers of the office."[42]

Even with the American military's impressive performance in ousting Saddam Hussein from power in Iraq, the Defense Department faces questions about how it can best meet the challenges of the twenty-first century. An immediate question is whether American troops should leave Iraq. Barack Obama pledged during the presidential campaign to withdraw American combat brigades from Iraq at a pace of one or two brigades a month—a brigade has roughly 5,000 soldiers—over 16 months. He proposed to leave behind a residual force of American soldiers in Iraq and the surrounding region to conduct counterterrorism missions, protect American diplomatic and civilian personnel, and help train Iraqi security forces. Once in office, Obama decided to withdraw combat troops over 19 months and to leave behind a large residual force. It remains to be seen whether the United States will be able to keep to this proposed timetable.

Another major question the Pentagon faces is how much the United States should spend on the military. As Figure 18–3 shows, total defense spending—which includes all Pentagon spending as well spending on defense-related nuclear activities in other government agencies—grew sharply in the 1980s, peaking at $304 billion in 1989. Spending fell during the first half of the 1990s, before increasing later in the decade, but these numbers do not take into account the effect of inflation. When inflation is considered, defense spending actually fell 25 percent between 1989 and

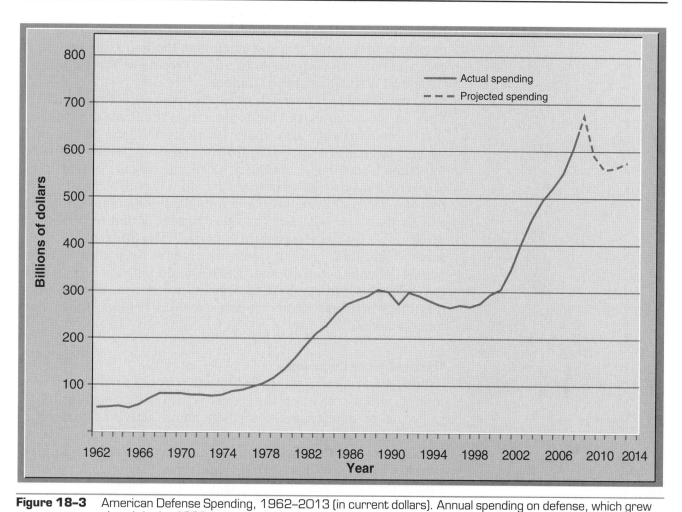

Figure 18–3 American Defense Spending, 1962–2013 (in current dollars). Annual spending on defense, which grew sharply in the 1980s as a result of the defense buildup during Ronald Reagan's presidency, dipped in the early 1990s before rising sharply after the September 11th attacks.

Source: *Data from Budget of the United States Government, Fiscal Year 2009: Historical Tables* (Washington, D.C.: U.S. Government Printing Office, 2008), 56–61.

2001.[43] And defense spending wasn't the only thing that fell with the end of the Cold War. The number of Americans in uniform did as well. The United States started the 1990s with 2.1 million people in uniform. By the end of the decade, only 1.4 million people were in uniform, a decline of roughly one-third.

American defense spending jumped once again after September 11th. In 2002 alone, American defense spending increased by $43 billion, or more than the total annual defense budget of either France or Britain. In 2008, the U.S. defense budget stood at $607 billion, and the Bush administration projected that defense spending would rise briefly before declining to $572 billion in 2013.[44] These projected budgets will need to cover the costs of the Iraq occupation, inflation, higher military health-care bills, better pay for the troops, and the bill for replacing aging weapons. Because it usually takes years to build major weapons systems like aircraft carriers and fighter planes, the benefits of new weapons programs begun during George W. Bush's presidency won't be seen for a decade or even longer. In the meantime, the Iraq War was fought and won with the weapons built under Presidents Ronald Reagan, George H. W. Bush, and Bill Clinton.

As important as how much money is spent on defense is what it buys. In recent years, the hot topic within the Pentagon has been *transformation*—the idea that American military forces must become faster and easier to deploy. One rationale for defense transformation is that the Soviet Union's collapse means that the United States no longer needs to prepare to fight a World-War II style war that emphasizes having heavily armored (and therefore big, bulky, and hard-to-move) forces. The other reason is that technology is revolutionizing many aspects of warfare.[45] The problem is that the services and their civilian overseers disagree over what weapons systems should be killed and which should be built to transform the American military. Defense experts are now busily analyzing the Iraq War trying to decide what lessons it holds for defense transformation.[46]

The Intelligence Community

A third major foreign-policy bureaucracy is the intelligence community, which consists of the sixteen organizations responsible for gathering or analyzing information about activities that might affect American interests around the world.[47] The best known intelligence organization, and the only one that exists as an independent agency, is the Central Intelligence Agency (CIA), established by the same 1947 legislation that created the Defense Department and the NSC.[48] Another major intelligence organization is the National Security Agency (NSA), which bears primary responsibility for monitoring the communications of other countries.[49] The National Reconnaissance Office (NRO)—an agency so secret that the government denied its very existence until 1992—oversees space reconnaissance systems, better known as spy satellites. NSA and NRO are both part of the Defense Department. Intelligence offices also exist within the Federal Bureau of Investigation and within the Departments of Defense, Energy, Homeland Security, State, and Treasury.

The budget for the intelligence community is secret, but it is believed to be more than $40 billion. Although mention of the intelligence community usually conjures up visions of covert operations, the primary task of the intelligence agencies is to track and analyze economic, military, and political events around the world. However, the intelligence agencies are discouraged from formulating policy. Officials worry that if the intelligence agencies become identified with particular policies, they will be tempted to distort their advice to serve their policy interests.

Like the Defense Department, the intelligence agencies saw their budgets jump after September 11th. Much of the new funding was intended to help the intelligence community better track terrorist organizations such as Al Qaeda. The intelligence agencies are also responsible for tracking traditional military threats to the United States as well as new threats such as nuclear proliferation, drug trafficking, environmental conflict, and economic espionage by foreign countries.[50]

September 11th prompted considerable criticism of the intelligence community. Many people, both inside and outside government, wondered why the intelligence agencies had failed to detect the Al Qaeda plot. The National Commission on Terrorist Attacks Upon the United States, an independent, bipartisan, government panel better known as the 9/11 Commission, was created in late 2002 to review the intelligence community's performance. When the panel released its final report in mid-2004, it sharply criticized the lack of communication and coordination within and between intelligence agencies. It recommended dozens of steps the government should take to prevent another terrorist attack.[51]

Many of the 9/11 Commission's recommendations were enacted into law with the passage in late 2004 of the Intelligence Reform and Terrorism Prevention Act (IRTPA). This law mandated the most dramatic changes in the organization and operation of the intelligence community since President Harry Truman signed the National Security Act of 1947, which (among other things) created the CIA. The general objective of IRTPA was to create a more unified, coordinated, and effective intelligence apparatus. The centerpiece reform was the creation of the new post of Director of National Intelligence (DNI) to be appointed by the president and confirmed by the Senate. The DNI is designated the president's principal adviser on intelligence matters and is responsible for overseeing all the national intelligence agencies. The Director of Central Intelligence, who had previously been designated as the president's principle intelligence adviser, oversees the CIA and reports to the DNI. Although IRTPA's supporters hoped that it would produce a more cohesive intelligence community, five years after the law was passed most observers doubted that it had fulfilled those hopes.

Other Agencies

In addition to the State Department, Defense Department, and the intelligence community, many agencies normally thought of as domestic bureaucracies play a role in foreign policy. The Treasury Department, for instance, handles international monetary matters. The Departments of Agriculture and Commerce administer programs that affect the agricultural and business interests of the United States abroad. The Justice Department plays a leading role in combating drug-producing operations overseas through its Drug Enforcement Agency. Although it might seem at first glance that the involvement of these and other agencies in foreign-policy making creates "too many cooks," their participation attests to the complexity and diversity of foreign-policy issues.

18-3c Congress

As we noted in Section 18-2a, the Constitution assigns to Congress considerable powers in foreign policy.[52] Yet the extent of congressional influence over foreign policy has varied greatly over the years as perceptions of external threats to the country have changed. In the second half of the nineteenth century, for example, a time when the United States faced few threats from abroad, Congress so dominated foreign policy that these years have been called the era of "congressional government," "congressional supremacy," "government-by-Congress," and "senatorial domination."[53] In contrast, at the height of the Cold War in the 1950s and 1960s, Congress became so willing to defer to presidential leadership on foreign policy that one senator complained that members of Congress responded to even the most far-reaching presidential decisions by "stumbling over each other to see who can say 'yea' the quickest and the loudest."[54] And when many members of Congress became convinced following the Vietnam War that American officials had exaggerated the threats facing the United States, Congress again became more active on foreign policy. That activism receded again immediately after September 11th, only to return in 2004 as the number of American soldiers killed in the occupation of Iraq mounted.

Increased congressional activism on foreign policy in the 1970s and 1980s prompted complaints that too many committees in Congress have a say in foreign policy.[55] As is true in the executive branch, the profusion of congressional committees with jurisdiction over some aspect of foreign policy owes more to the diversity and complexity of foreign-policy issues than to organizational inefficiency on the part of Congress. Moreover, most of Congress's activity on foreign and defense policy occurs within the confines of eight committees: the House International Relations Committee and the Senate Foreign Relations Committee (which oversee foreign aid programs), the House and Senate Armed Services Committees (which oversee defense programs), the House and Senate Intelligence Committees (which oversee intelligence programs), and the House and Senate Appropriations Committees (which appropriate the funds for all government spending).[56]

Congress influences foreign policy in three ways: with substantive legislation, procedural legislation, and efforts to shape public opinion.[57] In passing (or refusing to pass) substantive legislation, Congress specifies the substance or content of American foreign policy. When Congress uses substantive legislation, it often invokes its appropriations power.[58] Dollars are policy in Washington, D.C., and by law, the president generally cannot spend money unless Congress appropriates it. Thus, by deciding to fund some foreign-policy ventures and not others, Congress can steer the course of American foreign and defense policy. Congress also can specify the substance of foreign policy by virtue of its constitutional power to regulate foreign trade. One notable instance in which Congress used its trade power was the 1986 bill that placed sanctions on South

Africa to pressure Pretoria to end its policy of apartheid. In passing the legislation, Congress had to overcome several hurdles, including a presidential veto. The South Africa sanctions bill is the only time since 1973 that Congress has overridden a foreign-policy veto. And the Senate can specify the substance of foreign policy by approving or refusing to approve treaties the president has negotiated. In 1999, for instance, the Senate refused to give its approval to the Comprehensive Test Ban Treaty, which would have forever barred countries from testing nuclear weapons.

Along with passing substantive legislation, Congress can influence foreign policy by passing (or refusing to pass) procedural legislation, which are bills that change the procedures the executive branch uses to make decisions. Procedural legislation rests on the premise that changing the rules governing the decision-making process will change the policy that emerges from the executive branch. In trade policy, for example, legislation now requires the White House to consult with a wide range of consumer, industry, and labor groups whenever it is negotiating an international trade agreement. Sponsors of the law believe that including these groups in decision making makes it more likely that American trade policy will reflect American economic interests.[59]

In addition to passing substantive and procedural legislation, Congress can influence foreign policy by changing the climate of opinion in the country. When public opinion changes, policies frequently do as well. One example of a congressional effort to change public opinion and thereby American policy came in the late 1990s when many members of Congress believed the Clinton administration needed to push harder for Saddam Hussein's ouster in Iraq. Legislators favoring a tougher line toward Baghdad introduced bills, gave speeches, appeared on TV talk shows, and wrote articles for the opinion pages of newspapers, all in a bid to put public pressure on the administration. All these efforts played a major role in forcing President Clinton to make regime change in Iraq an official goal of American foreign policy. As this example suggests, members use a host of different techniques to influence public opinion. These diverse activities share a common goal, though—to set the terms of debate on an issue in a way that increases support for some policy options and decreases support for others.

18-3d The Public

Individual Americans have the potential to directly affect the course of American foreign policy. They can do so in two main ways: by becoming members of interest groups and by voting for presidential and congressional candidates who share their foreign-policy preferences.

As Chapter 10 notes, the number of interest groups in the United States has grown tremendously over the past several decades. Their growth in the area of foreign policy is no exception.[60] Many interest groups active on foreign policy are business and labor groups that wish to shape trade and foreign economic policy. Other groups are dedicated to representing ethnic interests, such as those of Jewish Americans, Greek Americans, or Arab Americans.[61] Still other interest groups active on foreign policy are citizen groups that champion issues such as defense spending, the environment, human rights, and immigration. As with any interest group, the ability of foreign-policy interest groups to influence policy making depends on external events, the existence of opposing groups, and their own internal characteristics.

Although interest groups are an important means by which the American public can express its views on foreign policy, most Americans do not belong to an interest group expressly devoted to foreign policy. Instead, the primary way the American public influences foreign policy occurs in the polling booth. Most studies of voting suggest that foreign policy usually plays a small role in presidential and congressional elections.[62] Still, when voters go to the polls, they determine who will set the country's foreign-policy agenda. John McCain no doubt would have made different foreign policy decisions in the White House than Barack Obama has.

Although the public determines who will sit in positions of political power, it seldom determines the course of day-to-day policy decisions. Quite often, policy makers pursue policies that a substantial portion of the public opposes. In 1977, for instance, President Jimmy Carter signed two treaties returning the Panama Canal to Panama, even though polls initially showed that more than 60 percent of the American public wanted the United States to retain control of the canal.[63] The Reagan administration provided aid to the Nicaraguan Contras despite the fact that most Americans opposed the policy.[64] The elder President Bush began the Gulf War even though polls showed that Americans were roughly split over whether to use economic sanctions or military force to dislodge Iraq from Kuwait.[65] President Clinton sent troops to Haiti and Bosnia even though most Americans opposed both peacekeeping missions.[66] The younger President Bush sent 22,000 additional American troops to Iraq in 2007 to combat the insurgency there even though polls showed that two-thirds of Americans opposed the idea.[67]

One reason policy makers can disregard public opinion was discussed in Chapter 6: The public lacks detailed knowledge about many policy areas, especially foreign policy.[68] Compared with the citizens of other countries, Americans know little about the world beyond their borders.[69] A second reason that public opinion does not guide American foreign policy is apathy. Americans usually care more about domestic issues than foreign ones, and the end of the Cold War strongly reinforced this tendency. In the 1990s, pollsters repeatedly found that when they asked people to identify the most important problem facing the country, less than 5 percent of respondents named a defense or foreign-policy issue. That changed after September 11th, when Americans realized they faced potentially grave threats from abroad. Even then, however, most people did not have detailed preferences about how they wanted President Bush to respond to these threats.

As with domestic policy, interest groups often lobby and demonstrate to influence foreign policy.

Because most Americans are uninformed and apathetic about foreign policy, public opinion can be swayed and may change dramatically in the span of a few days or weeks. For example, the Carter administration launched a major public relations effort to persuade the American public that the Panama Canal treaties would serve the interests of the United States. The campaign worked. By the time the Senate voted on the treaties, polls showed that a majority of the public had come to support them.[70] Likewise, the public typically rallies around the president during a crisis.[71] Polls taken in the first days after the start of the Iraq War showed that despite earlier misgivings, roughly 70 percent of the public supported the decision to invade. A year later, as the death toll for American troops topped one thousand, many Americans changed their minds yet again. Roughly half told pollsters that the Iraq War had not been worth fighting.[72]

In short, then, the main point of Chapter 6 holds particularly true for foreign affairs: Public opinion seldom provides government officials with direct guidance on policy making. Although the public's direct effect on foreign policy is usually limited, it has two important *indirect* effects. First, it constrains the policies officials can consider. How tight those constraints are varies over time and with changes in public opinion. Take the case of American military interventions in the Third World. During the 1960s, presidents essentially had a free hand to send American troops overseas; the Kennedy administration, for instance, sent more than 10,000 military advisers to South Vietnam without much thought about public reaction. After Vietnam, however, presidents had much less freedom to send troops overseas. The Clinton administration, for example, found itself embroiled in a bitter political debate when it proposed sending American troops as part of a NATO peacekeeping mission to the Balkans. What changed in the three decades from Kennedy to Clinton was that the public was less willing to support foreign military operations where American security interests were not directly threatened.[73]

Second, public opinion helps determine where foreign policy falls on the federal government's list of priorities. Why? Because politicians naturally gravitate toward issues the public cares about. When the public loses interest in foreign policy, as it did after the end of the Cold War, so too do many officials in Washington. This is why foreign policy only occasionally takes center stage in Washington debates. This neglect can have important consequences. As we saw in Chapter 10 narrow interests are most likely to influence policy when the broader public isn't looking. Conversely, when the public cares intensely about foreign policy—as it did after September 11th—so do most politicians. That is why the 2004 and 2006 elections turned largely on Iraq and the war on terrorism rather than on domestic issues.[74] In sum, then, public pressure affects Congress, the foreign-policy bureaucracy, and the president as they make decisions on foreign policy.

18-4 CHALLENGES TO THE UNITED STATES IN THE POST-COLD WAR ERA

The demise of the Soviet Union marked a watershed in American foreign policy. For the first time in nearly fifty years, Americans began rethinking their relations with the rest of the world. In the decade after the Berlin Wall fell, however, no consensus emerged on what should replace containment as the guiding principle of American foreign policy. September 11th looks to have provided an answer: combating what President Bush has called "terrorists with global reach" and the "rogue" states that support them.

Even if Americans continue to agree that counterterrorism should be the primary objective of American foreign policy, they will need to confront three fundamental challenges: (1) bridging disagreements about the proper strategies for defeating terrorists and rogue states, (2) mastering a foreign-policy agenda that encompasses many issues besides counterterrorism, and (3) reconciling the conflict between the preference of the United States for unilateral action and its frequent need to work with other countries to find solutions to common problems.

18-4a Disagreements about Strategies

One obstacle to sustaining a consensus that the top priority of American foreign policy should be defeating terrorist groups and rogue states is potential disagreement on what strategies are most likely to achieve those ends at an acceptable cost. In his 2002 State of the Union address, President Bush argued that rogue states like Iraq, Iran, and North Korea, "and their terrorist allies, constitute an axis of evil, arming to threaten the peace of the world." What he did not say in that speech, however, was how he intended to deal with this "axis of evil."

Over the next year, Bush's answer to that question became clear: It depends. In the case of Iraq, he ordered a military invasion that unseated Saddam Hussein. In the case of Iran and North Korea, however, he ruled out using military force in favor of diplomatic strategies. He reached this decision even though North Korea and Iran both had far more advanced nuclear weapons programs and Iran a far more extensive history of supporting terrorists. The reason Iraq was treated differently reflected a mix of factors: among them, suspicions (never borne out by the available evidence) that Baghdad had operational ties to Al Qaeda, the reality that twelve years of sanctions had weakened Iraq's military, and the fact that no country was going to come to Baghdad's aid.

The impressive American victory in Iraq initially led some observers to suggest that the Bush administration should use the military might of the United States to coerce Iran and North Korea into shutting down their nuclear weapons programs. Critics of such suggestions argued that it would almost certainly require far bloodier wars to compel regime change in either Tehran or Pyongyang. Some critics went even further and argued that the Iraq War had become a foreign-policy fiasco. The prospects that the United States would initiate a military confrontation against either Iran or North Korea receded as more of the American public came to doubt the wisdom of the Iraq War. Five years after the war began, more than four thousand American troops had died. Despite these losses, the Bush administration had failed in its goal of building a stable, democratic government in Iraq.

Although many discussions about how to deal with terrorists and rogue states focus on the utility of using military force, some experts argue for targeting broader societal problems that they believe that help breed terrorism. Then-Secretary of State Colin Powell observed shortly after the September 11th attacks that "Terrorism really flourishes in areas of poverty, despair, and hopelessness, where people see no future. We have to show people who might move in the direction of terrorism that there is a better way."[75] Such a strategy would emphasize foreign aid to poor countries and encourage them to move toward capitalist economies and democratic governance. Some critics of proposals to attack the so-called enabling causes of terrorism argue that it is wishful thinking that could be harmful. They point out that many Al Qaeda terrorists come from middle-class and upper-middle-class families. Other critics doubt that the United States has the capacity to promote democracy in countries that are not ready for it. They worry that the push for democratic governance will produce one-time elections that bring virulently anti-American governments to power in much of the Arab and Islamic world.

national missile defense (NMD)
A weapons system that, if it can be made to work, would potentially protect the United States and possibly its allies against attack by long-range ballistic missiles.

homeland security
Programs and initiatives designed to make it harder for terrorists to attack targets on American soil and to minimize the consequences of any attacks that do occur. Also, the name of the cabinet department established in 2003.

If it is too costly to attack every country that might threaten the United States and efforts to attack the enabling causes of terrorism are unlikely to work, what other options are available? One strategy is to limit the vulnerability of the United States to attack. This is the idea behind the Bush administration's pursuit of **national missile defense (NMD)**, which is a system designed to shoot down long-range ballistic missiles fired at the United States.[76] It is also behind the idea for better **homeland security**, which are initiatives designed to make it harder for terrorists to attack targets on American soil and to minimize the consequences of any attacks that do occur.[77] However, there are serious questions about how well such defensive strategies will work. Critics argue that despite years of research, the Pentagon has yet to make any NMD system work under real-world conditions, and in any event, a ballistic missile attack is one of the least likely threats facing the United States. As for homeland security, critics argue that the United States simply has too many targets to protect.

As Americans mull over the wisdom of these and other possible strategies for waging the war on terrorism, they must also confront questions of cost, both in terms of dollars and human lives. Money spent building an NMD system or protecting chemical facilities against terrorist attack is money that can't be used to fund domestic programs or cut taxes. Most Americans supported the Iraq War at least in part because they believed that American casualties would be light. Would they be willing to support a war against North Korea that most experts say could easily kill more than 10,000 American soldiers and more than 100,000 South Koreans? People's opinions vary greatly on the acceptable price for even the loftiest of foreign-policy goals.

It is not surprising, then, that debates over how to achieve a goal that most people accept as desirable—defeating terrorists and rogue states—could become heated. Many strategies offer uncertain chances for success. Even in instances where a strategy initially looks to have worked, as with Saddam Hussein's ouster, the long-term consequences may be perilous. Some strategies raise painful dilemmas. If pushing democracy in the Arab world runs the risk of producing anti-American governments, would the United States be wiser to forget its rhetoric about freedom and help friendly but authoritarian regimes stay in power? The human or financial cost of some strategies may also be higher than some Americans are willing to pay. Assessing these competing claims clearly involve subjective judgments. For that reason, foreign-policy debates can trigger considerable passion.

18-4b A Diverse Foreign-Policy Agenda

The second challenge facing the United States at the start of the twenty-first century is to master a foreign-policy agenda that encompasses many more issues than terrorists and rogue states. September 11th made counterterrorism America's number one priority. However, that did not mean that other foreign-policy issues ceased to matter. How well the United States handles the rest of its foreign-policy agenda is of great importance to most Americans. What happens abroad can affect their ability to earn a livelihood as well as the nature of the world their children will inherit.

One issue of great prominence is trade. During much of the Cold War era, the United States eagerly promoted **free trade**, which is an economic policy that holds that lowering trade barriers (such as tariffs, that is, taxes on imported goods) will benefit the economies of all the countries involved. For many years, most American industries supported free trade initiatives because they produced better quality goods at lower prices than their competitors abroad. Yet when foreign competition caught up to (and in some cases passed) Americans firms in the 1980s and early 1990s, many Americans lost their jobs. As a result, political support for free trade waned. In 1993, opponents of free trade came close to defeating the North American Free Trade Agreement (NAFTA), an accord that sought to reduce trade barriers among Canada, Mexico, and the United States. Antitrade sentiment moderated in the second half of the 1990s as the United States enjoyed an unprecedented economic boom, fueled in part by expanding American trade abroad. Hostility toward trade has grown again in recent years, however. Economists argue that trade benefits the American economy as a whole, and they have lots of evidence to back them up. Nonetheless, a majority of Americans sees trade as a threat to jobs.[78] Political opposition to trade in the United States (and elsewhere) was the main reason that the so-called Doha Round of global trade negotiations collapsed in failure in 2008.

As some long-neglected foreign issues have gained prominence following the end of the Cold War, some entirely new foreign-policy problems are appearing on the policy agenda. Because countries have become increasingly interconnected in the modern world as a result of **globalization**, the United States faces a host of new and pressing foreign-policy problems. Biodiversity, climate change, drug trafficking, energy dependence, and natural resource depletion are all problems unknown to Presidents Truman, Eisenhower, and Kennedy. Yet each of these issues is likely to consume considerable time and effort on the part of American officials in the twenty-first century.

Climate change (or global warming) may prove the most important of these new foreign-policy issues. No one disputes the basic theory of climate change: If the concentration of carbon dioxide and other heat-trapping gases in the atmosphere increases sufficiently, the earth's temperature will rise and its climate will change. The questions instead are whether human activity (primarily the burning of fossil fuels) is changing the climate significantly, and if so, whether it makes more sense to reduce emissions or adapt to a new climate. Most scientists and governments believe human activity is changing the climate and that reducing

free trade
An economic policy that holds that lowering trade barriers will benefit the economies of all the countries involved.

globalization
The process by which growing economic relations and technological change make countries increasingly interdependent.

emissions is essential for dealing with the problem. These beliefs led to the Kyoto Protocol, which is a treaty signed in 1997 that would require advanced industrialized nations to reduce their emissions of carbon dioxide. President George W. Bush withdrew the United States from the Kyoto process in 2001, however. He argued that more scientific study of the link between human activity and climate change was needed, and that in any event, the Kyoto Protocol was not a sensible approach to the problem of climate change.[79] President Barack Obama has pledged to reengage the United States in global climate change negotiations.

Foreign-policy issues such as trade and climate change present policy makers with unfamiliar challenges because, unlike traditional security problems, they are **intermestic issues** that straddle the line separating domestic policy from foreign policy.[80] In the case of trade, for instance, the president must negotiate with other heads of state as well as with domestic interest groups. For example, to convince Congress in 1993 to approve the North American Free Trade Agreement (NAFTA), President Clinton had to make numerous concessions to groups that claimed the agreement would hurt them.[81] Likewise, efforts to combat climate change require presidents to pursue both international and domestic initiatives. When both domestic and international interests are involved, the number and complexity of conflicting interests increase tremendously. It is clearly much more difficult to create rules that effectively manage the conflicts among all these competing interests.

Presidents also find it much harder to lead on intermestic issues than on pure foreign-policy issues because they cannot count on the automatic support of Congress or the American people. Congress is likely to be active because intermestic issues involve decisions traditionally considered part of domestic policy. Legislators will not suddenly defer to the White House on trade or environmental policy simply because the president says they are key foreign-policy problems. Moreover, intermestic issues directly affect the well-being of domestic groups; hence, a greater chance exists that any presidential or congressional initiative will face considerable constituent opposition and interest group activity. The foreign-policy agenda of the United States at the start of the twenty-first century is laced with intermestic issues that involve such potential problems.

18-4c Unilateralism versus Multilateralism

The third challenge the United States must meet as it grapples with its foreign-policy challenges is the increasing need to work with other countries to find multilateral solutions to common problems. A trademark characteristic of American foreign policy is **unilateralism**—that is, the tendency to act in foreign affairs without consulting other countries. When isolationism reigned supreme in the United States, one of the major arguments against joining an alliance with other countries was that the United

intermestic issues
Issues such as trade, the environment, and drug trafficking that affect both domestic and foreign interests.

unilateralism
The tendency of the United States to act alone in foreign affairs without consulting other countries.

States needed to have a free hand to choose its destiny. Even when the United States assumed a global role after World War II, the bias toward unilateralism continued because the country's great wealth enabled it to pursue policies without consulting other countries. In Korea, Vietnam, and elsewhere, the United States acted with relatively little help (and sometimes outright opposition) from its major allies. The collapse of the Soviet Union encouraged a surge of unilateralist sentiment in the United States, especially in the Republican Party. Unilateralists today argue that the United States is the lone superpower, and it should act as it sees fit, even if it upsets allies or former adversaries. Moreover, many unilateralists worry that international institutions and arrangements undermine American **sovereignty**, that is, the right of Americans to determine what laws they wish to live under.

Yet even as some people in the United States favor being able to act unilaterally, growing global interdependence puts pressure on American officials to move away from unilateralism and toward **multilateralism**—that is, an approach in which three or more countries cooperate in seeking solutions to foreign-policy problems. Fears about climate change illustrate the importance of multilateralism. The United States has historically emitted far more of the heat-trapping gases responsible for climate change than any other country. Yet because so many countries emit these gases, changes in American policy alone will not reverse the long-term potential for climate change.[82] Indeed, in 2008, China passed the United States to become the world's leading emitter of heat-trapping gases on an annual (but not historical) basis. In short, multilateral solutions are necessary to solve multilateral problems.

Of course, the United States has considerable experience with multilateralism. Washington drove the creation of both the UN and NATO. It also helped create the many multilateral institutions that devise and administer the rules of the international economy. One of the most important of these institutions is the **World Trade Organization (WTO)**.[83] The WTO operates as the successor to the General Agreement on Tariffs and Trade (GATT), which had dealt with international trade issues since its founding in 1947. In comparison with GATT, WTO was designed to have enhanced powers to enforce compliance with multilateral trade agreements. Washington has gone to the WTO when it thought that other countries were violating international trade rules. Although the WTO has ruled against the United States in a few instances, it more often has ruled in its favor. When the United States has lost, most American experts agreed that the American position violated world trade rules.

George W. Bush's presidency pushed the debate over the relative merits of unilateralism versus multilateralism to the top of the political agenda in the United States. In his first months in office, he withdrew the United States from the Kyoto Protocol and ended Washington's participation in a range of other multilateral efforts.

sovereignty
The power of self-rule.

multilateralism
An approach in which three or more countries cooperate for the purpose of solving some common problem.

World Trade Organization (WTO)
The international trade agency that began operation in 1995 as the successor to the General Agreement on Tariffs and Trade.

Source: © Fabrice Coffrini /Getty Images.

World Trade Organization headquarters in Geneva, Switzerland.

Bush's willingness to act unilaterally increased after September 11th, culminating in the decision to invade Iraq without an explicit UN authorization to use force. American and British forces, with small contributions from Australia and a few other countries, toppled Saddam Hussein. (The White House insisted that a broad "coalition" supported the Iraq War. However, most members of this coalition were countries such as Macedonia, Micronesia, and the Marshall Islands that had no real contribution to make.)

Bush's decision to ignore the UN on Iraq and his other unilateralist decisions alienated many of America's traditional allies. He argued that this was the price the United States had to pay to ensure its security. His critics argued that he had severely damaged America's ability to lead because even its closest allies were questioning its plans, purposes, and priorities. President Bush moderated his unilateralist rhetoric during his second term in office in an effort to repair his strained relations with American allies, but he still declined to embrace multilateral institutions. Barack Obama will undoubtedly champion multilateralist solutions during his presidency. It remains to be seen, however, whether the American public will be willing to follow.

Bridging disagreements over the proper strategies for counterterrorism, mastering a broad and diverse foreign-policy agenda, and deciding the relative merits of unilateralism versus multilateralism are three challenges the United States must confront as it charts its foreign policy at the start of the twenty-first century. As the United States struggles to meet these challenges, it faces a complex set of conflicting interests that span the globe. How the United States will decide to manage those conflicts, and how well it can manage them, remain to be seen.

SUMMARY

For the first 150 years of its history, the United States avoided foreign alliances. In the wake of World War II, however, the United States broke with its isolationist past and assumed the mantle of a global superpower. Containment of communism, and especially containment of the Soviet Union, became the cornerstone of American foreign policy. The eventual demise of the Soviet Union marked the triumph of containment. Having won the Cold War, the United States now struggles to define the role it will play in the world in the twenty-first century.

Presidents influence foreign policy to an extent not true of any other policy domain. Their influence stems from four factors. First, presidents enjoy inherent advantages in foreign affairs. Congress cannot hope to match the speed and secrecy of presidential decision making. Second, presidents have used precedents to expand their authority in foreign affairs. Third, the Supreme Court often hands down rulings that grant the president great freedom in foreign policy, and it generally declines to hear cases that challenge presidential authority. Fourth, partisan and institutional divisions make it difficult for Congress to act in the absence of consensus, and members of Congress frequently defer to the president for electoral reasons and because they believe that success in foreign policy requires strong presidential leadership.

Although presidents have the greatest say in foreign policy, they must continually struggle to control the bureaucracy and to maintain the support of Congress and the public. The foreign-policy bureaucracy exercises tremendous influence because it both formulates and implements policy. Congress makes its preferences felt through substantive and procedural legislation and by shaping public opinion. The public's great distance from the day-to-day affairs of government leaves it poorly positioned to affect most foreign-policy decisions. But the public's willingness to support foreign-policy initiatives places broad constraints on the actions the government can take.

At the beginning of the twenty-first century, the United States faces three major foreign-policy challenges. First, it must bridge disagreements over the proper strategies for achieving what most Americans agree is a top priority—defeating terrorists and rogue states. Second, it must master a foreign-policy agenda that encompasses many issues besides counterterrorism. Trade and climate change are among the foreign-policy problems Washington must tackle. Problems such as these have the potential to affect people's day-to-day lives; hence, they are likely to prove politically difficult to resolve. Third, the United States must decide the extent to which its foreign-policy goals can be accomplished by unilateralist versus multilateralist approaches. The traditional reliance on unilateral action offers the promise of being able to act free of constraints, but in an increasingly globalizing world, acting alone may mean forfeiting the chance to achieve important foreign-policy goals.

KEY TERMS

Bush Doctrine

Cold War

containment

détente

enlargement

executive agreements

foreign service officers

free trade

globalism

globalization

homeland security

intermestic issues

isolationism

Marshall Plan

Monroe Doctrine

multilateralism

national interest

national missile defense (NMD)

neoisolationism

North Atlantic Treaty
  Organization (NATO)

sovereignty

Third World

Truman Doctrine

two presidencies

unilateralism

World Trade Organization
  (WTO)

READINGS FOR FURTHER STUDY

Daalder, Ivo H., and I. M. Destler. *In the Shadow of the Oval Office—From JFK to Bush II: The Presidents' National Security Advisers* (New York: Simon & Schuster, 2009). Two leading foreign-policy analysts review how national security advisers operated from John F. Kennedy's administration to George W. Bush's.

Daalder, Ivo H., and James M. Lindsay. *America Unbound: The Bush Revolution in Foreign Policy,* 2nd ed (New York: Wiley, 2005). An award-winning analysis of President George W. Bush's approach to foreign policy.

Halperin, Morton H., and Priscilla Clapp, and Arnold Kantor (Collaborator). *Bureaucratic Politics and Foreign Policy,* 2nd ed (Washington, D.C.: Brookings Institution, 2006). An updated version of the classic discussion of the organizational politics that drive decision making within the American foreign-policy bureaucracy.

Herring, George C. *From Colony to Superpower: U.S. Foreign Relations Since 1776.* (New York: Oxford University Press, 2008). A comprehensive and lively history of American foreign policy from the days of George Washington to the presidency of George W. Bush.

Kagan, Robert. *Of Paradise and Power: America and Europe in the New World Order* (New York: Knopf, 2003). An illuminating and provocative discussion of why the United States and its European allies often see the world in strikingly different ways.

Lindsay, James M. *Congress and the Politics of U.S. Foreign Policy* (Baltimore, MD: Johns Hopkins University Press, 1994). A political scientist examines the tools Congress uses to influence foreign policy and shows how politics frequently drives members of Congress to discharge their constitutional duty to oversee the executive branch.

National Commission on Terrorist Attacks upon the United States. *9/11 Commission Report* (New York: Norton, 2004). Available at www.9-11commission.gov/report/911. The definitive account of how Al Qaeda masterminded the September 11 attacks and why the American government failed to detect them.

Packer, George. *The Assassin's Gate: America in Iraq* (New York: Farrar, Straus and Giroux, 2005). A journalist who supported the Iraq War explores the reasons why it did not deliver the political outcome that he (and the Bush administration) expected.

Zakaria, Fareed. *The Post-American World* (New York: Norton, 2008). A *Newsweek* columnist argues that the United States will no longer dominate the world economy, drive geopolitics, or overwhelm other cultures in the twenty-first century.

REVIEW QUESTIONS

1. A policy of neoisolationism suggests that the United States should
    a. isolate the People's Republic of China to prevent it from emerging as a threat to American interests in Asia.
    b. disengage from world affairs and turn inward.
    c. put a higher priority on commercial trade interest than on national security interests.
    d. minimize trade relations with developing nations.
2. The reasons the federal courts have given for dismissing congressional lawsuits that challenge presidential actions in foreign affairs include
    a. lack of ripeness.
    b. that the case in question raises political rather than legal questions.
    c. the contention that legislators do not have appropriate legal standing.
    d. all of the above.
3. The Bush Doctrine holds that
    a. the United States should withdraw from the United Nations.
    b. the United States should target terrorist groups and the states that aid or harbor them.
    c. the United States should build a national missile defense to protect itself against attack by long-range ballistic missiles.
    d. None of the above.

4. American diplomacy between 1942 and 1989 is referred to as the
   a. Truman era.
   b. New Frontier.
   c. isolationist era.
   d. globalist era.
5. The Clinton Administration proposed to replace the policy of containment with the policy of
   a. the Clinton Doctrine.
   b. enlargement.
   c. enrichment.
   d. neoisolationism.
6. _____ established the policy of détente.
   a. Lyndon Johnson
   b. Richard Nixon
   c. Gerald Ford
   d. Jimmy Carter
7. Which of the following does *not* explain why presidents typically have more say in foreign policy than in domestic policy?
   a. a literal reading of the Constitution
   b. precedents established by previous presidents
   c. rulings of the Supreme Court
   d. actions of the Congress
8. Which of the following was *not* granted to the president under the Constitution?
   a. commander in chief of the armed forces
   b. power to appoint foreign ambassadors
   c. power to make treaties
   d. power to declare war
9. In *U.S. v.*_____, the Supreme Court justices ruled that executive agreements are as binding as treaties.
   a. *Nixon*
   b. *Curtiss-Wright Export Corporation*
   c. *Belmont*
   d. *Truman*
10. Congress has formally declared war four times in American history. Which of the following summaries is correct?
    a. War of 1812, Spanish-American War, World War I, World War II
    b. American Revolution, Civil War, World War I, World War II
    c. War of 1812, Civil War, World War I, World War II
    d. World War I, World War II, Korean War, Vietnam War

NOTES

1. See Ivo H. Daalder and James M. Lindsay, *America Unbound: The Bush Revolution in Foreign Policy,* 2nd ed. (New York: Wiley, 2005).
2. Quoted in William Safire, *Lend Me Your Ears: Great Speeches in History* (New York: Norton, 1992), 727.

3. Quoted in Thomas G. Paterson and Dennis Merrill, eds., *Major Problems in American Foreign Relations*, Vol. I (Lexington, MA: Heath, 1995), 77. (Emphasis in the original.)

4. Quoted in ibid., 179–80.

5. See Ernest R. May, *The Making of the Monroe Doctrine* (Cambridge, MA: Harvard University Press, 1975); Dexter Perkins, *The Monroe Doctrine, 1823–1826* (Cambridge, MA: Harvard University Press, 1932).

6. Robert H. Ferrell, *American Diplomacy: A History,* 3rd ed. (New York: Norton, 1975), 169.

7. Among others, see Walter LaFeber, *The Cambridge History of American Foreign Relations, Volume II: The American Search for Opportunity, 1865–1913* (New York: Cambridge University Press, 1993).

8. Quoted in Ferrell, *American Diplomacy,* 457.

9. See Ralph Stone, *The Irreconcilables: The Fight Against the League of Nations* (Lexington: University of Kentucky Press, 1970); John Chalmers Vinson, *Referendum for Isolation: Defeat of Article Ten of the League of Nations Covenant* (Athens: University of Georgia Press, 1961); William C. Widenor, "The League of Nations Component of the Versailles Treaty," in *The Politics of Arms Control Treaty Ratification,* eds. Michael Krepon and Dan Caldwell (New York: St. Martin's, 1991).

10. Quoted in Ferrell, *American Diplomacy,* 631.

11. On the genesis of the Marshall Plan, see Joseph Marion Jones, *The Fifteen Weeks* (New York: Harcourt, Brace & World, 1955).

12. Organization for Economic Cooperation and Development, "Aid at a Glance Chart: United States," available at www.oecd.org/dataoecd/42/30/40039096.gif.

13. Among others, see George C. Herring, *America's Longest War: The United States and Vietnam, 1959–1975,* 3rd ed. (New York: Knopf, 1996); Stanley Karnow, *Vietnam, A History* (New York: Viking Penguin, 1991).

14. Herring, *America's Longest War,* 199.

15. Among others, see Bruce W. Jentleson, *With Friends Like These: Reagan, Bush, and Saddam, 1982–1990* (New York: Norton, 1994).

16. See, for example, Anthony Lake, "From Containment to Enlargement," *State Department Dispatch,* September 27, 1993, 658–64; *A National Security Strategy of Engagement and Enlargement,* February 1996, available at www.fas.org/spp/military/docops/national/1996stra.htm.

17. See Ivo H. Daalder and Michael E. O'Hanlon, *Winning Ugly: NATO's War to Save Kosovo* (Washington, D.C.: Brookings Institution, 2000).

18. Gov. George W. Bush, "A Period of Consequences." Speech delivered on September 23, 1999, available at www.externalaffairs.citadel.edu/pres_bush.

19. See Daalder and Lindsay, *America Unbound,* chaps. 8–10.

20. The term *two presidencies* was coined in Aaron Wildavsky, "The Two Presidencies," *Transaction* 4 (December 1966): 7–14. Wildavsky's article spawned a long line of research that has variously confirmed, modified, and challenged his original findings. Many of these studies are reprinted in Steven A. Shull, ed., *The Two Presidencies: A Quarter Century Assessment* (Chicago: Nelson-Hall, 1991). The relevance of these subsequent studies to the question of how presidential power varies across policy domains is limited, however, because of methodological problems. See James M. Lindsay and Wayne P. Steger, "The 'Two Presidencies' in Future Research: Moving Beyond Roll-Call Analysis," *Congress and the Presidency* 20 (Autumn 1993): 103–17.

21. See Michael J. Glennon, *Constitutional Diplomacy* (Princeton, NJ: Princeton University Press, 1990); Louis Henkin, *Foreign Affairs and the Constitution* (Mineola, NY: Foundation Press, 1972); Harold Hongju Koh, *The National Security Constitution: Sharing Power after the Iran-Contra Affair* (New Haven, CT: Yale University Press, 1990).

22. See David Gray Adler, "The Constitution and Presidential Warmaking," *Political Science Quarterly* 103 (Spring 1988): 8–13; Alexander Hamilton, "Federalist No. 69," in *The Federalist Papers,* ed. Garry Wills (New York: Bantam Books, 1982), 350; Henkin, *Foreign Affairs and the Constitution,* 50–51; Arthur M. Schlesinger, Jr., *The Imperial Presidency* (Boston: Houghton Mifflin, 1989), 6, 61–62.

23. Alexander Hamilton, "Federalist No. 70," in Alexander Hamilton, James Madison, and John Jay, *The Federalist Papers,* ed. Garry Wills (New York: Bantam Books, 1982), 356.

24. Among others, see Adler, "The Constitution and Presidential Warmaking," 3–17; John Hart Ely, *War and Responsibility: Constitutional Lessons of Vietnam and Its Aftermath* (Princeton, NJ: Princeton University Press, 1993); Louis Fisher, *Presidential War Power* (Lawrence: University of Kansas Press, 1995); Schlesinger, *Imperial Presidency,* chaps. 6–8; Abraham D. Sofaer, *War, Foreign Affairs, and Constitutional Power: The Origins* (Cambridge, MA: Ballinger, 1976); Francis D. Wormuth and Edwin B. Firmage, *To Chain the Dog of War: The War Powers of Congress in History and Law,* 2nd ed. (Urbana: University of Illinois Press, 1989).

25. See Gordon Silverstein, "Judicial Enhancement of Executive Power," in *The President, the Congress, and the Making of Foreign Policy,* ed. Paul E. Peterson (Norman: University of Oklahoma Press, 1994).

26. *Campbell v. Clinton,* 203 F.3d 19 (D.C. Cir. 2000). See also "Constitutional Law—Congressional Standing—D.C. Circuit Holds That Members of Congress May Not Challenge the President's Use of Troops in Kosovo," *Harvard Law Review* 113 (June 2000): 2134–39; Lori Fisler Damrosch, "The Clinton Administration and War Powers," *Law and Contemporary Problems* 63 (Winter/Spring 2001): 138–40; Louis Fisher, "The Law: Litigating the War Power with *Campbell v. Clinton,*" *Presidential Studies Quarterly* 30 (September 2000): 564–74.

27. See Thomas M. Franck, "Courts and Foreign Policy," *Foreign Policy* 83 (Summer 1991): 66–86; Thomas M. Franck, *Political Questions: Does the Rule of Law Apply to Foreign Affairs?* (Princeton, NJ: Princeton University Press, 1992); Glennon, *Constitutional Diplomacy,* 314–42; Koh, *National Security Constitution,* 134–49.

28. See James M. Lindsay, *Congress and Nuclear Weapons* (Baltimore, MD: Johns Hopkins University Press, 1991), 116–21, 145–59; Stephen R. Weissman, A *Culture of Deference: Congress's Failure of Leadership in Foreign Policy* (New York: Basic Books, 1995).

29. Among others, see Holbert N. Carroll, *The House of Representatives and Foreign Affairs,* rev. ed. (Boston: Little, Brown, 1966); Samuel P. Huntington, *The Common Defense: Strategic Programs in National Politics* (New York: Columbia University Press, 1961); James A. Robinson, *Congress and Foreign Policy-Making: A Study in Legislative Influence and Initiative,* rev. ed. (Homewood, IL: Dorsey Press, 1967); H. Bradford Westerfield, "Congress and Closed Politics in National Security Affairs," *Orbis* 10 (Fall 1966): 737–53.

30. See, for example, Jeremy D. Rosner, *The New Tug-of-War: Congress, the Executive Branch, and National Security* (Washington, D.C.: Carnegie Endowment, 1995).

31. For discussions of Powell's difficulties in influencing administration policy, see Bob Woodward, *Bush at War* (New York: Simon & Schuster, 2002); Bob Woodward, *Plan of Attack* (New York: Simon & Schuster, 2004); Bob Woodward, *State of Denial* (New York: Simon & Schuster, 2006); and Karen DeYoung, *Soldier: The Life of Colin Powell* (New York: Knopf, 2006).

32. Vincent A. Auger, "The National Security Council System after the Cold War," in *U.S. Foreign Policy after the Cold War: Processes, Structures, and Policies,* ed. Randall B. Ripley and James M. Lindsay (Pittsburgh, University of Pittsburgh Press, 1997); David Rothkopf, *Running the World* (New York: Public Affairs, 2005).

33. See I. M. Destler, "National Security Management: What Presidents Have Wrought," *Political Science Quarterly* 95 (Winter 1980/81): 578–80.

34. Seymour M. Hersh, *The Price of Power: Kissinger in the Nixon White House* (New York: Summit Books, 1983); Walter Isaacson, *Kissinger: A Biography* (New York: Simon & Schuster, 1992).

35. See Bert A. Rockman, "America's Departments of State: Irregular and Regular Syndromes of Policymaking," *American Political Science Review* 75 (December 1981): 911–27; Hedrick Smith, *The Power Game: How Washington Works* (New York: Random House, 1988), chaps. 15–16.

36. See Morton H. Halperin, *Bureaucratic Politics and Foreign Policy* (Washington, D.C.: Brookings Institution, 1974), 235–93.

37. Quoted in Marriner S. Eccles, *Beckoning Frontiers* (New York: Knopf, 1951), 336.

38. The classic works on bureaucratic politics are Graham Allison, *Essence of Decision: Explaining the Cuban Missile Crisis* (Boston: Little, Brown, 1971); Halperin, *Bureaucratic Politics and Foreign Policy*; John D. Steinbruner, *The Cybernetic Theory of Decision: New Dimensions of Political Analysis* (Princeton, NJ: Princeton University Press, 1974).

39. See Barry Rubin, *Secrets of State: The State Department and the Struggle over U.S. Foreign Policy* (New York: Oxford University Press, 1985).

40. See Duncan L. Clarke, "Why State Can't Lead," *Foreign Policy* 66 (Spring 1987): 128–42.

41. James Coates and Michael Kilian, *Heavy Losses: The Dangerous Decline of American Defense* (New York: Viking, 1985); Smith, *The Power Game,* chap. 8; Richard A. Stubbing with Richard A. Mendel, *The Defense Game: An Insider Explores the Astonishing Realities of America's Defense Establishment* (New York: Harper & Row, 1986).

42. James Schlesinger, "The Office of the Secretary of Defense," in *Reorganizing the Pentagon: Leadership in War and Peace,* eds. Robert J. Art, Vincent Davis, and Samuel P. Huntington (New York: Pergamon-Brassey's, 1985), 261.

43. *National Defense Budget Estimates for FY 2001,* Office of the Under Secretary of Defense (Comptroller), March 2000, Table 7–2, 206–7, available at www.dtic.mil/comptroller/fy2001 budget.

44. *Budget of the United States Government, Fiscal Year 2009: Historical Tables* (Washington, D.C.: U.S. Government Printing Office, 2008), 61.

45. See Michael E. O'Hanlon, *Technological Change and the Future of Warfare* (Washington, D.C.: Brookings Institution, 2000).

46. See, for example, Stephen Biddle, *Military Power: Explaining Victory and Defeat in Modern Battle* (Princeton, NJ: Princeton University Press, 2005); Michael O'Hanlon, "Military Policy: Getting the Best Bang for the Bucks," in *Agenda for the Nation,* eds. Henry J. Aaron, James M. Lindsay, and Pietro S. Nivola (Washington, D.C.: Brookings Institution, 2003), 389–92.

47. For discussions of the structure of the intelligence community, see Loch Johnson, *Secret Agencies: U.S. Intelligence in a Hostile World* (New Haven, CT: Yale University Press, 1996); Jeffrey T. Richelson, *The U.S. Intelligence Community,* 4th ed. (Boulder, CO: Westview, 1999).

48. See Robert M. Gates, "The CIA and American Foreign Policy," *Foreign Affairs* 66 (Winter 1987/88): 215–30; Loch K. Johnson, *America's Secret Power: The CIA in a Democratic Society* (New York: Oxford University Press, 1989); Loch K. Johnson, "Covert Action and Accountability: Decision-Making for America's Secret Foreign Policy," *International Studies Quarterly* 33 (March 1989): 81–109; Frank J. Smist, *Congress Oversees the United States Intelligence Community, 1947–1994,* 2nd ed. (Knoxville: University of Tennessee Press, 1994).

49. See James Bamford, *Body of Secrets: Anatomy of the Ultra-Secret National Security Agency* (New York: Anchor Books, 2002).

50. See Bruce D. Berkowitz and Allan E. Goodman, *Best Truth: Intelligence in the Information Age* (New Haven, CT: Yale University Press, 2002).

51. National Commission on Terrorist Attacks upon the United States, *9/11 Commission Report* (New York: Norton, 2004), available at www.9-11commission.gov/report/911Report.pdf.

52. For discussions of Congress's role in making foreign policy, see Cecil V. Crabb, Jr., and Pat M. Holt, *Invitation to Struggle: Congress, the President, and Foreign Policy,* 4th ed. (Washington, D.C.: CQ Press, 1992); Barbara Hinckley, *Less than Meets the Eye: Foreign Policy Making and the Myth of the Assertive Congress* (Chicago: University of Chicago Press, 1994); James M. Lindsay, *Congress and the Politics of U.S. Foreign Policy* (Baltimore, MD: Johns Hopkins University Press, 1994); Thomas E. Mann, ed., A *Question of Balance: The President, the Congress, and Foreign Policy* (Washington, D.C.: Brookings Institution, 1990); Paul E. Peterson, *The President, the Congress, and the Making of Foreign Policy* (Norman: University of Oklahoma Press, 1994); Randall B. Ripley and James M. Lindsay, eds., *Congress Resurgent: Foreign and Defense Policy on Capitol Hill* (Ann Arbor: University of Michigan Press, 1993); Gerard Felix Warburg, *Conflict and Consensus: The Struggle between Congress and the President over Foreign Policymaking* (New York: Harper & Row, 1989); Weissman, *A Culture of Deference.*

53. Daniel S. Cheever and H. Field Haviland, Jr., *American Foreign Policy and the Separation of Powers* (Cambridge, MA: Harvard University Press, 1952), 48; W. Stull Holt, *Treaties Defeated in the Senate* (Baltimore, MD: Johns Hopkins University Press, 1933), 121; Warburg, *Conflict and Consensus,* 20; Woodrow Wilson, *Congressional Government: A Study in American Politics* (Gloucester, MA: Peter Smith, 1973).

54. Quoted in James L. Sundquist, *The Decline and Resurgence of Congress* (Washington, D.C.: Brookings Institution, 1981), 125.

55. See, for example, John Lehman, *Making War: The 200-Year-Old Battle between the President and Congress over How America Goes to War* (New York: Scribner's, 1992), 214; Mackubin Thomas Owens, "Micromanaging the Defense Budget," *Public Interest* 100 (Summer 1990): 132.

56. On the International Relations and Foreign Relations committees, see James M. McCormick, "Decision Making in the Foreign Affairs and Foreign Relations Committees," in *Congress Resurgent: Foreign and Defense Policy on Capitol Hill,* eds. Randall B. Ripley and James M. Lindsay (Ann Arbor: University of Michigan Press, 1993). On the National Security and Armed Services committees, see Christopher J. Deering, "Decision Making in the Armed Services Committees," in *Congress Resurgent: Foreign and Defense Policy on Capitol Hill,* eds. Randall B. Ripley and James M. Lindsay (Ann Arbor: University of Michigan Press, 1993). On the Intelligence Committees, see Johnson, "Covert Action and Accountability," 81–109; Frederick M. Kaiser, "Congressional Rules and Conflict Resolution: Access to Information in the House Select Committee on Intelligence," *Congress and the Presidency* 15 (Spring 1988): 49–73. On the Appropriations Committees, see Joseph White, "Decision Making in the Appropriations Subcommittees on Defense and Foreign Operations," in *Congress Resurgent: Foreign and Defense Policy on Capitol Hill,* eds. Randall B. Ripley and James M. Lindsay (Ann Arbor: University of Michigan Press, 1993).

57. See James M. Lindsay, "Congress and Foreign Policy: Why the Hill Matters," *Political Science Quarterly* 107 (Winter 1992–93): 609–26; Lindsay, *Congress and the Politics of U.S. Foreign Policy,* chaps. 4–6; James M. Lindsay and Randall B. Ripley, "How Congress Influences Foreign and Defense Policy," in *Congress Resurgent: Foreign and Defense Policy on Capitol Hill,* eds. Randall B. Ripley and James M. Lindsay (Ann Arbor: University of Michigan Press, 1993), 22–35.

58. For extended legal analyses of the power of the purse, see William C. Banks and Peter Raven-Hansen, *National Security Law and the Power of the Purse* (New York: Oxford University Press, 1994); Kate Stith, "Congress' Power of the Purse," *Yale Law Journal* 97 (June 1988): 1343–96.

59. See Sharyn O'Halloran, "Congress and Foreign Trade Policy," in *Congress Resurgent: Foreign and Defense Policy on Capitol Hill,* eds. Randall B. Ripley and James M. Lindsay (Ann Arbor: University of Michigan Press, 1993).

60. See Norman Ornstein, "Interest Groups, Congress, and American Foreign Policy," in *American Foreign Policy in an Uncertain World,* ed. David P. Forsythe (Lincoln: University of Nebraska Press, 1984); John T. Tierney, "Congressional Activism in Foreign Policy: Its Varied Forms and Stimuli," in *The New Politics of American Foreign Policy,* ed. David A. Deese (New York: St. Martin's, 1994); John T. Tierney, "Interest Group Involvement in Congressional Foreign and Defense Policy," in *Congress Resurgent: Foreign and Defense Policy on Capitol Hill,* eds. Randall B. Ripley and James M. Lindsay (Ann Arbor: University of Michigan Press, 1993).

61. The literature on ethnic lobbies is large. Among others, see Mitchell Bard, *The Water's Edge and Beyond: Defining the Limits to Domestic Influence on United States Middle East Policy* (New Brunswick, NJ: Transaction, 1991); Rodolfo O. de la Garza and Harry P. Pachon, eds., *Latinos and U.S. Foreign Policy: Representing the "Homeland"?* (Lanham, MD: Rowman and Littlefield, 2000); David Howard Goldberg, *Foreign Policy and Ethnic Interest Groups* (Westport, CT: Greenwood, 1990); Tony Smith, *Foreign Attachments: The Power of Ethnic Groups in the Making of American Foreign Policy* (Cambridge, MA: Harvard University Press, 2000); Eric Uslaner, "A Tower of Babel on Foreign Policy?" in *Interest Group Politics,* 3rd ed., eds. Allan J. Cigler and Burdett A. Loomis (Washington, D.C.: CQ Press, 1991); Paul Y. Watanabe,

Ethnic Groups, Congress, and American Foreign Policy (Westport, CT: Greenwood, 1984).

62. For an exception to this view, see John H. Aldrich, John L. Sullivan, and Eugene Borgida, "Foreign Affairs and Issue Voting: Do Presidential Candidates 'Waltz before a Blind Audience?'" *American Political Science Review* 83 (March 1989): 123–42.

63. James M. McCormick and Michael Black, "Ideology and Senate Voting on the Panama Canal Treaty," *Legislative Studies Quarterly* 8 (February 1983): 45–64; George Moffett III, *The Limits of Victory: The Ratification of the Panama Canal Treaties* (Ithaca, NY: Cornell University Press, 1985).

64. See Richard Sobel, "Public Opinion about U.S. Intervention in Nicaragua: A Polling Addendum," in *Public Opinion in U.S. Foreign Policy,* ed. Richard Sobel (Lanham, MD: Rowman and Littlefield, 1993); Richard Sobel, "Public Opinion about United States Intervention in El Salvador and Nicaragua," *Public Opinion Quarterly* 53 (Spring 1990): 114–28.

65. Holly Idelson, "National Opinion Ambivalent as Winds of War Stir Gulf," *Congressional Quarterly Weekly Report,* January 5, 1991, 14–17; John Mueller, "American Public Opinion and the Gulf War: Some Polling Issues," *Public Opinion Quarterly* 57 (Spring 1993): 87; John Mueller, *Policy and Opinion in the Gulf War* (Chicago: University of Chicago Press, 1994).

66. See, for example, Michael R. Kagay, "Occupation Lifts Clinton's Standing in Poll, but Many Americans Are Skeptical," *New York Times,* September 21, 1994; Richard Morin, "How Do People Really Feel about Bosnia?" *Washington Post National Weekly Edition,* December 4–10, 1995, 34; "Opinion Outlook: Views on National Security," *National Journal,* July 30, 1994, 1822; "Opinion Outlook: Views on National Security," *National Journal,* November 25, 1995, 2945; "Opinion Outlook: Views on National Security," *National Journal,* December 23, 1995, 3174.

67. PollingReport.com, "Iraq," available at www.pollingreport.com/iraq6.htm.

68. Gabriel Almond, *The American People and Foreign Policy* (New York: Harcourt, Brace, 1950); Lloyd A. Cantril and Hadley Cantril, *The Political Beliefs of Americans: A Study of Public Opinion* (New York: Clarion Books, 1968); John E. Rielly, ed., *American Public Opinion and U.S. Foreign Policy* (Chicago: Chicago Council on Foreign Relations, 1991).

69. See, for example, "America's Grade on 20th-Century European Wars: F," *New York Times,* December 3, 1995; Gilbert M. Grosvenor, "Superpowers Not So Super in Geography," *National Geographic* 176 (December 1989): 817; Warren E. Leary, "Two Superpowers Failing in Geography," *New York Times,* November 9, 1989.

70. Mark G. McDonough, "Panama Canal Treaty Negotiations (B): Concluding a Treaty," Case no. C14-79-224, 1979, 11.

71. The classic treatment of the rally-'round-the-flag effect is John E. Mueller, *War, Presidents, and Public Opinion* (New York: Wiley, 1973). For more recent studies of the rally effect, see Bradley Lian and John R. O'Neal, "Presidents, the Use of Military Force, and Public Opinion," *Journal of Conflict Resolution* 37 (June 1993): 277–300; Suzanne L. Parker, "Toward an Understanding of 'Rally' Effects: Public Opinion in the Persian Gulf War," *Public Opinion Quarterly* 59 (Winter 1995): 526–46.

72. PollingReport.com, "Iraq."

73. See Bruce W. Jentleson, "The Pretty Prudent Public: Post Post-Vietnam American Opinion on the Use of Force," *International Studies Quarterly* 36 (March 1992): 49–74.

74. See James M. Lindsay, "The New Apathy," *Foreign Affairs* 79 (September/ October 2000): 2–8.

75. Quoted in Ivo H. Daalder and James M. Lindsay, "To Fight Terror, Increase Foreign Aid," *Newsday,* February 15, 2002.

76. See James M. Lindsay and Michael E. O'Hanlon, *Defending America: The Case for Limited National Missile Defense* (Washington, D.C.: Brookings Institution, 2001).

77. See Michael E. O'Hanlon, et al., *Protecting the American Homeland: One Year On* (Washington, D.C.: Brookings Institution, 2003).

78. CNN/Opinion Research Corporation Poll, June 26-29, 2008. Available at www.pollingreport.com/trade.htm.

79. Warrick J. McKibbin and Peter Wilcoxen, *Climate Change Policy after Kyoto: Blueprint for a Realistic Approach* (Washington, D.C.: Brookings Institution, 2003).

80. The term *intermestic issues* was coined in Bayless Manning, "The Congress, the Executive, and Intermestic Affairs: Three Proposals," *Foreign Affairs* 55 (January 1977): 306–24.

81. Keith Bradsher, "Administration Cuts Flurry of Deals," *New York Times,* November 16, 1993; Keith Bradsher, "Clinton's Shopping List for Votes Has Ring of Grocery Buyer's List," *New York Times,* November 17, 1993.

82. See National Academy of Sciences, *Policy Implications of Greenhouse Warming* (Washington, D.C.: National Academy Press, 1991).

83. See, for example, Bob Benenson, "Free Trade Carries the Day as GATT Easily Passes," *Congressional Quarterly Weekly Report,* December 3, 1994, 3446–50; Alissa J. Rubin, "Dole, Clinton Compromise Greases Wheels for GATT," *Congressional Quarterly Weekly Review,* November 26, 1994, 3405.

APPENDIX A
The Declaration of Independence

IN CONGRESS, 4 JULY 1776

The Unanimous Declaration of the Thirteen United States of America

When, in the course of human events, it becomes necessary for one people to dissolve the political bands which have connected them with another, and to assume, among the powers of the earth, the separate and equal station to which the laws of nature and of nature's God entitle them, a decent respect to the opinions of mankind requires that they should declare the causes which impel them to the separation.

We hold these truths to be self-evident: That all men are created equal; that they are endowed by their Creator with certain unalienable rights; that among these are life, liberty, and the pursuit of happiness; that, to secure these rights, governments are instituted among men, deriving their just powers from the consent of the governed; that whenever any form of government becomes destructive of these ends, it is the right of the people to alter or to abolish it, and to institute new government, laying its foundation on such principles, and organizing its powers in such form, as to them shall seem most likely to effect their safety and happiness. Prudence, indeed, will dictate that governments long established should not be changed for light and transient causes; and accordingly all experience hath shown that mankind are more disposed to suffer, while evils are sufferable, than to right themselves by abolishing the forms to which they are accustomed. But when a long train of abuses and usurpations, pursuing invariably the same object, evinces a design to reduce them under absolute despotism, it is their right, it is their duty, to throw off such government, and to provide new guards for their future security. Such has been the patient sufferance of these colonies; and such is now the necessity which constrains them to alter their former systems of government. The history of the present King of Great Britain is a history of repeated injuries and usurpations, all having in direct object the establishment of an absolute tyranny over these states. To prove this, let facts be submitted to a candid world.

He has refused his assent to laws, the most wholesome and necessary for the public good.

He has forbidden his governors to pass laws of immediate and pressing importance, unless suspended in their operation till his assent should be obtained; and, when so suspended, he has utterly neglected to attend to them.

He has refused to pass other laws for the accommodation of large districts of people, unless those people would relinquish the right of representation in the legislature, a right inestimable to them, and formidable to tyrants only.

He has called together legislative bodies at places unusual, uncomfortable, and distant from the depository of their public records, for the sole purpose of fatiguing them into compliance with his measures.

He has dissolved representative houses repeatedly, for opposing, with manly firmness, his invasions on the rights of the people.

He has refused for a long time, after such dissolutions, to cause others to be elected; whereby the legislative powers, incapable of annihilation, have returned to the people at large for their exercise; the state remaining, in the mean time, exposed to all the dangers of invasion from without and convulsions within.

He has endeavored to prevent the population of these states; for that purpose obstructing the laws for naturalization of foreigners; refusing to pass others to encourage their migration hither, and raising the conditions of new appropriations of lands.

He has obstructed the administration of justice, by refusing his assent to laws for establishing judiciary powers.

He has made judges dependent on his will alone, for the tenure of their offices, and the amount and payment of their salaries.

He has erected a multitude of new offices, and sent hither swarms of officers to harass our people and eat out their substance.

He has kept among us, in times of peace, standing armies, without the consent of our legislatures.

He has affected to render the military independent of, and superior to, the civil power.

He has combined with others to subject us to a jurisdiction foreign to our constitution, and unacknowledged by our laws, giving his assent to their acts of pretended legislation:

For quartering large bodies of armed troops among us;

For protecting them, by a mock trial, from punishment for any murders which they should commit on the inhabitants of these states;

For cutting off our trade with all parts of the world;

For imposing taxes on us without our consent;

For depriving us, in many cases, of the benefits of trial by jury;

For transporting us beyond seas, to be tried for pretended offenses;

For abolishing the free system of English laws in a neighboring province, establishing therein an arbitrary government, and enlarging its boundaries, so as to render it at once an example and fit instrument for introducing the same absolute rule into these colonies;

For taking away our charters, abolishing our most valuable laws, and altering fundamentally the forms of our governments;

For suspending our own legislatures, and declaring themselves invested with power to legislate for us in all cases whatsoever.

He has abdicated government here, by declaring us out of his protection and waging war against us.

He has plundered our seas, ravaged our coasts, burned our towns, and destroyed the lives of our people.

He is at this time transporting large armies of foreign mercenaries to complete the works of death, desolation, and tyranny already begun with circumstances of cruelty and perfidy scarcely paralleled in the most barbarous ages, and totally unworthy the head of a civilized nation.

He has constrained our fellow-citizens, taken captive on the high seas, to bear arms against their country, to become the executioners of their friends and brethren, or to fall themselves by their hands.

He has excited domestic insurrections among us, and has endeavored to bring on the inhabitants of our frontiers the merciless Indian savages, whose known rule of warfare is an undistinguished destruction of all ages, sexes, and conditions.

In every stage of these oppressions we have petitioned for redress in the most humble terms; our repeated petitions have been answered only by repeated injury. A prince, whose character is thus marked by every act which may define a tyrant, is unfit to be the ruler of a free people.

Nor have we been wanting in attentions to our British brethren. We have warned them, from time to time, of attempts by their legislature to extend an unwarrantable jurisdiction over us. We have reminded them of the circumstances of our emigration and settlement here. We have appealed to their native justice and magnanimity; and we have conjured them, by the ties of our common kindred, to disavow these usurpations, which would inevitably interrupt our connections and correspondence. They, too, have been deaf to the voice of justice and of consanguinity. We must, therefore, acquiesce in the necessity which denounces our separation, and hold them, as we hold the rest of mankind, enemies in war, in peace friends.

We, therefore, the representatives of the United States of America, in General Congress assembled, appealing to the Supreme Judge of the world for the rectitude of our intentions, do, in the name and by authority of the good people of these colonies, solemnly publish and declare, that these United Colonies are, and of right ought to be, FREE AND INDEPENDENT STATES, that they are absolved from all allegiance to the British crown, and that all political connection between them, and the state of Great Britain is, and ought to be, totally dissolved; and that, as free and independent states, they have full power to levy war, conclude peace, contract alliances, establish commerce, and do all other acts and things which independent states may of right do. And for the support of this declaration, with a firm reliance on the protection of Divine Providence, we mutually pledge to each other our lives, our fortunes, and our sacred honor.

Massachusetts John Hancock *[President]*

New Hampshire
Josiah Bartlett
William Whipple
Matthew Thornton

Massachusetts Bay
Samuel Adams
John Adams
Robert Treat Paine
Elbridge Gerry

Rhode Island
Stephen Hopkins
William Ellery

Connecticut
Roger Sherman
Samuel Huntington
William Williams
Oliver Wolcott

New York
William Floyd
Philip Livingston
Francis Lewis
Lewis Morris

New Jersey
Richard Stockton
John Witherspoon
Francis Hopkinson
John Hart
Abraham Clark

Pennsylvania
Robert Morris
Benjamin Rush
Benjamin Franklin
John Morton
George Clymer
James Smith

George Taylor
James Wilson
George Ross

Delaware
Caesar Rodney
George Read
Thomas McKean

Maryland
Samuel Chase
William Paca
Thomas Stone
Charles Carroll, of Carrollton

Virginia
George Wythe
Richard Henry Lee
Thomas Jefferson

Benjamin Harrison
Thomas Nelson, Jr.
Francis Lightfoot Lee
Carter Braxton

North Carolina
William Hooper
Joseph Hewes
John Penn

South Carolina
Edward Rutledge
Thomas Heyward, Jr.
Thomas Lynch, Jr.
Arthur Middleton

Georgia
Button Gwinnett
Lyman Hall
George Walton

Resolved. That copies of the Declaration be sent to the several assemblies, conventions, and committees, or councils of safety, and to the several commanding officers of the continental troops; that it be proclaimed in each of the United States, at the head of the army.

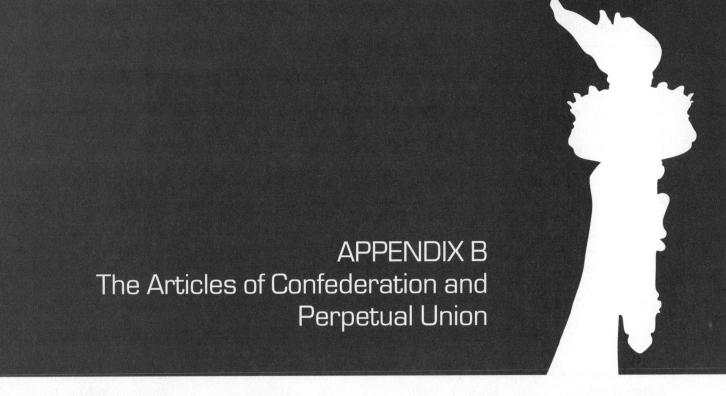

APPENDIX B
The Articles of Confederation and Perpetual Union

1 March 1781. To all to whom these Presents shall come, we the under signed Delegates of the States affixed to our Names, send greeting

Whereas the Delegates of the United States of America, in Congress assembled, did, on the 15th day of November, in the Year of Our Lord One thousand Seven Hundred and Seventy seven, and in the Second Year of the Independence of America, agree to certain articles of Confederation and perpetual Union between the States of New-hampshire, Massachusetts-bay, Rhode-island and Providence Plantations, Connecticut, New York, New Jersey, Pennsylvania, Delaware, Maryland, Virginia, North-Carolina, South-Carolina, and Georgia in the words following, viz. Articles of Confederation and perpetual Union between the states of New-hampshire, Massachusetts-bay, Rhode-island and Providence Plantations, Connecticut, New-York, New-Jersey, Pennsylvania, Delaware, Maryland, Virginia, North-Carolina, South-Carolina and Georgia.

Article I. The Stile of this confederacy shall be "The United States of America."

Article II. Each state retains its sovereignty, freedom, and independence, and every Power, Jurisdiction and right, which is not by this confederation expressly delegated to the United States, in Congress assembled.

Article III. The said states hereby severally enter into a firm league of friendship with each other, for their common defence, the security of their Liberties, and their mutual and general welfare, binding themselves to assist each other, against all force offered to, or attacks made upon them, or any of them, on account of religion, sovereignty, trade, or any other pretence whatever.

Article IV. The better to secure and perpetuate mutual friendship and intercourse among the people of the different states in this union, the free inhabitants of each of these states, paupers, vagabonds and fugitives from justice excepted, shall be entitled to all privileges and immunities of free citizens in the several states; and the people of each state shall have free ingress and regress to and from any other state, and shall enjoy therein all the privileges of trade and commerce, subject to the same duties, impositions and restrictions as the inhabitants thereof respectively, provided that such restriction shall not extend so far as to prevent the removal of property imported into any state, to any other state, of which the Owner is an inhabitant; provided also that no imposition, duties or restriction shall be laid by any state, on the property of the united states, or either of them.

If any Person guilty of, or charged with treason, felony, or other high misdemeanor in any state, shall flee from Justice, and be found in any of the united states, he shall, upon demand of the

Governor or executive power, of the state from which he fled, be delivered up and removed to the state having jurisdiction of his offence.

Full faith and credit shall be given in each of these states to the records, acts and judicial proceedings of the courts and magistrates of every other state.

Article V. For the more convenient management of the general interests of the united states, delegates shall be annually appointed in such manner as the legislature of each state shall direct, to meet in Congress on the first Monday in November, in every year, with a power reserved to each state, to recall its delegates, or any of them, at any time within the year, and to send others in their stead, for the remainder of the Year.

No state shall be represented in Congress by less than two, nor by more than seven Members; and no person shall be capable of being a delegate for more than three years in any term of six years; nor shall any person, being a delegate, be capable of holding any office under the united states, for which he, or another for his benefit receives any salary, fees or emolument of any kind.

Each state shall maintain its own delegates in a meeting of the states, and while they act as members of the committee of the states.

In determining questions in the united states in Congress assembled, each state shall have one vote.

Freedom of speech and debate in Congress shall not be impeached or questioned in any Court, or place out of Congress, and the members of congress shall be protected in their persons from arrests and imprisonments, during the time of their going to and from, and attendance on congress, except for treason, felony, or breach of the peace.

Article VI. No state, without the Consent of the united states in congress assembled, shall send any embassy to, or receive any embassy from, or enter into any conference, agreement, alliance or treaty with any King, prince or state; nor shall any person holding any office of profit or trust under the united states, or any of them, accept of any present, emolument, office or title of any kind whatever from any king, prince or foreign state, nor shall the united states in congress assembled, or any of them, grant any title of nobility.

No two or more states shall enter into any treaty, confederation or alliance whatever between them, without the consent of the united states in congress assembled, specifying accurately the purposes for which the same is to be entered into, and how long it shall continue.

No state shall lay any imposts or duties, which may interfere with any stipulations in treaties, entered into by the united states in congress assembled, with any king, prince or state, in pursuance of any treaties already proposed by congress, to the courts of France and Spain.

No vessels of war shall be kept up in time of peace by any state, except such number only, as shall be deemed necessary by the united states in congress assembled, for the defence of such state, or its trade; nor shall any body of forces be kept up by any state, in time of peace, except such number only, as in the judgment of the united states, in congress assembled, shall be deemed requisite to garrison the forts necessary for the defence of such state; but every state shall always keep up a well regulated and disciplined militia, sufficiently armed and accoutred, and shall provide and constantly have ready for use, in public stores, a due number of field pieces and tents, and a proper quantity of arms, ammunition and camp equipage.

No state shall engage in any war without the consent of the united states in congress assembled, unless such state be actually invaded by enemies, or shall have received certain advice of a resolution being formed by some nation of Indians to invade such state, and the danger is so imminent as not to admit of a delay till the united states in congress assembled can be consulted: nor shall any state grant commissions to any ships or vessels of war, nor letters of marque or reprisal, except it be after a declaration of war by the united states in congress assembled, and then only against the kingdom or state and the subjects thereof, against which war has been so declared, and under such regulations as shall be established by the united states in congress assembled, unless such state be infested by pirates, in which case vessels of war may be fitted out for that occasion, and kept so long as the danger shall continue, or until the united states in congress assembled, shall determine otherwise.

Article VII. When land-forces are raised by any state for the common defence, all officers of or under the rank of colonel, shall be appointed by the legislature of each state respectively, by whom such forces shall be raised, or in such manner as such state shall direct, and all vacancies shall be filled up by the State which first made the appointment.

Article VIII. All charges of war, and all other expenses that shall be incurred for the common defence or general welfare, and allowed by the united states in congress assembled, shall be defrayed out of a common treasury, which shall be supplied by the several states in proportion to the value of all land within each state, granted to or surveyed for any Person, as such land and the buildings and improvements thereon shall be estimated according to such mode as the united states in congress assembled, shall from time to time direct and appoint.

The taxes for paying that proportion shall be laid and levied by the authority and direction of the legislatures of the several states within the time agreed upon by the united states in congress assembled.

Article IX. The united states in congress assembled, shall have the sole and exclusive right and power of determining on peace and war, except in the cases mentioned in the sixth article—or sending and receiving ambassadors—entering into treaties and alliances, provided that no treaty of commerce shall be made whereby the legislative power of the respective states shall be restrained from imposing such imposts and duties on foreigners as their own people are subjected to, or from prohibiting the exportation or importation of any species of goods or commodities whatsoever—of establishing rules for deciding in all cases, what captures on land or water shall be legal, and in what manner prizes taken by land or naval forces in the service of the united states shall be divided or appropriated—or granting letters of marque and reprisal in times of peace—appointing courts for the trial of piracies and felonies committed on the high seas and establishing courts for receiving and determining finally appeals in all cases of captures, provided that no member of congress shall be appointed a judge of any of the said courts.

The united states in congress assembled shall also be the last resort on appeal in all disputes and differences now subsisting or that hereafter

may arise between two or more states concerning boundary, jurisdiction or any other cause whatever; which authority shall always be exercised in the manner following. Whenever the legislative or executive authority or lawful agent of any state in controversy with another shall present a petition to congress stating the matter in question and praying for a hearing, notice thereof shall be given by order of congress to the legislative or executive authority of the other state in controversy, and a day assigned for the appearance of the parties by their lawful agents, who shall then be directed to appoint by joint consent, commissioners or judges to constitute a court for hearing and determining the matter in question: but if they cannot agree, congress shall name three persons out of each of the united states, and from the list of such persons each party shall alternately strike out one, the petitioners beginning, until the number shall be reduced to thirteen; and from that number not less than seven, nor more than nine names as congress shall direct, shall in the presence of congress be drawn out by lot, and the person whose name shall be so drawn or any five of them, shall be commissioners or judges, to hear and finally determine the controversy, so always as a major part of the judges who shall hear the cause shall agree in the determination: and if either party shall neglect to attend at the day appointed, without showing reasons, which congress shall judge sufficient, or being present shall refuse to strike, the congress shall proceed to nominate three persons out of each state, and the secretary of congress shall strike in behalf of such party absent or refusing; and the judgment and sentence of the court to be appointed, in the manner before prescribed, shall be final and conclusive; and if any of the parties shall refuse to submit to the authority of such court, or to appear or defend their claim or cause, the court shall nevertheless proceed to pronounce sentence, or judgment, which shall in like manner be final and decisive, the judgment or sentence and other proceedings being in either case transmitted to congress, and lodged among the acts of congress for the security of the parties concerned: provided that every commissioner, before he sits in judgment, shall take an oath to be administered by one of the judges of the supreme or superior court of the state, where the cause shall be tried, "well and truly to hear and determine the matter in question, according to the best of his judgment, without favour, affection or hope of reward:" provided also, that no state shall be deprived of territory for the benefit of the united states.

All controversies concerning the private right of soil claimed under different grants of two or more states, whose jurisdictions as they may respect such lands, and the states which passed such grants are adjusted, the said grants or either of them being at the same time claimed to have originated antecedent to such settlement of jurisdiction, shall on the petition of either party to the congress of the united states, be finally determined as near as may be in the same manner as is before prescribed for deciding disputes respecting territorial jurisdiction between different states.

The united states in congress assembled shall also have the sole and exclusive right and power of regulating the alloy and value of coin struck by their own authority, or by that of the respective states—fixing the standards of weights and measures throughout the united states—regulating the trade and managing all affairs with the Indians, not members of any of the states, provided that the legislative right of any state within its own limits be not infringed or violated—establishing and regulating post-offices from one state to another, throughout all the united states, and exacting such postage on the papers passing thro' the same as may be requisite to defray the expenses of the said office—appointing all officers of the land forces, in the service of the united states, excepting regimental officers—appointing all the officers of the naval forces, and commissioning all officers whatever in the service of the united states—making rules for the government and regulation of the said land and naval forces, and directing their operations.

The united states in congress assembled shall have authority to appoint a committee, to sit in the recess of congress, to be denominated "A Committee of the States," and to consist of one delegate from each state; and to appoint such other committees and civil officers as may be necessary for managing the general affairs of the united states under their direction—to appoint

one of their number to preside, provided that no person be allowed to serve in the office of president more than one year in any term of three years; to ascertain the necessary sums of money to be raised for the service of the united states, and to appropriate and apply the same for defraying the public expenses—to borrow money, or emit bills on the credit of the united states, transmitting every half year to the respective states an account of the sums of money so borrowed or emitted—to build and equip a navy—to agree upon the number of land forces, and to make requisitions from each state for its quota, in proportion to the number of white inhabitants in such state; which requisition shall be binding, and thereupon the legislature of each state shall appoint the regimental officers, raise the men and cloath, arm and equip them in a soldier like manner, at the expence of the united states; and the officers and men so cloathed, armed and equipped shall march to the place appointed, and within the time agreed on by the united states in congress assembled: But if the united states in congress assembled shall, on consideration of circumstances judge proper that any state should not raise men, or should raise a smaller number than its quota, and that any other state should raise a greater number of men than the quota thereof, such extra number shall be raised, officered, cloathed, armed and equipped in the same manner as the quota of such state, unless the legislature of such state shall judge that such extra number cannot be safely spared out of the same, in which case they shall raise officer, cloath, arm and equip as many of such extra number as they judge can be safely spared. And the officers and men so cloathed, armed and equipped, shall march to the place appointed, and within the time agreed on by the united states in congress assembled.

The united states in congress assembled shall never engage in a war, not grant letters of marque and reprisal in time of peace, nor enter into any treaties or alliances, nor coin money, nor regulate the value thereof, nor ascertain the sums and expenses necessary for the defence and welfare of the united states, or any of them, nor emit bills, nor borrow money on the credit of the united states, nor appropriate money, nor agree upon the number of vessels of war, to be built or purchased, or the number of land or sea forces to be raised, nor appoint a commander in chief of the army or navy, unless nine states assent to the same: nor shall a question on any other point, except for adjourning from day to day be determined, unless by the votes of a majority of the united states in congress assembled.

The congress of the united states shall have power to adjourn to any time within the year, and to any place within the united states, so that no period of adjournment be for a longer duration than the space of six Months, and shall publish the Journal of their proceedings monthly, except such parts thereof relating to treaties, alliances or military operations, as in their judgment require secrecy; and the yeas and nays of the delegates of each state on any question shall be entered on the Journal, when it is desired by any delegate; and the delegates of a state, or any of them, at his or their request shall be furnished with a transcript of the said Journal, except such parts as are above excepted, to lay before the legislatures of the several states.

Article X. The committee of the states, or any nine of them, shall be authorized to execute, in the recess of congress, such of the powers of congress as the united states in congress assembled, by the consent of nine states, shall from time to time think expedient to vest them with; provided that no power be delegated to the said committee, for the exercise of which, by the articles of confederation, the voice of nine states in the congress of the united states assembled is requisite.

Article XI. Canada acceding to this confederation, and joining in the measures of the united states, shall be admitted into, and entitled to all the advantages of this union: but no other colony shall be admitted into the same, unless such admission be agreed to by nine states.

Article XII. All bills of credit emitted, monies borrowed and debts contracted by, or under the authority of congress, before the assembling of the united states, in pursuance of the present confederation, shall be deemed and considered as a charge against the united states, for payment and satisfaction whereof the said united states, and the public faith are hereby solemnly pledged.

Article XIII. Every state shall abide by the determinations of the united states in congress assembled, on all questions which by this confederation are submitted to them. And the Articles of this confederation shall be inviolably observed by every state, and the union shall be perpetual; nor shall any alteration at any time hereafter be made in any of them; unless such alteration be agreed to in a congress of the united states, and be afterwards confirmed by the legislatures of every state.

And Whereas it hath pleased the Great Governor of the World to incline the hearts of the legislatures we respectively represent in congress, to approve of, and to authorize us to ratify the said articles of confederation and perpetual union. Know Ye that we the undersigned delegates, by virtue of the power and authority to us given for that purpose, do by these presents, in the name and in behalf of our respective constituents, fully and entirely ratify and confirm each and every of the said articles of confederation and perpetual union, and all and singular the matters and things therein contained: And we do further solemnly plight and engage the faith of our respective constituents, that they shall abide by the determinations of the united states in congress assembled, on all questions, which by the said confederation are submitted to them. And that the articles thereof shall be inviolably observed by the states we respectively represent, and that the union shall be perpetual. In Witness whereof we have here-unto set our hands in Congress. Done at Philadelphia in the state of Pennsylvania the ninth day of July, in the Year of our Lord one Thousand seven Hundred and Seventy-eight, and in the third year of the independence of America.

Josiah Bartlett,
John Wentworth, Junr
August 8th, 1778,
⎤
⎦ On the part and behalf of the State of New Hampshire.

John Hanson,
March 1, 1781,
Daniel Carroll, DO
⎤
⎦ On the part and behalf of the State of Maryland.

John Hancock,
Samuel Adams,
Elbridge Gerry,
Francis Dana,
James Lovell,
Samuel Holten,
⎤
⎦ On the part and behalf of the State of Massachusetts Bay.

Thos McKean,
Feby 22d, 1779,
John Dickinson,
May 5th, 1779
Nicholas Van Dyke,
⎤
⎦ On the part and behalf of the State of Delaware.

William Ellery,
Henry Marchant,
John Collins,
⎤
⎦ On the part and behalf of the State of Rhode-Island and Providence Plantations.

Richard Henry Lee,
John Banister,
Thomas Adams,
Jno Harvic,
Francis Lightfoot Lee,
⎤
⎦ On the part and behalf of the State of Virginia.

Roger Sherman,
Samuel Huntington,
Oliver Wolcott,
Titus Hosmer,
Andrew Adams,
⎤
⎦ On the part and behalf of the State of Connecticut.

John Penn,
July 21st 1778,
Corn^s Harnett,
Jno Williams,
⎤
⎦ On the part and behalf of the State of North Carolina.

Ja^s Duane,
Fra: Lewis,
Wm Duer,
Gouv^r Morris,
⎤
⎦ On the part and behalf of the State of New York.

Henry Laurens,
William Henry Drayton,
Jno Mathews,
Richd Hutson
Thos Heyward, Junr.
⎤
⎦ On the part and behalf of the State of South Carolina.

Jno Witherspoon,
Nathl Scudder
⎤
⎦ On the part and behalf of the State of New Jersey, 26, 1778.

Jno Walton,
24th July, 1778,
Edwd Telfair,
Edwd Lanworthy,
⎤
⎦ On the part and behalf of the State of Georgia.[1]

Robert Morris,
Daniel Roberdeau,
Jon. Bayard Smith,
William Clingar,
Joseph Reed,
22d July, 1778,
⎤
⎦ On the part and behalf of the State of Pennsylvania.

Note: These Articles of Confederation are taken from *Journals of the Continental Congress,* Library of Congress edition, Vol. XIX (1912), 214.

The Articles of Confederation were agreed to by the Congress, 15 November 1777. They were, as appears from the list of signatures affixed to these Articles, signed at different times by the delegates of the different American states. On 1 March 1781, the delegates from Maryland, the last of the states to take action, "did, in behalf of the said state of Maryland, sign and ratify the said articles, by which act the Confederation of the United States of America was completed, each and every of the Thirteen United States, from New Hampshire to Georgia, both included, having adopted and confirmed, and by their delegates in Congress, ratified the same."

[1]The proceedings of this day with respect to the signing of the Articles of Confederation, the Articles themselves, and the signers are entered in the *Papers of the Continental Congress,* No. 9 (History of the Confederation), but not in the Journal itself. The Articles are printed here from the original roll in the Bureau of Rolls and Library, Department of State.

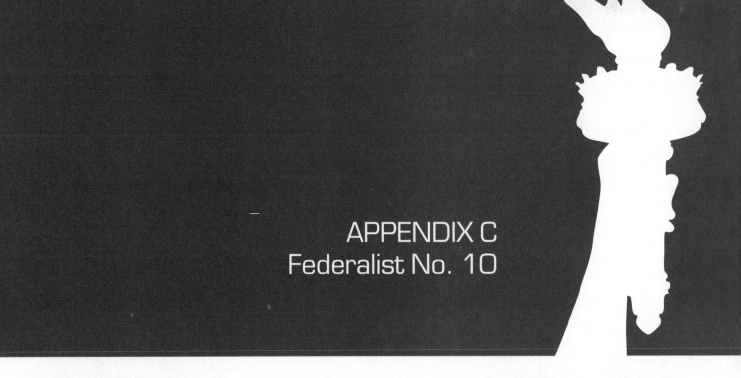

APPENDIX C
Federalist No. 10

JAMES MADISON
22 NOVEMBER 1787

To the People of the State of New York

Among the numerous advantages promised by a well constructed Union, none deserves to be more accurately developed than its tendency to break and control the violence of faction. The friend of popular governments, never finds himself so much alarmed for their character and fate, as when he contemplates their propensity to this dangerous vice. He will not fail therefore to set a due value on any plan which, without violating the principles to which he is attached, provides a proper cure for it. The instability, injustice and confusion introduced into the public councils, have in truth been the mortal diseases under which popular governments have every where perished; as they continue to be the favorite and fruitful topics from which the adversaries to liberty derive their most specious declamations. The valuable improvements made by the American Constitutions on the popular models, both ancient and modern, cannot certainly be too much admired; but it would be an unwarrantable partiality, to contend that they have as effectually obviated the danger on this side as was wished and expected. Complaints are every where heard from our most considerate and virtuous citizens, equally the friends of public and private faith, and of public and personal liberty; that our governments are too unstable; that the public good is disregarded in the conflicts of rival parties; and that measures are too often decided, not according to the rules of justice, and the rights of the minor party; but by the superior force of an interested and over-bearing majority. However anxiously we may wish that these complaints had no foundation, the evidence of known facts will not permit us to deny that they are in some degree true. It will be found indeed, on a candid review of our situation, that some of the distresses under which we labor, have been erroneously charged on the operation of our governments; but it will be found, at the same time, that other causes will not alone account for many of our heaviest misfortunes; and particularly, for that prevailing and increasing distrust of public engagements, and alarm for private rights, which are echoed from one end of the continent to the other. These must be chiefly, if not wholly, effects of the unsteadiness and injustice, with which a factious spirit has tainted our public administrations.

By a faction I understand a number of citizens, whether amounting to a majority or minority of the whole, who are united and actuated by some common impulse of passion, or of interest, adverse to the rights of other citizens, or to the permanent and aggregate interests of the community.

There are two methods of curing the mischiefs of faction: the one, by removing its causes; the other, by controlling its effects.

There are again two methods of removing the causes of faction: the one by destroying the liberty which is essential to its existence; the other, by giving to every citizen the same opinions, the same passions, and the same interests.

It could never be more truly said than of the first remedy, that it is worse than the disease. Liberty is to faction, what air is to fire, an ailment without which it instantly expires. But it could not be a less folly to abolish liberty, which is essential to political life, because it nourishes faction, than it would be to wish the annihilation of air, which is essential to animal life, because it imparts to fire its destructive agency.

The second expedient is as impracticable, as the first would be unwise. As long as the reason of man continues fallible, and he is at liberty to exercise it, different opinions will be formed. As long as the connection subsists between his reason and his self-love, his opinions and his passions will have a reciprocal influence on each other; and the former will be objects to which the latter will attach themselves. The diversity in the faculties of men from which the rights of property originate, is not less an insuperable obstacle to a uniformity of interests. The protection of these faculties is the first object of Government. From the protection of different and unequal faculties of acquiring property, the possession of different degrees and kinds of property immediately results: and from the influence of these on the sentiments and views of the respective proprietors, ensues a division of the society into different interests and parties.

The latent causes of faction are thus sown in the nature of man; and we see them every where brought into different degrees of activity, according to the different circumstances of civil society. A zeal for different opinions concerning religion, concerning Government and many other points, as well of speculation as of practice; an attachment to different leaders ambitiously contending for pre-eminence and power; or to persons of other descriptions whose fortunes have been interesting to the human passions, have in turn divided #mankind into parties, inflamed them with mutual animosity, and rendered them much more disposed to vex and oppress each other, than to cooperate for their common good. So strong is this propensity of mankind to fall into mutual animosities, that where no substantial occasion presents itself, the most frivolous and fanciful distinctions have been sufficient to kindle their unfriendly passions, and excite their most violent conflicts. But the most common and durable sources of factions, has been the various and unequal distribution of property. Those who hold, and those who are without property, have ever formed distinct interests in society. Those who are creditors, and those who are debtors, fall under a like discrimination. A landed interest, a manufacturing interest, a mercantile interest, a monied interest, with many lesser interests, grow up of necessity in civilized nations, and divide them into different classes, actuated by different sentiments and views. The regulation of these various and interfering interests forms the principal task of modern Legislation and involves the spirit of party and faction in the necessary and ordinary operations of Government.

No man is allowed to be a judge in his own cause; because his interest would certainly bias his judgment, and, not improbably, corrupt his integrity. With equal, nay with greater reason, a body of men, are unfit to be both judges and parties, at the same time; yet, what are many of the most important acts of legislation, but so many judicial determinations, not indeed concerning the rights of single persons, but concerning the rights of large bodies of citizens, and what are the different classes of legislators, but advocates and parties to the causes which they determine? Is a law proposed concerning private debts? It is a question to which the creditors are parties on one side, and the debtors on the other. Justice ought to hold the balance between them. Yet the parties are and must be themselves the judges; and the most numerous party, or, in other words, the most powerful faction must be expected to prevail. Shall domestic manufactures be encouraged, and in what degree, by restrictions on foreign manufactures? are questions which would be differently decided by the landed and the manufacturing classes; and probably by neither, with a sole regard to justice and the public good. The apportionment of taxes on the various descriptions of property, is an act which seems to require the most exact impartiality; yet, there is perhaps no legislative act in which greater opportunity and temptation are given to a predominant party, to trample on the rules of justice. Every shilling with which they over-burden the inferior number, is a shilling saved to their own pockets.

It is in vain to say, that enlightened statesmen will be able to adjust these clashing interests, and render them all subservient to the public good. Enlightened statesmen will not always be at the helm: Nor, in many cases, can such an adjustment be made at all, without taking into view indirect and remote considerations, which will rarely prevail over the immediate interest which one party may find in disregarding the rights of another, or the good of the whole.

The inference to which we are brought, is, that the causes of faction cannot be removed; and that relief is only to be sought in the means of controlling its *effects.*

If a faction consists of less than a majority, relief is supplied by the republican principle, which enables the majority to defeat its sinister views by regular vote: It may clog the administration, it may convulse the society; but it will be unable to execute and mask its violence under the forms of the Constitution. When a majority is included in a faction, the form of popular government on the other hand enables it to sacrifice to its ruling passion or interest, both the public good and the rights of other citizens. To secure the public good, and private rights, against the danger of such a faction, and at the same time to preserve the spirit and the form of popular government, is then the great object to which our enquiries are directed: Let me add that it is the great desideratum, by which alone this form of government can be rescued from the opprobrium under which it has so long labored, and be recommended to the esteem and adoption of mankind.

By what means is this object attainable? Evidently by one of two only. Either the existence of the same passion or interest in a majority at the same time, must be prevented; or the majority, having such co-existent passion or interest, must be rendered, by their number and local situation, unable to concert and carry into effect schemes of oppression. If the impulse and the opportunity be suffered to coincide, we well know that neither moral nor religious motives can be relied on as an adequate control. They are not found to be such on the injustice and violence of individuals, and lose their efficacy in proportion to the number combined together; that is, in proportion as their efficacy becomes needful.

From this view of the subject, it may be concluded, that a pure Democracy, by which I mean, a Society, consisting of a small number of citizens, who assemble and administer the Government in person, can admit of no cure for the mischiefs of faction. A common passion or interest will, in almost every case, be felt by a majority of the whole; a communication and concert results from the form of Government itself; and there is nothing to check the inducements to sacrifice the weaker party, or an obnoxious individual. Hence it is, that such Democracies have ever been spectacles of turbulence and contention; have ever been found incompatible with personal security, or the rights of property; and have in general been as short in their lives, as they have been violent in their deaths. Theoretic politicians, who have patronized this species of Government, have erroneously supposed, that by reducing mankind to a perfect equality in their political rights, they would, at the same time, be perfectly equalized and assimilated in their possessions, their opinions, and their passions.

A republic, by which I mean a government in which the scheme of representation takes place, opens a different prospect, and promises the cure for which we are seeking. Let us examine the points in which it varies from pure democracy, and we shall comprehend both the nature of the cure and the efficacy which it must derive from the union.

The two great points of difference, between a democracy and a republic, are, first, the delegation of the government, in the latter, to a small number of citizens, elected by the rest; secondly, the greater number of citizens, and greater sphere of country, over which the latter may be extended.

The effect of the first difference is, on the one hand, to refine and enlarge the public views, by passing them through the medium of a chosen body of citizens, whose wisdom may best discern the true interest of their country, and whose patriotism and love of justice, will be least likely to sacrifice it to temporary or partial considerations. Under such a regulation, it may well happen, that the public voice, pronounced by the representatives of the people, will be more consonant to the public good, than if pronounced by the people themselves, convened for the purpose. On the other hand the effect may be inverted. Men of factious tempers, of local prejudices, or of sinister designs, may by intrigue, by corruption, or by other means, first obtain the suffrages, and then betray the interest of the people. The question resulting is, whether small or extensive republics are most favorable to the election of proper guardians of the public weal, and it is clearly decided in favor of the latter by two obvious considerations.

In the first place, it is to be remarked that, however small the republic may be, the representatives must be raised to a certain number, in order to guard against the cabals of a few; and that however large it may be, they must be limited to a certain number, in order to guard against the confusion of a multitude. Hence, the number of representatives in the two cases not being in proportion to that of the constituents, and being proportionally greatest in the small republic, it follows, that if the proportion of fit characters be not less in the large than in the small republic, the former will present a greater option, and consequently a greater probability of a fit choice.

In the next place, as each Representative will be chosen by a greater number of citizens in the large than in the small Republic, it will be more difficult for unworthy candidates to practise with success the vicious arts, by which elections are too often carried; and the suffrages of the people being more free, will be more likely to center on men who possess the most attractive merit, and the most diffusive and established characters.

It must be confessed, that in this, as in most other cases, there is a mean, on both sides of which inconveniences will be found to lie. By enlarging too much the number of electors, you render the representative too little acquainted with all their local circumstances and lesser interests; as by reducing it too much, you render him unduly attached to these, and too little fit to comprehend and pursue great and national objects. The Federal Constitution forms a happy combination in this respect; the great and aggregate interests being referred to the national, the local and particular, to the state legislatures.

The other point of difference is, the greater number of citizens and extent of territory which may be brought within the compass of Republican, than of Democratic Government; and it is this circumstance principally which renders factious combinations less to be dreaded in the former, than in the latter. The smaller the society, the fewer probably will be the distinct parties and interests composing it; the fewer the distinct parties and interests, the more frequently will a majority be found of the same party; and the smaller the number of individuals composing a majority, and the smaller the compass within which they are placed, the more easily will they concert and execute their plans of oppression. Extend the sphere, and you take in a greater variety of parties and interests; you make it less probable that a majority of the whole will have a common motive to invade the rights of other citizens; or if such a common motive exists, it will be more difficult for all who feel it to discover their own strength, and to act in unison with each other. Besides other impediments, it may be remarked, that where there is a consciousness of unjust or dishonorable purposes, communication is always checked by distrust, in proportion to the number whose concurrence is necessary.

Hence it clearly appears, that the same advantage, which a Republic has over a Democracy, in controlling the effects of faction, is enjoyed by a large over a small Republic—is enjoyed by the Union over the States composing it. Does this advantage consist in the substitution of Representatives, whose enlightened views and virtuous sentiments render them superior to local prejudices, and to schemes of injustice? It will not be denied, that the Representation of the Union will be most likely to possess these requisite endowments. Does it consist in the greater security afforded by a greater variety of parties, against the event of any one party being able to outnumber and oppress the rest? In an equal degree does the increased variety of parties, comprised within the Union, increase this security? Does it, in fine, consist in the greater obstacles opposed to the concert and accomplishment of the secret wishes of an unjust and interested majority? Here, again, the extent of the Union gives it the most palpable advantage.

The influence of factious leaders may kindle a flame within their particular States, but will be unable to spread a general conflagration through the other States: a religious sect, may degenerate into a political faction in a part of the Confederacy but the variety of sects dispersed over the entire face of it, must secure the national Councils against any danger from that source: a rage for paper money, for an abolition of debts, for an equal division of property, or for any other improper or wicked project, will be less apt to pervade the whole body of the Union, than a particular member of it; in the same proportion as such a malady is more likely to taint a particular county or district, than an entire State.

In the extent and proper structure of the Union, therefore, we behold a Republican remedy for the diseases most incident to Republican Government. And according to the degree of pleasure and pride, we feel in being Republicans, ought to be our zeal in cherishing the spirit, and supporting the character of Federalists.

Publius

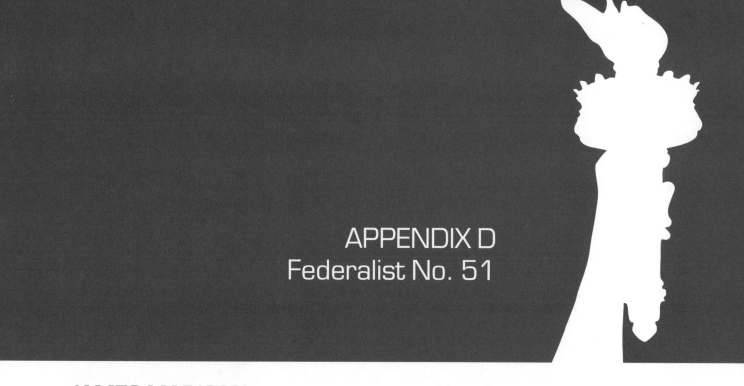

APPENDIX D
Federalist No. 51

JAMES MADISON
6 FEBRUARY 1788

To the People of the State of New York

To what expedient then shall we finally resort for maintaining in practice the necessary partition of power among the several departments, as laid down in the constitution? The only answer that can be given is, that as all these exterior provisions are found to be inadequate, the defect must be supplied, by so contriving the interior structure of the government, as that its several constituent parts may, by their mutual relations, be the means of keeping each other in their proper places. Without presuming to undertake a full development of this important idea, I will hazard a few general observations, which may perhaps place it in a clearer light, and enable us to form a more correct judgment of the principles and structure of the government planned by the convention.

In order to lay a due foundation for that separate and distinct exercise of the different powers of government, which to a certain extent, is admitted on all hands to be essential to the preservation of liberty, it is evident that each department should have a will of its own; and consequently should be so constituted, that the members of each should have as little agency as possible in the appointment of the members of the others. Were this principle rigorously adhered to, it would require that all the appointments for the supreme executive, legislative, and judiciary magistracies, should be drawn from the same fountain of authority, the people, through channels, having no communication whatever with one another. Perhaps such a plan of constructing the several departments would be less difficult in practice than it may in contemplation appear. Some difficulties however, and some additional expense, would attend the execution of it. Some deviations therefore from the principle must be admitted. In the constitution of the judiciary department in particular, it might be inexpedient to insist rigorously on the principle; first, because peculiar qualifications being essential in the members, the primary consideration ought to be to select that mode of choice, which best secures these qualifications; secondly, because the permanent tenure by which the appointments are held in that department, must soon destroy all sense of dependence on the authority conferring them.

It is equally evident that the members of each department should be as little dependent as possible on those of the others, for the emoluments annexed to their offices. Were the executive magistrate, or the judges, not independent of the legislature in this particular, their independence in every other would be merely nominal.

But the great security against a gradual concentration of the several powers in the same department, consists in giving to those who administer each department, the necessary constitutional means, and personal motives, to resist encroachments of the others. The provision for defense must in this, as in all other cases, be made commensurate to the danger of attack. Ambition must be made to counteract ambition. The interest of the man must be connected with the constitutional right of the place. It may be a reflection on human nature, that such devices should be necessary to control the abuses of government. But what is government itself but the greatest of all reflections on human nature? If men were angels, no government would be necessary. If angels were to govern men, neither external nor internal controls on government would be necessary. In framing a government which is to be administered by men over men, the great difficulty lies in this: You must first enable the government to control the governed; and in the next place, oblige it to control itself. A dependence on the people is no doubt the primary control on the government; but experience has taught mankind the necessity of auxiliary precautions.

This policy of supplying by opposite and rival interests, the defect of better motives, might be traced through the whole system of human affairs, private as well as public. We see it particularly displayed in all the subordinate distributions of power; where the constant aim is to divide and arrange the several offices in such a manner as that each may be a check on the other; that the private interest of every individual, may be a sentinel over the public rights. These inventions of prudence cannot be less requisite in the distribution of the supreme powers of the state.

But it is not possible to give to each department an equal power of self defense. In republican government the legislative authority, necessarily, predominates. The remedy for this inconveniency is, to divide the legislature into different branches; and to render them by different modes of election, and different principles of action, as little connected with each other, as the nature of their common functions, and their common dependence on the society, will admit. It may even be necessary to guard against dangerous encroachments by still further precautions. As the weight of #the legislative authority

requires that it should be thus divided, the weakness of the executive may require, on the other hand, that it should be fortified. An absolute negative, on the legislature, appears at first view to be the natural defense with which the executive magistrate should be armed. But perhaps it would be neither altogether safe, nor alone sufficient. On ordinary occasions, it might not be exerted with the requisite firmness; and on extraordinary occasions, it might be perfidiously abused. May not this defect of an absolute negative be supplied, by some qualified connection between this weaker department, and the weaker branch of the stronger department, by which the latter may be led to support the constitutional rights of the former, without being too much detached from the rights of its own department?

If the principles on which these observations are founded be just, as I persuade myself they are, and they be applied as a criterion, to the several state constitutions, and to the federal constitution, it will be found, that if the latter does not perfectly correspond with them, the former are infinitely less able to bear such a test.

There are moreover two considerations particularly applicable to the federal system of America, which place that system in a very interesting point of view.

First. In a single republic, all the power surrendered by the people, is submitted to the administration of a single government; and usurpations are guarded against by a division of the government into distinct and separate departments. In the compound republic of America, the power surrendered by the people, is first divided between two distinct governments, and then the portion allotted to each, subdivided among distinct and separate departments. Hence a double security arises to the rights of the people. The different governments will control each other; at the same time that each will be controlled by itself.

Second. It is of great importance in a republic, not only to guard the society against the oppression of its rulers; but to guard one part of the society against the injustice of the other part. Different interests necessarily exist in different classes of citizens. If a majority be united by a common interest, the rights of the minority will be insecure. There are but two methods of providing against this evil: The one by creating a will in the community independent of the majority, that is, of the society itself, the other by comprehending in the society so many separate descriptions of citizens, as will render an unjust combination of a majority of the whole, very improbable, if not impracticable. The first method prevails in all governments possessing an hereditary or self appointed authority. This at best is but a precarious security; because a power independent of the society may as well espouse the unjust views of the major, as the rightful interests, of the minor party, and may possibly be turned against both parties. The second method will be exemplified in the federal republic of the United States. While all authority in it will be derived from and dependent on the society, the society itself will be broken into so many parts, interests and classes of citizens, that the rights of individuals or of the minority, will be in little danger from interested combinations of the majority. In a free government, the security for civil rights must be the same as for religious rights. It consists in the one case in the multiplicity of interests, and in the other, in the multiplicity of sects. The degree of security in both cases will depend on the number of interests and sects; and this may be presumed to depend on the extent of country and number of people comprehended under the same government. This view of the subject must particularly recommend a proper federal system to all the sincere and considerate friends of republican government: Since it shows that in exact proportion as the territory of the union may be formed into more circumscribed confederacies or states, oppressive combinations of a majority will be facilitated, the best security under the republican form, for the rights of every class of citizens, will be diminished; and consequently, the stability and independence of some member of the government, the only other security, must be proportionally increased. Justice is the end of government. It is the end of civil society. It ever has been, and ever will be pursued, until it be obtained, or until liberty be lost in the pursuit. In a society under the forms of which the stronger faction can readily unite and oppress the weaker, anarchy may as truly be said to reign, as in a state of nature where the weaker individual is not secured against the violence of the stronger. And as in the latter state even the stronger individuals are prompted by the uncertainty of their condition, to submit to a government which may protect the weak as well as themselves: So in the former state, will the more powerful factions or parties be gradually induced by a like motive, to wish for a government which will protect all parties, the weaker as well as the more powerful. It can be little doubted, that if the state of Rhode Island was separated from the confederacy, and left to itself, the insecurity of rights under the popular form of government within such narrow limits, would be displayed by such reiterated oppressions of factious majorities, that some power altogether independent of the people would soon be called for by the voice of the very factions whose misrule had proved the necessity of it. In the extended republic of the United States, and among the great variety of interests, parties and sects which it embraces, a coalition of a majority of the whole society could seldom take place on any other principles than those of justice and the general good; and there being thus less danger to a minor from the will of the major party, there must be less pretext also, to provide for the security of the former, by introducing into the government a will not dependent on the latter; or in other words, a will independent of the society itself. It is no less certain than it is important, notwithstanding the contrary opinions which have been entertained, that the larger the society, provided it lie within a practicable sphere, the more duly capable it will be of self government. And happily for the *republican cause*, the practicable sphere may be carried to a very great extent, by a judicious modification and mixture of the federal principle.

Publius

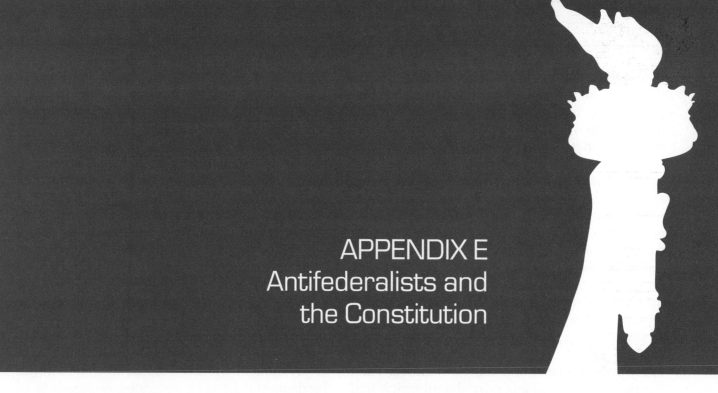

Antifederalists opposed ratification of the Constitution because they feared it would create a strong national government that would trample the rights of individual citizens. In the following selection, George Mason, a leading Antifederalist who participated in the Constitutional Convention but who refused to sign the final document, systematically details his objections to the Constitution. Like most Antifederalists, Mason concentrates his criticisms on the risks of giving too much power to the national government. James Madison, a leading Federalist, responded to Mason's objections in a letter to George Washington.

GEORGE MASON, "OBJECTIONS TO THE CONSTITUTION"

CIRCULATED EARLY OCTOBER 1787, PUBLISHED IN FULL IN THE VIRGINIA JOURNAL (ALEXANDRIA), NOVEMBER 22, 1787

Objections to the Constitution of Government formed by the Convention

There is no declaration of rights; and the laws of the general government being paramount to the laws and constitutions of the several States, the declarations of rights in the separate States are no security. Nor are the people secured even in the enjoyment of the benefits of the common law, which stands here upon no other foundation than its having been adopted by the respective acts forming the constitutions of the several States.

In the House of Representatives there is not the substance, but the shadow only of representation; which can never produce proper information in the Legislature, or inspire confidence in the people; the laws will therefore be generally made by men little concerned in, and unacquainted with their effects and consequences.

The Senate have the power of altering all money-bills, and of originating appropriations of money, and the salaries of the officers of their own appointment in conjunction with the President of the United States; although they are not the representatives of the people, or amenable to them.

These with their other great powers (viz. their power in the appointment of ambassadors and other public officers, in making treaties, and in trying all impeachments) their influence upon and connection with the supreme executive from these causes, their duration of office, and their being a constant existing body almost continually sitting, joined with their being one complete branch of the Legislature, will destroy any balance in the government, and enable them to accomplish what usurpations they please upon the rights and liberties of the people.

The judiciary of the United States is so constructed and extended as to absorb and destroy the judiciaries of the several States; thereby rendering law as tedious, intricate and expensive, and justice as unattainable by a great part of the community, as in England, and enabling the rich to oppress and ruin the poor.

The President of the United States has no constitutional council (a thing unknown in any safe and regular government) he will therefore be unsupported by proper information and advice; and will be generally directed by minions and favorites—or he will become a tool to the Senate—or a Council of State will grow out of the principal officers of the great departments; the worst and most dangerous of all ingredients for such a council in a free country; for they may be induced to join in any dangerous or oppressive measures, to shelter themselves, and prevent an inquiry into their own misconduct in office; whereas had a constitutional council been formed (as was proposed) of six member, viz. two from the eastern, two from the middle, and two from the southern States, to be appointed by vote of the States in the House of Representatives, with the same duration and rotation in office as the Senate, the Executive would always have had safe and proper information and advice, the President of such a council might have acted as Vice-President of the United States, pro tempore, upon any vacancy or disability of the chief Magistrate; and long continued sessions of the Senate would in a great measure have been prevented.

From this fatal defect of a constitutional council has arisen the improper power of the Senate, in the appointment of public officers, and the alarming dependance and connection between that branch of the Legislature and the supreme Executive.

Hence also sprung that unnecessary and dangerous officer the Vice-President; who for want of other employment is made President of the Senate; thereby dangerously blending the executive and legislative powers; besides always giving to some one of the States an unnecessary and unjust preminence over the others.

The President of the United States has the unrestrained power of granting pardons for treason; which may be sometimes exercised to screen from punishment those whom he had secretly instigated to commit the crime, and thereby prevent a discovery of his own guilt.

By declaring all treaties supreme laws of the land, the Executive and the Senate have, in many cases, an exclusive power of legislation; which might have been avoided by proper distinctions with respect to treaties, and requiring the assent of the House of Representatives, where it could be done with safety.

By requiring only a majority to make all commercial and navigation laws, the five southern States (whose produce and circumstances are totally different from that of the eight northern and eastern States) will be ruined; for such rigid and premature regulations may be made, as will enable the merchants of the northern and eastern States not only to demand an exorbitant freight, but to monopolize the purchase of the commodities at their own price, for many years: To the great injury of the landed interest, and impoverishment of the people: And the danger is the greater, as the gain on one side will be in proportion to the loss on the other. Whereas requiring two-thirds of the members present in both houses would have produced mutual moderation, promoted the general interest and removed an insuperable objection to the adoption of the government.

Under their own construction of the general clause at the end of the enumerated powers, the Congress may grant monopolies in trade and commerce, constitute new crimes, inflict unusual and severe punishments, and extend their power as far as they shall think proper; so that the State Legislatures have no security for the powers now presumed to remain to them; or the people for their rights.

There is no declaration of any kind for preserving the liberty of the press, the trial by jury in civil causes; nor against the danger of standing armies in time of peace.

The State Legislatures are restrained from laying export duties on their own produce.

The general Legislature is restrained from prohibiting the further importation of slaves for twenty odd years; though such importations render the United States weaker, and more vulnerable, and less capable of defence.

Both the general Legislature and the State Legislatures are expressly prohibited making ex post facto laws; though there never was nor can be a Legislature but must and will make such laws, when necessity and the public safety require them, which will hereafter be a breach of all the constitutions in the Union, and afford precedents for other innovations.

This government will commence in a moderate aristocracy; it is at present impossible to foresee whether it will, in its operation, produce a monarchy, or a corrupt oppressive aristocracy; it will most probably vibrate some years between the two, and then terminate between the one and the other.

JAMES MADISON TO GEORGE WASHINGTON, "A 'PROLIX' COMMENT ON MASON'S OBJECTIONS"

NEW YORK, OCTOBER 18, 1787

I have been this day honoured with your favor of the 10th instant, under the same cover with which is a copy of Col. Mason's objections to the Work of the Convention. As he persists in the temper which produced his dissent it is no small satisfaction to find him reduced to such distress for a proper gloss on it; for no other consideration surely could have led him to dwell on an objection which he acknowledged to have been in some degree removed by the Convention themselves—on the paltry right of the Senate to propose alterations in money bills—on the appointment of the vice President—President of the Senate instead of making the President of the Senate the vice President, which seemed to be the alternative—and on the *possibility*, that the Congress may misconstrue their powers & betray their trust so far as to grant monopolies in trade &c. If I do not forget too some of his other reasons were either not at all or very faintly urged at the time when alone they ought to have been urged; such as the power of the Senate in the case of treaties & of impeachments; and their duration in office. With respect to the latter point I recollect well that he more than once disclaimed opposition to it. My memory fails me also if he did not acquiesce in if not vote for, the term allowed for the further importation of slaves;

and the prohibition of duties on exports by the States. What he means by the dangerous tendency of the Judiciary I am at some loss to comprehend. It never was intended, nor can it be supposed that in ordinary cases the inferior tribunals will not have final jurisdiction in order to prevent the evils of which he complains. The great mass of suits in every State lie between Citizen & Citizen, and relate to matters not of federal cognizance. Notwithstanding the stress laid on the necessity of a Council to the President I strongly suspect, though I was a friend to the thing, that if such an one as Col. Mason proposed, had been established, and the power of the Senate in appointments to offices transferred to it, that as great a clamour would have been heard from some quarters which in general echo his Objections. What can he mean by saying that the Common law is not secured by the new Constitution, though it has been adopted by the State Constitutions. The Common law is nothing more than the unwritten law, and is left by all the Constitutions equally liable to legislative alterations. I am not sure that any notice is particularly taken of it in the Constitutions of the States. If there is, nothing more is provided than a general declaration that it shall continue along with other branches of law to be in force till legally changed. The Constitution of Virga. drawn up by Col. Mason himself, is absolutely silent on the subject. An *ordinance* passed during the same Session, declared the Common law as heretofore & all Statutes of prior date to the 4 of James I. to be still the law of the land, merely to obviate pretexts that the separation from G. Britain threw us into a State of nature, and abolished all civil rights and obligations. Since the Revolution every State has made great inroads & with great propriety in many instances on this *monarchical* code. The "revisal of the laws" by a Committe of wch. Col. Mason was a member, though not an acting one, abounds with such innovations. The abolition of the *right of primogeniture*, which I am sure Col. Mason does not disapprove, falls under this head. What could the Convention have done? If they had in general terms declared the Common law to be in force, they would have broken in upon the legal Code of every State in the most material points: they would have done more, they would have brought over from G.B. a thousand heterogeneous & antirepublican doctrines, and even the *ecclesiastical Hierarchy itself*, for that is a part of the Common law. If they had undertaken a discrimination, they must have formed a digest of laws, instead of a Constitution. This objection surely was not brought forward in the Convention, or it wd. have been placed in such a light that a repetition of it out of doors would scarcely have been hazarded. Were it allowed the weight which Col. M. may suppose it deserves, it would remain to be decided whether it be candid to arraign the Convention for omissions which were never suggested to them—or prudent to vindicate the dissent by reasons which either were not previously thought of, or must have been willfully concealed—But I am running into a comment as prolix, as it is out of place.

I find by a letter from the Chancellor (Mr. Pendleton) that he views the act of the Convention in its true light, and gives it his unequivocal approbation. His support will have great effect. The accounts we have here of some other respectable characters vary considerably. Much will depend on Mr. Henry, and I am glad to find by your letter that his favorable decision on the subject may yet be hoped for.—The Newspapers here begin to teem with vehement & virulent calumniations of the proposed Govt. As they are chiefly borrowed from the Pennsylvania papers, you see them of course. The reports however from different quarters continue to be rather flattering.

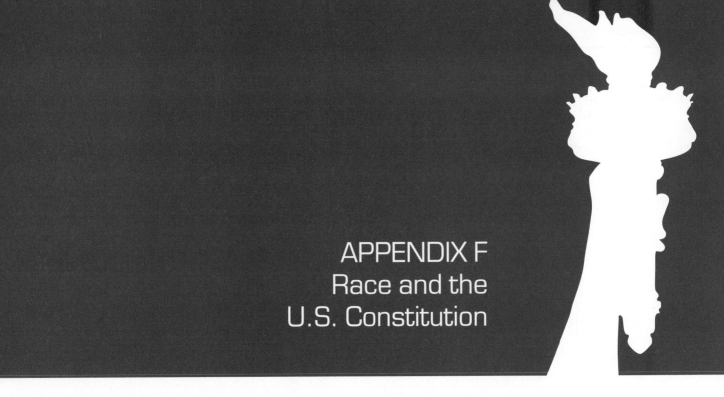

Race has been a fundamental issue in American politics since the founding of the Republic. As the following excerpts from the Supreme Court's rulings in four landmark cases show, our understanding of the civil rights guaranteed by the Constitution has changed dramatically over the past two centuries.

DRED SCOTT V. SANDFORD

19 HOW. 393; 15 L. ED. 691 (1857)

[Dred Scott was an African-American slave who moved with his owner from Missouri, a slave state, first to Illinois, a free state, and then to the Wisconsin territory, where slavery was illegal under the terms of the Missouri Compromise of 1820. In 1846, Scott asked a state court in Missouri to grant him his freedom on the ground that he had lived for two years in a free state and a free territory. Scott initially won his case, but the judgment was overturned on appeal and eventually made its way to the Supreme Court. In 1857, the Court's southern majority ruled against Scott, arguing that the Missouri Compromise was unconstitutional because Congress had no power to ban slavery in federal territories. As the following excerpt shows, the Court went even further and argued that African Americans descended from slaves were not

American citizens and thus had no right to sue in court.]

MR. CHIEF JUSTICE TANEY delivered the opinion of the Court:

. . . .

The question is simply this: Can a Negro, whose ancestors were imported into this country, and sold as slaves, become a member of the political community formed and brought into existence by the Constitution of the United States, and as such become entitled to all the rights, and privileges, and immunities, guaranteed by that instrument to the citizen? One of which rights is the privilege of suing in a court of the United States in the cases specified in the Constitution . . . .

The words "people of the United States" and "citizens" are synonymous terms, and mean the same thing. They both describe the political body who, according to our republican institutions, form the sovereignty, and who hold the power and conduct the Government through their representatives. They are what we familiarly call the "sovereign people," and every citizen is one of this people, and a constituent member of this sovereignty. The question before us is, whether the class of persons described in the plea in abatement compose a portion of this people, and are constituent members of this sovereignty? We think they are not, and that they are not included, and were not intended to be included, under the word "citizens" in the Constitution, and can therefore claim none of the rights and privileges which that instrument provides for and secures to citizens of the United States. On the contrary, they were at that time considered as a subordinate and inferior class of beings, who had been subjugated by the dominant race, and, whether emancipated or not, yet remained subject to their authority, and had no rights or privileges but such as those who held the power and the government might choose to grant them. . . .

[A review of] the legislation of the States . . . shows, in a manner not to be mistaken, the inferior and subject condition of that race at the time the Constitution was adopted, and long afterward, throughout the thirteen States by which that instrument was framed . . . . It cannot be supposed that they intended to secure to them rights, and privileges, and rank, in the new political body throughout the Union, which every one of them denied within the limits of its own dominion. More especially, it cannot be believed that the large slaveholding States regarded them as included in the word citizens, or would have consented to a Constitution which might compel them to receive them in that character from another State. For if they were so received, and entitled to the privileges and immunities of citizens, it would exempt them from the operation of the special laws and from the police regulations which they considered to be necessary for their own safety. It would give to persons of the Negro race, who were recognised as citizens in any one State of the Union, the right to enter every other State whenever they pleased, singly or in companies, without pass or passport, and without obstruction to sojourn there as long as they pleased, to go where they pleased at every hour of the day or night without molestation, unless they committed some violation of law for which a white man would be punished; and it would give them the full liberty of speech in public and in private upon all subjects upon which its own citizens might speak; to hold public meetings upon political affairs, and to keep and carry arms wherever they went. And all of this would be done in the face of the subject race of the same color, both free and slaves, and inevitably producing discontent and insubordination among them, and endangering the peace and safety of the State. . . .

Undoubtedly, a person may be a citizen, that is, a member of the community who form the sovereignty, although he exercises no share of the political power, and is incapacitated from holding particular offices. Women and minors, who form a part of the political family, cannot vote; and when a property qualification is required to vote or hold a particular office, those who have not the necessary qualification cannot vote or hold the office, yet they are citizens.

So, too, a person may be entitled to vote by the law of the State, who is not a citizen even of the State itself. And in some of the States of the Union foreigners not naturalized are allowed to vote. And the State may give the right to free negroes and mulattoes, but that does not make them citizens of the State, and still less of the United States. And the provision in the Constitution giving privileges and immunities in other States does not apply to them. . . .

No one, we presume, supposes that any change in public opinion or feeling, in relation to this unfortunate race, in the civilized nations of Europe or in this country, should induce the court to give to the words of the Constitution a more liberal construction in their favor than they were intended to bear when the instrument was framed and adopted. Such an argument would be altogether inadmissible in any tribunal called on to interpret it. If any of its provisions are deemed unjust, there is a mode prescribed in the instrument itself by which it may be amended; but while it remains unaltered, it must be construed now as it was understood at the time of its adoption. It is not only the same in words, but the same in meaning, and delegates the same powers to the Government, and reserves and secures the same rights and privileges to the citizen; and as long as it continues to exist in its present form, it speaks not only in the same words, but with the same meaning and intent with which it spoke when it came from the hands of its framers, and was voted on and adopted by the people of the United States. Any other rule of construction would abrogate the judicial character of this court, and make it the mere reflex of the popular opinion or passion of the day. This court was not created by the Constitution for such purposes. Higher and graver trusts have been confided to it, and it must not falter in the path of duty. . . .

[T]he court is of opinion, that, ... Dred Scott was not a citizen of Missouri within the meaning of the Constitution of the United States, and not entitled as such to sue in its courts....

PLESSY V. FERGUSON

163 U.S. 537; 16 SUP. CT. 1138; 41 L. ED. 256 (1896)

[In 1890, the Louisiana state legislature followed the lead of several other southern states and passed a law requiring that "all railway companies carrying passengers in their coaches in this State, shall provide equal but separate accommodations for the white, and colored, races." Homer Adolph Plessy, who was one-eighth African American by descent, was arrested for violating the statute. He was tried in the Criminal District Court of New Orleans, where Judge John H. Ferguson found him guilty. In 1896, the Supreme Court upheld Ferguson's verdict, finding that "separate but equal" laws did not violate the Fourteenth Amendment, as Plessy had argued.]

MR. JUSTICE BROWN delivered the opinion of the Court:

. . . .

The constitutionality of this act is attacked upon the ground that it conflicts both with the Thirteenth Amendment of the Constitution, abolishing slavery, and the Fourteenth Amendment, which prohibits certain restrictive legislation on the part of the States.

1. That it does not conflict with the Thirteenth Amendment, which abolished slavery and involuntary servitude, except as a punishment for crime, is too clear for argument....

A statute which implies merely a legal distinction between the white and colored races—a distinction which is founded in the color of the two races, and which must always exist so long as white men are distinguished from the other race by color—has no tendency to destroy the legal equality of the two races, or reestablish a state of involuntary servitude. Indeed, we do not understand that the Thirteenth Amendment is strenuously relied upon by the plaintiff in error in this connection.

2. By the Fourteenth Amendment, all persons born or naturalized in the United States, and subject to the jurisdiction thereof, are made citizens of the United States and of the State wherein they reside; and the States are forbidden from making or enforcing any law which shall abridge the privileges or immunities of citizens of the United States, or shall deprive any person of life, liberty, or property without due process of law, or deny to any person within their jurisdiction the equal protection of the laws....

The object of the amendment was undoubtedly to enforce the absolute equality of the two races before the law, but in the nature of things it could not have been intended to abolish distinctions based upon color, or to enforce social, as distinguished from political equality, or a commingling of the two races upon terms unsatisfactory to either. Laws permitting, and even requiring, their separation in places where they are liable to be brought into contact do not necessarily imply the inferiority of either race to the other, and have been generally, if not universally, recognized as within the competency of the state legislatures in the exercise of their police power. The most common instance of this is connected with the establishment of separate schools for white and colored children, which has been held to be a valid exercise of the legislative power even by courts of States where the political rights of the colored race have been longest and most earnestly enforced.

It is ... suggested by the learned counsel for the plaintiff in error that the same argument that will justify the state legislature in requiring railways to provide separate accommodation for the two races will also authorize them to require separate cars to be provided for people whose hair is of a certain color, or who are aliens, or who belong to certain nationalities, or to enact laws requiring colored people to walk upon one side of the street, and white people upon the other, or requiring white men's houses to be painted white, and colored men's black, or their vehicles or business signs to be of different colors, upon the theory that one side of the street is as good as the other, or that a house or vehicle of one color is as good as one of another color. The reply to all this is that every exercise of the police power must be reasonable, and extend only to such laws as are enacted in good faith for the promotion of the public good, and not for the annoyance or oppression of a particular class. . . .

So far, then, as a conflict with the Fourteenth Amendment is concerned, the case reduces itself to the question whether the statute of Louisiana is a reasonable regulation, and with respect to this there must necessarily be a large discretion on the part of the legislature. In determining the question of reasonableness it is at liberty to act with reference to the established usages, customs, and traditions of the people, and with a view to the promotion of their comfort, and the preservation of the public peace and good order. Gauged by this standard, we cannot say that a law which authorizes or even requires the separation of the two races in public conveyances is unreasonable, or more obnoxious to the Fourteenth Amendment than the acts of Congress requiring separate schools for colored children in the District of Columbia, the constitutionality of which does not seem to have been questioned, or the corresponding acts of state legislatures.

We consider the underlying fallacy of the plaintiff's argument to consist in the assumption that the enforced separation of the two races stamps the colored race with a badge of inferiority. If this be so, it is not by reason of anything found in the act, but solely because the colored race chooses to put that construction upon it. The argument necessarily assumes that if, as has been more than once the case, and is not unlikely to be so again, the colored race should become the dominant power in the state legislature, and should enact a law in precisely similar terms, it would thereby relegate the white race to an inferior position. We imagine that the white race, at least, would not acquiesce in this assumption. The argument also assumes that social prejudices may be overcome by legislation, and that equal rights cannot be secured to the Negro except by an enforced commingling of the two races. We cannot accept this proposition. If the two races are to meet upon terms of social equality, it must be the result of natural affinities, a mutual appreciation of each other's merits, and a voluntary consent of individuals. . . . Legislation is powerless to eradicate racial instincts or to abolish distinctions based upon physical differences, and the attempt to do so can only result in accentuating the difficulties of the present situation. If the civil and political rights of both races be equal

one cannot be inferior to the other civilly or politically. If one race be inferior to the other socially, the Constitution of the United States cannot put them upon the same plane. . . .

[Justice John Marshall Harlan dissented from the majority's ruling in **Plessy v. Ferguson**. *He argued that the "Constitution is color-blind" and requires that all citizens be treated equally under the law.]*

MR. JUSTICE HARLAN, dissenting:

. . . .

. . . It was said in argument that the statute of Louisiana does not discriminate against either race, but prescribes a rule applicable alike to white and colored citizens. But this argument does not meet the difficulty. Everyone knows that the statute in question had its origin in the purpose, not so much to exclude white persons from railroad cars occupied by blacks, as to exclude colored people from coaches occupied by or assigned to white persons . . . No one would be so wanting in candor as to assert the contrary. The fundamental objection, therefore, to the statute is that it interferes with the personal freedom of citizens . . . If a white man and a black man choose to occupy the same public conveyance on a public highway, it is their right to do so, and no government, proceeding alone on grounds of race, can prevent it without infringing the personal liberty of each.

. . . In view of the Constitution, in the eye of the law, there is in this country no superior, dominant, ruling class of citizens. There is no caste here. Our Constitution is color-blind, and neither knows nor tolerates classes among citizens. In respect of civil rights, all citizens are equal before the law. The humblest is the peer of the most powerful. The law regards man as man, and takes no account of his surroundings or of his color when his civil rights as guaranteed by the supreme law of the land are involved.

. . . The sure guaranty of the peace and security of each race is the clear, distinct, unconditional recognition by our governments, National and State, of every right that inheres in civil freedom, and of the equality before the law of all citizens of the United States without regard to race. State enactments regulating the enjoyment of civil rights upon the basis of race, and cunningly devised to defeat legitimate results of the war, under the pretence of recognizing equality of rights, can have no other result than to render permanent peace impossible, and to keep alive a conflict of races, the continuance of which must do harm to all concerned.

... The arbitrary separation of citizens, on the basis of race, while they are on a public highway, is a badge of servitude wholly inconsistent with the civil freedom and the equality before the law established by the Constitution. It cannot be justified upon any legal grounds.

... We boast of the freedom enjoyed by our people above all other peoples. But it is difficult to reconcile that boast with a state of the law which, practically, puts the brand of servitude and degradation upon a large class of our fellow-citizens, our equals before the law. The thin disguise of "equal" accommodations for passengers in railroad coaches will not mislead anyone, nor atone for the wrong this day done....

I am of opinion that the statute of Louisiana is inconsistent with the personal liberty of citizens, white and black, in that State, and hostile to both the spirit and letter of the Constitution of the United States....

BROWN ET AL. V. BOARD OF EDUCATION

347 U.S. 483; 74 SUP. CT. 693; 98 L. ED. 591 (1954)

*[In 1950, Oliver Brown, a railroad worker in Topeka, Kansas, attempted to enroll his daughter Linda in the third grade at the Sumner School, a public school for whites located only four blocks from his home. When school officials refused to admit Linda because she was African American, Brown sued the Board of Education for the city of Topeka. Brown's lawsuit eventually reached the Supreme Court, where it was considered along with several other cases challenging the constitutionality of segregated public schools. In 1954, a unanimous Court ruled that segregated school systems denied African-American children equal protection under the law, thereby violating the Fourteenth Amendment. The Court's decision in **Brown et al. v. Board of Education***

*effectively overturned the decision it had reached fifty years earlier in **Plessy v. Ferguson**.]*

MR. CHIEF JUSTICE WARREN delivered the opinion of the Court:

· · · ·

These cases come to us from the States of Kansas, South Carolina, Virginia, and Delaware. They are premised on different facts and different local conditions, but a common legal question justifies their consideration together in this consolidated opinion.

In each of the cases minors of the Negro race, through their legal representatives, seek the aid of the courts in obtaining admission to the public schools of their community on a nonsegregated basis. In each instance, they had been denied admission to schools attended by white children under laws requiring or permitting segregation according to race. This segregation was alleged to deprive the plaintiffs of the equal protection of the laws under the Fourteenth Amendment. In each of the cases other than the Delaware case, a three-judge federal district court denied relief to the plaintiffs on the so-called "separate but equal" doctrine announced by this Court in *Plessy v. Ferguson*....

The plaintiffs contend that segregated public schools are not "equal" and cannot be made "equal," and that hence they are deprived of the equal protection of the laws. Because of the obvious importance of the question presented, the Court took jurisdiction. Argument was heard in the 1952 Term, and reargument was heard this Term on certain questions propounded by the Court.

Reargument was largely devoted to the circumstances surrounding the adoption of the Fourteenth Amendment in 1868. It covered exhaustively consideration of the Amendment in Congress, ratification by the states, then existing practices in racial segregation, and the view of the proponents and opponents of the Amendment. This discussion and our own investigation convince us that, although these sources cast some light, it is not enough to resolve the problem with which we are faced. At best, they are inconclusive. The most avid proponents of the postwar Amendments undoubtedly intended them to remove all legal distinctions among "all persons born or naturalized in the United States." Their opponents, just as certainly, were antagonistic to both the letter and the spirit of the Amendments and wished them to have the most limited effect. What others in Congress and the state legislatures had in mind cannot be determined with any degree of certainty.

An additional reason for the inclusive nature of the Amendment's history, with respect to segregated schools, is the status of public education at that time. In the South, the movement toward free common schools, supported by general taxation, had not yet taken hold. Education of white children was largely in the hands of private groups. Education of Negroes was almost nonexistent, and practically all of the race were illiterate. In fact, any education of Negroes was forbidden by law in some states. Today, in contrast, many Negroes have achieved outstanding success in the arts and science as well as in the business and professional world. It is true that public education had already advanced further in the North, but the effect of the Amendment on northern states was generally ignored in the congressional debates. Even in the North, the conditions of public education did not approximate those existing today. The curriculum was usually rudimentary; ungraded schools were common in rural areas; the school term was but three months a year in many states; and compulsory school attendance was virtually unknown. As a consequence, it is not surprising that there should be so little in the history of the Fourteenth Amendment relating to its intended effect on public education.

In the first cases in this Court construing the Fourteenth Amendment, decided shortly after its adoption, the Court interpreted it as proscribing all state-imposed discriminations against the Negro race. The doctrine of "separate but equal" did not make its appearance in this Court until 1896 in the case of *Plessy v. Ferguson* ... involving not education but transportation. American courts have since labored with the doctrine for over half a century ... in the field of public education. In *Cumming v. County Board of Education* ... and *Gong Lum v. Rice* ... the validity of the doctrine itself was not challenged. In more recent cases, all on the graduate-school level, inequality was found in that specific benefits enjoyed by white students were denied to Negro students of the same educational qualifications ... In none of these cases was it necessary to

re-examine the doctrine to grant relief to the Negro plaintiff. And in *Sweatt v. Painter* ... the Court expressly reserved decision on the question whether *Plessy v. Ferguson* should be held inapplicable to public education.

In the instant cases, that question is directly presented. Here, unlike *Sweatt v. Painter*, there are findings below that the Negro and white schools involved have been equalized, or are being equalized, with respect to buildings, curricula, qualifications and salaries of teachers, and other "tangible" factors. Our decision, therefore, cannot turn on merely a comparison of these tangible factors in the Negro and white schools involved in each of the cases. We must look instead to the effect of segregation itself on public education ...

We come then to the question presented: Does segregation of children in public schools solely on the basis of race, even though the physical facilities and other "tangible" factors may be equal, deprive the children of the minority group of equal educational opportunities? We believe that it does.

... [I]n finding [in *Sweatt v. Painter*] that a segregated law school for Negroes could not provide them equal educational opportunities, this Court relied in large part on "those qualities which are incapable of objective measurement but which make for greatness in a law school." In *McLaurin v. Oklahoma State Regents* ... the Court, in requiring that a Negro admitted to a white graduate school be treated like all other students, again resorted to intangible considerations: "... his ability to study, to engage in discussions and exchange views with other students, and, in general, to learn his profession." Such considerations apply with added force to children in grade and high schools. To separate them from others of similar age and qualifications solely because of their race generates a feeling of inferiority as to their status in the community that may affect their hearts and minds in a way unlikely ever to be undone. The effect of this separation on their educational opportunities was well stated by a finding in the Kansas case by a court which nevertheless felt compelled to rule against the Negro plaintiffs:

"Segregation of white and colored children in public schools has a detrimental effect upon the colored children. The impact is greater when it has the sanction of the law; for the policy of separating the races is usually interpreted as denoting the inferiority of the Negro group. A sense of inferiority affects the motivation of a child to learn. Segregation with the sanction of law, therefore, has a tendency to retard the educational and mental development of Negro children and to deprive them of some of the benefits they would receive in a racially integrated school system."

Whatever may have been the extent of psychological knowledge at the time of *Plessy v. Ferguson*, this finding is amply supported by modern authority. Any language in *Plessy v. Ferguson* contrary to this finding is rejected.

We conclude that in the field of public education the doctrine of "separate but equal" has no place. Separate educational facilities are inherently unequal. Therefore, we hold that the plaintiffs and others similarly situated for whom the actions have been brought are, by reason of the segregation complained of, deprived of the equal protection of the laws guaranteed by the Fourteenth Amendment....

BROWN V. BOARD OF EDUCATION [BROWN II—THE IMPLEMENTATION DECISION]

349 U.S. 294; 75 S. CT. 753; 99 L.ED. 1083(1955)

*[Although Brown et al. v. **Board of Education** held that segregated public schools violated the Fourteenth Amendment, the case did not address the question of relief, that is, how the nation should desegregate its public schools. Instead, the Supreme Court scheduled further arguments on the question of relief. After hearing new arguments from the original parties to the lawsuit as well as from the Attorney General of the United States and the attorneys general of six states, the Court ruled in 1955 that the federal courts should oversee desegregation efforts. While recognizing that practical considerations made it impossible to end segregation immediately, the Court ruled that desegregation should proceed with "all deliberate speed."]*

MR. CHIEF JUSTICE WARREN delivered the opinion of the Court:

. . . .

These cases were decided on May 17, 1954. The opinions of that date, declaring the fundamental principle that racial discrimination in public education is unconstitutional, are incorporated herein by reference. All provisions of federal, state, or local law requiring or permitting such discrimination must yield to this principle. There remains for consideration the manner in which relief is to be accorded....

Full implementation of these constitutional principles may require solution of varied local school problems. School authorities have the primary responsibility for elucidating, assessing, and solving these problems; courts will have to consider whether the action of school authorities constitutes good faith implementation of the governing constitutional principles. Because of their proximity to local conditions and the possible need for further hearings, the courts which originally heard these cases can best perform this judicial appraisal. Accordingly, we believe it appropriate to remand the cases to those courts.

In fashioning and effectuating the decrees, the courts will be guided by equitable principles. Traditionally, equity has been characterized by a practical flexibility in shaping its remedies and by a facility for adjusting and reconciling public and private needs. These cases call for the exercise of these traditional attributes of equity power. At stake is the personal interest of the plaintiffs in admission to public schools as soon as practicable on a nondiscriminatory basis. To effectuate this interest may call for elimination of a variety of obstacles in making the transition to school systems operated in accordance with the constitutional principles set forth in our May 17, 1954, decision. Courts of equity may properly take into account the public interest in the elimination of such obstacles in a systematic and effective manner. But it should go without saying that the vitality of these constitutional principles cannot be allowed to yield simply because of disagreement with them.

While giving weight to these public and private considerations, the courts will require that the defendants make a prompt and reasonable start toward full compliance with our May 17, 1954, ruling. Once such a start has been made, the courts may find that additional time is necessary to carry out the ruling in an effective manner. The burden rests upon the defendants to establish that such time is necessary in the public interest and is consistent with good faith compliance at the earliest practicable date. To that end, the courts may consider problems related to administration, arising from the physical condition of the school plant, the school transportation system, personnel, revision of school districts and attendance areas into compact units to achieve a system of determining admission to the public schools on a nonracial basis, and revision of local laws and regulations which may be necessary in solving the foregoing problems. They will also consider the adequacy of any plans the defendants may propose to meet these problems and to effectuate a transition to a racially nondiscriminatory school system. During this period of transition, the courts will retain jurisdiction of these cases.

The [cases are accordingly remanded to the lower courts] to take such proceedings and enter such orders and decrees consistent with this opinion as are necessary and proper to admit to public schools on a racially nondiscriminatory basis with all deliberate speed the parties to these cases . . . .

APPENDIX G
The Presidents and Vice Presidents of the United States

Year	President and Vice President	Party of President
1789–1797	**George Washington**	None
	John Adams	
1797–1801	**John Adams**	Federalist
	Thomas Jefferson	
1801–1809	**Thomas Jefferson**	Democratic-Republican
	Aaron Burr (to 1805)	
	George Clinton (to 1809)	
1809–1817	**James Madison**	Democratic-Republican
	George Clinton (to 1813)	
	Elbridge Gerry (to 1817)	
1817–1825	**James Monroe**	Democratic-Republican
	Daniel D. Tompkins	
1825–1829	**John Quincy Adams**	Democratic-Republican
	John C. Calhoun	
1829–1837	**Andrew Jackson**	Democratic
	John C. Calhoun (to 1833)	

Year	President and Vice President	Party of President
	Martin Van Buren (to 1837)	
1837–1841	**Martin Van Buren**	Democratic
	Richard M. Johnson	
1841	**William H. Harrison***	Whig
	John Tyler	
1841–1845	**John Tyler**	Whig
	(VP vacant)	
1845–1849	**James K. Polk**	Democratic
	George M. Dallas	
1849–1850	**Zachary Taylor***	Whig
	Millard Fillmore	
1850–1853	**Millard Fillmore**	Whig
	(VP vacant)	
1853–1857	**Franklin Pierce**	Democratic
	William R. King	
1857–1861	**James Buchanan**	Democratic
	John C. Breckinridge	
1861–1865	**Abraham Lincoln***	Republican
	Hannibal Hamlin (to 1865)	
	Andrew Johnson (1865)	

Year	President and Vice President	Party of President
1865–1869	**Andrew Johnson**	Democratic
	(VP vacant)	
1869–1877	**Ulysses S. Grant**	Republican
	Schuyler Colfax (to 1873)	
	Henry Wilson (to 1877)	
1877–1881	**Rutherford B. Hayes**	Republican
	William A. Wheeler	
1881	**James A. Garfield** *	Republican
	Chester A. Arthur	
1881–1885	**Chester A. Arthur**	Republican
	(VP vacant)	
1885–1889	**Grover Cleveland**	Democratic
	Thomas A. Hendricks	
1889–1893	**Benjamin Harrison**	Republican
	Levi P. Morton	
1893–1897	**Grover Cleveland**	Democratic
	Adlai E. Stevenson	
1897–1901	**William McKinley** *	Republican
	Garret A. Hobart (to 1901)	
	Theodore Roosevelt (1901)	
1901–1909	**Theodore Roosevelt**	Republican
	(VP vacant, 1901–1905)	
	Charles W. Fairbanks (1905–1909)	
1909–1913	**William Howard Taft**	Republican
	James S. Sherman	
1913–1921	**Woodrow Wilson**	Democratic
	Thomas R. Marshall	
1921–1923	**Warren G. Harding** *	Republican
	Calvin Coolidge	

Year	President and Vice President	Party of President
1923–1929	**Calvin Coolidge**	Republican
	(VP vacant, 1923–1925)	
	Charles G. Dawes (1925–1929)	
1929–1933	**Herbert Hoover**	Republican
	Charles Curtis	
1933–1945	**Franklin D. Roosevelt** *	Democratic
	John N. Garner (1933–1941)	
	Henry A. Wallace (1941–1945)	
	Harry S. Truman (1945)	
1945–1953	**Harry S. Truman**	Democratic
	(VP vacant, 1945–1949)	
	Alben W. Barkley (1949–1953)	
1953–1961	**Dwight D. Eisenhower**	Republican
	Richard M. Nixon	
1961–1963	**John F. Kennedy** *	Democratic
	Lyndon B. Johnson	
1963–1969	**Lyndon B. Johnson**	Democratic
	(VP vacant, 1963–1965)	
	Hubert H. Humphrey (1965–1969)	
1969–1974	**Richard M. Nixon** [†]	Republican
	Spiro T. Agnew [††] (1969–1973)	
	Gerald R. Ford [§] (1973–1974)	
1974–1977	**Gerald R. Ford**	Republican
	Nelson A. Rockefeller [§]	

(Continued)

Year	President and Vice President	Party of President	Year	President and Vice President	Party of President
1977–1981	**Jimmy Carter**	Democratic	1993–2001	**William J. Clinton**	Democratic
	Walter Mondale			Albert Gore, Jr.	
1981–1989	**Ronald Reagan**	Republican	2001–2008	**George W. Bush**	Republican
	George Bush			Richard Cheney	
1989–1993	**George Bush**	Republican	2008–	**Barack Obama**	Democratic
	J. Danforth Quayle			Joseph R. Biden	

* Died in office.
† Resigned from the presidency.
†† Resigned from the vice presidency.
§ Appointed vice president.

APPENDIX H
Presidential Election Results, 1789–2008

Year	Candidates	Party	Popular Vote	Electoral Vote
1789	**George Washington**			69
	John Adams			34
	Others			35
1792	**George Washington**			132
	John Adams			77
	George Clinton			50
	Others			5
1796	**John Adams**	Federalist		71
	Thomas Jefferson	Democrat-Republican		68
	Thomas Pinckney	Federalist		59
	Aaron Burr	Democrat-Republican		30
	Others			48
1800	**Thomas Jefferson**	Democrat-Republican		73
	Aaron Burr	Democrat-Republican		73
	John Adams	Federalist		65
	Charles C. Pinckney	Federalist		64
1804	**Thomas Jefferson**	Democrat-Republican		162
	Charles C. Pinckney	Federalist		14
1808	**James Madison**	Democrat-Republican		122
	Charles C. Pinckney	Federalist		47
	George Clinton	Independent-Republican		6

Year	Candidates	Party	Popular Vote	Electoral Vote
1812	**James Madison**	Democrat-Republican		128
	DeWitt Clinton	Federalist		89
1816	**James Monroe**	Democrat-Republican		183
	Rufus King	Federalist		34
1820	**James Monroe**	Democrat-Republican		231
	John Quincy Adams	Independent-Republican		1
1824	**John Quincy Adams**	Democrat-Republican	108,740 (30.5%)	84
	Andrew Jackson	Democrat-Republican	153,544 (43.1%)	99
	Henry Clay	Democrat-Republican	47,136 (13.2%)	37
	William H. Crawford	Democrat-Republican	46,618 (13.1%)	41
1828	**Andrew Jackson**	Democratic	647,231 (56.0%)	178
	John Quincy Adams	National Republican	509,097 (44.0%)	83
1832	**Andrew Jackson**	Democratic	687,502 (55.0%)	219
	Henry Clay	National Republican	530,189 (42.4%)	49
	William Wirt	Anti-Masonic		7
	John Floyd	National Republican	33,108 (2.6%)	11
1836	**Martin Van Buren**	Democratic	761,549 (50.9%)	170
	William H. Harrison	Whig	549,567 (36.7%)	73
	Hugh L. White	Whig	145,396 (9.7%)	26
	Daniel Webster	Whig	41,287 (2.7%)	14
1840	**William H. Harrison**	Whig	1,275,017 (53.1%)	234
	Martin Van Buren	Democratic	1,128,702 (46.9%)	60
1844	**James K. Polk**	Democratic	1,337,243 (49.6%)	170
	Henry Clay	Whig	1,299,068 (48.1%)	105
	James G. Birney	Liberty	63,300 (2.3%)	0
1848	**Zachary Taylor**	Whig	1,360,101 (47.4%)	163
	Lewis Cass	Democratic	1,220,544 (42.5%)	127
	Martin Van Buren	Free Soil	291,163 (10.1%)	0
1852	**Franklin Pierce**	Democratic	1,601,474 (50.9%)	254
	Winfield Scott	Whig	1,386,578 (44.1%)	42
1856	**James Buchanan**	Democratic	1,838,169 (45.4%)	174
	John C. Fremont	Republican	1,335,264 (33.0%)	114
	Millard Fillmore	American	874,534 (21.6%)	8
1860	**Abraham Lincoln**	Republican	1,865,593 (39.8%)	180
	Stephen A. Douglas	Democratic	1,381,713 (29.5%)	12

Year	Candidates	Party	Popular Vote	Electoral Vote
	John C. Breckinridge	Democratic	848,356 (18.1%)	72
	John Bell	Constitutional Union	592,906 (12.6%)	79
1864	**Abraham Lincoln**	Republican	2,206,938 (55.0%)	212
	George B. McClellan	Democratic	1,803,787 (45.0%)	21
1868	**Ulysses S. Grant**	Republican	3,013,421 (52.7%)	214
	Horatio Seymour	Democratic	2,706,829 (47.3%)	80
1872	**Ulysses S. Grant**	Republican	3,596,745 (55.6%)	286
	Horace Greeley	Democratic	2,843,446 (43.9%)	66
1876	**Rutherford B. Hayes**	Republican	4,036,571 (48.0%)	185
	Samuel J. Tilden	Democratic	4,284,020 (51.0%)	184
1880	**James A. Garfield**	Republican	4,449,053 (48.3%)	214
	Winfield S. Hancock	Democratic	4,442,035 (48.2%)	155
	James B. Weaver	Greenback-Labor	308,578 (3.4%)	0
1884	**Grover Cleveland**	Democratic	4,874,986 (48.5%)	219
	James G. Blaine	Republican	4,851,931 (48.2%)	182
	Benjamin F. Butler	Greenback-Labor	175,370 (1.8%)	0
1888	**Benjamin Harrison**	Republican	5,444,337 (47.8%)	233
	Grover Cleveland	Democratic	5,540,050 (48.6%)	168
1892	**Grover Cleveland**	Democratic	5,554,414 (46.0%)	277
	Benjamin Harrison	Republican	5,190,802 (43.0%)	145
	James B. Weaver	People's	1,027,329 (8.5%)	22
1896	**William McKinley**	Republican	7,035,638 (50.8%)	271
	William J. Bryan	Democratic; Populist	6,467,946 (46.7%)	176
1900	**William McKinley**	Republican	7,219,530 (51.7%)	292
	William J. Bryan	Democratic; Populist	6,356,734 (45.5%)	155
1904	**Theodore Roosevelt**	Republican	7,628,834 (56.4%)	336
	Alton B. Parker	Democratic	5,084,401 (37.6%)	140
	Eugene V. Debs	Socialist	402,460 (3.0%)	0
1908	**William H. Taft**	Republican	7,679,006 (51.6%)	321
	William J. Bryan	Democratic	6,409,106 (43.1%)	162
	Eugene V. Debs	Socialist	420,820 (2.8%)	0
1912	**Woodrow Wilson**	Democratic	6,286,820 (41.8%)	435
	Theodore Roosevelt	Progressive	4,126,020 (27.4%)	88
	William H. Taft	Republican	3,483,922 (23.2%)	8
	Eugene V. Debs	Socialist	897,011 (6.0%)	0

Year	Candidates	Party	Popular Vote	Electoral Vote
1916	**Woodrow Wilson**	Democratic	9,129,606 (49.3%)	277
	Charles E. Hughes	Republican	8,538,211 (46.1%)	254
1920	**Warren G. Harding**	Republican	16,152,200 (61.0%)	404
	James M. Cox	Democratic	9,147,353 (34.6%)	127
	Eugene V. Debs	Socialist	919,799 (3.5%)	0
1924	**Calvin Coolidge**	Republican	15,725,016 (54.1%)	382
	John W. Davis	Democratic	8,385,586 (28.8%)	136
	Robert M. La Follette	Progressive	4,822,856 (16.6%)	13
1928	**Herbert C. Hoover**	Republican	21,392,190 (58.2%)	444
	Alfred E. Smith	Democratic	15,016,443 (40.8%)	87
1932	**Franklin D. Roosevelt**	Democratic	22,809,638 (57.3%)	472
	Herbert C. Hoover	Republican	15,758,901 (39.6%)	59
	Norman Thomas	Socialist	881,951 (2.2%)	0
1936	**Franklin D. Roosevelt**	Democratic	27,751,612 (60.7%)	523
	Alfred M. Landon	Republican	16,681,913 (36.4%)	8
	William Lemke	Union	891,858 (1.9%)	0
1940	**Franklin D. Roosevelt**	Democratic	27,243,466 (54.7%)	449
	Wendell L. Wilkie	Republican	22,304,755 (44.8%)	82
1944	**Franklin D. Roosevelt**	Democratic	25,602,505 (52.8%)	432
	Thomas E. Dewey	Republican	22,006,278 (44.5%)	99
1948	**Harry S. Truman**	Democratic	24,105,812 (49.5%)	303
	Thomas E. Dewey	Republican	21,970,065 (45.1%)	189
	J. Strom Thurmond	States' Rights	1,169,063 (2.4%)	39
	Henry A. Wallace	Progressive	1,157,172 (2.4%)	0
1952	**Dwight D. Eisenhower**	Republican	33,936,234 (55.2%)	442
	Adlai E. Stevenson	Democratic	27,314,992 (44.5%)	89
1956	**Dwight D. Eisenhower**	Republican	35,590,472 (57.4%)	457
	Adlai E. Stevenson	Democratic	26,022,752 (42.0%)	73
1960	**John F. Kennedy**	Democratic	34,227,096 (49.9%)	303
	Richard M. Nixon	Republican	34,108,546 (49.6%)	219
1964	**Lyndon B. Johnson**	Democratic	43,126,233 (61.1%)	486
	Barry M. Goldwater	Republican	27,174,989 (38.5%)	52
1968	**Richard M. Nixon**	Republican	31,783,783 (43.4%)	301
	Hubert H. Humphrey	Democratic	31,271,839 (42.7%)	191
	George C. Wallace	American Independent	9,899,557 (13.5%)	46

Year	Candidates	Party	Popular Vote	Electoral Vote
1972	**Richard M. Nixon**	Republican	46,632,189 (61.3%)	520
	George McGovern	Democratic	28,422,015 (37.3%)	17
1976	**Jimmy Carter**	Democratic	40,828,587 (50.1%)	297
	Gerald R. Ford	Republican	39,147,613 (48.0%)	240
1980	**Ronald Reagan**	Republican	42,941,145 (50.7%)	489
	Jimmy Carter	Democratic	34,663,037 (41.0%)	49
	John B. Anderson	Independent	5,551,551 (6.6%)	0
1984	**Ronald Reagan**	Republican	53,428,357 (58.8%)	525
	Walter F. Mondale	Democratic	36,930,923 (40.6%)	13
1988	**George Bush**	Republican	48,881,011 (53.4%)	426
	Michael Dukakis	Democratic	41,828,350 (45.6%)	111
1992	**Bill Clinton**	Democratic	44,908,233 (43.0%)	370
	George Bush	Republican	39,102,282 (37.4%)	168
	Ross Perot	Independent	19,741,048 (18.9%)	0
1996	**Bill Clinton**	Democratic	45,628,667 (49.2%)	379
	Robert Dole	Republican	37,869,435 (40.8%)	159
	Ross Perot	Reform	7,874,283 (8.5%)	0
2000	**George W. Bush**	Republican	50,456,141 (47.87%)	271
	Albert Gore	Democrat	50,996,039 (48.38%)	266
	Ralph Nader	Green	2,882,807 (2.73%)	0
2004	**George W. Bush**	Republican	62,039,073 (50.7%)	286
	John Kerry	Democrat	59,027,678 (48.3%)	251
2008	**Barak Obama**	Democrat	69,456,897 (52.9%)	365
	John McCain	Republican	59,943,814 (45.7%)	173

APPENDIX I
Party Control of the Presidency, Senate, and House of Representatives, 1901–2011

Congress	Years	President	Senate			House		
			D	R	Other*	D	R	Other*
57th	1901–1903	McKinley	29	56	3	153	198	5
		T. Roosevelt						
58th	1903–1905	T. Roosevelt	32	58	—	178	207	—
59th	1905–1907	T. Roosevelt	32	58	—	136	250	—
60th	1907–1909	T. Roosevelt	29	61	—	164	222	—
61st	1909–1911	Taft	32	59	—	172	219	—
62d	1911–1913	Taft	42	49	—	228††	162	1
63d	1913–1915	Wilson	51	44	1	290	127	18
64th	1915–1917	Wilson	56	39	1	231	193	8
65th	1917–1919	Wilson	53	42	1	210	216	9
66th	1919–1921	Wilson	47	48††	1	191	237††	7
67th	1921–1923	Harding	37	59	—	132	300	1
68th	1923–1925	Coolidge	43	51	2	207	225	3
69th	1925–1927	Coolidge	40	54	1	183	247	5
70th	1927–1929	Coolidge	47	48	1	195	237	3
71st	1929–1931	Hoover	39	56	1	163	267	1
72d	1931–1933	Hoover	47	48	1	216††	218	1
73d	1933–1935	F. Roosevelt	59	36	1	313	117	5
74th	1935–1937	F. Roosevelt	69	25	2	322	103	10
75th	1937–1939	F. Roosevelt	75	17	4	333	89	13

Congress	Years	President	Senate			House		
			D	R	Other*	D	R	Other*
76th	1939–1941	F. Roosevelt	69	23	4	262	169	4
77th	1941–1943	F. Roosevelt	66	28	2	267	162	6
78th	1943–1945	F. Roosevelt	57	38	1	222	209	4
79th	1945–1947	Truman	57	38	1	243	190	2
80th	1947–1949	Truman	45	51††	—	188	246††	1
81st	1949–1951	Truman	54	42	—	263	171	1
82d	1951–1953	Truman	48	47	1	234	199	2
83d	1953–1955	Eisenhower	46	48	2	213	221	1
84th	1955–1957	Eisenhower	48††	47	1	232††	203	—
85th	1957–1959	Eisenhower	49††	47	—	234††	201	—
86th†	1959–1961	Eisenhower	64††	34	—	283††	154	—
87th	1961–1963	Kennedy	64	36	—	262	175	—
88th	1963–1965	Kennedy	67	33	—	258	176	—
		Johnson						
89th	1965–1967	Johnson	68	32	—	295	140	—
90th	1967–1969	Johnson	64	36	—	248	187	—
91st	1969–1971	Nixon	58††	42	—	243††	192	—
92d	1971–1973	Nixon	54††	44	2	255††	180	—
93d	1973–1975	Nixon	56††	42	2	242††	192	—
		Ford						
94th	1975–1977	Ford	61††	37	2	291††	144	—
95th	1977–1979	Carter	61	38	1	292	143	—
96th	1979–1981	Carter	58	41	1	277	158	—
97th	1981–1983	Reagan	46	53	1	243††	192	—
98th	1983–1985	Reagan	46	54	—	268††	167	—
99th	1985–1987	Reagan	47	53	—	253††	182	—
100th	1987–1989	Reagan	55††	45	—	258††	177	—
101st	1989–1991	Bush	55††	45	—	260††	175	—
102d	1991–1993	Bush	56††	44	—	267††	167	1
103d	1993–1995	Clinton	57	43	—	258	176	1
104th	1995–1997	Clinton	47	53††		204	230††	1
105th	1997–1999	Clinton	45	55††	—	207	227††	1
106th	1999–2001	Clinton	45	55††	—	211	223	1
107th	2001–2003	G. W. Bush	50	49	1	212	221	2

Congress	Years	President	Senate			House		
			D	R	Other*	D	R	Other*
108th	2003–2005	G. W. Bush	48	51	1	205	229	1
109th	2005–2007	G. W. Bush	44	55	1	202	232	1
110th	2007–2009	G. W. Bush	49	49	2	233	202	0
111th	2009–2011	Obama	56	41	2	254	178	0

* Excludes vacancies at beginning of each session. Party balance immediately following election.
† The 437 members of the House in the 86th and 87th Congresses are attributable to the at-large representative given to both Alaska (January 3, 1959) and Hawaii (August 21, 1959) prior to redistricting in 1962.
†† Chamber controlled by party other than that of the president.
D= Democrat; R = Republican

APPENDIX J
Justices of the Supreme Court
since 1900

Name	Nominated by	Service
John M. Harlan	Hayes	1877–1911
Horace Gray	Arthur	1882–1902
Melville W. Fuller	Cleveland	1888–1910
David J. Brewer	Harrison	1890–1910
Henry B. Brown	Harrison	1890–1906
George Shiras, Jr.	Harrison	1892–1903
Edward D. White	Cleveland	1894–1910
Rufus W. Peckham	Cleveland	1895–1909
Joseph McKenna	McKinley	1898–1925
Oliver W. Holmes	T. Roosevelt	1902–1932
William R. Day	T. Roosevelt	1903–1922
William H. Moody	T. Roosevelt	1906–1910
Horace H. Lurton	Taft	1910–1914
Edward D. White	Taft	1910–1921
Charles E. Hughes	Taft	1910–1916
Willis Van Devanter	Taft	1911–1937
Joseph R. Lamar	Taft	1911–1916
Mahlon Pitney	Taft	1912–1922
James C. McReynolds	Wilson	1914–1941
Louis D. Brandeis	Wilson	1916–1939
John H. Clarke	Wilson	1916–1922

Name	Nominated by	Service
William H. Taft	Harding	1921–1930
George Sutherland	Harding	1922–1938
Pierce Butler	Harding	1922–1939
Edward T. Sanford	Harding	1923–1930
Harlan F. Stone	Coolidge	1925–1941
Charles E. Hughes	Hoover	1930–1941
Owen J. Roberts	Hoover	1930–1945
Benjamin N. Cardozo	Hoover	1932–1938
Hugo L. Black	F. Roosevelt	1937–1971
Stanley F. Reed	F. Roosevelt	1938–1957
Felix Frankfurter	F. Roosevelt	1939–1962
William O. Douglas	F. Roosevelt	1939–1975
Frank Murphy	F. Roosevelt	1940–1949
Harlan F. Stone	F. Roosevelt	1941–1946
James F. Byrnes	F. Roosevelt	1941–1942
Robert H. Jackson	F. Roosevelt	1941–1954
Wiley B. Rutledge	F. Roosevelt	1943–1949
Harold H. Burton	Truman	1945–1958
Fred M. Vinson	Truman	1946–1953
Tom C. Clark	Truman	1949–1967
Sherman Minton	Truman	1949–1956

Name	Nominated by	Service
Earl Warren	Eisenhower	1953–1969
John M. Harlan	Eisenhower	1955–1971
William J. Brennan, Jr.	Eisenhower	1956–1990
Charles E. Whittaker	Eisenhower	1957–1962
Potter Stewart	Eisenhower	1958–1981
Byron R. White	Kennedy	1962–1993
Arthur J. Goldberg	Kennedy	1962–1965
Abe Fortas	Johnson	1965–1969
Thurgood Marshall	Johnson	1967–1991
Warren E. Burger	Nixon	1969–1986
Harry A. Blackmun	Nixon	1970–1994
Lewis F. Powell, Jr.	Nixon	1971–1987

Name	Nominated by	Service
William H. Rehnquist	Nixon	1971–1986
John Paul Stevens	Ford	1975–
Sandra Day O'Connor	Reagan	1981–2006
William H. Rehnquist	Reagan	1986–2005
Antonin Scalia	Reagan	1986–
Anthony M. Kennedy	Reagan	1988–
David H. Souter	Bush	1990–
Clarence Thomas	Bush	1991–
Ruth Bader Ginsburg	Clinton	1993–
Stephen G. Breyer	Clinton	1994–
John G. Roberts, Jr.	Bush	2005–
Samuel A. Alito, Jr.	Bush	2006–

Note: *Boldface type indicates service as chief justice.*

APPENDIX K
Presidential General Election Returns by State, 2008

	Popular Vote				Electoral Vote	
	Barak Obama (Democrat)		*John McCain (Republican)*			
	Vote	*Percent*	*Vote*	*Percent*	*D*	*R*
Alabama	813,479	39%	1,266,546	60%	0	9
Alaska	123,594	38%	193,841	59%	0	3
Arizona	1,034,707	45%	1,230,111	53%	0	10
Arkansas	422,310	39%	638,017	59%	0	6
California	8,274,473	61%	5,011,781	37%	55	0
Colorado	1,288,576	54%	1,073,589	45%	9	0
Connecticut	997,773	61%	629,428	38%	7	0
Delaware	255,459	62%	152,374	37%	3	0
District of Columbia	245,800	92%	17,367	7%	3	0
Florida	4,282,074	51%	4,045,624	48%	27	0
Georgia	1,844,123	47%	2,048,759	52%	0	15
Hawaii	325,871	72%	120,566	27%	4	0
Idaho	236,440	36%	403,012	61%	0	4
Illinois	3,419,348	62%	2,031,179	37%	21	0
Indiana	1,374,039	50%	1,345,648	49%	11	0
Iowa	828,940	54%	682,379	44%	7	0
Kansas	514,765	42%	699,655	57%	0	6
Kentucky	751,985	41%	1,048,462	57%	0	8
Louisiana	782,989	40%	1,148,275	59%	0	9

	Popular Vote				Electoral Vote	
	Barak Obama (Democrat)		**John McCain (Republican)**			
	Vote	*Percent*	*Vote*	*Percent*	**D**	**R**
Maine	421,923	58%	295,273	40%	4	0
Maryland	1,629,467	62%	959,862	36%	10	0
Massachusetts	1,904,097	62%	1,108,854	36%	12	0
Michigan	2,872,579	57%	2,048,639	41%	17	0
Minnesota	1,573,354	54%	1,275,409	44%	10	0
Mississippi	554,662	43%	724,597	56%	0	6
Missouri	1,441,911	49%	1,445,814	49%	0	11
Montana	231,667	47%	242,763	49%	0	3
Nebraska	333,319	42%	452,979	57%	1	4
Nevada	533,736	55%	412,827	43%	5	0
New Hampshire	384,826	54%	316,534	45%	4	0
New Jersey	2,215,422	57%	1,613,207	42%	15	0
New Mexico	472,422	57%	346,832	42%	5	0
New York	4,804,701	63%	2,752,728	36%	31	0
North Carolina	2,142,651	50%	2,128,474	49%	15	0
North Dakota	141,278	45%	168,601	53%	0	3
Ohio	2,940,044	51%	2,677,820	47%	20	0
Oklahoma	502,496	34%	960,165	66%	0	7
Oregon	1,037,291	57%	738,475	40%	7	0
Pennsylvania	3,276,363	54%	2,655,885	44%	21	0
Rhode Island	296,571	63%	165,391	35%	4	0
South Carolina	862,449	45%	1,034,896	54%	0	8
South Dakota	170,924	45%	203,054	53%	0	3
Tennessee	1,087,437	42%	1,479,178	57%	0	11
Texas	3,528,633	44%	4,479,328	55%	0	34
Utah	327,670	34%	596,030	62%	0	5
Vermont	219,262	67%	98,974	30%	3	0
Virginia	1,959,532	53%	1,725,005	46%	13	0
Washington	1,750,848	57%	1,229,216	40%	11	0
West Virginia	303,857	43%	397,466	57%	0	5
Wisconsin	1,677,211	56%	1,262,393	42%	10	0
Wyoming	82,868	33%	164,958	65%	0	3
Total	69,498,216	53%	59,948,240	46%	365	173

APPENDIX L
Portrait of the Electorate, 1996–2008

This portrait of Americans at the polls shows how different groups have voted in the last four presidential elections, measuring the ebbs and flows of political alliances that have elected and defeated presidents. The vast size of each sample makes it possible to study the preferences of some groups, such as Jewish, Asian-American, and Hispanic-American voters, whose small numbers make them almost invisible in typical national telephone polls.

Percentage of 2008 Total Vote		1996			2000			2004		2008	
		Clinton	Dole	Perot	Gore	Bush	Nader	Bush	Kerry	Obama	McCain
	Total vote	49	41	8	48	48	2			53	46
Sex											
47%	Men	43	44	10	42	53	3	55	44	49	48
53%	Women	54	38	7	54	43	2	48	51	56	43
Race											
74%	White	43	46	9	42	54	3	58	41	43	55
13%	African American	84	12	4	90	8	1	11	88	95	4
9%	Hispanic American	72	21	6	67	31	2	44	53	67	31
2%	Asian American	43	48	8	54	41	4	44	56	62	35
Age											
18%	18–29 years old	53	34	10	48	46	5	45	54	66	32
29%	30–44 years old	48	41	9	48	49	2	53	46	52	46
30%	45–59 years old	49	41	9	48	49	2	51	48	48	49
23%	60 and older	48	44	7	51	47	2	54	46	47	51

Percentage of 2008 Total Vote		1996			2000			2004		2008	
		Clinton	Dole	Perot	Gore	Bush	Nader	Bush	Kerry	Obama	McCain
	Party										
32%	Republican	13	80	6	8	91	1	93	6	10	89
39%	Democratic	43	35	17	45	47	6	48	49	89	10
29%	Independent	84	10	5	86	11	2	11	89	52	44
	Ideology										
22%	Liberal	78	11	7	80	13	6	13	85	89	10
44%	Moderate	57	33	9	52	44	2	45	54	60	39
34%	Conservative	20	71	8	17	81	1	84	15	20	78
	Region										
21%	From the East	55	34	9	56	39	3	43	56	59	40
24%	From the Midwest	48	41	10	48	49	2	51	48	54	44
32%	From the South	46	46	7	43	55	1	58	42	45	54
23%	From the West	48	40	8	48	46	4	49	50	57	40
	Education										
4%	Not a high school graduate	59	28	11	59	39	1	49	50	63	35
20%	High school graduate	51	35	13	48	49	1	52	47	52	46
31%	Some college education	48	40	10	45	51	3	54	46	51	47
28%	College Graduate	44	46	8	45	51	3	52	46	50	48
17%	Post-graduate education	52	40	5	52	44	3	44	55	58	40
	Religion										
42%	White Protestant	36	53	10	34	63	2	59	40	34	65
19%	Catholic	53	37	9	49	47	2	52	47	47	45
2%	Jewish	78	16	3	79	19	1	25	74	78	21
	Union Membership										
12%	Union household	59	30	9	59	37	3	40	59	59	39
	Family income is:										
6%	Under $15,000	59	28	11	57	37	4	36	63	73	25
12%	$15,000–$29,999	53	36	9	54	41	3	42	57	60	37
19%	$30,000–$49,000	48	40	10	49	48	2	49	50	55	43
52%	Over $50,000	44	48	7	45	52	2	56	43	48	49
41%	Over $75,000	41	51	7	44	53	2	57	43	51	48
26%	Over $100,000	38	54	6	43	54	2	58	41	49	49

Percentage of 2008 Total Vote		1996			2000			2004		2008	
		Clinton	Dole	Perot	Gore	Bush	Nader	Bush	Kerry	Obama	McCain
	Family's financial situation is:										
24%	Better today	66	26	6	61	36	2	80	19	37	60
34%	Same today	46	45	8	35	60	3	49	50	45	53
42%	Worse today	27	57	13	33	63	4	20	79	71	28
11%	**First time voters**	54	34	11	52	43	4	46	53	69	30

Source: http://elections.nytimes.com/2008/results/president/national-exit-polls.html.

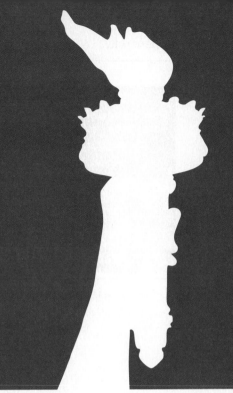

APPENDIX M
American Political Parties Since 1789

Although the Democratic and Republican parties have existed for more than a century, the party system has witnessed the rise and fall of many other parties, as shown in the illustration on the opposite page.

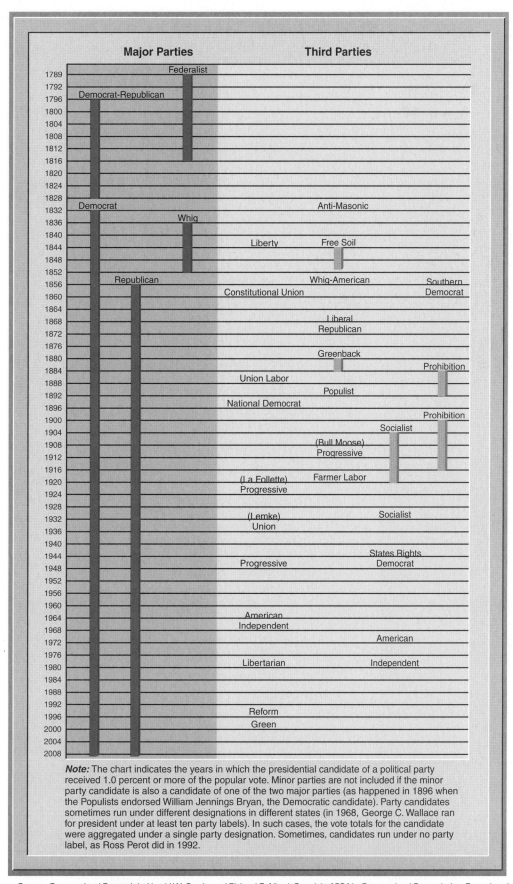

Note: The chart indicates the years in which the presidential candidate of a political party received 1.0 percent or more of the popular vote. Minor parties are not included if the minor party candidate is also a candidate of one of the two major parties (as happened in 1896 when the Populists endorsed William Jennings Bryan, the Democratic candidate). Party candidates sometimes run under different designations in different states (in 1968, George C. Wallace ran for president under at least ten party labels). In such cases, the vote totals for the candidate were aggregated under a single party designation. Sometimes, candidates run under no party label, as Ross Perot did in 1992.

Source: *Congressional Quarterly* by Harold W. Stanley and Richard G. Niemi. Copyright 1994 by Congressional Quarterly, Inc. Reproduced with permission of Congressional Quarterly, Inc. via Copyright Clearance Center. Additional years added by the authors.

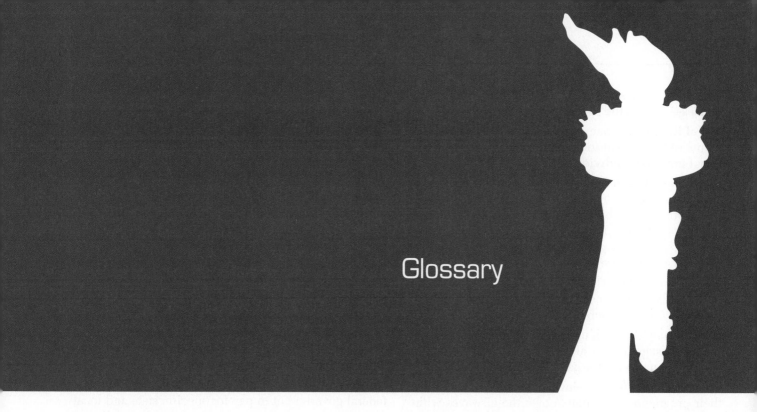

Glossary

A

advice and consent The requirement that the president gain the Senate's approval of appointees to a variety of government positions, as per the provision in Article II of the Constitution.

advocacy advertising Newspaper, television, and radio advertisements that promote an interest group's political views.

affirmative action Programs designed to take positive actions to increase the number of women and minorities in jobs and educational programs.

Americans with Disabilities Act of 1990 An act of Congress that seeks to minimize job discrimination, maximize access to government programs, and ensure access to public accommodations for people with disabilities.

amicus curiae Literally, friend of the court. A brief filed with the court by a person or group who is not directly involved in the legal action but who has views on the matter.

Antifederalists The label describing those who opposed adoption of the Constitution. While opponents gave a variety of reasons for rejecting the Constitution, their main concern was that a strong national government would jeopardize individual rights.

Articles of Confederation The document written by the states following their declaration of independence from England and adopted in 1781. It established a system of strong states and a weak national government with a legislative branch but no separate executive or judicial branches and few powers beyond the sphere of foreign relations.

astroturf lobbying Efforts, usually led by interest groups with deep financial pockets, to create synthetic grass-roots movements by aggressively encouraging voters to contact their elected officials about specific issues.

attentive publics or issue publics People who follow a particular issue closely, are well informed about it, and have strong opinions on it.

attitude consistency The degree to which a person's political opinions all fall at about the same point on the liberal-conservative dimension.

attitudes or opinions Preferences on specific issues.

Australian ballot A government-printed ballot (as opposed to one distributed by political parties) that allows people to vote in secret.

B

baby boomers The generation of Americans born between 1946 and 1964.

bad tendency doctrine The doctrine that speech need only be likely to lead to negative consequences, in Congress's judgment, for it to be illegal.

balanced budget A federal budget in which spending and revenues are equal.

bandwagon effect Candidates who do well in early primary elections find it easier to raise campaign funds, receive media coverage, and gain additional public support

bargaining strategy Direct negotiations the White House conducts with other political actors, such as members of Congress and leaders of interest groups, that attempt to reach mutually beneficial agreements.

bicameral legislature A legislature with two houses—such as the House and the Senate.

Bill of Rights The name given to the first ten amendments of the Constitution. They outline a large number of important individual rights.

Bipartisan Campaign Reform Act (BCRA) Also known as McCain-Feingold. A law passed in 2002 that restricts the ability of interest groups to donate funds to national political parties and bars interest groups from running ads promoting or attacking federal candidates close to an election.

blanket primaries Direct primaries in which voters may cast ballots for candidates of any party but may vote only once for each office.

block grants Grants of money from the federal government that state and local governments may spend on any program serving the general purpose of the grant.

broadcast television Television stations that make their programming available over the airwaves without charge. Most local cable companies include broadcast television channels as part of their basic package of services.

Brown v. Board of Education The landmark 1954 Supreme Court decision holding that separate was not equal and public schools must be desegregated.

Brown v. Board of Education II The 1955 Supreme Court decision which stated that the nation's entrenched system of segregated schools should desegregate with "all deliberate speed."

Budget and Accounting Act of 1921 An act of Congress that created the Bureau of the Budget and allowed the president to review and coordinate the spending proposals of federal agencies and departments.

budget deficits The amount by which government spending exceeds government revenues in a single year.

budget surplus The amount by which government revenues exceed government spending in a single year.

bureaucracy In general usage, the set of government agencies that carries out government policies. The bureaucracy is characterized by formalized structures, specialized duties, a hierarchical system of authority, routine recordkeeping, and a permanent staff.

bureaucrats A term used generally to identify people who work within a large, formal organization. More specifically, it refers to career civil service employees of the government.

Bush Doctrine A policy, announced by President George W. Bush in 2001, stating that the United States would target terrorist groups and the states that aided them.

C

cabinet An informal designation that refers to the collective body of individuals appointed by the president to head the executive departments. The cabinet can, but rarely does, function as an advisory body to the president.

cable television Television programming not originally transmitted over the air, as with broadcast television, but rather carried via coaxial or fiber-optic cable into the homes of people who pay a monthly fee.

candidate characteristics The candidate's character, personality, experiences, past record, and physical appearance.

candidate-centered campaigns Campaigns in which candidates set up campaign organizations, raise money, and campaign independently of other candidates in their party.

categorical grants-in-aid Grants of money from the federal government to pay for specific state and local government activities under strict federal guidelines.

caucus A closed meeting of members of a political party to discuss matters of public policy and political strategy, and in some cases, to select candidates for office.

caucus/convention system A nomination method in which registered party members attend a party caucus, or meeting, to choose a nominee. In large districts, local caucuses send delegates to represent them at a convention.

central legislative clearance The power the Budget and Accounting Act of 1921 granted to the president to create a package of legislative proposals and budgets for congressional consideration.

centrist parties Parties close to the political center.

checks and balances The powers each branch of government can use to block the actions of other branches.

citizen groups Interest groups, also known as public interest groups, dedicated to promoting a vision of good public policy rather than the economic interests of their members.

civic voluntarism model A theory claiming that political activism can be explained by the time, money, and civic skills that people have.

civil disobedience The nonviolent refusal to obey what one perceives to be unjust laws.

civil liberties The freedoms guaranteed to all Americans in the Bill of Rights (although some are in the body of the Constitution). These liberties include freedom of speech, freedom of religion, and the right to assemble peaceably.

civil rights The equality of rights for all people regardless of race, sex, ethnicity, religion, and sexual orientation. Civil rights are rooted in the courts' interpretation of the Fourteenth Amendment and in laws that Congress and the state legislatures pass.

Civil Rights Act of 1964 An act of Congress that outlaws racial segregation in public accommodations and employment and prevents tax dollars from going to organizations that discriminate on the basis of race, color, or national origin.

civil rights movement The mobilization of people to push for racial equality.

civil service The method by which most government employees have been hired, promoted, and fired since the 1880s. Personnel decisions are based on merit, or the competence of the individual to do the job, rather than the individual's political loyalties.

classical liberalism A political philosophy, particularly strong in the eighteenth century, that claims that the rights of the individual predate the existence of government and take priority over government policy. This philosophy advocates the protection of individual freedoms from the government.

clear and present danger standard The doctrine that Congress may limit speech if it causes a clear and present danger to the interests of the country.

clientele The recipients of the services a government agency's programs provide.

closed primaries Direct primaries in which voters must register their party affiliations before Election Day.

closing date The last day before the election when one can register to vote—usually described in number of days before Election Day.

cloture The procedure to stop a filibuster, which requires a supermajority of sixty votes.

coercive force The ability of a government to compel its citizens to obey its decisions.

Cold War A phrase used to describe the high level of tension and distrust that characterized relations between the Soviet Union and the United States from the late 1940s until the early 1990s.

collective goods dilemma A dilemma created when people can obtain the benefits of interest group activity without paying any of the costs associated with it. In this situation, the interest group may not form because everyone has an incentive to let someone else pay the costs of group formation.

concurring opinion A statement from one or more Supreme Court justices agreeing with a decision in a case but giving an alternative explanation for it.

conference committee An ad hoc committee of House and Senate members formed to resolve the differences in a bill that passes each body with different provisions.

Congressional Budget and Impoundment Control Act of 1974 An act of Congress that created the new budget process and the Congressional Budget Office and that curtailed the president's power to impound funds.

Congressional Budget Office (CBO) A nonpartisan congressional agency in charge of assisting Congress in reviewing and coordinating budget requests to Congress.

Connecticut Compromise A plan the Connecticut delegation proposed at the Constitutional Convention. This plan sought to manage the dispute between large- and small-population states by creating a two-house legislature with representation in one house based on population and representation in the second house set at two seats per state.

conservatism The political philosophy that government should play a minimal role in society (except in the area of traditional moral values) with the goal of ensuring all its citizens economic freedom.

Conservative Coalition The Conservative Coalition appears when a majority of southern Democrats votes with a majority of Republicans against a majority of northern Democrats.

constituent service Favors members of Congress do for constituents—usually in the form of help in dealing with the federal bureaucracy.

constitutional courts The three-tiered system of federal district courts, courts of appeals (originally circuit courts), and the Supreme Court. Article III of the Constitution provides for the creation of these courts.

containment A bedrock principle of U.S. foreign policy from the 1940s to the 1980s that emphasized the need to prevent communist countries, especially the Soviet Union, from expanding the territory they controlled.

continuing resolutions Temporary laws Congress passes to keep the government running when Congress misses the deadline for passing the budget.

corporate welfare Government subsidies or tax breaks of questionable value to private corporations.

cost-of-living adjustment (COLA) An increase in Social Security or other benefits designed to keep pace with inflation.

counter-cyclical programs Government programs that automatically increase spending when the economy slows down and unemployment rises, and decrease spending when the economy speeds up.

critical elections Elections that disrupt party coalitions and create new ones in a party realignment.

cross-cutting cleavages Divisions that split society into small groups so that in different policy areas, people have different allies and opponents, and so that no group forms a majority on all issues.

D

de facto segregation Segregation that results from the actions of individuals rather than the government.

de jure segregation Government-imposed laws that required African Americans to live and work separately from white Americans.

democracy A form of government in which the people (defined broadly to include all adults or narrowly to exclude women or slaves, for example) are the ultimate political authority.

détente A policy the Nixon administration followed to develop more cordial relations with the Soviet Union.

direct democracy Mechanisms such as the initiative, referendum, and recall—powers that enable voters to use the ballot box to set government policy.

direct lobbying Trying to influence public policy through direct contact with government officials.

direct primary An election in which voters and not party leaders directly choose a party's nominees for political office.

discretionary spending Federal spending on programs that can be controlled through the regular budget process.

dissenting opinion A statement from one or more Supreme Court justices explaining why they disagree with a decision in a case.

divided government The type of government experienced when the president is of one party and the other party has a majority in at least one house of Congress.

dual federalism An interpretation of federalism that held that the national government was supreme within those areas specifically assigned to it in the Constitution, and the states were supreme in all other areas of public policy.

Duverger's Law The generalization that if a nation has a single-member, plurality electoral system, it will develop a two-party system.

E

easy issues Simple issues that allow voters to make quick, emotional decisions without much information.

economic issues Issues relating to the distribution of income and wealth in society.

economic regulation Laws and governmental rules that affect the competitive practices of private business.

electoral college The body of electors, whose composition is determined by the results of the general election, that chooses the president and vice president. To win in the electoral college, candidates must secure a majority of the electoral vote.

embedding A program under which the Defense Department allowed journalists to travel with the U.S. military during the Iraq War.

enlargement The policy President Bill Clinton proposed as a substitute for containment. It called on the United States to promote the emergence of market democracies, that is, countries that combine a free market economic system with a democratic political system.

entitlement programs Programs, created by legislation, that require the government to pay a benefit directly to any individual who meets the eligibility requirements the law establishes.

enumerated powers Powers explicitly identified in the text of the Constitution.

environmental impact statement A document federal agencies must issue that analyzes the environmental impact of any significant actions they plan to take.

Equal Pay Act of 1963 An act of Congress that banned wage discrimination based on sex, race, religion, and national origin.

equal-time provision A federal law that stipulates that if a radio or television station gives or sells air time to a candidate for political office, it must provide all candidates for public office with access to the airwaves under the same conditions.

establishment clause The provision in the First Amendment of the Constitution that "Congress shall make no law respecting an establishment of religion."

exclusionary rule The doctrine, stemming from the Fourth Amendment, that the government cannot use illegally obtained evidence in court.

executive agreements International agreements that, unlike treaties, do not require the approval of two-thirds of the Senate to become binding on the United States.

executive amendment A procedure allowing governors to reject a bill by returning it to the legislature with changes that would make it acceptable; the legislature must agree to the changes for the bill to become law.

executive order A presidential directive to an agency of the federal government that tells the agency to take some specified action.

expertise Specialized knowledge acquired through work experience or training and education.

expressive benefits The feelings of satisfaction people derive from working for an interest group cause they believe is just and right. Also known as purposive benefits.

F

fairness doctrine A regulation the FCC adopted in 1949 and repealed in 1987. It required broadcasters to provide "reasonable opportunities for the expression of opposing views on controversial issues of public importance."

Federal Communications Commission (FCC) An independent federal agency that regulates interstate and international communication by radio, television, telephone, telegraph, cable, and satellite.

Federal Reserve System An independent regulatory commission that Congress created in 1913 to oversee the nation's money supply.

federalism A two-tiered form of government in which governments on both levels are sovereign and share authority over the same geographic jurisdiction.

Federalists The label describing those who supported adoption of the Constitution. They believed in the need for a national government stronger than the one provided under the Articles of Confederation.

feminization of poverty The trend in the United States in which families headed by women account for a growing share of the people who live below the poverty line.

filibuster The tactic of stalling a bill in the Senate by talking endlessly about the bill in order to win changes in it or kill it.

fire-alarm oversight Congressional oversight hearings designed to investigate a problem after it has become highly visible.

fiscal federalism The principle that the federal government should play a major role in financing some of the activities of state and local governments.

fiscal policy Using the federal government's control over taxes and spending to influence the condition of the national economy.

527 groups Tax-exempt organizations that engage in political activities, often funded with unlimited contributions. Most 527s try to influence federal elections through voter mobilization efforts and issue ads that praise or attack a candidate's record. These groups must publicly identify their contributors and expenditures.

flat tax Any income tax system in which taxable income is taxed at the same percentage rate regardless of the taxpayer's income.

Food Stamp program A public assistance program established in 1964 that provides stamps (or coupons) to low-income people to buy food.

foreign service officers Career professional diplomats who work for the Department of State.

franchise The right to vote.

franking privilege The right of a member of Congress to send official mail without paying postage.

free exercise clause The provision in the First Amendment of the Constitution that "Congress shall make no law ... prohibiting the free exercise" of religion.

free riders People or groups who benefit from the efforts of others without bearing any of the costs.

free trade An economic policy that holds that lowering trade barriers will benefit the economies of all the countries involved.

Freedom of Information Act An act of Congress passed in 1966 that created a system through which anyone can petition the government to declassify secret documents.

frontloading The decision states make to move their primaries and caucuses to earlier dates to increase their impact on the nomination process.

G

gender gap The difference between men's and women's voting rates for either a Democratic or Republican candidate.

general revenue sharing A program giving federal money to state and local governments with no restrictions on how it will be spent.

gerrymandering Drawing congressional district boundaries to favor one party over the other.

globalism The idea that the United States should be prepared to use military force around the globe to defend its political and economic interests.

globalization The process by which growing economic relations and technological change make countries increasingly interdependent.

going public strategy Direct presidential appeals to the public for support. Presidents use public support to pressure other political actors to accept their policies.

grass-roots lobbying Trying to influence public policy indirectly by mobilizing an interest group's membership and the broader public to contact elected officials.

Great Depression The worst economic crisis in U.S. history, with unemployment rates reaching 25 percent. It began in 1929 and lasted until the start of World War II.

Great Society The economic and social programs Congress enacted during Lyndon Johnson's presidency, from 1963 to 1969.

gross domestic product (GDP) A measure of a country's total economic output in any given year.

group consciousness Identification with one's social group (for instance, African-American consciousness).

H

hard issues Complicated issues that require voters to have information about the policy and to spend time considering their choices.

home style The way in which members of Congress present themselves to their constituents in the district.

homeland security Programs and initiatives designed to make it harder for terrorists to attack targets on American soil and to minimize the consequences of any attacks that do occur. Also, the name of the cabinet department established in 2003.

horse-race journalism News coverage of elections that focuses on which candidate is leading in the polls rather than on the substantive issues in the campaign.

I

ideology An elaborate set of interrelated beliefs with overarching, abstract principles that make people's political philosophies coherent.

impeachment Formally charging a government official with having committed "Treason, Bribery, or other High Crimes and Misdemeanors." Officials convicted of such charges are removed from office.

implied powers Governmental powers not enumerated in the Constitution; authority the government is assumed to have in order to carry out its enumerated powers.

incitement standard The doctrine that speech must cause listeners to be likely to commit immediate illegal acts for the speech itself to be illegal.

independent expenditures Funds raised and spent without contact with the supported candidate.

industrial policy The policy of seeking to strengthen selected industries by targeting them for governmental aid rather than letting the forces of the free market determine their fates.

initiative A proposed law or amendment placed on the ballot by citizens, usually through a petition.

interest group An organized group of people who share some goals and try to influence public policy.

intermediate scrutiny A legal standard for judging whether a discriminatory law is unconstitutional. Intermediate scrutiny lies somewhere between the rational and strict scrutiny standards. It requires the government to show that a discriminatory law serves important governmental interests and is substantially related to the achievement of those objectives, or a group to show that the law does not meet these two standards.

intermestic issues Issues such as trade, the environment, and drug trafficking that affect both domestic and foreign interests.

interstate commerce clause The provision in Article I of the Constitution granting Congress the power to "regulate commerce . . . among the several states."

iron triangles The alliance of a government agency, congressional committee or subcommittee, and political interest group for the purpose of directing government policy within the agency's jurisdiction to the mutual benefit of the three partners.

isolationism A foreign policy built on the principle of avoiding formal military and political alliances with other countries.

issue networks A loose collection of groups or people in and out of government who interact on a policy issue on the basis of their interest and knowledge rather than just on the basis of economic interests.

issue publics or attentive publics People who follow a particular issue closely, are well informed about it, and have strong opinions on it.

J

Jim Crow laws Laws that discriminated against African Americans, usually by enforcing segregation.

judicial activism The vigorous use of judicial review to overturn laws and make public policy from the federal bench.

judicial review The doctrine allowing the Supreme Court to review and overturn decisions made by Congress and the president.

K

Keynesian economics An economic theory, based on the work of British economist John Maynard Keynes, that contends that the national government can manage the economy by running budget surpluses and budget deficits.

L

laissez faire An economic theory, dominant at the start of the twentieth century, that argued that the federal government's only role in the economy was to ensure a stable supply of money.

lame duck An officeholder whose political power is weakened because his or her term is coming to an end.

leak Confidential government information surreptitiously given to journalists.

left The liberal end of the political spectrum.

legislative courts Various administrative courts and tribunals that Congress establishes, as Article I of the Constitution provides.

legitimacy A self-imposed willingness of citizens to respect and obey the decisions of their government.

libel law Laws governing written or visual publications that unjustly injure a person's reputation.

liberalism The political philosophy that government should play an expansive role in society (except in the area of personal morality) with the goal of protecting its weaker citizens and ensuring political and social equality for all citizens.

line-item veto The ability of an executive to delete or veto some provisions of a bill, while allowing the rest of the bill to become law.

literacy tests Tests of ability to read and write, used in the South to prevent people from voting.

lobbying Trying to influence governmental decisions, especially the voting decisions legislators make on proposed legislation.

lobbyists People who make their living trying to influence public policy.

Lucas critique An economic theory which contends that if people act rationally, then their reactions to changes in government policy will often negate the intent of those changes.

lynching The unlawful killing, usually by hanging, of a person by a mob.

M

majority opinion The document announcing and usually explaining the Supreme Court's decision in a case.

majority tyranny A situation in which the majority uses its advantage in numbers to suppress the rights of the minority.

mandates Laws Congress passes that require state and local governments to undertake specified actions.

Marbury v. Madison The Supreme Court decision in 1803 that established the principle of judicial review.

Marshall Plan A multibillion-dollar U.S. aid program in the late 1940s and early 1950s that helped Western European countries rebuild their economies in the wake of World War II.

massive resistance The policy many southern states followed in the wake of the first Brown decision of fiercely resisting desegregation.

material benefits Goods and services with real, monetary value.

material scarcity The inability of a society to provide its citizens with all the goods and services they may want or need.

McCain-Feingold Also known as the Bipartisan Campaign Reform Act (BCRA). A law passed in 2002 that restricts the ability of interest groups to donate funds to national political parties and bars interest groups from running ads promoting or attacking federal candidates close to an election.

means test A requirement that people must fall below certain income and wealth requirements to qualify for government benefits.

median voter hypothesis The theory that the best possible position for a politician who cares only about winning elections is the center—that is, in the position of the median voter.

Medicaid A public assistance program that provides publicly subsidized health care to low-income Americans.

Medicare A social insurance program that provides basic hospital insurance and supplementary insurance for doctors' bills and other health-care expenses for people over the age of sixty-five.

merit civil service system A system of hiring government employees on the basis of merit, or the competence of the individual to do the job, rather than the individual's political loyalties.

Merit System Also called the Missouri Plan. The system some states use to select judges, appointing them but requiring them to stand for periodic reelection.

midterm elections The congressional elections that take place midway through a president's four-year term.

Miranda rights The rights against self-incrimination that the Fifth Amendment guarantees. Miranda rights include the right to remain silent during questioning, the right to know that any statements suspects make may be used as evidence against them, and the right to speak to an attorney before questioning.

Missouri Plan The system some states use to select judges, appointing them but requiring them to stand for periodic reelection.

monetary theory An economic theory which contends that a nation's money supply, or the amount of money in circulation, is the primary if not sole determinant of the health of the national economy.

Monroe Doctrine A basic principle of U.S. foreign policy that dates back to a warning President James Monroe issued in 1823 that the United States would resist further European efforts to intervene in the affairs of the Western Hemisphere.

muckraking An early form of investigative journalism popular at the beginning of the twentieth century.

multilateralism An approach in which three or more countries cooperate for the purpose of solving some common problem.

N

national debt The total amount of money the federal government owes to pay for accumulated deficits.

national interest The idea that the United States has certain interests in international relations that most Americans agree on.

national missile defense (NMD) A weapons system that, if it can be made to work, would potentially protect the United States and possibly its allies against attack by long-range ballistic missiles.

national supremacy An interpretation of federalism that holds that the national government's laws should take precedence over state law. This idea is based on the provision in Article VI of the Constitution that the national government's laws are the "supreme law of the land."

necessary and proper clause The provision in Article I of the Constitution that states that Congress possesses whatever additional and unspecified powers it needs to fulfill its responsibilities.

neoisolationism The idea that the United States should reduce its role in world affairs and return to a foreign policy similar to the one it pursued before World War II.

netroots lobbying Using blogs, wikis and social networking sites on the Internet to pressure elected officials on political issues.

neutral competence The belief that staff members (usually career civil servants) should be able to work competently for any president, regardless of partisan affiliation or policy preferences and without advocating the policies of individual presidents.

New Deal The economic and social programs Congress enacted during Franklin Roosevelt's presidency before World War II.

New Deal coalition The Democratic Party coalition that formed in 1932. It got its name from President Franklin Delano Roosevelt's New Deal policies.

New Jersey Plan A plan for a new national government that the New Jersey delegation proposed at the Constitutional Convention in 1787. Its key feature consisted of giving each state equal representation in the national legislature, regardless of its population.

nondiscretionary spending Federal spending on programs such as Social Security that cannot be controlled through the regular budget process.

North Atlantic Treaty Organization (NATO) A military alliance founded in 1949 for the purpose of defending Western Europe from attack. Members of NATO now include the United States, Canada, and twenty-six European countries.

objective press A form of journalism that developed in the 1920s and which continues to predominate today. It emphasizes that journalists should strive to keep their opinions out of their coverage of the news.

obscenity law Laws governing materials whose predominant appeal is to a prurient interest in nudity, sex, or excretion.

Office of Management and Budget (OMB) The agency in charge of assisting the president in reviewing and coordinating budget requests to Congress from federal agencies and departments. Formerly the Bureau of the Budget.

One Hundred Days A benchmark period for assessing a new president's performance, based on the first three months of Franklin Roosevelt's presidency, when he gained passage of more than a dozen major bills as part of his New Deal agenda.

open primaries Direct primaries in which voters may choose which party primary they will vote in on Election Day.

opinions or attitudes Preferences on specific issues.

original intent The theory that judges should interpret the Constitution by determining what the Founders intended when they wrote it.

P

pack journalism The tendency of journalists to cover stories because other journalists are covering them and to ignore stories that other journalists aren't covering.

party dealignment A trend in which voter loyalties to the two major parties weaken.

party identification The psychological feeling of belonging to a particular political party, which influences voting behavior.

party machine A party organization built on the use of selective, material incentives for participation.

party platforms Official statements of beliefs, values, and policy positions that national party conventions issue.

party realignments Long-term shifts in the electoral balance between the major parties.

patronage The practice of rewarding partisan supporters with government jobs. Also known as the spoils system.

patronage jobs Jobs given as a reward for loyal party service.

Pentagon Papers A set of secret government documents—leaked to the press in 1971—showing that Presidents Kennedy and Johnson misled the public about U.S. involvement in Vietnam.

photo opportunities Events that political candidates and government officials stage to allow newspaper photographers and television news crews to take flattering photos.

picket-fence federalism The tendency of federal, state, and local agencies concerned with the same issues to coordinate their efforts with each other and to be insulated from other government agencies that deal with different issues.

pluralism The theory that political power is spread widely and that on different issues different groups of people exercise power.

pocket veto The power of the president to veto a bill passed during the last ten days of a session of Congress simply by failing to sign it.

police-patrol oversight Congressional oversight hearings designed to take a wide-ranging look for possible problems.

policy oversight Efforts by Congress to see that the legislation it passes is implemented, that the expected results have come about, and whether new laws are needed.

policy rule A decision a government institution reaches on a specific political question within its jurisdiction.

political action committees (PACs) Organizations that solicit contributions from members of interest groups and channel those contributions to election campaigns.

political agenda The list of issues that people think are important and that government officials are actively debating.

political cleavages Divisions in society around which parties organize.

political efficacy The feeling that one can have an effect on politics and political decision makers.

political party A coalition of people seeking to control the government by contesting elections and winning office.

poll taxes Before 1964, the taxes that people paid in some states if they chose to vote.

pool reporting A system the Defense Department instituted in the 1980s for reporting from a combat zone during wartime. With pool reporting, military officials escort small groups of reporters when they interview American troops.

pork barrel Legislation that appropriates government money for local projects of questionable value that may ingratiate a legislator with his or her constituents.

Presidential signing statement A statement issued by the President about a bill, in conjunction with signing that bill into law.

prior restraint An act of government preventing publication or broadcast of a story or document.

privatization Turning government programs over to private companies to run or selling government assets to the private sector.

pro-choice Favoring the policy of allowing women to choose whether to have abortions.

Progressive movement An early twentieth-century political movement that sought to advance the public interest by reducing the power of political parties in the selection of candidates and the administration of government.

progressive tax A tax system in which those with high incomes pay a higher percentage of their income in taxes than those with low incomes.

pro-life Favoring the policy of making abortion illegal.

proportional representation system A system in which legislators are elected at large and each party wins legislative seats in proportion to the number of votes it receives.

prospective issue voting Deciding how to vote on the basis of a candidate's likely future policies.

public assistance Government programs, such as Medicaid and food stamps, that are funded out of general tax revenues and that are designed to provide benefits only to low-income people.

R

rainy day funds Surplus revenues a state government holds in reserve for budget emergencies and shortfalls.

rational scrutiny A legal standard for judging whether a discriminatory law is unconstitutional. Rational scrutiny requires the government only to show that a law is reasonable and not arbitrary.

reapportionment The redistribution of seats in the House of Representatives among the states, which occurs every ten years following the census, so that the size of each state's delegation is proportional to its share of the total population.

referendum An election held allowing voters to accept or reject a proposed law or amendment passed by a legislative body.

regressive tax A tax system in which those with high incomes pay a lower percentage of their income in taxes than those with low incomes.

regulatory policy Laws and government rules targeting private business for the purpose of (1) protecting consumers and other businesses from what the government deems unfair business practices, (2) protecting workers from unsafe or unhealthy working conditions, (3) protecting consumers from unsafe products, and (4) protecting a number of groups from discrimination.

Republicanism A system of government in which the people's selected representatives run the government.

retrospective issue voting Deciding how to vote on the basis of past policy outcomes.

revenue neutral A quality of any tax reform plan that will neither increase nor decrease government revenue.

reverse discrimination Laws and policies that discriminate against whites, especially white males.

right The conservative end of the political spectrum.

Roe v. Wade A 1973 Supreme Court decision that a woman's right to privacy prevents states from barring her from having an abortion during the first trimester of pregnancy. States can impose reasonable regulations on abortions during the second trimester and can prohibit abortions under most circumstances in the third trimester.

rule adjudication Determining whether an agency's rules have been violated.

rule administration The core function of the bureaucracy—to carry out the decisions of Congress, the president, or the courts.

rule making Formulating the rules for carrying out the programs a bureaucratic agency administers.

Rule of Four The Supreme Court rule that at least four justices must decide that a case merits a review before it goes on the Court's schedule.

Rust Belt The major industrial states of the Northeast and Midwest that did not enjoy great population or economic growth in the second half of the twentieth century.

S

select committees Congressional committees that typically are created for only specific lengths of time and that lack authority to report legislation.

selective benefits Any benefit given to a member of a group but denied to nonmembers.

selective perception A phenomenon in which people perceive the same event differently because they have different beliefs and personal experiences.

senatorial courtesy The practice a president follows in choosing a nominee for a district or appeals court judgeship. The president selects a nominee from a list supplied by the senior senator of the president's party from the state or region where the vacancy occurs.

seniority rule The congressional norm of making the member of the majority party with the longest continuous service on a committee the chair of that committee.

separate-but-equal standard The now-rejected Supreme Court doctrine that separation of the races was acceptable as long as each race was treated equally.

separation of powers The principle that each of the three powers of government—legislative, executive, and judicial—should be held by a separate branch of government.

Shays's Rebellion A protest, staged by small farmers from western Massachusetts and led by Daniel Shays, an officer in the American Revolutionary War, against the state's taxes and policy of foreclosing on debtor farmers.

single-member districts A legislative district in which only one legislator is elected.

single-member, plurality electoral system A system in which each district elects a single member as its representative; the winner in each district is the candidate who receives a plurality of the vote.

social insurance Government programs, such as Social Security and Medicare, that require future beneficiaries to make contributions (otherwise known as taxes) and that distribute benefits without regard to the recipient's income.

social issues Issues based on moral or value judgments.

social regulation Laws and governmental rules designed to protect Americans from dangers or unfair practices associated with the way private businesses produce their products or with the products themselves.

Social Security Act of 1935 The act of Congress that created the Social Security tax (Federal Insurance Contribution Act—FICA) and Social Security programs.

social welfare policy Government programs that provide goods and services to citizens to improve the quality of their lives.

socialization The process by which people acquire values and opinions from their societies.

socioeconomic status Social status as measured by one's education, income, and occupation.

sociotropic voters People who vote on the basis of their community's economic interests, rather than their personal economic interests.

soft money Expenditures political parties make during an election for any activity that serves the purpose of increasing voter turnout.

solidary benefits The emotional and psychological enjoyment that comes from belonging to an interest group whose members share common interests and goals.

sound bite A short excerpt from a person's speech or conversation that appears on radio or television news.

sovereignty The power of self-rule.

spin control The practice of trying to persuade journalists to cover news stories in ways that put policies one likes in the most favorable light.

spoils system The method used to hire and fire government employees during most of the 1800s. Government employees of the new president's choosing would replace those a previous president had appointed. Government jobs were the "spoils" (or rewards) of the electoral "wars." This system was also known as patronage.

standing committee A permanent committee in Congress with jurisdiction over a specific policy area. Such a committee has tremendous say over the details of legislation within its jurisdiction.

stare decisis The doctrine that previous Supreme Court decisions should be allowed to stand.

states' rights An interpretation of federalism which claimed that states possessed the right to accept or reject federal laws.

strict scrutiny A legal standard for judging whether a discriminatory law is unconstitutional. Strict scrutiny requires the government to show a compelling reason for a discriminatory law.

structural rules Rules that establish the organization, procedures, and powers of government.

subcommittees The smaller units of a standing committee that oversee one part of the committee's jurisdiction.

suffrage The right to vote.

Sun Belt The states in the South, Southwest, and West Coast—areas that have experienced tremendous population and economic growth since 1950.

supply-side economics An economic theory which argues that if the government cuts taxes, reduces spending, and eliminates regulations, resources will be freed up to fuel the economy to produce even more goods and services.

T

talk radio Political talk shows on radio. Since the early 1990s, talk radio has emerged as an important force in American politics.

Temporary Assistance for Needy Families (TANF) A public assistance program that provides government aid to low-income families with children for a limited amount of time.

Third World A term loosely defined to mean the developing countries in Asia, Africa, and Latin America.

Truman Doctrine A policy, announced by President Truman in 1947, that the United States would oppose communist attempts to overthrow or conquer non-communist countries.

turnover Change in membership of Congress between elections.

two presidencies The argument that presidents have much greater influence over the content of foreign policy than the content of domestic policy.

two-party system A political system in which two major parties dominate.

U

unilateralism The tendency of the United States to act alone in foreign affairs without consulting other countries.

unit rule A winner-take-all system which requires that the candidate with the most popular votes receive all of that state's electoral votes.

V

values Basic principles that lead people to form opinions on specific issues.

Virginia Plan A plan for a new national government that the Virginia delegation proposed at the Constitutional Convention in 1787. It called for a strong, essentially unitary national government, with separate executive and judicial branches, and a two-house legislative branch with representation based on each state's population.

voter turnout The percentage of people who actually vote.

Voting Rights Act of 1965 An act of Congress that bars states from creating voting and registration practices that discriminate against African Americans and other minorities.

W

winnowing effect Candidates who do poorly in early primary elections usually lose the ability to raise campaign funds, attract media attention, or hold their public support, which dooms them to eventual defeat.

women's movement The mobilization of people to push for equality between the sexes.

World Trade Organization (WTO) The international trade agency that began operation in 1995 as the successor to the General Agreement on Tariffs and Trade.

writ of certiorari A Supreme Court order for a lower court to send it the records of a case—the first step in reviewing a lower court case.

Y

yellow journalism A form of journalism, popular at the end of the nineteenth century, that emphasized sensational and sometimes lurid news coverage.

Name Index

Subject Index